KEKKAISHI 3-in-1

Volumes 1-2-3
Shonen Sunday 3-in-1 Edition

Story and Art by YELLOW TANABE

© 2004 Yellow TANABE/Shogakukan
All rights reserved.
Original Japanese edition "KEKKAISHI" published by SHOGAKUKAN Inc.
Logo and cover design created by Bay Bridge Studio

English Adaptation/Shaenon Garrity
Translation/Yuko Sawada
Touch-up Art & Lettering/Stephen Dutro
Cover Design & Graphic Layout/Yukiko Whitley (3-in-1 edition); Amy Martin (graphic novels 1–3)
Editors/Megan Bates (vol. 1 and 2), Eric Searleman (vol. 3), Annette Roman (3-in-1 edition)

Printed in the U.S.A.

Published by VIZ Media, LLC
P.O. Box 77010
San Francisco, CA 94107

10 9 8 7 6 5 4 3 2
3-in-1 edition first printing, May 2011
Second printing, September 2011

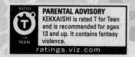

PARENTAL ADVISORY
KEKKAISHI is rated T for Teen and is recommended for ages 13 and up. It contains fantasy violence.
ratings.viz.com

www.viz.com

WWW.SHONENSUNDAY.COM

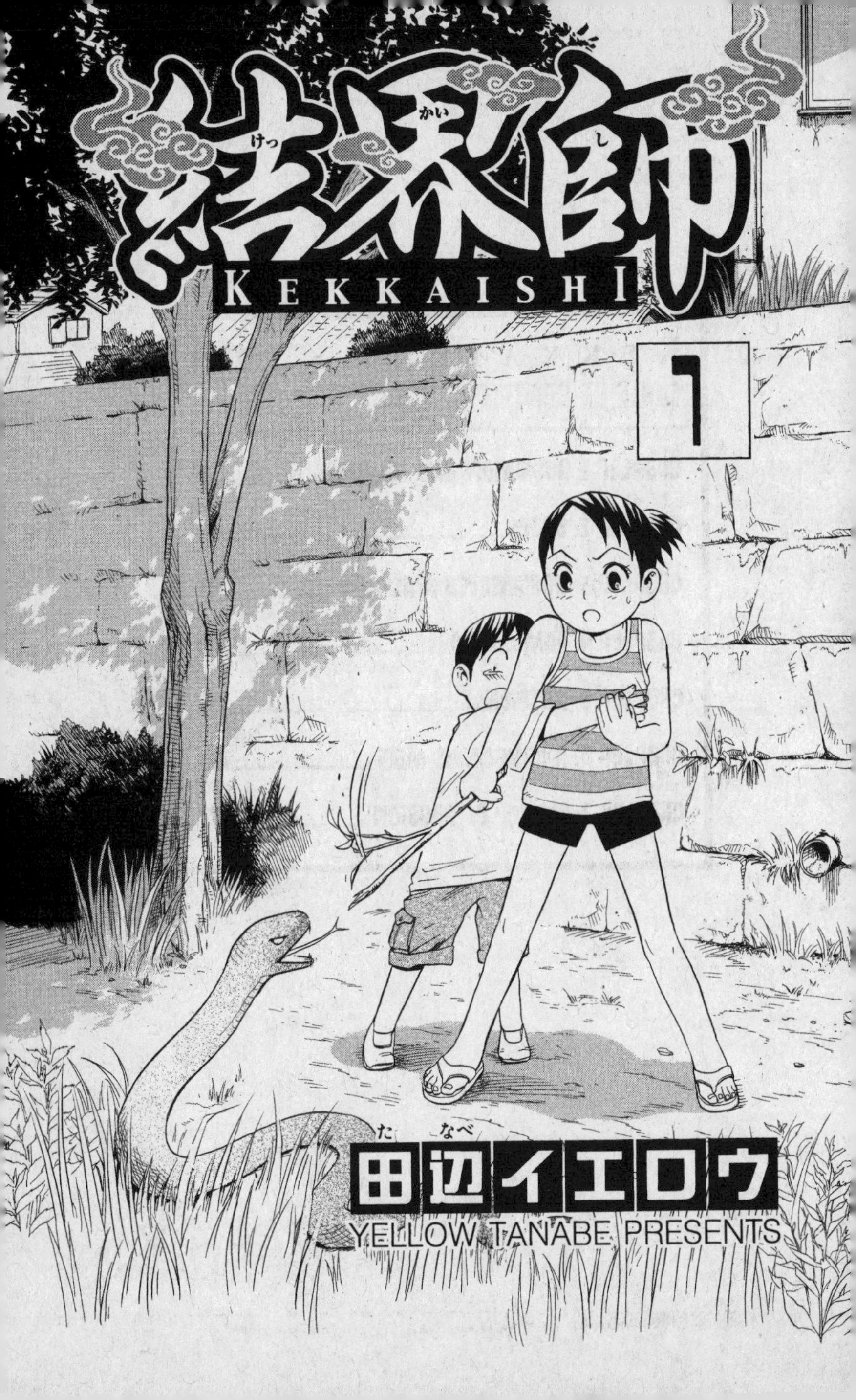
結界師
KEKKAISHI
1
田辺イエロウ
YELLOW TANABE PRESENTS

K E K K A I S H I VOL. 1

TABLE OF CONTENTS

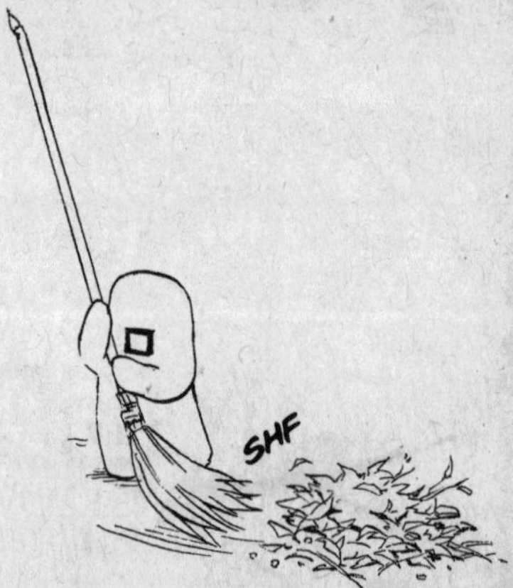

SHF

Chapter 1: Yoshimori and Tokine

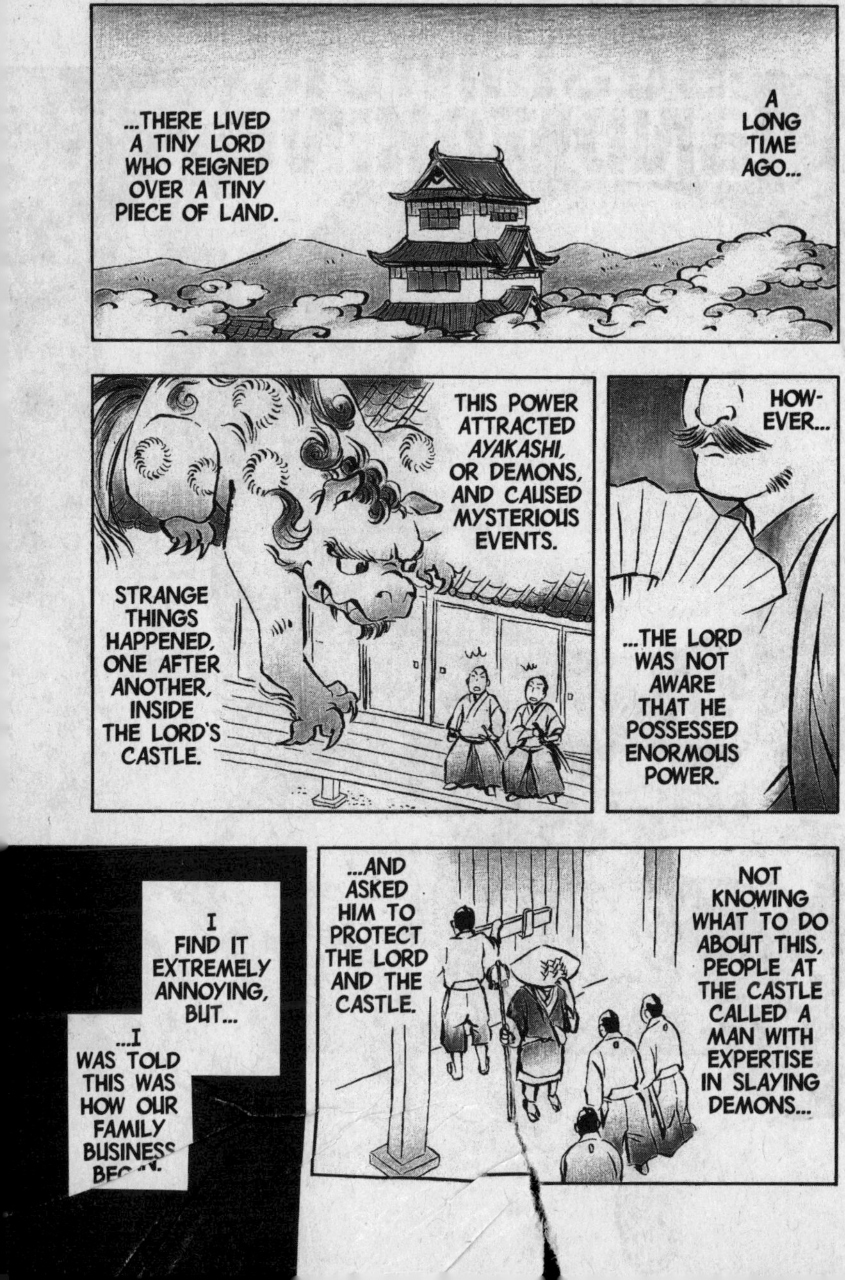
A LONG TIME AGO...
...THERE LIVED A TINY LORD WHO REIGNED OVER A TINY PIECE OF LAND.
HOW-EVER...
...THE LORD WAS NOT AWARE THAT HE POSSESSED ENORMOUS POWER.
THIS POWER ATTRACTED *AYAKASHI*, OR DEMONS, AND CAUSED MYSTERIOUS EVENTS.
STRANGE THINGS HAPPENED, ONE AFTER ANOTHER, INSIDE THE LORD'S CASTLE.
NOT KNOWING WHAT TO DO ABOUT THIS, PEOPLE AT THE CASTLE CALLED A MAN WITH EXPERTISE IN SLAYING DEMONS...
...AND ASKED HIM TO PROTECT THE LORD AND THE CASTLE.
I FIND IT EXTREMELY ANNOYING, BUT...
...I WAS TOLD THIS WAS HOW OUR FAMILY BUSINESS

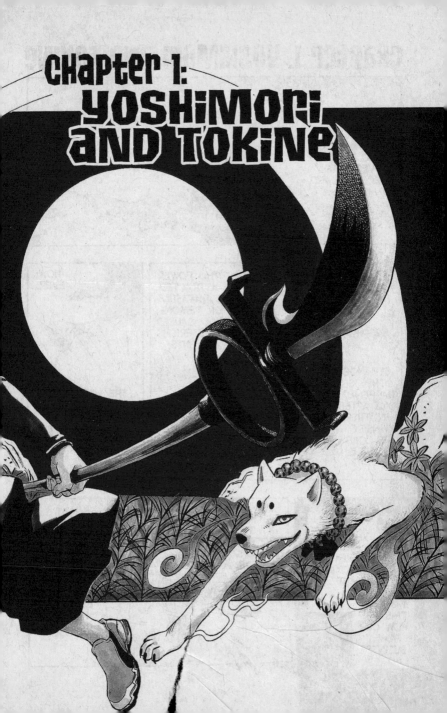

CHAPTER 1: YOSHIMORI AND TOKINE

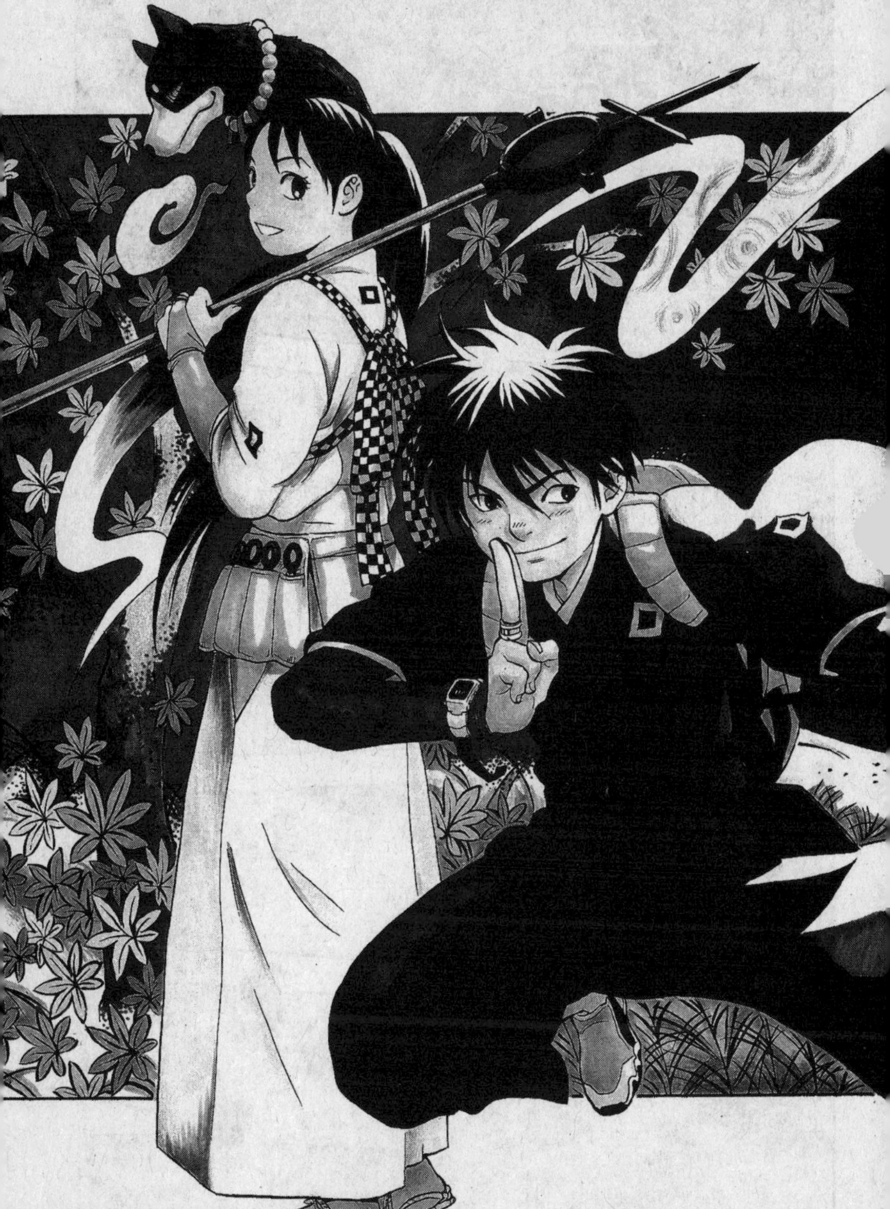

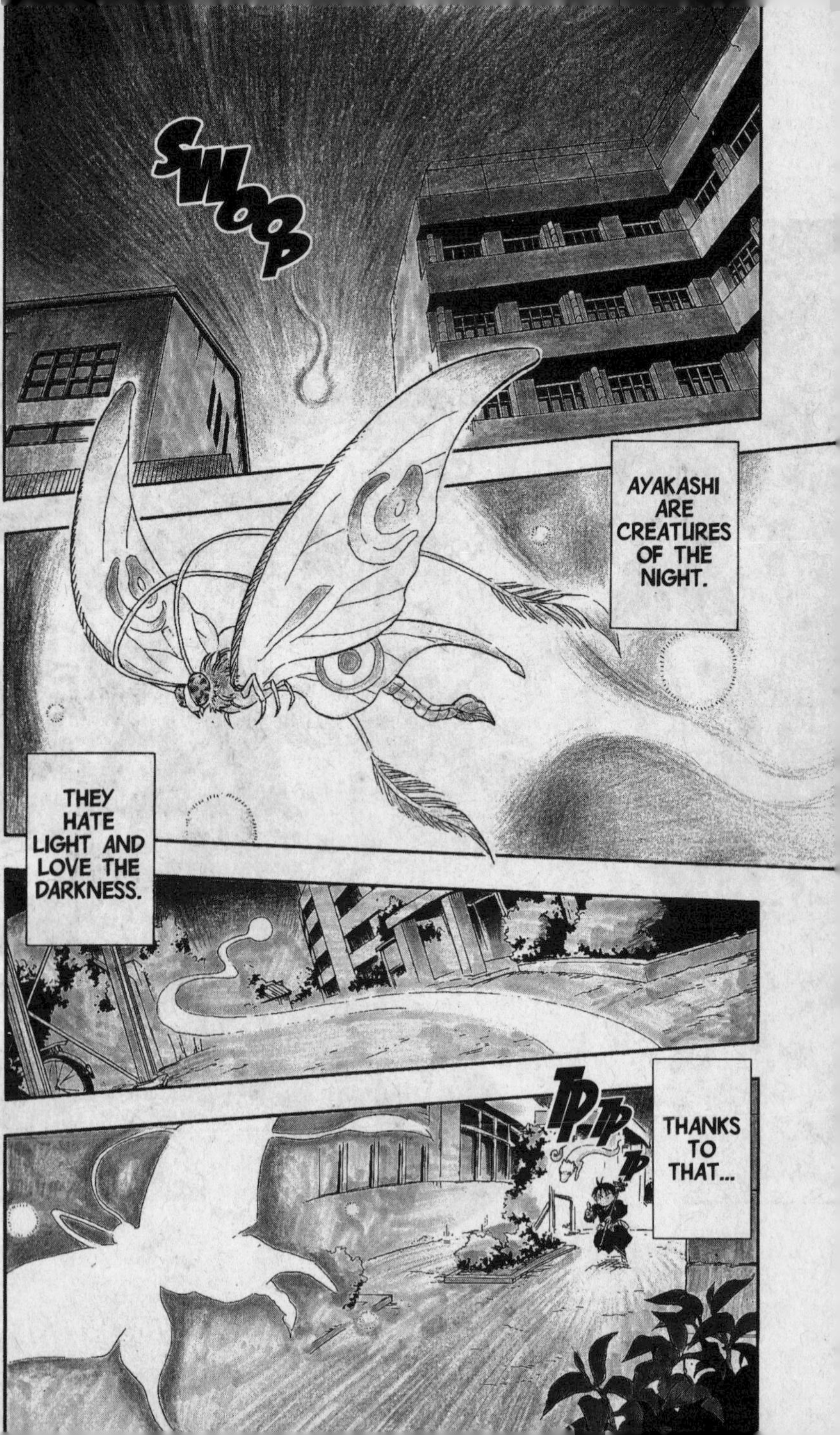
SWOOP
AYAKASHI ARE CREATURES OF THE NIGHT.
THEY HATE LIGHT AND LOVE THE DARKNESS.
THANKS TO THAT...
TP TP TP

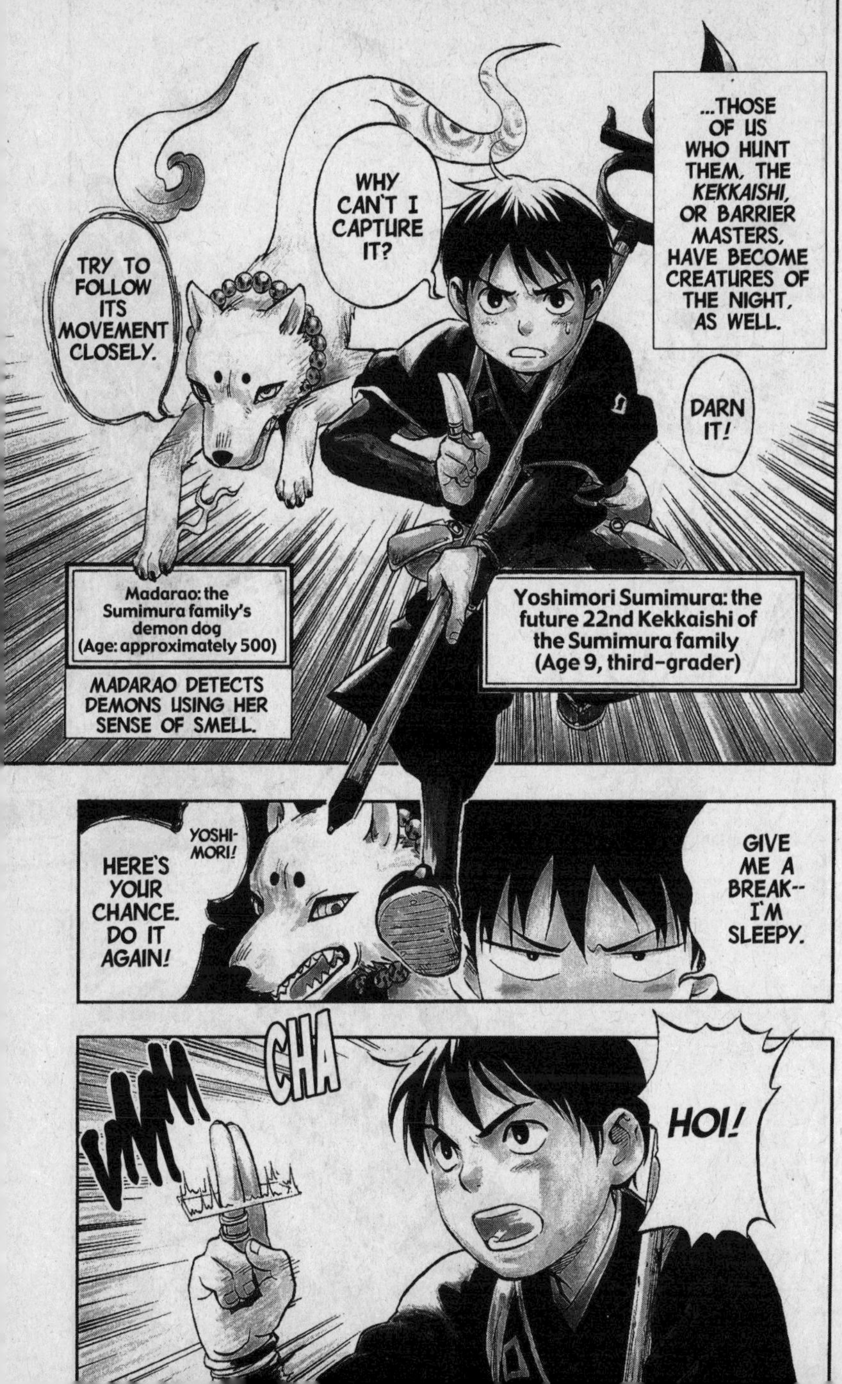
...THOSE OF US WHO HUNT THEM, THE *KEKKAISHI*, OR BARRIER MASTERS, HAVE BECOME CREATURES OF THE NIGHT, AS WELL.
WHY CAN'T I CAPTURE IT?
DARN IT!
TRY TO FOLLOW ITS MOVEMENT CLOSELY.
Yoshimori Sumimura: the future 22nd Kekkaishi of the Sumimura family (Age 9, third-grader)
Madarao: the Sumimura family's demon dog (Age: approximately 500)
MADARAO DETECTS DEMONS USING HER SENSE OF SMELL.
GIVE ME A BREAK-- I'M SLEEPY.
YOSHI-MORI!
HERE'S YOUR CHANCE. DO IT AGAIN!
HOI!
CHA
VMM

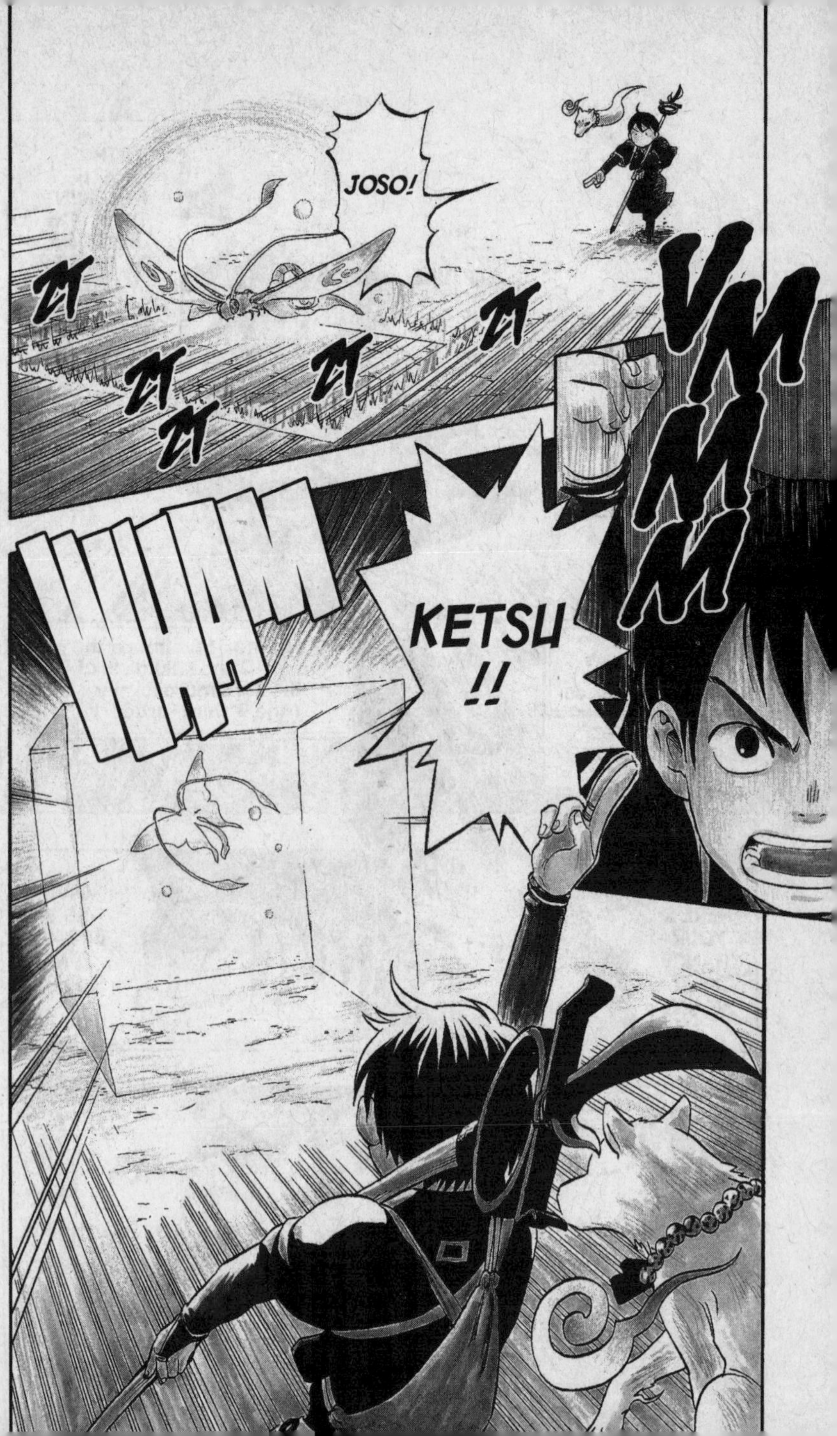

JOSO!
ZZT
ZZT
ZZT
ZZT
ZZT
VMMM
KETSU !!
WHAM

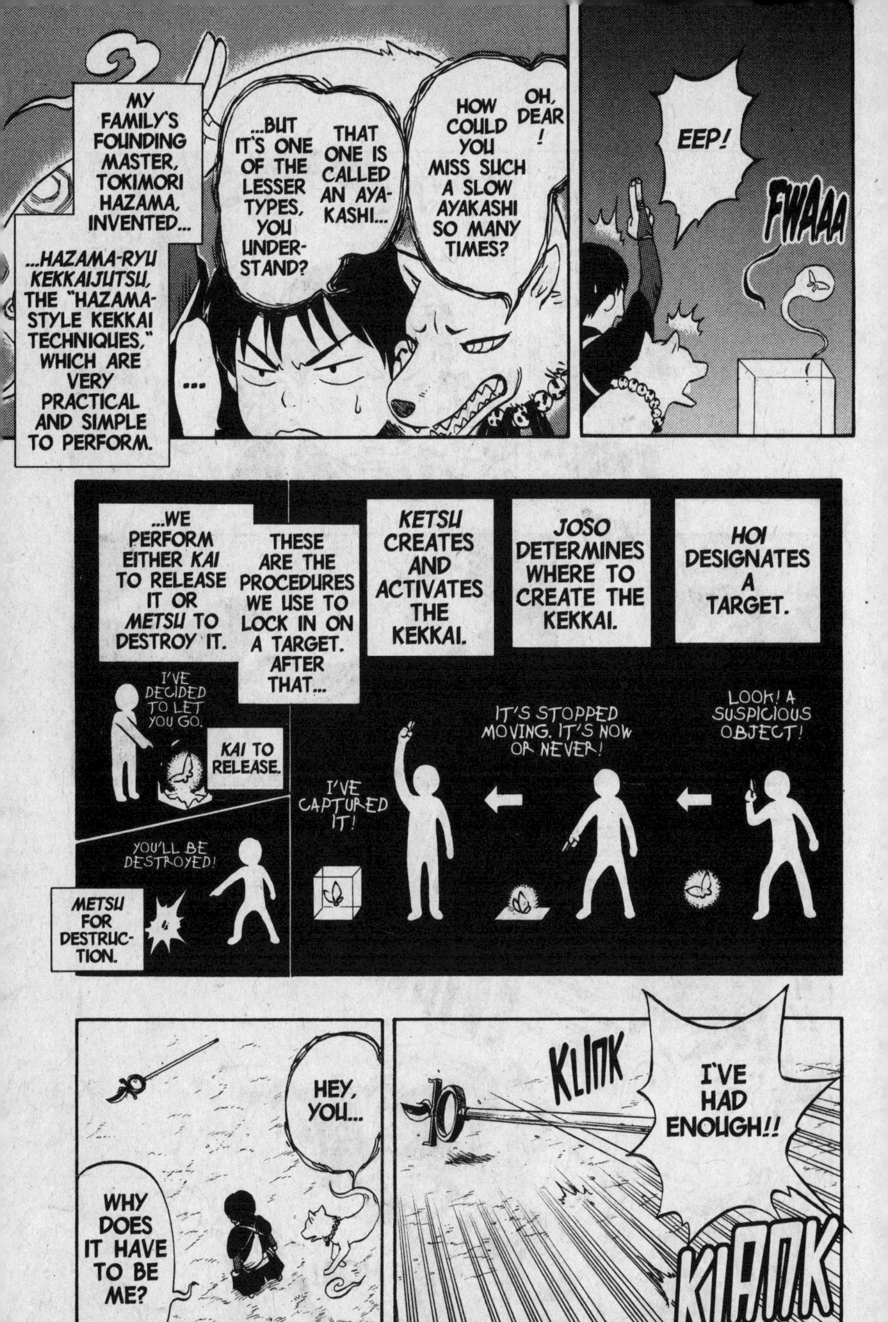
EEP!
FWAAA
OH, DEAR!
HOW COULD YOU MISS SUCH A SLOW AYAKASHI SO MANY TIMES?
THAT ONE IS CALLED AN AYA-KASHI...
...BUT IT'S ONE OF THE LESSER TYPES, YOU UNDER-STAND?
MY FAMILY'S FOUNDING MASTER, TOKIMORI HAZAMA, INVENTED...
...*HAZAMA-RYU KEKKAIJUTSU*, THE "HAZAMA-STYLE KEKKAI TECHNIQUES," WHICH ARE VERY PRACTICAL AND SIMPLE TO PERFORM.
...
HOI DESIGNATES A TARGET.
JOSO DETERMINES WHERE TO CREATE THE KEKKAI.
KETSU CREATES AND ACTIVATES THE KEKKAI.
THESE ARE THE PROCEDURES WE USE TO LOCK IN ON A TARGET. AFTER THAT...
...WE PERFORM EITHER *KAI* TO RELEASE IT OR *METSU* TO DESTROY IT.
LOOK! A SUSPICIOUS OBJECT!
IT'S STOPPED MOVING. IT'S NOW OR NEVER!
I'VE CAPTURED IT!
KAI TO RELEASE.
I'VE DECIDED TO LET YOU GO.
METSU FOR DESTRUC-TION.
YOU'LL BE DESTROYED!
KLINK
I'VE HAD ENOUGH!!
KLANK
HEY, YOU...
WHY DOES IT HAVE TO BE ME?

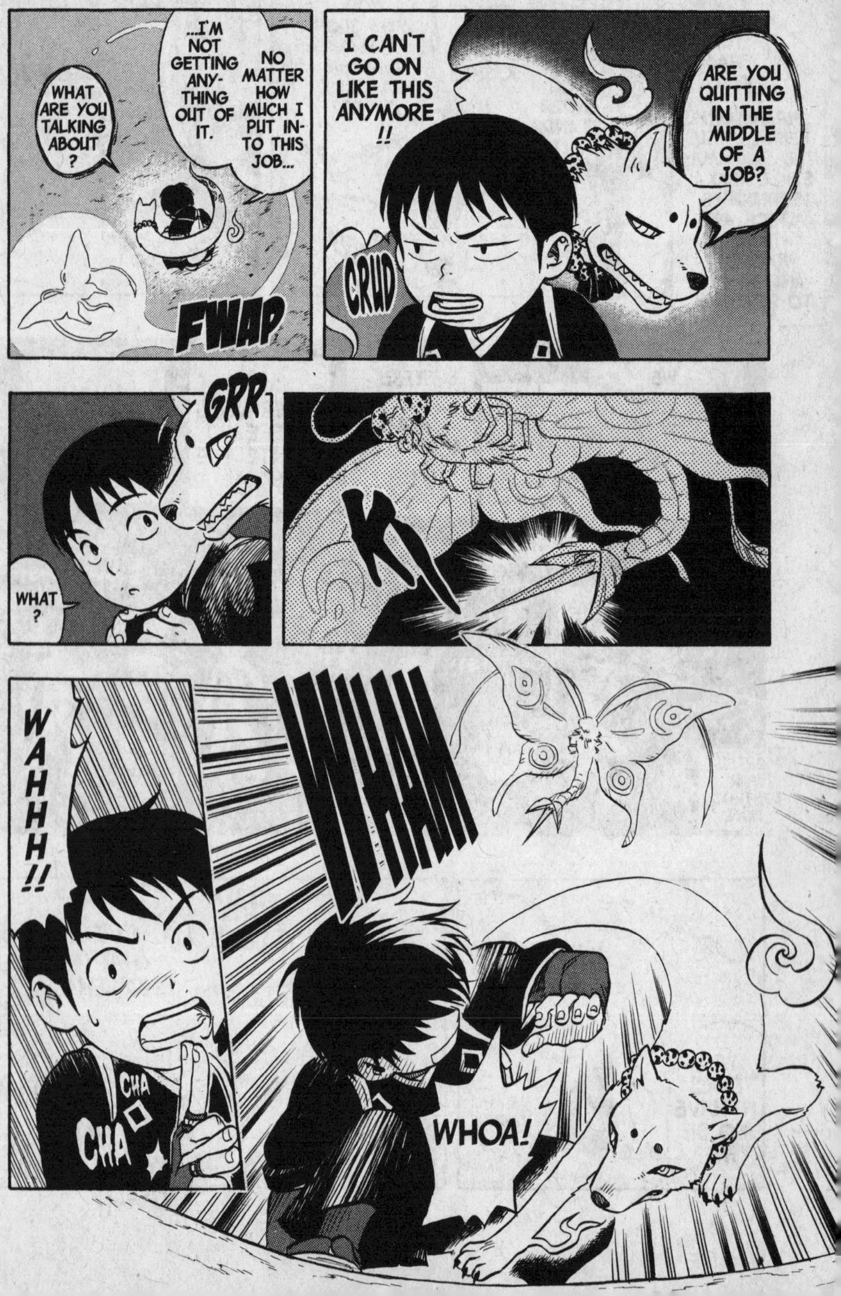
ARE YOU QUITTING IN THE MIDDLE OF A JOB?
I CAN'T GO ON LIKE THIS ANYMORE!!
CRUD
NO MATTER HOW MUCH I PUT INTO THIS JOB...
...I'M NOT GETTING ANYTHING OUT OF IT.
WHAT ARE YOU TALKING ABOUT?
FWAP
K
GRR
WHAT?
WHAM
WHOA!
WAHHHH!!
CHA
CHA

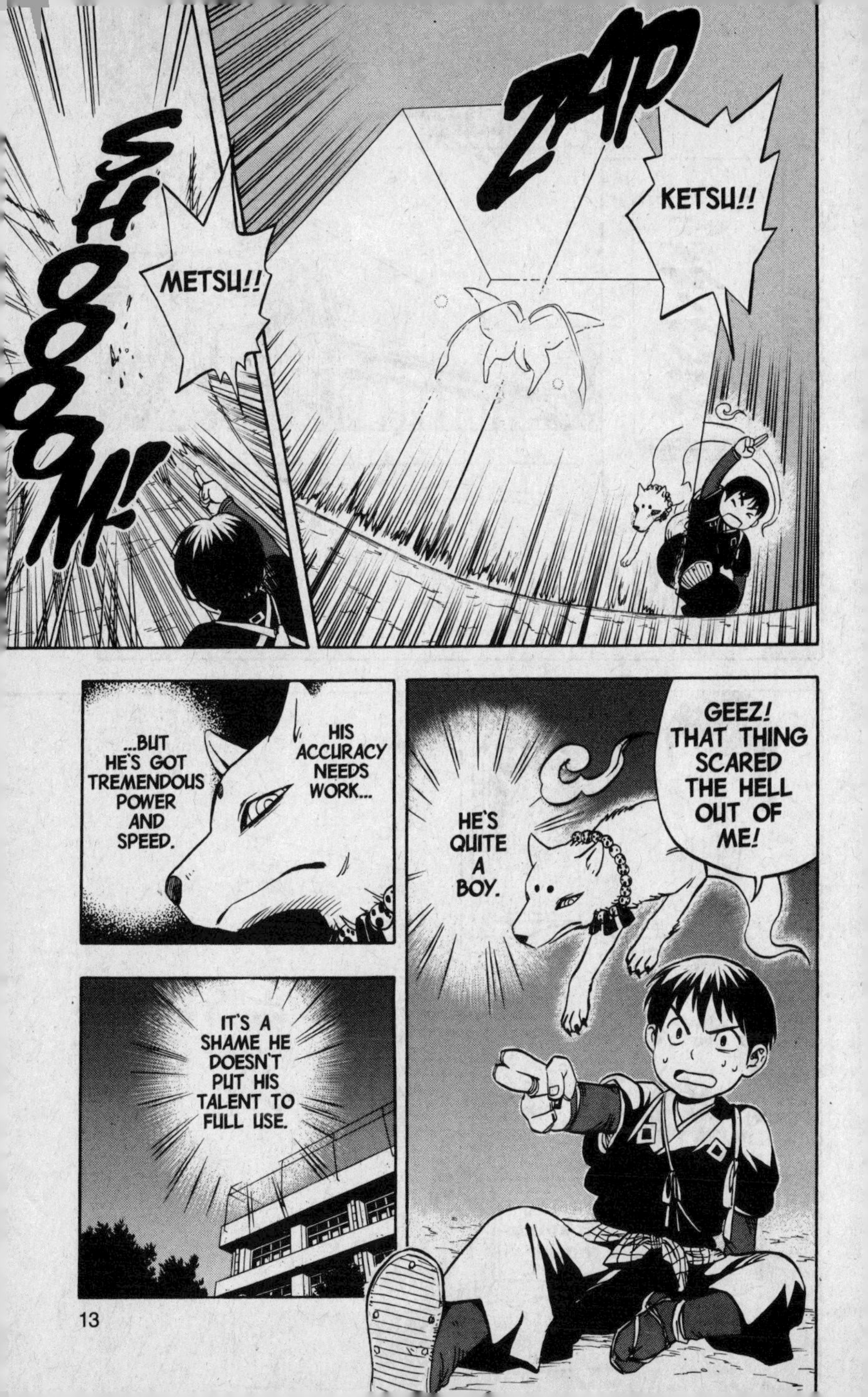
ZAP
KETSU!!
METSU!!
SHOOOOOM!
GEEZ! THAT THING SCARED THE HELL OUT OF ME!
HE'S QUITE A BOY.
HIS ACCURACY NEEDS WORK...
...BUT HE'S GOT TREMENDOUS POWER AND SPEED.
IT'S A SHAME HE DOESN'T PUT HIS TALENT TO FULL USE.

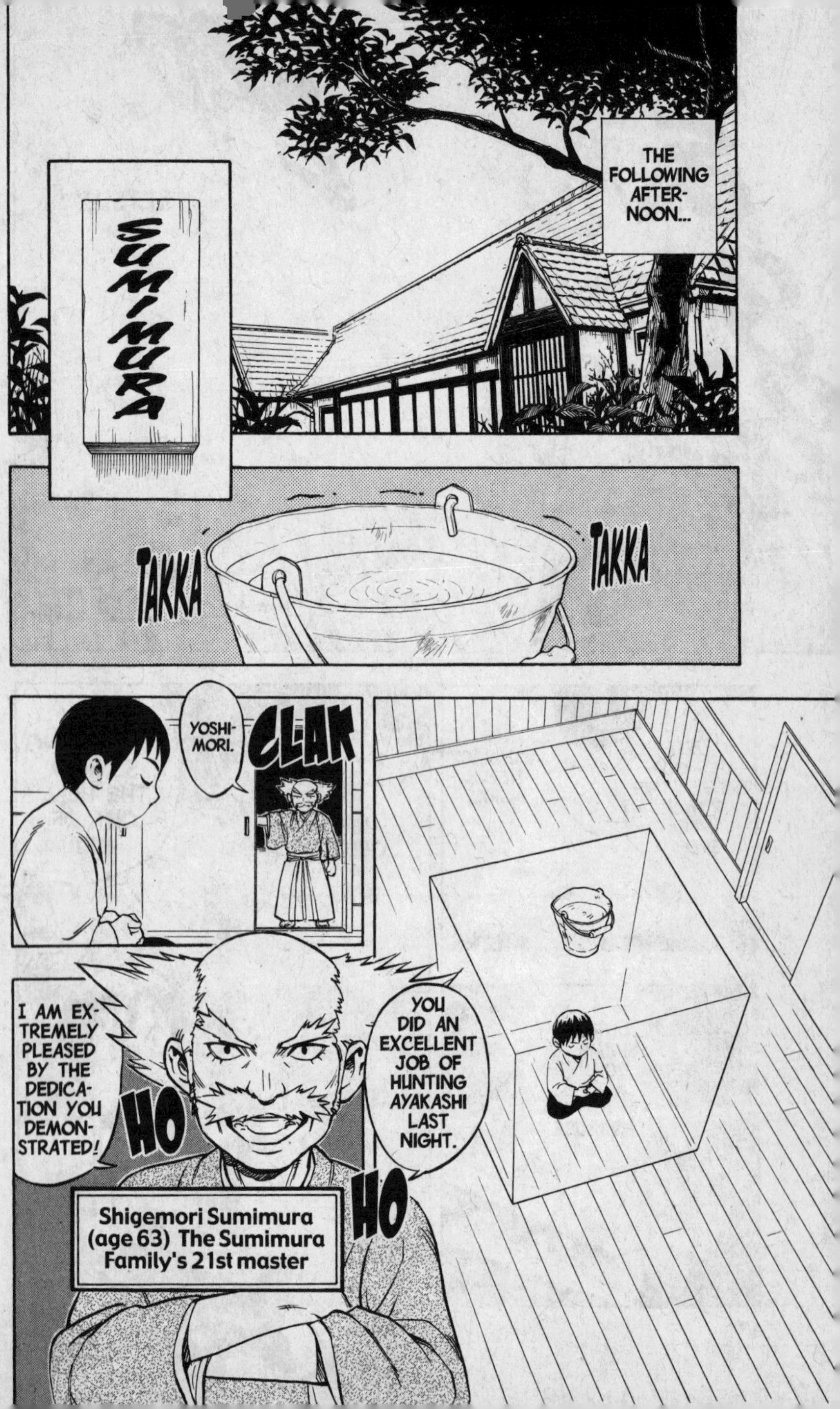
THE FOLLOWING AFTER-NOON...
SUMIMURA
TAKKA
TAKKA
CLAK
YOSHI-MORI.
YOU DID AN EXCELLENT JOB OF HUNTING AYAKASHI LAST NIGHT.
I AM EX-TREMELY PLEASED BY THE DEDICA-TION YOU DEMON-STRATED!
HO
HO
Shigemori Sumimura (age 63) The Sumimura Family's 21st master

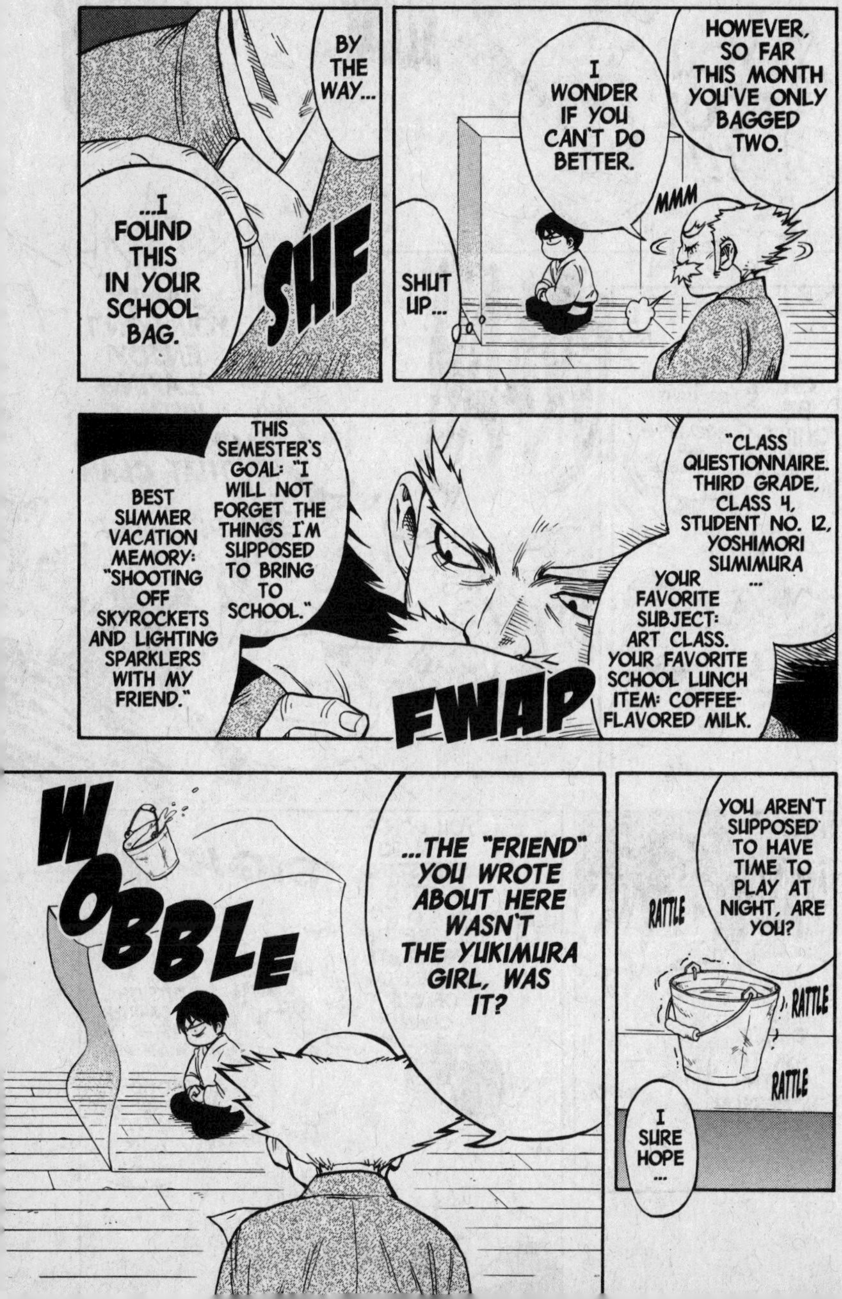
HOWEVER, SO FAR THIS MONTH YOU'VE ONLY BAGGED TWO.
I WONDER IF YOU CAN'T DO BETTER.
MMM
SHUT UP...
BY THE WAY...
SHF
...I FOUND THIS IN YOUR SCHOOL BAG.
"CLASS QUESTIONNAIRE. THIRD GRADE, CLASS 4, STUDENT NO. 12, YOSHIMORI SUMIMURA ...
YOUR FAVORITE SUBJECT: ART CLASS. YOUR FAVORITE SCHOOL LUNCH ITEM: COFFEE-FLAVORED MILK.
THIS SEMESTER'S GOAL: "I WILL NOT FORGET THE THINGS I'M SUPPOSED TO BRING TO SCHOOL."
BEST SUMMER VACATION MEMORY: "SHOOTING OFF SKYROCKETS AND LIGHTING SPARKLERS WITH MY FRIEND."
FWAP
YOU AREN'T SUPPOSED TO HAVE TIME TO PLAY AT NIGHT, ARE YOU?
RATTLE
RATTLE
RATTLE
I SURE HOPE ...
...THE "FRIEND" YOU WROTE ABOUT HERE WASN'T THE YUKIMURA GIRL, WAS IT?
WOBBLE

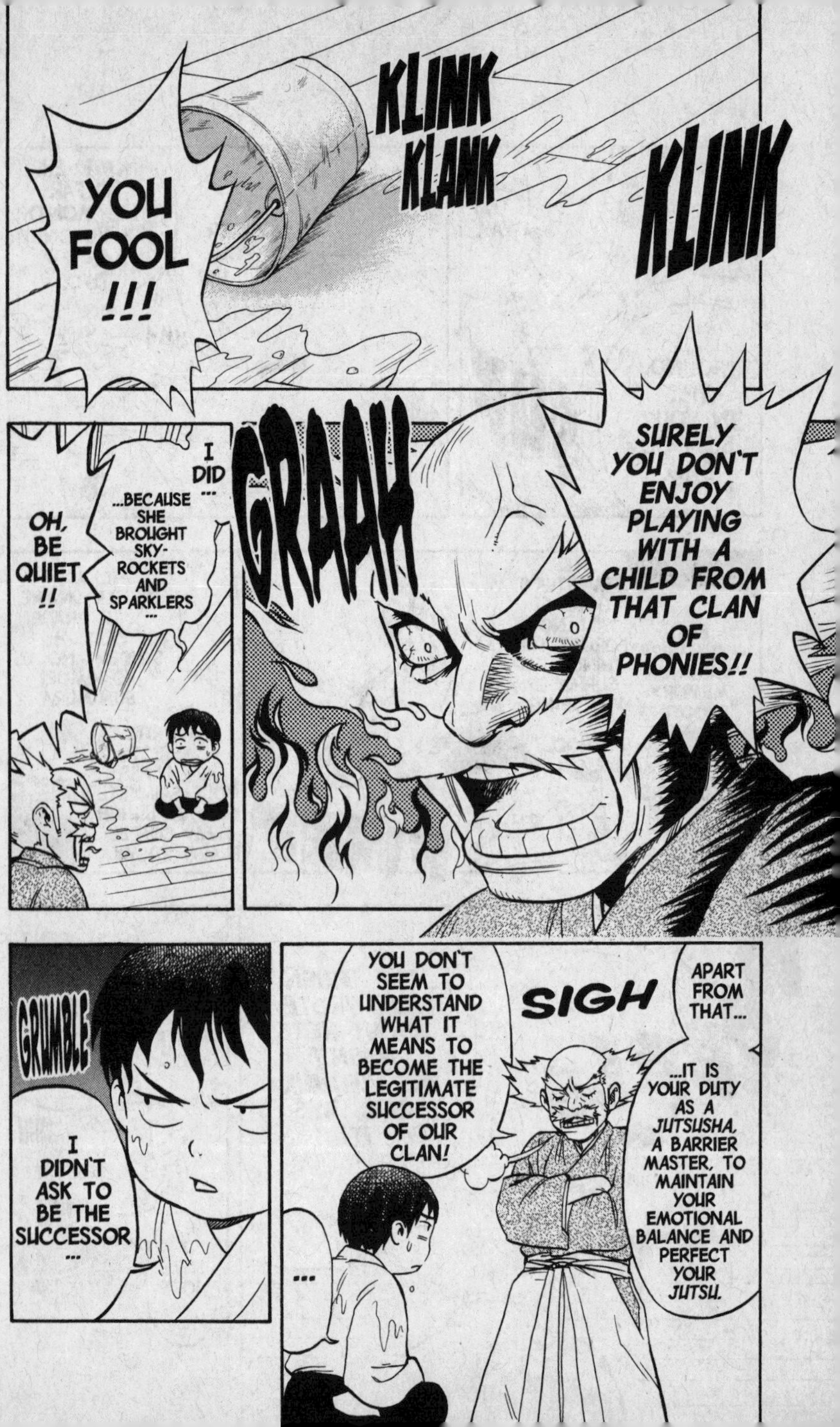
KLINK
KLINK KLANK
YOU FOOL!!!
SURELY YOU DON'T ENJOY PLAYING WITH A CHILD FROM THAT CLAN OF PHONIES!!
GRAAH
I DID...
...BECAUSE SHE BROUGHT SKY-ROCKETS AND SPARKLERS...
OH, BE QUIET!!
APART FROM THAT...
SIGH
YOU DON'T SEEM TO UNDERSTAND WHAT IT MEANS TO BECOME THE LEGITIMATE SUCCESSOR OF OUR CLAN!
...IT IS YOUR DUTY AS A JUTSUSHA, A BARRIER MASTER, TO MAINTAIN YOUR EMOTIONAL BALANCE AND PERFECT YOUR JUTSU.
...
GRUMBLE
I DIDN'T ASK TO BE THE SUCCESSOR...

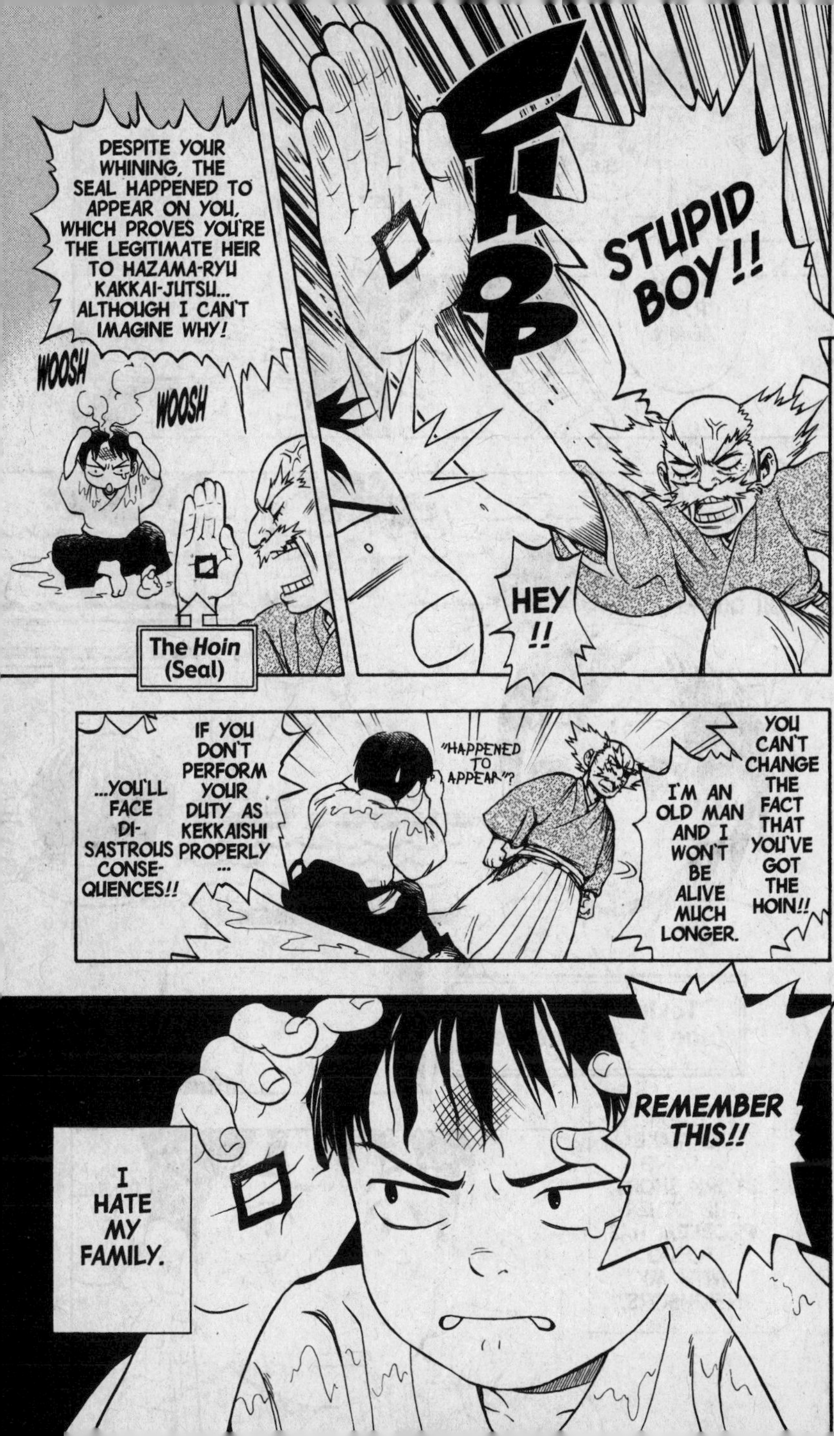
STUPID BOY!!
HEY!!
DESPITE YOUR WHINING, THE SEAL HAPPENED TO APPEAR ON YOU, WHICH PROVES YOU'RE THE LEGITIMATE HEIR TO HAZAMA-RYU KAKKAI-JUTSU... ALTHOUGH I CAN'T IMAGINE WHY!
WOOSH
WOOSH
The Hoin (Seal)
YOU CAN'T CHANGE THE FACT THAT YOU'VE GOT THE HOIN!!
I'M AN OLD MAN AND I WON'T BE ALIVE MUCH LONGER.
"HAPPENED TO APPEAR"?
IF YOU DON'T PERFORM YOUR DUTY AS KEKKAISHI PROPERLY...
...YOU'LL FACE DI-SASTROUS CONSE-QUENCES!!
REMEMBER THIS!!
I HATE MY FAMILY.

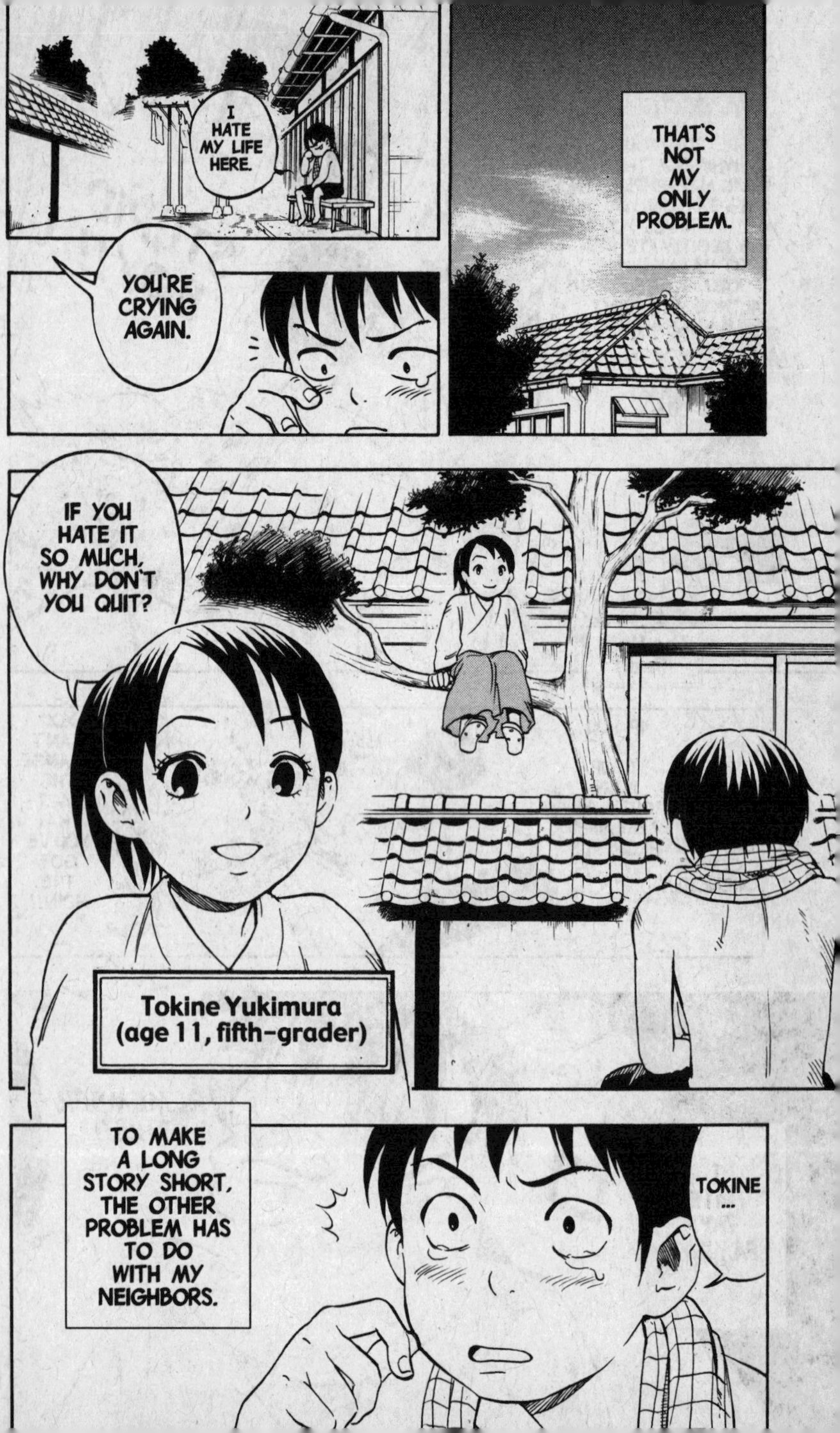
THAT'S NOT MY ONLY PROBLEM.
I HATE MY LIFE HERE.
YOU'RE CRYING AGAIN.
IF YOU HATE IT SO MUCH, WHY DON'T YOU QUIT?
Tokine Yukimura (age 11, fifth-grader)
TOKINE...
TO MAKE A LONG STORY SHORT, THE OTHER PROBLEM HAS TO DO WITH MY NEIGHBORS.

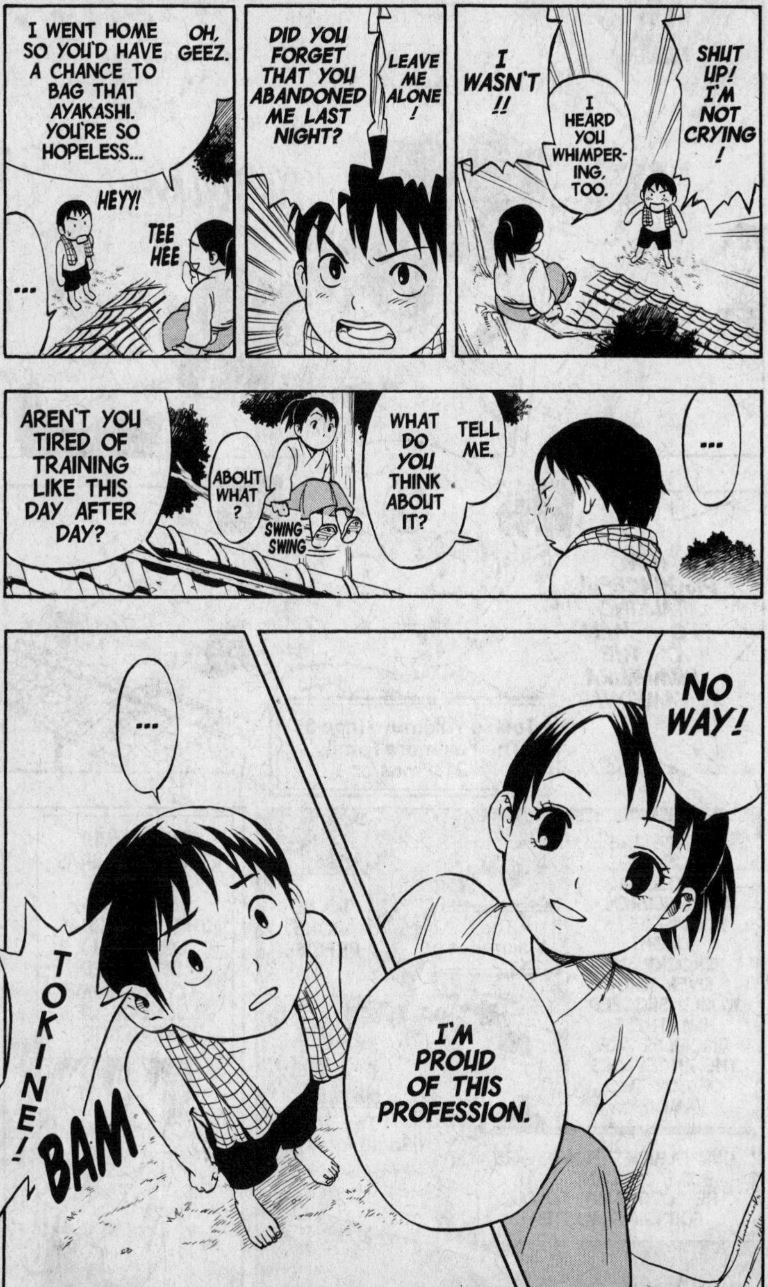
SHUT UP! I'M NOT CRYING!
I WASN'T!!
I HEARD YOU WHIMPERING, TOO.
LEAVE ME ALONE!
DID YOU FORGET THAT YOU ABANDONED ME LAST NIGHT?
OH, GEEZ.
I WENT HOME SO YOU'D HAVE A CHANCE TO BAG THAT AYAKASHI. YOU'RE SO HOPELESS...
HEYY!
TEE HEE
...
...
TELL ME.
WHAT DO YOU THINK ABOUT IT?
ABOUT WHAT?
SWING SWING
AREN'T YOU TIRED OF TRAINING LIKE THIS DAY AFTER DAY?
NO WAY!
I'M PROUD OF THIS PROFESSION.
...
TOKINE!
BAM

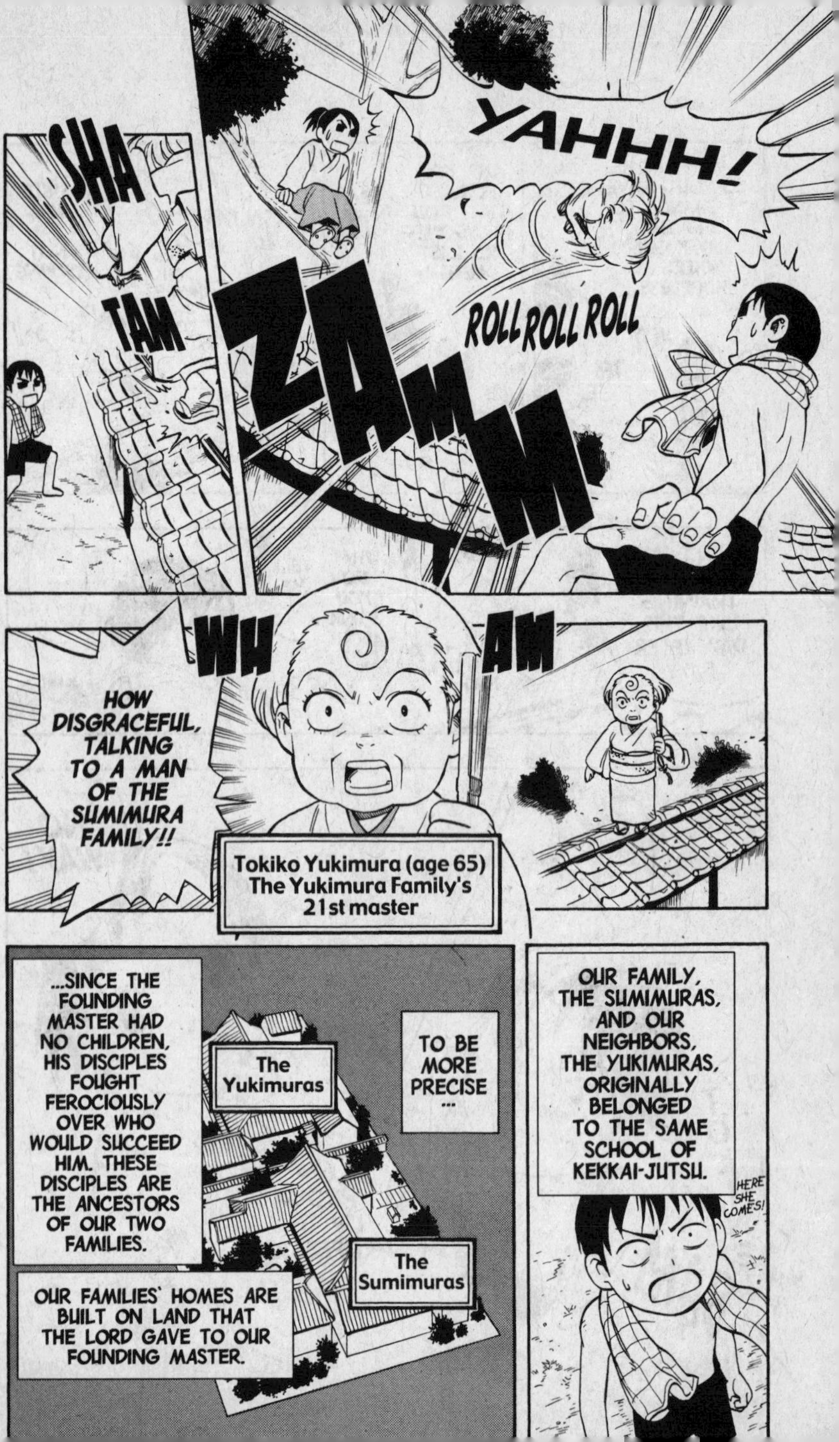
YAHHH!
ROLL ROLL ROLL
ZAMM
SHA
TAM
WHAM
Tokiko Yukimura (age 65)
The Yukimura Family's
21st master
HOW DISGRACEFUL, TALKING TO A MAN OF THE SUMIMURA FAMILY!!
OUR FAMILY, THE SUMIMURAS, AND OUR NEIGHBORS, THE YUKIMURAS, ORIGINALLY BELONGED TO THE SAME SCHOOL OF KEKKAI-JUTSU.
HERE SHE COMES!
TO BE MORE PRECISE ...
...SINCE THE FOUNDING MASTER HAD NO CHILDREN, HIS DISCIPLES FOUGHT FEROCIOUSLY OVER WHO WOULD SUCCEED HIM. THESE DISCIPLES ARE THE ANCESTORS OF OUR TWO FAMILIES.
The Yukimuras
The Sumimuras
OUR FAMILIES' HOMES ARE BUILT ON LAND THAT THE LORD GAVE TO OUR FOUNDING MASTER.

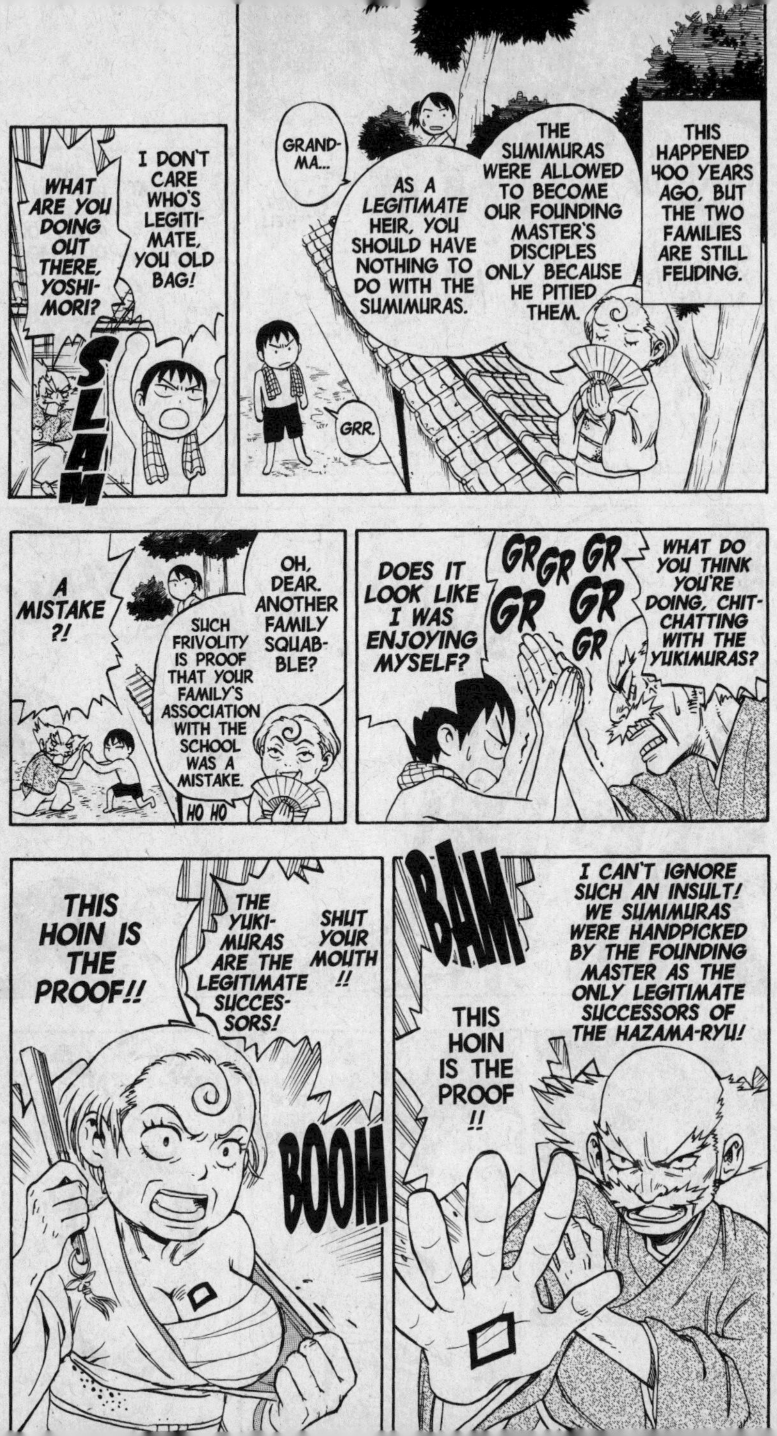
THIS HAPPENED 400 YEARS AGO, BUT THE TWO FAMILIES ARE STILL FEUDING.
THE SUMIMURAS WERE ALLOWED TO BECOME OUR FOUNDING MASTER'S DISCIPLES ONLY BECAUSE HE PITIED THEM.
AS A LEGITIMATE HEIR, YOU SHOULD HAVE NOTHING TO DO WITH THE SUMIMURAS.
GRAND-MA...
GRR.
I DON'T CARE WHO'S LEGITI-MATE, YOU OLD BAG!
WHAT ARE YOU DOING OUT THERE, YOSHI-MORI?
SLAM
WHAT DO YOU THINK YOU'RE DOING, CHIT-CHATTING WITH THE YUKIMURAS?
GR GR GR GR GR GR
DOES IT LOOK LIKE I WAS ENJOYING MYSELF?
OH, DEAR. ANOTHER FAMILY SQUAB-BLE?
SUCH FRIVOLITY IS PROOF THAT YOUR FAMILY'S ASSOCIATION WITH THE SCHOOL WAS A MISTAKE.
HO HO
A MISTAKE ?!
I CAN'T IGNORE SUCH AN INSULT! WE SUMIMURAS WERE HANDPICKED BY THE FOUNDING MASTER AS THE ONLY LEGITIMATE SUCCESSORS OF THE HAZAMA-RYU!
BAM
THIS HOIN IS THE PROOF !!
SHUT YOUR MOUTH !!
THE YUKI-MURAS ARE THE LEGITIMATE SUCCES-SORS!
THIS HOIN IS THE PROOF!!
BOOM

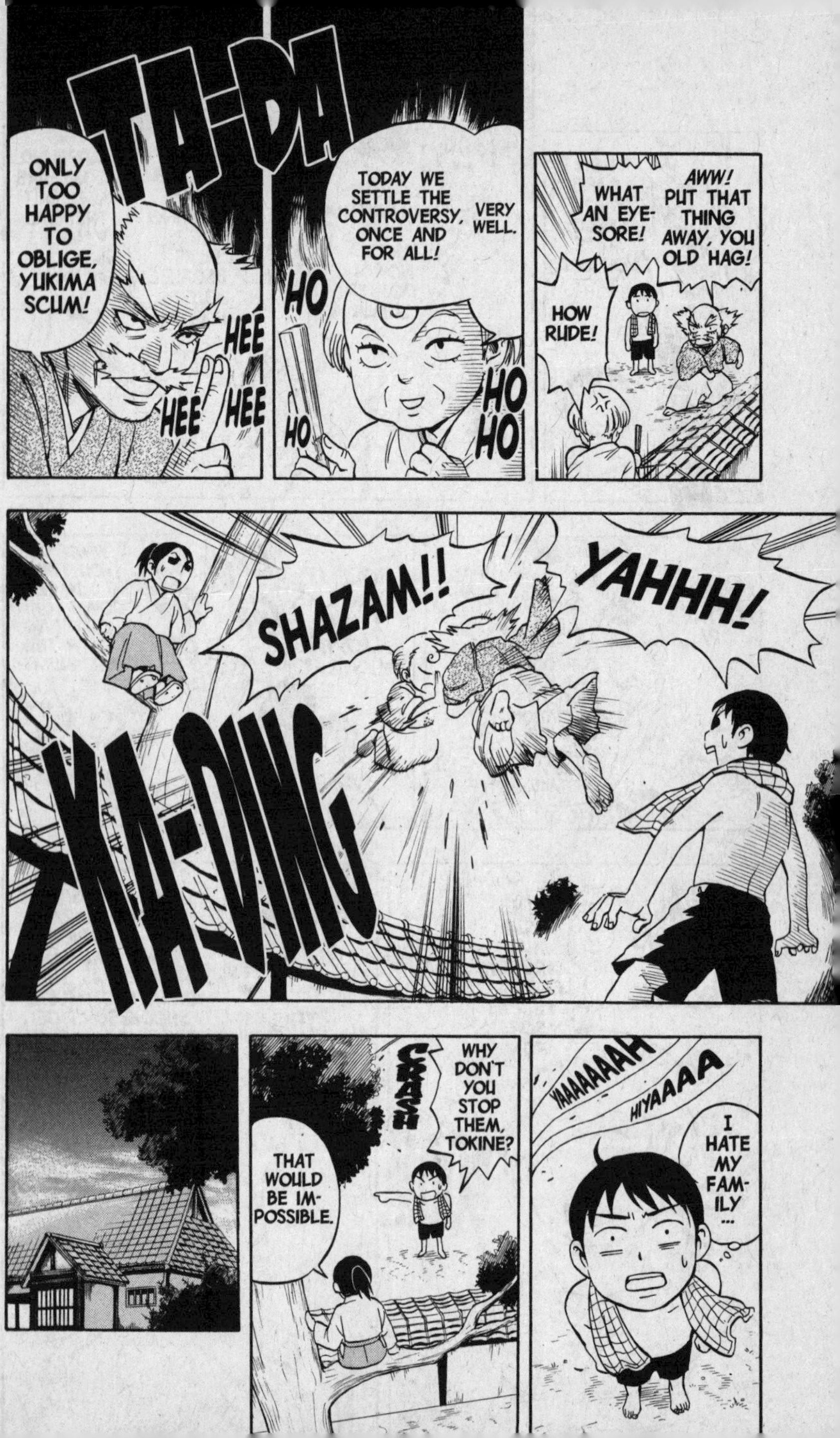
AWW! PUT THAT THING AWAY, YOU OLD HAG!
WHAT AN EYE-SORE!
HOW RUDE!
VERY WELL.
TODAY WE SETTLE THE CONTROVERSY, ONCE AND FOR ALL!
HO HO
HO HO
TA-DA
ONLY TOO HAPPY TO OBLIGE, YUKIMA SCUM!
HEE HEE
HEE HEE
YAHHH!
SHAZAM!!
KA-DING
YAAAAAAAH
HIYAAAA
I HATE MY FAM-ILY...
WHY DON'T YOU STOP THEM, TOKINE?
CRASH
THAT WOULD BE IM-POSSIBLE.

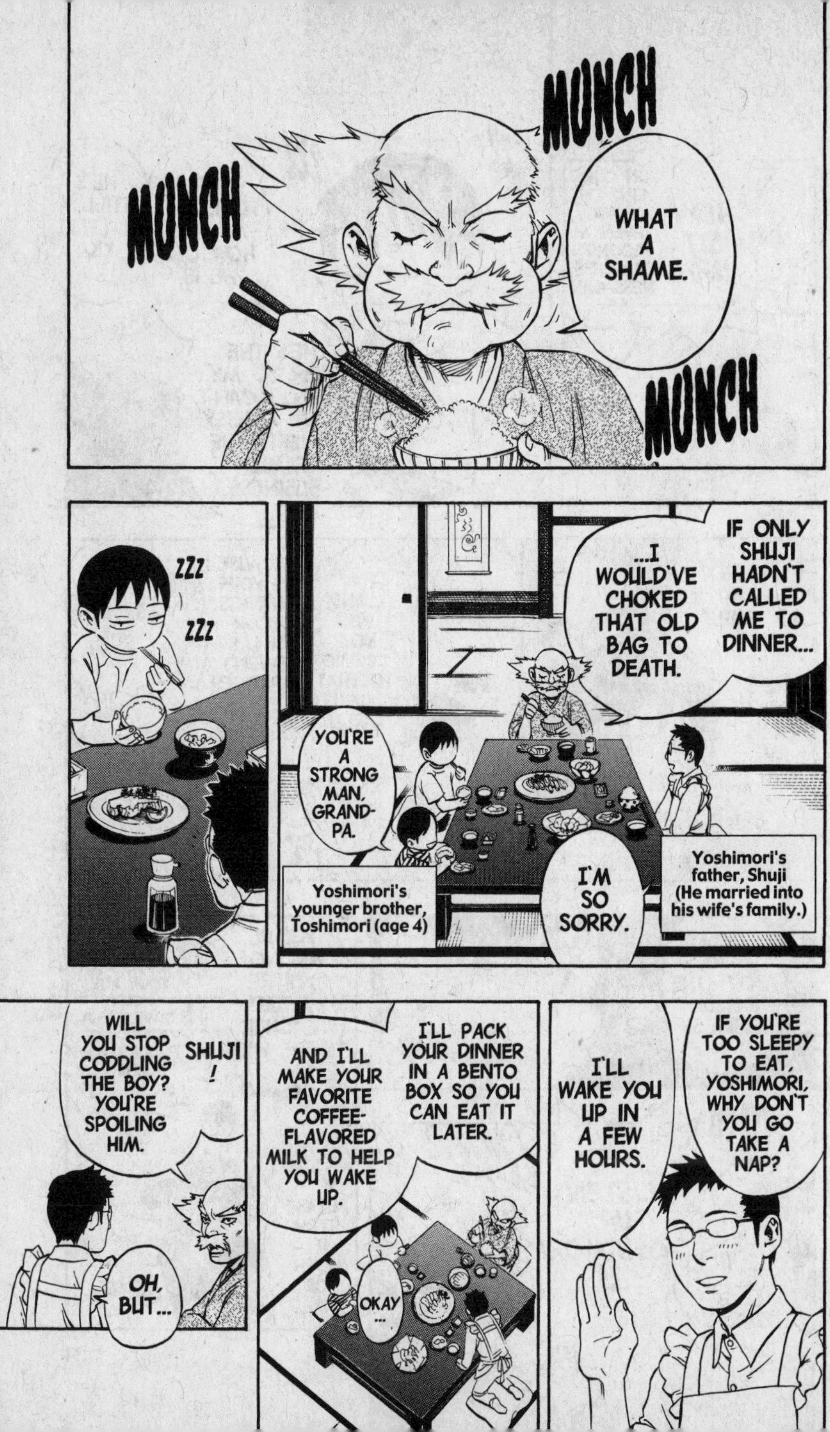
MUNCH
WHAT A SHAME.
MUNCH
MUNCH
IF ONLY SHUJI HADN'T CALLED ME TO DINNER...
...I WOULD'VE CHOKED THAT OLD BAG TO DEATH.
YOU'RE A STRONG MAN, GRANDPA.
Yoshimori's father, Shuji (He married into his wife's family.)
I'M SO SORRY.
Yoshimori's younger brother, Toshimori (age 4)
ZZZ
ZZZ
IF YOU'RE TOO SLEEPY TO EAT, YOSHIMORI, WHY DON'T YOU GO TAKE A NAP?
I'LL WAKE YOU UP IN A FEW HOURS.
I'LL PACK YOUR DINNER IN A BENTO BOX SO YOU CAN EAT IT LATER.
AND I'LL MAKE YOUR FAVORITE COFFEE-FLAVORED MILK TO HELP YOU WAKE UP.
OKAY...
SHUJI!
WILL YOU STOP CODDLING THE BOY? YOU'RE SPOILING HIM.
OH, BUT...

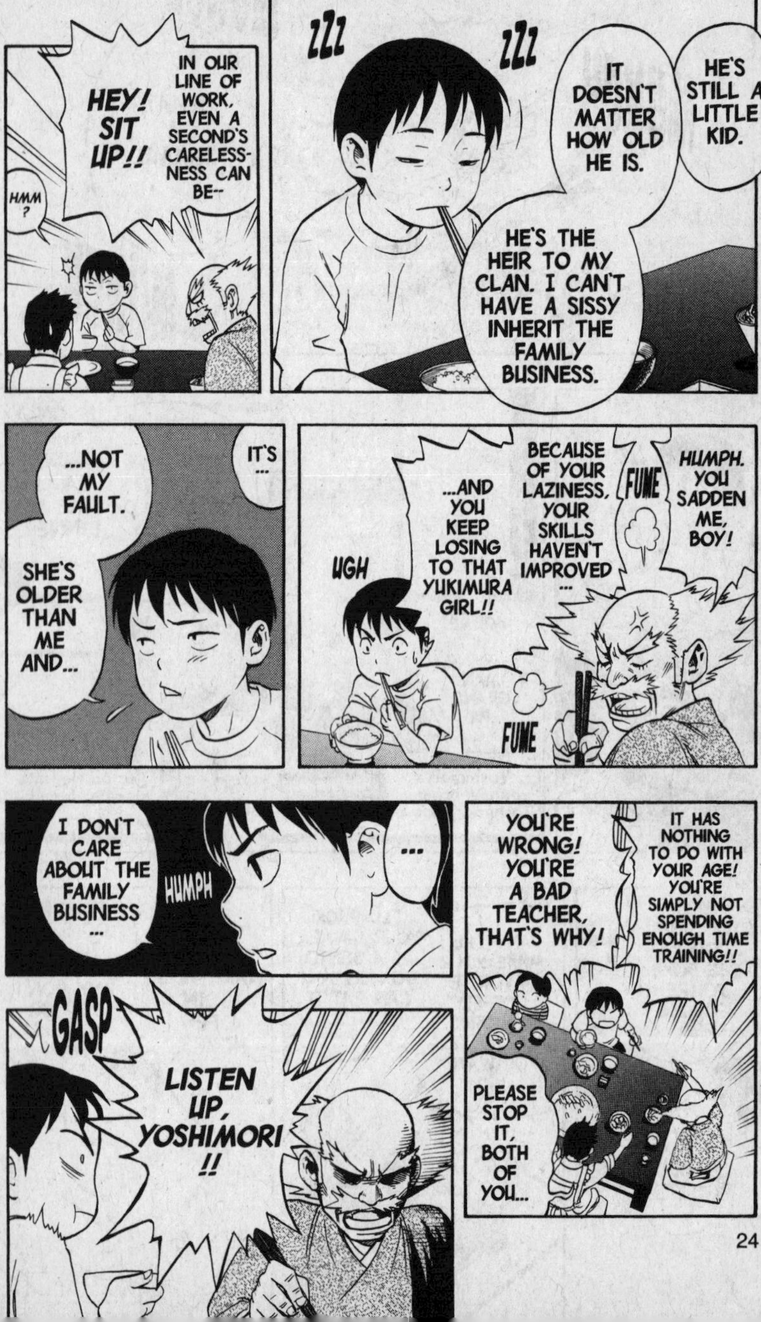
ZZZ
ZZZ
HE'S STILL A LITTLE KID.
IT DOESN'T MATTER HOW OLD HE IS.
HE'S THE HEIR TO MY CLAN. I CAN'T HAVE A SISSY INHERIT THE FAMILY BUSINESS.
IN OUR LINE OF WORK, EVEN A SECOND'S CARELESSNESS CAN BE--
HEY! SIT UP!!
HMM ?
HUMPH. YOU SADDEN ME, BOY!
FUME
BECAUSE OF YOUR LAZINESS, YOUR SKILLS HAVEN'T IMPROVED ...
...AND YOU KEEP LOSING TO THAT YUKIMURA GIRL!!
UGH
FUME
IT'S ...
...NOT MY FAULT.
SHE'S OLDER THAN ME AND...
IT HAS NOTHING TO DO WITH YOUR AGE! YOU'RE SIMPLY NOT SPENDING ENOUGH TIME TRAINING!!
YOU'RE WRONG! YOU'RE A BAD TEACHER, THAT'S WHY!
PLEASE STOP IT, BOTH OF YOU...
...
HUMPH
I DON'T CARE ABOUT THE FAMILY BUSINESS ...
GASP
LISTEN UP, YOSHIMORI !!

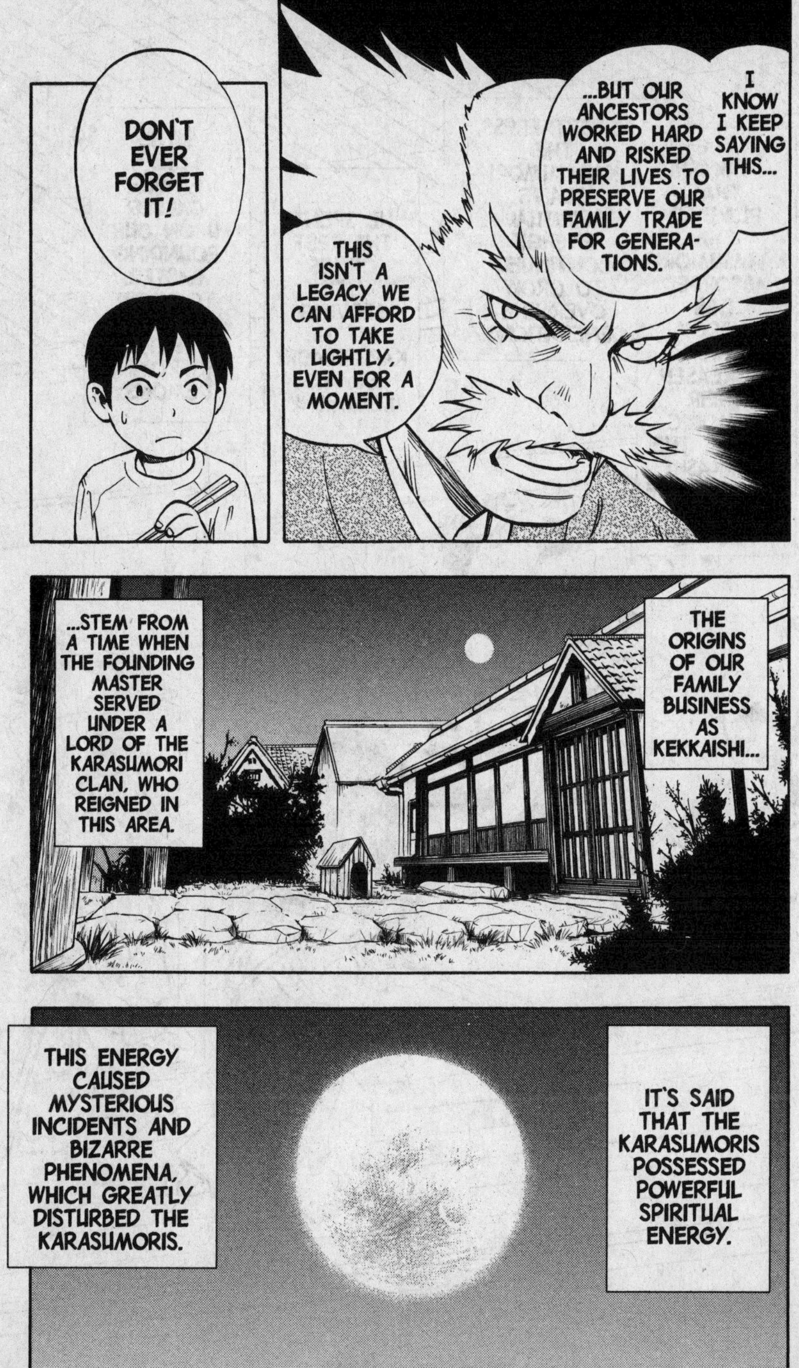
I KNOW I KEEP SAYING THIS...
...BUT OUR ANCESTORS WORKED HARD AND RISKED THEIR LIVES TO PRESERVE OUR FAMILY TRADE FOR GENERATIONS.
THIS ISN'T A LEGACY WE CAN AFFORD TO TAKE LIGHTLY, EVEN FOR A MOMENT.
DON'T EVER FORGET IT!
THE ORIGINS OF OUR FAMILY BUSINESS AS KEKKAISHI...
...STEM FROM A TIME WHEN THE FOUNDING MASTER SERVED UNDER A LORD OF THE KARASUMORI CLAN, WHO REIGNED IN THIS AREA.
IT'S SAID THAT THE KARASUMORIS POSSESSED POWERFUL SPIRITUAL ENERGY.
THIS ENERGY CAUSED MYSTERIOUS INCIDENTS AND BIZARRE PHENOMENA, WHICH GREATLY DISTURBED THE KARASUMORIS.

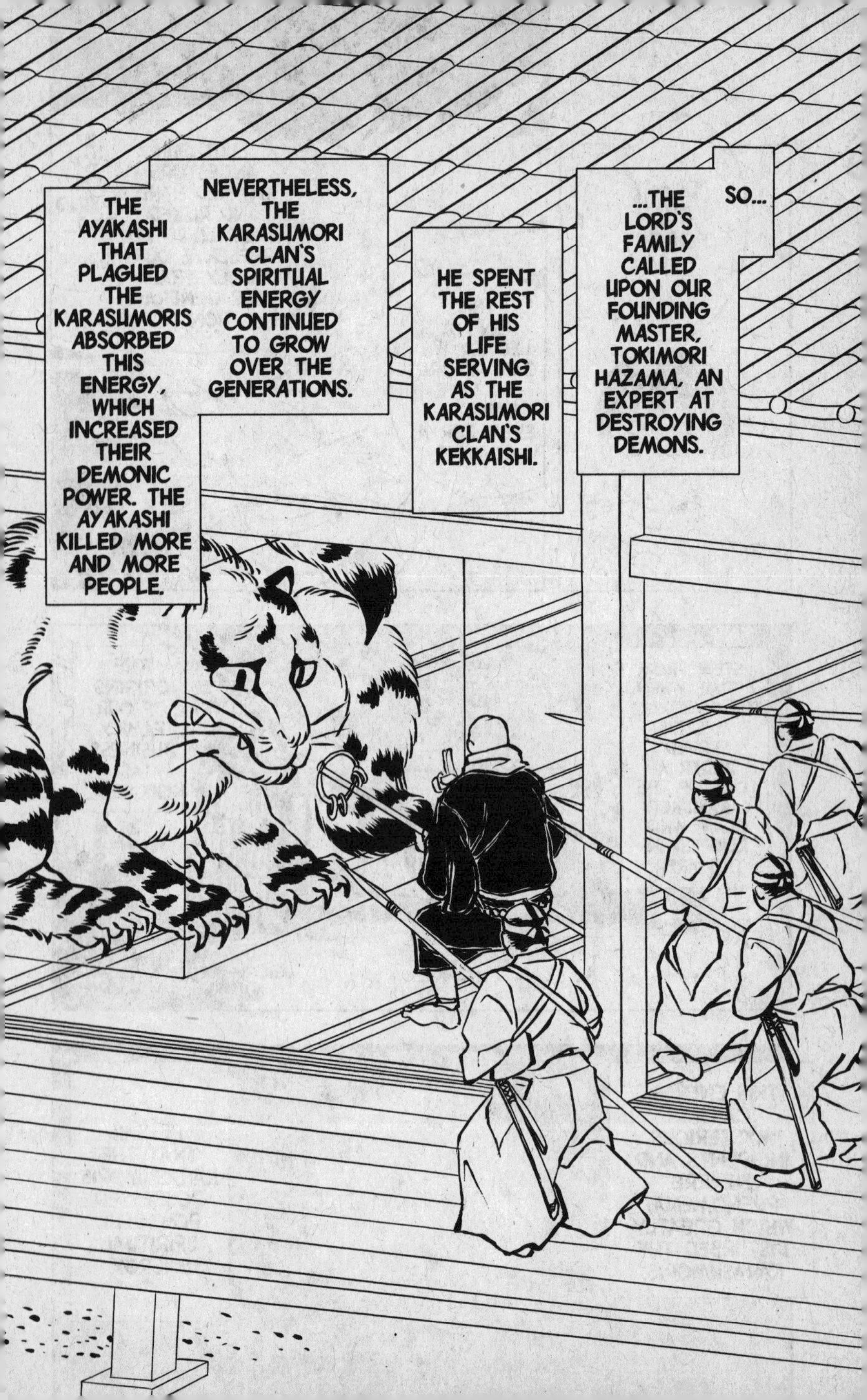
SO...
...THE LORD'S FAMILY CALLED UPON OUR FOUNDING MASTER, TOKIMORI HAZAMA, AN EXPERT AT DESTROYING DEMONS.
HE SPENT THE REST OF HIS LIFE SERVING AS THE KARASUMORI CLAN'S KEKKAISHI.
NEVERTHELESS, THE KARASUMORI CLAN'S SPIRITUAL ENERGY CONTINUED TO GROW OVER THE GENERATIONS.
THE AYAKASHI THAT PLAGUED THE KARASUMORIS ABSORBED THIS ENERGY, WHICH INCREASED THEIR DEMONIC POWER. THE AYAKASHI KILLED MORE AND MORE PEOPLE.

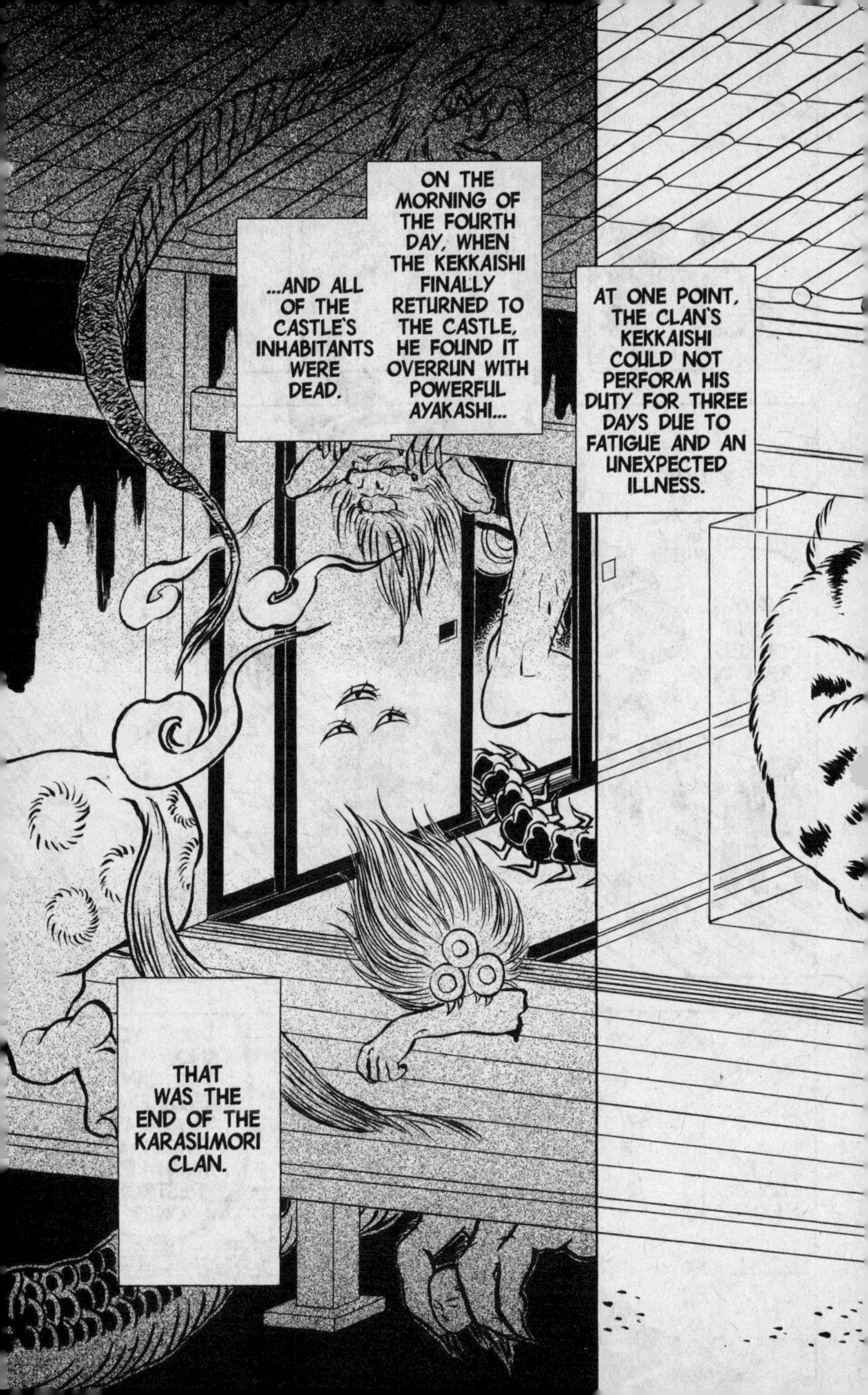
AT ONE POINT, THE CLAN'S KEKKAISHI COULD NOT PERFORM HIS DUTY FOR THREE DAYS DUE TO FATIGUE AND AN UNEXPECTED ILLNESS.
ON THE MORNING OF THE FOURTH DAY, WHEN THE KEKKAISHI FINALLY RETURNED TO THE CASTLE, HE FOUND IT OVERRUN WITH POWERFUL AYAKASHI...
...AND ALL OF THE CASTLE'S INHABITANTS WERE DEAD.
THAT WAS THE END OF THE KARASUMORI CLAN.

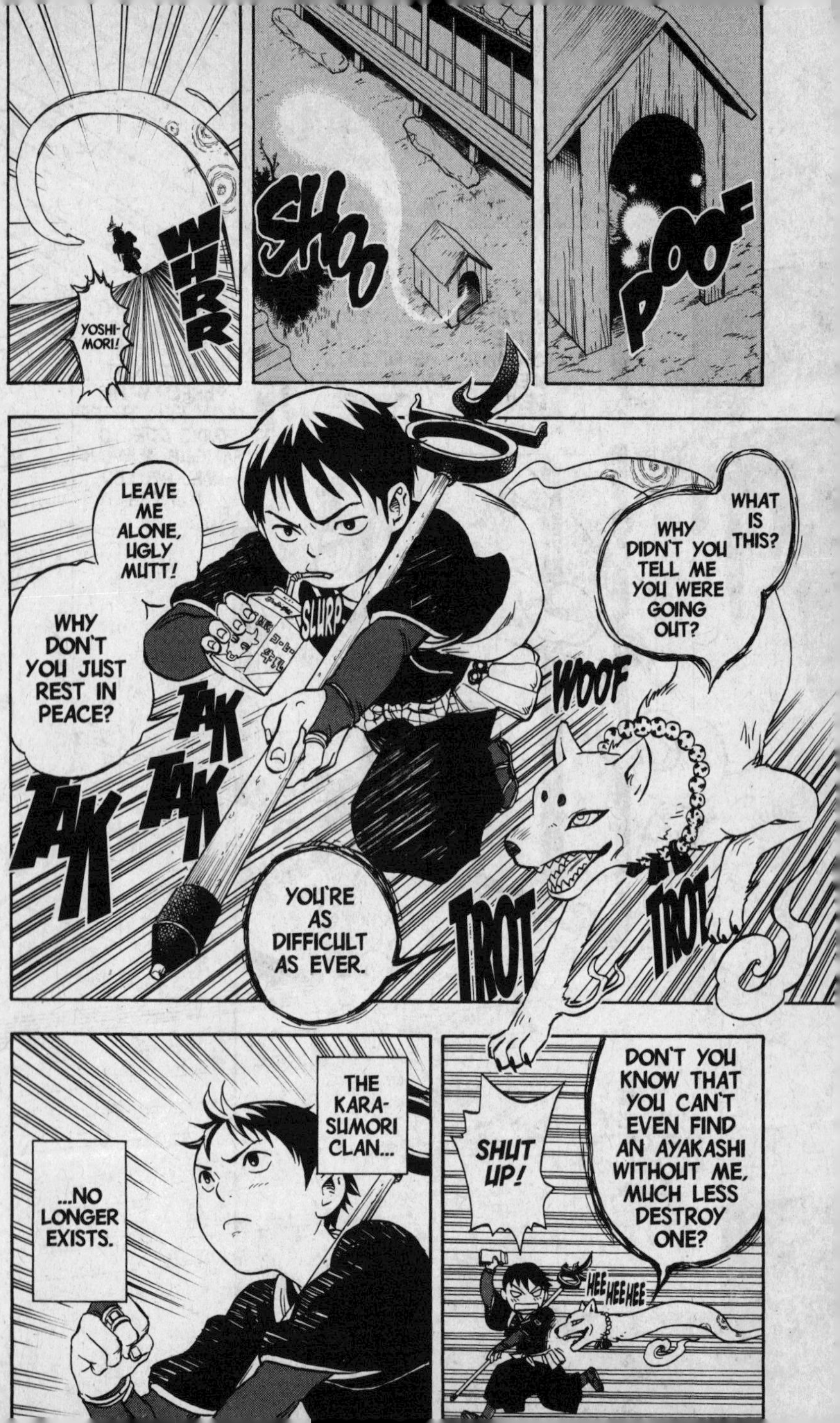
POOF
SHOOO
WHRR
YOSHIMORI!
WHAT IS THIS?
WHY DIDN'T YOU TELL ME YOU WERE GOING OUT?
WOOF
LEAVE ME ALONE, UGLY MUTT!
SLURP
WHY DON'T YOU JUST REST IN PEACE?
TROT
TROT
YOU'RE AS DIFFICULT AS EVER.
TAK
TAK
TAK
DON'T YOU KNOW THAT YOU CAN'T EVEN FIND AN AYAKASHI WITHOUT ME, MUCH LESS DESTROY ONE?
SHUT UP!
HEE HEE HEE
THE KARASUMORI CLAN...
...NO LONGER EXISTS.

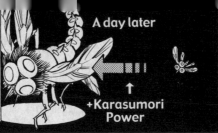

THEIR SPIRITUAL POWER, HOWEVER, IS STILL ALIVE AND KICKING.
A day later
+Karasumori Power
IF YOU LEAVE THE SMALL AYAKASHI ALONE, THEY WILL EVOLVE INTO SOMETHING VERY DANGEROUS.
THEREFORE, ACCORDING TO GRANDPA, MY FAMILY GETS SUPPORT FROM A SHADOWY RESIDENTS' ASSOCIATION...
...AND CONTINUES TO PLY THE FAMILY TRADE EVERY SINGLE DAY.
A SMALL SHRINE DEDICATED TO THE SOULS OF THE KARASUMORI CLAN--THE SOURCE OF THEIR SPIRITUAL ENERGY--IS LOCATED...
ALLEY-OOP.
...DEEP UNDERGROUND...
...BENEATH MY SCHOOL...
...WHERE THE CASTLE ONCE STOOD.
Private School
Karasumori Academy of Junior and Senior High Schools
Entrance to High School Building
Entrance to Junior High School
UH.
TOKINE!
DID YOU NOTICE ANYTHING OUT OF THE ORDINARY?
TK
TK TK

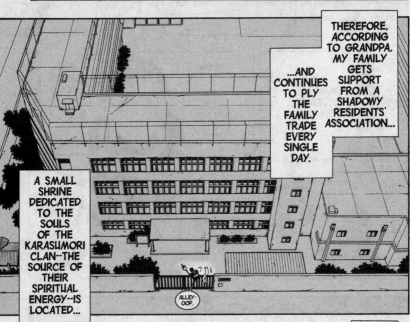

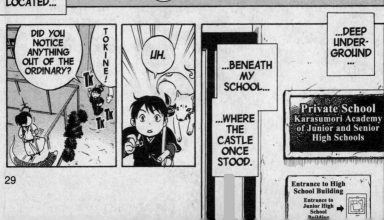

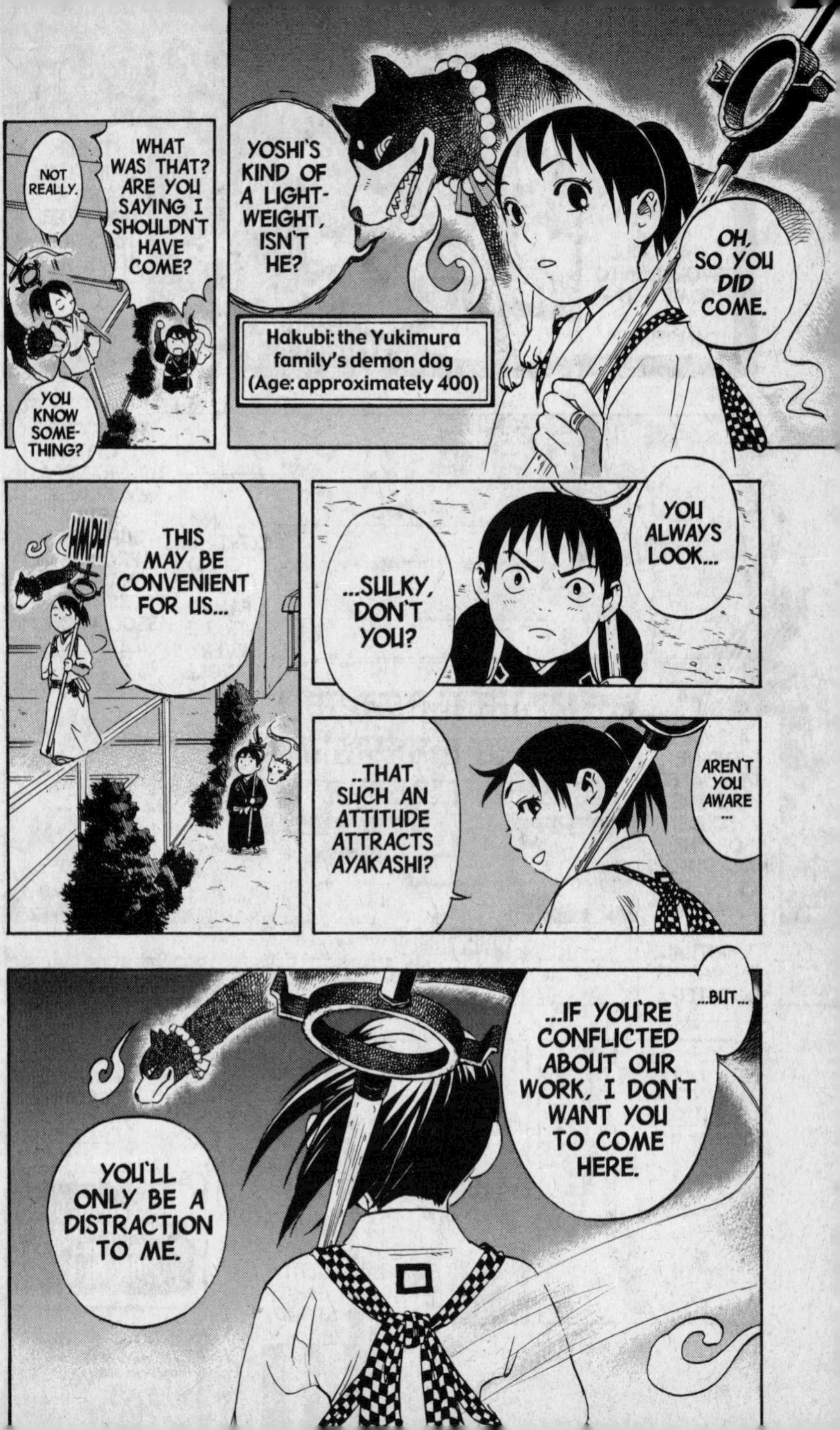
OH, SO YOU DID COME.
YOSHI'S KIND OF A LIGHTWEIGHT, ISN'T HE?
Hakubi: the Yukimura family's demon dog (Age: approximately 400)
WHAT WAS THAT? ARE YOU SAYING I SHOULDN'T HAVE COME?
NOT REALLY.
YOU KNOW SOMETHING?
YOU ALWAYS LOOK...
...SULKY, DON'T YOU?
AREN'T YOU AWARE...
..THAT SUCH AN ATTITUDE ATTRACTS AYAKASHI?
HMPH
THIS MAY BE CONVENIENT FOR US...
...BUT...
...IF YOU'RE CONFLICTED ABOUT OUR WORK, I DON'T WANT YOU TO COME HERE.
YOU'LL ONLY BE A DISTRACTION TO ME.

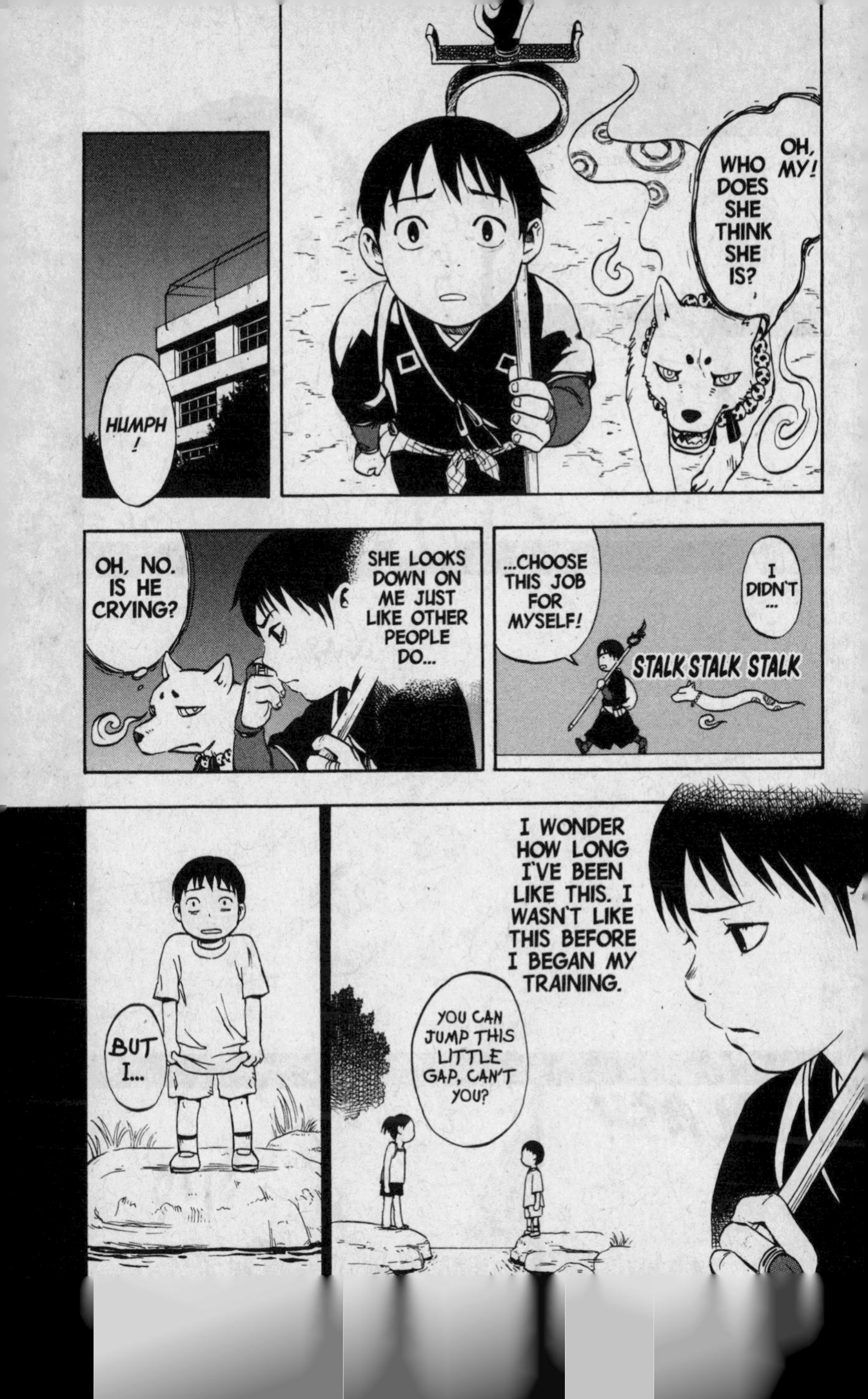
OH, MY! WHO DOES SHE THINK SHE IS?
HUMPH!
I DIDN'T ...
...CHOOSE THIS JOB FOR MYSELF!
STALK STALK STALK
SHE LOOKS DOWN ON ME JUST LIKE OTHER PEOPLE DO...
OH, NO. IS HE CRYING?
I WONDER HOW LONG I'VE BEEN LIKE THIS. I WASN'T LIKE THIS BEFORE I BEGAN MY TRAINING.
YOU CAN JUMP THIS LITTLE GAP, CAN'T YOU?
BUT I...

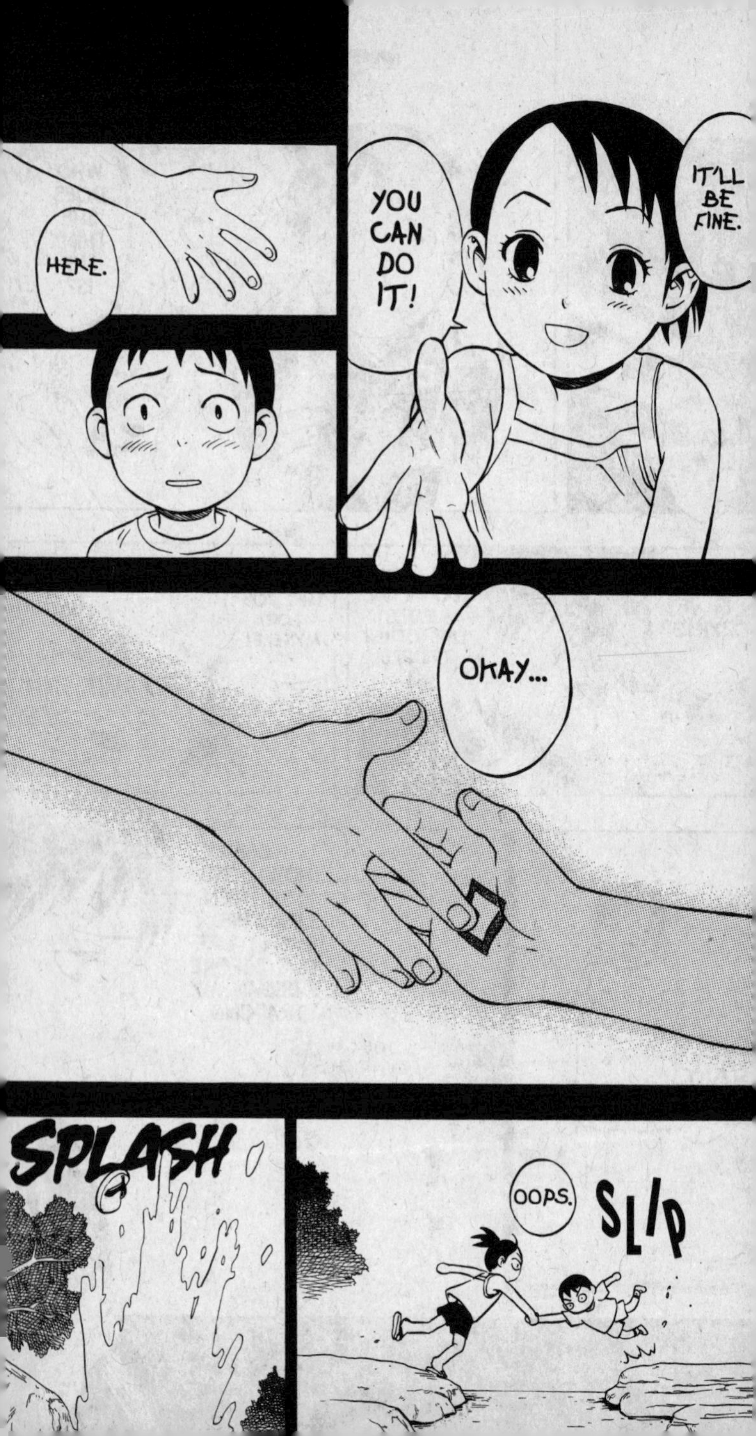
IT'LL BE FINE.
YOU CAN DO IT!
HERE.
OKAY...
OOPS.
SLIP
SPLASH

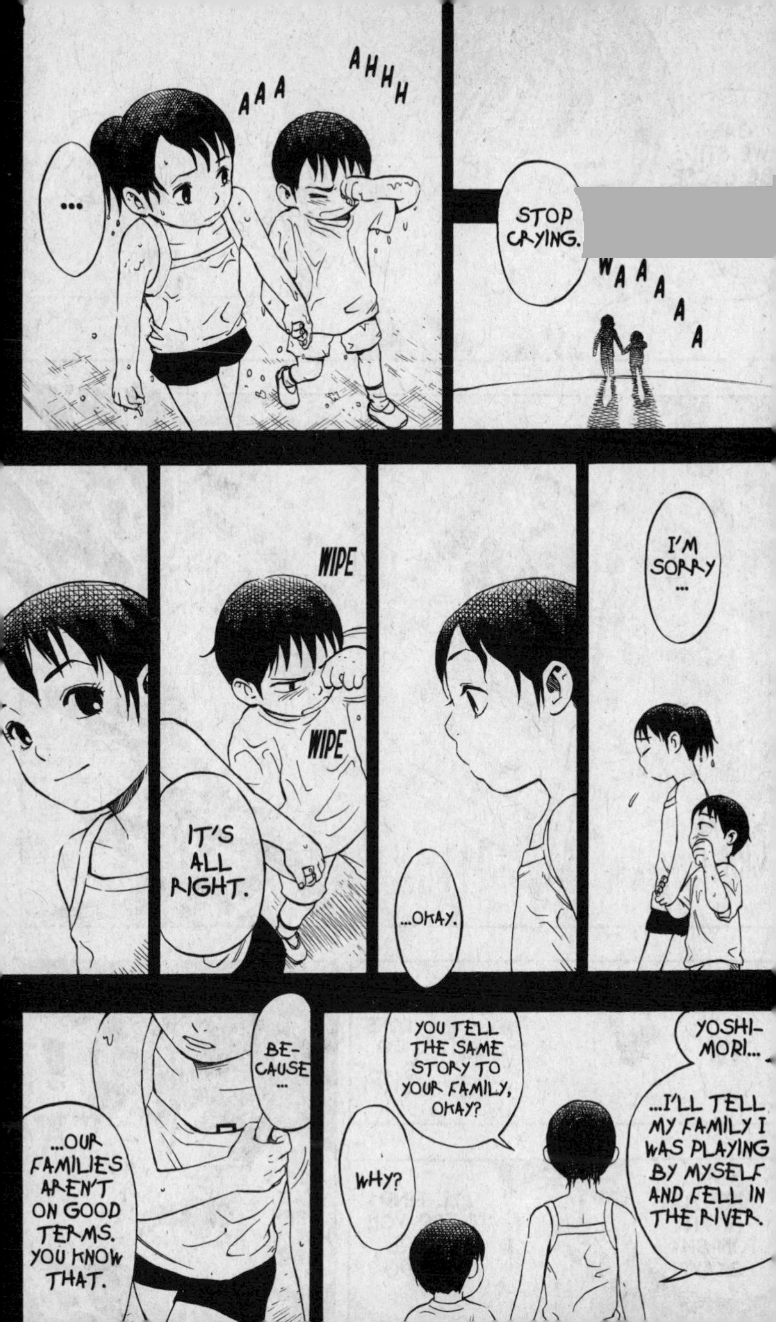
STOP CRYING.
WAAAAAA
AHHH
AAA
...
I'M SORRY...
...OKAY.
WIPE
WIPE
IT'S ALL RIGHT.
YOSHI-MORI...
...I'LL TELL MY FAMILY I WAS PLAYING BY MYSELF AND FELL IN THE RIVER.
YOU TELL THE SAME STORY TO YOUR FAMILY, OKAY?
WHY?
BE-CAUSE...
...OUR FAMILIES AREN'T ON GOOD TERMS. YOU KNOW THAT.

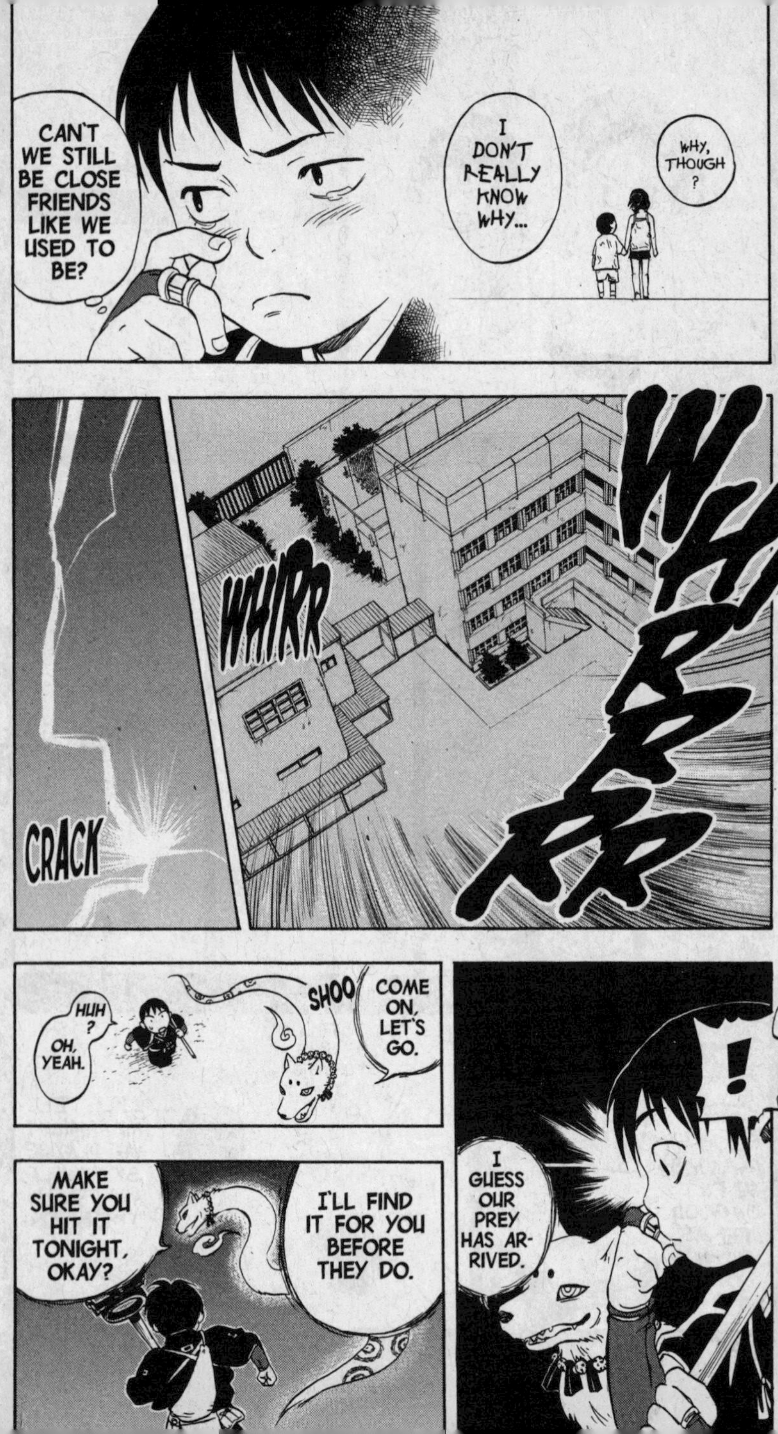
WHY, THOUGH?
I DON'T REALLY KNOW WHY...
CAN'T WE STILL BE CLOSE FRIENDS LIKE WE USED TO BE?
WHIRRR
WHIRR
CRACK
!
I GUESS OUR PREY HAS AR-RIVED.
COME ON, LET'S GO.
SHOO
HUH? OH, YEAH.
I'LL FIND IT FOR YOU BEFORE THEY DO.
MAKE SURE YOU HIT IT TONIGHT, OKAY?

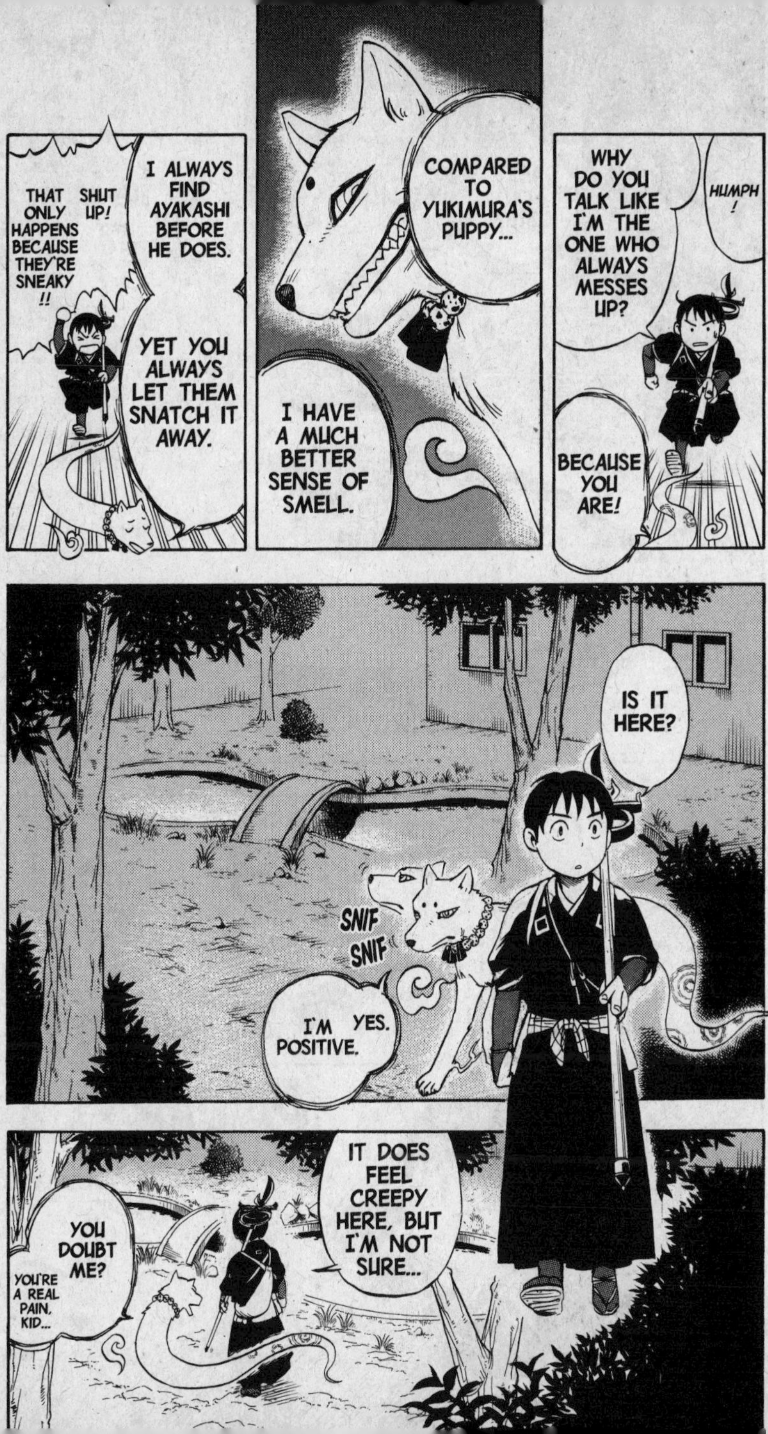
HUMPH!
WHY DO YOU TALK LIKE I'M THE ONE WHO ALWAYS MESSES UP?
BECAUSE YOU ARE!
COMPARED TO YUKIMURA'S PUPPY...
I HAVE A MUCH BETTER SENSE OF SMELL.
I ALWAYS FIND AYAKASHI BEFORE HE DOES.
YET YOU ALWAYS LET THEM SNATCH IT AWAY.
SHUT UP!
THAT ONLY HAPPENS BECAUSE THEY'RE SNEAKY!!
IS IT HERE?
SNIF SNIF
YES.
I'M POSITIVE.
IT DOES FEEL CREEPY HERE, BUT I'M NOT SURE...
YOU DOUBT ME?
YOU'RE A REAL PAIN, KID...

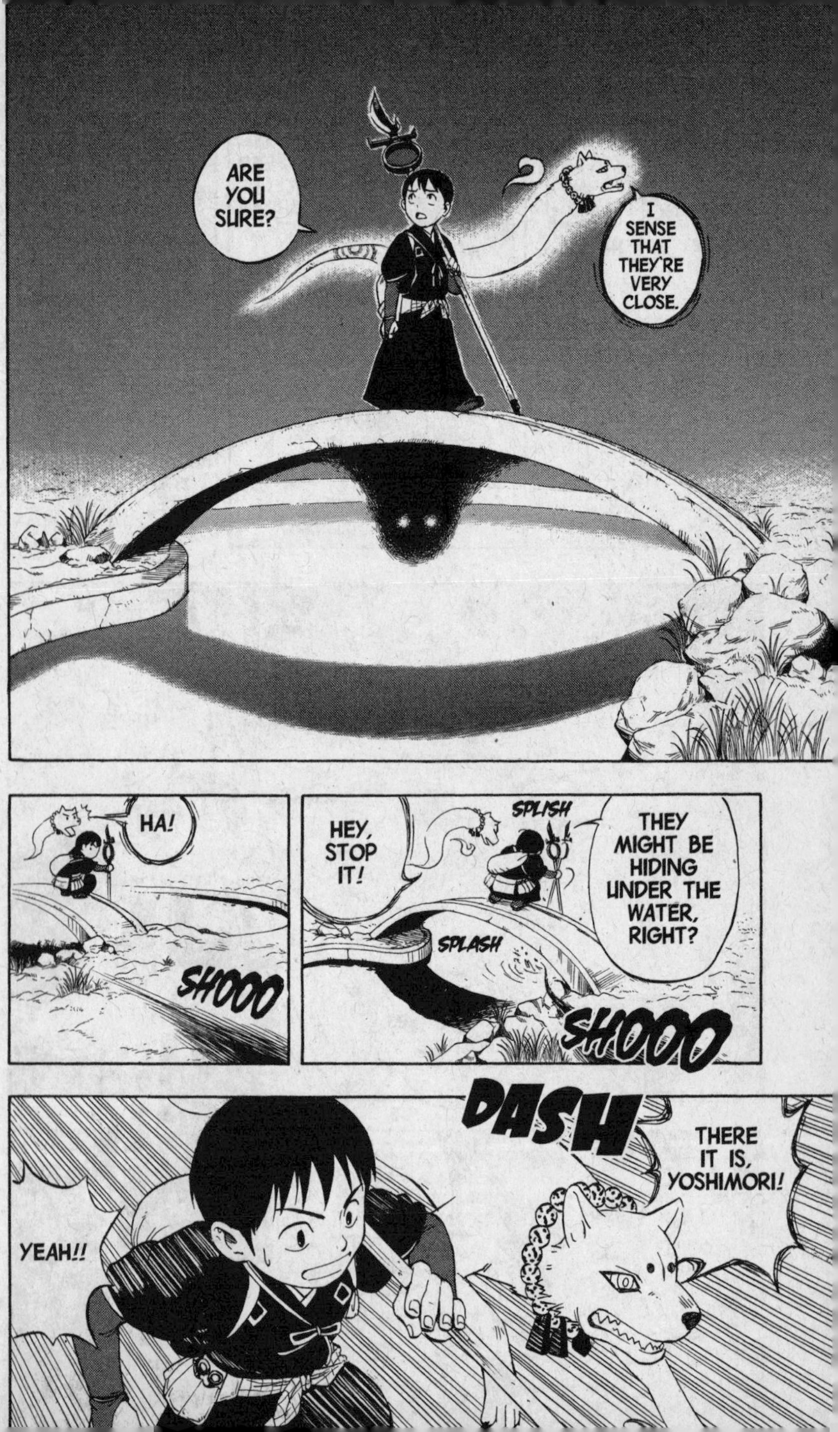
I SENSE THAT THEY'RE VERY CLOSE.
ARE YOU SURE?
SPLISH
THEY MIGHT BE HIDING UNDER THE WATER, RIGHT?
HEY, STOP IT!
SPLASH
SHOOO
HA!
SHOOO
DASH
THERE IT IS, YOSHIMORI!
YEAH!!

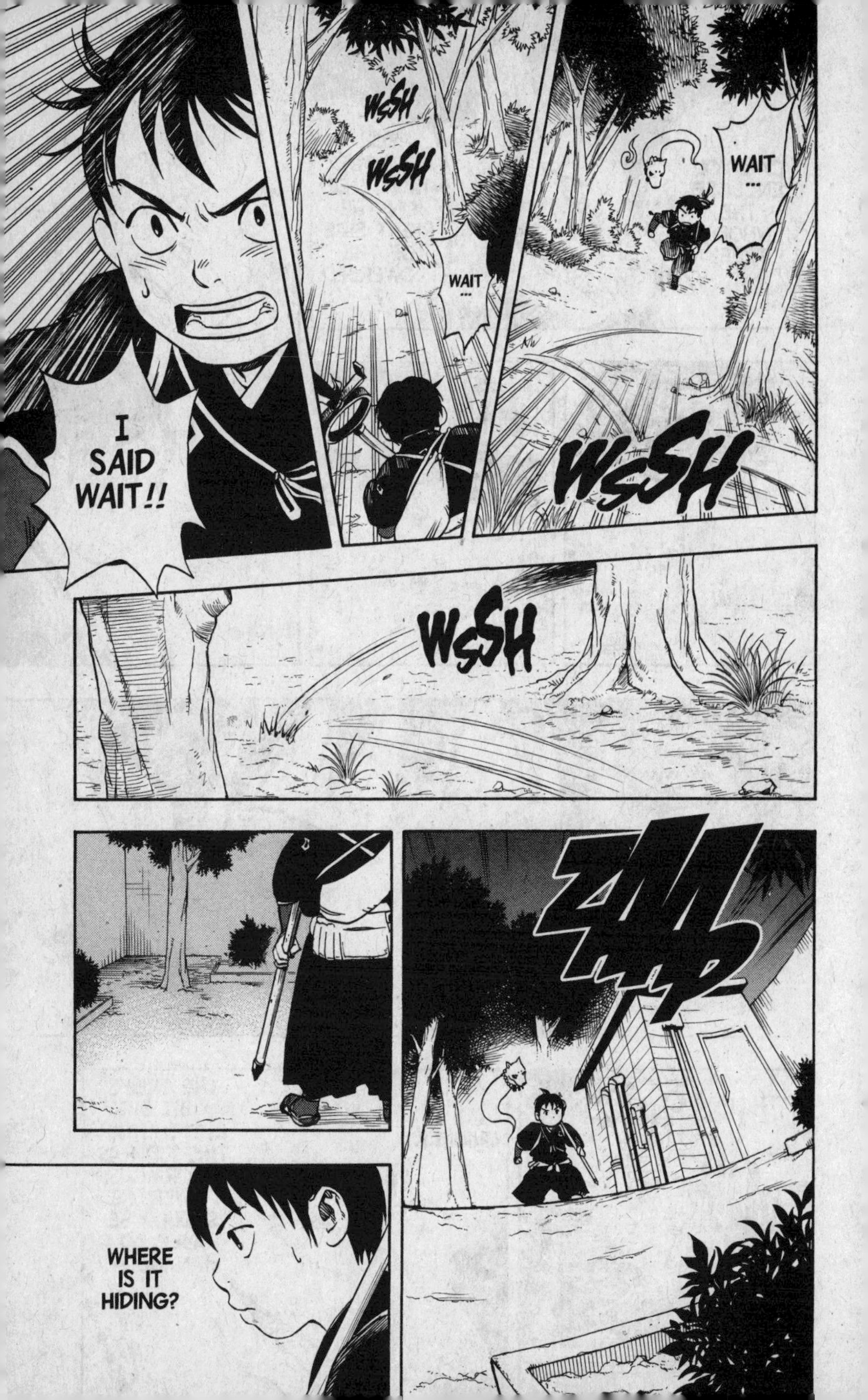
WAIT ...
WSSH
WSSH
WSSH
WAIT ...
I SAID WAIT!!
WSSH
ZIP
WHERE IS IT HIDING?

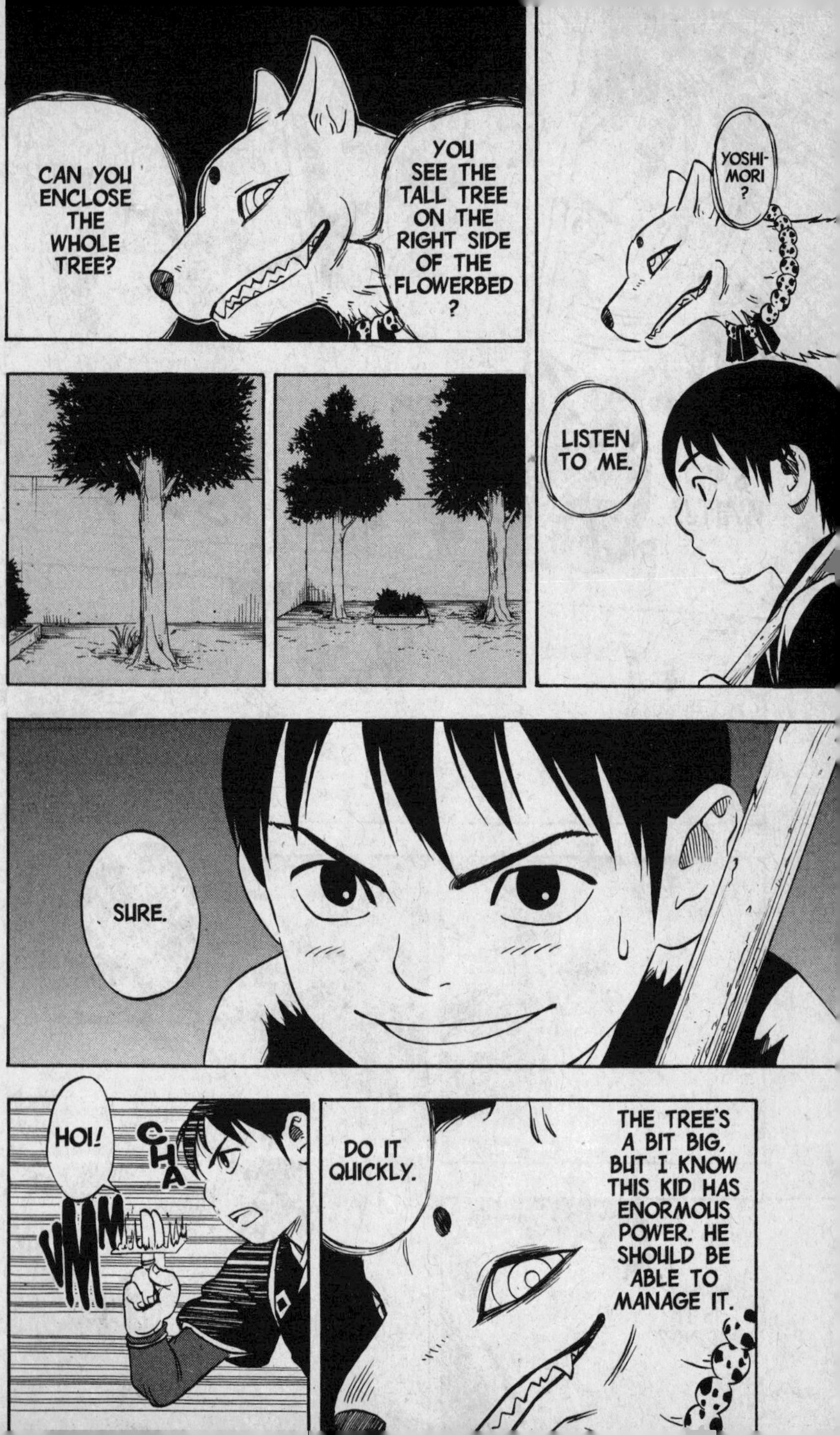
YOSHIMORI?
LISTEN TO ME.
YOU SEE THE TALL TREE ON THE RIGHT SIDE OF THE FLOWERBED?
CAN YOU ENCLOSE THE WHOLE TREE?
SURE.
THE TREE'S A BIT BIG, BUT I KNOW THIS KID HAS ENORMOUS POWER. HE SHOULD BE ABLE TO MANAGE IT.
DO IT QUICKLY.
HOI!
CHA
VMM

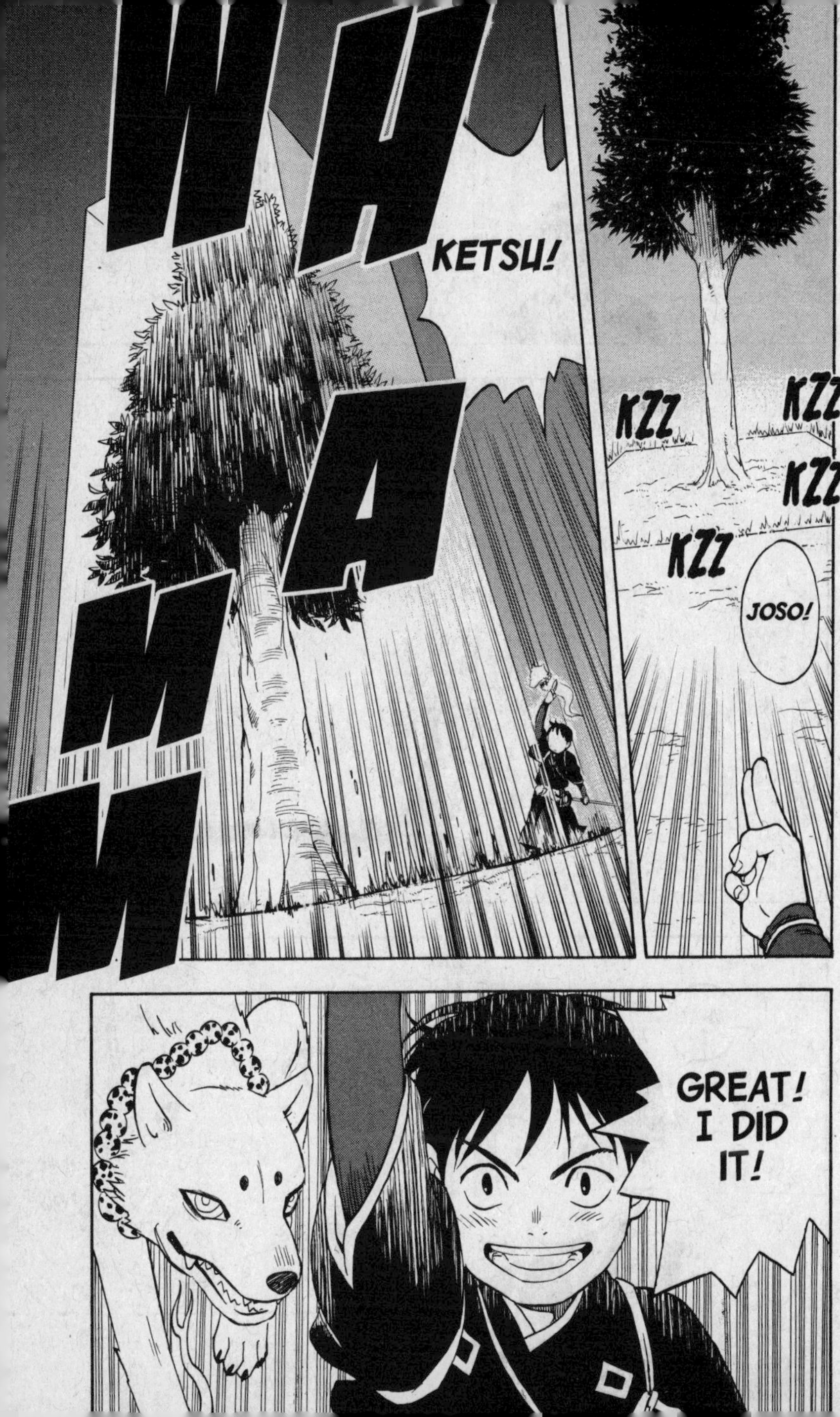
KZZ
KZZ
KZZ
KZZ
JOSO!
WHAMM
KETSU!
GREAT! I DID IT!

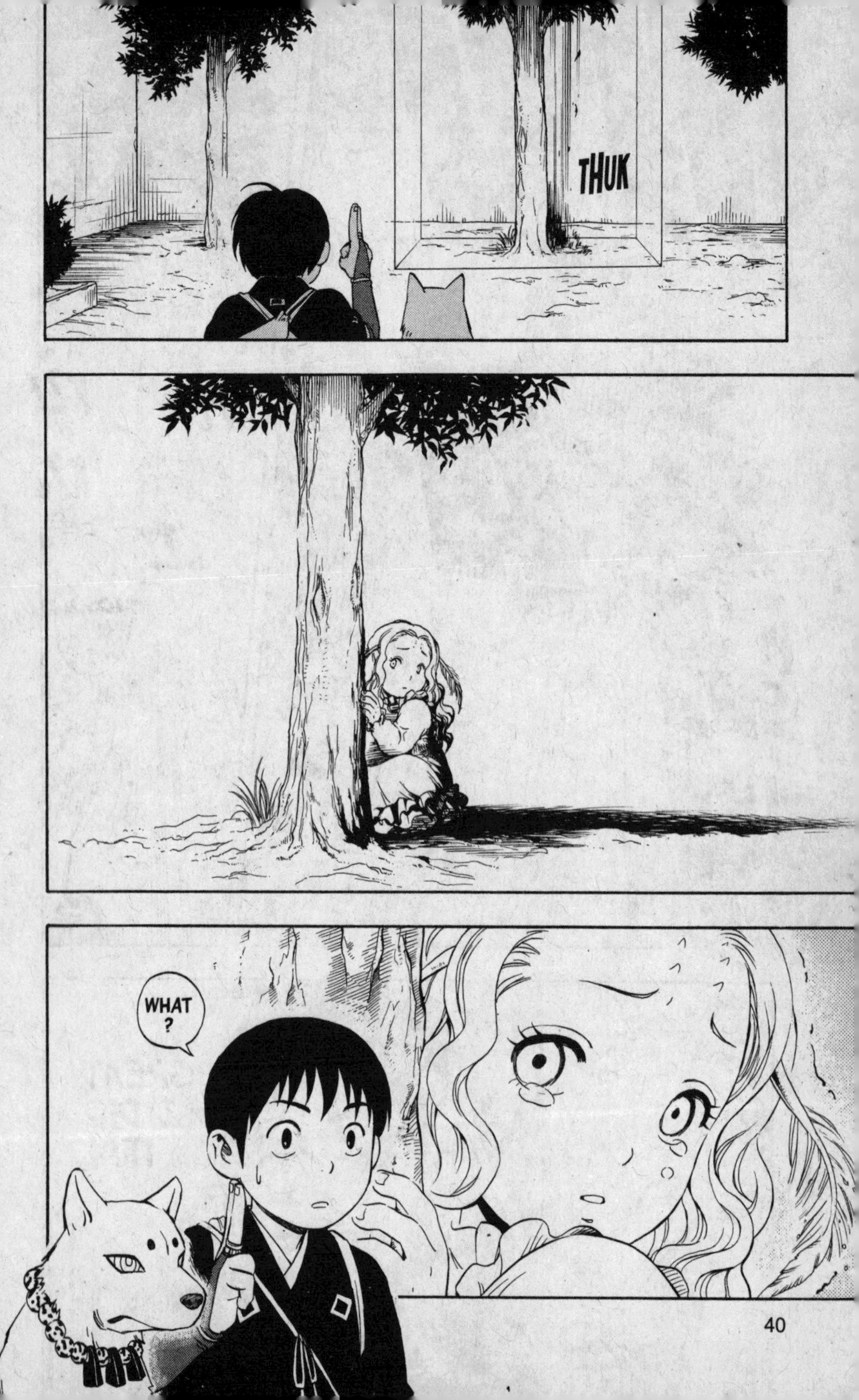
THUK
WHAT?

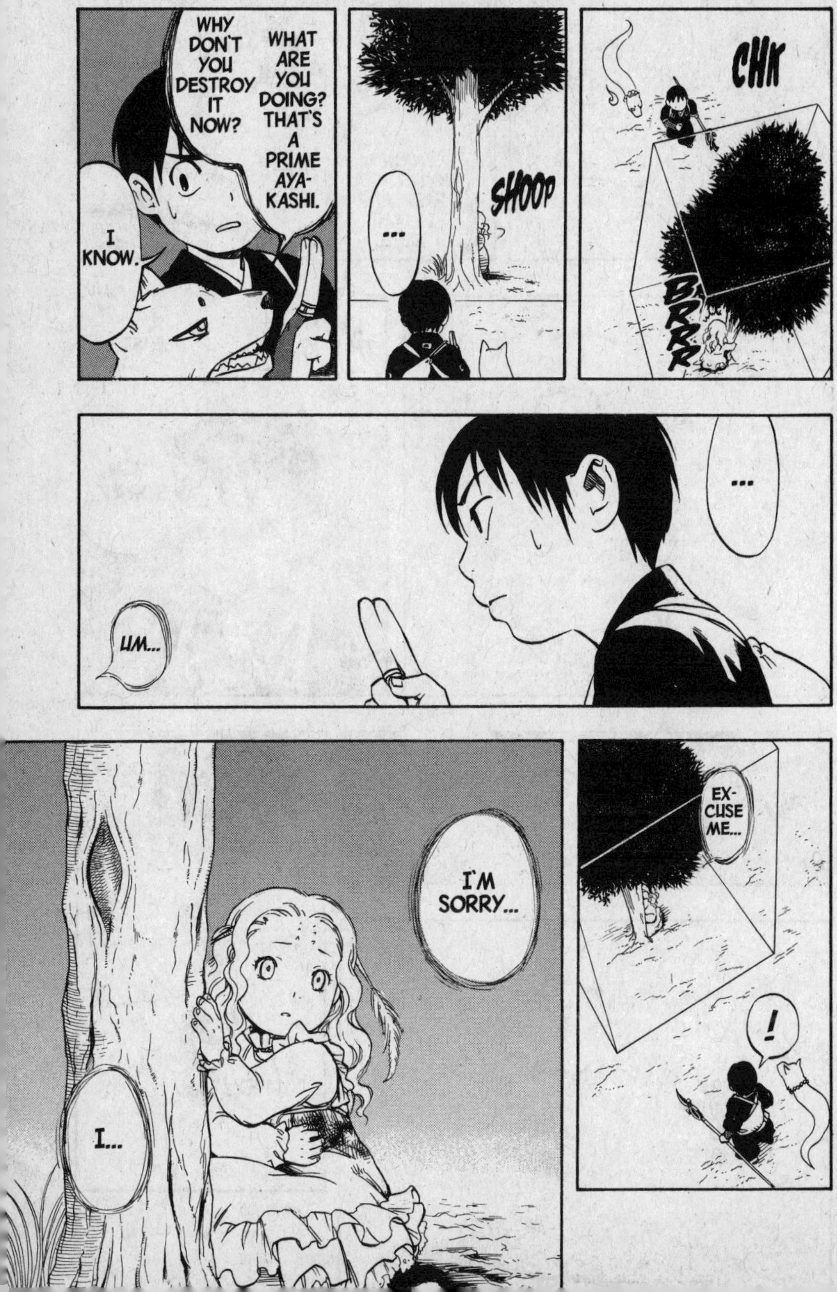
CHK
BRRR
SHOOP
...
WHAT ARE YOU DOING? THAT'S A PRIME AYA-KASHI.
WHY DON'T YOU DESTROY IT NOW?
I KNOW.
...
UM...
EX-CUSE ME...
!
I'M SORRY...
I...

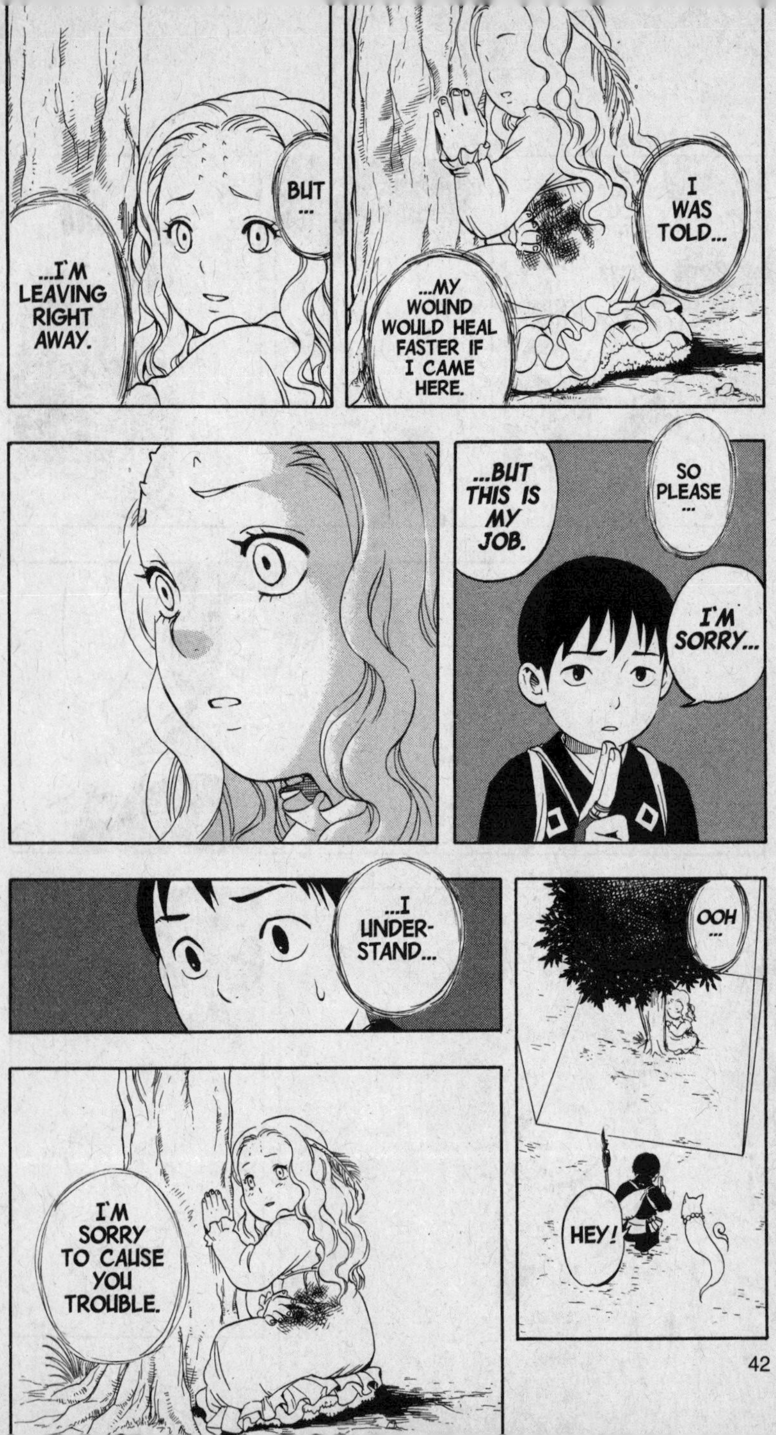
I WAS TOLD...
...MY WOUND WOULD HEAL FASTER IF I CAME HERE.
BUT ...
...I'M LEAVING RIGHT AWAY.
SO PLEASE ...
...BUT THIS IS MY JOB.
I'M SORRY...
OOH ...
HEY!
...I UNDER-STAND...
I'M SORRY TO CAUSE YOU TROUBLE.

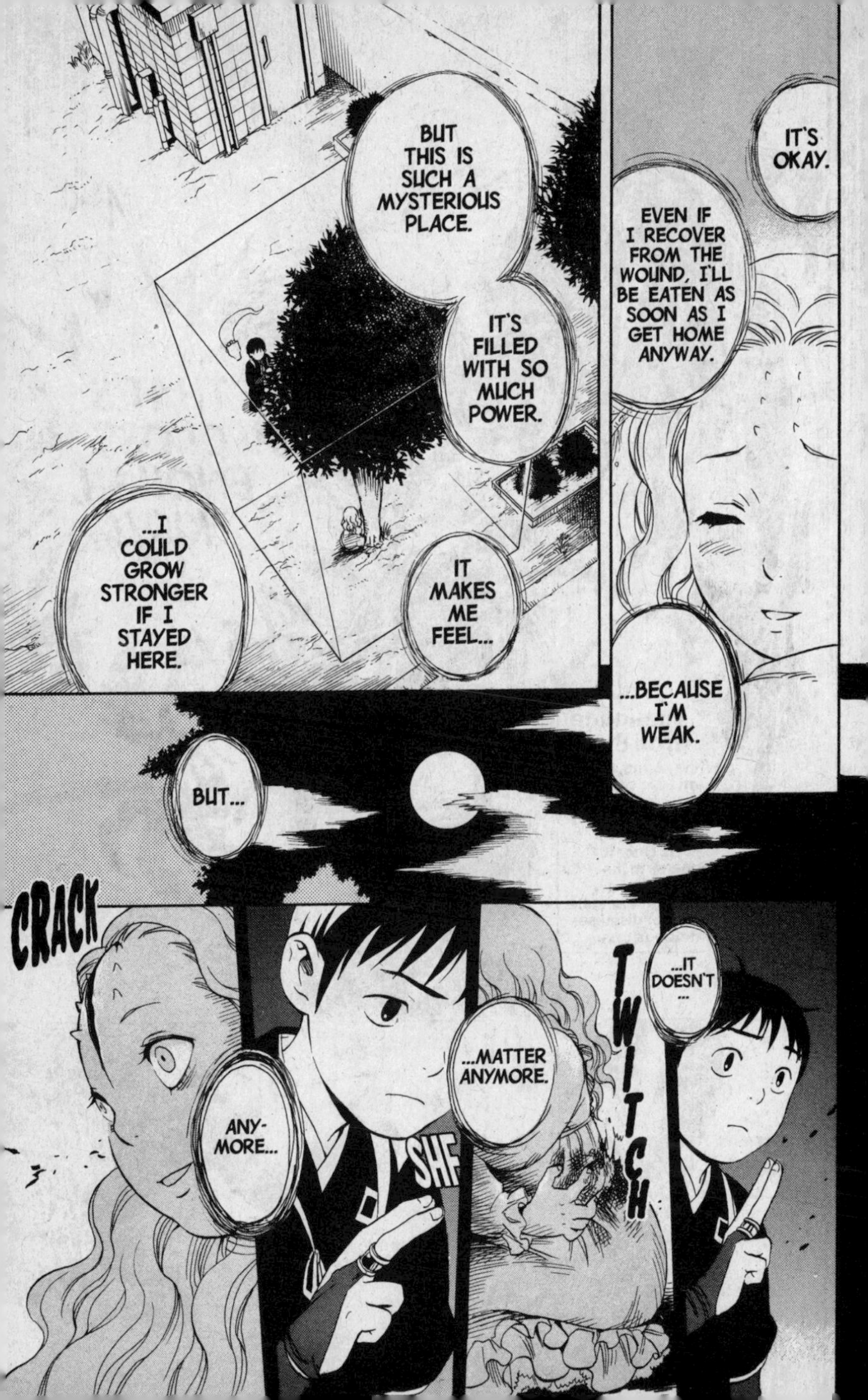
IT'S OKAY.
EVEN IF I RECOVER FROM THE WOUND, I'LL BE EATEN AS SOON AS I GET HOME ANYWAY.
...BECAUSE I'M WEAK.
BUT THIS IS SUCH A MYSTERIOUS PLACE.
IT'S FILLED WITH SO MUCH POWER.
IT MAKES ME FEEL...
...I COULD GROW STRONGER IF I STAYED HERE.
BUT...
...IT DOESN'T ...
TWITCH
...MATTER ANYMORE.
SHF
ANY-MORE...
CRACK

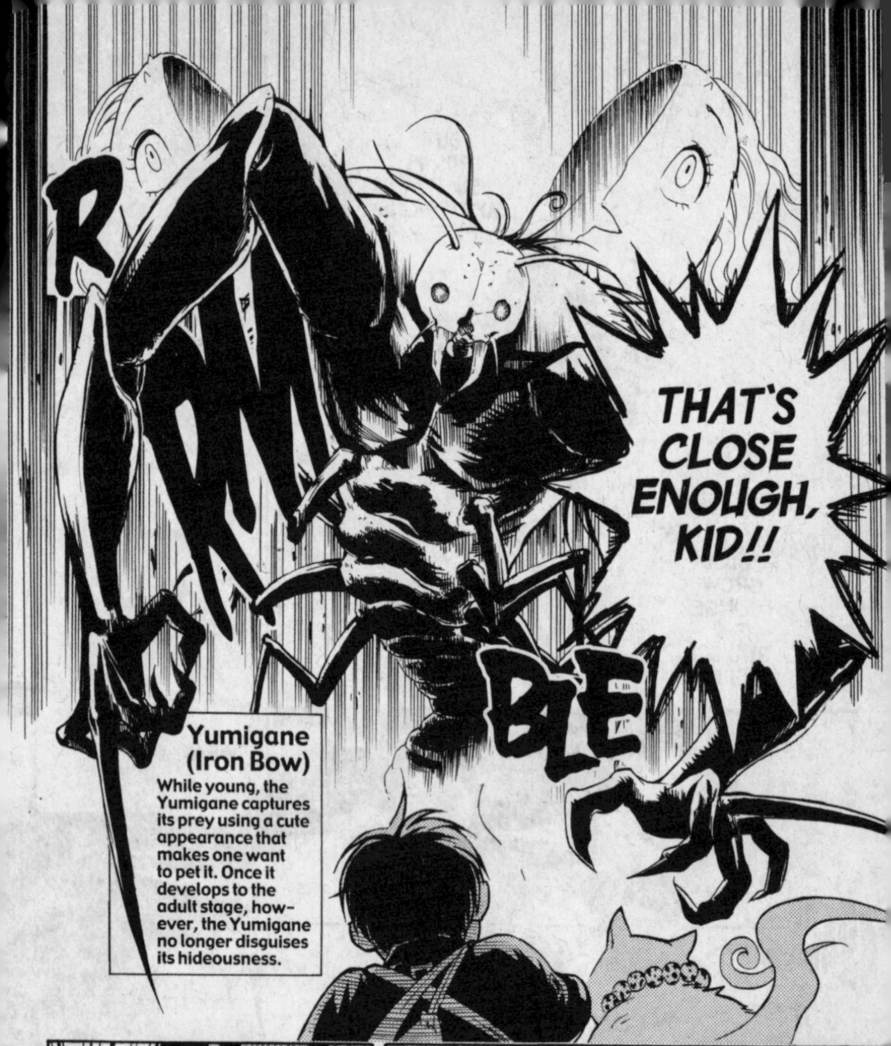
RRRR
THAT'S CLOSE ENOUGH, KID!!
BLEAAAA
Yumigane (Iron Bow)
While young, the Yumigane captures its prey using a cute appearance that makes one want to pet it. Once it develops to the adult stage, however, the Yumigane no longer disguises its hideousness.
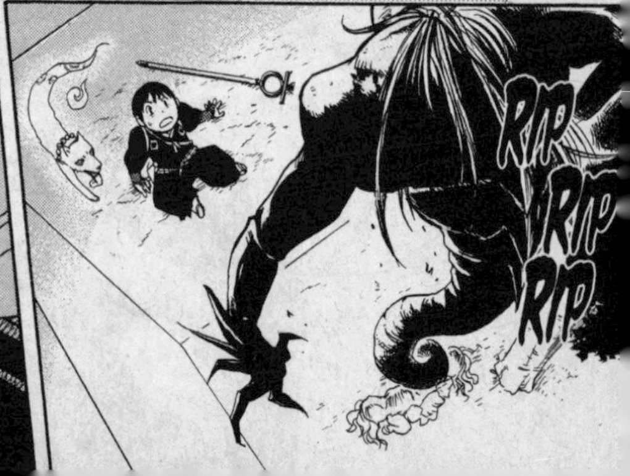
RIP RIP RIP RIP
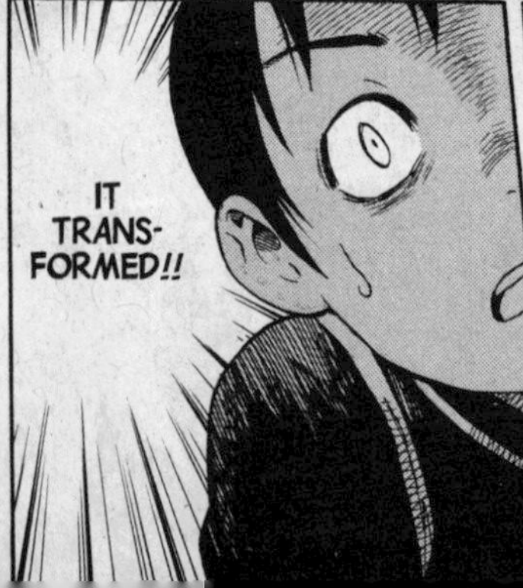
IT TRANS-FORMED!!

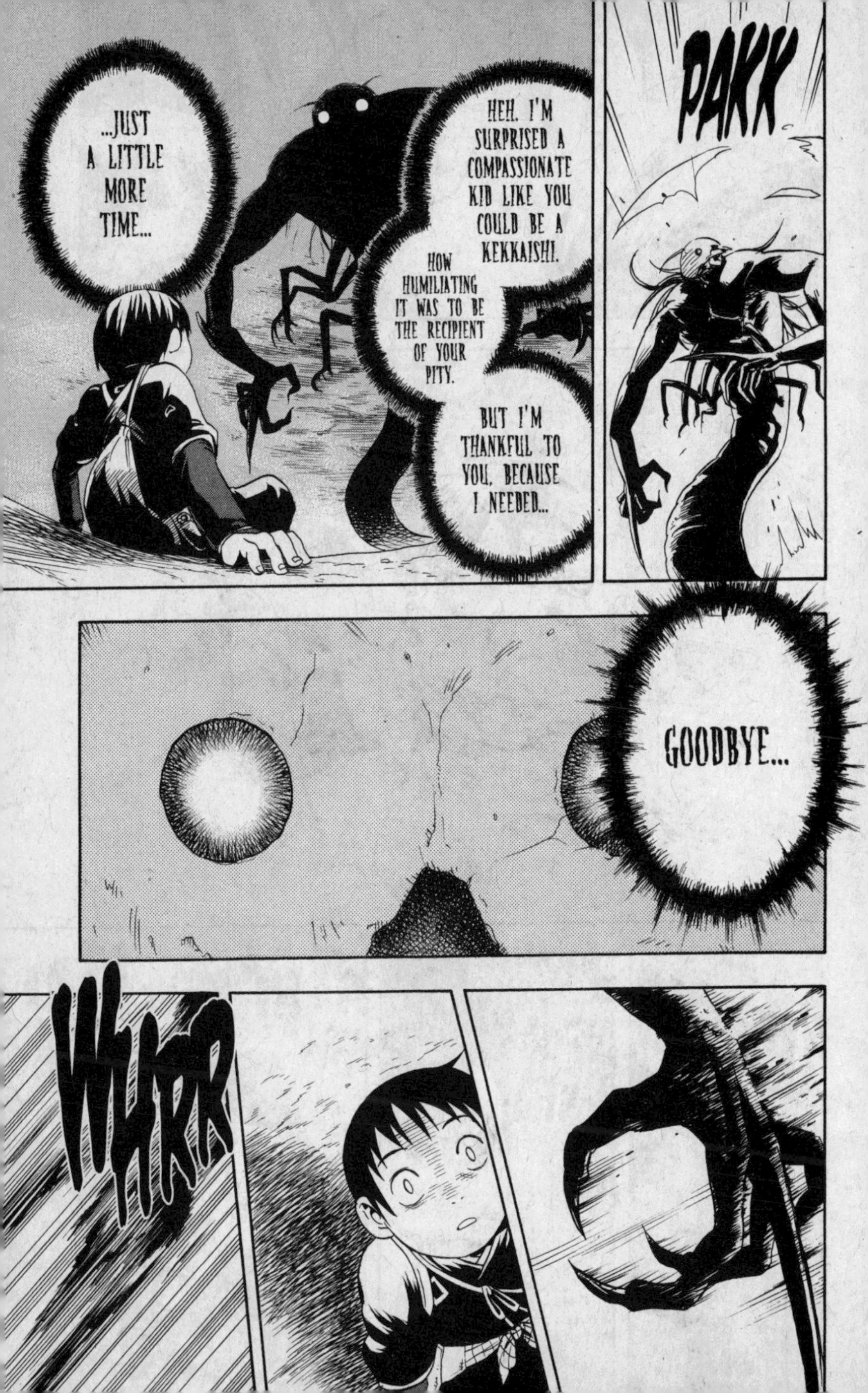
PAKK
HEH. I'M SURPRISED A COMPASSIONATE KID LIKE YOU COULD BE A KEKKAISHI.
HOW HUMILIATING IT WAS TO BE THE RECIPIENT OF YOUR PITY.
BUT I'M THANKFUL TO YOU, BECAUSE I NEEDED...
...JUST A LITTLE MORE TIME...
GOODBYE...
WHRR

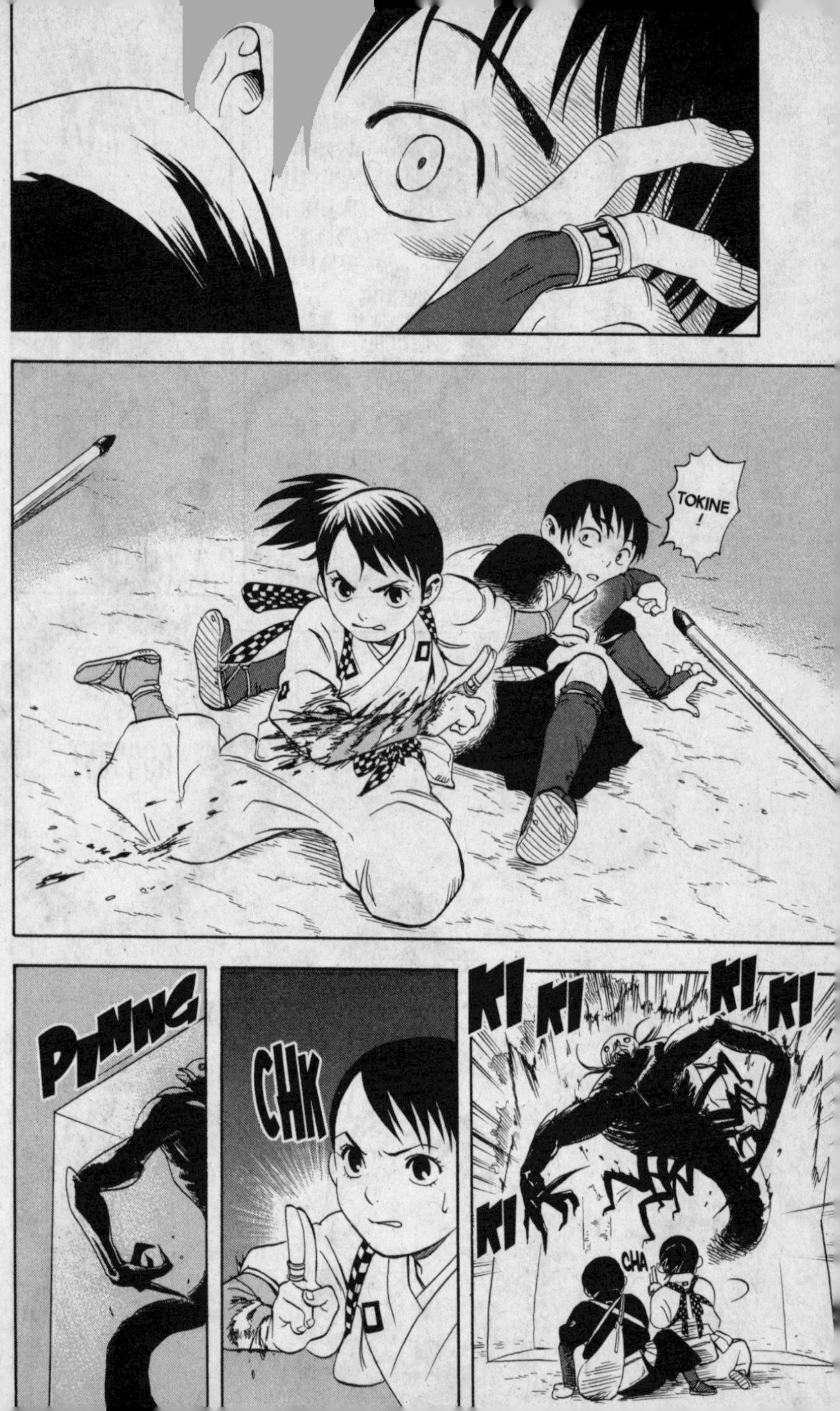
TOKINE!
KI KI KI KI
KI
CHA
CHK
PTWNG

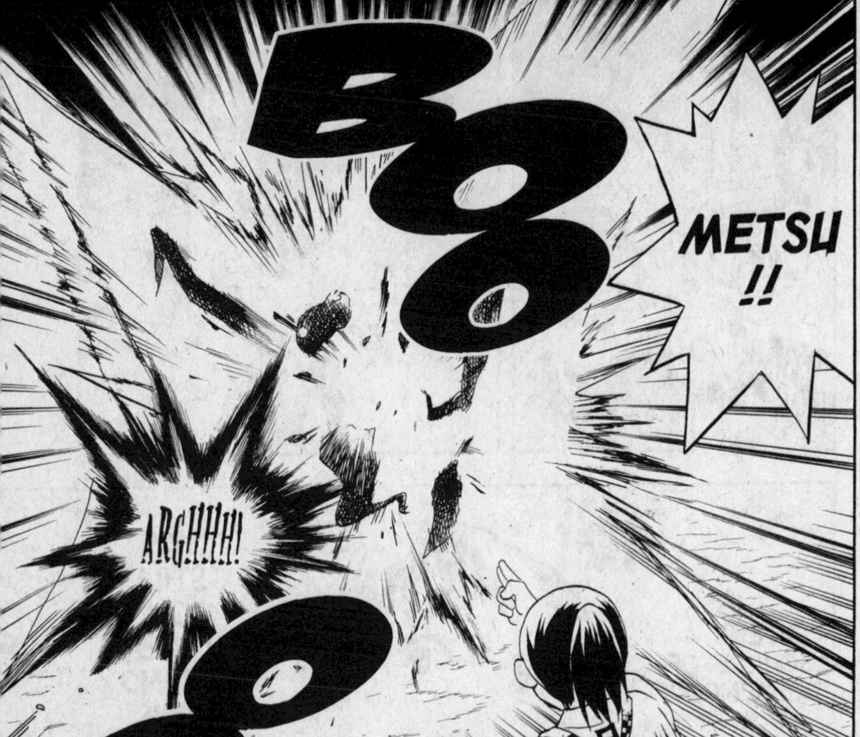
METSU !!
ARGHHH!
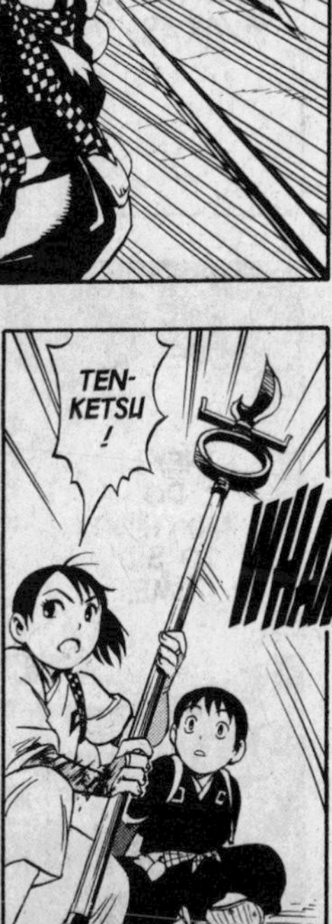
TEN-
KETSU
!
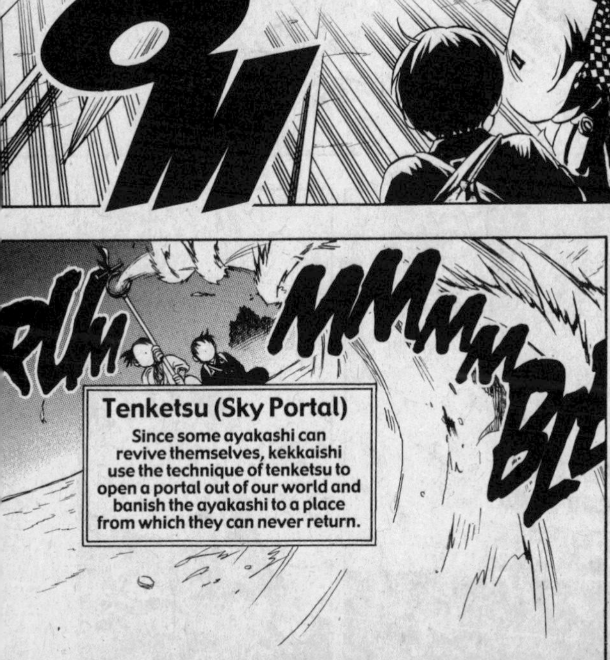
Tenketsu (Sky Portal)
Since some ayakashi can revive themselves, kekkaishi use the technique of tenketsu to open a portal out of our world and banish the ayakashi to a place from which they can never return.

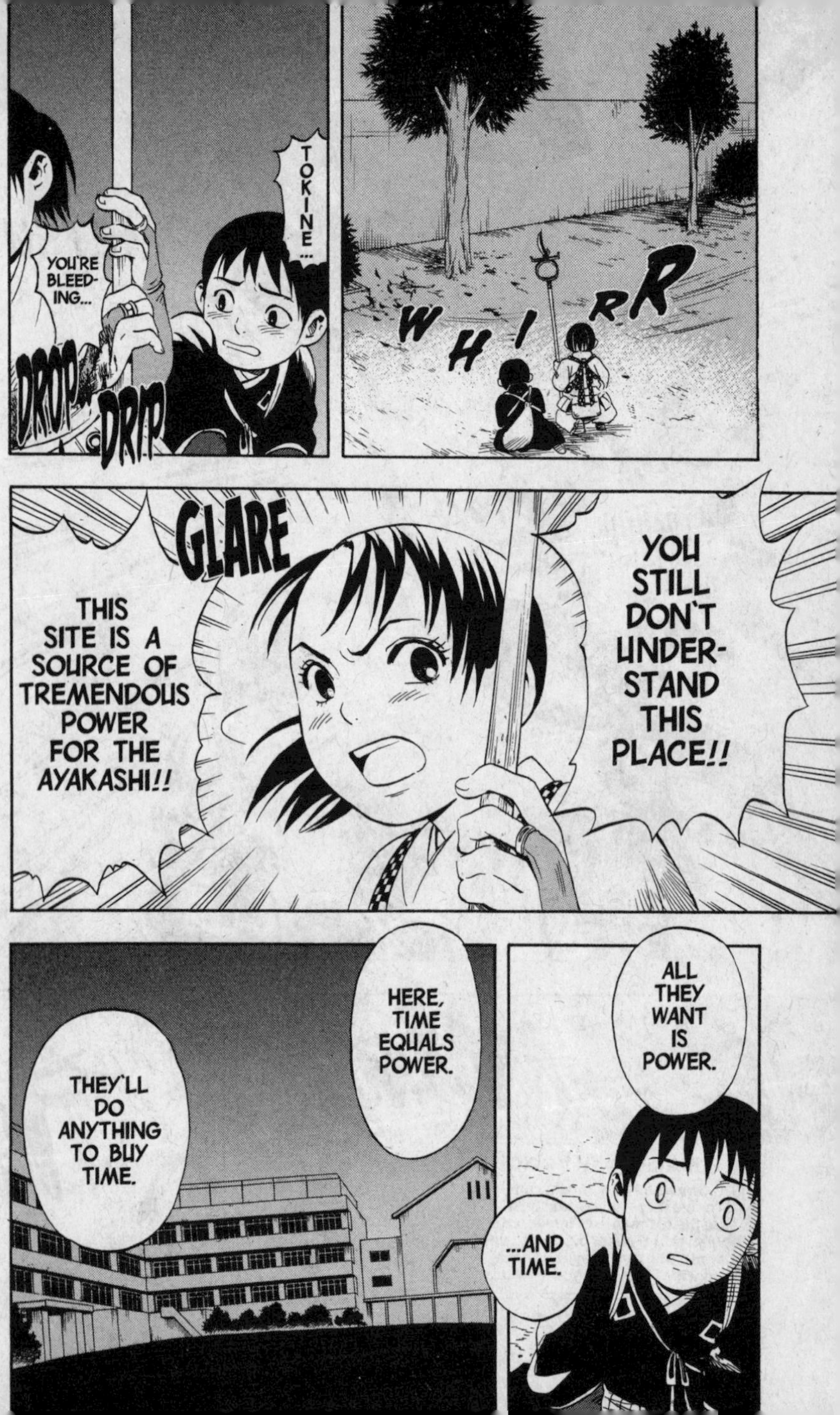
WHIRRR
TOKINE...
YOU'RE BLEED-ING...
DROP
DRIP
YOU STILL DON'T UNDER-STAND THIS PLACE!!
GLARE
THIS SITE IS A SOURCE OF TREMENDOUS POWER FOR THE AYAKASHI!!
ALL THEY WANT IS POWER.
...AND TIME.
HERE, TIME EQUALS POWER.
THEY'LL DO ANYTHING TO BUY TIME.

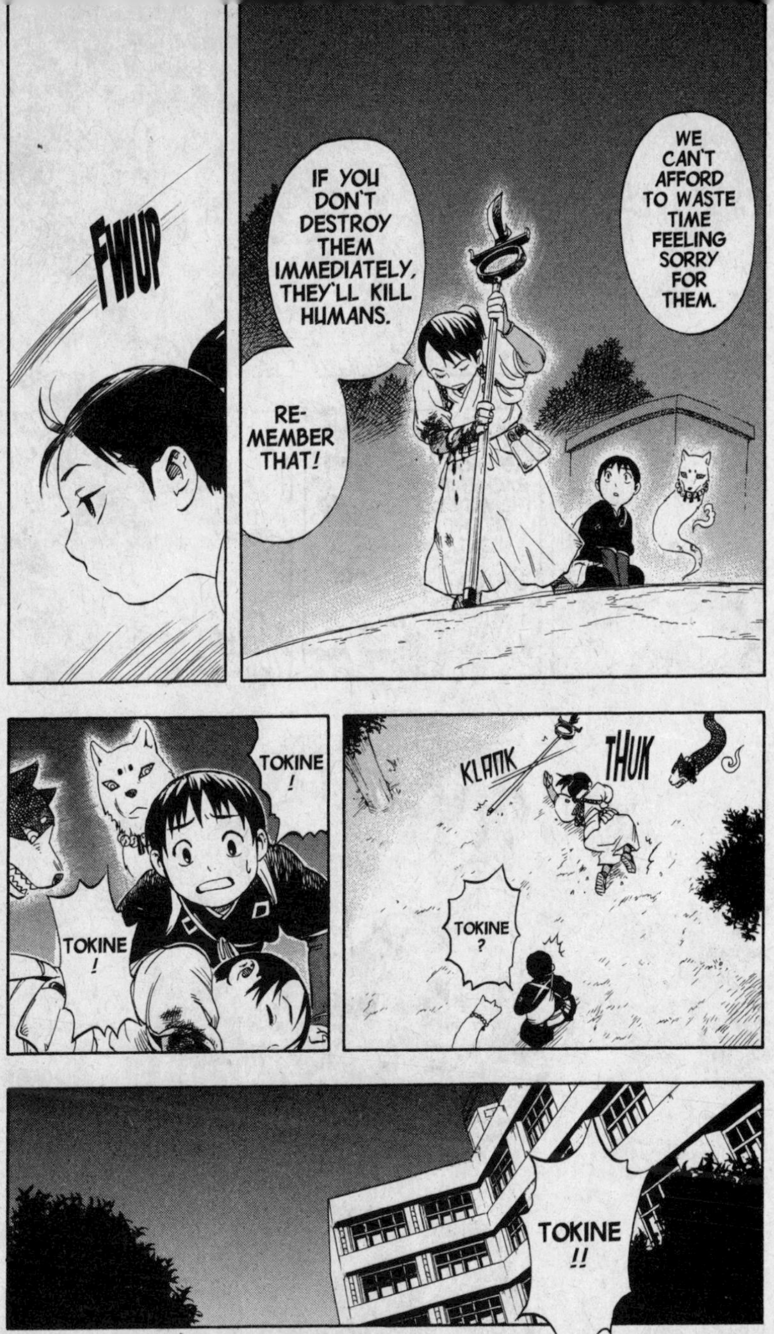
WE CAN'T AFFORD TO WASTE TIME FEELING SORRY FOR THEM.
IF YOU DON'T DESTROY THEM IMMEDIATELY, THEY'LL KILL HUMANS.
RE-MEMBER THAT!
FWUP
THUK
KLANK
TOKINE?
TOKINE!
TOKINE!
TOKINE!!

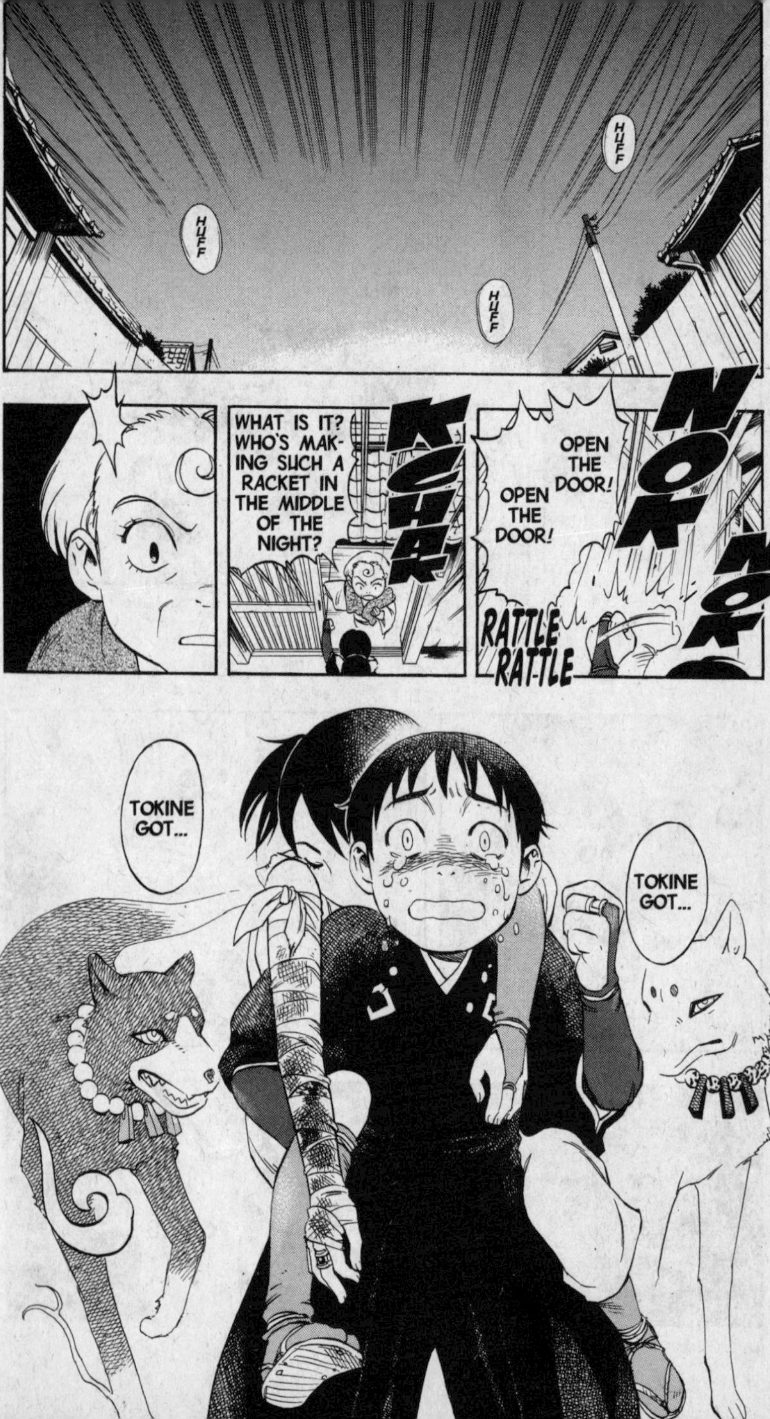
HUFF
HUFF
HUFF
NOK NOK
OPEN THE DOOR!
OPEN THE DOOR!
RATTLE RATTLE RATTLE
KCHAK
WHAT IS IT? WHO'S MAKING SUCH A RACKET IN THE MIDDLE OF THE NIGHT?
TOKINE GOT...
TOKINE GOT...

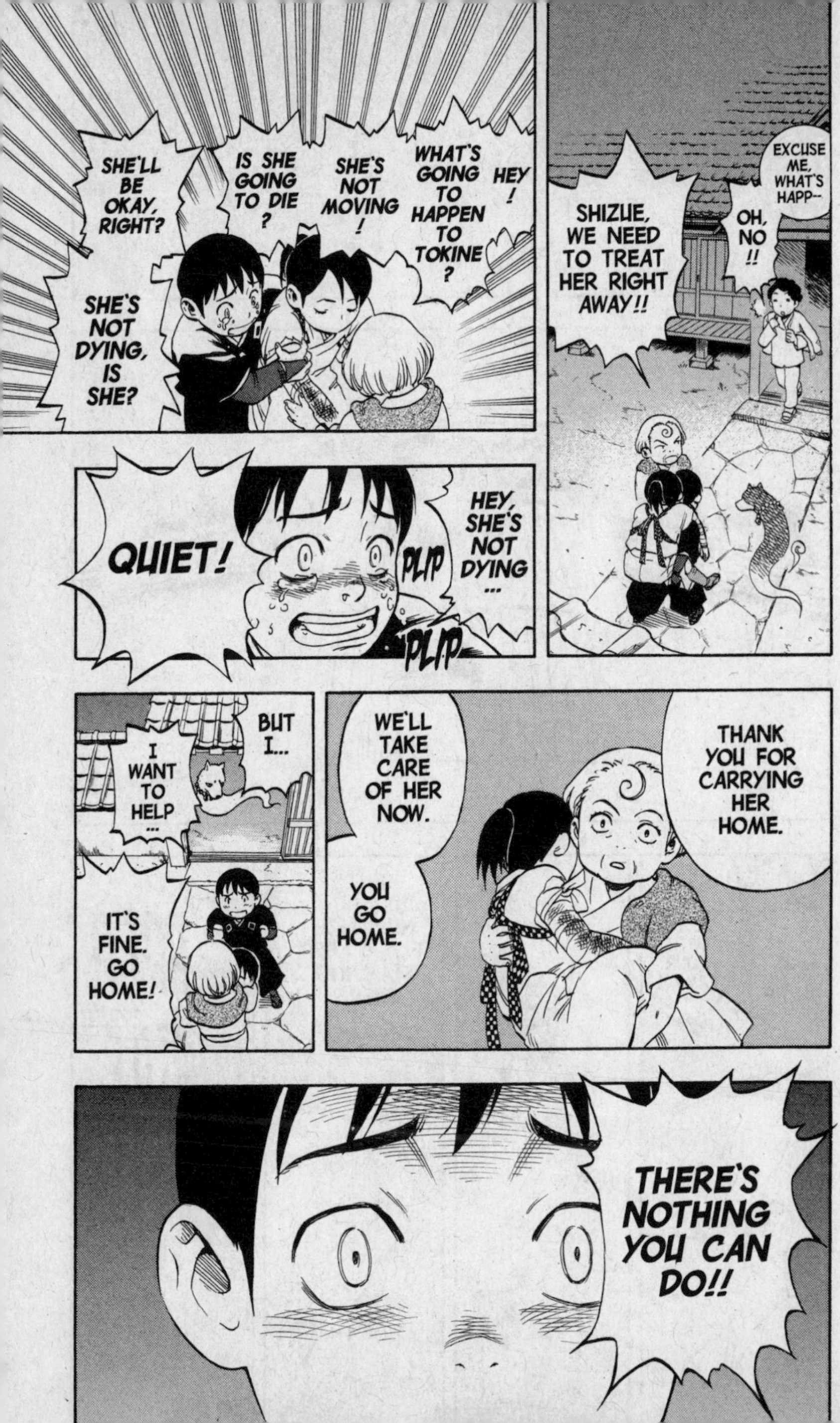
EXCUSE ME, WHAT'S HAPP--
OH, NO!!
SHIZUE, WE NEED TO TREAT HER RIGHT AWAY!!
HEY!
WHAT'S GOING TO HAPPEN TO TOKINE?
SHE'S NOT MOVING!
IS SHE GOING TO DIE?
SHE'LL BE OKAY, RIGHT?
SHE'S NOT DYING, IS SHE?
HEY, SHE'S NOT DYING...
PLIP
PLIP
QUIET!
THANK YOU FOR CARRYING HER HOME.
WE'LL TAKE CARE OF HER NOW.
YOU GO HOME.
BUT I...
I WANT TO HELP...
IT'S FINE. GO HOME!
THERE'S NOTHING YOU CAN DO!!

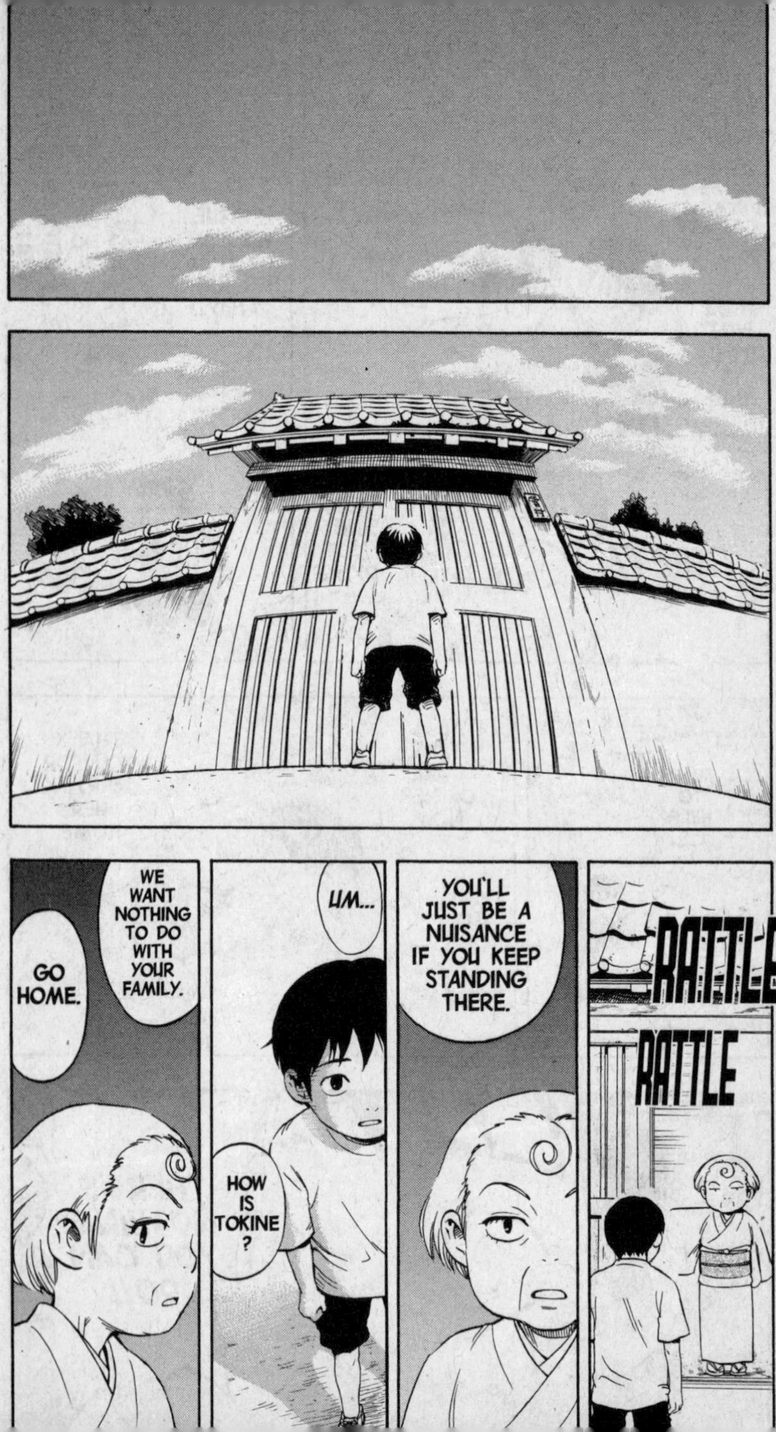
RATTLE
RATTLE
YOU'LL JUST BE A NUISANCE IF YOU KEEP STANDING THERE.
UM...
HOW IS TOKINE?
WE WANT NOTHING TO DO WITH YOUR FAMILY.
GO HOME.

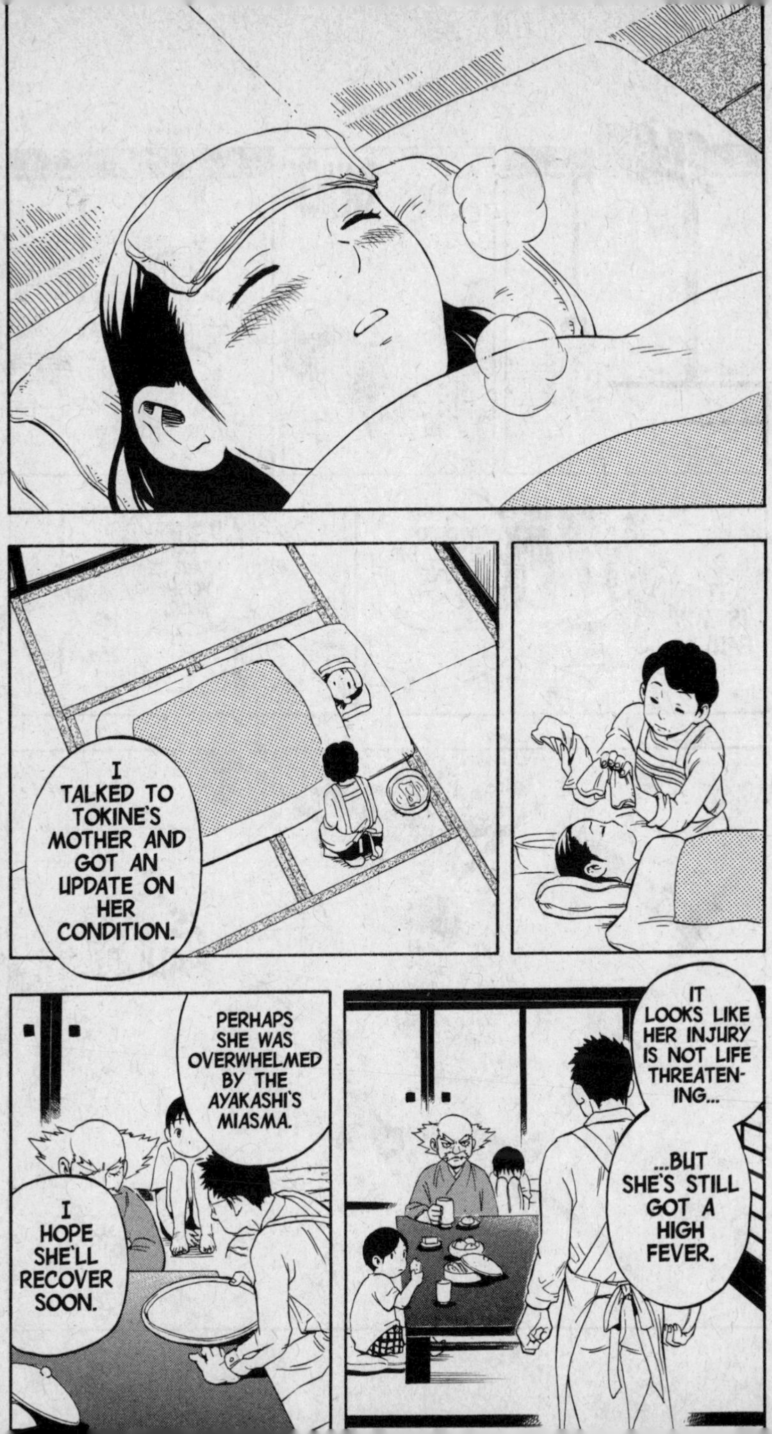
I TALKED TO TOKINE'S MOTHER AND GOT AN UPDATE ON HER CONDITION.
IT LOOKS LIKE HER INJURY IS NOT LIFE THREATEN-ING...
...BUT SHE'S STILL GOT A HIGH FEVER.
PERHAPS SHE WAS OVERWHELMED BY THE AYAKASHI'S MIASMA.
I HOPE SHE'LL RECOVER SOON.

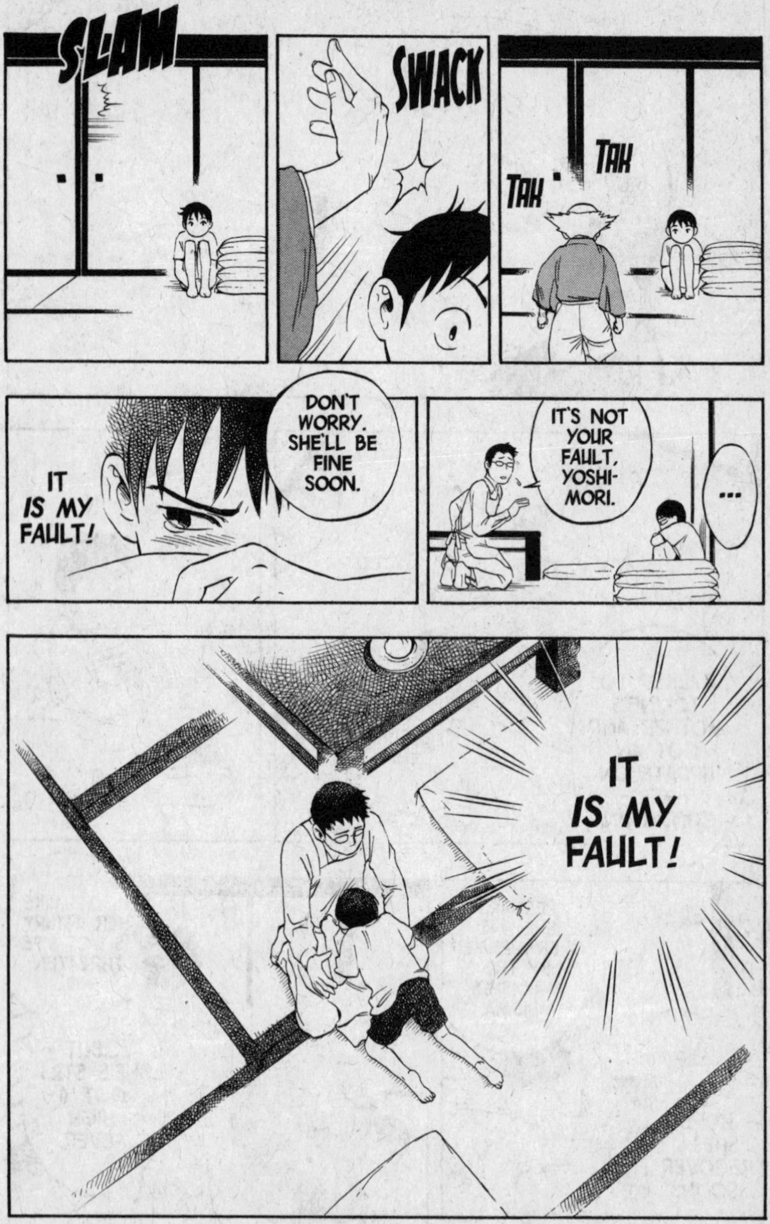
TAK
TAK
SWACK
SLAM
IT'S NOT YOUR FAULT, YOSHIMORI.
...
DON'T WORRY. SHE'LL BE FINE SOON.
IT *IS* MY FAULT!
IT *IS* MY FAULT!

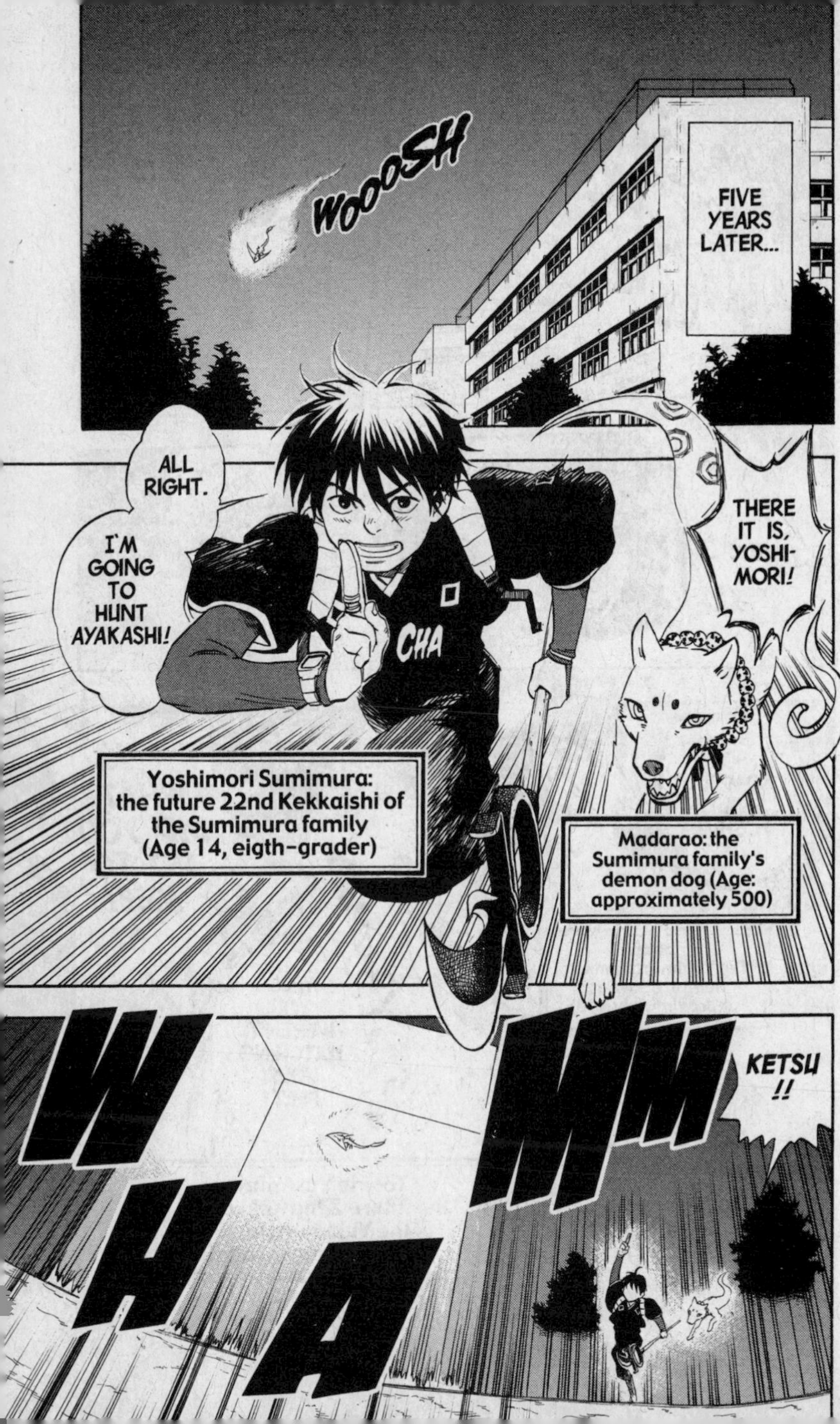
FIVE YEARS LATER...
WOOOSH
THERE IT IS, YOSHIMORI!
ALL RIGHT.
I'M GOING TO HUNT AYAKASHI!
Madarao: the Sumimura family's demon dog (Age: approximately 500)
Yoshimori Sumimura: the future 22nd Kekkaishi of the Sumimura family (Age 14, eigth-grader)
CHA
KETSU !!
WHHAMM

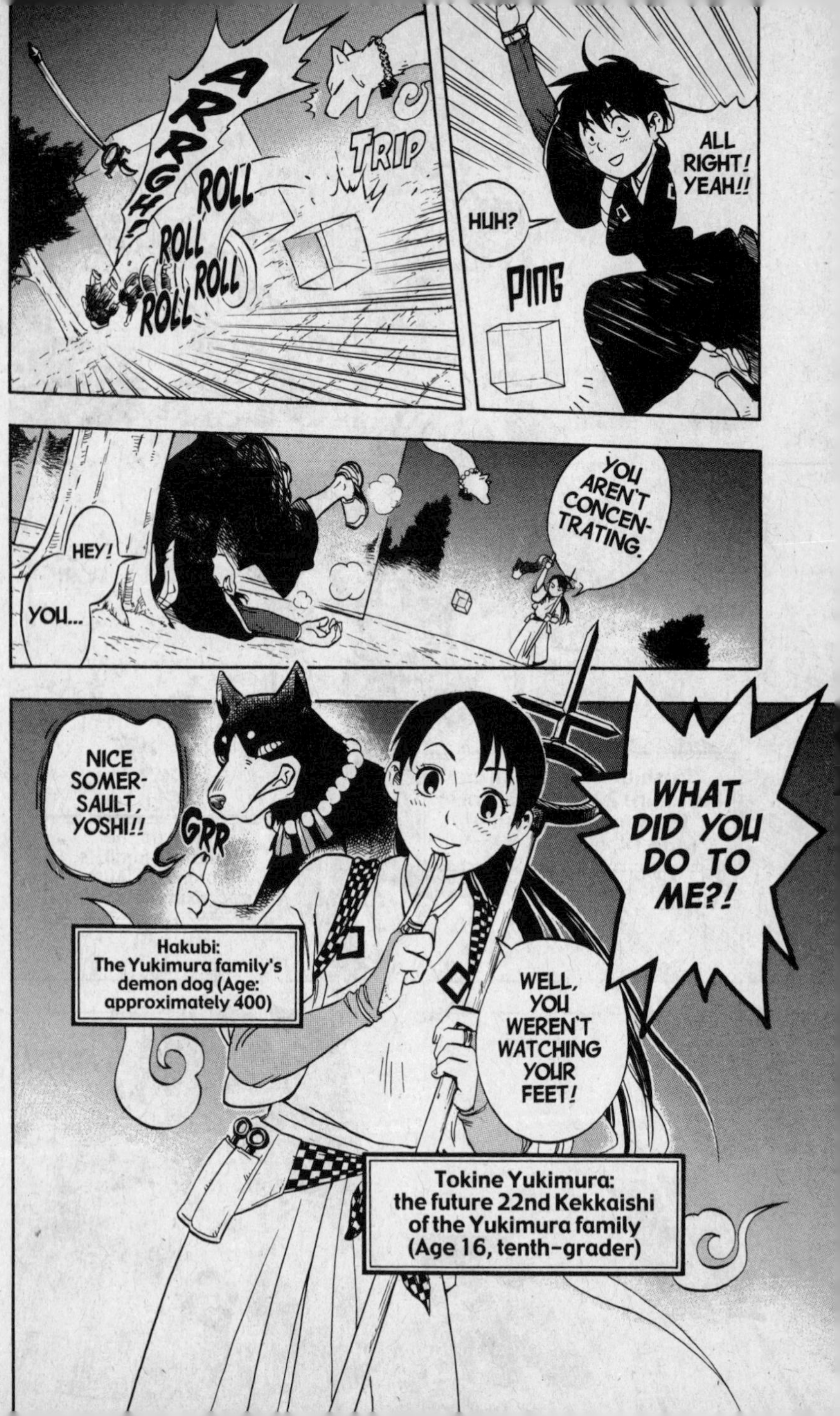
ALL RIGHT! YEAH!!
HUH?
PING
TRIP
ARRGH!
ROLL
ROLL
ROLL
ROLL
YOU AREN'T CONCENTRATING.
HEY!
YOU...
WHAT DID YOU DO TO ME?!
WELL, YOU WEREN'T WATCHING YOUR FEET!
NICE SOMERSAULT, YOSHI!!
GRR
Hakubi: The Yukimura family's demon dog (Age: approximately 400)
Tokine Yukimura: the future 22nd Kekkaishi of the Yukimura family (Age 16, tenth-grader)

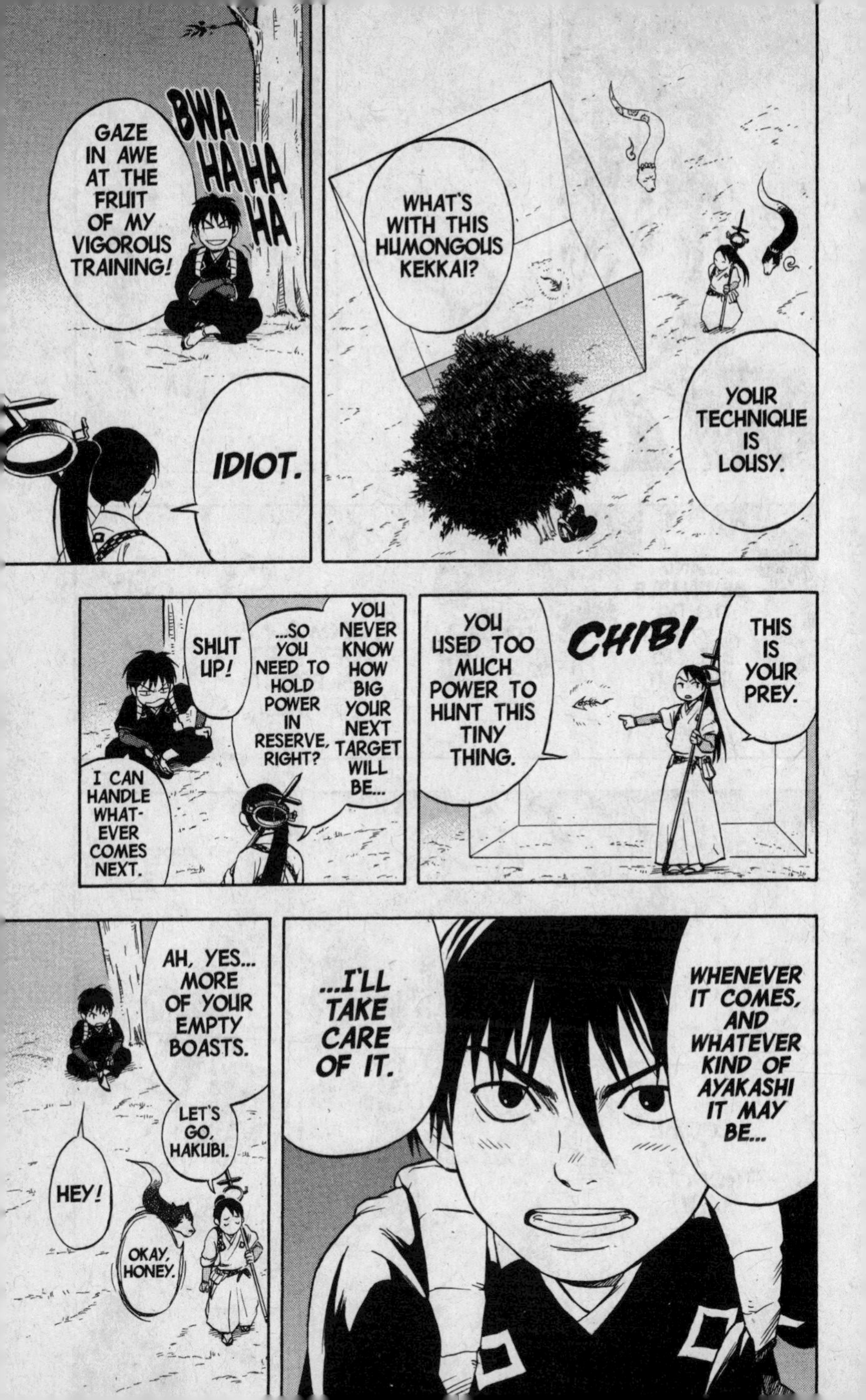
WHAT'S WITH THIS HUMONGOUS KEKKAI?
YOUR TECHNIQUE IS LOUSY.
GAZE IN AWE AT THE FRUIT OF MY VIGOROUS TRAINING!
BWA HA HA HA HA
IDIOT.
THIS IS YOUR PREY.
CHIBI
YOU USED TOO MUCH POWER TO HUNT THIS TINY THING.
YOU NEVER KNOW HOW BIG YOUR NEXT TARGET WILL BE...
...SO YOU NEED TO HOLD POWER IN RESERVE, RIGHT?
SHUT UP!
I CAN HANDLE WHATEVER COMES NEXT.
WHENEVER IT COMES, AND WHATEVER KIND OF AYAKASHI IT MAY BE...
...I'LL TAKE CARE OF IT.
AH, YES... MORE OF YOUR EMPTY BOASTS.
LET'S GO, HAKUBI.
HEY!
OKAY, HONEY.

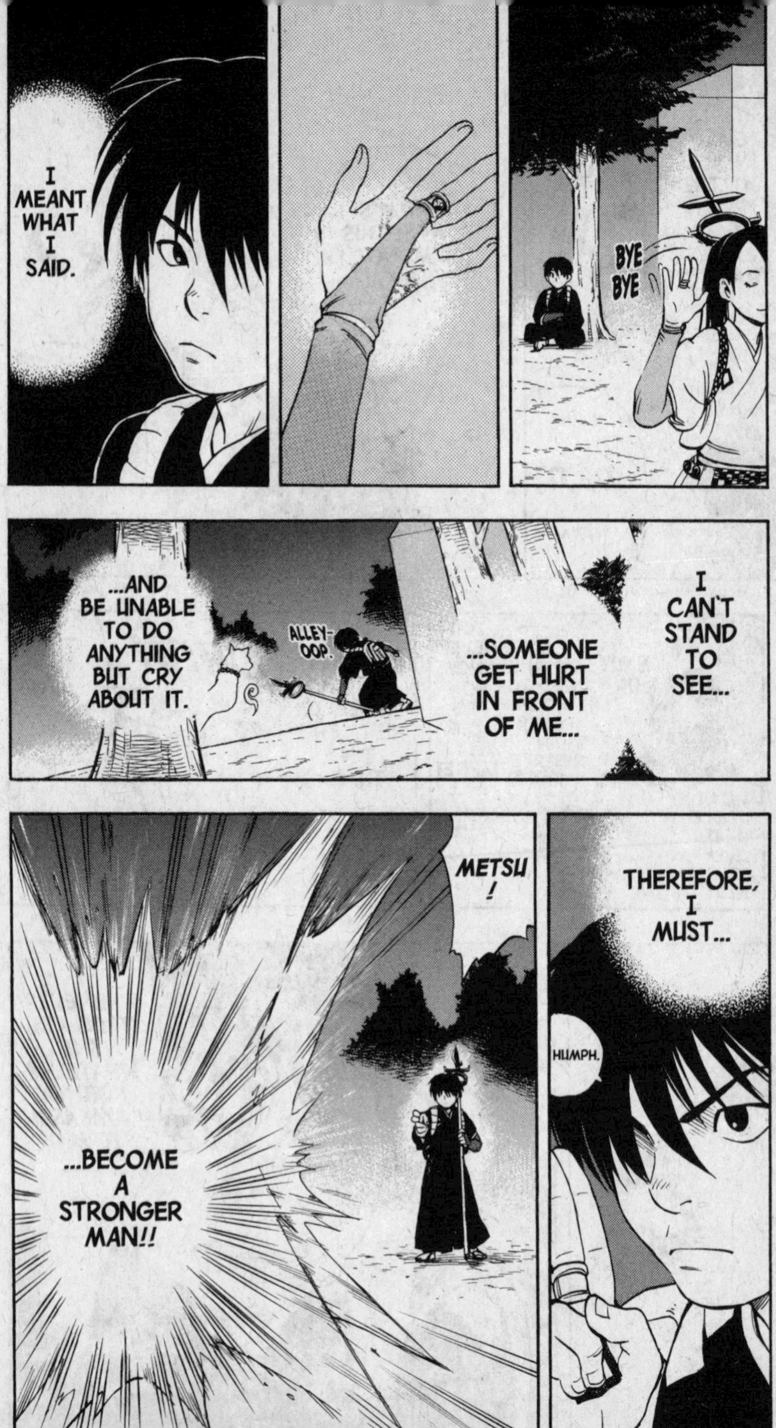
BYE BYE
I MEANT WHAT I SAID.
I CAN'T STAND TO SEE...
...SOMEONE GET HURT IN FRONT OF ME...
ALLEY-OOP.
...AND BE UNABLE TO DO ANYTHING BUT CRY ABOUT IT.
THEREFORE, I MUST...
HUMPH.
METSU!
...BECOME A STRONGER MAN!!

結界師

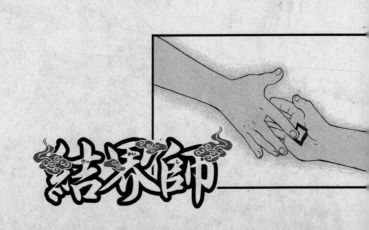

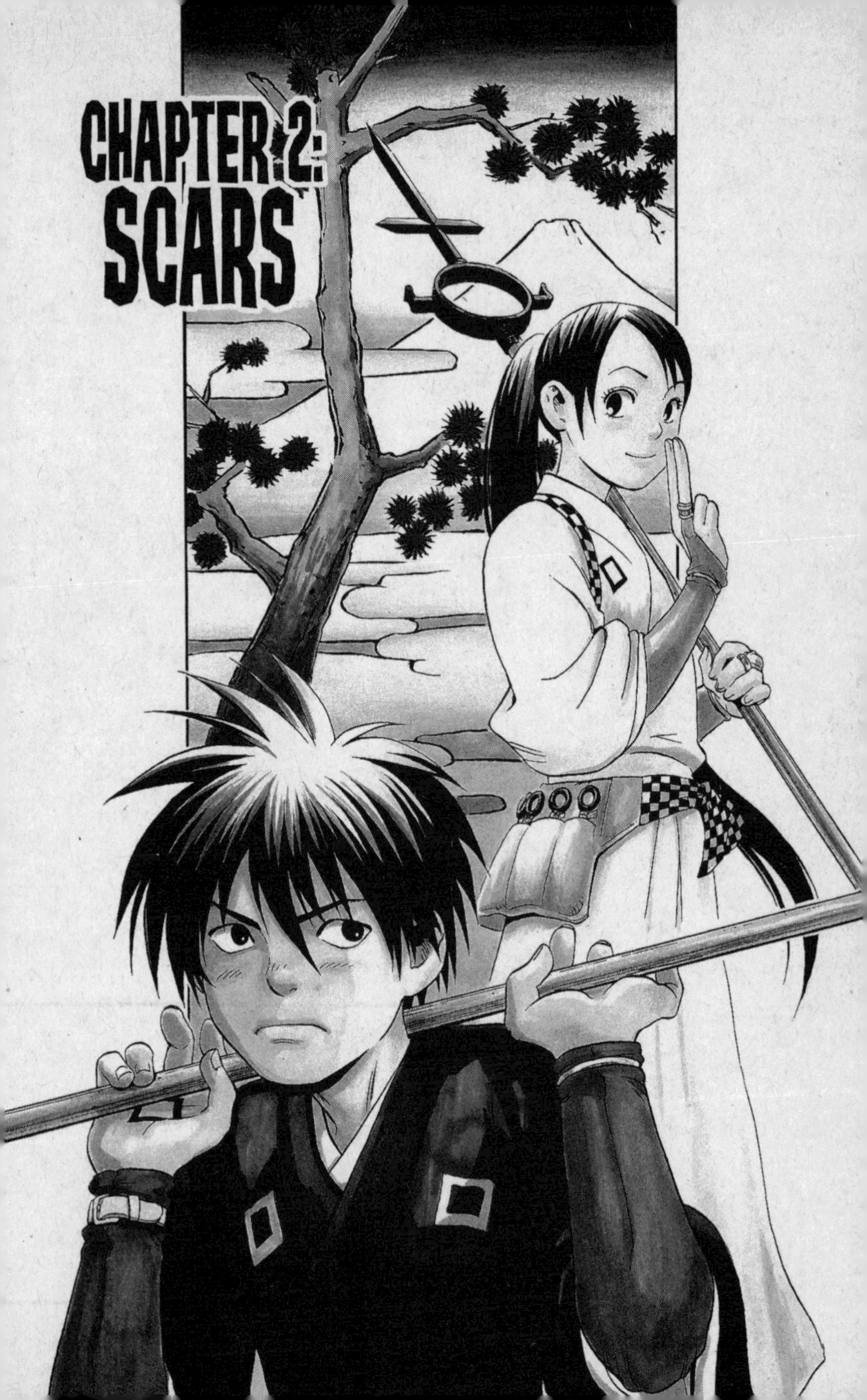
CHAPTER 2:
SCARS

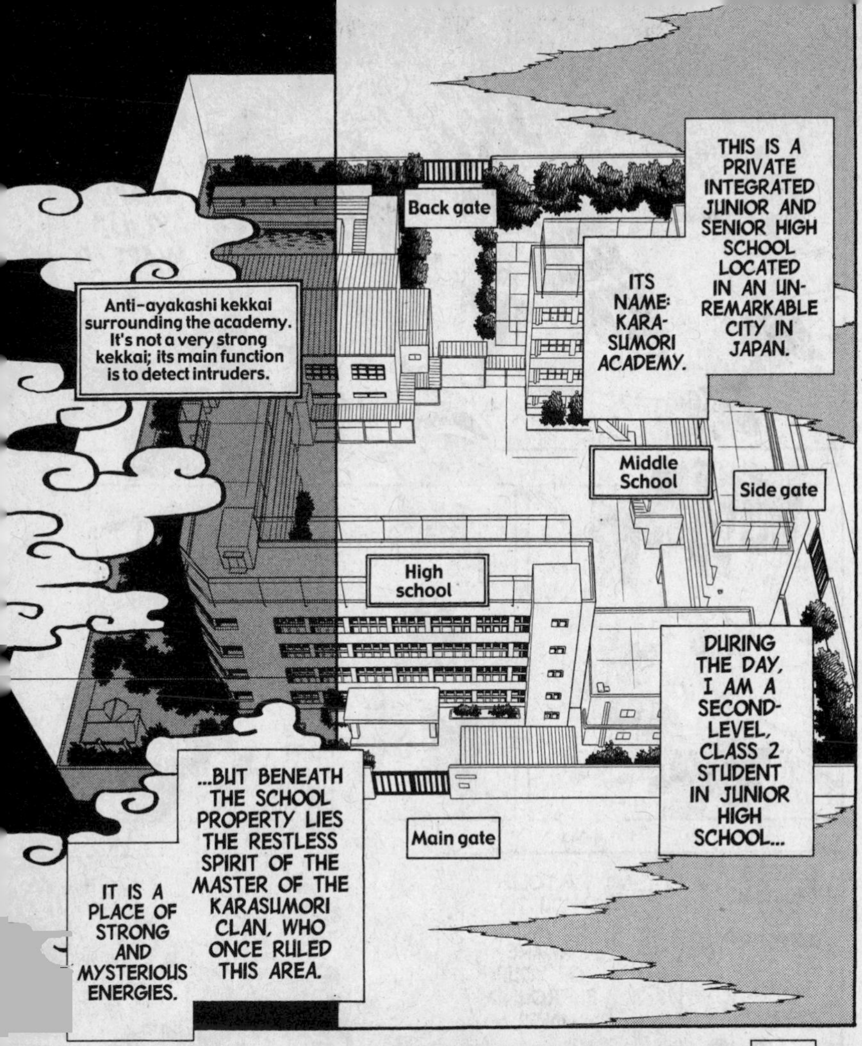
THIS IS A PRIVATE INTEGRATED JUNIOR AND SENIOR HIGH SCHOOL LOCATED IN AN UNREMARKABLE CITY IN JAPAN.
ITS NAME: KARASUMORI ACADEMY.
Back gate
Anti-ayakashi kekkai surrounding the academy. It's not a very strong kekkai; its main function is to detect intruders.
Middle School
Side gate
High school
DURING THE DAY, I AM A SECOND-LEVEL, CLASS 2 STUDENT IN JUNIOR HIGH SCHOOL...
Main gate
IT IS A PLACE OF STRONG AND MYSTERIOUS ENERGIES.
...BUT BENEATH THE SCHOOL PROPERTY LIES THE RESTLESS SPIRIT OF THE MASTER OF THE KARASUMORI CLAN, WHO ONCE RULED THIS AREA.
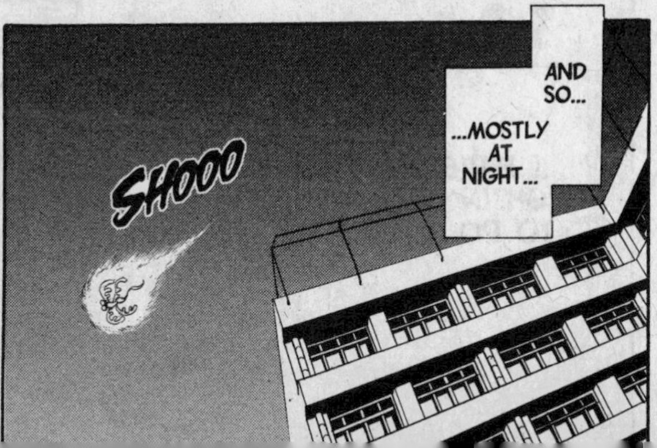
AND SO...
...MOSTLY AT NIGHT...
SHOOO
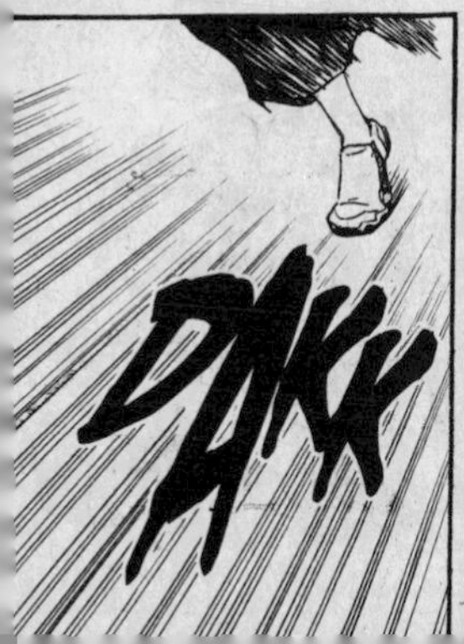
DAKK

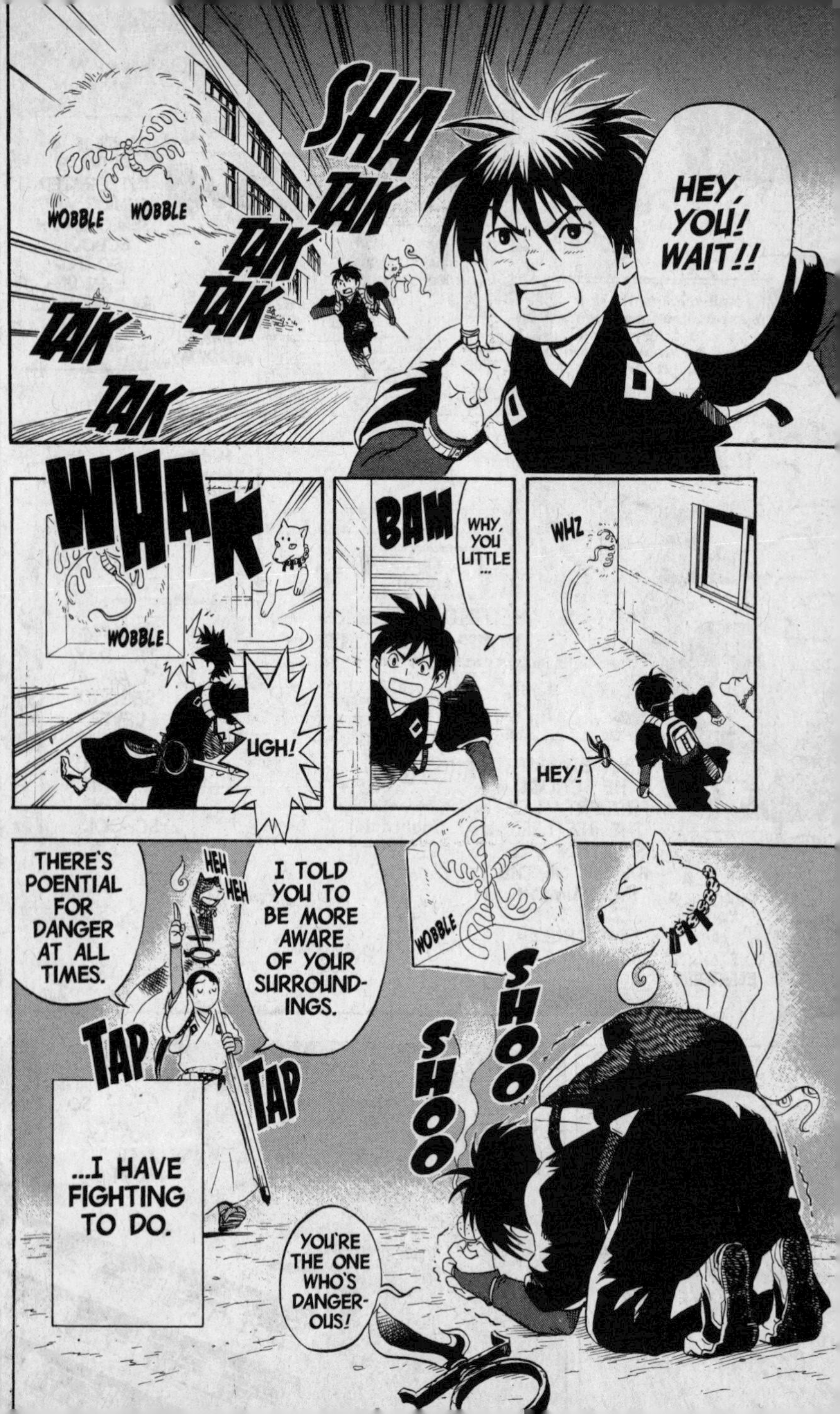
HEY, YOU! WAIT!!
SHA
TAK TAK TAK
TAK
TAK
WOBBLE WOBBLE
WHZ
HEY!
BAM
WHY, YOU LITTLE ...
WHAK
WOBBLE
UGH!
WOBBLE
SHOO SHOO
SHOO SHOO
YOU'RE THE ONE WHO'S DANGEROUS!
I TOLD YOU TO BE MORE AWARE OF YOUR SURROUNDINGS.
HEH HEH
THERE'S POTENTIAL FOR DANGER AT ALL TIMES.
TAP TAP
...I HAVE FIGHTING TO DO.

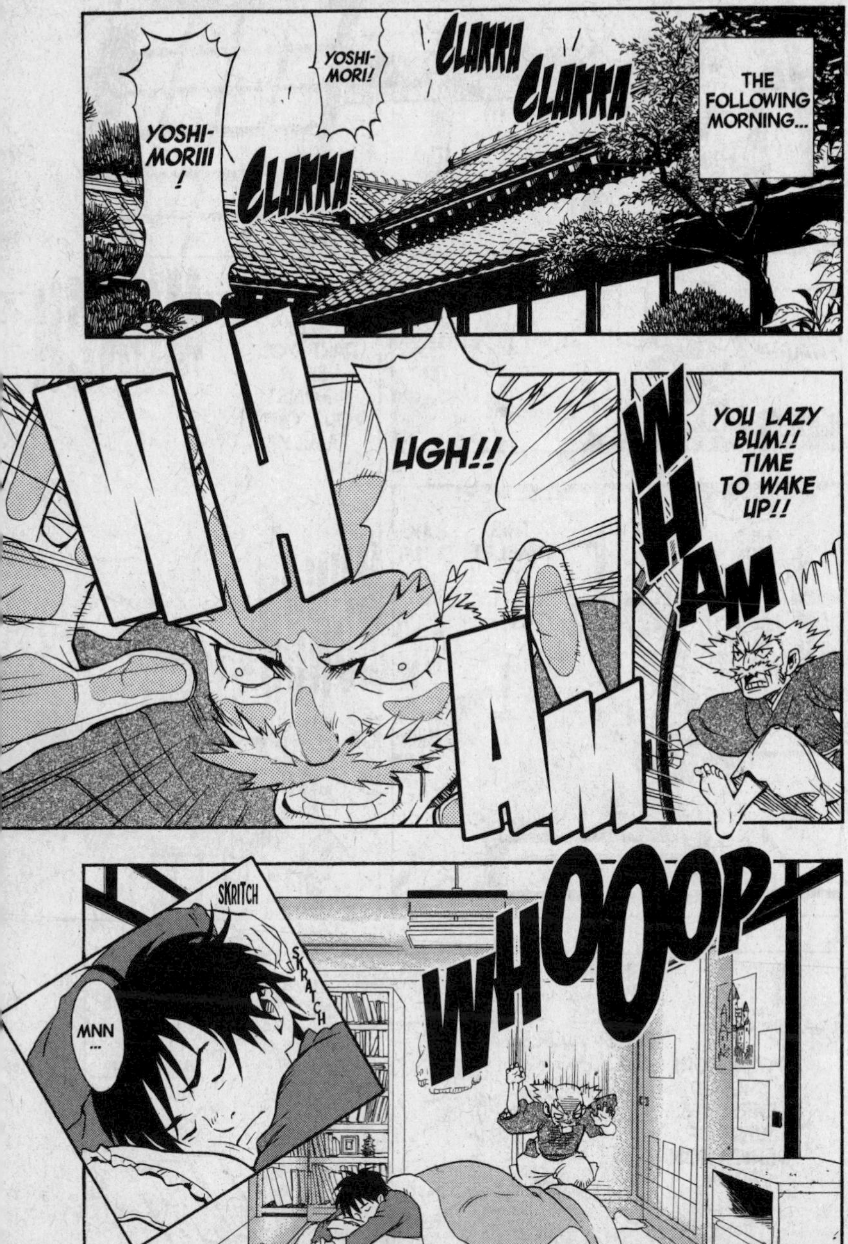
THE FOLLOWING MORNING...
CLARRA
CLARRA
YOSHI-MORI!
CLARRA
YOSHI-MORIII!
YOU LAZY BUM!! TIME TO WAKE UP!!
WHAM
UGH!!
WHAM
WHOOOP
SKRITCH
SKRATCH
MNN...

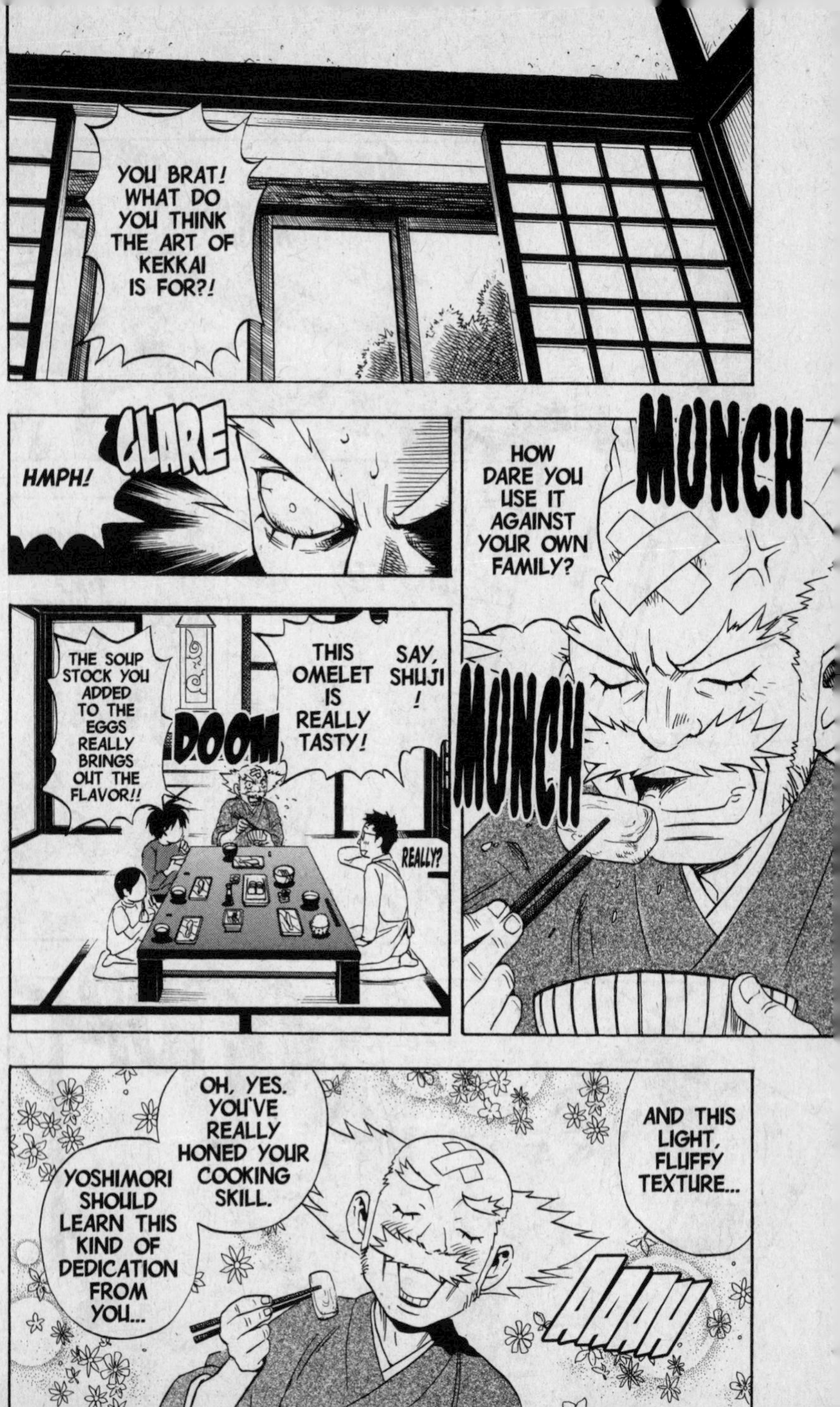
YOU BRAT! WHAT DO YOU THINK THE ART OF KEKKAI IS FOR?!
MUNCH
HOW DARE YOU USE IT AGAINST YOUR OWN FAMILY?
MUNCH
GLARE
HMPH!
SAY, SHUJI!
THIS OMELET IS REALLY TASTY!
THE SOUP STOCK YOU ADDED TO THE EGGS REALLY BRINGS OUT THE FLAVOR!!
DOOM
REALLY?
AND THIS LIGHT, FLUFFY TEXTURE...
AAAH
OH, YES. YOU'VE REALLY HONED YOUR COOKING SKILL.
YOSHIMORI SHOULD LEARN THIS KIND OF DEDICATION FROM YOU...

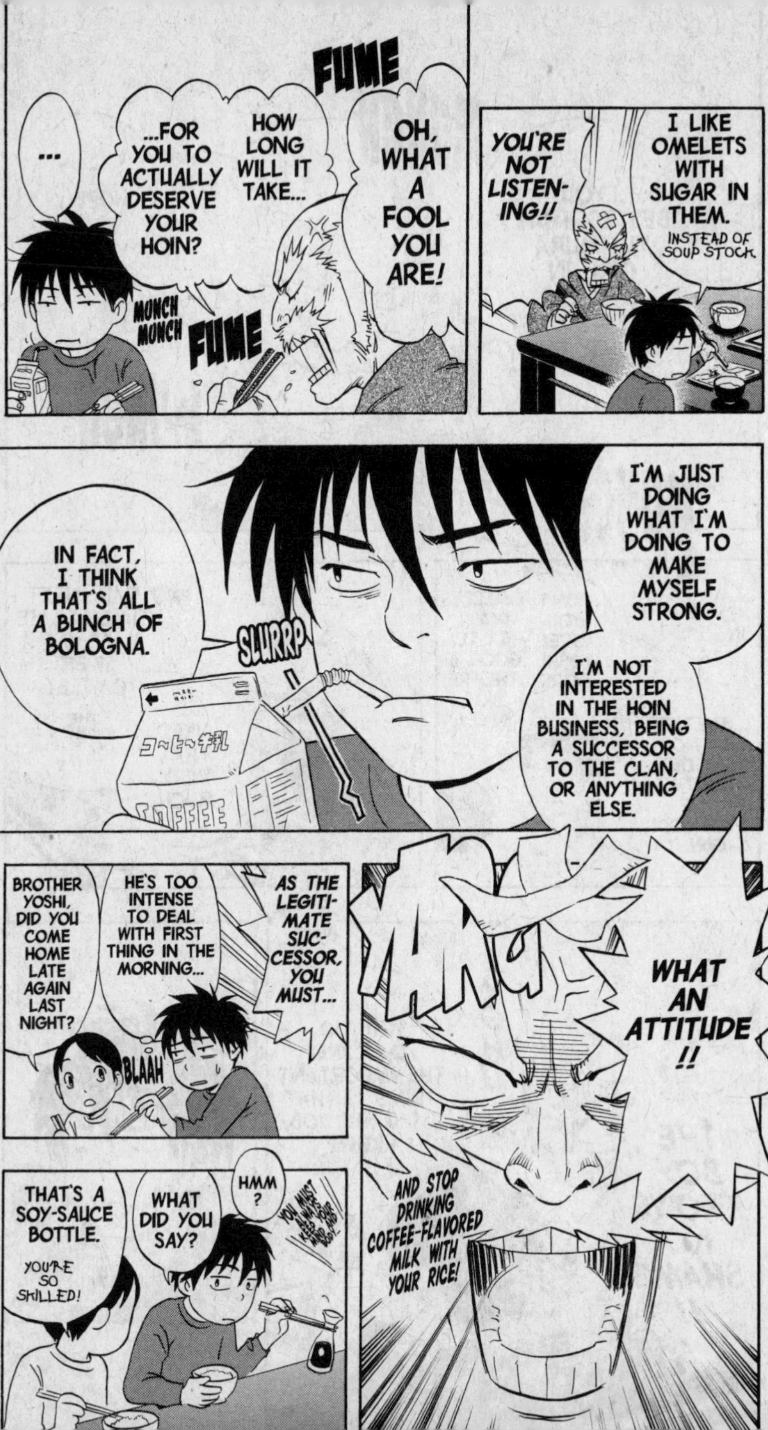

I LIKE OMELETS WITH SUGAR IN THEM.
INSTEAD OF SOUP STOCK
YOU'RE NOT LISTEN-ING!!
FUME
OH, WHAT A FOOL YOU ARE!
HOW LONG WILL IT TAKE...
...FOR YOU TO ACTUALLY DESERVE YOUR HOIN?
FUME
MUNCH MUNCH
...
I'M JUST DOING WHAT I'M DOING TO MAKE MYSELF STRONG.
I'M NOT INTERESTED IN THE HOIN BUSINESS, BEING A SUCCESSOR TO THE CLAN, OR ANYTHING ELSE.
SLURRP
IN FACT, I THINK THAT'S ALL A BUNCH OF BOLOGNA.
コ〜ヒ〜牛乳
COFFEE
YANK
WHAT AN ATTITUDE!!
AND STOP DRINKING COFFEE-FLAVORED MILK WITH YOUR RICE!
AS THE LEGITIMATE SUC-CESSOR, YOU MUST...
HE'S TOO INTENSE TO DEAL WITH FIRST THING IN THE MORNING...
BROTHER YOSHI, DID YOU COME HOME LATE AGAIN LAST NIGHT?
BLAAH
HMM?
YOU MUST ALWAYS KEEP YOUR MIND AND BODY...
WHAT DID YOU SAY?
THAT'S A SOY-SAUCE BOTTLE.
YOU'RE SO SKILLED!

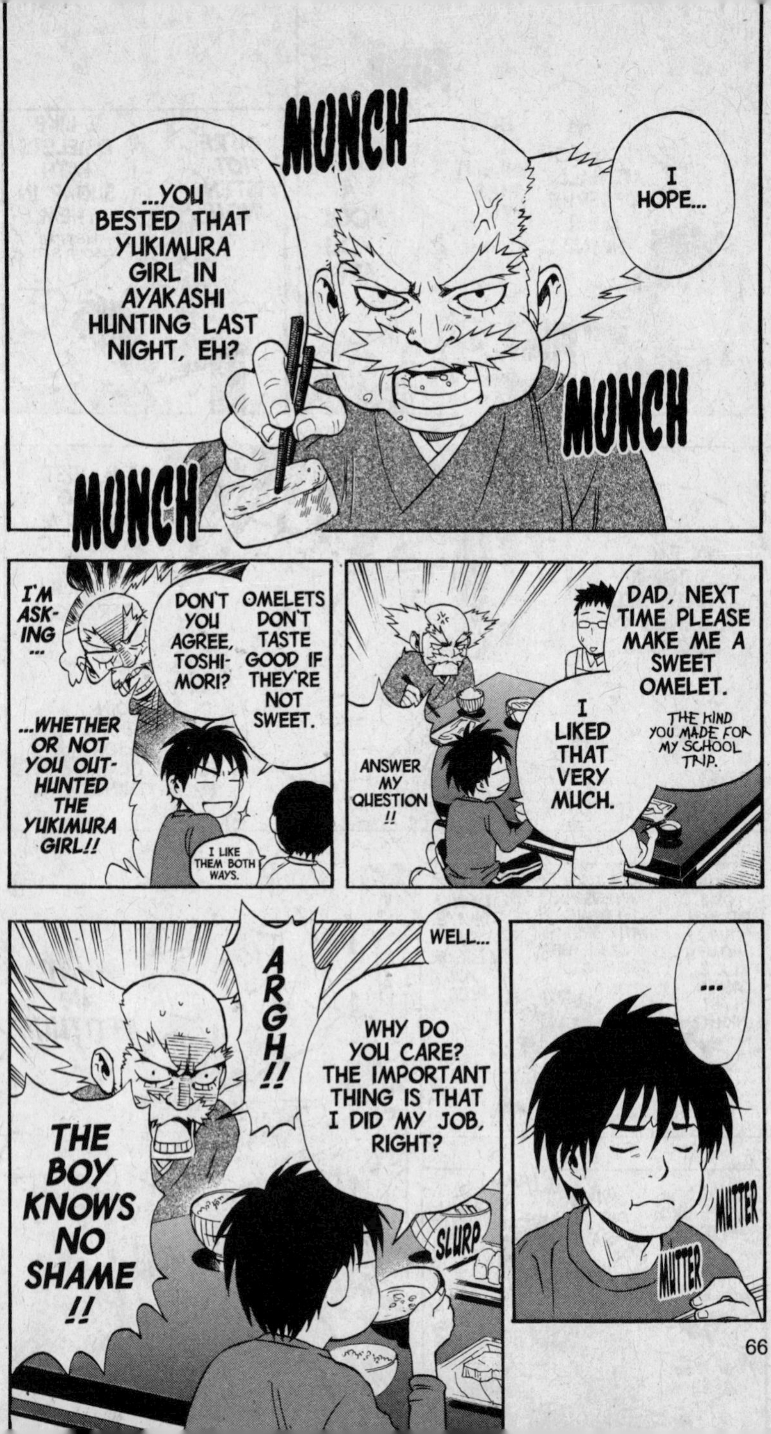
I HOPE...
MUNCH
...YOU BESTED THAT YUKIMURA GIRL IN AYAKASHI HUNTING LAST NIGHT, EH?
MUNCH
MUNCH
DAD, NEXT TIME PLEASE MAKE ME A SWEET OMELET.
THE KIND YOU MADE FOR MY SCHOOL TRIP.
I LIKED THAT VERY MUCH.
ANSWER MY QUESTION!!
OMELETS DON'T TASTE GOOD IF THEY'RE NOT SWEET.
DON'T YOU AGREE, TOSHIMORI?
I'M ASKING...
...WHETHER OR NOT YOU OUT-HUNTED THE YUKIMURA GIRL!!
I LIKE THEM BOTH WAYS.
...
MUTTER
MUTTER
WELL...
WHY DO YOU CARE? THE IMPORTANT THING IS THAT I DID MY JOB, RIGHT?
ARGH!!
THE BOY KNOWS NO SHAME!!
SLURP

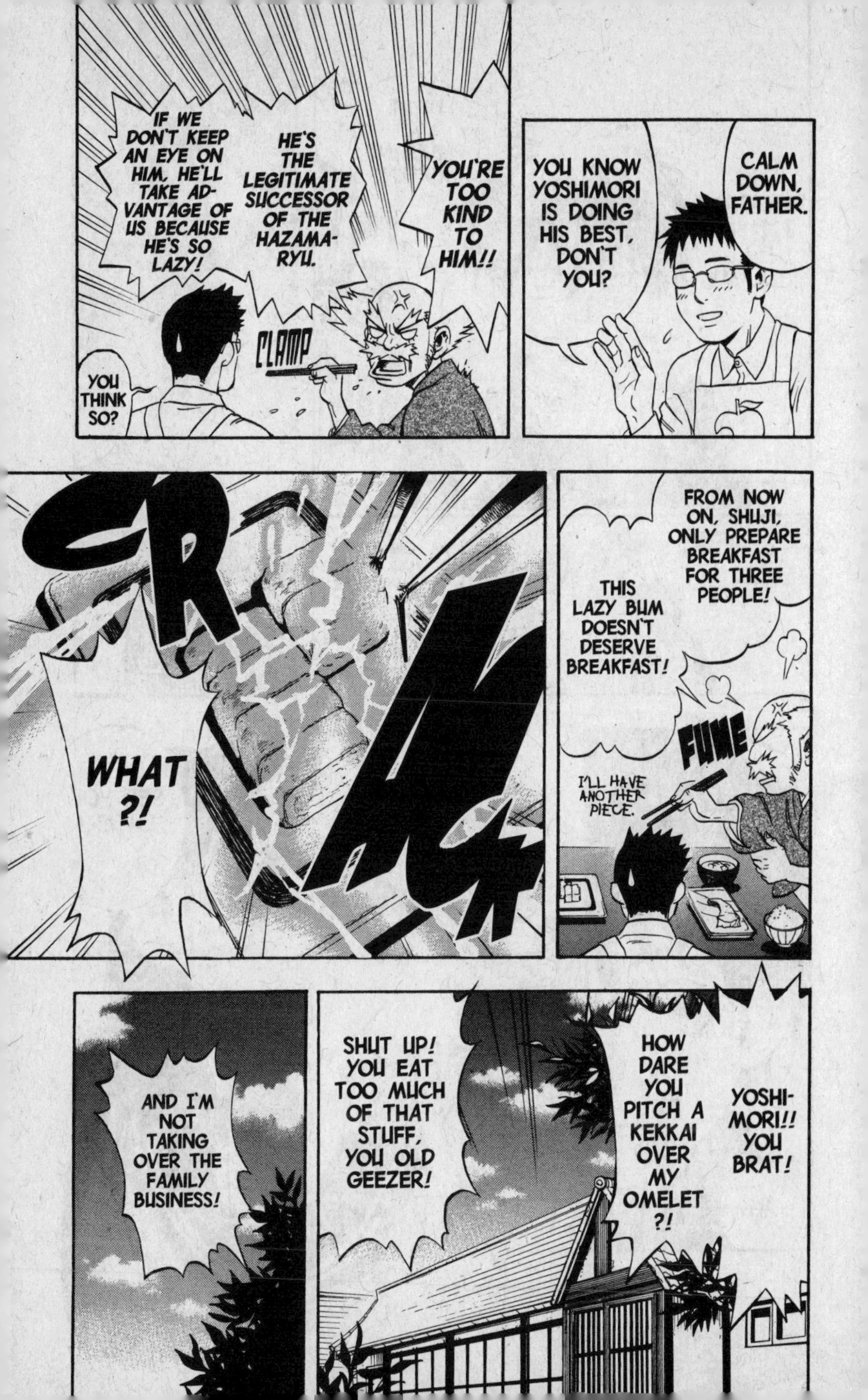
CALM DOWN, FATHER.
YOU KNOW YOSHIMORI IS DOING HIS BEST, DON'T YOU?
YOU'RE TOO KIND TO HIM!!
HE'S THE LEGITIMATE SUCCESSOR OF THE HAZAMA-RYU.
IF WE DON'T KEEP AN EYE ON HIM, HE'LL TAKE AD-VANTAGE OF US BECAUSE HE'S SO LAZY!
CLAMP
YOU THINK SO?
FROM NOW ON, SHUJI, ONLY PREPARE BREAKFAST FOR THREE PEOPLE!
THIS LAZY BUM DOESN'T DESERVE BREAKFAST!
FUME
I'LL HAVE ANOTHER PIECE.
CR
WHAT ?!
YOSHI-MORI!! YOU BRAT!
HOW DARE YOU PITCH A KEKKAI OVER MY OMELET ?!
SHUT UP! YOU EAT TOO MUCH OF THAT STUFF, YOU OLD GEEZER!
AND I'M NOT TAKING OVER THE FAMILY BUSINESS!

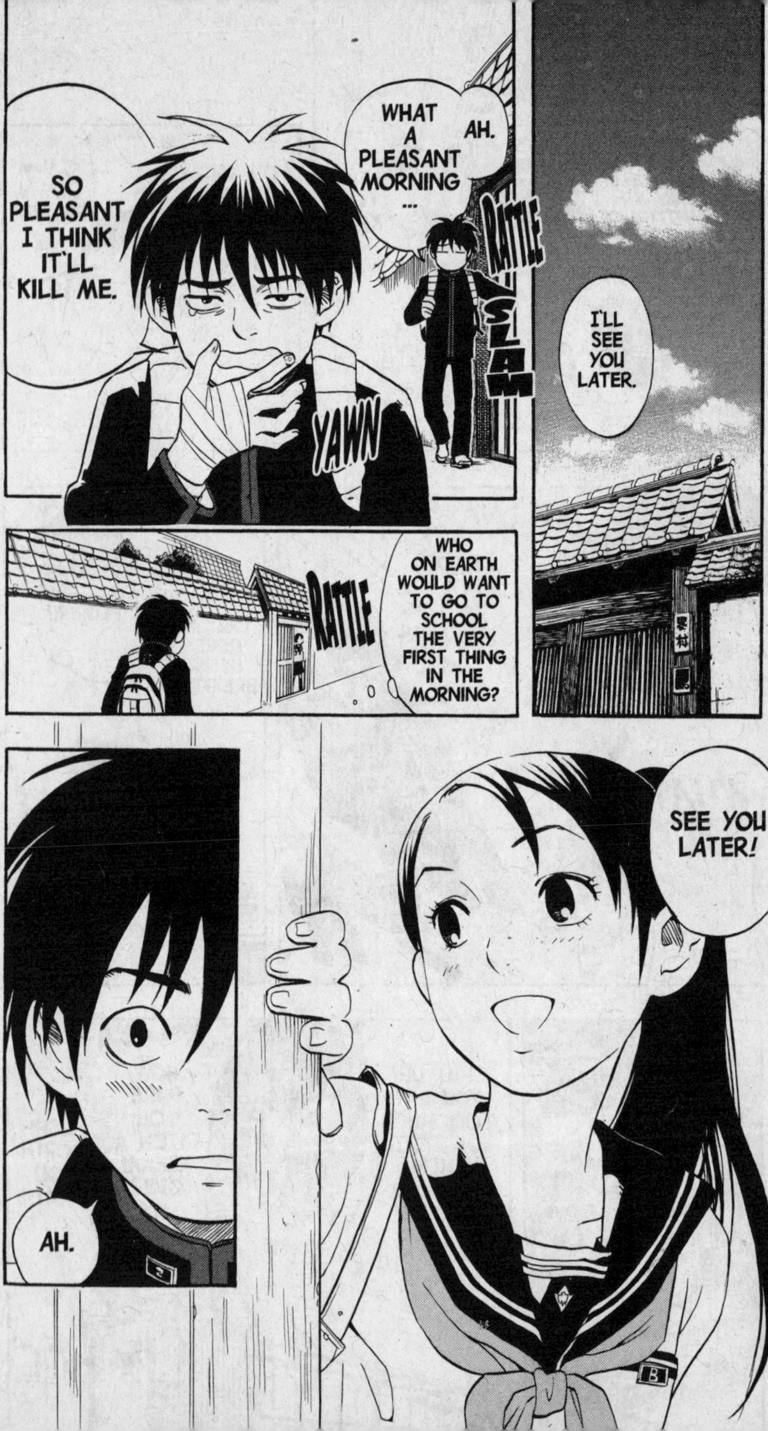
I'LL SEE YOU LATER.
RATTLE
SLAM
WHAT A PLEASANT MORNING ... AH.
YAWN
SO PLEASANT I THINK IT'LL KILL ME.
WHO ON EARTH WOULD WANT TO GO TO SCHOOL THE VERY FIRST THING IN THE MORNING?
RATTLE
SEE YOU LATER!
AH.

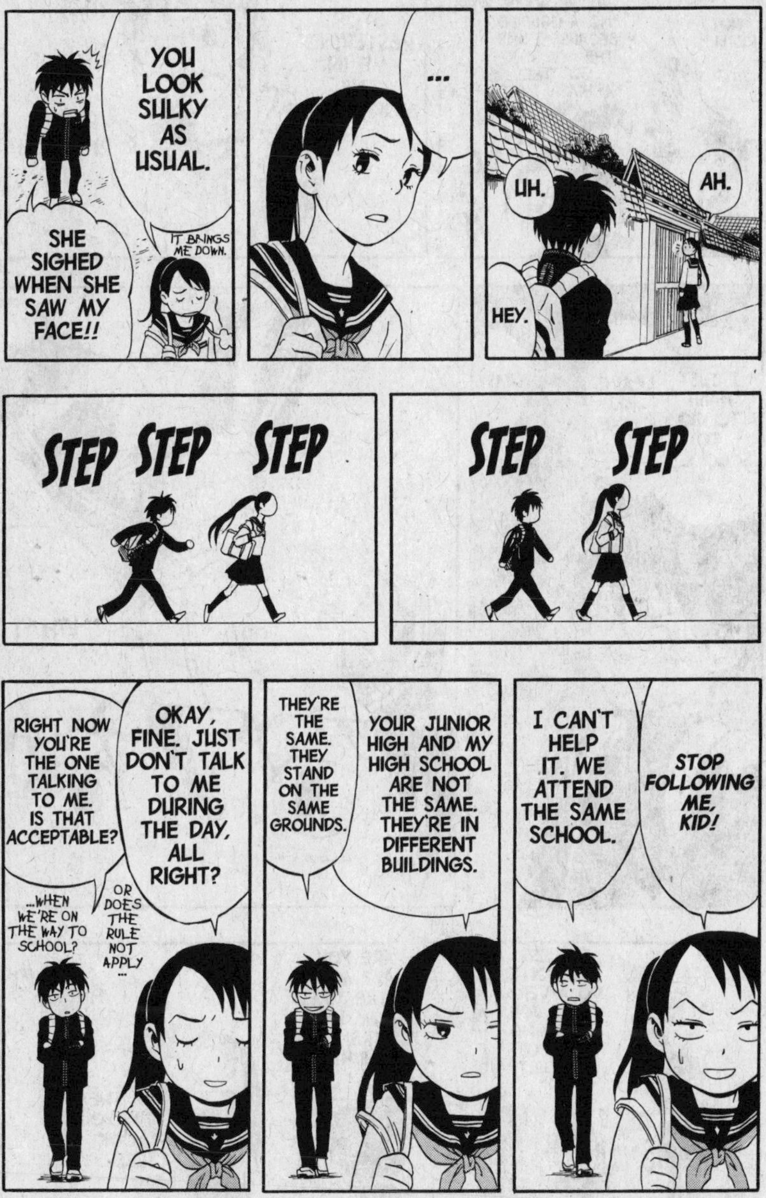
AH.
UH.
HEY.
...
YOU LOOK SULKY AS USUAL.
SHE SIGHED WHEN SHE SAW MY FACE!!
IT BRINGS ME DOWN.
STEP STEP
STEP STEP STEP
STOP FOLLOWING ME, KID!
I CAN'T HELP IT. WE ATTEND THE SAME SCHOOL.
YOUR JUNIOR HIGH AND MY HIGH SCHOOL ARE NOT THE SAME. THEY'RE IN DIFFERENT BUILDINGS.
THEY'RE THE SAME. THEY STAND ON THE SAME GROUNDS.
OKAY, FINE. JUST DON'T TALK TO ME DURING THE DAY, ALL RIGHT?
RIGHT NOW YOU'RE THE ONE TALKING TO ME. IS THAT ACCEPTABLE?
OR DOES THE RULE NOT APPLY...
...WHEN WE'RE ON THE WAY TO SCHOOL?

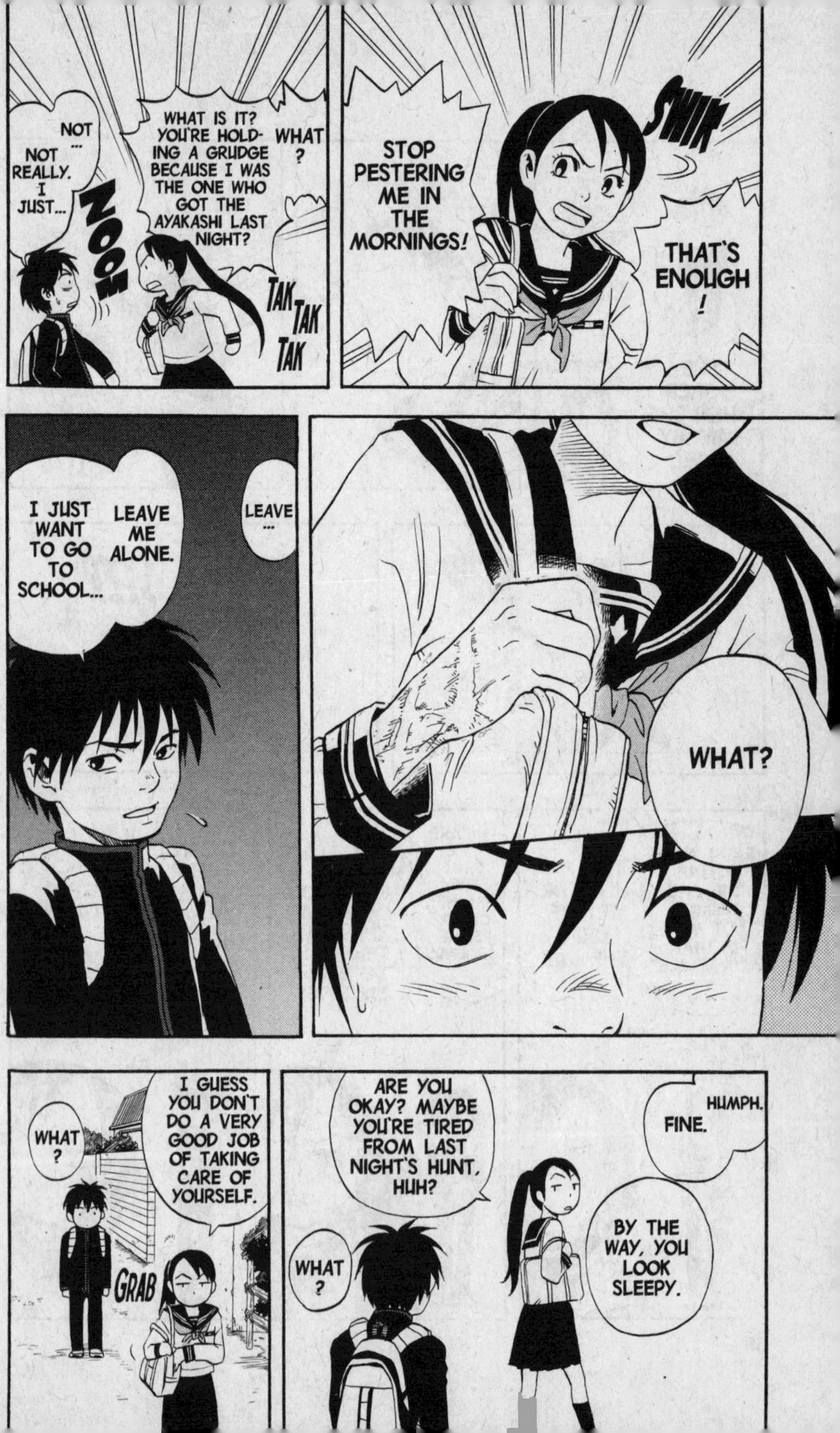
SNIK
THAT'S ENOUGH!
STOP PESTERING ME IN THE MORNINGS!
WHAT?
WHAT IS IT? YOU'RE HOLDING A GRUDGE BECAUSE I WAS THE ONE WHO GOT THE AYAKASHI LAST NIGHT?
TAK TAK TAK
NOT... NOT REALLY. I JUST...
ZOOM
WHAT?
LEAVE...
LEAVE ME ALONE.
I JUST WANT TO GO TO SCHOOL...
HUMPH. FINE.
BY THE WAY, YOU LOOK SLEEPY.
ARE YOU OKAY? MAYBE YOU'RE TIRED FROM LAST NIGHT'S HUNT, HUH?
WHAT?
I GUESS YOU DON'T DO A VERY GOOD JOB OF TAKING CARE OF YOURSELF.
WHAT?
GRAB

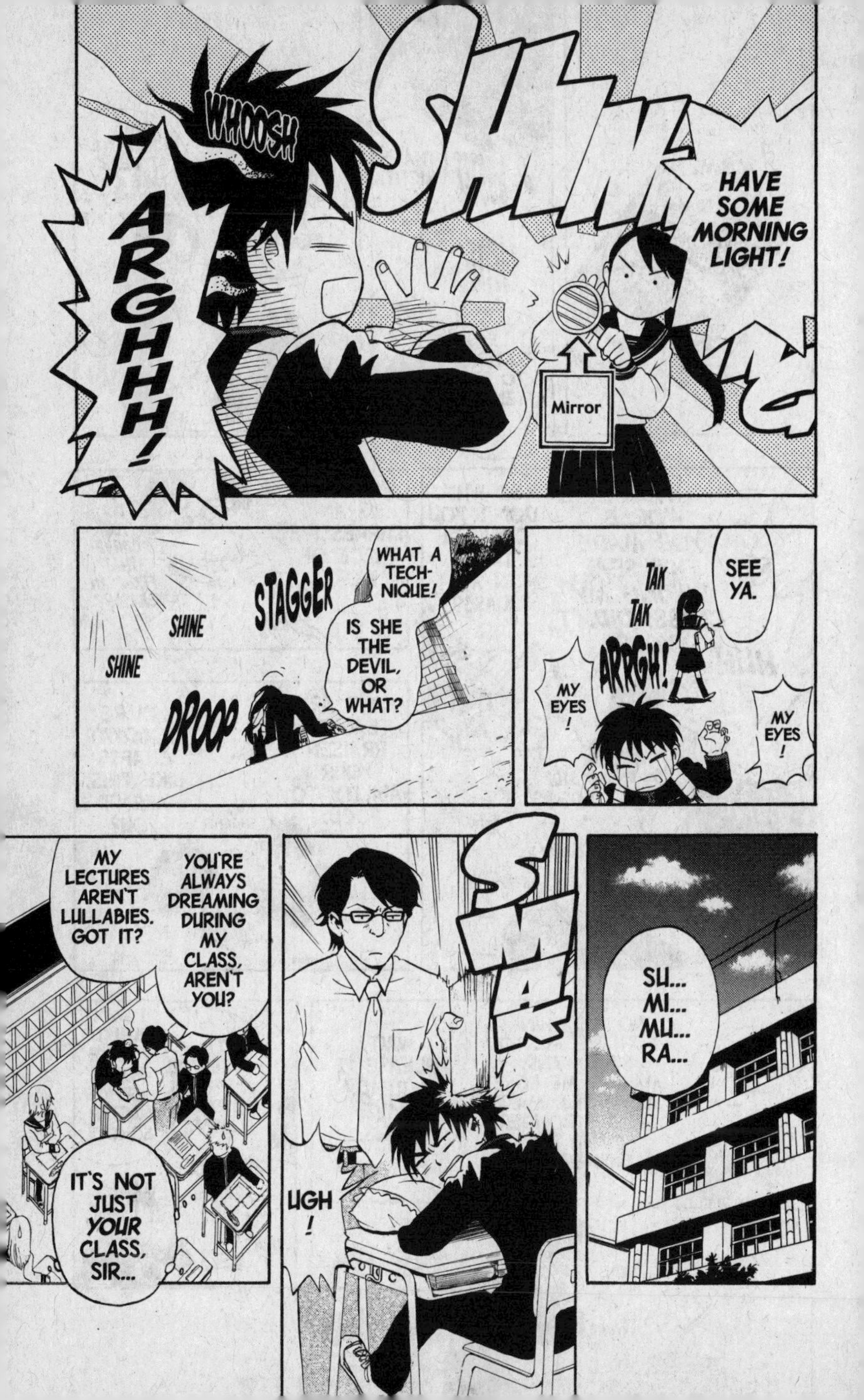
HAVE SOME MORNING LIGHT!
Mirror
WHOOSH
ARGHHH!
SEE YA.
TAK TAK
ARRGH!
MY EYES!
MY EYES!
WHAT A TECHNIQUE!
IS SHE THE DEVIL, OR WHAT?
STAGGER
SHINE
SHINE
DROOP
SU... MI... MU... RA...
SMAK
UGH!
YOU'RE ALWAYS DREAMING DURING MY CLASS, AREN'T YOU?
MY LECTURES AREN'T LULLABIES. GOT IT?
IT'S NOT JUST YOUR CLASS, SIR...

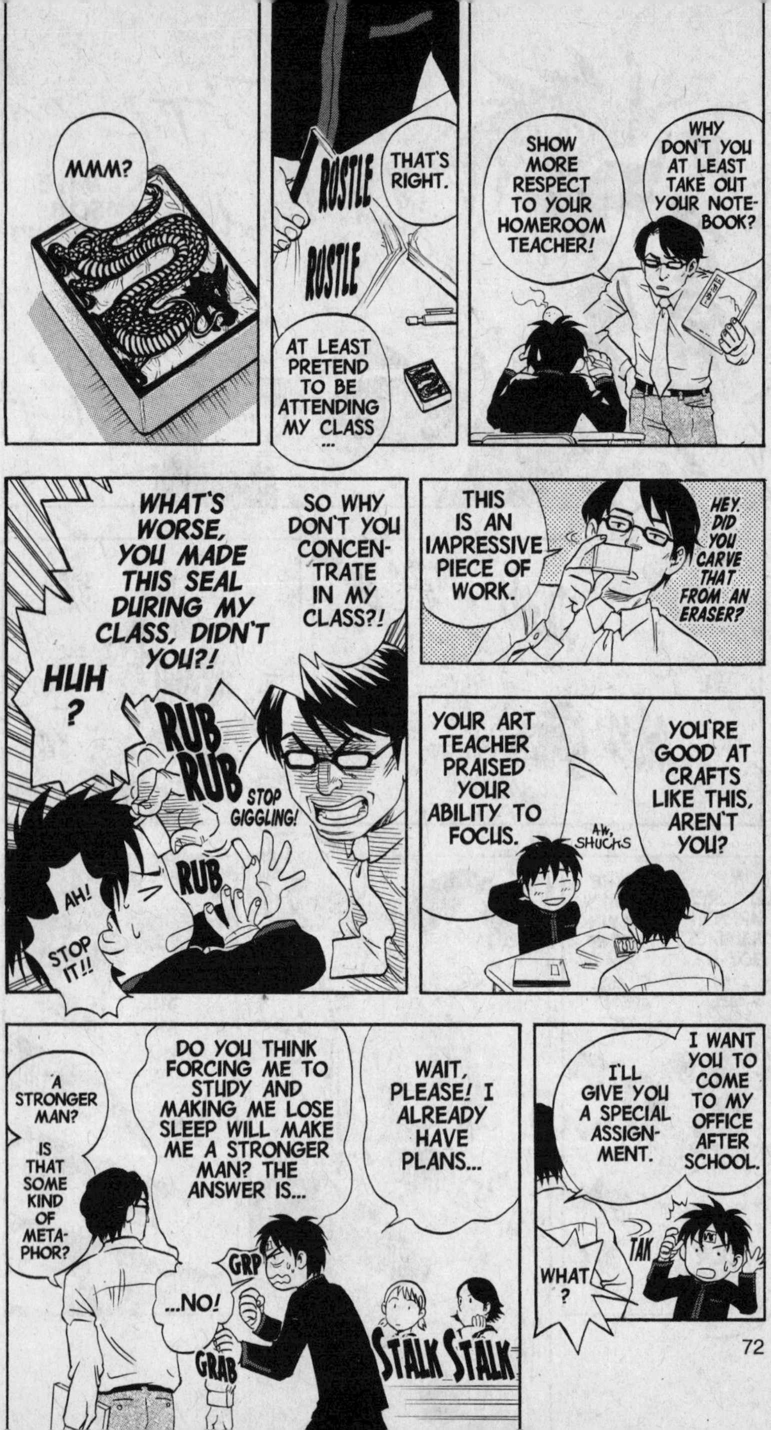
WHY DON'T YOU AT LEAST TAKE OUT YOUR NOTE-BOOK?
SHOW MORE RESPECT TO YOUR HOMEROOM TEACHER!
THAT'S RIGHT.
RUSTLE
RUSTLE
AT LEAST PRETEND TO BE ATTENDING MY CLASS ...
MMM?
HEY. DID YOU CARVE THAT FROM AN ERASER?
THIS IS AN IMPRESSIVE PIECE OF WORK.
YOU'RE GOOD AT CRAFTS LIKE THIS, AREN'T YOU?
YOUR ART TEACHER PRAISED YOUR ABILITY TO FOCUS.
AW, SHUCKS
SO WHY DON'T YOU CONCEN-TRATE IN MY CLASS?!
WHAT'S WORSE, YOU MADE THIS SEAL DURING MY CLASS, DIDN'T YOU?!
HUH ?
RUB RUB
STOP GIGGLING!
RUB
AH!
STOP IT!!
I WANT YOU TO COME TO MY OFFICE AFTER SCHOOL.
I'LL GIVE YOU A SPECIAL ASSIGN-MENT.
TAK
WHAT ?
WAIT, PLEASE! I ALREADY HAVE PLANS...
DO YOU THINK FORCING ME TO STUDY AND MAKING ME LOSE SLEEP WILL MAKE ME A STRONGER MAN? THE ANSWER IS...
GRP
...NO!
GRAB
STALK STALK
A STRONGER MAN? IS THAT SOME KIND OF META-PHOR?

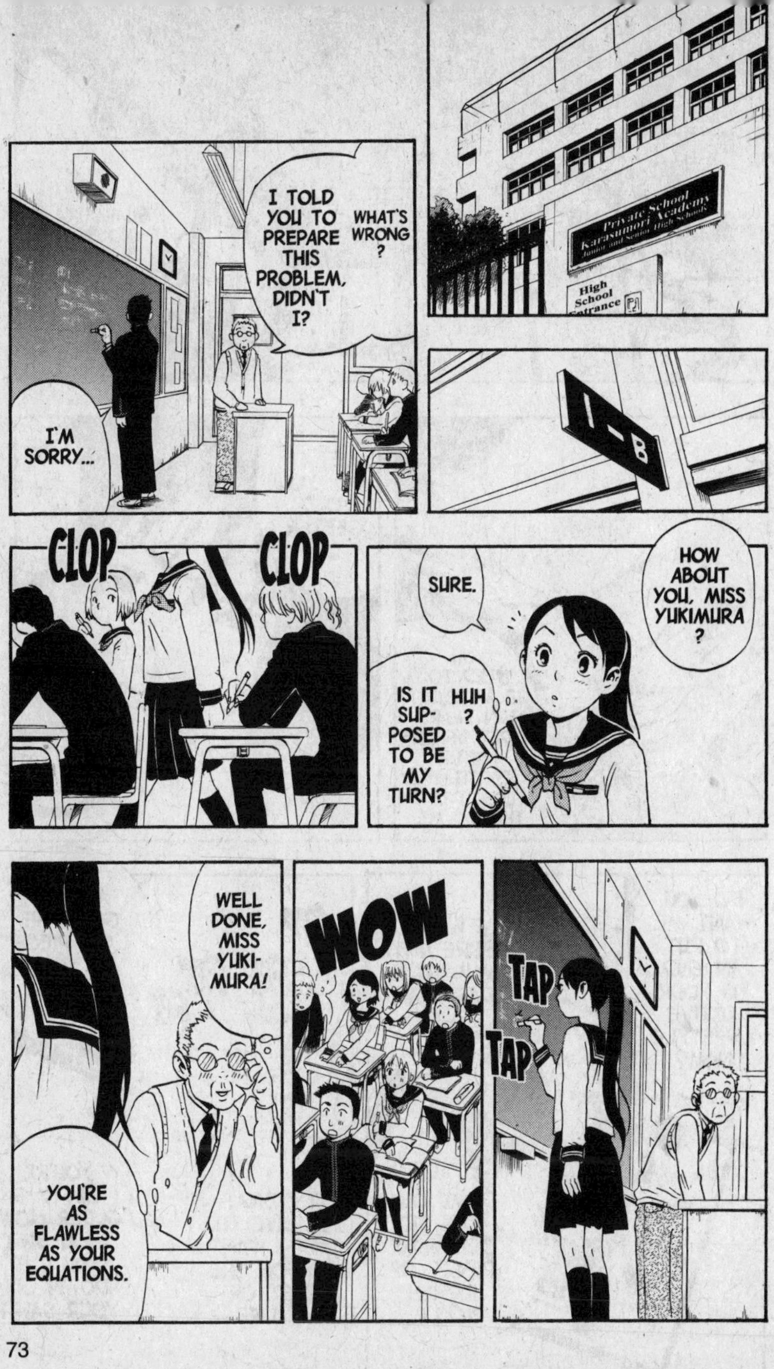
Private School
Karasumori Academy
Junior and Senior High School
High School
1-B
WHAT'S WRONG?
I TOLD YOU TO PREPARE THIS PROBLEM, DIDN'T I?
I'M SORRY...
HOW ABOUT YOU, MISS YUKIMURA?
HUH?
IS IT SUPPOSED TO BE MY TURN?
SURE.
CLOP
CLOP
TAP
TAP
WOW
WELL DONE, MISS YUKIMURA!
YOU'RE AS FLAWLESS AS YOUR EQUATIONS.

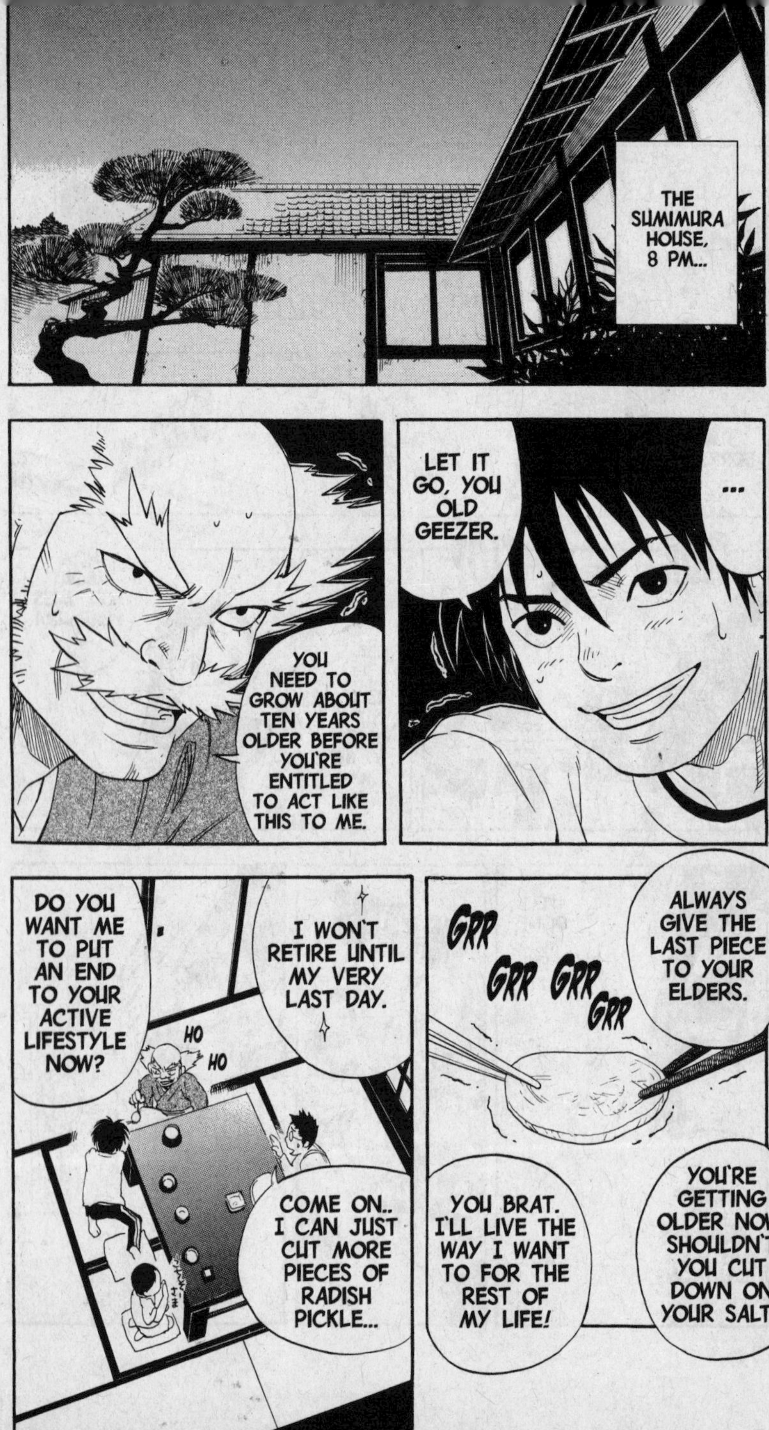
THE SUMIMURA HOUSE, 8 PM...
...
LET IT GO, YOU OLD GEEZER.
YOU NEED TO GROW ABOUT TEN YEARS OLDER BEFORE YOU'RE ENTITLED TO ACT LIKE THIS TO ME.
ALWAYS GIVE THE LAST PIECE TO YOUR ELDERS.
GRR GRR GRR GRR
YOU'RE GETTING OLDER NOW. SHOULDN'T YOU CUT DOWN ON YOUR SALT?
YOU BRAT. I'LL LIVE THE WAY I WANT TO FOR THE REST OF MY LIFE!
I WON'T RETIRE UNTIL MY VERY LAST DAY.
DO YOU WANT ME TO PUT AN END TO YOUR ACTIVE LIFESTYLE NOW?
HO HO
COME ON.. I CAN JUST CUT MORE PIECES OF RADISH PICKLE...

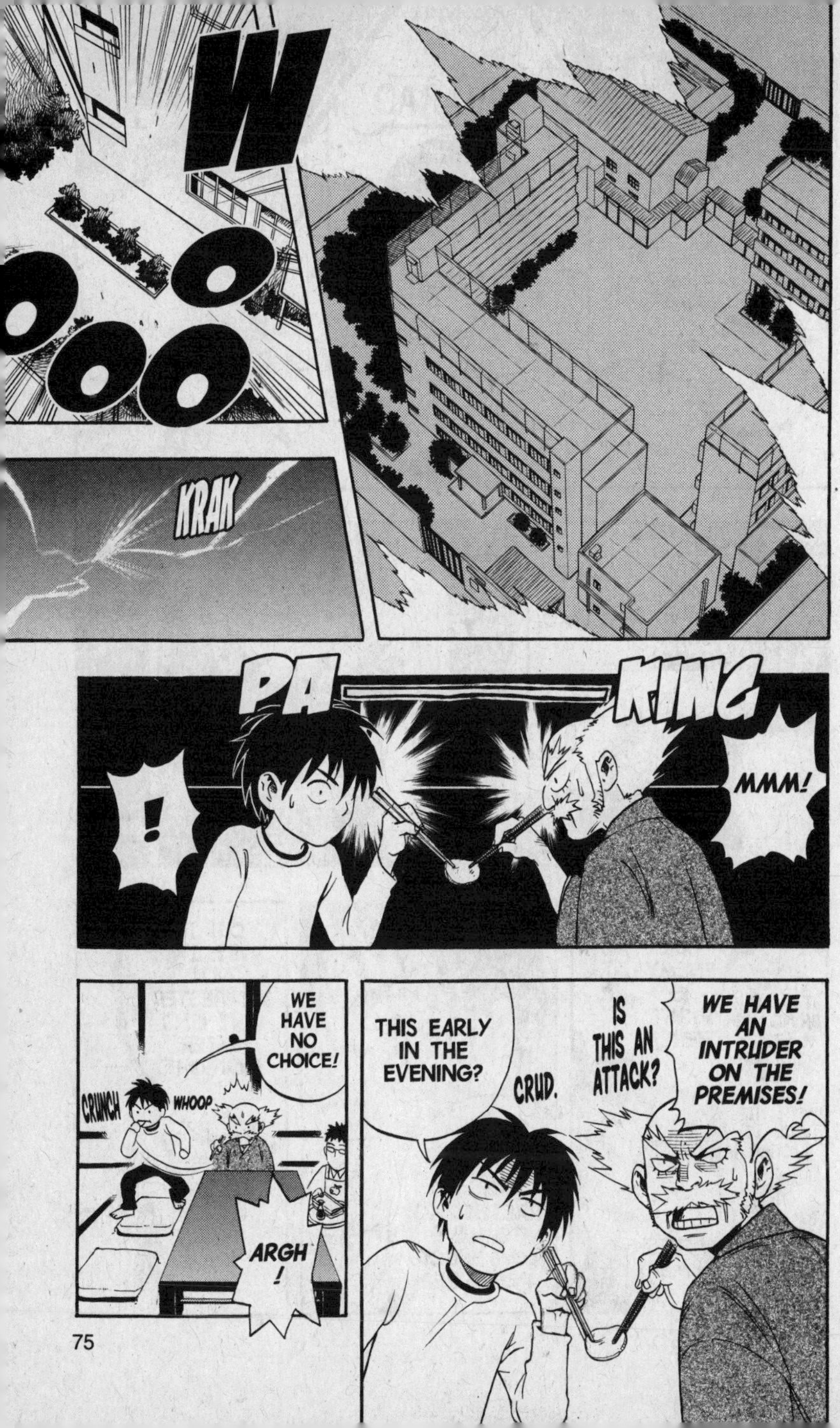
WHOOOOO
KRAK
PA—KING
MMM!
!
WE HAVE AN INTRUDER ON THE PREMISES!
IS THIS AN ATTACK?
CRUD.
THIS EARLY IN THE EVENING?
WE HAVE NO CHOICE!
WHOOP
CRUNCH
ARGH!

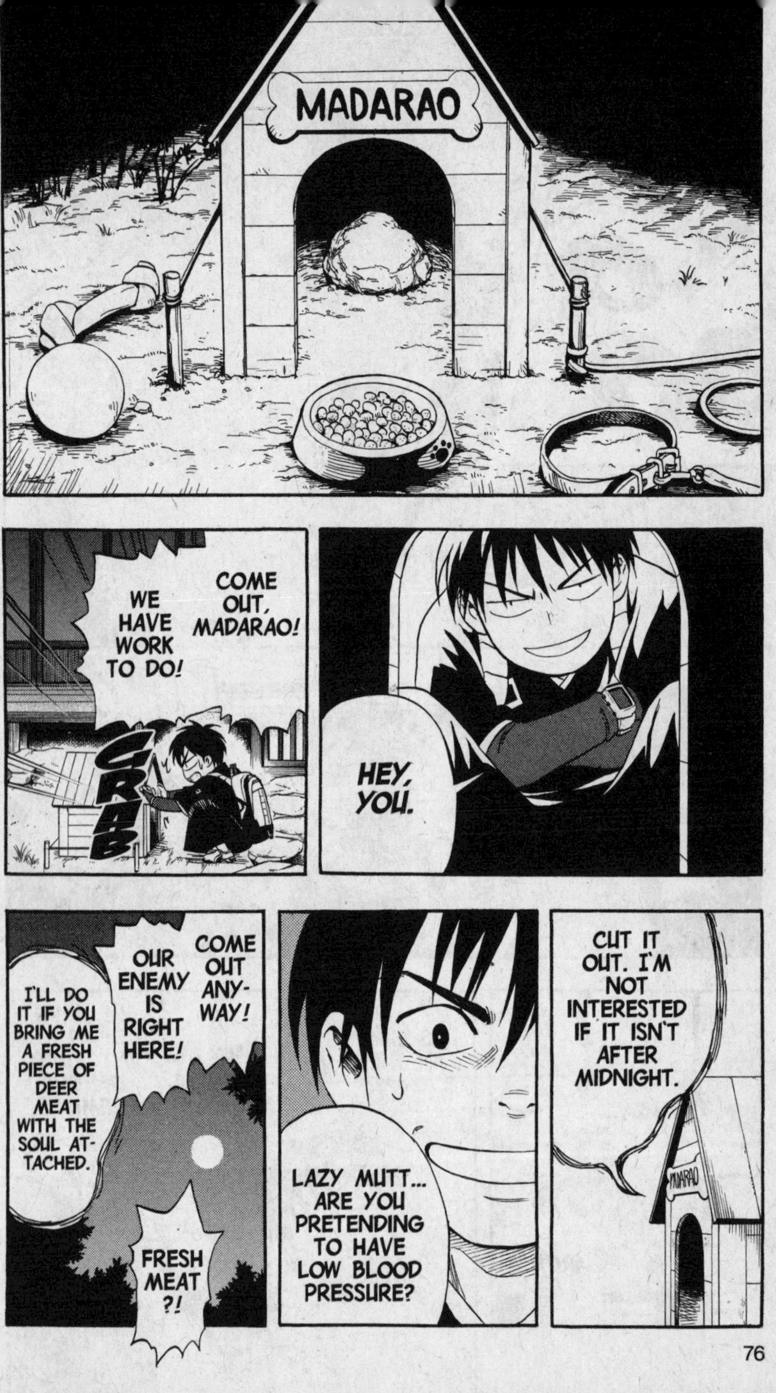
MADARAO
HEY, YOU.
COME OUT, MADARAO!
WE HAVE WORK TO DO!
GRAB
CUT IT OUT. I'M NOT INTERESTED IF IT ISN'T AFTER MIDNIGHT.
MADARAO
LAZY MUTT... ARE YOU PRETENDING TO HAVE LOW BLOOD PRESSURE?
COME OUT ANY-WAY!
OUR ENEMY IS RIGHT HERE!
I'LL DO IT IF YOU BRING ME A FRESH PIECE OF DEER MEAT WITH THE SOUL AT-TACHED.
FRESH MEAT ?!

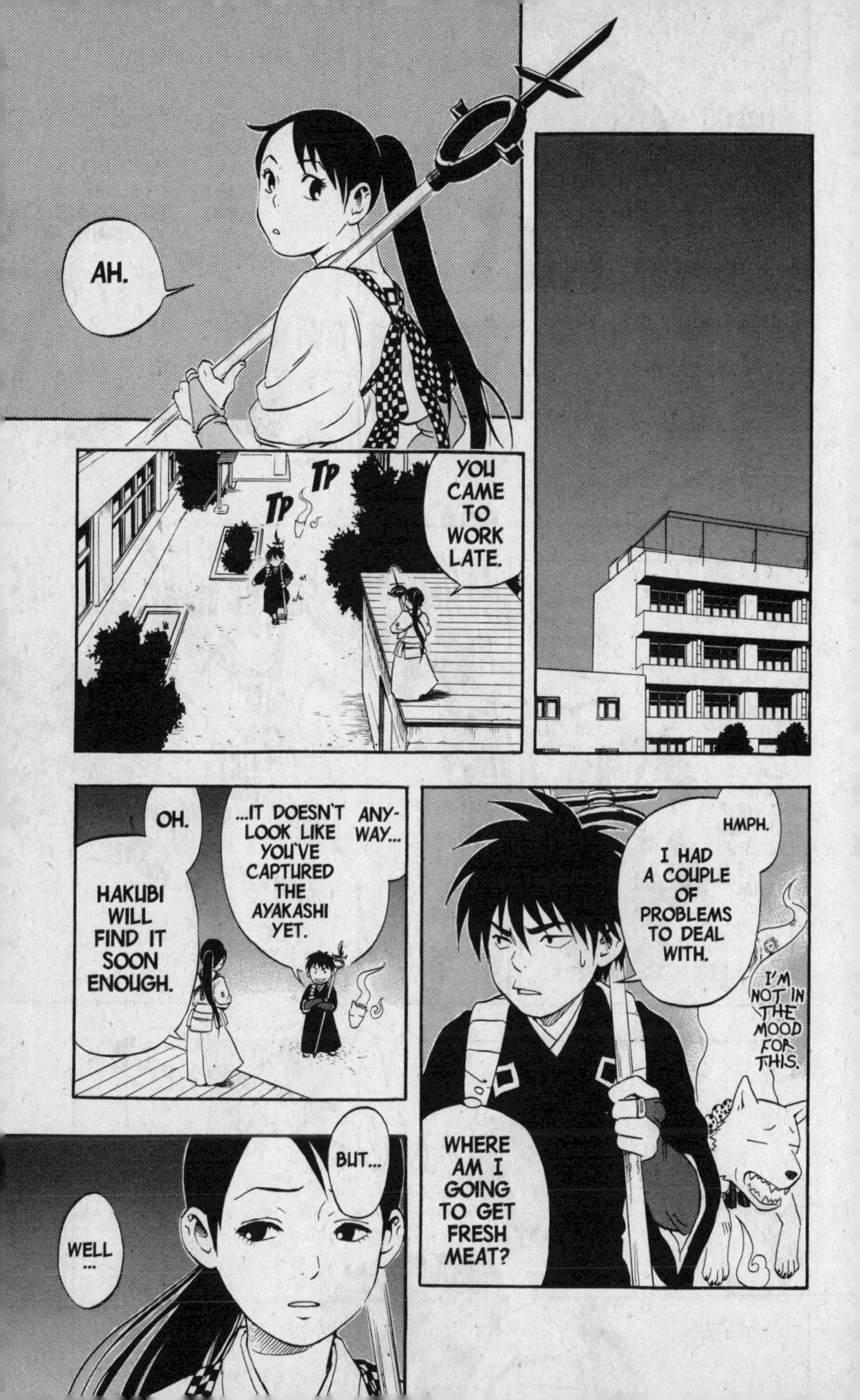
AH.
YOU CAME TO WORK LATE.
HMPH.
I HAD A COUPLE OF PROBLEMS TO DEAL WITH.
I'M NOT IN THE MOOD FOR THIS.
WHERE AM I GOING TO GET FRESH MEAT?
ANY-WAY...
...IT DOESN'T LOOK LIKE YOU'VE CAPTURED THE AYAKASHI YET.
OH.
HAKUBI WILL FIND IT SOON ENOUGH.
BUT...
WELL ...

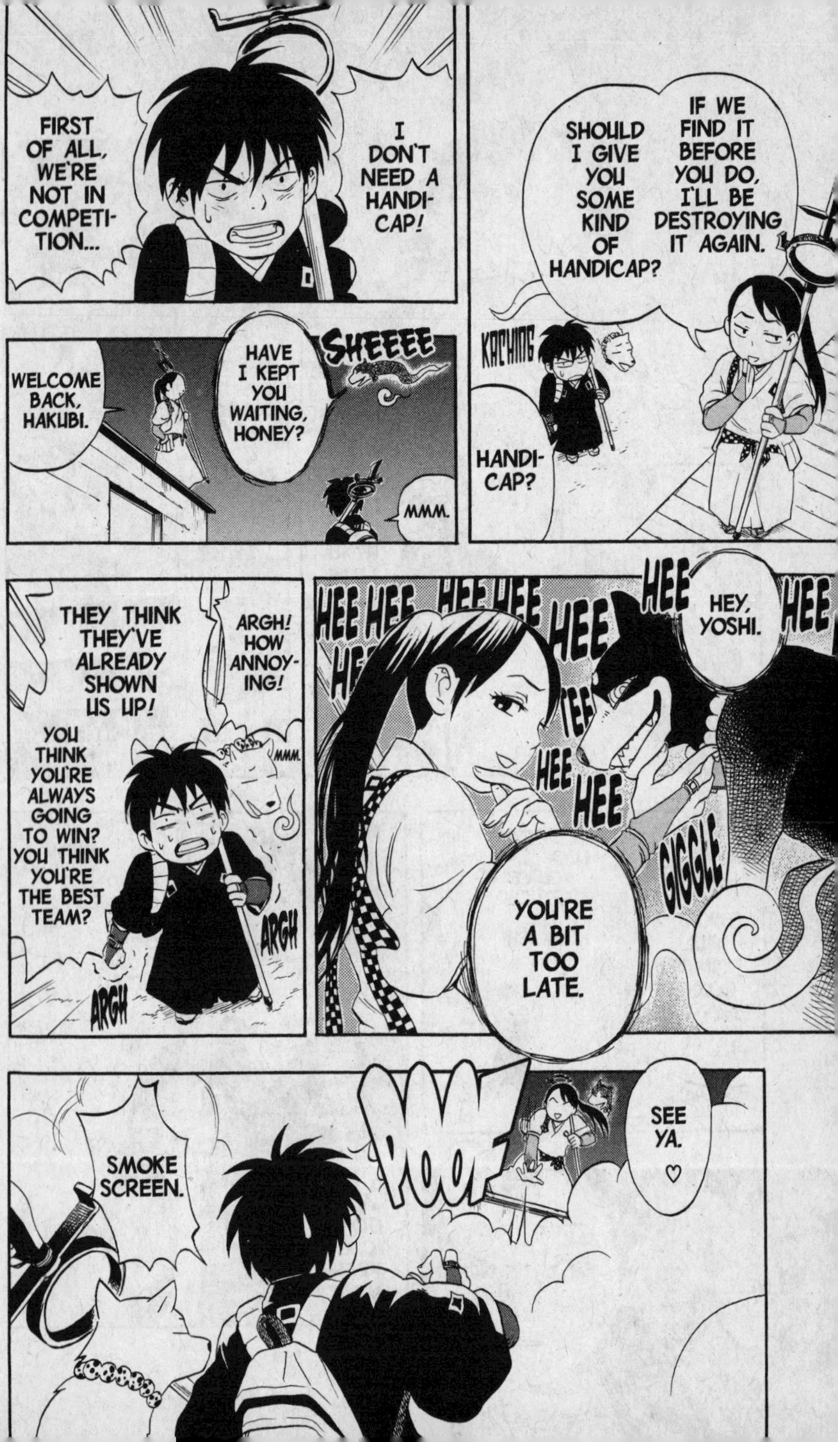
SHOULD I GIVE YOU SOME KIND OF HANDICAP? IF WE FIND IT BEFORE YOU DO, I'LL BE DESTROYING IT AGAIN.
KACHING
HANDICAP?
I DON'T NEED A HANDICAP!
FIRST OF ALL, WE'RE NOT IN COMPETITION...
SHEEEEE
HAVE I KEPT YOU WAITING, HONEY?
WELCOME BACK, HAKUBI.
MMM.
HEE
HEY, YOSHI.
HEE
HEE HEE HEE HEE
HEE
HEE HEE
YOU'RE A BIT TOO LATE.
GIGGLE
ARGH! HOW ANNOYING!
THEY THINK THEY'VE ALREADY SHOWN US UP!
MMM.
YOU THINK YOU'RE ALWAYS GOING TO WIN? YOU THINK YOU'RE THE BEST TEAM?
ARGH
ARGH
SEE YA. ♡
POOF
SMOKE SCREEN.

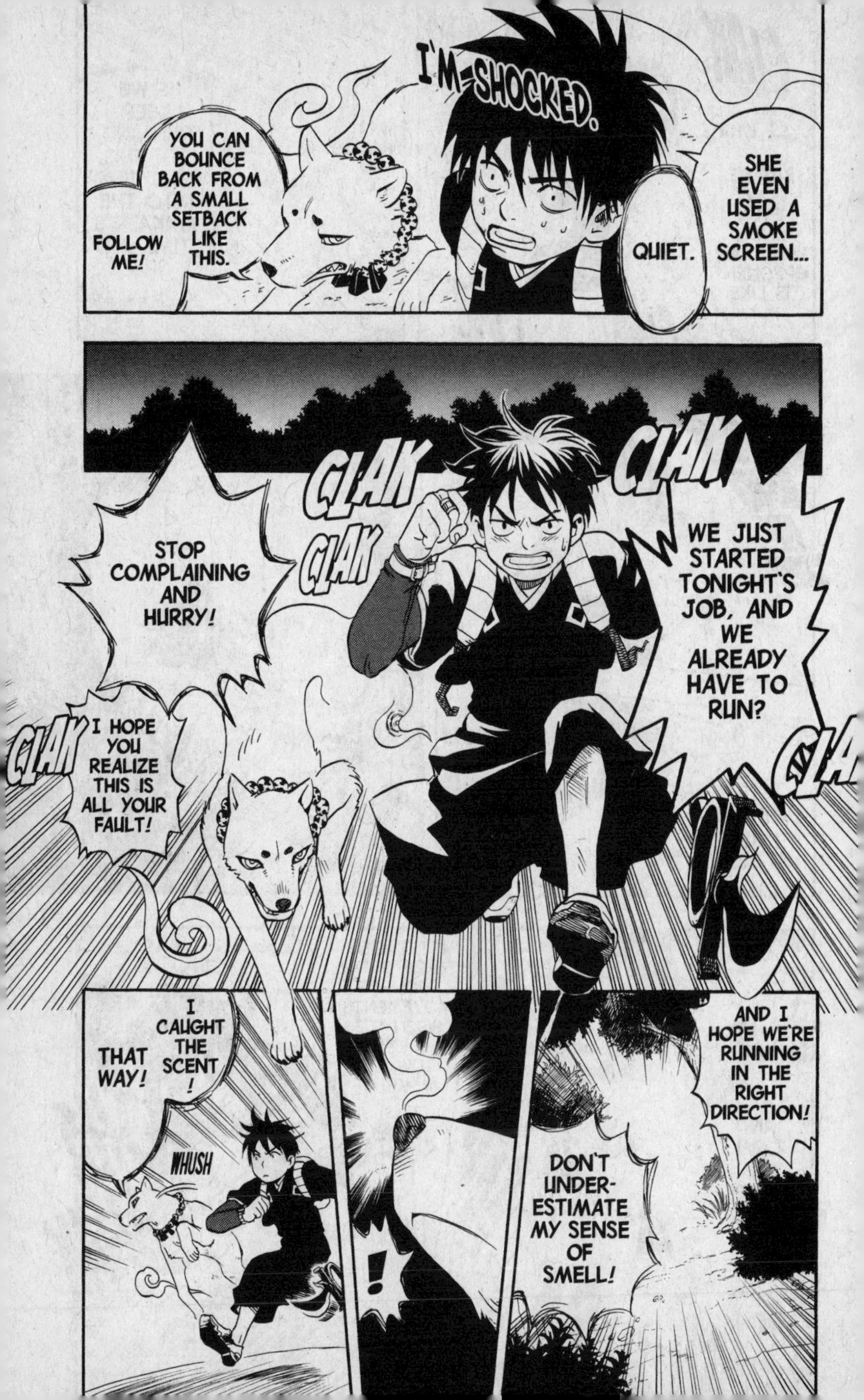
SHE EVEN USED A SMOKE SCREEN...
QUIET.
I'M SHOCKED.
YOU CAN BOUNCE BACK FROM A SMALL SETBACK LIKE THIS.
FOLLOW ME!
CLAK
WE JUST STARTED TONIGHT'S JOB, AND WE ALREADY HAVE TO RUN?
CLAK
CLAK
STOP COMPLAINING AND HURRY!
CLAK
I HOPE YOU REALIZE THIS IS ALL YOUR FAULT!
AND I HOPE WE'RE RUNNING IN THE RIGHT DIRECTION!
DON'T UNDER-ESTIMATE MY SENSE OF SMELL!
!
I CAUGHT THE SCENT!
THAT WAY!
WHUSH

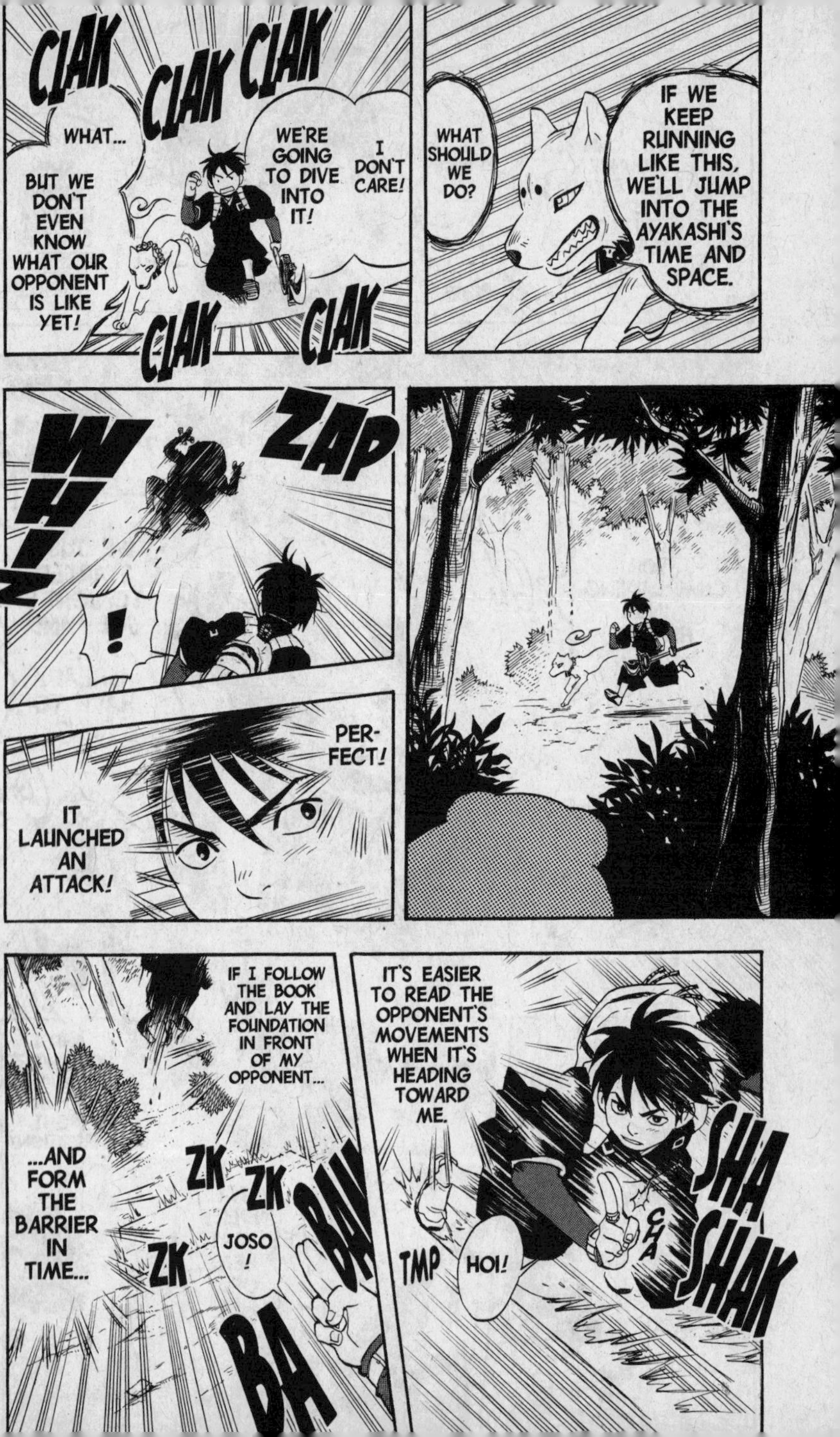
IF WE KEEP RUNNING LIKE THIS, WE'LL JUMP INTO THE AYAKASHI'S TIME AND SPACE.
WHAT SHOULD WE DO?
CLAK CLAK
I DON'T CARE!
WE'RE GOING TO DIVE INTO IT!
CLAK
WHAT...
BUT WE DON'T EVEN KNOW WHAT OUR OPPONENT IS LIKE YET!
CLAK CLAK
ZAP
WHIZ
!
PER-FECT!
IT LAUNCHED AN ATTACK!
IT'S EASIER TO READ THE OPPONENT'S MOVEMENTS WHEN IT'S HEADING TOWARD ME.
SHA SHAK
CHA
HOI!
TMP
IF I FOLLOW THE BOOK AND LAY THE FOUNDATION IN FRONT OF MY OPPONENT...
ZK ZK
JOSO!
ZK
...AND FORM THE BARRIER IN TIME...
BA

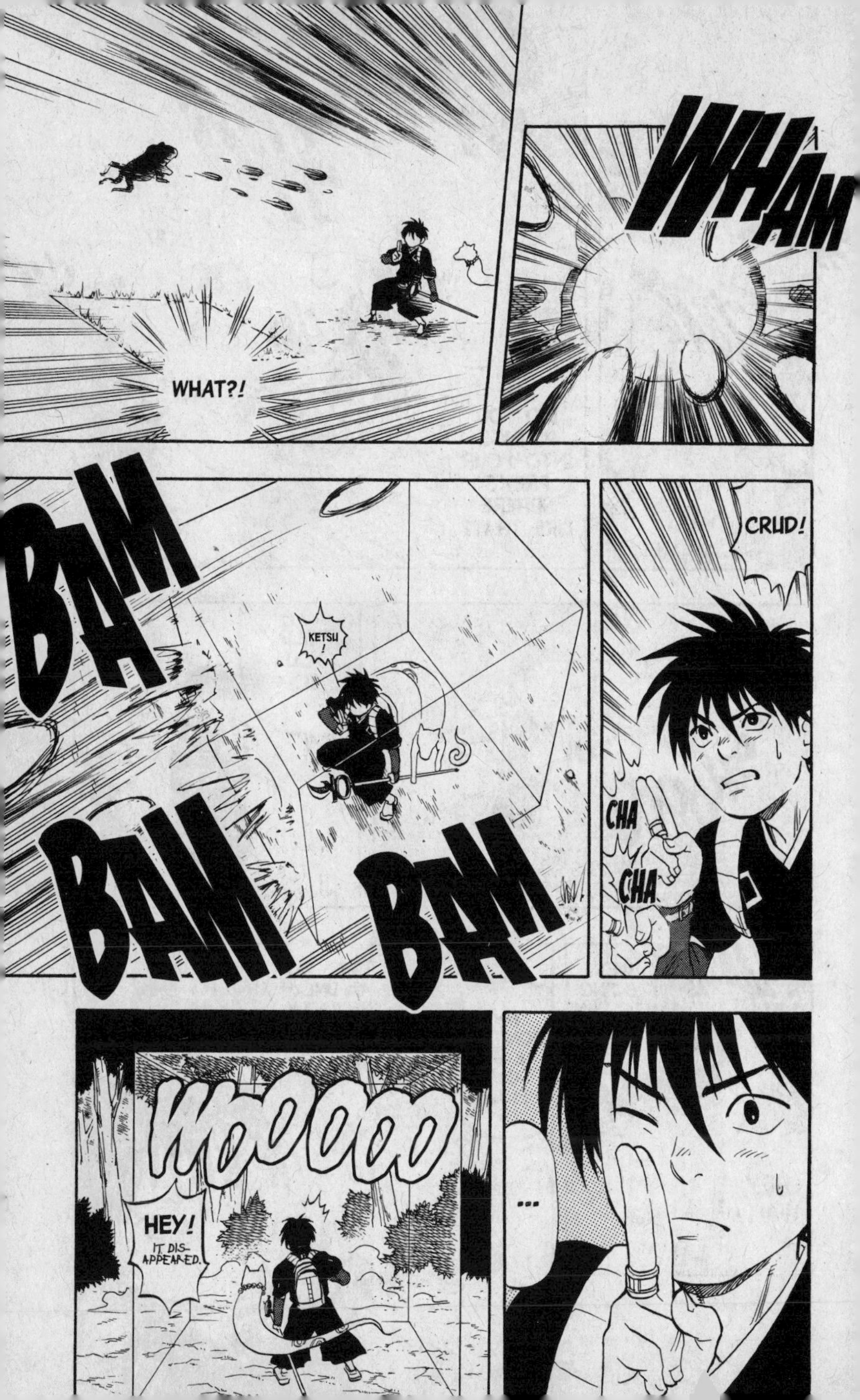
WHAM
WHAT?!
CRUD!
CHA
CHA
BAM
KETSU!
BAM
BAM
...
WOOOOO
HEY!
IT DIS-APPEARED.

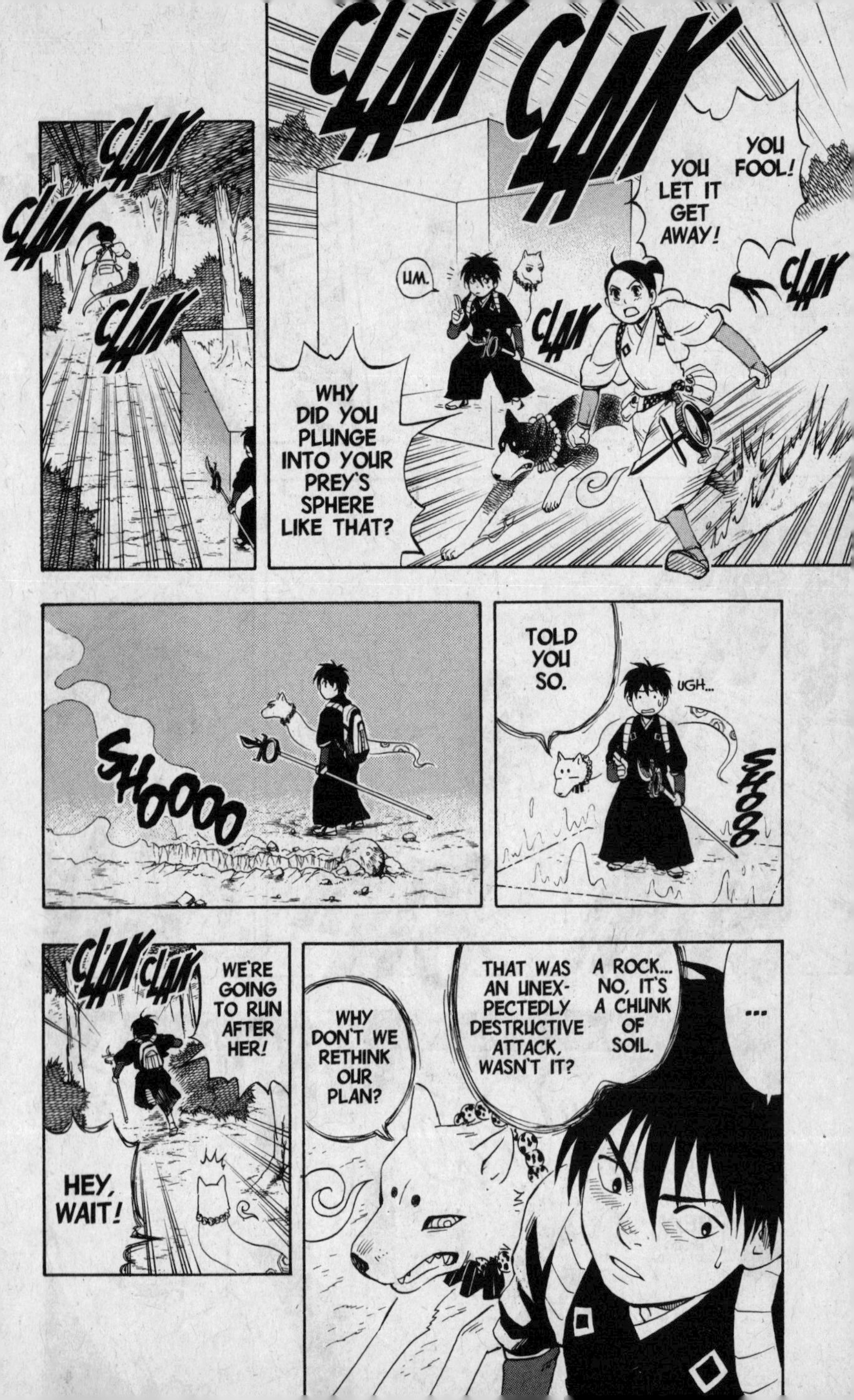
CLAK CLAK
YOU FOOL!
YOU LET IT GET AWAY!
CLAK
CLAK
UM.
WHY DID YOU PLUNGE INTO YOUR PREY'S SPHERE LIKE THAT?
CLAK
CLAK
CLAK
TOLD YOU SO.
UGH...
SHOOOO
SHOOOO
...
A ROCK... NO, IT'S A CHUNK OF SOIL.
THAT WAS AN UNEXPECTEDLY DESTRUCTIVE ATTACK, WASN'T IT?
WHY DON'T WE RETHINK OUR PLAN?
CLAK CLAK
WE'RE GOING TO RUN AFTER HER!
HEY, WAIT!

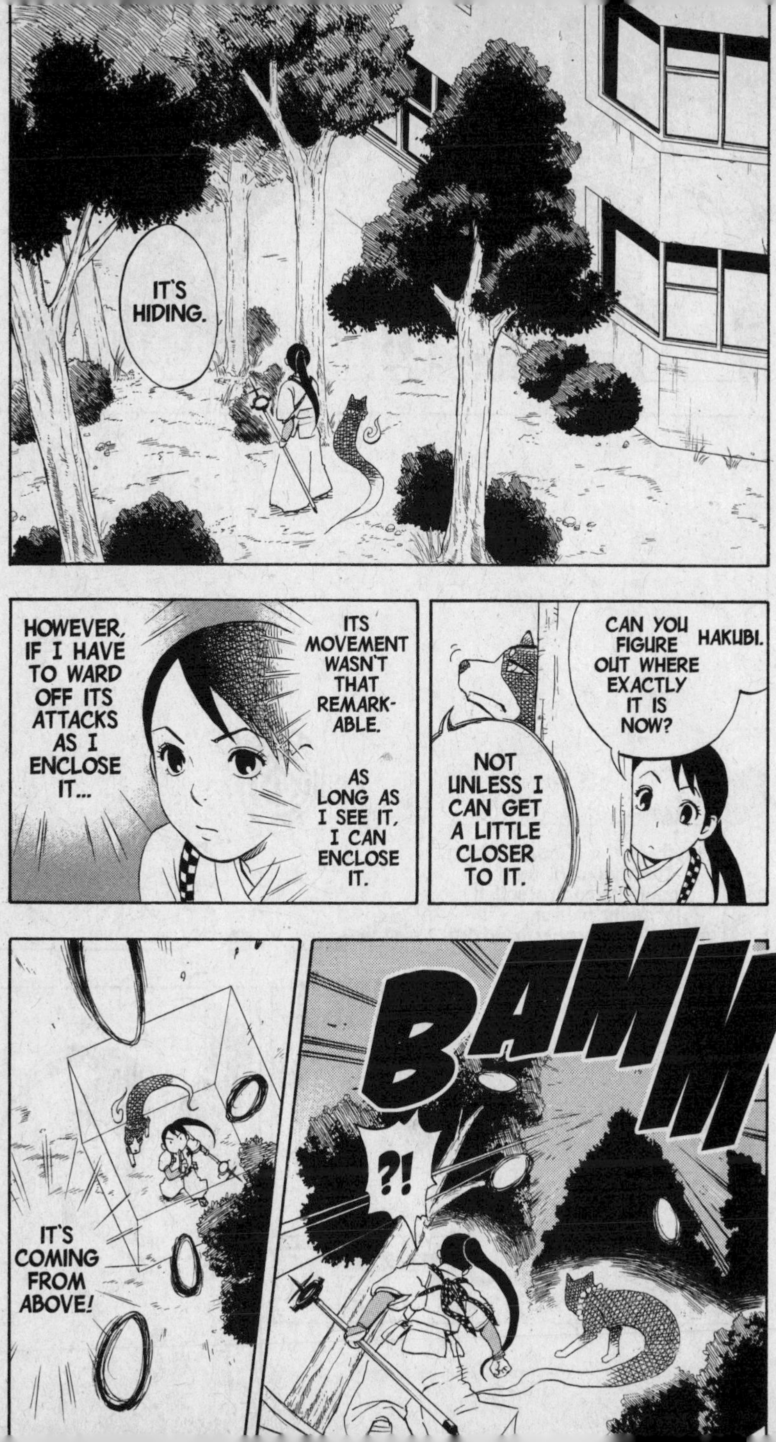
IT'S HIDING.
HAKUBI.
CAN YOU FIGURE OUT WHERE EXACTLY IT IS NOW?
NOT UNLESS I CAN GET A LITTLE CLOSER TO IT.
ITS MOVEMENT WASN'T THAT REMARKABLE.
AS LONG AS I SEE IT, I CAN ENCLOSE IT.
HOWEVER, IF I HAVE TO WARD OFF ITS ATTACKS AS I ENCLOSE IT...
BAMM
?!
IT'S COMING FROM ABOVE!

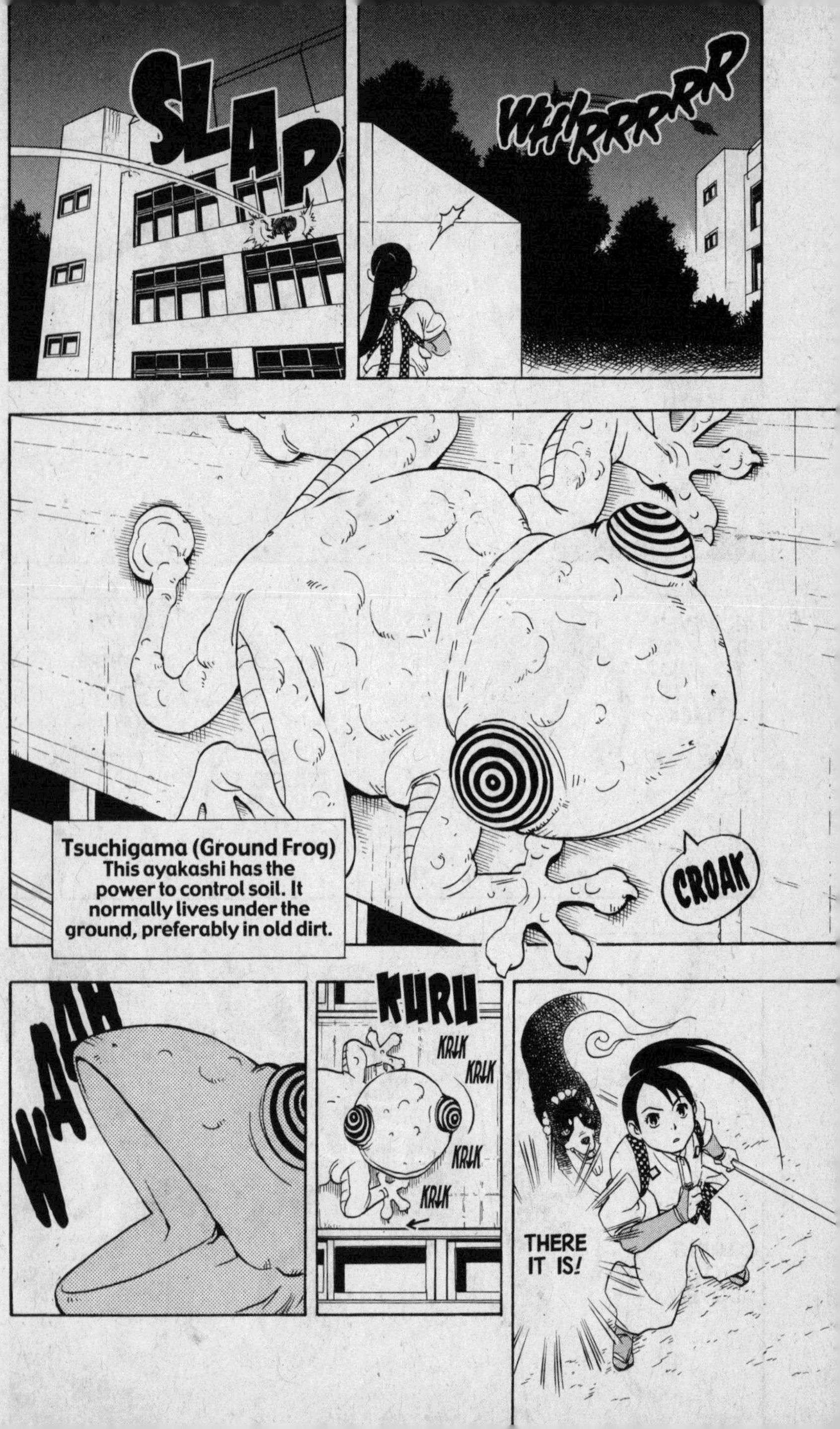
WHIRRRRRR
SLAP
CROAK
Tsuchigama (Ground Frog)
This ayakashi has the power to control soil. It normally lives under the ground, preferably in old dirt.
THERE IT IS!
KURU
KRLK
KRLK
KRLK
KRLK
WAAH

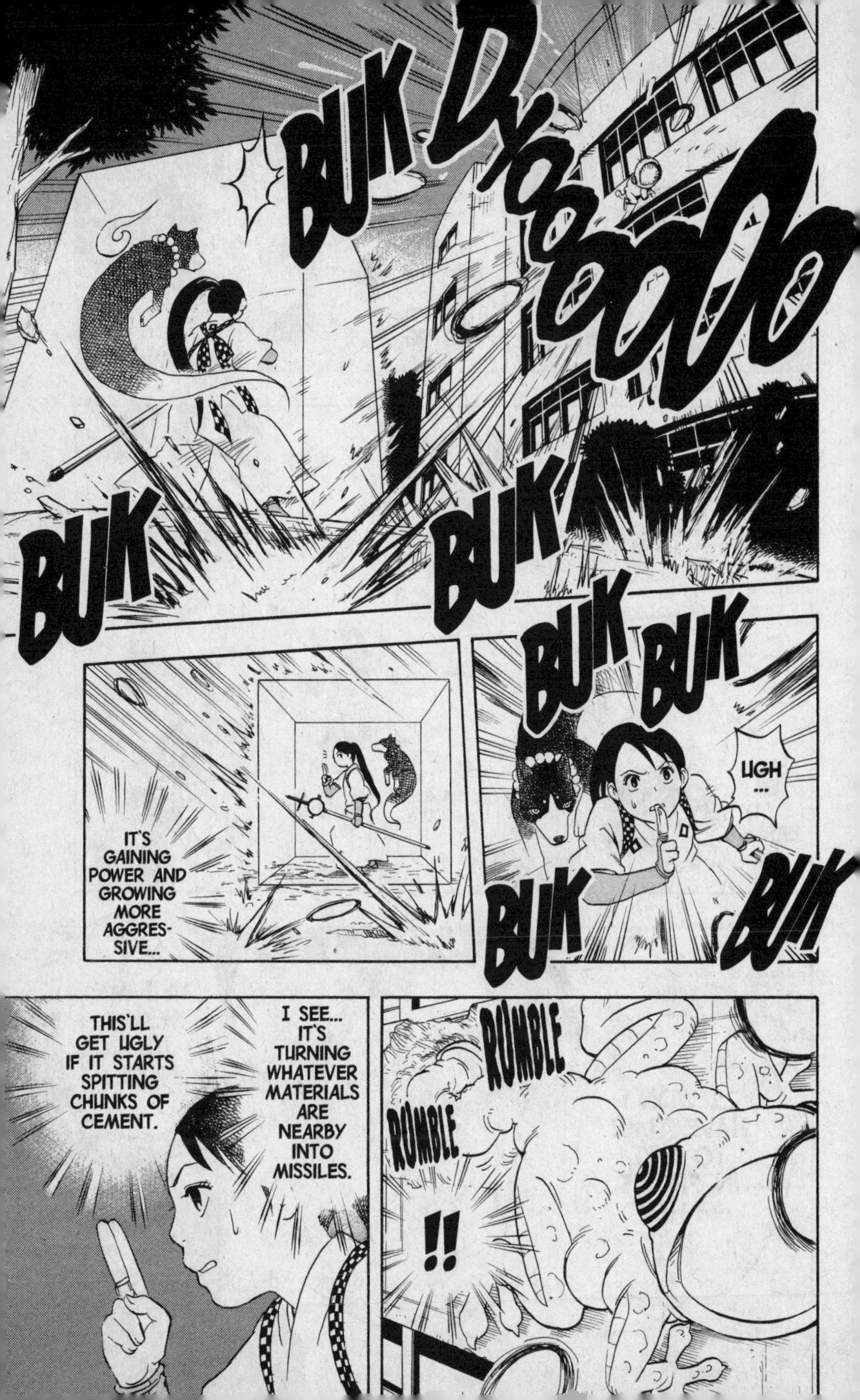
BUK
BUK
BUK
BUK
UGH ...
BUK
BUK
IT'S GAINING POWER AND GROWING MORE AGGRES-SIVE...
RUMBLE
RUMBLE
!!
I SEE... IT'S TURNING WHATEVER MATERIALS ARE NEARBY INTO MISSILES.
THIS'LL GET UGLY IF IT STARTS SPITTING CHUNKS OF CEMENT.

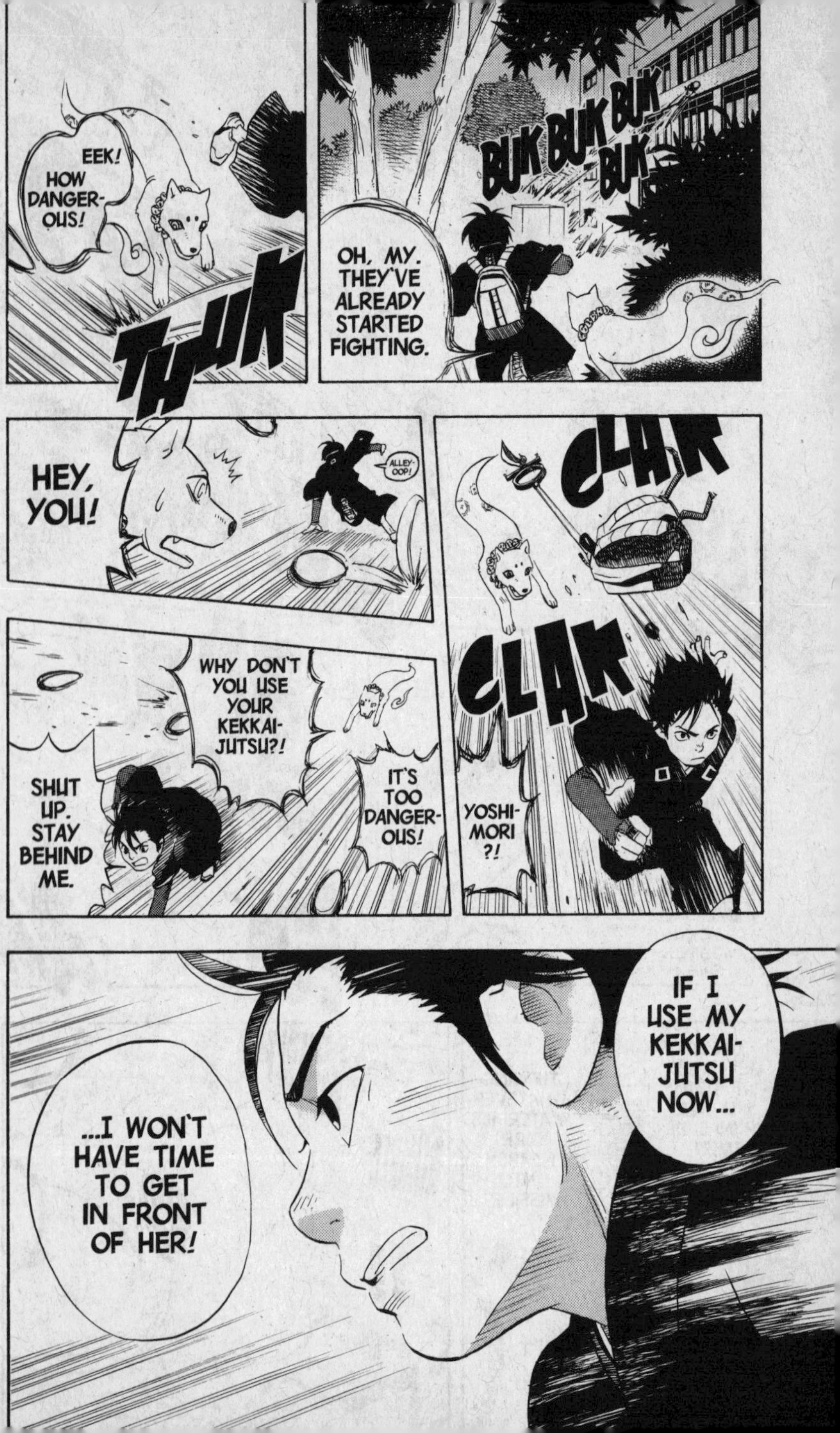
BUK BUK BUK BUK
OH, MY. THEY'VE ALREADY STARTED FIGHTING.
EEK! HOW DANGER-OUS!
THUNK
CLAK
CLAK
YOSHI-MORI ?!
HEY, YOU!
ALLEY-OOP!
WHY DON'T YOU USE YOUR KEKKAI-JUTSU?!
IT'S TOO DANGER-OUS!
SHUT UP. STAY BEHIND ME.
IF I USE MY KEKKAI-JUTSU NOW...
...I WON'T HAVE TIME TO GET IN FRONT OF HER!

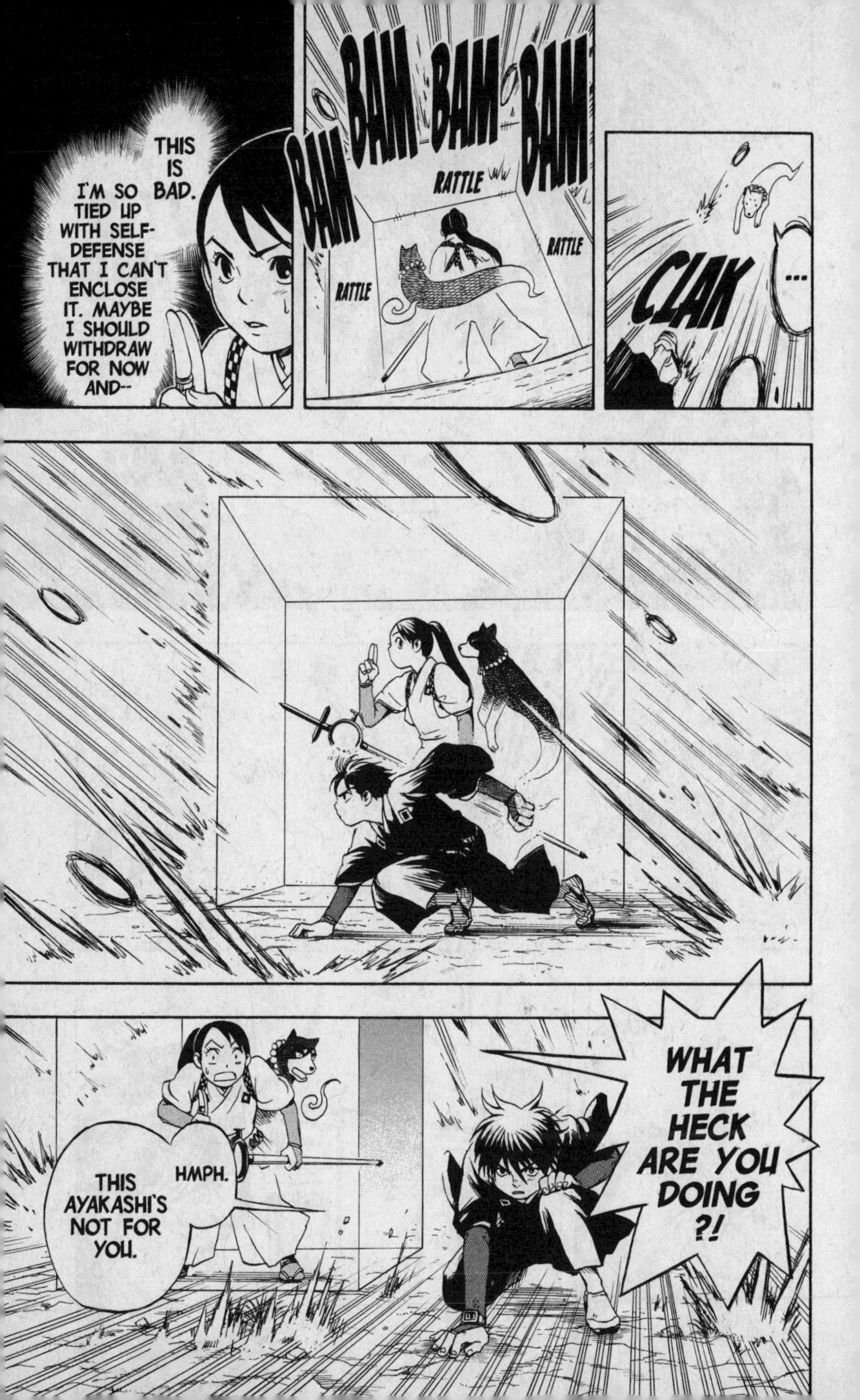
CLAK
...
BAM BAM BAM BAM BAM
RATTLE
RATTLE
RATTLE
THIS IS BAD.
I'M SO TIED UP WITH SELF-DEFENSE THAT I CAN'T ENCLOSE IT. MAYBE I SHOULD WITHDRAW FOR NOW AND--
WHAT THE HECK ARE YOU DOING ?!
HMPH.
THIS AYAKASHI'S NOT FOR YOU.

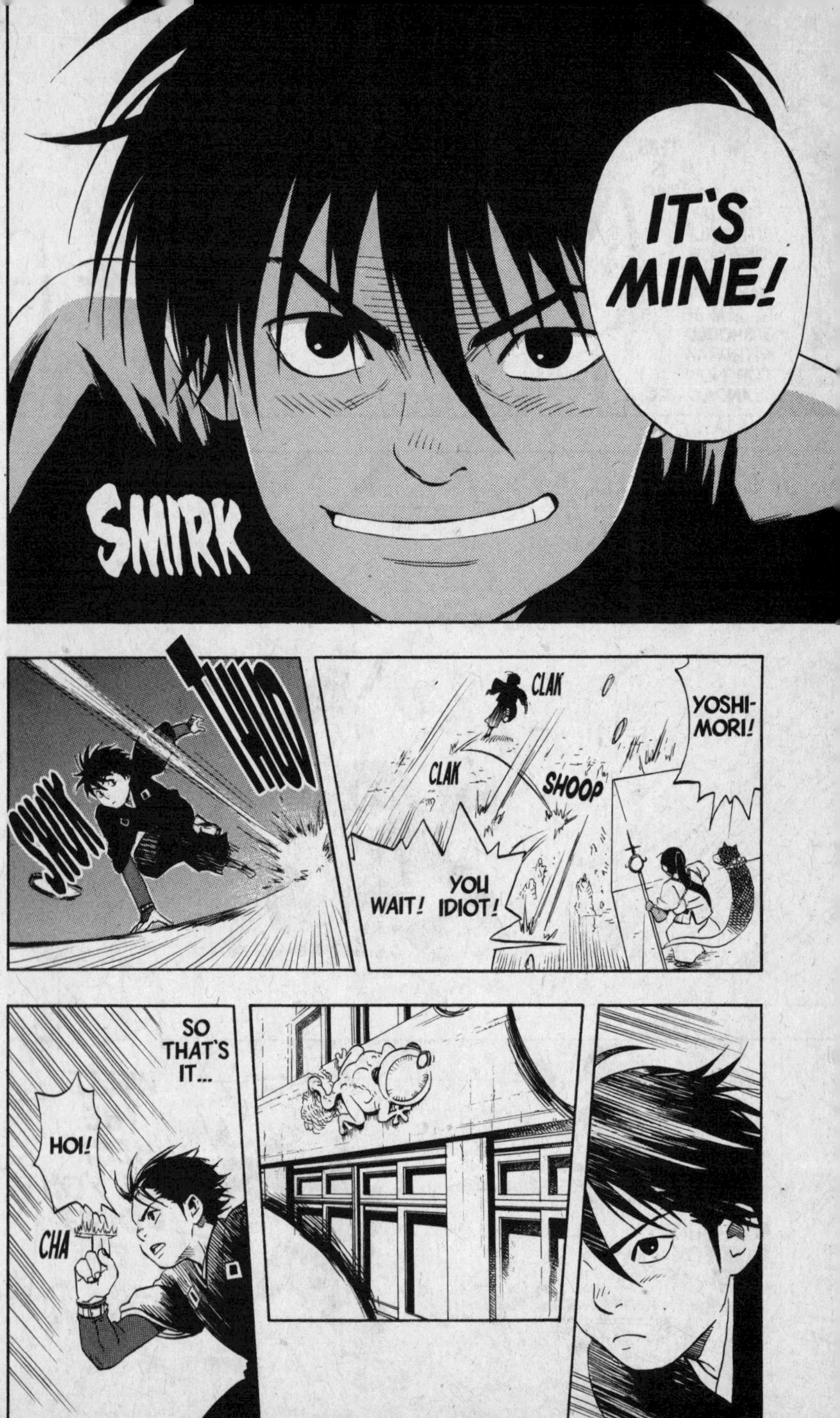
IT'S MINE!
SMIRK
YOSHI-MORI!
CLAK
CLAK
SHOOP
YOU IDIOT!
WAIT!
SO THAT'S IT...
HOI!
CHA

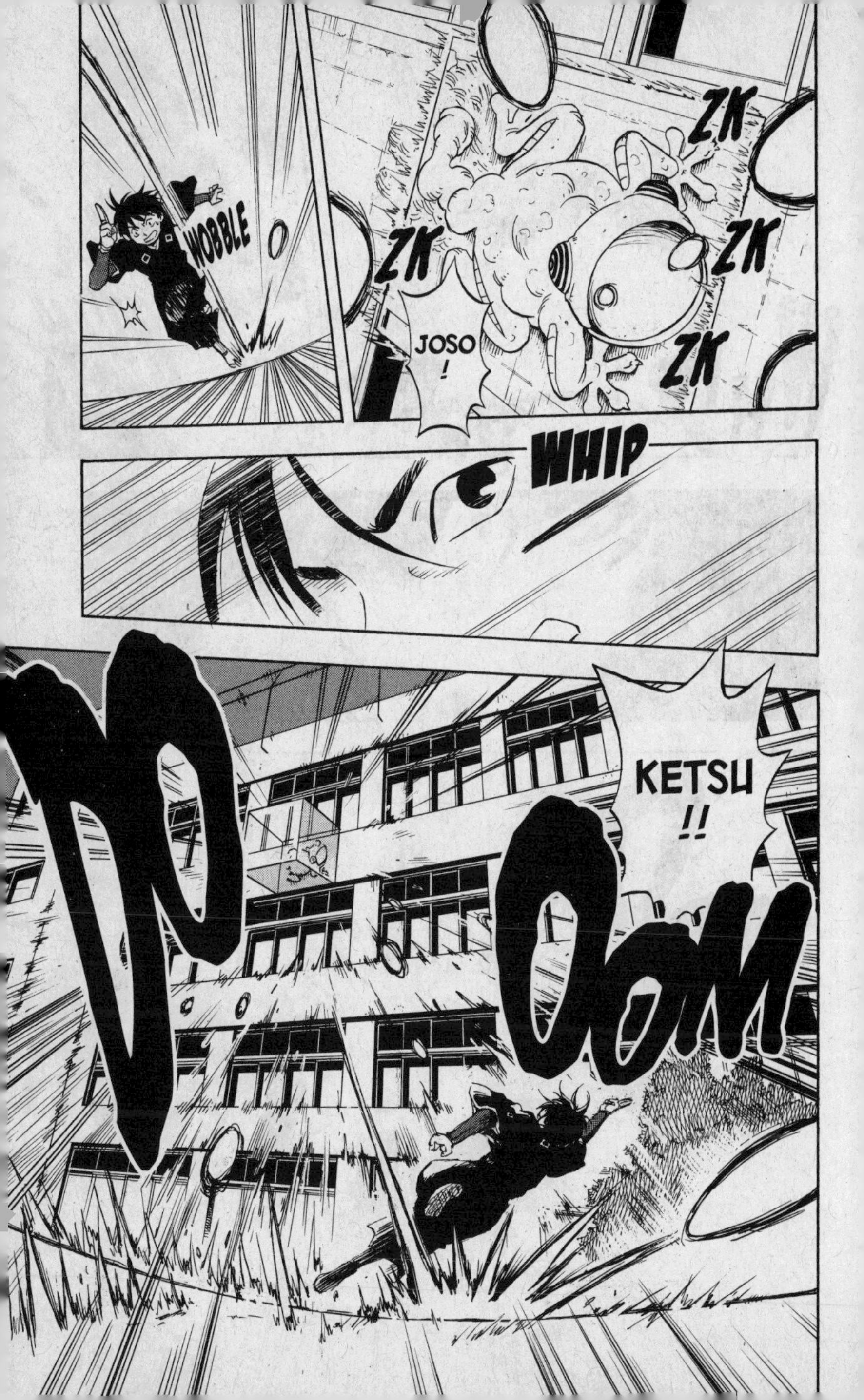
ZK
ZK
ZK
ZK
JOSO!
WOBBLE
WHIP
KETSU!!
DOOM

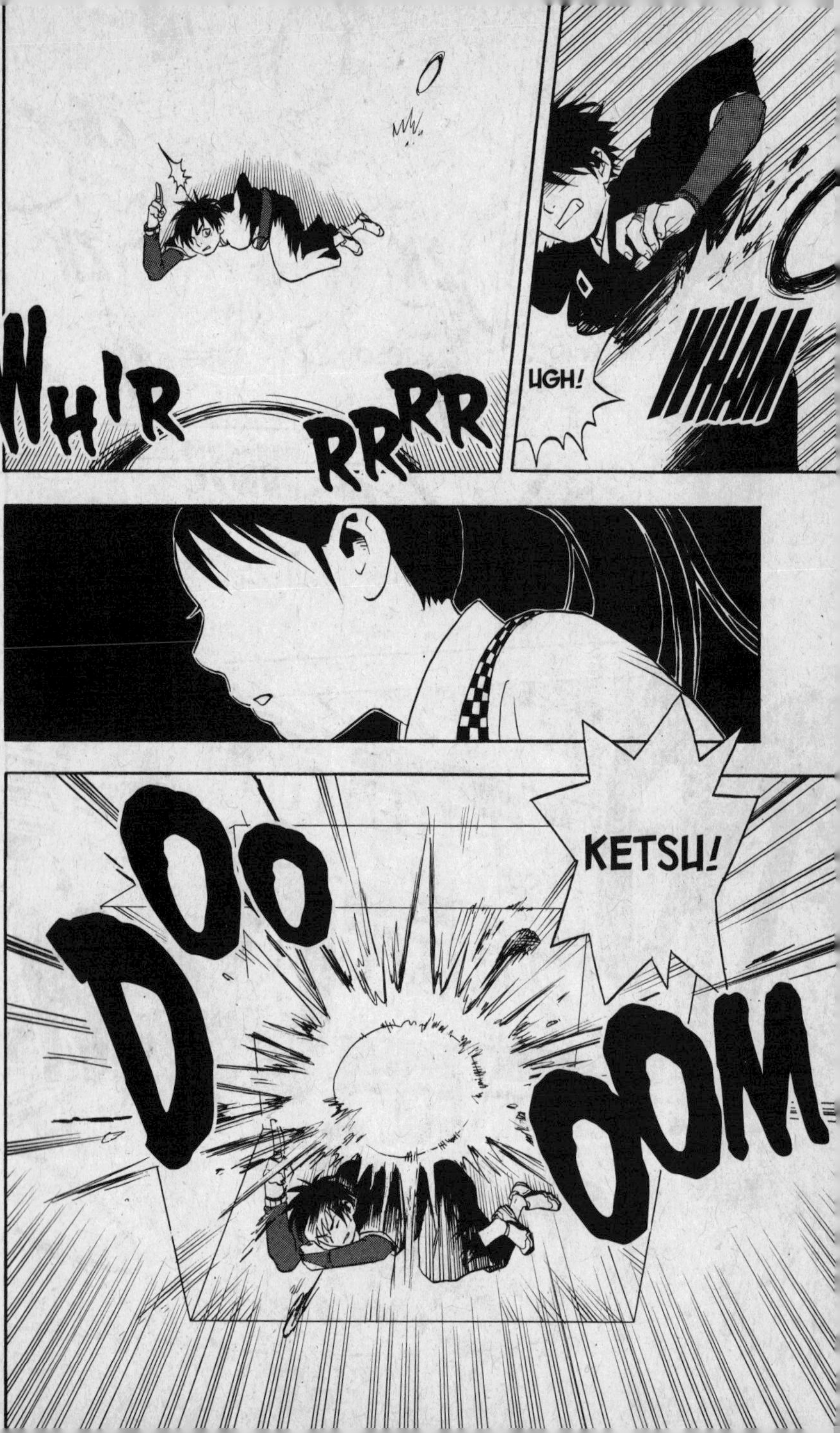
UGH!
WHAM
WHIR
RRRR
KETSU!
DOO
OOM

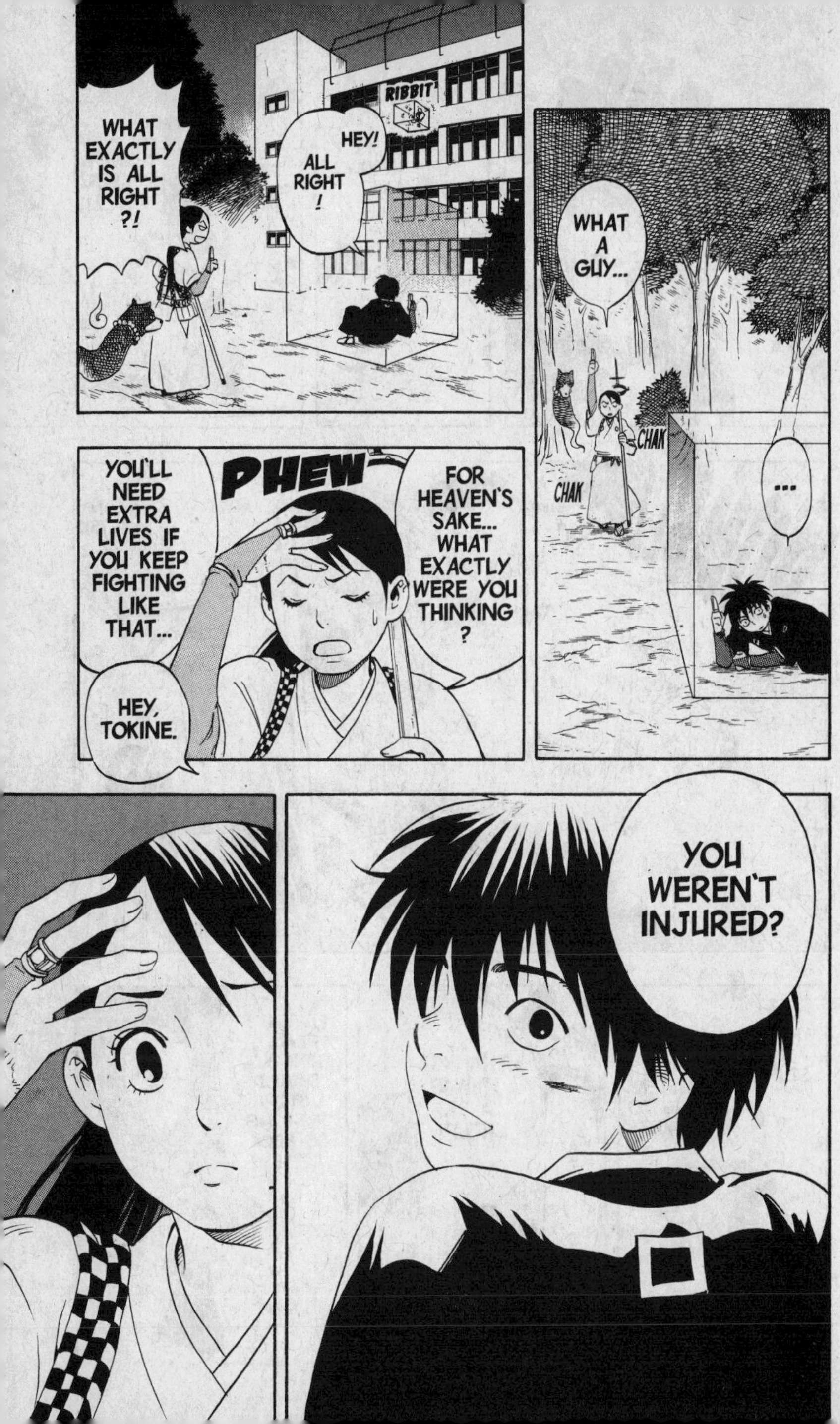
RIBBIT
HEY! ALL RIGHT!
WHAT EXACTLY IS ALL RIGHT?!
WHAT A GUY...
CHAK
CHAK
...
PHEW
FOR HEAVEN'S SAKE... WHAT EXACTLY WERE YOU THINKING?
YOU'LL NEED EXTRA LIVES IF YOU KEEP FIGHTING LIKE THAT...
HEY, TOKINE.
YOU WEREN'T INJURED?

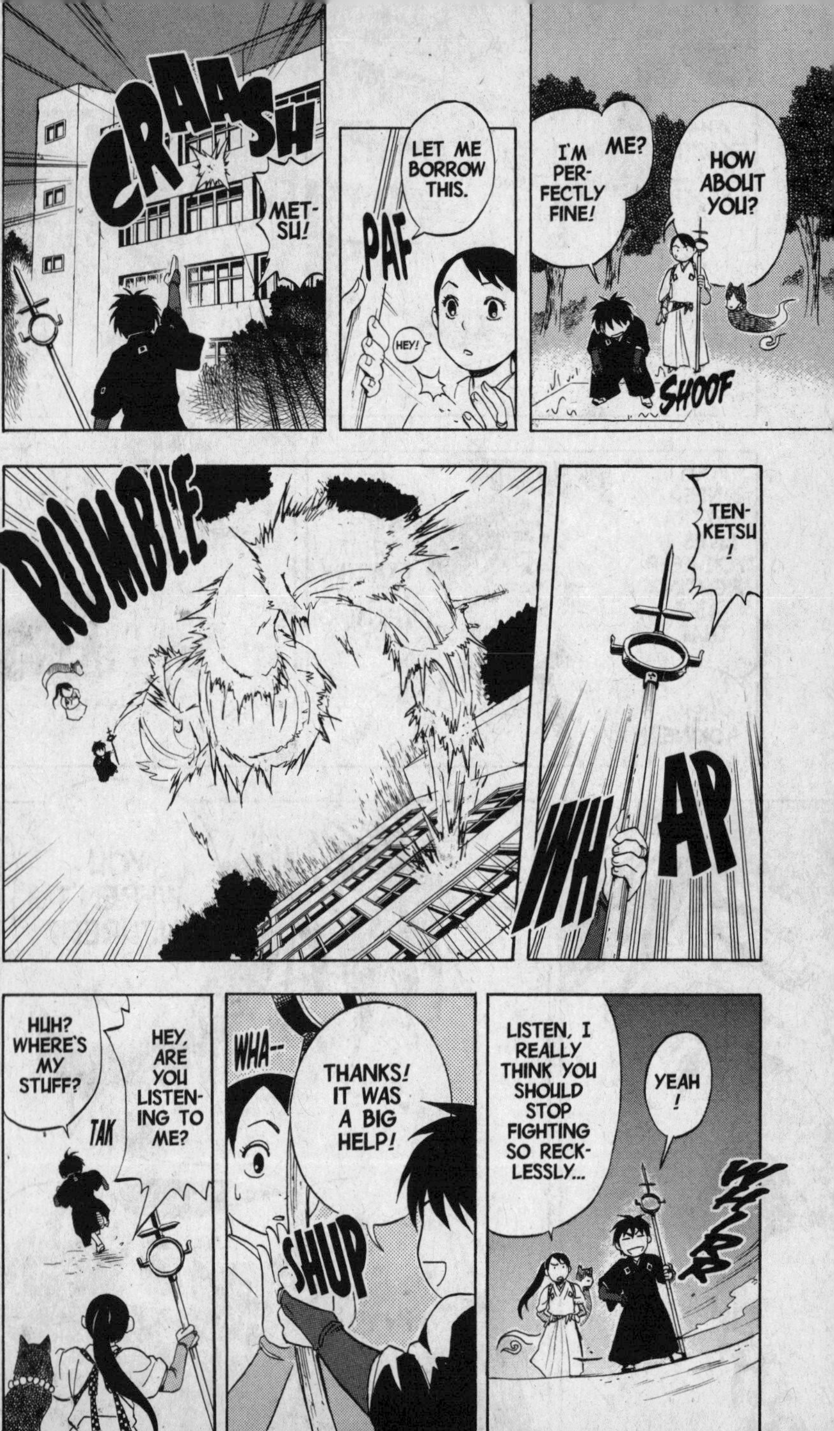
HOW ABOUT YOU?
ME?
I'M PER-FECTLY FINE!
SHOOF
LET ME BORROW THIS.
PAF
HEY!
CRAASH
MET-SU!
TEN-KETSU!
WHAP
RUMBLE
YEAH!
LISTEN, I REALLY THINK YOU SHOULD STOP FIGHTING SO RECK-LESSLY...
WHA--
THANKS! IT WAS A BIG HELP!
SHUP
HEY, ARE YOU LISTEN-ING TO ME?
HUH? WHERE'S MY STUFF?
TAK

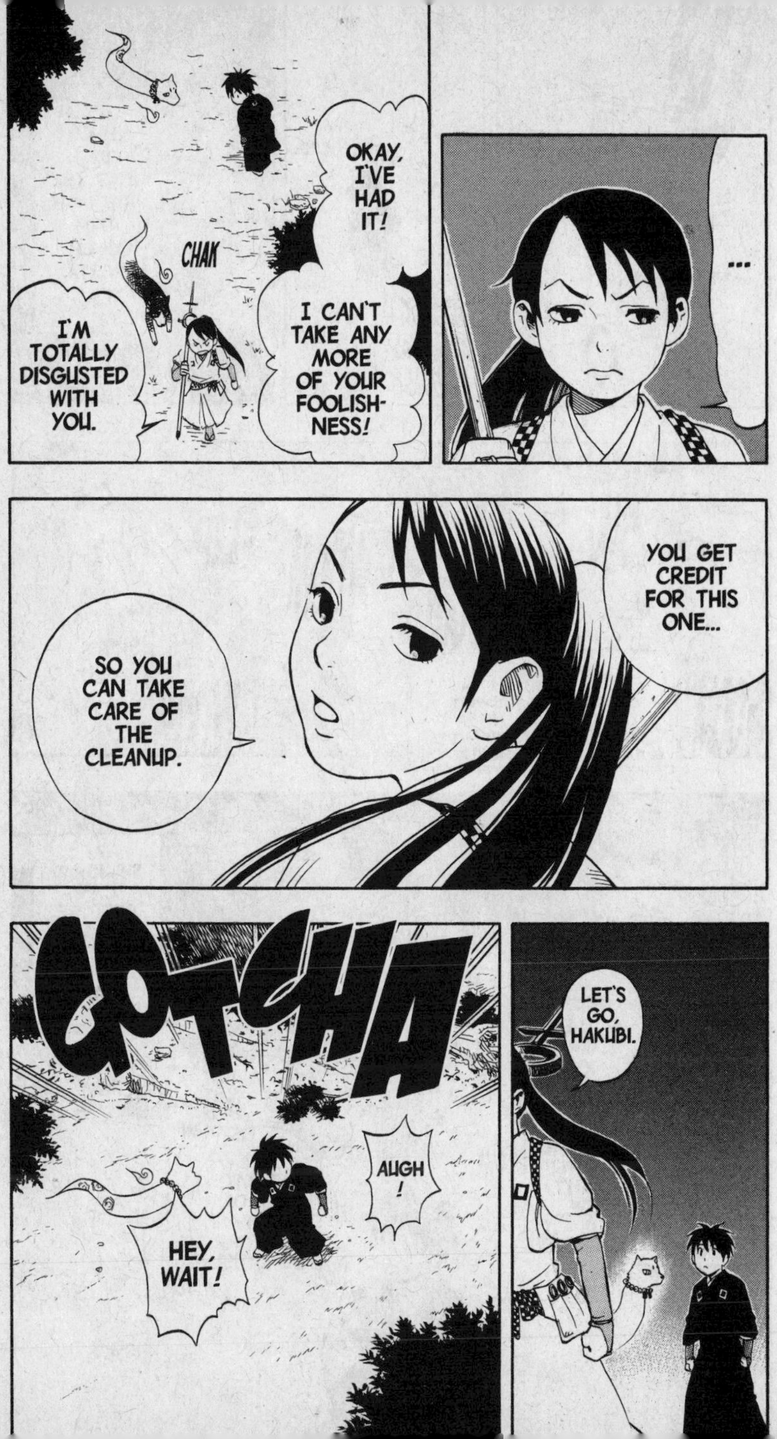
...
OKAY, I'VE HAD IT!
I CAN'T TAKE ANY MORE OF YOUR FOOLISHNESS!
CHAK
I'M TOTALLY DISGUSTED WITH YOU.
YOU GET CREDIT FOR THIS ONE...
SO YOU CAN TAKE CARE OF THE CLEANUP.
LET'S GO, HAKUBI.
GOTCHA
AUGH!
HEY, WAIT!

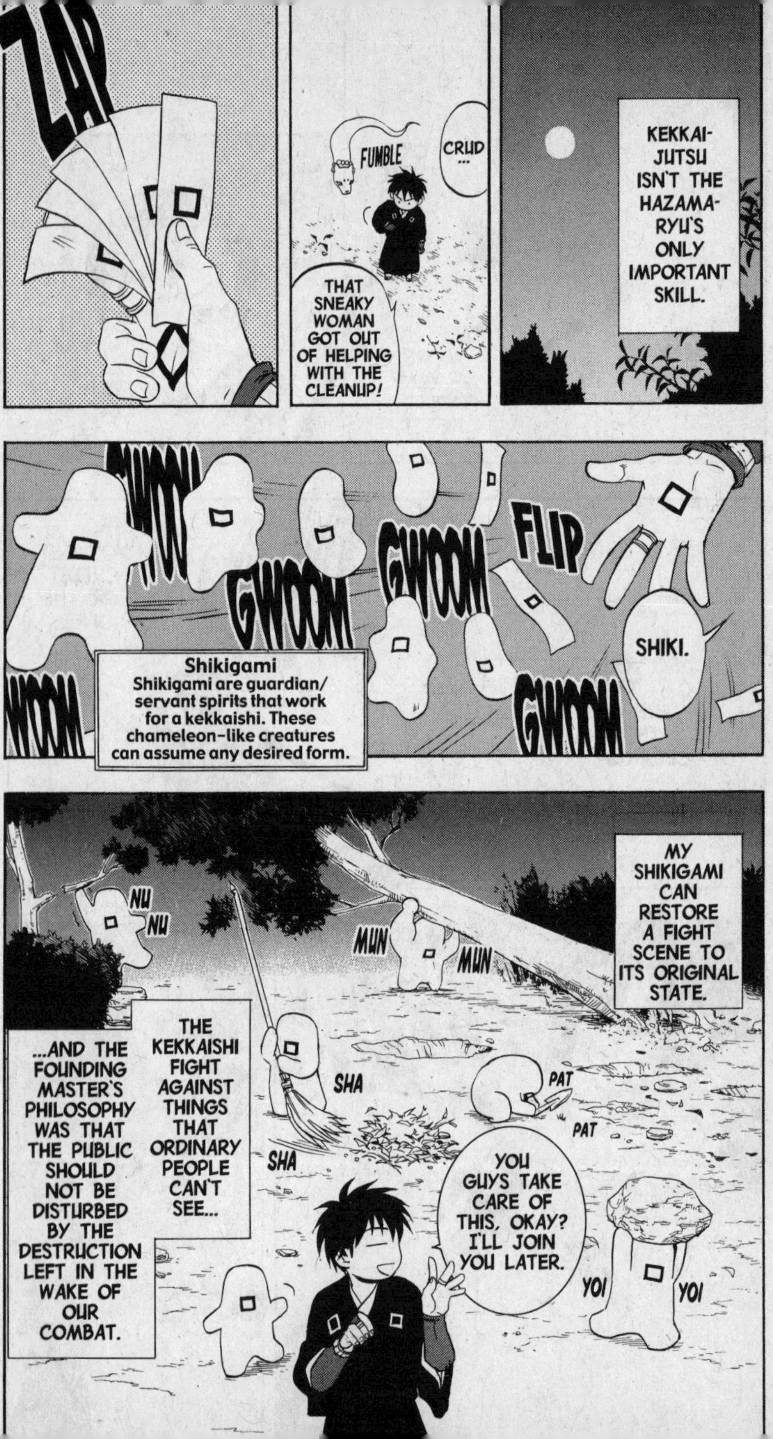
KEKKAI-JUTSU ISN'T THE HAZAMA-RYU'S ONLY IMPORTANT SKILL.
CRUD...
FUMBLE
THAT SNEAKY WOMAN GOT OUT OF HELPING WITH THE CLEANUP!
ZAP
SHIKI.
FLIP
GWOOM
GWOOM
GWOOM
GWOOM
Shikigami
Shikigami are guardian/servant spirits that work for a kekkaishi. These chameleon-like creatures can assume any desired form.
MY SHIKIGAMI CAN RESTORE A FIGHT SCENE TO ITS ORIGINAL STATE.
MUN MUN
NU NU
PAT PAT
SHA SHA
THE KEKKAISHI FIGHT AGAINST THINGS THAT ORDINARY PEOPLE CAN'T SEE...
...AND THE FOUNDING MASTER'S PHILOSOPHY WAS THAT THE PUBLIC SHOULD NOT BE DISTURBED BY THE DESTRUCTION LEFT IN THE WAKE OF OUR COMBAT.
YOU GUYS TAKE CARE OF THIS, OKAY? I'LL JOIN YOU LATER.
YOI YOI

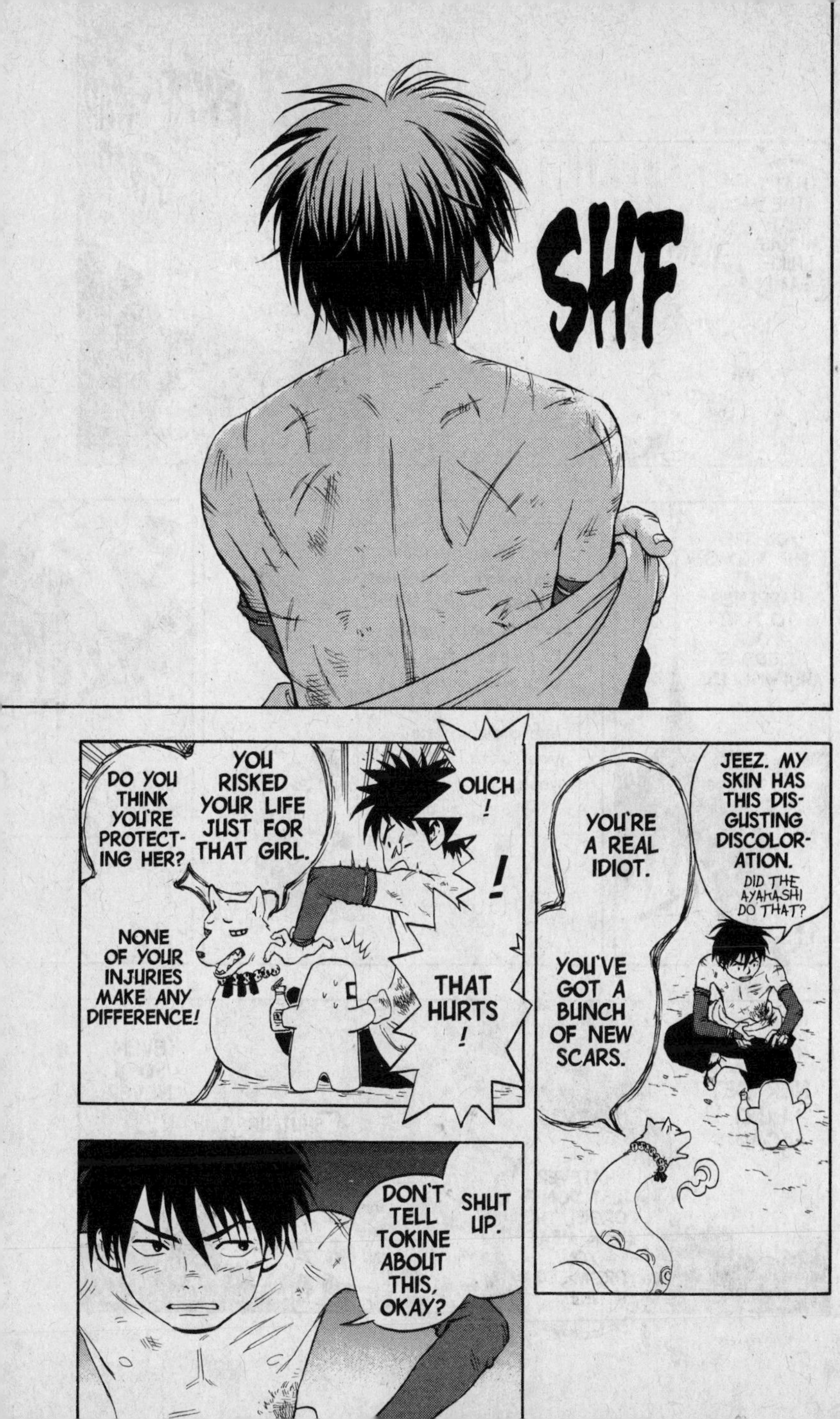
SHF
JEEZ. MY SKIN HAS THIS DISGUSTING DISCOLORATION.
DID THE AYAKASHI DO THAT?
YOU'RE A REAL IDIOT.
YOU'VE GOT A BUNCH OF NEW SCARS.
OUCH!
!
YOU RISKED YOUR LIFE JUST FOR THAT GIRL.
DO YOU THINK YOU'RE PROTECTING HER?
THAT HURTS!
NONE OF YOUR INJURIES MAKE ANY DIFFERENCE!
SHUT UP.
DON'T TELL TOKINE ABOUT THIS, OKAY?

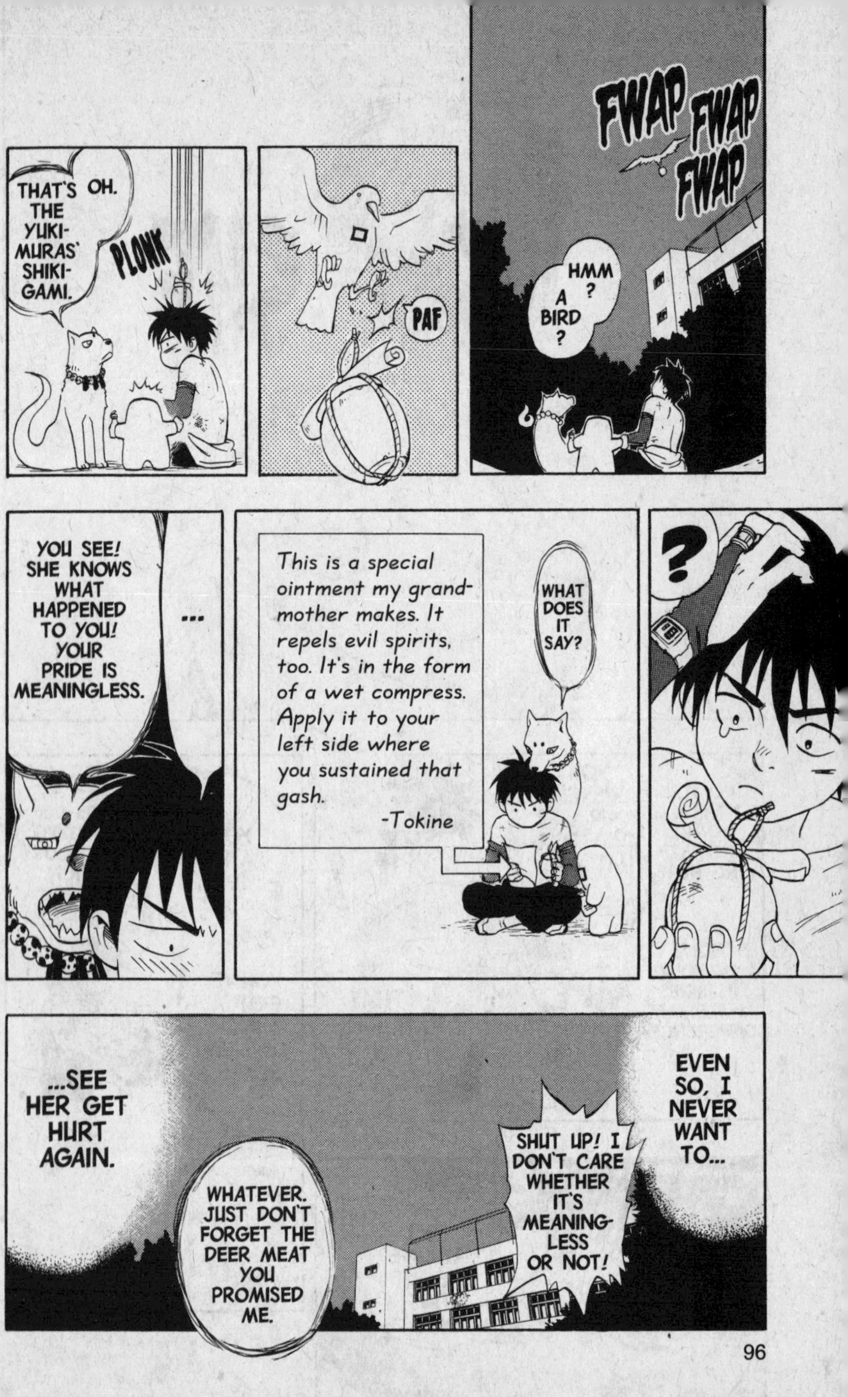
FWAP FWAP FWAP
HMM? A BIRD?
PAF
PLONK
OH.
THAT'S THE YUKI-MURAS' SHIKI-GAMI.
?
WHAT DOES IT SAY?
This is a special ointment my grand-mother makes. It repels evil spirits, too. It's in the form of a wet compress. Apply it to your left side where you sustained that gash. -Tokine
...
YOU SEE! SHE KNOWS WHAT HAPPENED TO YOU! YOUR PRIDE IS MEANINGLESS.
EVEN SO, I NEVER WANT TO...
SHUT UP! I DON'T CARE WHETHER IT'S MEANING-LESS OR NOT!
WHATEVER. JUST DON'T FORGET THE DEER MEAT YOU PROMISED ME.
...SEE HER GET HURT AGAIN.

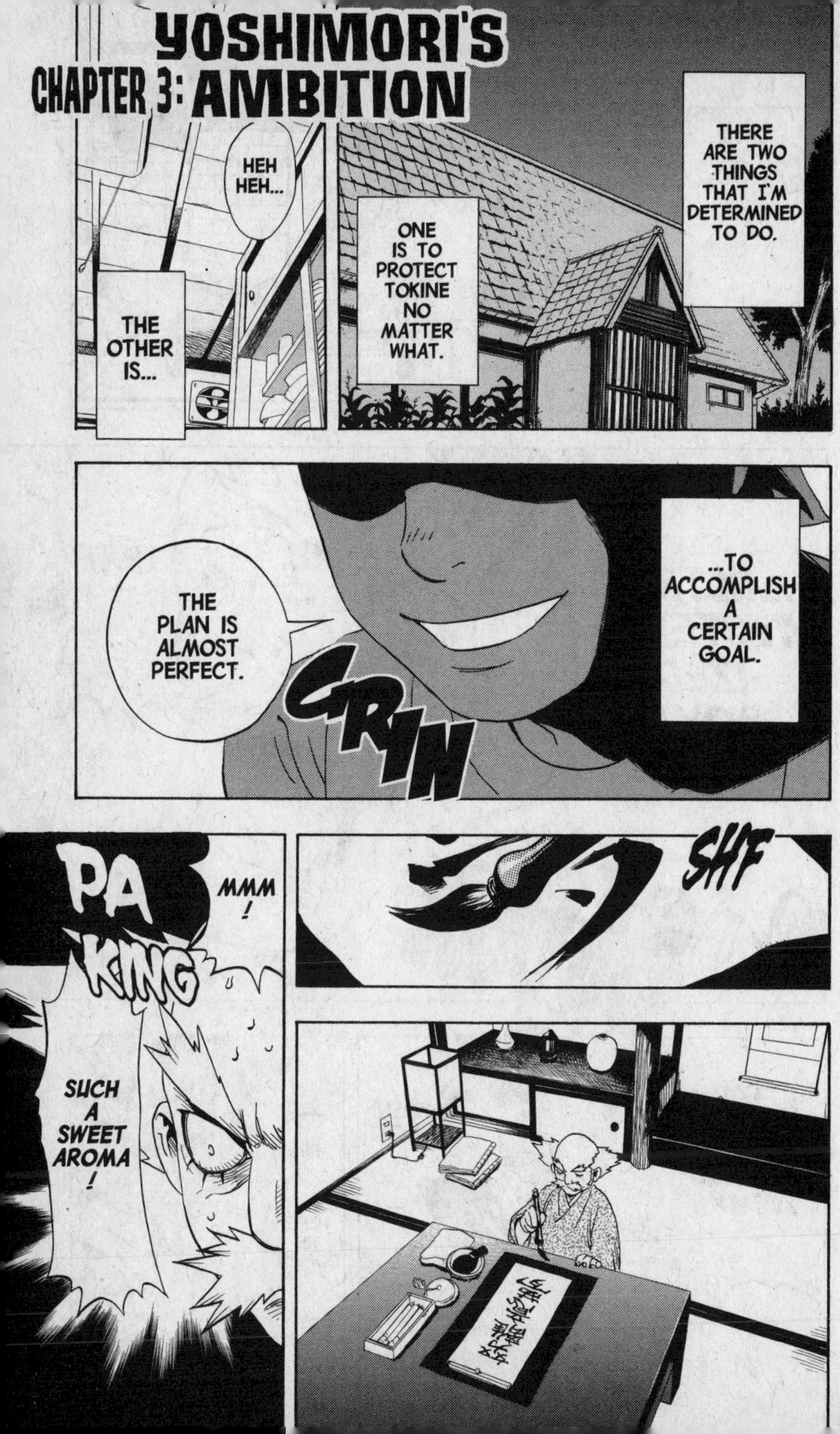
CHAPTER 3: YOSHIMORI'S AMBITION
THERE ARE TWO THINGS THAT I'M DETERMINED TO DO.
ONE IS TO PROTECT TOKINE NO MATTER WHAT.
HEH HEH...
THE OTHER IS...
...TO ACCOMPLISH A CERTAIN GOAL.
THE PLAN IS ALMOST PERFECT.
GRIN
SHF
PA KING
MMM!
SUCH A SWEET AROMA!

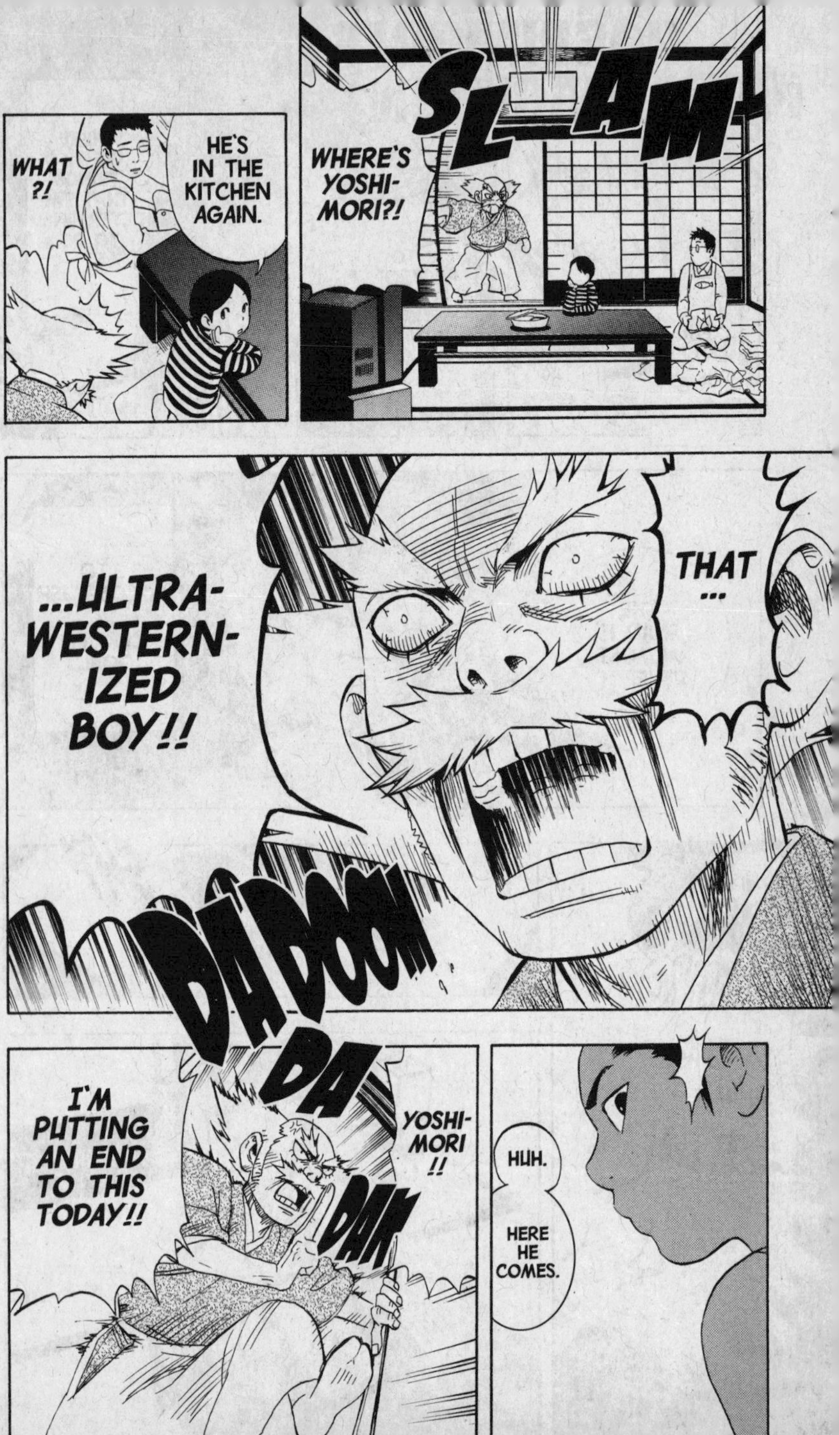
SLAM
WHERE'S YOSHIMORI?!
HE'S IN THE KITCHEN AGAIN.
WHAT ?!
THAT ...
...ULTRA-WESTERNIZED BOY!!
DA BOOM
DA
DAK
HUH.
HERE HE COMES.
YOSHIMORI !!
I'M PUTTING AN END TO THIS TODAY!!

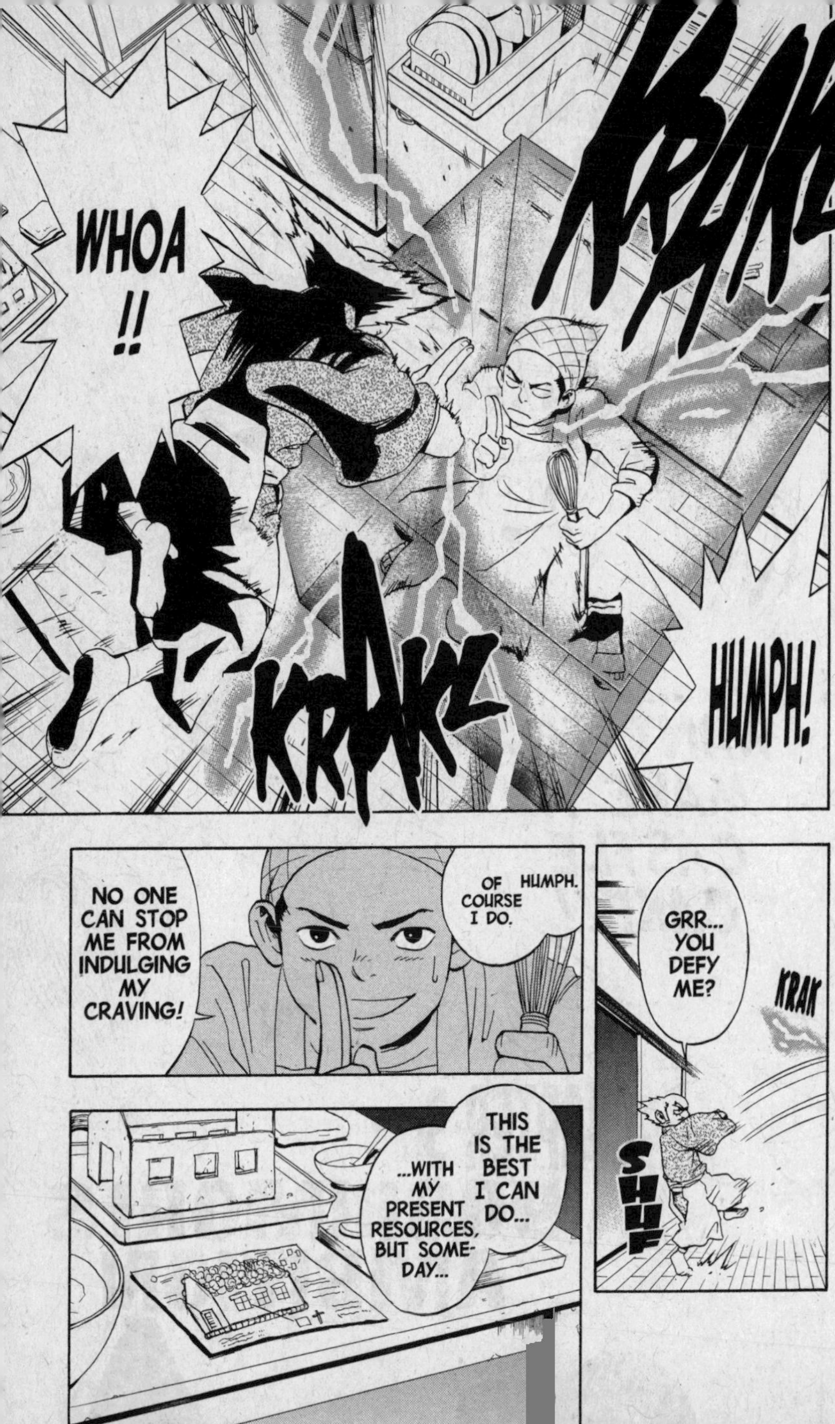
KRAK
WHOA !!
HUMPH!
KRAK
GRR... YOU DEFY ME?
KRAK
SHUF
HUMPH.
OF COURSE I DO.
NO ONE CAN STOP ME FROM INDULGING MY CRAVING!
THIS IS THE BEST I CAN DO...
...WITH MY PRESENT RESOURCES, BUT SOME-DAY...

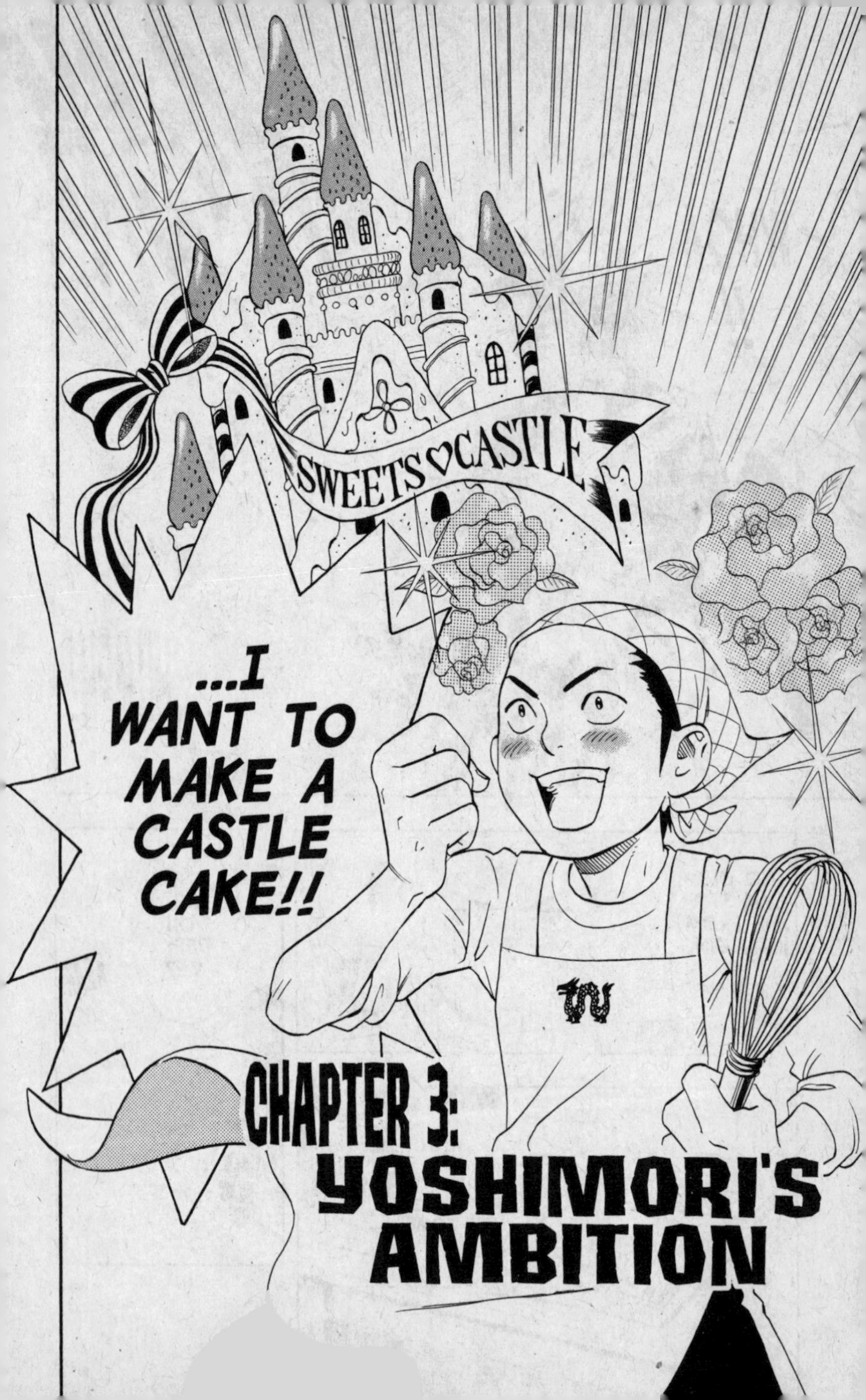
SWEETS♡CASTLE
...I WANT TO MAKE A CASTLE CAKE!!
CHAPTER 3: YOSHIMORI'S AMBITION

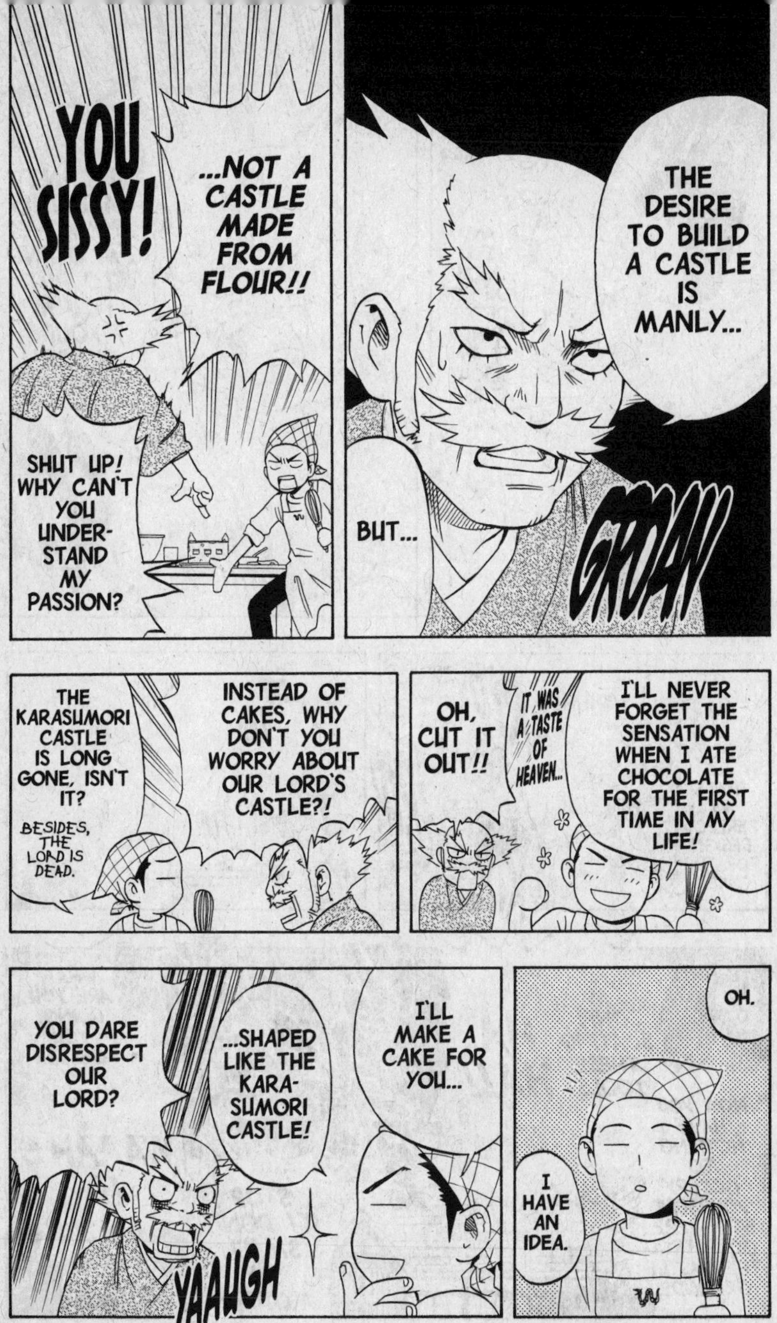
THE DESIRE TO BUILD A CASTLE IS MANLY...
BUT...
GROAN
...NOT A CASTLE MADE FROM FLOUR!!
YOU SISSY!
SHUT UP! WHY CAN'T YOU UNDER-STAND MY PASSION?
I'LL NEVER FORGET THE SENSATION WHEN I ATE CHOCOLATE FOR THE FIRST TIME IN MY LIFE!
IT WAS A TASTE OF HEAVEN...
OH, CUT IT OUT!!
INSTEAD OF CAKES, WHY DON'T YOU WORRY ABOUT OUR LORD'S CASTLE?!
THE KARASUMORI CASTLE IS LONG GONE, ISN'T IT?
BESIDES, THE LORD IS DEAD.
OH.
I HAVE AN IDEA.
I'LL MAKE A CAKE FOR YOU...
...SHAPED LIKE THE KARA-SUMORI CASTLE!
YOU DARE DISRESPECT OUR LORD?
YAAUGH

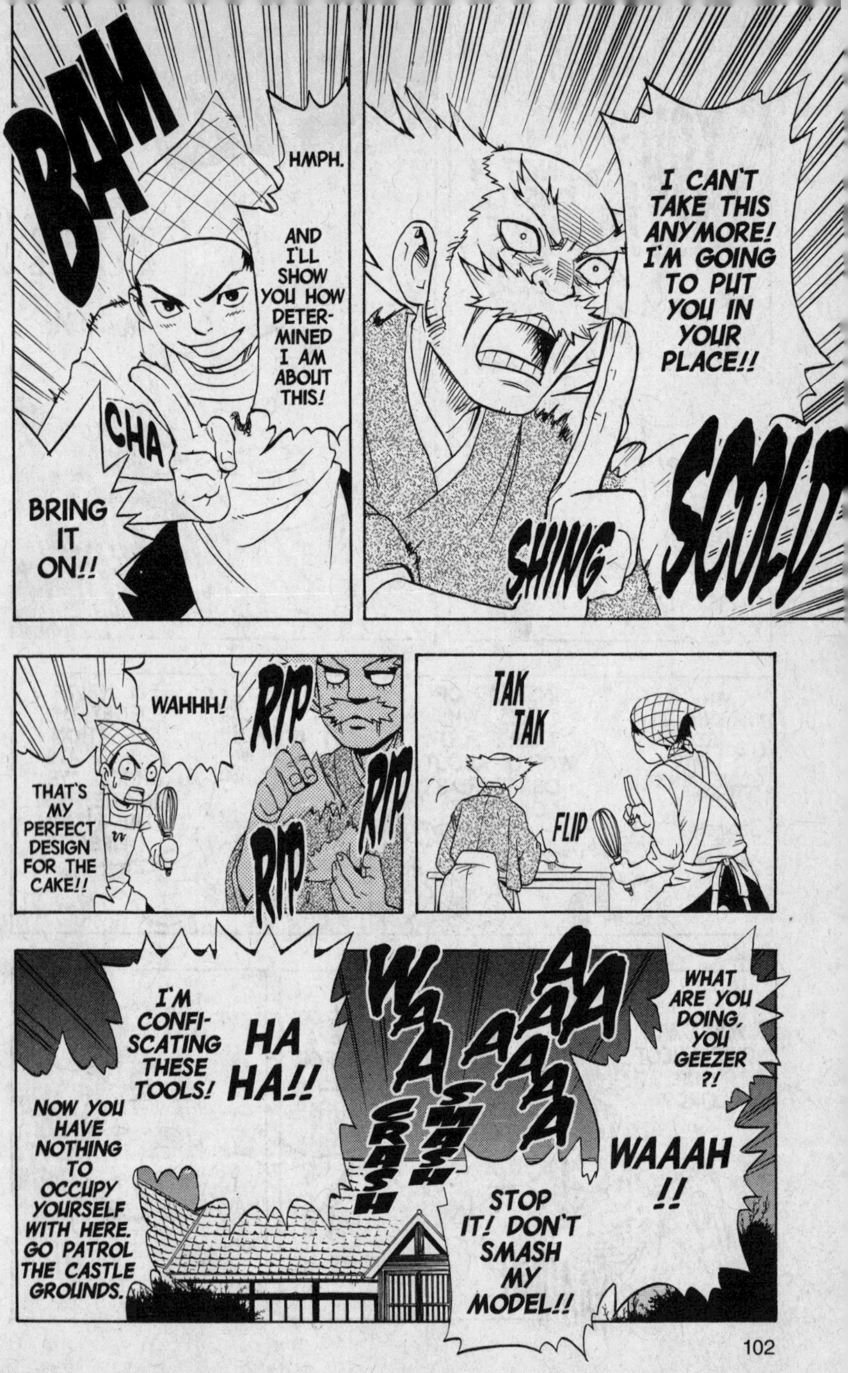
I CAN'T TAKE THIS ANYMORE! I'M GOING TO PUT YOU IN YOUR PLACE!!
SCOLD
SHING
HMPH.
AND I'LL SHOW YOU HOW DETER-MINED I AM ABOUT THIS!
BAM
CHA
BRING IT ON!!
TAK TAK
FLIP
WAHHH!
RIP
RIP
RIP
THAT'S MY PERFECT DESIGN FOR THE CAKE!!
WHAT ARE YOU DOING, YOU GEEZER?!
WAAAH!!
AAAAAAAA
WAAA
SMASH
CRASH
STOP IT! DON'T SMASH MY MODEL!!
HA HA!!
I'M CONFI-SCATING THESE TOOLS!
NOW YOU HAVE NOTHING TO OCCUPY YOURSELF WITH HERE. GO PATROL THE CASTLE GROUNDS.

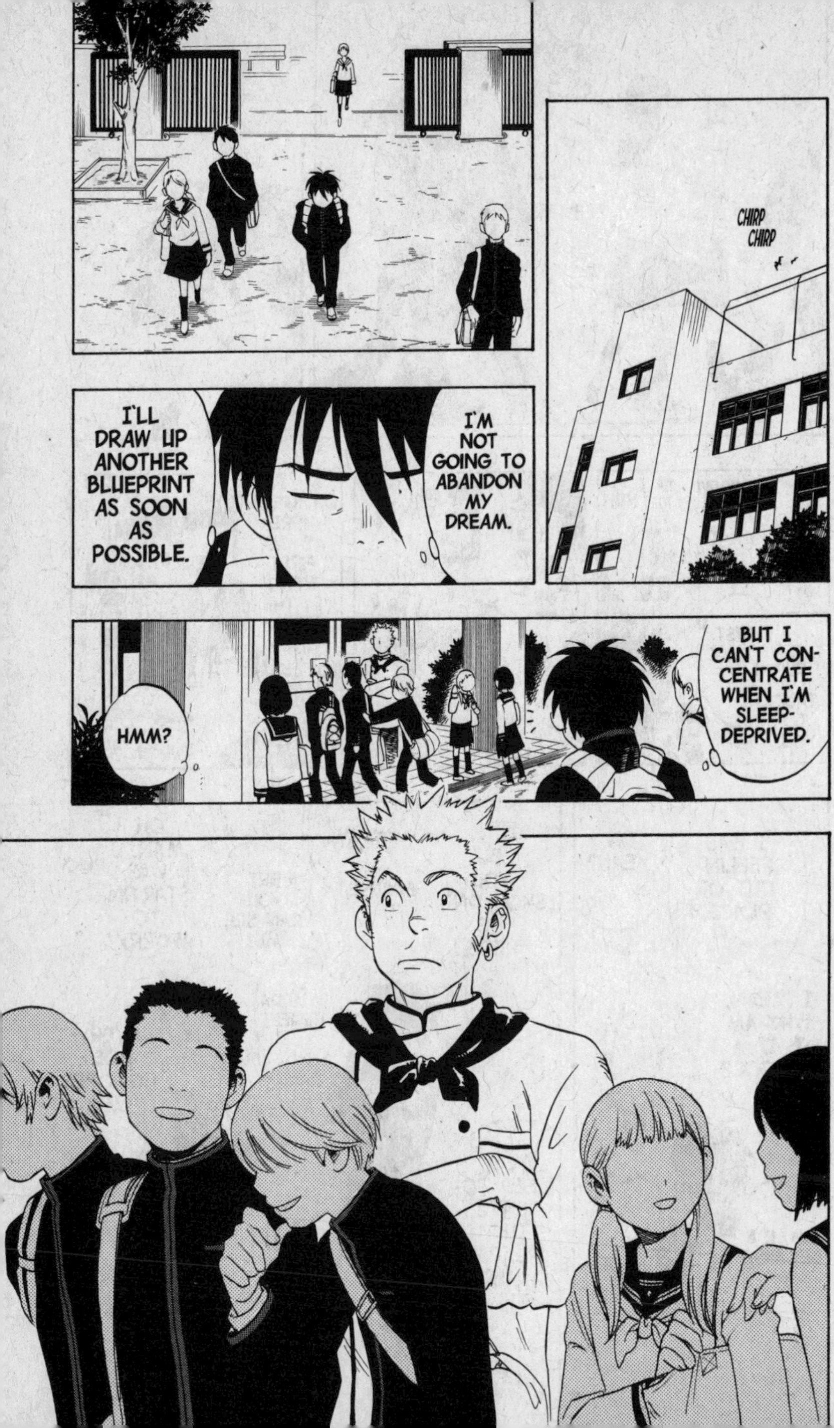
CHIRP CHIRP
I'M NOT GOING TO ABANDON MY DREAM.
I'LL DRAW UP ANOTHER BLUEPRINT AS SOON AS POSSIBLE.
BUT I CAN'T CONCENTRATE WHEN I'M SLEEP-DEPRIVED.
HMM?

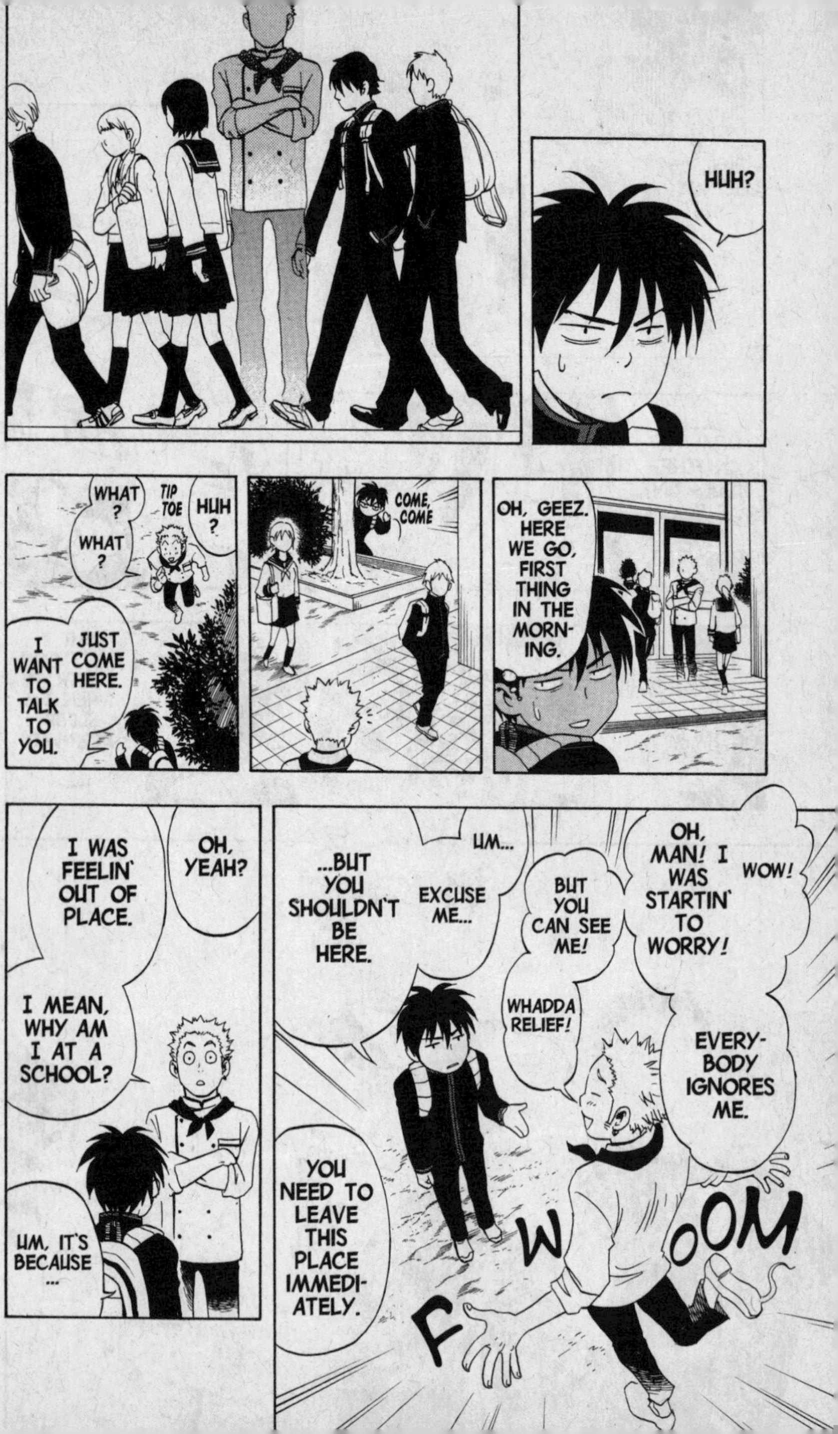
HUH?
OH, GEEZ. HERE WE GO, FIRST THING IN THE MORNING.
COME, COME
HUH ?
TIP TOE
WHAT ? WHAT ?
JUST COME HERE.
I WANT TO TALK TO YOU.
WOW!
OH, MAN! I WAS STARTIN' TO WORRY!
BUT YOU CAN SEE ME!
WHADDA RELIEF!
EVERYBODY IGNORES ME.
UM...
EXCUSE ME...
...BUT YOU SHOULDN'T BE HERE.
YOU NEED TO LEAVE THIS PLACE IMMEDIATELY.
FWOOM
OH, YEAH?
I WAS FEELIN' OUT OF PLACE.
I MEAN, WHY AM I AT A SCHOOL?
UM, IT'S BECAUSE ...

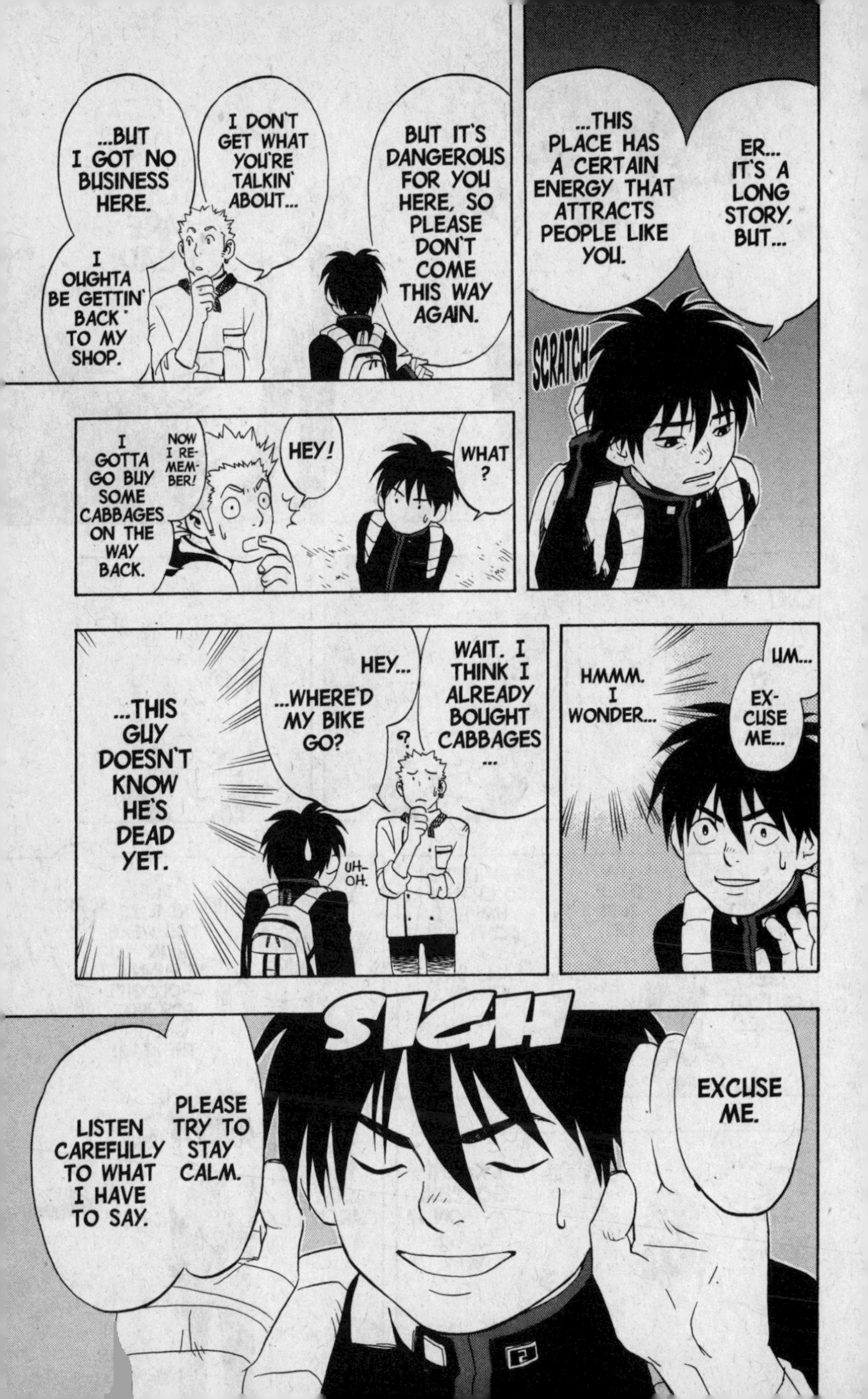
ER... IT'S A LONG STORY, BUT...
...THIS PLACE HAS A CERTAIN ENERGY THAT ATTRACTS PEOPLE LIKE YOU.
SCRATCH
BUT IT'S DANGEROUS FOR YOU HERE, SO PLEASE DON'T COME THIS WAY AGAIN.
I DON'T GET WHAT YOU'RE TALKIN' ABOUT...
...BUT I GOT NO BUSINESS HERE.
I OUGHTA BE GETTIN' BACK TO MY SHOP.
WHAT?
HEY!
NOW I RE-MEM-BER!
I GOTTA GO BUY SOME CABBAGES ON THE WAY BACK.
UM... EX-CUSE ME...
HMMM. I WONDER...
WAIT. I THINK I ALREADY BOUGHT CABBAGES...
HEY... ...WHERE'D MY BIKE GO?
?
UH-OH.
...THIS GUY DOESN'T KNOW HE'S DEAD YET.
SIGH
EXCUSE ME.
PLEASE TRY TO STAY CALM.
LISTEN CAREFULLY TO WHAT I HAVE TO SAY.

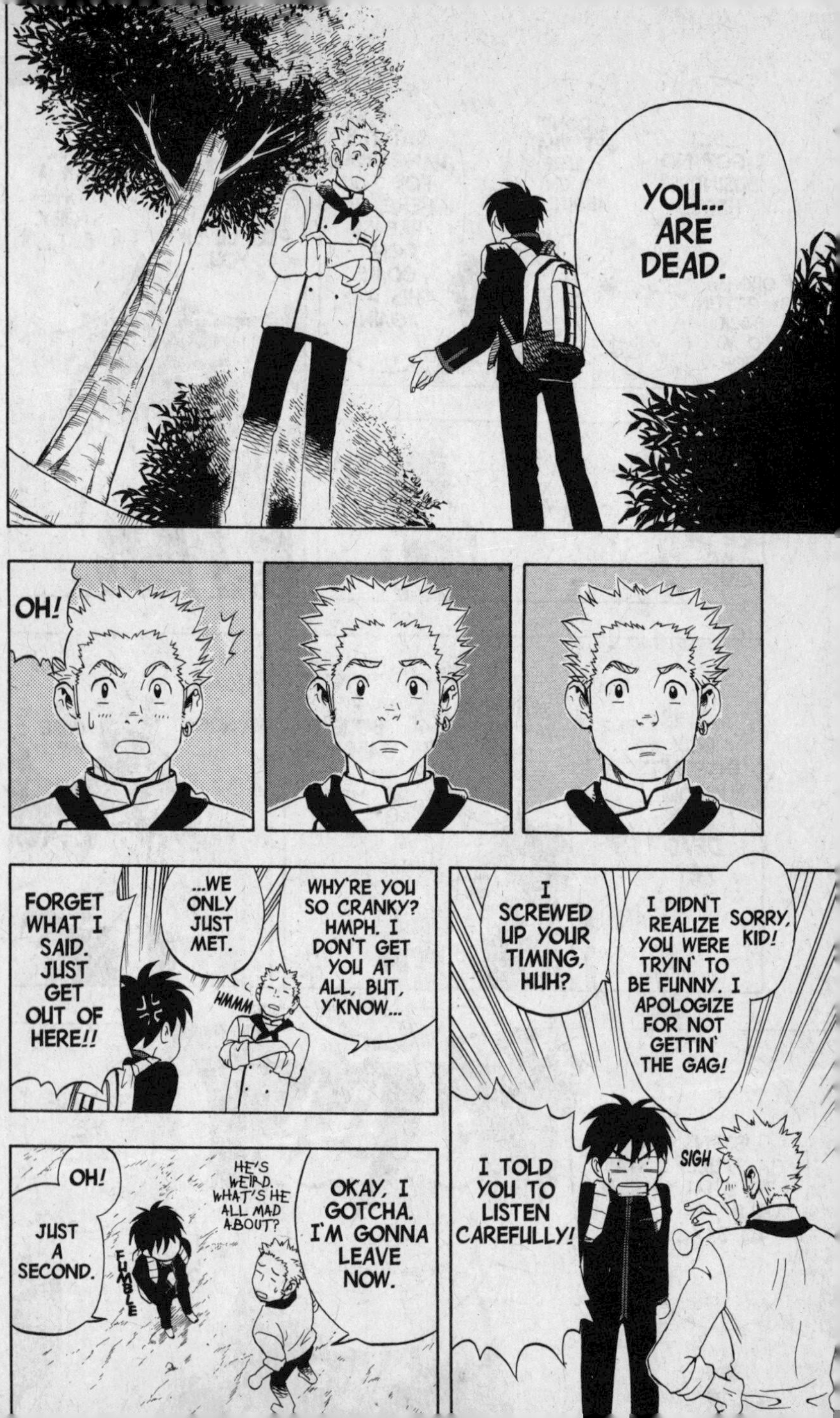
YOU... ARE DEAD.
OH!
SORRY, KID!
I DIDN'T REALIZE YOU WERE TRYIN' TO BE FUNNY. I APOLOGIZE FOR NOT GETTIN' THE GAG!
I SCREWED UP YOUR TIMING, HUH?
SIGH
I TOLD YOU TO LISTEN CAREFULLY!
WHY'RE YOU SO CRANKY? HMPH. I DON'T GET YOU AT ALL, BUT, Y'KNOW...
...WE ONLY JUST MET.
HMMM
FORGET WHAT I SAID. JUST GET OUT OF HERE!!
OKAY, I GOTCHA. I'M GONNA LEAVE NOW.
HE'S WEIRD. WHAT'S HE ALL MAD ABOUT?
OH!
JUST A SECOND.
FUMBLE

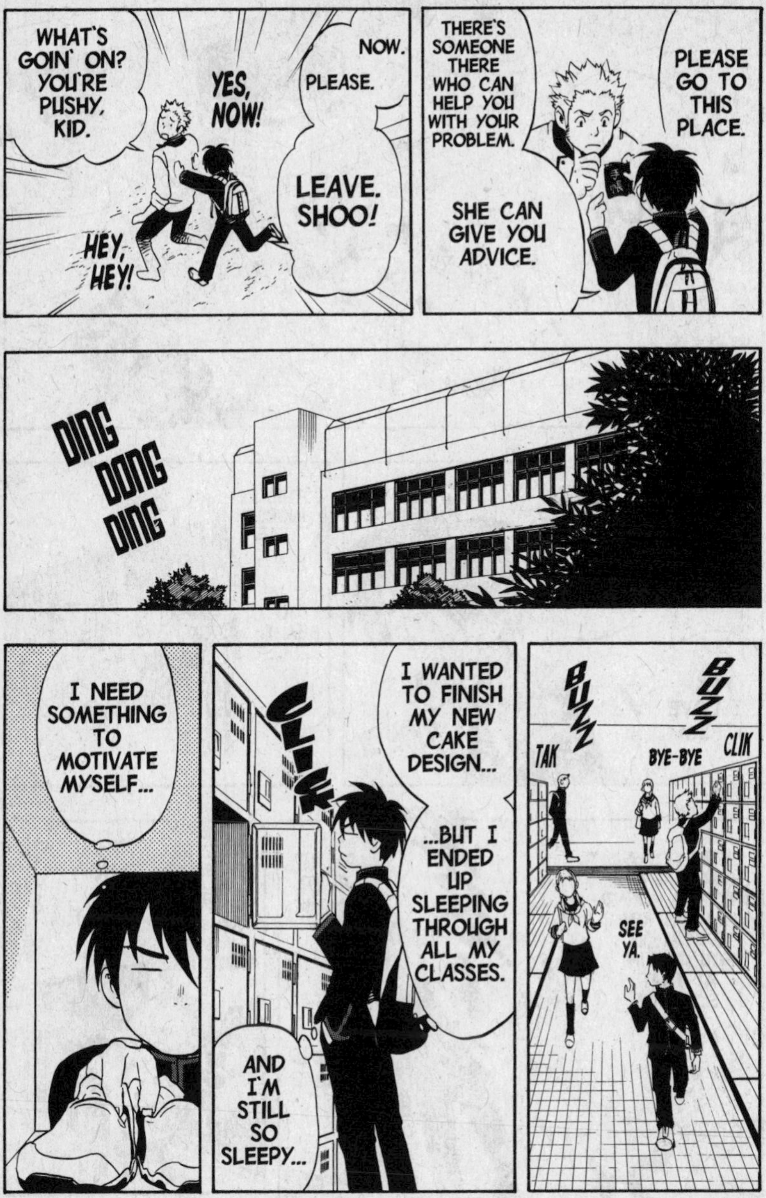
PLEASE GO TO THIS PLACE.
THERE'S SOMEONE THERE WHO CAN HELP YOU WITH YOUR PROBLEM.
SHE CAN GIVE YOU ADVICE.
NOW.
PLEASE.
LEAVE. SHOO!
YES, NOW!
WHAT'S GOIN' ON? YOU'RE PUSHY, KID.
HEY, HEY!
DING DONG DING
BUZZ
BUZZ
CLIK
BYE-BYE
TAK
SEE YA.
I WANTED TO FINISH MY NEW CAKE DESIGN...
...BUT I ENDED UP SLEEPING THROUGH ALL MY CLASSES.
CLICK
AND I'M STILL SO SLEEPY...
I NEED SOMETHING TO MOTIVATE MYSELF...

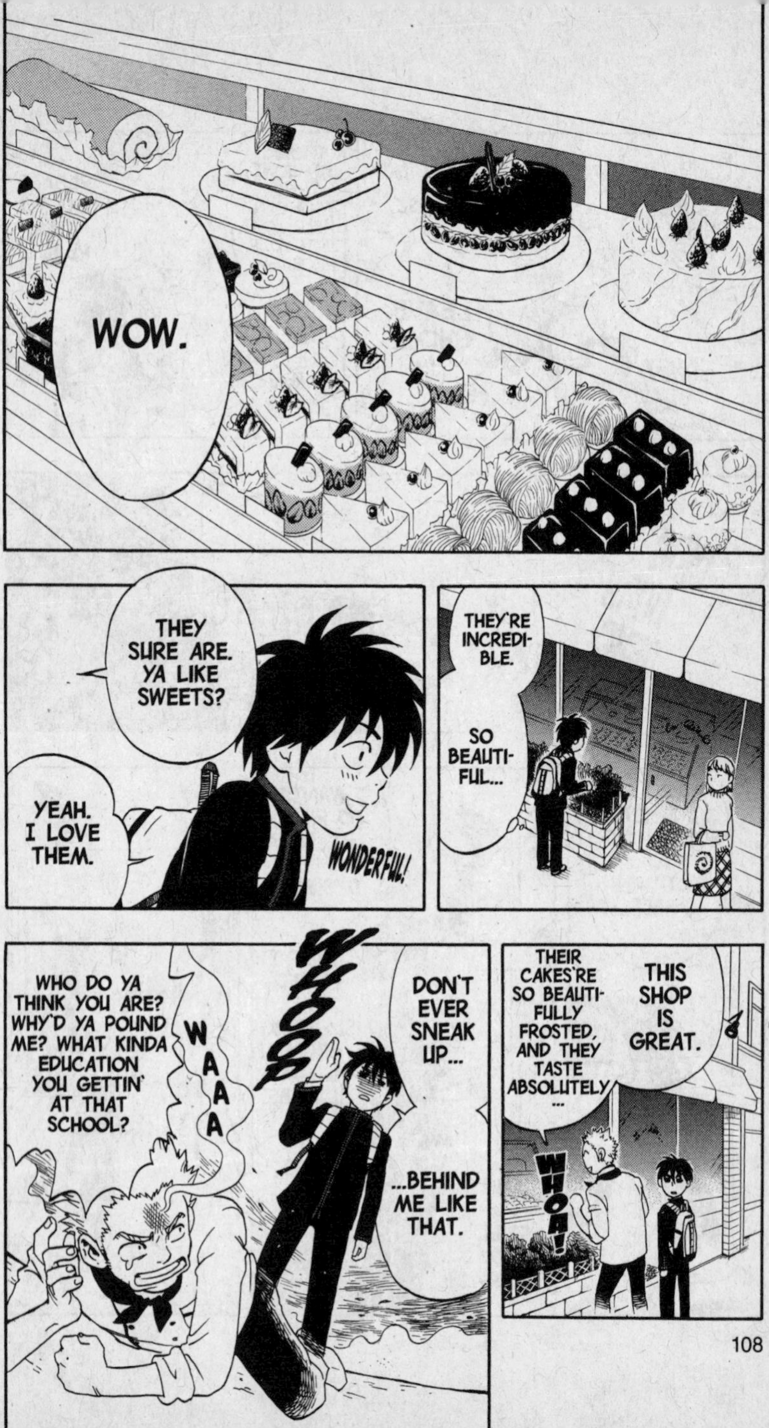
WOW.
THEY'RE INCREDI-BLE.
SO BEAUTI-FUL...
THEY SURE ARE. YA LIKE SWEETS?
YEAH. I LOVE THEM.
WONDERFUL!
THIS SHOP IS GREAT.
THEIR CAKES'RE SO BEAUTI-FULLY FROSTED, AND THEY TASTE ABSOLUTELY ...
WHOA!
DON'T EVER SNEAK UP...
...BEHIND ME LIKE THAT.
WAAA
WHO DO YA THINK YOU ARE? WHY'D YA POUND ME? WHAT KINDA EDUCATION YOU GETTIN' AT THAT SCHOOL?

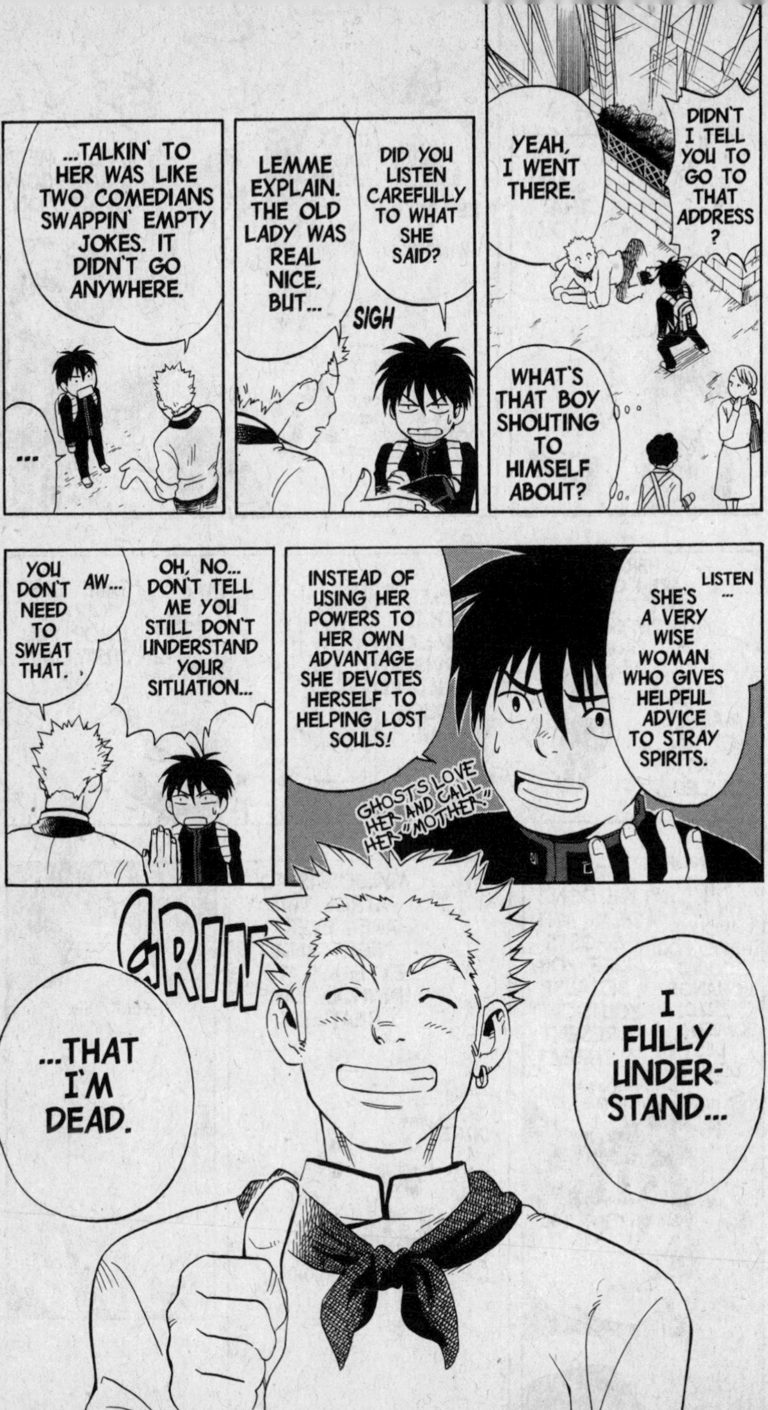
DIDN'T I TELL YOU TO GO TO THAT ADDRESS?
YEAH, I WENT THERE.
WHAT'S THAT BOY SHOUTING TO HIMSELF ABOUT?
DID YOU LISTEN CAREFULLY TO WHAT SHE SAID?
SIGH
LEMME EXPLAIN. THE OLD LADY WAS REAL NICE, BUT...
...TALKIN' TO HER WAS LIKE TWO COMEDIANS SWAPPIN' EMPTY JOKES. IT DIDN'T GO ANYWHERE.
...
LISTEN...
SHE'S A VERY WISE WOMAN WHO GIVES HELPFUL ADVICE TO STRAY SPIRITS.
INSTEAD OF USING HER POWERS TO HER OWN ADVANTAGE SHE DEVOTES HERSELF TO HELPING LOST SOULS!
GHOSTS LOVE HER AND CALL HER "MOTHER."
OH, NO... DON'T TELL ME YOU STILL DON'T UNDERSTAND YOUR SITUATION...
AW...
YOU DON'T NEED TO SWEAT THAT.
GRIN
I FULLY UNDER-STAND...
...THAT I'M DEAD.

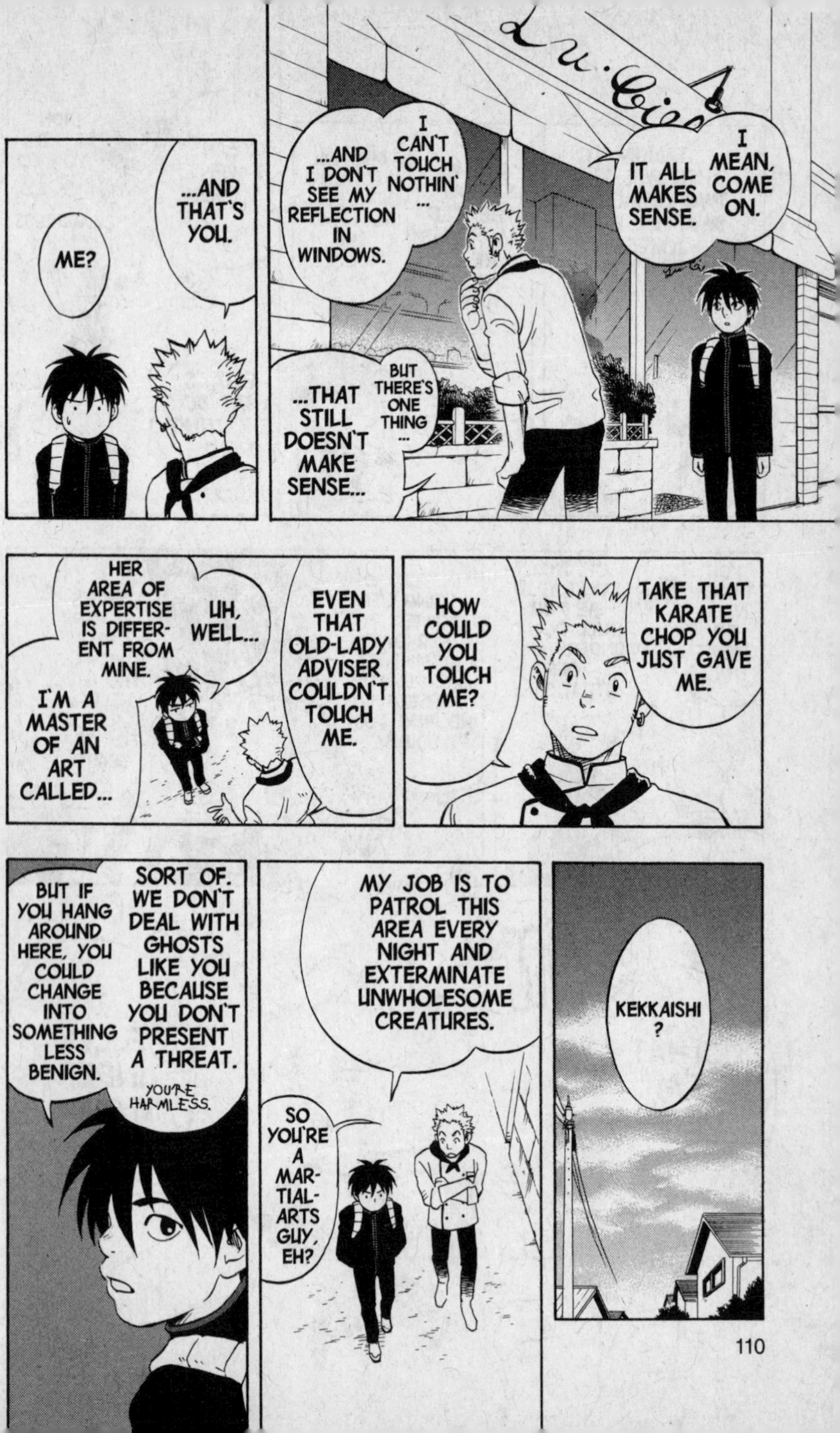
I MEAN, COME ON.
IT ALL MAKES SENSE.
I CAN'T TOUCH NOTHIN'...
...AND I DON'T SEE MY REFLECTION IN WINDOWS.
BUT THERE'S ONE THING...
...THAT STILL DOESN'T MAKE SENSE...
...AND THAT'S YOU.
ME?
TAKE THAT KARATE CHOP YOU JUST GAVE ME.
HOW COULD YOU TOUCH ME?
EVEN THAT OLD-LADY ADVISER COULDN'T TOUCH ME.
UH, WELL...
HER AREA OF EXPERTISE IS DIFFER-ENT FROM MINE.
I'M A MASTER OF AN ART CALLED...
KEKKAISHI?
SO YOU'RE A MAR-TIAL-ARTS GUY, EH?
MY JOB IS TO PATROL THIS AREA EVERY NIGHT AND EXTERMINATE UNWHOLESOME CREATURES.
SORT OF. WE DON'T DEAL WITH GHOSTS LIKE YOU BECAUSE YOU DON'T PRESENT A THREAT.
YOU'RE HARMLESS.
BUT IF YOU HANG AROUND HERE, YOU COULD CHANGE INTO SOMETHING LESS BENIGN.

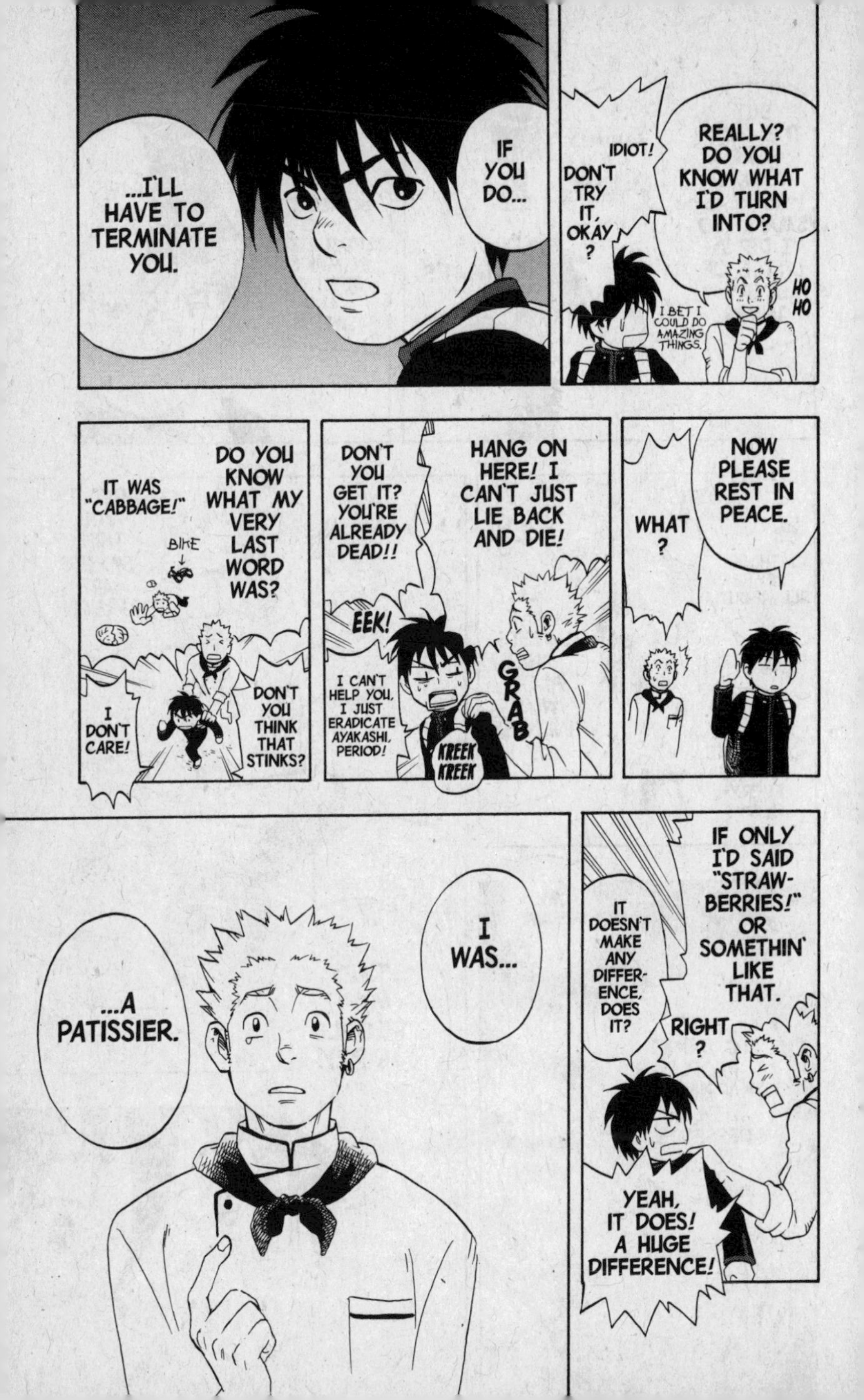
REALLY? DO YOU KNOW WHAT I'D TURN INTO?
HO HO
I BET I COULD DO AMAZING THINGS.
IDIOT! DON'T TRY IT, OKAY?
IF YOU DO...
...I'LL HAVE TO TERMINATE YOU.
NOW PLEASE REST IN PEACE.
WHAT?
HANG ON HERE! I CAN'T JUST LIE BACK AND DIE!
GRAB
DON'T YOU GET IT? YOU'RE ALREADY DEAD!!
EEK!
I CAN'T HELP YOU, I JUST ERADICATE AYAKASHI, PERIOD!
KREEK KREEK
DO YOU KNOW WHAT MY VERY LAST WORD WAS?
IT WAS "CABBAGE!"
BIKE
DON'T YOU THINK THAT STINKS?
I DON'T CARE!
IF ONLY I'D SAID "STRAWBERRIES!" OR SOMETHIN' LIKE THAT.
RIGHT?
IT DOESN'T MAKE ANY DIFFERENCE, DOES IT?
YEAH, IT DOES! A HUGE DIFFERENCE!
I WAS...
...A PATISSIER.

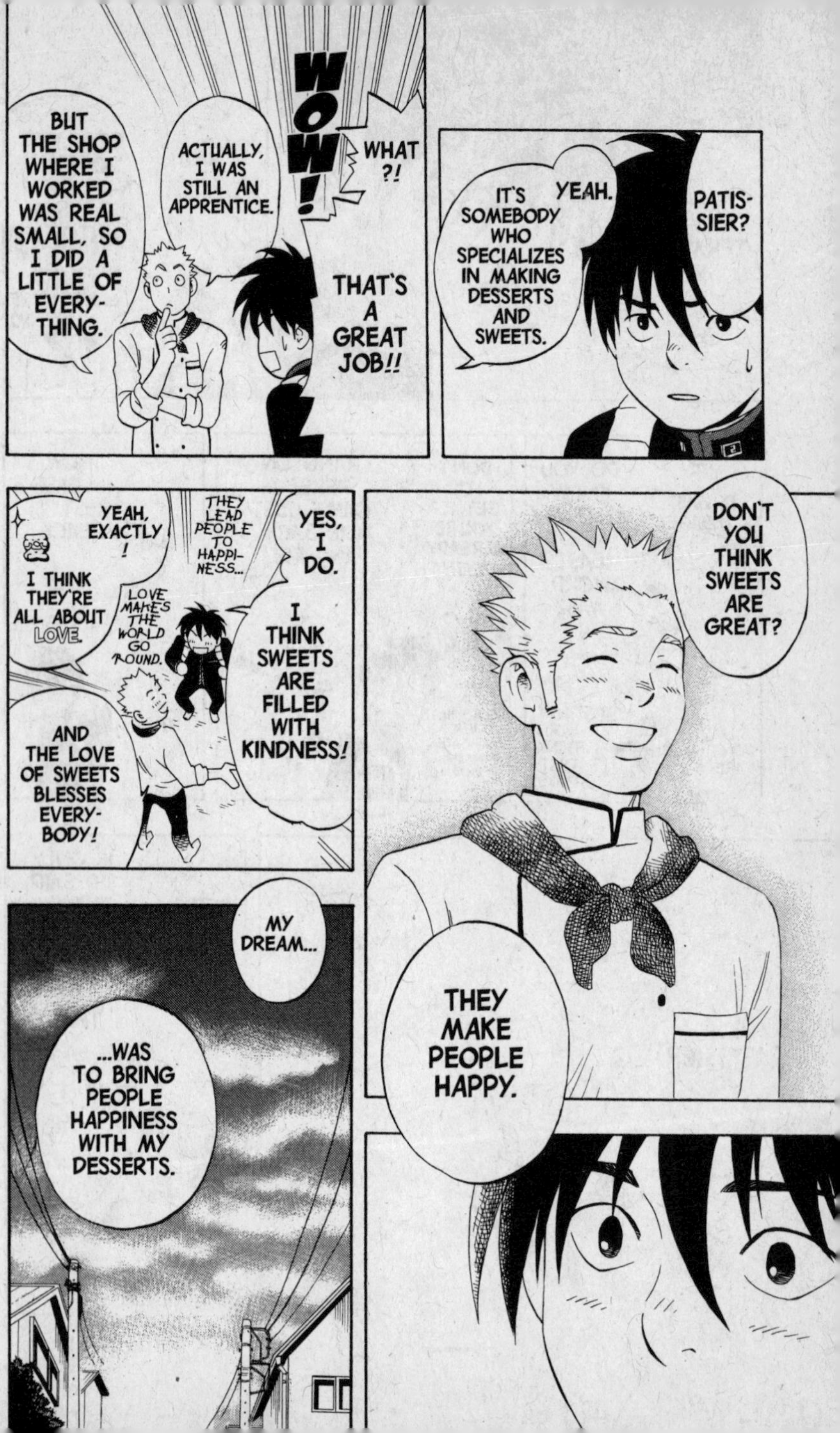
PATIS-SIER?
YEAH.
IT'S SOMEBODY WHO SPECIALIZES IN MAKING DESSERTS AND SWEETS.
WHAT ?!
WOW!
THAT'S A GREAT JOB!!
ACTUALLY, I WAS STILL AN APPRENTICE.
BUT THE SHOP WHERE I WORKED WAS REAL SMALL, SO I DID A LITTLE OF EVERY-THING.
DON'T YOU THINK SWEETS ARE GREAT?
THEY MAKE PEOPLE HAPPY.
YES, I DO.
I THINK SWEETS ARE FILLED WITH KINDNESS!
THEY LEAD PEOPLE TO HAPPI-NESS...
YEAH, EXACTLY!
I THINK THEY'RE ALL ABOUT LOVE.
LOVE MAKES THE WORLD GO ROUND.
AND THE LOVE OF SWEETS BLESSES EVERY-BODY!
MY DREAM...
...WAS TO BRING PEOPLE HAPPINESS WITH MY DESSERTS.

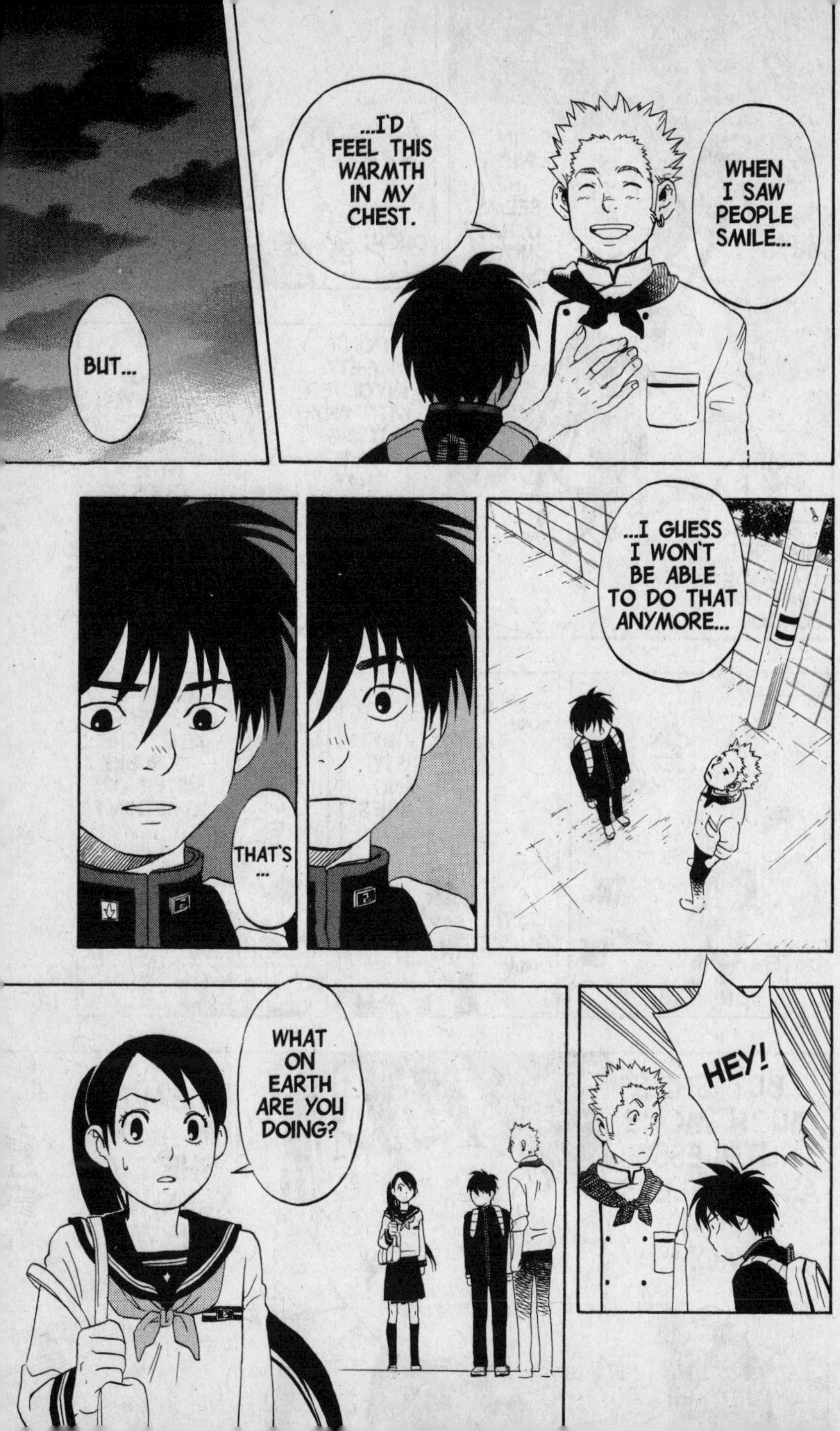
WHEN I SAW PEOPLE SMILE...
...I'D FEEL THIS WARMTH IN MY CHEST.
BUT...
...I GUESS I WON'T BE ABLE TO DO THAT ANYMORE...
THAT'S ...
HEY!
WHAT ON EARTH ARE YOU DOING?

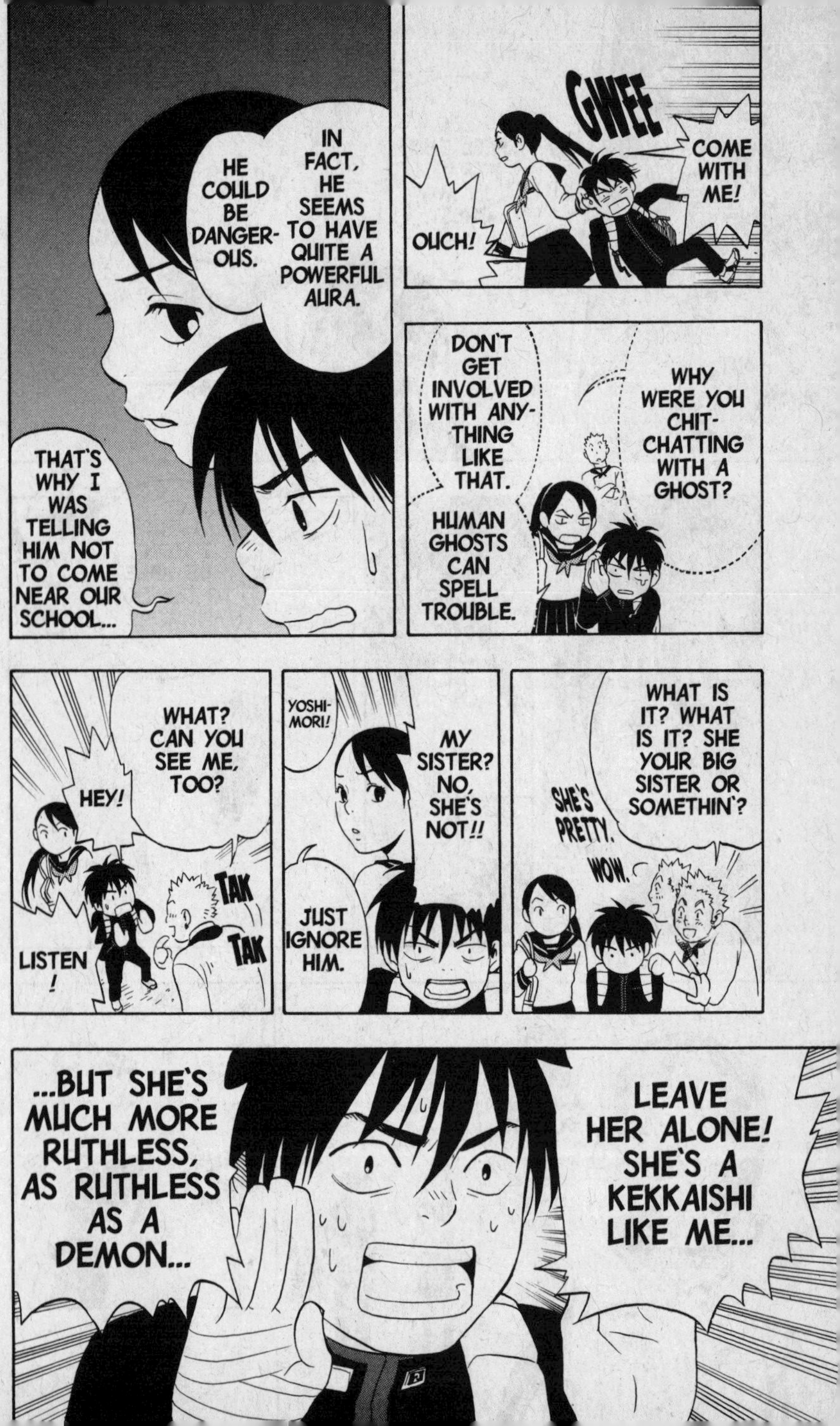
GWEE
COME WITH ME!
OUCH!
WHY WERE YOU CHIT-CHATTING WITH A GHOST?
DON'T GET INVOLVED WITH ANYTHING LIKE THAT.
HUMAN GHOSTS CAN SPELL TROUBLE.
IN FACT, HE SEEMS TO HAVE QUITE A POWERFUL AURA.
HE COULD BE DANGEROUS.
THAT'S WHY I WAS TELLING HIM NOT TO COME NEAR OUR SCHOOL...
WHAT IS IT? WHAT IS IT? SHE YOUR BIG SISTER OR SOMETHIN'?
SHE'S PRETTY.
WOW.
MY SISTER? NO, SHE'S NOT!!
YOSHIMORI!
JUST IGNORE HIM.
WHAT? CAN YOU SEE ME, TOO?
HEY!
TAK
TAK
LISTEN!
LEAVE HER ALONE! SHE'S A KEKKAISHI LIKE ME...
...BUT SHE'S MUCH MORE RUTHLESS, AS RUTHLESS AS A DEMON...

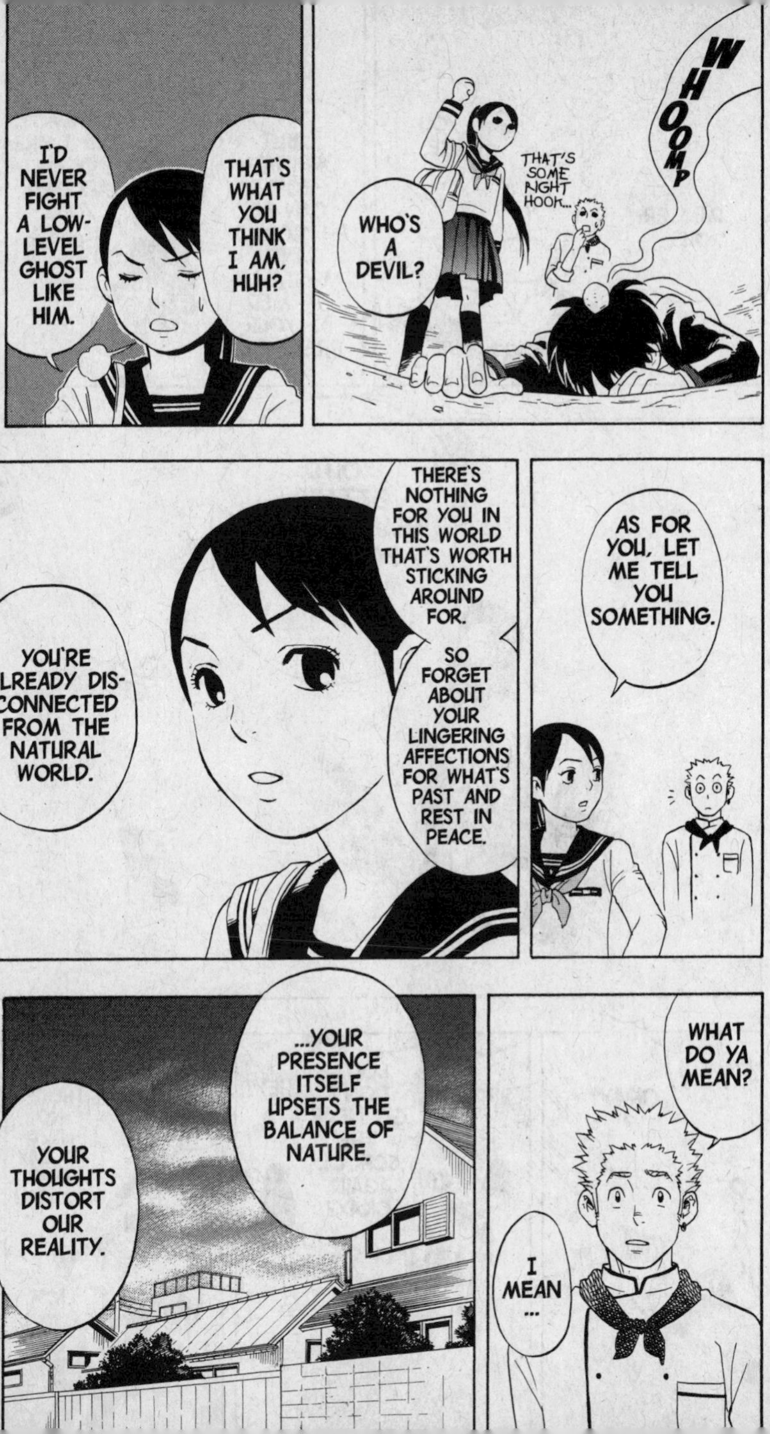
WHOOOMP
THAT'S SOME RIGHT HOOK...
WHO'S A DEVIL?
THAT'S WHAT YOU THINK I AM, HUH?
I'D NEVER FIGHT A LOW-LEVEL GHOST LIKE HIM.
AS FOR YOU, LET ME TELL YOU SOMETHING.
THERE'S NOTHING FOR YOU IN THIS WORLD THAT'S WORTH STICKING AROUND FOR.
SO FORGET ABOUT YOUR LINGERING AFFECTIONS FOR WHAT'S PAST AND REST IN PEACE.
YOU'RE ALREADY DIS-CONNECTED FROM THE NATURAL WORLD.
WHAT DO YA MEAN?
I MEAN...
...YOUR PRESENCE ITSELF UPSETS THE BALANCE OF NATURE.
YOUR THOUGHTS DISTORT OUR REALITY.

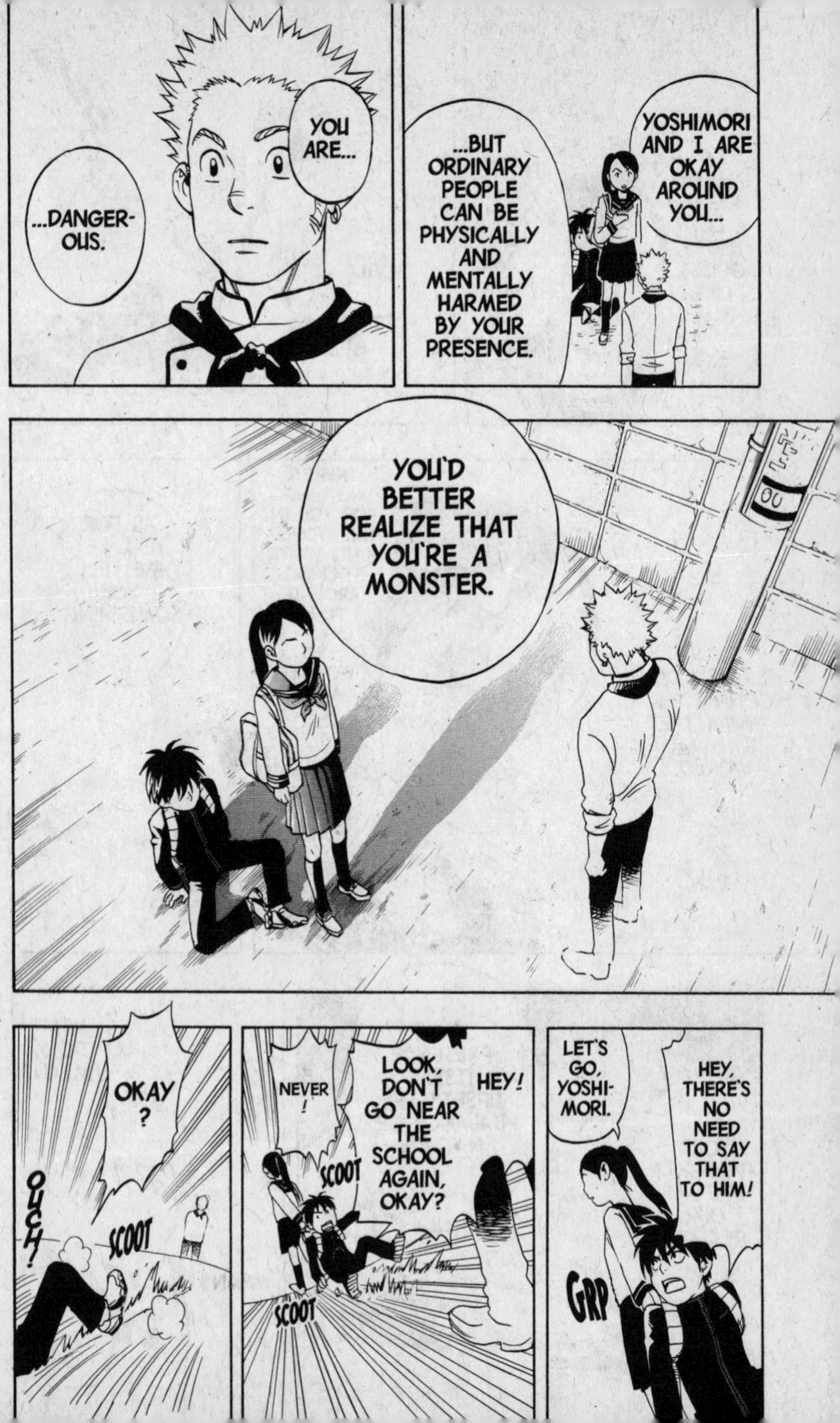
YOSHIMORI AND I ARE OKAY AROUND YOU...
...BUT ORDINARY PEOPLE CAN BE PHYSICALLY AND MENTALLY HARMED BY YOUR PRESENCE.
YOU ARE...
...DANGER-OUS.
YOU'D BETTER REALIZE THAT YOU'RE A MONSTER.
HEY, THERE'S NO NEED TO SAY THAT TO HIM!
LET'S GO, YOSHI-MORI.
GRP
HEY!
LOOK, DON'T GO NEAR THE SCHOOL AGAIN, OKAY?
NEVER!
SCOOT
SCOOT
OKAY?
OUCH!
SCOOT

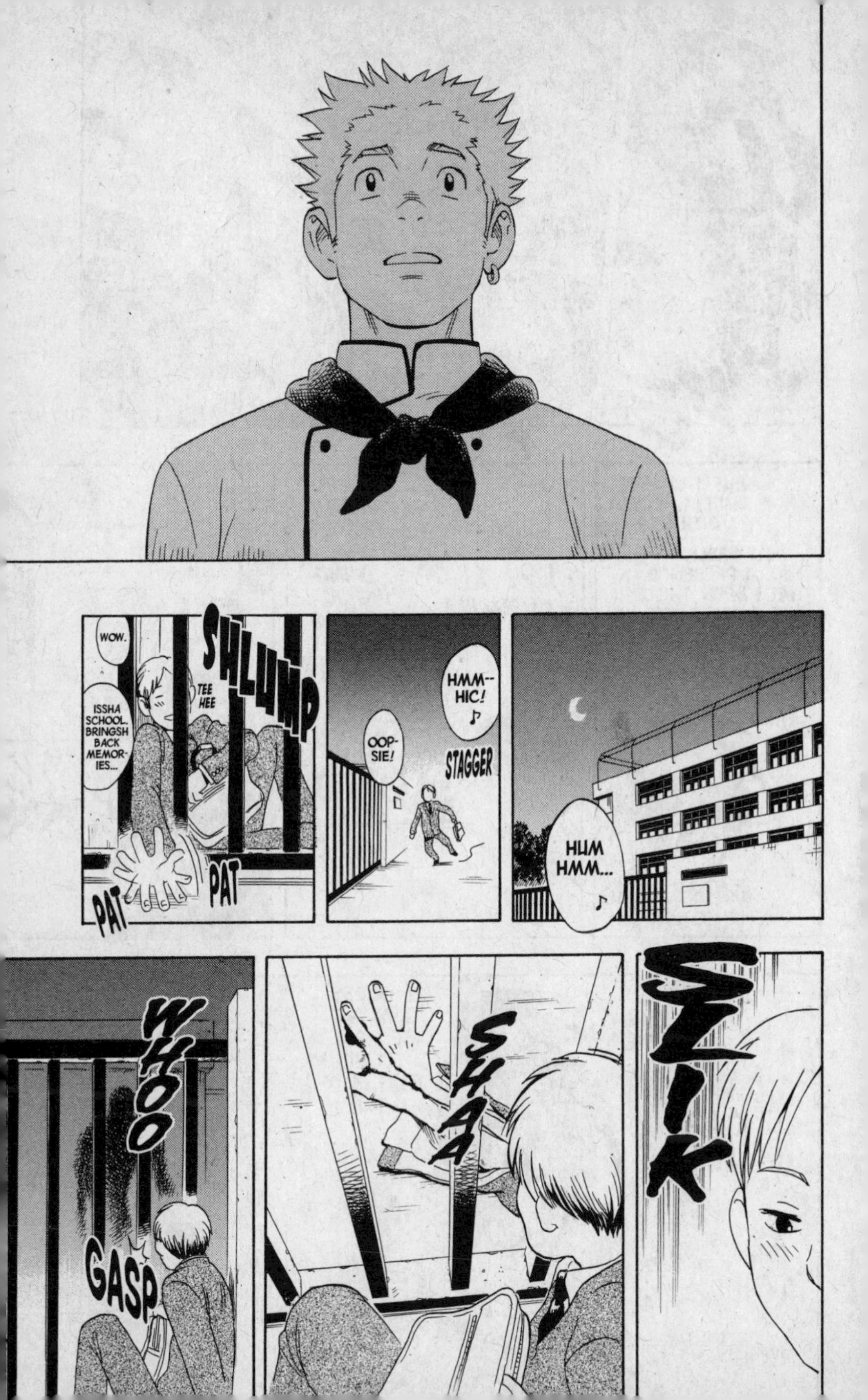
HUM HMM... ♪
HMM--HIC! ♪
OOP-SIE!
STAGGER
WOW.
SHLUMP
TEE HEE
ISSHA SCHOOL. BRINGSH BACK MEMOR-IES...
PAT
PAT
SLIK
SHAA
WHOOO
GASP

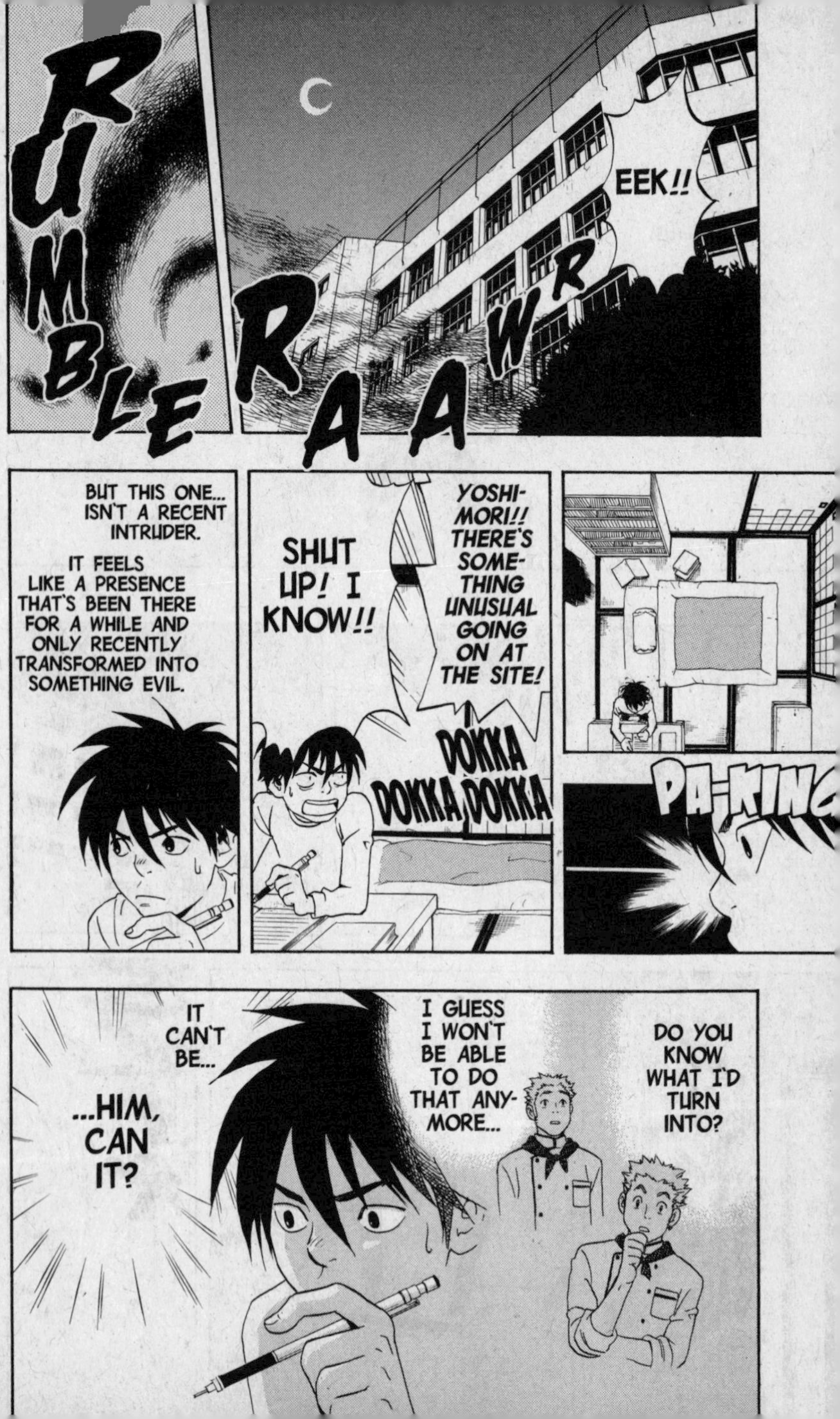
EEK!!
RAAAWR
RUMBLE
PA-KING
YOSHIMORI!! THERE'S SOMETHING UNUSUAL GOING ON AT THE SITE!
SHUT UP! I KNOW!!
DOKKA DOKKA DOKKA
BUT THIS ONE... ISN'T A RECENT INTRUDER.
IT FEELS LIKE A PRESENCE THAT'S BEEN THERE FOR A WHILE AND ONLY RECENTLY TRANSFORMED INTO SOMETHING EVIL.
DO YOU KNOW WHAT I'D TURN INTO?
I GUESS I WON'T BE ABLE TO DO THAT ANYMORE...
IT CAN'T BE...
...HIM, CAN IT?

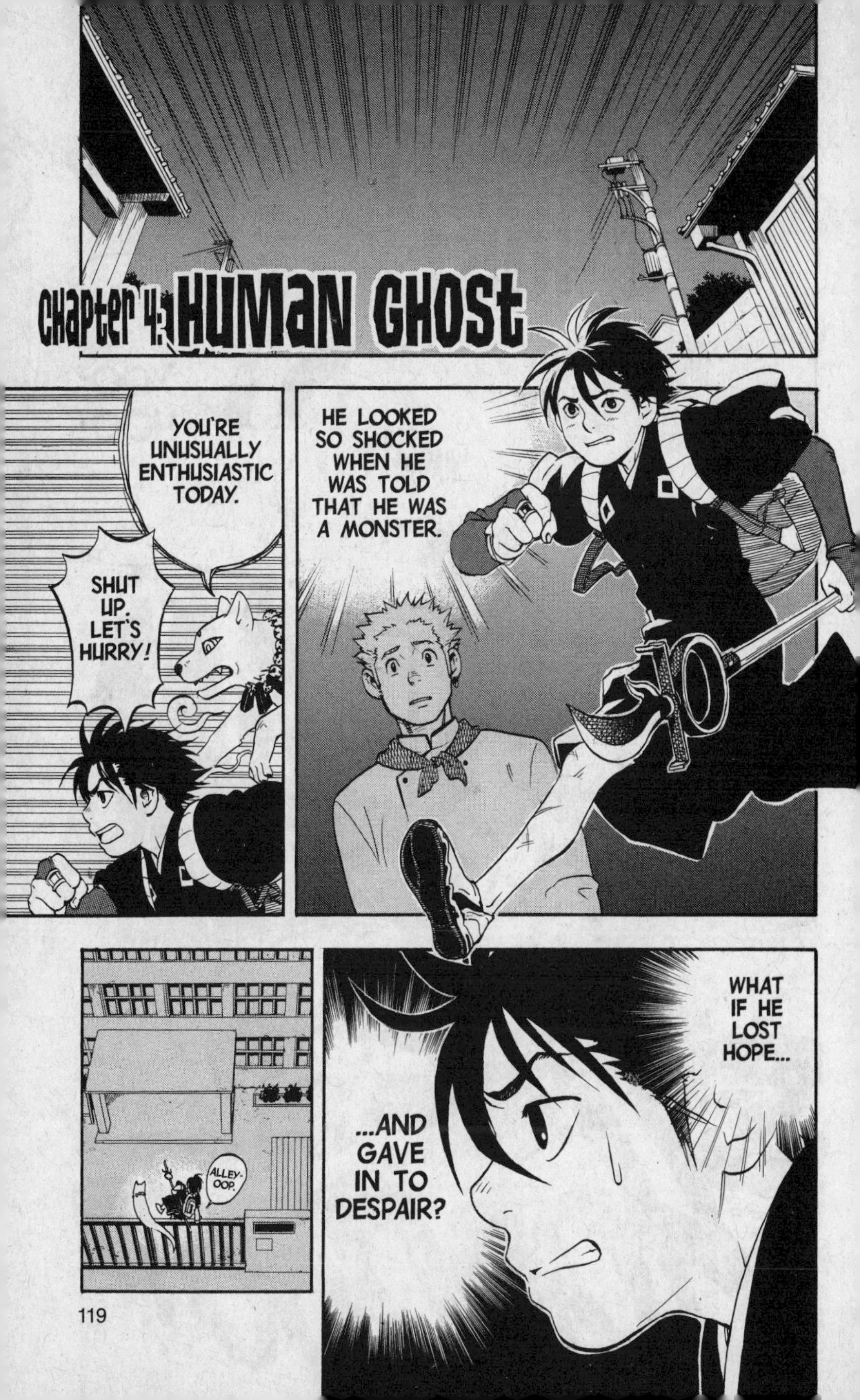
Chapter 4: Human Ghost
HE LOOKED SO SHOCKED WHEN HE WAS TOLD THAT HE WAS A MONSTER.
YOU'RE UNUSUALLY ENTHUSIASTIC TODAY.
SHUT UP. LET'S HURRY!
WHAT IF HE LOST HOPE...
...AND GAVE IN TO DESPAIR?
ALLEY-OOP.

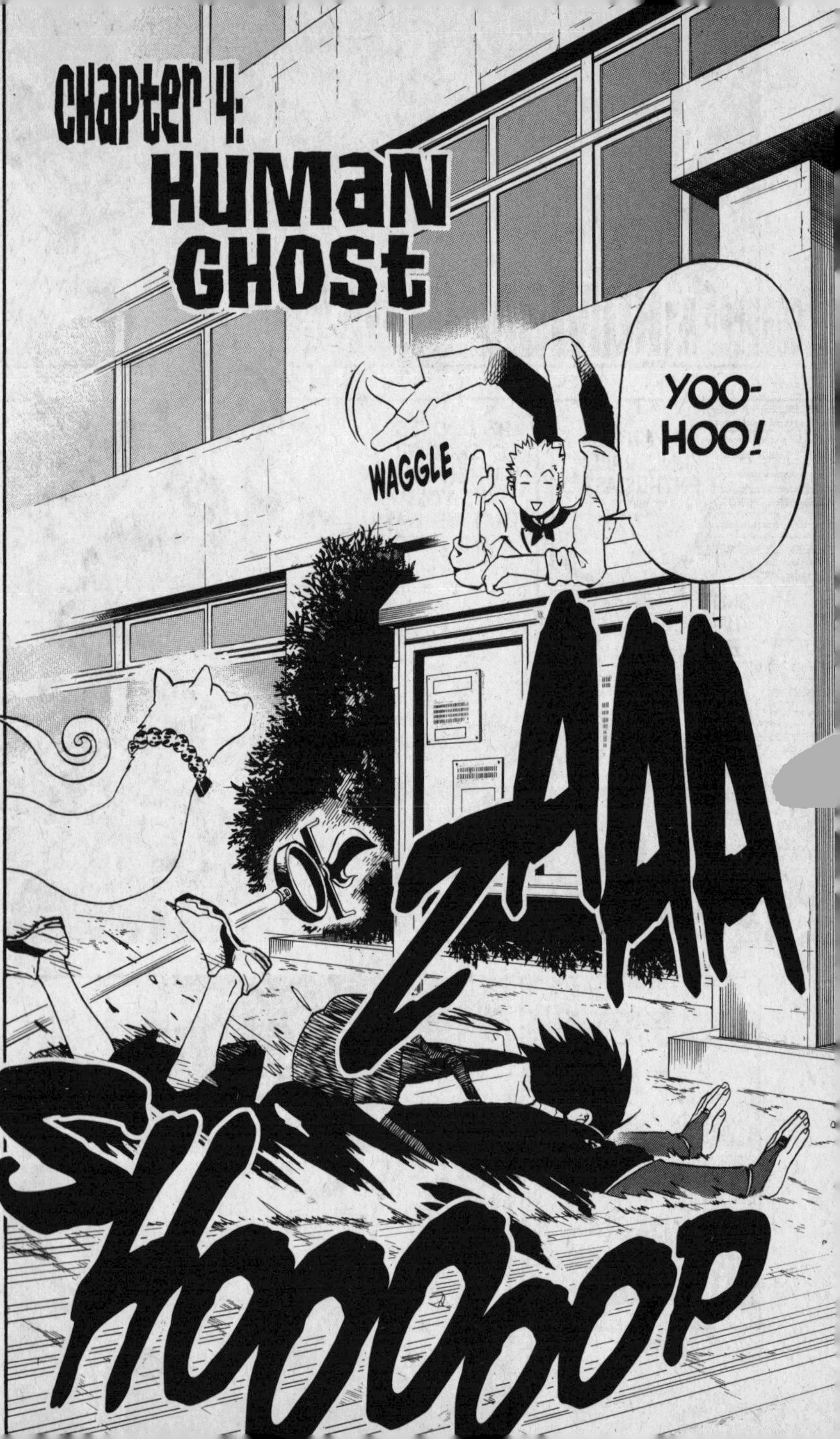
CHAPTER 4:
HUMAN GHOST
YOO-HOO!
WAGGLE
ZAAA
SHOOOOP

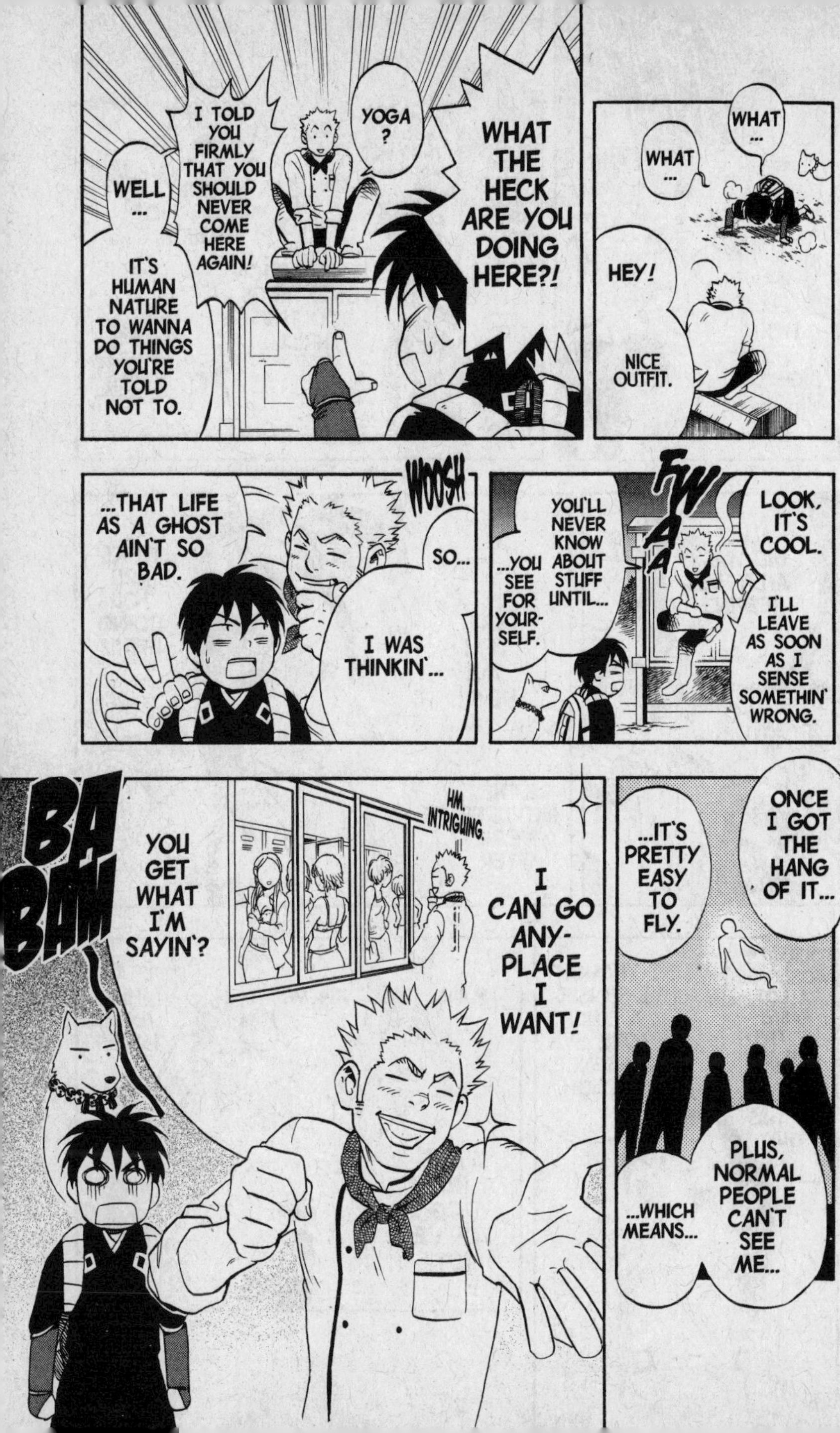
WHAT ...
WHAT ...
HEY!
NICE OUTFIT.
WHAT THE HECK ARE YOU DOING HERE?!
YOGA ?
I TOLD YOU FIRMLY THAT YOU SHOULD NEVER COME HERE AGAIN!
WELL ...
IT'S HUMAN NATURE TO WANNA DO THINGS YOU'RE TOLD NOT TO.
FWAA
LOOK, IT'S COOL.
I'LL LEAVE AS SOON AS I SENSE SOMETHIN' WRONG.
YOU'LL NEVER KNOW ABOUT STUFF UNTIL...
...YOU SEE FOR YOURSELF.
WOOSH
SO...
I WAS THINKIN'...
...THAT LIFE AS A GHOST AIN'T SO BAD.
ONCE I GOT THE HANG OF IT...
...IT'S PRETTY EASY TO FLY.
PLUS, NORMAL PEOPLE CAN'T SEE ME...
...WHICH MEANS...
I CAN GO ANY-PLACE I WANT!
HM. INTRIGUING.
YOU GET WHAT I'M SAYIN'?
BA BAM

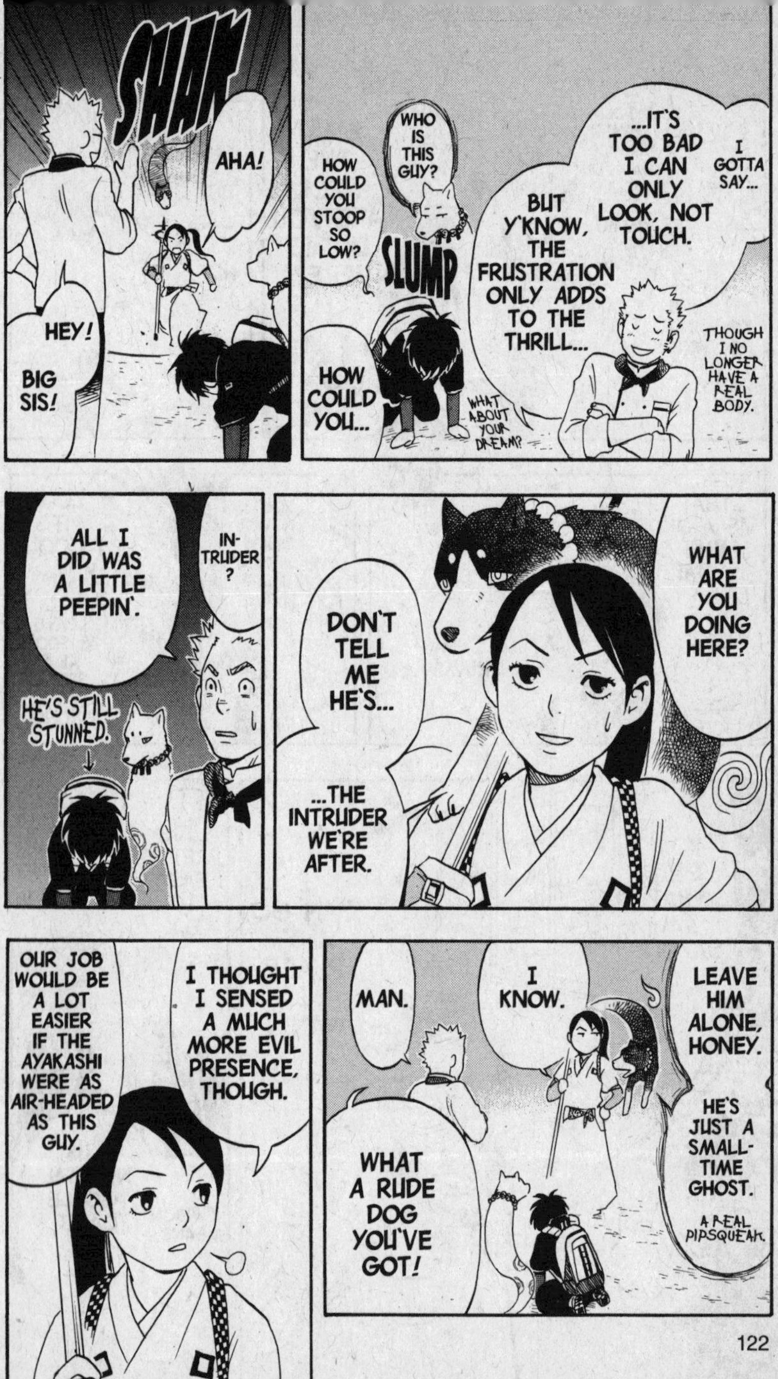
I GOTTA SAY...
...IT'S TOO BAD I CAN ONLY LOOK, NOT TOUCH.
BUT Y'KNOW, THE FRUSTRATION ONLY ADDS TO THE THRILL...
THOUGH I NO LONGER HAVE A REAL BODY.
WHO IS THIS GUY?
HOW COULD YOU STOOP SO LOW?
SLUMP
HOW COULD YOU...
WHAT ABOUT YOUR DREAM?
SHAK
AHA!
HEY!
BIG SIS!
WHAT ARE YOU DOING HERE?
DON'T TELL ME HE'S...
...THE INTRUDER WE'RE AFTER.
IN-TRUDER?
ALL I DID WAS A LITTLE PEEPIN'.
HE'S STILL STUNNED.
LEAVE HIM ALONE, HONEY.
HE'S JUST A SMALL-TIME GHOST.
A REAL PIPSQUEAK.
I KNOW.
MAN.
WHAT A RUDE DOG YOU'VE GOT!
I THOUGHT I SENSED A MUCH MORE EVIL PRESENCE, THOUGH.
OUR JOB WOULD BE A LOT EASIER IF THE AYAKASHI WERE AS AIR-HEADED AS THIS GUY.

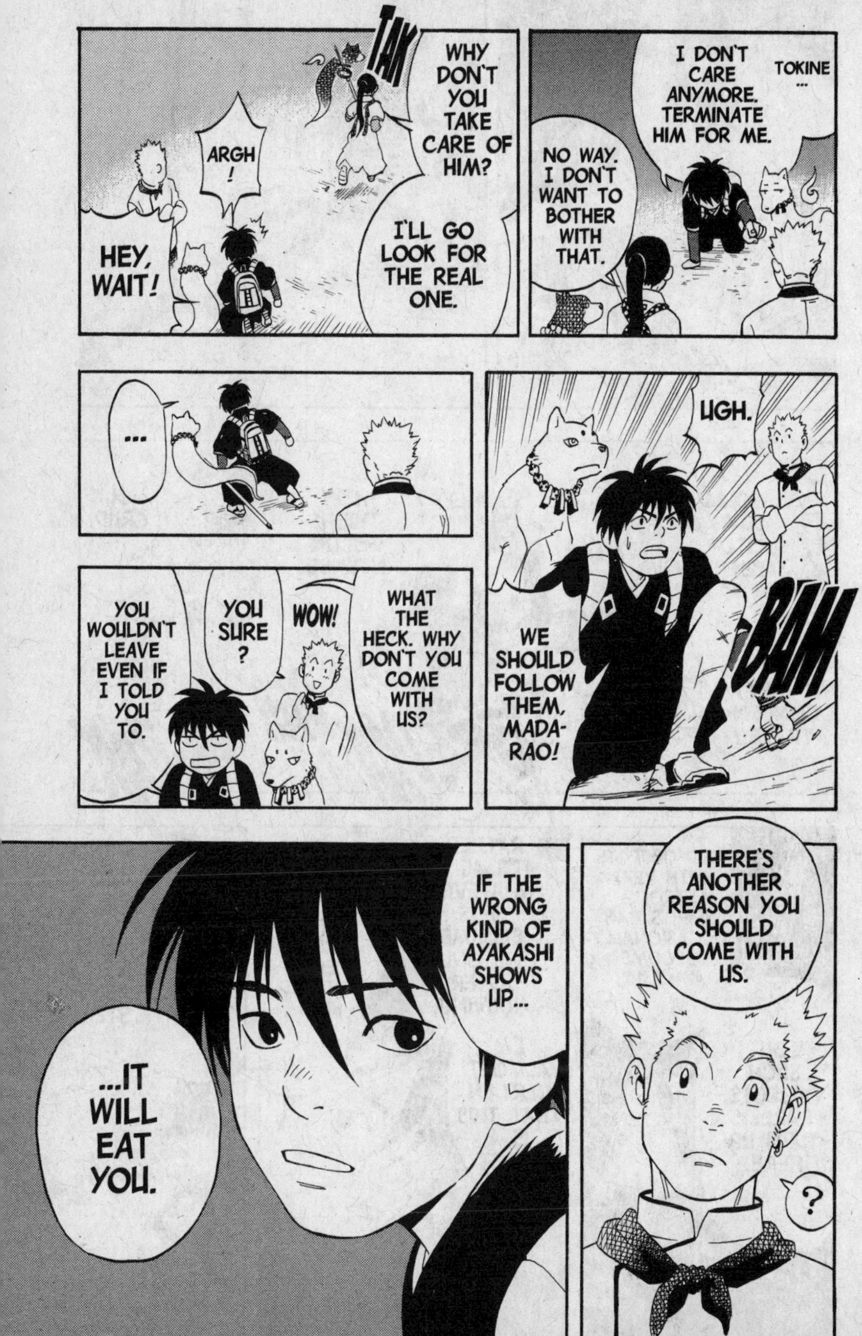
I DON'T CARE ANYMORE. TERMINATE HIM FOR ME.
TOKINE...
NO WAY. I DON'T WANT TO BOTHER WITH THAT.
WHY DON'T YOU TAKE CARE OF HIM?
TAK
I'LL GO LOOK FOR THE REAL ONE.
ARGH!
HEY, WAIT!
UGH.
BAM
WE SHOULD FOLLOW THEM, MADARAO!
...
WHAT THE HECK. WHY DON'T YOU COME WITH US?
WOW!
YOU SURE?
YOU WOULDN'T LEAVE EVEN IF I TOLD YOU TO.
THERE'S ANOTHER REASON YOU SHOULD COME WITH US.
?
IF THE WRONG KIND OF AYAKASHI SHOWS UP...
...IT WILL EAT YOU.

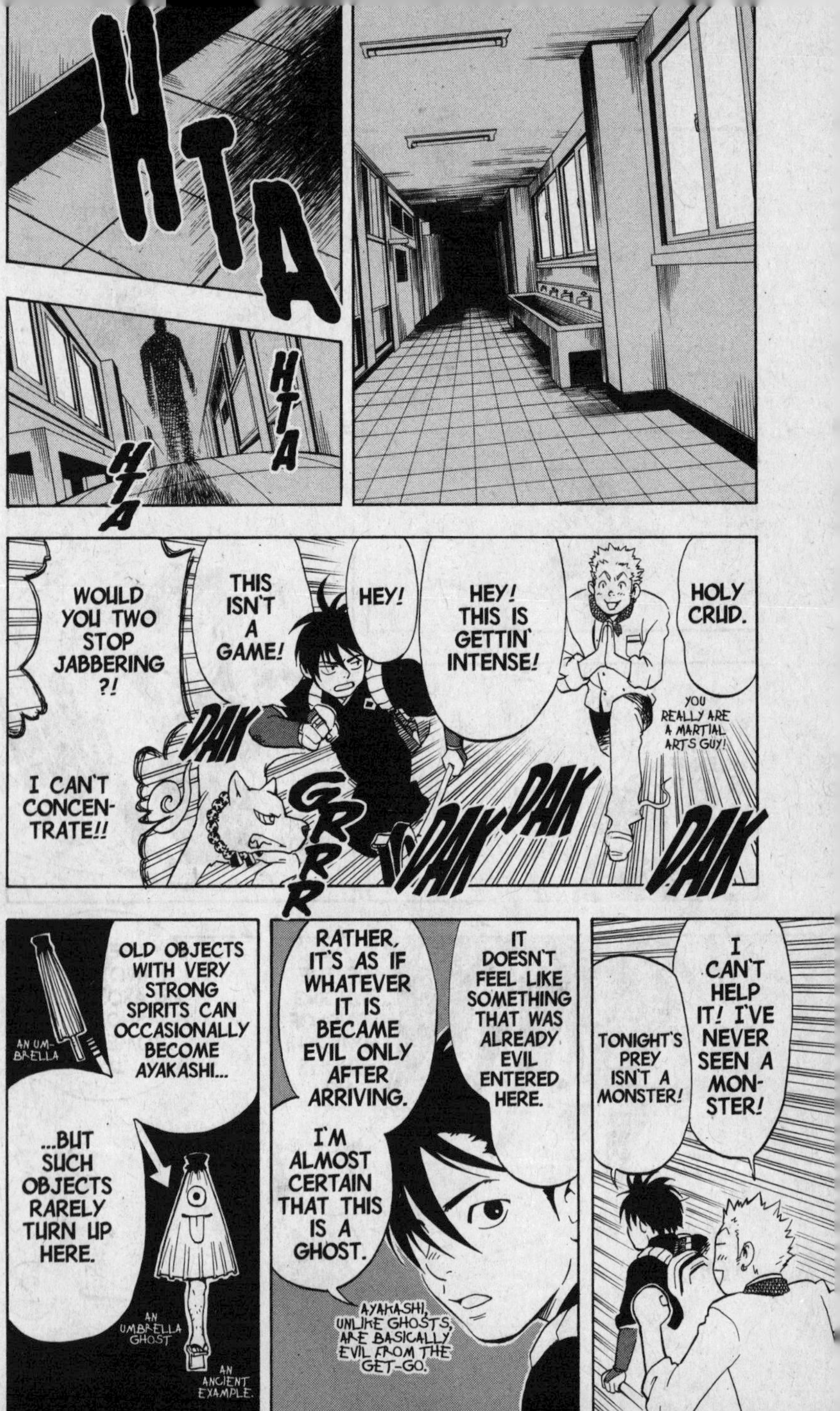
HTA
HTA
HTA
HOLY CRUD.
YOU REALLY ARE A MARTIAL ARTS GUY!
HEY! THIS IS GETTIN' INTENSE!
HEY!
THIS ISN'T A GAME!
WOULD YOU TWO STOP JABBERING?!
I CAN'T CONCENTRATE!!
DAK
DAK
DAK
DAK
DAK
GRRR
I CAN'T HELP IT! I'VE NEVER SEEN A MONSTER!
TONIGHT'S PREY ISN'T A MONSTER!
IT DOESN'T FEEL LIKE SOMETHING THAT WAS ALREADY EVIL ENTERED HERE.
RATHER, IT'S AS IF WHATEVER IT IS BECAME EVIL ONLY AFTER ARRIVING.
I'M ALMOST CERTAIN THAT THIS IS A GHOST.
AYAKASHI, UNLIKE GHOSTS, ARE BASICALLY EVIL FROM THE GET-GO.
OLD OBJECTS WITH VERY STRONG SPIRITS CAN OCCASIONALLY BECOME AYAKASHI...
AN UMBRELLA
...BUT SUCH OBJECTS RARELY TURN UP HERE.
AN UMBRELLA GHOST
AN ANCIENT EXAMPLE.

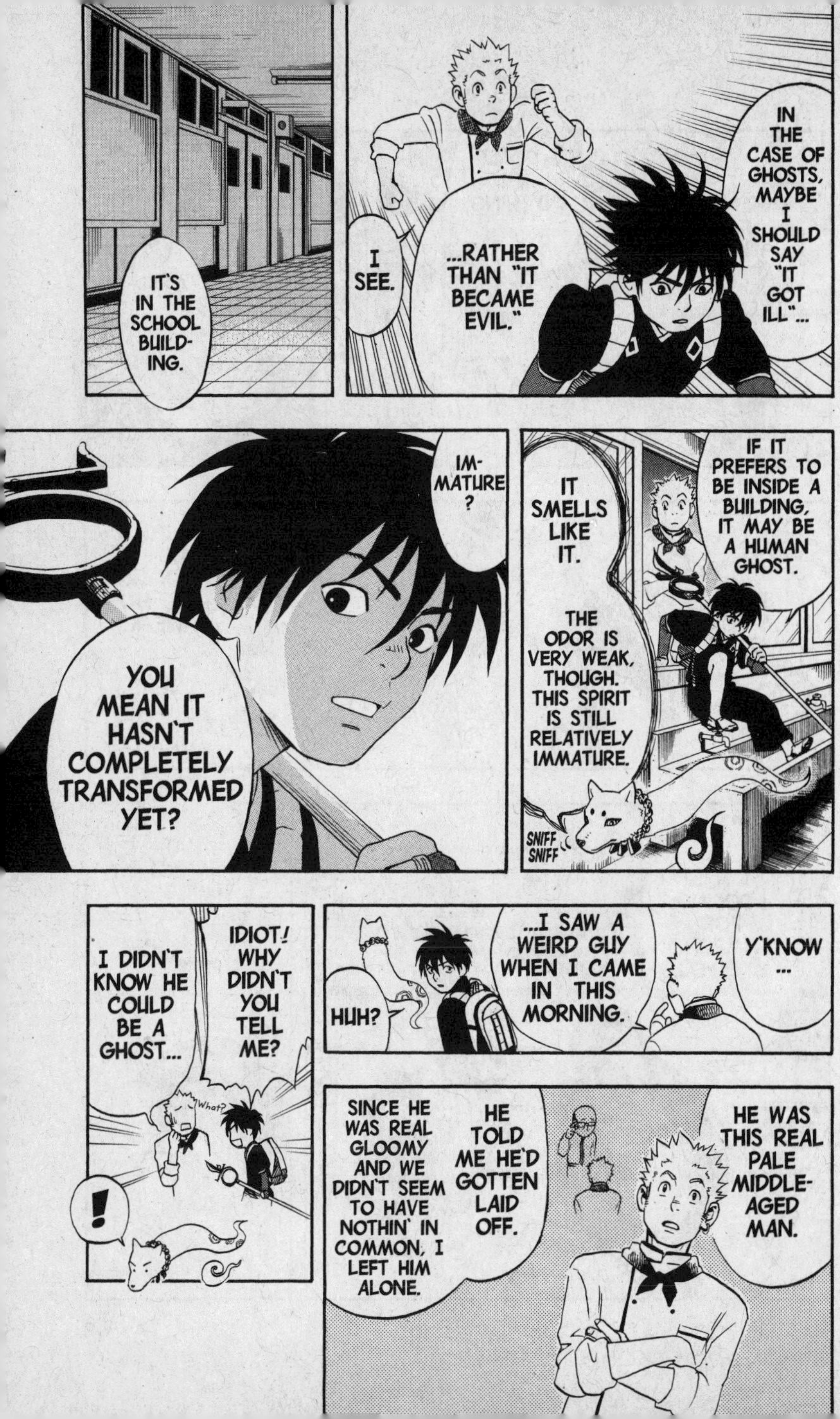
IN THE CASE OF GHOSTS, MAYBE I SHOULD SAY "IT GOT ILL"...
...RATHER THAN "IT BECAME EVIL."
I SEE.
IT'S IN THE SCHOOL BUILD-ING.
IF IT PREFERS TO BE INSIDE A BUILDING, IT MAY BE A HUMAN GHOST.
IT SMELLS LIKE IT.
THE ODOR IS VERY WEAK, THOUGH. THIS SPIRIT IS STILL RELATIVELY IMMATURE.
SNIFF SNIFF
IM-MATURE?
YOU MEAN IT HASN'T COMPLETELY TRANSFORMED YET?
Y'KNOW...
...I SAW A WEIRD GUY WHEN I CAME IN THIS MORNING.
HUH?
HE WAS THIS REAL PALE MIDDLE-AGED MAN.
HE TOLD ME HE'D GOTTEN LAID OFF.
SINCE HE WAS REAL GLOOMY AND WE DIDN'T SEEM TO HAVE NOTHIN' IN COMMON, I LEFT HIM ALONE.
IDIOT! WHY DIDN'T YOU TELL ME?
I DIDN'T KNOW HE COULD BE A GHOST...
What?
!

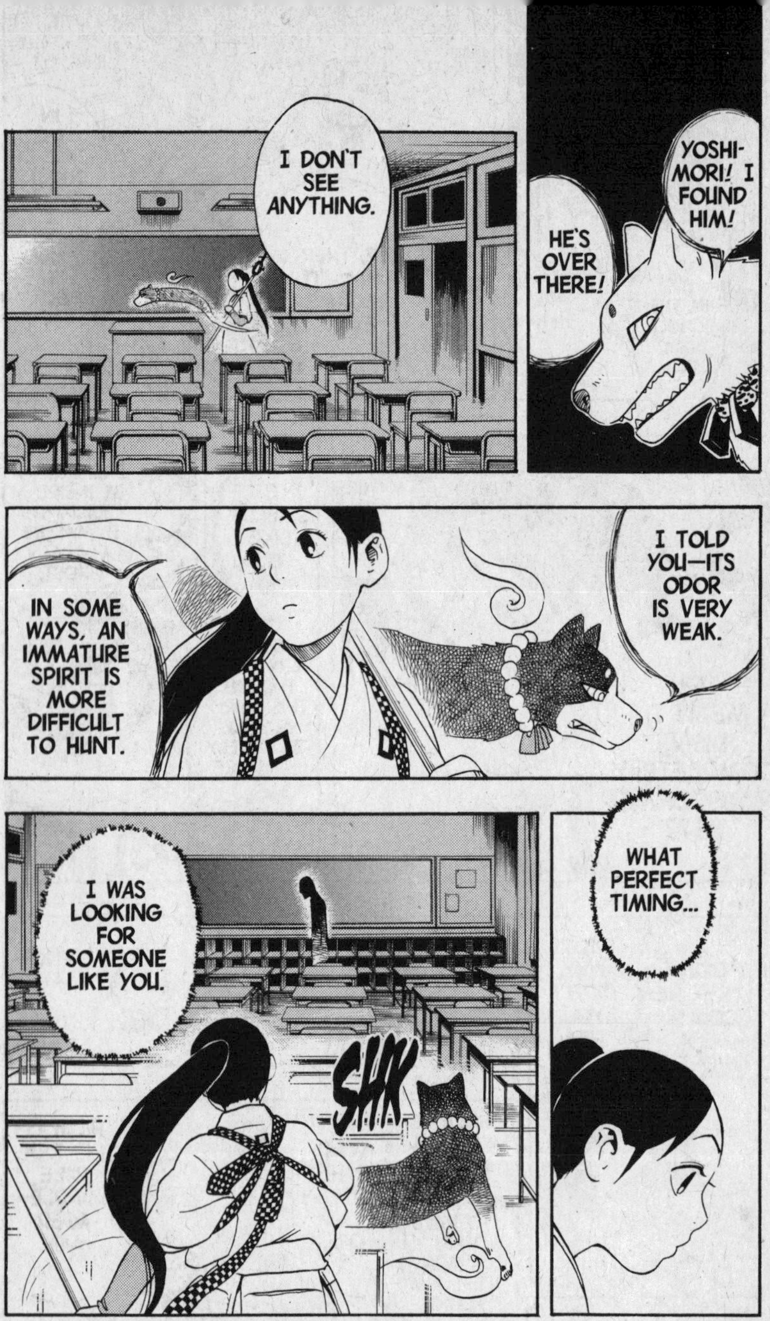
YOSHI-MORI! I FOUND HIM!
HE'S OVER THERE!
I DON'T SEE ANYTHING.
I TOLD YOU—ITS ODOR IS VERY WEAK.
IN SOME WAYS, AN IMMATURE SPIRIT IS MORE DIFFICULT TO HUNT.
WHAT PERFECT TIMING...
I WAS LOOKING FOR SOMEONE LIKE YOU.
SHK

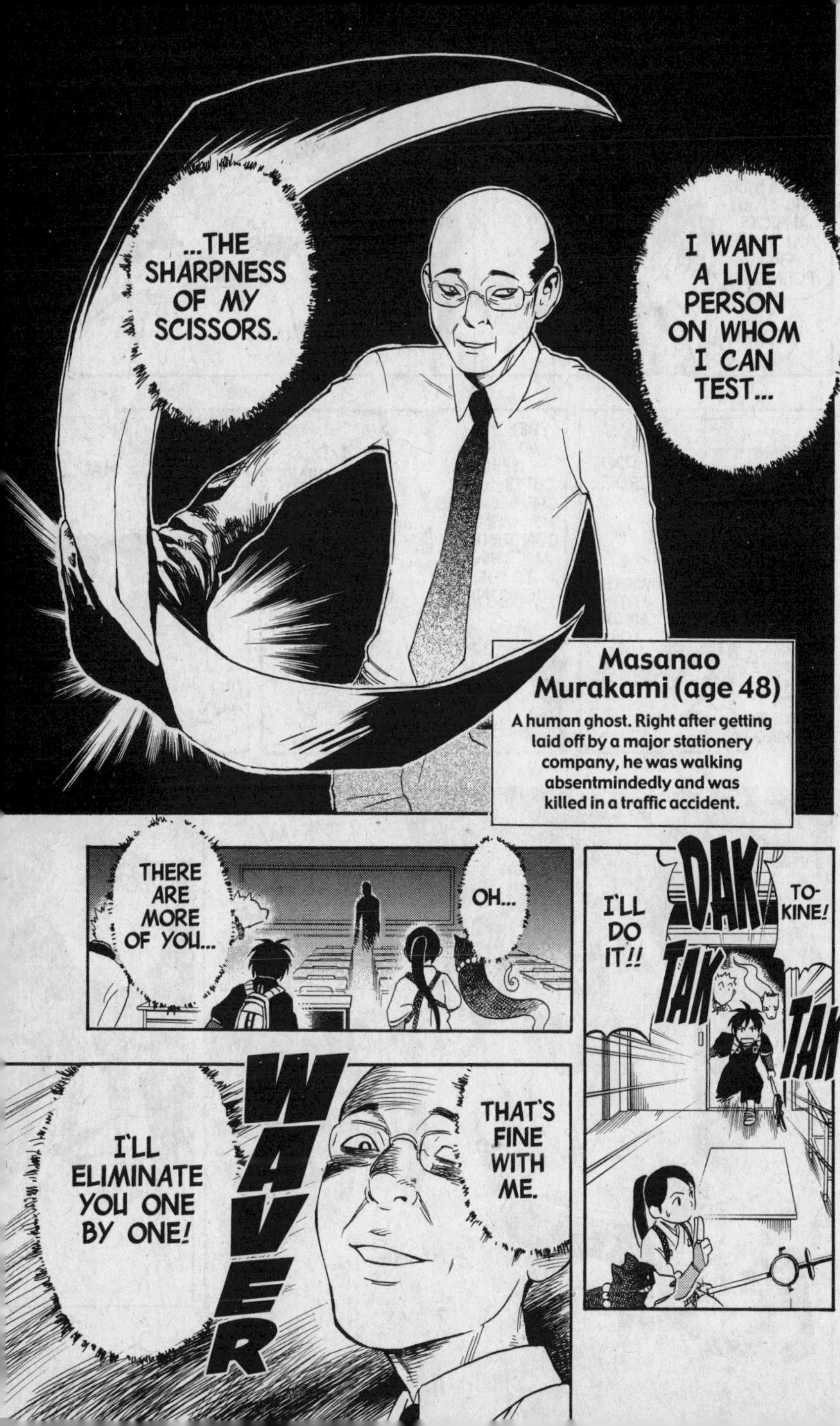
I WANT A LIVE PERSON ON WHOM I CAN TEST...
...THE SHARPNESS OF MY SCISSORS.
Masanao Murakami (age 48)
A human ghost. Right after getting laid off by a major stationery company, he was walking absentmindedly and was killed in a traffic accident.
TO-KINE!
DAK
I'LL DO IT!!
TAK
TAK
OH...
THERE ARE MORE OF YOU...
THAT'S FINE WITH ME.
WAVER
I'LL ELIMINATE YOU ONE BY ONE!

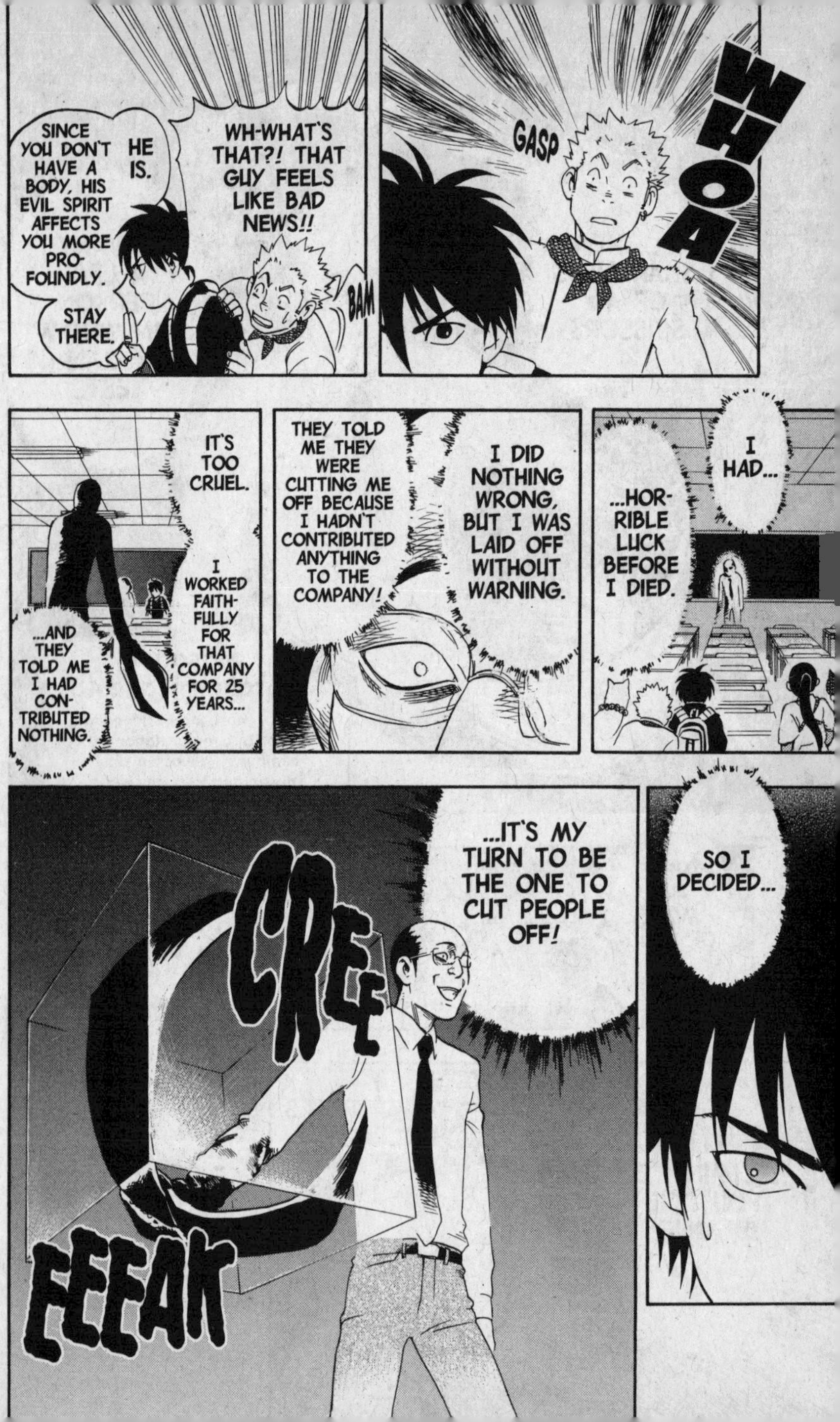
WHOA
GASP
WH-WHAT'S THAT?! THAT GUY FEELS LIKE BAD NEWS!!
HE IS.
SINCE YOU DON'T HAVE A BODY, HIS EVIL SPIRIT AFFECTS YOU MORE PRO-FOUNDLY.
STAY THERE.
BAM
I HAD...
...HOR-RIBLE LUCK BEFORE I DIED.
I DID NOTHING WRONG, BUT I WAS LAID OFF WITHOUT WARNING.
THEY TOLD ME THEY WERE CUTTING ME OFF BECAUSE I HADN'T CONTRIBUTED ANYTHING TO THE COMPANY!
IT'S TOO CRUEL.
I WORKED FAITH-FULLY FOR THAT COMPANY FOR 25 YEARS...
...AND THEY TOLD ME I HAD CON-TRIBUTED NOTHING.
SO I DECIDED...
...IT'S MY TURN TO BE THE ONE TO CUT PEOPLE OFF!
CREE
EEEAK

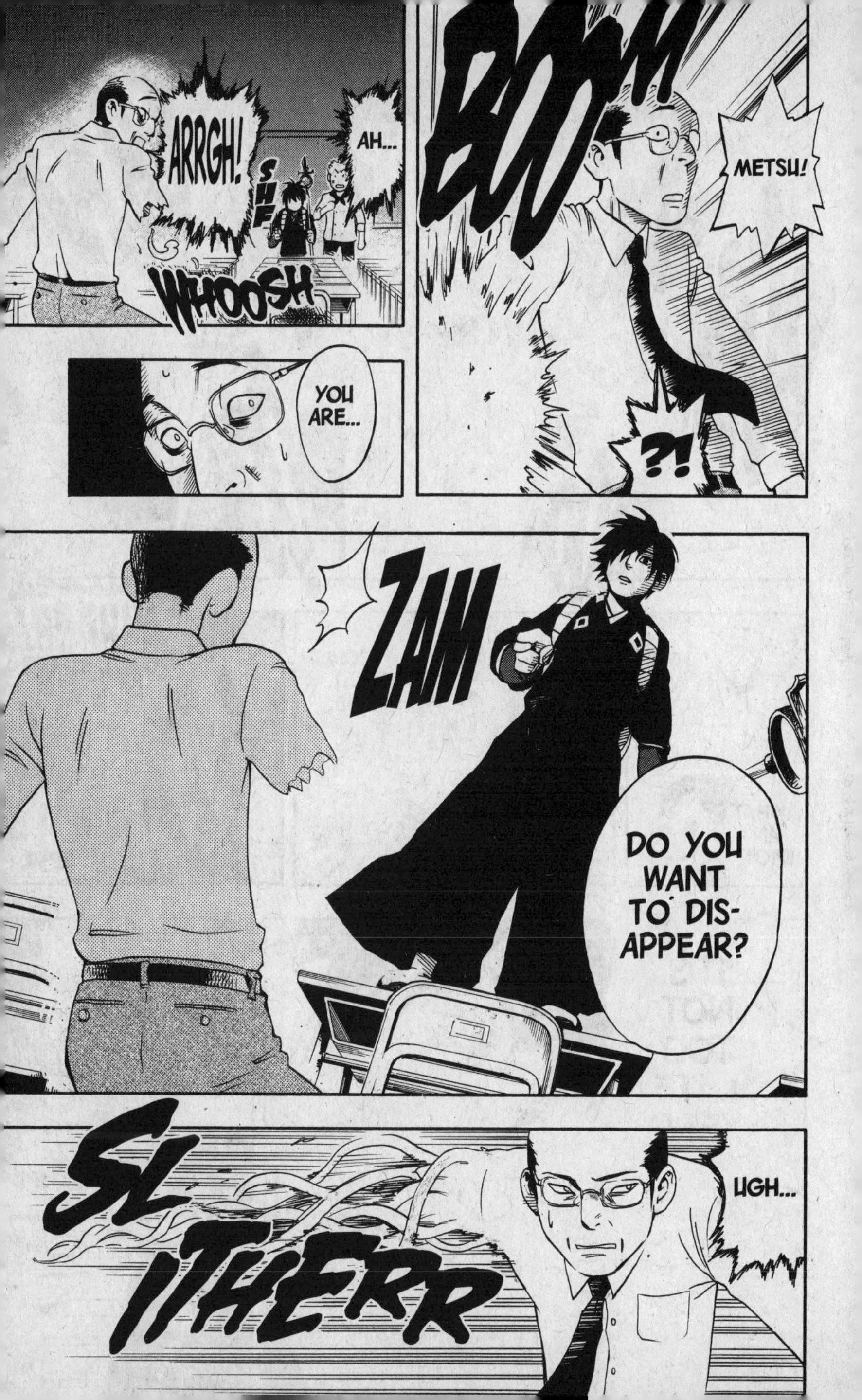
METSU!
BOOM
?!
AH...
SHF
ARRGH!
WHOOSH
YOU ARE...
ZAM
DO YOU WANT TO DIS-APPEAR?
UGH...
SLITHERR

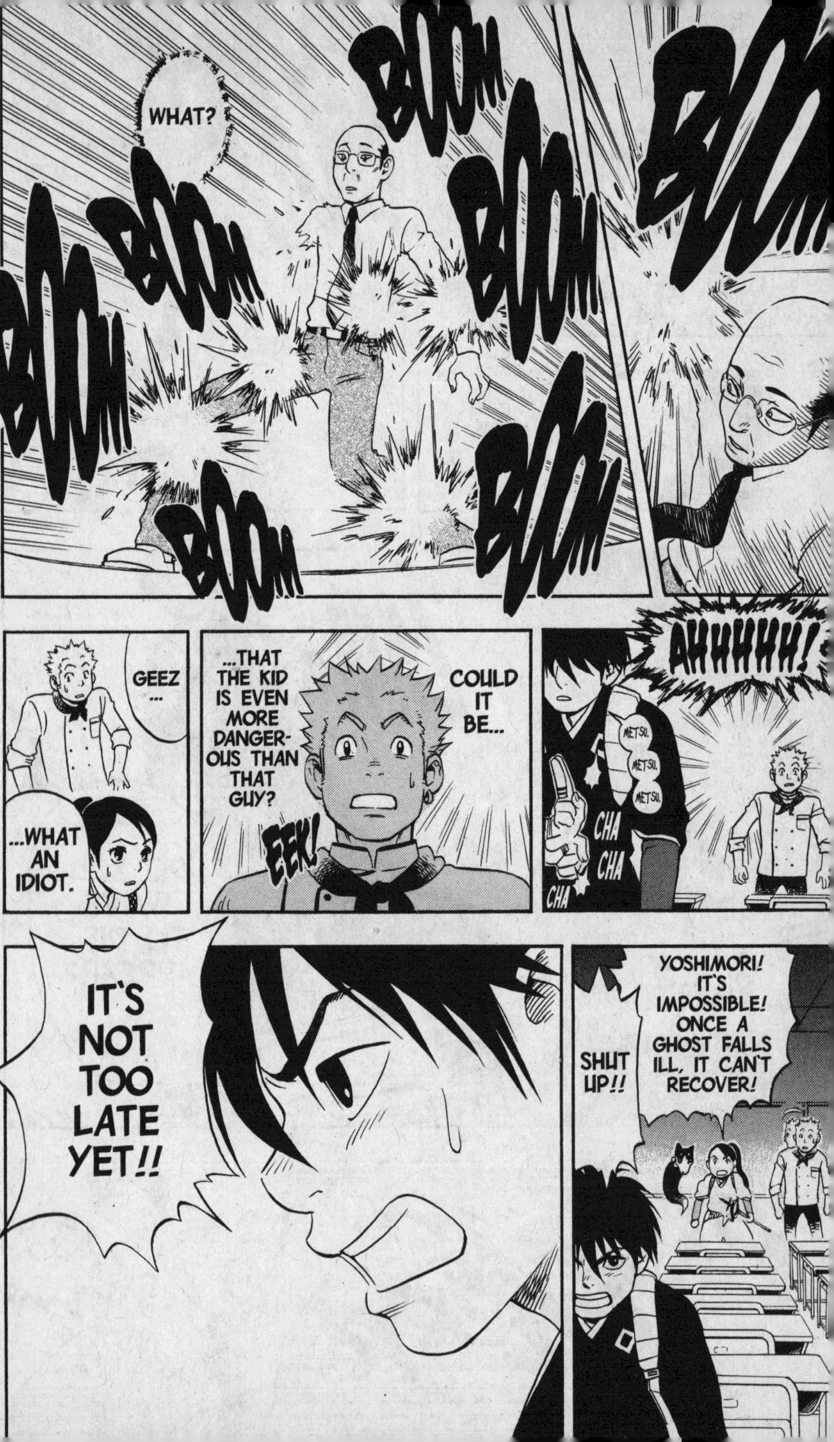
BOOM
BOOM
BOOM
WHAT?
BOOM
BOOM
BOOM
BOOM
BOOM
AHHHHH!
METSU
METSU
METSU
CHA
CHA
CHA
COULD IT BE...
...THAT THE KID IS EVEN MORE DANGER-OUS THAN THAT GUY?
EEK!
GEEZ...
...WHAT AN IDIOT.
YOSHIMORI! IT'S IMPOSSIBLE! ONCE A GHOST FALLS ILL, IT CAN'T RECOVER!
SHUT UP!!
IT'S NOT TOO LATE YET!!

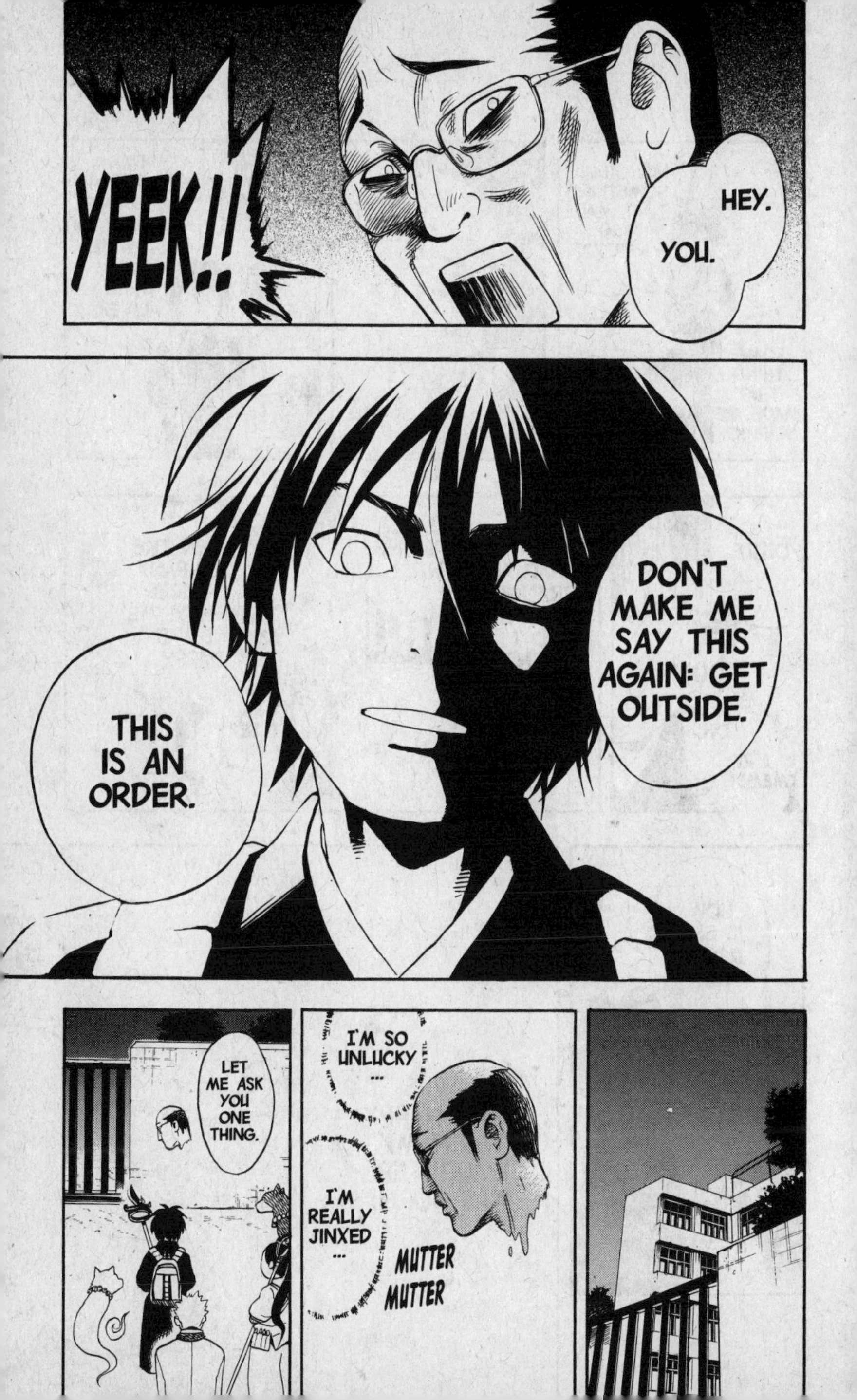
HEY. YOU.
YEEK!!
DON'T MAKE ME SAY THIS AGAIN: GET OUTSIDE.
THIS IS AN ORDER.
I'M SO UNLUCKY ...
I'M REALLY JINXED ...
MUTTER MUTTER
LET ME ASK YOU ONE THING.

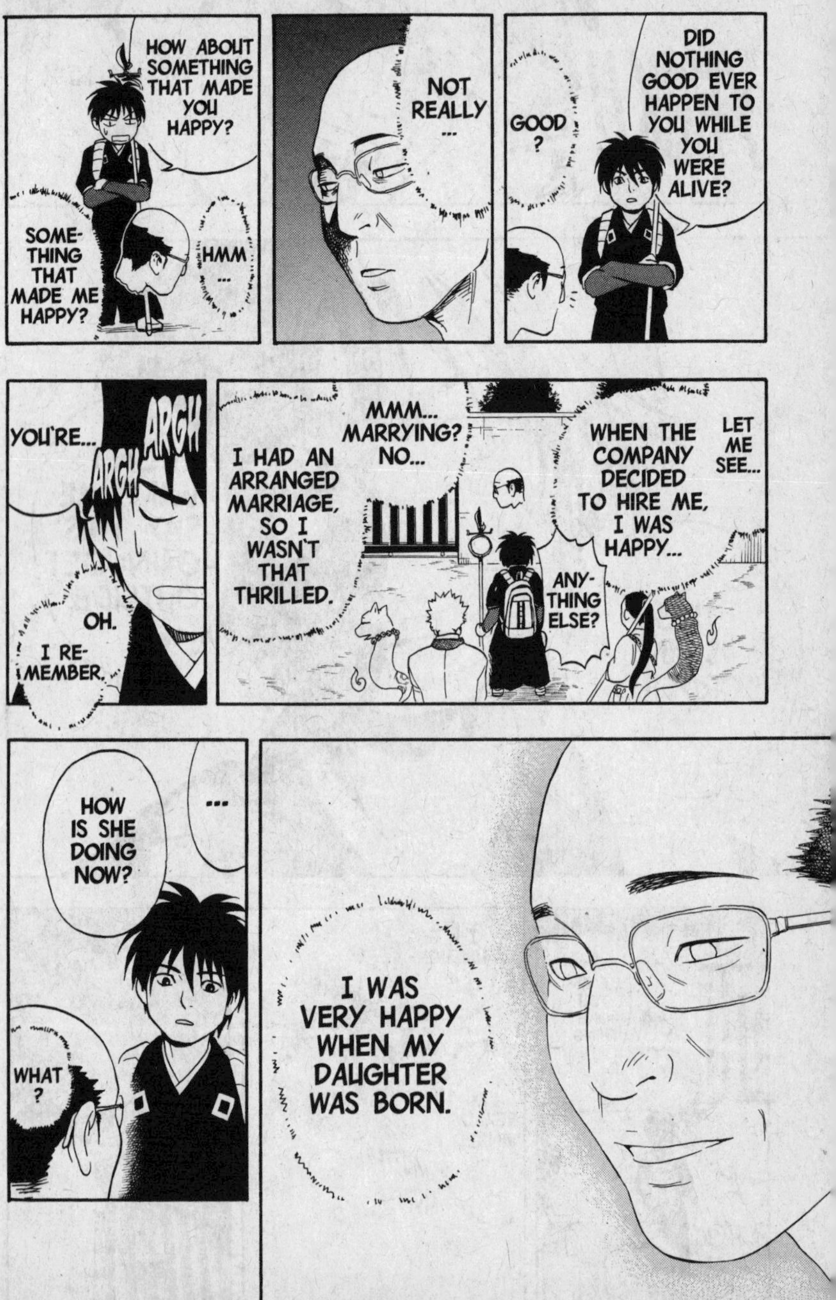
DID NOTHING GOOD EVER HAPPEN TO YOU WHILE YOU WERE ALIVE?
GOOD ?
NOT REALLY ...
HOW ABOUT SOMETHING THAT MADE YOU HAPPY?
HMM ...
SOMETHING THAT MADE ME HAPPY?
LET ME SEE...
WHEN THE COMPANY DECIDED TO HIRE ME, I WAS HAPPY...
ANYTHING ELSE?
MMM... MARRYING? NO...
I HAD AN ARRANGED MARRIAGE, SO I WASN'T THAT THRILLED.
YOU'RE...
ARGH
ARGH
OH.
I REMEMBER.
I WAS VERY HAPPY WHEN MY DAUGHTER WAS BORN.
...
HOW IS SHE DOING NOW?
WHAT ?

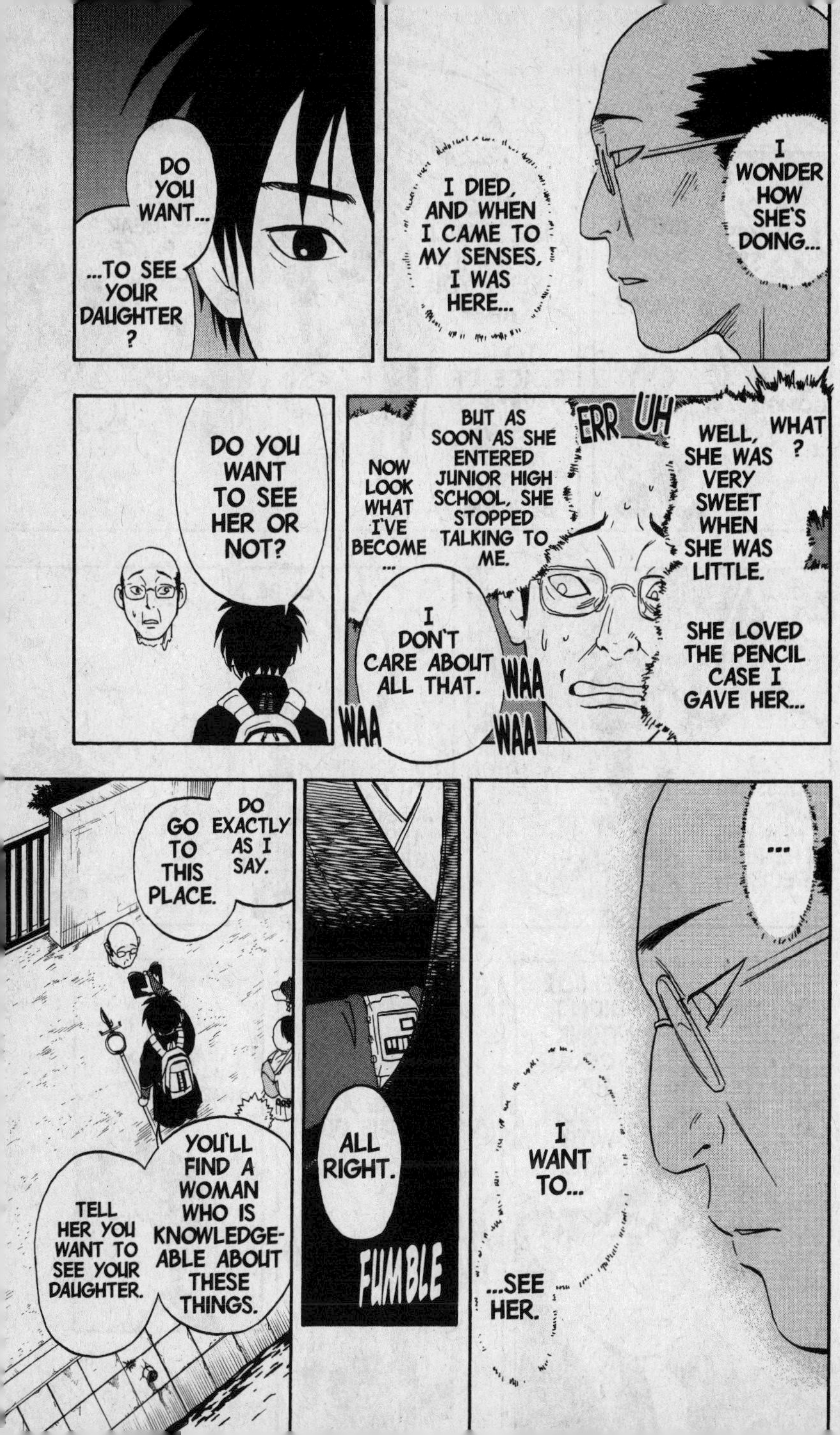
I WONDER HOW SHE'S DOING...
I DIED, AND WHEN I CAME TO MY SENSES, I WAS HERE...
DO YOU WANT...
...TO SEE YOUR DAUGHTER?
WHAT?
UH
ERR
WELL, SHE WAS VERY SWEET WHEN SHE WAS LITTLE.
SHE LOVED THE PENCIL CASE I GAVE HER...
BUT AS SOON AS SHE ENTERED JUNIOR HIGH SCHOOL, SHE STOPPED TALKING TO ME.
NOW LOOK WHAT I'VE BECOME...
WAA
I DON'T CARE ABOUT ALL THAT.
WAA
WAA
DO YOU WANT TO SEE HER OR NOT?
...
I WANT TO...
...SEE HER.
ALL RIGHT.
FUMBLE
DO EXACTLY AS I SAY.
GO TO THIS PLACE.
YOU'LL FIND A WOMAN WHO IS KNOWLEDGE-ABLE ABOUT THESE THINGS.
TELL HER YOU WANT TO SEE YOUR DAUGHTER.

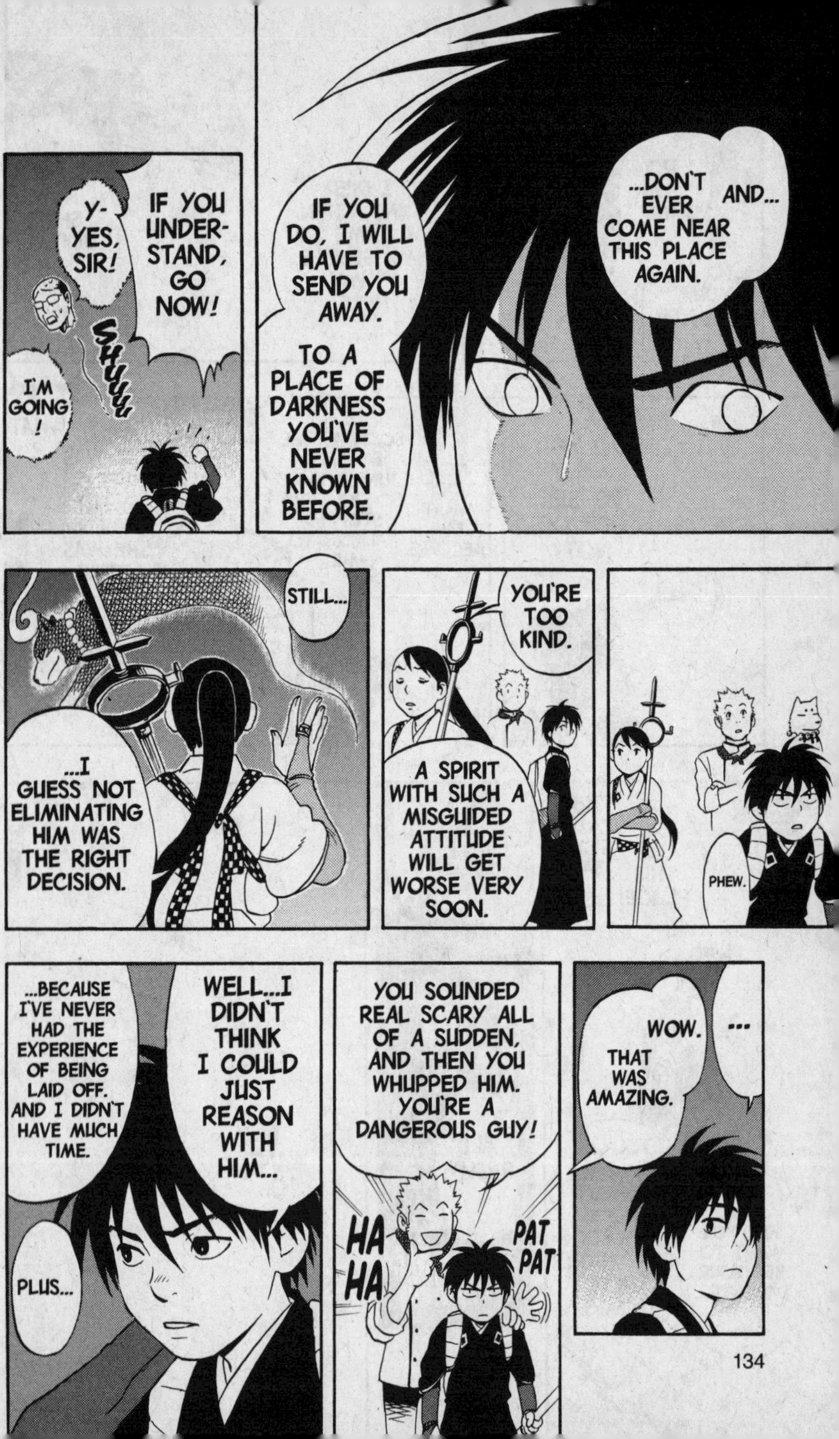
AND...
...DON'T EVER COME NEAR THIS PLACE AGAIN.
IF YOU DO, I WILL HAVE TO SEND YOU AWAY.
TO A PLACE OF DARKNESS YOU'VE NEVER KNOWN BEFORE.
IF YOU UNDERSTAND, GO NOW!
Y-YES, SIR!
SHUUUU
I'M GOING!
PHEW.
YOU'RE TOO KIND.
A SPIRIT WITH SUCH A MISGUIDED ATTITUDE WILL GET WORSE VERY SOON.
STILL...
...I GUESS NOT ELIMINATING HIM WAS THE RIGHT DECISION.
...
WOW.
THAT WAS AMAZING.
YOU SOUNDED REAL SCARY ALL OF A SUDDEN, AND THEN YOU WHUPPED HIM. YOU'RE A DANGEROUS GUY!
HA HA
PAT PAT
WELL...I DIDN'T THINK I COULD JUST REASON WITH HIM...
...BECAUSE I'VE NEVER HAD THE EXPERIENCE OF BEING LAID OFF. AND I DIDN'T HAVE MUCH TIME.
PLUS...

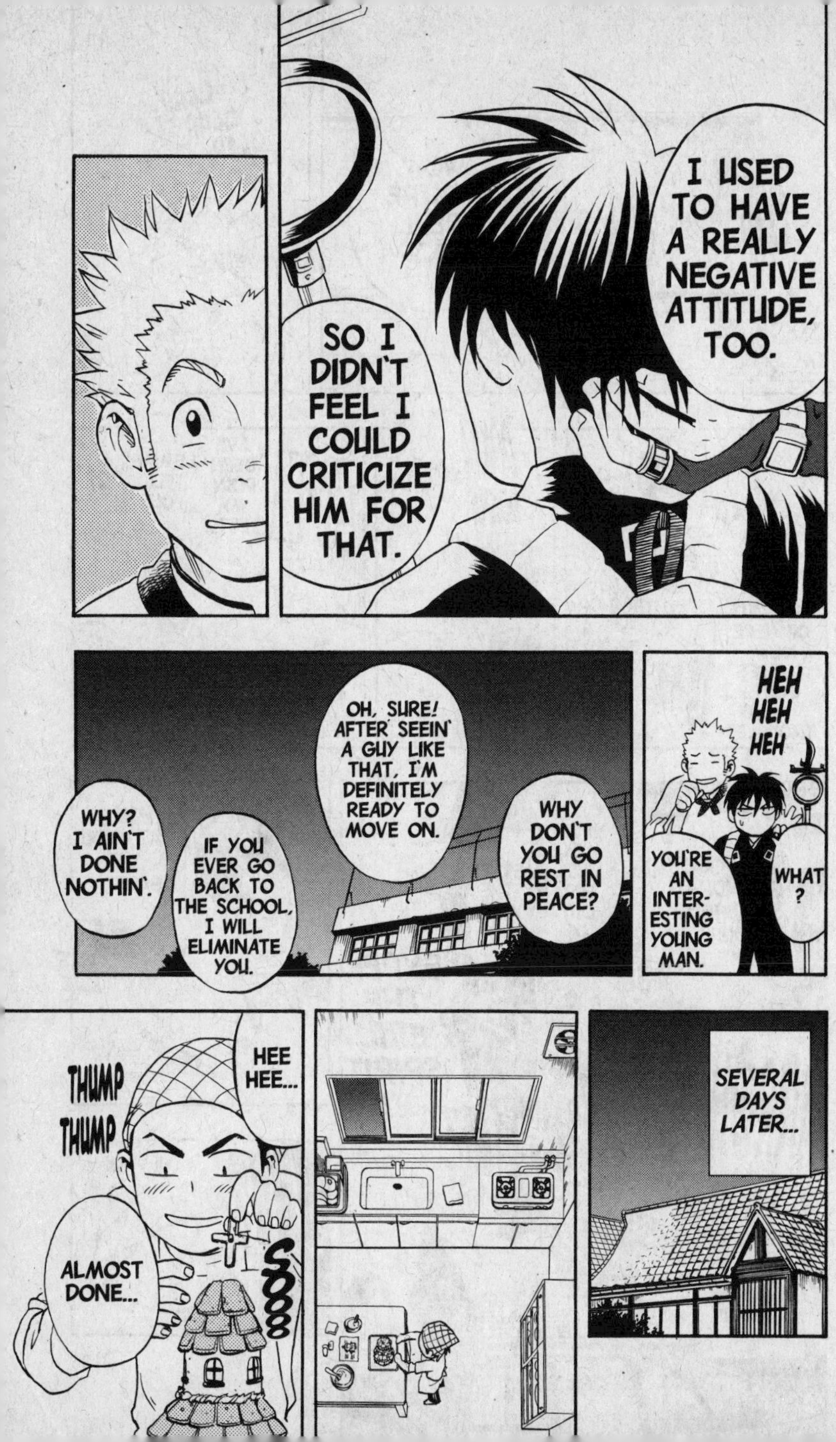
I USED TO HAVE A REALLY NEGATIVE ATTITUDE, TOO.
SO I DIDN'T FEEL I COULD CRITICIZE HIM FOR THAT.
HEH HEH HEH
YOU'RE AN INTER-ESTING YOUNG MAN.
WHAT?
WHY DON'T YOU GO REST IN PEACE?
OH, SURE! AFTER SEEIN' A GUY LIKE THAT, I'M DEFINITELY READY TO MOVE ON.
IF YOU EVER GO BACK TO THE SCHOOL, I WILL ELIMINATE YOU.
WHY? I AIN'T DONE NOTHIN'.
SEVERAL DAYS LATER...
HEE HEE...
THUMP THUMP
SOOOO
ALMOST DONE...

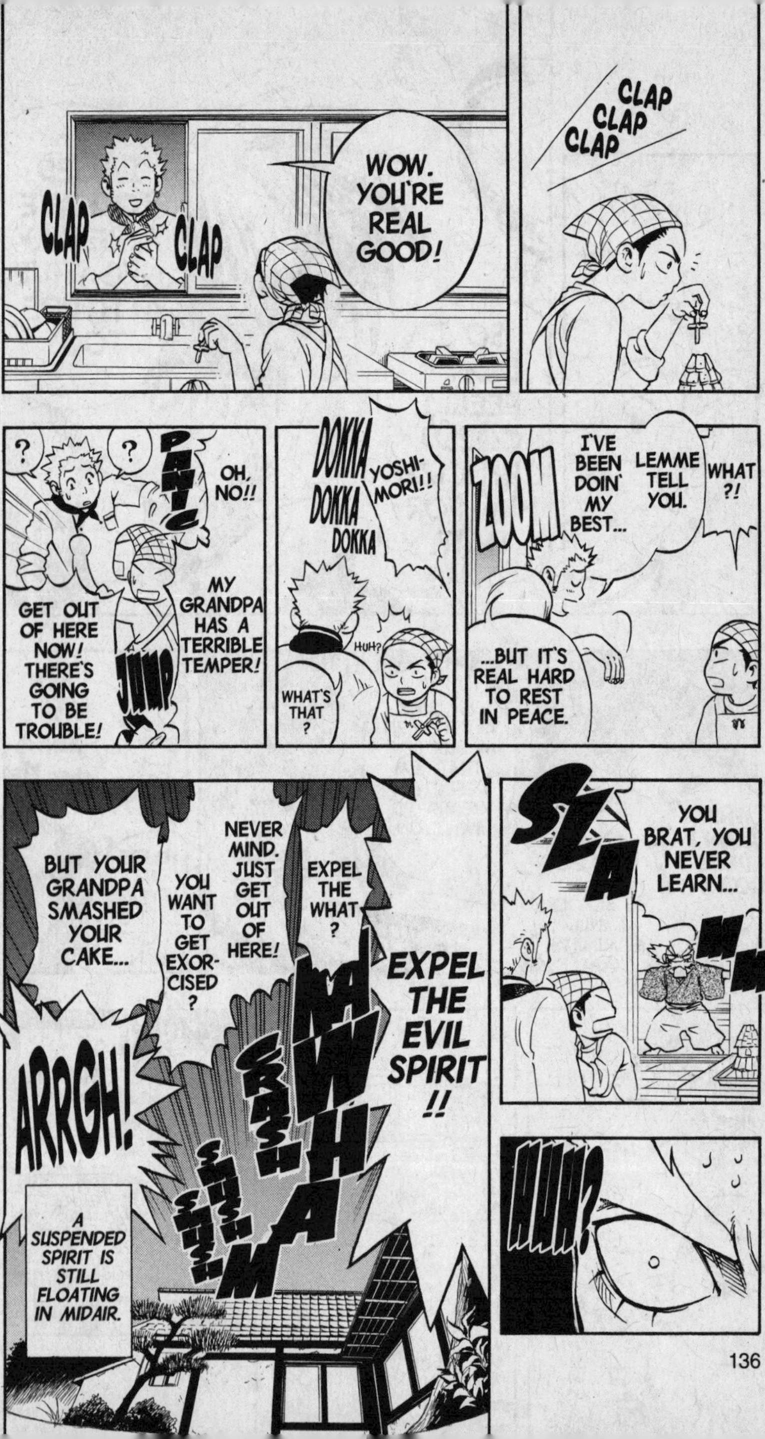
CLAP
CLAP
CLAP
WOW. YOU'RE REAL GOOD!
CLAP
CLAP
WHAT?!
LEMME TELL YOU.
I'VE BEEN DOIN' MY BEST...
ZOOM
...BUT IT'S REAL HARD TO REST IN PEACE.
YOSHI-MORI!!
DOKKA
DOKKA
DOKKA
HUH?
WHAT'S THAT?
PANIC
OH, NO!!
?
?
MY GRANDPA HAS A TERRIBLE TEMPER!
GET OUT OF HERE NOW! THERE'S GOING TO BE TROUBLE!
JUMP
SLA
YOU BRAT, YOU NEVER LEARN...
HUH?
EXPEL THE EVIL SPIRIT!!
EXPEL THE WHAT?
NEVER MIND. JUST GET OUT OF HERE!
YOU WANT TO GET EXOR-CISED?
BUT YOUR GRANDPA SMASHED YOUR CAKE...
WHAM
CRASH
SMASH
SMASH
SMASH
ARRGH!
A SUSPENDED SPIRIT IS STILL FLOATING IN MIDAIR.

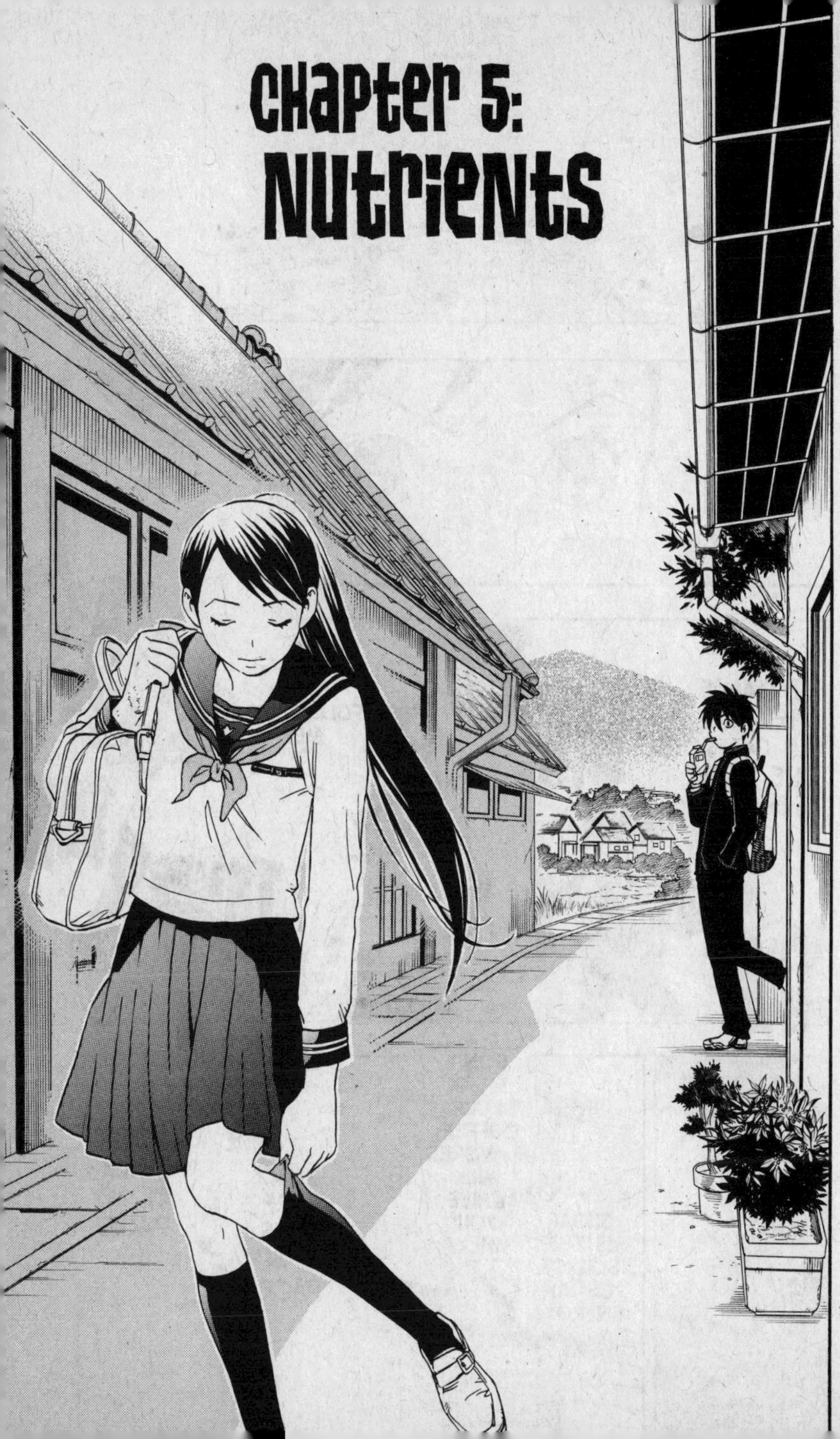
Chapter 5:
Nutrients

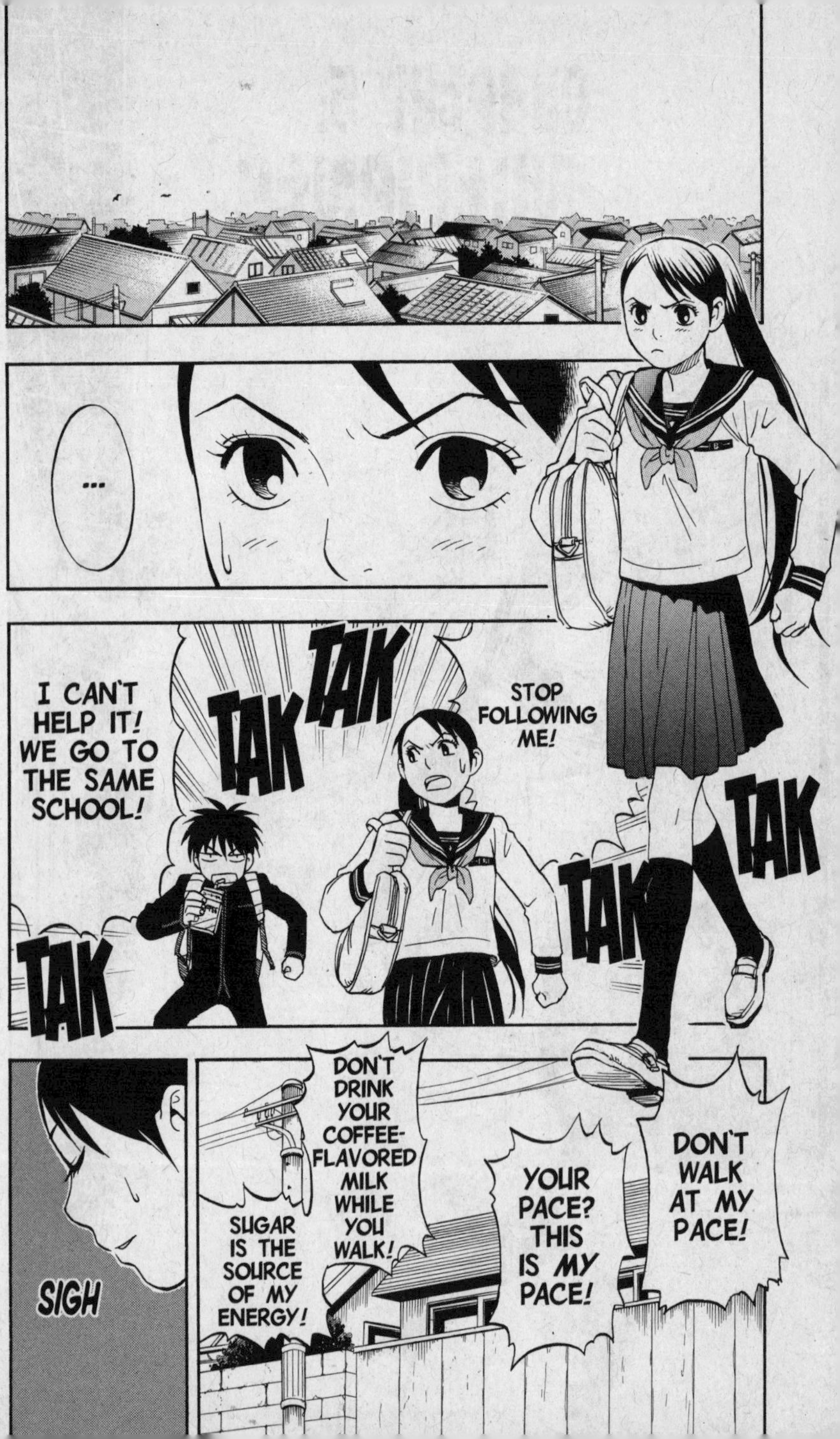
...
TAK TAK
STOP FOLLOWING ME!
TAK TAK
I CAN'T HELP IT! WE GO TO THE SAME SCHOOL!
TAK TAK
DON'T WALK AT MY PACE!
YOUR PACE? THIS IS MY PACE!
DON'T DRINK YOUR COFFEE-FLAVORED MILK WHILE YOU WALK!
SUGAR IS THE SOURCE OF MY ENERGY!
SIGH

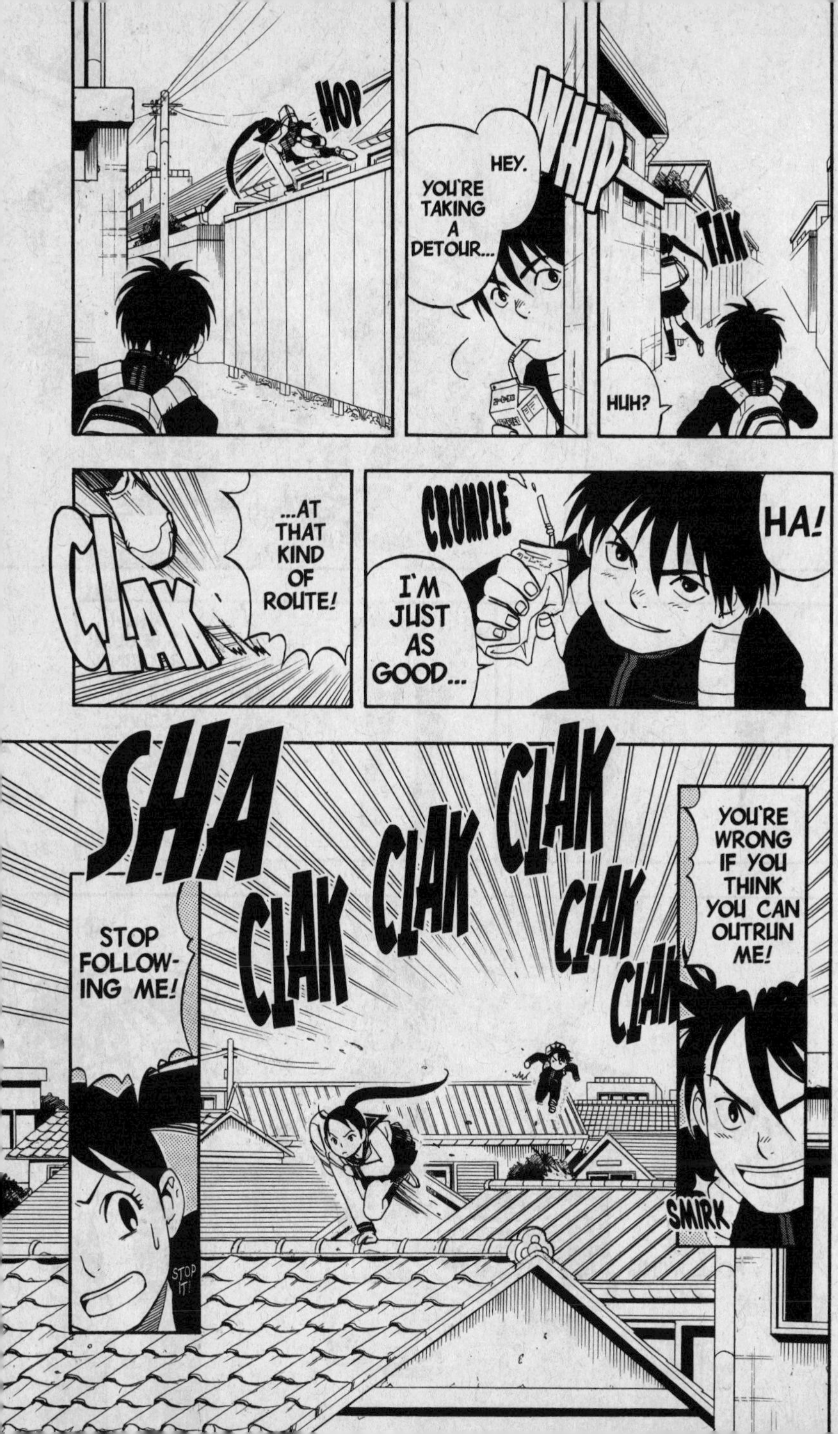

TAK
HUH?
WHIP
HEY.
YOU'RE TAKING A DETOUR...
HOP
HA!
CRUMPLE
I'M JUST AS GOOD...
...AT THAT KIND OF ROUTE!
CLAK
SHA
CLAK
CLAK
CLAK
CLAK
CLAK
YOU'RE WRONG IF YOU THINK YOU CAN OUTRUN ME!
SMIRK
STOP FOLLOWING ME!
STOP IT!

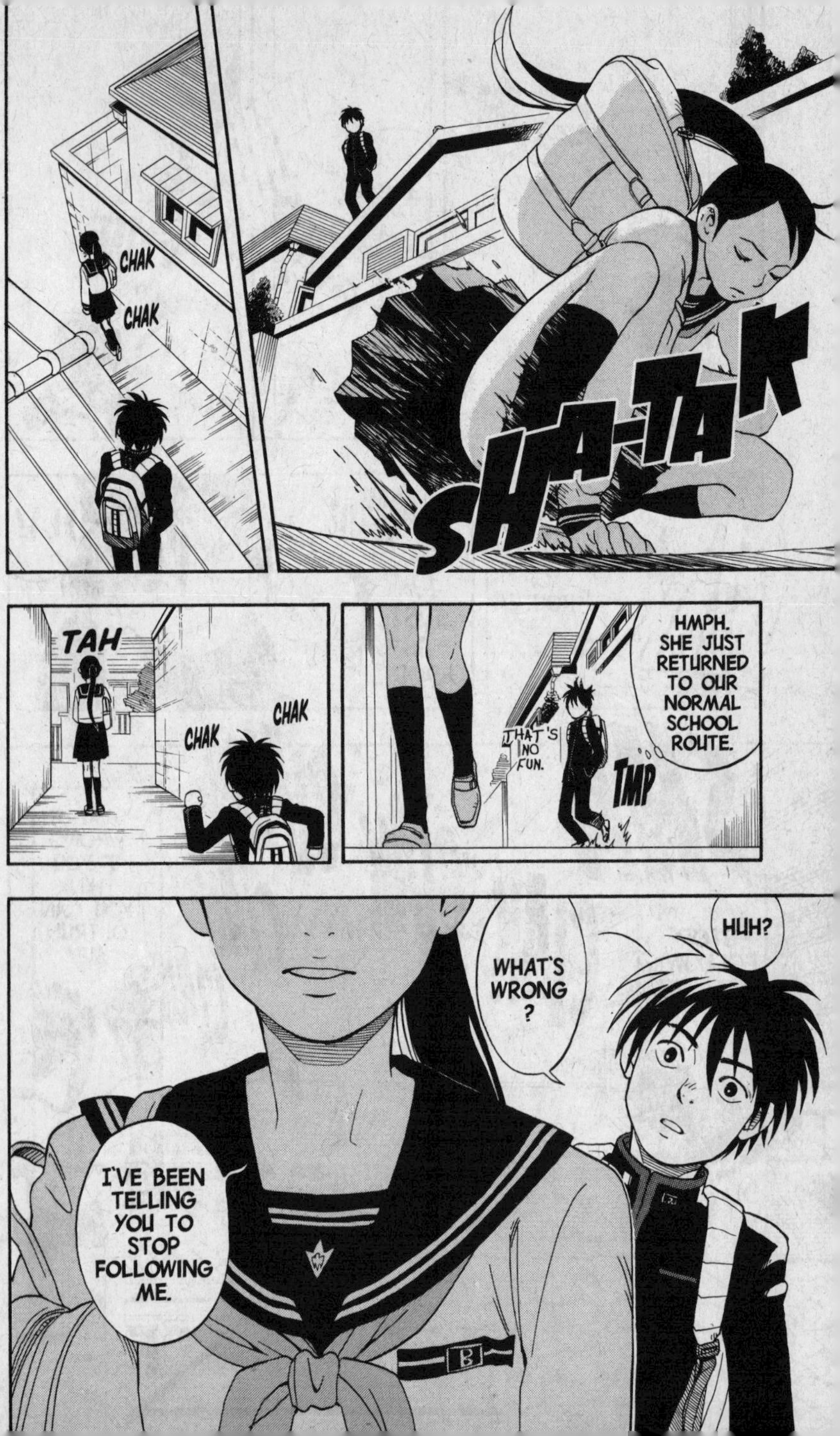
SHA-TAK
CHAK
CHAK
HMPH. SHE JUST RETURNED TO OUR NORMAL SCHOOL ROUTE.
THAT'S NO FUN.
TMP
TAH
CHAK
CHAK
WHAT'S WRONG?
HUH?
I'VE BEEN TELLING YOU TO STOP FOLLOWING ME.

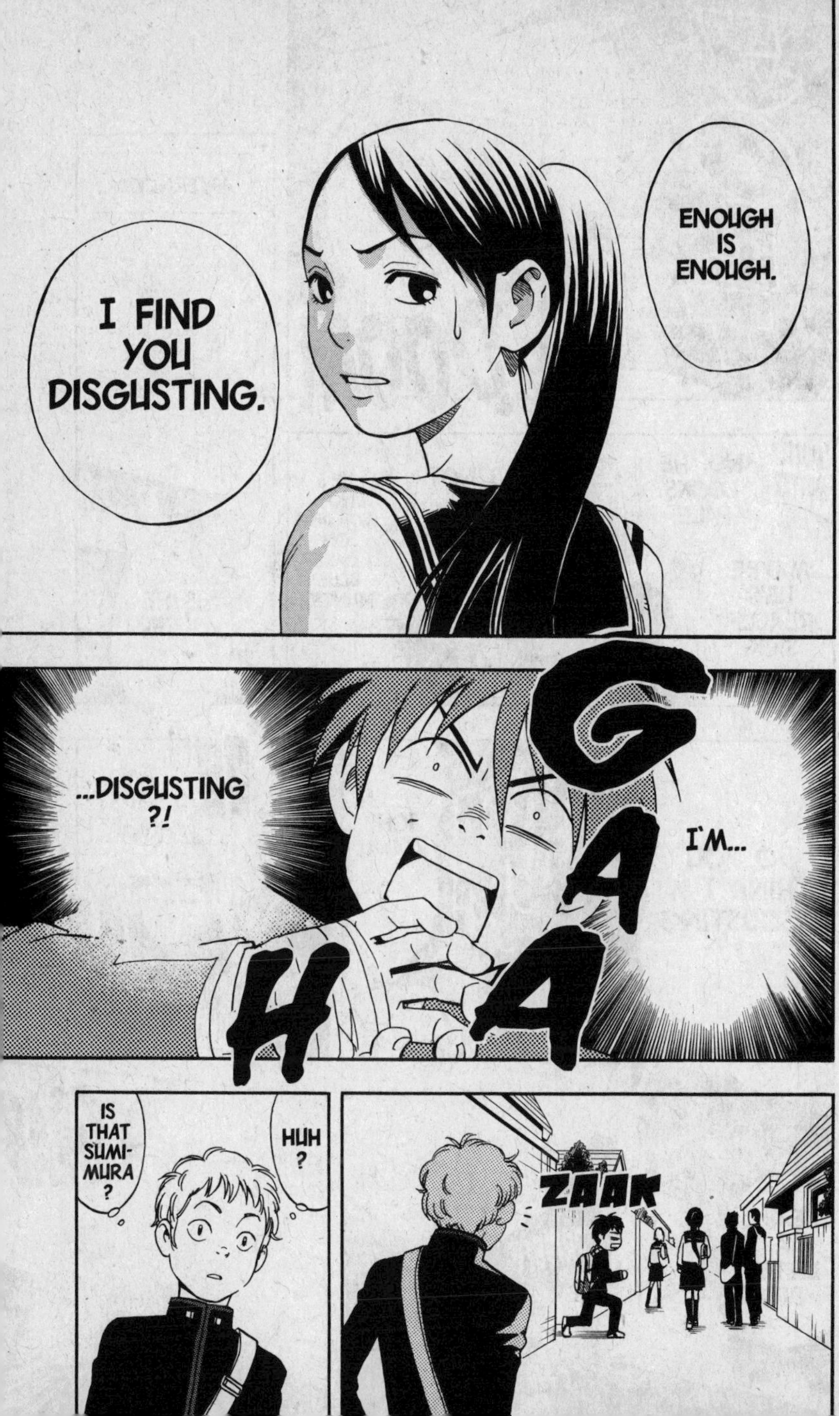
ENOUGH IS ENOUGH.
I FIND YOU DISGUSTING.
I'M...
GAAH
...DISGUSTING ?!
ZAAK
HUH ?
IS THAT SUMI-MURA ?

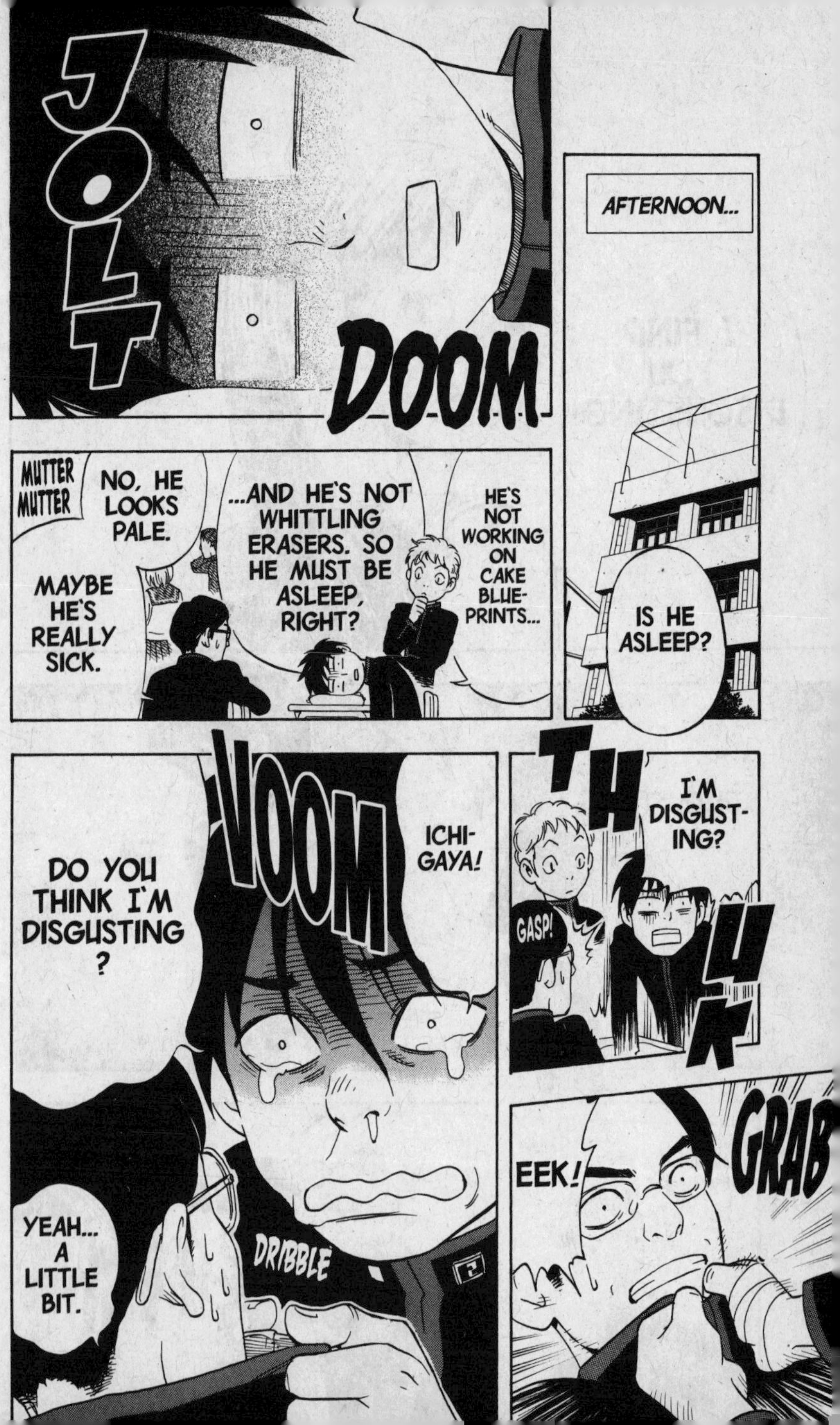
AFTERNOON...
IS HE ASLEEP?
HE'S NOT WORKING ON CAKE BLUE-PRINTS...
...AND HE'S NOT WHITTLING ERASERS. SO HE MUST BE ASLEEP, RIGHT?
NO, HE LOOKS PALE.
MAYBE HE'S REALLY SICK.
MUTTER MUTTER
JOLT
DOOM
ICHI-GAYA!
VOOM
DO YOU THINK I'M DISGUSTING?
YEAH... A LITTLE BIT.
DRIBBLE
TH
I'M DISGUST-ING?
GASP!
UK
GRAB
EEK!

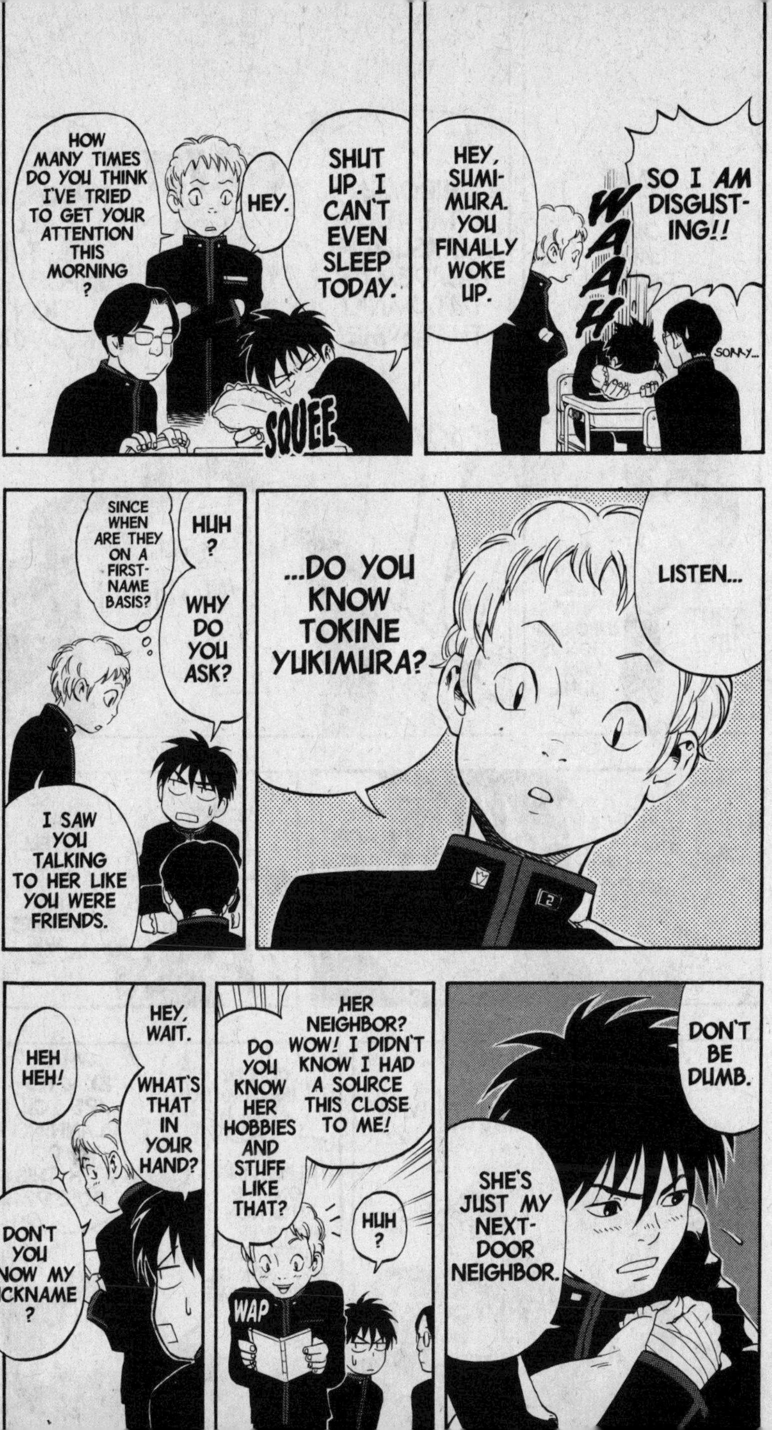
SO I AM DISGUSTING!!
WAAH
HEY, SUMIMURA. YOU FINALLY WOKE UP.
SORRY...
SHUT UP. I CAN'T EVEN SLEEP TODAY.
HEY.
HOW MANY TIMES DO YOU THINK I'VE TRIED TO GET YOUR ATTENTION THIS MORNING?
SQUEE
LISTEN...
...DO YOU KNOW TOKINE YUKIMURA?
HUH? WHY DO YOU ASK?
SINCE WHEN ARE THEY ON A FIRST-NAME BASIS?
I SAW YOU TALKING TO HER LIKE YOU WERE FRIENDS.
DON'T BE DUMB.
SHE'S JUST MY NEXT-DOOR NEIGHBOR.
HER NEIGHBOR? WOW! I DIDN'T KNOW I HAD A SOURCE THIS CLOSE TO ME!
DO YOU KNOW HER HOBBIES AND STUFF LIKE THAT?
HUH?
WAP
HEY, WAIT. WHAT'S THAT IN YOUR HAND?
HEH HEH!
DON'T YOU KNOW MY NICKNAME?

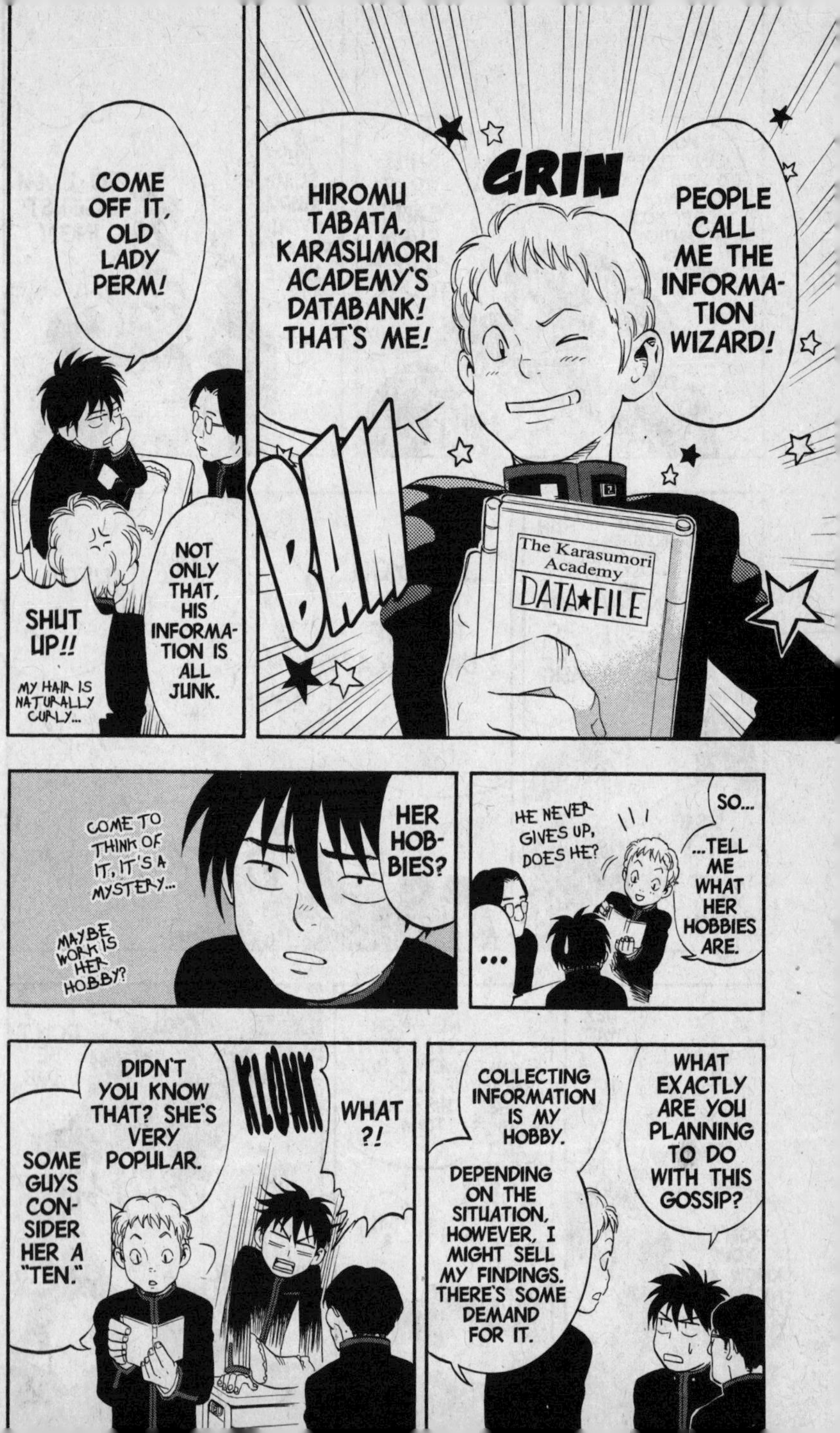
PEOPLE CALL ME THE INFORMATION WIZARD!
GRIN
HIROMU TABATA, KARASUMORI ACADEMY'S DATABANK! THAT'S ME!
BAM
The Karasumori Academy DATA★FILE
COME OFF IT, OLD LADY PERM!
NOT ONLY THAT, HIS INFORMATION IS ALL JUNK.
SHUT UP!!
MY HAIR IS NATURALLY CURLY...
SO...
...TELL ME WHAT HER HOBBIES ARE.
HE NEVER GIVES UP, DOES HE?
...
HER HOBBIES?
COME TO THINK OF IT, IT'S A MYSTERY...
MAYBE WORK IS HER HOBBY?
WHAT EXACTLY ARE YOU PLANNING TO DO WITH THIS GOSSIP?
COLLECTING INFORMATION IS MY HOBBY.
DEPENDING ON THE SITUATION, HOWEVER, I MIGHT SELL MY FINDINGS. THERE'S SOME DEMAND FOR IT.
WHAT?!
KLONK
DIDN'T YOU KNOW THAT? SHE'S VERY POPULAR.
SOME GUYS CONSIDER HER A "TEN."

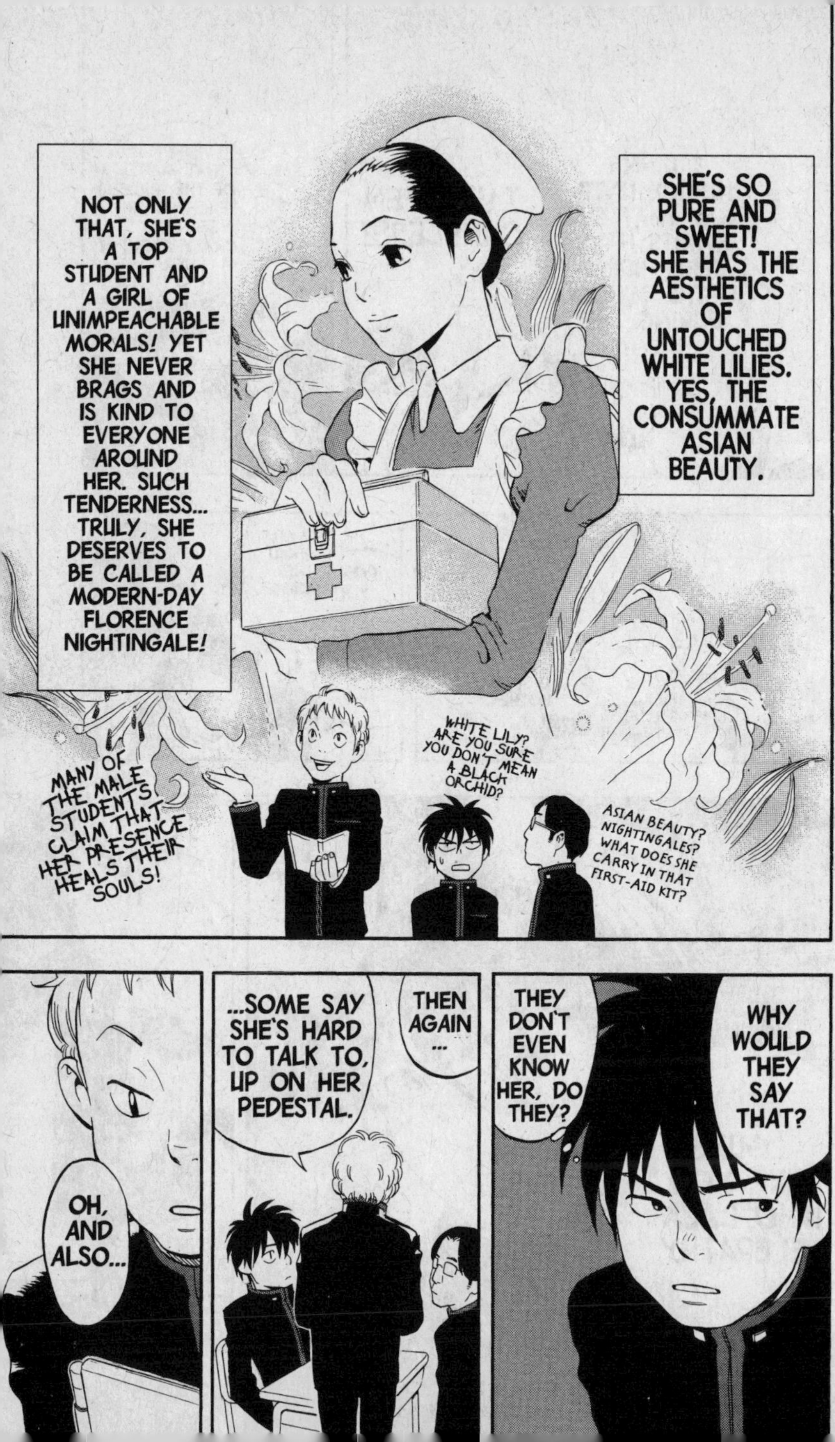
SHE'S SO PURE AND SWEET! SHE HAS THE AESTHETICS OF UNTOUCHED WHITE LILIES. YES, THE CONSUMMATE ASIAN BEAUTY.
NOT ONLY THAT, SHE'S A TOP STUDENT AND A GIRL OF UNIMPEACHABLE MORALS! YET SHE NEVER BRAGS AND IS KIND TO EVERYONE AROUND HER. SUCH TENDERNESS... TRULY, SHE DESERVES TO BE CALLED A MODERN-DAY FLORENCE NIGHTINGALE!
MANY OF THE MALE STUDENTS CLAIM THAT HER PRESENCE HEALS THEIR SOULS!
WHITE LILY? ARE YOU SURE YOU DON'T MEAN A BLACK ORCHID?
ASIAN BEAUTY? NIGHTINGALES? WHAT DOES SHE CARRY IN THAT FIRST-AID KIT?
WHY WOULD THEY SAY THAT?
THEY DON'T EVEN KNOW HER, DO THEY?
THEN AGAIN...
...SOME SAY SHE'S HARD TO TALK TO, UP ON HER PEDESTAL.
OH, AND ALSO...

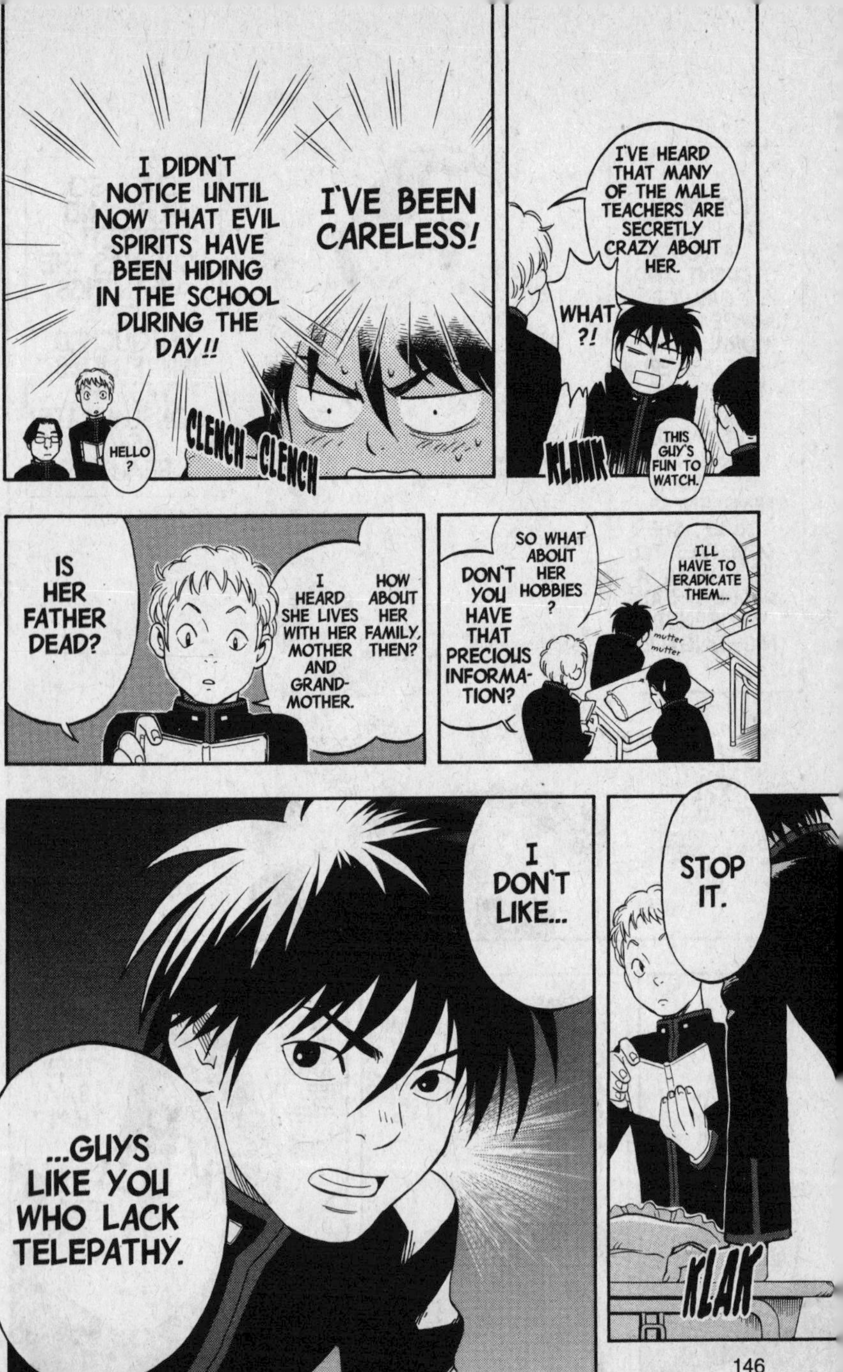
I'VE HEARD THAT MANY OF THE MALE TEACHERS ARE SECRETLY CRAZY ABOUT HER.
WHAT?!
KLANK
THIS GUY'S FUN TO WATCH.
I'VE BEEN CARELESS!
I DIDN'T NOTICE UNTIL NOW THAT EVIL SPIRITS HAVE BEEN HIDING IN THE SCHOOL DURING THE DAY!!
CLENCH CLENCH
HELLO?
I'LL HAVE TO ERADICATE THEM...
mutter mutter
SO WHAT ABOUT HER HOBBIES?
DON'T YOU HAVE THAT PRECIOUS INFORMATION?
HOW ABOUT HER FAMILY, THEN?
I HEARD SHE LIVES WITH HER MOTHER AND GRANDMOTHER.
IS HER FATHER DEAD?
STOP IT.
KLAK
I DON'T LIKE...
...GUYS LIKE YOU WHO LACK TELEPATHY.

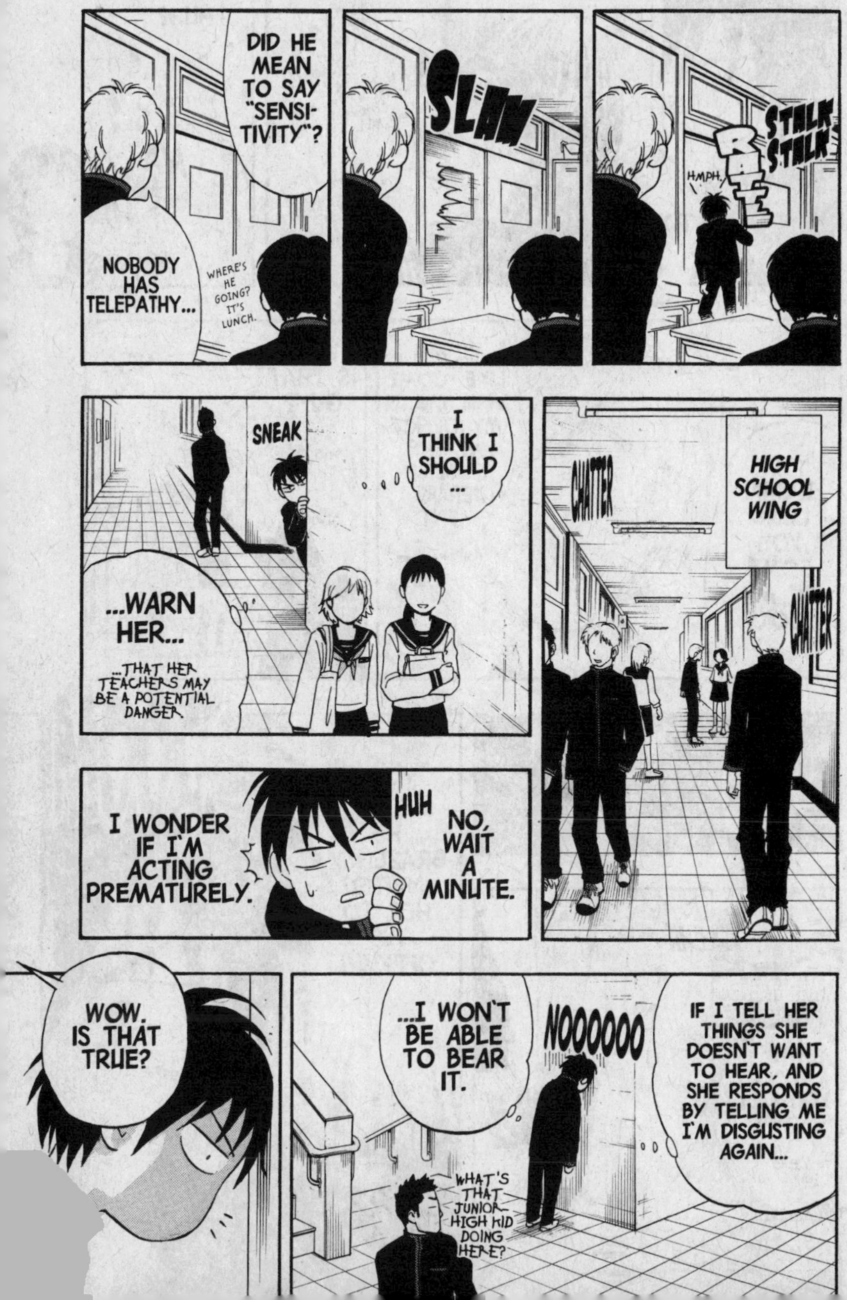
STALK STALK
RATTLE
HMPH.
SLAM
DID HE MEAN TO SAY "SENSITIVITY"?
NOBODY HAS TELEPATHY...
WHERE'S HE GOING? IT'S LUNCH.
HIGH SCHOOL WING
CHATTER
CHATTER
I THINK I SHOULD ...
SNEAK
...WARN HER...
...THAT HER TEACHERS MAY BE A POTENTIAL DANGER.
NO, WAIT A MINUTE.
HUH
I WONDER IF I'M ACTING PREMATURELY.
IF I TELL HER THINGS SHE DOESN'T WANT TO HEAR, AND SHE RESPONDS BY TELLING ME I'M DISGUSTING AGAIN...
NOOOOOO
...I WON'T BE ABLE TO BEAR IT.
WHAT'S THAT JUNIOR HIGH KID DOING HERE?
WOW. IS THAT TRUE?

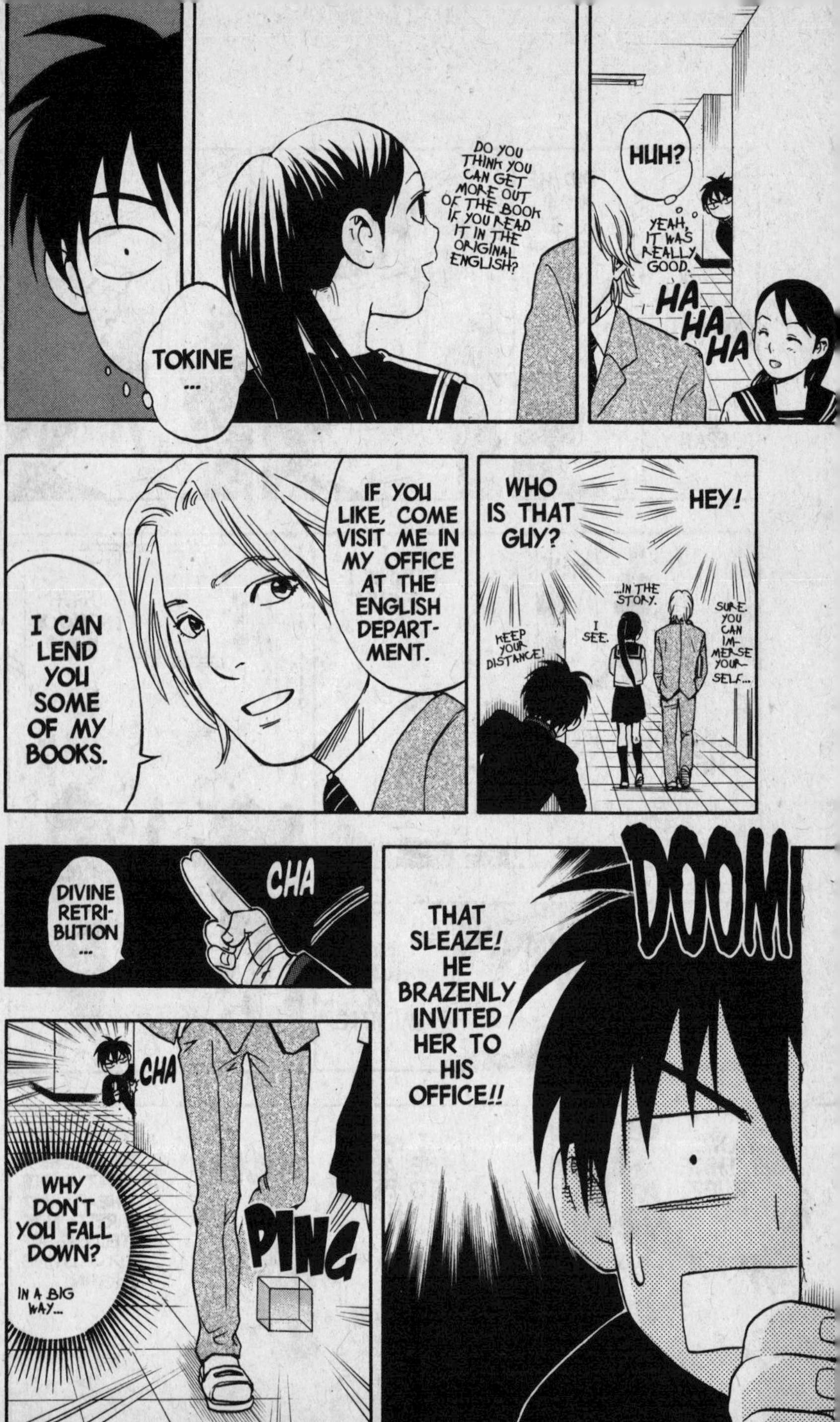
HUH?
YEAH, IT WAS REALLY GOOD.
HA HA HA
DO YOU THINK YOU CAN GET MORE OUT OF THE BOOK IF YOU READ IT IN THE ORIGINAL ENGLISH?
TOKINE ...
HEY!
WHO IS THAT GUY?
SURE. YOU CAN IM-MERSE YOUR-SELF...
...IN THE STORY.
I SEE.
KEEP YOUR DISTANCE!
IF YOU LIKE, COME VISIT ME IN MY OFFICE AT THE ENGLISH DEPART-MENT.
I CAN LEND YOU SOME OF MY BOOKS.
DOOM
THAT SLEAZE! HE BRAZENLY INVITED HER TO HIS OFFICE!!
CHA
DIVINE RETRI-BUTION ...
CHA
PING
WHY DON'T YOU FALL DOWN?
IN A BIG WAY...

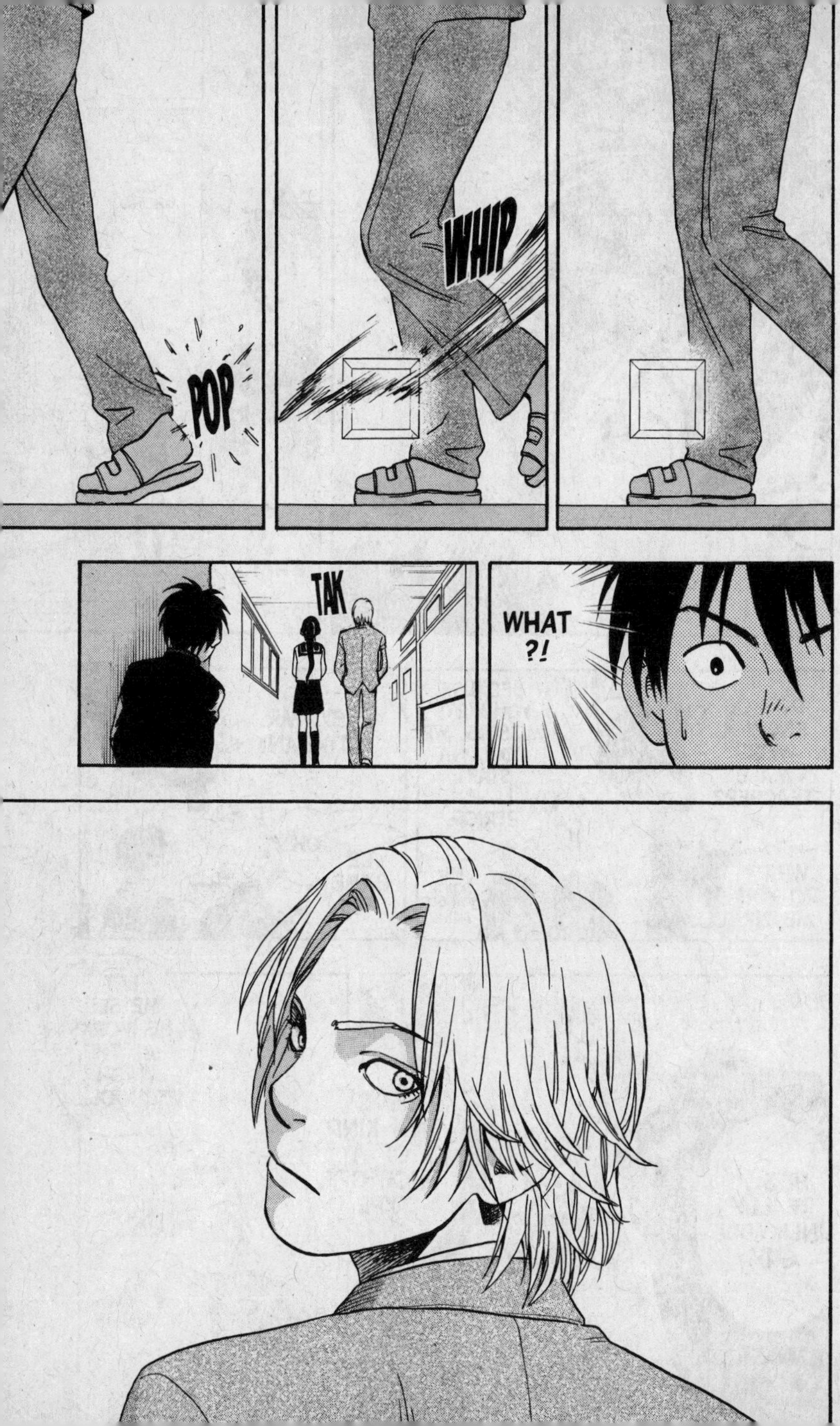
WHIP
POP
WHAT ?!
TAK

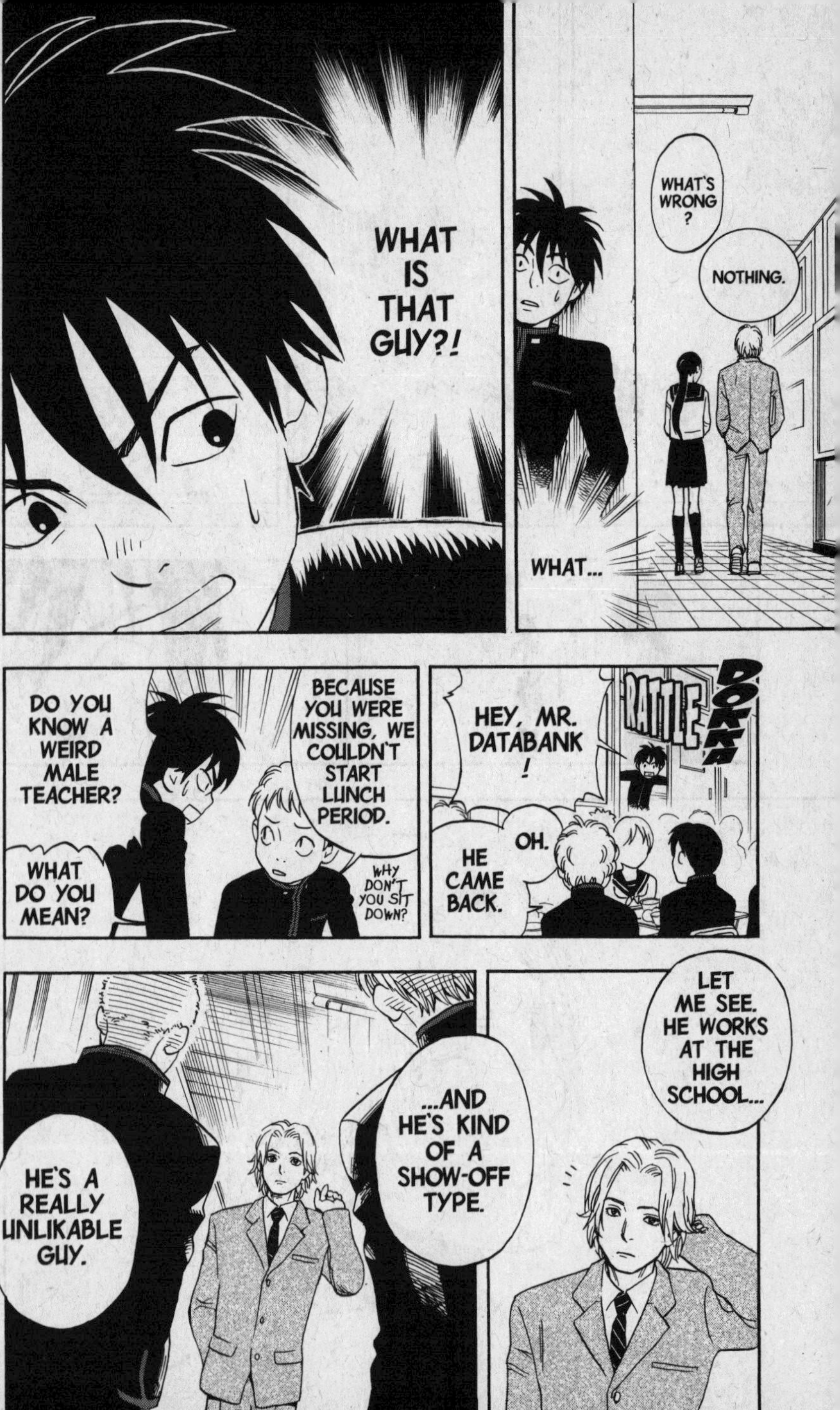
WHAT'S WRONG ?
NOTHING.
WHAT...
WHAT IS THAT GUY?!
DOKA
RATTLE
HEY, MR. DATABANK !
OH.
HE CAME BACK.
BECAUSE YOU WERE MISSING, WE COULDN'T START LUNCH PERIOD.
DO YOU KNOW A WEIRD MALE TEACHER?
WHY DON'T YOU SIT DOWN?
WHAT DO YOU MEAN?
LET ME SEE. HE WORKS AT THE HIGH SCHOOL...
...AND HE'S KIND OF A SHOW-OFF TYPE.
HE'S A REALLY UNLIKABLE GUY.

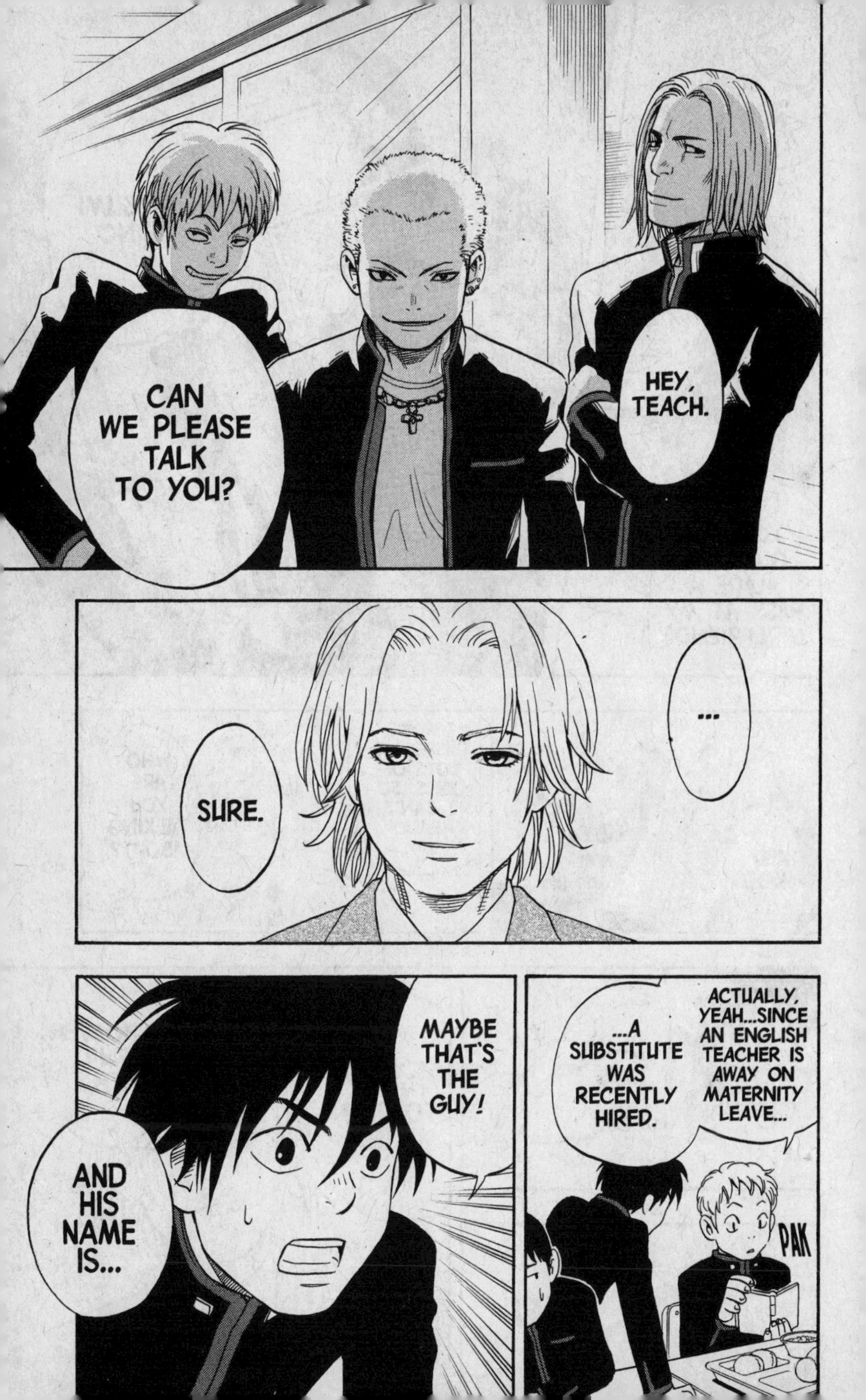
HEY, TEACH.
CAN WE PLEASE TALK TO YOU?
...
SURE.
ACTUALLY, YEAH...SINCE AN ENGLISH TEACHER IS AWAY ON MATERNITY LEAVE...
...A SUBSTITUTE WAS RECENTLY HIRED.
PAK
MAYBE THAT'S THE GUY!
AND HIS NAME IS...

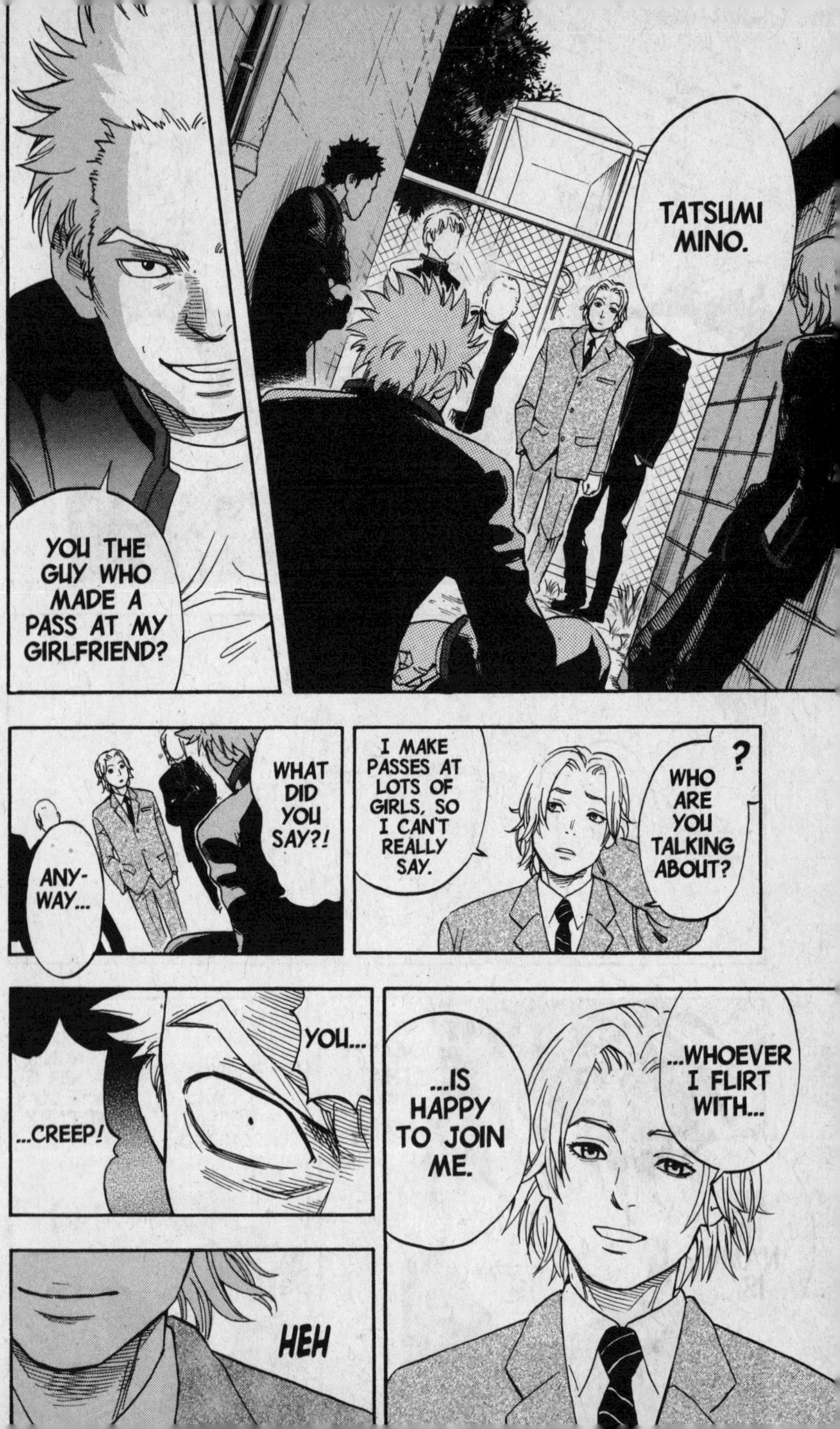
TATSUMI MINO.
YOU THE GUY WHO MADE A PASS AT MY GIRLFRIEND?
?
WHO ARE YOU TALKING ABOUT?
I MAKE PASSES AT LOTS OF GIRLS, SO I CAN'T REALLY SAY.
WHAT DID YOU SAY?!
ANY-WAY...
...WHOEVER I FLIRT WITH...
...IS HAPPY TO JOIN ME.
YOU...
...CREEP!
HEH

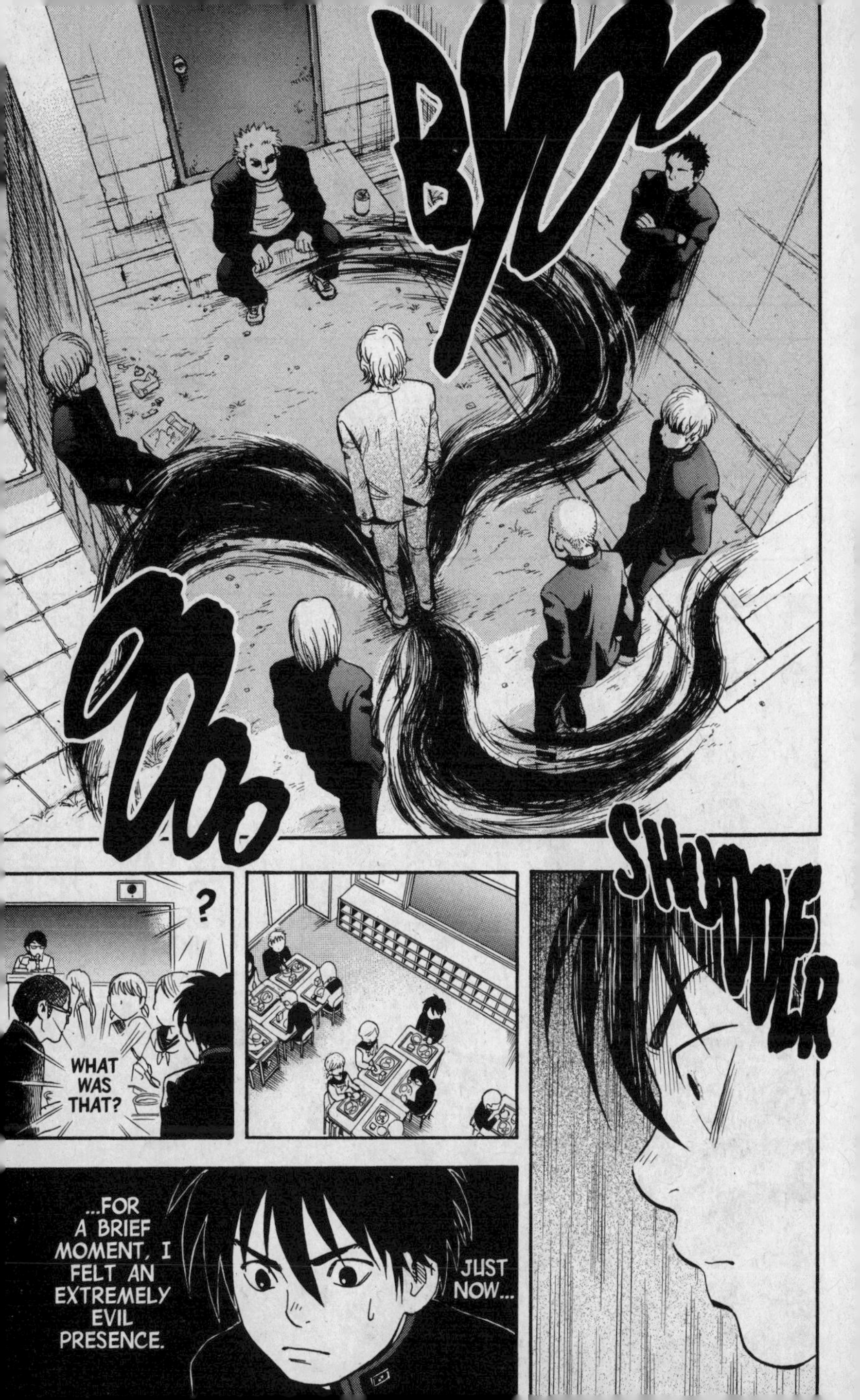
SHUDDER
?
WHAT WAS THAT?
JUST NOW...
...FOR A BRIEF MOMENT, I FELT AN EXTREMELY EVIL PRESENCE.

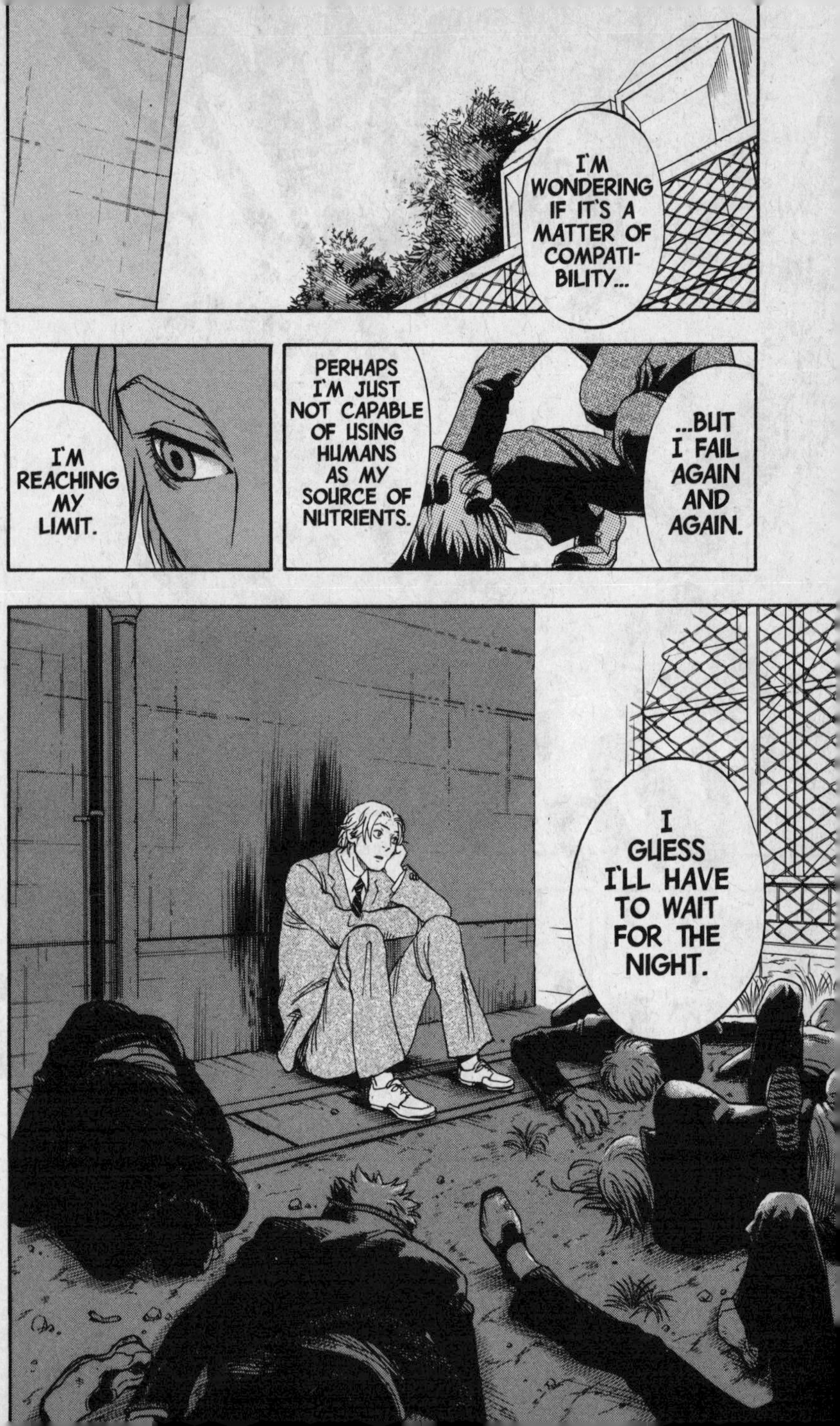
I'M WONDERING IF IT'S A MATTER OF COMPATI-BILITY...
...BUT I FAIL AGAIN AND AGAIN.
PERHAPS I'M JUST NOT CAPABLE OF USING HUMANS AS MY SOURCE OF NUTRIENTS.
I'M REACHING MY LIMIT.
I GUESS I'LL HAVE TO WAIT FOR THE NIGHT.

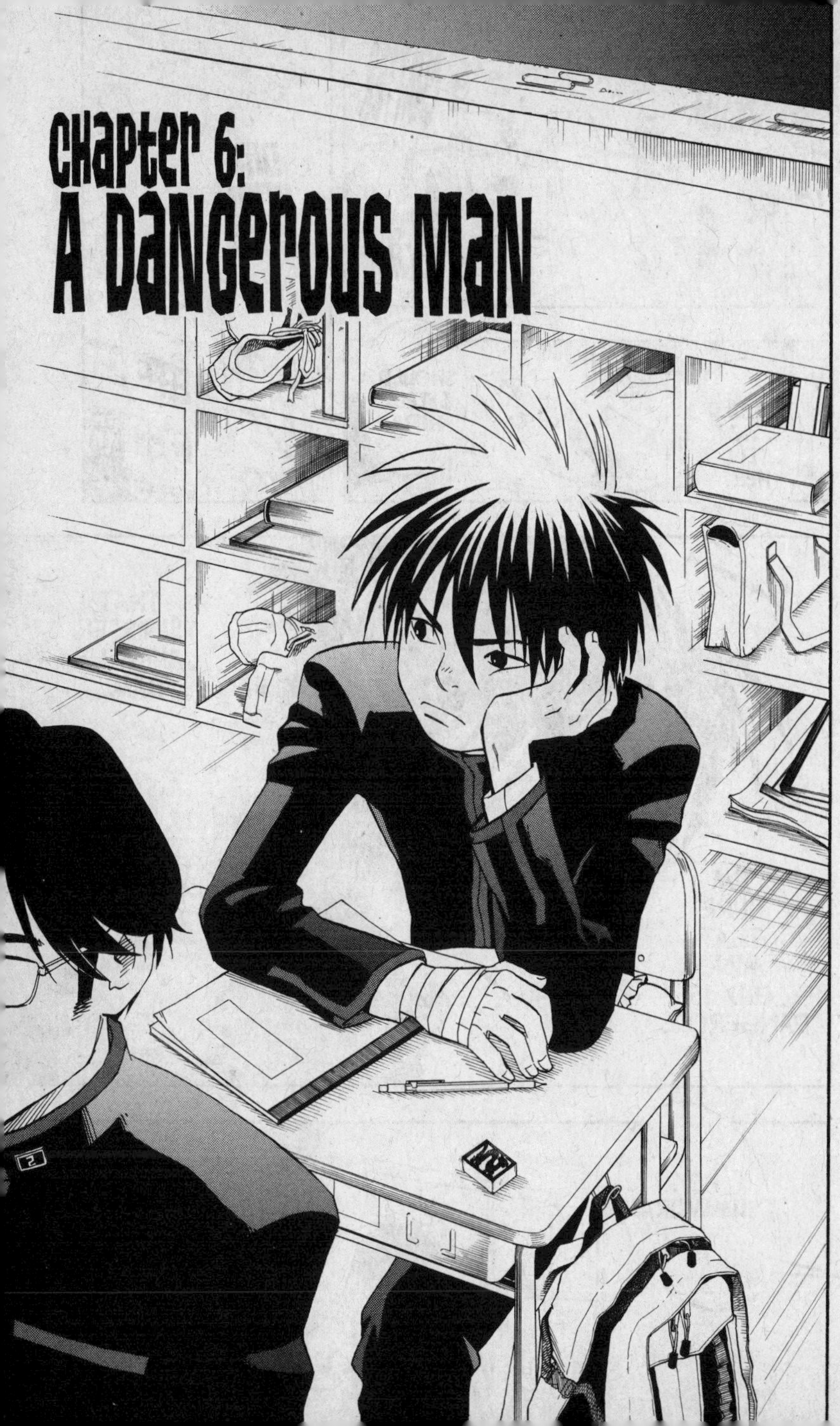
Chapter 6:
A Dangerous Man

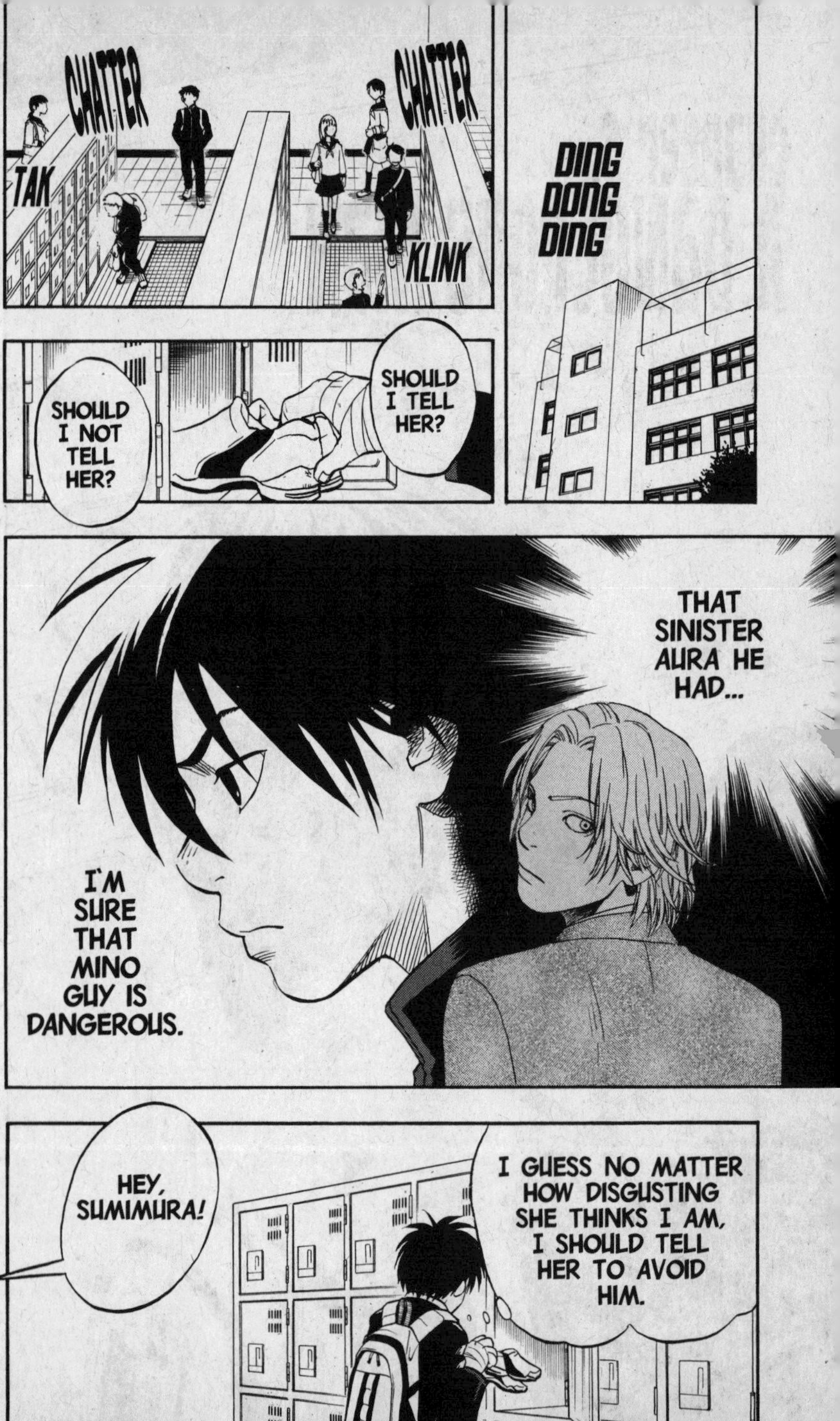
DING DONG DING
CHATTER
KLINK
CHATTER
TAK
SHOULD I TELL HER?
SHOULD I NOT TELL HER?
THAT SINISTER AURA HE HAD...
I'M SURE THAT MINO GUY IS DANGEROUS.
I GUESS NO MATTER HOW DISGUSTING SHE THINKS I AM, I SHOULD TELL HER TO AVOID HIM.
HEY, SUMIMURA!

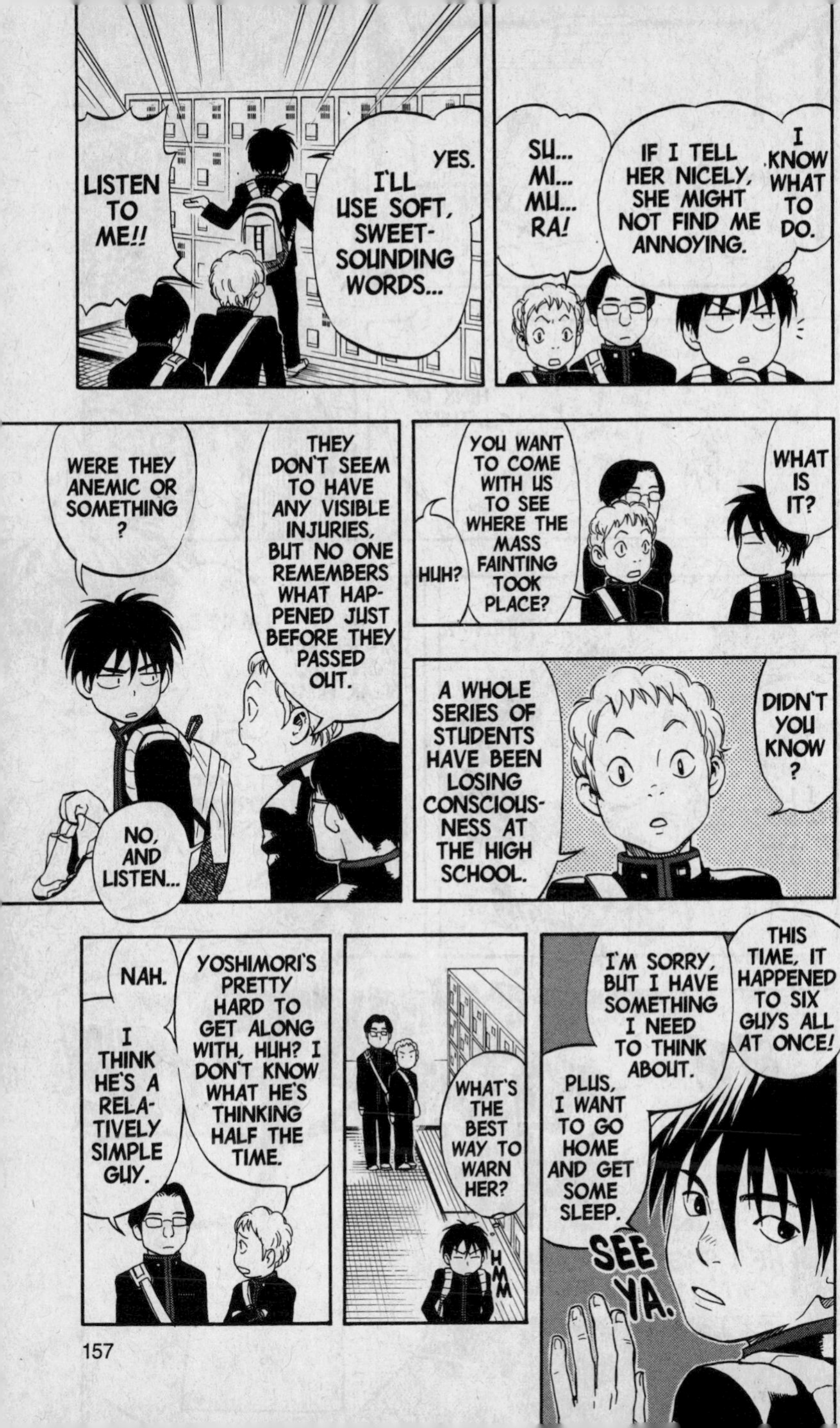
I KNOW WHAT TO DO.
IF I TELL HER NICELY, SHE MIGHT NOT FIND ME ANNOYING.
SU... MI... MU... RA!
YES.
I'LL USE SOFT, SWEET-SOUNDING WORDS...
LISTEN TO ME!!
WHAT IS IT?
YOU WANT TO COME WITH US TO SEE WHERE THE MASS FAINTING TOOK PLACE?
HUH?
DIDN'T YOU KNOW?
A WHOLE SERIES OF STUDENTS HAVE BEEN LOSING CONSCIOUSNESS AT THE HIGH SCHOOL.
THEY DON'T SEEM TO HAVE ANY VISIBLE INJURIES, BUT NO ONE REMEMBERS WHAT HAPPENED JUST BEFORE THEY PASSED OUT.
WERE THEY ANEMIC OR SOMETHING?
NO, AND LISTEN...
THIS TIME, IT HAPPENED TO SIX GUYS ALL AT ONCE!
I'M SORRY, BUT I HAVE SOMETHING I NEED TO THINK ABOUT.
PLUS, I WANT TO GO HOME AND GET SOME SLEEP.
SEE YA.
WHAT'S THE BEST WAY TO WARN HER?
HMM
YOSHIMORI'S PRETTY HARD TO GET ALONG WITH, HUH? I DON'T KNOW WHAT HE'S THINKING HALF THE TIME.
NAH.
I THINK HE'S A RELATIVELY SIMPLE GUY.

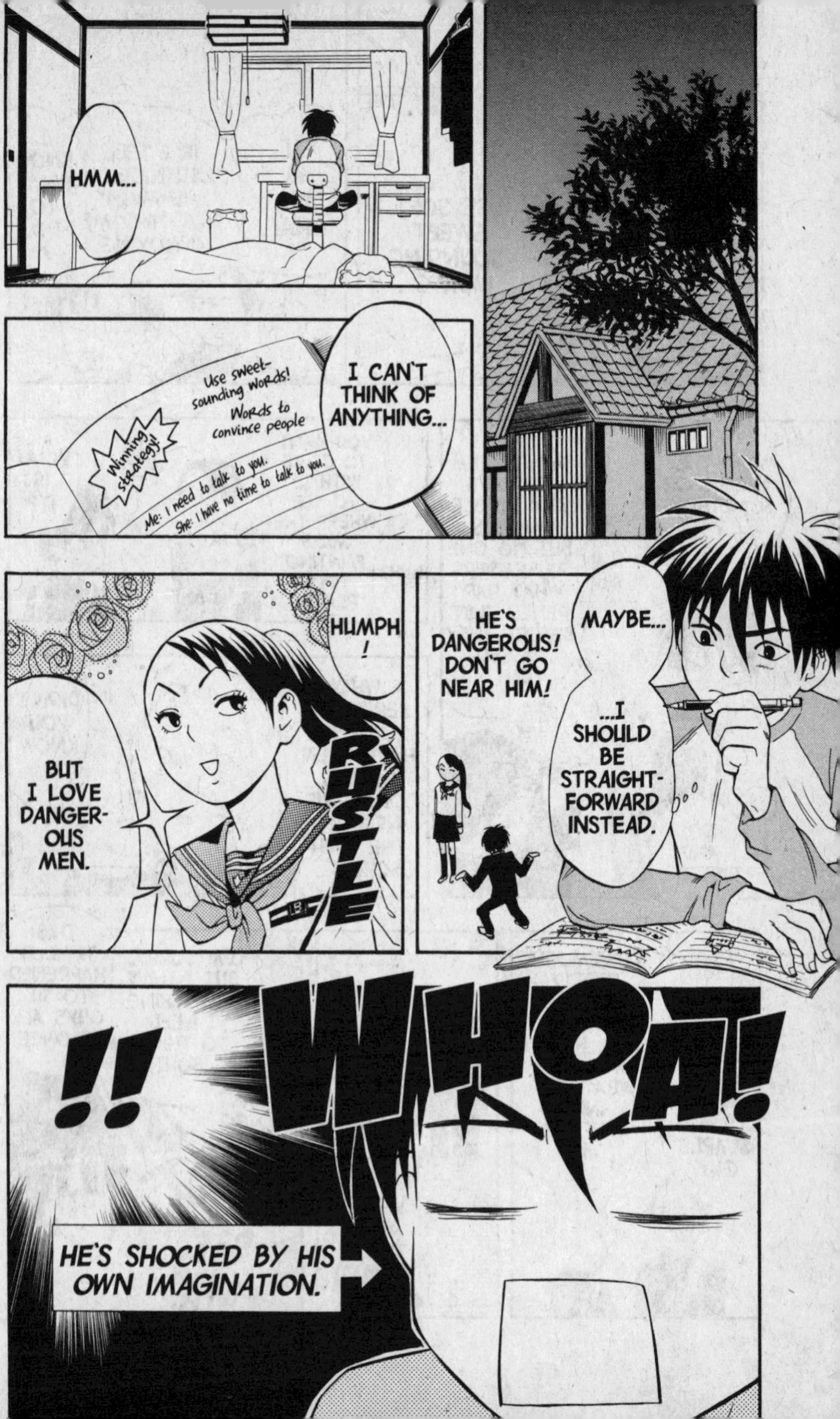
HMM...
I CAN'T THINK OF ANYTHING...
Winning strategy!
Use sweet-sounding words!
Words to convince people
Me: I need to talk to you.
She: I have no time to talk to you.
MAYBE...
...I SHOULD BE STRAIGHT-FORWARD INSTEAD.
HE'S DANGEROUS! DON'T GO NEAR HIM!
HUMPH!
RUSTLE
BUT I LOVE DANGER-OUS MEN.
WHOA!
!!
HE'S SHOCKED BY HIS OWN IMAGINATION.

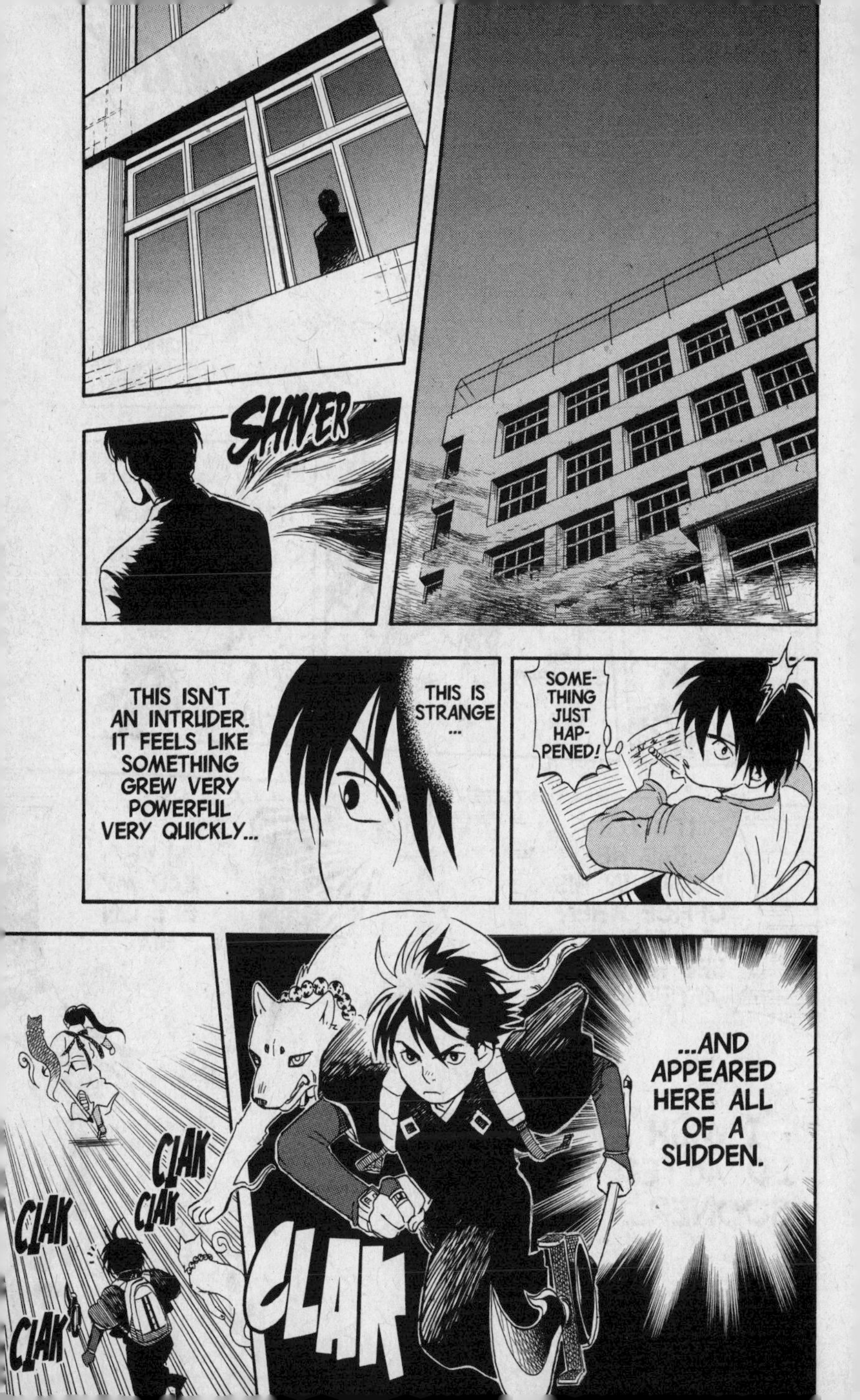
SHIVER
SOMETHING JUST HAPPENED!
THIS IS STRANGE...
THIS ISN'T AN INTRUDER. IT FEELS LIKE SOMETHING GREW VERY POWERFUL VERY QUICKLY...
...AND APPEARED HERE ALL OF A SUDDEN.
CLAK
CLAK
CLAK
CLAK
CLAK

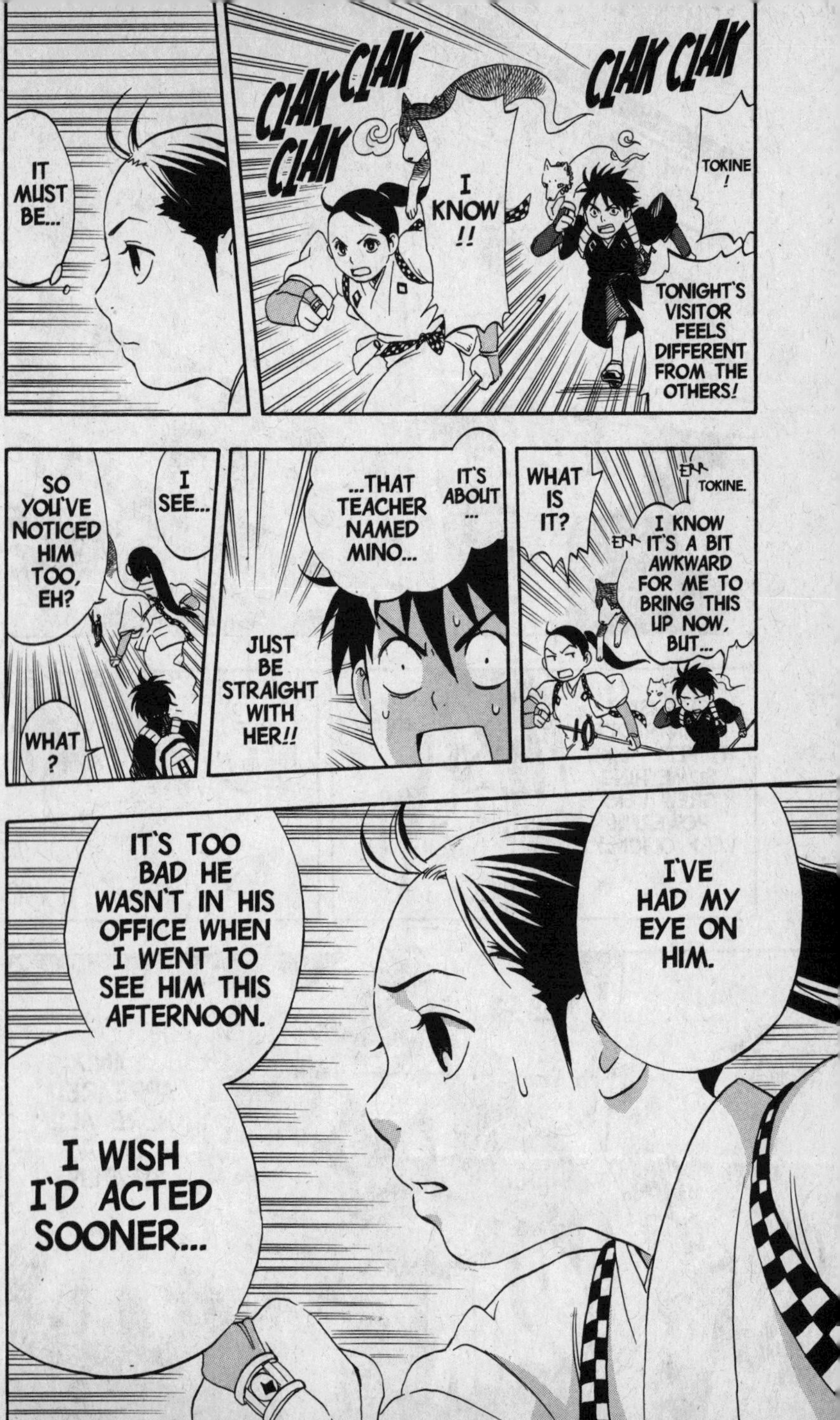
CLAK CLAK
TOKINE!
TONIGHT'S VISITOR FEELS DIFFERENT FROM THE OTHERS!
CLAK CLAK CLAK
I KNOW!!
IT MUST BE...
TOKINE.
I KNOW IT'S A BIT AWKWARD FOR ME TO BRING THIS UP NOW, BUT...
WHAT IS IT?
IT'S ABOUT...
...THAT TEACHER NAMED MINO...
JUST BE STRAIGHT WITH HER!!
I SEE...
SO YOU'VE NOTICED HIM TOO, EH?
WHAT?
I'VE HAD MY EYE ON HIM.
IT'S TOO BAD HE WASN'T IN HIS OFFICE WHEN I WENT TO SEE HIM THIS AFTERNOON.
I WISH I'D ACTED SOONER...

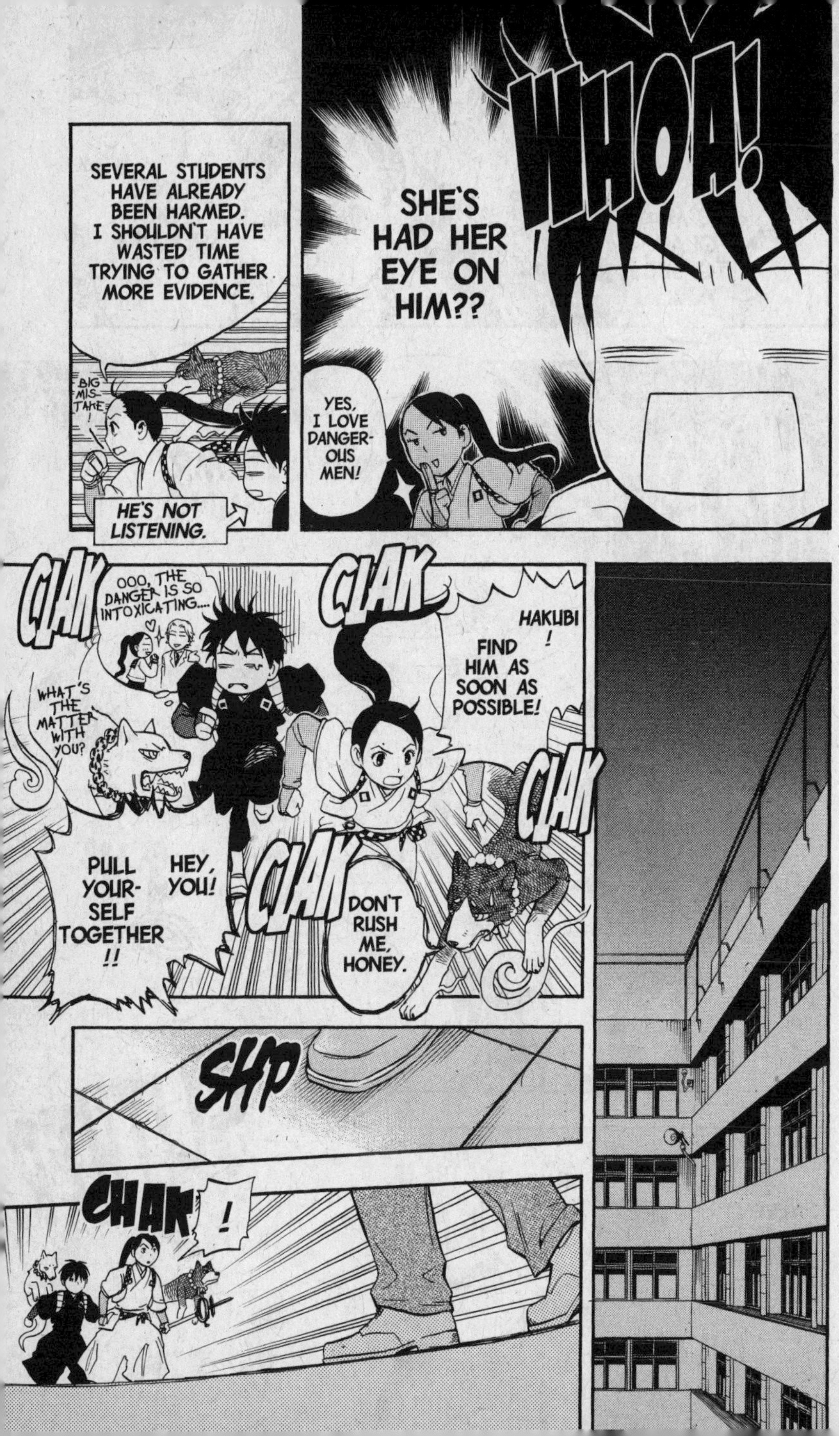
WHOA!
SHE'S HAD HER EYE ON HIM??
YES, I LOVE DANGEROUS MEN!
SEVERAL STUDENTS HAVE ALREADY BEEN HARMED. I SHOULDN'T HAVE WASTED TIME TRYING TO GATHER MORE EVIDENCE.
BIG MISTAKE!
HE'S NOT LISTENING.
HAKUBI! FIND HIM AS SOON AS POSSIBLE!
CLAK
CLAK
OOO, THE DANGER IS SO INTOXICATING....
CLAK
WHAT'S THE MATTER WITH YOU?
CLAK
DON'T RUSH ME, HONEY.
HEY, YOU!
PULL YOURSELF TOGETHER!!
SHP
CHAK!

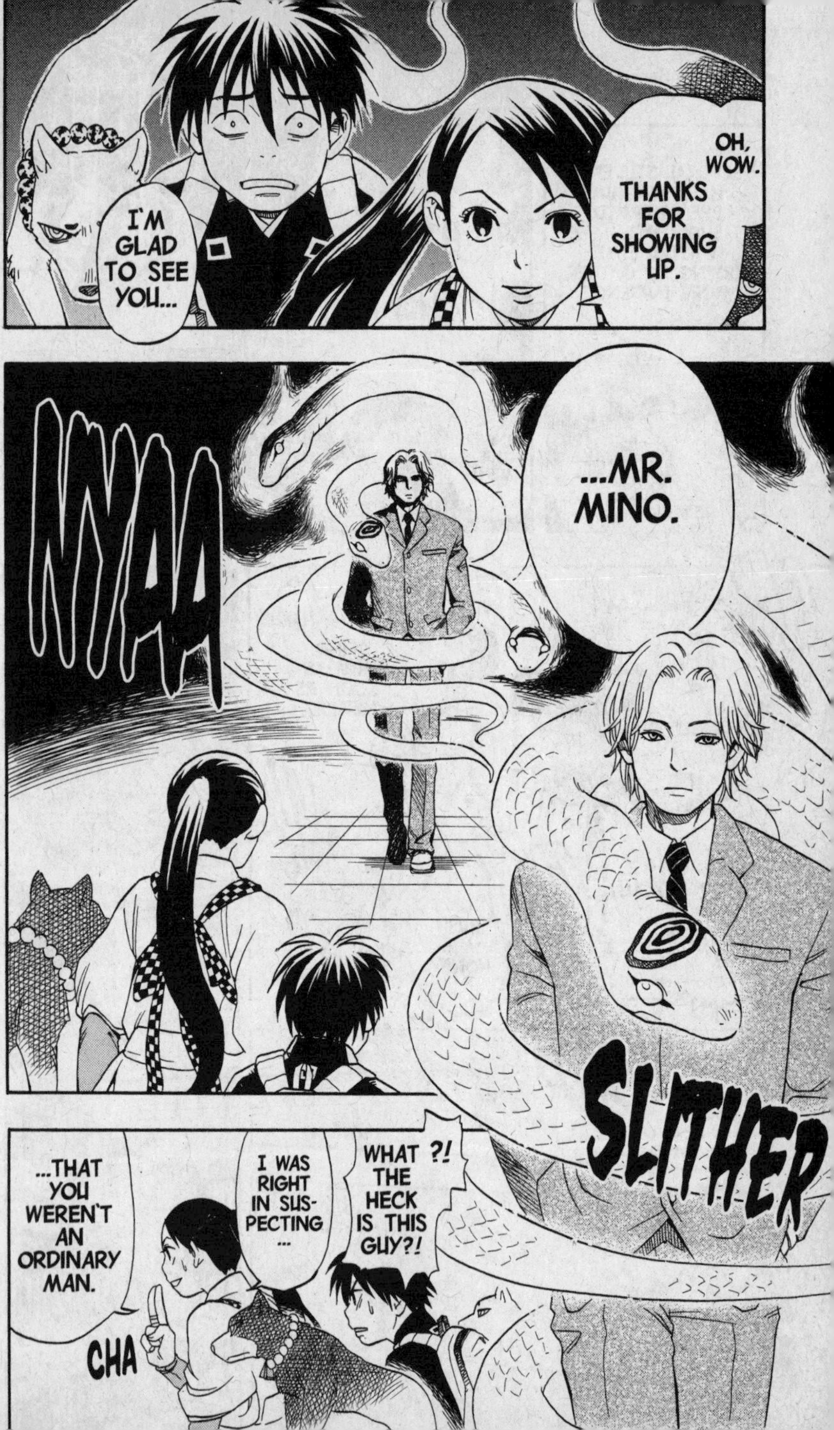
OH, WOW. THANKS FOR SHOWING UP.
I'M GLAD TO SEE YOU...
...MR. MINO.
NYAA
SLITHER
WHAT ?! THE HECK IS THIS GUY?!
I WAS RIGHT IN SUS-PECTING ...
...THAT YOU WEREN'T AN ORDINARY MAN.
CHA

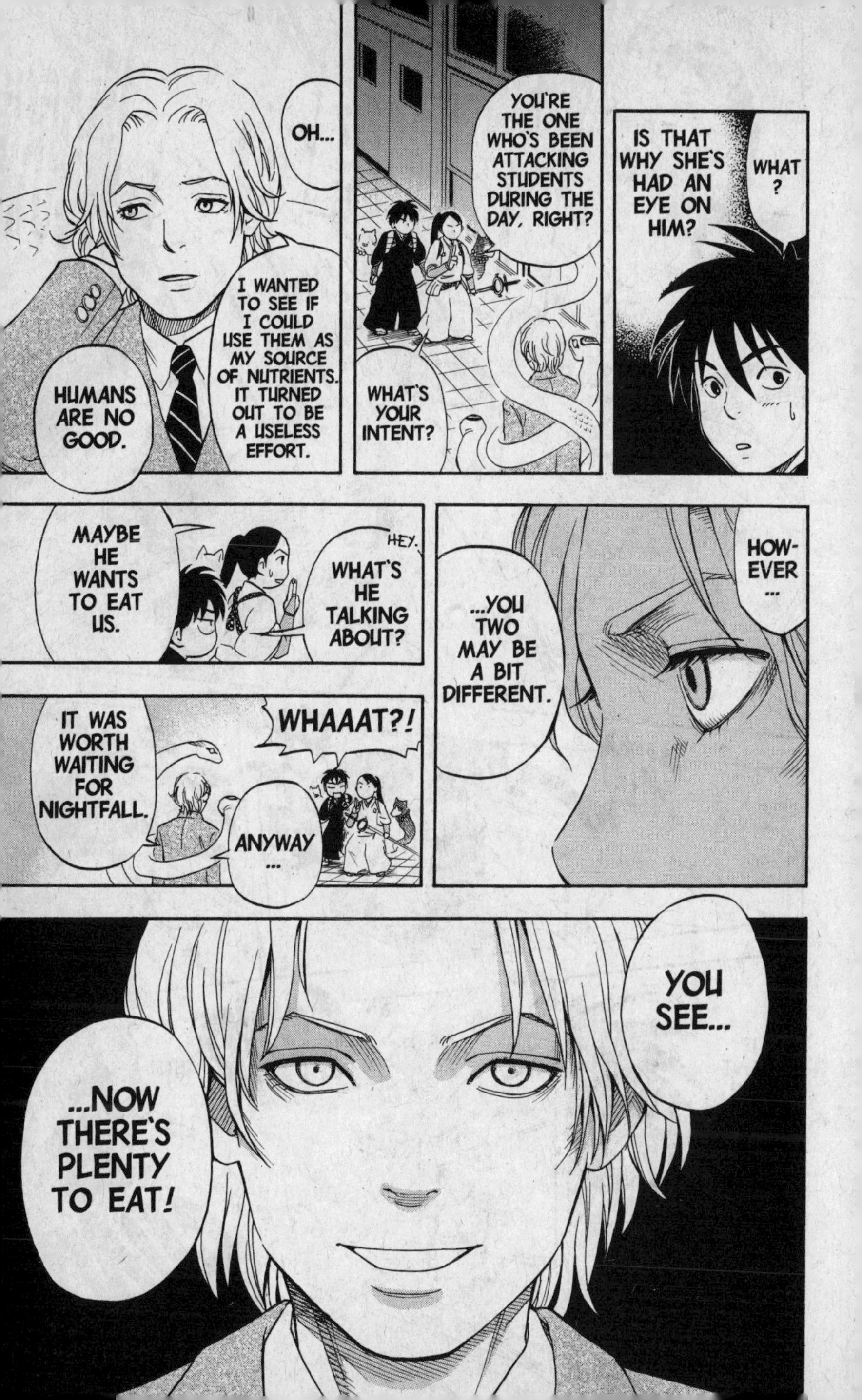
WHAT ?
IS THAT WHY SHE'S HAD AN EYE ON HIM?
YOU'RE THE ONE WHO'S BEEN ATTACKING STUDENTS DURING THE DAY, RIGHT?
WHAT'S YOUR INTENT?
OH...
I WANTED TO SEE IF I COULD USE THEM AS MY SOURCE OF NUTRIENTS. IT TURNED OUT TO BE A USELESS EFFORT.
HUMANS ARE NO GOOD.
HOW-EVER ...
...YOU TWO MAY BE A BIT DIFFERENT.
HEY.
WHAT'S HE TALKING ABOUT?
MAYBE HE WANTS TO EAT US.
WHAAAT?!
ANYWAY ...
IT WAS WORTH WAITING FOR NIGHTFALL.
YOU SEE...
...NOW THERE'S PLENTY TO EAT!

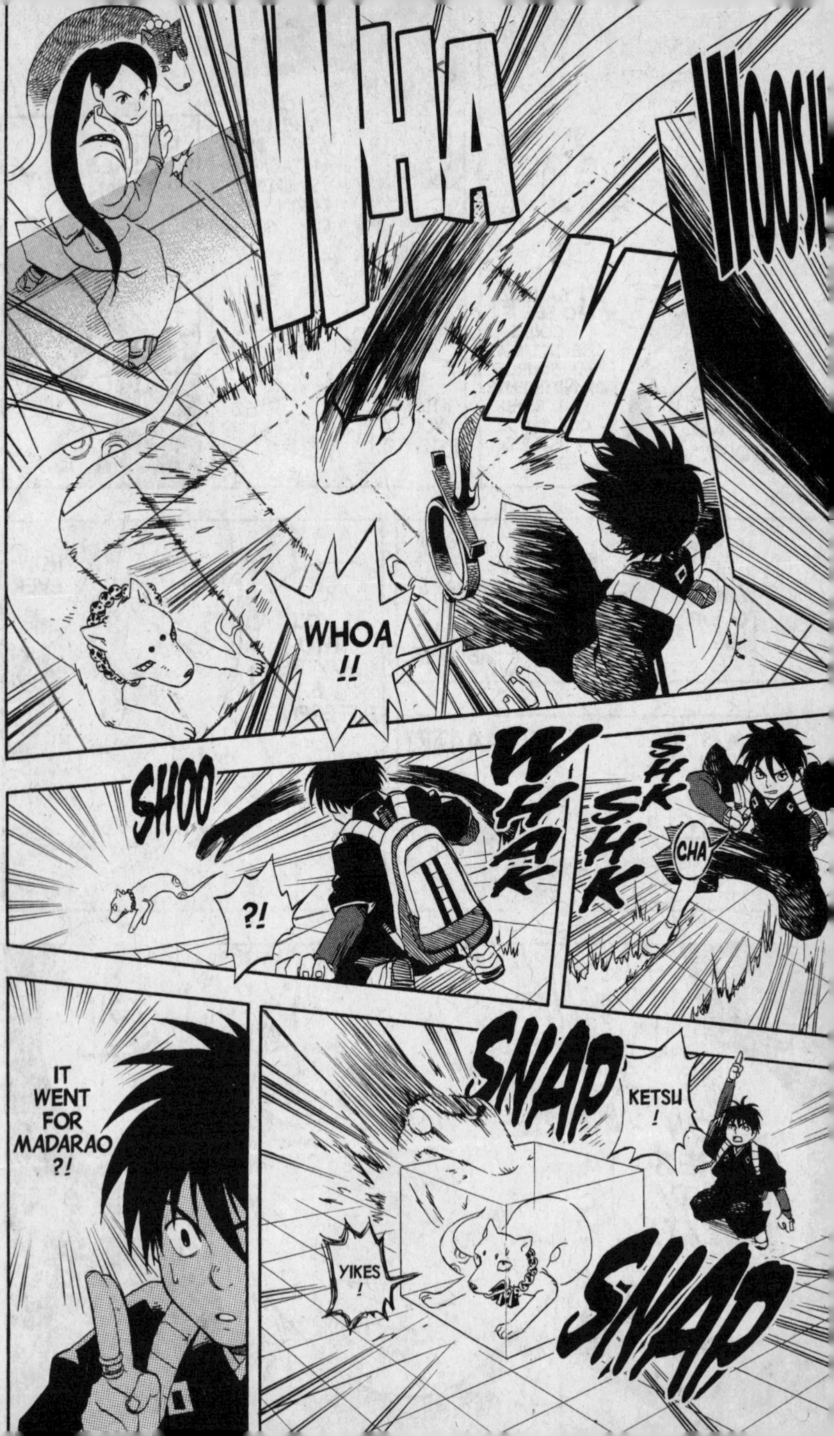
WOOSH
WHAM
WHOA !!
SHK SHK
CHA
WHAK
SHOO
?!
SNAP
KETSU !
SNAP
YIKES !
IT WENT FOR MADARAO ?!

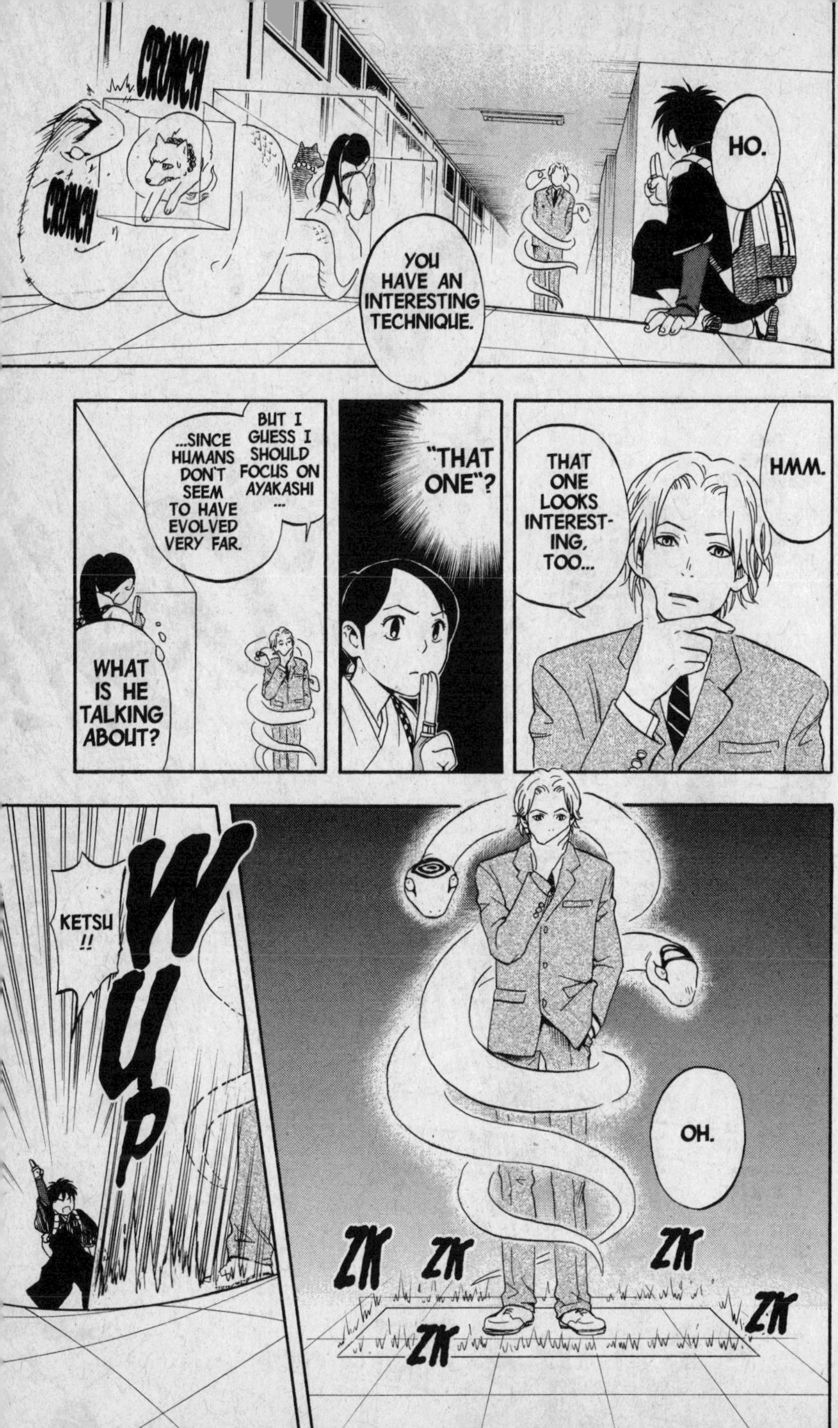
HO.
YOU HAVE AN INTERESTING TECHNIQUE.
CRUNCH
CRUNCH
HMM.
THAT ONE LOOKS INTEREST-ING, TOO...
"THAT ONE"?
BUT I GUESS I SHOULD FOCUS ON AYAKASHI...
...SINCE HUMANS DON'T SEEM TO HAVE EVOLVED VERY FAR.
WHAT IS HE TALKING ABOUT?
OH.
ZK
ZK
ZK
ZK
ZK
KETSU!!
WUP

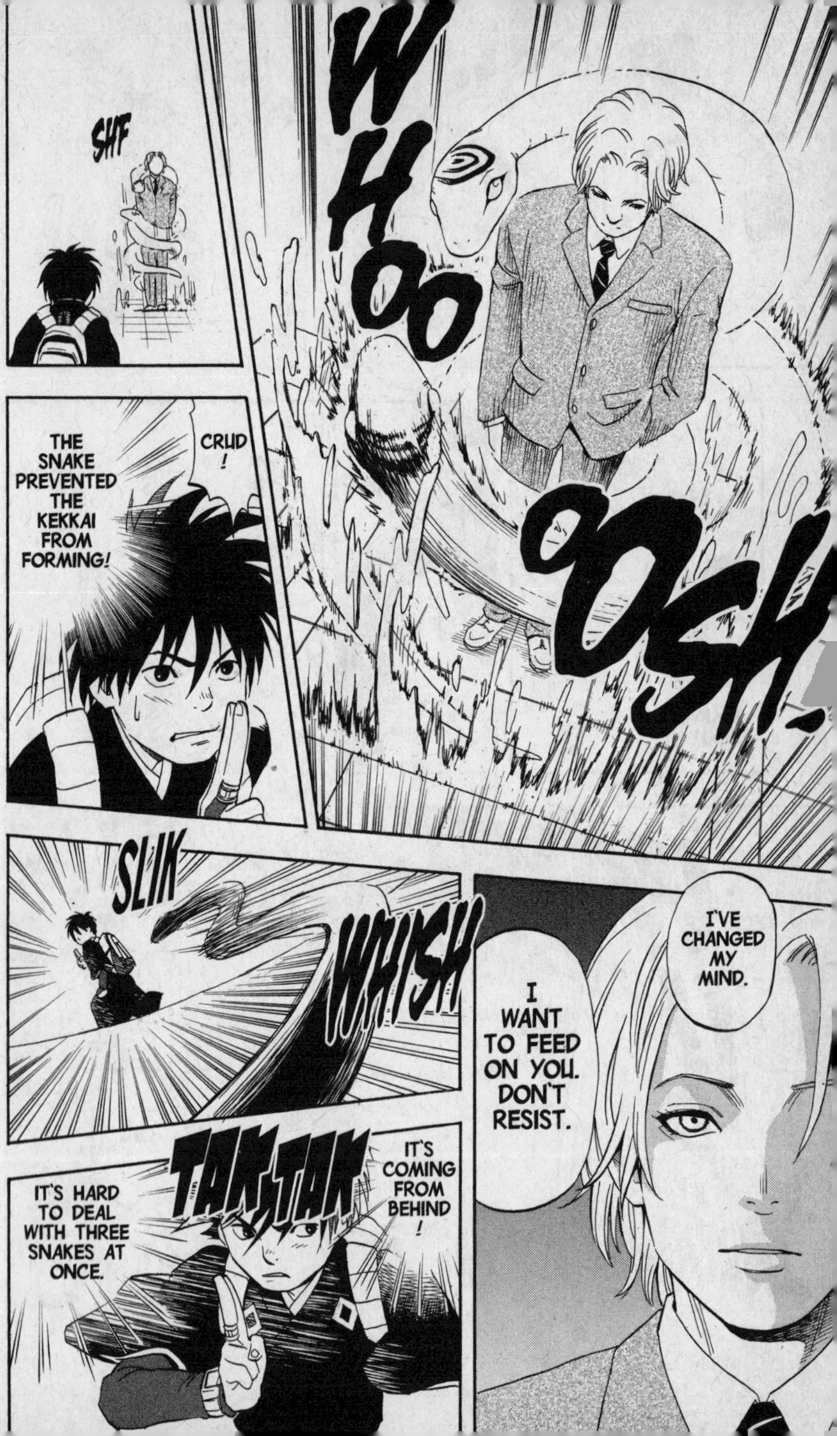
WHOOOOSH!
SHF
CRUD!
THE SNAKE PREVENTED THE KEKKAI FROM FORMING!
I'VE CHANGED MY MIND.
I WANT TO FEED ON YOU. DON'T RESIST.
SLIK
WHISH
TAK TAK
IT'S COMING FROM BEHIND!
IT'S HARD TO DEAL WITH THREE SNAKES AT ONCE.

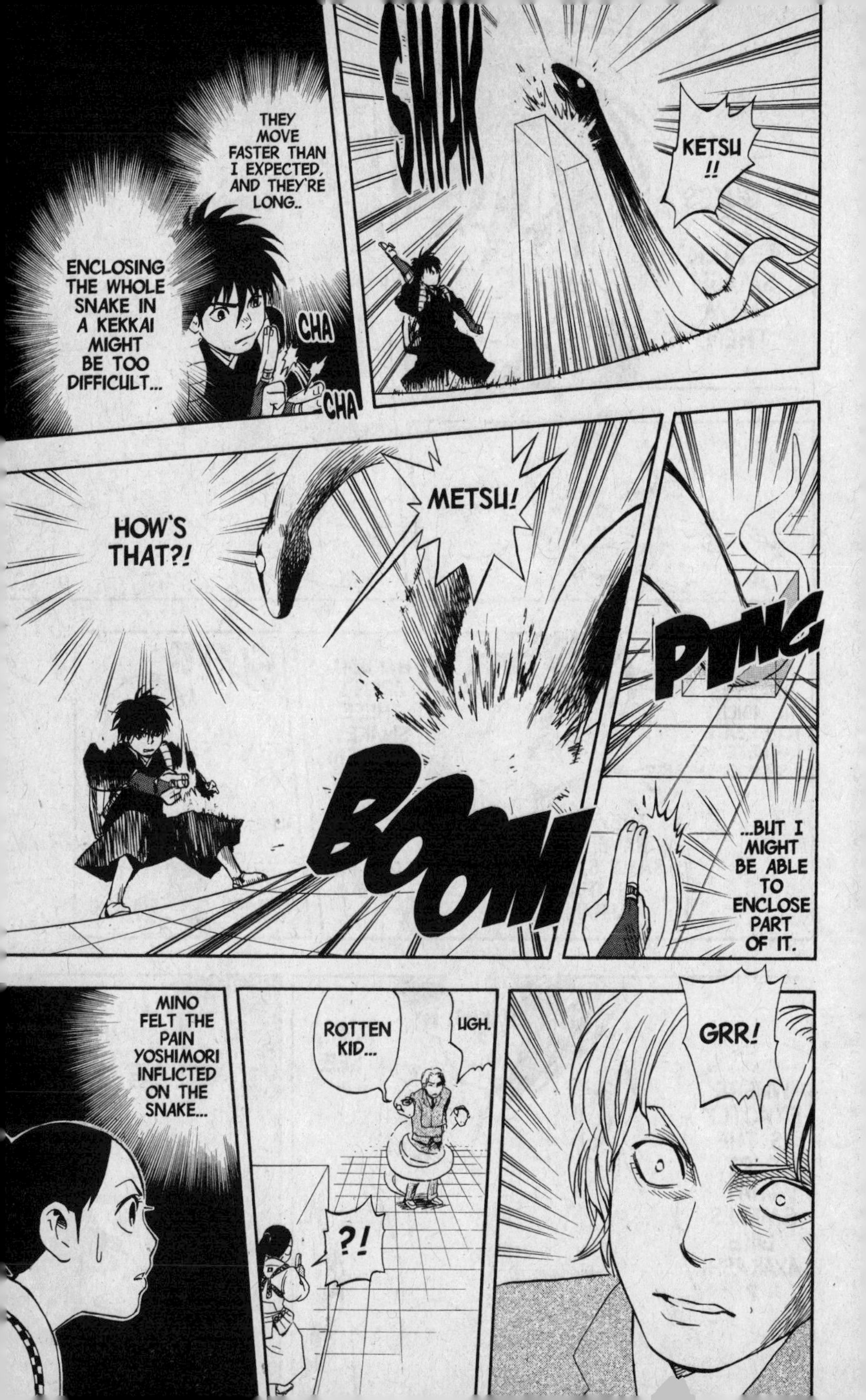
SNAK
KETSU !!
THEY MOVE FASTER THAN I EXPECTED, AND THEY'RE LONG..
ENCLOSING THE WHOLE SNAKE IN A KEKKAI MIGHT BE TOO DIFFICULT...
CHA
CHA
...BUT I MIGHT BE ABLE TO ENCLOSE PART OF IT.
PING
METSU!
HOW'S THAT?!
BOOM
GRR!
UGH.
ROTTEN KID...
?!
MINO FELT THE PAIN YOSHIMORI INFLICTED ON THE SNAKE...

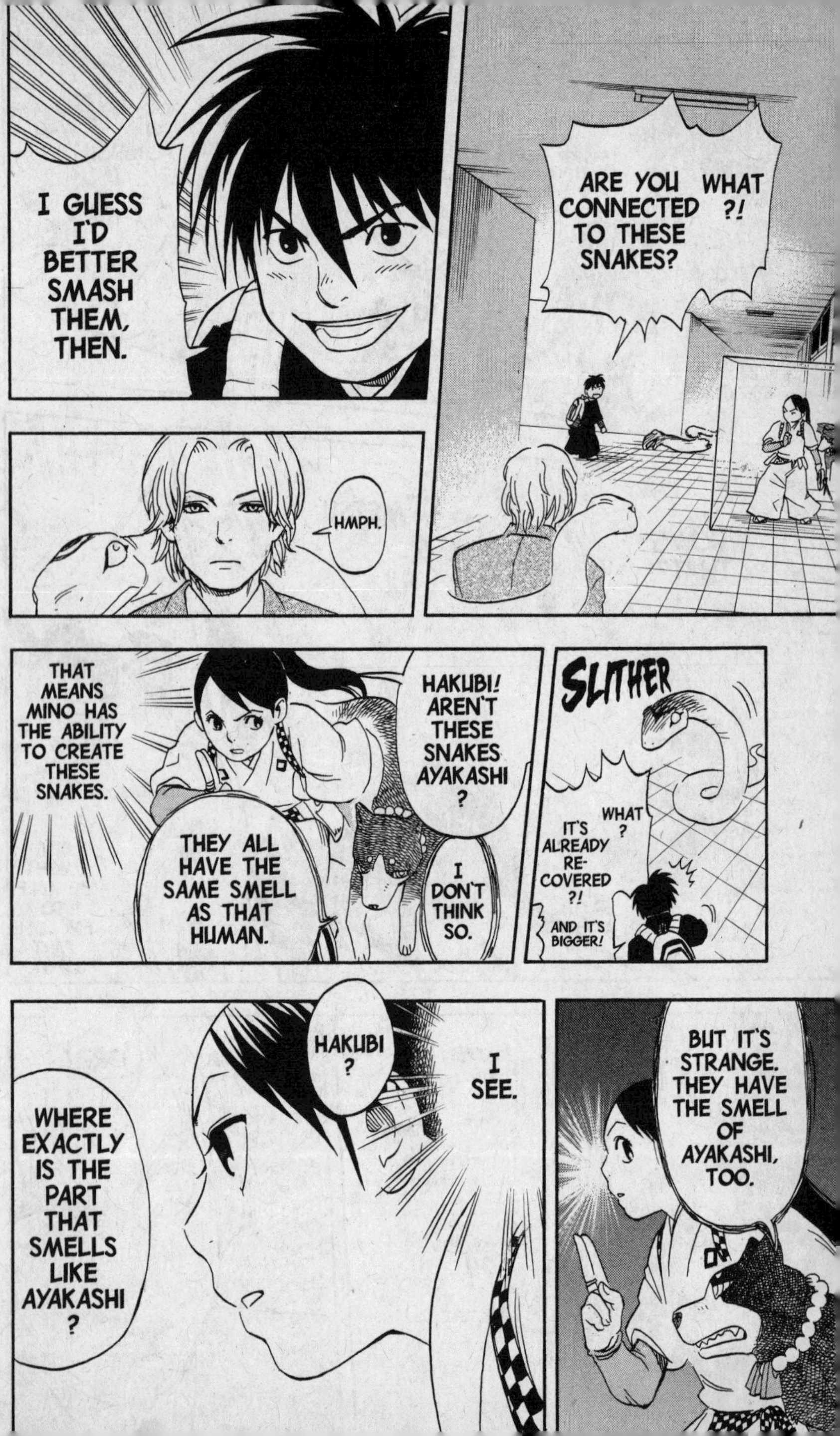
WHAT ?!
ARE YOU CONNECTED TO THESE SNAKES?
I GUESS I'D BETTER SMASH THEM, THEN.
HMPH.
SLITHER
WHAT ?
IT'S ALREADY RE-COVERED ?!
AND IT'S BIGGER!
HAKUBI! AREN'T THESE SNAKES AYAKASHI ?
I DON'T THINK SO.
THEY ALL HAVE THE SAME SMELL AS THAT HUMAN.
THAT MEANS MINO HAS THE ABILITY TO CREATE THESE SNAKES.
BUT IT'S STRANGE. THEY HAVE THE SMELL OF AYAKASHI, TOO.
I SEE.
HAKUBI ?
WHERE EXACTLY IS THE PART THAT SMELLS LIKE AYAKASHI ?

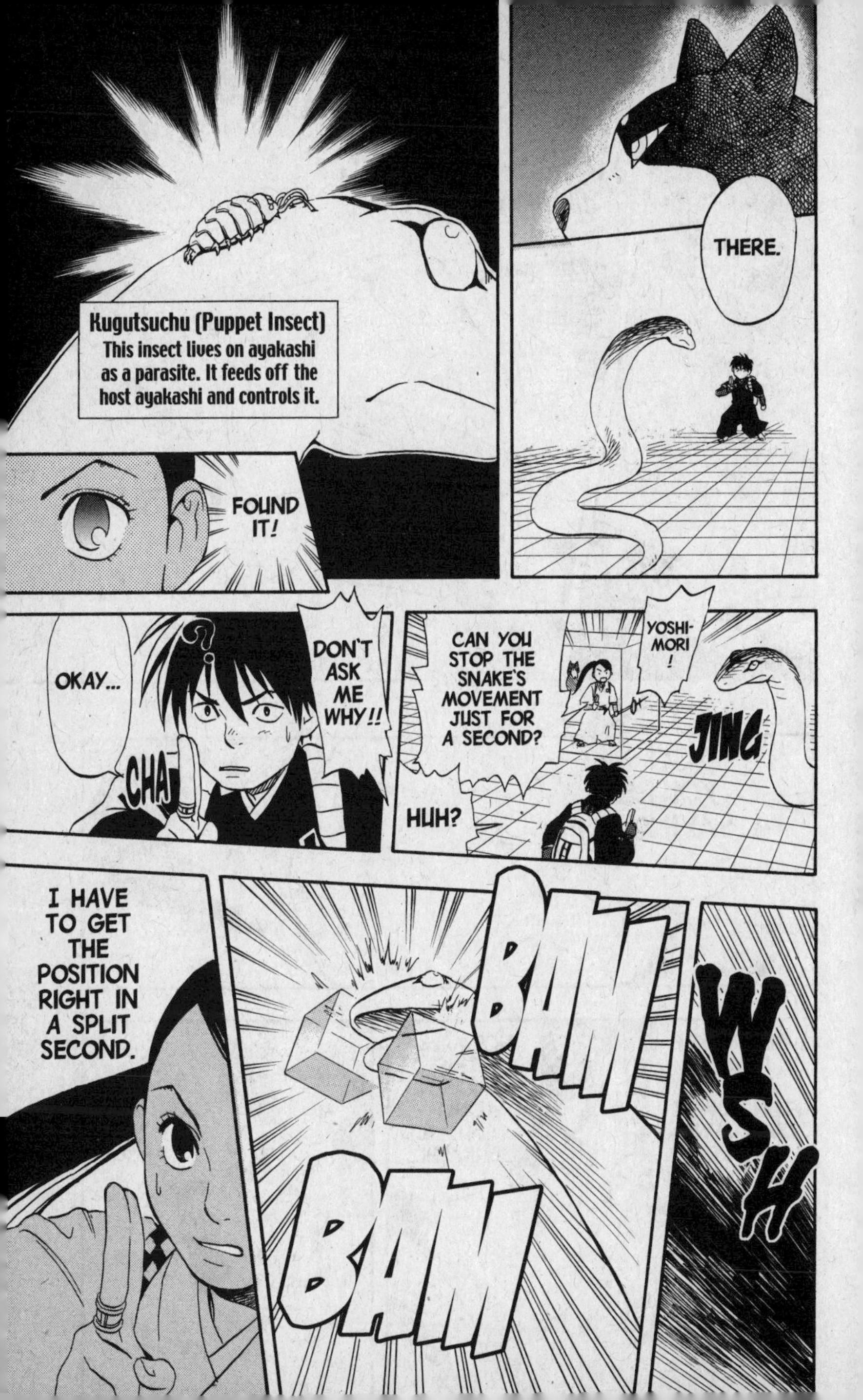

THERE.
Kugutsuchu (Puppet Insect)
This insect lives on ayakashi as a parasite. It feeds off the host ayakashi and controls it.
FOUND IT!
YOSHI-MORI!
CAN YOU STOP THE SNAKE'S MOVEMENT JUST FOR A SECOND?
JING
HUH?
DON'T ASK ME WHY!!
OKAY...
CHA
WSH
BAM
BAM
I HAVE TO GET THE POSITION RIGHT IN A SPLIT SECOND.

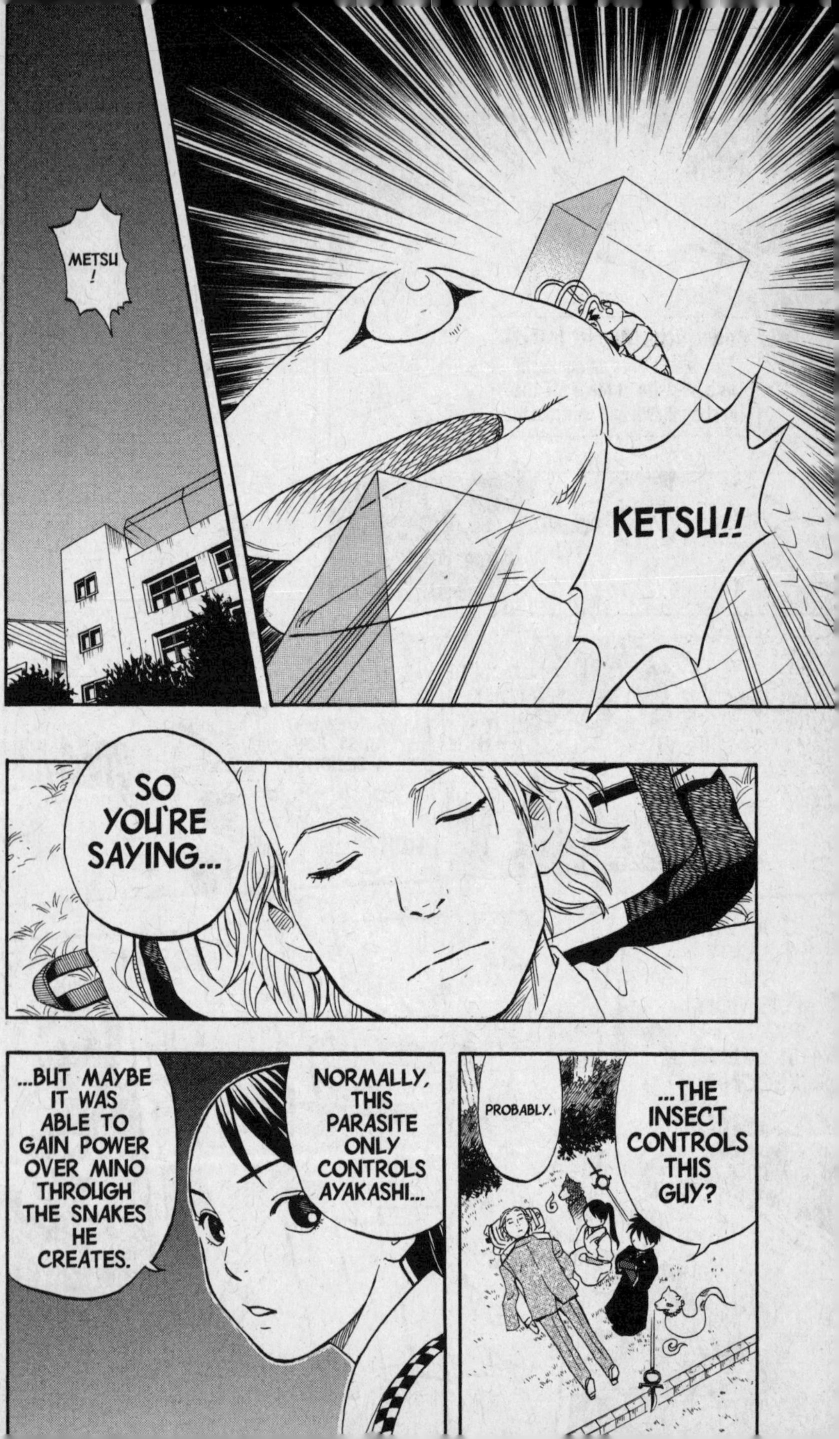
KETSU!!
METSU!
SO YOU'RE SAYING...
...THE INSECT CONTROLS THIS GUY?
PROBABLY.
NORMALLY, THIS PARASITE ONLY CONTROLS AYAKASHI...
...BUT MAYBE IT WAS ABLE TO GAIN POWER OVER MINO THROUGH THE SNAKES HE CREATES.

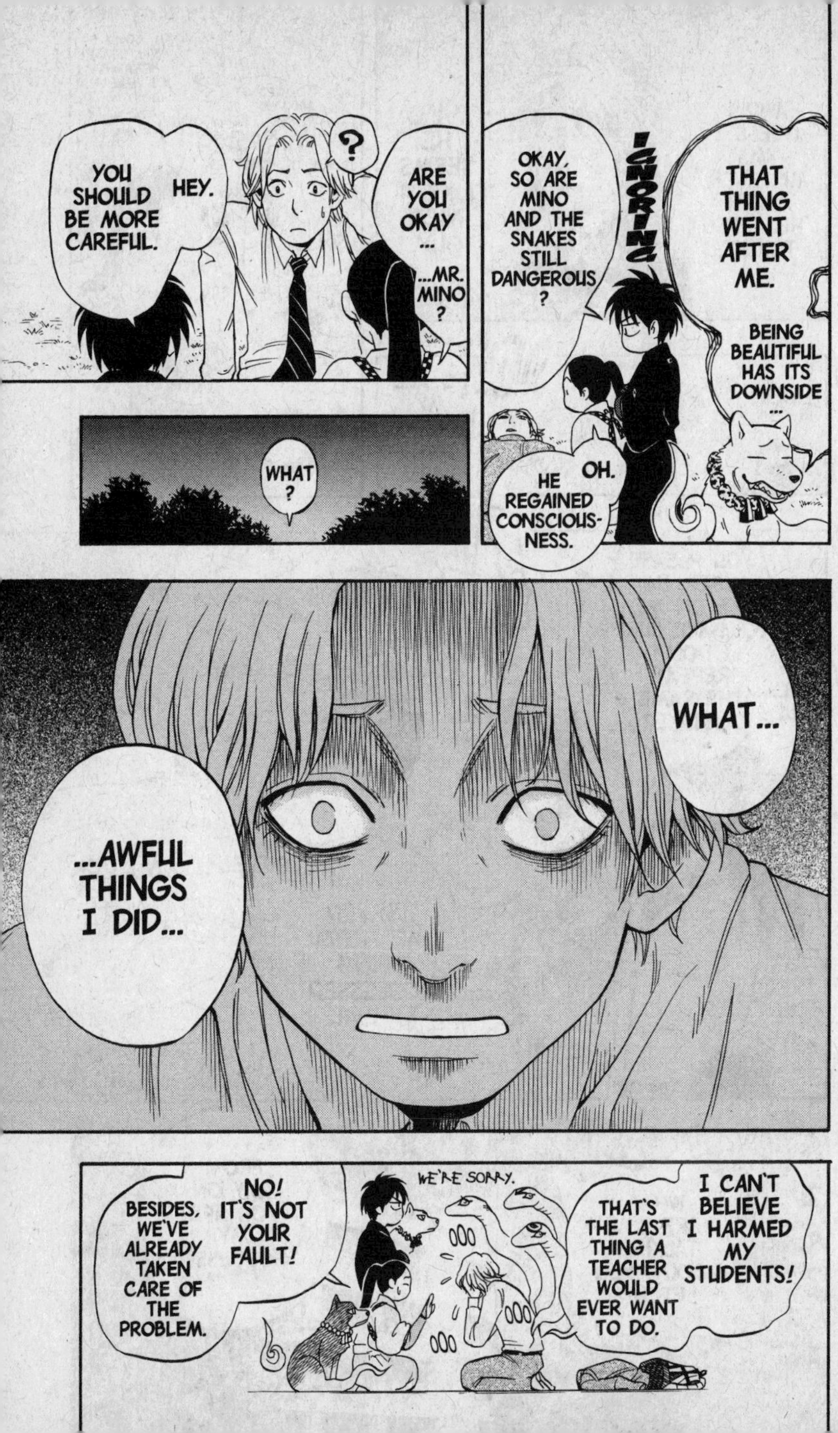
THAT THING WENT AFTER ME.
BEING BEAUTIFUL HAS ITS DOWNSIDE...
IGNORING
OKAY, SO ARE MINO AND THE SNAKES STILL DANGEROUS?
OH. HE REGAINED CONSCIOUSNESS.
ARE YOU OKAY... ...MR. MINO?
?
HEY.
YOU SHOULD BE MORE CAREFUL.
WHAT?
WHAT...
...AWFUL THINGS I DID...
I CAN'T BELIEVE I HARMED MY STUDENTS!
THAT'S THE LAST THING A TEACHER WOULD EVER WANT TO DO.
WE'RE SORRY.
NO! IT'S NOT YOUR FAULT!
BESIDES, WE'VE ALREADY TAKEN CARE OF THE PROBLEM.

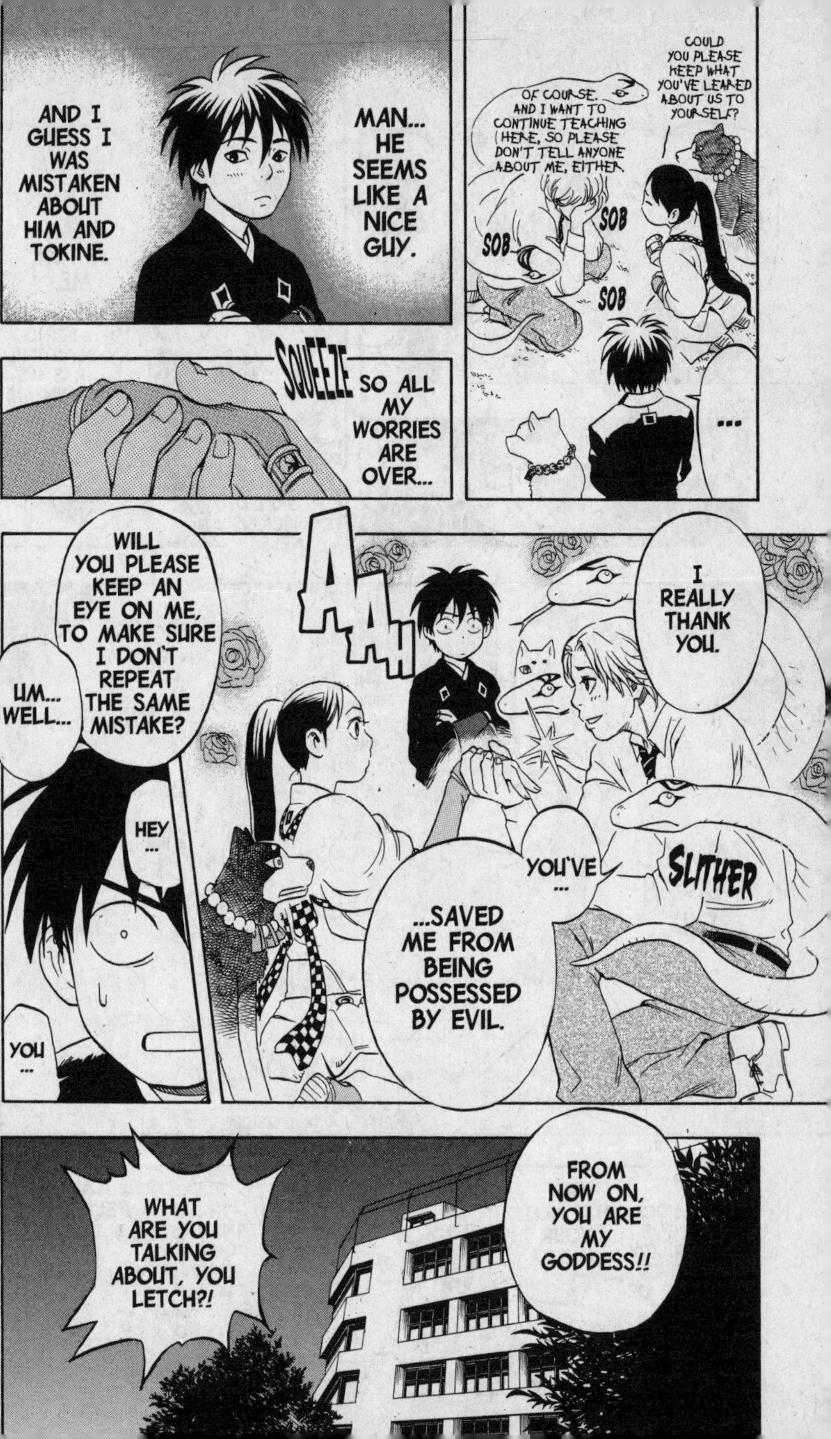
COULD YOU PLEASE KEEP WHAT YOU'VE LEARED ABOUT US TO YOURSELF?
OF COURSE. AND I WANT TO CONTINUE TEACHING HERE, SO PLEASE DON'T TELL ANYONE ABOUT ME, EITHER.
SOB
SOB
SOB
MAN... HE SEEMS LIKE A NICE GUY.
AND I GUESS I WAS MISTAKEN ABOUT HIM AND TOKINE.
...
SO ALL MY WORRIES ARE OVER...
SQUEEZE
I REALLY THANK YOU.
YOU'VE...
...SAVED ME FROM BEING POSSESSED BY EVIL.
SLITHER
AAH
WILL YOU PLEASE KEEP AN EYE ON ME, TO MAKE SURE I DON'T REPEAT THE SAME MISTAKE?
UM... WELL...
HEY...
YOU...
FROM NOW ON, YOU ARE MY GODDESS!!
WHAT ARE YOU TALKING ABOUT, YOU LETCH?!

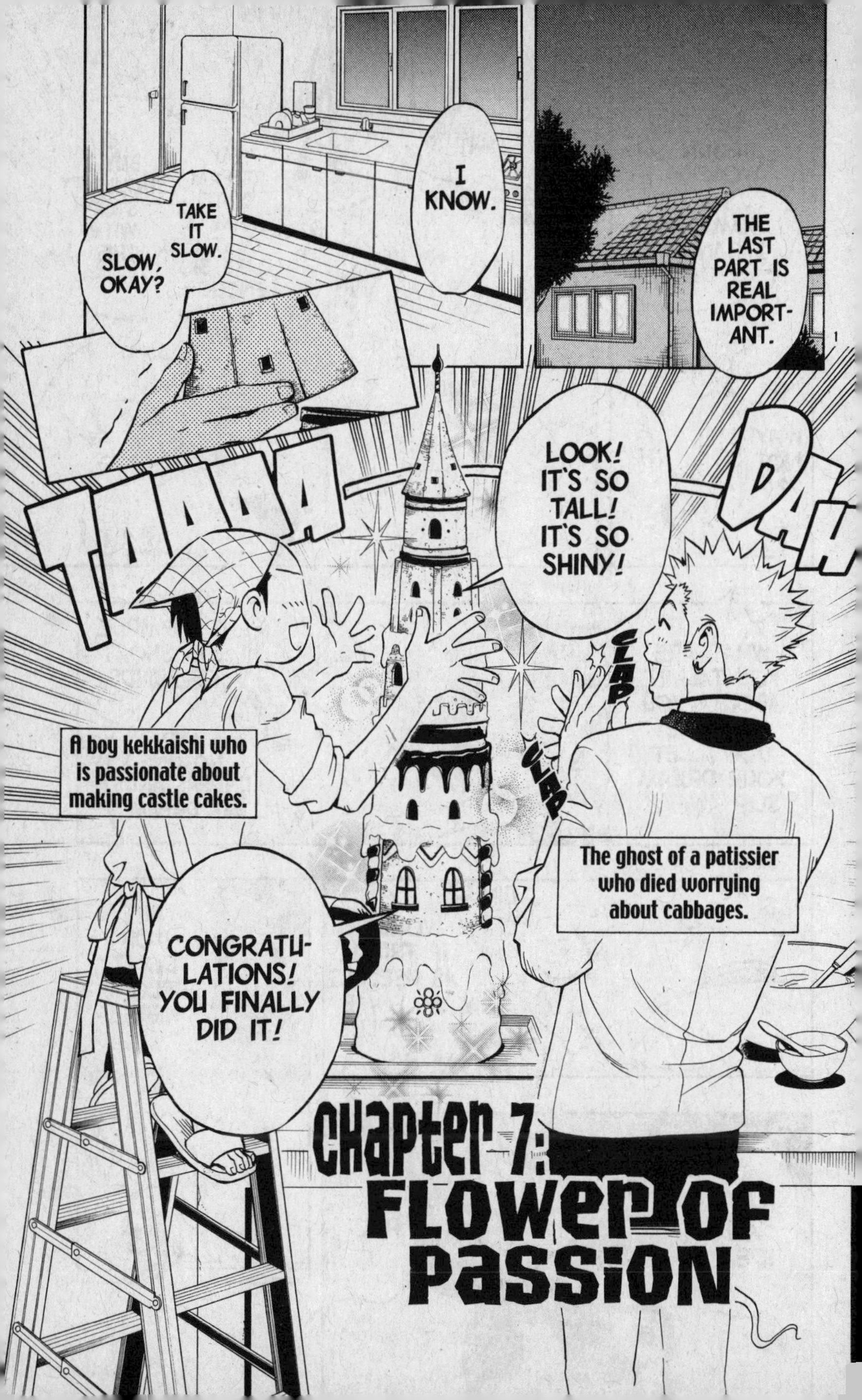
THE LAST PART IS REAL IMPORTANT.
TAKE IT SLOW. SLOW, OKAY?
I KNOW.
TADAA
DAH
LOOK! IT'S SO TALL! IT'S SO SHINY!
CLAP
CLAP
The ghost of a patissier who died worrying about cabbages.
A boy kekkaishi who is passionate about making castle cakes.
CONGRATULATIONS! YOU FINALLY DID IT!

Chapter 7: Flower of Passion

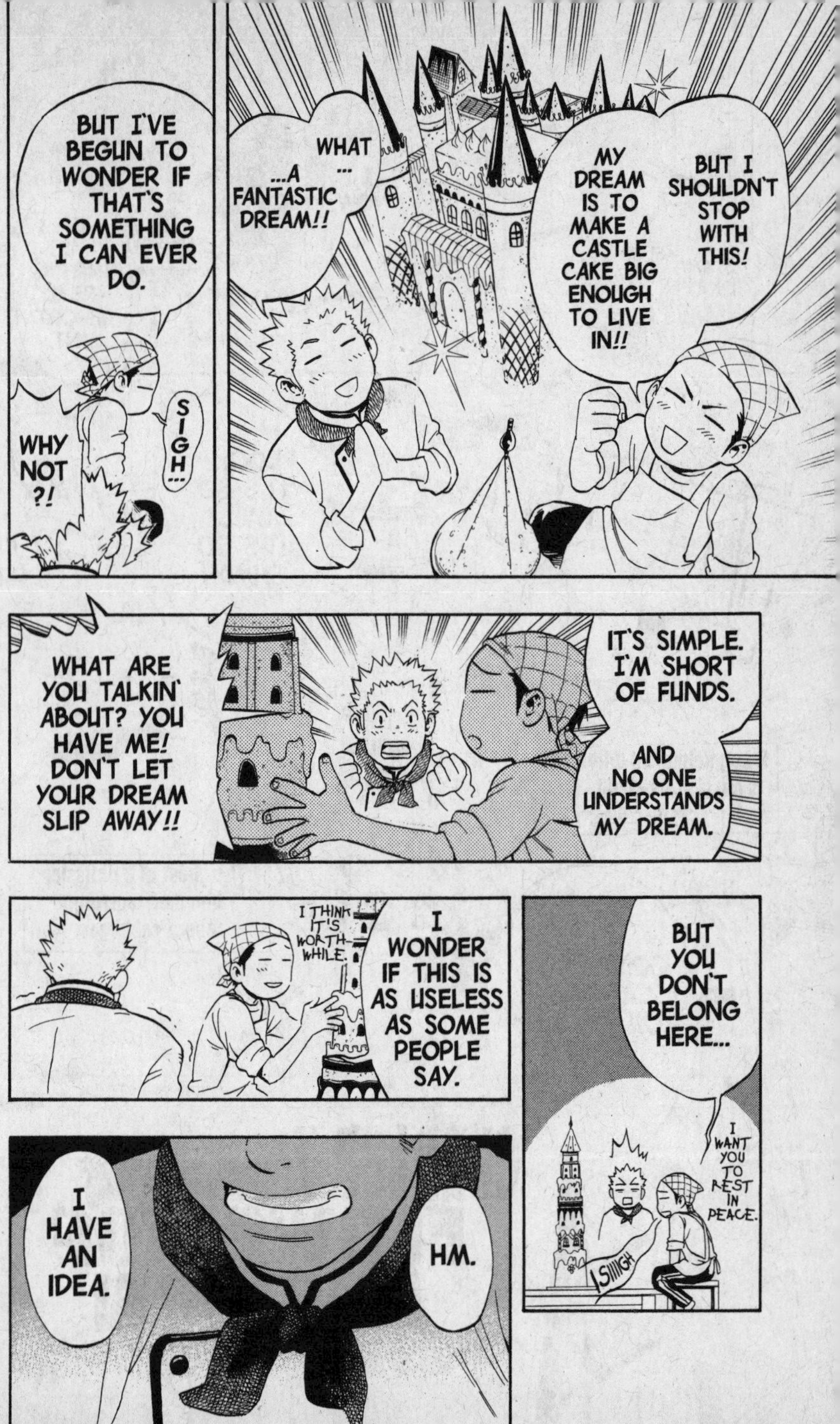
BUT I SHOULDN'T STOP WITH THIS!
MY DREAM IS TO MAKE A CASTLE CAKE BIG ENOUGH TO LIVE IN!!
WHAT ...A ... FANTASTIC DREAM!!
BUT I'VE BEGUN TO WONDER IF THAT'S SOMETHING I CAN EVER DO.
SIGH...
WHY NOT ?!
IT'S SIMPLE. I'M SHORT OF FUNDS.
AND NO ONE UNDERSTANDS MY DREAM.
WHAT ARE YOU TALKIN' ABOUT? YOU HAVE ME! DON'T LET YOUR DREAM SLIP AWAY!!
I WONDER IF THIS IS AS USELESS AS SOME PEOPLE SAY.
I THINK IT'S WORTHWHILE.
BUT YOU DON'T BELONG HERE...
I WANT YOU TO REST IN PEACE.
SIIIIGH
HM.
I HAVE AN IDEA.

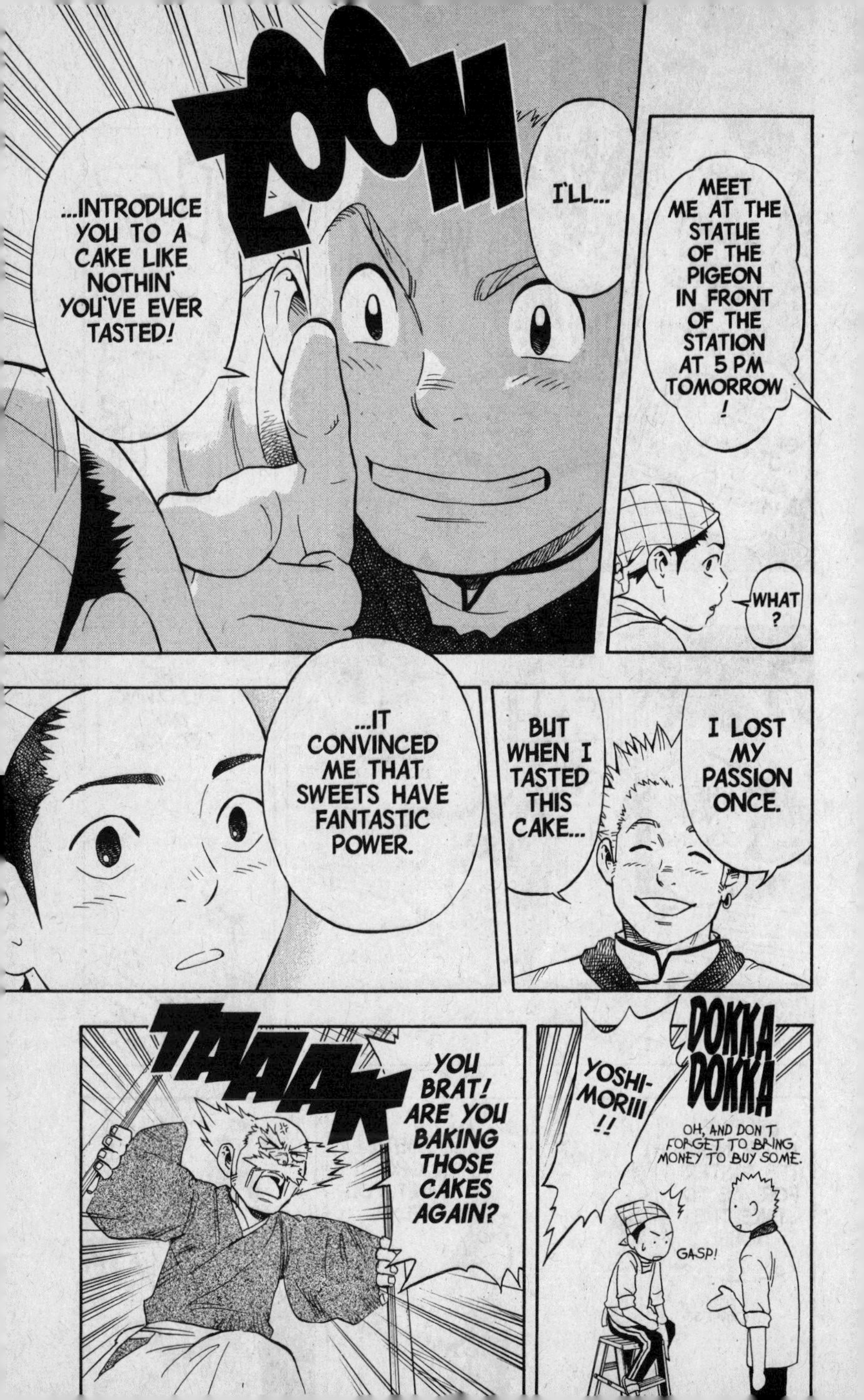
MEET ME AT THE STATUE OF THE PIGEON IN FRONT OF THE STATION AT 5 PM TOMORROW!
WHAT?
I'LL...
ZOOM
...INTRODUCE YOU TO A CAKE LIKE NOTHIN' YOU'VE EVER TASTED!
I LOST MY PASSION ONCE.
BUT WHEN I TASTED THIS CAKE...
...IT CONVINCED ME THAT SWEETS HAVE FANTASTIC POWER.
DOKKA DOKKA
YOSHI-MORIII!!
OH, AND DON'T FORGET TO BRING MONEY TO BUY SOME.
GASP!
TAAAK
YOU BRAT! ARE YOU BAKING THOSE CAKES AGAIN?

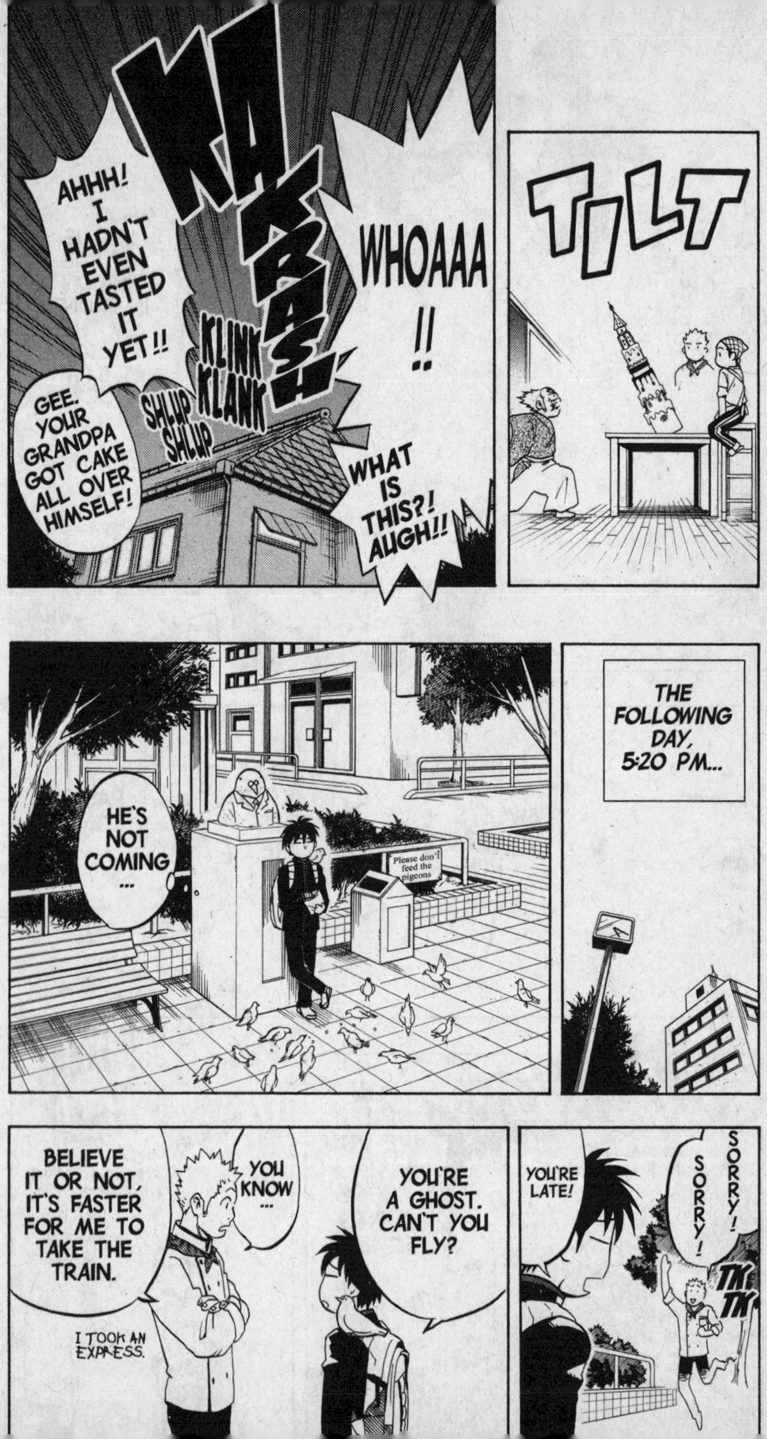
TILT
WHOAAA !!
KA-KRASH
AHHH! I HADN'T EVEN TASTED IT YET!!
KLINK KLANK
SHLUP SHLUP
GEE. YOUR GRANDPA GOT CAKE ALL OVER HIMSELF!
WHAT IS THIS?! AUGH!!
THE FOLLOWING DAY, 5:20 PM...
HE'S NOT COMING ...
Please don't feed the pigeons
SORRY! SORRY!
TK TK
YOU'RE LATE!
YOU'RE A GHOST. CAN'T YOU FLY?
YOU KNOW ...
BELIEVE IT OR NOT, IT'S FASTER FOR ME TO TAKE THE TRAIN.
I TOOK AN EXPRESS.

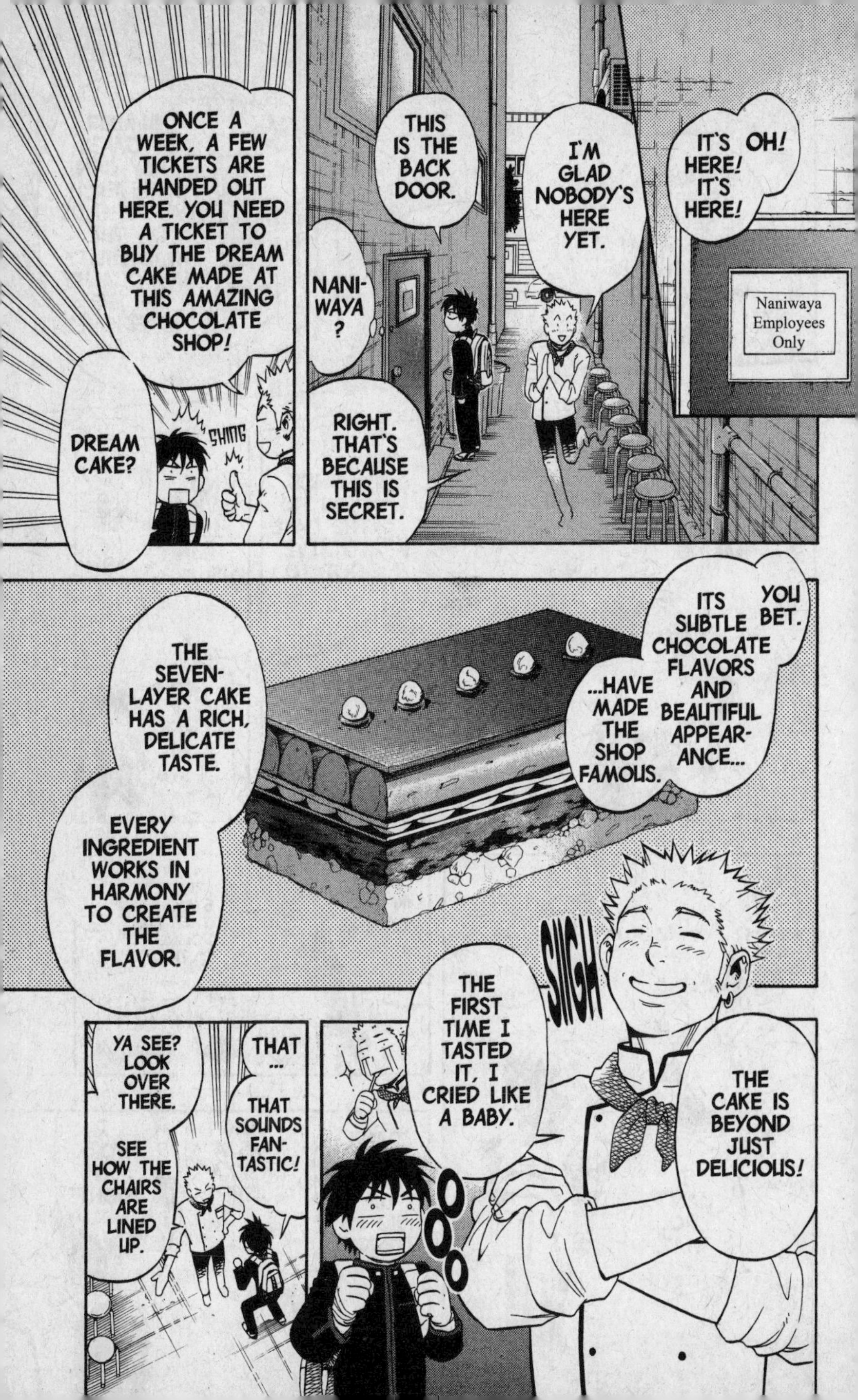
OH!
IT'S HERE! IT'S HERE!
I'M GLAD NOBODY'S HERE YET.
Naniwaya Employees Only
THIS IS THE BACK DOOR.
NANIWAYA?
RIGHT. THAT'S BECAUSE THIS IS SECRET.
ONCE A WEEK, A FEW TICKETS ARE HANDED OUT HERE. YOU NEED A TICKET TO BUY THE DREAM CAKE MADE AT THIS AMAZING CHOCOLATE SHOP!
SHING
DREAM CAKE?
YOU BET.
ITS SUBTLE CHOCOLATE FLAVORS AND BEAUTIFUL APPEARANCE...
...HAVE MADE THE SHOP FAMOUS.
THE SEVEN-LAYER CAKE HAS A RICH, DELICATE TASTE.
EVERY INGREDIENT WORKS IN HARMONY TO CREATE THE FLAVOR.
SIGH
THE CAKE IS BEYOND JUST DELICIOUS!
THE FIRST TIME I TASTED IT, I CRIED LIKE A BABY.
THAT... THAT SOUNDS FANTASTIC!
YA SEE? LOOK OVER THERE.
SEE HOW THE CHAIRS ARE LINED UP.

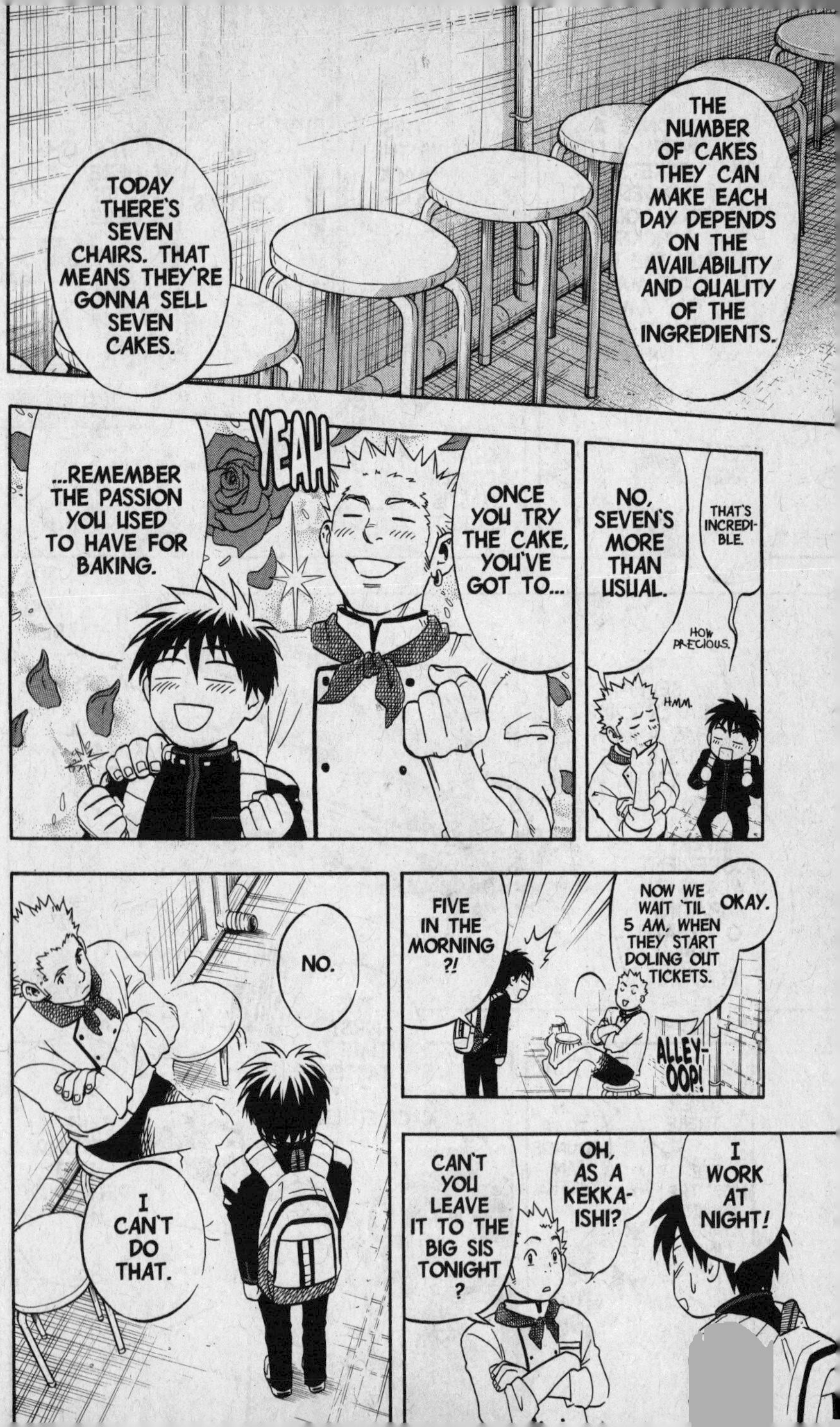
THE NUMBER OF CAKES THEY CAN MAKE EACH DAY DEPENDS ON THE AVAILABILITY AND QUALITY OF THE INGREDIENTS.
TODAY THERE'S SEVEN CHAIRS. THAT MEANS THEY'RE GONNA SELL SEVEN CAKES.
THAT'S INCREDI-BLE.
HOW PRECIOUS.
NO, SEVEN'S MORE THAN USUAL.
HMM.
ONCE YOU TRY THE CAKE, YOU'VE GOT TO...
YEAH
...REMEMBER THE PASSION YOU USED TO HAVE FOR BAKING.
OKAY.
NOW WE WAIT 'TIL 5 AM, WHEN THEY START DOLING OUT TICKETS.
ALLEY-OOP!
FIVE IN THE MORNING?!
I WORK AT NIGHT!
OH, AS A KEKKA-ISHI?
CAN'T YOU LEAVE IT TO THE BIG SIS TONIGHT?
NO.
I CAN'T DO THAT.

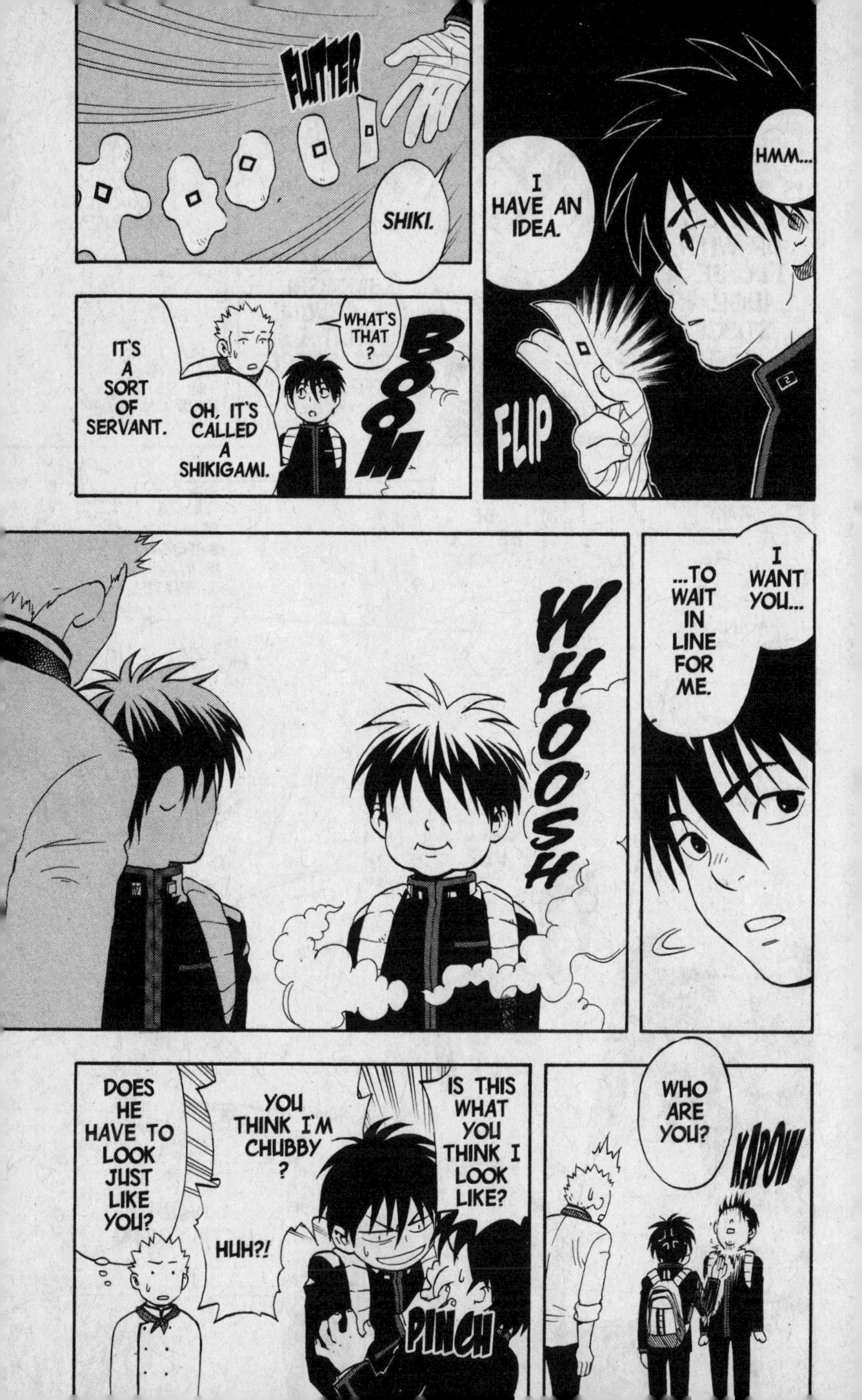
HMM...
I HAVE AN IDEA.
FLIP
FLUTTER
SHIKI.
WHAT'S THAT?
BOOM
OH, IT'S CALLED A SHIKIGAMI.
IT'S A SORT OF SERVANT.
I WANT YOU...
...TO WAIT IN LINE FOR ME.
WHOOOSH
WHO ARE YOU?
KAPOW
IS THIS WHAT YOU THINK I LOOK LIKE?
YOU THINK I'M CHUBBY?
HUH?!
DOES HE HAVE TO LOOK JUST LIKE YOU?
PINCH

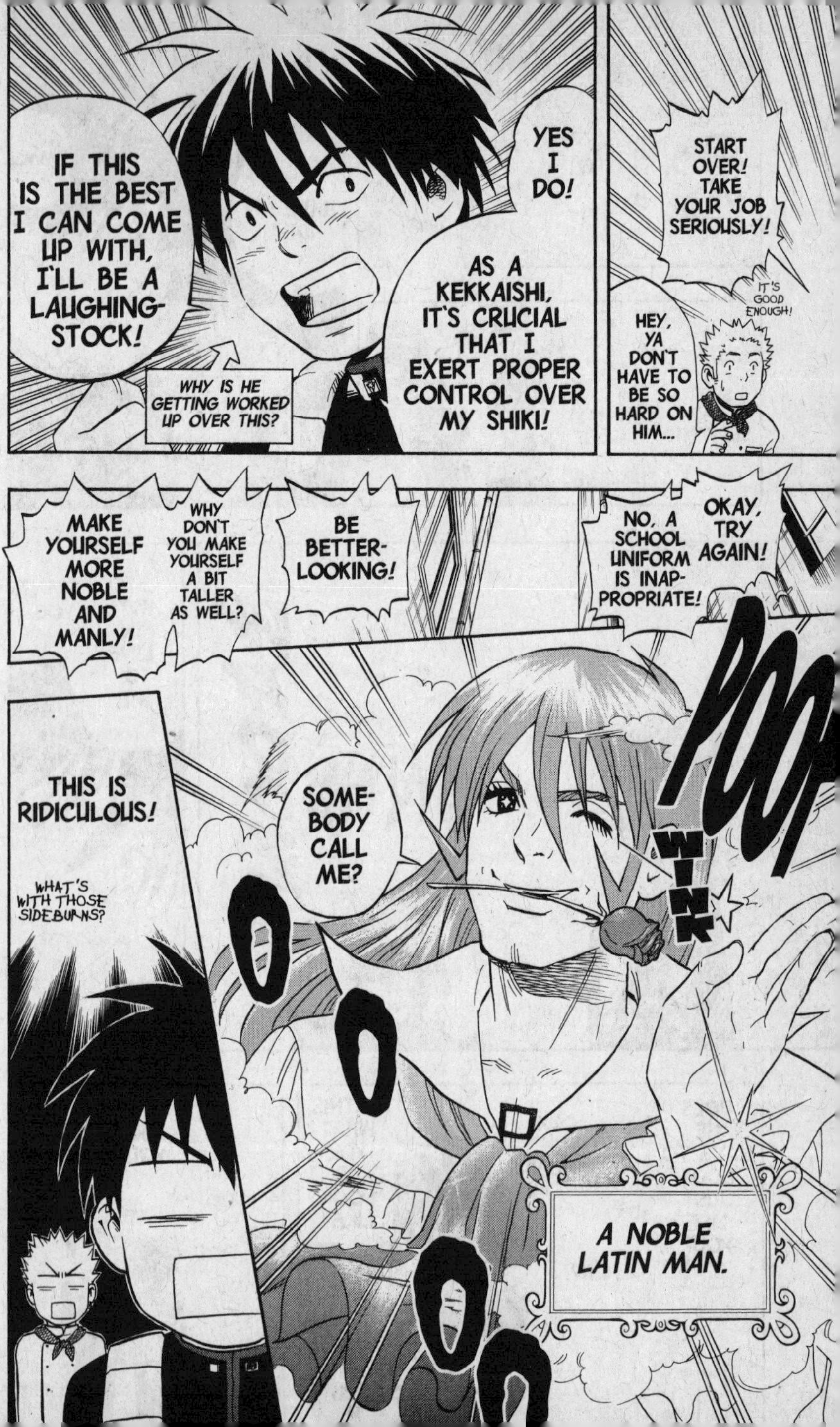
START OVER! TAKE YOUR JOB SERIOUSLY!
IT'S GOOD ENOUGH!
HEY, YA DON'T HAVE TO BE SO HARD ON HIM...
YES I DO!
AS A KEKKAISHI, IT'S CRUCIAL THAT I EXERT PROPER CONTROL OVER MY SHIKI!
IF THIS IS THE BEST I CAN COME UP WITH, I'LL BE A LAUGHING-STOCK!
WHY IS HE GETTING WORKED UP OVER THIS?
OKAY, TRY AGAIN!
NO, A SCHOOL UNIFORM IS INAPPROPRIATE!
BE BETTER-LOOKING!
WHY DON'T YOU MAKE YOURSELF A BIT TALLER AS WELL?
MAKE YOURSELF MORE NOBLE AND MANLY!
POOF
SOMEBODY CALL ME?
WINK
THIS IS RIDICULOUS!
WHAT'S WITH THOSE SIDEBURNS?
A NOBLE LATIN MAN.

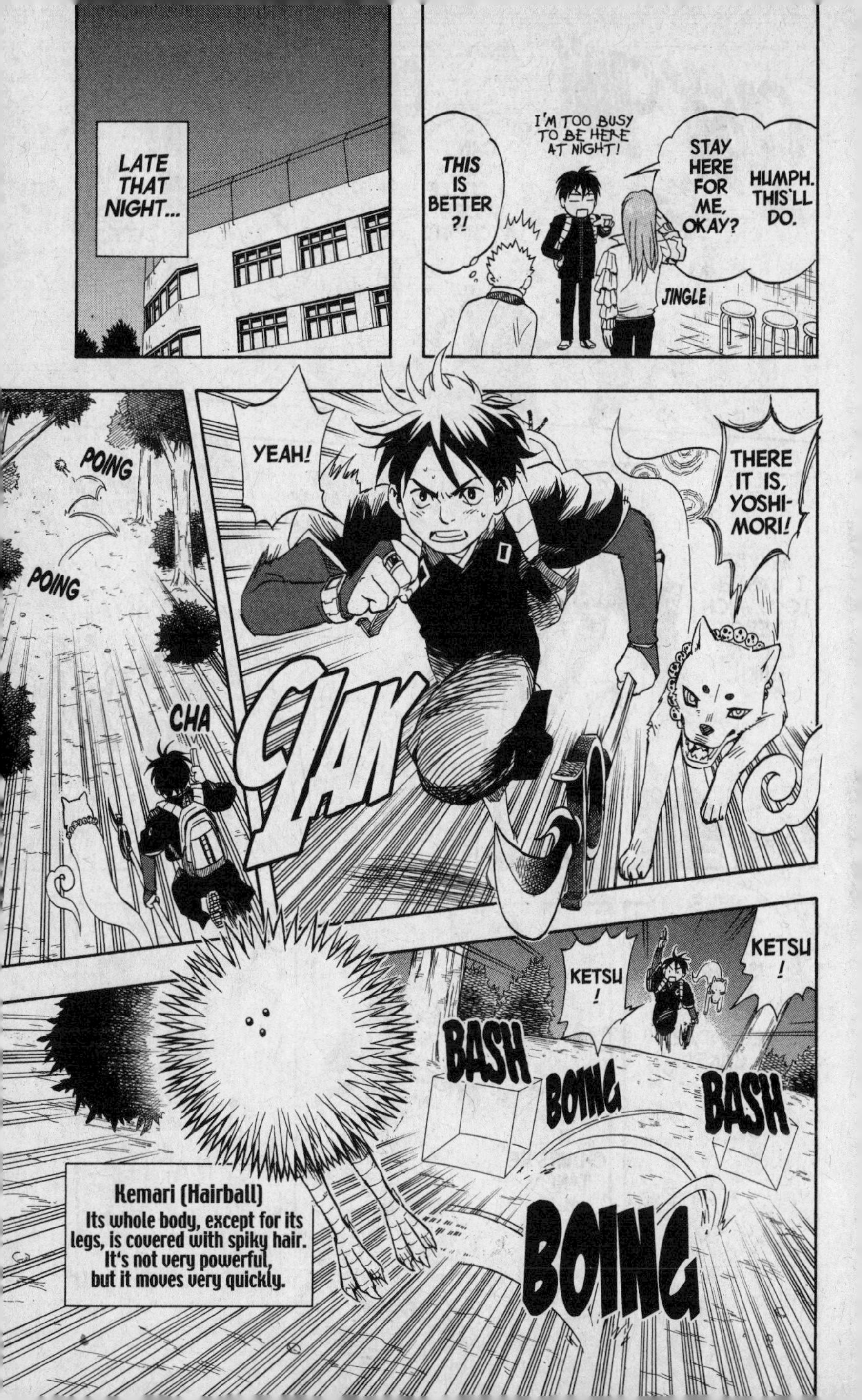
STAY HERE FOR ME, OKAY?
HUMPH. THIS'LL DO.
I'M TOO BUSY TO BE HERE AT NIGHT!
THIS IS BETTER ?!
JINGLE
LATE THAT NIGHT...
THERE IT IS, YOSHI-MORI!
YEAH!
CLAK
POING
POING
CHA
KETSU !
KETSU !
BASH
BOING
BASH
BOING
Kemari (Hairball)
Its whole body, except for its legs, is covered with spiky hair. It's not very powerful, but it moves very quickly.

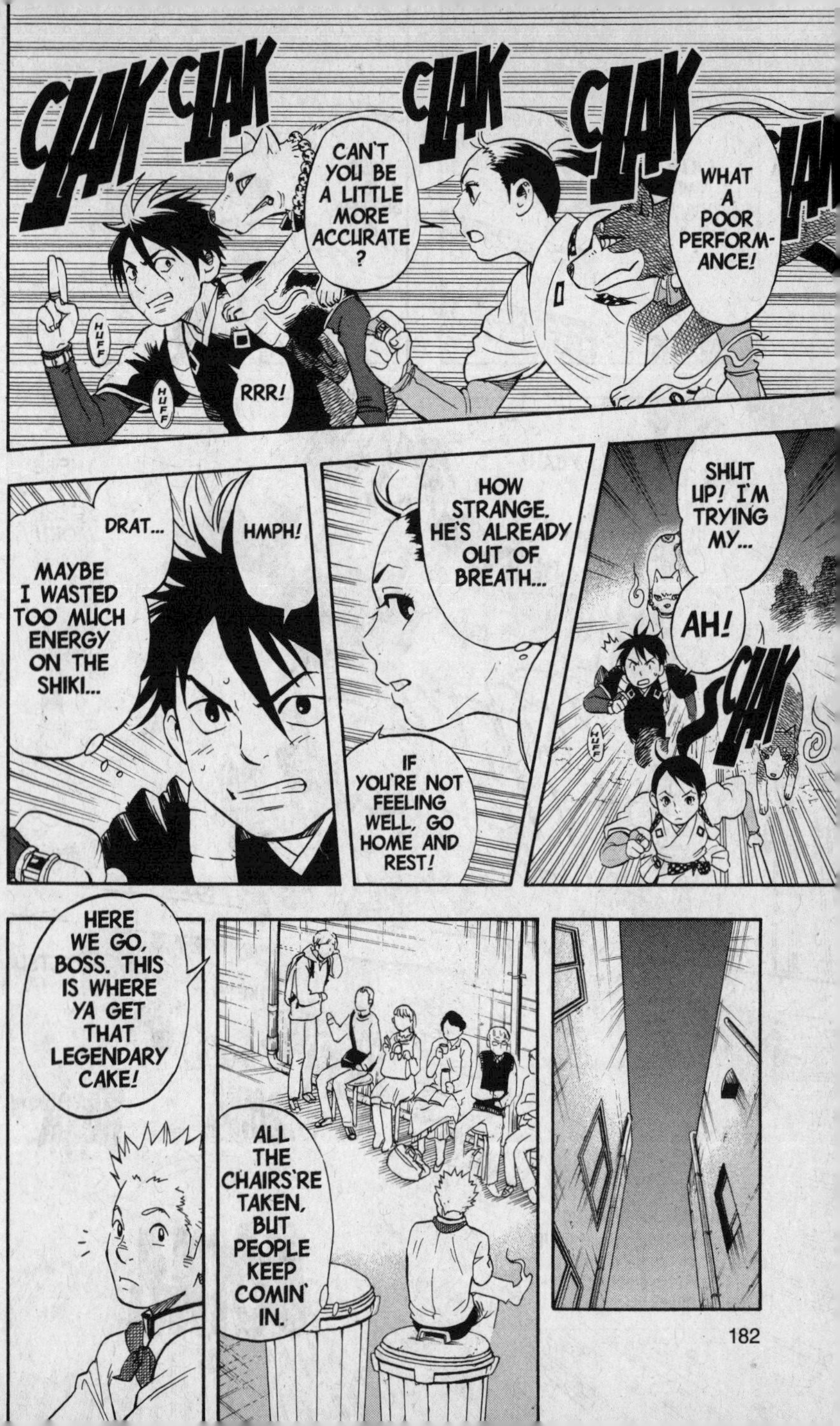
CIAK CIAK CIAK CIAK CIAK
WHAT A POOR PERFORMANCE!
CAN'T YOU BE A LITTLE MORE ACCURATE?
RRR!
HUFF HUFF
SHUT UP! I'M TRYING MY...
AH!
CIAK
HUFF
HOW STRANGE. HE'S ALREADY OUT OF BREATH...
IF YOU'RE NOT FEELING WELL, GO HOME AND REST!
HMPH!
DRAT...
MAYBE I WASTED TOO MUCH ENERGY ON THE SHIKI...
ALL THE CHAIRS'RE TAKEN, BUT PEOPLE KEEP COMIN' IN.
HERE WE GO, BOSS. THIS IS WHERE YA GET THAT LEGENDARY CAKE!

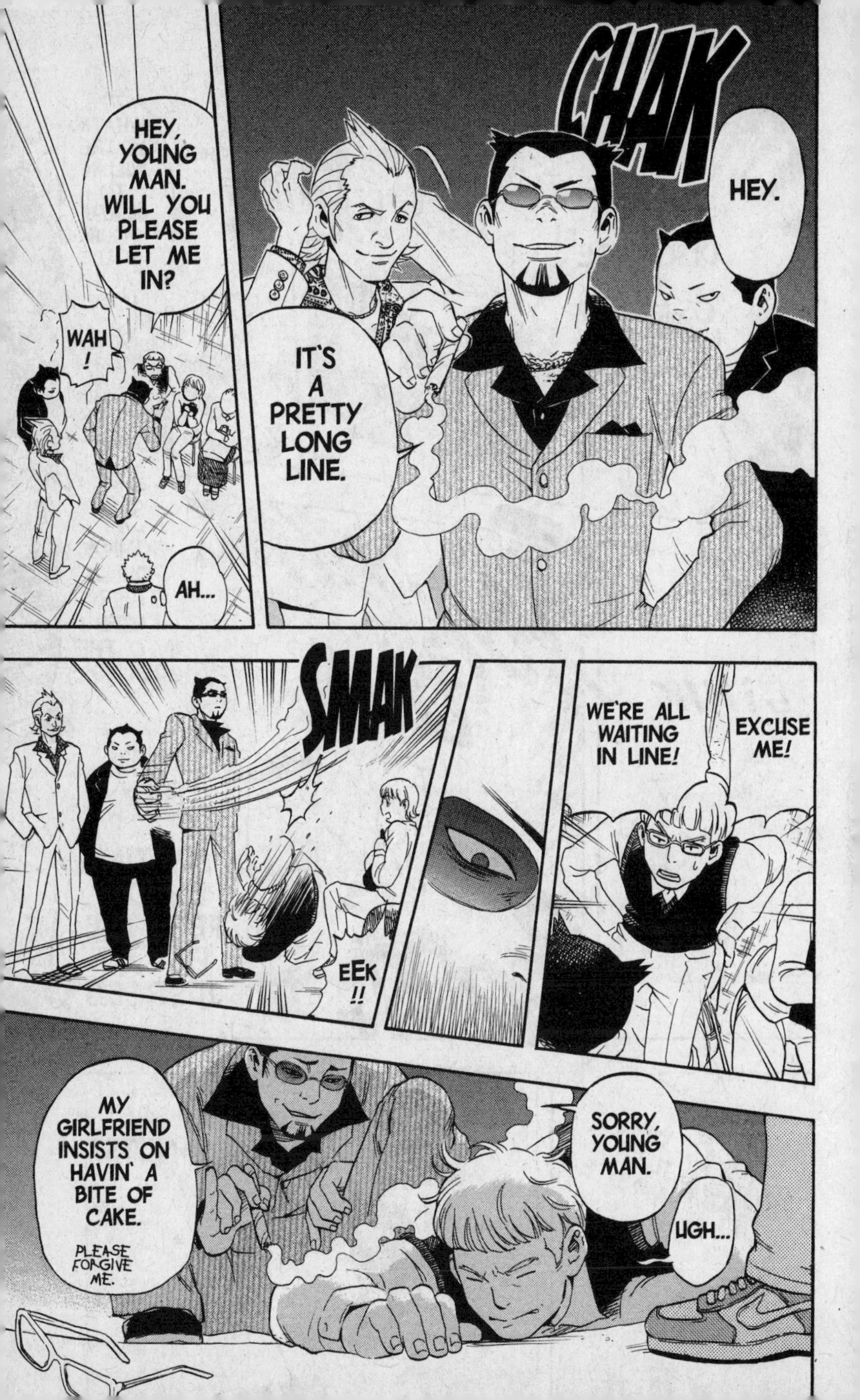
CHAK
HEY.
IT'S A PRETTY LONG LINE.
HEY, YOUNG MAN. WILL YOU PLEASE LET ME IN?
WAH!
AH...
EXCUSE ME!
WE'RE ALL WAITING IN LINE!
SMAK
EEK!!
SORRY, YOUNG MAN.
UGH...
MY GIRLFRIEND INSISTS ON HAVIN' A BITE OF CAKE.
PLEASE FORGIVE ME.

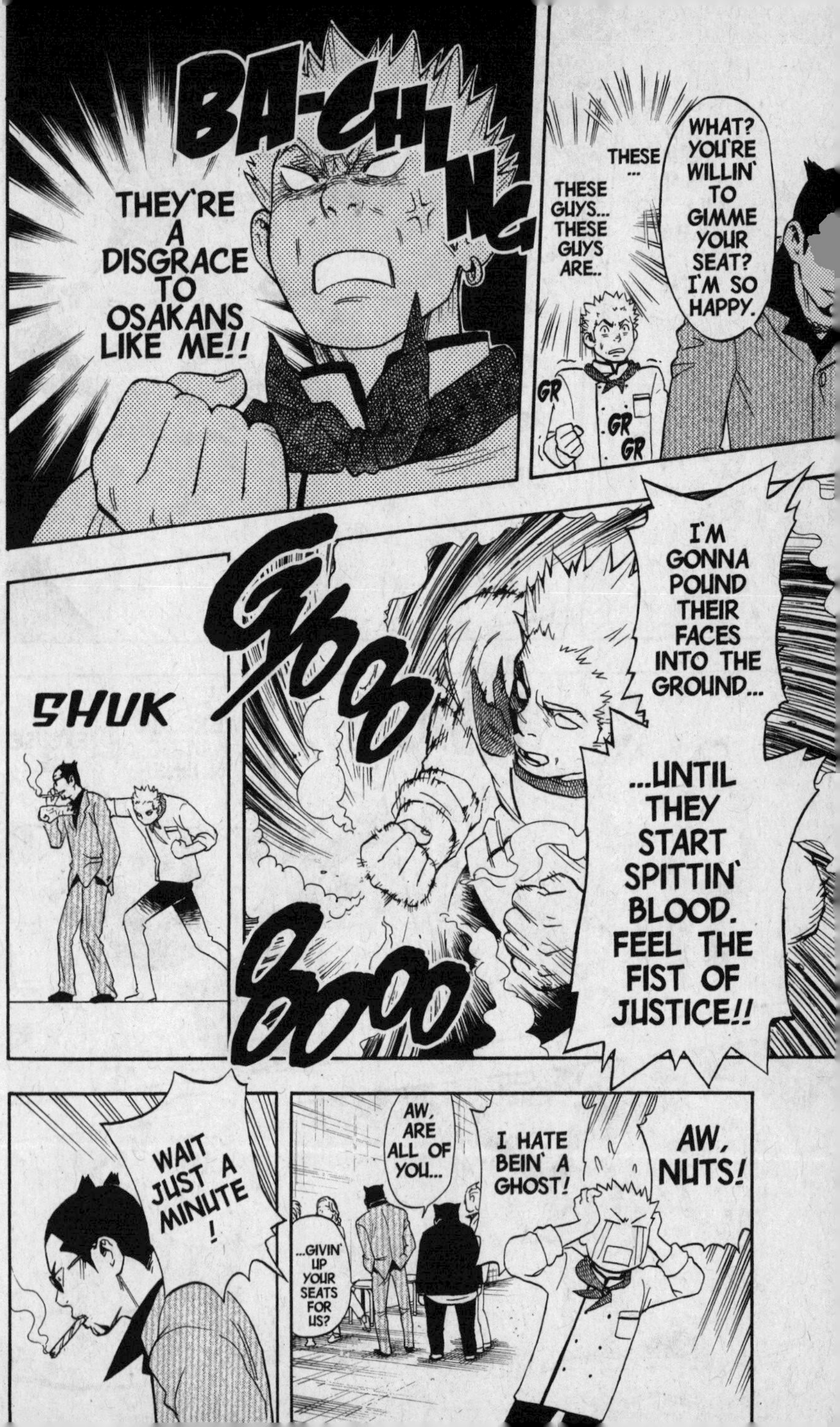
WHAT? YOU'RE WILLIN' TO GIMME YOUR SEAT? I'M SO HAPPY.
THESE ...
THESE GUYS... THESE GUYS ARE..
GR
GR
GR
BA-CHING
THEY'RE A DISGRACE TO OSAKANS LIKE ME!!
I'M GONNA POUND THEIR FACES INTO THE GROUND...
...UNTIL THEY START SPITTIN' BLOOD. FEEL THE FIST OF JUSTICE!!
GOOOOOOOO
SHUK
AW, NUTS!
I HATE BEIN' A GHOST!
AW, ARE ALL OF YOU...
...GIVIN' UP YOUR SEATS FOR US?
WAIT JUST A MINUTE!

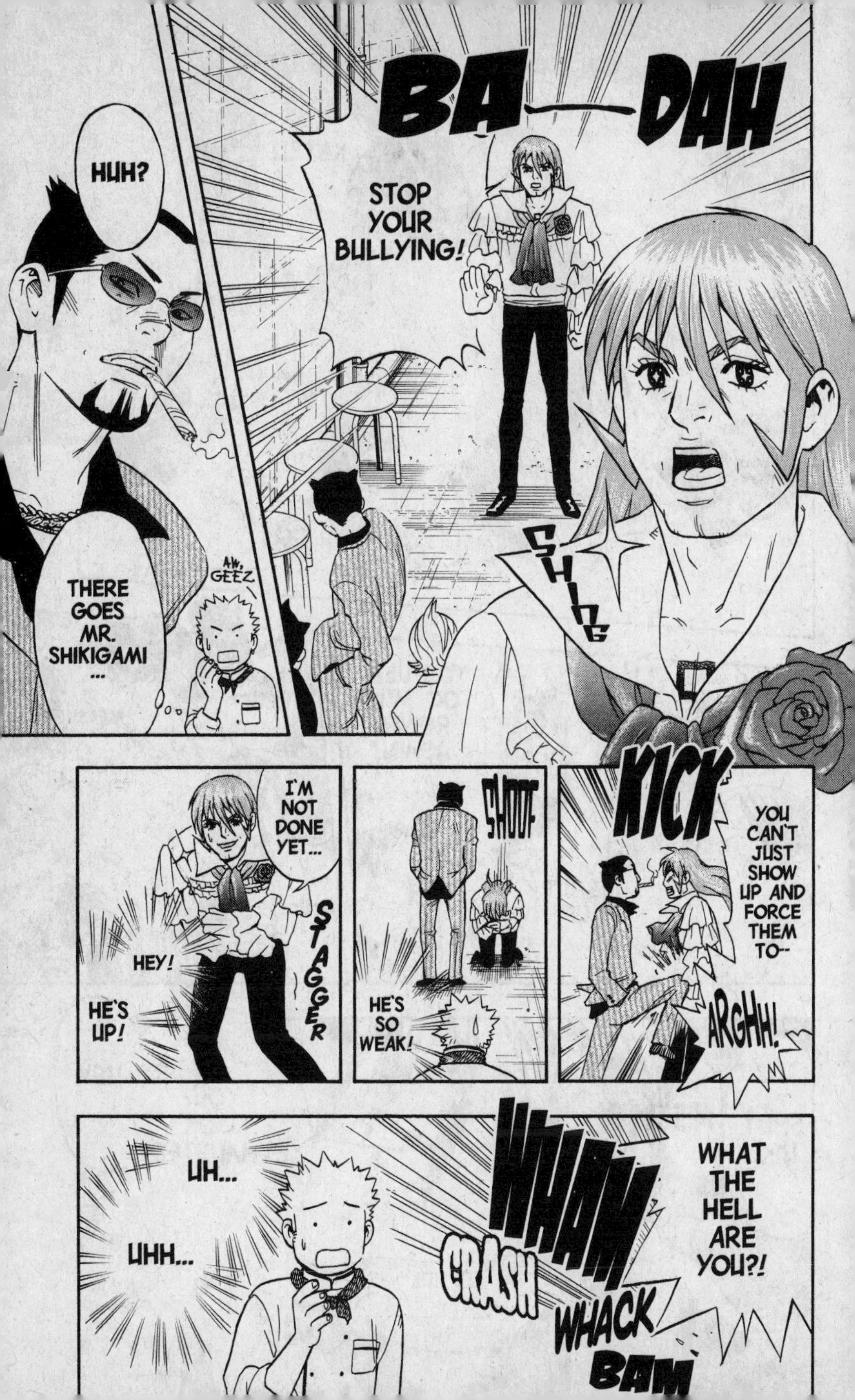
BA—DAH
STOP YOUR BULLYING!
SHING
HUH?
A-W, GEEZ.
THERE GOES MR. SHIKIGAMI ...
KICK
YOU CAN'T JUST SHOW UP AND FORCE THEM TO--
ARGHH!
SHOOF
HE'S SO WEAK!
I'M NOT DONE YET...
STAGGER
HEY!
HE'S UP!
WHAT THE HELL ARE YOU?!
WHAM
CRASH
WHACK
BAM
UH...
UHH...

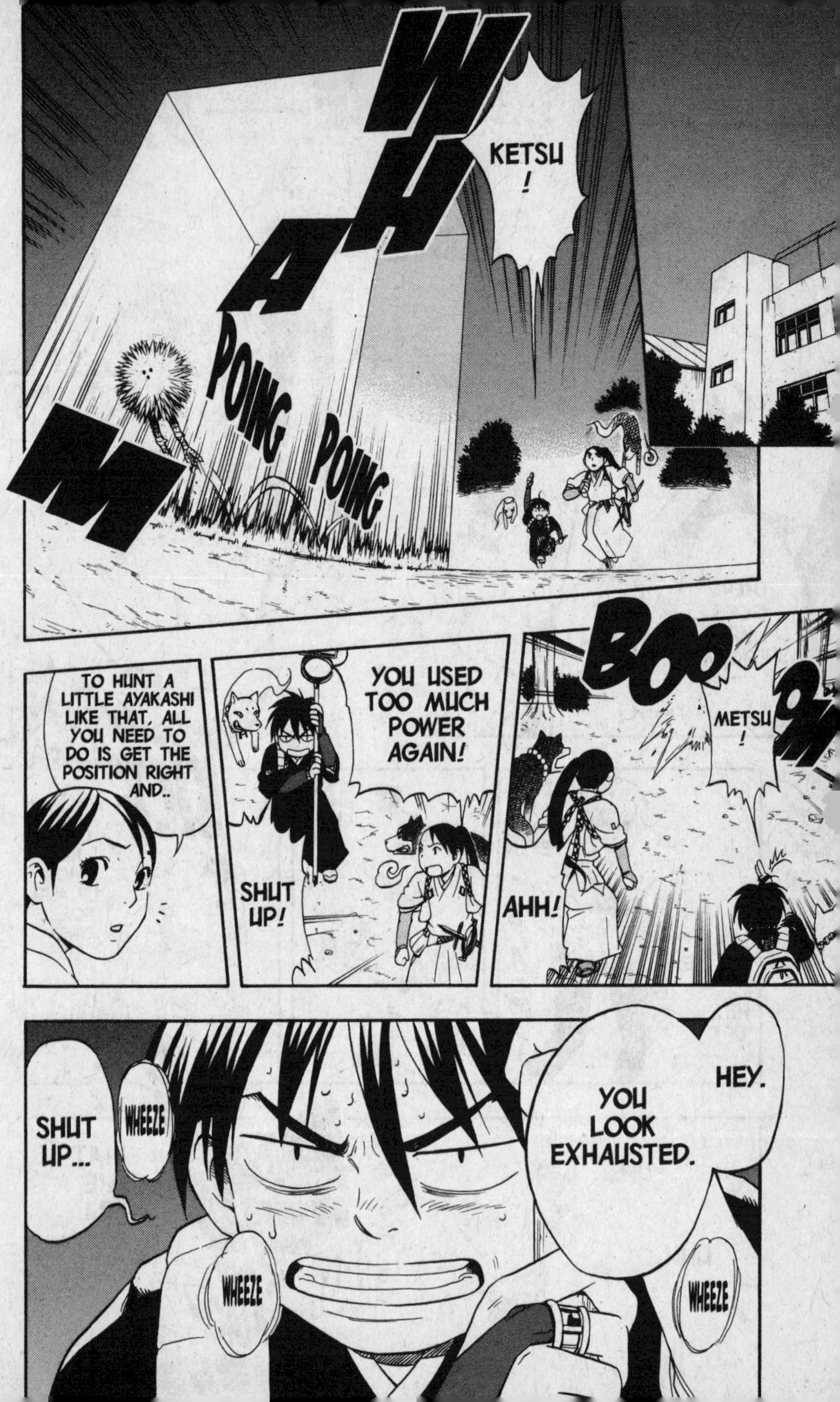
KETSU!
WHAM
POING POING
METSU!
BOOOM
AHH!
YOU USED TOO MUCH POWER AGAIN!
SHUT UP!
TO HUNT A LITTLE AYAKASHI LIKE THAT, ALL YOU NEED TO DO IS GET THE POSITION RIGHT AND..
HEY.
YOU LOOK EXHAUSTED.
WHEEZE
WHEEZE
WHEEZE
SHUT UP...

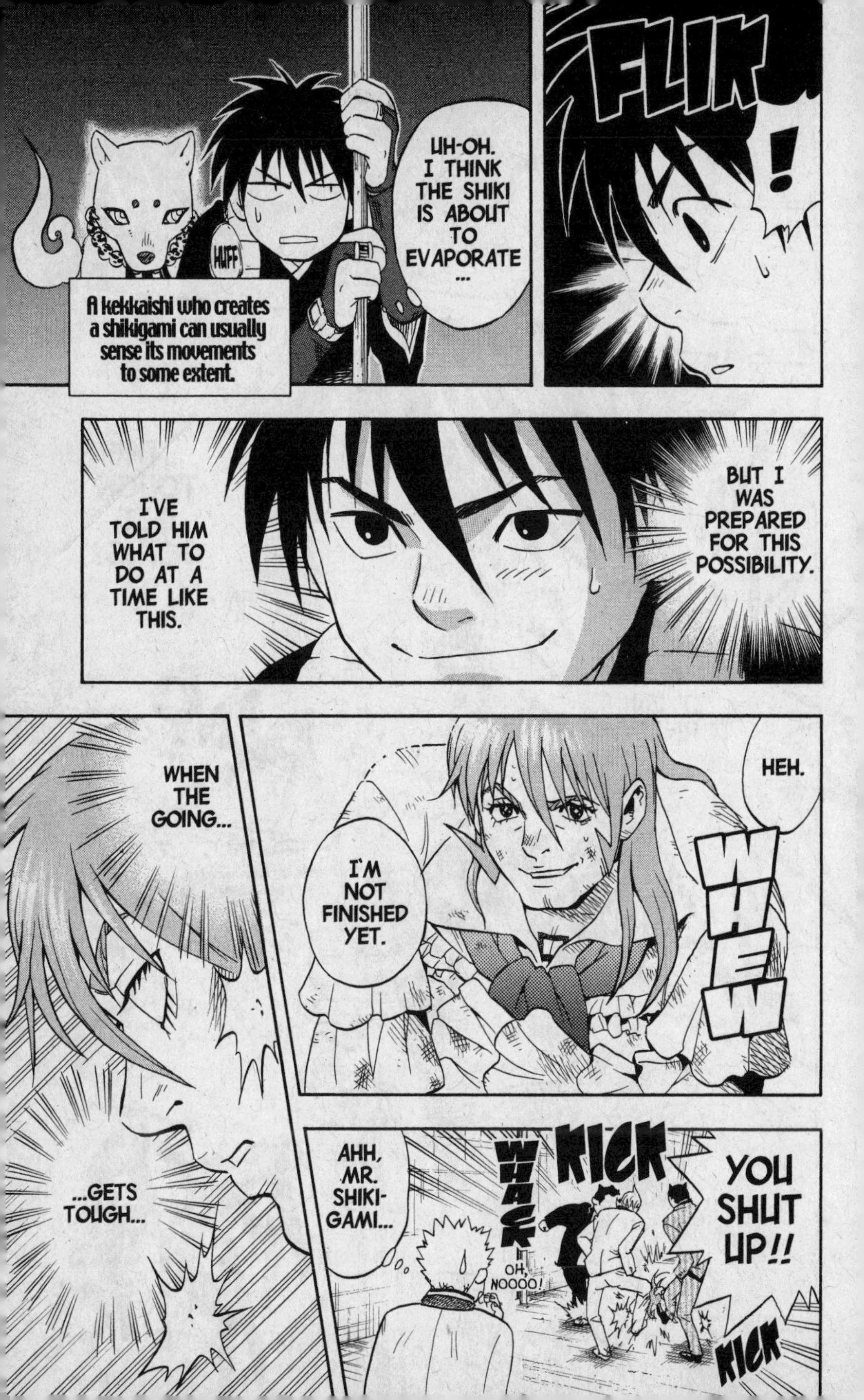
FLIK
!
UH-OH. I THINK THE SHIKI IS ABOUT TO EVAPORATE ...
HUFF
A kekkaishi who creates a shikigami can usually sense its movements to some extent.
BUT I WAS PREPARED FOR THIS POSSIBILITY.
I'VE TOLD HIM WHAT TO DO AT A TIME LIKE THIS.
HEH.
WHEW
I'M NOT FINISHED YET.
YOU SHUT UP!!
KICK
WHACK
AHH, MR. SHIKI-GAMI...
OH, NOOOO!
KICK
WHEN THE GOING...
...GETS TOUGH...

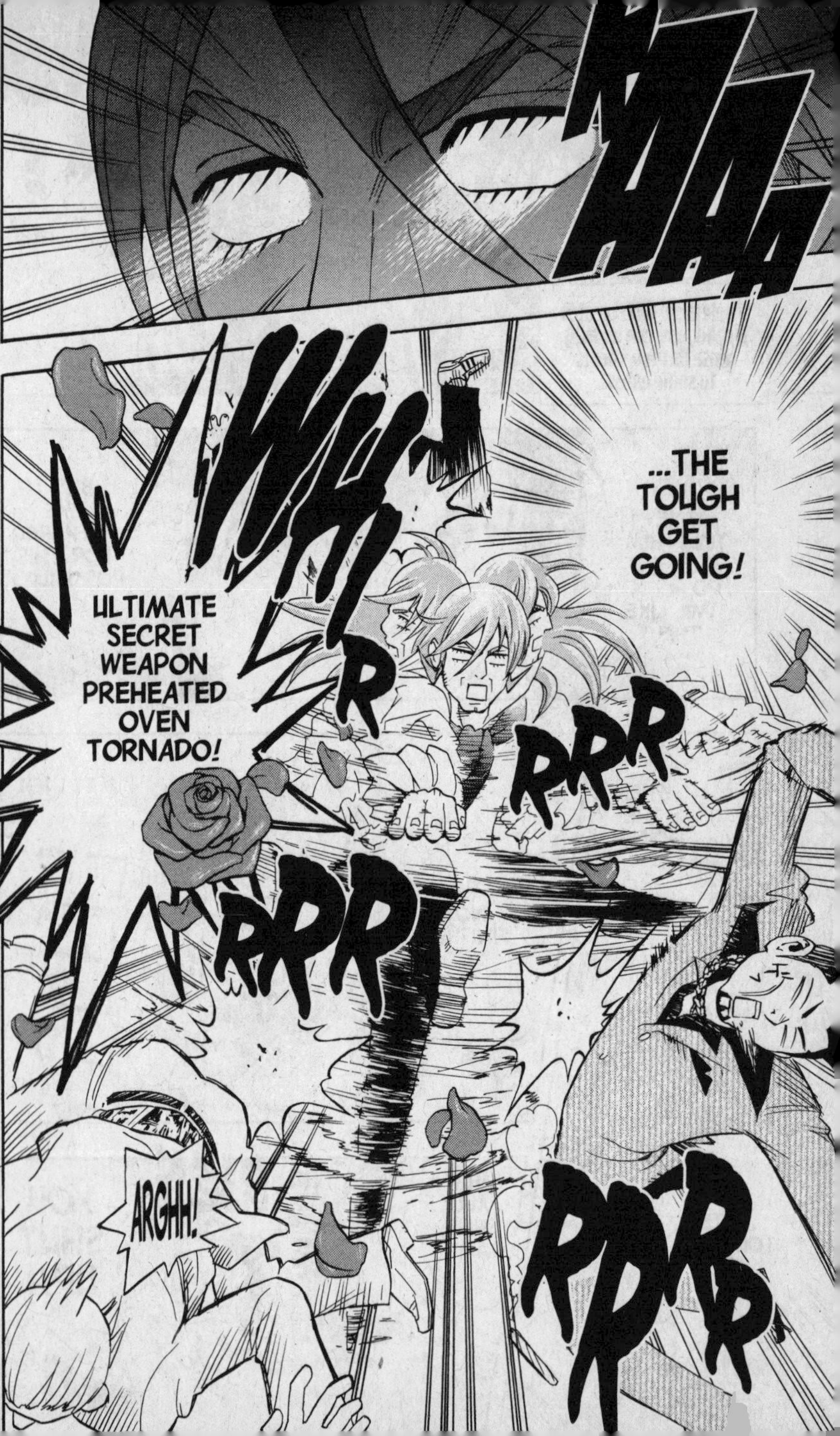
...THE TOUGH GET GOING!
ULTIMATE SECRET WEAPON PREHEATED OVEN TORNADO!
ARGHH!

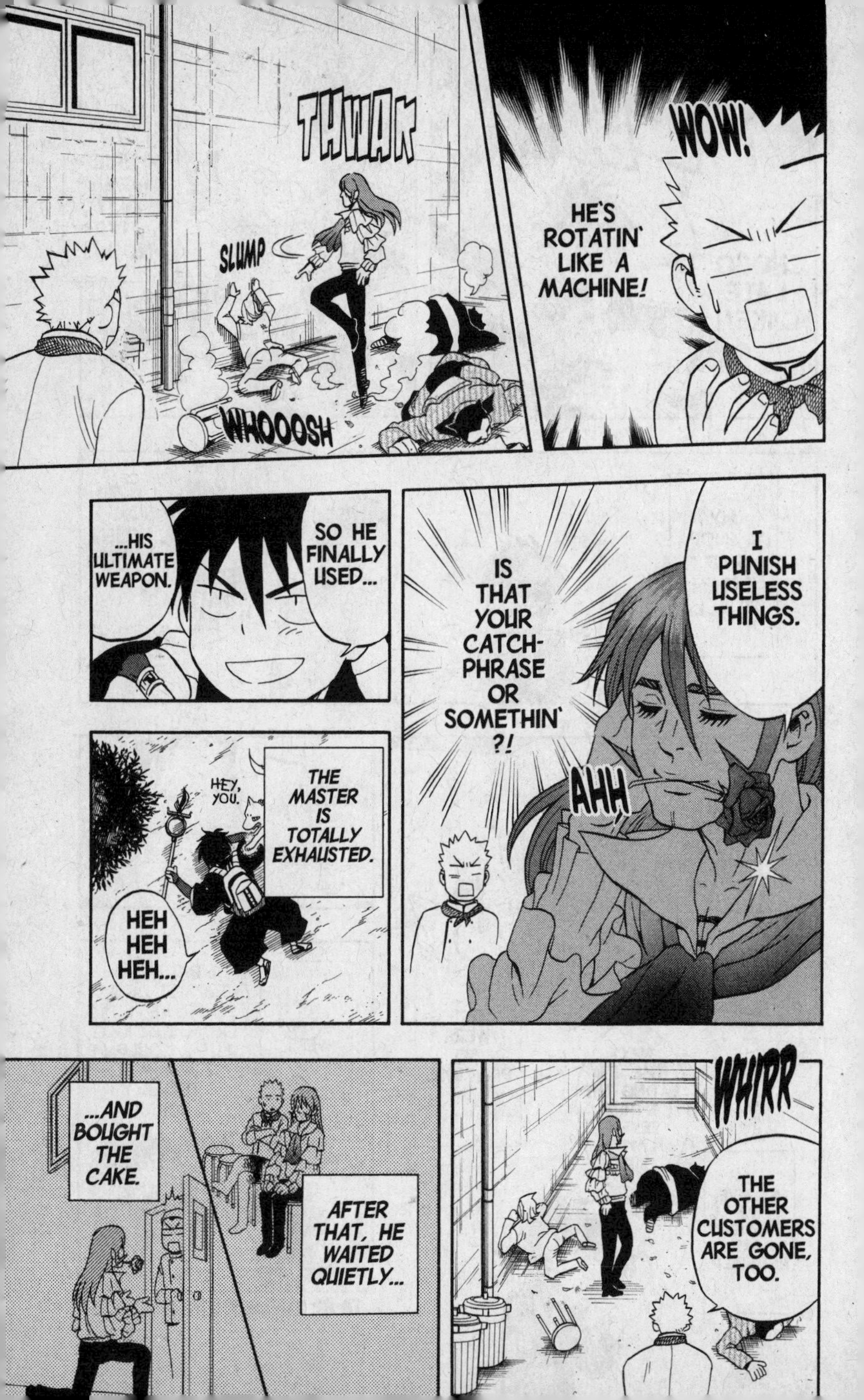
WOW!
HE'S ROTATIN' LIKE A MACHINE!
THWAK
SLUMP
WHOOOSH
I PUNISH USELESS THINGS.
IS THAT YOUR CATCH-PHRASE OR SOMETHIN' ?!
AHH
SO HE FINALLY USED...
...HIS ULTIMATE WEAPON.
THE MASTER IS TOTALLY EXHAUSTED.
HEY, YOU.
HEH HEH HEH...
WHIRR
THE OTHER CUSTOMERS ARE GONE, TOO.
AFTER THAT, HE WAITED QUIETLY...
...AND BOUGHT THE CAKE.

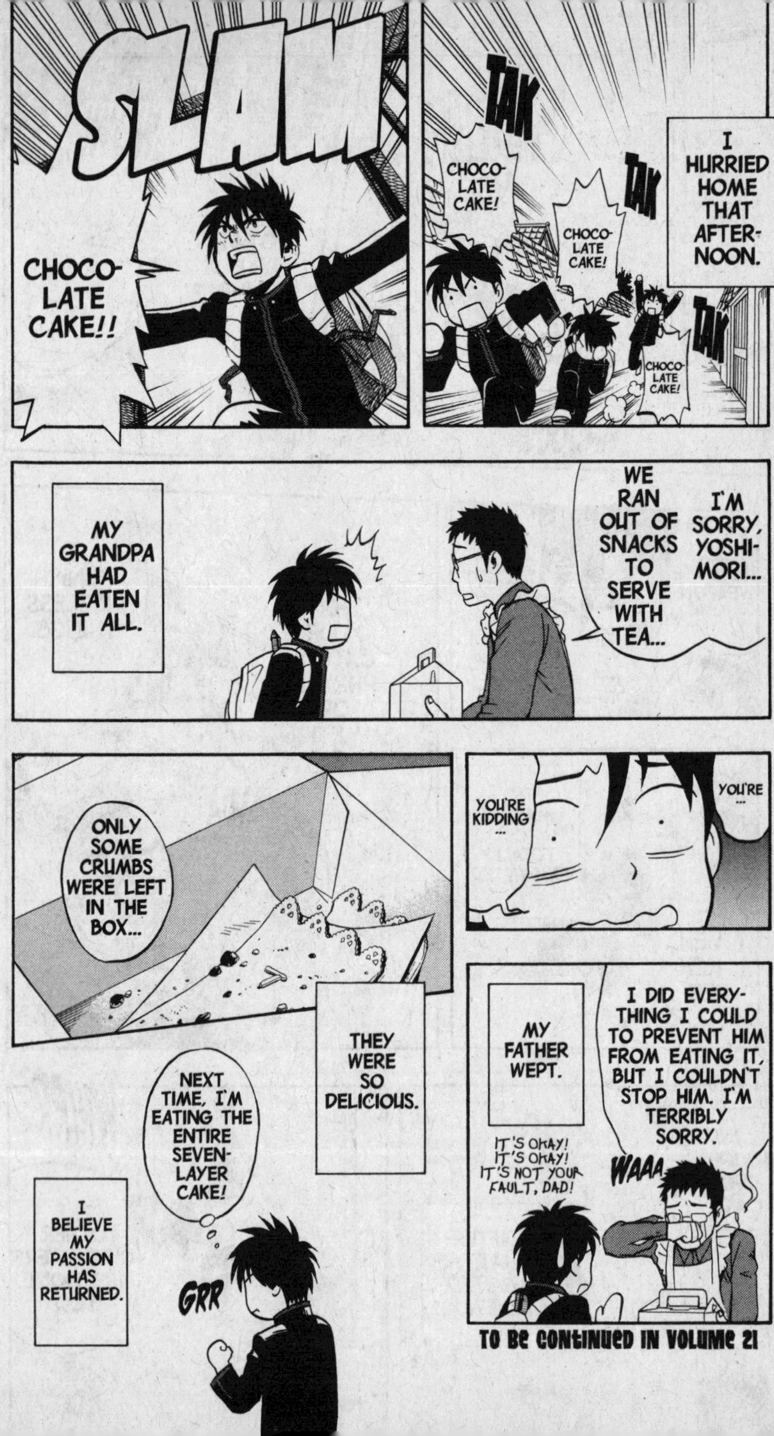
I HURRIED HOME THAT AFTER-NOON.
TAK
CHOCO-LATE CAKE!
TAK
CHOCO-LATE CAKE!
TAK
CHOCO-LATE CAKE!
SLAM
CHOCO-LATE CAKE!!
I'M SORRY, YOSHI-MORI...
WE RAN OUT OF SNACKS TO SERVE WITH TEA...
MY GRANDPA HAD EATEN IT ALL.
YOU'RE ...
YOU'RE KIDDING ...
ONLY SOME CRUMBS WERE LEFT IN THE BOX...
I DID EVERY-THING I COULD TO PREVENT HIM FROM EATING IT, BUT I COULDN'T STOP HIM. I'M TERRIBLY SORRY.
MY FATHER WEPT.
WAAA
IT'S OKAY! IT'S OKAY! IT'S NOT YOUR FAULT, DAD!
THEY WERE SO DELICIOUS.
NEXT TIME, I'M EATING THE ENTIRE SEVEN-LAYER CAKE!
GRR
I BELIEVE MY PASSION HAS RETURNED.

TO BE CONTINUED IN VOLUME 21

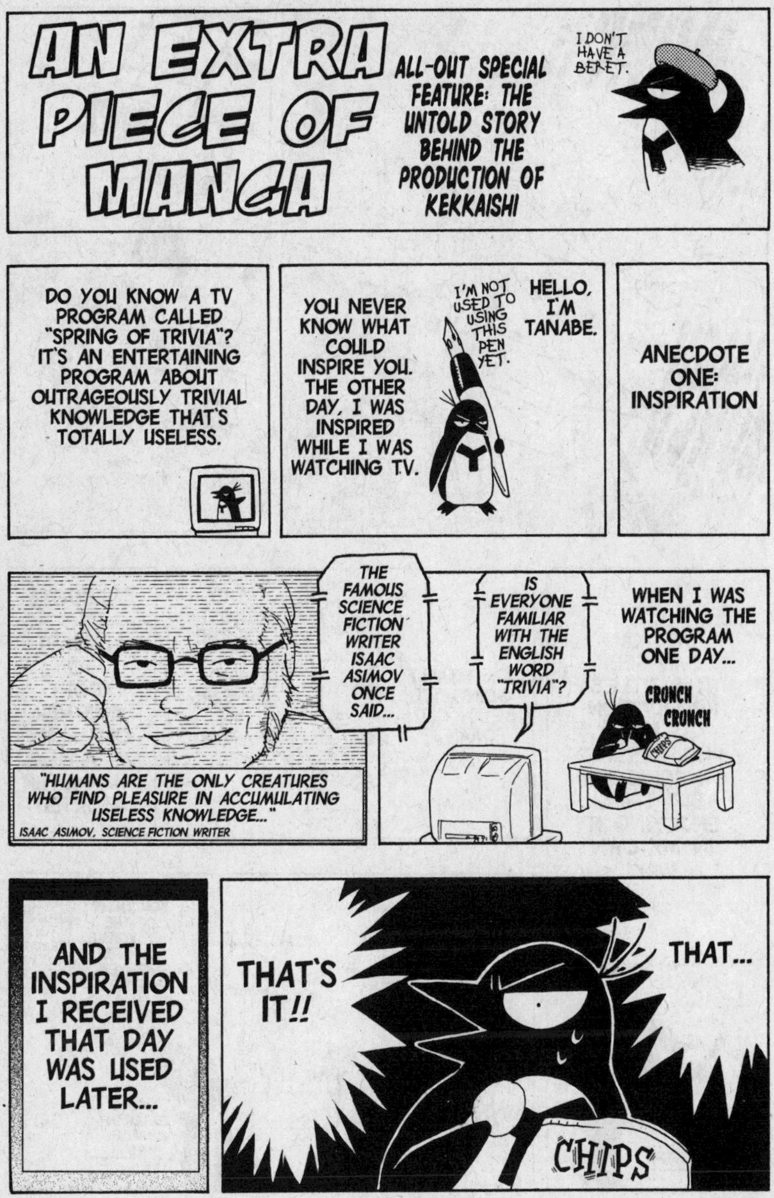
AN EXTRA PIECE OF MANGA
ALL-OUT SPECIAL FEATURE: THE UNTOLD STORY BEHIND THE PRODUCTION OF KEKKAISHI
I DON'T HAVE A BERET.
ANECDOTE ONE: INSPIRATION
HELLO, I'M TANABE.
I'M NOT USED TO USING THIS PEN YET.
YOU NEVER KNOW WHAT COULD INSPIRE YOU. THE OTHER DAY, I WAS INSPIRED WHILE I WAS WATCHING T.V.
DO YOU KNOW A TV PROGRAM CALLED "SPRING OF TRIVIA"? IT'S AN ENTERTAINING PROGRAM ABOUT OUTRAGEOUSLY TRIVIAL KNOWLEDGE THAT'S TOTALLY USELESS.
WHEN I WAS WATCHING THE PROGRAM ONE DAY...
CRUNCH
CRUNCH
CHIPS
IS EVERYONE FAMILIAR WITH THE ENGLISH WORD "TRIVIA"?
THE FAMOUS SCIENCE FICTION WRITER ISAAC ASIMOV ONCE SAID...
"HUMANS ARE THE ONLY CREATURES WHO FIND PLEASURE IN ACCUMULATING USELESS KNOWLEDGE..."
ISAAC ASIMOV, SCIENCE FICTION WRITER
THAT...
THAT'S IT!!
CHIPS
AND THE INSPIRATION I RECEIVED THAT DAY WAS USED LATER...

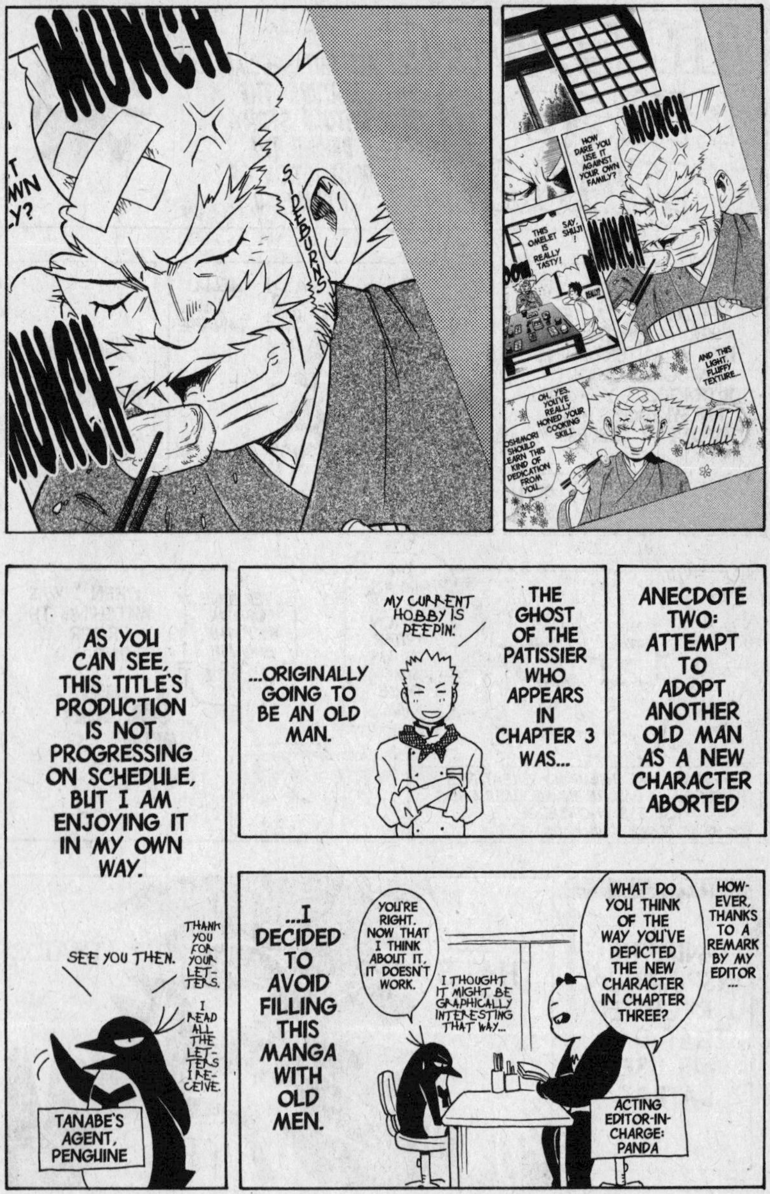
MUNCH
HOW DARE YOU USE IT AGAINST YOUR OWN FAMILY?
SAY, SHUJI!
THIS OMELET IS REALLY TASTY!
MUNCH
AND THIS LIGHT, FLUFFY TEXTURE...
OH, YES. YOU'VE REALLY HONED YOUR COOKING SKILL.
OSHIMORI SHOULD LEARN THIS KIND OF DEDICATION FROM YOU.
AAAH
MUNCH
SIDEBURNS
MUNCH
ANECDOTE TWO: ATTEMPT TO ADOPT ANOTHER OLD MAN AS A NEW CHARACTER ABORTED
THE GHOST OF THE PATISSIER WHO APPEARS IN CHAPTER 3 WAS...
MY CURRENT HOBBY IS PEEPIN'.
...ORIGINALLY GOING TO BE AN OLD MAN.
HOWEVER, THANKS TO A REMARK BY MY EDITOR...
WHAT DO YOU THINK OF THE WAY YOU'VE DEPICTED THE NEW CHARACTER IN CHAPTER THREE?
I THOUGHT IT MIGHT BE GRAPHICALLY INTERESTING THAT WAY...
YOU'RE RIGHT. NOW THAT I THINK ABOUT IT, IT DOESN'T WORK.
...I DECIDED TO AVOID FILLING THIS MANGA WITH OLD MEN.
ACTING EDITOR-IN-CHARGE: PANDA
AS YOU CAN SEE, THIS TITLE'S PRODUCTION IS NOT PROGRESSING ON SCHEDULE, BUT I AM ENJOYING IT IN MY OWN WAY.
THANK YOU FOR YOUR LETTERS. I READ ALL THE LETTERS I RECEIVE.
SEE YOU THEN.
TANABE'S AGENT, PENGUINE

I want
to be a
dashing
fellow.

Skating ← ♀

MESSAGE FROM YELLOW TANABE

When I was a kid, I didn't know the word
kekkai (protective ward), but my friends
and I used to play a game in which we
pretended that we could create invisible
walls. We'd declare, "I stretched the barrier
from here to there!" If someone stepped
into that barrier, ignoring a friend's
declaration, he'd be given the cold shoulder
as if he'd done something insensitive.
I feel it is far more difficult to undo a
kekkai, a barrier, than to create one.

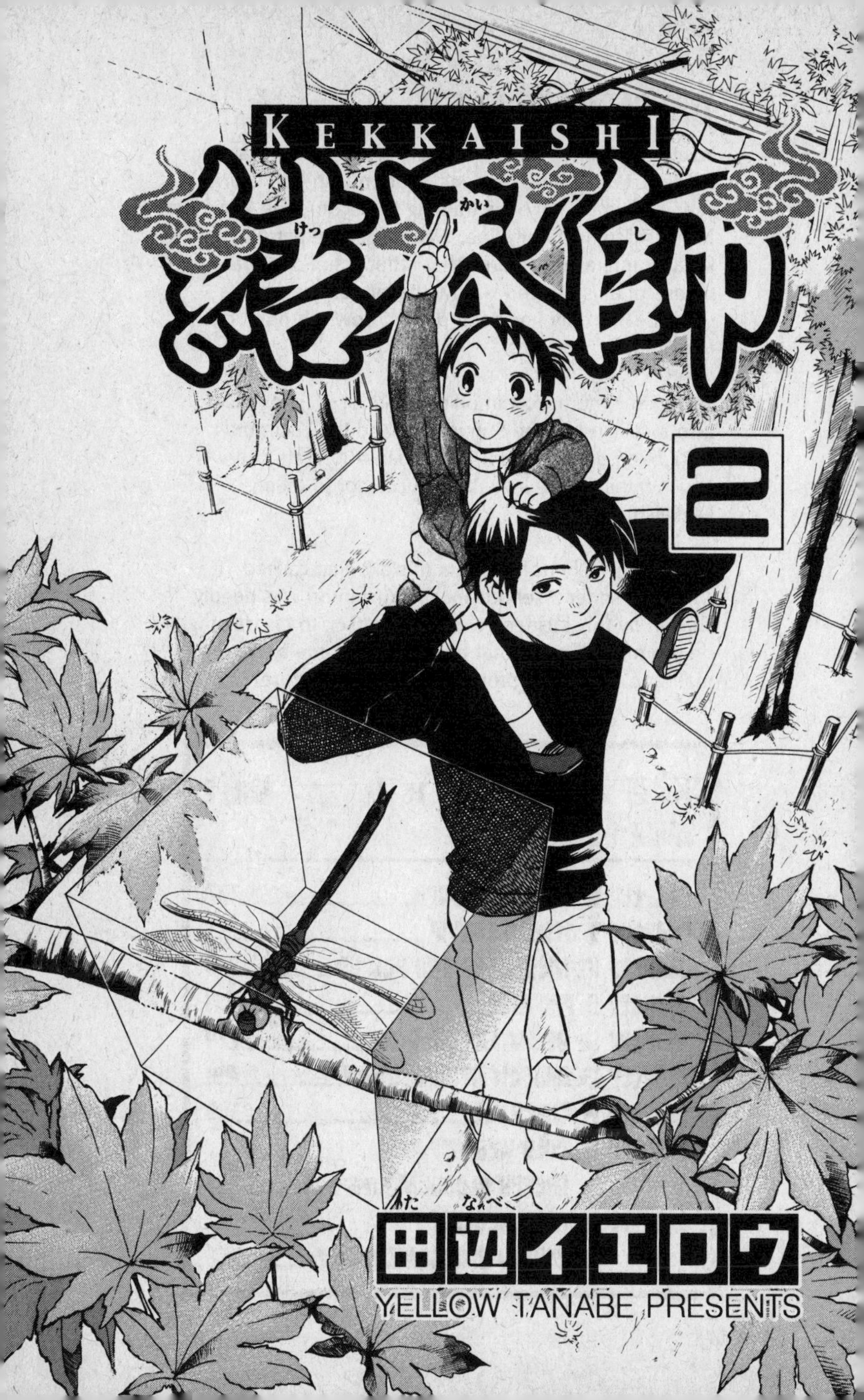
KEKKAISHI
結界師
2
田辺イエロウ
YELLOW TANABE PRESENTS

The Story Thus Far

Yoshimori Sumimura is a *kekkaishi*, or barrier master, an expert in fighting demons. Currently in his second year at junior high, he is training to become the 22nd kekkaishi in his family line. Each night, he patrols Karasumori, a cursed area that attracts supernatural beings of all sorts and is now the site of Yoshimori's school. This duty has been passed down through his family for generations.

Tokine Yukimura, Yoshimori's next-door neighbor, is also a kekkaishi. The Sumimuras and the Yukimuras have been quarreling for more than 400 years over which family is the legitimate successor to their kekkaishi school.

As a child, Yoshimori made a mistake that caused Tokine to suffer a serious injury. Yoshimori was deeply shaken by this incident. Devoting himself to his training, he promised himself that he would become a strong man and be able to protect Tokine in the future.

KEKKAISHI VOL. 2

TABLE OF CONTENTS

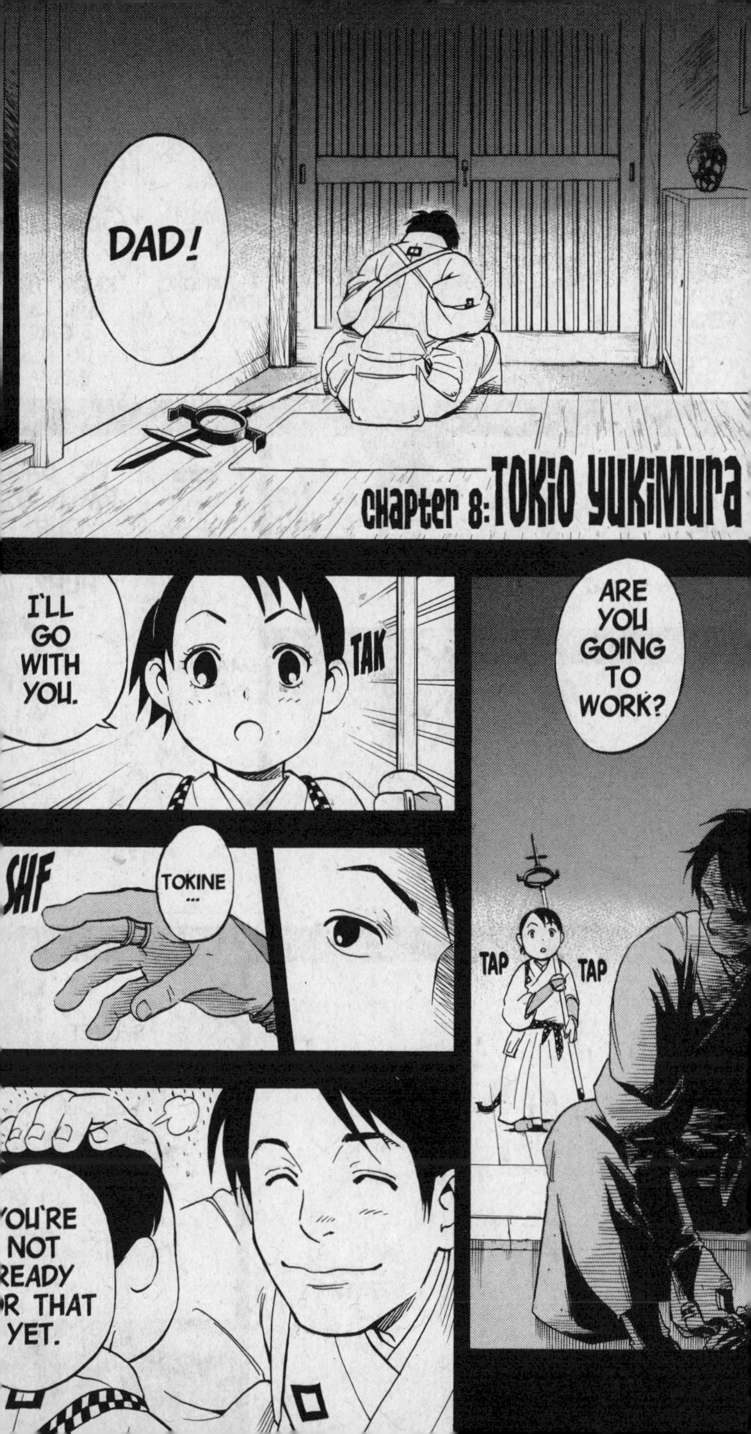
DAD!
Chapter 8: TOKIO YUKIMURA
ARE YOU GOING TO WORK?
TAP TAP
I'LL GO WITH YOU.
TAK
TOKINE...
SHF
YOU'RE NOT READY R THAT YET.

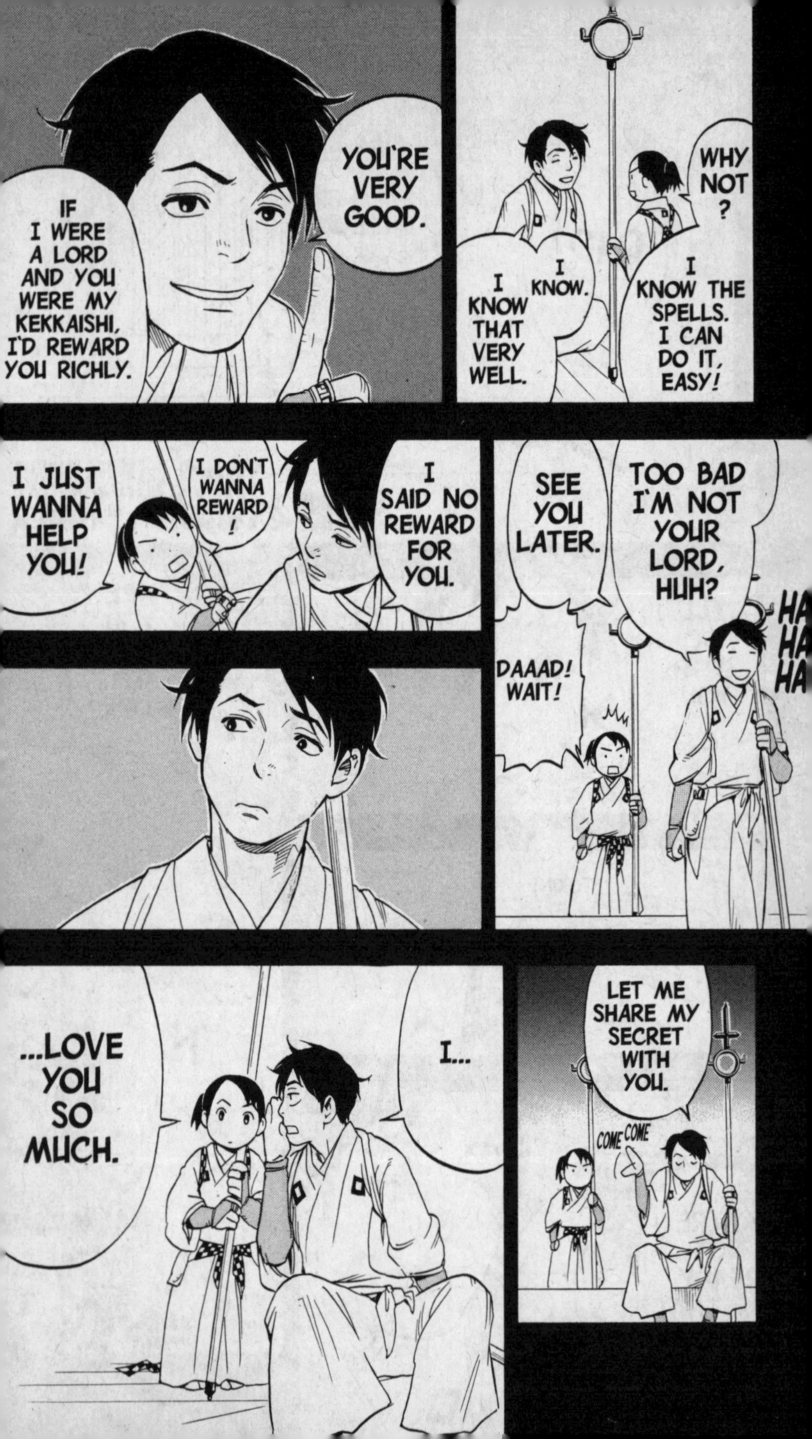
WHY NOT?
I KNOW THE SPELLS. I CAN DO IT, EASY!
I KNOW.
I KNOW THAT VERY WELL.
YOU'RE VERY GOOD.
IF I WERE A LORD AND YOU WERE MY KEKKAISHI, I'D REWARD YOU RICHLY.
TOO BAD I'M NOT YOUR LORD, HUH?
SEE YOU LATER.
HA HA HA
DAAAD! WAIT!
I SAID NO REWARD FOR YOU.
I DON'T WANNA REWARD!
I JUST WANNA HELP YOU!
LET ME SHARE MY SECRET WITH YOU.
COME COME
I...
...LOVE YOU SO MUCH.

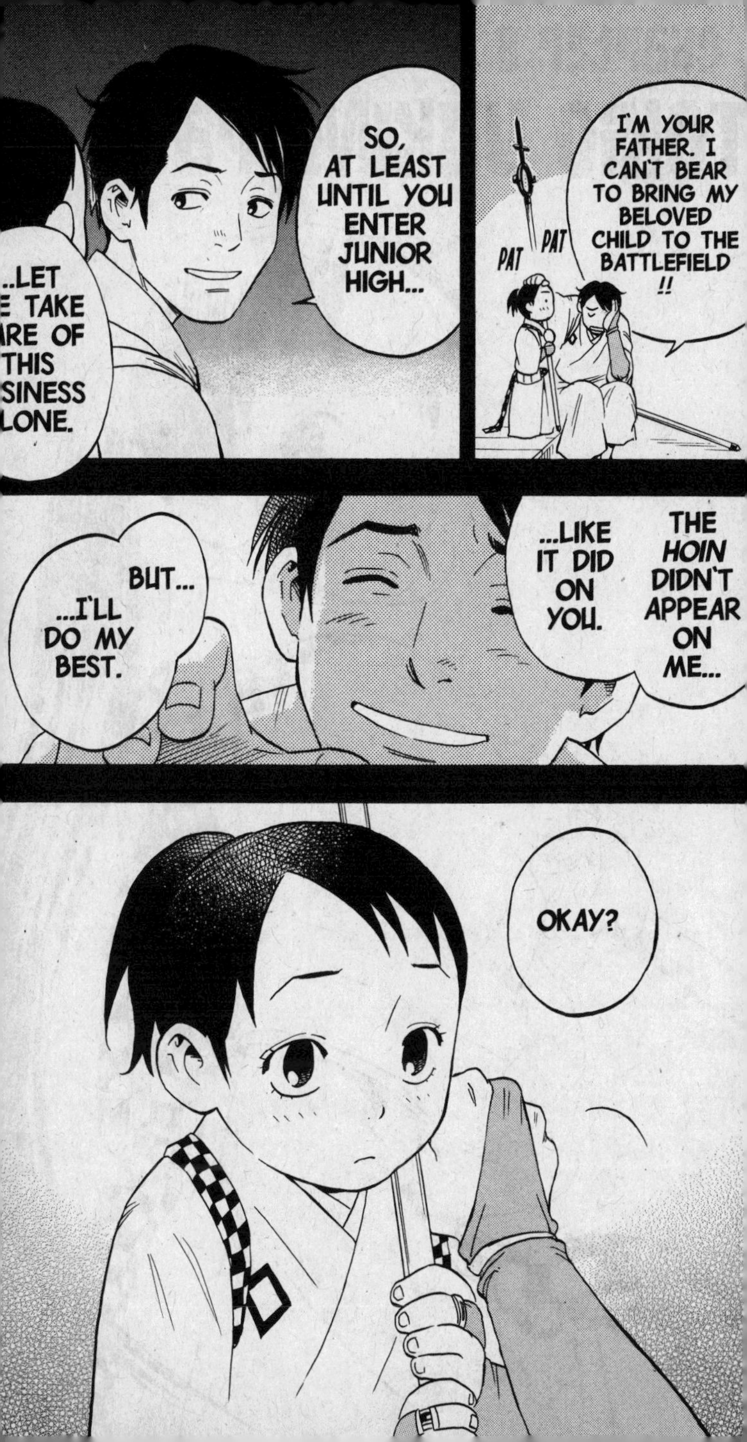
I'M YOUR FATHER. I CAN'T BEAR TO BRING MY BELOVED CHILD TO THE BATTLEFIELD !!
PAT PAT
SO, AT LEAST UNTIL YOU ENTER JUNIOR HIGH...
..LET E TAKE RE OF THIS SINESS LONE.
THE *HOIN* DIDN'T APPEAR ON ME...
...LIKE IT DID ON YOU.
BUT... ...I'LL DO MY BEST.
OKAY?

Chapter 8: Tokio Yukimura

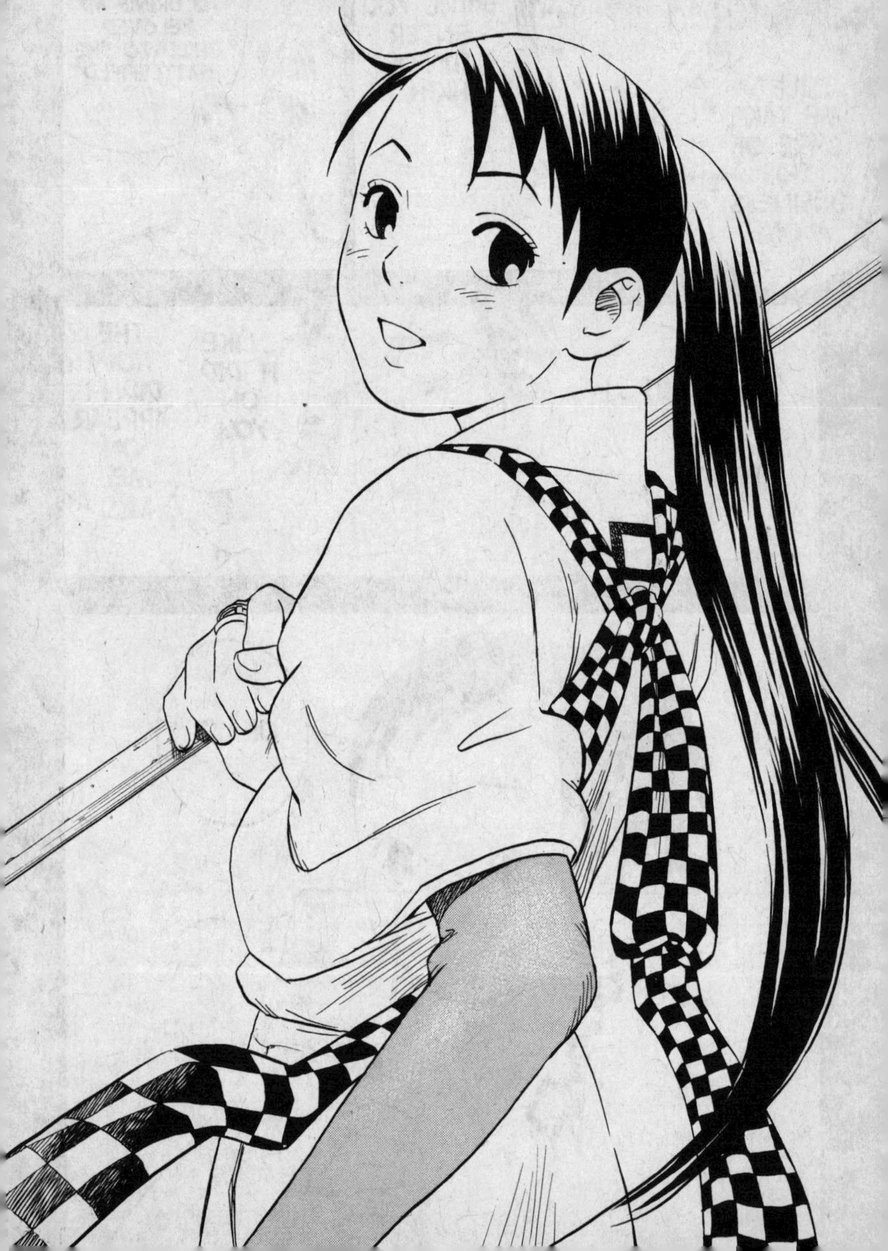

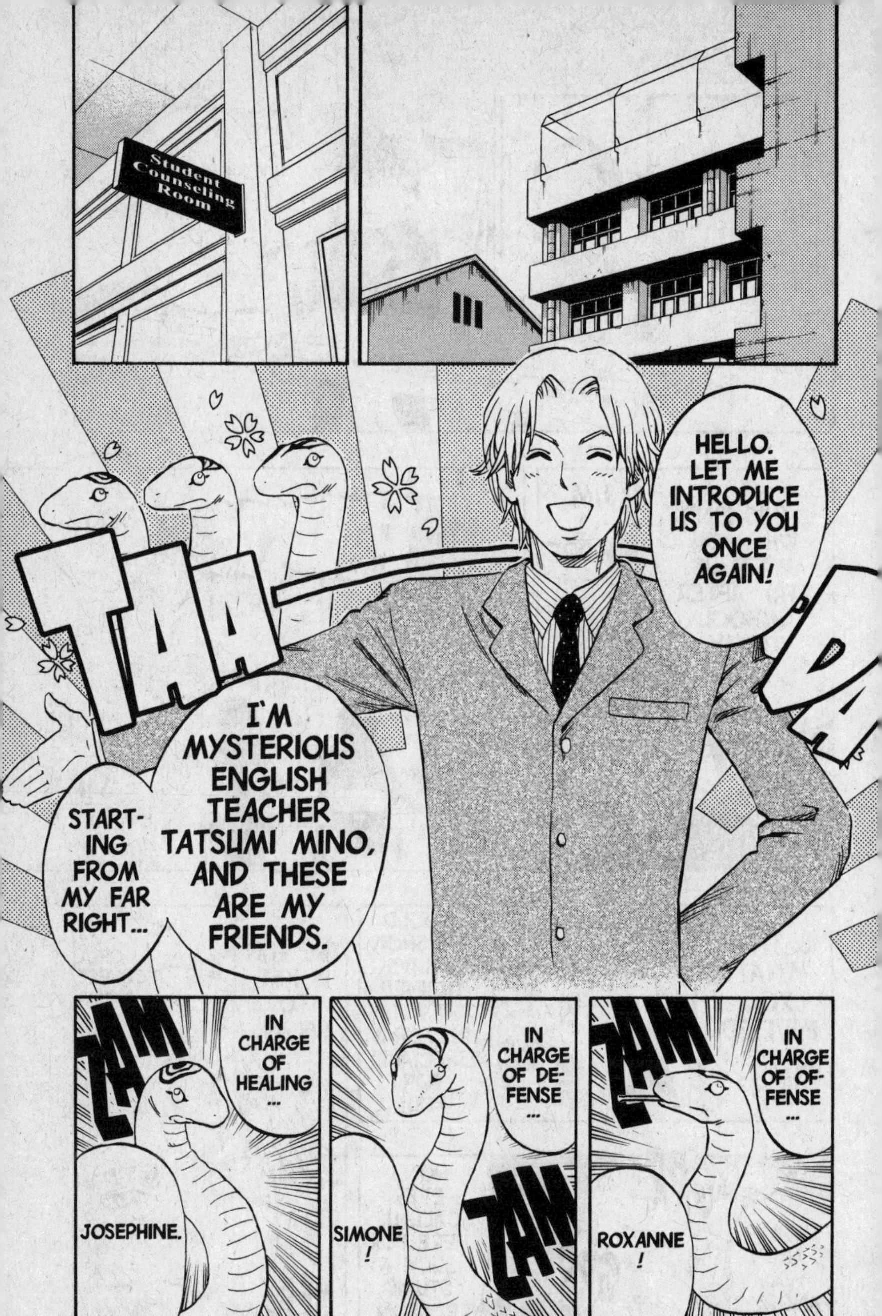
Student Counseling Room
HELLO. LET ME INTRODUCE US TO YOU ONCE AGAIN!
TAA
DA
I'M MYSTERIOUS ENGLISH TEACHER TATSUMI MINO, AND THESE ARE MY FRIENDS.
STARTING FROM MY FAR RIGHT...
IN CHARGE OF OFFENSE...
ROXANNE!
ZAM
IN CHARGE OF DEFENSE...
SIMONE!
ZAM
IN CHARGE OF HEALING...
JOSEPHINE.
ZAM

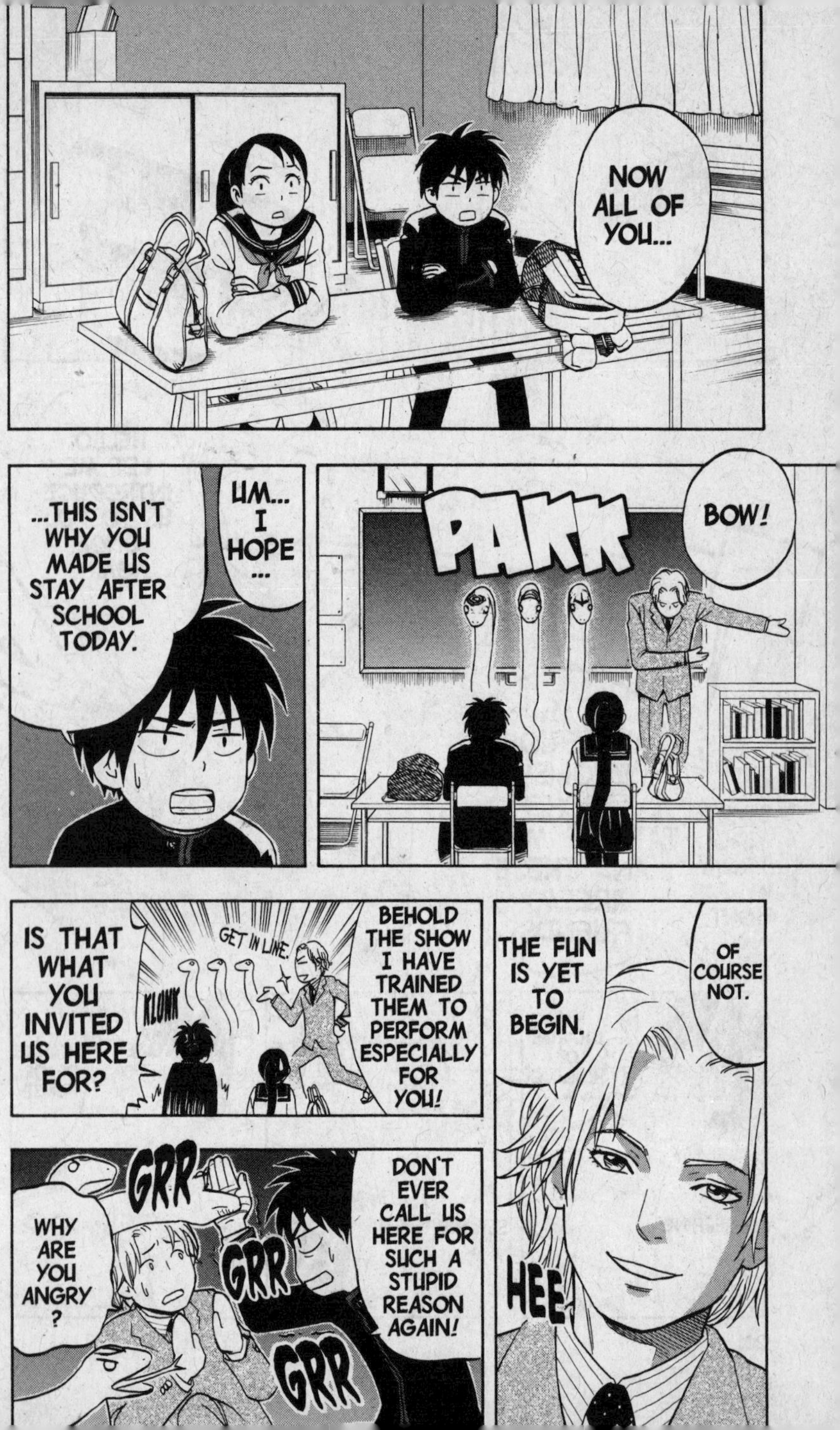
NOW ALL OF YOU...
BOW!
PAKK
UM... I HOPE ...
...THIS ISN'T WHY YOU MADE US STAY AFTER SCHOOL TODAY.
OF COURSE NOT.
THE FUN IS YET TO BEGIN.
HEE
BEHOLD THE SHOW I HAVE TRAINED THEM TO PERFORM ESPECIALLY FOR YOU!
GET IN LINE.
KLUNK
IS THAT WHAT YOU INVITED US HERE FOR?
DON'T EVER CALL US HERE FOR SUCH A STUPID REASON AGAIN!
GRR
GRR
GRR
WHY ARE YOU ANGRY ?

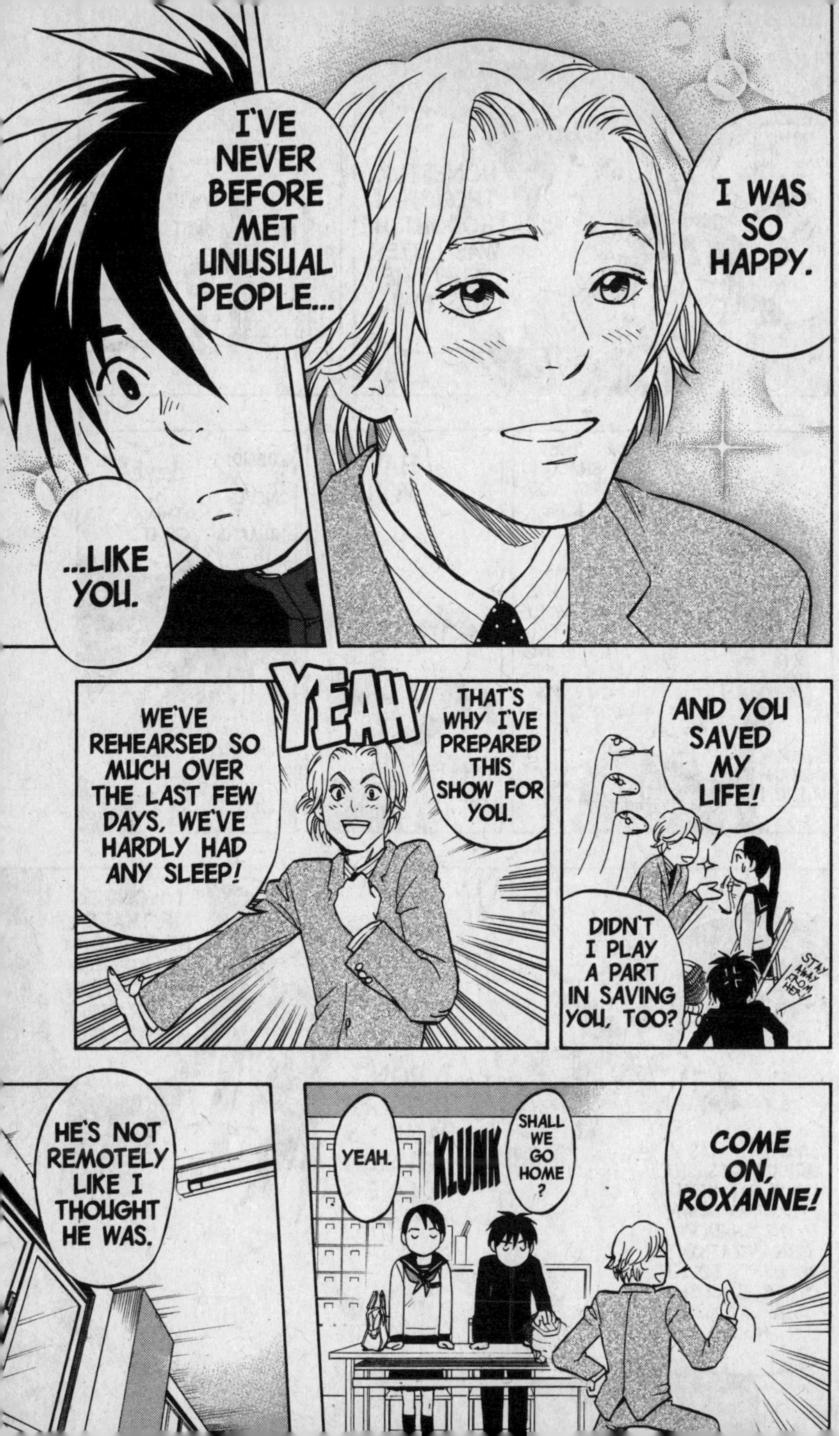
I WAS SO HAPPY.
I'VE NEVER BEFORE MET UNUSUAL PEOPLE...
...LIKE YOU.
AND YOU SAVED MY LIFE!
DIDN'T I PLAY A PART IN SAVING YOU, TOO?
STAY AWAY FROM HER!
YEAH
THAT'S WHY I'VE PREPARED THIS SHOW FOR YOU.
WE'VE REHEARSED SO MUCH OVER THE LAST FEW DAYS, WE'VE HARDLY HAD ANY SLEEP!
COME ON, ROXANNE!
SHALL WE GO HOME?
KLUNK
YEAH.
HE'S NOT REMOTELY LIKE I THOUGHT HE WAS.

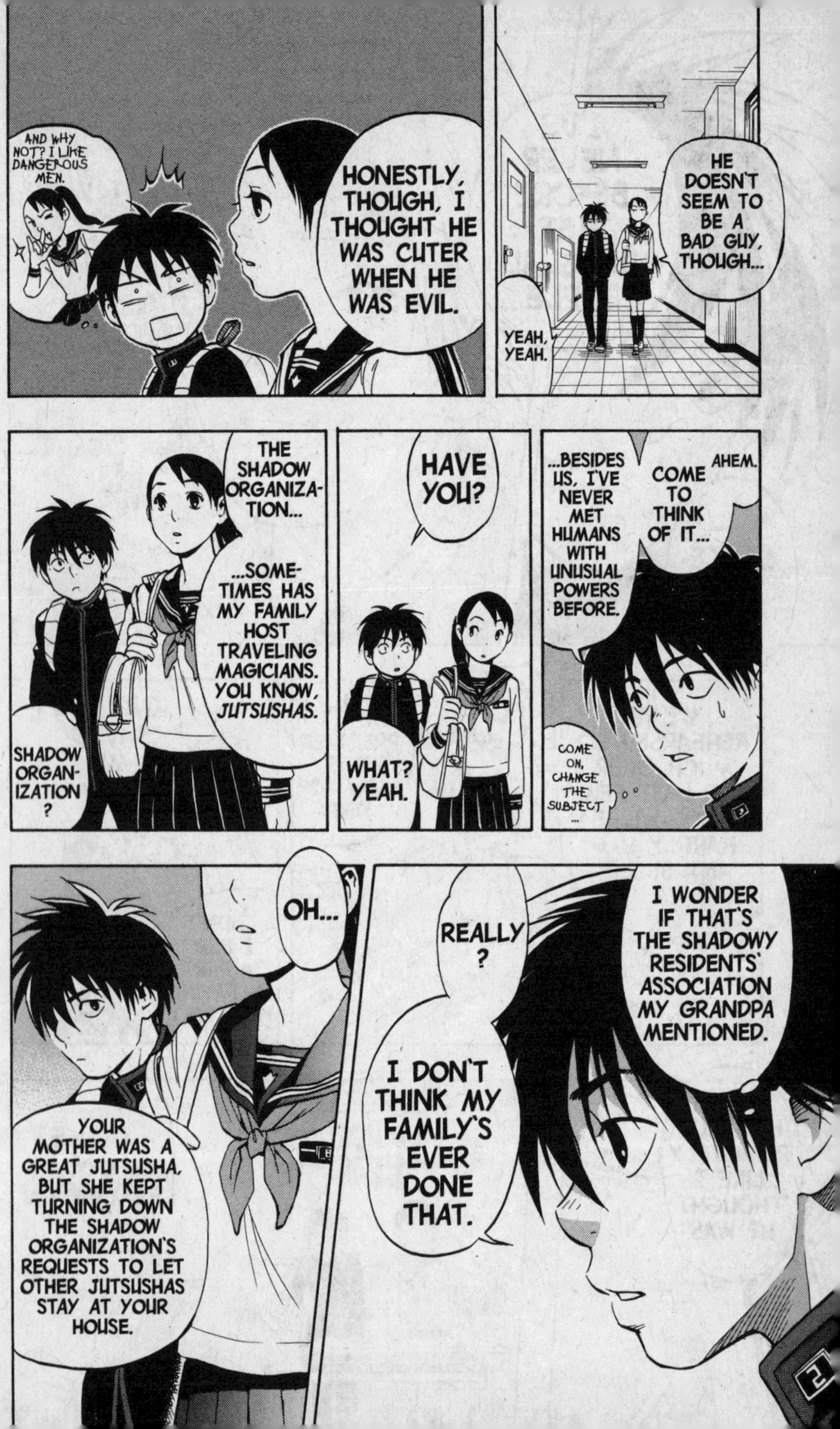
HE DOESN'T SEEM TO BE A BAD GUY, THOUGH...
YEAH, YEAH.
HONESTLY, THOUGH, I THOUGHT HE WAS CUTER WHEN HE WAS EVIL.
AND WHY NOT? I LIKE DANGEROUS MEN.
AHEM.
COME TO THINK OF IT...
...BESIDES US, I'VE NEVER MET HUMANS WITH UNUSUAL POWERS BEFORE.
COME ON, CHANGE THE SUBJECT ...
HAVE YOU?
WHAT? YEAH.
THE SHADOW ORGANIZATION...
...SOMETIMES HAS MY FAMILY HOST TRAVELING MAGICIANS. YOU KNOW, JUTSUSHAS.
SHADOW ORGANIZATION?
I WONDER IF THAT'S THE SHADOWY RESIDENTS' ASSOCIATION MY GRANDPA MENTIONED.
REALLY?
I DON'T THINK MY FAMILY'S EVER DONE THAT.
OH...
YOUR MOTHER WAS A GREAT JUTSUSHA, BUT SHE KEPT TURNING DOWN THE SHADOW ORGANIZATION'S REQUESTS TO LET OTHER JUTSUSHAS STAY AT YOUR HOUSE.

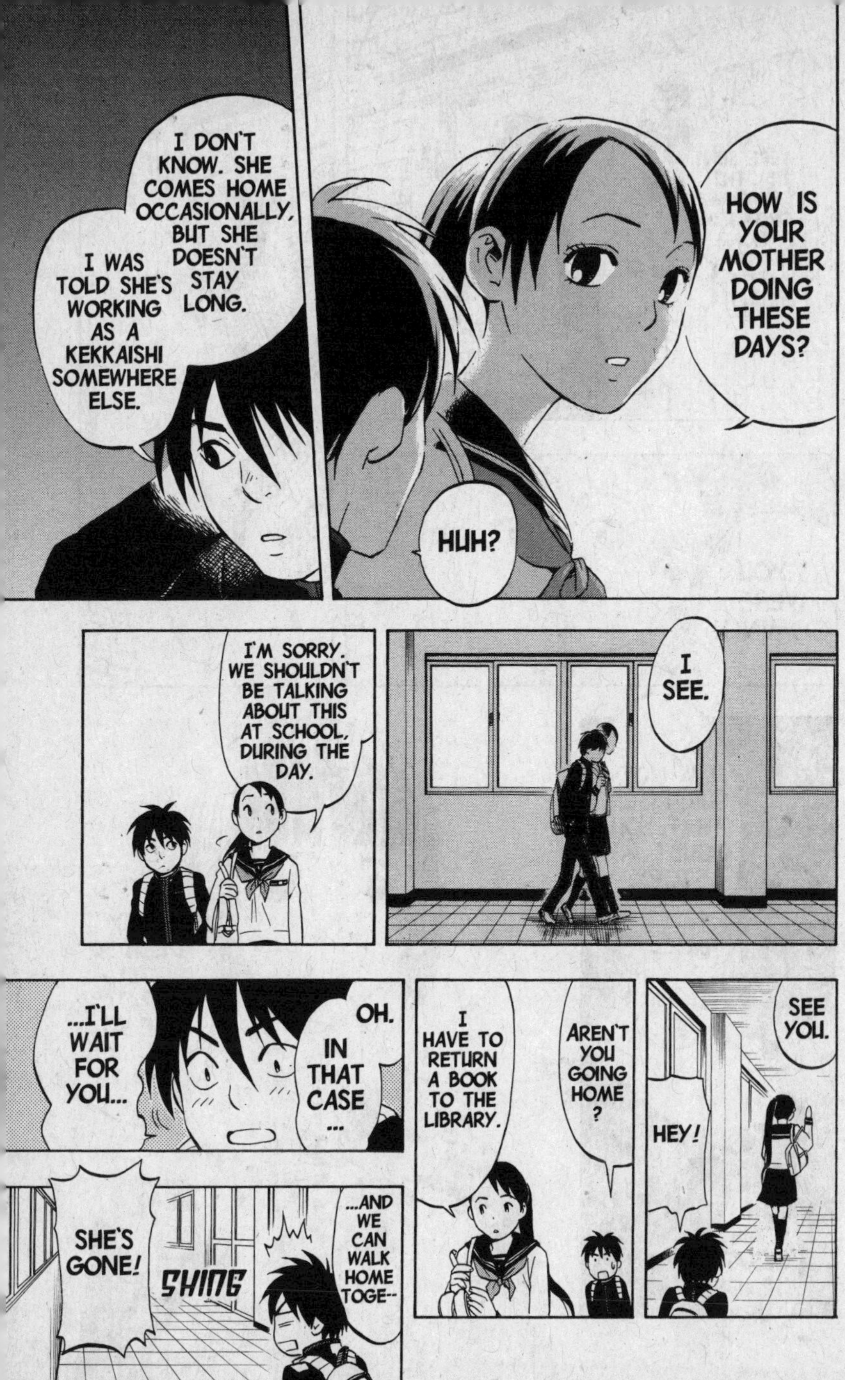
HOW IS YOUR MOTHER DOING THESE DAYS?
HUH?
I DON'T KNOW. SHE COMES HOME OCCASIONALLY, BUT SHE DOESN'T STAY LONG.
I WAS TOLD SHE'S WORKING AS A KEKKAISHI SOMEWHERE ELSE.
I SEE.
I'M SORRY. WE SHOULDN'T BE TALKING ABOUT THIS AT SCHOOL, DURING THE DAY.
SEE YOU.
HEY!
AREN'T YOU GOING HOME?
I HAVE TO RETURN A BOOK TO THE LIBRARY.
OH. IN THAT CASE...
...I'LL WAIT FOR YOU...
...AND WE CAN WALK HOME TOGE--
SHING
SHE'S GONE!

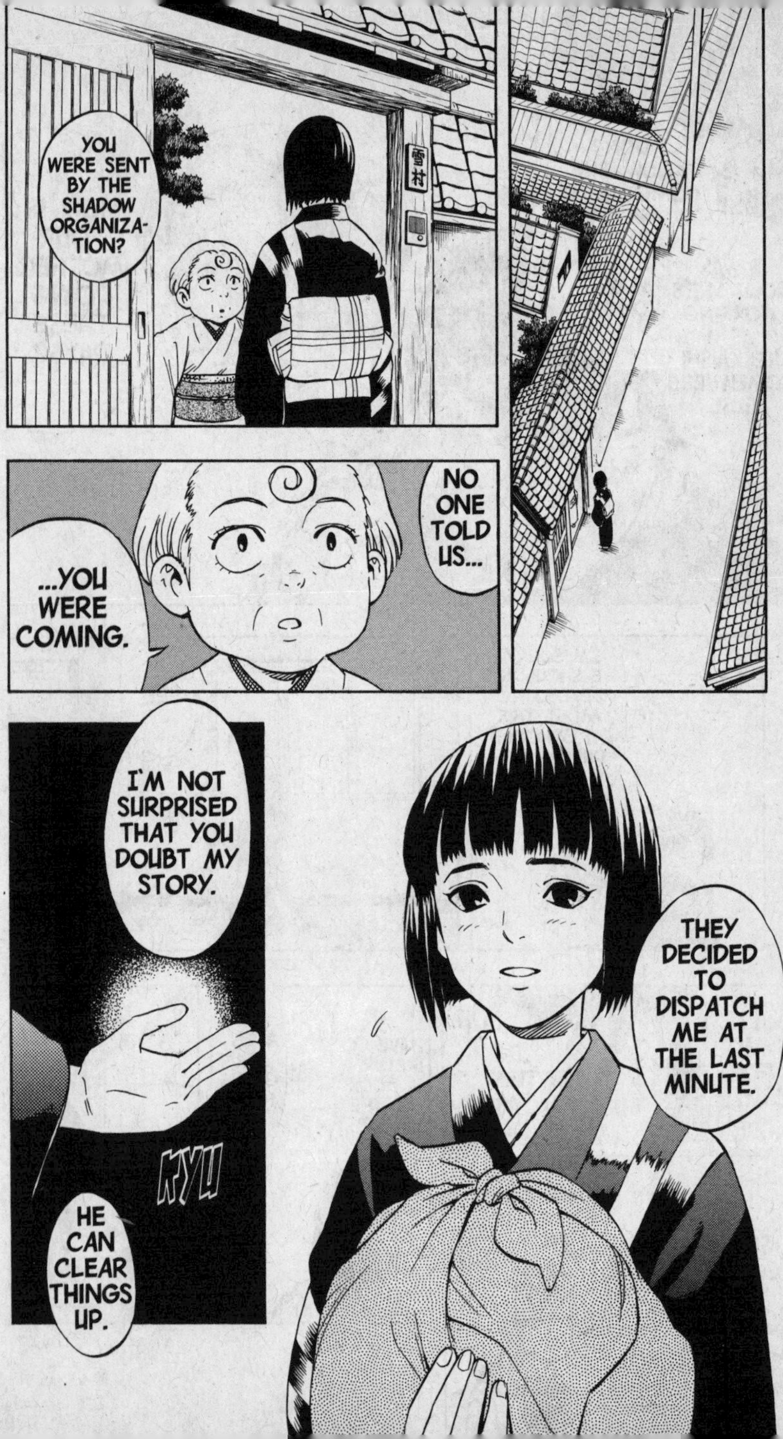
雪村
YOU WERE SENT BY THE SHADOW ORGANIZATION?
NO ONE TOLD US...
...YOU WERE COMING.
THEY DECIDED TO DISPATCH ME AT THE LAST MINUTE.
I'M NOT SURPRISED THAT YOU DOUBT MY STORY.
KYU
HE CAN CLEAR THINGS UP.

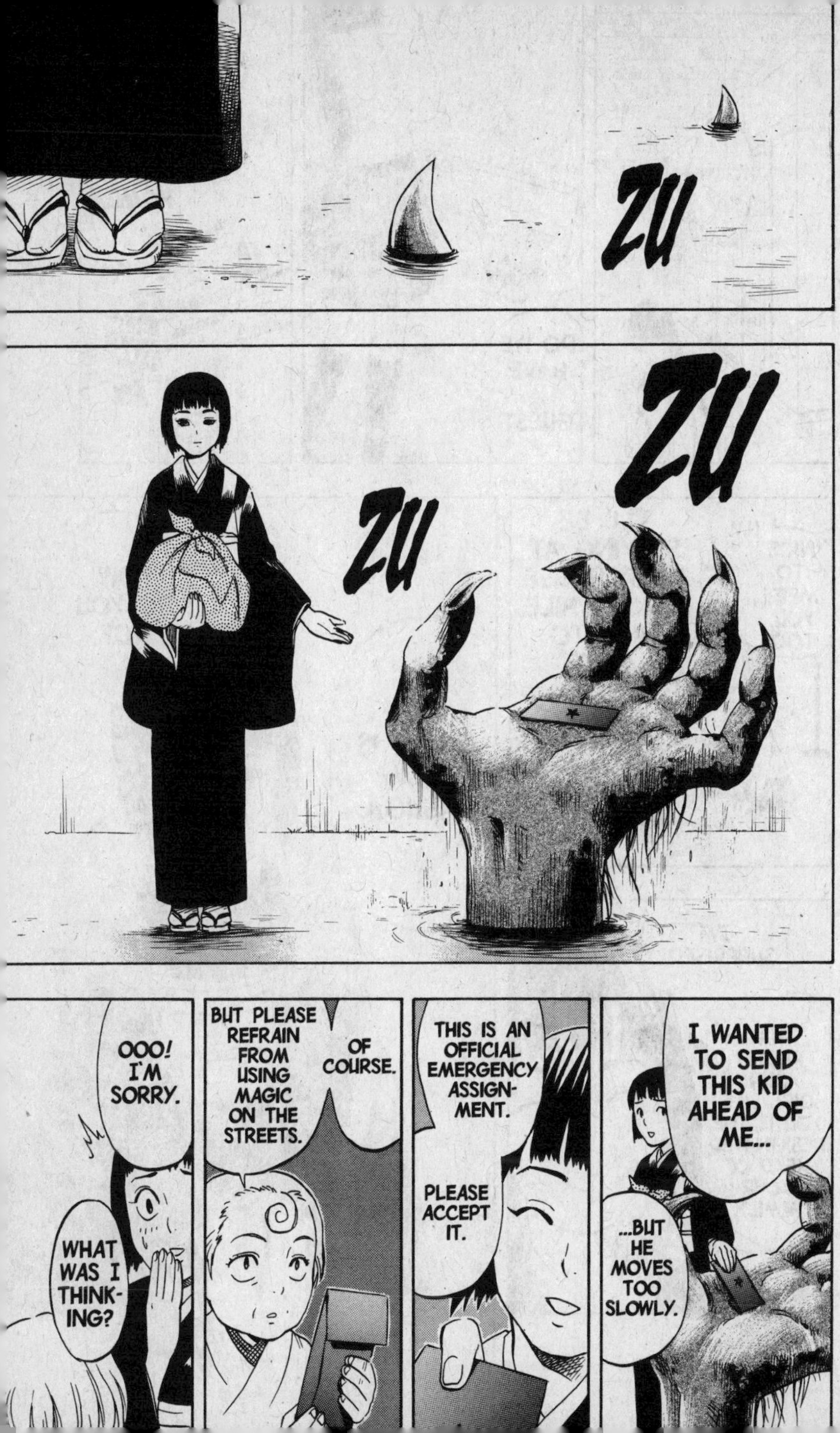
ZU
ZU
ZU
I WANTED TO SEND THIS KID AHEAD OF ME...
...BUT HE MOVES TOO SLOWLY.
THIS IS AN OFFICIAL EMERGENCY ASSIGN-MENT.
PLEASE ACCEPT IT.
OF COURSE.
BUT PLEASE REFRAIN FROM USING MAGIC ON THE STREETS.
OOO! I'M SORRY.
WHAT WAS I THINK-ING?

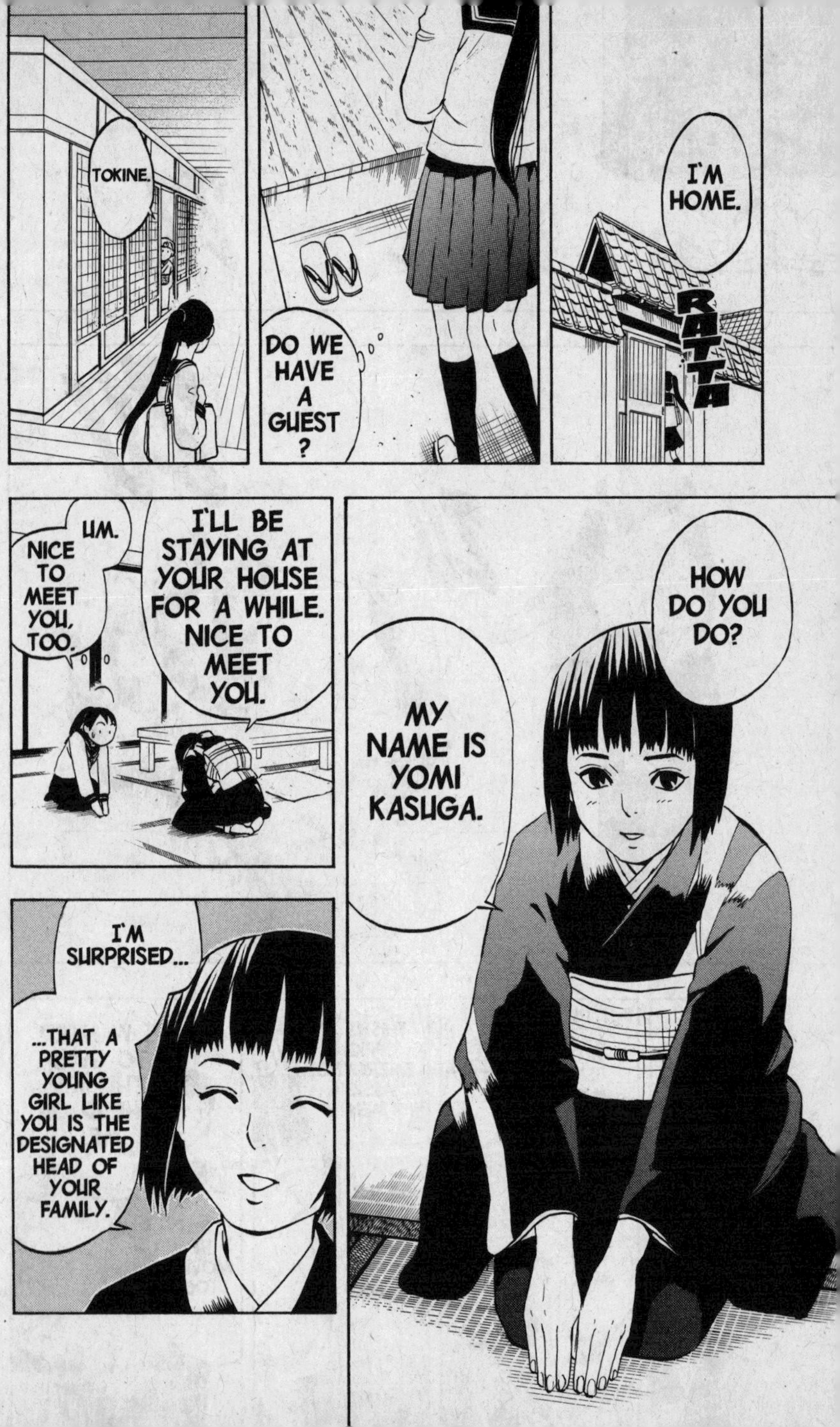
I'M HOME.
RATTA
DO WE HAVE A GUEST?
TOKINE.
HOW DO YOU DO?
MY NAME IS YOMI KASUGA.
I'LL BE STAYING AT YOUR HOUSE FOR A WHILE. NICE TO MEET YOU.
UM.
NICE TO MEET YOU, TOO.
I'M SURPRISED...
...THAT A PRETTY YOUNG GIRL LIKE YOU IS THE DESIGNATED HEAD OF YOUR FAMILY.

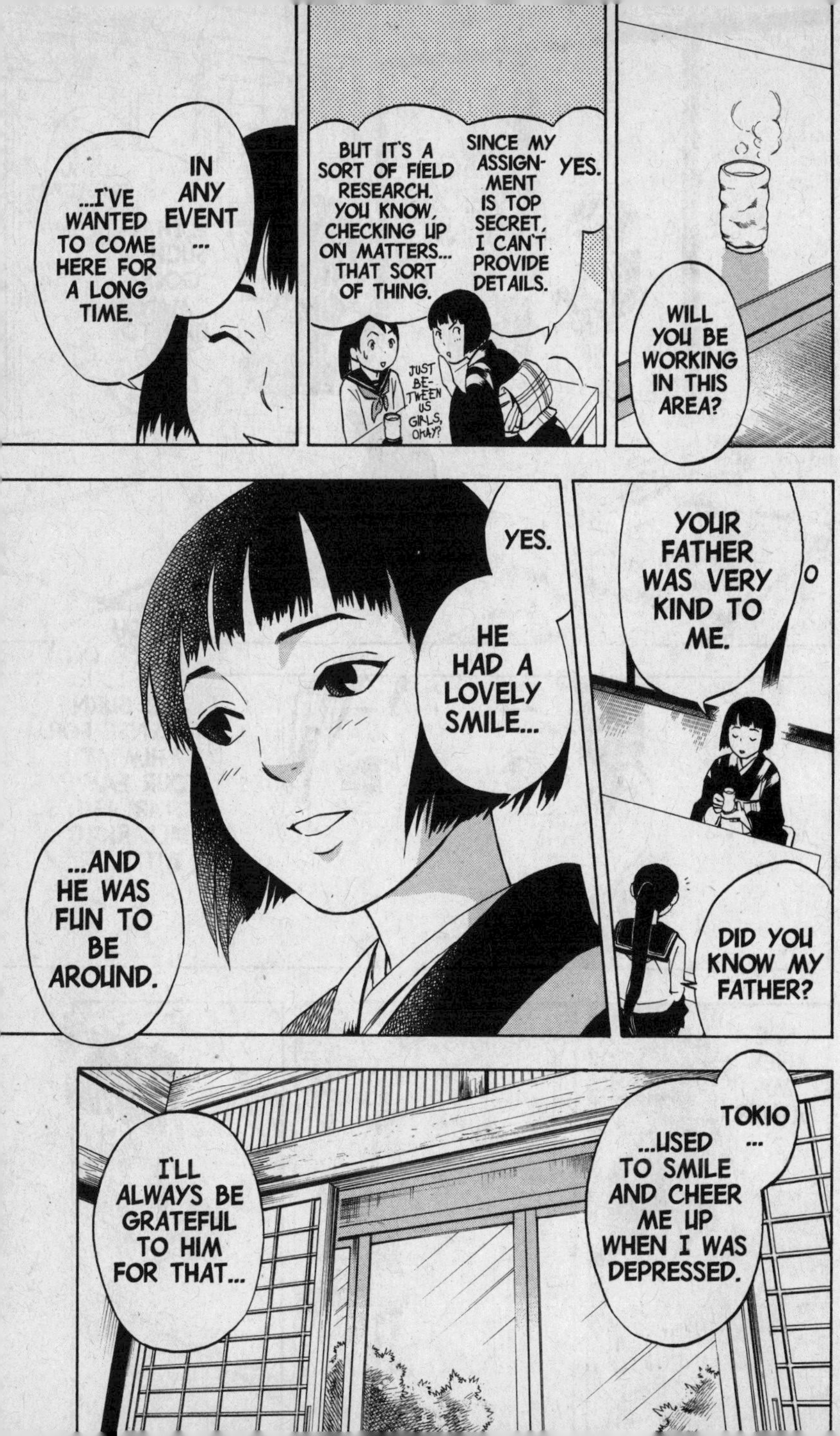
WILL YOU BE WORKING IN THIS AREA?
YES.
SINCE MY ASSIGN-MENT IS TOP SECRET, I CAN'T PROVIDE DETAILS.
BUT IT'S A SORT OF FIELD RESEARCH. YOU KNOW, CHECKING UP ON MATTERS... THAT SORT OF THING.
JUST BE-TWEEN US GIRLS, OKAY?
IN ANY EVENT...
...I'VE WANTED TO COME HERE FOR A LONG TIME.
YOUR FATHER WAS VERY KIND TO ME.
DID YOU KNOW MY FATHER?
YES.
HE HAD A LOVELY SMILE...
...AND HE WAS FUN TO BE AROUND.
TOKIO...
...USED TO SMILE AND CHEER ME UP WHEN I WAS DEPRESSED.
I'LL ALWAYS BE GRATEFUL TO HIM FOR THAT...

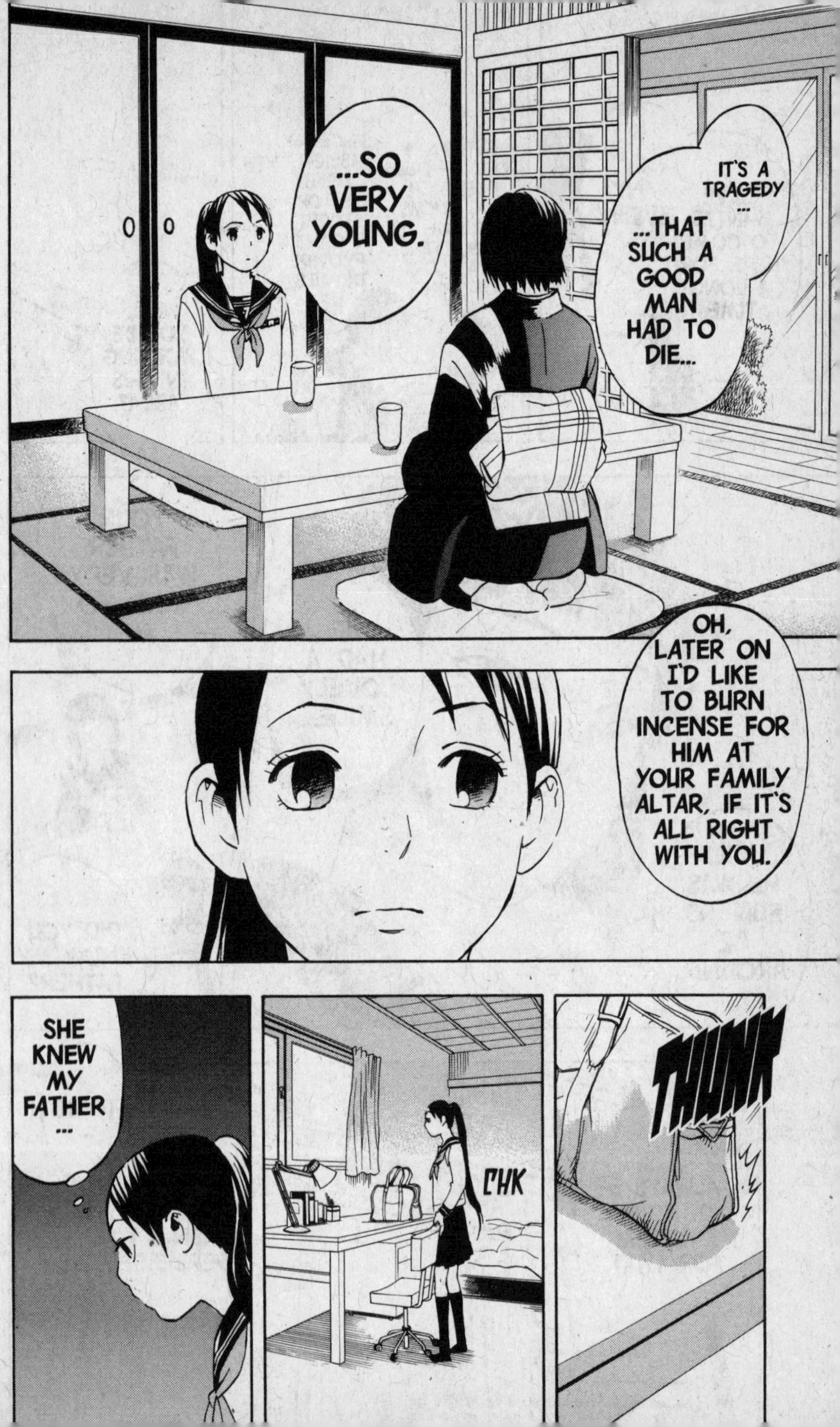
IT'S A TRAGEDY... ...THAT SUCH A GOOD MAN HAD TO DIE...
...SO VERY YOUNG.
OH, LATER ON I'D LIKE TO BURN INCENSE FOR HIM AT YOUR FAMILY ALTAR, IF IT'S ALL RIGHT WITH YOU.
THUNK
CHK
SHE KNEW MY FATHER...

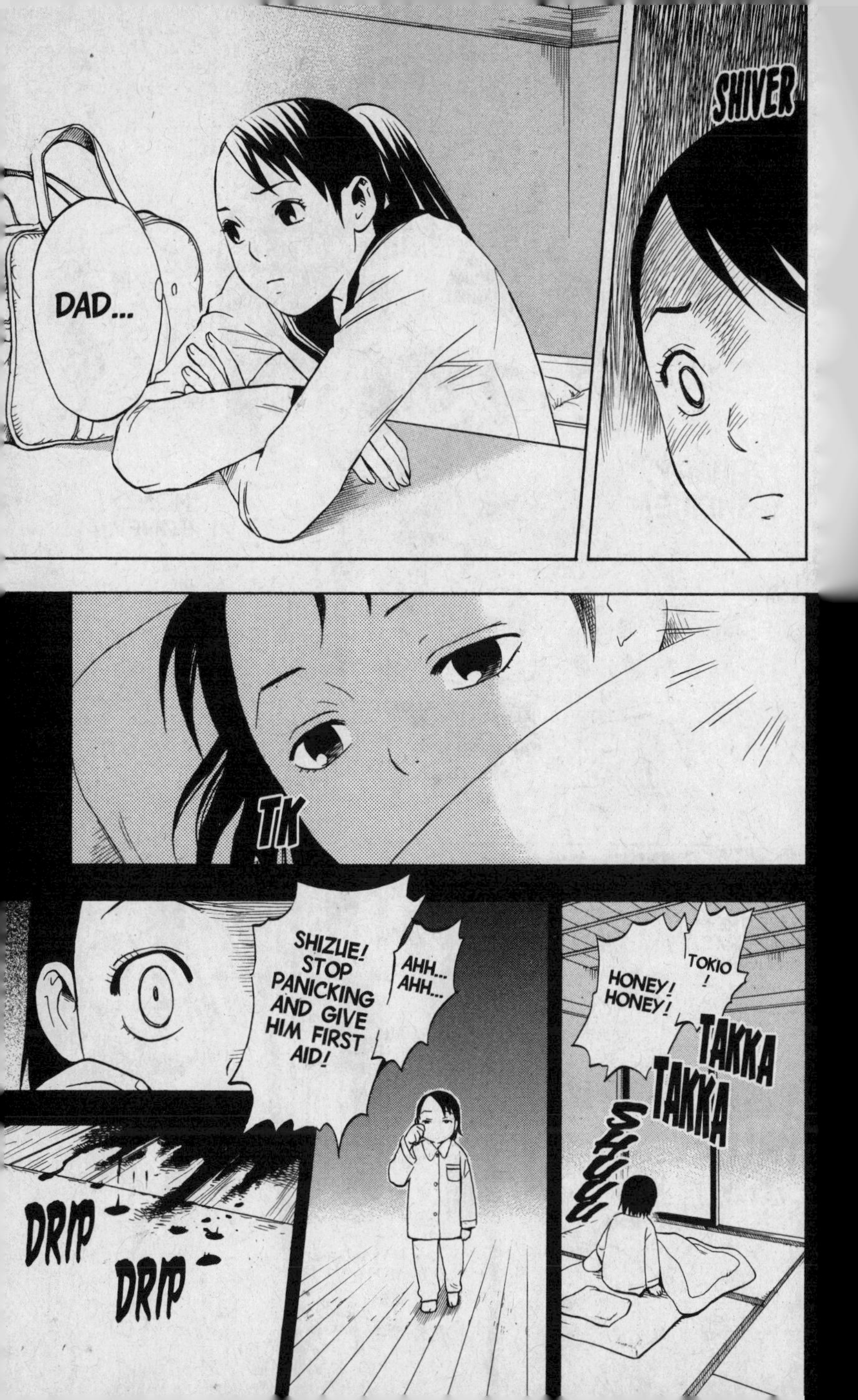
SHIVER
DAD...
TK
TOKIO!
HONEY! HONEY!
TAKKA TAKKA
SHUUU
AHH... AHH...
SHIZUE! STOP PANICKING AND GIVE HIM FIRST AID!
DRIP
DRIP

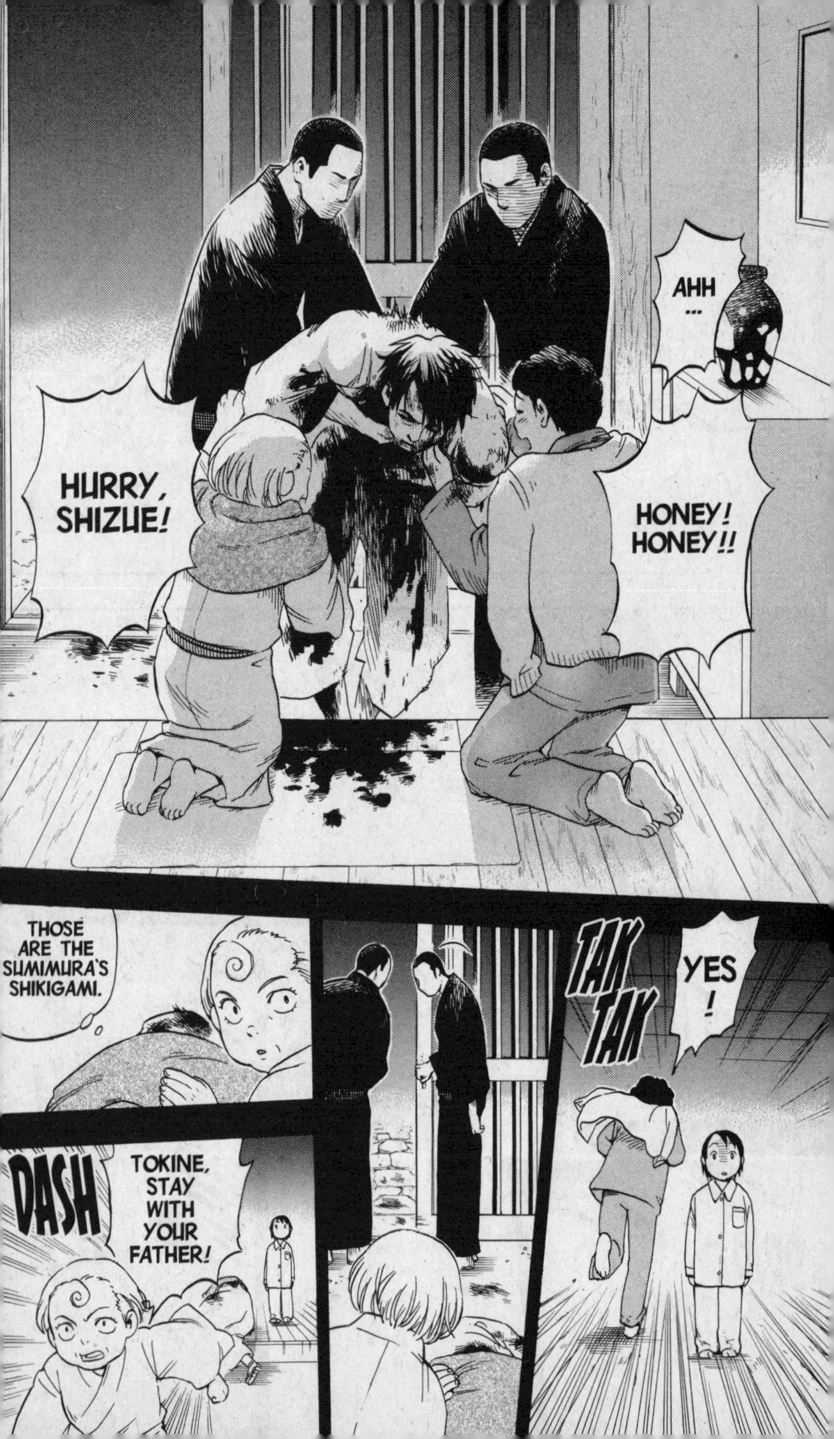
AHH ...
HONEY! HONEY!!
HURRY, SHIZUE!
TAK TAK
YES!
THOSE ARE THE SUMIMURA'S SHIKIGAMI.
DASH
TOKINE, STAY WITH YOUR FATHER!

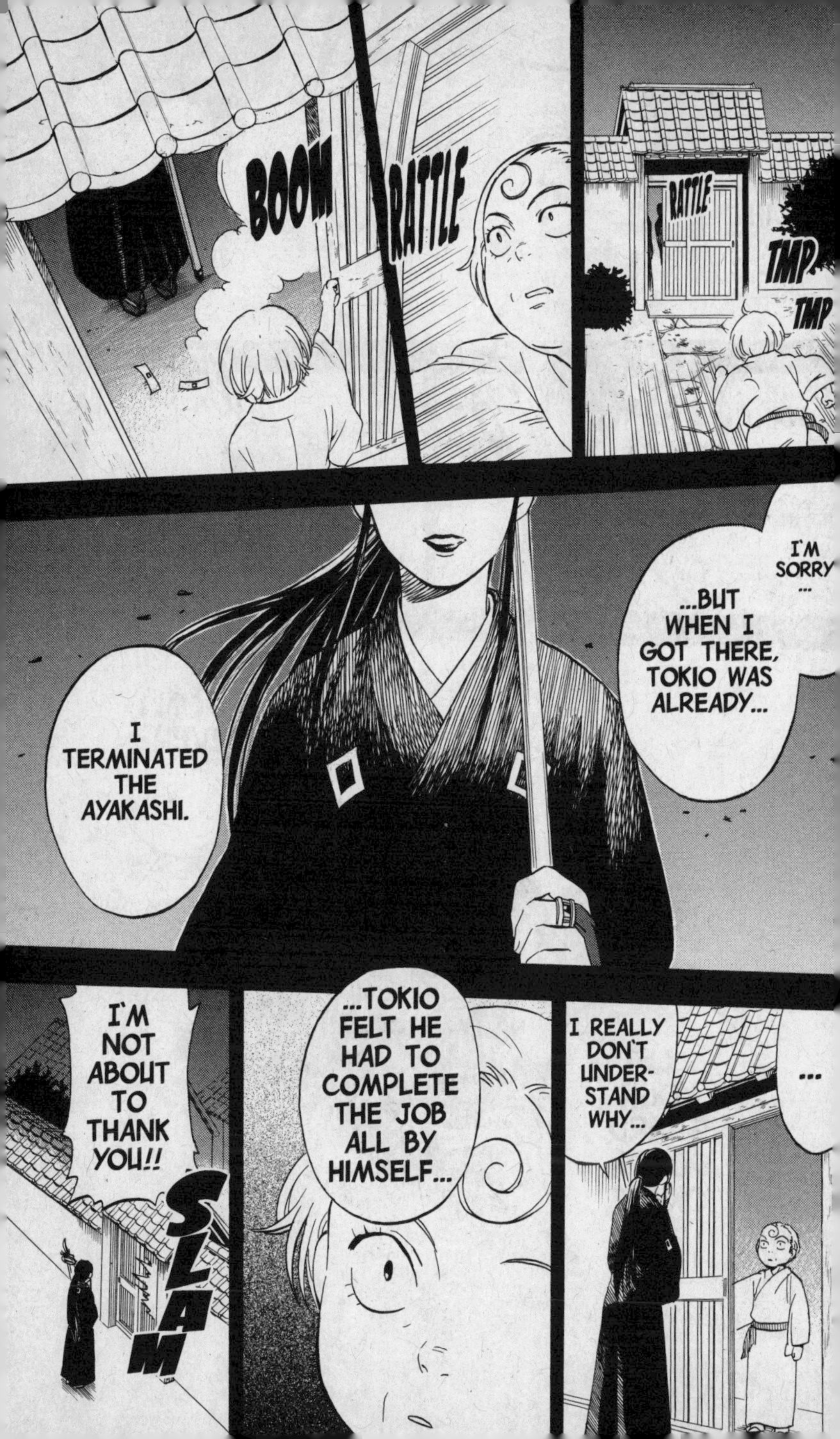
RATTLE
TMP
TMP
RATTLE
BOOM
I'M SORRY...
...BUT WHEN I GOT THERE, TOKIO WAS ALREADY...
I TERMINATED THE AYAKASHI.
...
I REALLY DON'T UNDER-STAND WHY...
...TOKIO FELT HE HAD TO COMPLETE THE JOB ALL BY HIMSELF...
I'M NOT ABOUT TO THANK YOU!!
SLAM

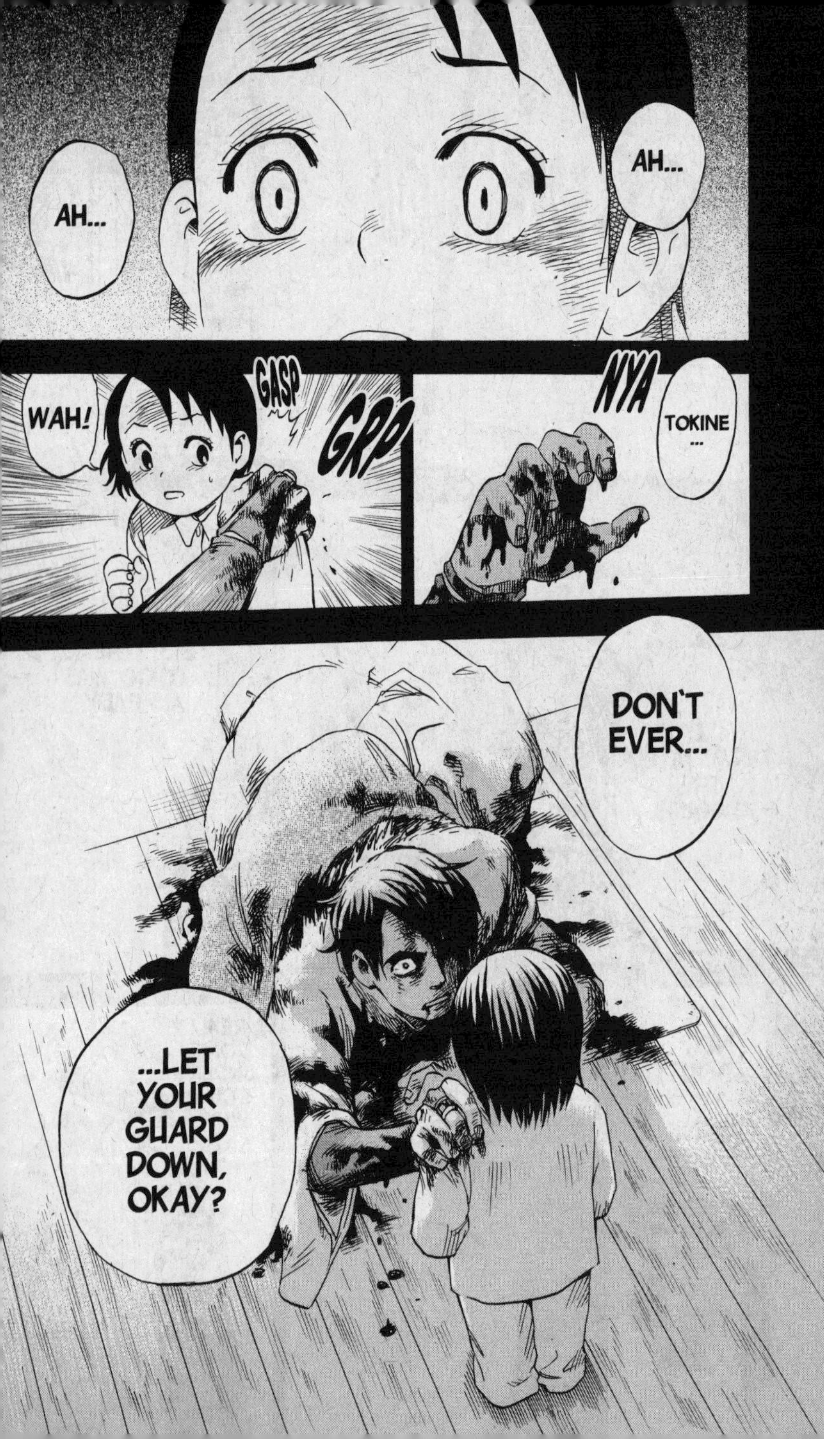
AH...
AH...
NYA
TOKINE ...
GASP
GRP
WAH!
DON'T EVER...
...LET YOUR GUARD DOWN, OKAY?

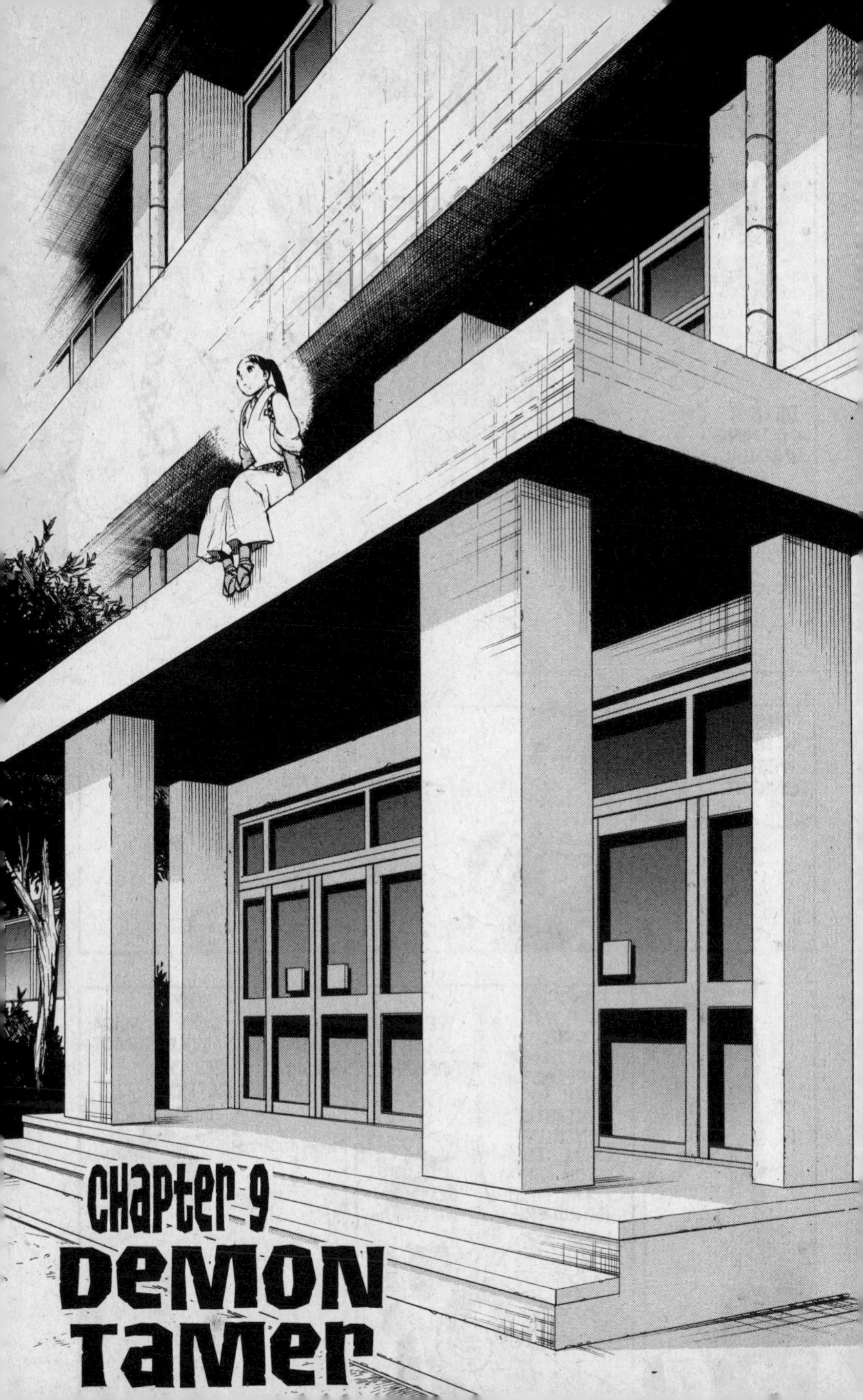
Chapter 9
Demon Tamer

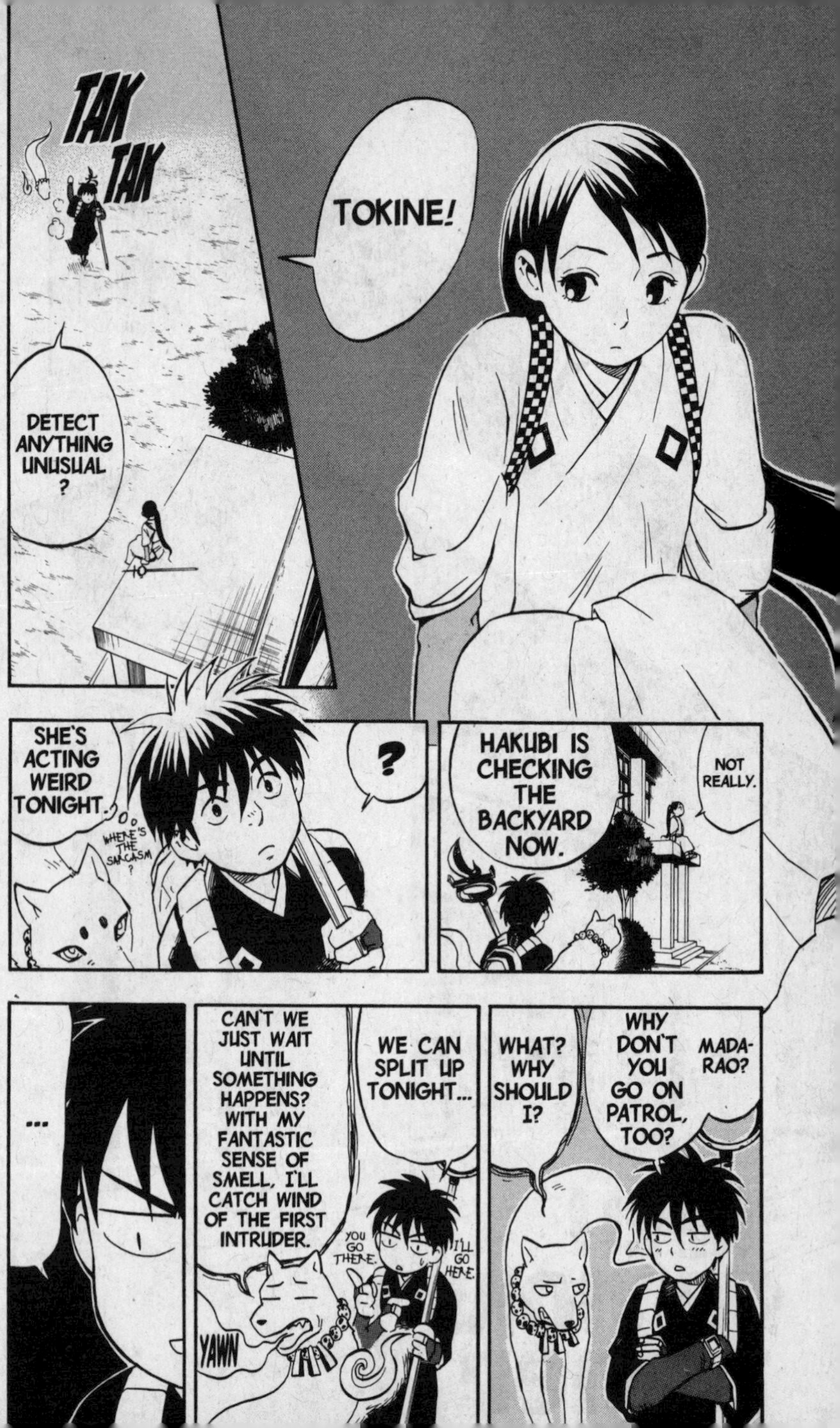
TOKINE!
TAK TAK
DETECT ANYTHING UNUSUAL?
NOT REALLY.
HAKUBI IS CHECKING THE BACKYARD NOW.
?
SHE'S ACTING WEIRD TONIGHT.
WHERE'S THE SARCASM?
MADARAO?
WHY DON'T YOU GO ON PATROL, TOO?
WHAT? WHY SHOULD I?
WE CAN SPLIT UP TONIGHT...
I'LL GO HERE.
YOU GO THERE.
CAN'T WE JUST WAIT UNTIL SOMETHING HAPPENS? WITH MY FANTASTIC SENSE OF SMELL, I'LL CATCH WIND OF THE FIRST INTRUDER.
YAWN
...

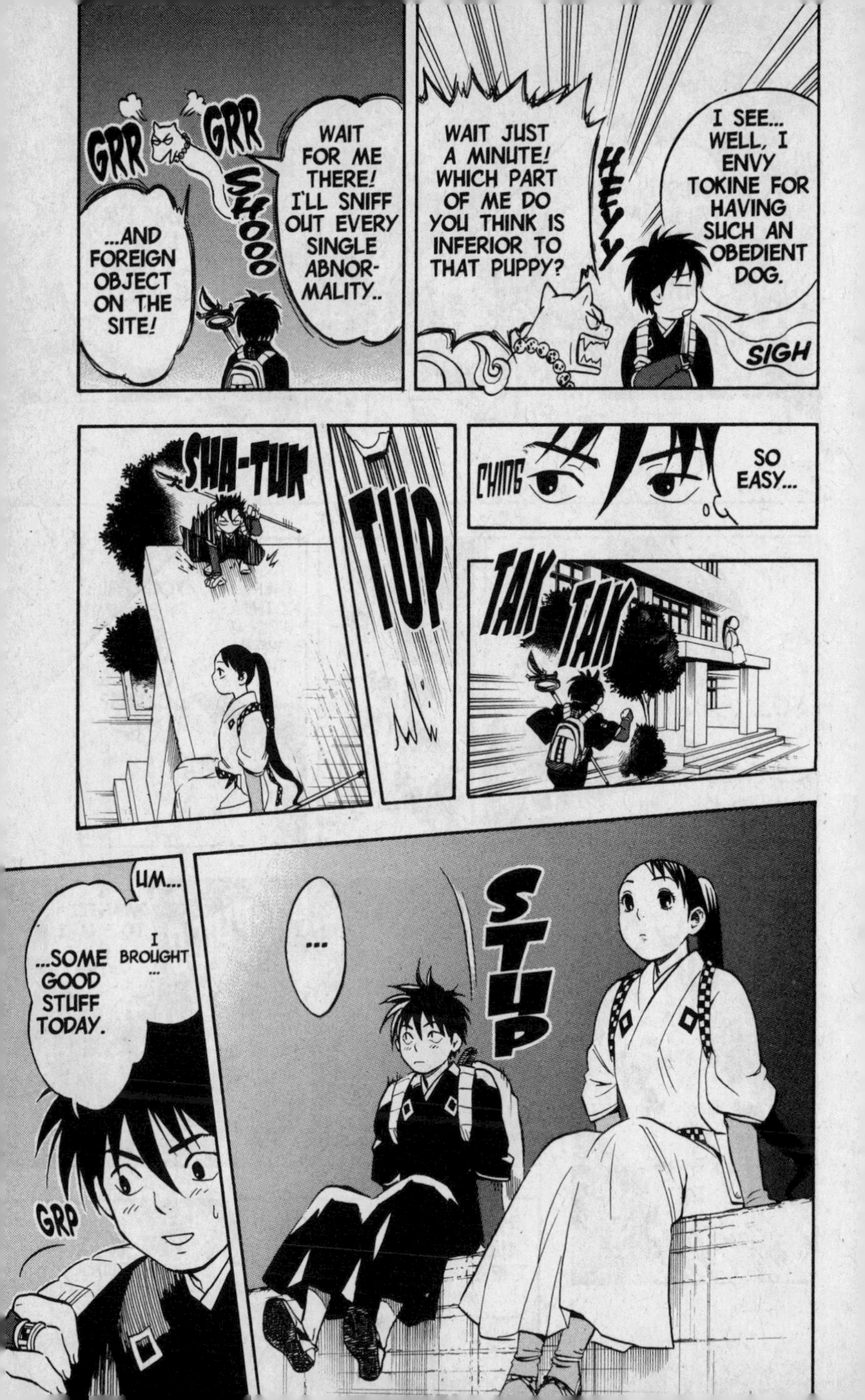
I SEE... WELL, I ENVY TOKINE FOR HAVING SUCH AN OBEDIENT DOG.
SIGH
HEYY
WAIT JUST A MINUTE! WHICH PART OF ME DO YOU THINK IS INFERIOR TO THAT PUPPY?
WAIT FOR ME THERE! I'LL SNIFF OUT EVERY SINGLE ABNORMALITY..
GRR
GRR
SHOOOO
...AND FOREIGN OBJECT ON THE SITE!
SO EASY...
CHING
TAK
TAK
TUP
SHA-TUK
STUP
...
UM...
I BROUGHT ...
...SOME GOOD STUFF TODAY.
GRP

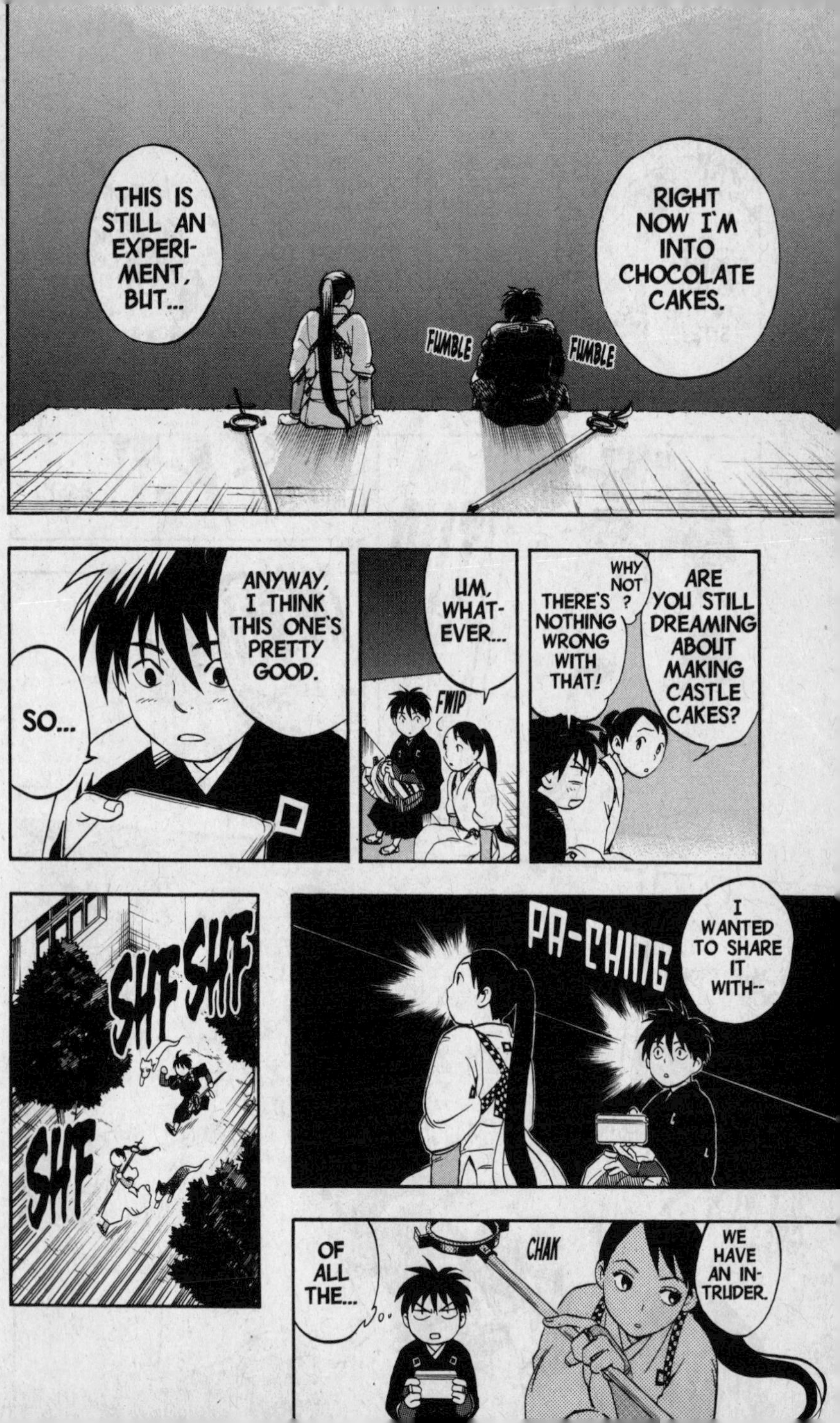
RIGHT NOW I'M INTO CHOCOLATE CAKES.
FUMBLE
FUMBLE
THIS IS STILL AN EXPERI-MENT, BUT...
ARE YOU STILL DREAMING ABOUT MAKING CASTLE CAKES?
WHY NOT?
THERE'S NOTHING WRONG WITH THAT!
UM, WHAT-EVER...
FWIP
ANYWAY, I THINK THIS ONE'S PRETTY GOOD.
SO...
I WANTED TO SHARE IT WITH--
PA-CHING
WE HAVE AN IN-TRUDER.
CHAK
OF ALL THE...
SHF SHF
SHF

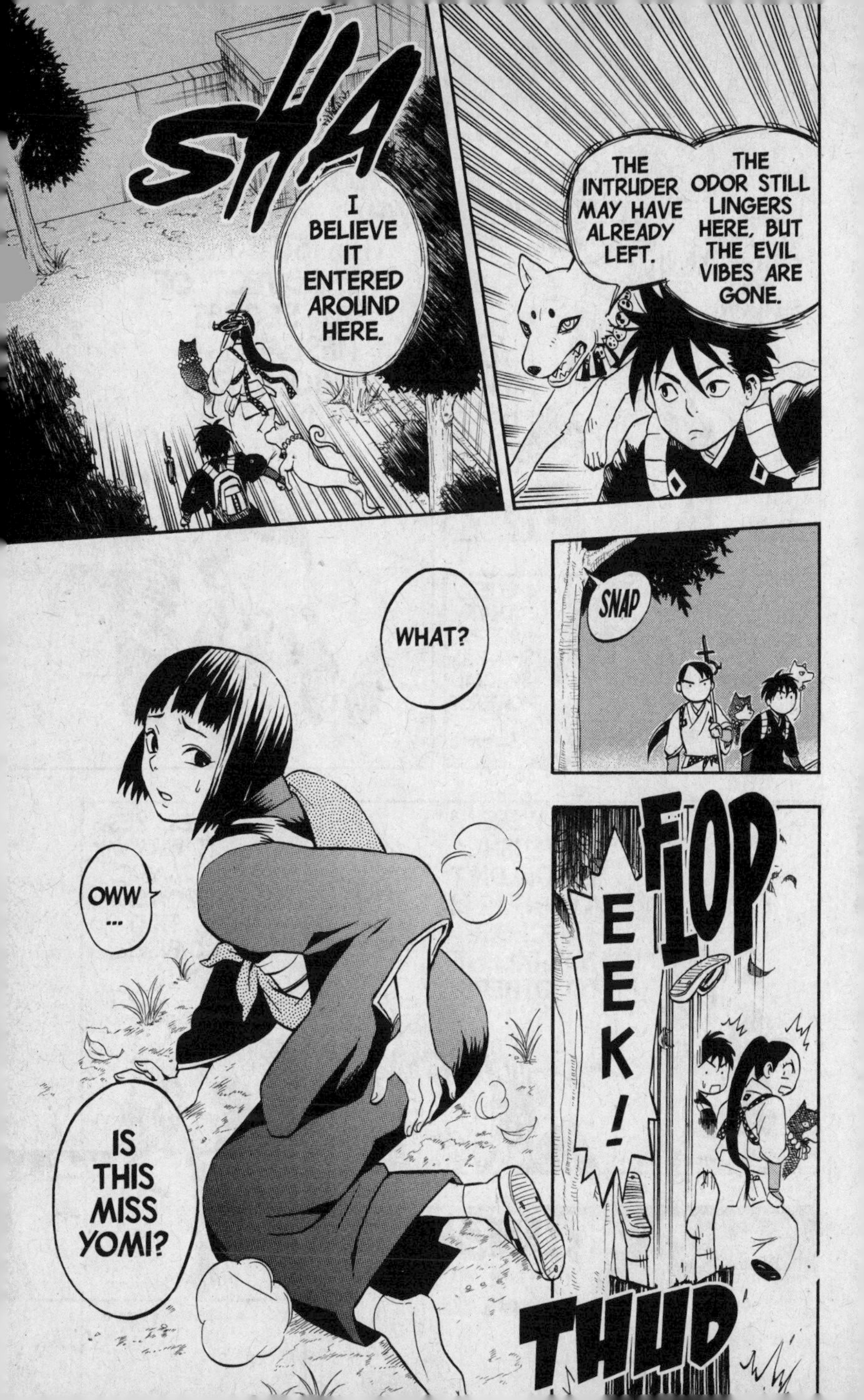

THE ODOR STILL LINGERS HERE, BUT THE EVIL VIBES ARE GONE.
THE INTRUDER MAY HAVE ALREADY LEFT.
SHA
I BELIEVE IT ENTERED AROUND HERE.
SNAP
FLOP
EEK!
THUD
WHAT?
OWW ...
IS THIS MISS YOMI?

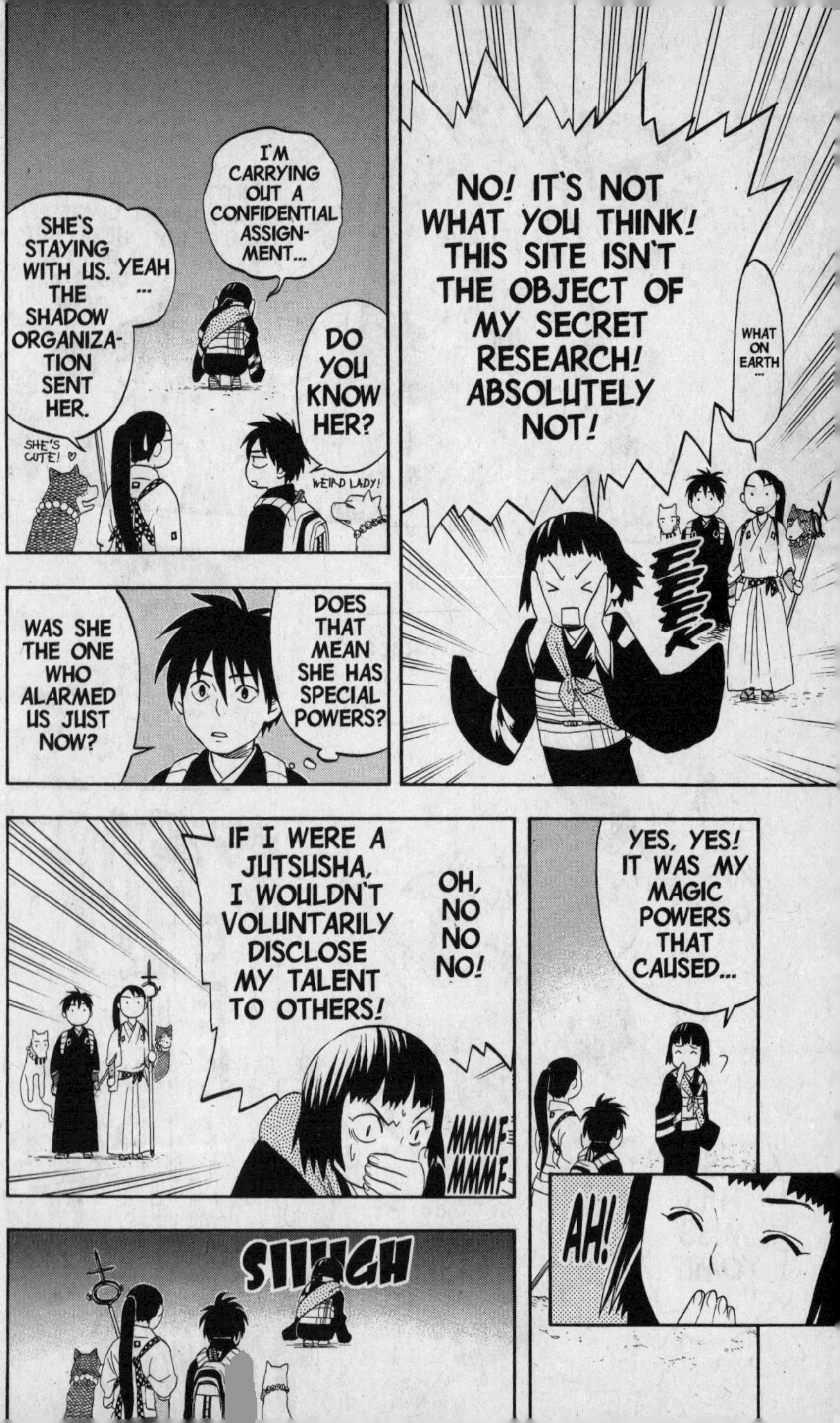
NO! IT'S NOT WHAT YOU THINK! THIS SITE ISN'T THE OBJECT OF MY SECRET RESEARCH! ABSOLUTELY NOT!
WHAT ON EARTH ...
I'M CARRYING OUT A CONFIDENTIAL ASSIGN- MENT...
DO YOU KNOW HER?
WEIRD LADY!
YEAH ...
SHE'S STAYING WITH US. THE SHADOW ORGANIZA- TION SENT HER.
SHE'S CUTE! ♡
DOES THAT MEAN SHE HAS SPECIAL POWERS?
WAS SHE THE ONE WHO ALARMED US JUST NOW?
YES, YES! IT WAS MY MAGIC POWERS THAT CAUSED...
AH!
OH, NO NO NO!
IF I WERE A JUTSUSHA, I WOULDN'T VOLUNTARILY DISCLOSE MY TALENT TO OTHERS!
MMMF MMMF
SIIIGH

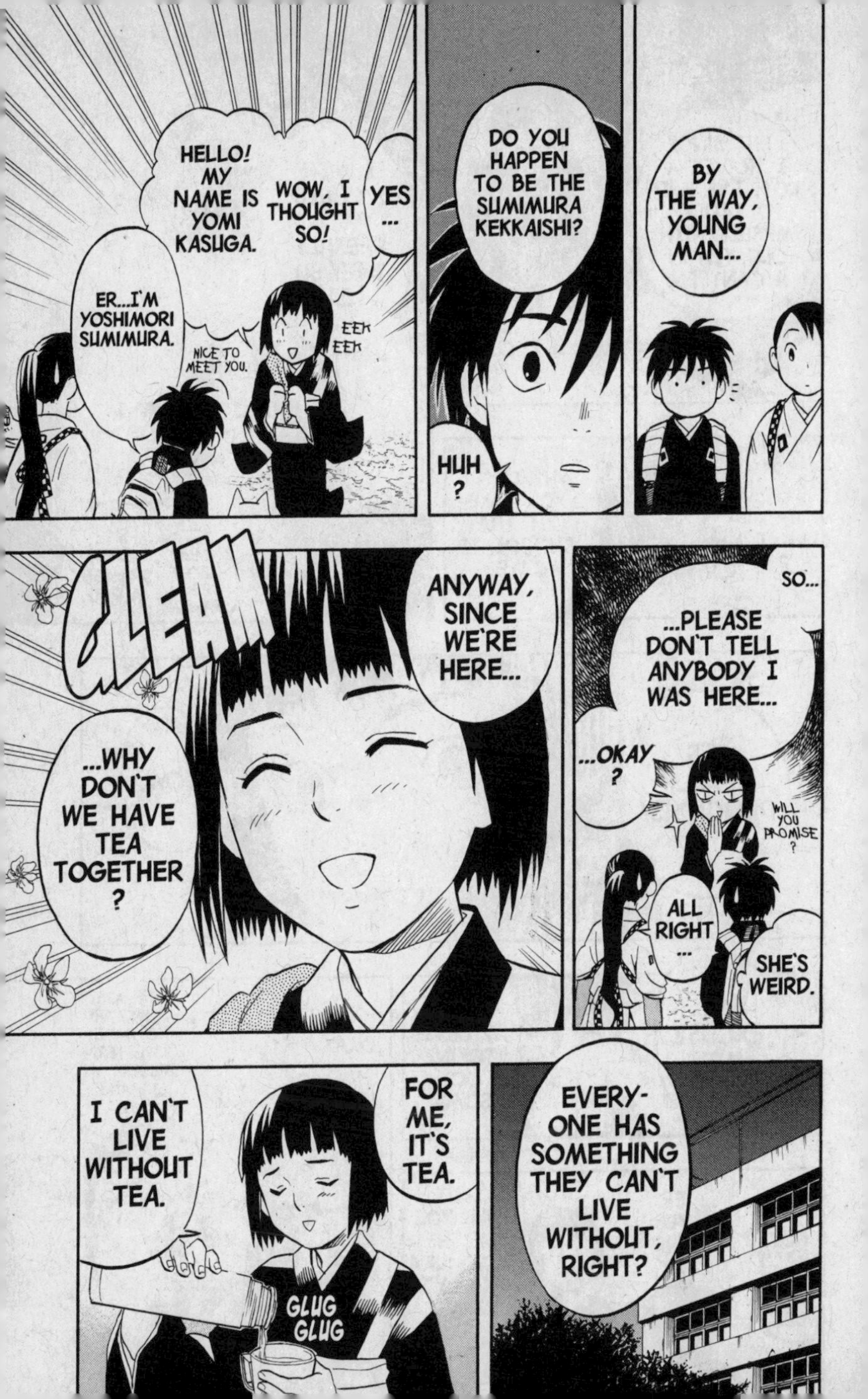
BY THE WAY, YOUNG MAN...
DO YOU HAPPEN TO BE THE SUMIMURA KEKKAISHI?
HUH?
YES...
WOW, I THOUGHT SO!
HELLO! MY NAME IS YOMI KASUGA.
EEK EEK
NICE TO MEET YOU.
ER...I'M YOSHIMORI SUMIMURA.
SO...
...PLEASE DON'T TELL ANYBODY I WAS HERE...
WILL YOU PROMISE?
...OKAY?
ALL RIGHT...
SHE'S WEIRD.
GLEAM
ANYWAY, SINCE WE'RE HERE...
...WHY DON'T WE HAVE TEA TOGETHER?
EVERY-ONE HAS SOMETHING THEY CAN'T LIVE WITHOUT, RIGHT?
FOR ME, IT'S TEA.
I CAN'T LIVE WITHOUT TEA.
GLUG GLUG

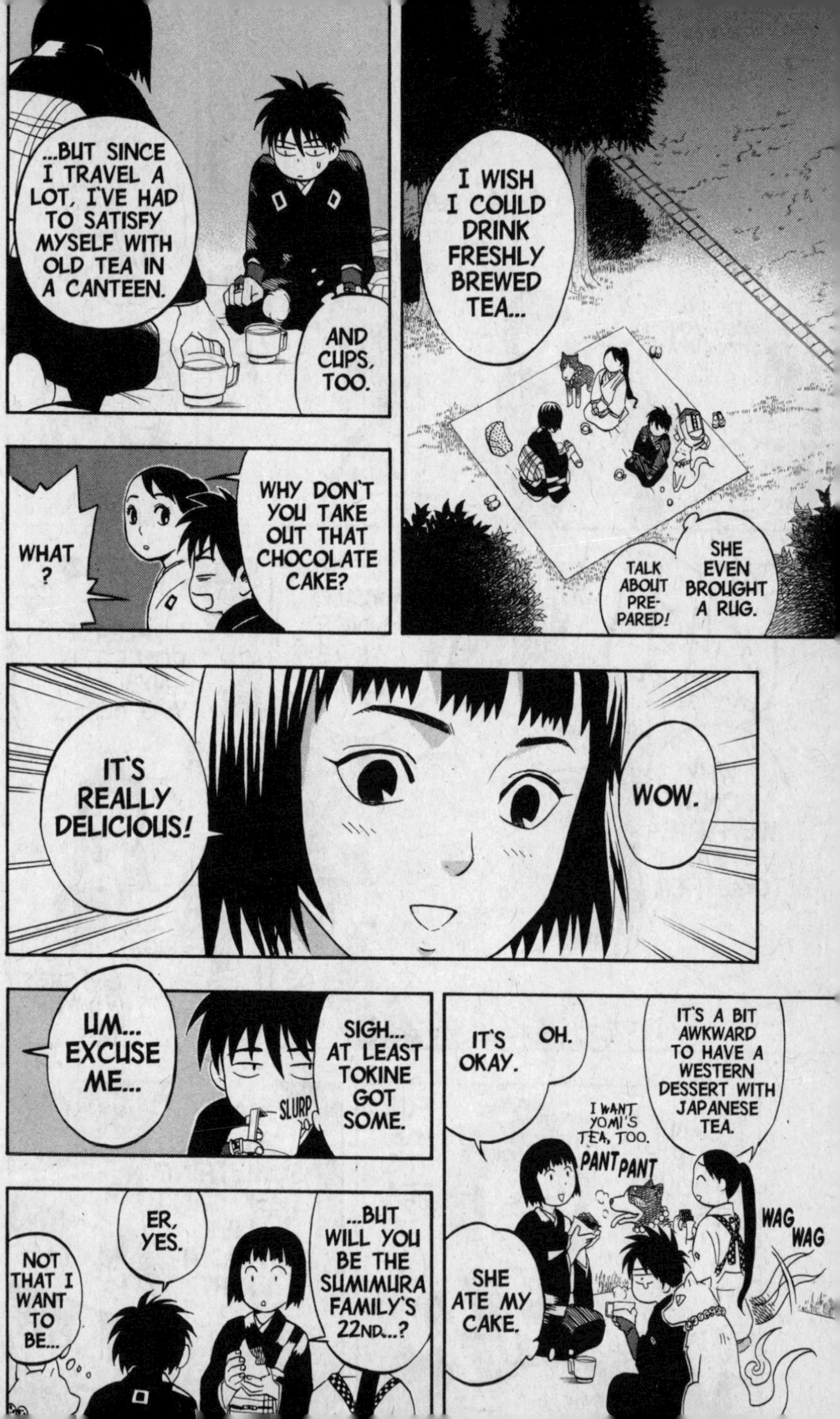
I WISH I COULD DRINK FRESHLY BREWED TEA...
SHE EVEN BROUGHT A RUG.
TALK ABOUT PRE-PARED!
...BUT SINCE I TRAVEL A LOT, I'VE HAD TO SATISFY MYSELF WITH OLD TEA IN A CANTEEN.
AND CUPS, TOO.
WHY DON'T YOU TAKE OUT THAT CHOCOLATE CAKE?
WHAT?
WOW.
IT'S REALLY DELICIOUS!
IT'S A BIT AWKWARD TO HAVE A WESTERN DESSERT WITH JAPANESE TEA.
OH.
IT'S OKAY.
I WANT YOMI'S TEA, TOO.
PANT PANT
WAG WAG
SHE ATE MY CAKE.
SIGH... AT LEAST TOKINE GOT SOME.
SLURP
UM... EXCUSE ME...
...BUT WILL YOU BE THE SUMIMURA FAMILY'S 22ND...?
ER, YES.
NOT THAT I WANT TO BE...

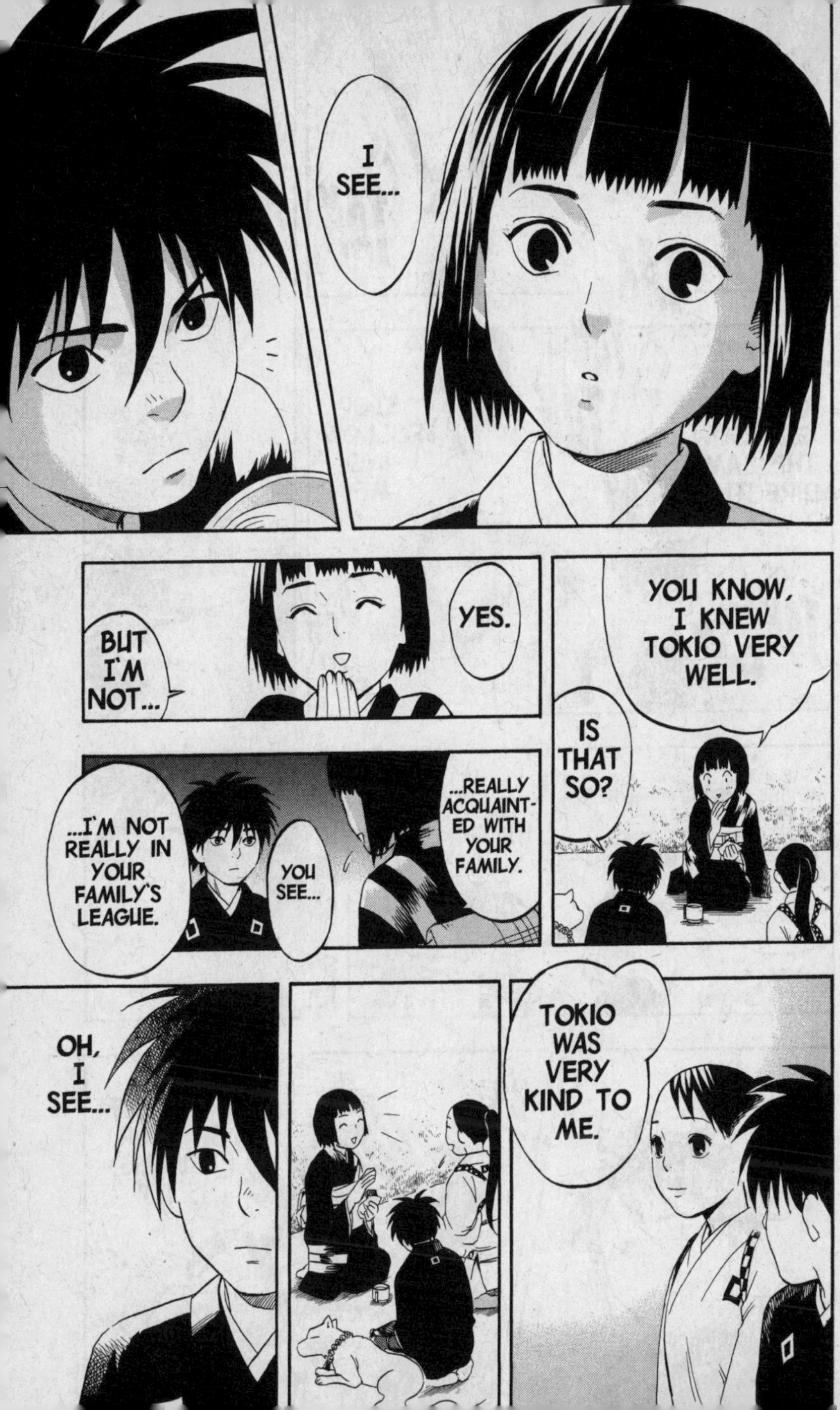
I SEE...
YOU KNOW, I KNEW TOKIO VERY WELL.
IS THAT SO?
YES.
BUT I'M NOT...
...REALLY ACQUAINT-ED WITH YOUR FAMILY.
YOU SEE...
...I'M NOT REALLY IN YOUR FAMILY'S LEAGUE.
TOKIO WAS VERY KIND TO ME.
OH, I SEE...

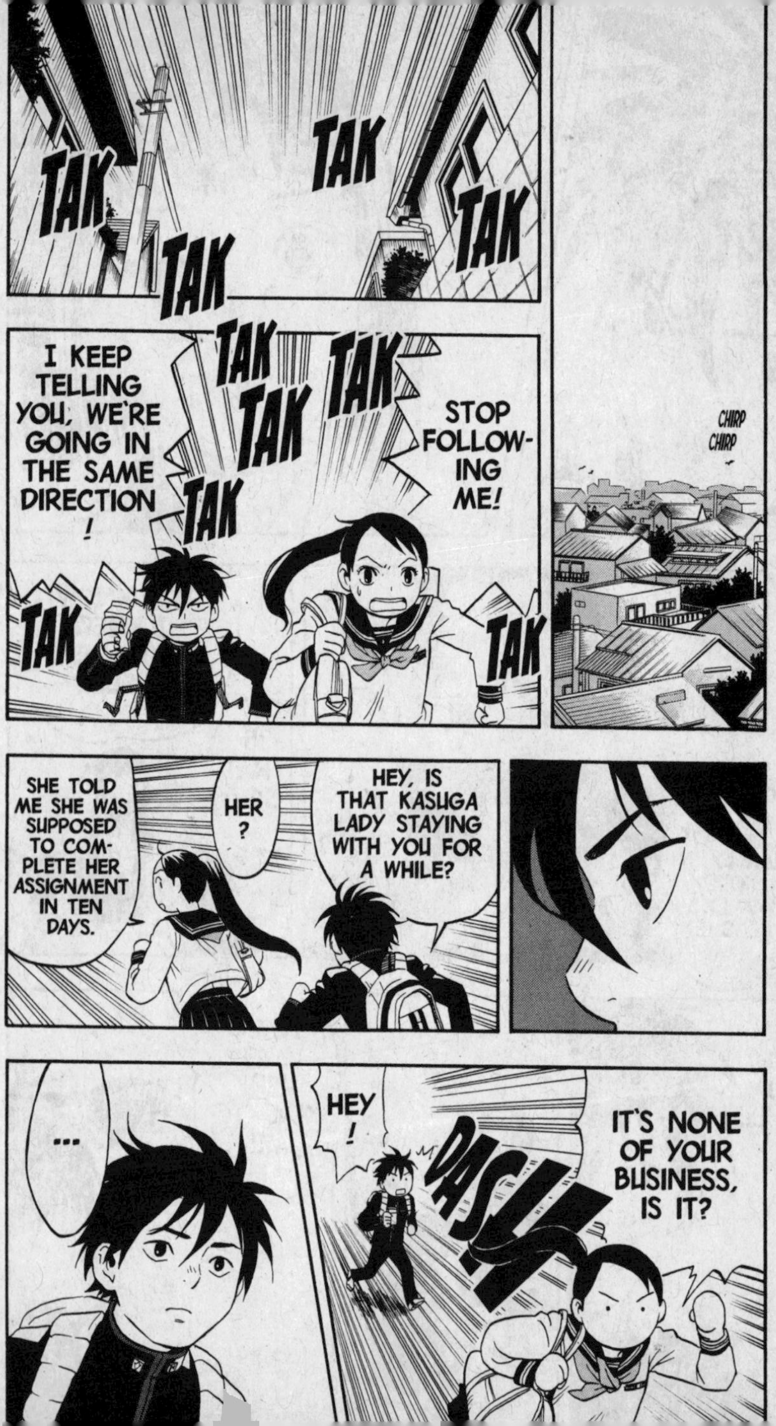
CHIRP CHIRP
TAK
TAK
TAK
TAK
STOP FOLLOWING ME!
TAK
TAK
TAK
I KEEP TELLING YOU, WE'RE GOING IN THE SAME DIRECTION!
TAK
TAK
TAK
HEY, IS THAT KASUGA LADY STAYING WITH YOU FOR A WHILE?
HER?
SHE TOLD ME SHE WAS SUPPOSED TO COMPLETE HER ASSIGNMENT IN TEN DAYS.
IT'S NONE OF YOUR BUSINESS, IS IT?
DASH
HEY!
...

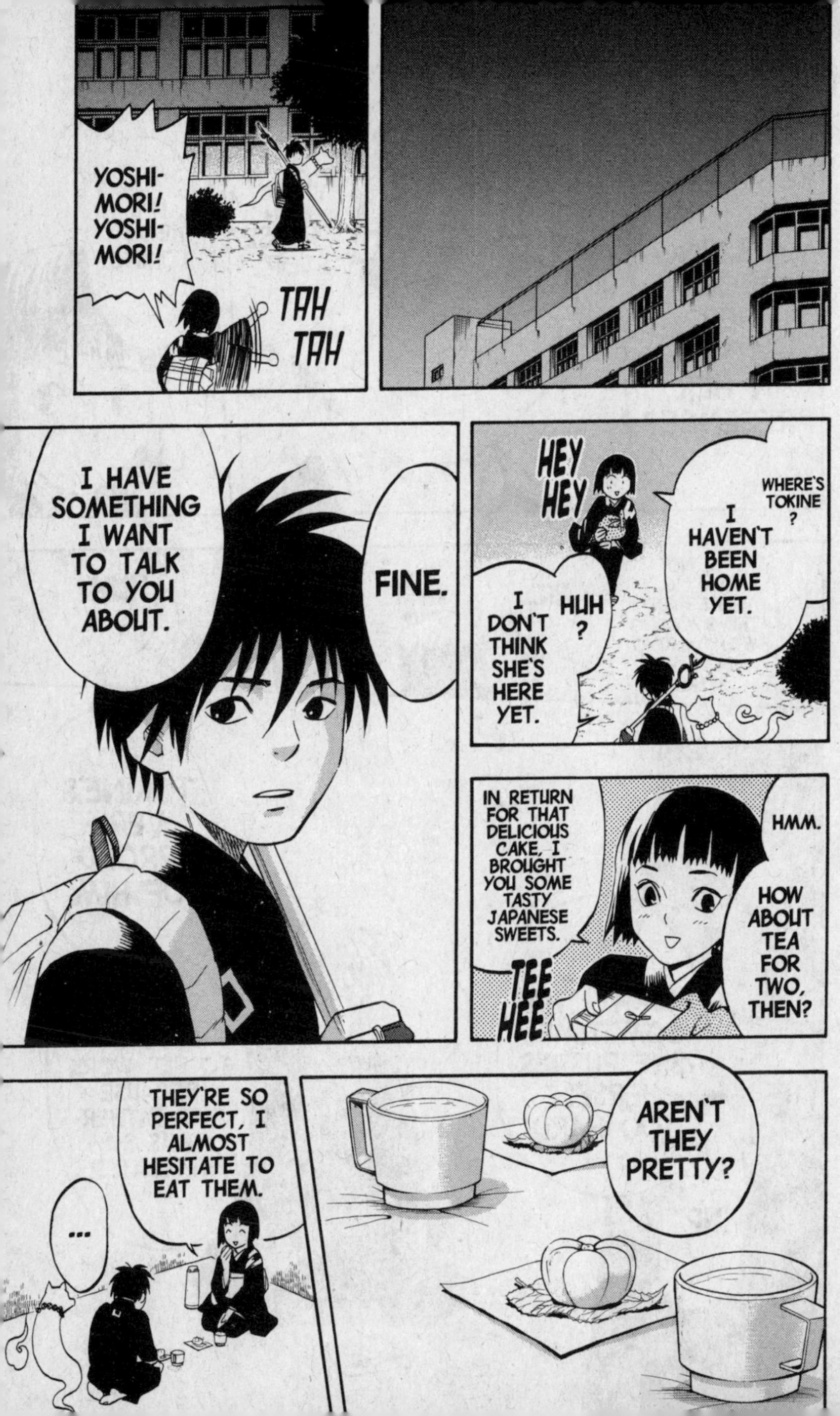
YOSHIMORI! YOSHIMORI!
TAH TAH
HEY HEY
WHERE'S TOKINE?
I HAVEN'T BEEN HOME YET.
HUH?
I DON'T THINK SHE'S HERE YET.
HMM.
HOW ABOUT TEA FOR TWO, THEN?
IN RETURN FOR THAT DELICIOUS CAKE, I BROUGHT YOU SOME TASTY JAPANESE SWEETS.
TEE HEE
I HAVE SOMETHING I WANT TO TALK TO YOU ABOUT.
FINE.
AREN'T THEY PRETTY?
THEY'RE SO PERFECT, I ALMOST HESITATE TO EAT THEM.
...

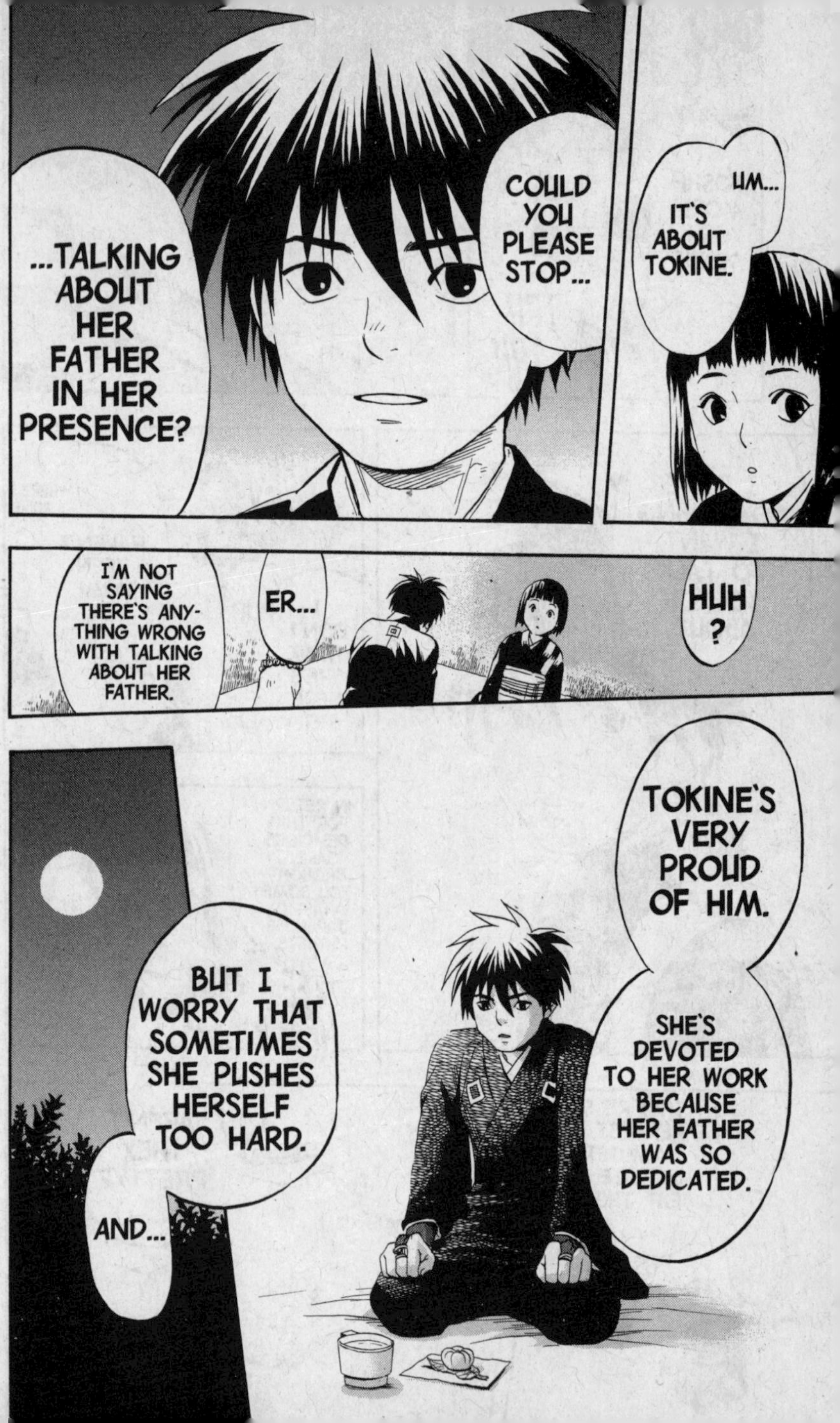
UM... IT'S ABOUT TOKINE.
COULD YOU PLEASE STOP...
...TALKING ABOUT HER FATHER IN HER PRESENCE?
HUH?
ER...
I'M NOT SAYING THERE'S ANYTHING WRONG WITH TALKING ABOUT HER FATHER.
TOKINE'S VERY PROUD OF HIM.
SHE'S DEVOTED TO HER WORK BECAUSE HER FATHER WAS SO DEDICATED.
BUT I WORRY THAT SOMETIMES SHE PUSHES HERSELF TOO HARD.
AND...

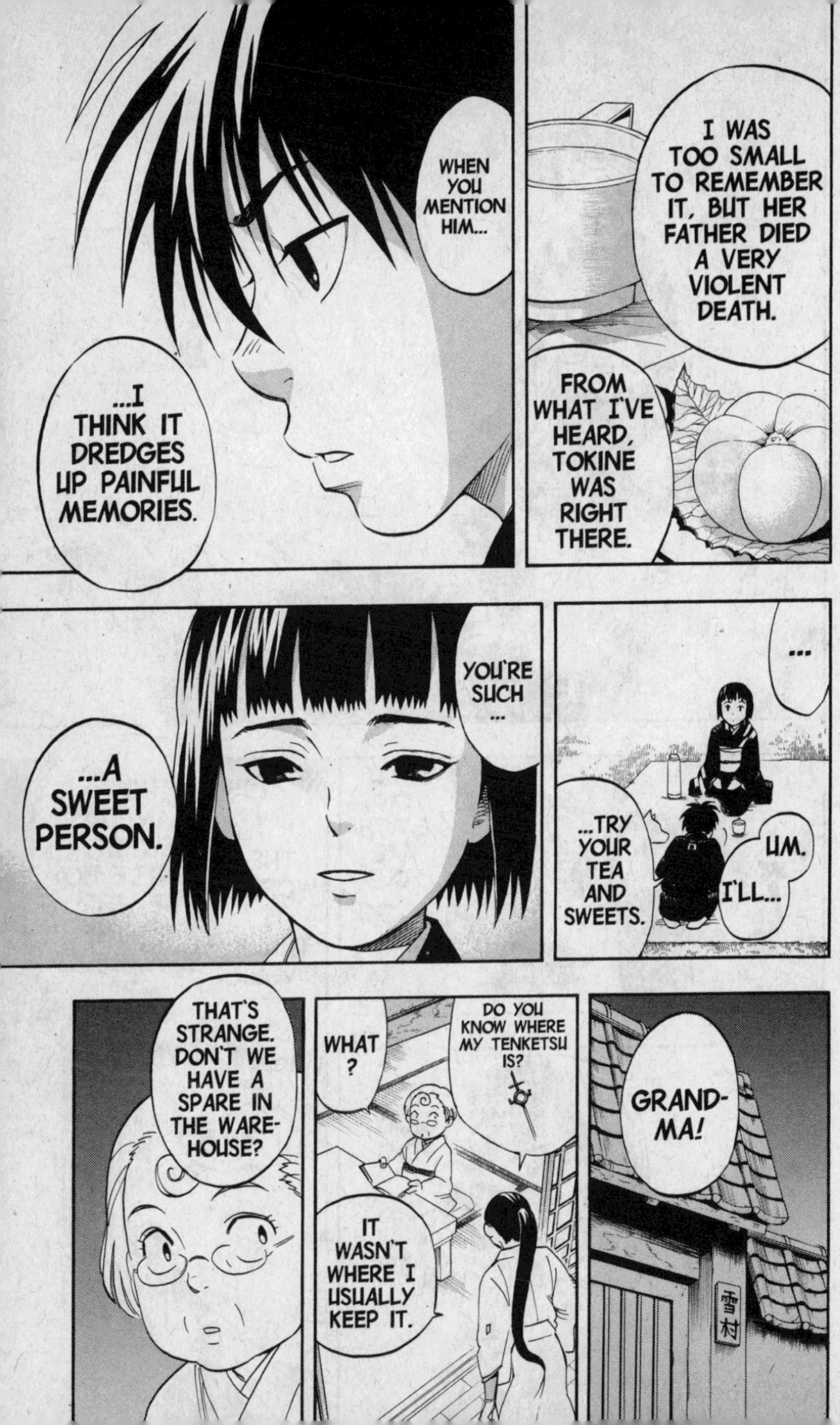
I WAS TOO SMALL TO REMEMBER IT, BUT HER FATHER DIED A VERY VIOLENT DEATH.
FROM WHAT I'VE HEARD, TOKINE WAS RIGHT THERE.
WHEN YOU MENTION HIM...
...I THINK IT DREDGES UP PAINFUL MEMORIES.
...
UM. I'LL...
...TRY YOUR TEA AND SWEETS.
YOU'RE SUCH...
...A SWEET PERSON.
GRAND-MA!
雪村
DO YOU KNOW WHERE MY TENKETSU IS?
WHAT?
IT WASN'T WHERE I USUALLY KEEP IT.
THAT'S STRANGE. DON'T WE HAVE A SPARE IN THE WARE-HOUSE?

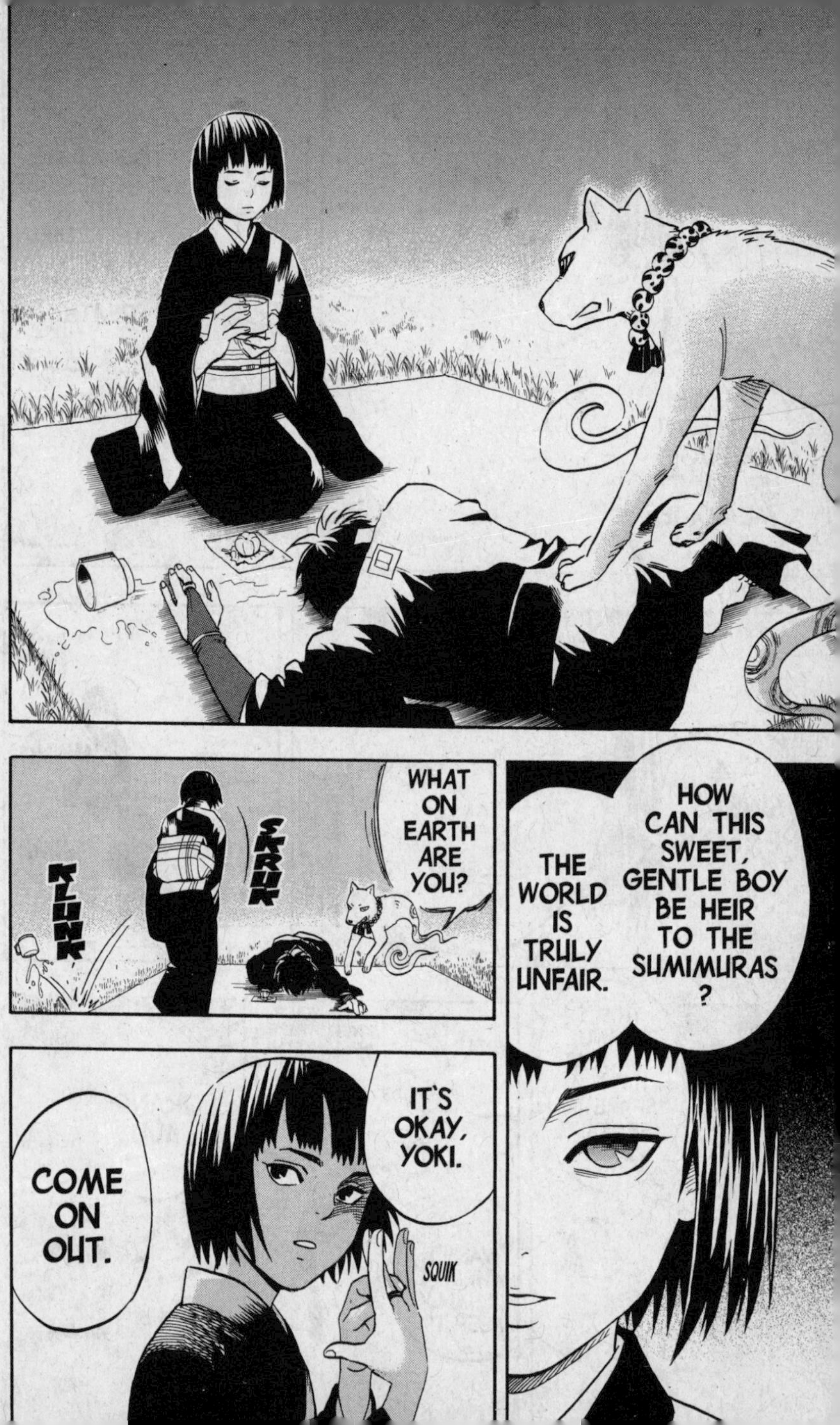
HOW CAN THIS SWEET, GENTLE BOY BE HEIR TO THE SUMIMURAS?
THE WORLD IS TRULY UNFAIR.
WHAT ON EARTH ARE YOU?
SKRUK
KLUNK
IT'S OKAY, YOKI.
COME ON OUT.
SQUIK

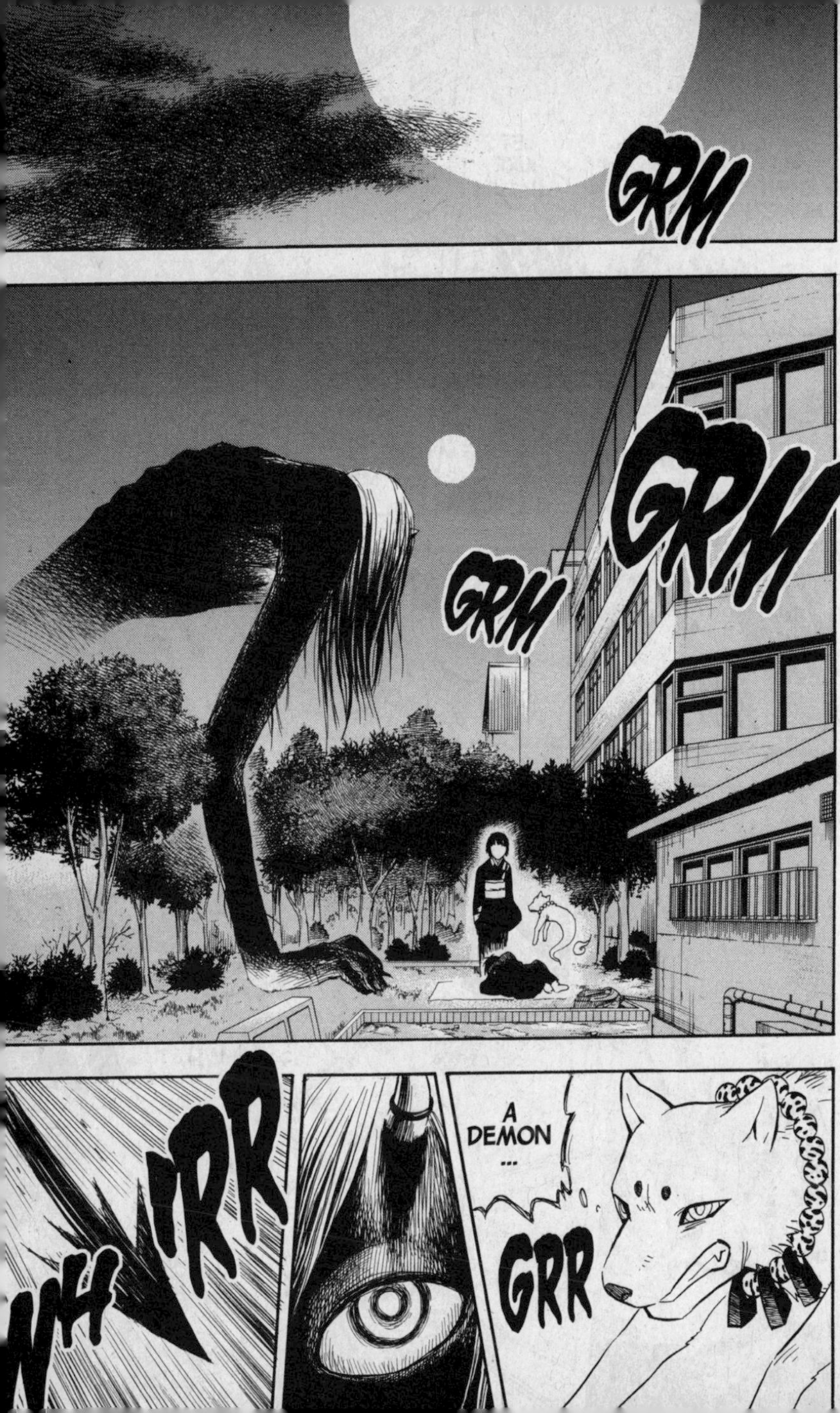
GRM
GRM
GRM
A DEMON ...
GRR
WHIRR

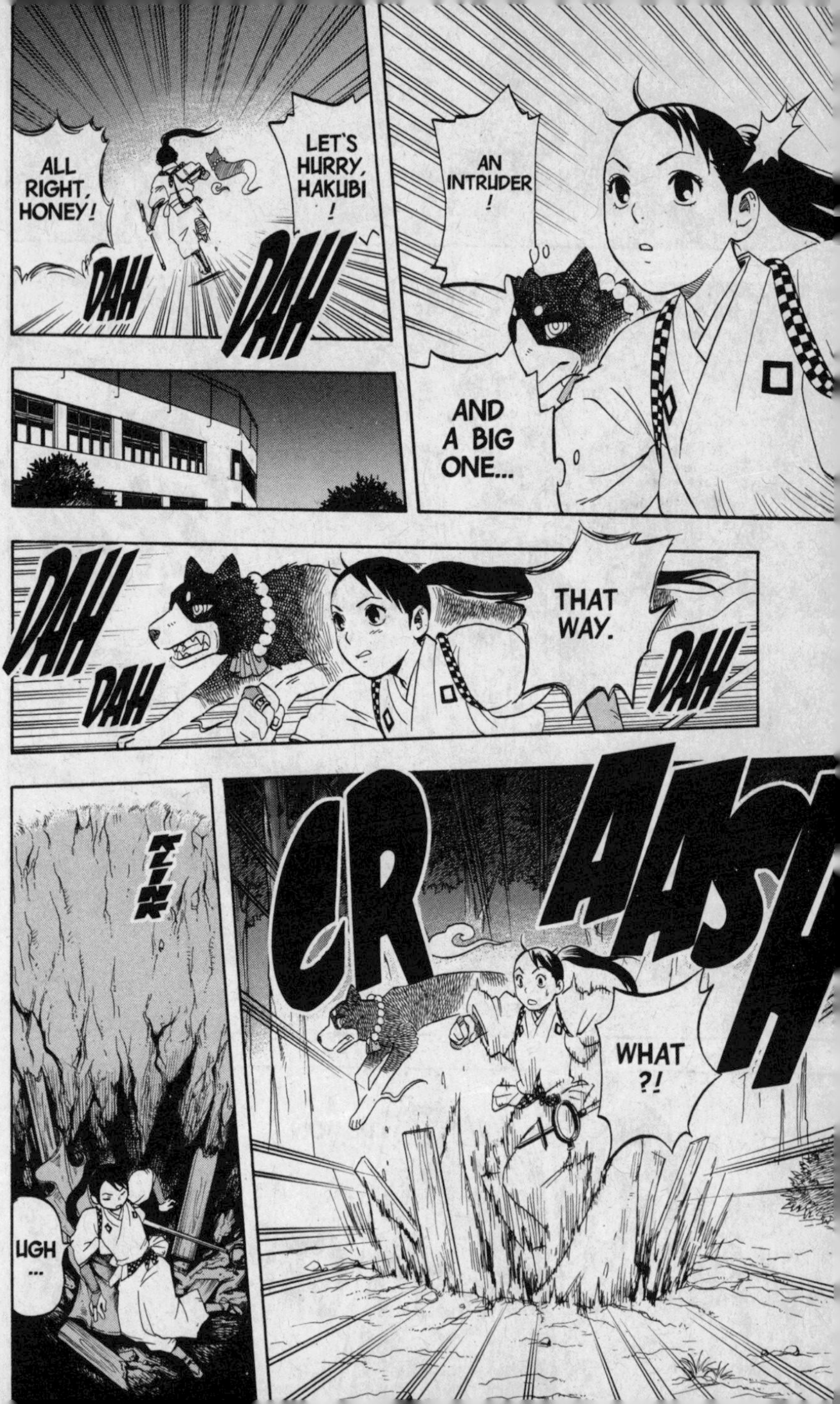
AN INTRUDER!
AND A BIG ONE...
LET'S HURRY, HAKUBI!
DAH
ALL RIGHT, HONEY!
DAH
DAH
THAT WAY.
DAH
DAH
CRAASH
WHAT?!
KLINK
UGH...

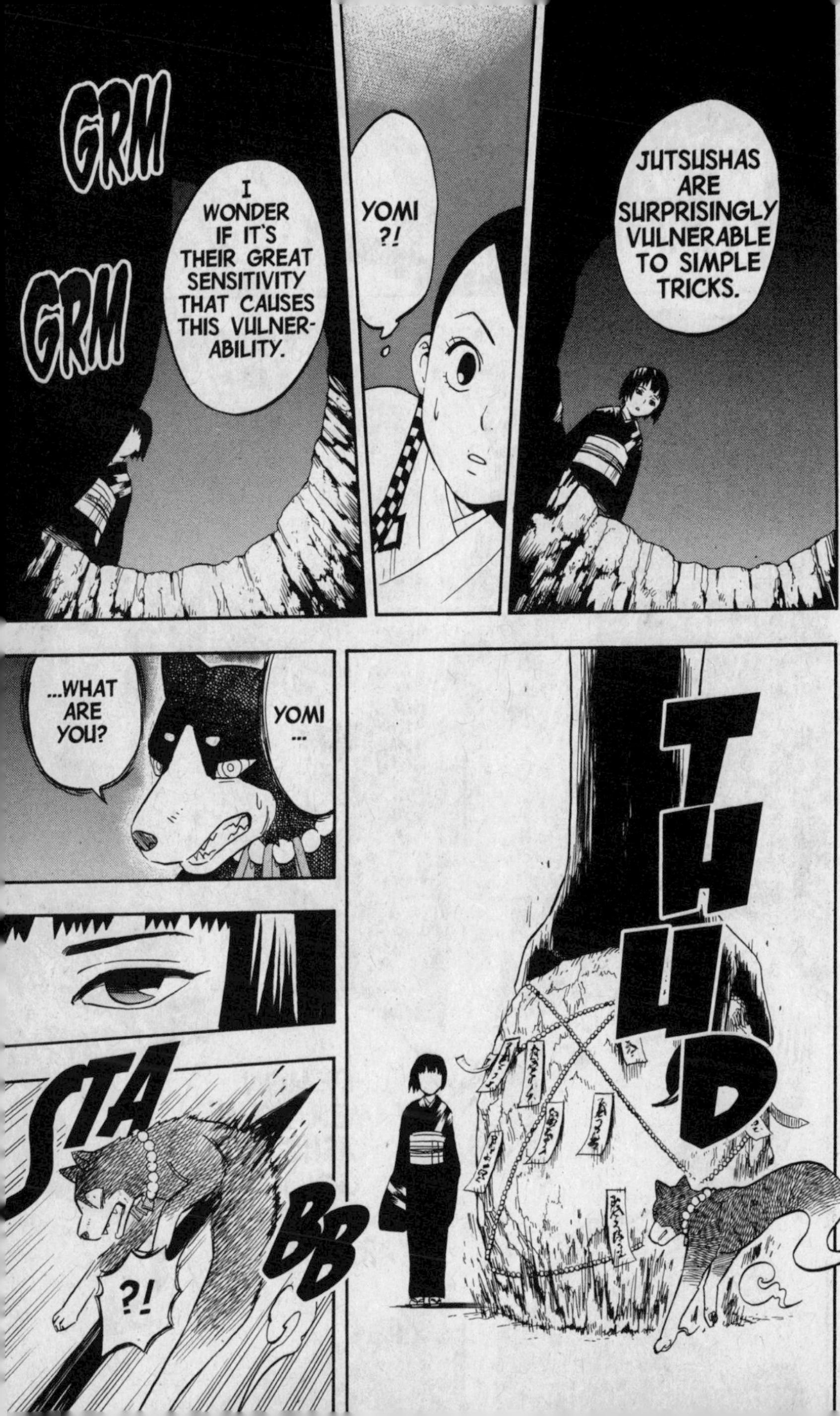
JUTSUSHAS ARE SURPRISINGLY VULNERABLE TO SIMPLE TRICKS.
YOMI ?!
I WONDER IF IT'S THEIR GREAT SENSITIVITY THAT CAUSES THIS VULNER-ABILITY.
GRM
GRM
THUD
YOMI ...
...WHAT ARE YOU?
STABB
?!

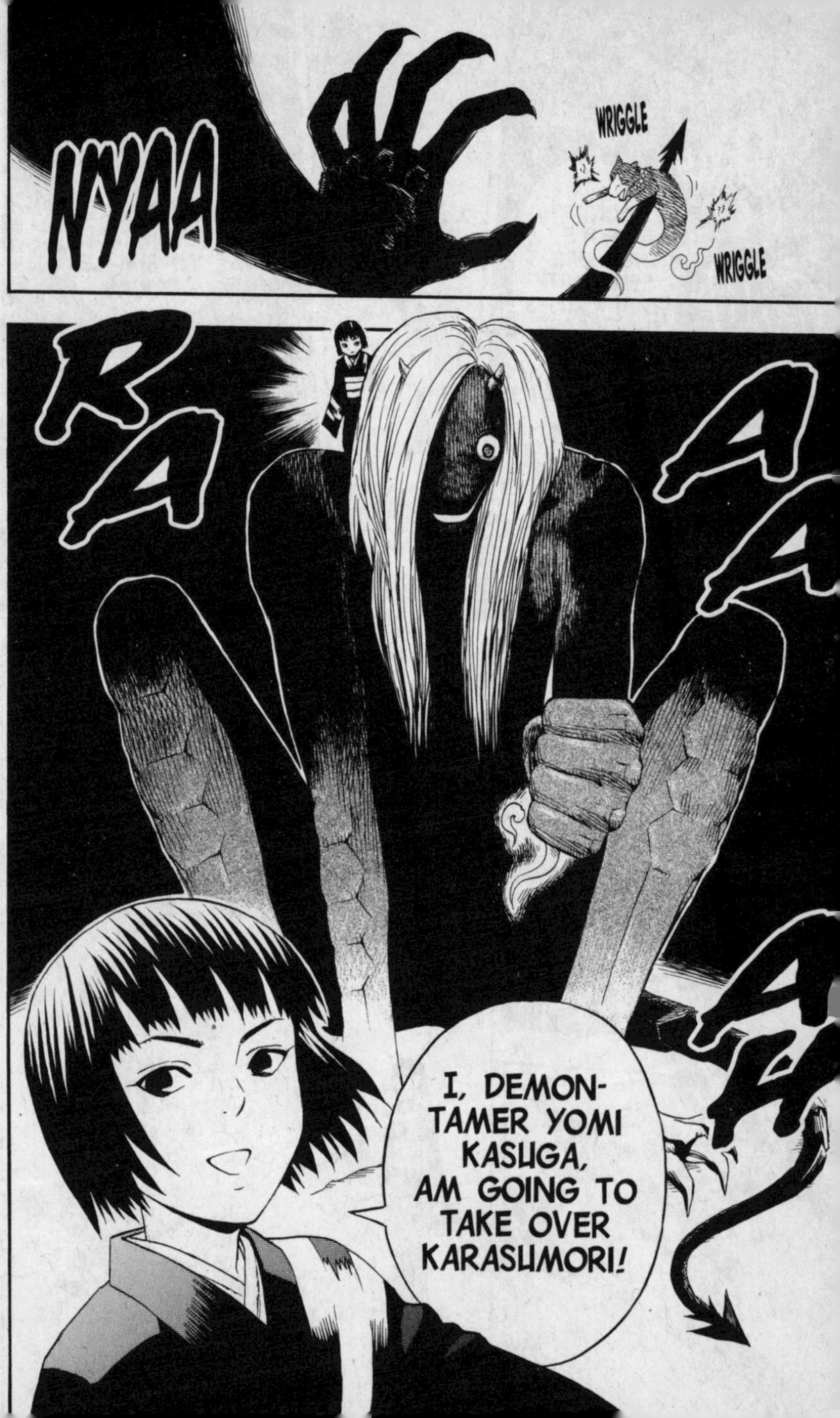
WRIGGLE
WRIGGLE
NYAA
RAAAA
I, DEMON-TAMER YOMI KASUGA, AM GOING TO TAKE OVER KARASUMORI!

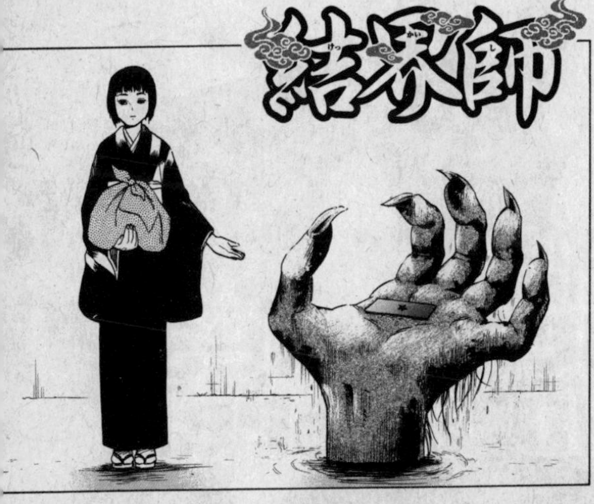
結界師

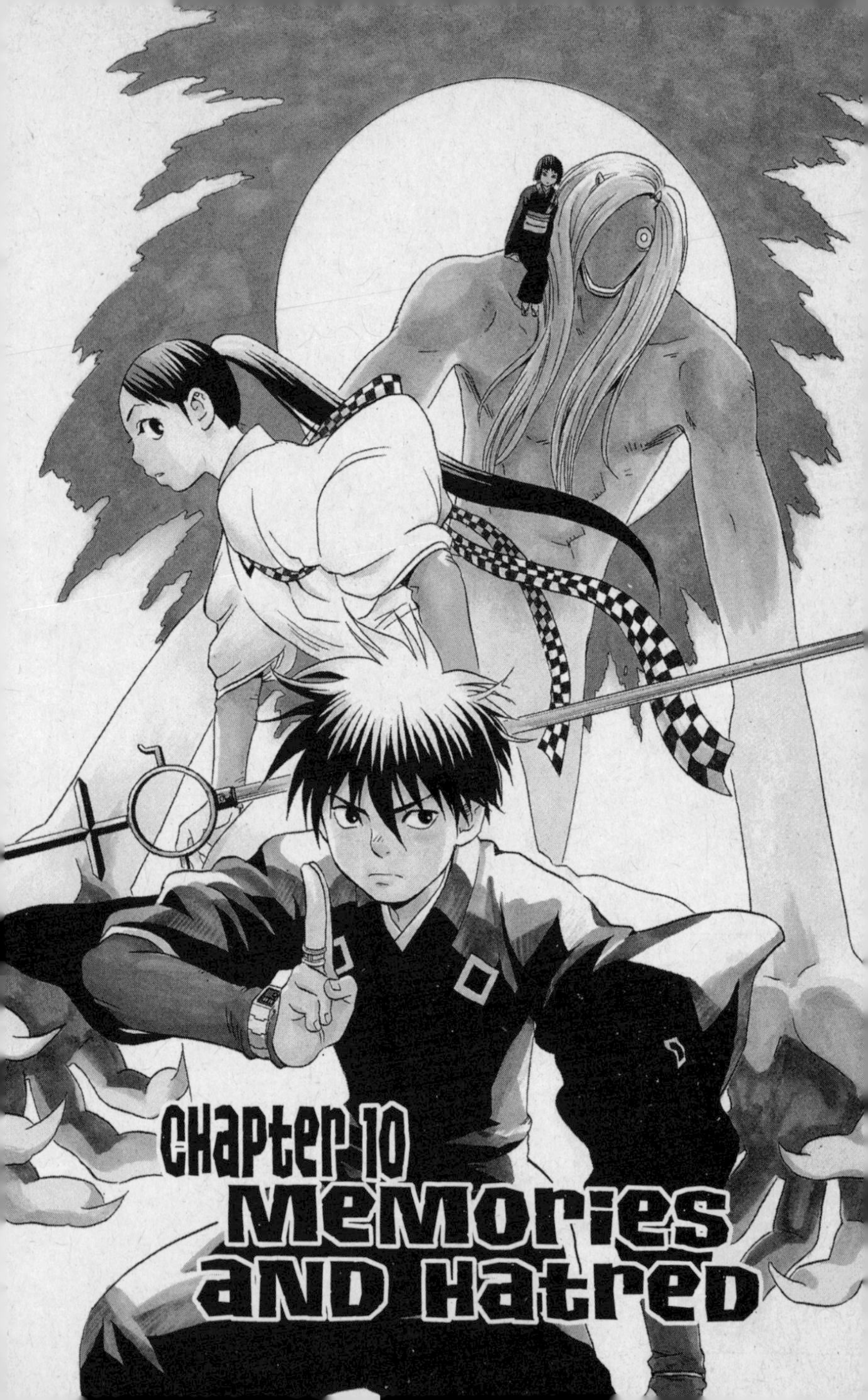
CHAPTER 10
MEMORIES AND HATRED

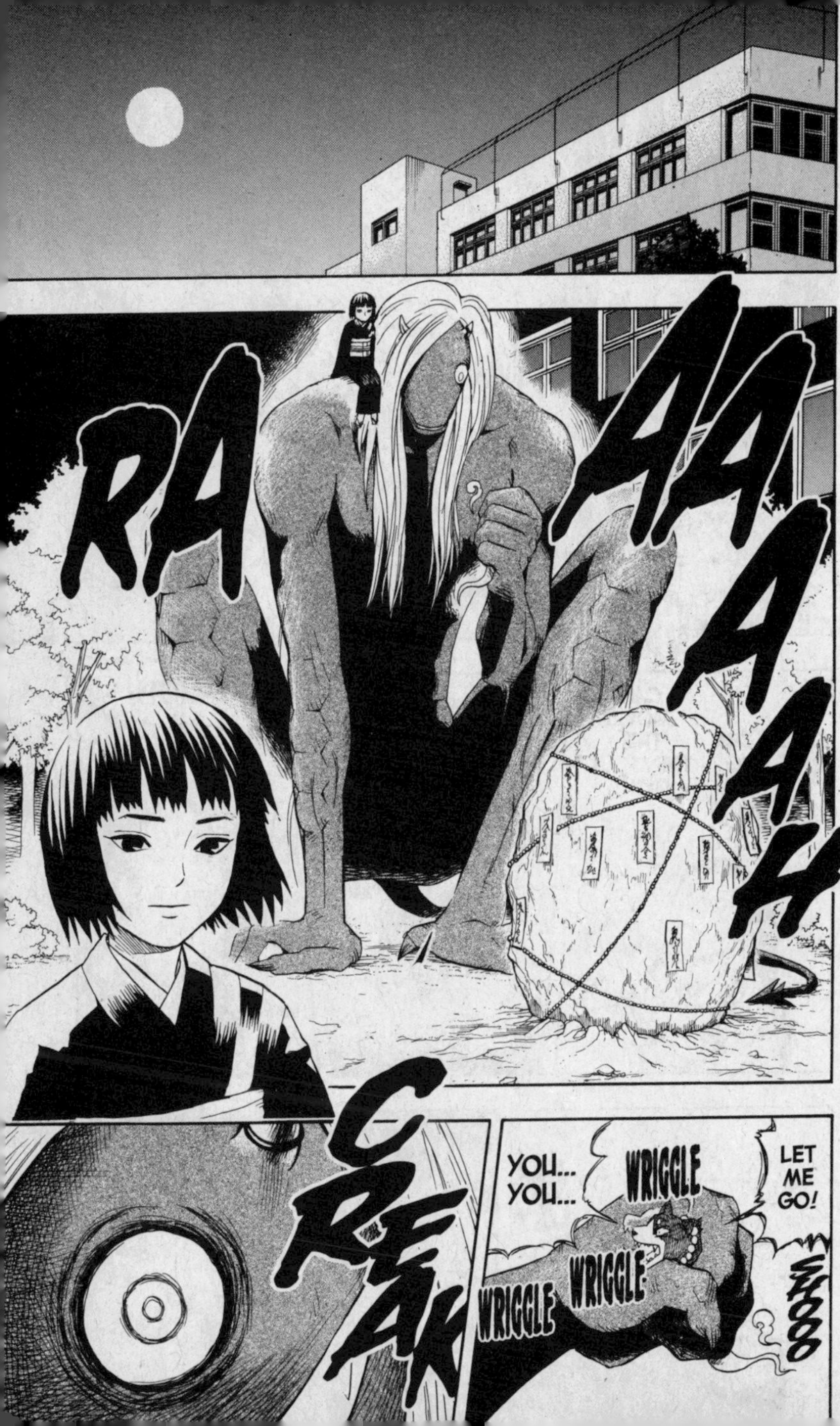
RAAAAAAAH
CREAK
LET ME GO!
WRIGGLE
YOU... YOU...
WRIGGLE
WRIGGLE
SHOOOO

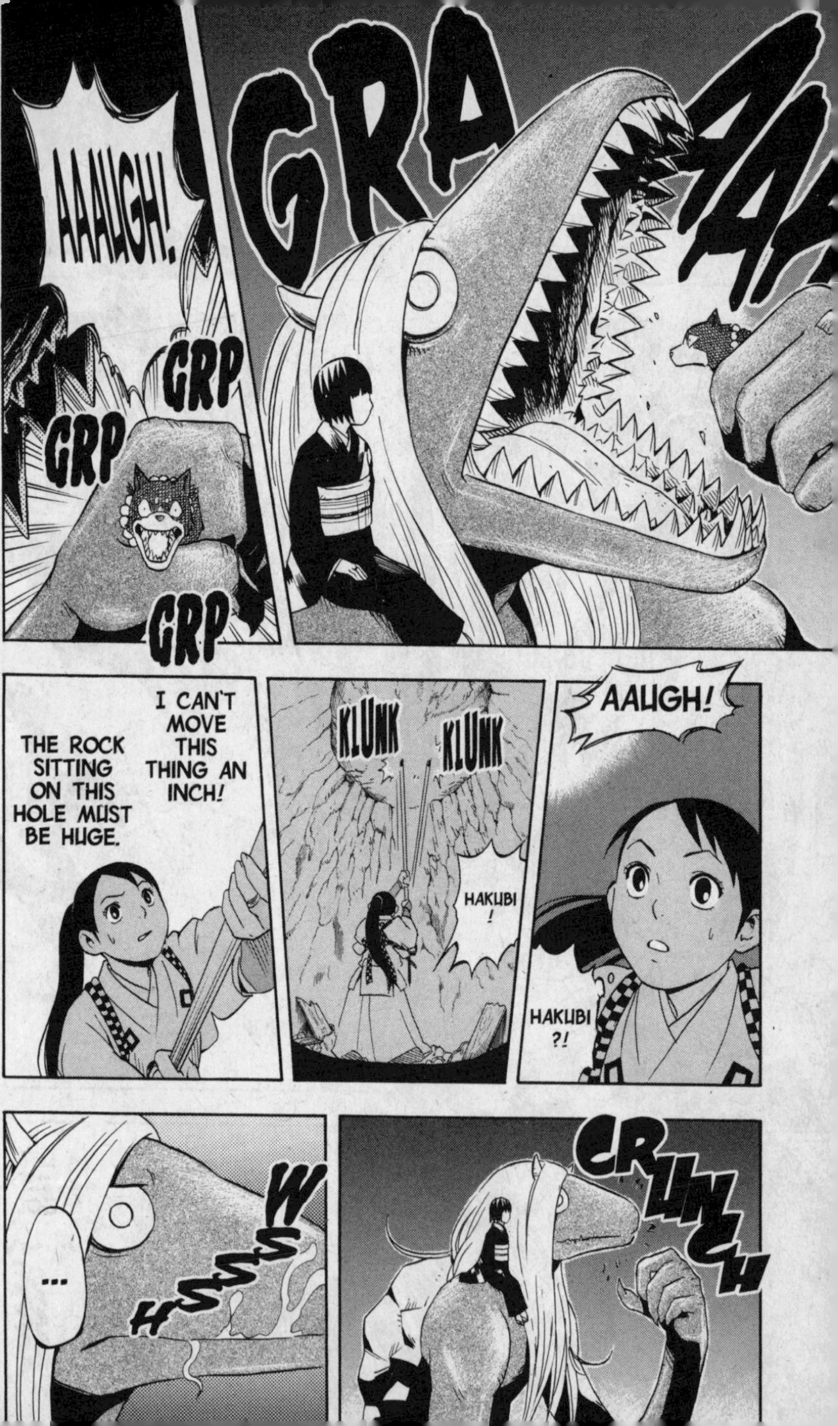
GRA
AA
AAAUGH!
GRP
GRP
GRP
AAUGH!
HAKUBI?!
KLUNK
KLUNK
HAKUBI!
I CAN'T MOVE THIS THING AN INCH!
THE ROCK SITTING ON THIS HOLE MUST BE HUGE.
CRUNCH
HSSSW
...

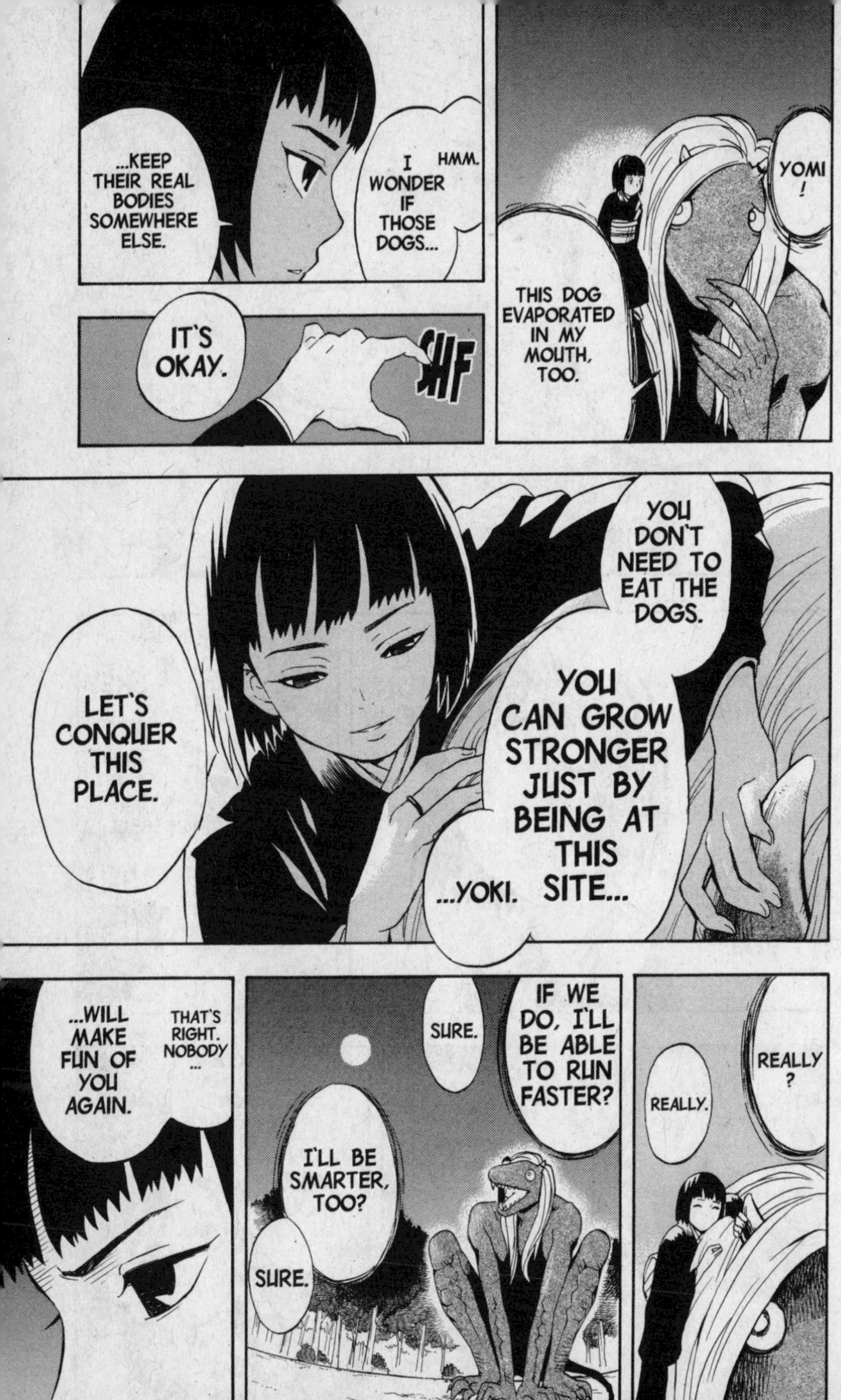
YOMI!
THIS DOG EVAPORATED IN MY MOUTH, TOO.
HMM. I WONDER IF THOSE DOGS...
...KEEP THEIR REAL BODIES SOMEWHERE ELSE.
SHF
IT'S OKAY.
YOU DON'T NEED TO EAT THE DOGS.
YOU CAN GROW STRONGER JUST BY BEING AT THIS SITE...
...YOKI.
LET'S CONQUER THIS PLACE.
REALLY?
REALLY.
IF WE DO, I'LL BE ABLE TO RUN FASTER?
SURE.
I'LL BE SMARTER, TOO?
SURE.
THAT'S RIGHT. NOBODY...
...WILL MAKE FUN OF YOU AGAIN.

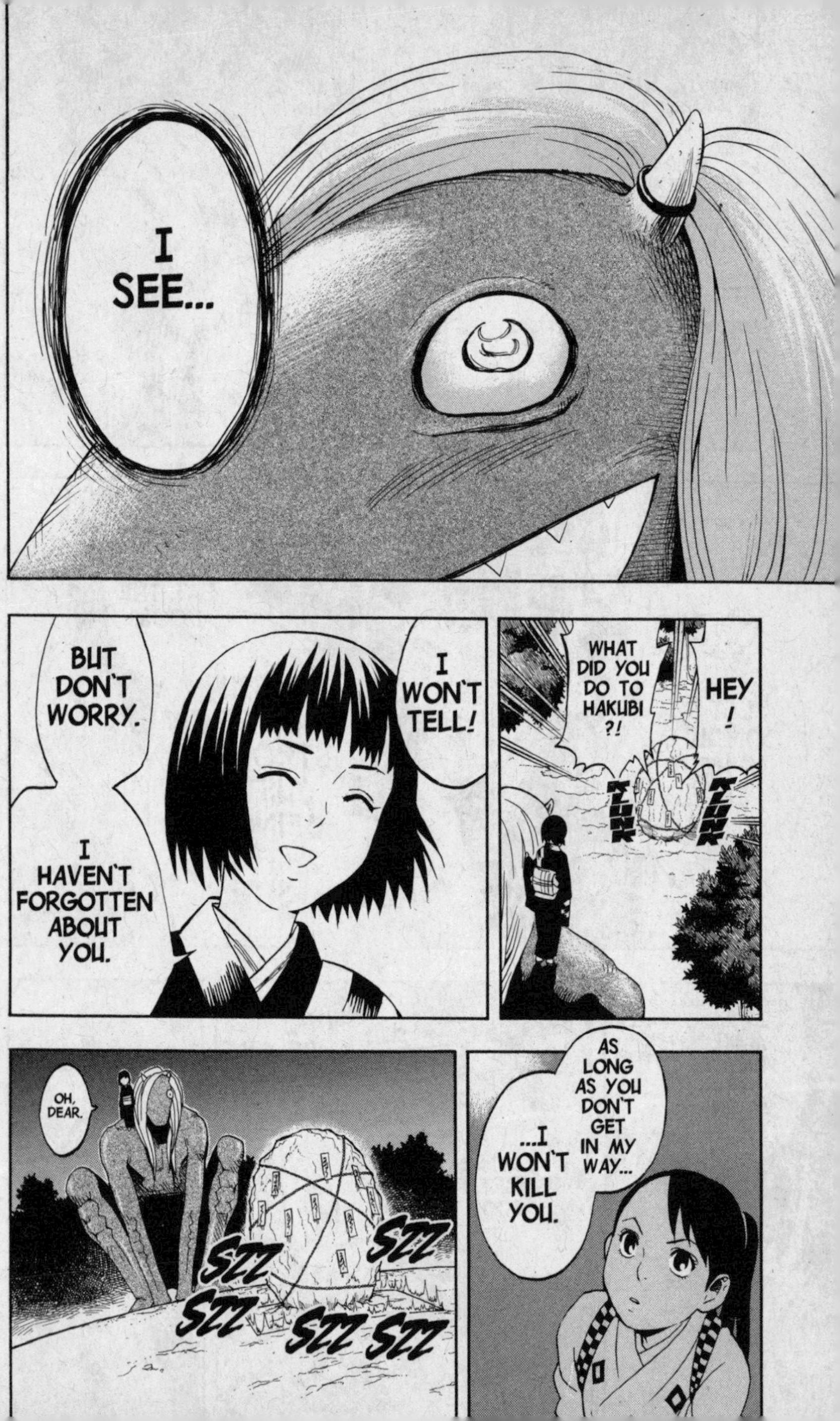
I SEE...
HEY!
WHAT DID YOU DO TO HAKUBI?!
TUNK
TUNK
I WON'T TELL!
BUT DON'T WORRY.
I HAVEN'T FORGOTTEN ABOUT YOU.
AS LONG AS YOU DON'T GET IN MY WAY...
...I WON'T KILL YOU.
OH, DEAR.
SZZ
SZZ
SZZ
SZZ
SZZ
SZZ

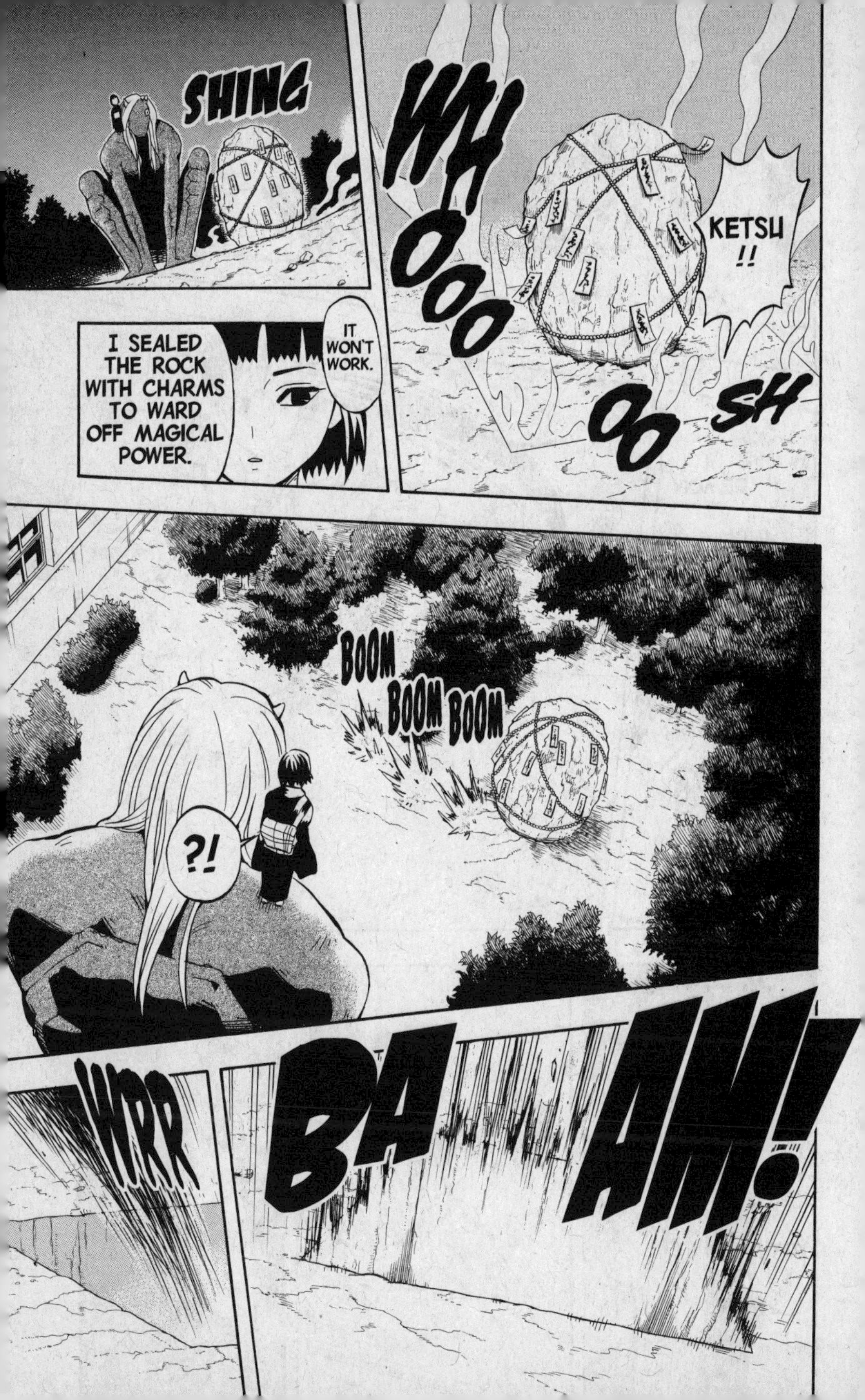
WHOOOOOOSH
KETSU!!
SHING
IT WON'T WORK.
I SEALED THE ROCK WITH CHARMS TO WARD OFF MAGICAL POWER.
BOOM BOOM BOOM
?!
BAAM!
WRR

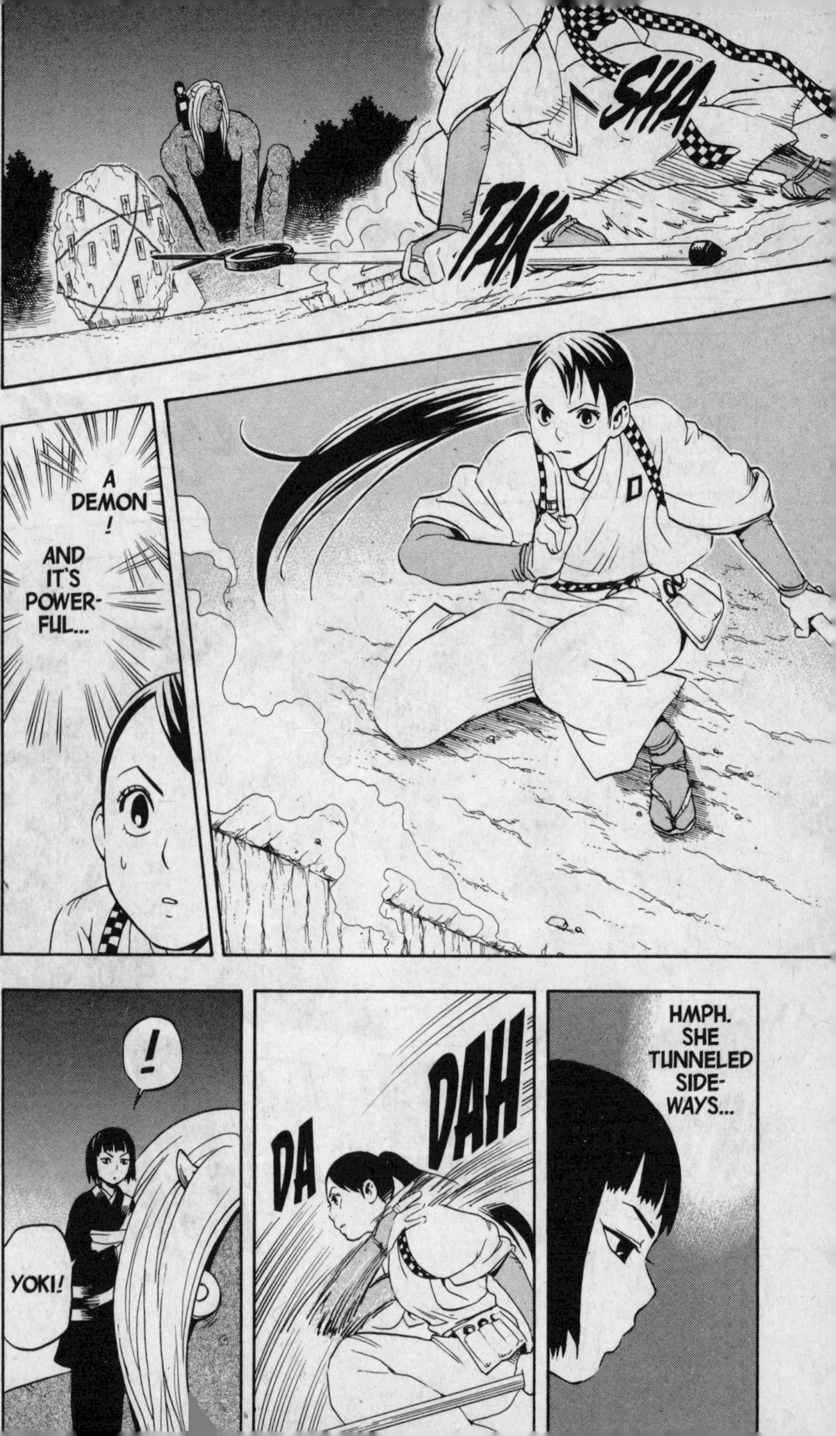
SHA
TAK
A DEMON!
AND IT'S POWERFUL...
HMPH. SHE TUNNELED SIDEWAYS...
DAH
DA
!
YOKI!

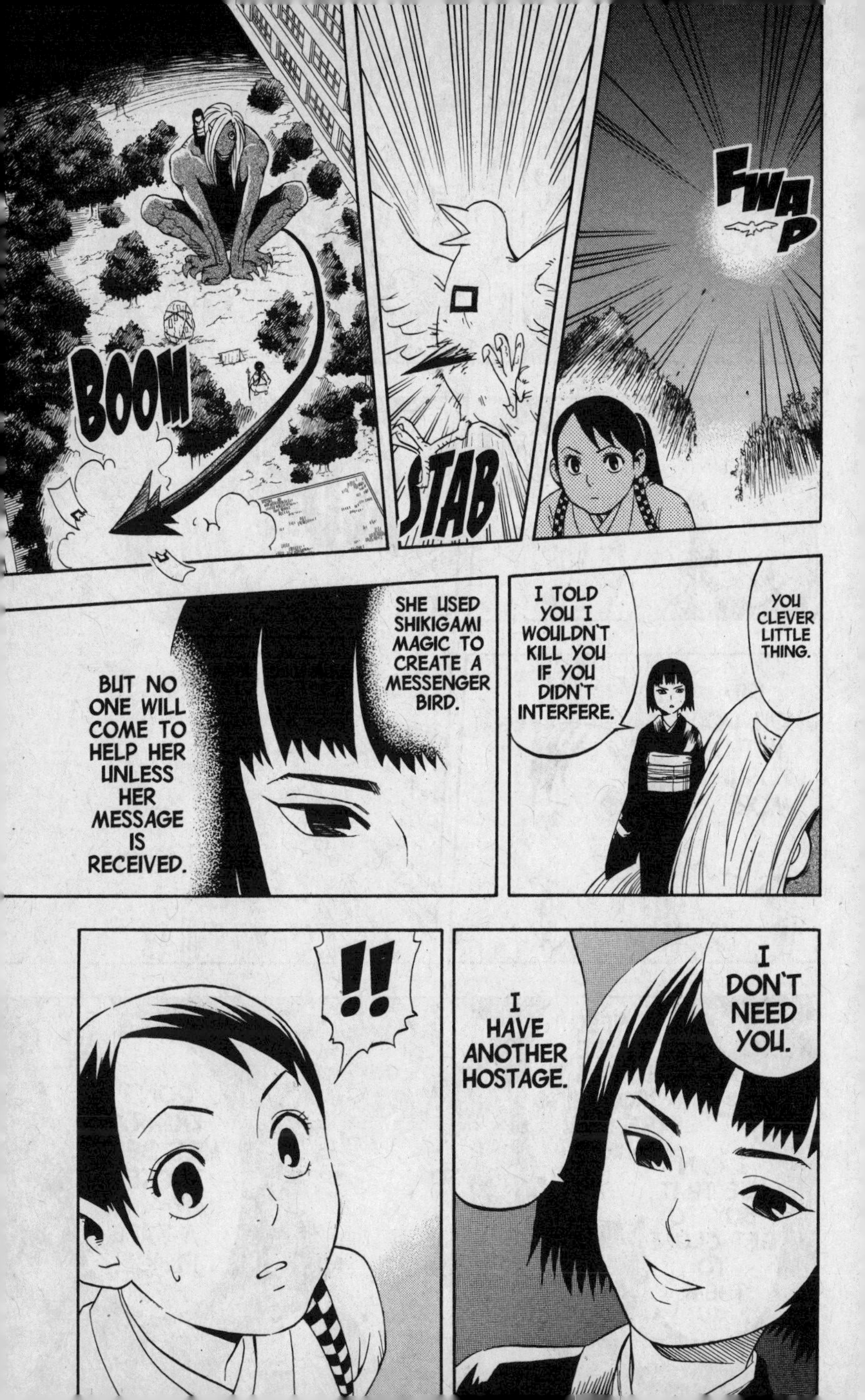
FWAP
STAB
BOOM
YOU CLEVER LITTLE THING.
I TOLD YOU I WOULDN'T KILL YOU IF YOU DIDN'T INTERFERE.
SHE USED SHIKIGAMI MAGIC TO CREATE A MESSENGER BIRD.
BUT NO ONE WILL COME TO HELP HER UNLESS HER MESSAGE IS RECEIVED.
I DON'T NEED YOU.
I HAVE ANOTHER HOSTAGE.
!!

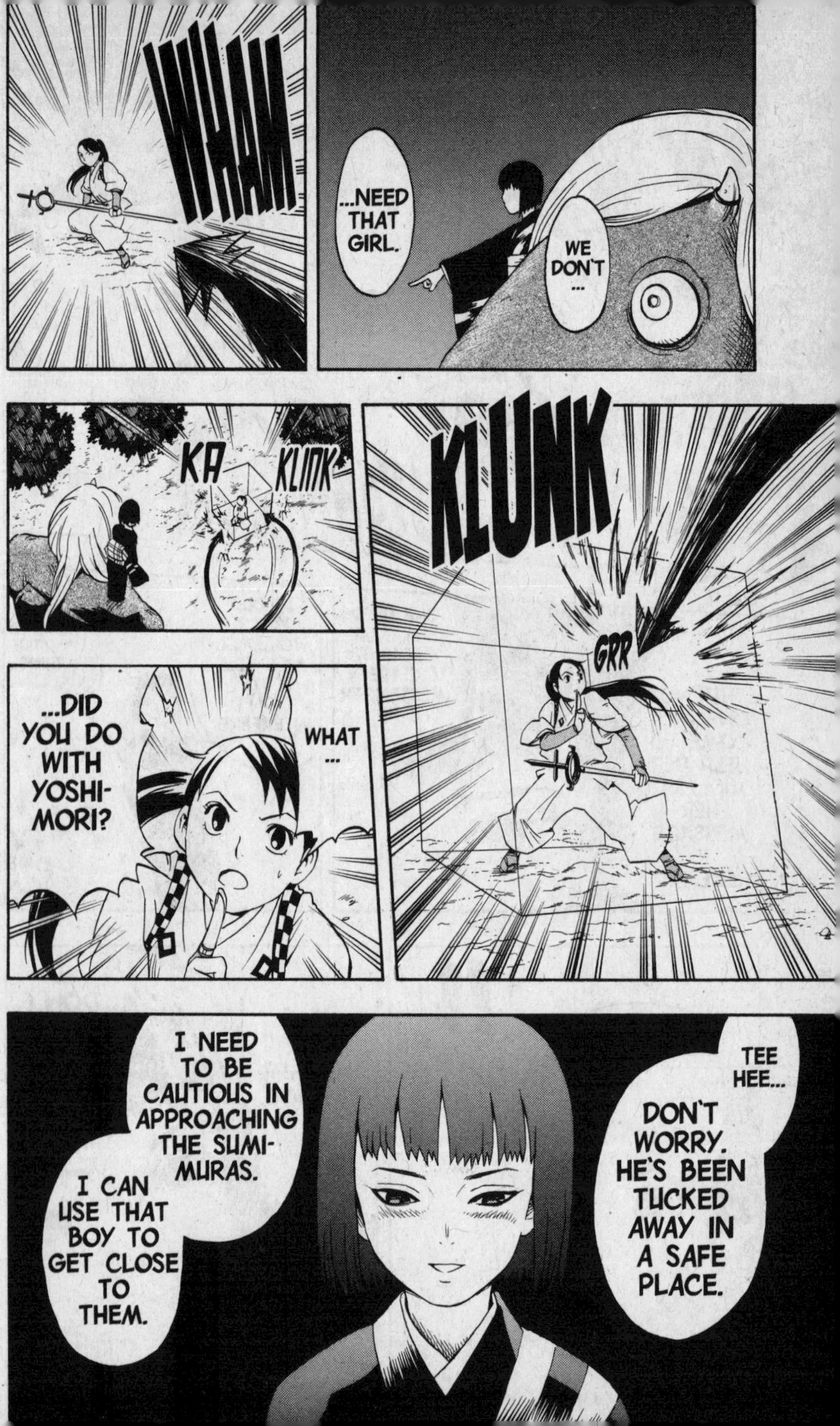
WE DON'T ...
...NEED THAT GIRL.
WHAM
KLUNK
GRR
KA KLINK
WHAT ...
...DID YOU DO WITH YOSHI-MORI?
TEE HEE...
DON'T WORRY. HE'S BEEN TUCKED AWAY IN A SAFE PLACE.
I NEED TO BE CAUTIOUS IN APPROACHING THE SUMI-MURAS.
I CAN USE THAT BOY TO GET CLOSE TO THEM.

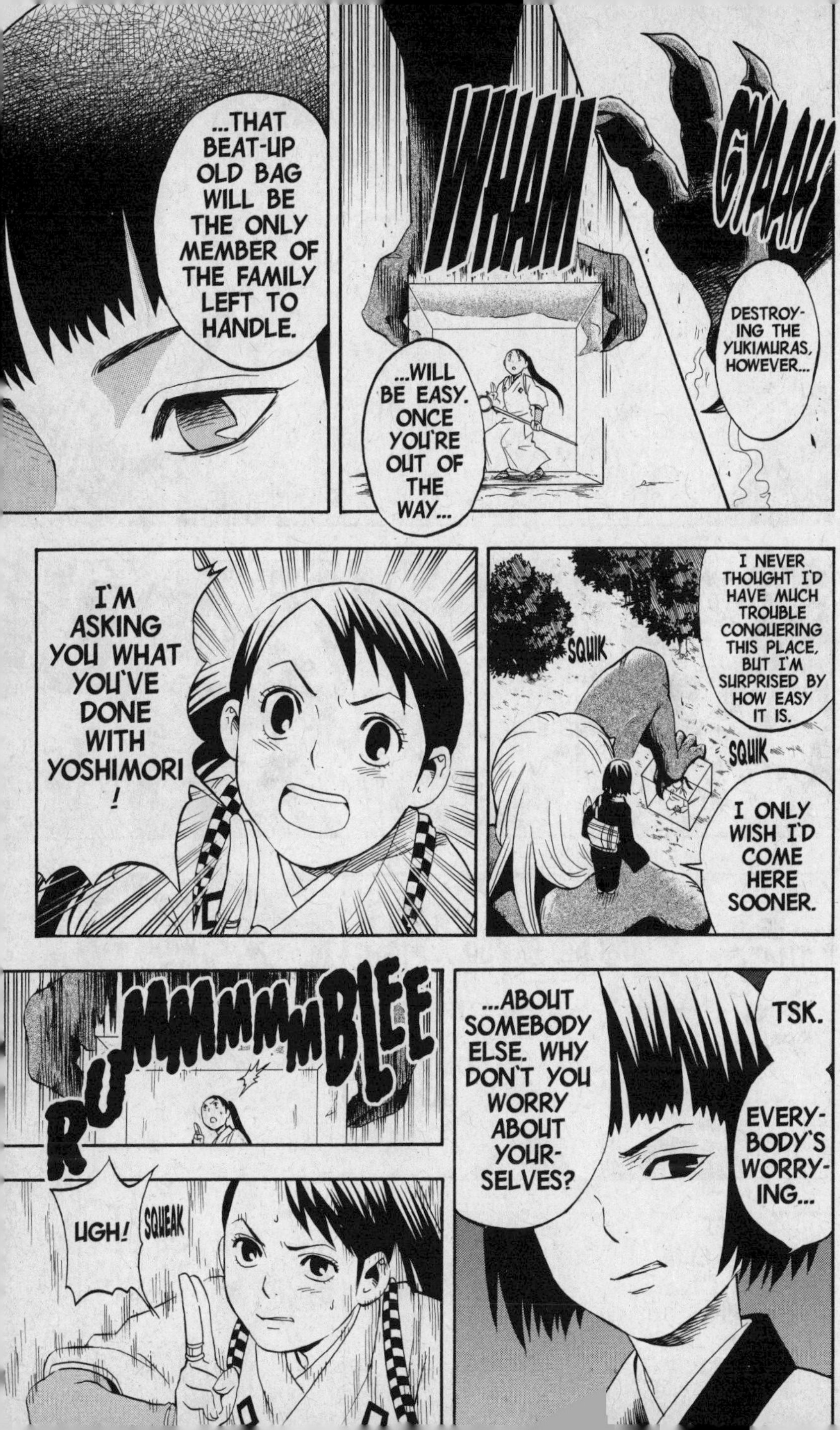
GYAAH
WHAM
DESTROYING THE YUKIMURAS, HOWEVER...
...WILL BE EASY. ONCE YOU'RE OUT OF THE WAY...
...THAT BEAT-UP OLD BAG WILL BE THE ONLY MEMBER OF THE FAMILY LEFT TO HANDLE.
I NEVER THOUGHT I'D HAVE MUCH TROUBLE CONQUERING THIS PLACE, BUT I'M SURPRISED BY HOW EASY IT IS.
SQUIK
SQUIK
I ONLY WISH I'D COME HERE SOONER.
I'M ASKING YOU WHAT YOU'VE DONE WITH YOSHIMORI!
TSK.
EVERYBODY'S WORRYING...
...ABOUT SOMEBODY ELSE. WHY DON'T YOU WORRY ABOUT YOURSELVES?
RUMMMMMMBLEE
UGH!
SQUEAK

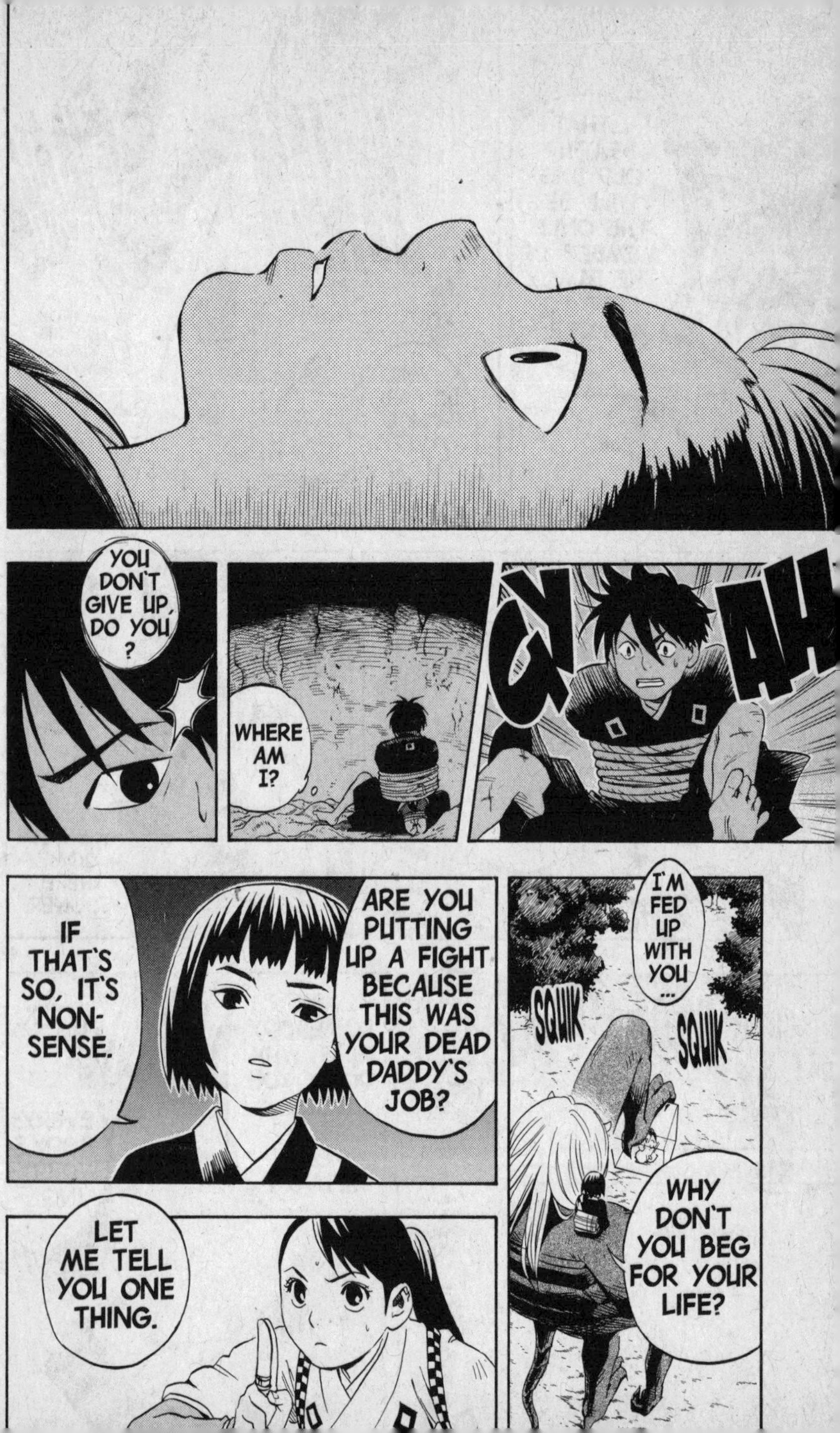
AH
WHERE AM I?
YOU DON'T GIVE UP, DO YOU?
I'M FED UP WITH YOU ...
SQUIK
SQUIK
WHY DON'T YOU BEG FOR YOUR LIFE?
ARE YOU PUTTING UP A FIGHT BECAUSE THIS WAS YOUR DEAD DADDY'S JOB?
IF THAT'S SO, IT'S NON-SENSE.
LET ME TELL YOU ONE THING.

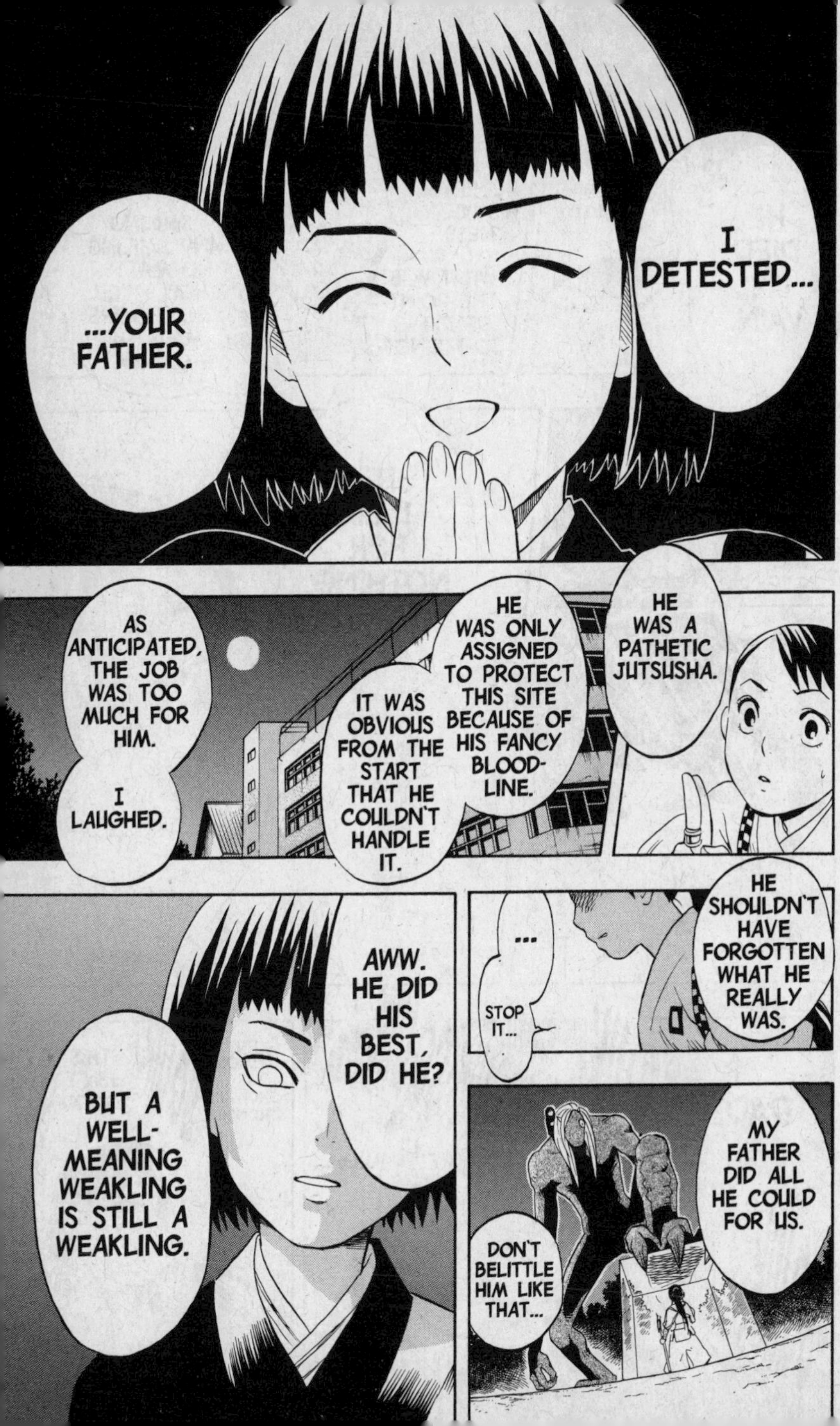
I DETESTED...
...YOUR FATHER.
HE WAS A PATHETIC JUTSUSHA.
HE WAS ONLY ASSIGNED TO PROTECT THIS SITE BECAUSE OF HIS FANCY BLOODLINE.
IT WAS OBVIOUS FROM THE START THAT HE COULDN'T HANDLE IT.
AS ANTICIPATED, THE JOB WAS TOO MUCH FOR HIM.
I LAUGHED.
HE SHOULDN'T HAVE FORGOTTEN WHAT HE REALLY WAS.
...
STOP IT...
MY FATHER DID ALL HE COULD FOR US.
DON'T BELITTLE HIM LIKE THAT...
AWW. HE DID HIS BEST, DID HE?
BUT A WELL-MEANING WEAKLING IS STILL A WEAKLING.

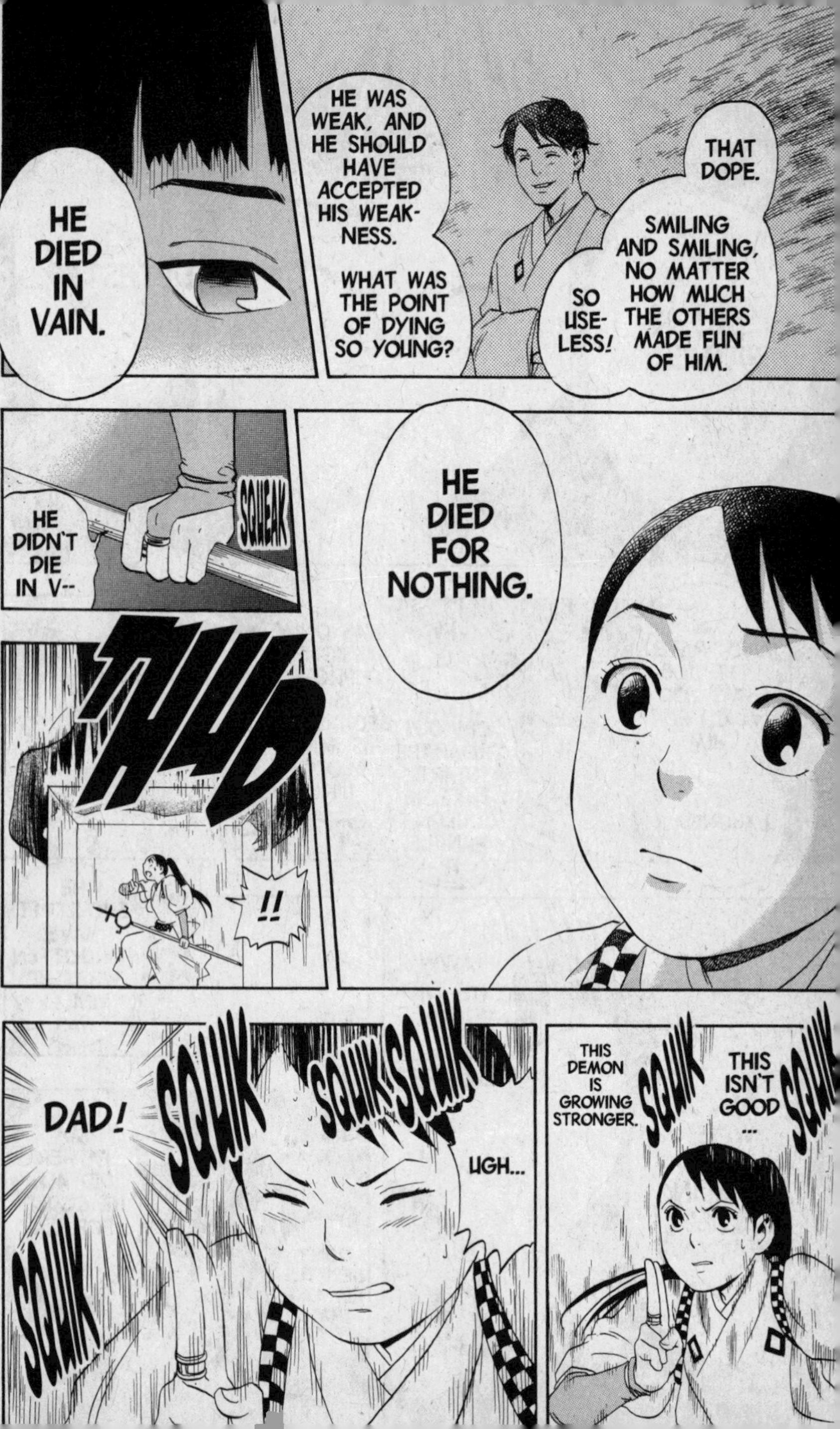
THAT DOPE.
SMILING AND SMILING, NO MATTER HOW MUCH THE OTHERS MADE FUN OF HIM.
SO USELESS!
HE WAS WEAK, AND HE SHOULD HAVE ACCEPTED HIS WEAKNESS.
WHAT WAS THE POINT OF DYING SO YOUNG?
HE DIED IN VAIN.
HE DIED FOR NOTHING.
HE DIDN'T DIE IN V--
SQUEAK
THUD
!!
SQUIK
THIS ISN'T GOOD...
SQUIK
THIS DEMON IS GROWING STRONGER.
SQUIK SQUIK
UGH...
SQUIK
DAD!
SQUIK

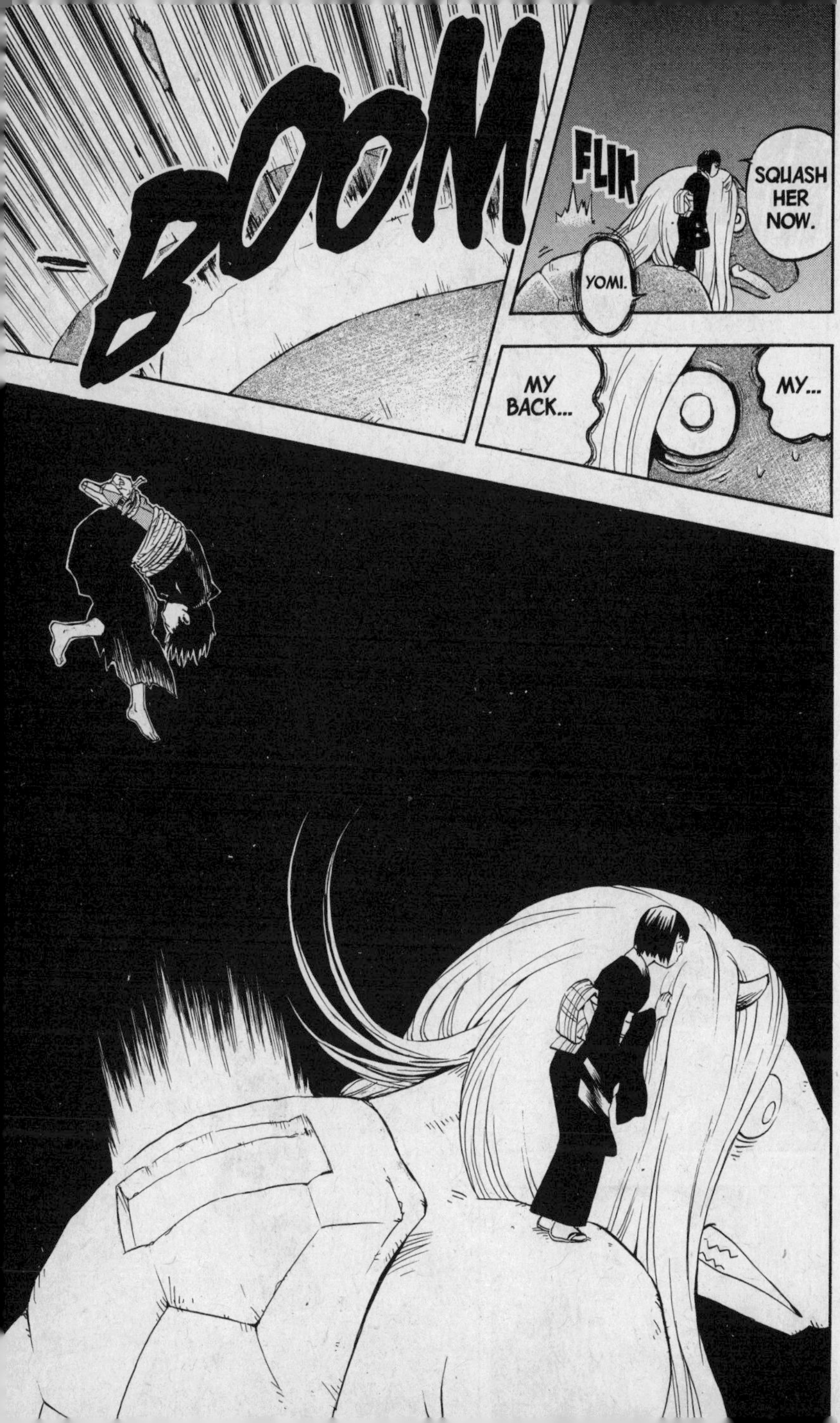
SQUASH HER NOW.
YOMI.
FLIK
MY...
MY BACK...
BOOM

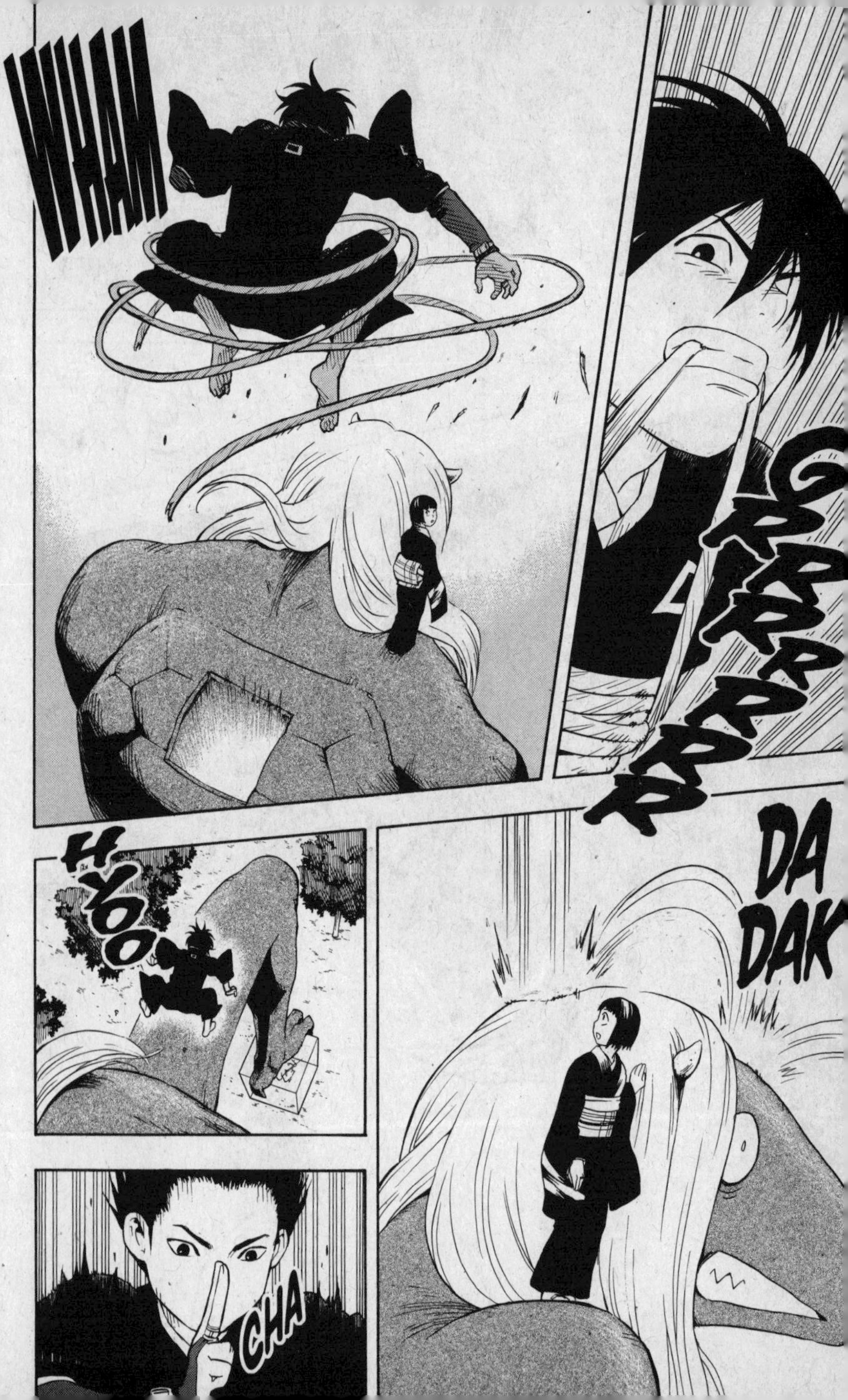
GRRRRRR
WHAM
DA DAK
HYOO
CHA

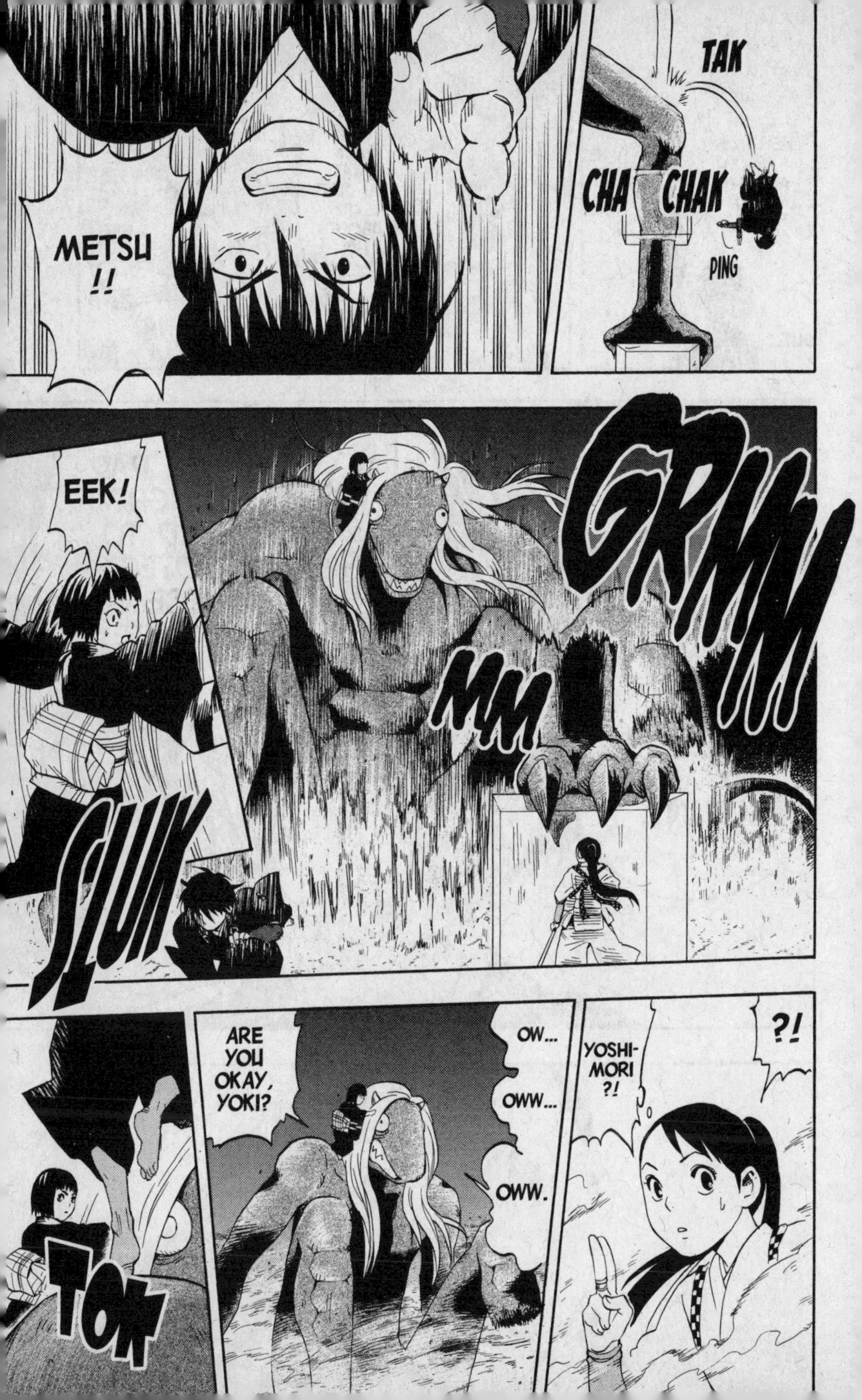
TAK
CHA CHAK
PING
METSU !!
GRMMMM
EEK!
SLUK
?!
YOSHIMORI?!
OW... OWW... OWW.
ARE YOU OKAY, YOKI?
TOK

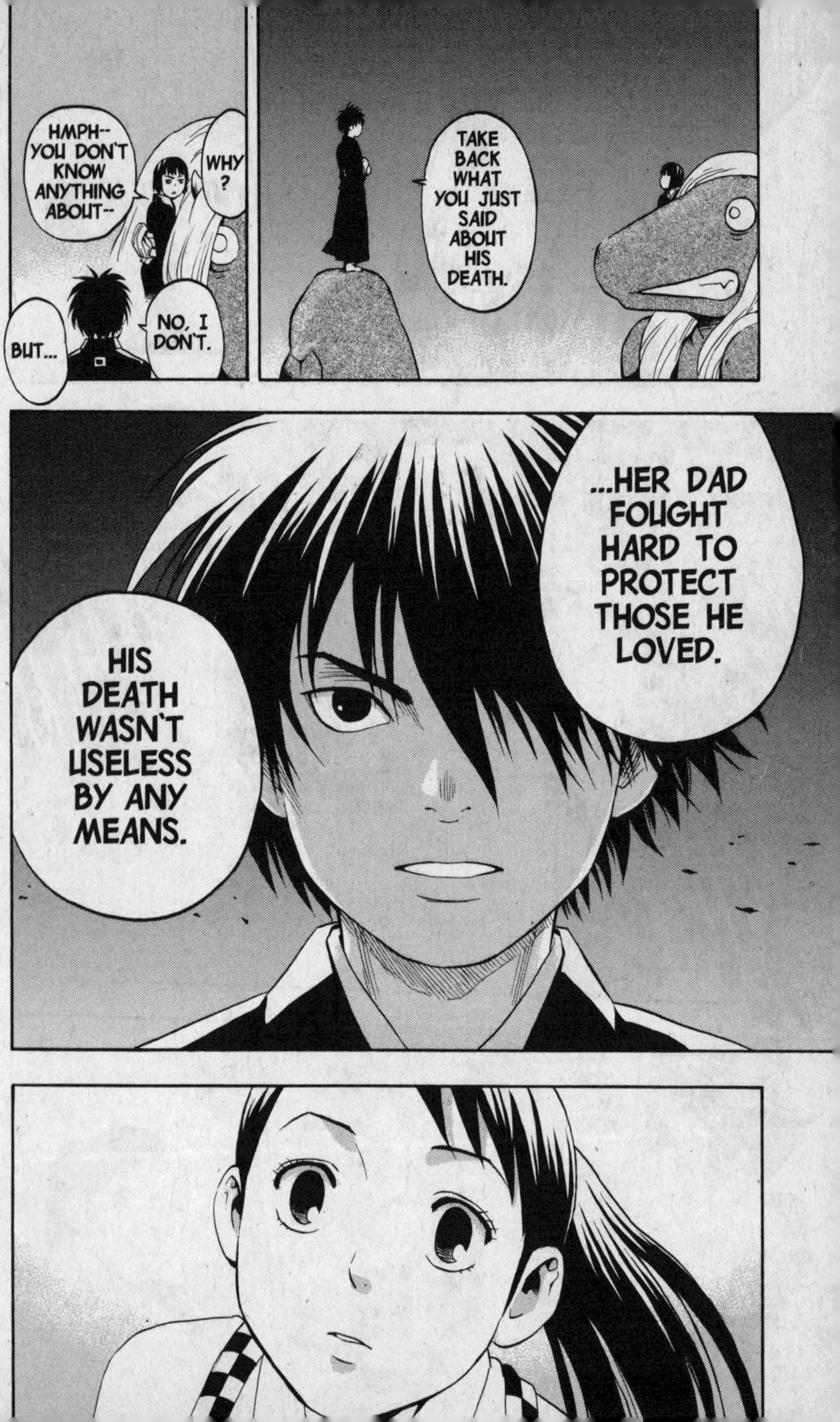
TAKE BACK WHAT YOU JUST SAID ABOUT HIS DEATH.
WHY?
HMPH-- YOU DON'T KNOW ANYTHING ABOUT--
NO, I DON'T.
BUT...
...HER DAD FOUGHT HARD TO PROTECT THOSE HE LOVED.
HIS DEATH WASN'T USELESS BY ANY MEANS.

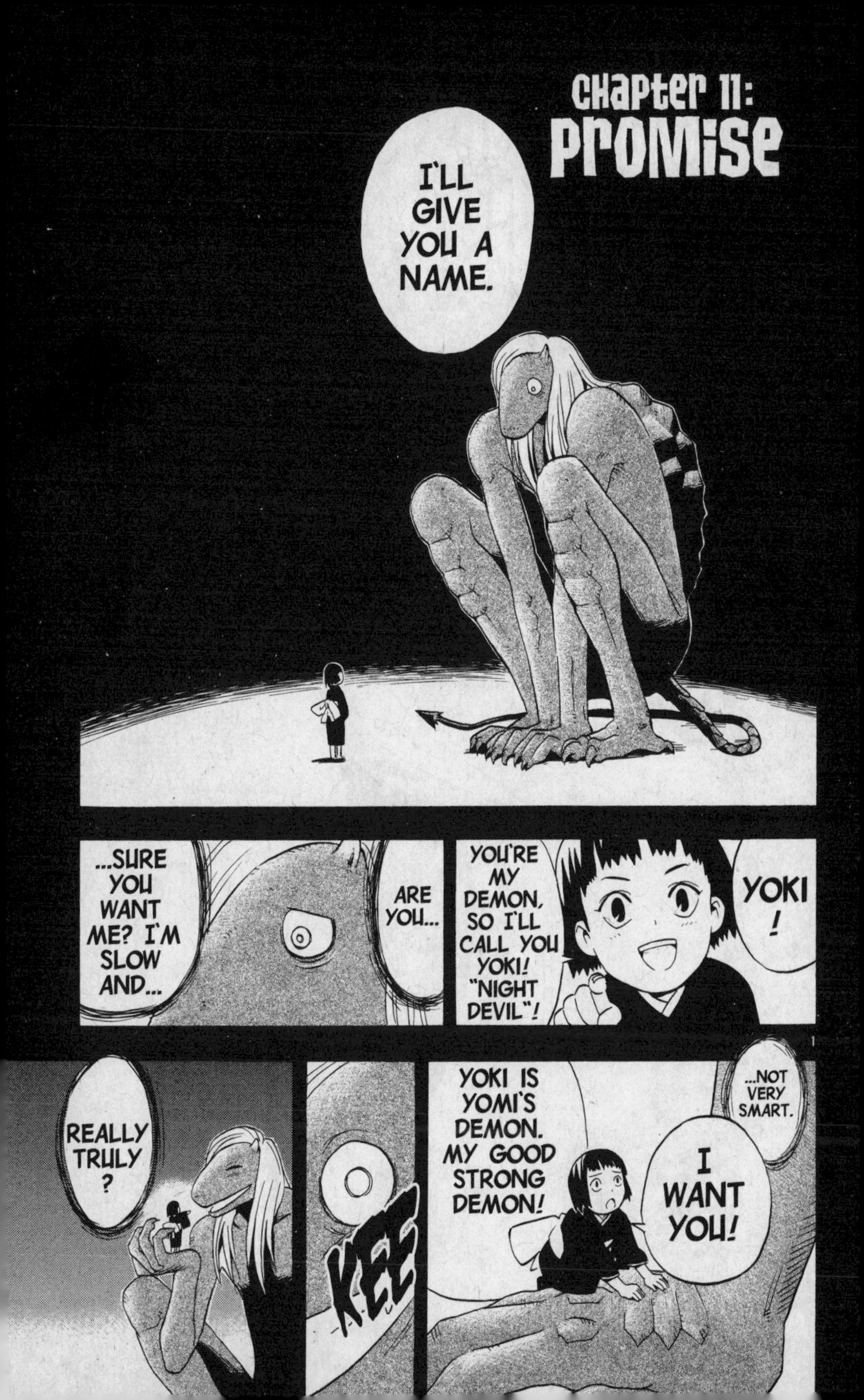
Chapter 11: Promise
I'LL GIVE YOU A NAME.
YOKI!
YOU'RE MY DEMON, SO I'LL CALL YOU YOKI! "NIGHT DEVIL"!
ARE YOU...
...SURE YOU WANT ME? I'M SLOW AND...
...NOT VERY SMART.
I WANT YOU!
YOKI IS YOMI'S DEMON. MY GOOD STRONG DEMON!
KEE
REALLY TRULY?

CHAPTER 11:
PROMISE

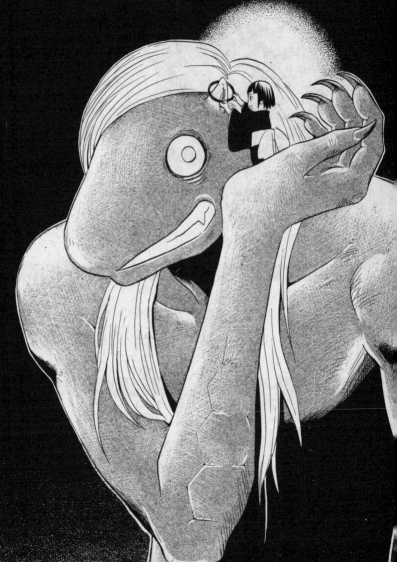

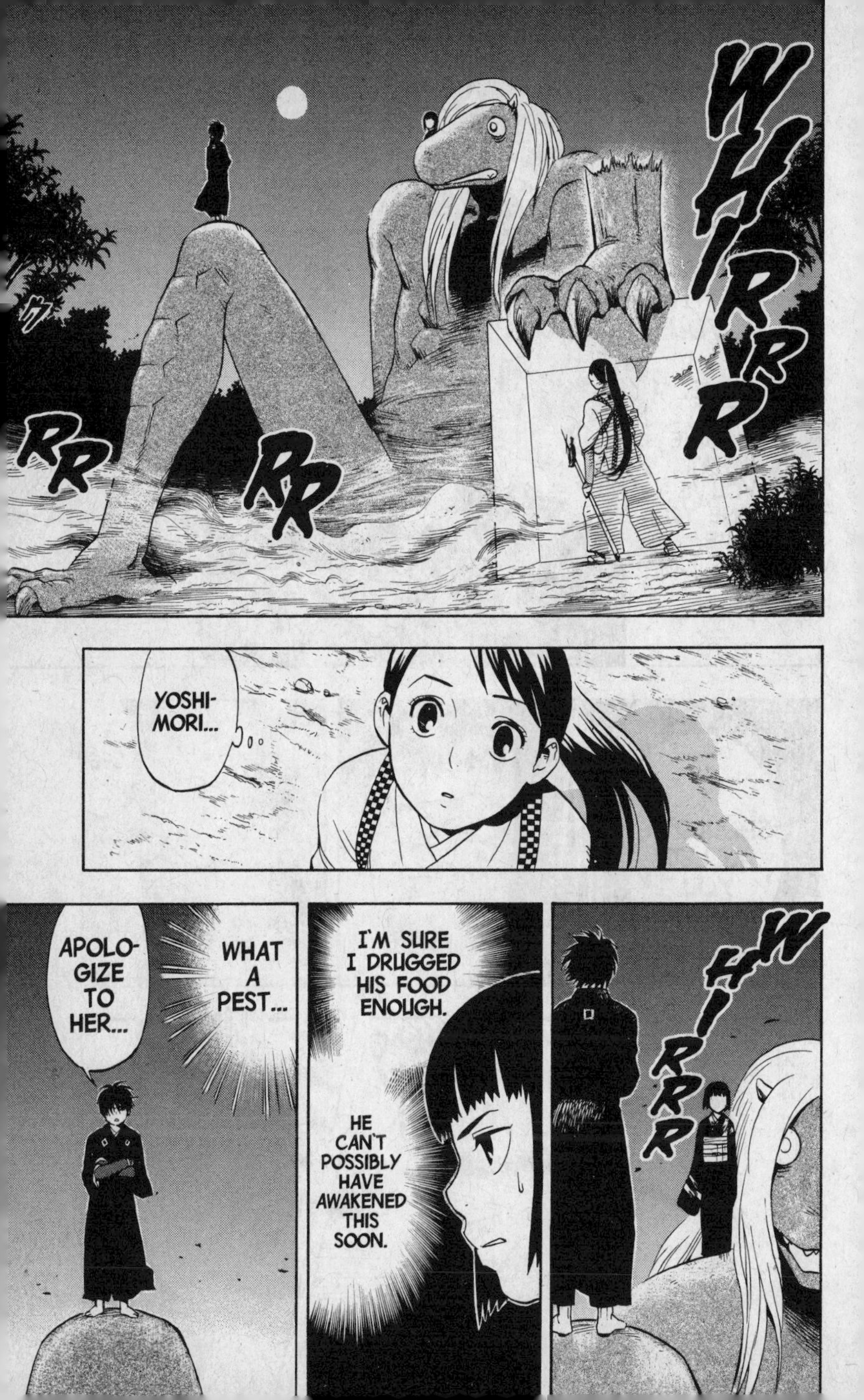
WHIRRRR
RR
RR
YOSHI-MORI...
WHIRRR
I'M SURE I DRUGGED HIS FOOD ENOUGH.
HE CAN'T POSSIBLY HAVE AWAKENED THIS SOON.
WHAT A PEST...
APOLO-GIZE TO HER...

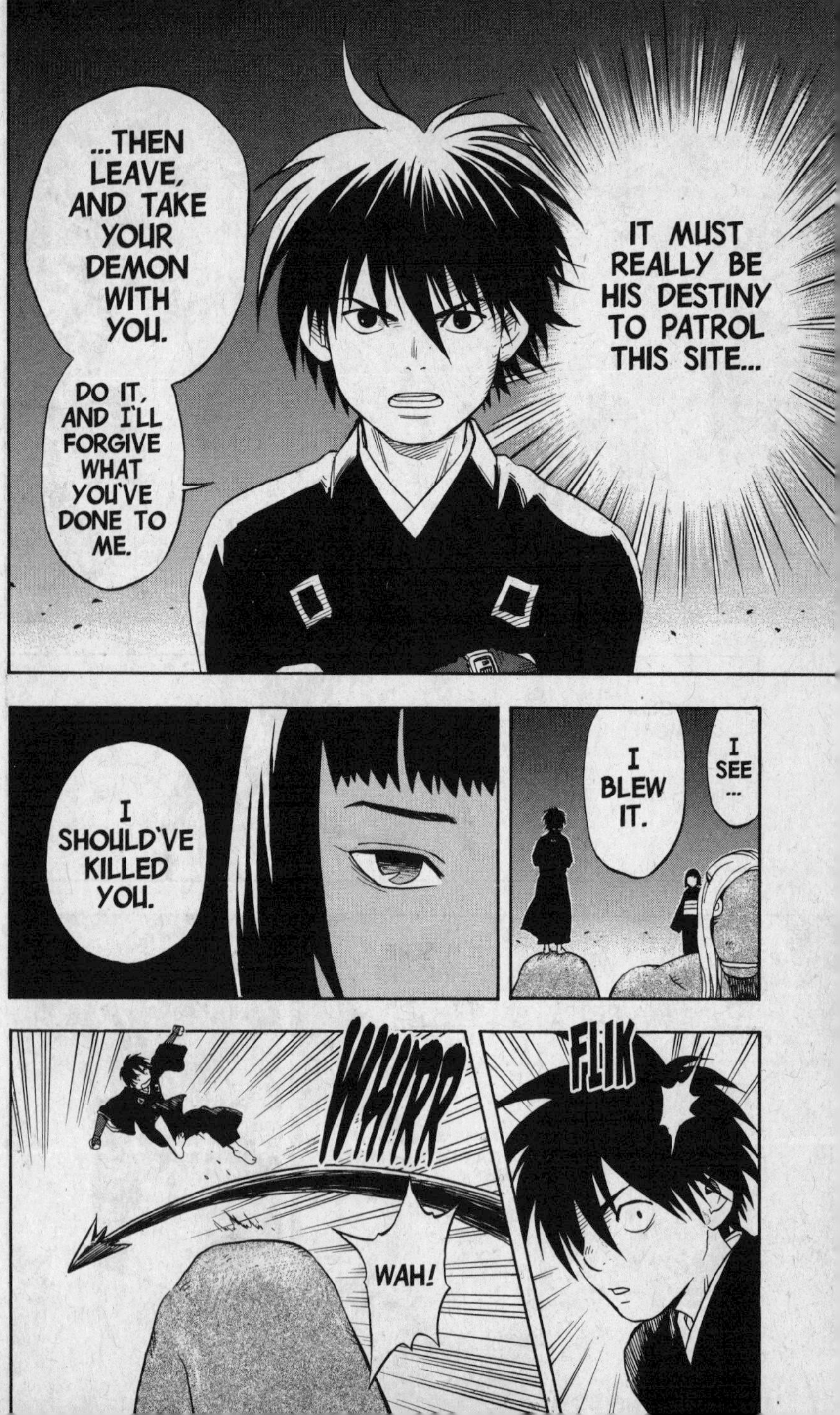
IT MUST REALLY BE HIS DESTINY TO PATROL THIS SITE...
...THEN LEAVE, AND TAKE YOUR DEMON WITH YOU.
DO IT, AND I'LL FORGIVE WHAT YOU'VE DONE TO ME.
I SEE...
I BLEW IT.
I SHOULD'VE KILLED YOU.
FLIK
WHIRR
WAH!

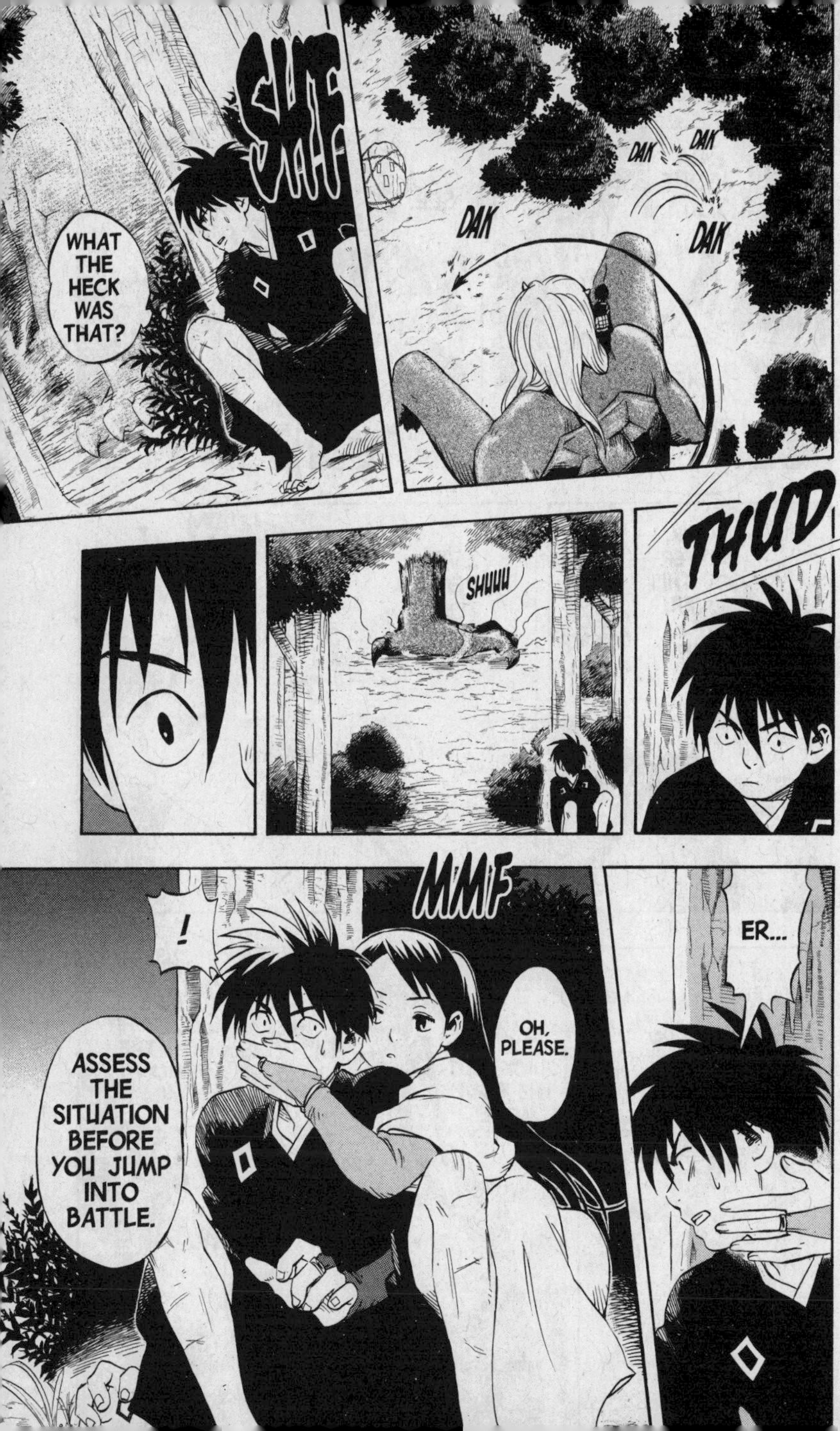
DAK
DAK
DAK
DAK
WHAT THE HECK WAS THAT?
THUD
SHUUU
ER...
MMF
!
OH, PLEASE.
ASSESS THE SITUATION BEFORE YOU JUMP INTO BATTLE.

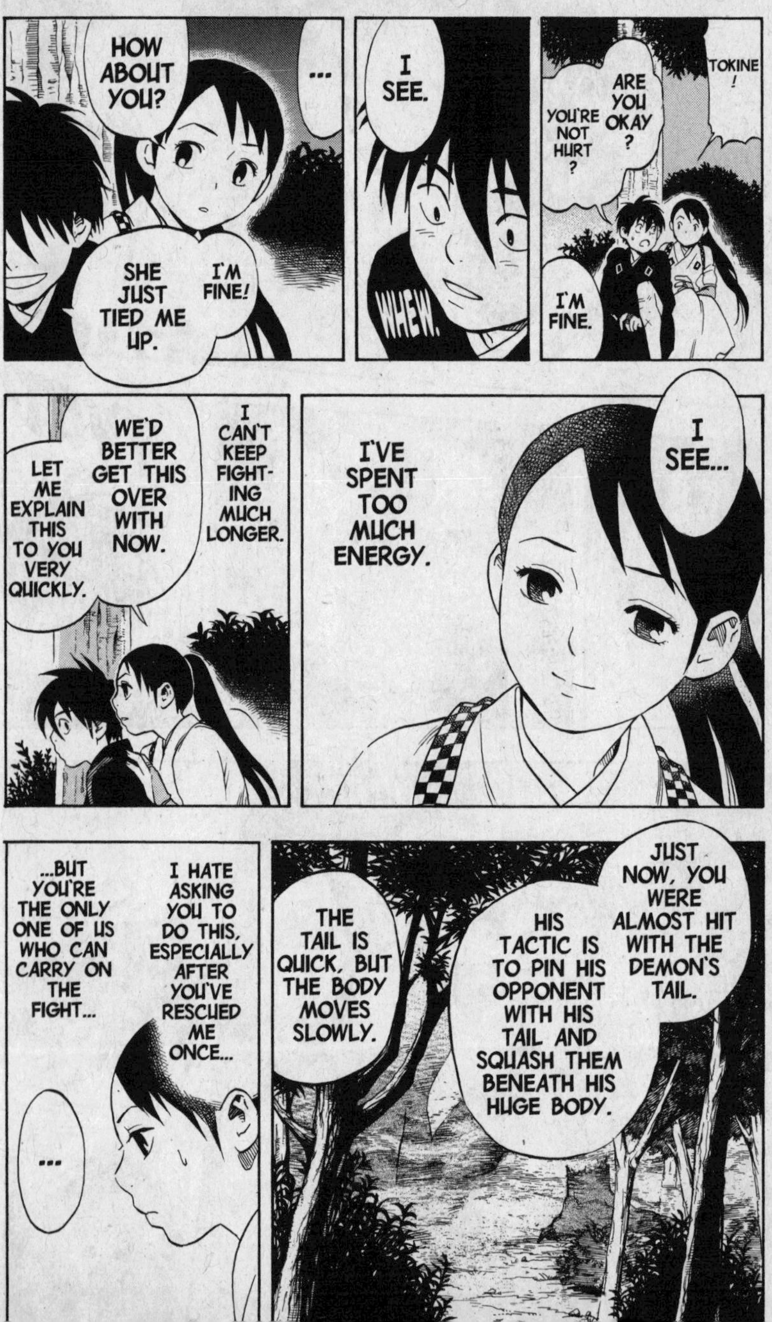
TOKINE!
ARE YOU OKAY?
YOU'RE NOT HURT?
I'M FINE.
I SEE.
WHEW.
...
HOW ABOUT YOU?
I'M FINE!
SHE JUST TIED ME UP.
I SEE...
I'VE SPENT TOO MUCH ENERGY.
I CAN'T KEEP FIGHT-ING MUCH LONGER.
WE'D BETTER GET THIS OVER WITH NOW.
LET ME EXPLAIN THIS TO YOU VERY QUICKLY.
JUST NOW, YOU WERE ALMOST HIT WITH THE DEMON'S TAIL.
HIS TACTIC IS TO PIN HIS OPPONENT WITH HIS TAIL AND SQUASH THEM BENEATH HIS HUGE BODY.
THE TAIL IS QUICK, BUT THE BODY MOVES SLOWLY.
I HATE ASKING YOU TO DO THIS, ESPECIALLY AFTER YOU'VE RESCUED ME ONCE...
...BUT YOU'RE THE ONLY ONE OF US WHO CAN CARRY ON THE FIGHT...
...

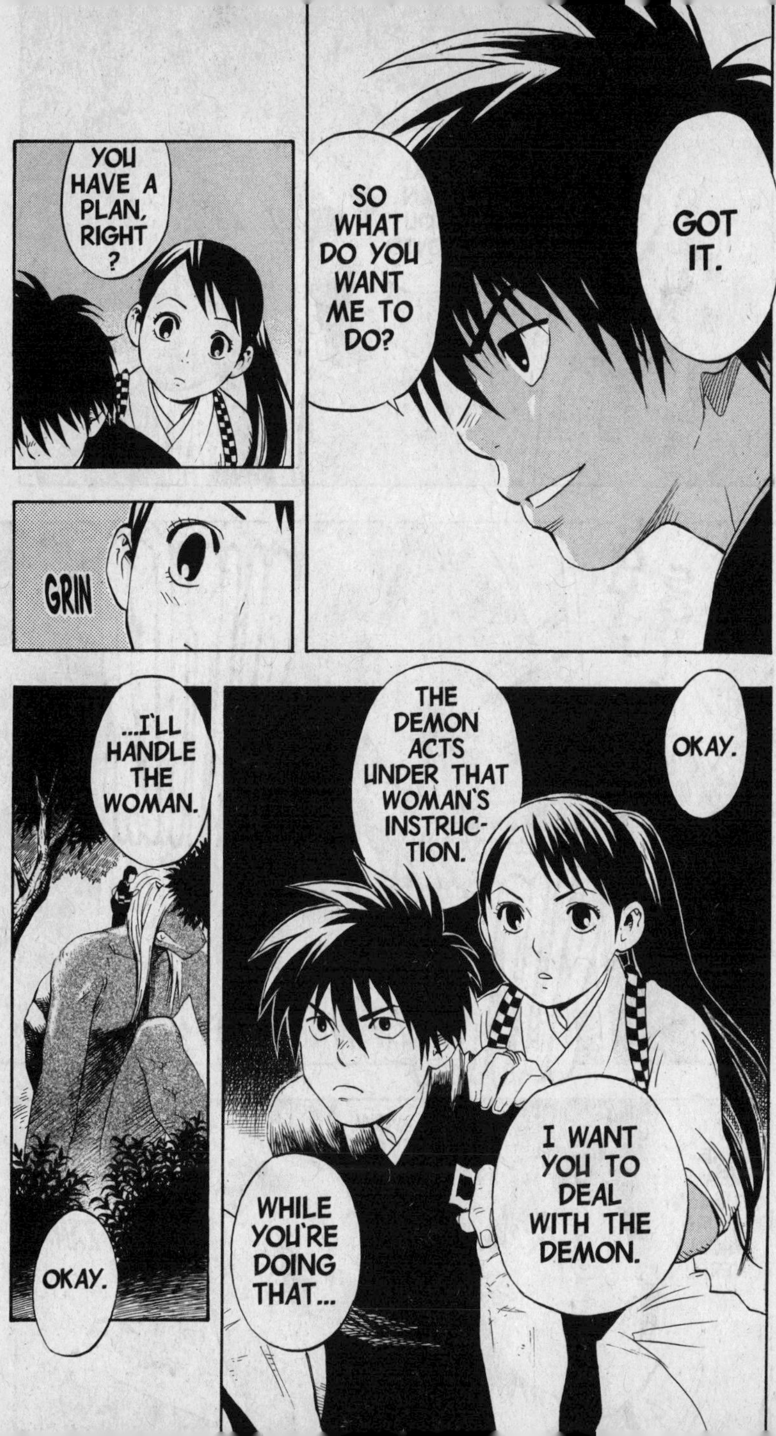
GOT IT.
SO WHAT DO YOU WANT ME TO DO?
YOU HAVE A PLAN, RIGHT?
GRIN
OKAY.
THE DEMON ACTS UNDER THAT WOMAN'S INSTRUC-TION.
I WANT YOU TO DEAL WITH THE DEMON.
WHILE YOU'RE DOING THAT...
...I'LL HANDLE THE WOMAN.
OKAY.

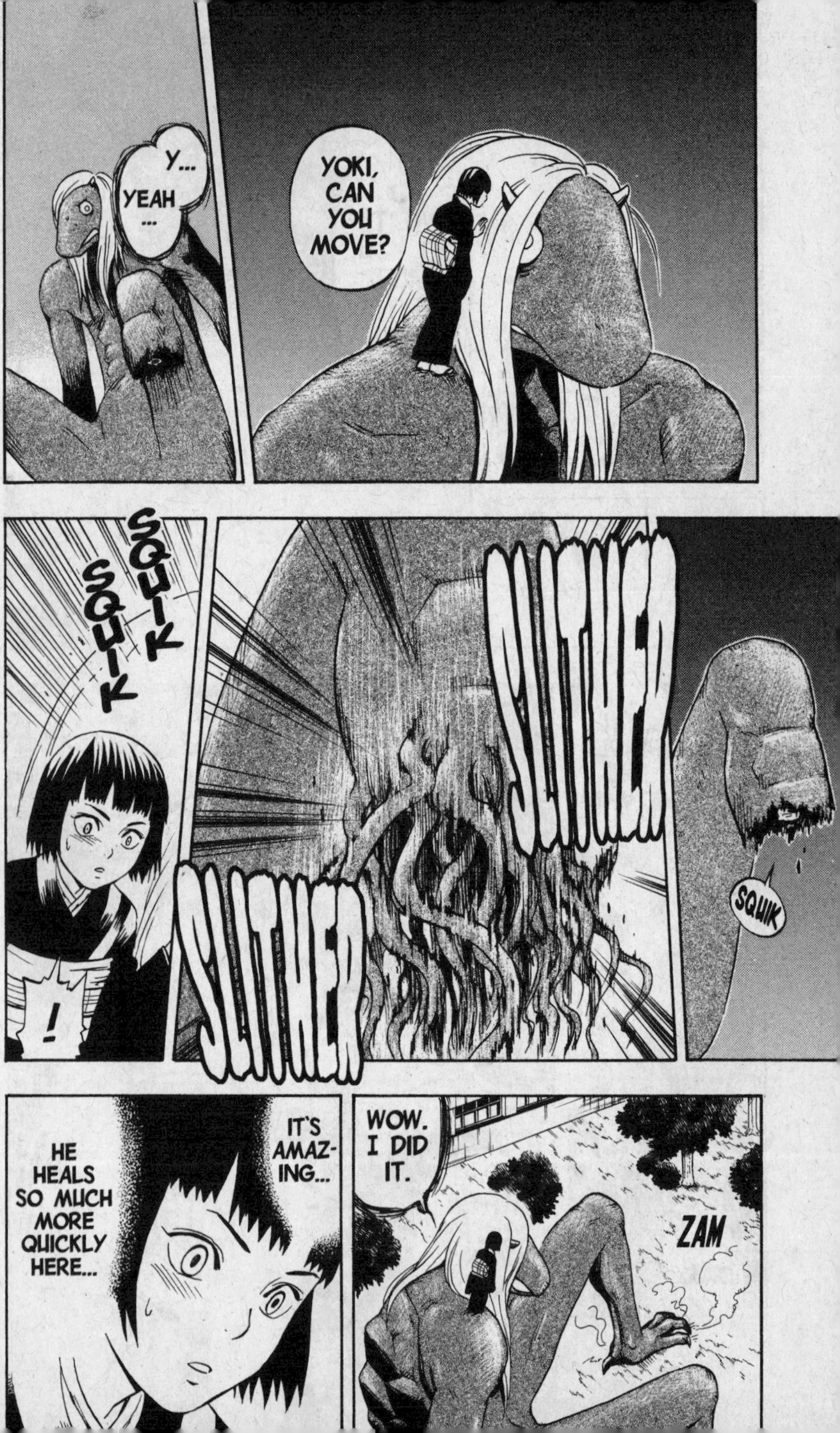
YOKI, CAN YOU MOVE?
Y...
YEAH ...
SQUIK
SLITHER
SLITHER
SQUIK
SQUIK
!
WOW. I DID IT.
ZAM
IT'S AMAZ-ING...
HE HEALS SO MUCH MORE QUICKLY HERE...

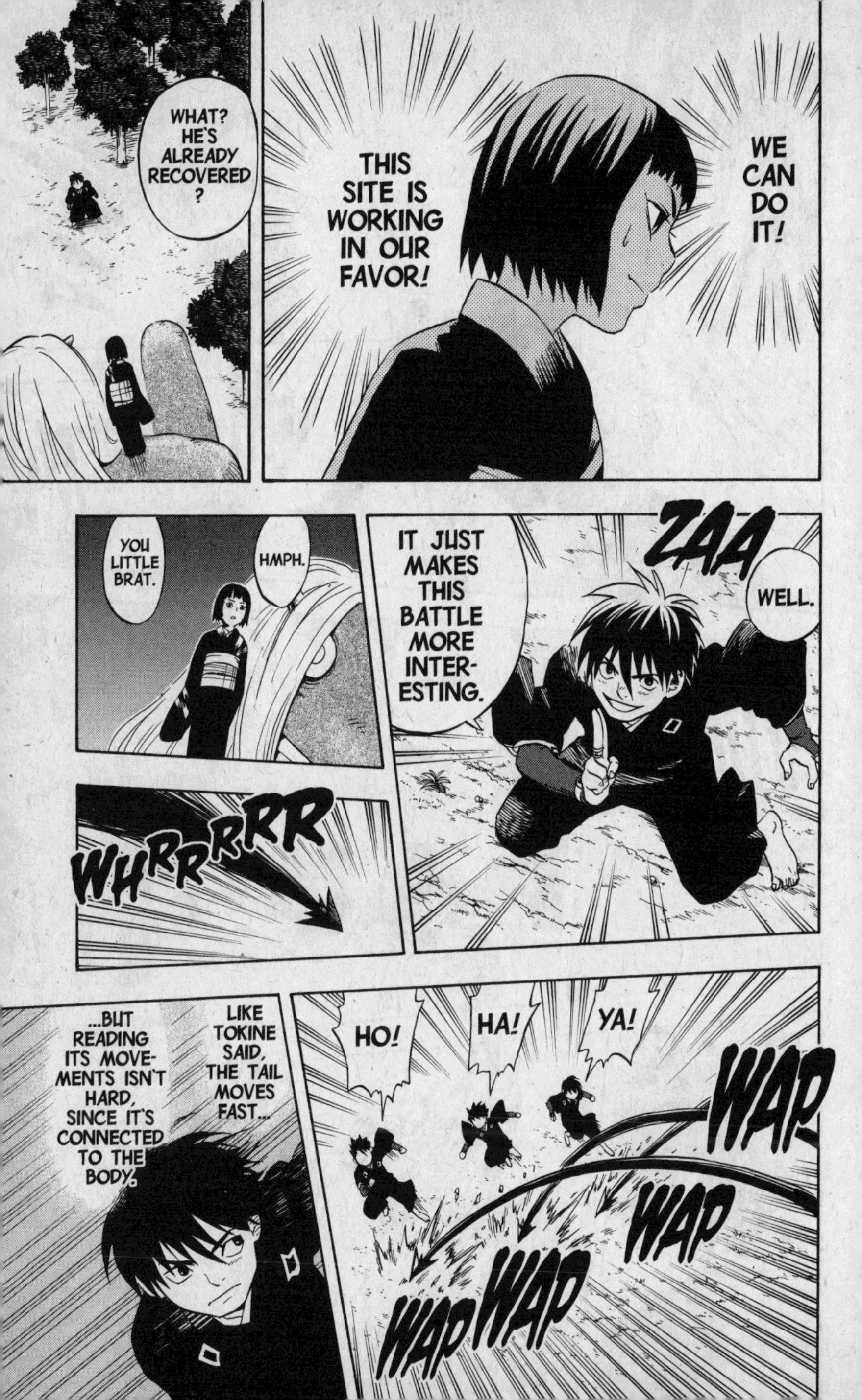
THIS SITE IS WORKING IN OUR FAVOR!
WE CAN DO IT!
WHAT? HE'S ALREADY RECOVERED?
ZAA
WELL.
IT JUST MAKES THIS BATTLE MORE INTER-ESTING.
HMPH.
YOU LITTLE BRAT.
WHRRRRR
YA!
HA!
HO!
WAP
WAP
WAP
WAP
LIKE TOKINE SAID, THE TAIL MOVES FAST...
...BUT READING ITS MOVE-MENTS ISN'T HARD, SINCE IT'S CONNECTED TO THE BODY.

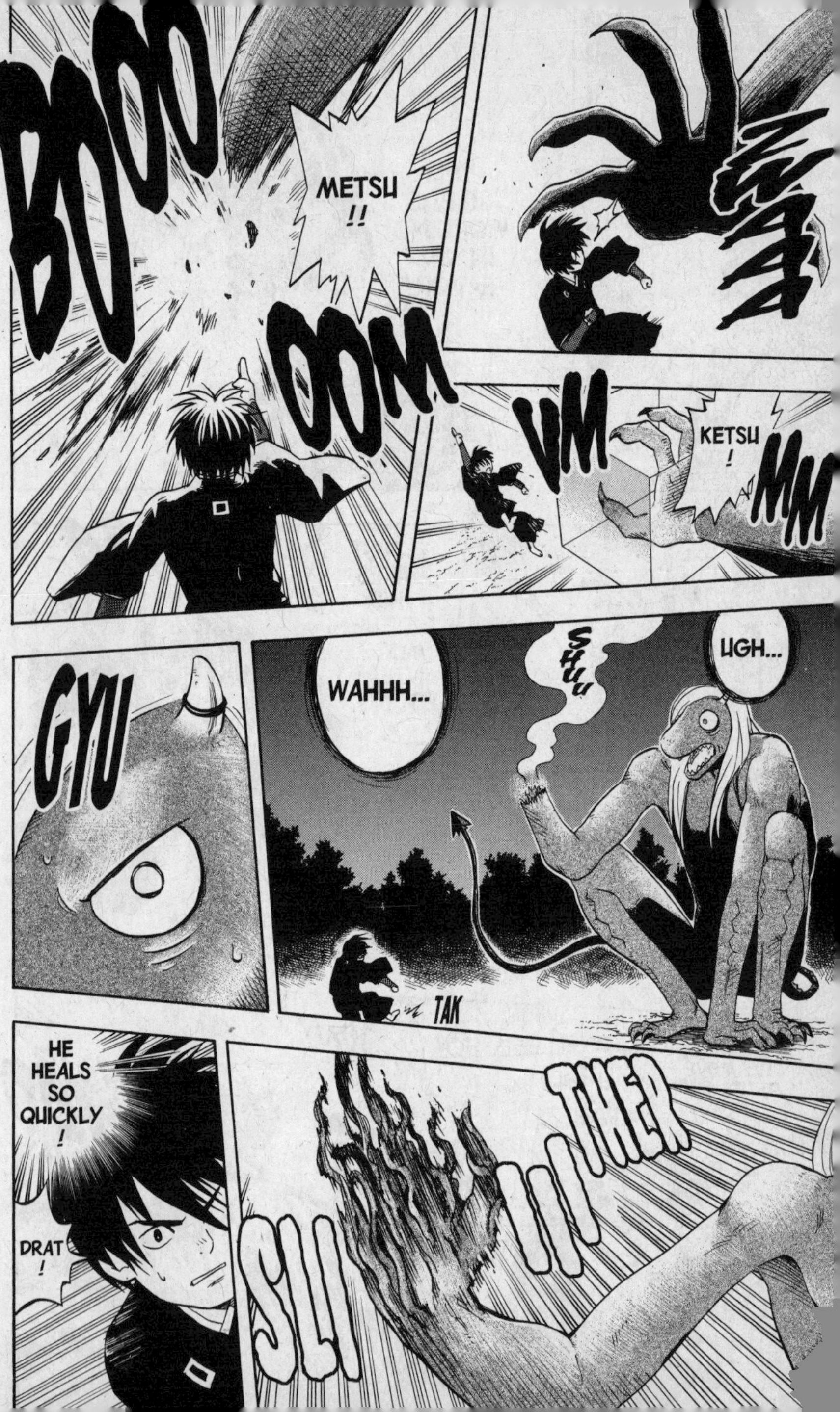
VM
KETSU!
MM
BOOO
METSU!!
OOM
SHUU
UGH...
WAHHH...
TAK
GYU
SLI
II
THER
HE HEALS SO QUICKLY!
DRAT!

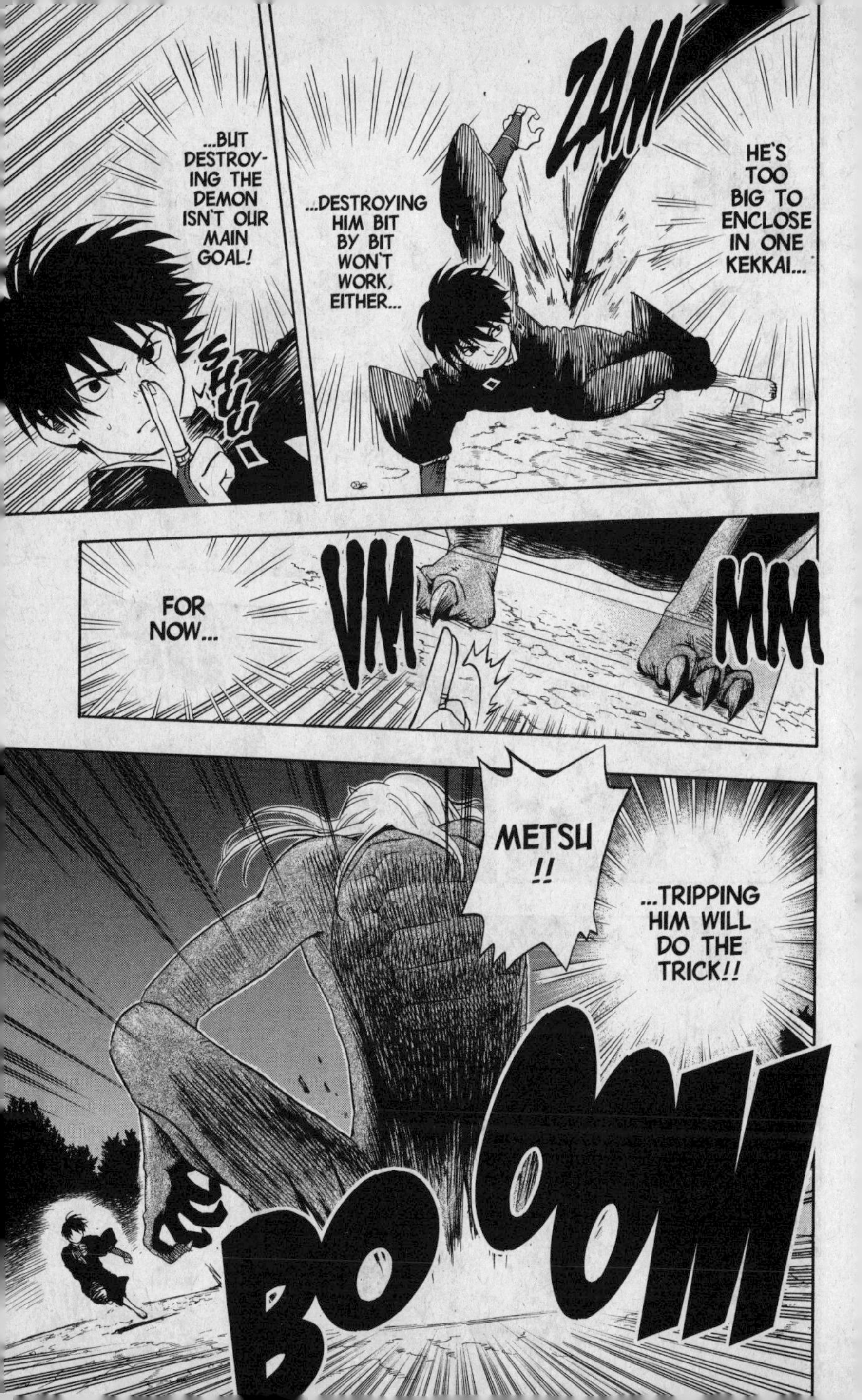
ZAM
HE'S TOO BIG TO ENCLOSE IN ONE KEKKAI...
...DESTROYING HIM BIT BY BIT WON'T WORK, EITHER...
...BUT DESTROYING THE DEMON ISN'T OUR MAIN GOAL!
SHUU
MM
VM
FOR NOW...
...TRIPPING HIM WILL DO THE TRICK!!
METSU!!
BOOOM

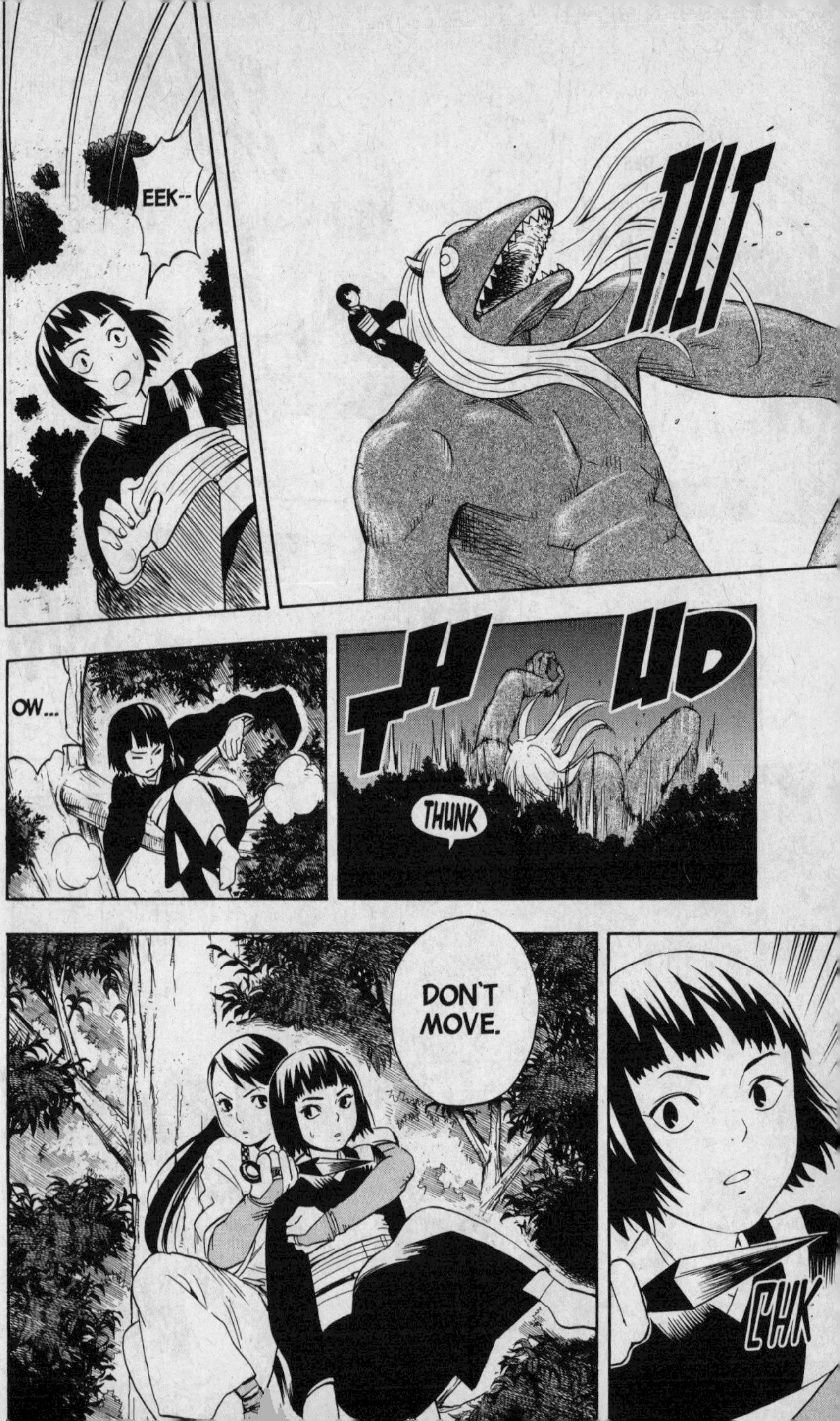
TILT
EEK--
THUD
THUNK
OW...
CHK
DON'T MOVE.

YOMI!

YOMI!

SHUFF

ORDER YOUR DEMON TO STOP FIGHTING AND LEAVE HERE IMMEDIATELY.

AND IF I REFUSE?

...

I DON'T REALLY WANT TO DO IT...

...BUT I'LL HAVE TO TAKE YOU HOSTAGE.

LET ME SEE...

?!

SQUEEEAK

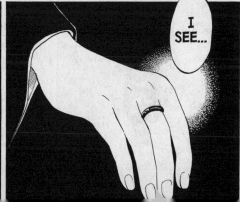

I SEE...

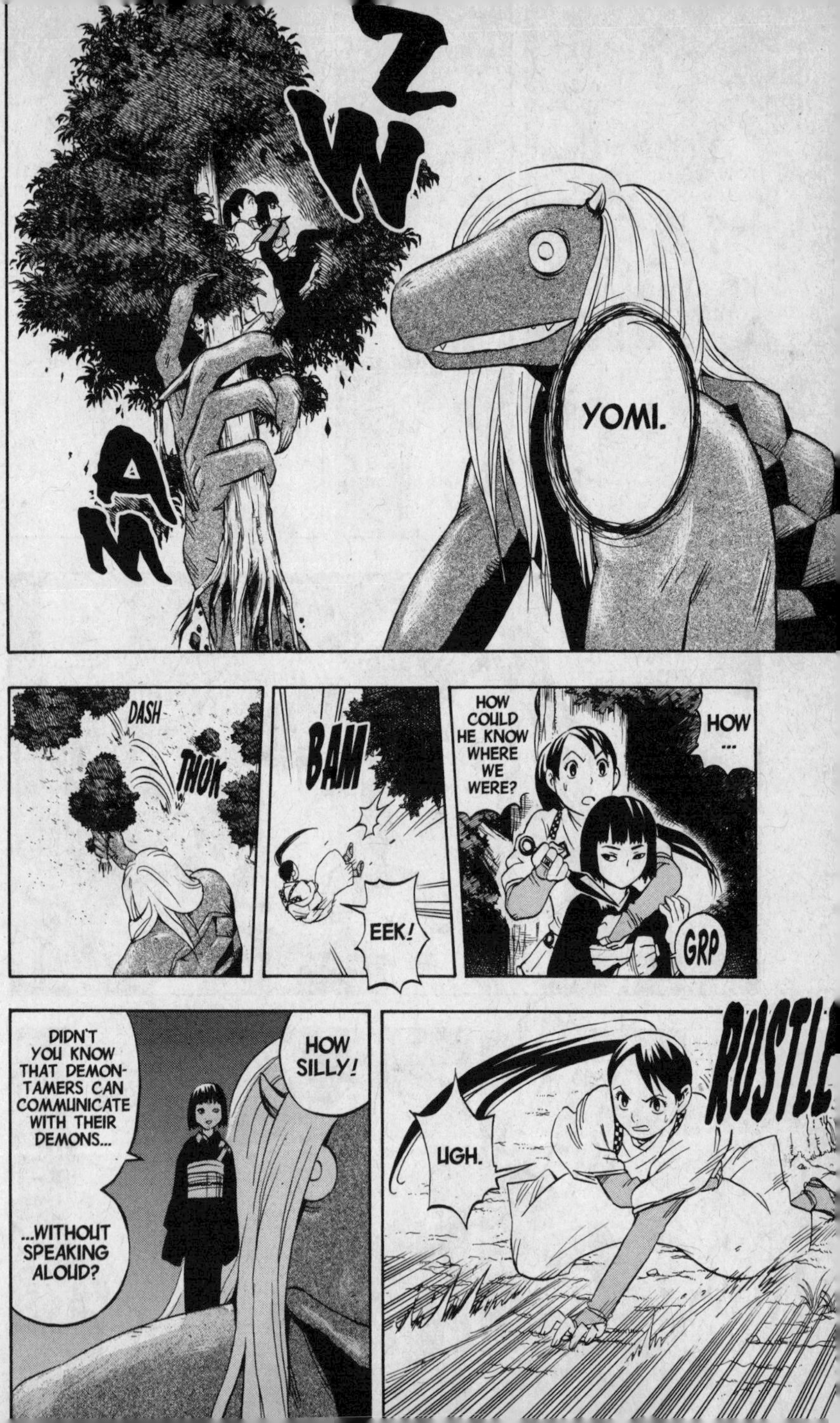
ZWAM
YOMI.
HOW ...
HOW COULD HE KNOW WHERE WE WERE?
GRP
BAM
EEK!
DASH
THUK
RUSTLE
UGH.
HOW SILLY!
DIDN'T YOU KNOW THAT DEMON-TAMERS CAN COMMUNICATE WITH THEIR DEMONS...
...WITHOUT SPEAKING ALOUD?

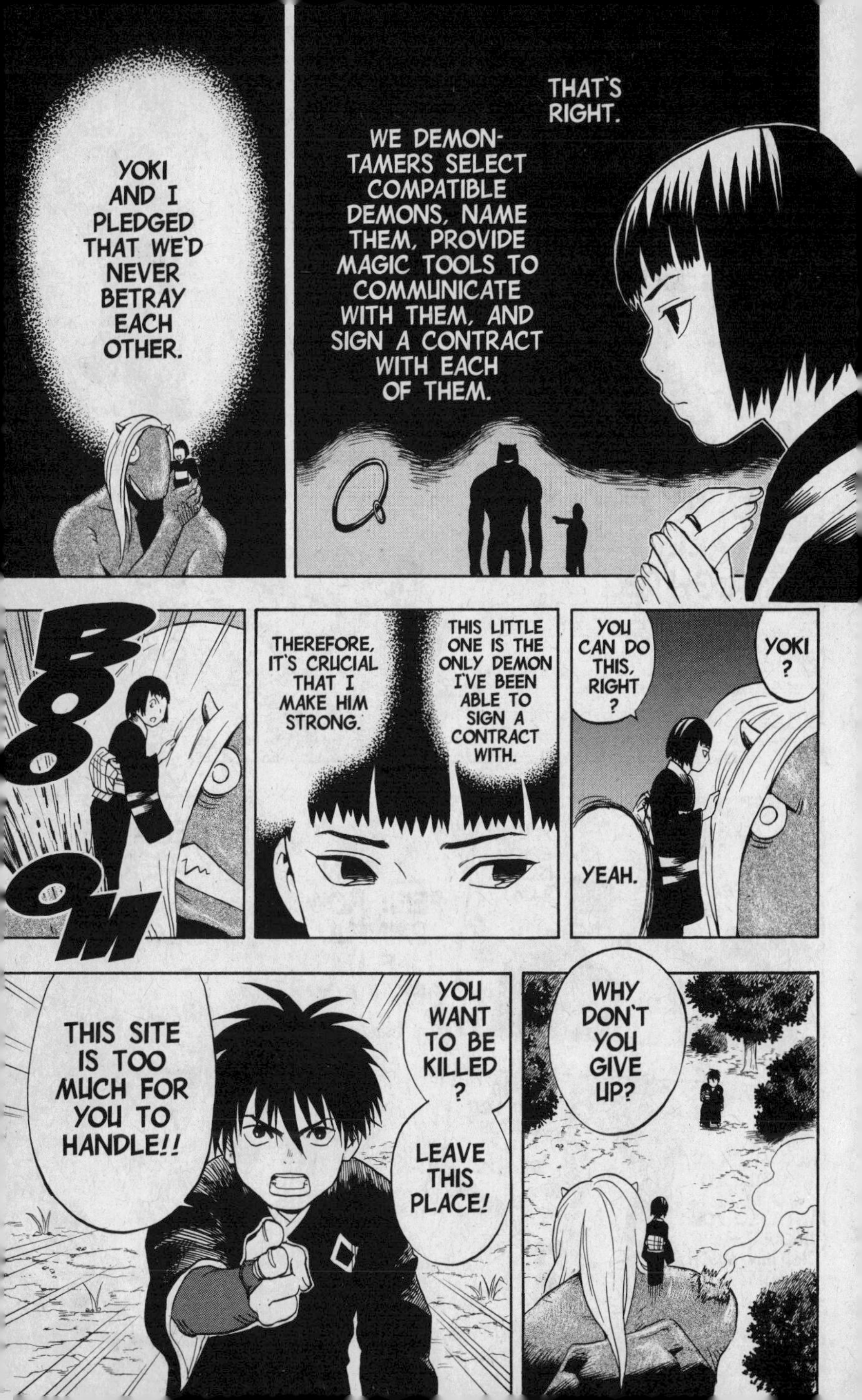

THAT'S RIGHT.
WE DEMON-TAMERS SELECT COMPATIBLE DEMONS, NAME THEM, PROVIDE MAGIC TOOLS TO COMMUNICATE WITH THEM, AND SIGN A CONTRACT WITH EACH OF THEM.
YOKI AND I PLEDGED THAT WE'D NEVER BETRAY EACH OTHER.
YOKI?
YOU CAN DO THIS, RIGHT?
YEAH.
THIS LITTLE ONE IS THE ONLY DEMON I'VE BEEN ABLE TO SIGN A CONTRACT WITH.
THEREFORE, IT'S CRUCIAL THAT I MAKE HIM STRONG.
BOOOM
WHY DON'T YOU GIVE UP?
YOU WANT TO BE KILLED?
LEAVE THIS PLACE!
THIS SITE IS TOO MUCH FOR YOU TO HANDLE!!

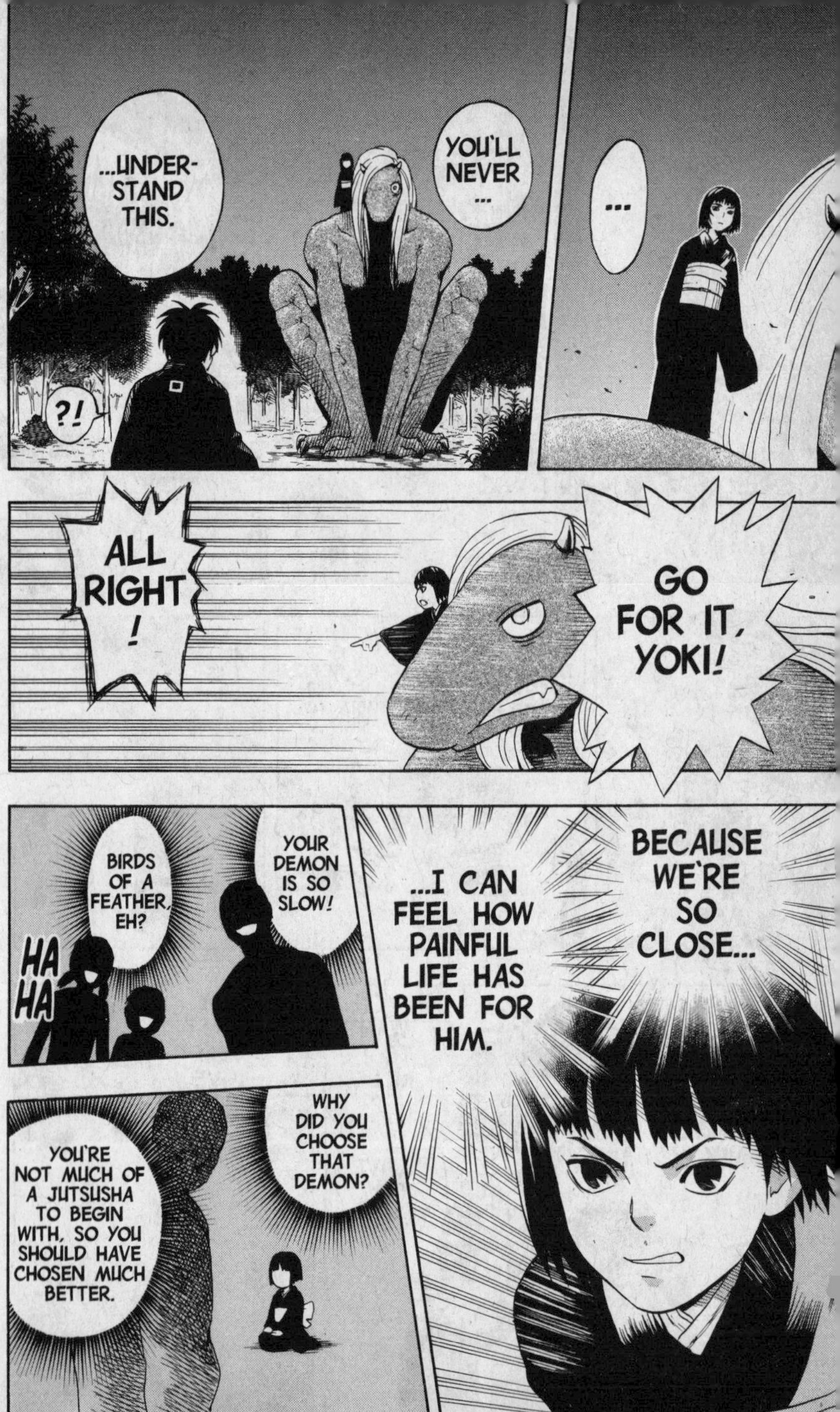
...
YOU'LL NEVER ...
...UNDER-STAND THIS.
?!
GO FOR IT, YOKI!
ALL RIGHT!
BECAUSE WE'RE SO CLOSE...
...I CAN FEEL HOW PAINFUL LIFE HAS BEEN FOR HIM.
YOUR DEMON IS SO SLOW!
BIRDS OF A FEATHER, EH?
HA HA
WHY DID YOU CHOOSE THAT DEMON?
YOU'RE NOT MUCH OF A JUTSUSHA TO BEGIN WITH, SO YOU SHOULD HAVE CHOSEN MUCH BETTER.

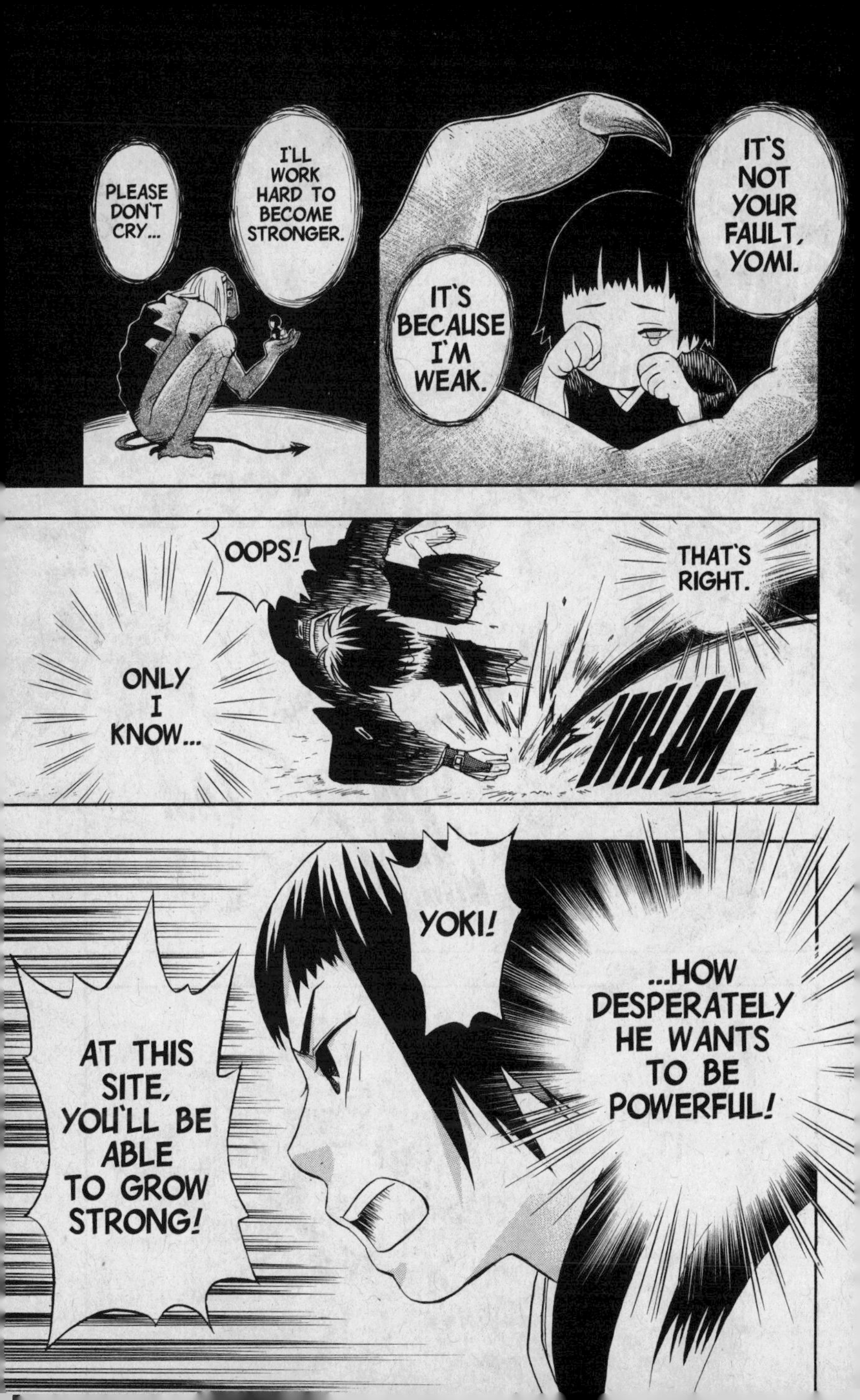
IT'S NOT YOUR FAULT, YOMI.
IT'S BECAUSE I'M WEAK.
I'LL WORK HARD TO BECOME STRONGER.
PLEASE DON'T CRY...
THAT'S RIGHT.
OOPS!
ONLY I KNOW...
YOKI!
...HOW DESPERATELY HE WANTS TO BE POWERFUL!
AT THIS SITE, YOU'LL BE ABLE TO GROW STRONG!

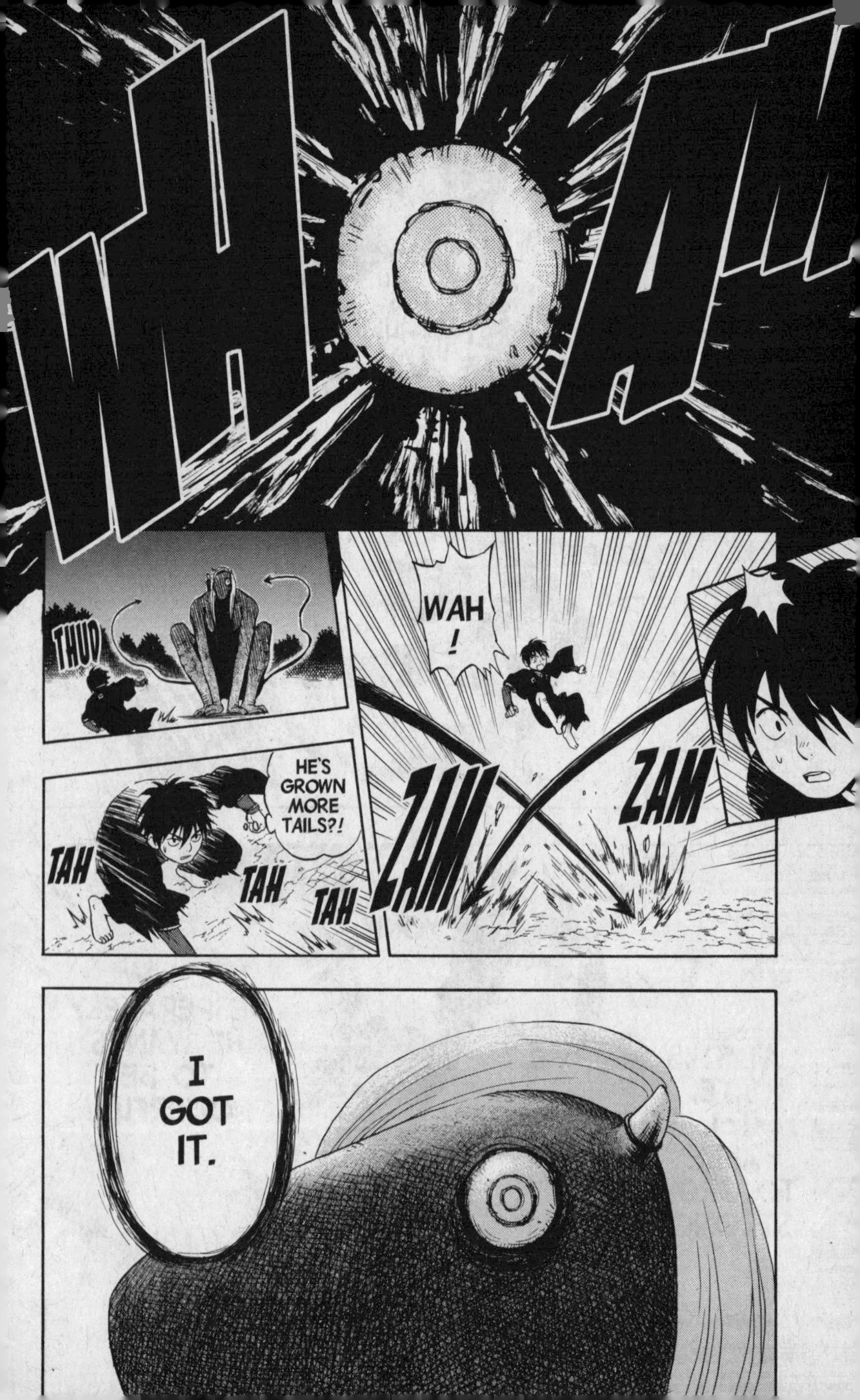
WHAM
WAH!
ZAM
ZAM
THUD
HE'S GROWN MORE TAILS?!
TAH
TAH
TAH
I GOT IT.

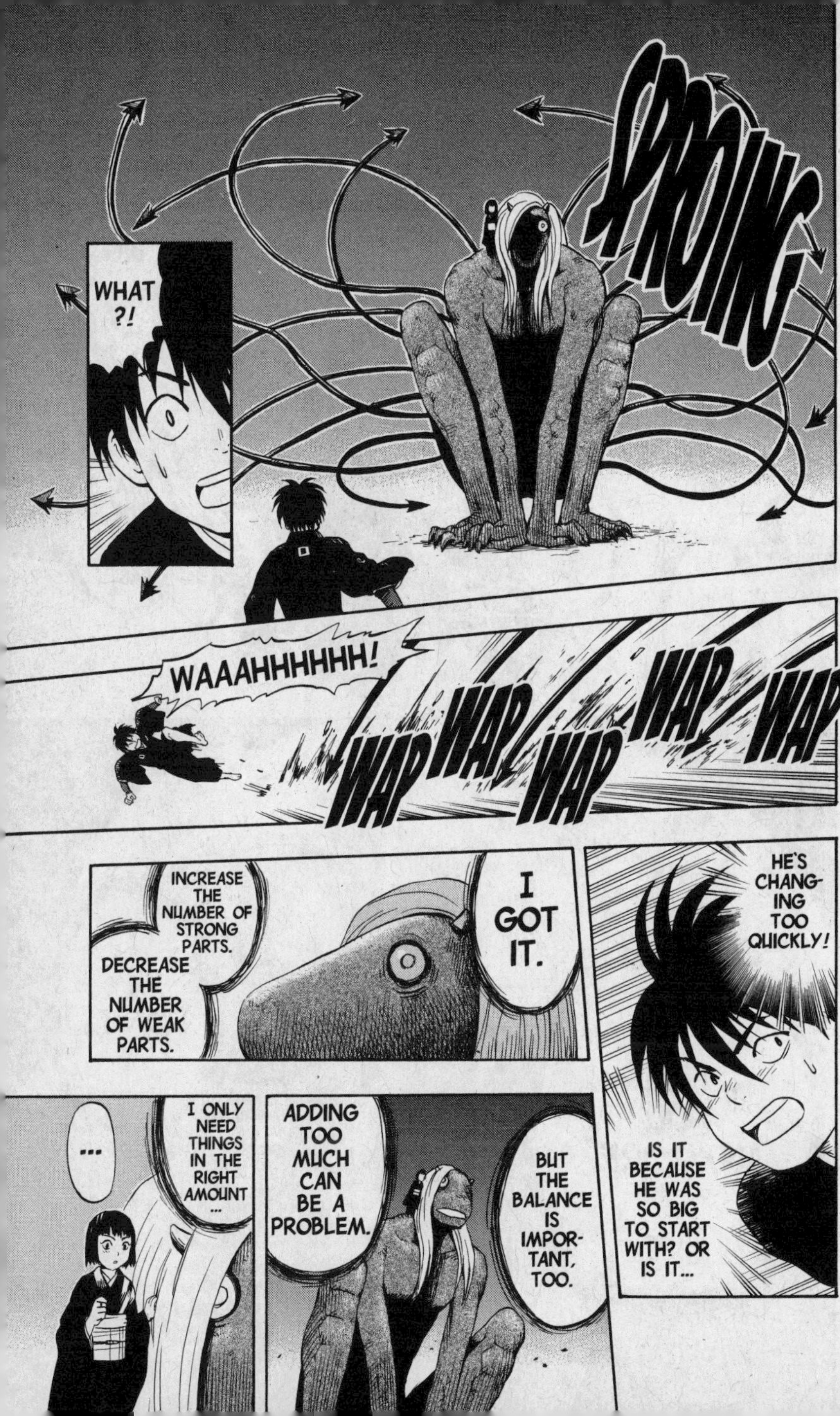
SPROING
WHAT ?!
WAP WAP WAP WAP WAP
WAAAHHHHH!
HE'S CHANGING TOO QUICKLY!
IS IT BECAUSE HE WAS SO BIG TO START WITH? OR IS IT...
I GOT IT.
INCREASE THE NUMBER OF STRONG PARTS.
DECREASE THE NUMBER OF WEAK PARTS.
BUT THE BALANCE IS IMPORTANT, TOO.
ADDING TOO MUCH CAN BE A PROBLEM.
I ONLY NEED THINGS IN THE RIGHT AMOUNT...
...

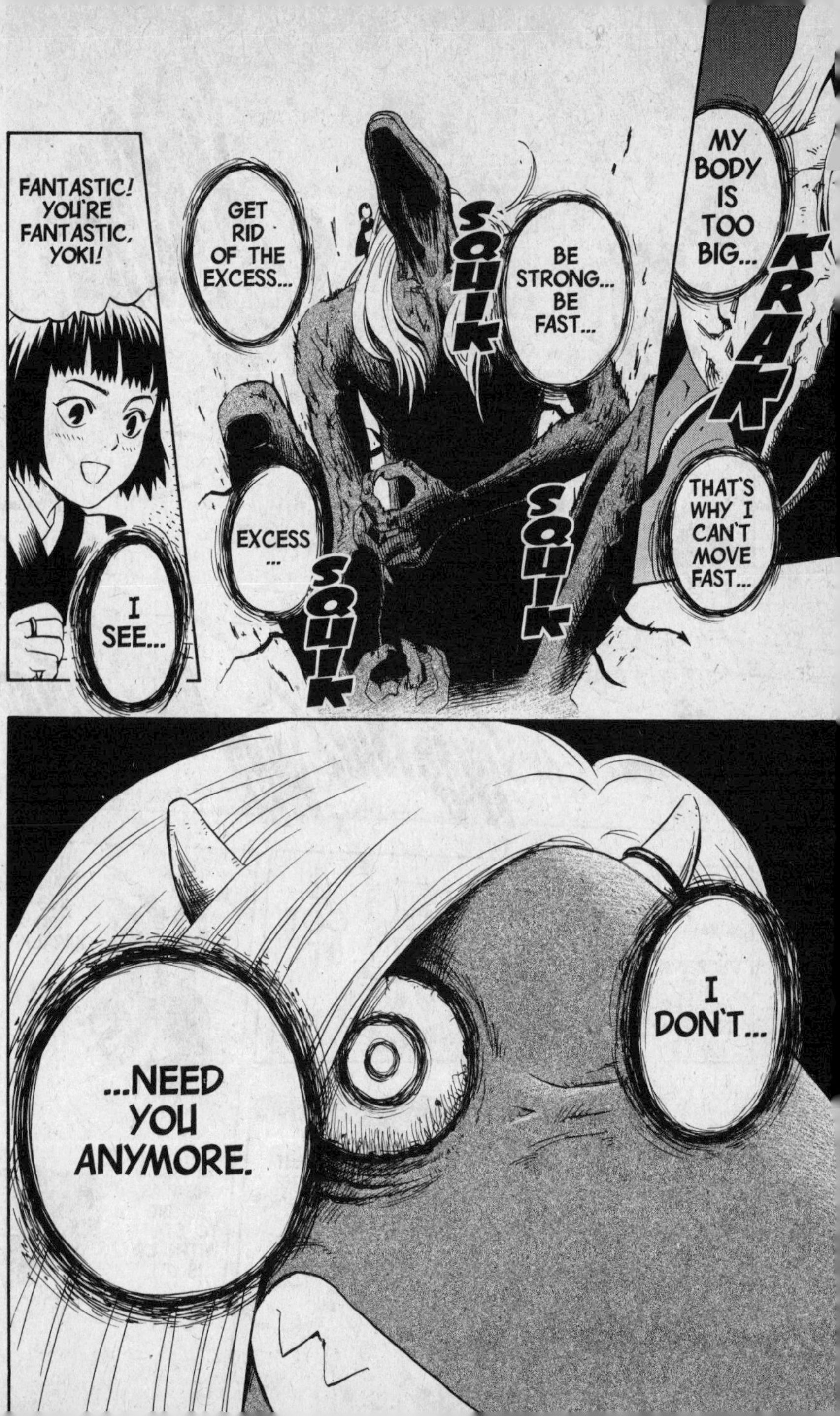
MY BODY IS TOO BIG...
KRAK
THAT'S WHY I CAN'T MOVE FAST...
BE STRONG... BE FAST...
SQUIK
GET RID OF THE EXCESS...
SQUIK
EXCESS...
SQUIK
FANTASTIC! YOU'RE FANTASTIC, YOKI!
I SEE...
I DON'T...
...NEED YOU ANYMORE.

WHAT
?

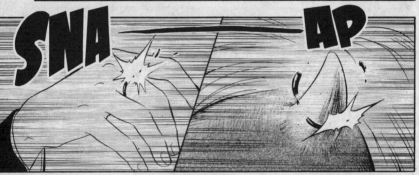

SNA AP

YOKI...

WHY?

YOKI...

SMACK

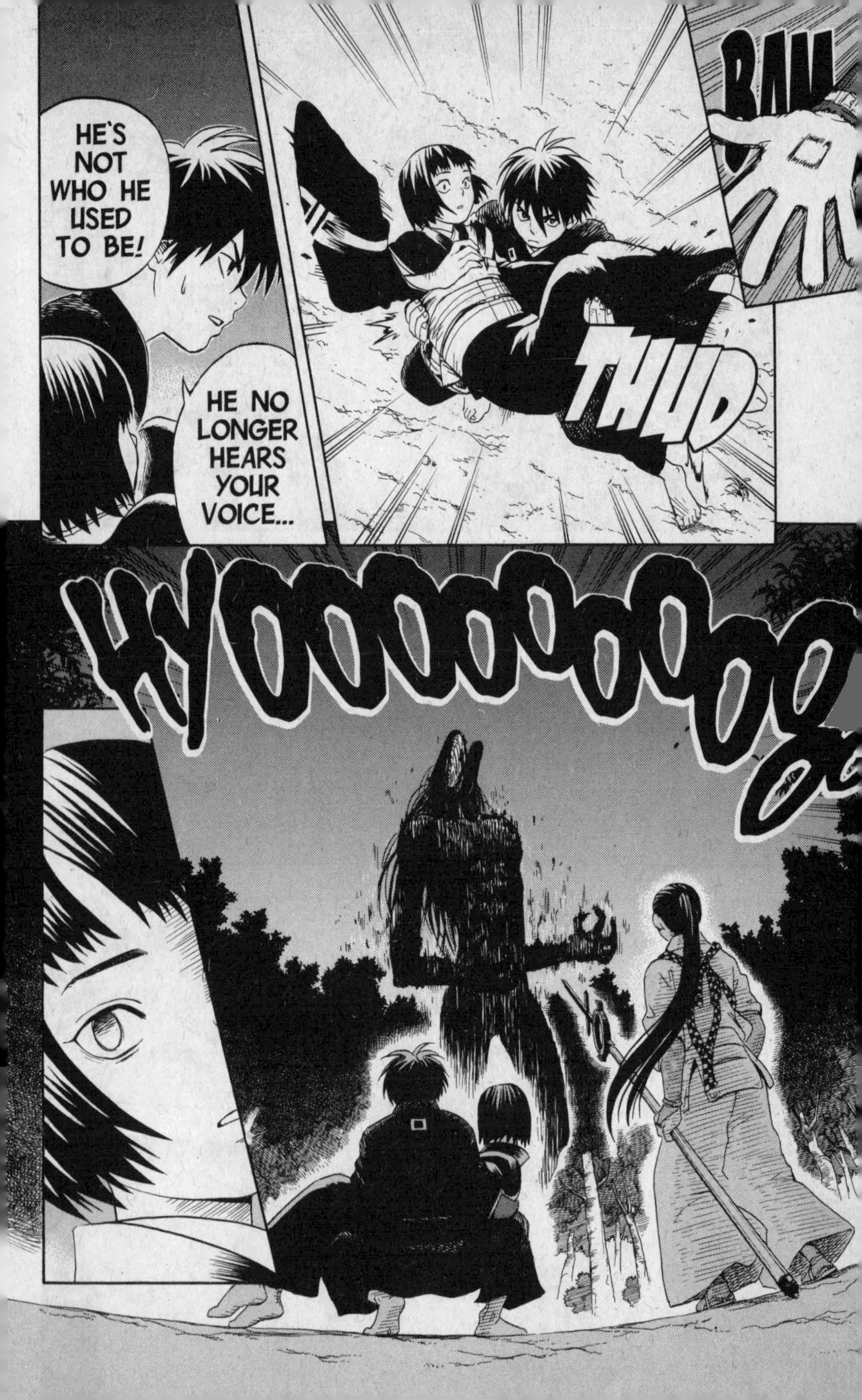
THUD
HE'S NOT WHO HE USED TO BE!
HE NO LONGER HEARS YOUR VOICE...
HYOOOOOOOO

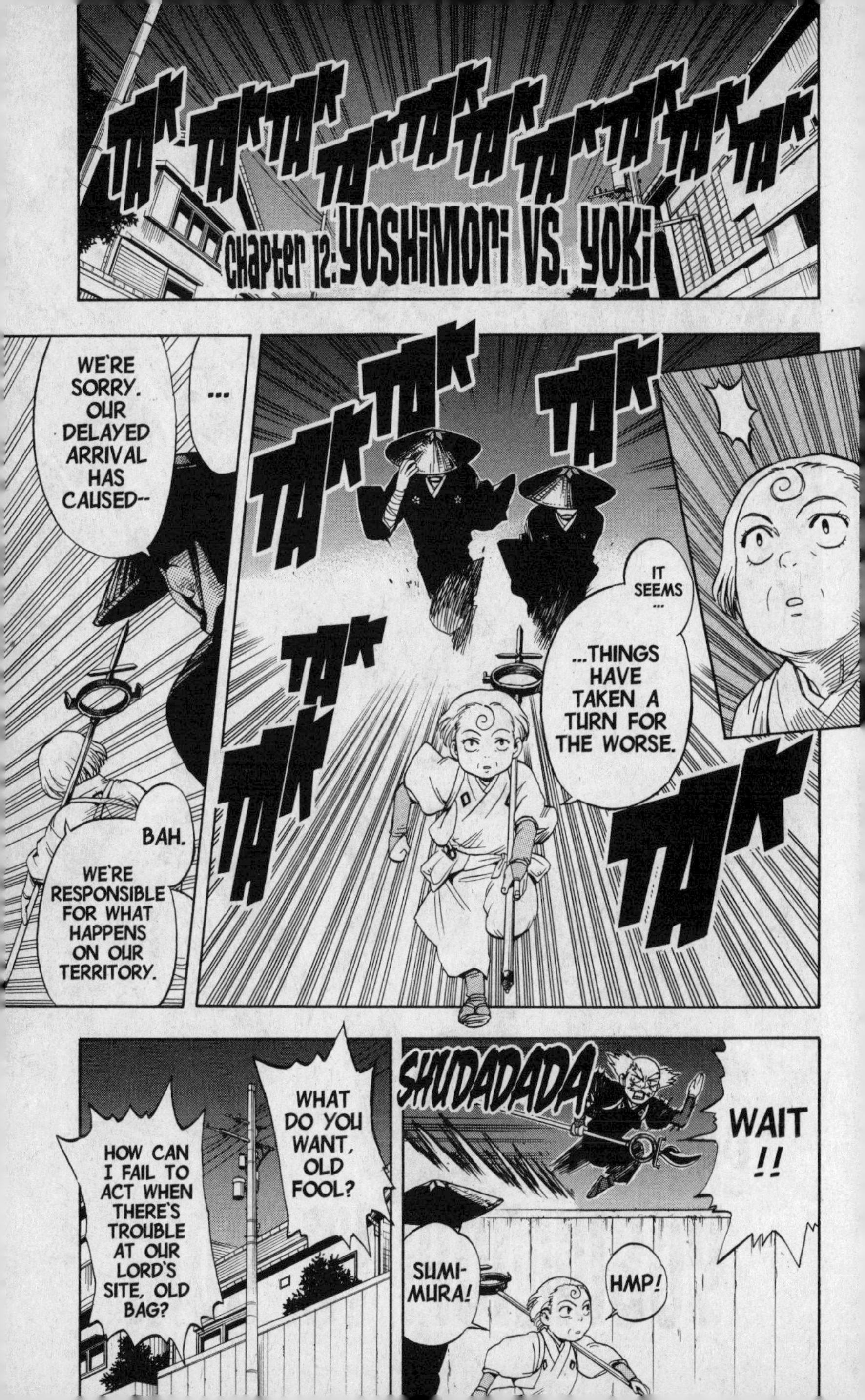
TAK TAK TAK TAK TAK TAK TAK TAK TAK TAK TAK TAK
Chapter 12: YOSHIMORI VS. YOKI
TAK TAK TAK TAK TAK
IT SEEMS...
...THINGS HAVE TAKEN A TURN FOR THE WORSE.
TAK
...
WE'RE SORRY. OUR DELAYED ARRIVAL HAS CAUSED--
BAH.
WE'RE RESPONSIBLE FOR WHAT HAPPENS ON OUR TERRITORY.
WAIT !!
SHUDADADA
HMP!
SUMI-MURA!
WHAT DO YOU WANT, OLD FOOL?
HOW CAN I FAIL TO ACT WHEN THERE'S TROUBLE AT OUR LORD'S SITE, OLD BAG?

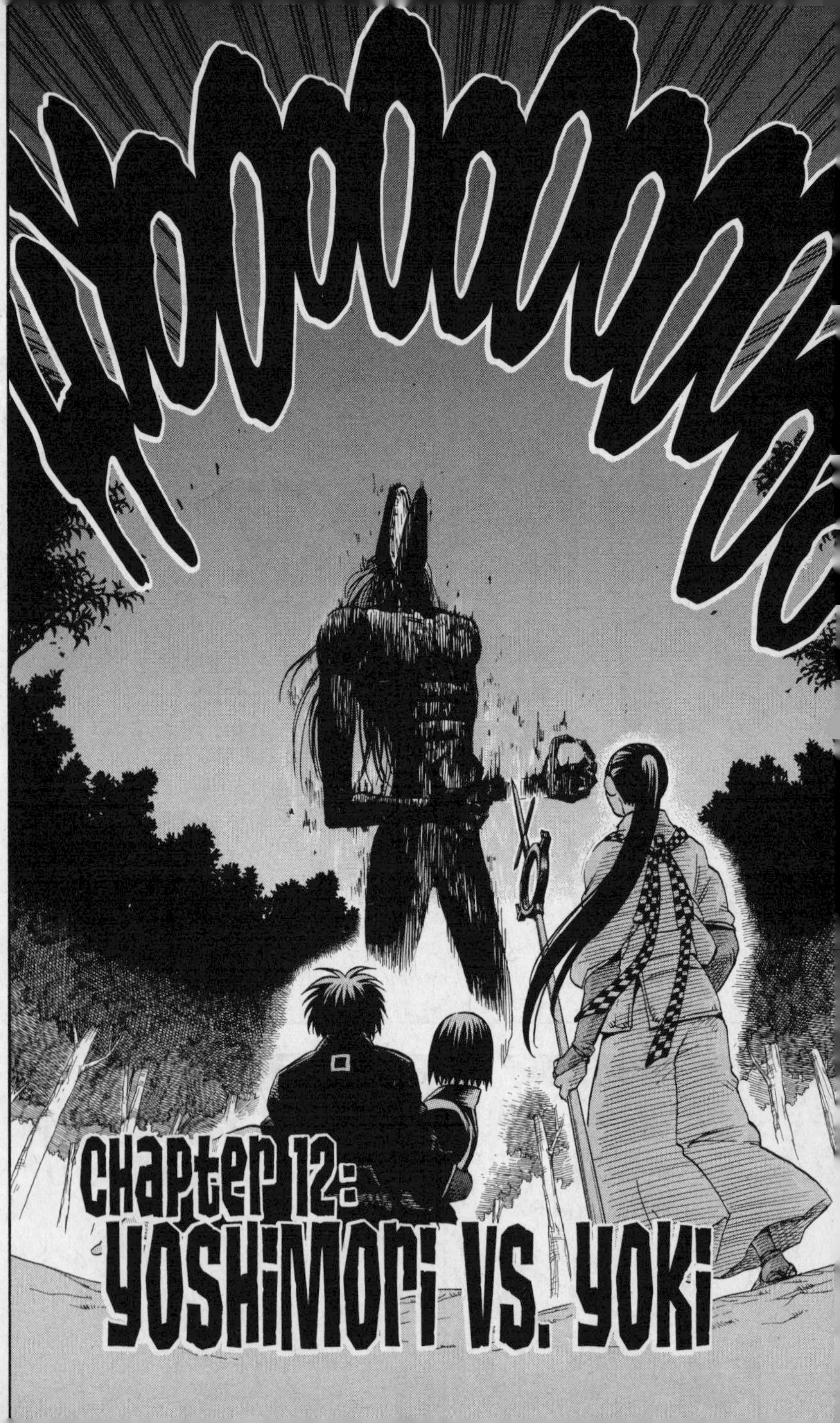
CHAPTER 12:
YOSHIMORI VS. YOKI

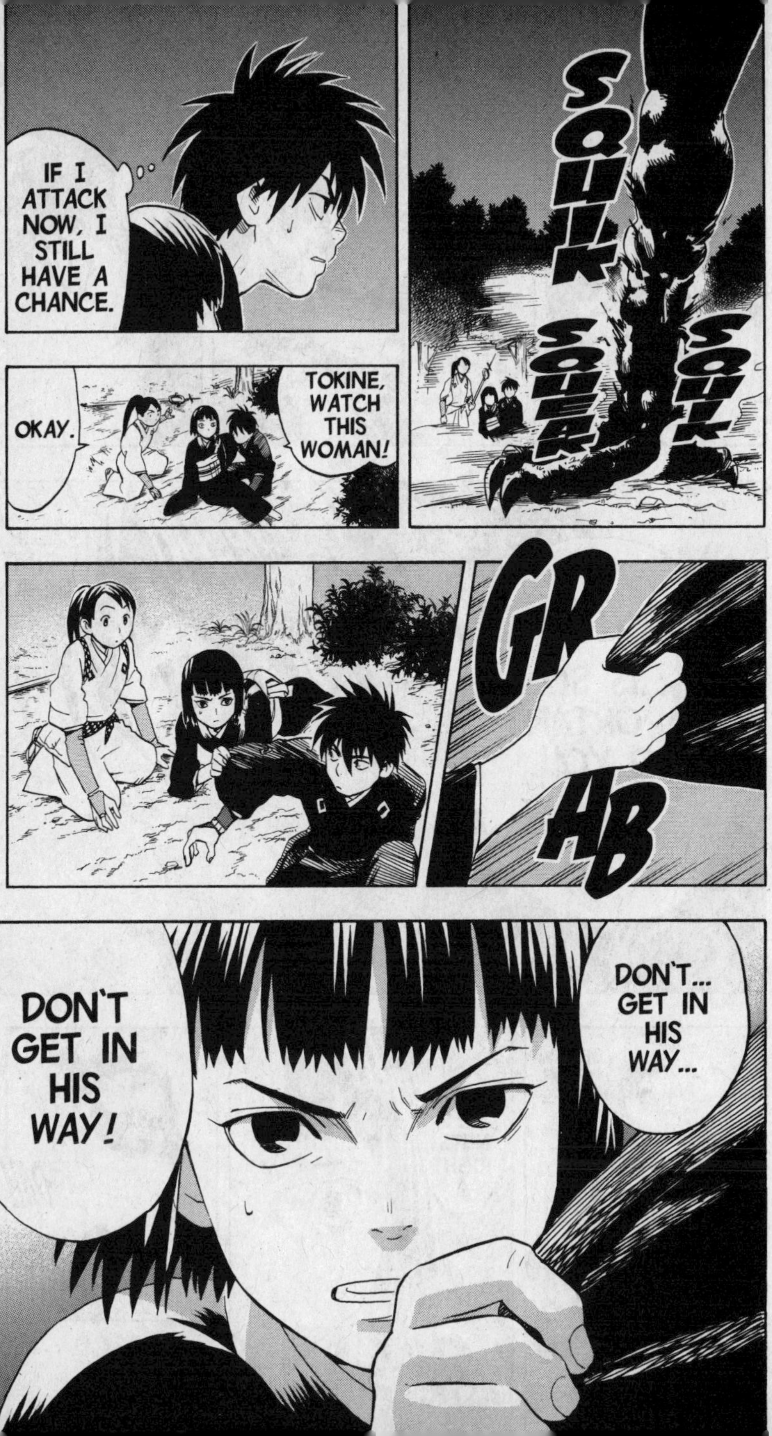
SQUIK
SQUIK
SQUEAK
IF I ATTACK NOW, I STILL HAVE A CHANCE.
TOKINE, WATCH THIS WOMAN!
OKAY.
GRAB
DON'T... GET IN HIS WAY...
DON'T GET IN HIS WAY!

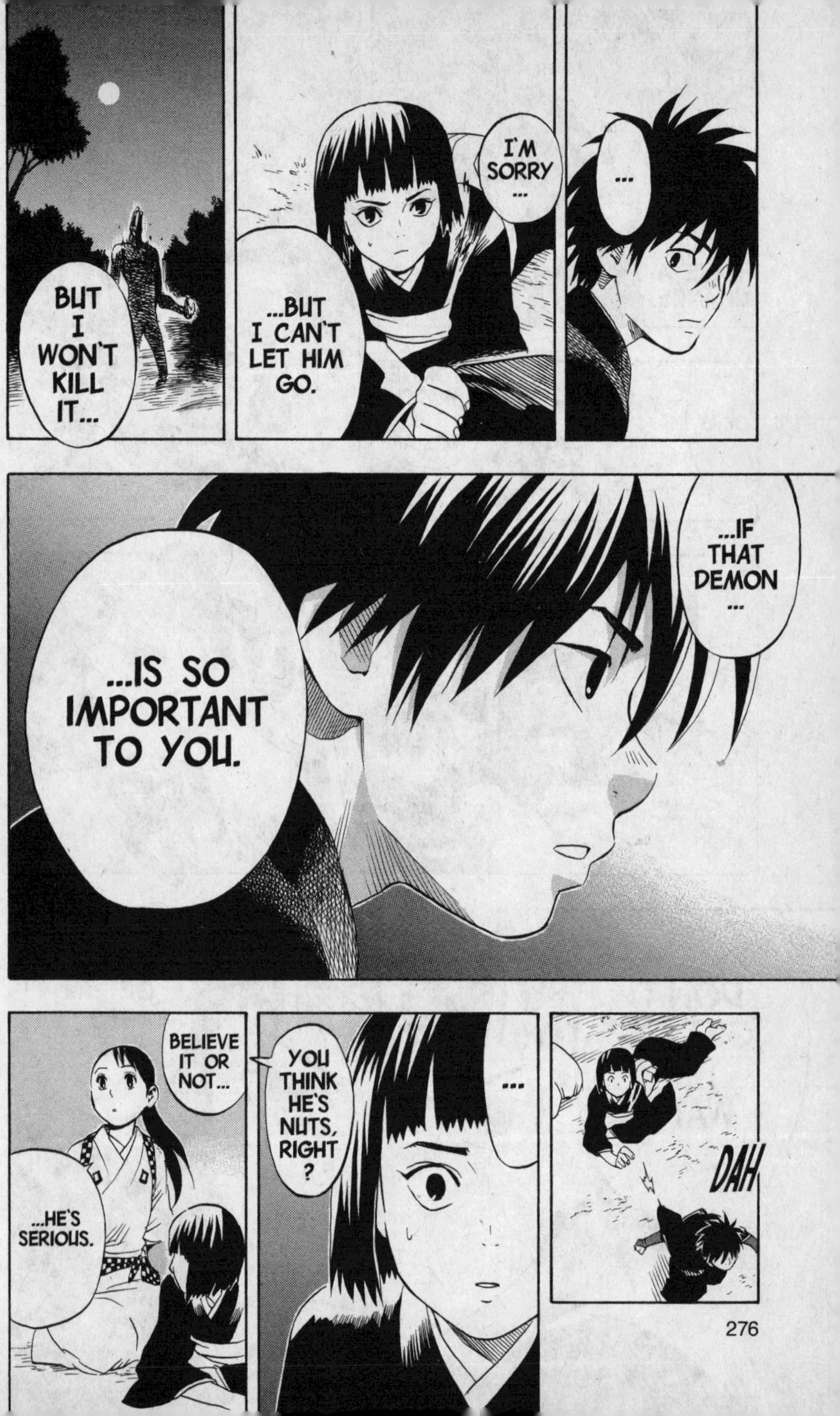
...
I'M SORRY ...
...BUT I CAN'T LET HIM GO.
BUT I WON'T KILL IT...
...IF THAT DEMON ...
...IS SO IMPORTANT TO YOU.
DAH
...
YOU THINK HE'S NUTS, RIGHT?
BELIEVE IT OR NOT...
...HE'S SERIOUS.

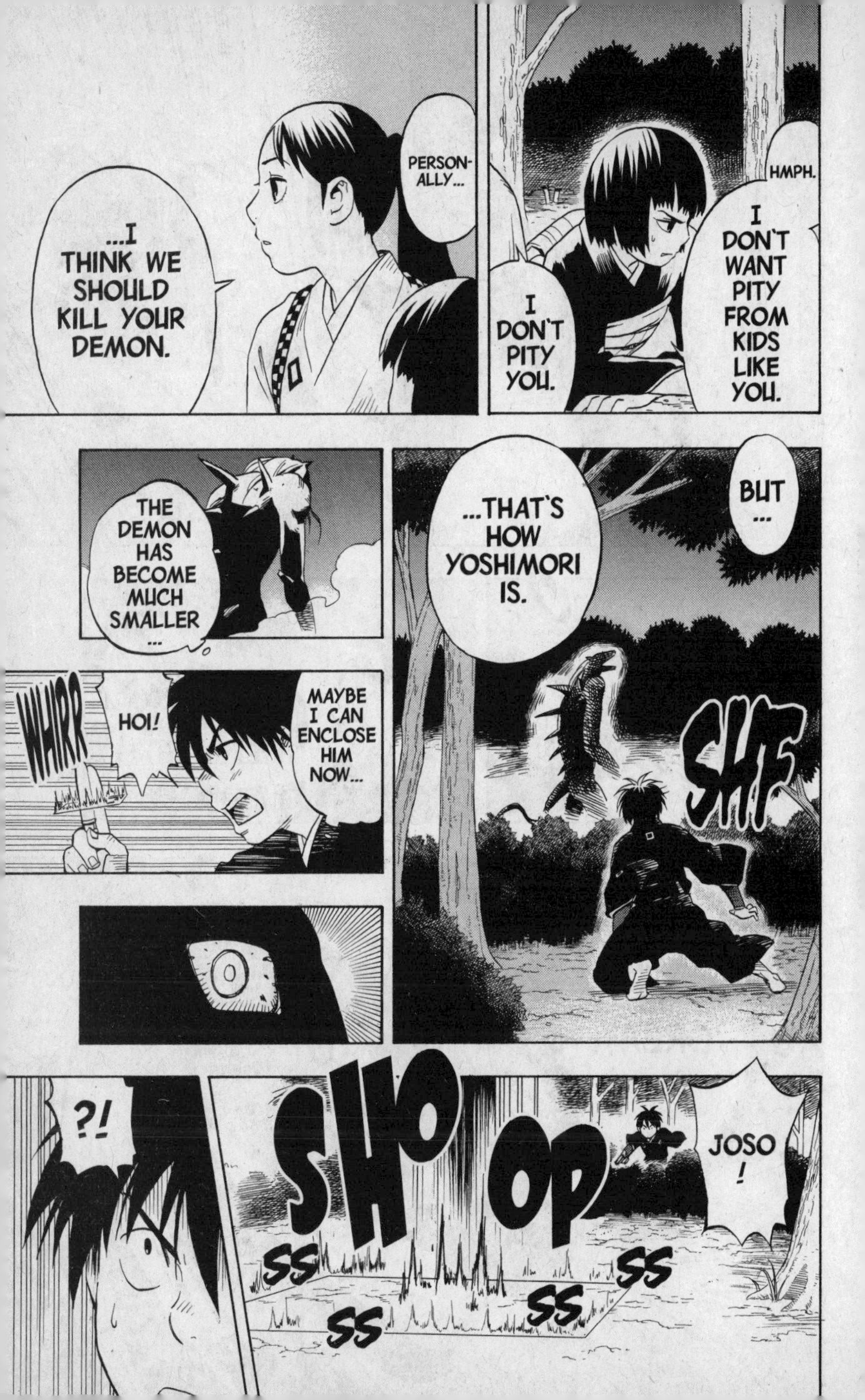
HMPH.
I DON'T WANT PITY FROM KIDS LIKE YOU.
I DON'T PITY YOU.
PERSON-ALLY...
...I THINK WE SHOULD KILL YOUR DEMON.
BUT ...
...THAT'S HOW YOSHIMORI IS.
SHF
THE DEMON HAS BECOME MUCH SMALLER ...
MAYBE I CAN ENCLOSE HIM NOW...
HOI!
WHIRR
JOSO!
SHOOP
SS
SS
SS
SS
?!

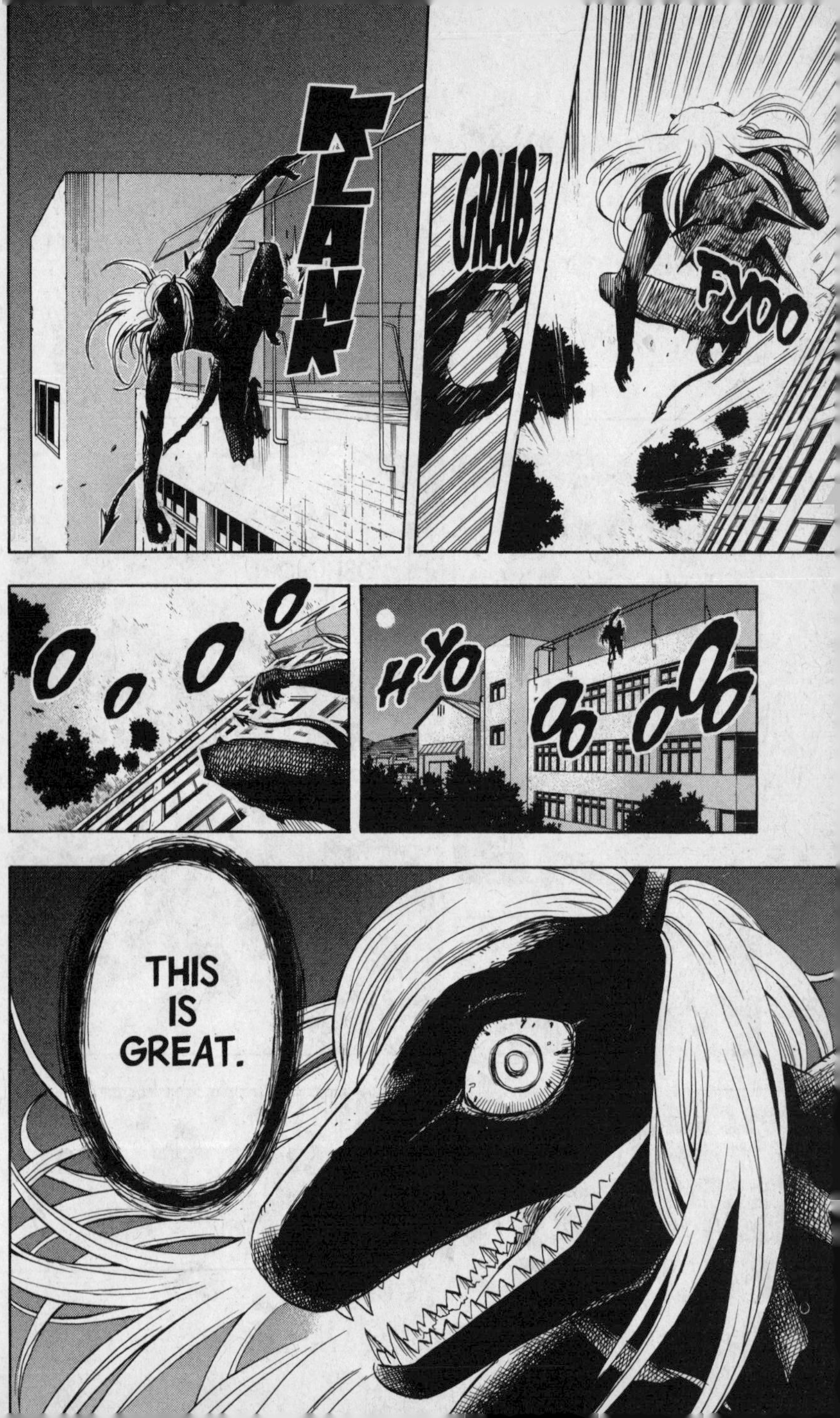
FYOO
GRAB
KLANK
HYO
OOOO
OOOOO
THIS IS GREAT.

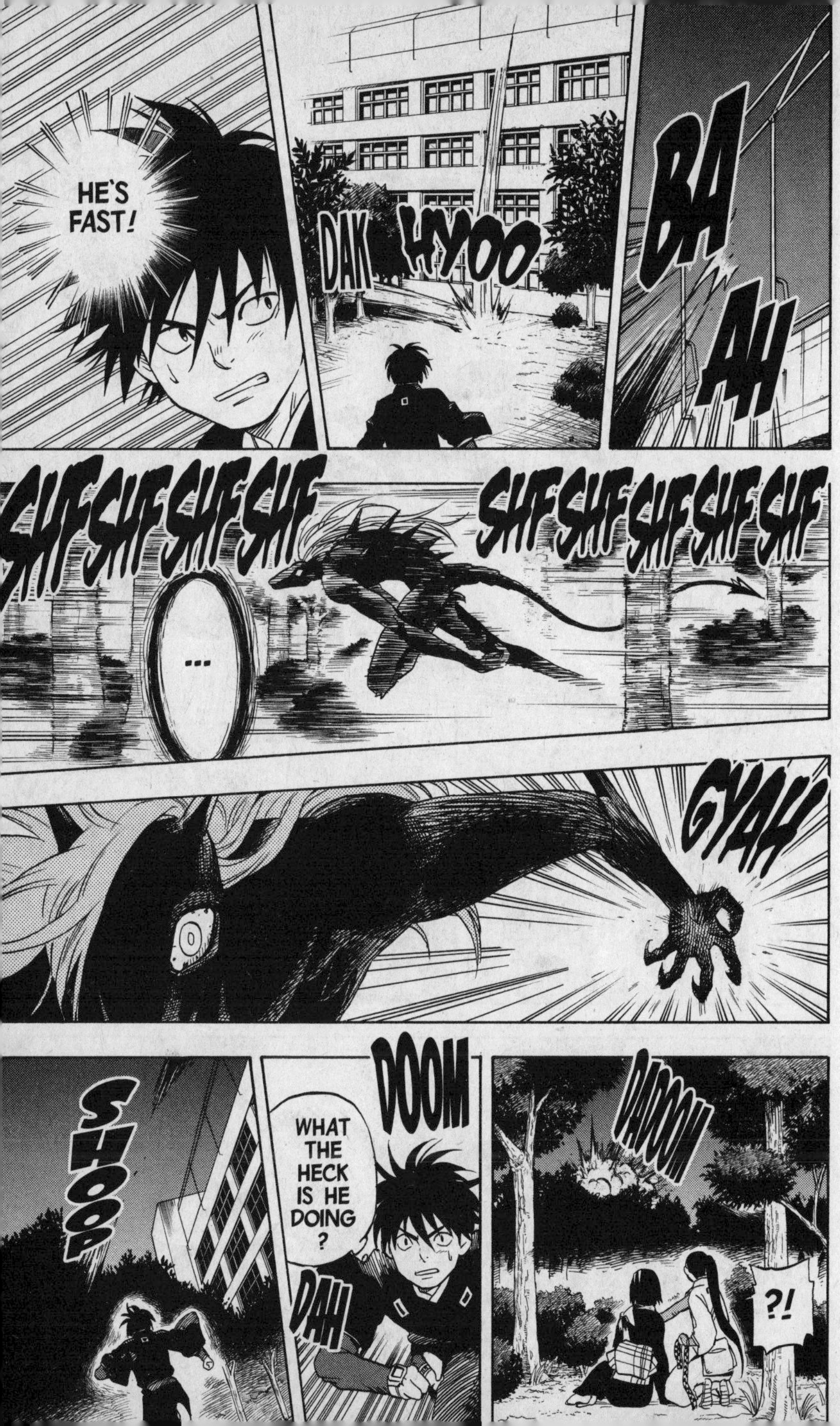
BA
AH
DAK
HYOO
HE'S FAST!
SHF SHF SHF SHF SHF
SHF SHF SHF SHF
...
GYAH
DAVOOM
?!
DOOM
WHAT THE HECK IS HE DOING?
DAH
SHOOP

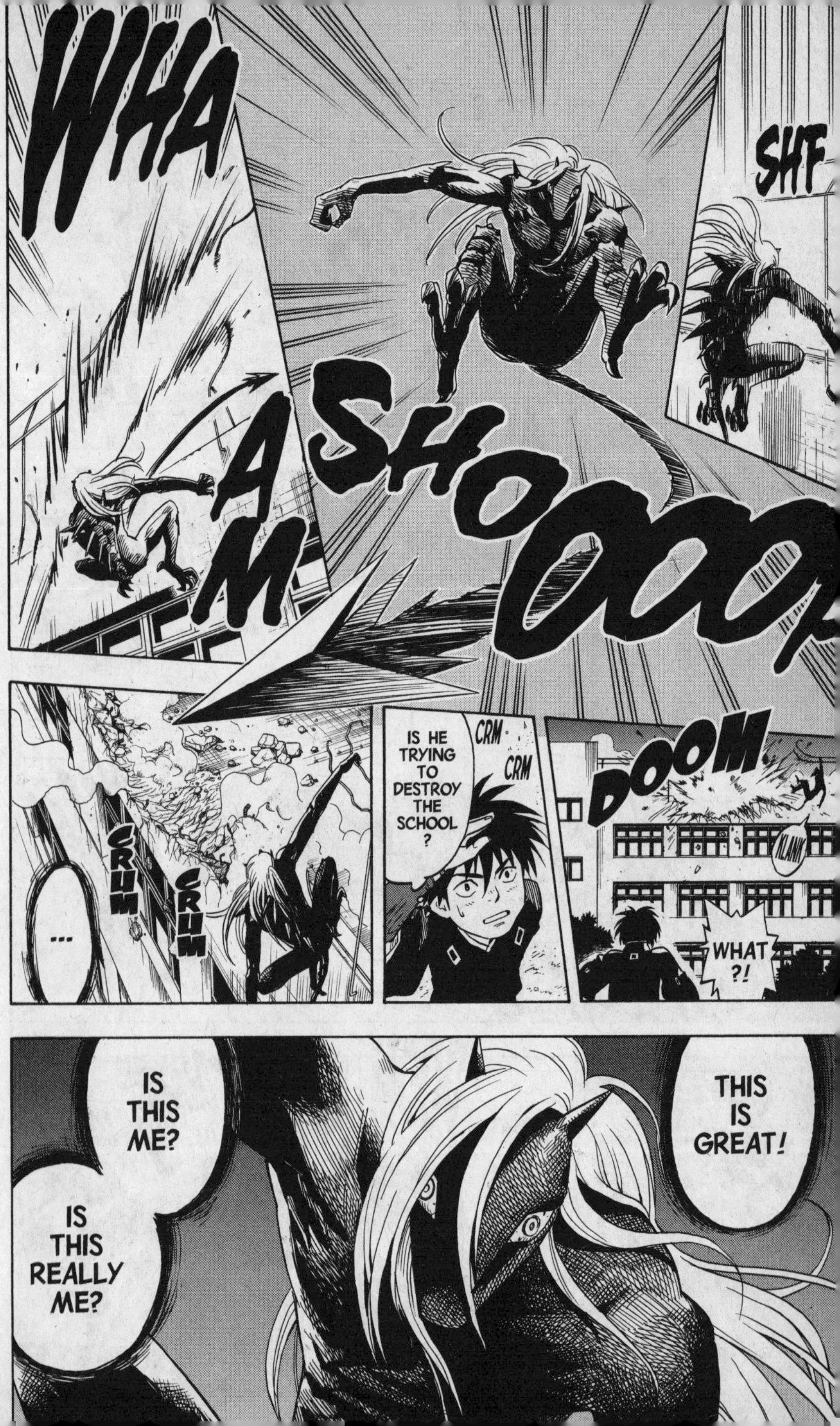
SHF
WHA
AM
SHOOOO
DOOM
KLANK
WHAT ?!
CRM
CRM
IS HE TRYING TO DESTROY THE SCHOOL ?
CRUM
CRUM
...
THIS IS GREAT!
IS THIS ME?
IS THIS REALLY ME?

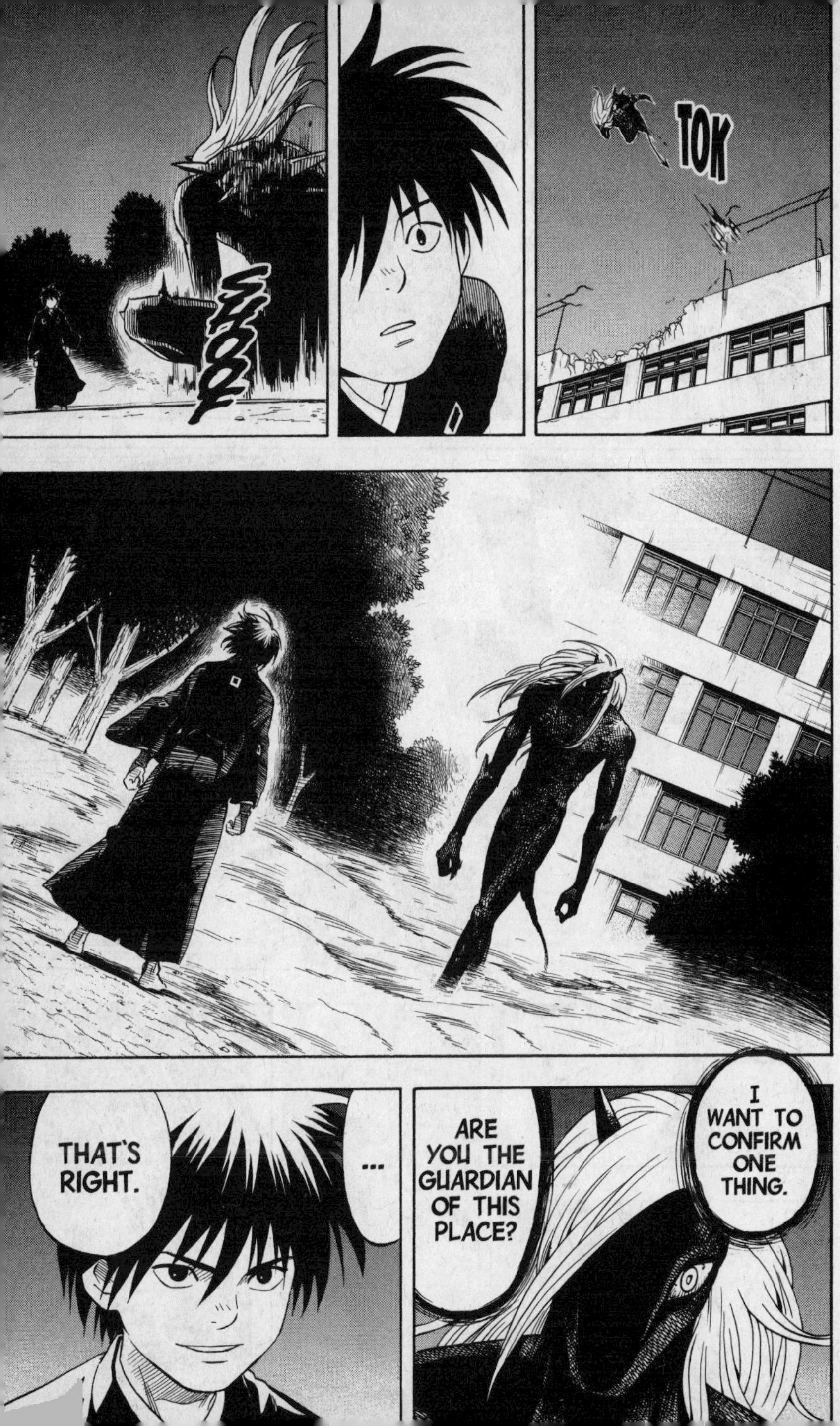
TOK
I WANT TO CONFIRM ONE THING.
ARE YOU THE GUARDIAN OF THIS PLACE?
...
THAT'S RIGHT.

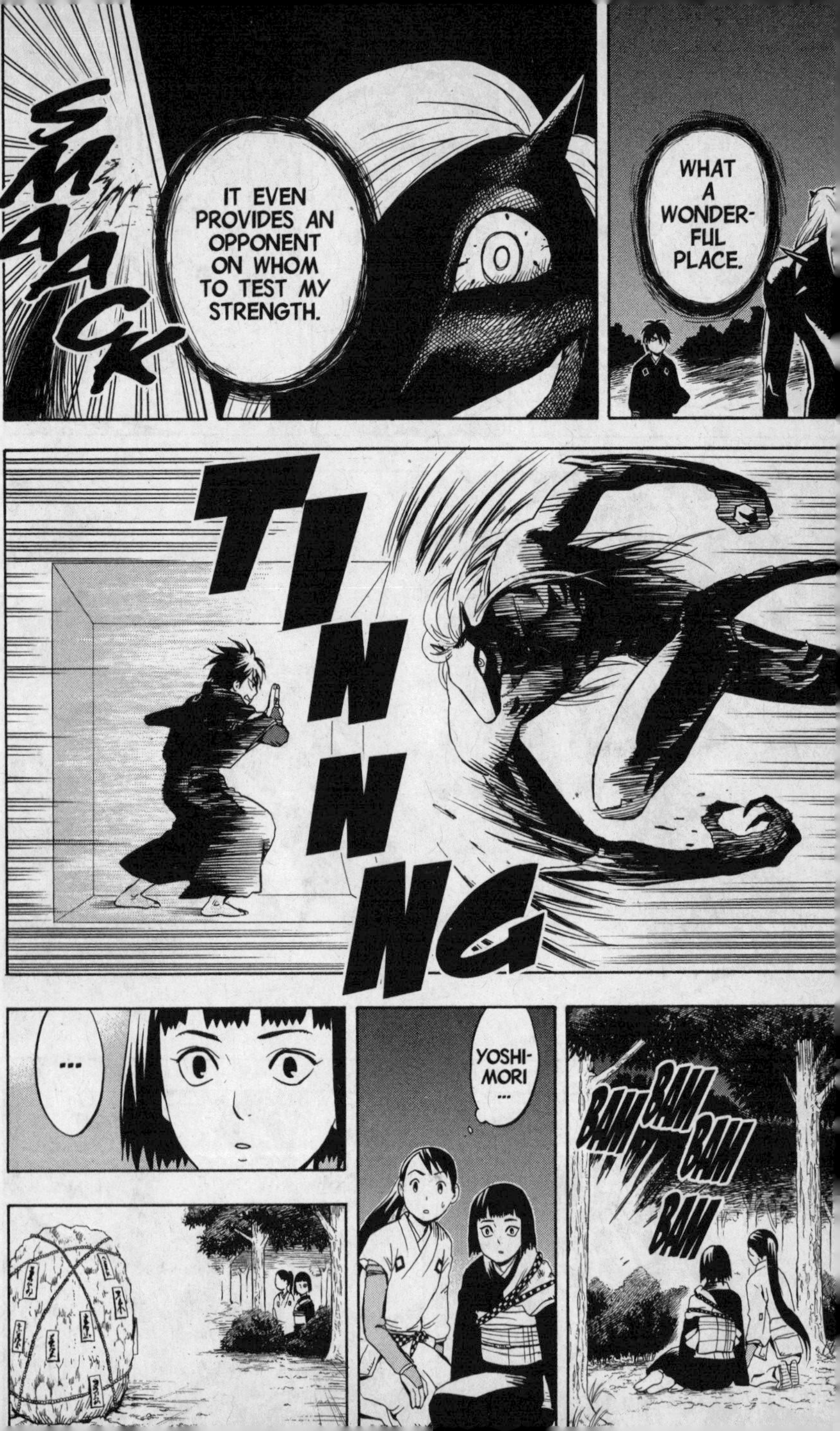
WHAT A WONDERFUL PLACE.
IT EVEN PROVIDES AN OPPONENT ON WHOM TO TEST MY STRENGTH.
SMAACK
TINNNG
BAM BAM BAM BAM BAM
YOSHIMORI...
...

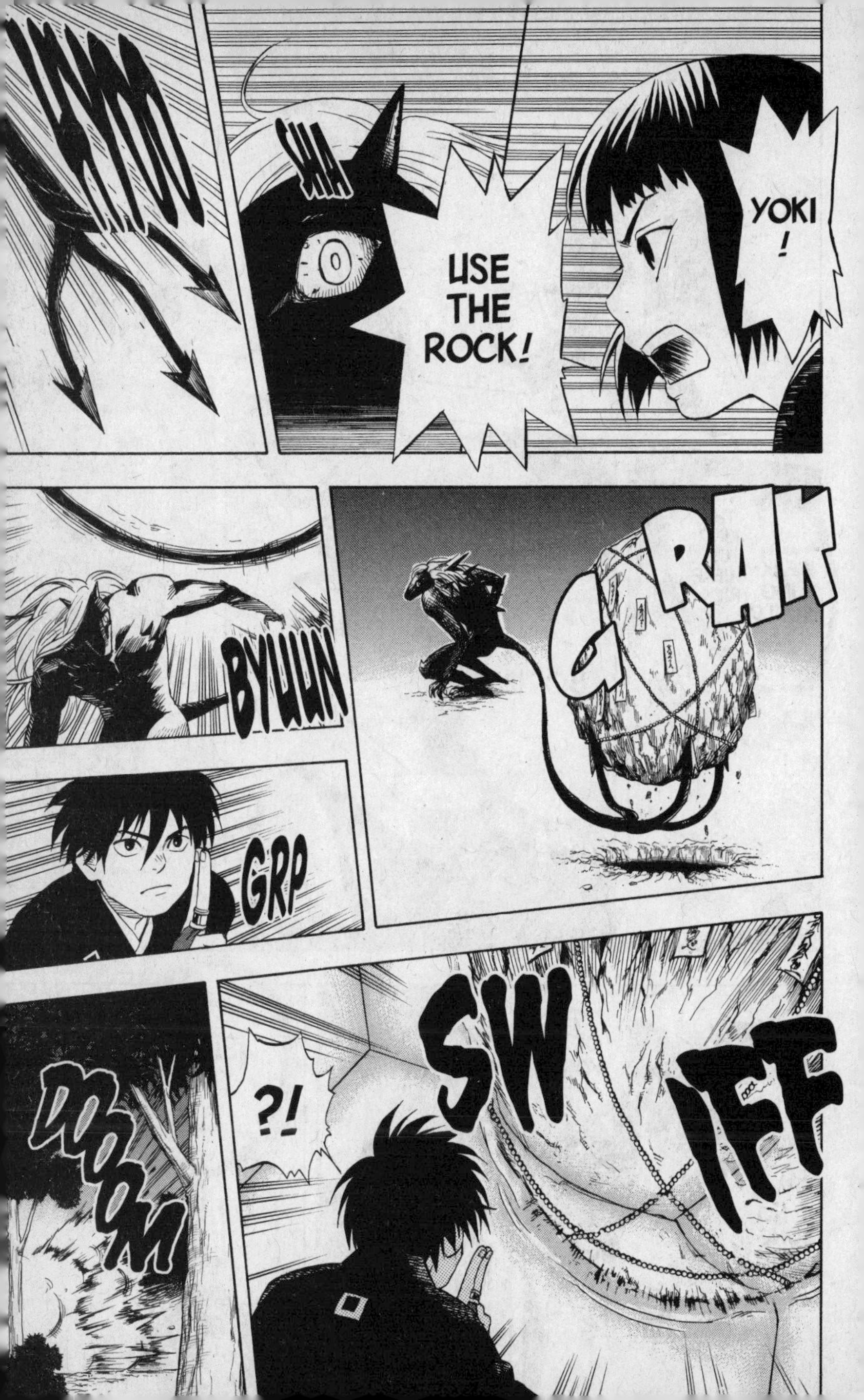
YOKI!
USE THE ROCK!
SHA
GRAK
BYUUN
GRP
SWIFF
?!
DOOOM

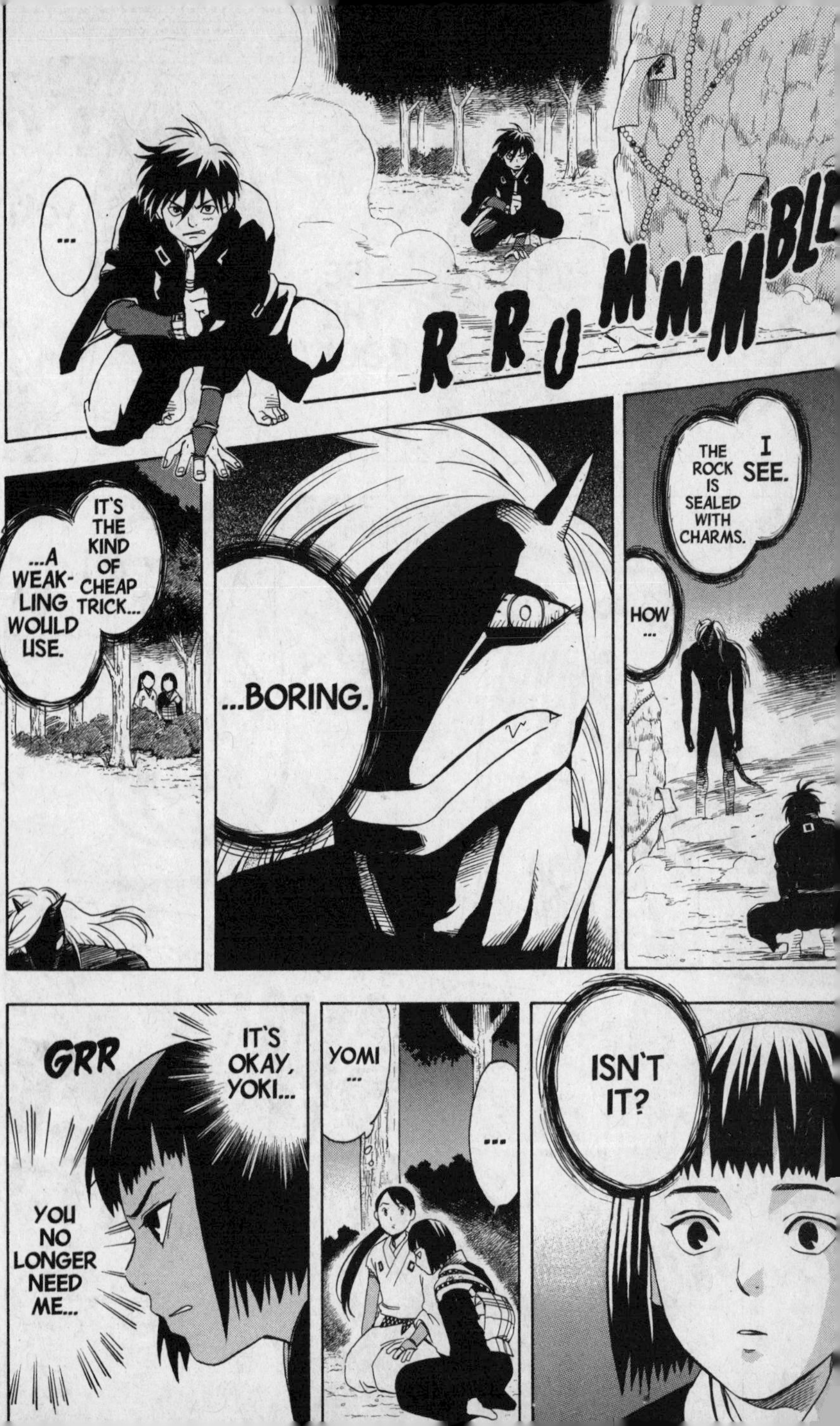
RRUMMMMBLE
...
I SEE.
THE ROCK IS SEALED WITH CHARMS.
HOW...
...BORING.
IT'S THE KIND OF CHEAP TRICK...
...A WEAKLING WOULD USE.
ISN'T IT?
YOMI...
...
IT'S OKAY, YOKI...
GRR
YOU NO LONGER NEED ME...

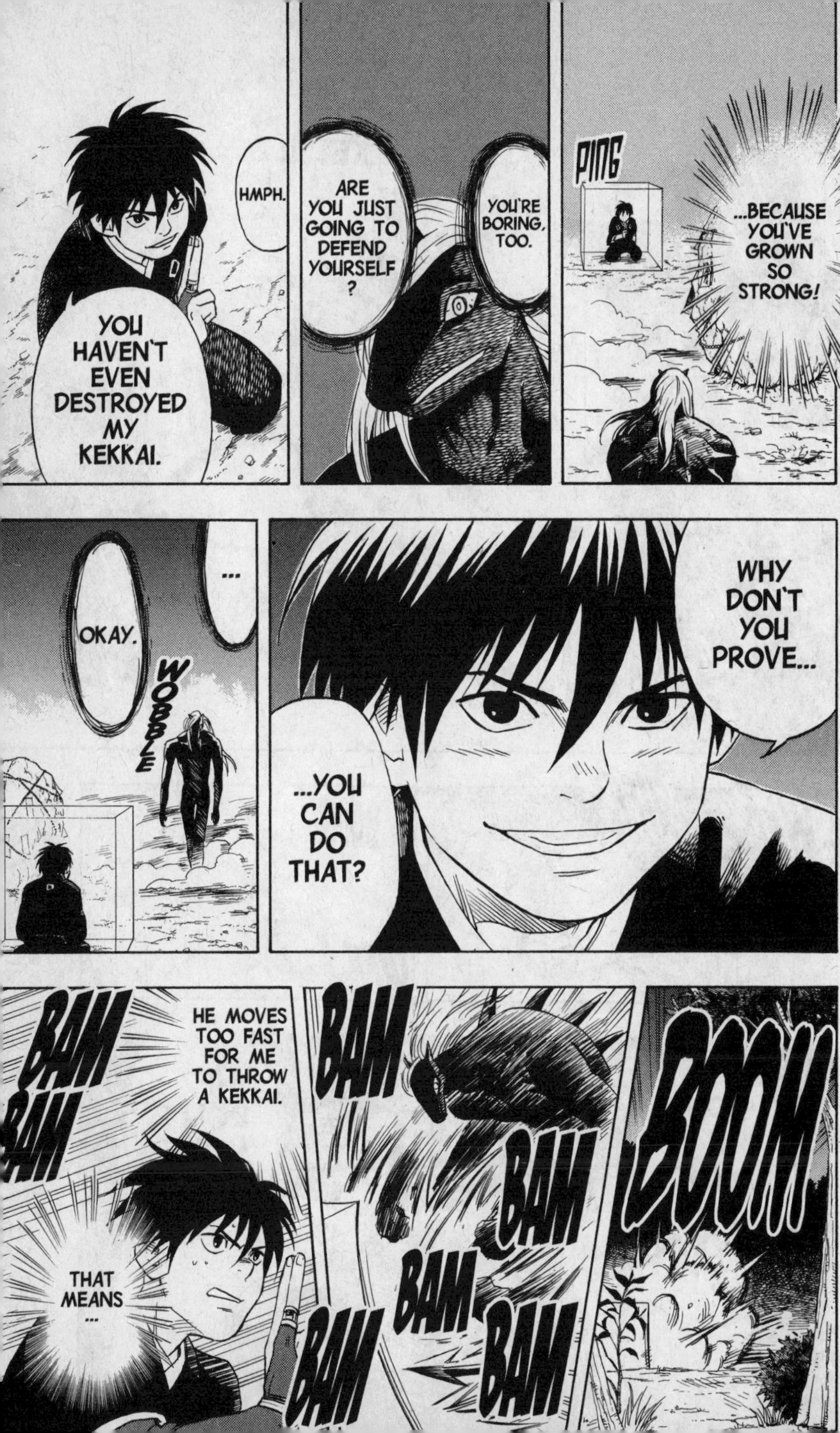
PING
...BECAUSE YOU'VE GROWN SO STRONG!
YOU'RE BORING, TOO.
ARE YOU JUST GOING TO DEFEND YOURSELF?
HMPH.
YOU HAVEN'T EVEN DESTROYED MY KEKKAI.
WHY DON'T YOU PROVE...
...YOU CAN DO THAT?
...
OKAY.
WOBBLE
BOOM
BAM
BAM
BAM
BAM
BAM
BAM
BAM
BAM
HE MOVES TOO FAST FOR ME TO THROW A KEKKAI.
THAT MEANS ...

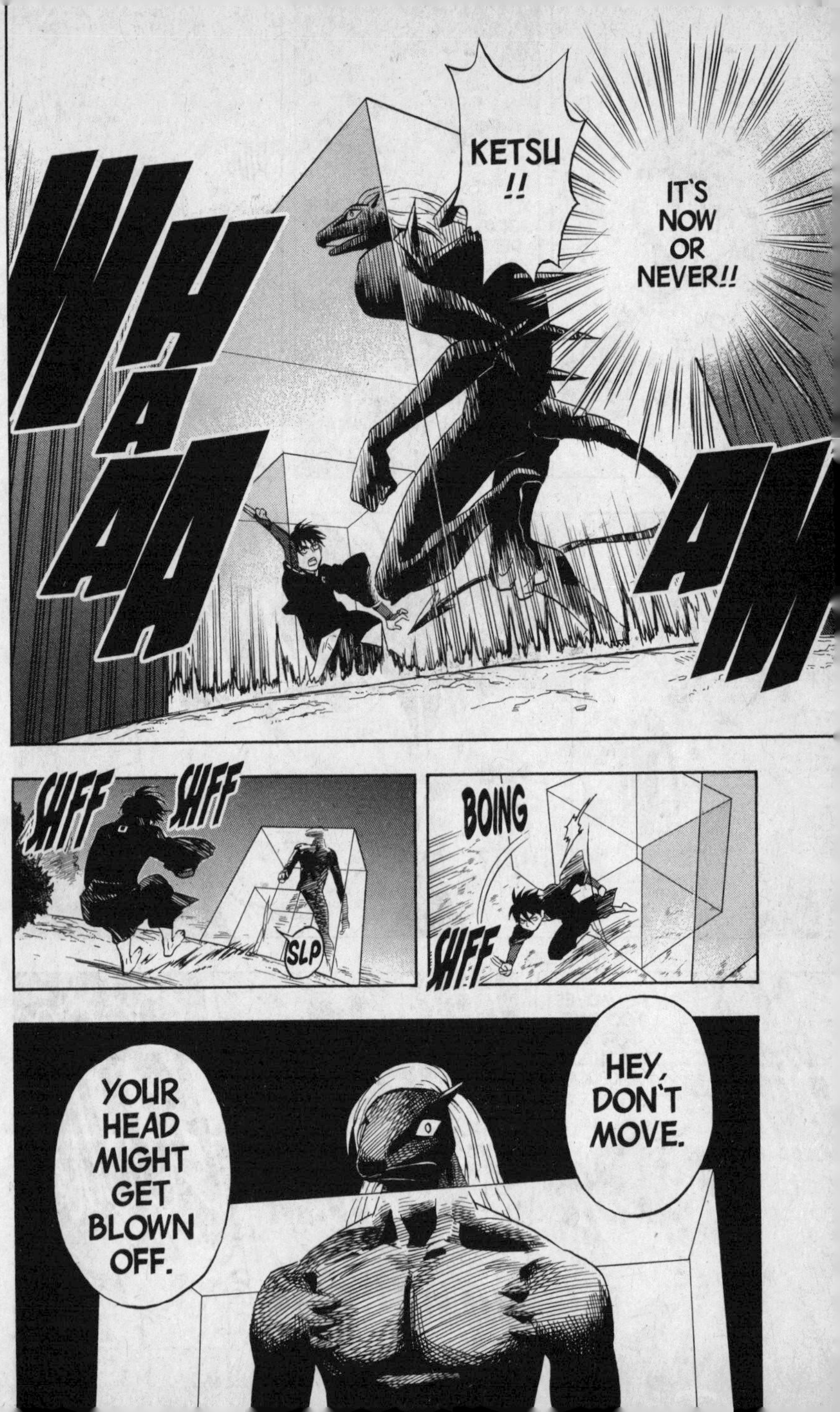
IT'S NOW OR NEVER!!
KETSU!!
WHAAAAAH
BOING
SHFF
SHFF SHFF
SLP
HEY, DON'T MOVE.
YOUR HEAD MIGHT GET BLOWN OFF.

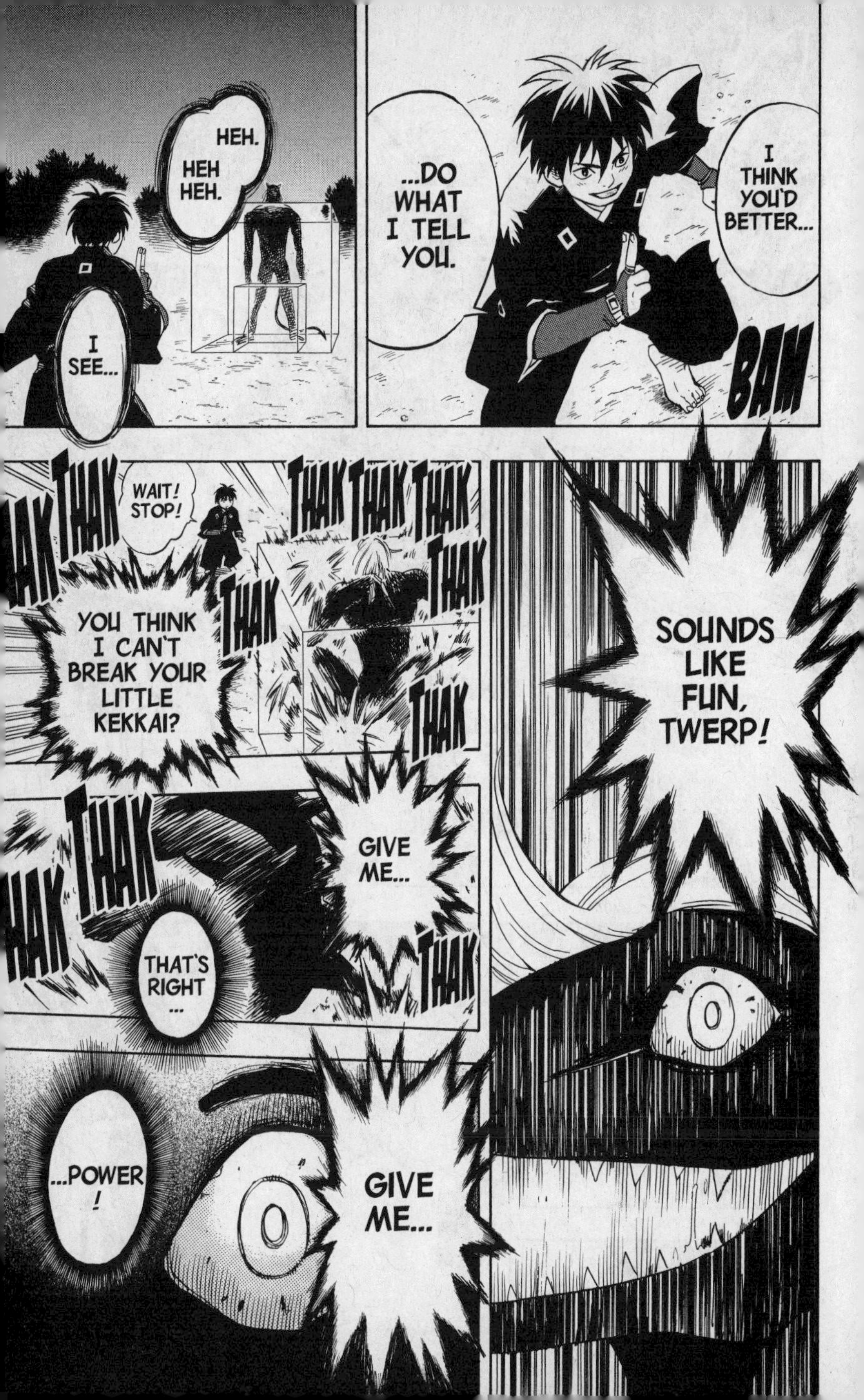
I THINK YOU'D BETTER...
...DO WHAT I TELL YOU.
BAM
HEH. HEH HEH.
I SEE...
SOUNDS LIKE FUN, TWERP!
THAK THAK THAK
THAK
WAIT! STOP!
THAK THAK
THAK
YOU THINK I CAN'T BREAK YOUR LITTLE KEKKAI?
THAK
GIVE ME...
THAK THAK
THAT'S RIGHT...
THAK
GIVE ME...
...POWER!

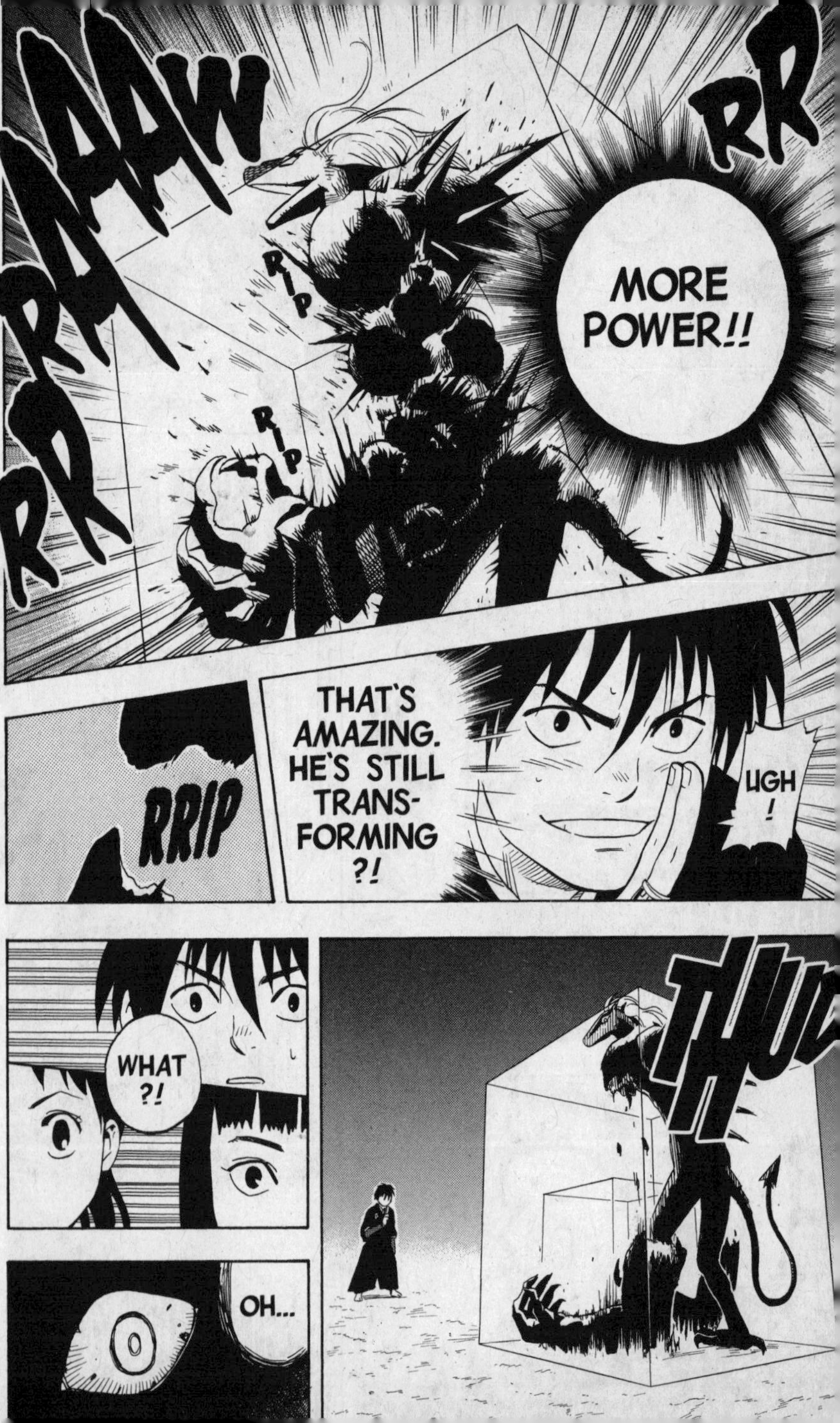
RR
MORE POWER!!
RAAAW RRR
RIP
RIP
UGH!
THAT'S AMAZING. HE'S STILL TRANS-FORMING?!
RRIP
THUD
WHAT?!
OH...

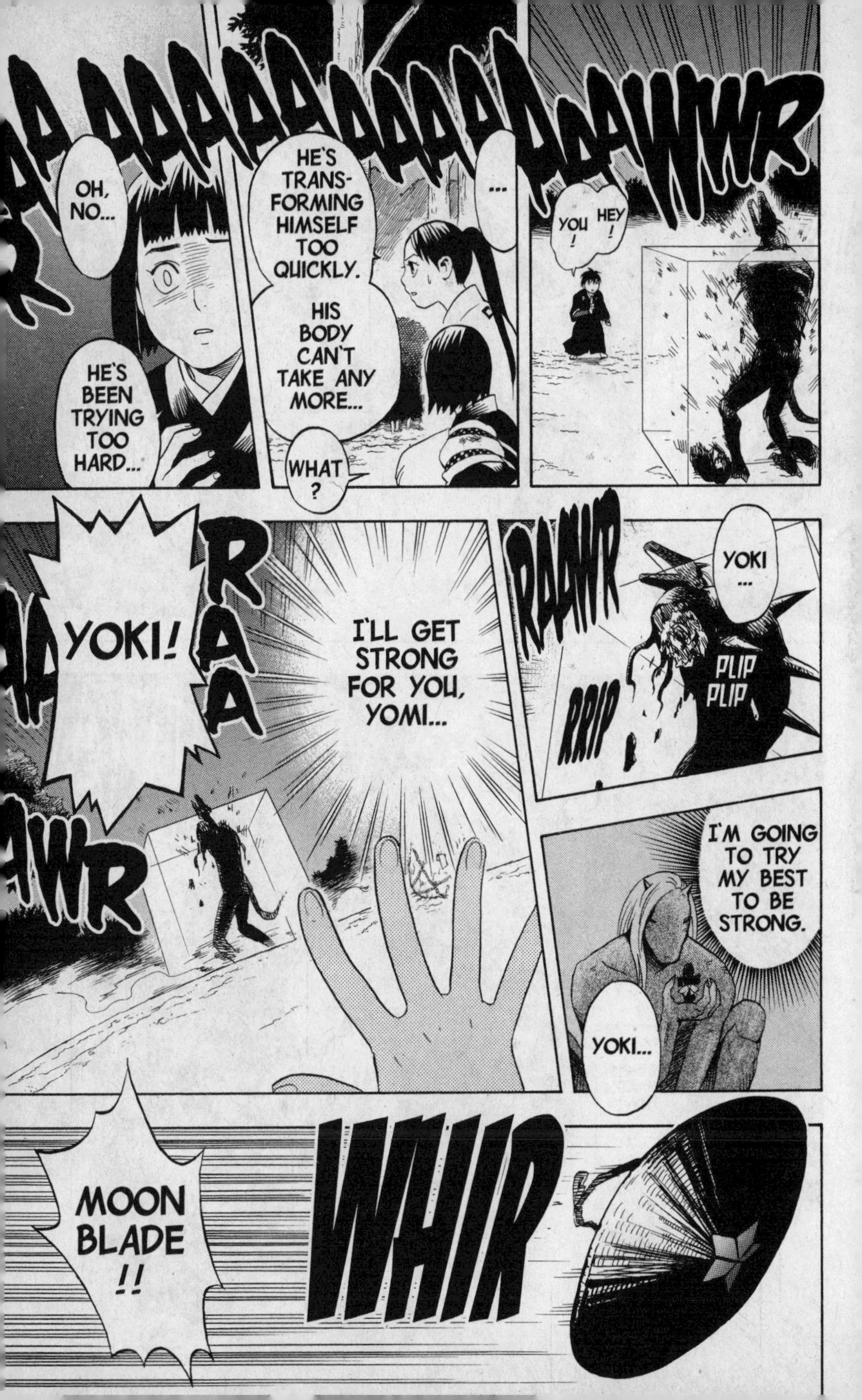
AAAAAAAAAAAAAAWWR
HEY!
YOU!
...
HE'S TRANSFORMING HIMSELF TOO QUICKLY.
HIS BODY CAN'T TAKE ANY MORE...
WHAT?
OH, NO...
HE'S BEEN TRYING TOO HARD...
RAAWR
YOKI...
PLIP PLIP
RRIP
I'M GOING TO TRY MY BEST TO BE STRONG.
YOKI...
RAAAAWR
I'LL GET STRONG FOR YOU, YOMI...
YOKI!
WHIR
MOON BLADE!!

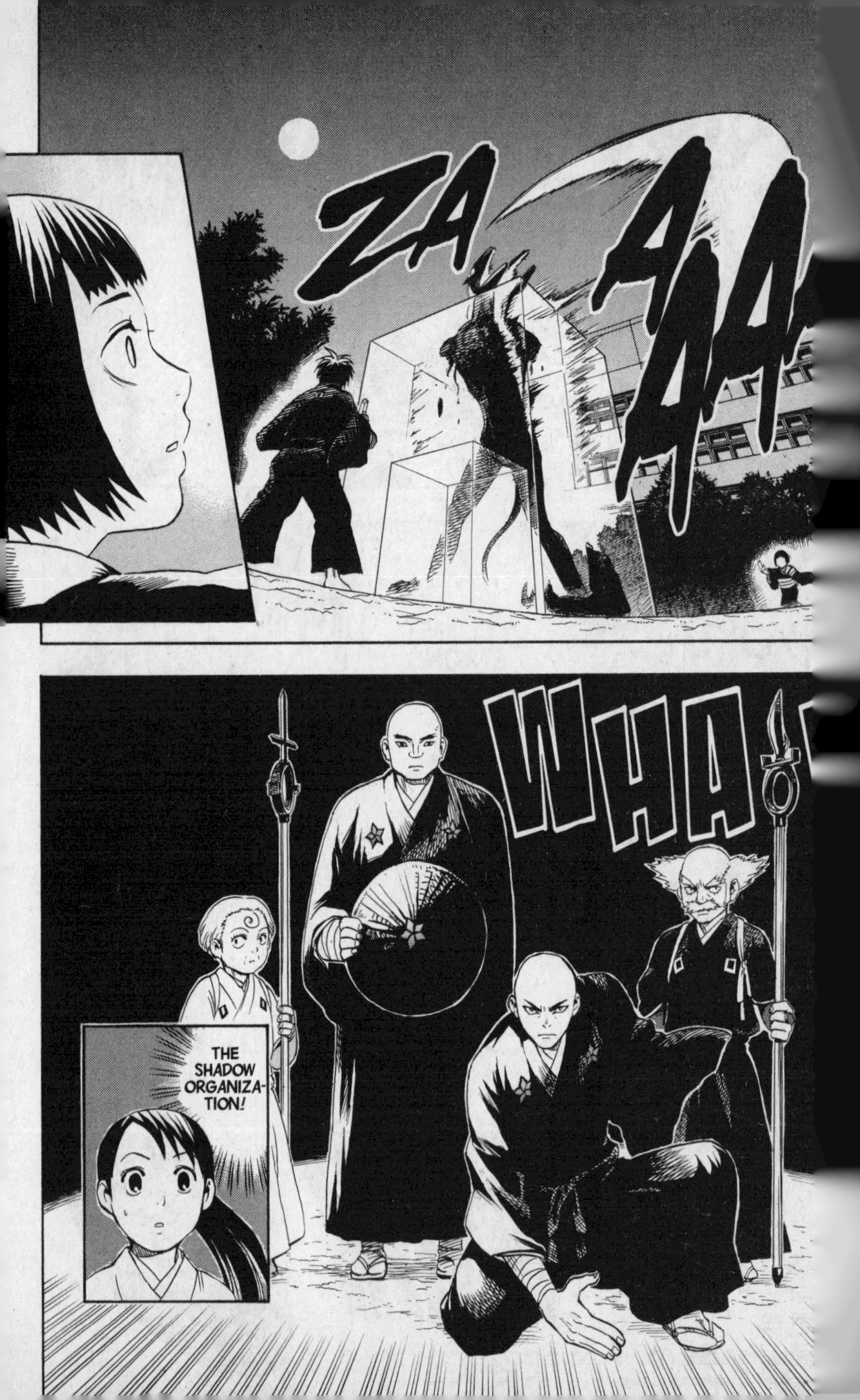
ZAAAA
WHA
THE SHADOW ORGANIZATION!

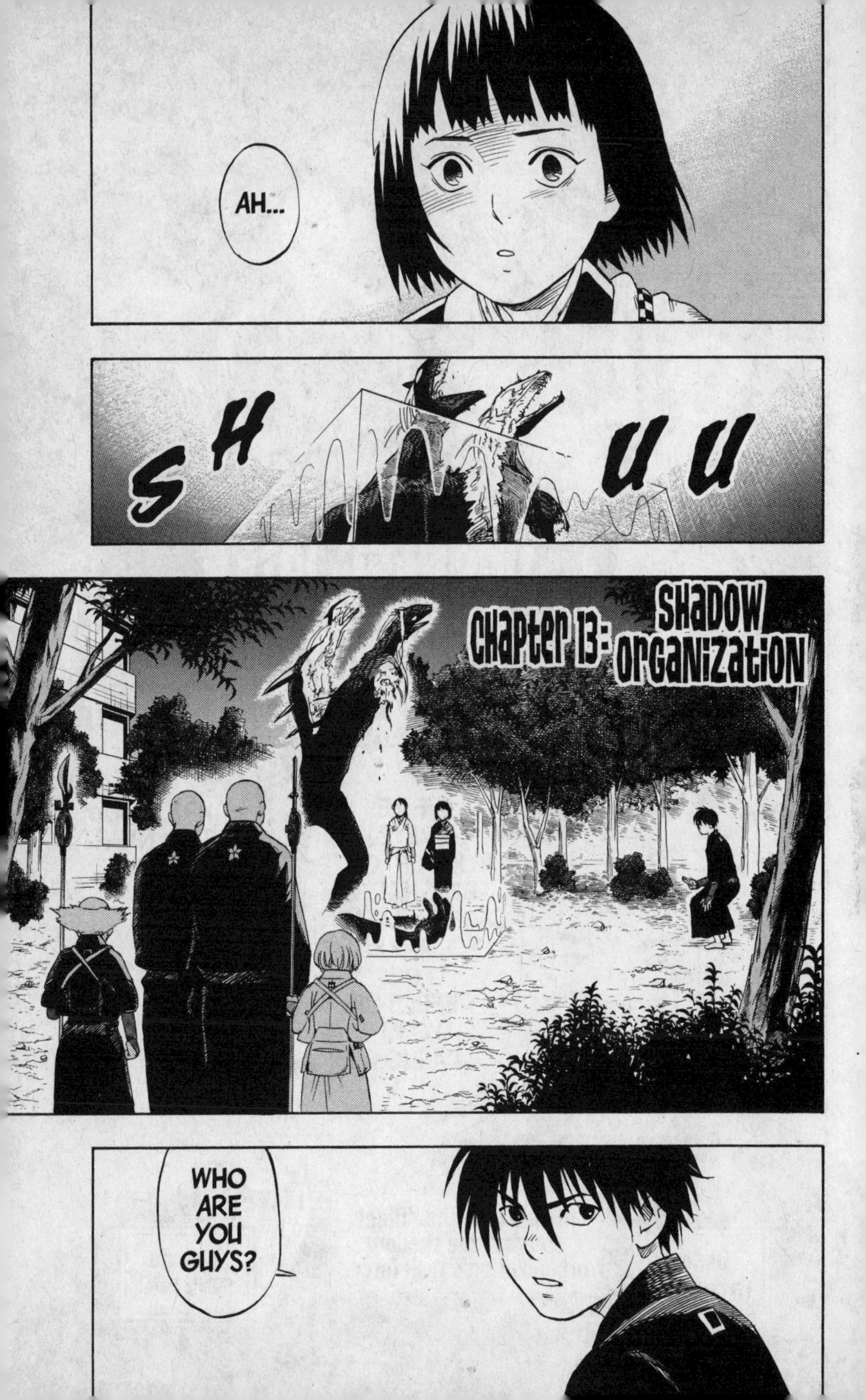
AH...
SHUUU
Chapter 13: Shadow Organization
WHO ARE YOU GUYS?

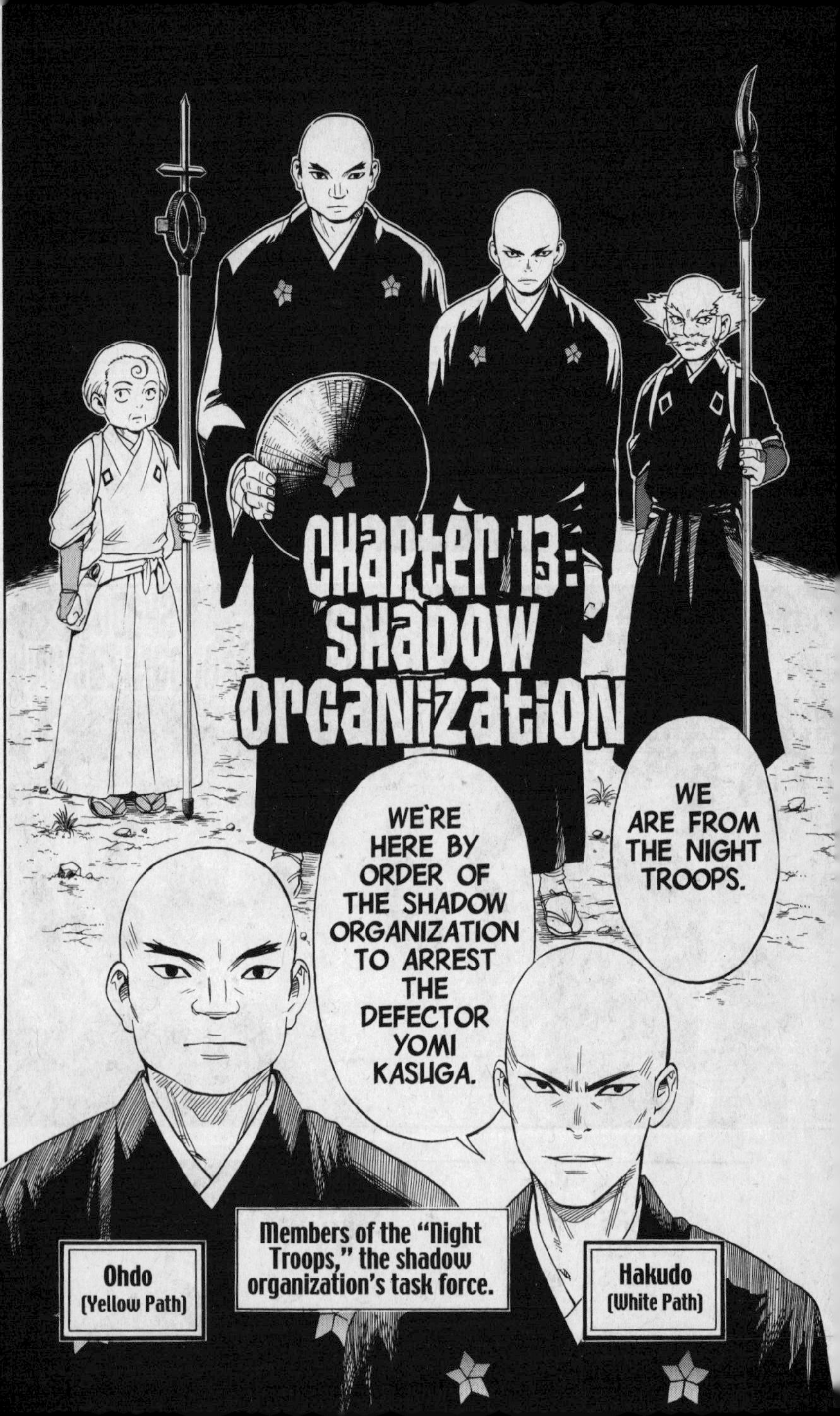
CHAPTER 13: SHADOW ORGANIZATION
WE ARE FROM THE NIGHT TROOPS.
WE'RE HERE BY ORDER OF THE SHADOW ORGANIZATION TO ARREST THE DEFECTOR YOMI KASUGA.
Hakudo (White Path)
Members of the "Night Troops," the shadow organization's task force.
Ohdo (Yellow Path)

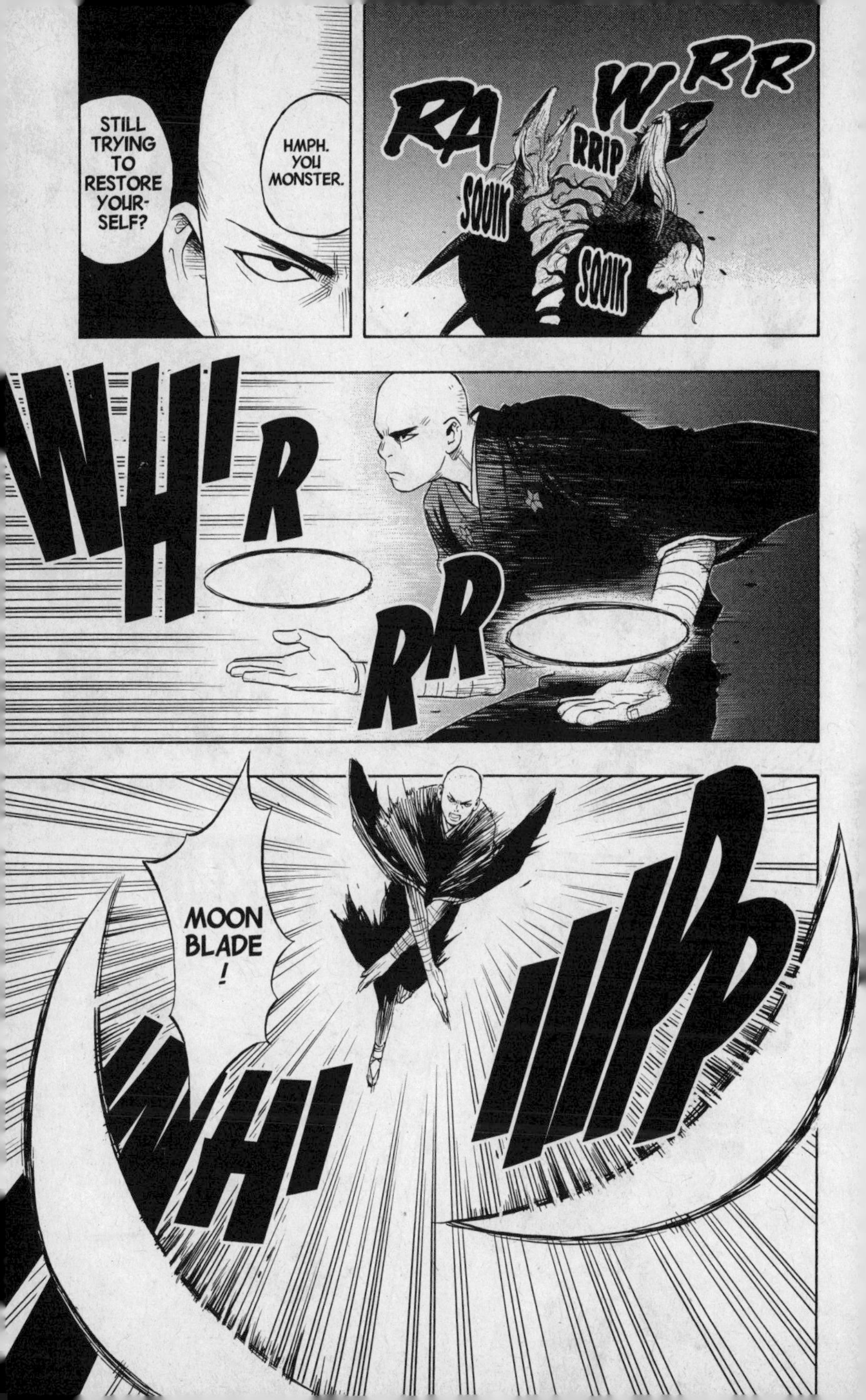
RAWRR
RRIP
SQUIK
SQUIK
HMPH. YOU MONSTER.
STILL TRYING TO RESTORE YOUR-SELF?
WHIR
RR
MOON BLADE!
WHI
IIR

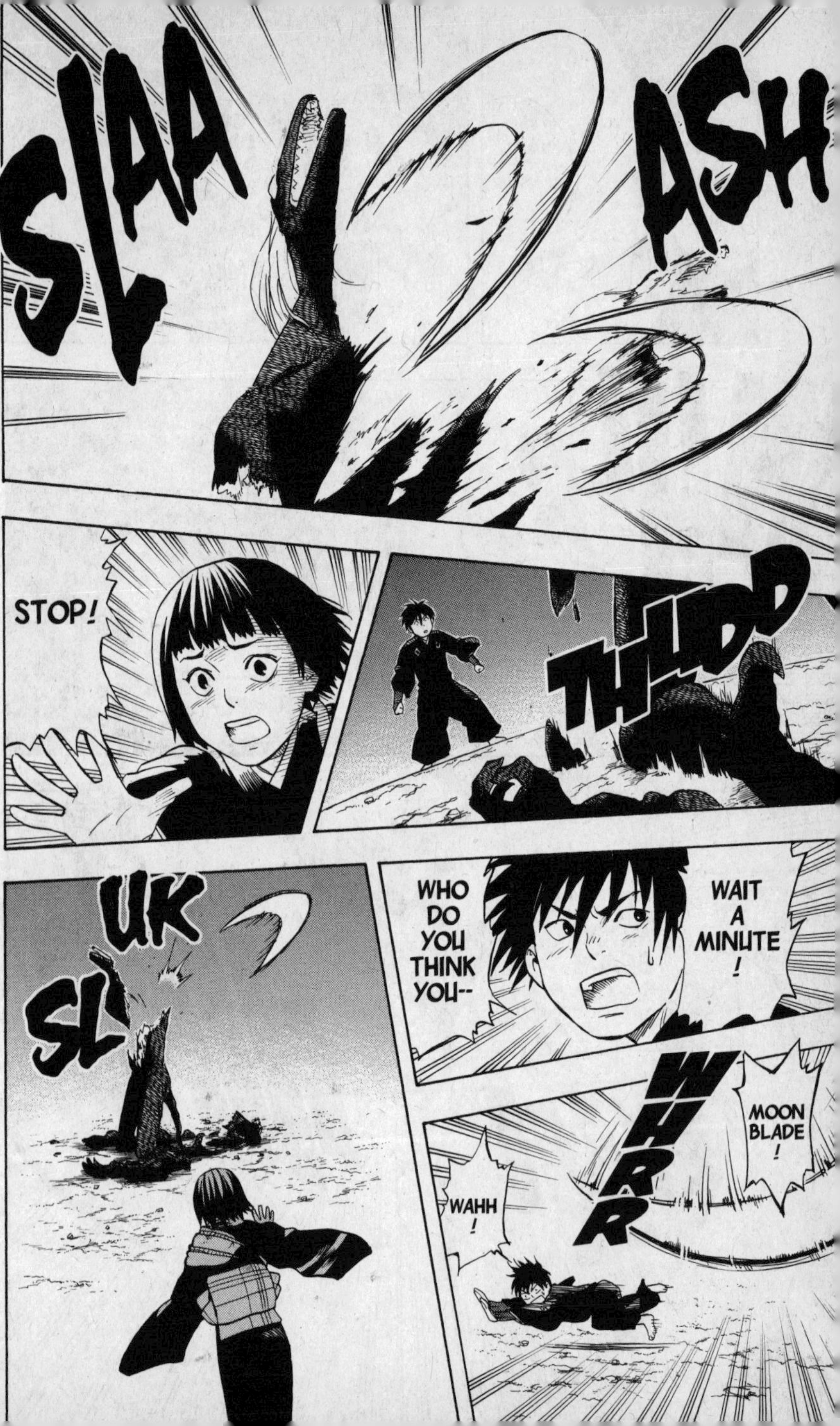
SLAA
ASH
THUDD
STOP!
WAIT A MINUTE!
WHO DO YOU THINK YOU--
MOON BLADE!
WHRR
WAHH!
SLUK

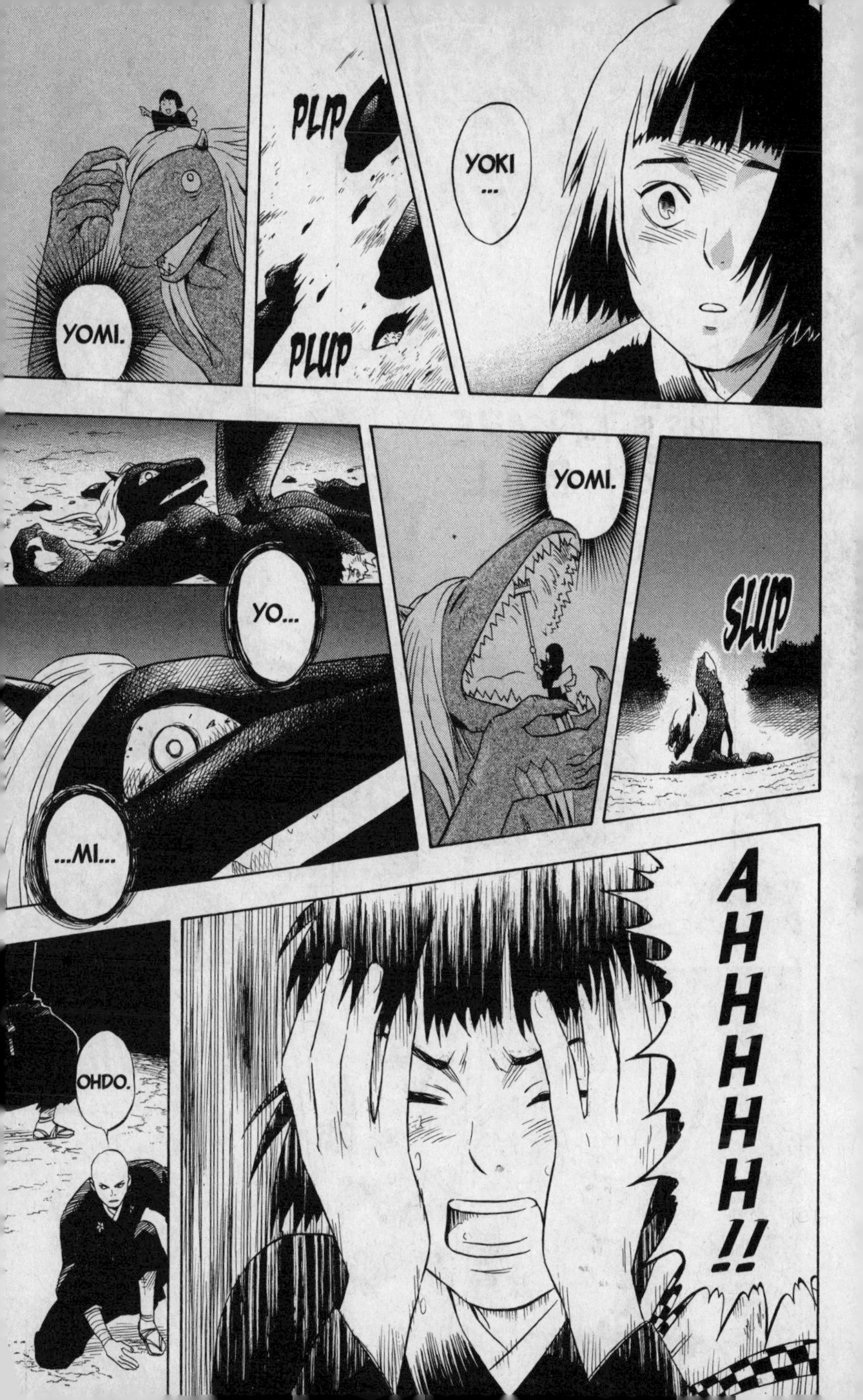
YOKI ...
PLIP
PLUP
YOMI.
SLUP
YOMI.
YO...
...MI...
AHHHHHH!!
OHDO.

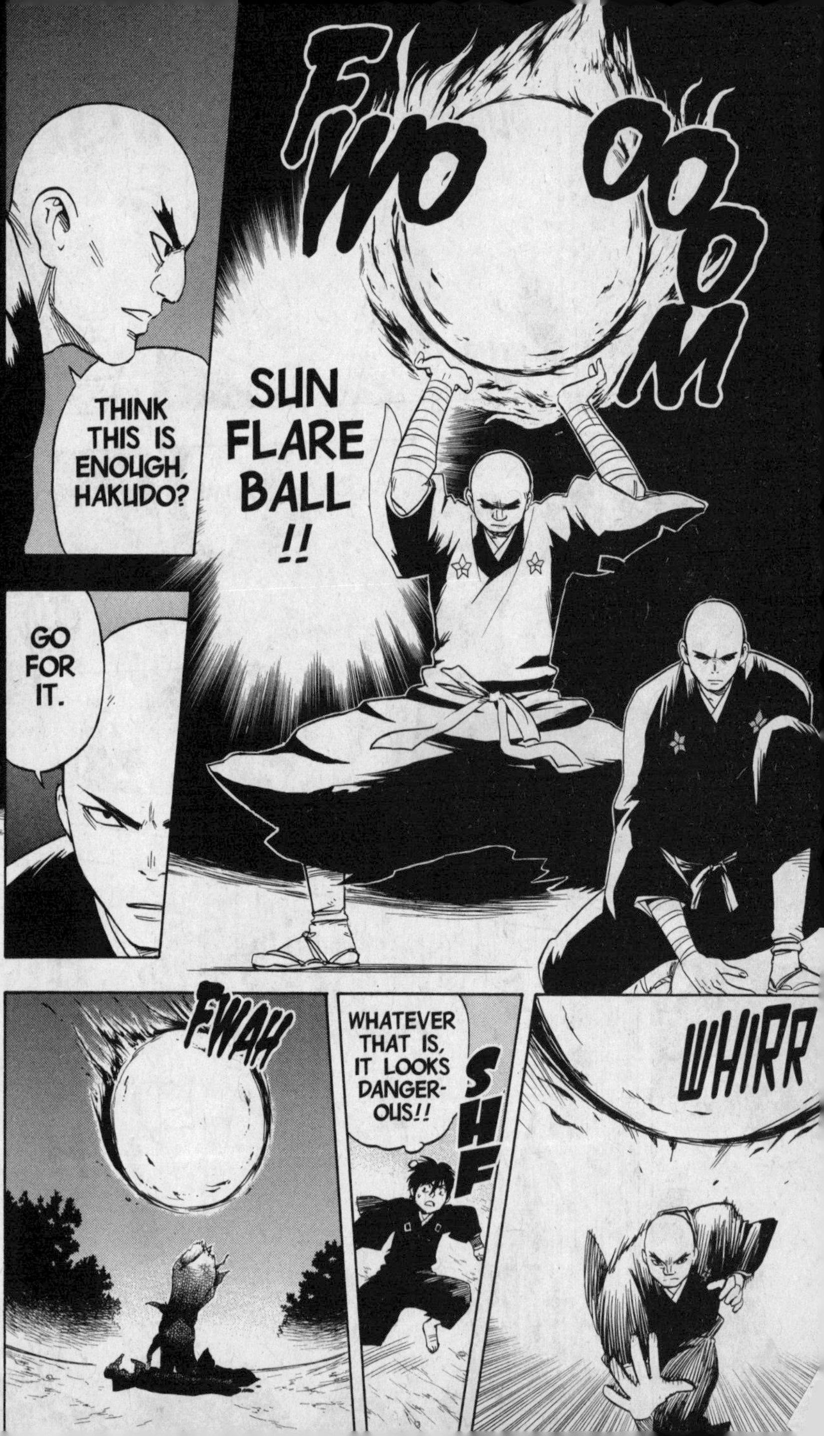
FWOOOM
SUN FLARE BALL!!
THINK THIS IS ENOUGH, HAKUDO?
GO FOR IT.
WHIRR
WHATEVER THAT IS, IT LOOKS DANGER-OUS!!
SHF
FWAH

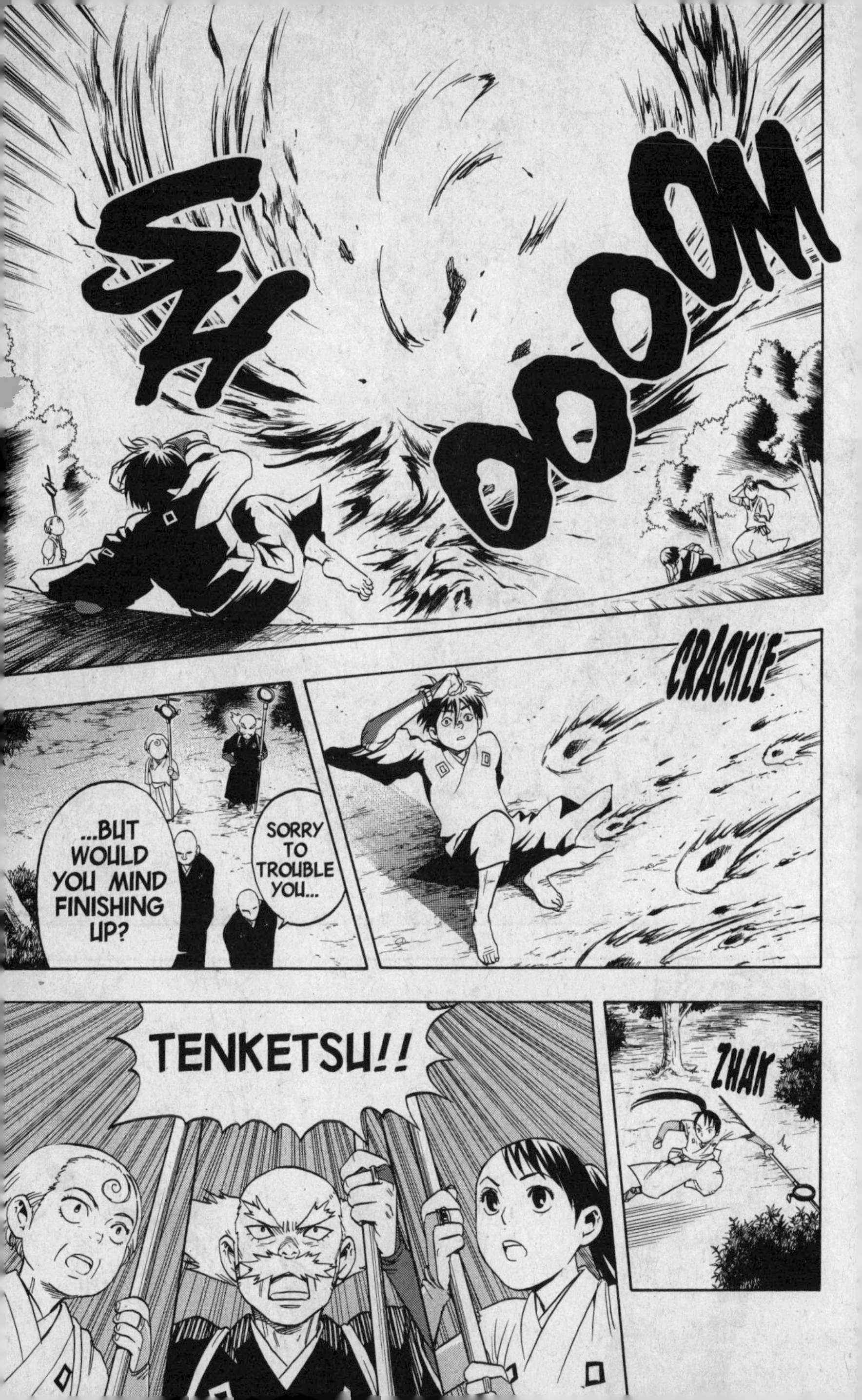
SHOOOOOM
CRACKLE
SORRY TO TROUBLE YOU...
...BUT WOULD YOU MIND FINISHING UP?
ZHAK
TENKETSU!!

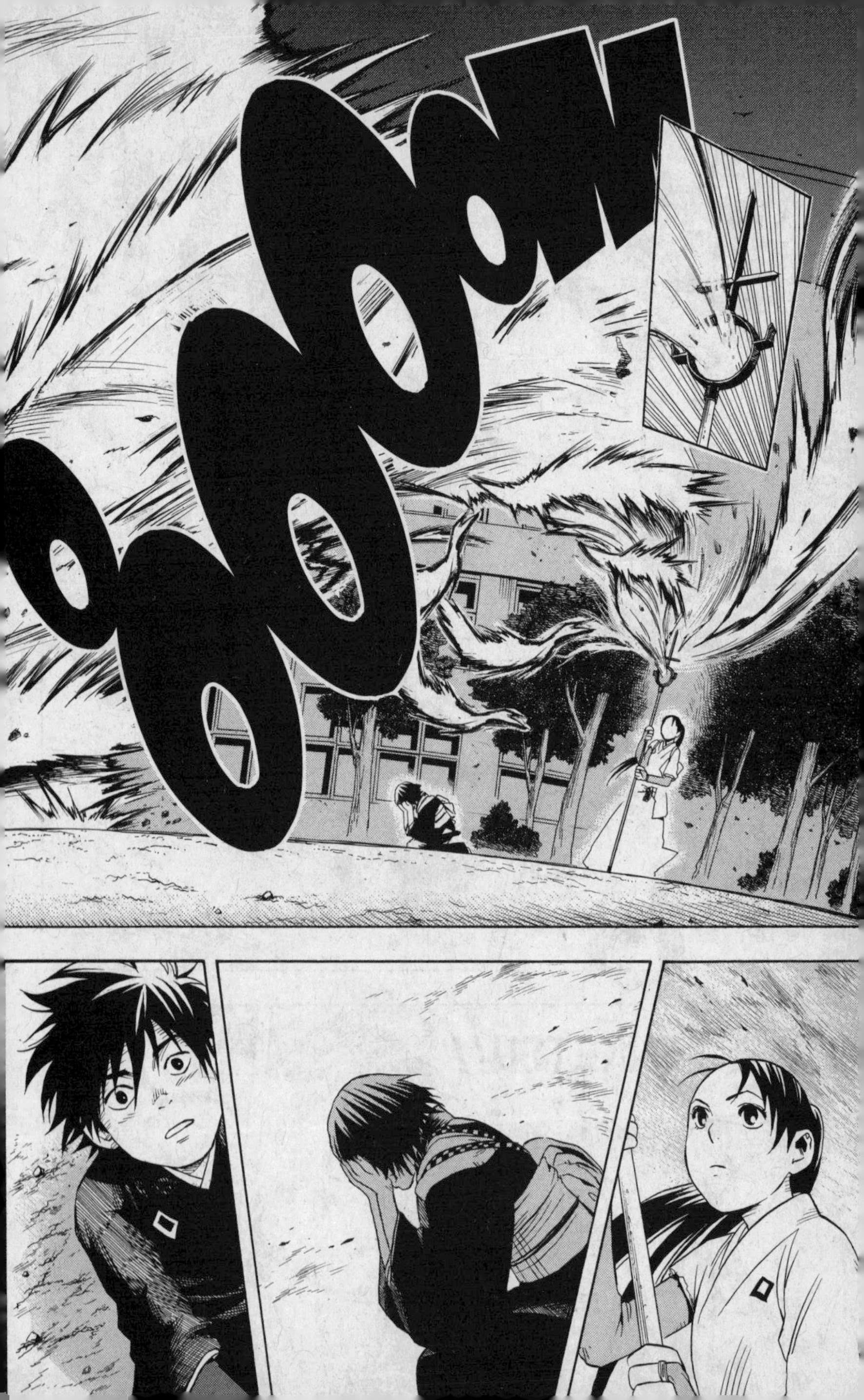

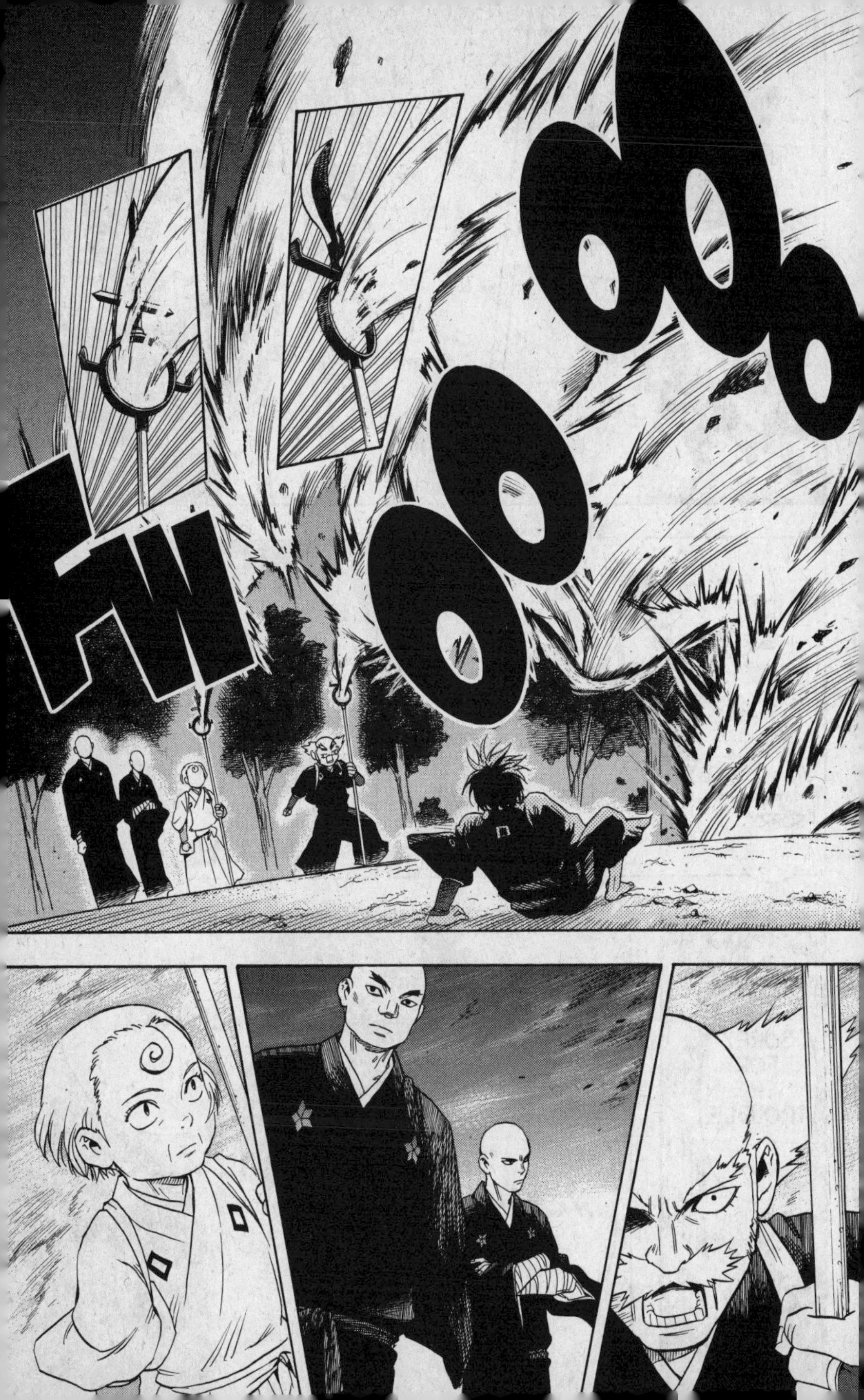
FWOOOOO

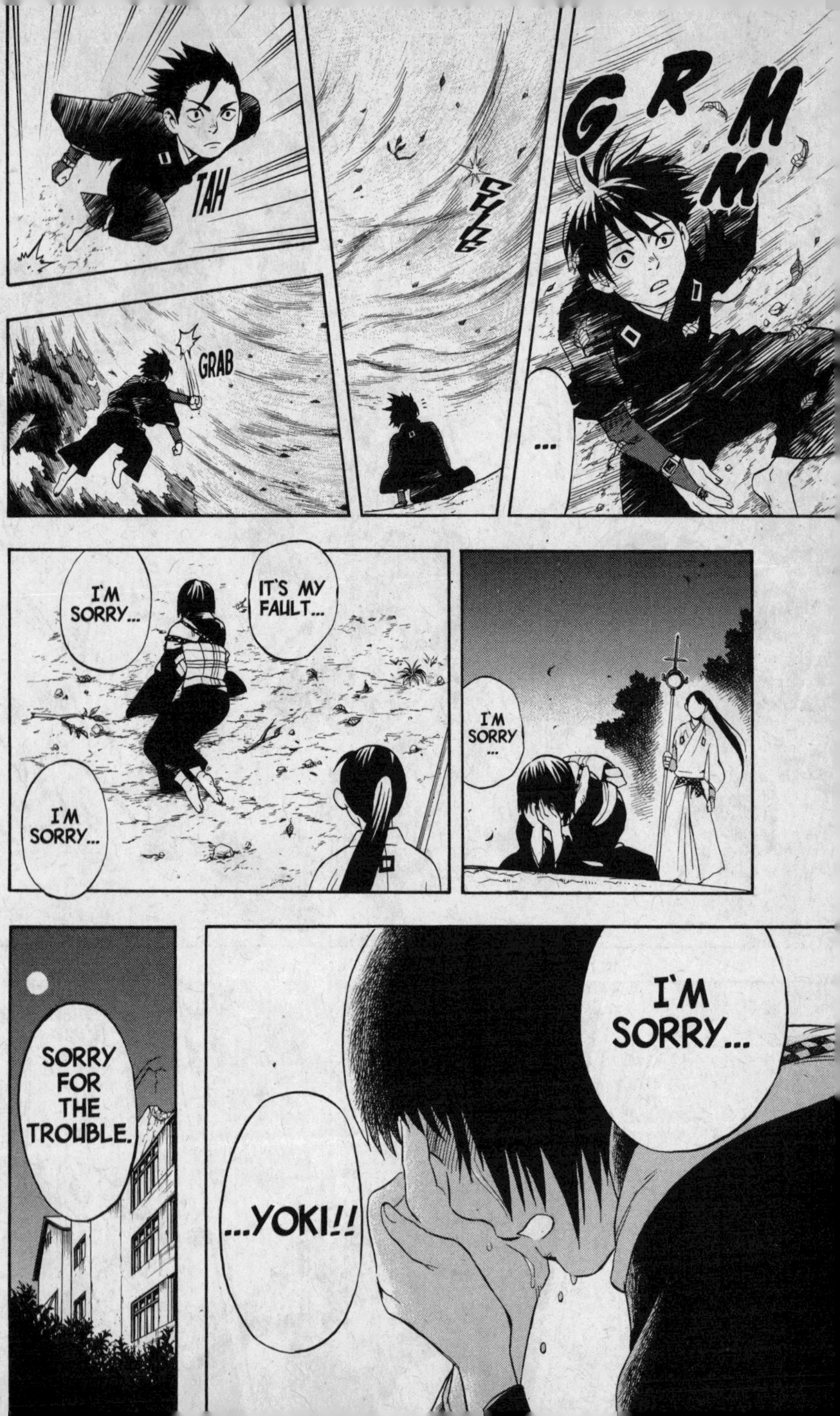
GRMM
...
TAH
GRAB
I'M SORRY ...
IT'S MY FAULT...
I'M SORRY...
I'M SORRY...
I'M SORRY...
...YOKI!!
SORRY FOR THE TROUBLE.

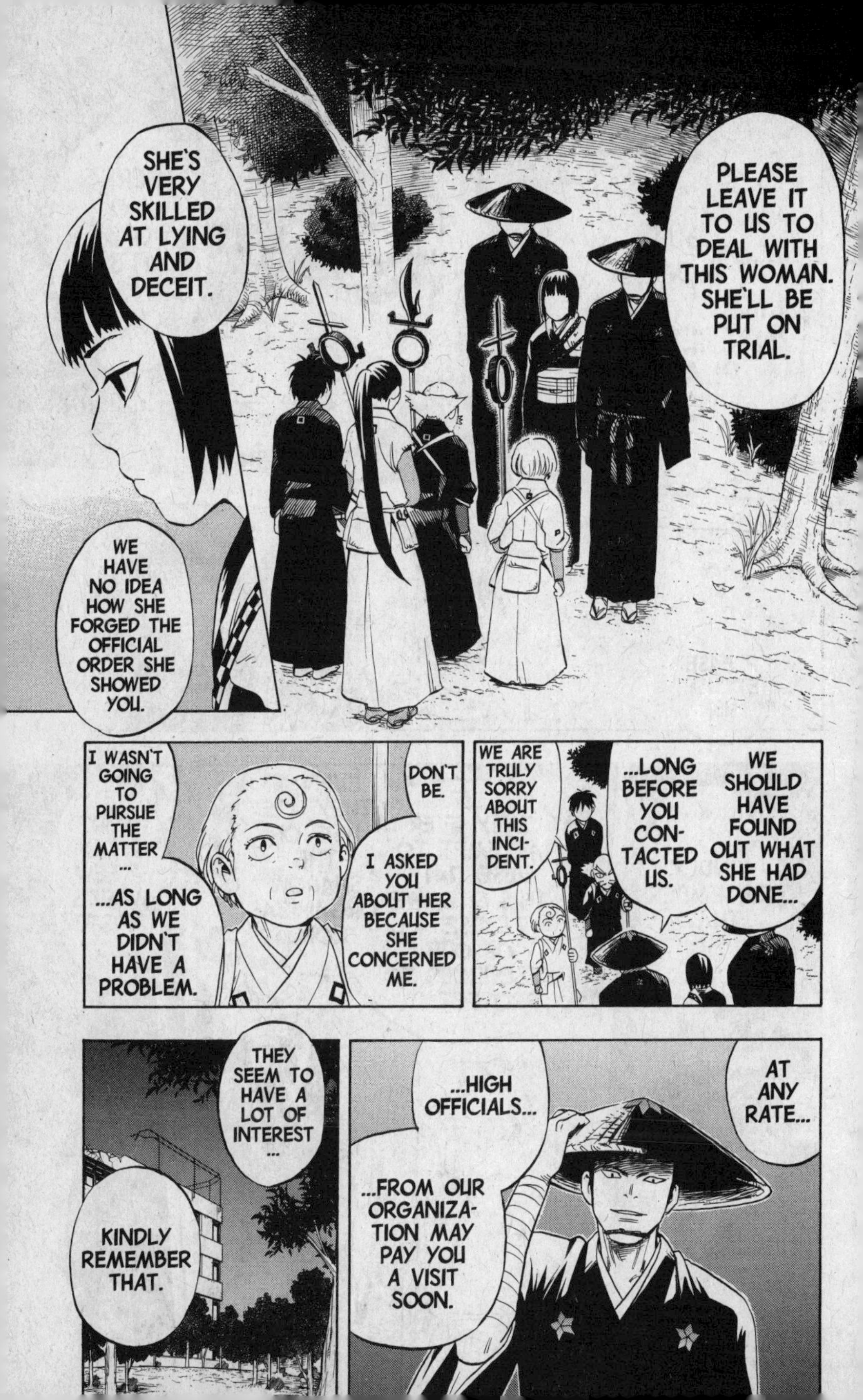
PLEASE LEAVE IT TO US TO DEAL WITH THIS WOMAN. SHE'LL BE PUT ON TRIAL.
SHE'S VERY SKILLED AT LYING AND DECEIT.
WE HAVE NO IDEA HOW SHE FORGED THE OFFICIAL ORDER SHE SHOWED YOU.
WE SHOULD HAVE FOUND OUT WHAT SHE HAD DONE...
...LONG BEFORE YOU CON-TACTED US.
WE ARE TRULY SORRY ABOUT THIS INCI-DENT.
DON'T BE.
I ASKED YOU ABOUT HER BECAUSE SHE CONCERNED ME.
I WASN'T GOING TO PURSUE THE MATTER...
...AS LONG AS WE DIDN'T HAVE A PROBLEM.
AT ANY RATE...
...HIGH OFFICIALS...
...FROM OUR ORGANIZA-TION MAY PAY YOU A VISIT SOON.
THEY SEEM TO HAVE A LOT OF INTEREST...
KINDLY REMEMBER THAT.

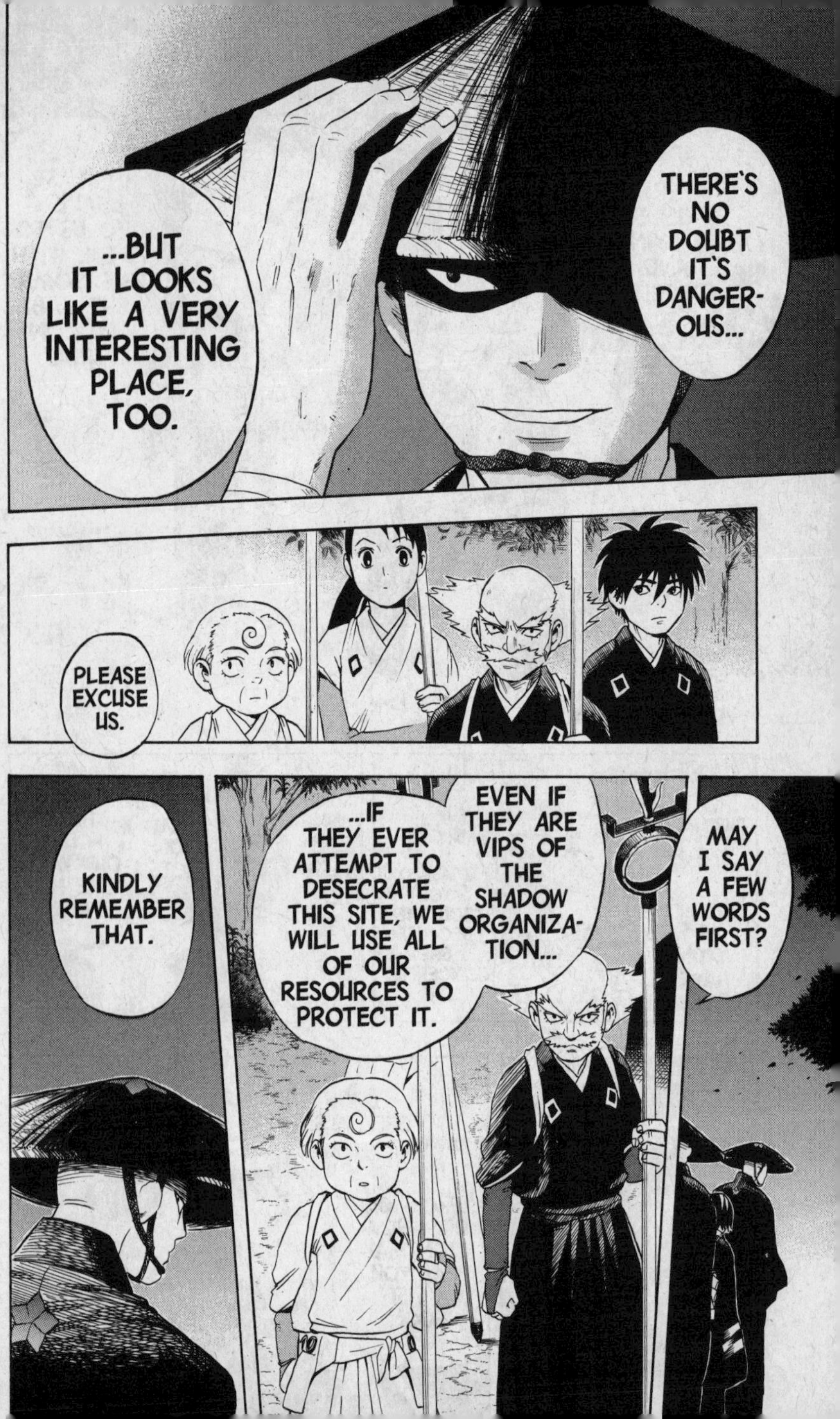
THERE'S NO DOUBT IT'S DANGEROUS...
...BUT IT LOOKS LIKE A VERY INTERESTING PLACE, TOO.
PLEASE EXCUSE US.
MAY I SAY A FEW WORDS FIRST?
EVEN IF THEY ARE VIPS OF THE SHADOW ORGANIZATION...
...IF THEY EVER ATTEMPT TO DESECRATE THIS SITE, WE WILL USE ALL OF OUR RESOURCES TO PROTECT IT.
KINDLY REMEMBER THAT.

STUPID WOMAN.

HURRY UP.

DON'T WORRY. THEY'LL SHOW UP WITH CANDY AND FLOWERS.

HA HA HA

COULDN'T YOU SEE YOUR MONSTER HAD LIMITS NO MATTER HOW HARD YOU TRIED TO STRENGTHEN HIM?

I KNOW I'M NOT SUPPOSED TO HAVE SPARED HIM, BUT...

TAK TAK

PSST

SWUP

...

EXCUSE ME!

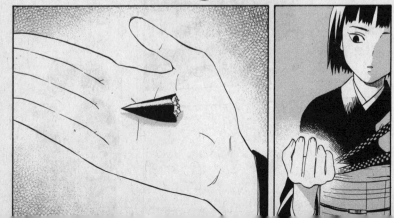

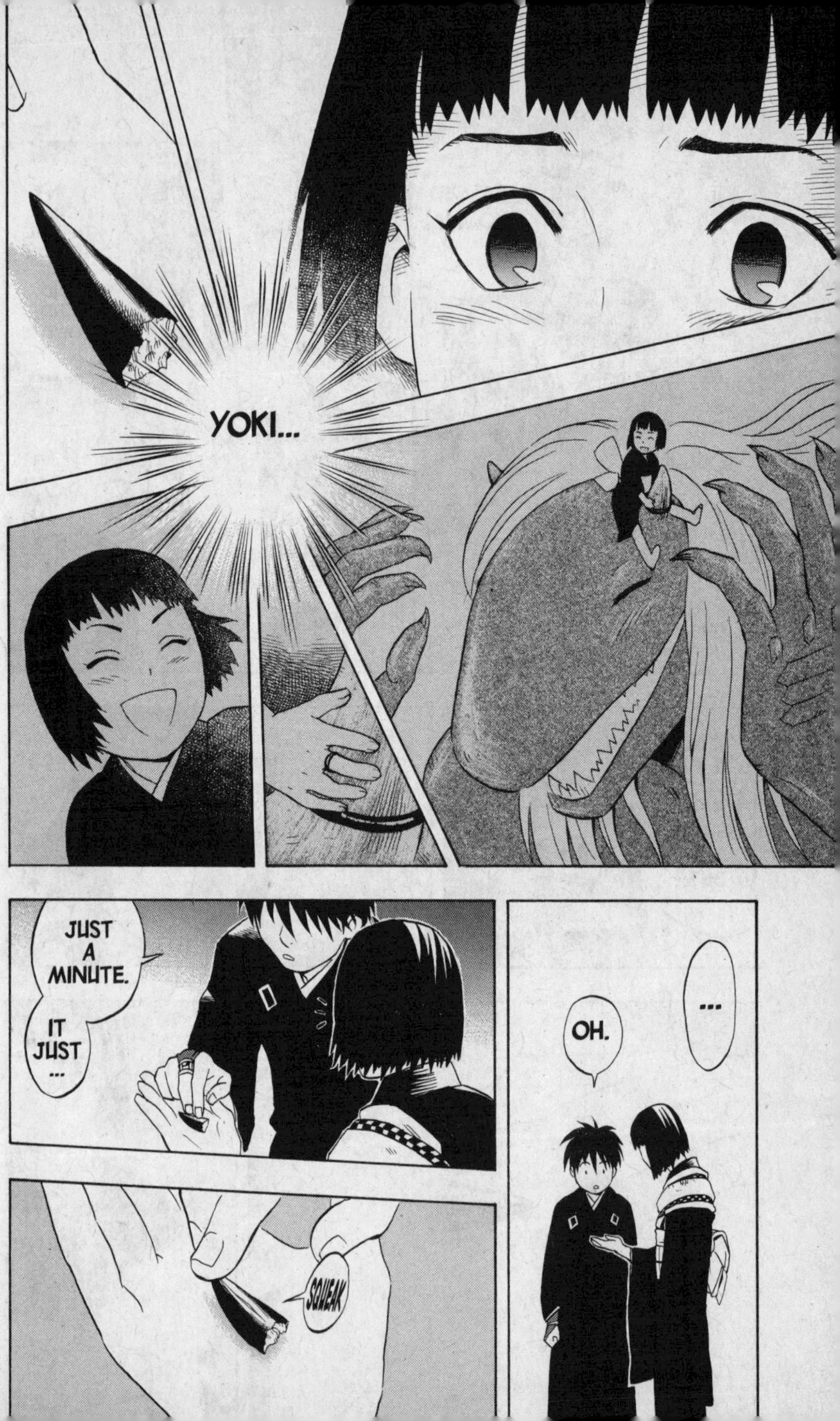
YOKI...
...
OH.
JUST A MINUTE.
IT JUST ...
SQUEAK

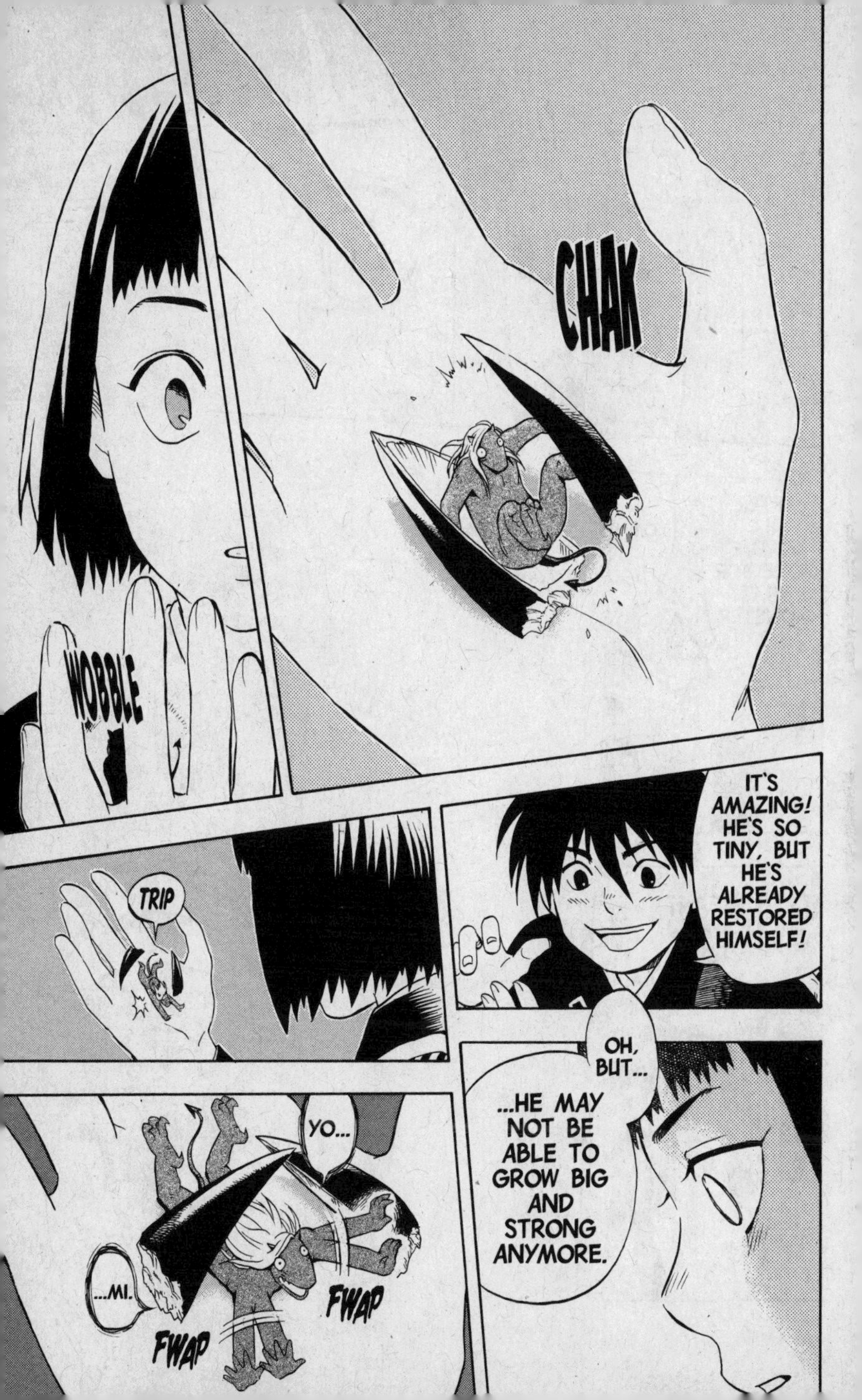
CHAK
WOBBLE
IT'S AMAZING! HE'S SO TINY, BUT HE'S ALREADY RESTORED HIMSELF!
TRIP
OH, BUT...
...HE MAY NOT BE ABLE TO GROW BIG AND STRONG ANYMORE.
YO...
...MI.
FWAP
FWAP

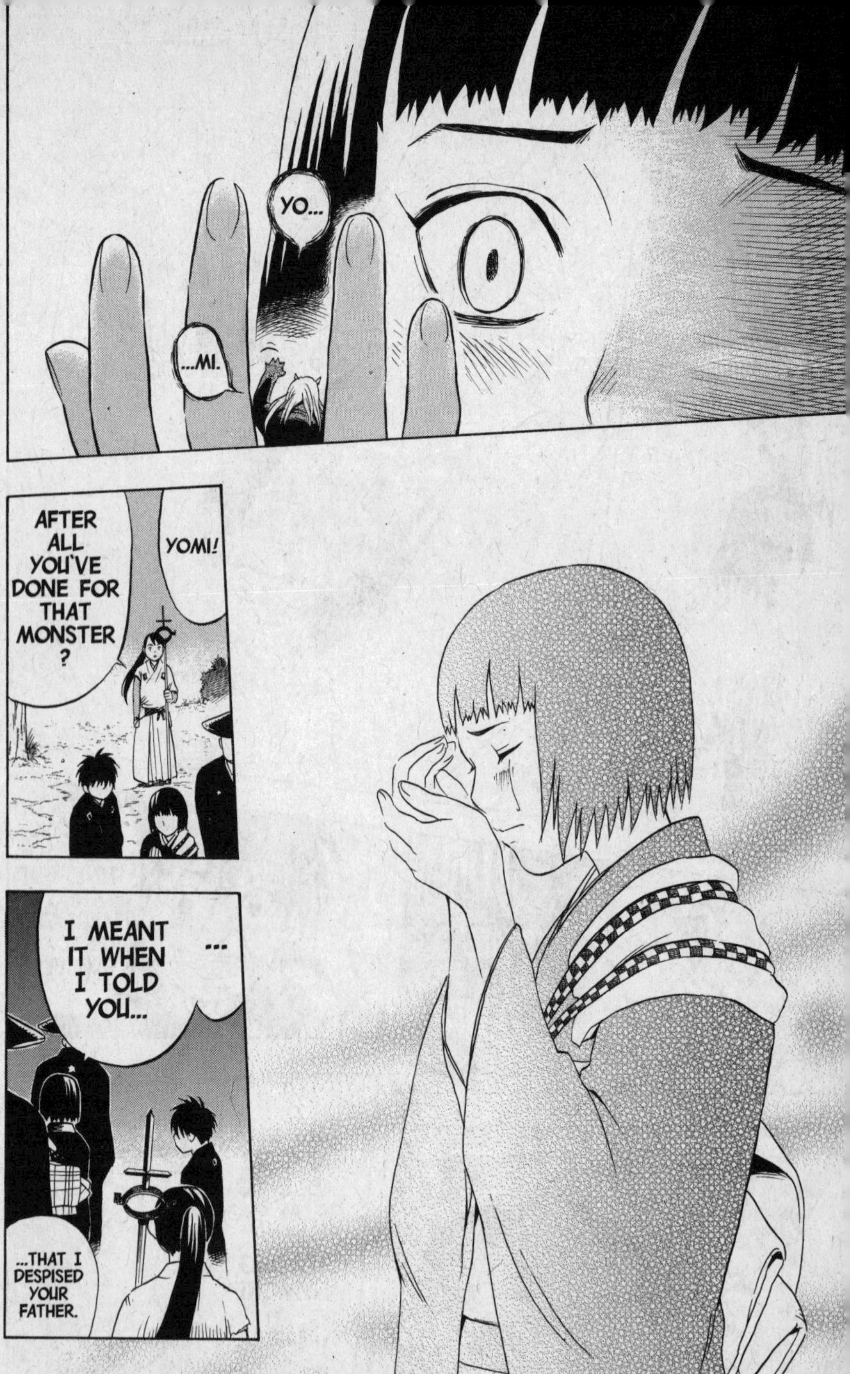
YO...
...MI.
YOMI!
AFTER ALL YOU'VE DONE FOR THAT MONSTER?
...
I MEANT IT WHEN I TOLD YOU...
...THAT I DESPISED YOUR FATHER.

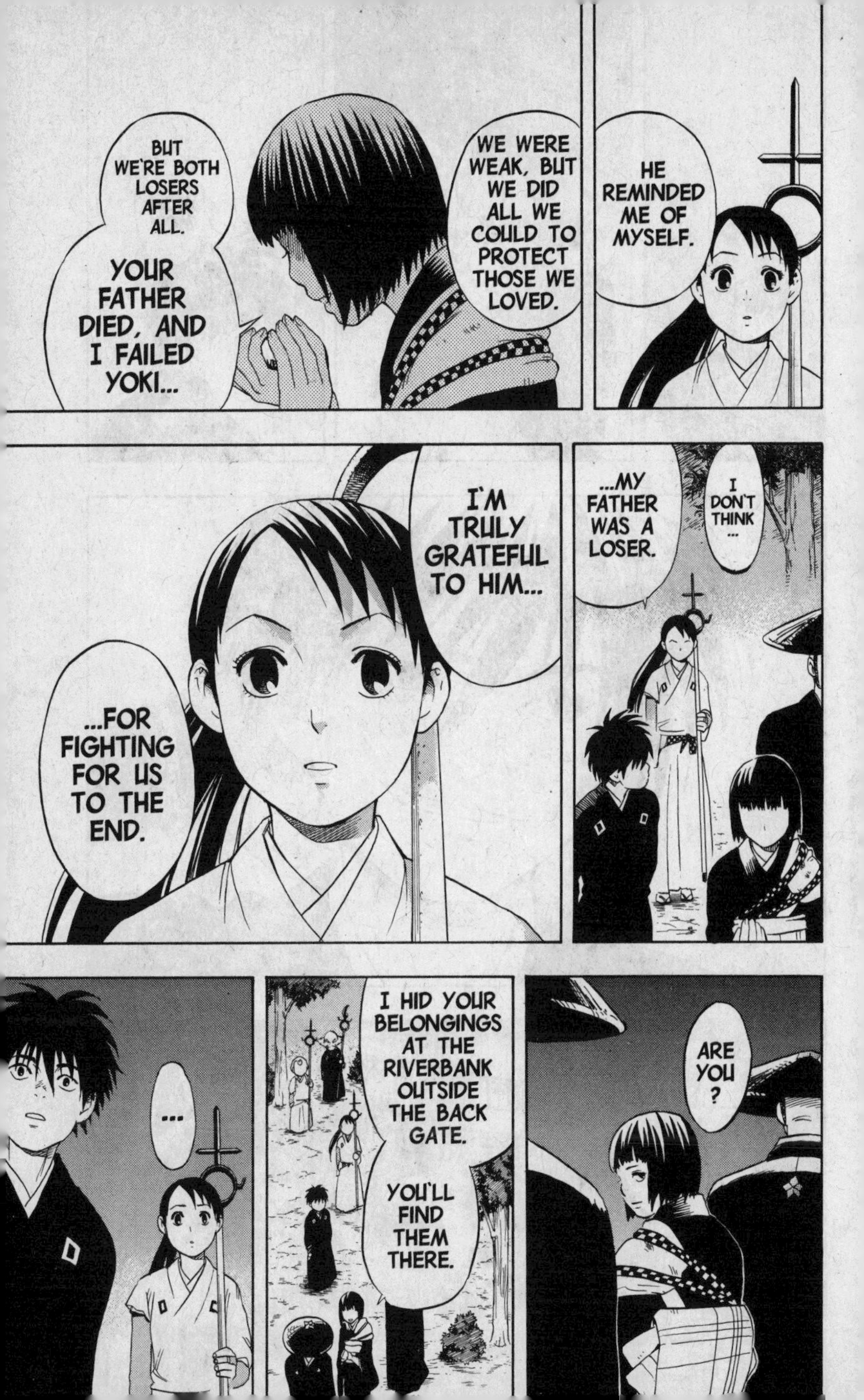
HE REMINDED ME OF MYSELF.
WE WERE WEAK, BUT WE DID ALL WE COULD TO PROTECT THOSE WE LOVED.
BUT WE'RE BOTH LOSERS AFTER ALL.
YOUR FATHER DIED, AND I FAILED YOKI...
I DON'T THINK...
...MY FATHER WAS A LOSER.
I'M TRULY GRATEFUL TO HIM...
...FOR FIGHTING FOR US TO THE END.
ARE YOU ?
I HID YOUR BELONGINGS AT THE RIVERBANK OUTSIDE THE BACK GATE.
YOU'LL FIND THEM THERE.
...

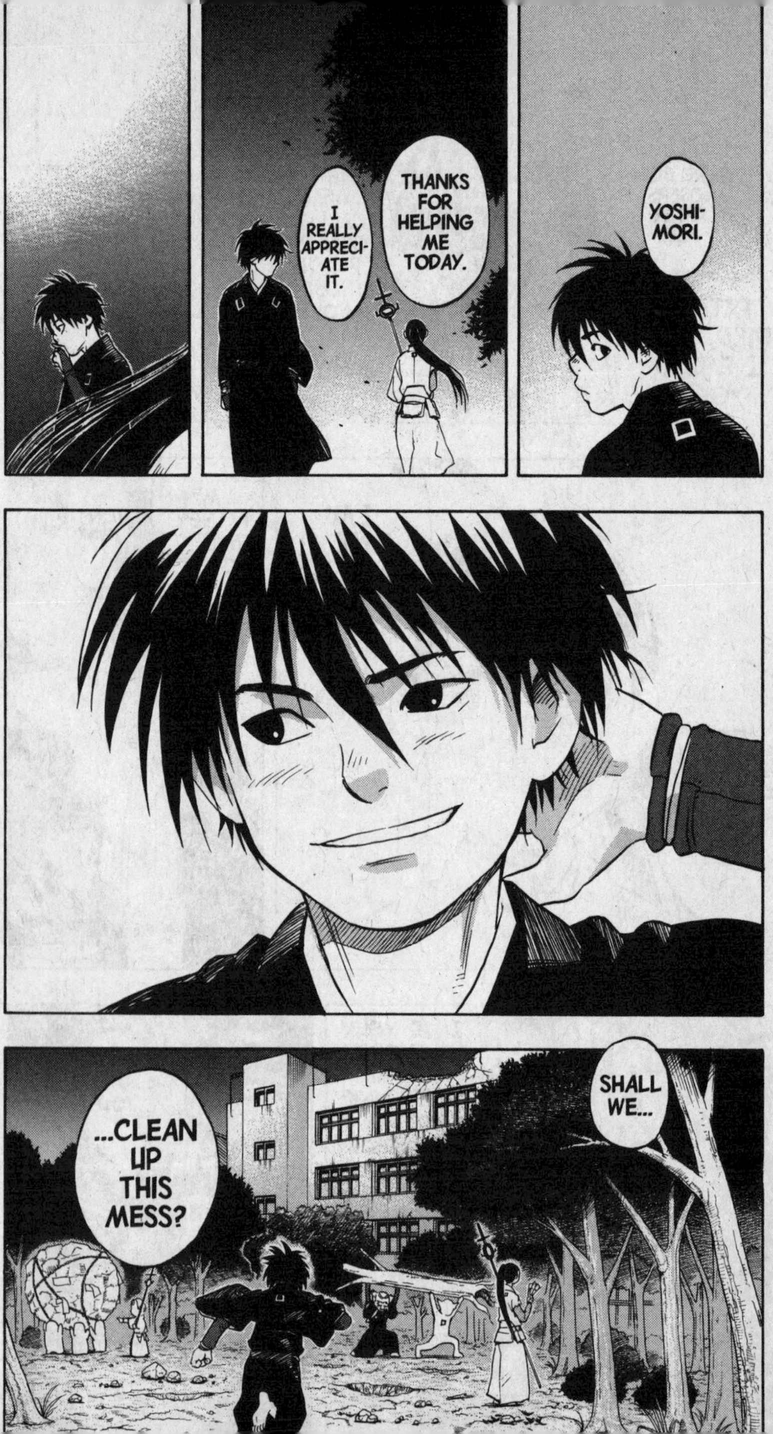
YOSHI-MORI.
THANKS FOR HELPING ME TODAY.
I REALLY APPRECI-ATE IT.
SHALL WE...
...CLEAN UP THIS MESS?

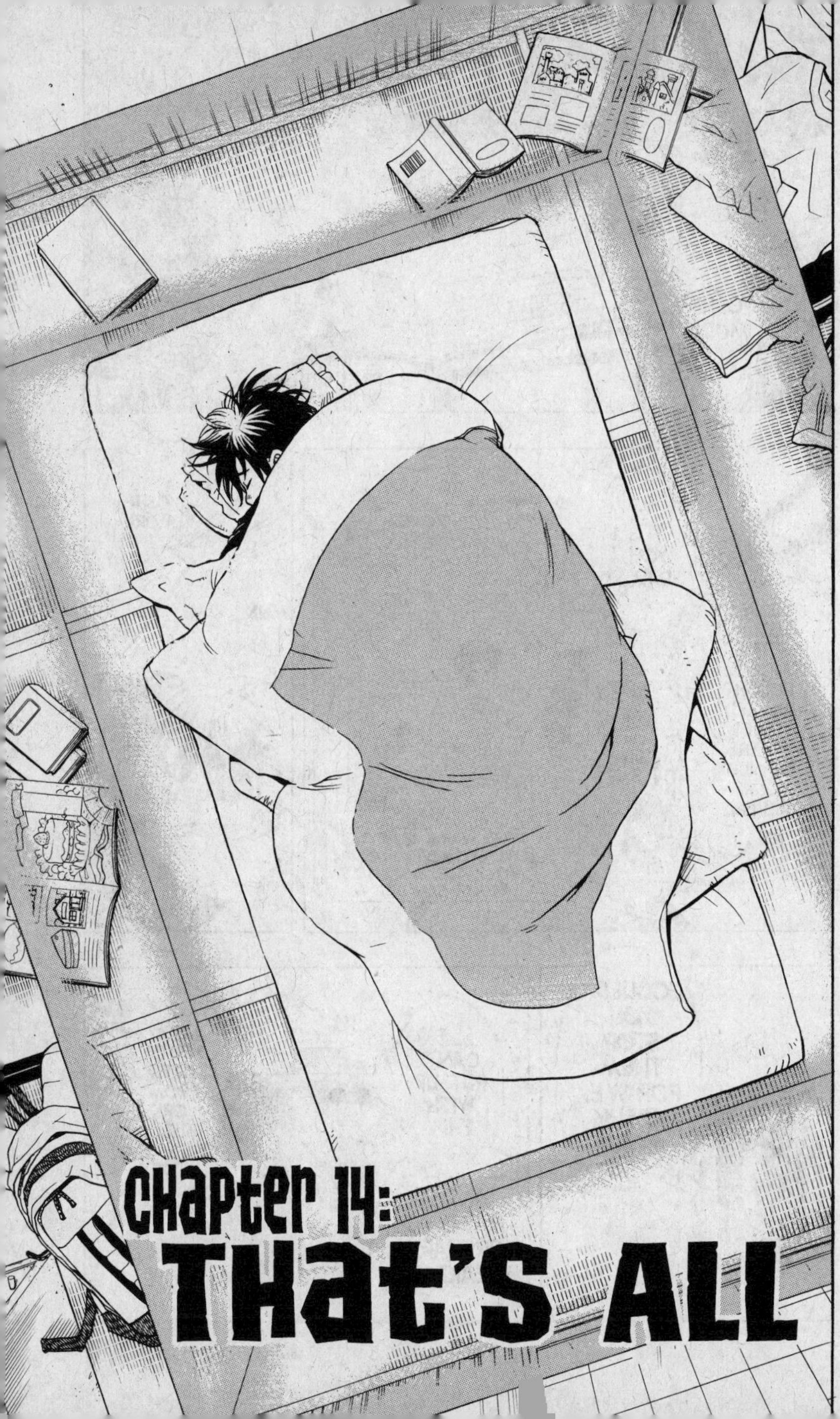
CHAPTER 14:
THAT'S ALL

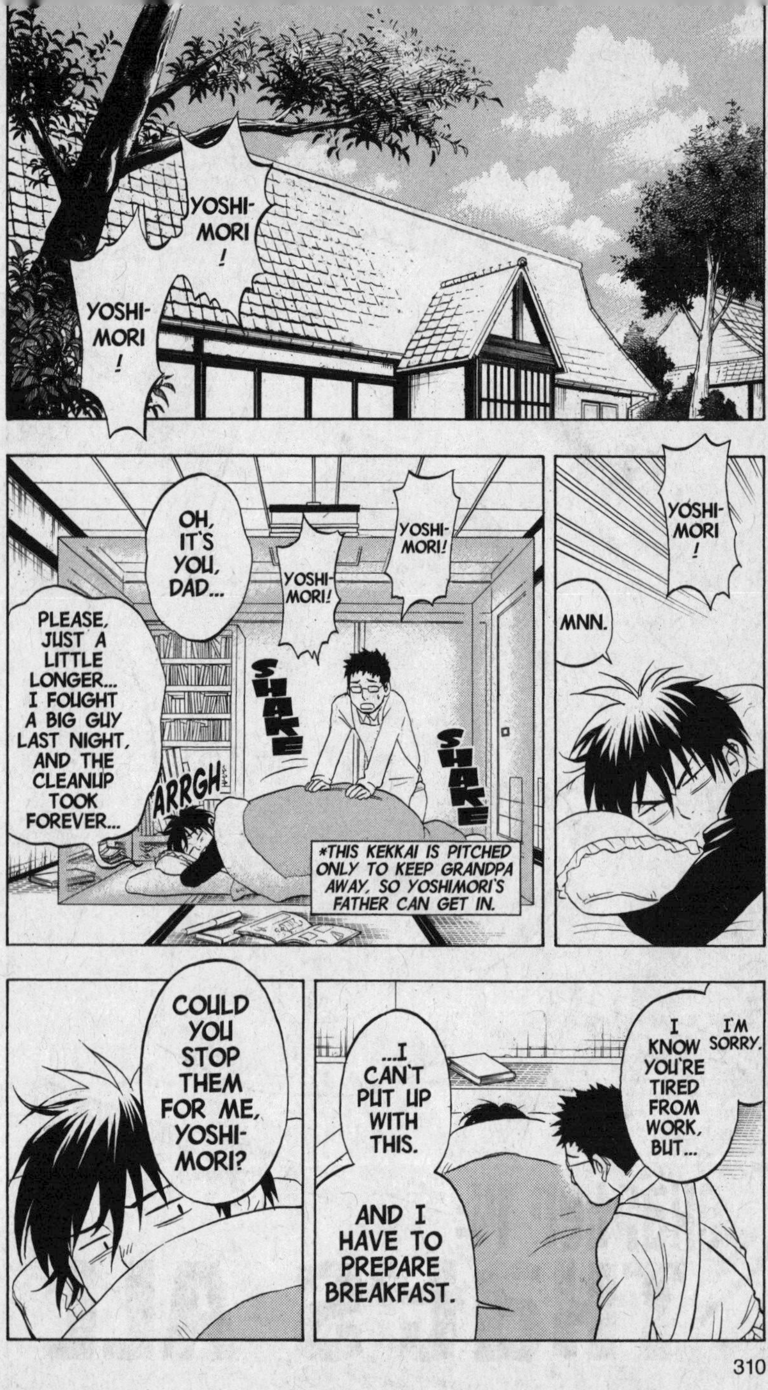
YOSHI-MORI!
YOSHI-MORI!
YOSHI-MORI!
MNN.
YOSHI-MORI!
YOSHI-MORI!
OH, IT'S YOU, DAD...
PLEASE, JUST A LITTLE LONGER... I FOUGHT A BIG GUY LAST NIGHT, AND THE CLEANUP TOOK FOREVER...
SHAKE
SHAKE
ARRGH
*THIS KEKKAI IS PITCHED ONLY TO KEEP GRANDPA AWAY, SO YOSHIMORI'S FATHER CAN GET IN.
I'M SORRY.
I KNOW YOU'RE TIRED FROM WORK, BUT...
...I CAN'T PUT UP WITH THIS.
AND I HAVE TO PREPARE BREAKFAST.
COULD YOU STOP THEM FOR ME, YOSHI-MORI?

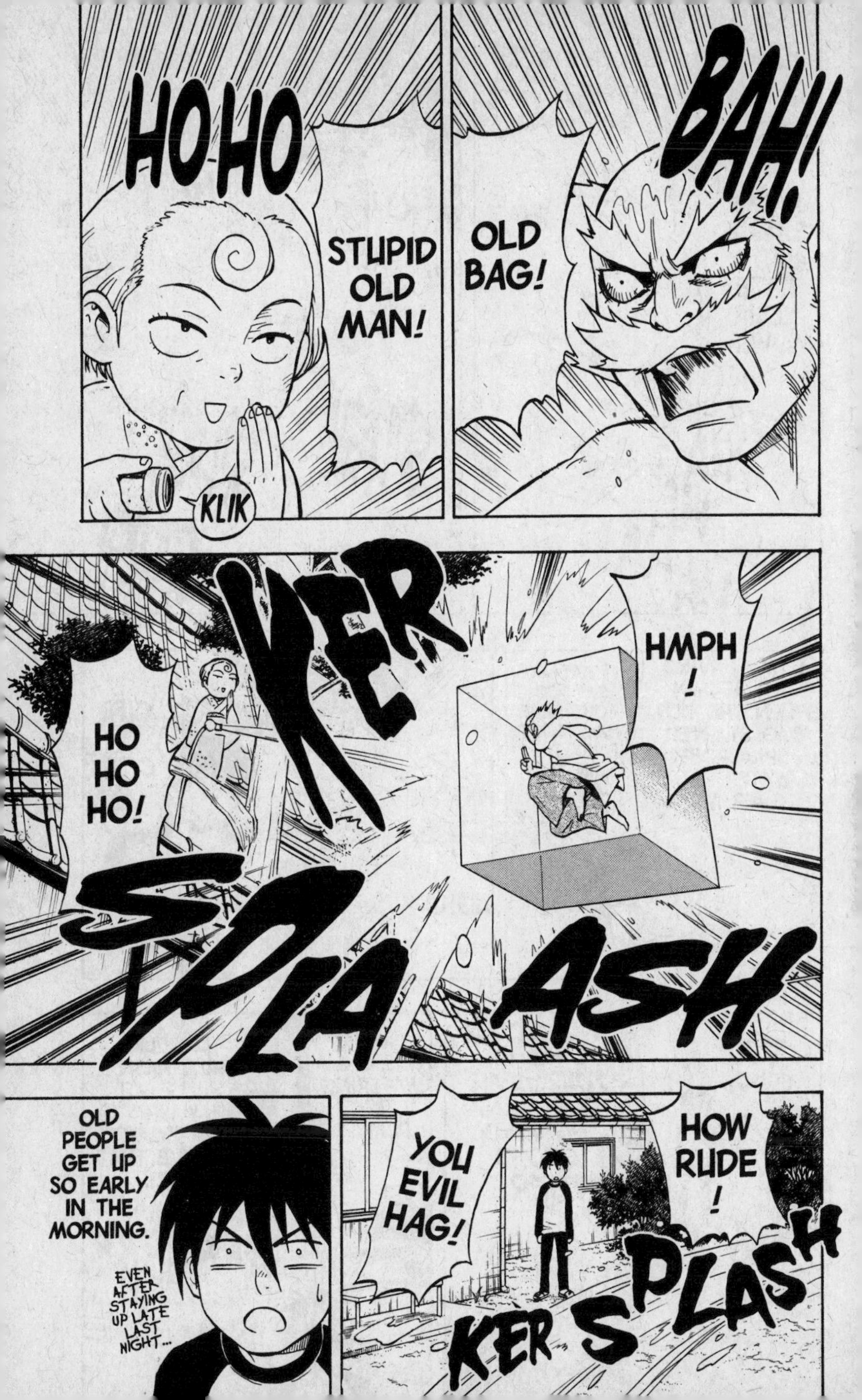
BAH!
OLD BAG!
HO-HO
STUPID OLD MAN!
KLIK
HMPH!
KER
SPLA ASH
HO HO HO!
HOW RUDE!
YOU EVIL HAG!
KER SPLASH
OLD PEOPLE GET UP SO EARLY IN THE MORNING.
EVEN AFTER STAYING UP LATE LAST NIGHT...

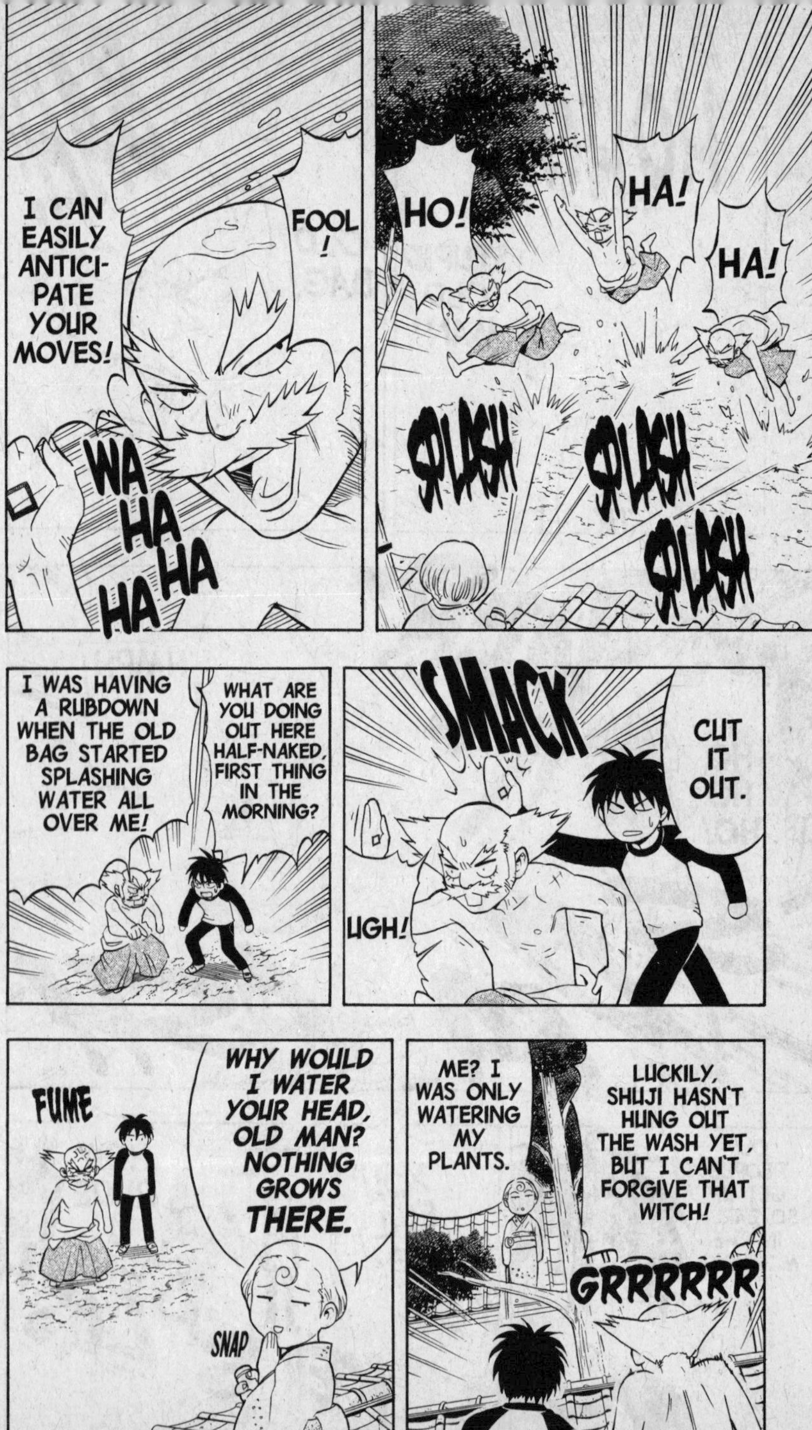
HA!
HA!
HO!
SPLASH
SPLASH
SPLASH
FOOL!
I CAN EASILY ANTICIPATE YOUR MOVES!
WA HA HA HA HA
SMACK
CUT IT OUT.
UGH!
WHAT ARE YOU DOING OUT HERE HALF-NAKED, FIRST THING IN THE MORNING?
I WAS HAVING A RUBDOWN WHEN THE OLD BAG STARTED SPLASHING WATER ALL OVER ME!
LUCKILY, SHUJI HASN'T HUNG OUT THE WASH YET, BUT I CAN'T FORGIVE THAT WITCH!
ME? I WAS ONLY WATERING MY PLANTS.
GRRRRRR
WHY WOULD I WATER YOUR HEAD, OLD MAN? NOTHING GROWS THERE.
FUME
SNAP

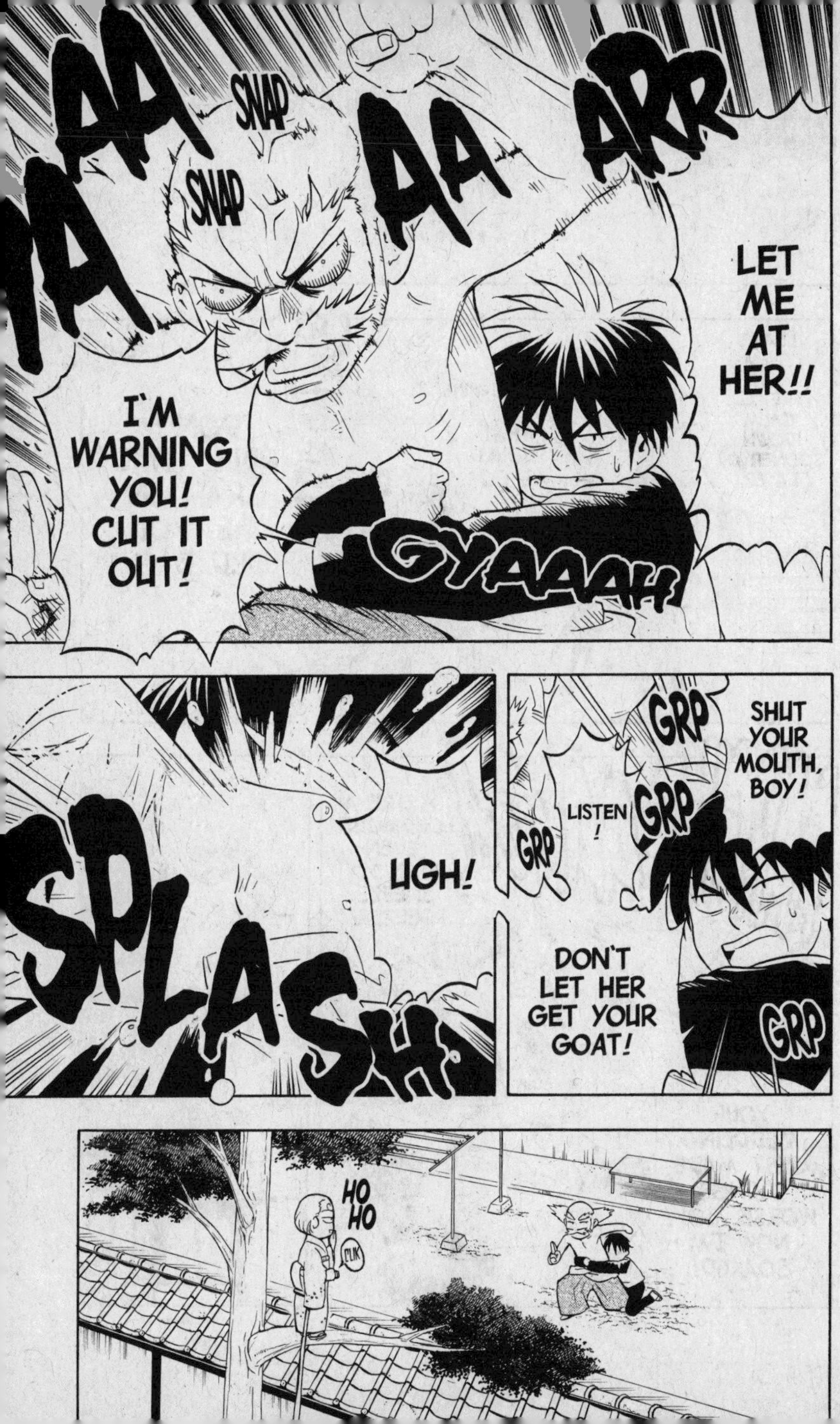
AA AA ARR
SNAP
SNAP
LET ME AT HER!!
I'M WARNING YOU! CUT IT OUT!
GYAAAH
GRP
SHUT YOUR MOUTH, BOY!
GRP
LISTEN!
GRP
DON'T LET HER GET YOUR GOAT!
GRP
UGH!
SPLASH
HO HO
CLIK

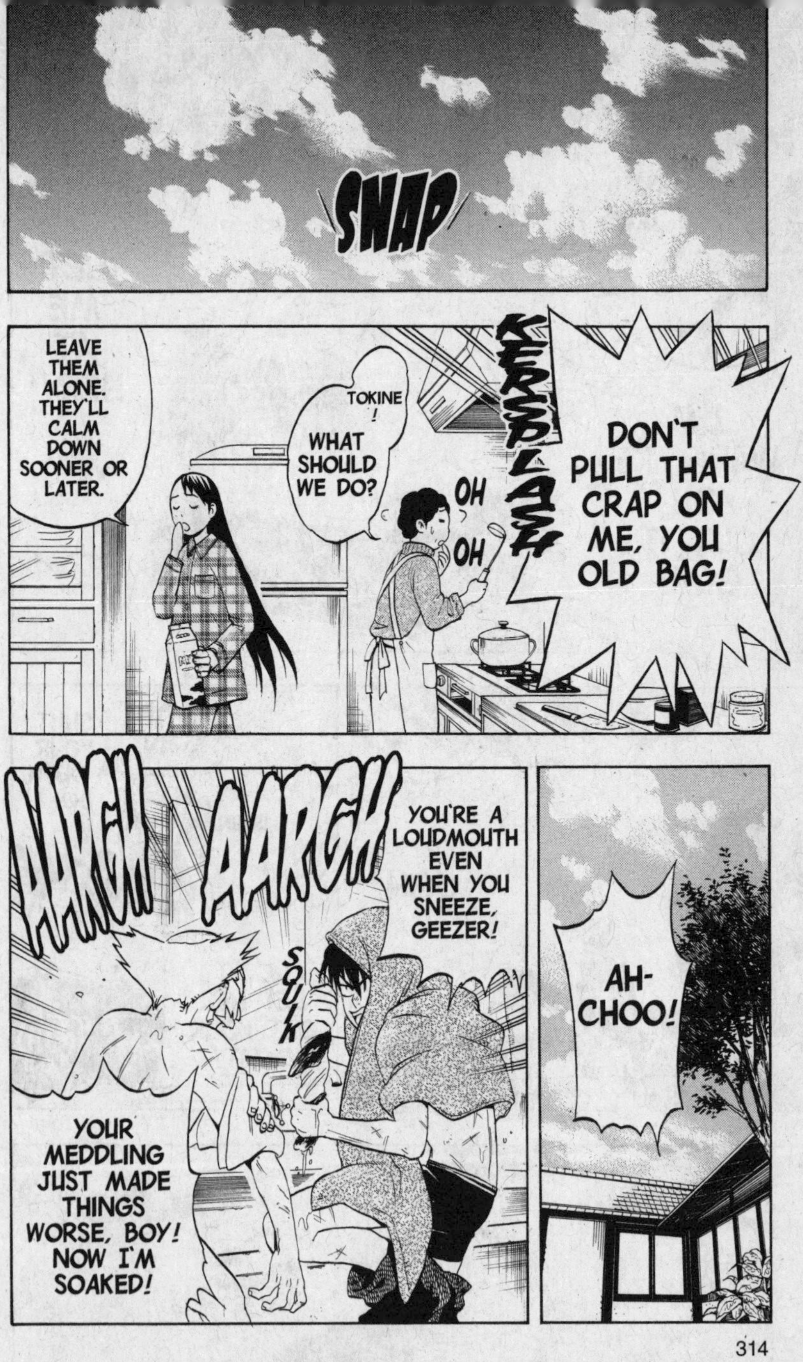
SNAP
DON'T PULL THAT CRAP ON ME, YOU OLD BAG!
KERSPLASH
OH
OH
TOKINE! WHAT SHOULD WE DO?
LEAVE THEM ALONE. THEY'LL CALM DOWN SOONER OR LATER.
AH-CHOO!
YOU'RE A LOUDMOUTH EVEN WHEN YOU SNEEZE, GEEZER!
AARGH
AARGH
SQUIK
YOUR MEDDLING JUST MADE THINGS WORSE, BOY! NOW I'M SOAKED!

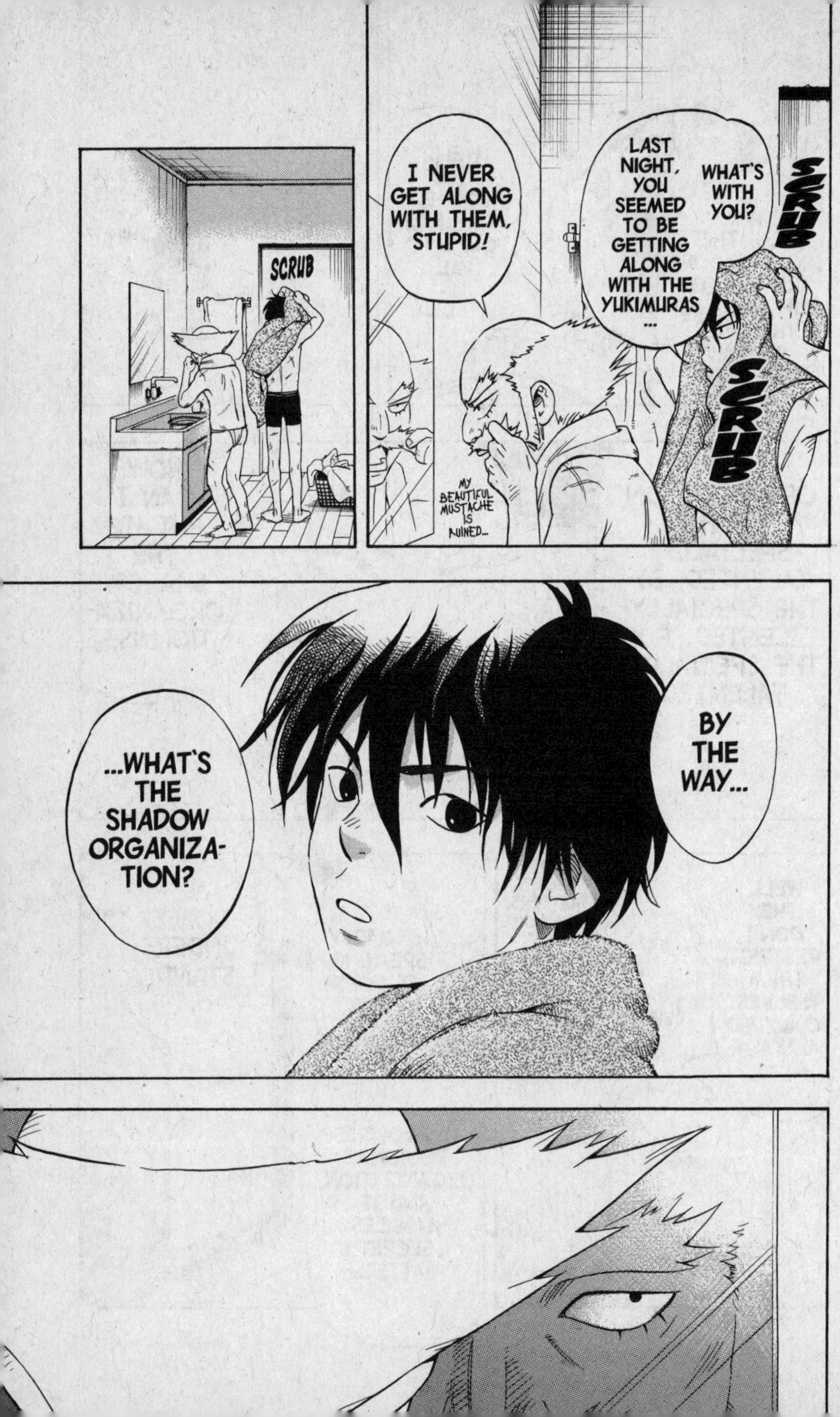
SCRUB
WHAT'S WITH YOU?
LAST NIGHT, YOU SEEMED TO BE GETTING ALONG WITH THE YUKIMURAS ...
SCRUB
I NEVER GET ALONG WITH THEM, STUPID!
MY BEAUTIFUL MUSTACHE IS RUINED...
SCRUB
BY THE WAY...
...WHAT'S THE SHADOW ORGANIZA-TION?

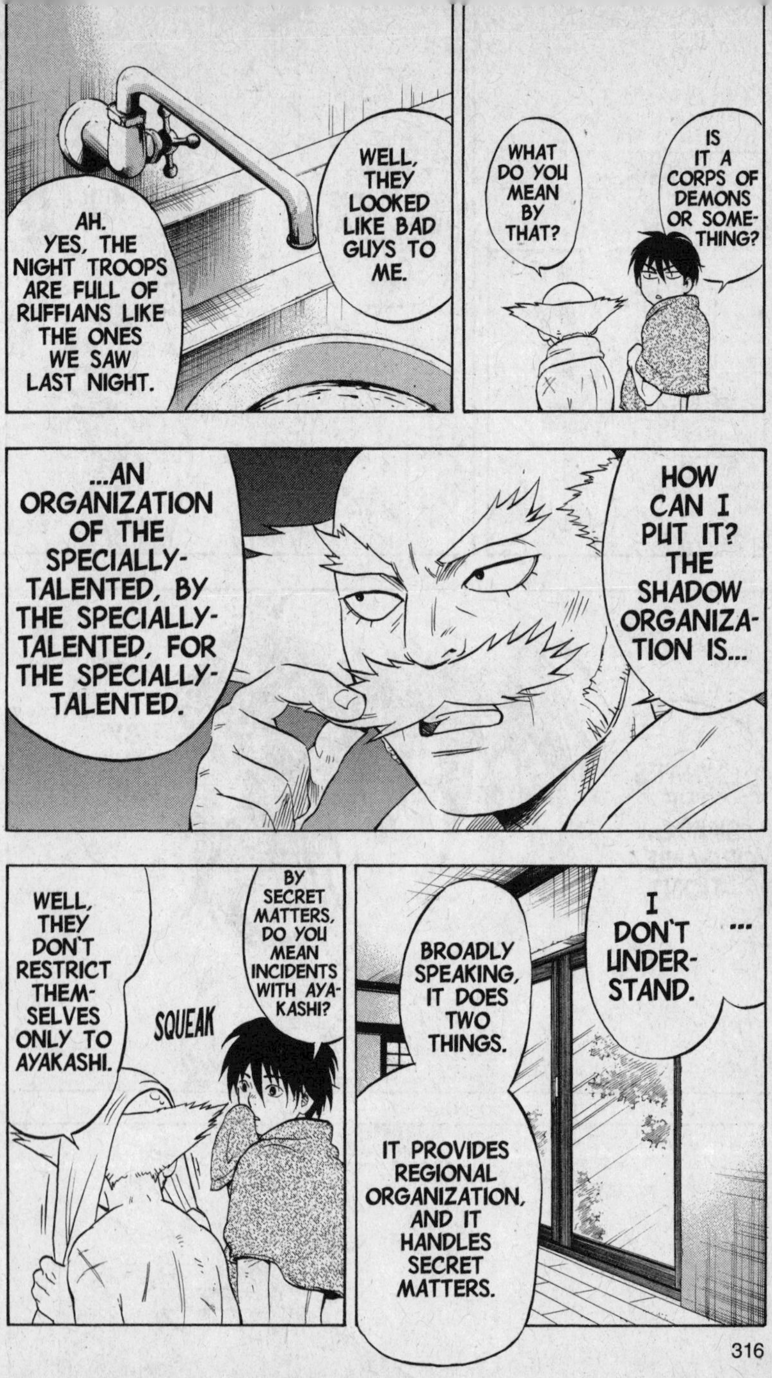
IS IT A CORPS OF DEMONS OR SOMETHING?
WHAT DO YOU MEAN BY THAT?
WELL, THEY LOOKED LIKE BAD GUYS TO ME.
AH. YES, THE NIGHT TROOPS ARE FULL OF RUFFIANS LIKE THE ONES WE SAW LAST NIGHT.
HOW CAN I PUT IT? THE SHADOW ORGANIZATION IS...
...AN ORGANIZATION OF THE SPECIALLY-TALENTED, BY THE SPECIALLY-TALENTED, FOR THE SPECIALLY-TALENTED.
I DON'T UNDERSTAND.
...
BROADLY SPEAKING, IT DOES TWO THINGS.
IT PROVIDES REGIONAL ORGANIZATION, AND IT HANDLES SECRET MATTERS.
BY SECRET MATTERS, DO YOU MEAN INCIDENTS WITH AYAKASHI?
SQUEAK
WELL, THEY DON'T RESTRICT THEMSELVES ONLY TO AYAKASHI.

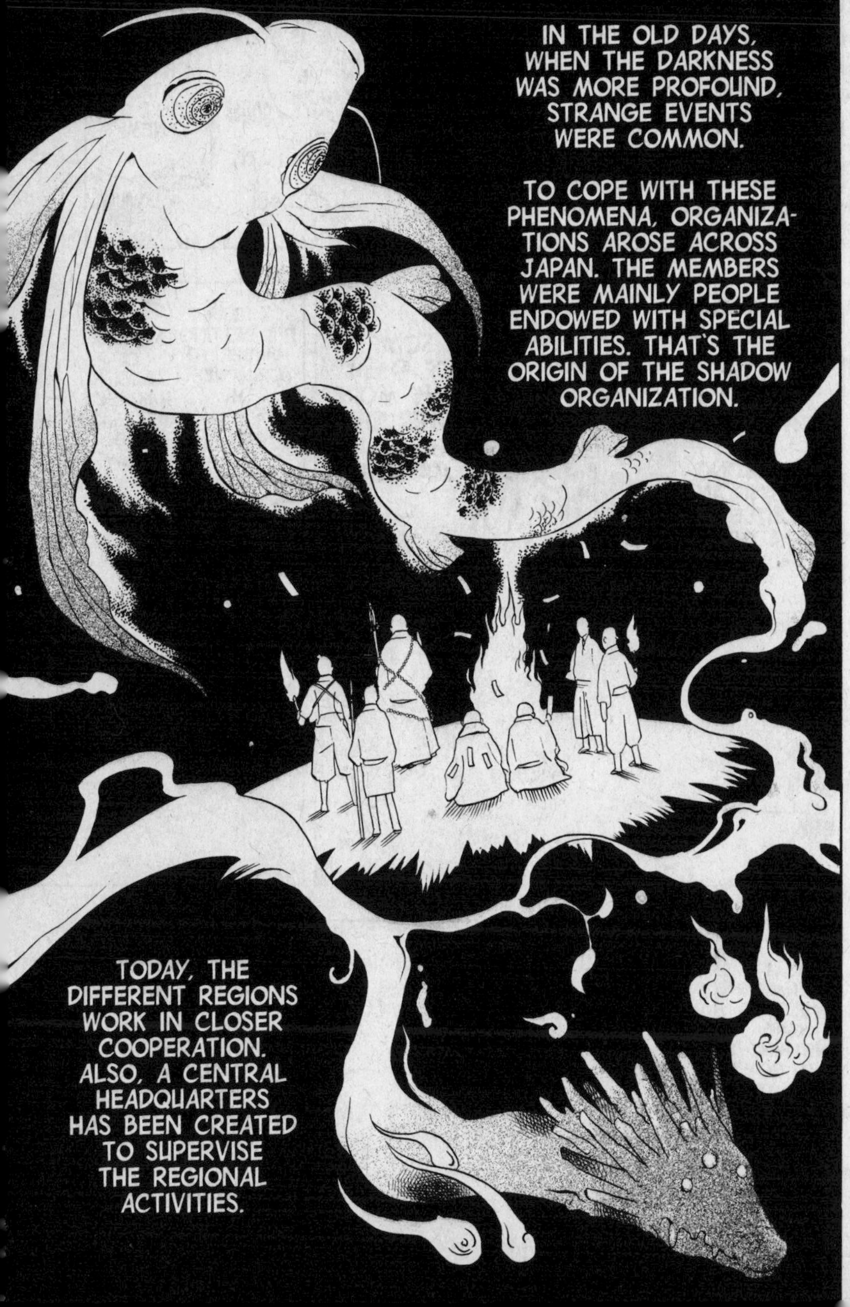
IN THE OLD DAYS, WHEN THE DARKNESS WAS MORE PROFOUND, STRANGE EVENTS WERE COMMON.
TO COPE WITH THESE PHENOMENA, ORGANIZATIONS AROSE ACROSS JAPAN. THE MEMBERS WERE MAINLY PEOPLE ENDOWED WITH SPECIAL ABILITIES. THAT'S THE ORIGIN OF THE SHADOW ORGANIZATION.
TODAY, THE DIFFERENT REGIONS WORK IN CLOSER COOPERATION. ALSO, A CENTRAL HEADQUARTERS HAS BEEN CREATED TO SUPERVISE THE REGIONAL ACTIVITIES.

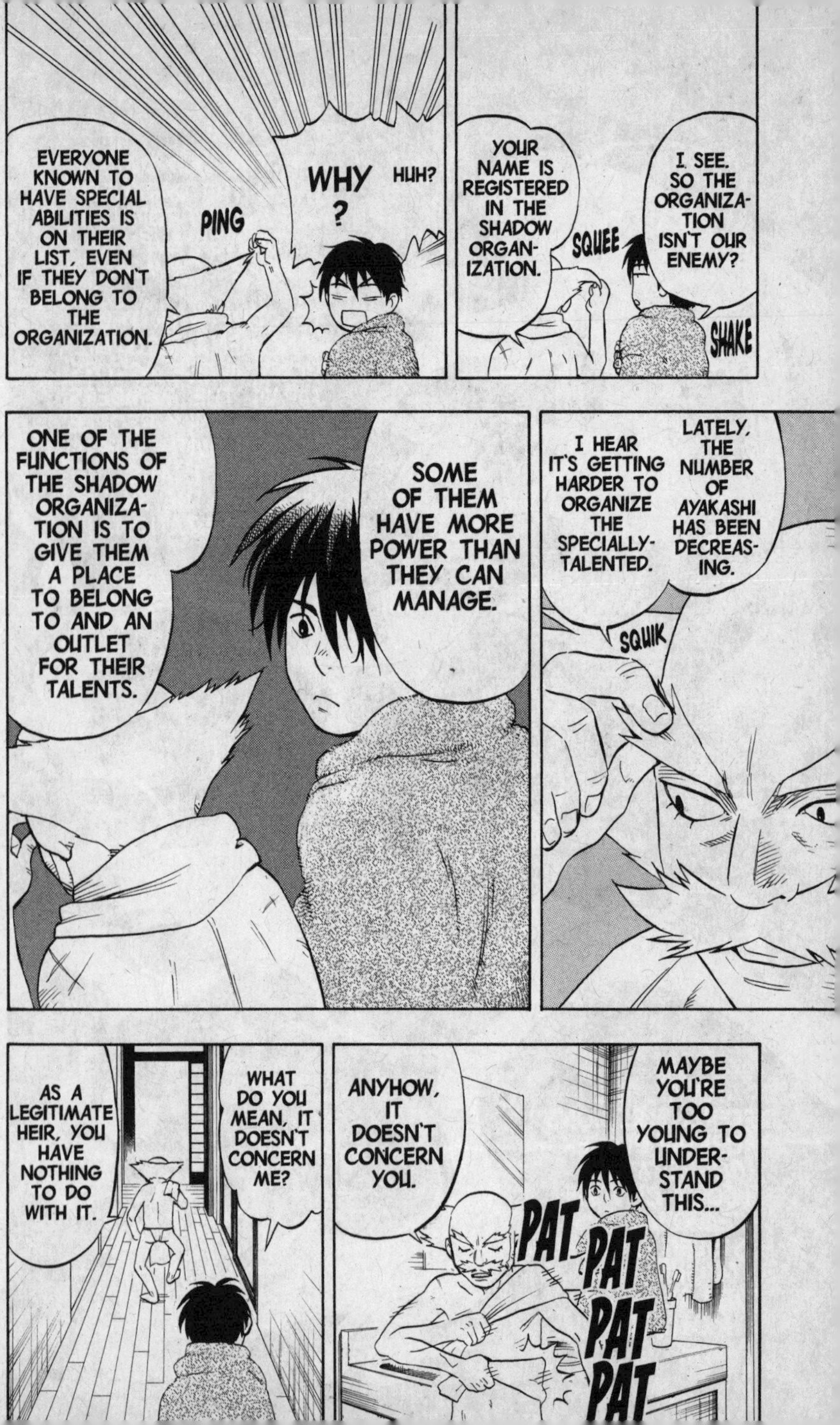
I SEE. SO THE ORGANIZATION ISN'T OUR ENEMY?
SQUEE
YOUR NAME IS REGISTERED IN THE SHADOW ORGANIZATION.
SHAKE
HUH?
WHY ?
PING
EVERYONE KNOWN TO HAVE SPECIAL ABILITIES IS ON THEIR LIST, EVEN IF THEY DON'T BELONG TO THE ORGANIZATION.
LATELY, THE NUMBER OF AYAKASHI HAS BEEN DECREASING.
I HEAR IT'S GETTING HARDER TO ORGANIZE THE SPECIALLY-TALENTED.
SQUIK
SOME OF THEM HAVE MORE POWER THAN THEY CAN MANAGE.
ONE OF THE FUNCTIONS OF THE SHADOW ORGANIZATION IS TO GIVE THEM A PLACE TO BELONG TO AND AN OUTLET FOR THEIR TALENTS.
MAYBE YOU'RE TOO YOUNG TO UNDERSTAND THIS...
ANYHOW, IT DOESN'T CONCERN YOU.
PAT PAT PAT PAT
WHAT DO YOU MEAN, IT DOESN'T CONCERN ME?
AS A LEGITIMATE HEIR, YOU HAVE NOTHING TO DO WITH IT.

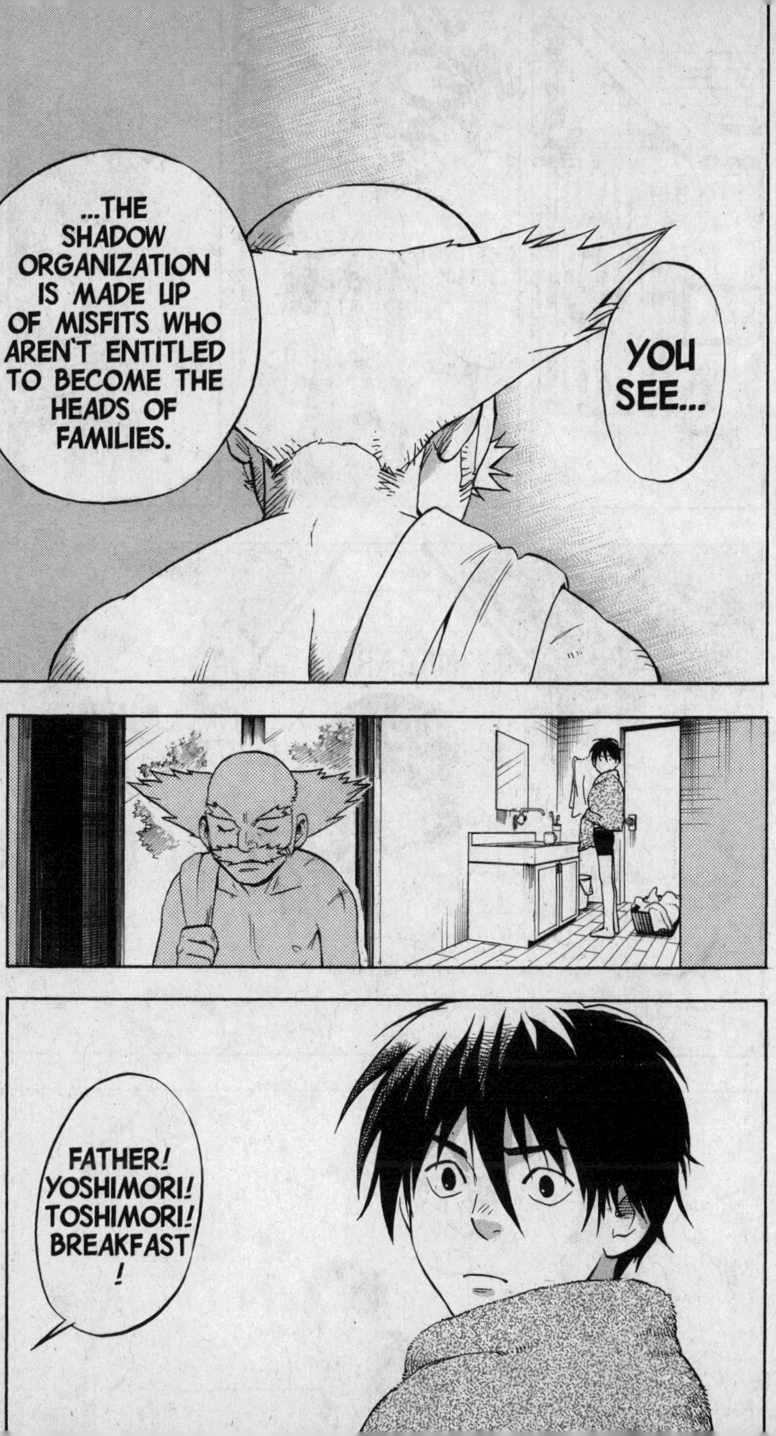
YOU SEE...
...THE SHADOW ORGANIZATION IS MADE UP OF MISFITS WHO AREN'T ENTITLED TO BECOME THE HEADS OF FAMILIES.
FATHER! YOSHIMORI! TOSHIMORI! BREAKFAST!

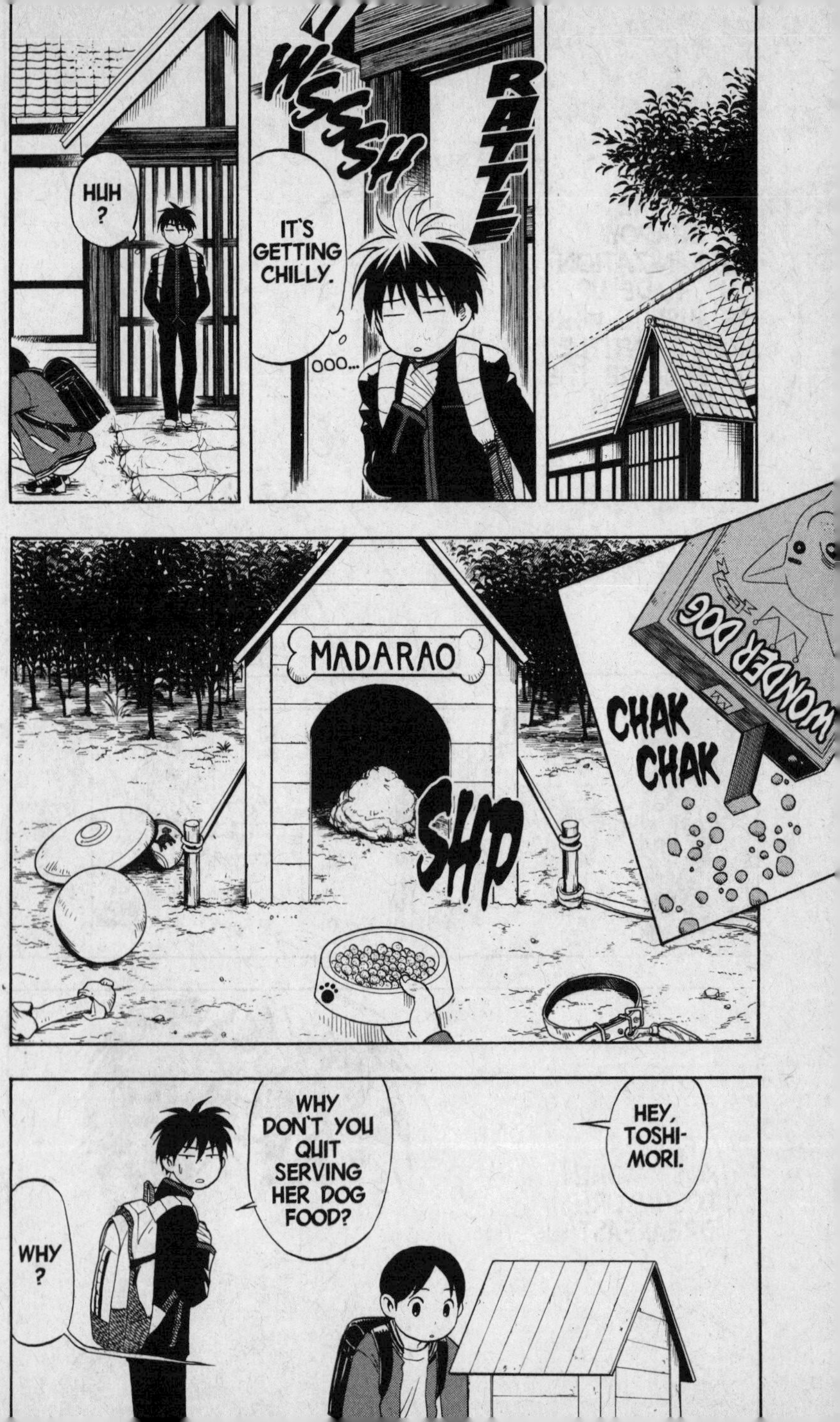
WSSSH
RATTLE
IT'S GETTING CHILLY.
OOO...
HUH?
WONDER DOG
CHAK CHAK
MADARAO
SHP
HEY, TOSHI-MORI.
WHY DON'T YOU QUIT SERVING HER DOG FOOD?
WHY?

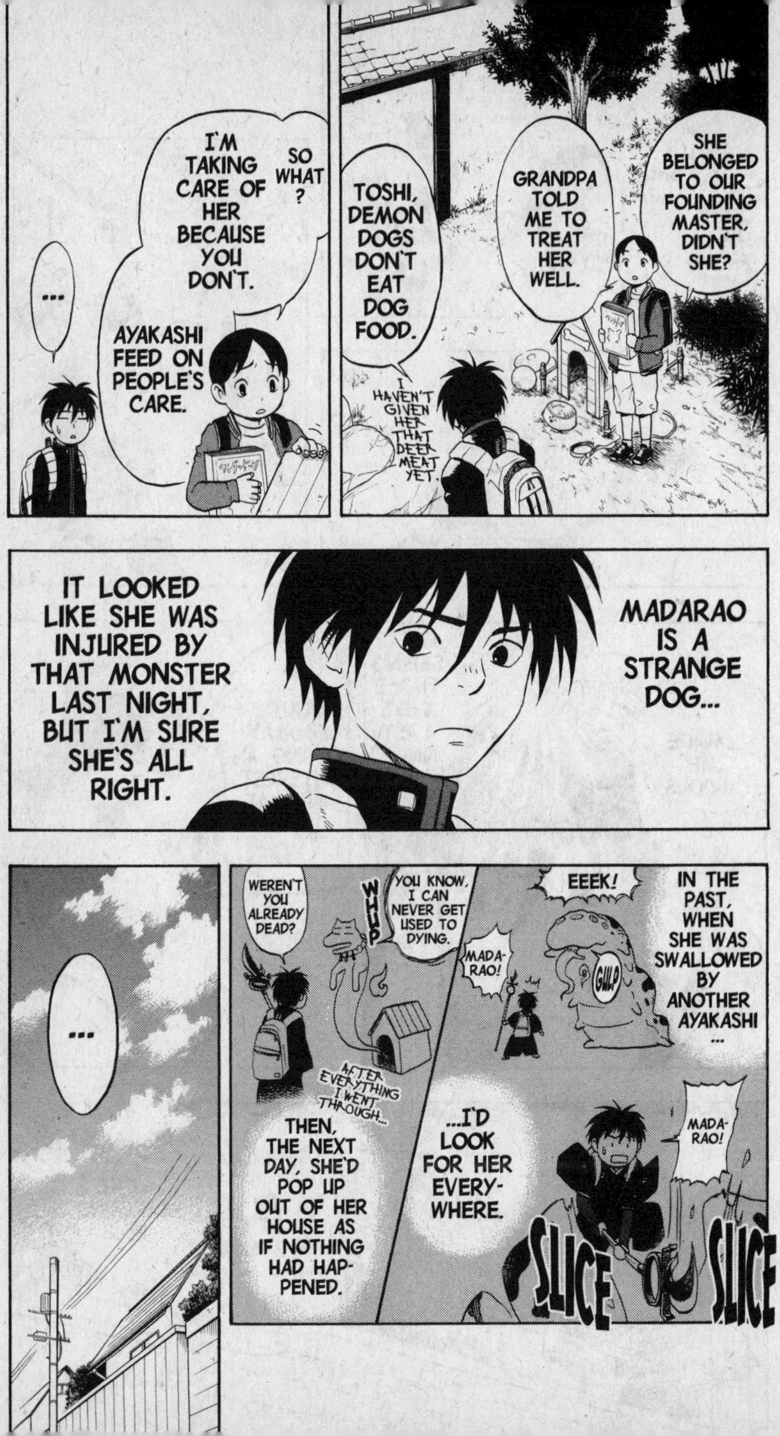

SHE BELONGED TO OUR FOUNDING MASTER, DIDN'T SHE?
GRANDPA TOLD ME TO TREAT HER WELL.
TOSHI, DEMON DOGS DON'T EAT DOG FOOD.
I HAVEN'T GIVEN HER THAT DEER MEAT YET.
SO WHAT?
I'M TAKING CARE OF HER BECAUSE YOU DON'T.
AYAKASHI FEED ON PEOPLE'S CARE.
...
MADARAO IS A STRANGE DOG...
IT LOOKED LIKE SHE WAS INJURED BY THAT MONSTER LAST NIGHT, BUT I'M SURE SHE'S ALL RIGHT.
IN THE PAST, WHEN SHE WAS SWALLOWED BY ANOTHER AYAKASHI...
EEEK!
GULP
MADA-RAO!
MADA-RAO!
SLICE
SLICE
...I'D LOOK FOR HER EVERY-WHERE.
THEN, THE NEXT DAY, SHE'D POP UP OUT OF HER HOUSE AS IF NOTHING HAD HAP-PENED.
YOU KNOW, I CAN NEVER GET USED TO DYING.
WHUP
WEREN'T YOU ALREADY DEAD?
AFTER EVERYTHING I WENT THROUGH...
...

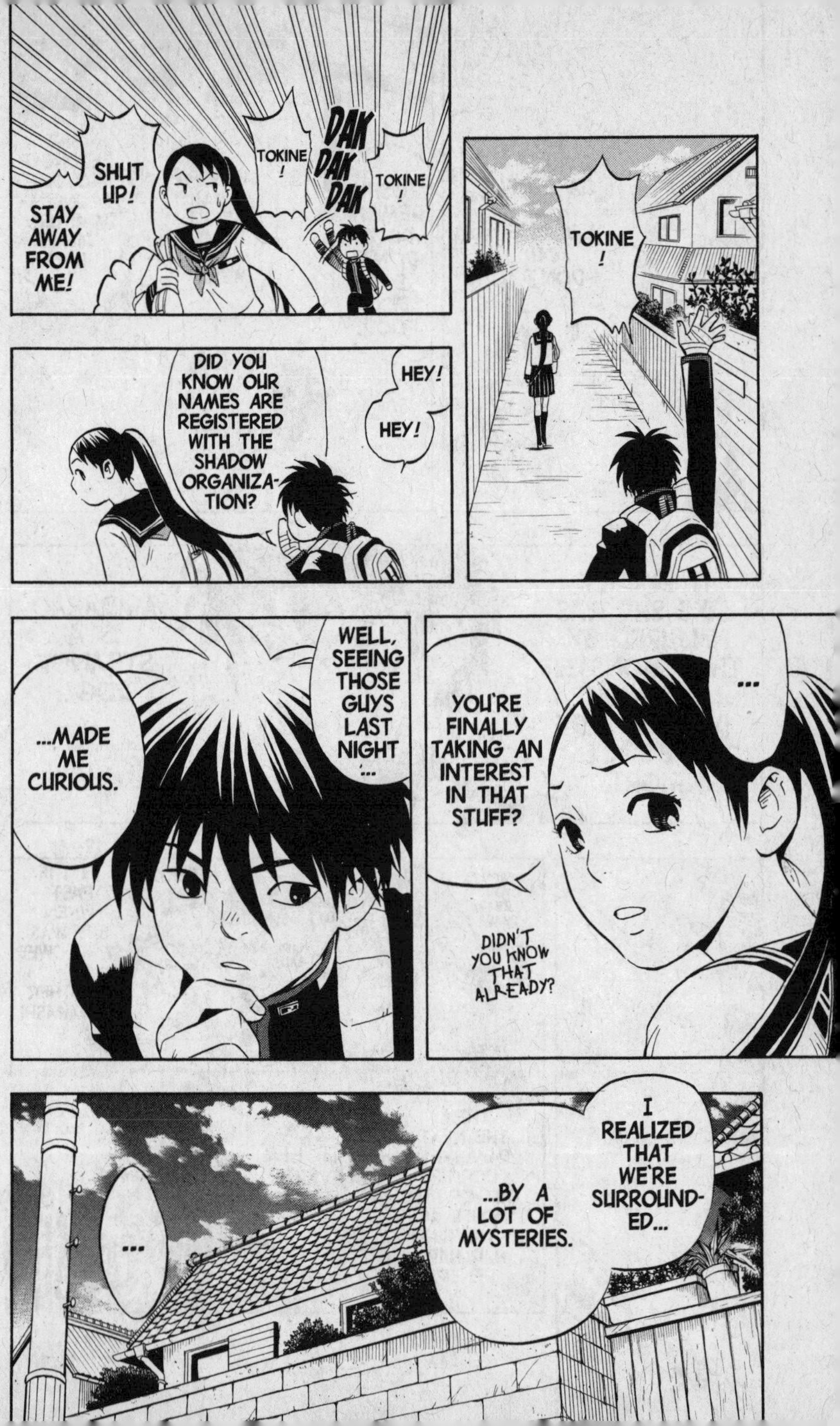
TOKINE!
TOKINE!
DAK DAK DAK
TOKINE!
SHUT UP!
STAY AWAY FROM ME!
HEY!
HEY!
DID YOU KNOW OUR NAMES ARE REGISTERED WITH THE SHADOW ORGANIZA-TION?
...
YOU'RE FINALLY TAKING AN INTEREST IN THAT STUFF?
DIDN'T YOU KNOW THAT ALREADY?
WELL, SEEING THOSE GUYS LAST NIGHT...
...MADE ME CURIOUS.
I REALIZED THAT WE'RE SURROUND-ED...
...BY A LOT OF MYSTERIES.
...

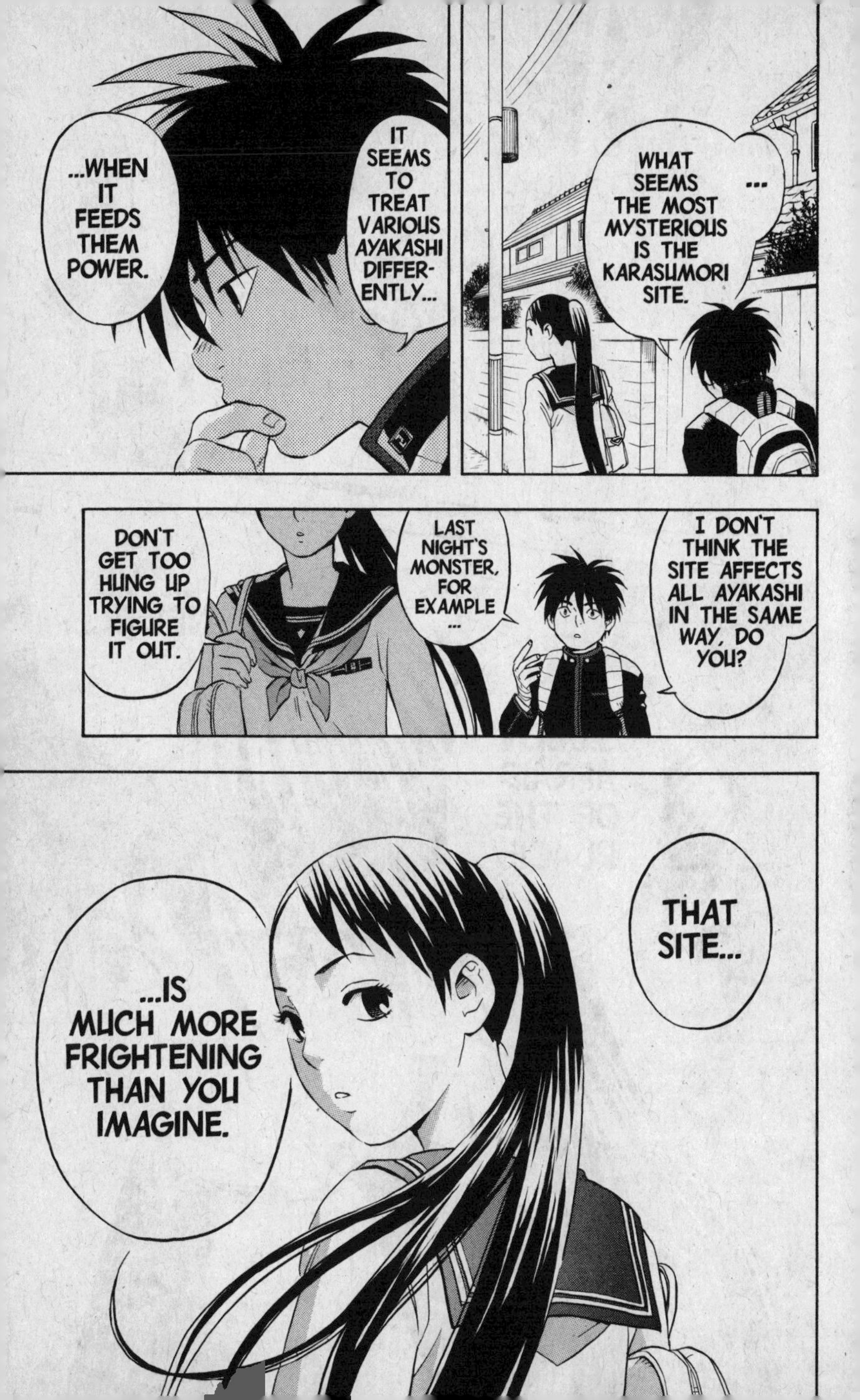
...
WHAT SEEMS THE MOST MYSTERIOUS IS THE KARASUMORI SITE.
IT SEEMS TO TREAT VARIOUS AYAKASHI DIFFER-ENTLY...
...WHEN IT FEEDS THEM POWER.
I DON'T THINK THE SITE AFFECTS ALL AYAKASHI IN THE SAME WAY, DO YOU?
LAST NIGHT'S MONSTER, FOR EXAMPLE ...
DON'T GET TOO HUNG UP TRYING TO FIGURE IT OUT.
THAT SITE...
...IS MUCH MORE FRIGHTENING THAN YOU IMAGINE.

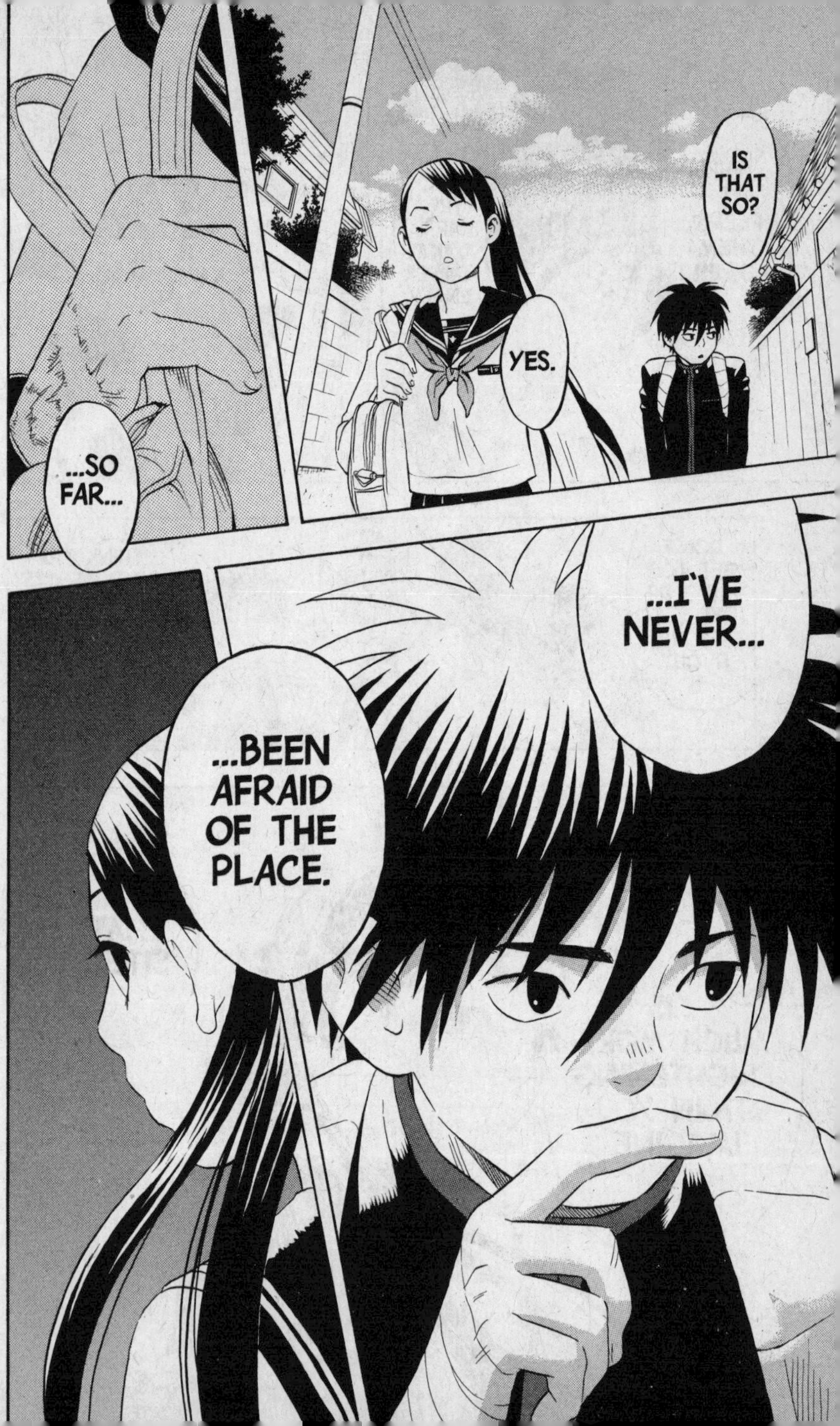
IS THAT SO?
YES.
...SO FAR...
...I'VE NEVER...
...BEEN AFRAID OF THE PLACE.

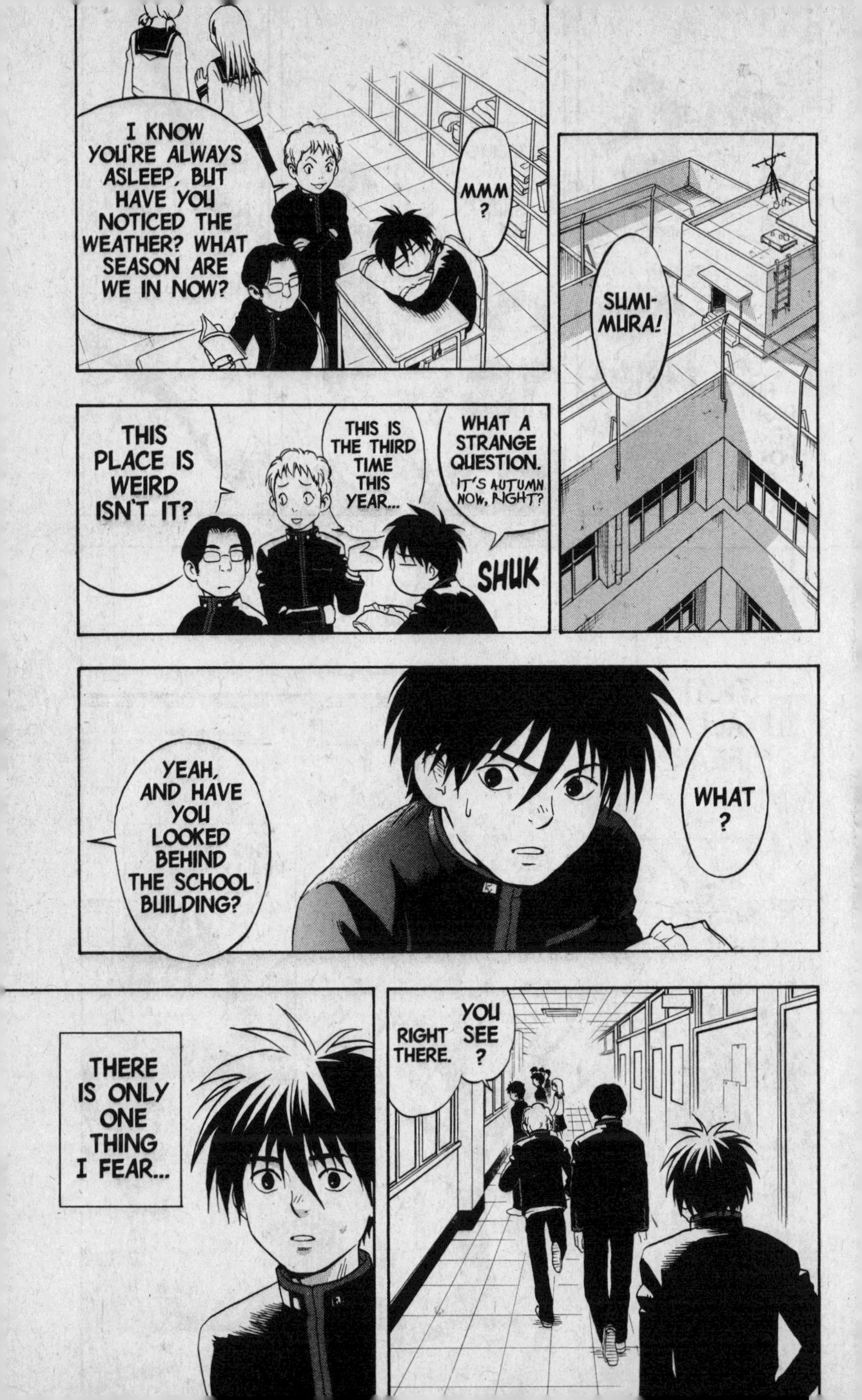
SUMI-MURA!
MMM?
I KNOW YOU'RE ALWAYS ASLEEP, BUT HAVE YOU NOTICED THE WEATHER? WHAT SEASON ARE WE IN NOW?
WHAT A STRANGE QUESTION. IT'S AUTUMN NOW, RIGHT?
SHUK
THIS IS THE THIRD TIME THIS YEAR...
THIS PLACE IS WEIRD ISN'T IT?
WHAT?
YEAH, AND HAVE YOU LOOKED BEHIND THE SCHOOL BUILDING?
YOU SEE?
RIGHT THERE.
THERE IS ONLY ONE THING I FEAR...

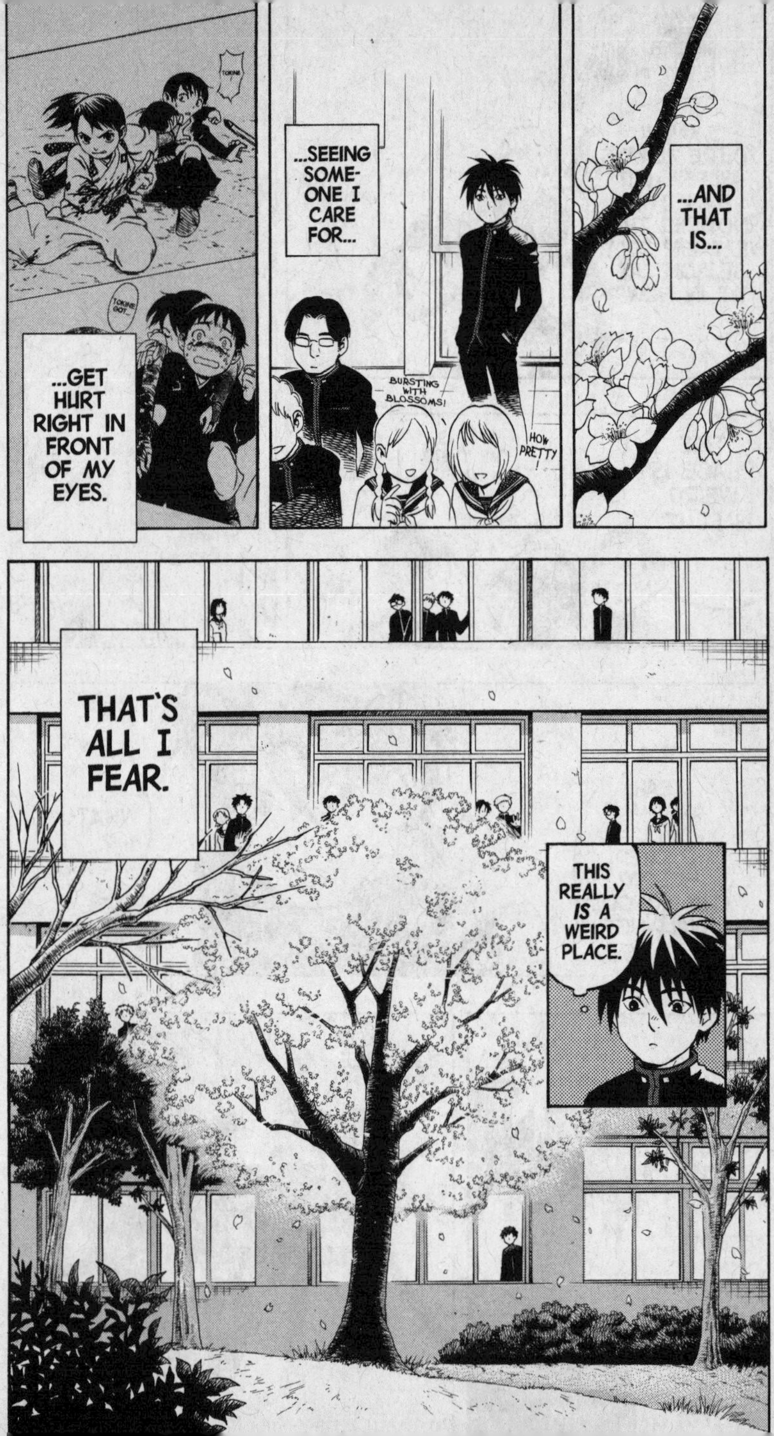
...AND THAT IS...
...SEEING SOMEONE I CARE FOR...
BURSTING WITH BLOSSOMS!
HOW PRETTY!
TOKINE!
TOKINE GOT...
...GET HURT RIGHT IN FRONT OF MY EYES.
THIS REALLY IS A WEIRD PLACE.
THAT'S ALL I FEAR.

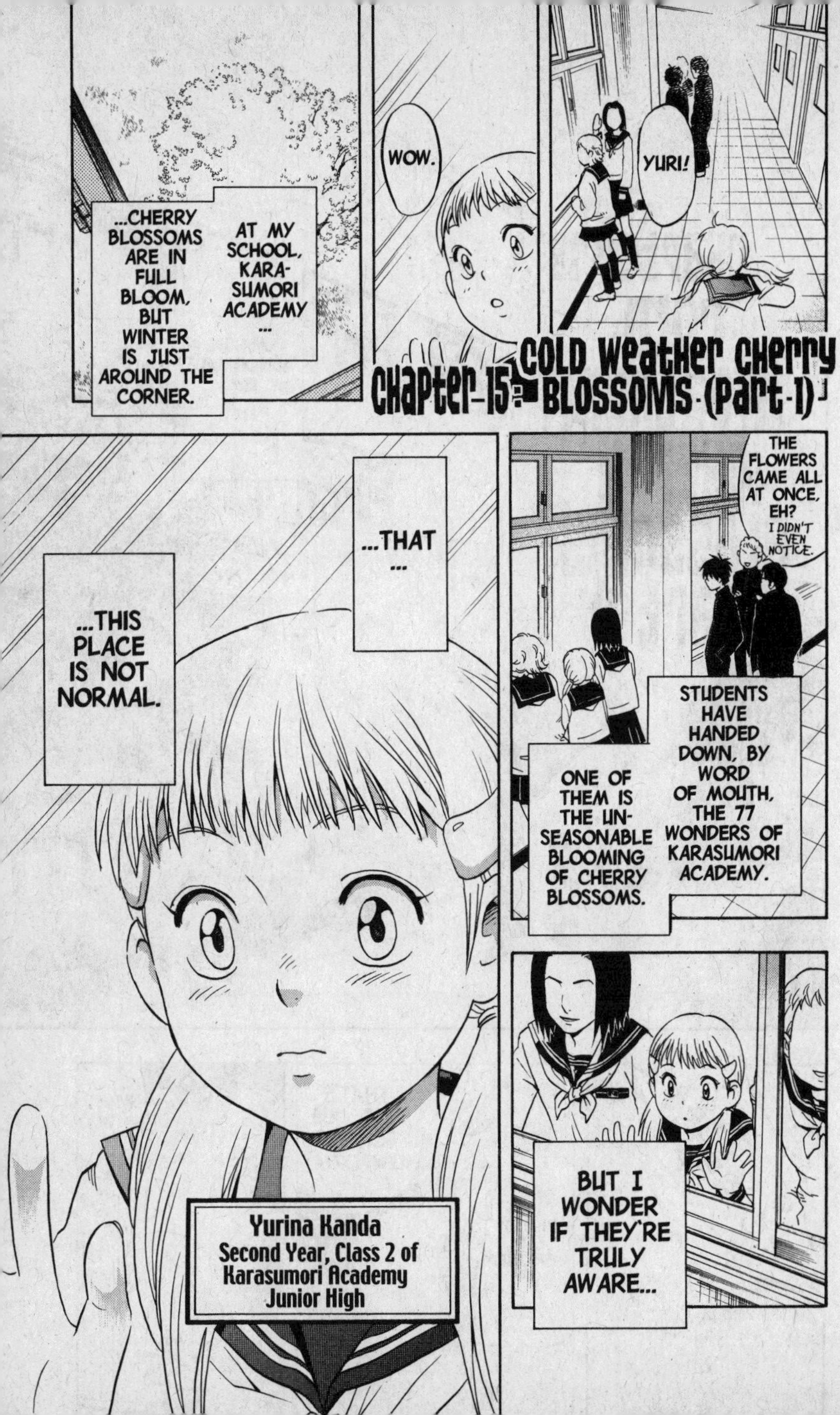
YURI!
WOW.
AT MY SCHOOL, KARASUMORI ACADEMY...
...CHERRY BLOSSOMS ARE IN FULL BLOOM, BUT WINTER IS JUST AROUND THE CORNER.
Chapter 15: Cold Weather Cherry Blossoms (Part 1)
THE FLOWERS CAME ALL AT ONCE, EH?
I DIDN'T EVEN NOTICE.
STUDENTS HAVE HANDED DOWN, BY WORD OF MOUTH, THE 77 WONDERS OF KARASUMORI ACADEMY.
ONE OF THEM IS THE UNSEASONABLE BLOOMING OF CHERRY BLOSSOMS.
BUT I WONDER IF THEY'RE TRULY AWARE...
...THAT...
...THIS PLACE IS NOT NORMAL.
Yurina Kanda
Second Year, Class 2 of Karasumori Academy Junior High

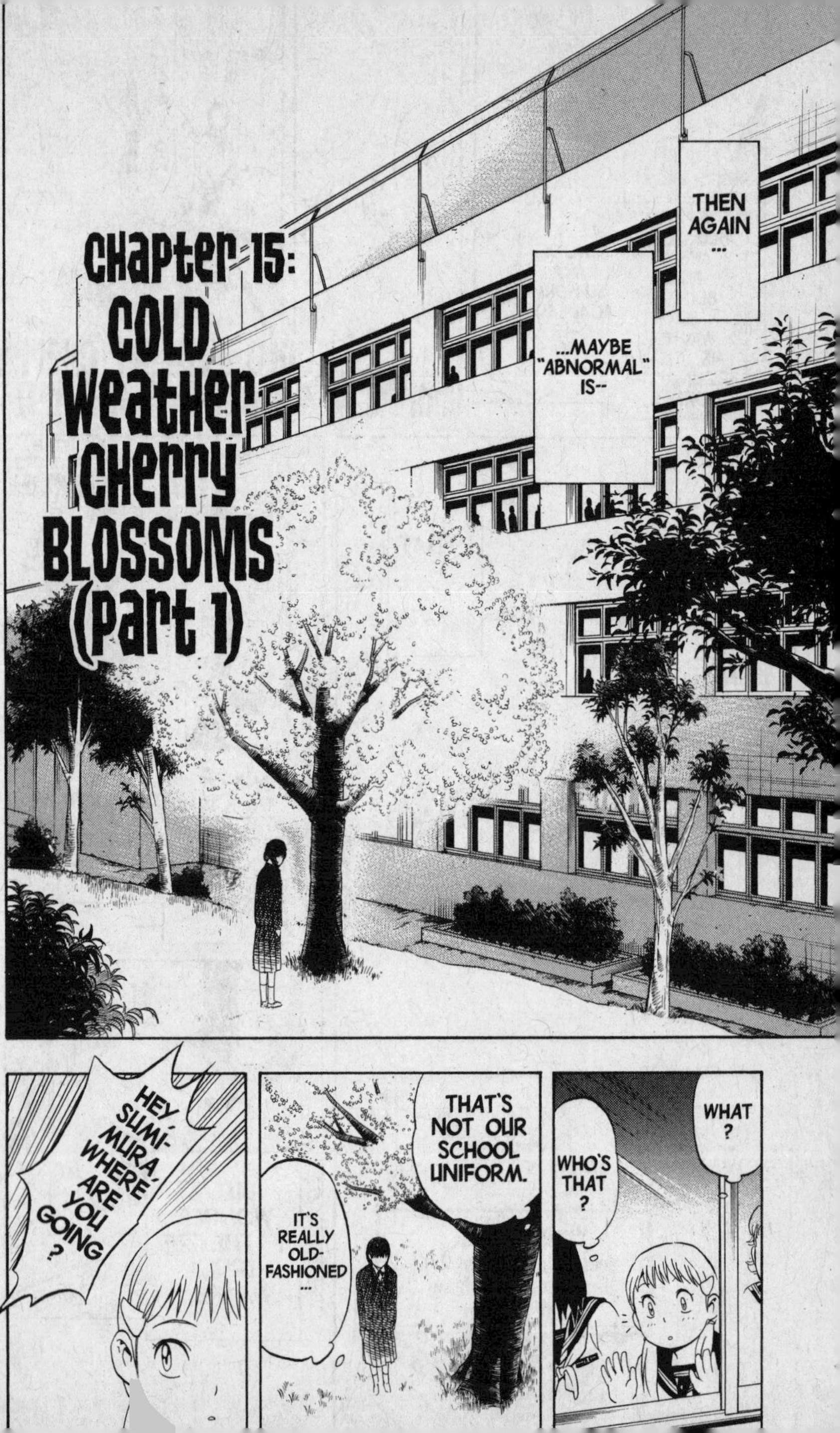
THEN AGAIN ...
...MAYBE "ABNORMAL" IS--
Chapter 15: COLD Weather Cherry BLOSSOMS (Part 1)
WHAT?
WHO'S THAT?
THAT'S NOT OUR SCHOOL UNIFORM.
IT'S REALLY OLD-FASHIONED ...
HEY SUMIMURA, WHERE ARE YOU GOING?

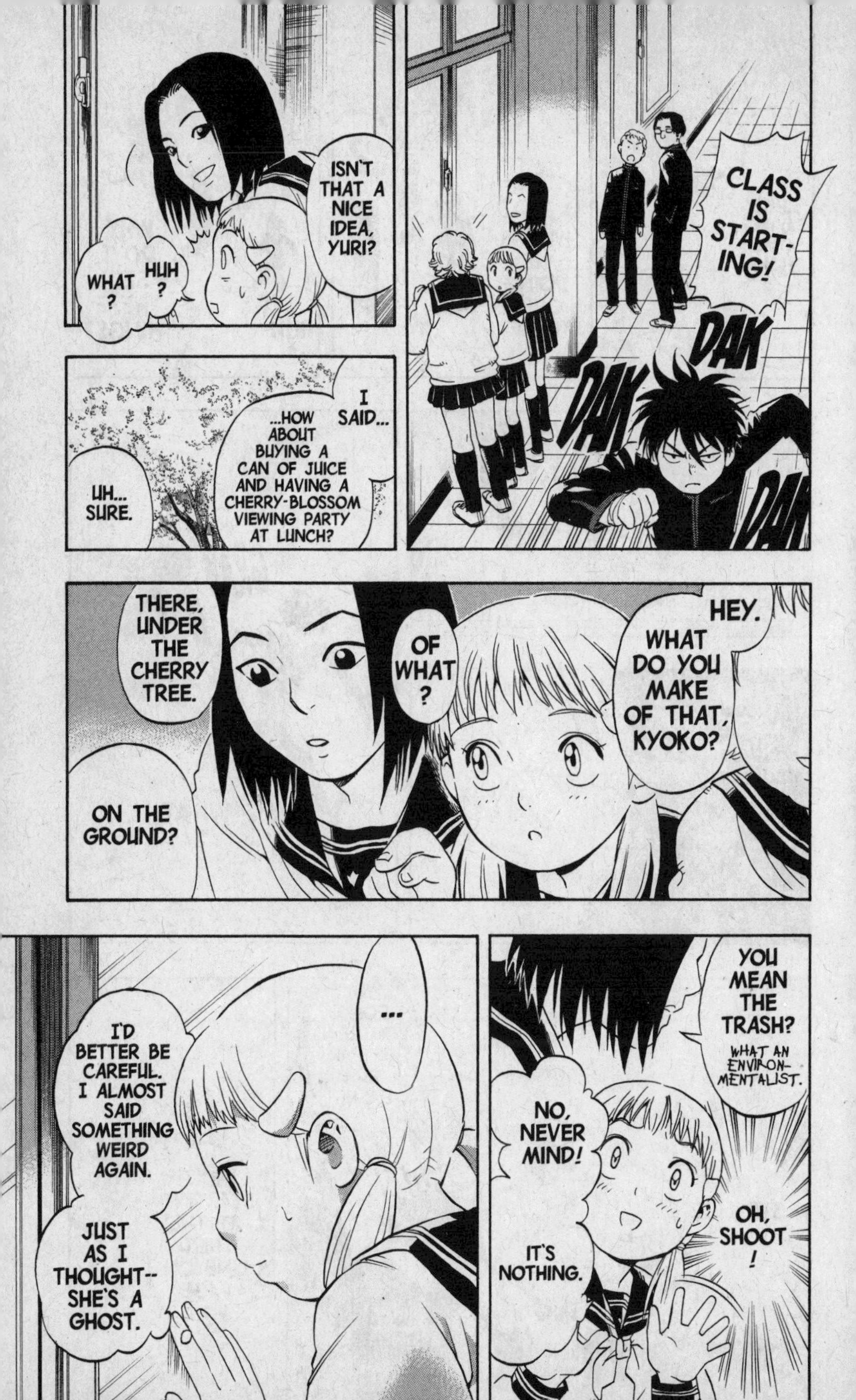
CLASS IS STARTING!
DAK
DAK
DAK
ISN'T THAT A NICE IDEA, YURI?
HUH?
WHAT?
I SAID...
...HOW ABOUT BUYING A CAN OF JUICE AND HAVING A CHERRY-BLOSSOM VIEWING PARTY AT LUNCH?
UH... SURE.
HEY.
WHAT DO YOU MAKE OF THAT, KYOKO?
OF WHAT?
THERE, UNDER THE CHERRY TREE.
ON THE GROUND?
YOU MEAN THE TRASH?
WHAT AN ENVIRONMENTALIST.
OH, SHOOT!
NO, NEVER MIND!
IT'S NOTHING.
...
I'D BETTER BE CAREFUL. I ALMOST SAID SOMETHING WEIRD AGAIN.
JUST AS I THOUGHT--SHE'S A GHOST.

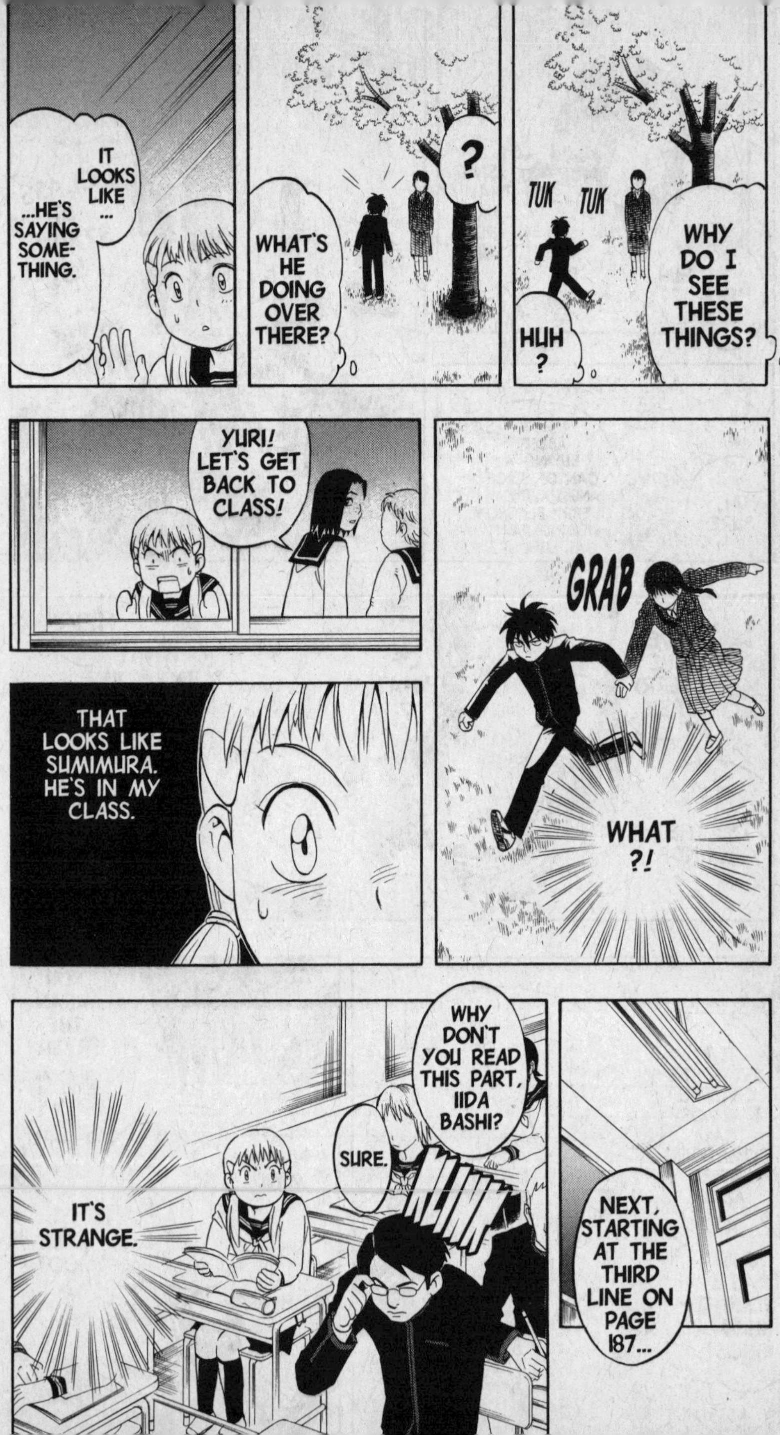
TUK
TUK
WHY DO I SEE THESE THINGS?
HUH?
?
WHAT'S HE DOING OVER THERE?
IT LOOKS LIKE...
...HE'S SAYING SOMETHING.
GRAB
WHAT?!
YURI! LET'S GET BACK TO CLASS!
THAT LOOKS LIKE SUMIMURA. HE'S IN MY CLASS.
NEXT, STARTING AT THE THIRD LINE ON PAGE 187...
WHY DON'T YOU READ THIS PART, IIDA BASHI?
SURE.
KLINK
IT'S STRANGE.

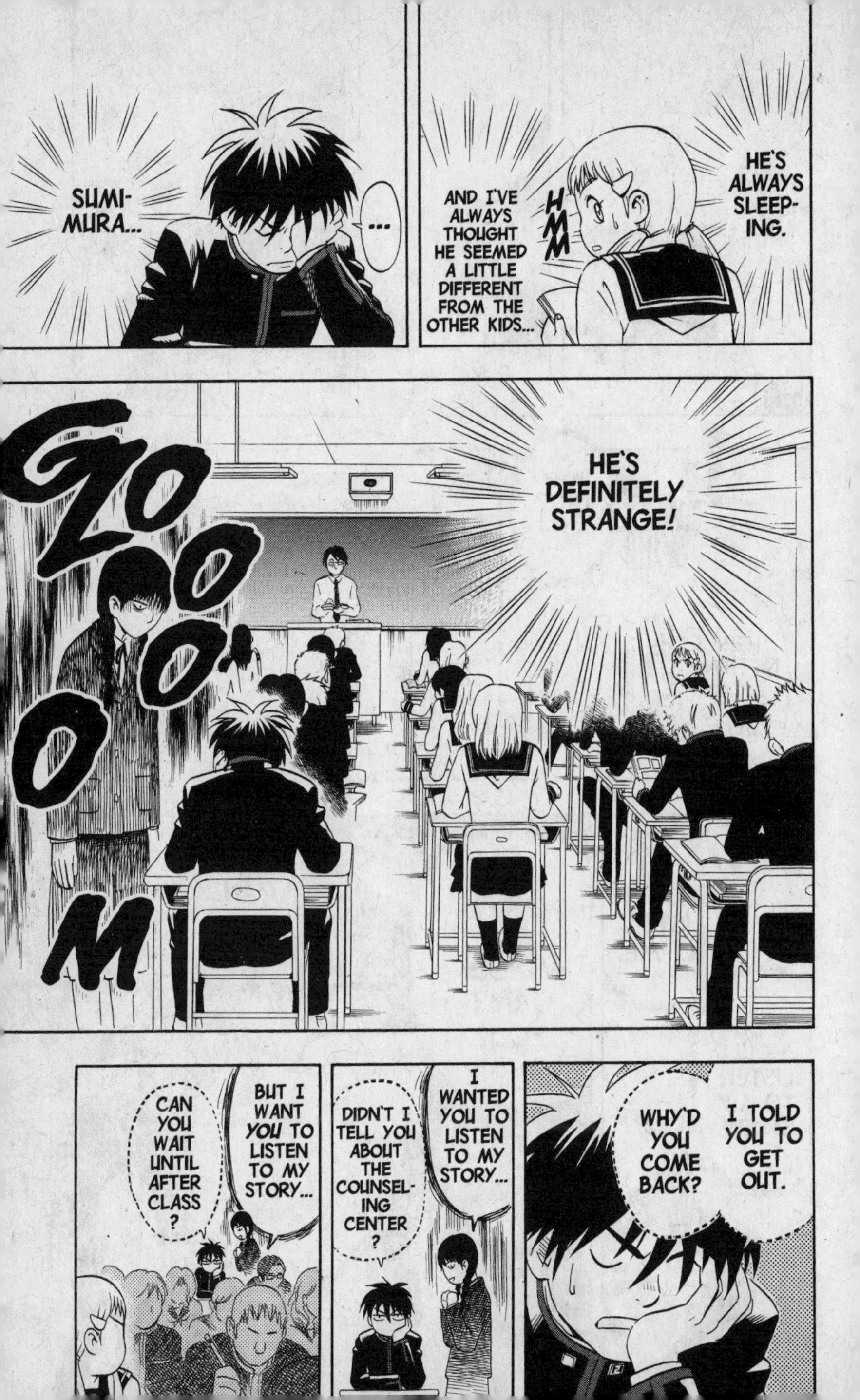
HE'S ALWAYS SLEEPING.
HMM
AND I'VE ALWAYS THOUGHT HE SEEMED A LITTLE DIFFERENT FROM THE OTHER KIDS...
SUMI-MURA...
...
HE'S DEFINITELY STRANGE!
GOOOOOM
I TOLD YOU TO GET OUT.
WHY'D YOU COME BACK?
I WANTED YOU TO LISTEN TO MY STORY...
DIDN'T I TELL YOU ABOUT THE COUNSEL-ING CENTER?
BUT I WANT *YOU* TO LISTEN TO MY STORY...
CAN YOU WAIT UNTIL AFTER CLASS?

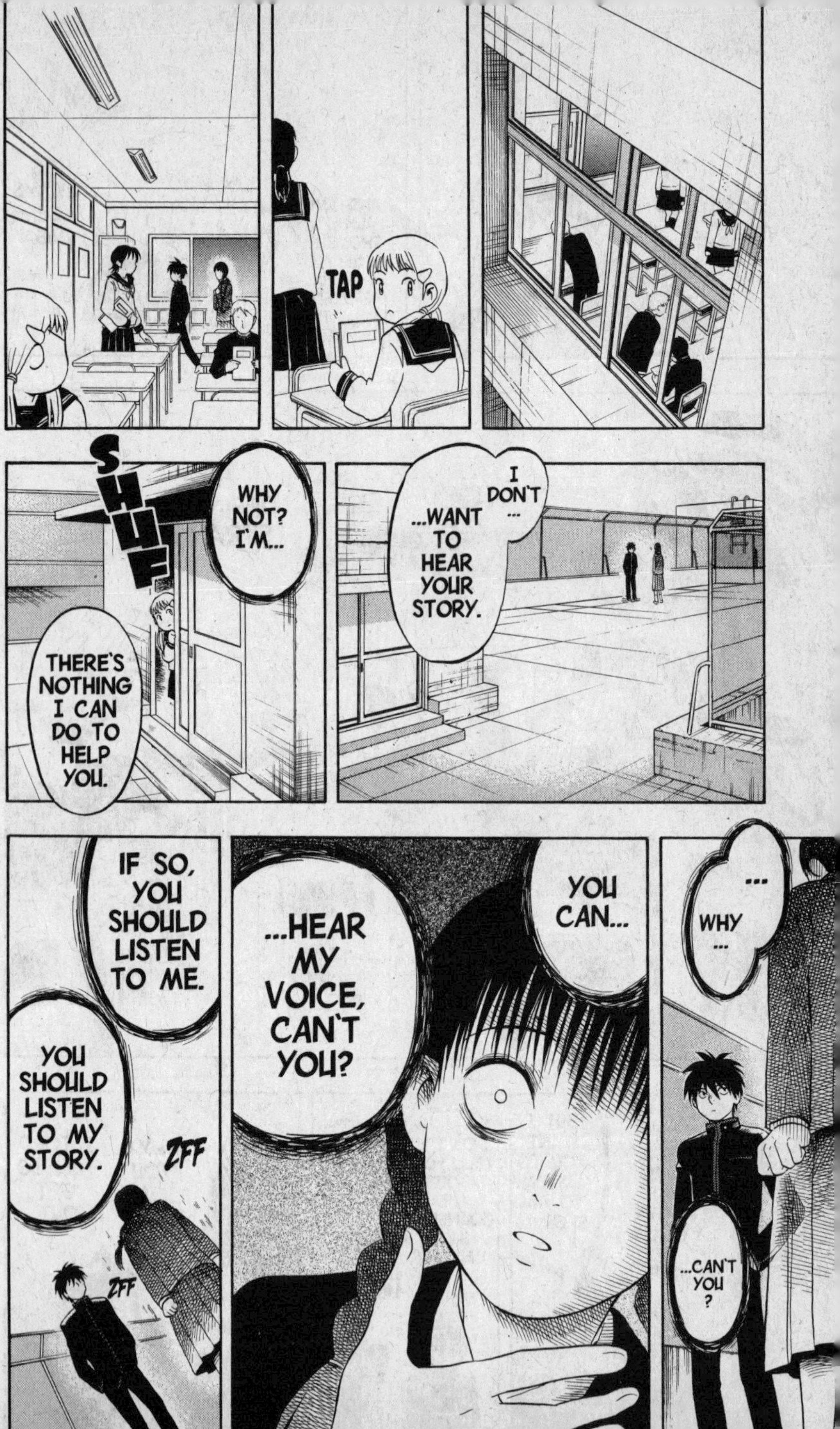
TAP
I DON'T ...
...WANT TO HEAR YOUR STORY.
SHUF
WHY NOT? I'M...
THERE'S NOTHING I CAN DO TO HELP YOU.
... WHY ...
...CAN'T YOU ?
YOU CAN...
...HEAR MY VOICE, CAN'T YOU?
IF SO, YOU SHOULD LISTEN TO ME.
YOU SHOULD LISTEN TO MY STORY.
ZFF
ZFF

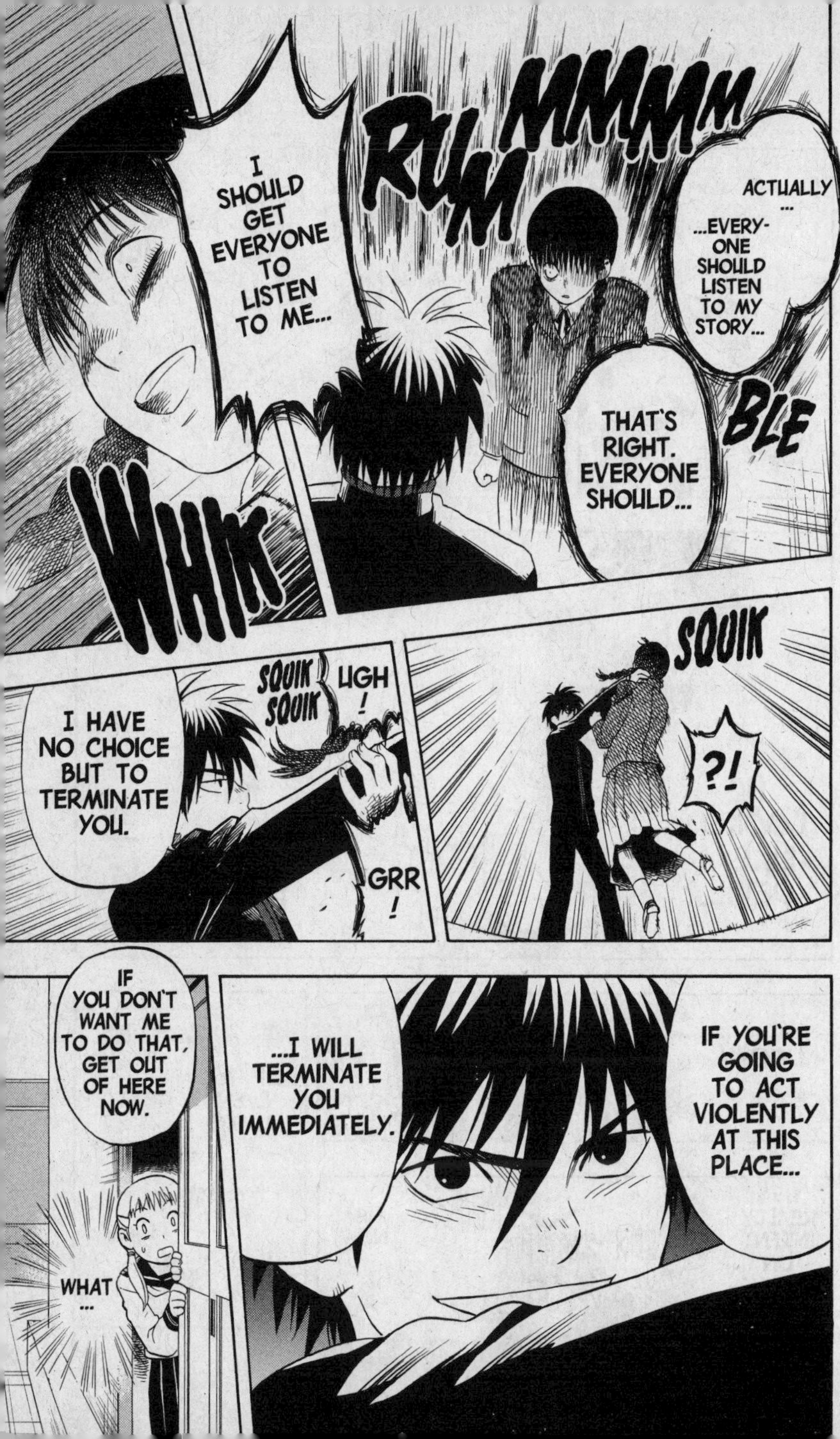

RUMMMMM
ACTUALLY ...
...EVERYONE SHOULD LISTEN TO MY STORY...
BLE
THAT'S RIGHT. EVERYONE SHOULD...
I SHOULD GET EVERYONE TO LISTEN TO ME...
WHIK
SQUIK
?!
UGH!
SQUIK SQUIK
I HAVE NO CHOICE BUT TO TERMINATE YOU.
GRR!
IF YOU'RE GOING TO ACT VIOLENTLY AT THIS PLACE...
...I WILL TERMINATE YOU IMMEDIATELY.
IF YOU DON'T WANT ME TO DO THAT, GET OUT OF HERE NOW.
WHAT ...

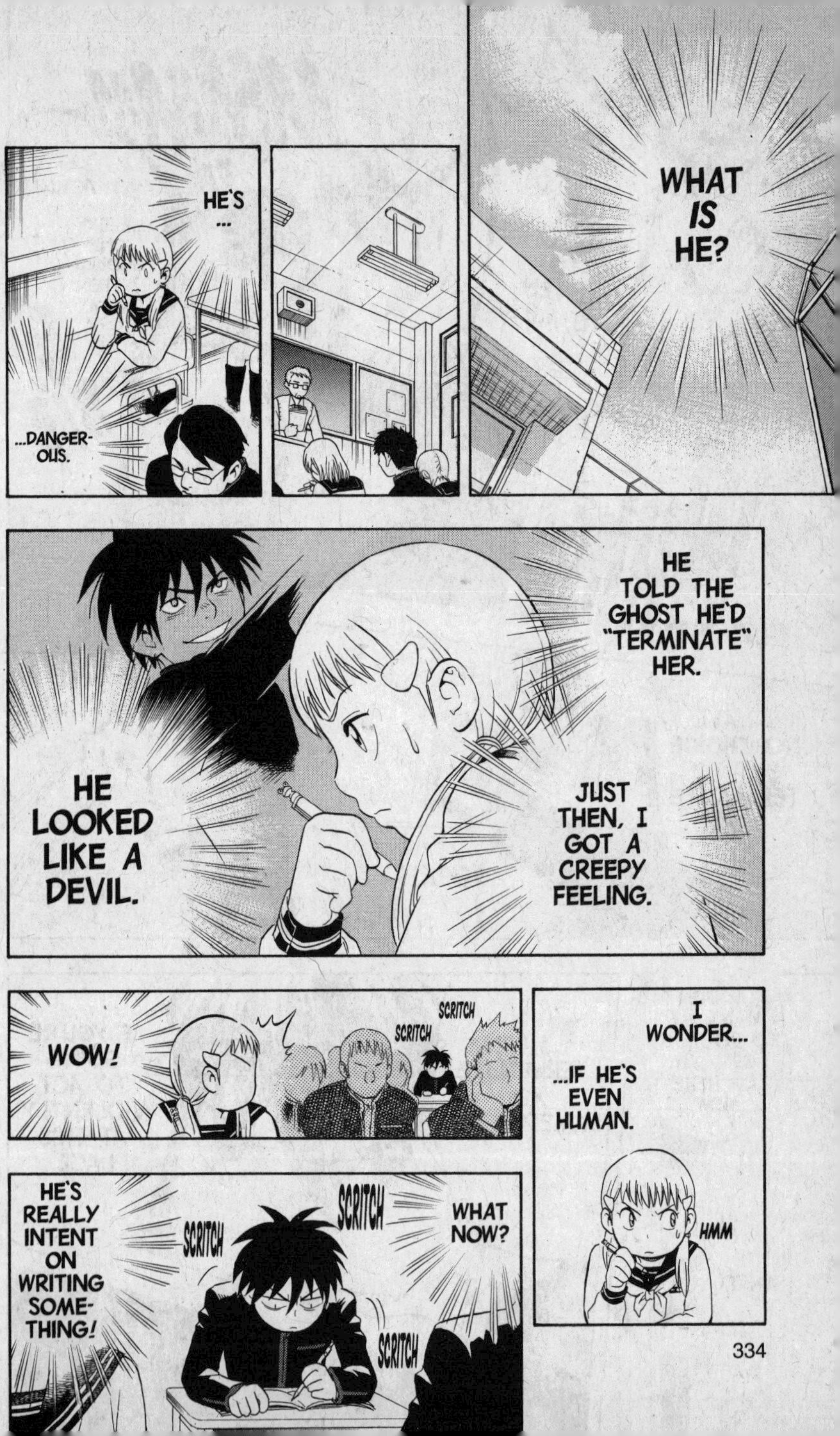
WHAT IS HE?
HE'S ...
...DANGER-OUS.
HE TOLD THE GHOST HE'D "TERMINATE" HER.
JUST THEN, I GOT A CREEPY FEELING.
HE LOOKED LIKE A DEVIL.
I WONDER...
...IF HE'S EVEN HUMAN.
HMM
SCRITCH
SCRITCH
WOW!
WHAT NOW?
SCRITCH
SCRITCH
HE'S REALLY INTENT ON WRITING SOME-THING!
SCRITCH

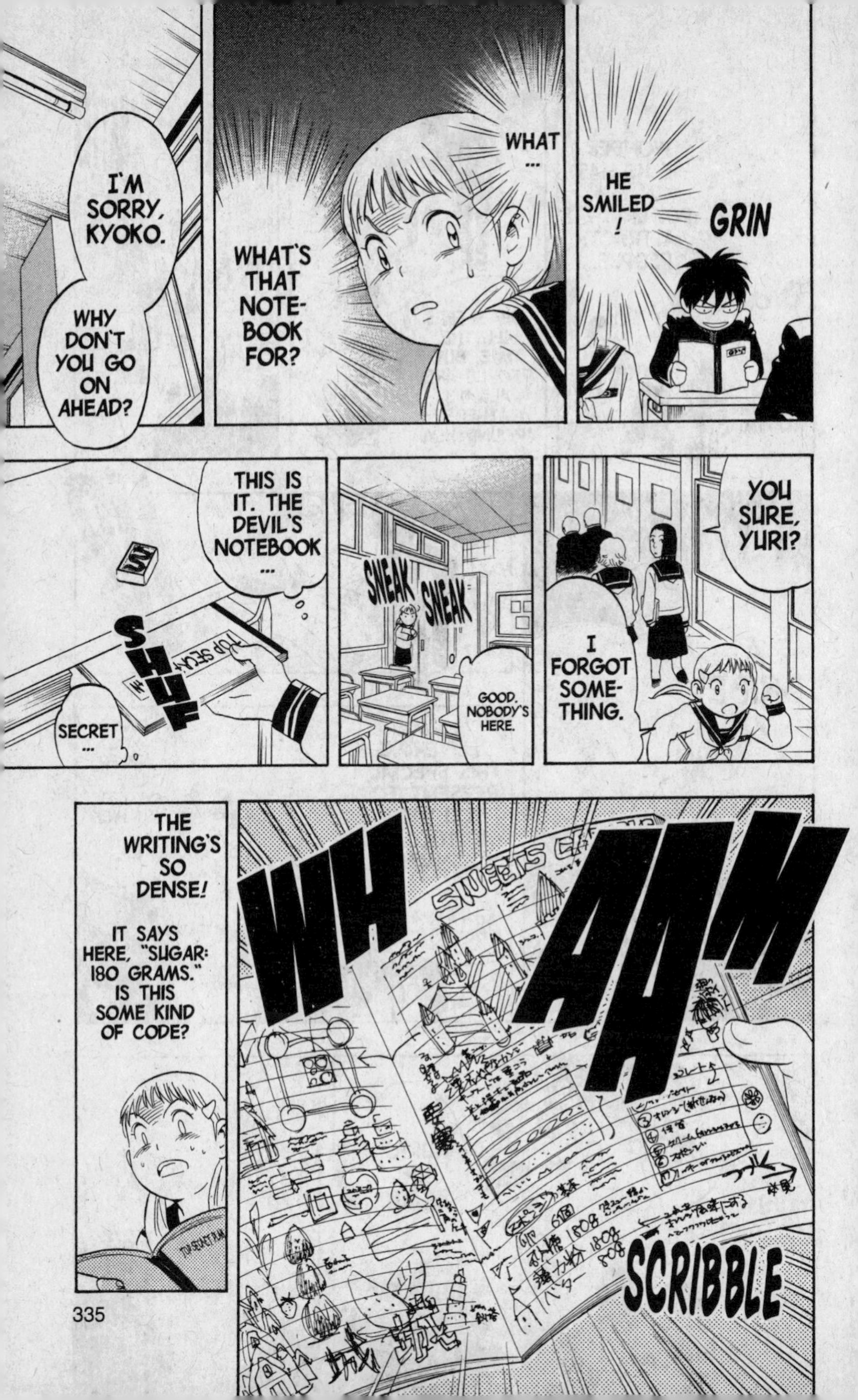

HE SMILED!
GRIN
WHAT...
WHAT'S THAT NOTEBOOK FOR?
I'M SORRY, KYOKO.
WHY DON'T YOU GO ON AHEAD?
YOU SURE, YURI?
I FORGOT SOMETHING.
SNEAK SNEAK
GOOD. NOBODY'S HERE.
THIS IS IT. THE DEVIL'S NOTEBOOK...
SHUF
SECRET...
WHAAAH
SCRIBBLE
THE WRITING'S SO DENSE!
IT SAYS HERE, "SUGAR: 180 GRAMS." IS THIS SOME KIND OF CODE?

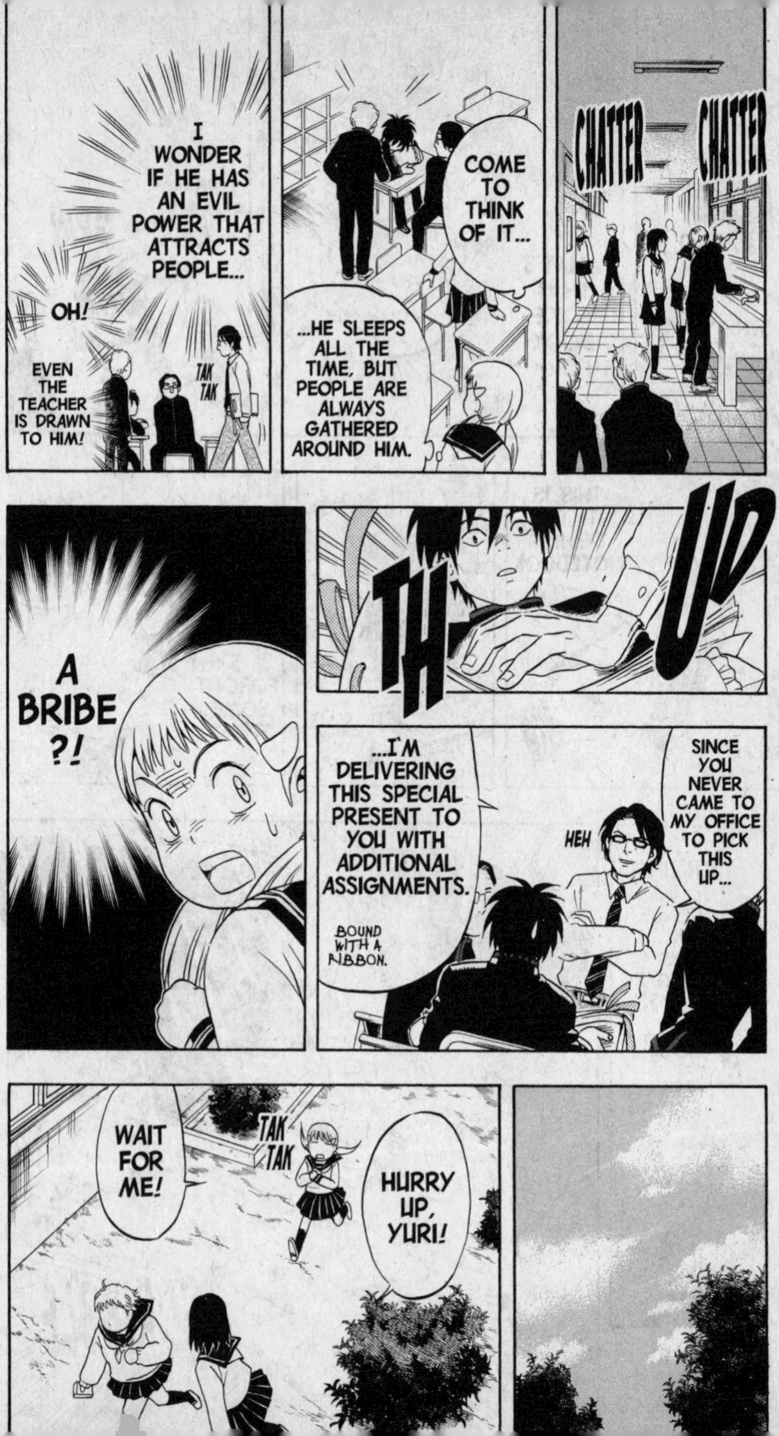
CHATTER
CHATTER
COME TO THINK OF IT...
...HE SLEEPS ALL THE TIME, BUT PEOPLE ARE ALWAYS GATHERED AROUND HIM.
I WONDER IF HE HAS AN EVIL POWER THAT ATTRACTS PEOPLE...
OH!
TAK TAK
EVEN THE TEACHER IS DRAWN TO HIM!
THUD
SINCE YOU NEVER CAME TO MY OFFICE TO PICK THIS UP...
HEH
...I'M DELIVERING THIS SPECIAL PRESENT TO YOU WITH ADDITIONAL ASSIGNMENTS.
BOUND WITH A RIBBON.
A BRIBE?!
HURRY UP, YURI!
TAK TAK
WAIT FOR ME!

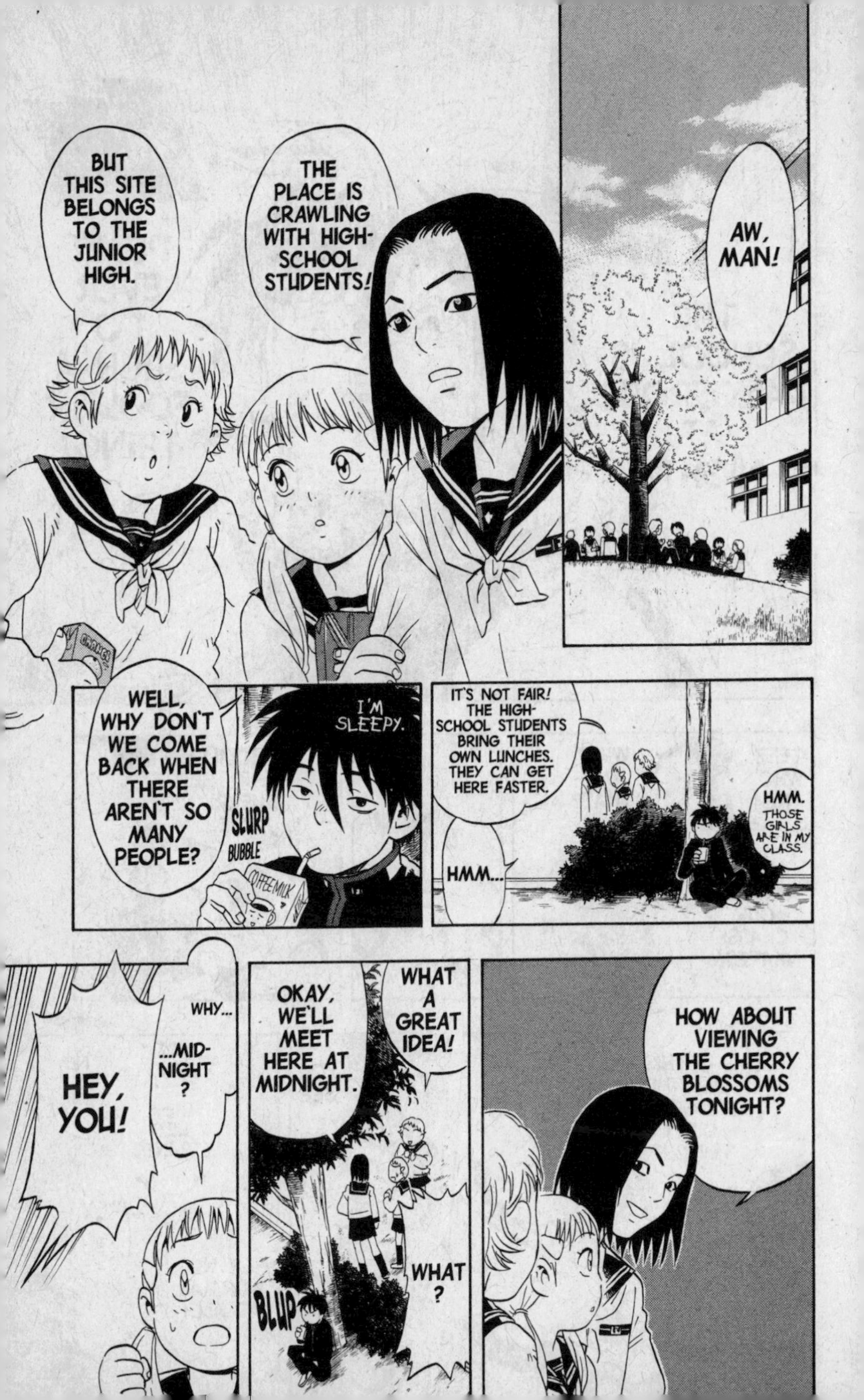
AW, MAN!
THE PLACE IS CRAWLING WITH HIGH-SCHOOL STUDENTS!
BUT THIS SITE BELONGS TO THE JUNIOR HIGH.
HMM. THOSE GIRLS ARE IN MY CLASS.
IT'S NOT FAIR! THE HIGH-SCHOOL STUDENTS BRING THEIR OWN LUNCHES. THEY CAN GET HERE FASTER.
HMM...
I'M SLEEPY.
SLURP
BUBBLE
COFFEE MILK
WELL, WHY DON'T WE COME BACK WHEN THERE AREN'T SO MANY PEOPLE?
HOW ABOUT VIEWING THE CHERRY BLOSSOMS TONIGHT?
WHAT A GREAT IDEA!
OKAY, WE'LL MEET HERE AT MIDNIGHT.
WHAT?
BLUP
WHY...
...MID-NIGHT?
HEY, YOU!

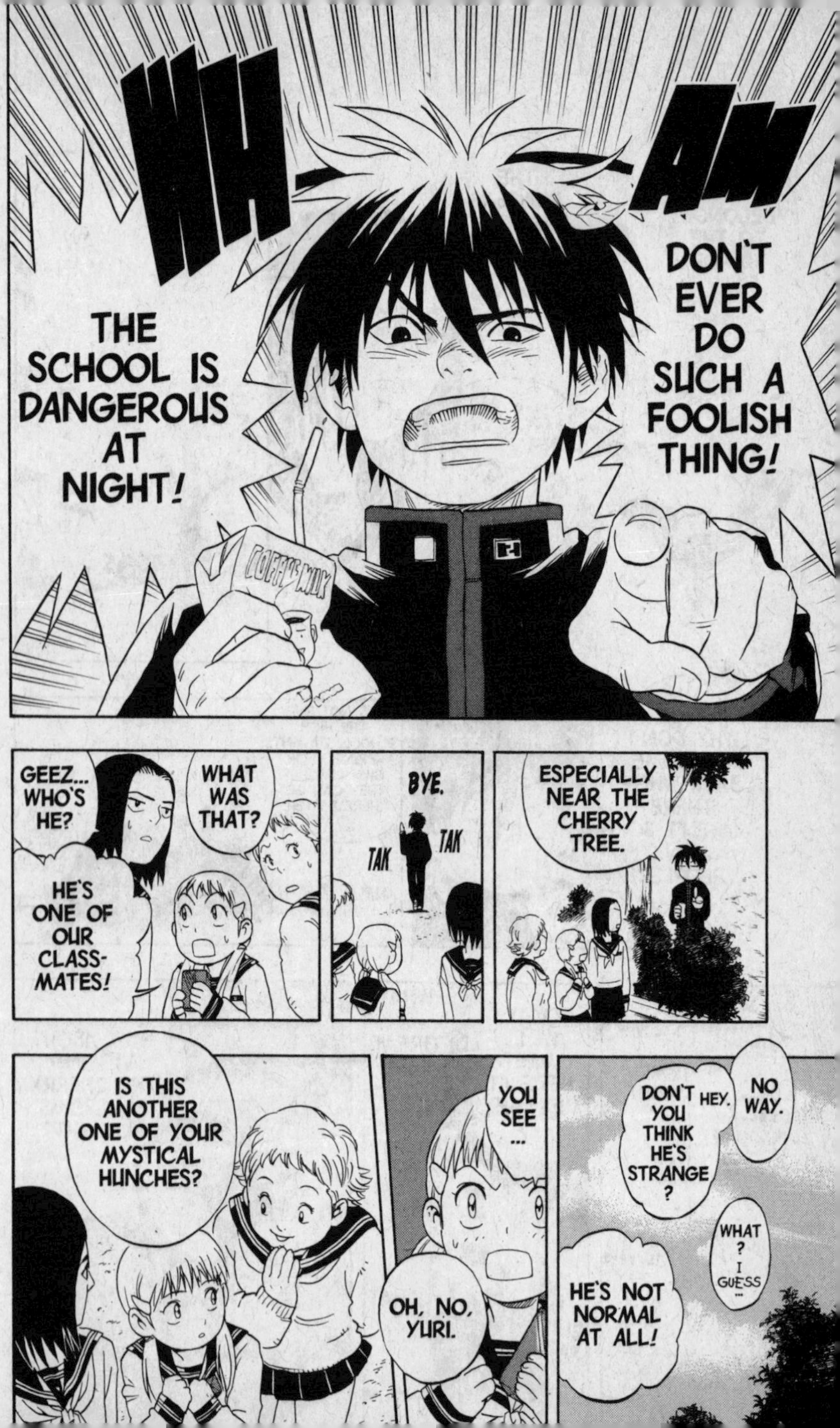
WH-
AM
DON'T EVER DO SUCH A FOOLISH THING!
THE SCHOOL IS DANGEROUS AT NIGHT!
ESPECIALLY NEAR THE CHERRY TREE.
BYE.
TAK
TAK
WHAT WAS THAT?
GEEZ... WHO'S HE?
HE'S ONE OF OUR CLASS-MATES!
NO WAY.
HEY.
DON'T YOU THINK HE'S STRANGE?
WHAT? I GUESS...
HE'S NOT NORMAL AT ALL!
YOU SEE...
OH, NO, YURI.
IS THIS ANOTHER ONE OF YOUR MYSTICAL HUNCHES?

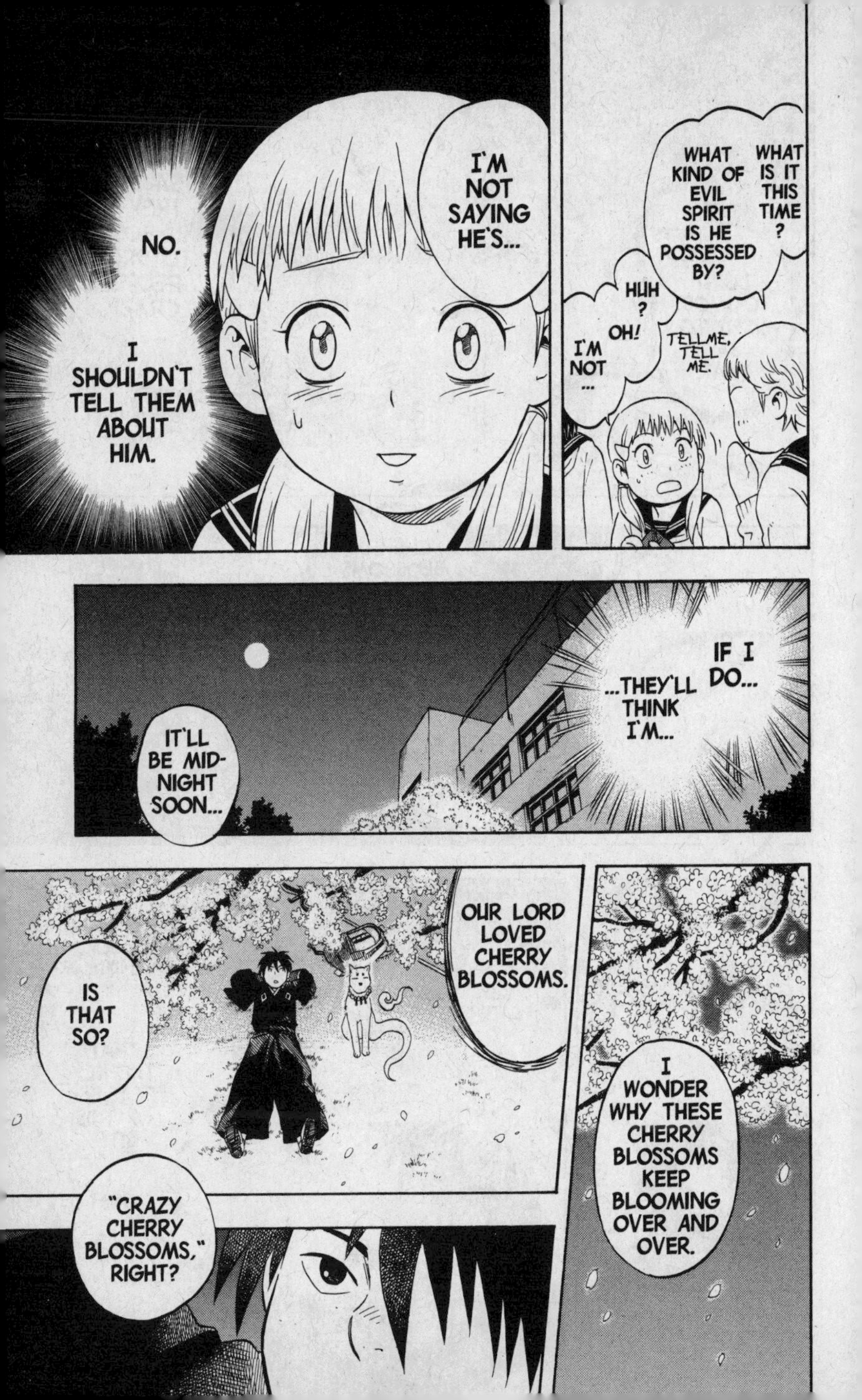
WHAT IS IT THIS TIME?
WHAT KIND OF EVIL SPIRIT IS HE POSSESSED BY?
TELLME, TELL ME.
HUH? OH!
I'M NOT ...
I'M NOT SAYING HE'S...
NO.
I SHOULDN'T TELL THEM ABOUT HIM.
IF I DO...
...THEY'LL THINK I'M...
IT'LL BE MID-NIGHT SOON...
I WONDER WHY THESE CHERRY BLOSSOMS KEEP BLOOMING OVER AND OVER.
OUR LORD LOVED CHERRY BLOSSOMS.
IS THAT SO?
"CRAZY CHERRY BLOSSOMS," RIGHT?

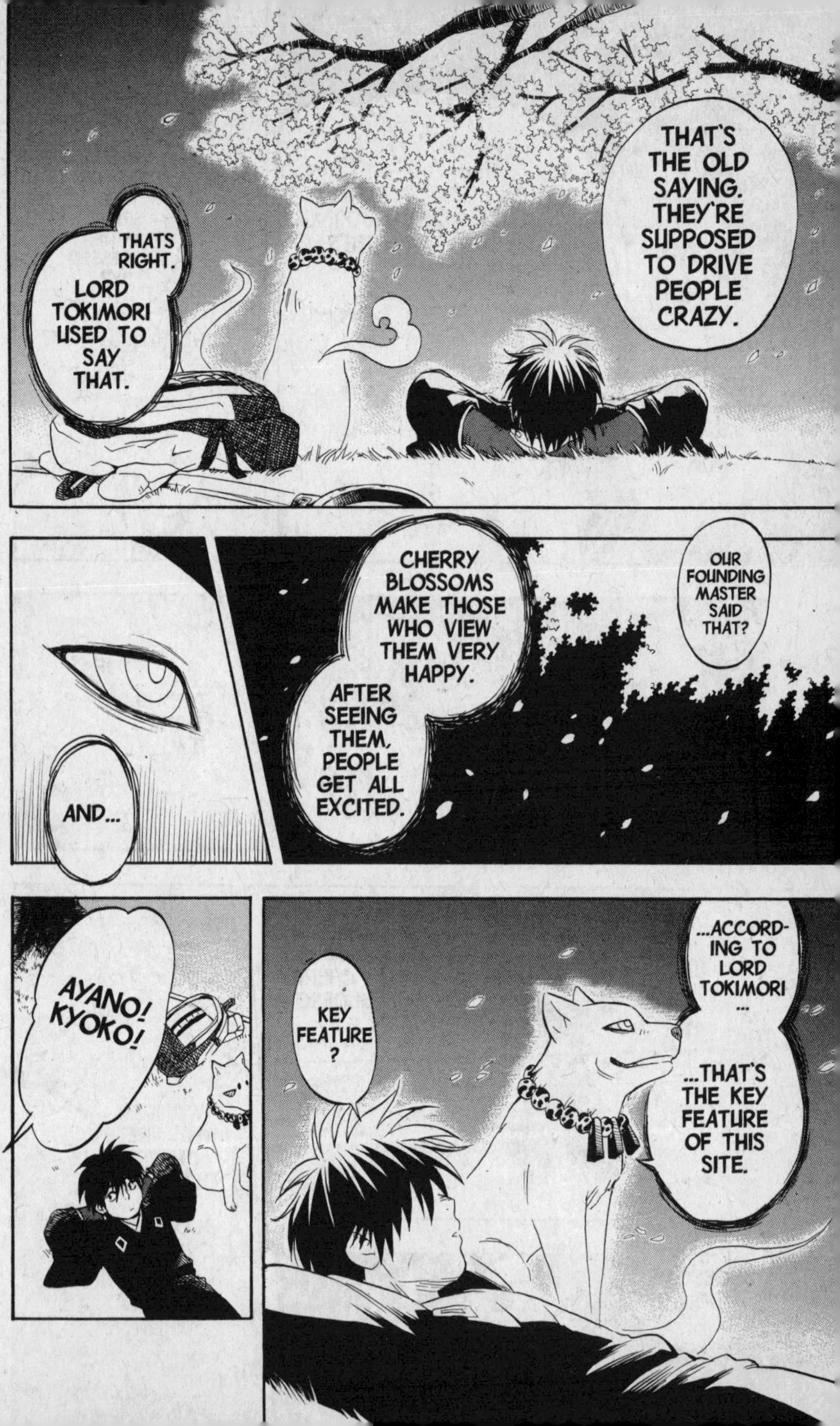
THAT'S THE OLD SAYING. THEY'RE SUPPOSED TO DRIVE PEOPLE CRAZY.
THATS RIGHT.
LORD TOKIMORI USED TO SAY THAT.
OUR FOUNDING MASTER SAID THAT?
CHERRY BLOSSOMS MAKE THOSE WHO VIEW THEM VERY HAPPY.
AFTER SEEING THEM, PEOPLE GET ALL EXCITED.
AND...
...ACCORDING TO LORD TOKIMORI...
...THAT'S THE KEY FEATURE OF THIS SITE.
KEY FEATURE?
AYANO! KYOKO!

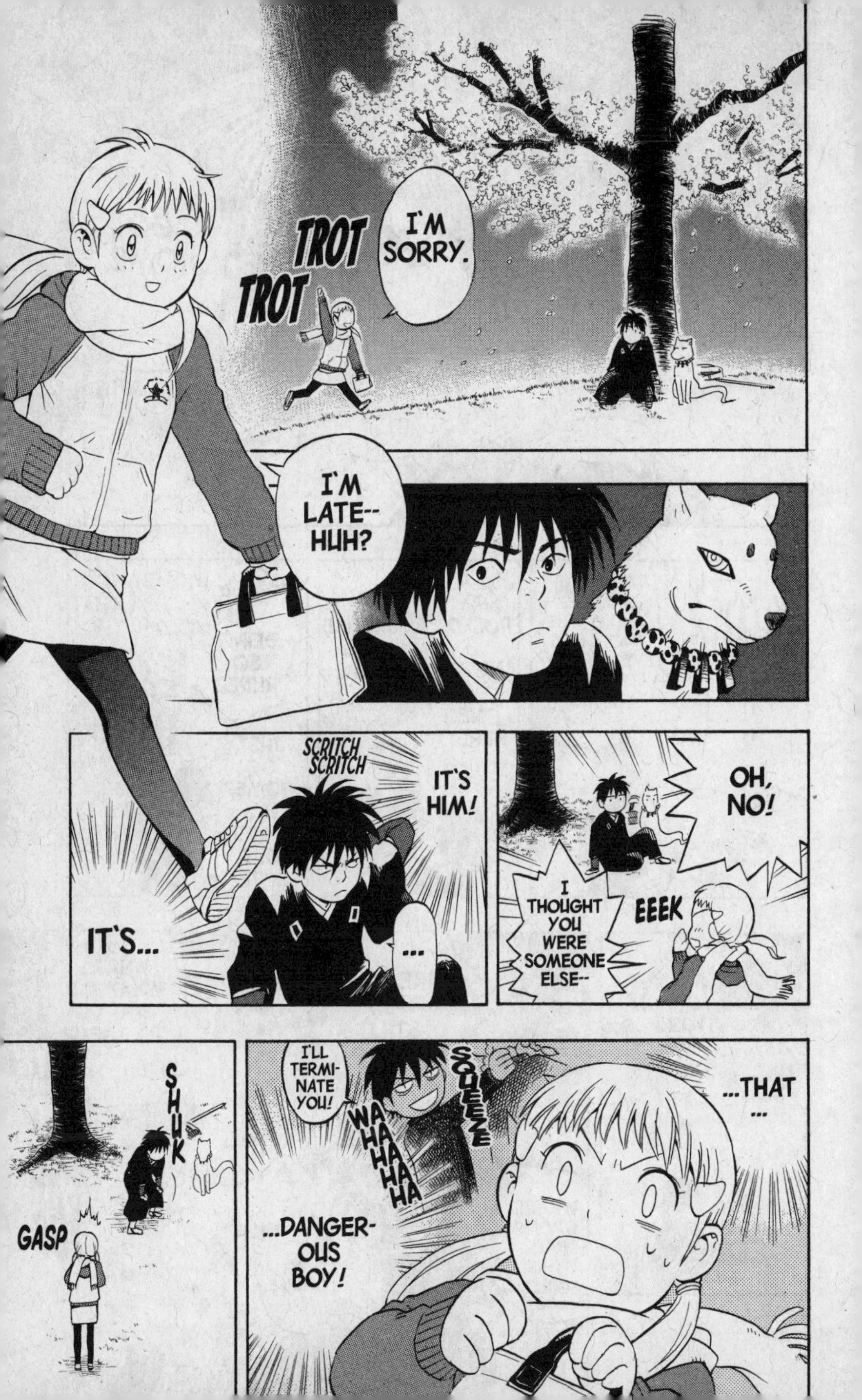
TROT
TROT
I'M SORRY.
I'M LATE-- HUH?
OH, NO!
I THOUGHT YOU WERE SOMEONE ELSE--
EEEK
SCRITCH SCRITCH
IT'S HIM!
IT'S...
...
...THAT ...
I'LL TERMINATE YOU!
WAHAHAHAHA
SQUEEZE
...DANGEROUS BOY!
SHUK
GASP

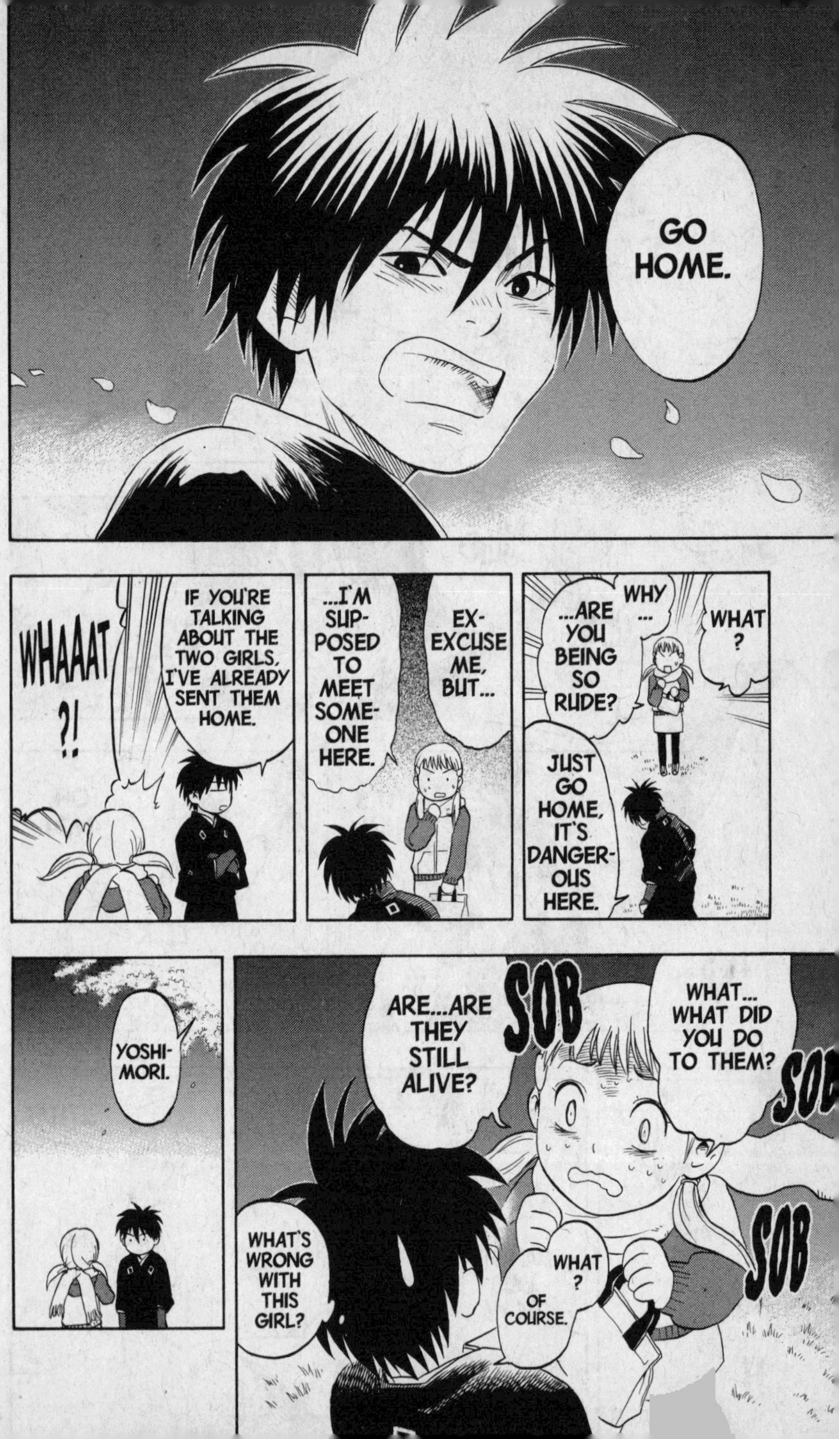
GO HOME.
WHAT?
WHY... ...ARE YOU BEING SO RUDE?
JUST GO HOME, IT'S DANGEROUS HERE.
EX-EXCUSE ME, BUT...
...I'M SUPPOSED TO MEET SOMEONE HERE.
IF YOU'RE TALKING ABOUT THE TWO GIRLS, I'VE ALREADY SENT THEM HOME.
WHAAAT?!
SOB
WHAT... WHAT DID YOU DO TO THEM?
SOB
ARE...ARE THEY STILL ALIVE?
SOB
WHAT?
OF COURSE.
WHAT'S WRONG WITH THIS GIRL?
YOSHIMORI.

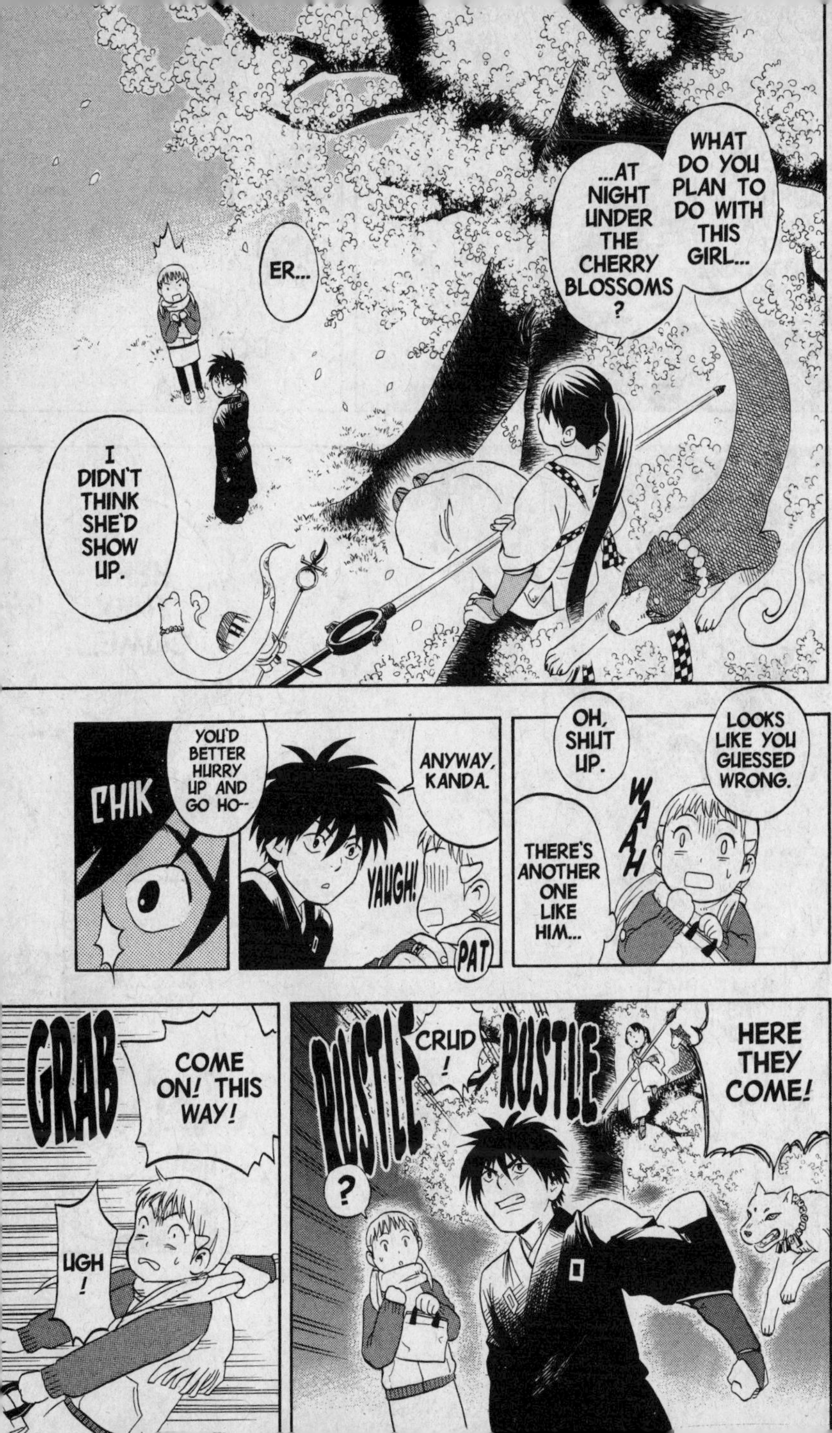
WHAT DO YOU PLAN TO DO WITH THIS GIRL...
...AT NIGHT UNDER THE CHERRY BLOSSOMS?
ER...
I DIDN'T THINK SHE'D SHOW UP.
LOOKS LIKE YOU GUESSED WRONG.
OH, SHUT UP.
WAAH
THERE'S ANOTHER ONE LIKE HIM...
ANYWAY, KANDA.
YOU'D BETTER HURRY UP AND GO HO-
YAUGH!
PAT
CHIK
HERE THEY COME!
RUSTLE
CRUD!
RUSTLE
?
GRAB
COME ON! THIS WAY!
UGH!

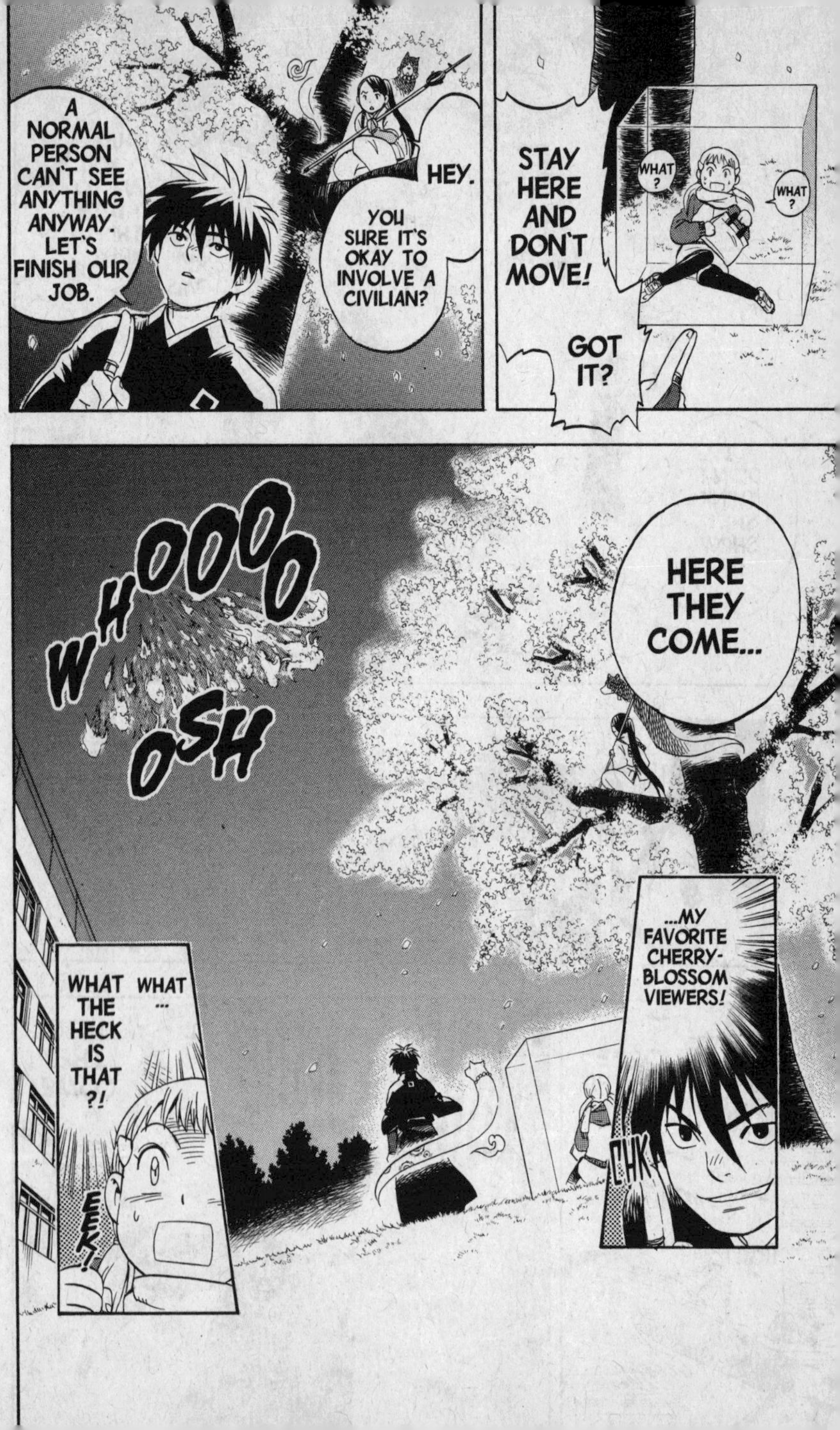
STAY HERE AND DON'T MOVE!
WHAT?
WHAT?
GOT IT?
HEY.
YOU SURE IT'S OKAY TO INVOLVE A CIVILIAN?
A NORMAL PERSON CAN'T SEE ANYTHING ANYWAY. LET'S FINISH OUR JOB.
HERE THEY COME...
...MY FAVORITE CHERRY-BLOSSOM VIEWERS!
CHK
WHOOOOOSH
WHAT WHAT...
WHAT THE HECK IS THAT?!
EEK!

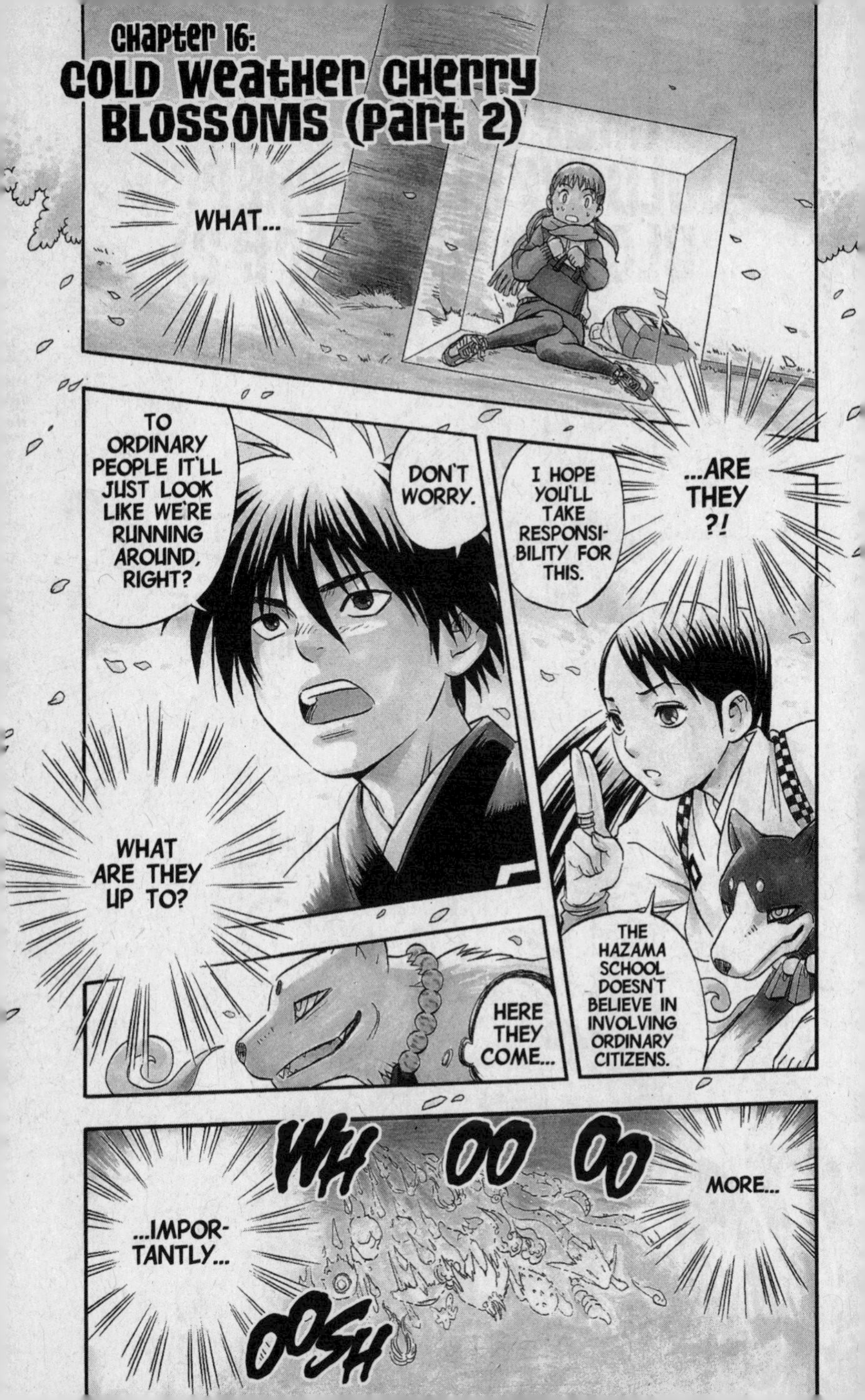
Chapter 16:
Cold Weather Cherry Blossoms (Part 2)
WHAT...
...ARE THEY ?!
I HOPE YOU'LL TAKE RESPONSIBILITY FOR THIS.
DON'T WORRY.
TO ORDINARY PEOPLE IT'LL JUST LOOK LIKE WE'RE RUNNING AROUND, RIGHT?
WHAT ARE THEY UP TO?
THE HAZAMA SCHOOL DOESN'T BELIEVE IN INVOLVING ORDINARY CITIZENS.
HERE THEY COME...
MORE...
...IMPORTANTLY...
WHOOOOOOSH

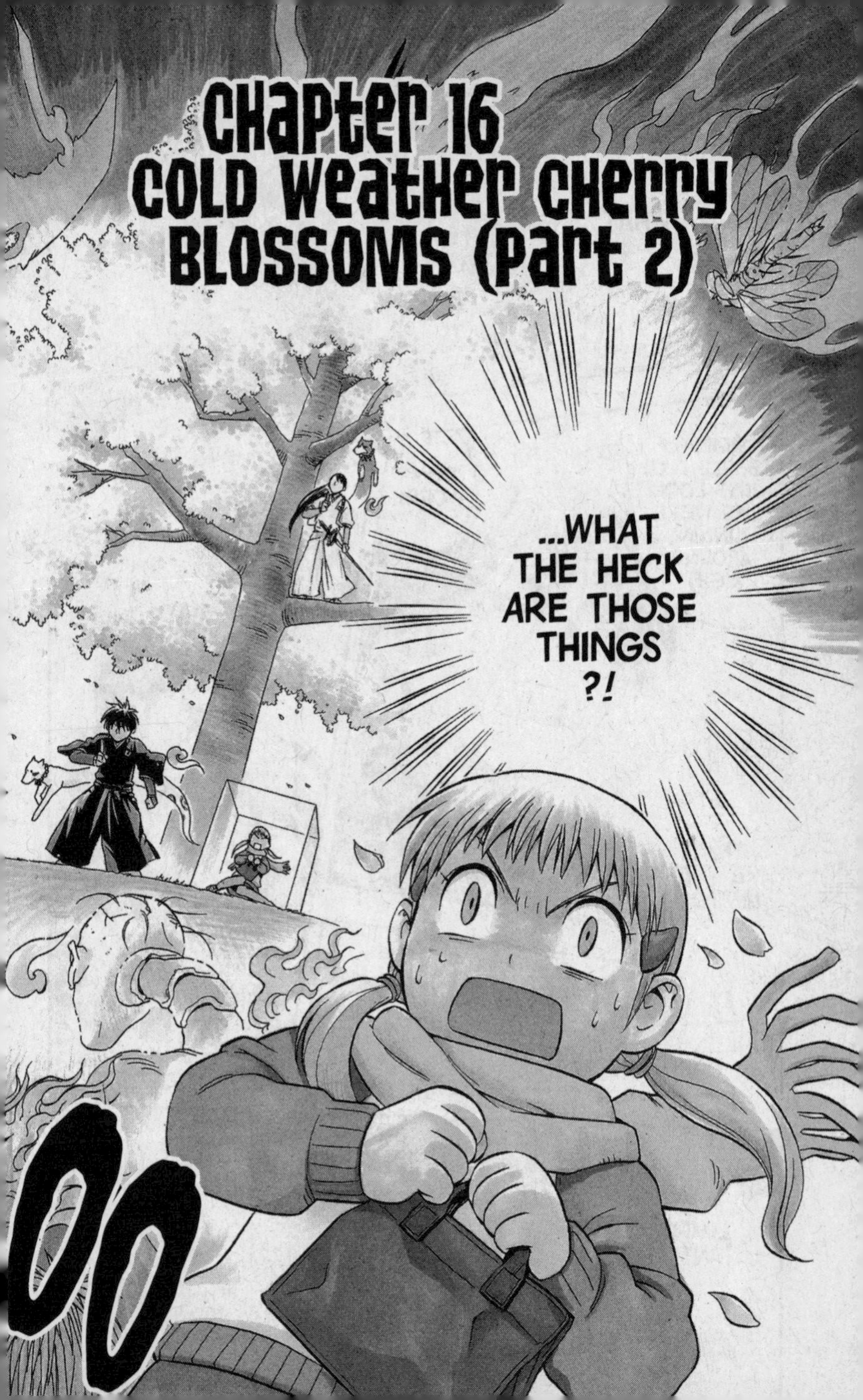
CHAPTER 16
COLD WEATHER CHERRY BLOSSOMS (PART 2)
...WHAT THE HECK ARE THOSE THINGS ?!

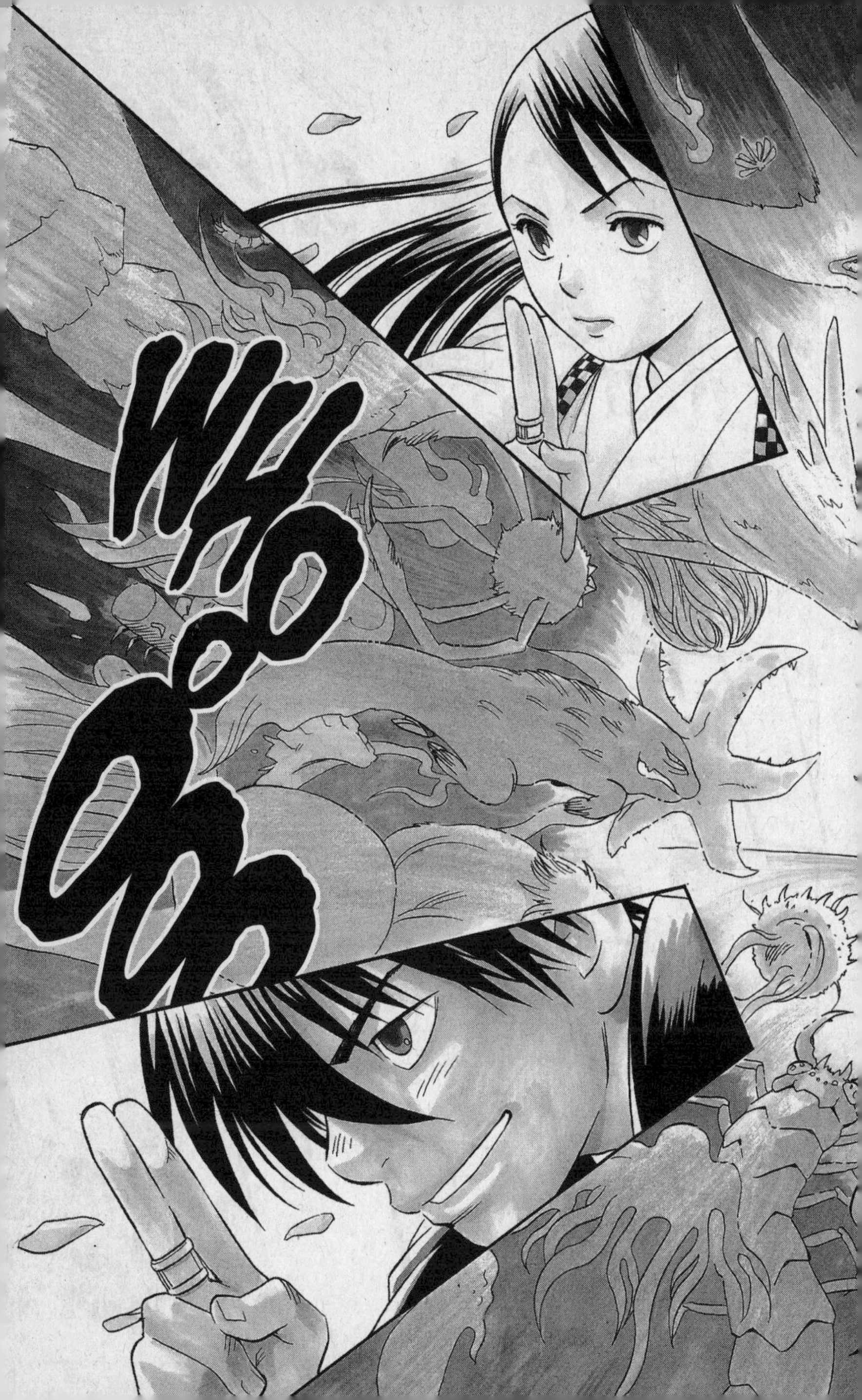
WHOOSH

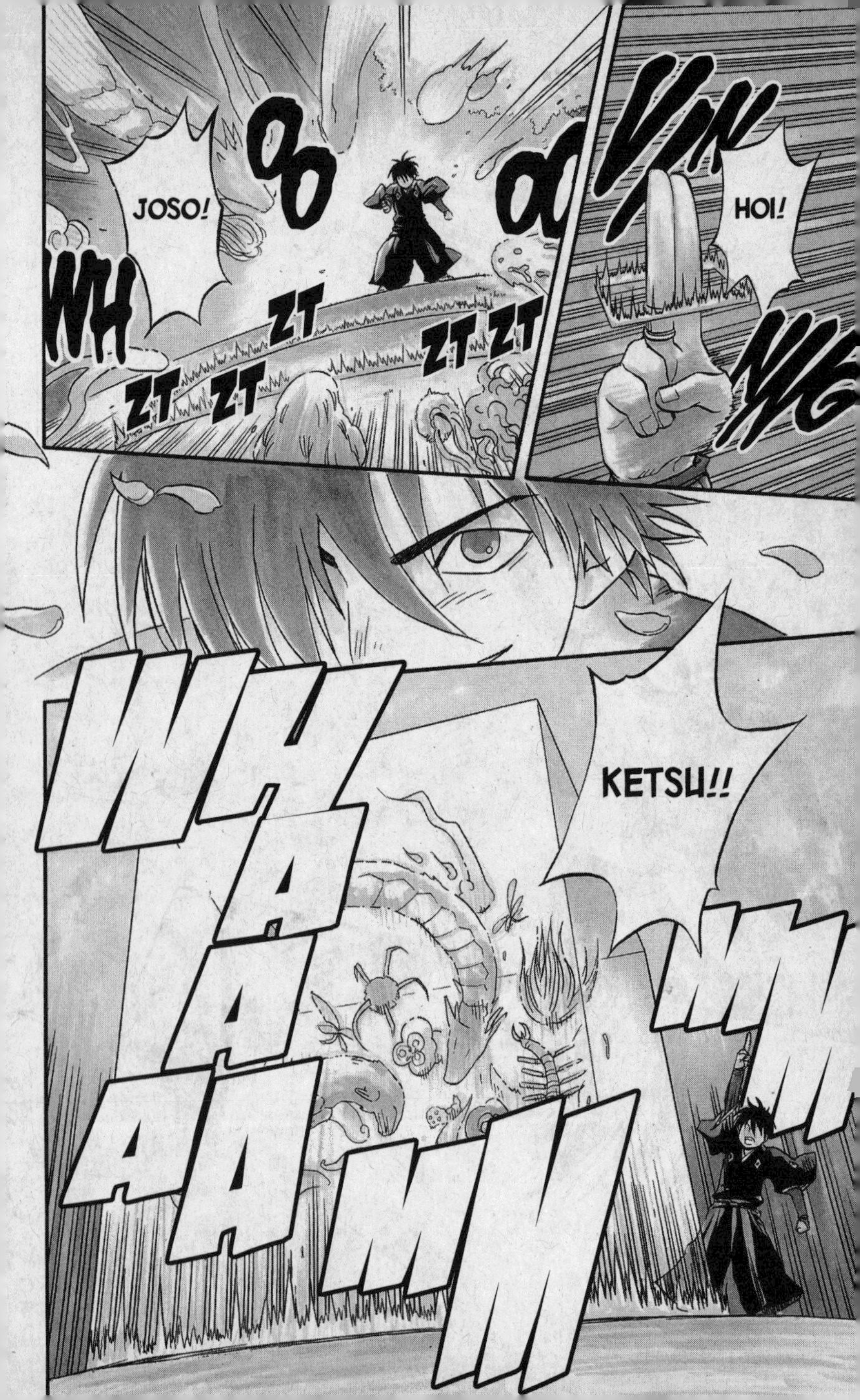
HOI!
JOSO!
ZT
ZT
ZT
ZT
ZT
KETSU!!
WHAAAMM

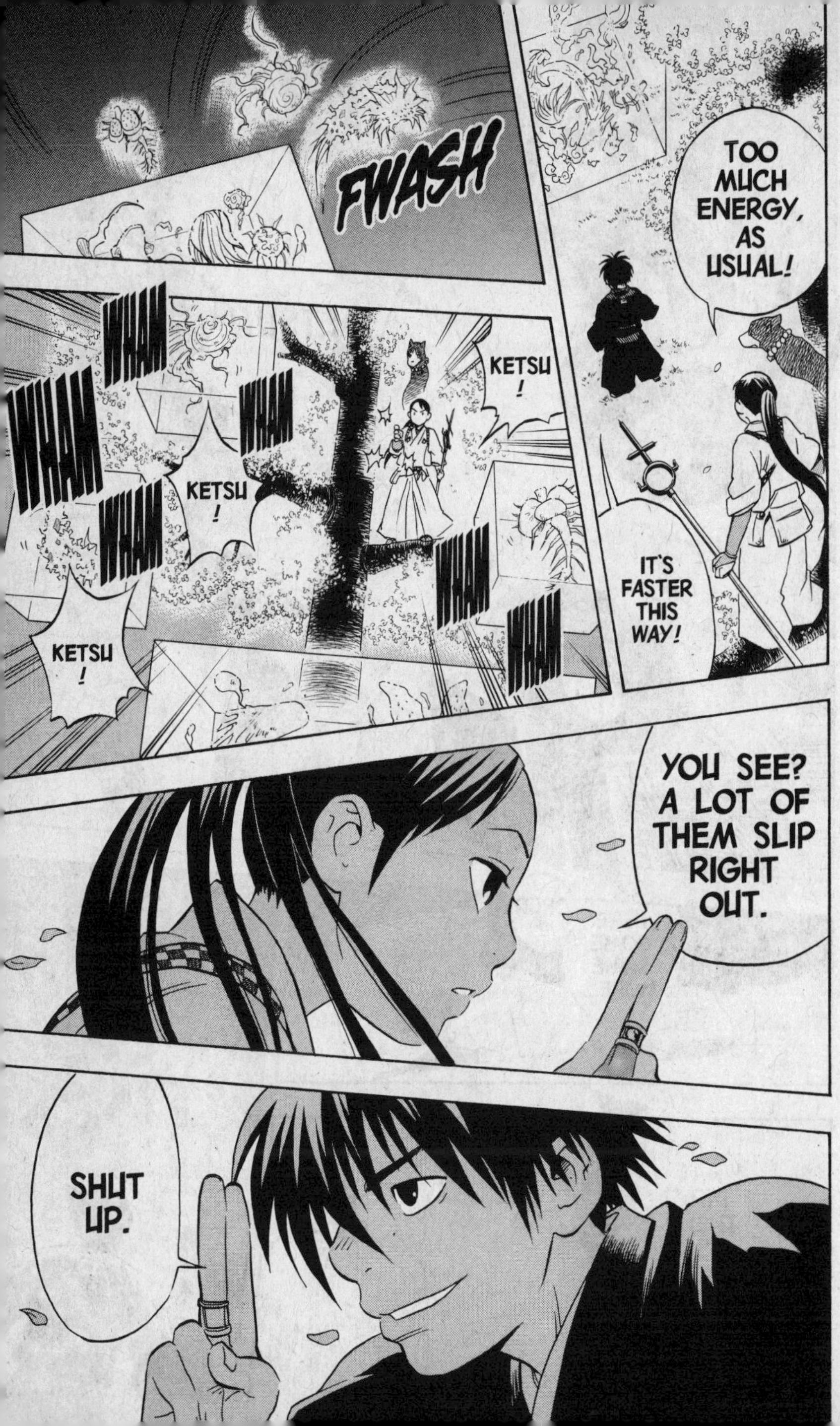

TOO MUCH ENERGY, AS USUAL!
IT'S FASTER THIS WAY!
FWASH
KETSU!
WHAM
WHAM
WHAM
WHAM
WHAM
WHAM
KETSU!
KETSU!
YOU SEE? A LOT OF THEM SLIP RIGHT OUT.
SHUT UP.

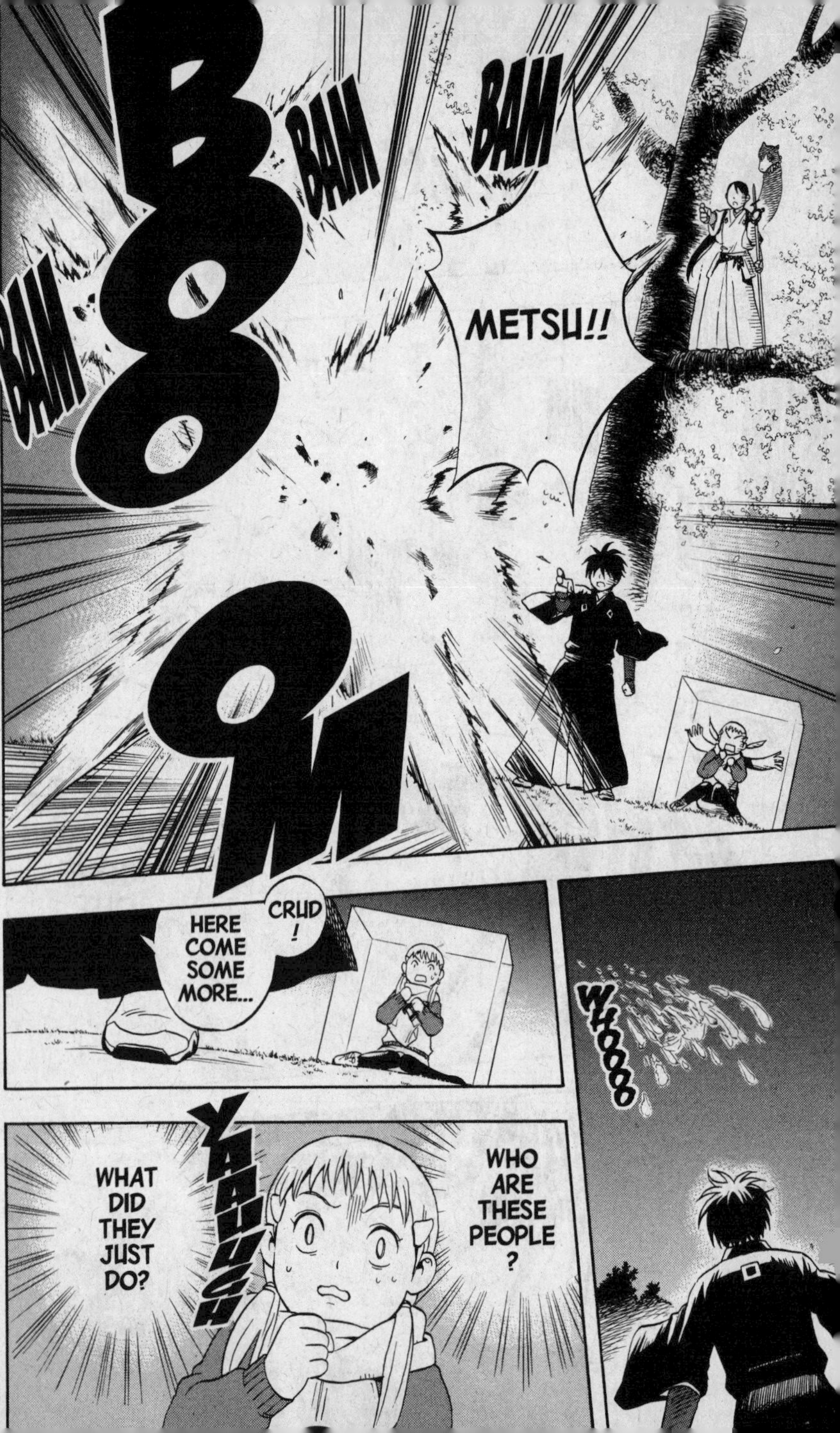
BAM
BAM
METSU!!
BAM
BOOM
WHOOOO
CRUD!
HERE COME SOME MORE...
WHO ARE THESE PEOPLE?
YAAUGH
WHAT DID THEY JUST DO?

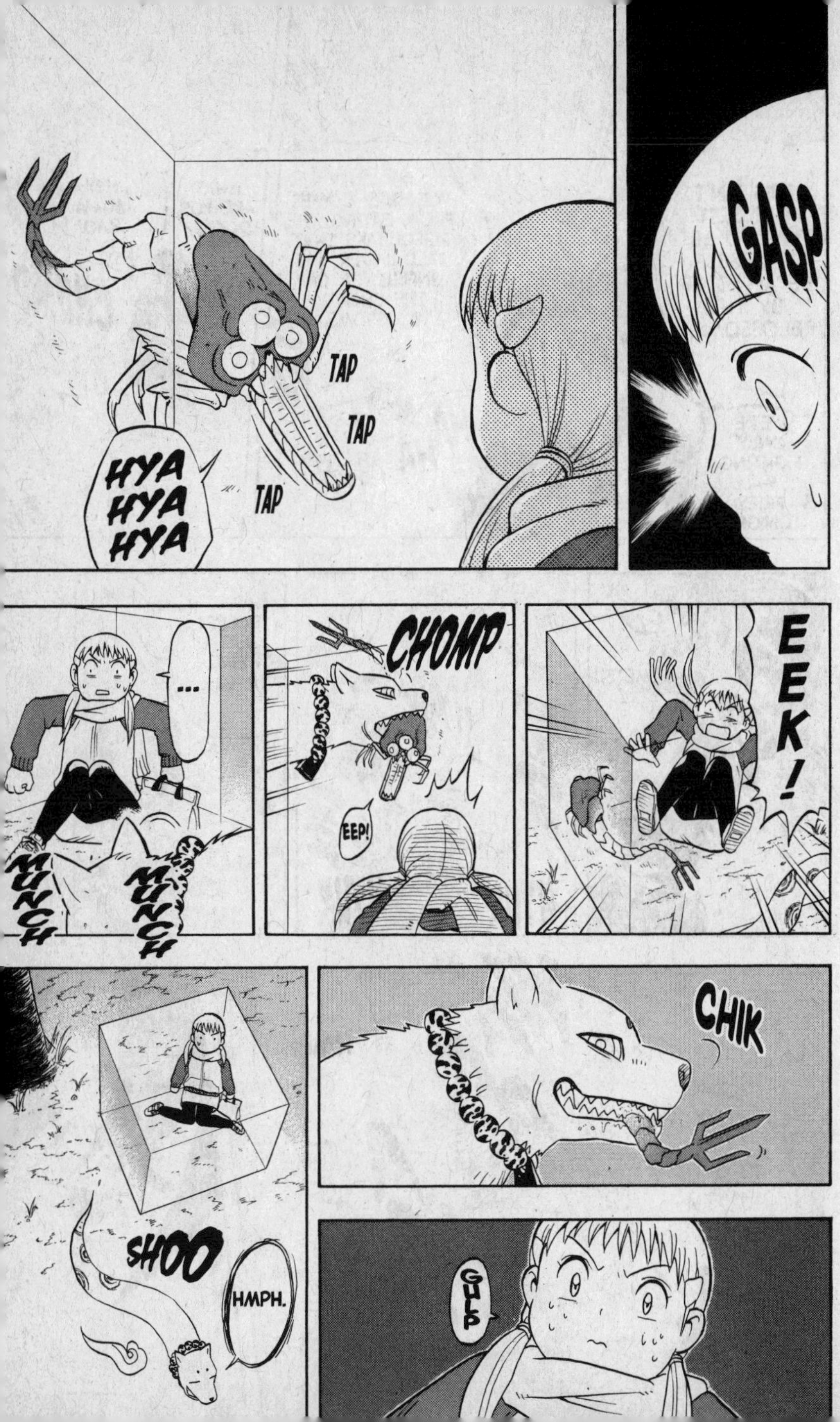

GASP
TAP
TAP
TAP
HYA HYA HYA
EEK!
CHOMP
EEP!
...
MUNCH MUNCH
CHIK
GULP
SHOO
HMPH.

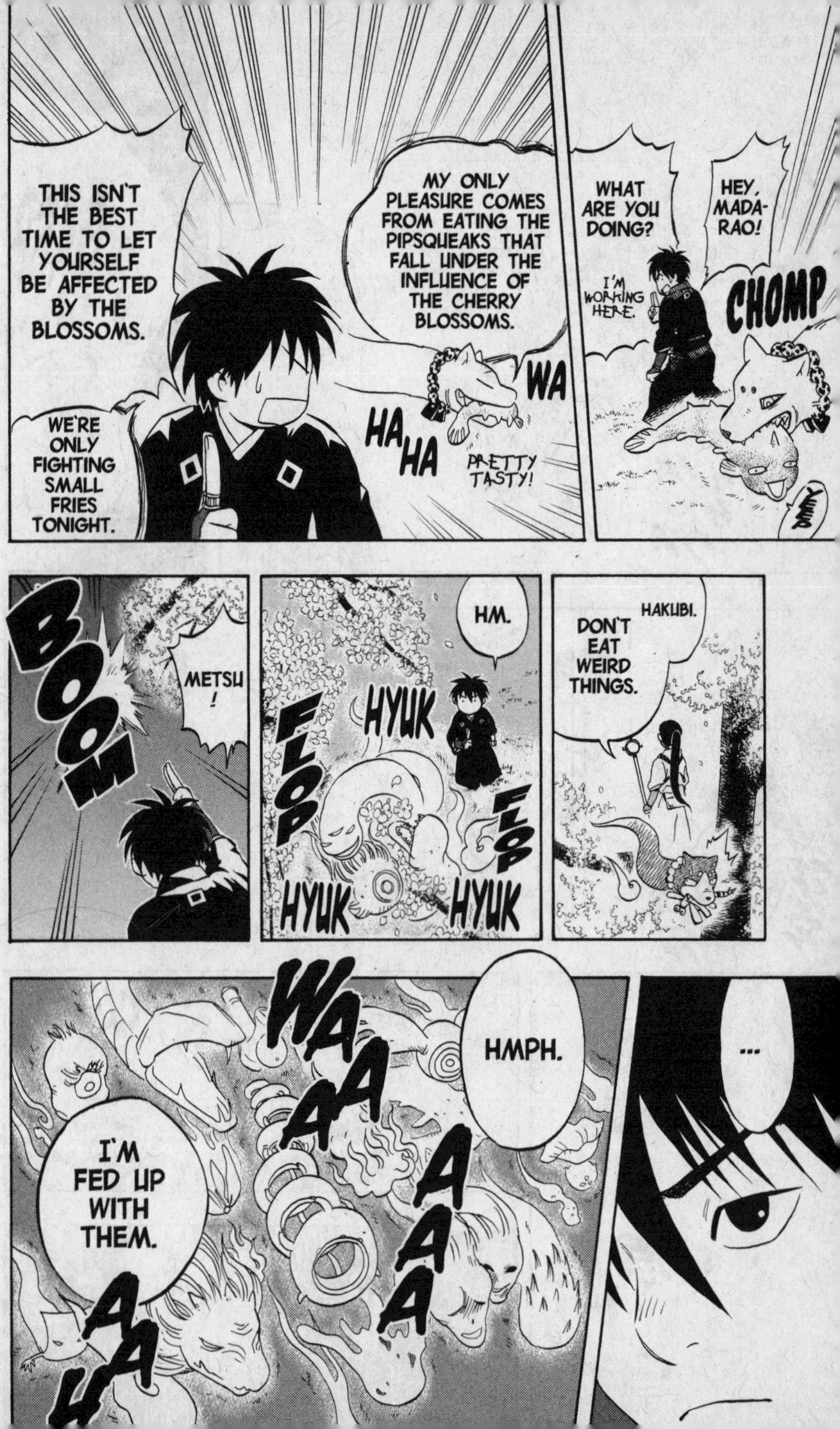
HEY, MADA-RAO!
WHAT ARE YOU DOING?
I'M WORKING HERE.
CHOMP
MY ONLY PLEASURE COMES FROM EATING THE PIPSQUEAKS THAT FALL UNDER THE INFLUENCE OF THE CHERRY BLOSSOMS.
WA
HA HA
PRETTY TASTY!
THIS ISN'T THE BEST TIME TO LET YOURSELF BE AFFECTED BY THE BLOSSOMS.
WE'RE ONLY FIGHTING SMALL FRIES TONIGHT.
HAKUBI.
DON'T EAT WEIRD THINGS.
HM.
HYUK
FLOP
FLOP
HYUK HYUK
METSU!
BOOM
...
HMPH.
WAAAAAAA
I'M FED UP WITH THEM.
AAH

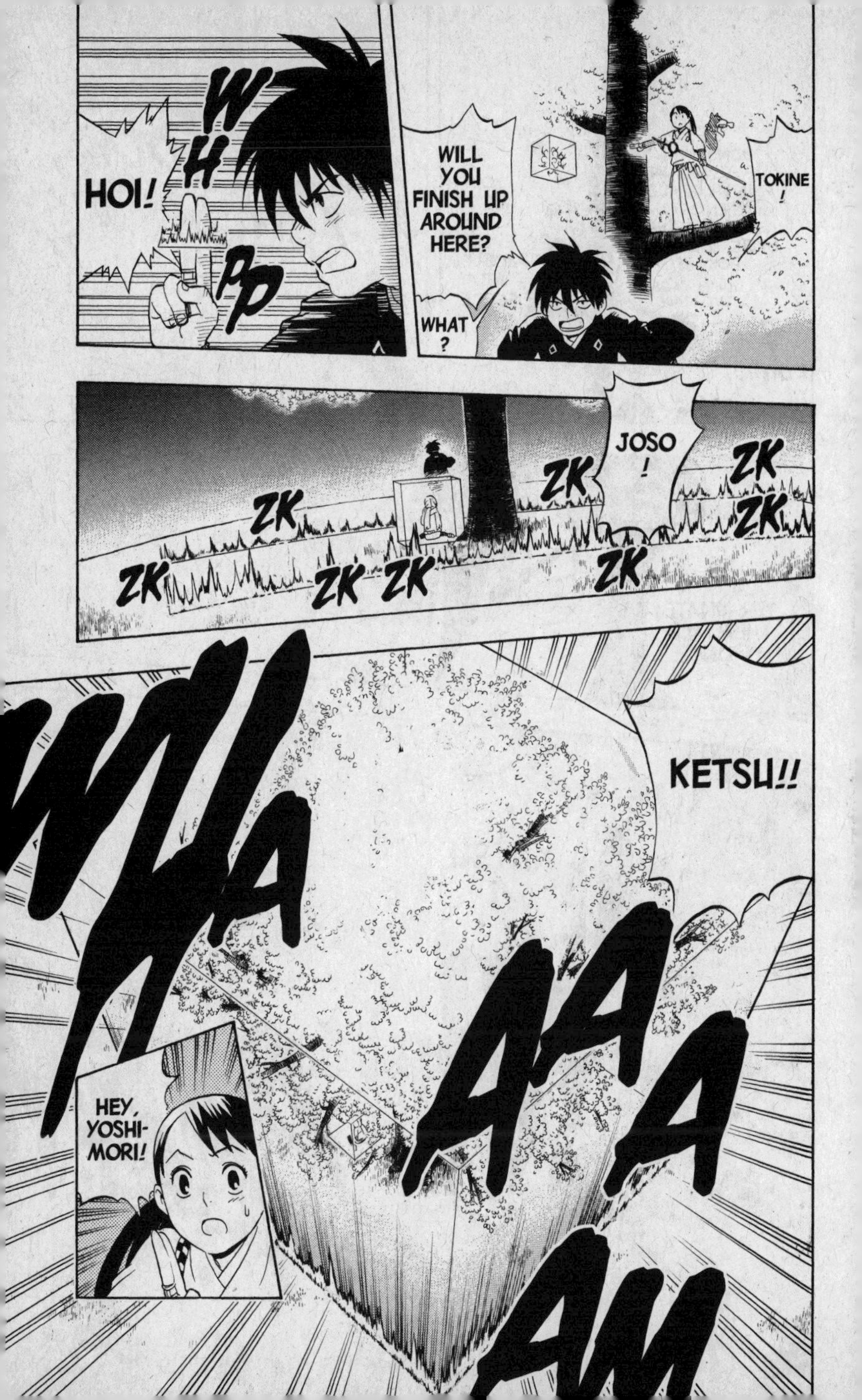
TOKINE!
WILL YOU FINISH UP AROUND HERE?
WHAT?
WHPP
HOI!
JOSO!
ZK ZK ZK ZK ZK ZK ZK ZK
KETSU!!
WHAAAAAAM
HEY, YOSHI-MORI!

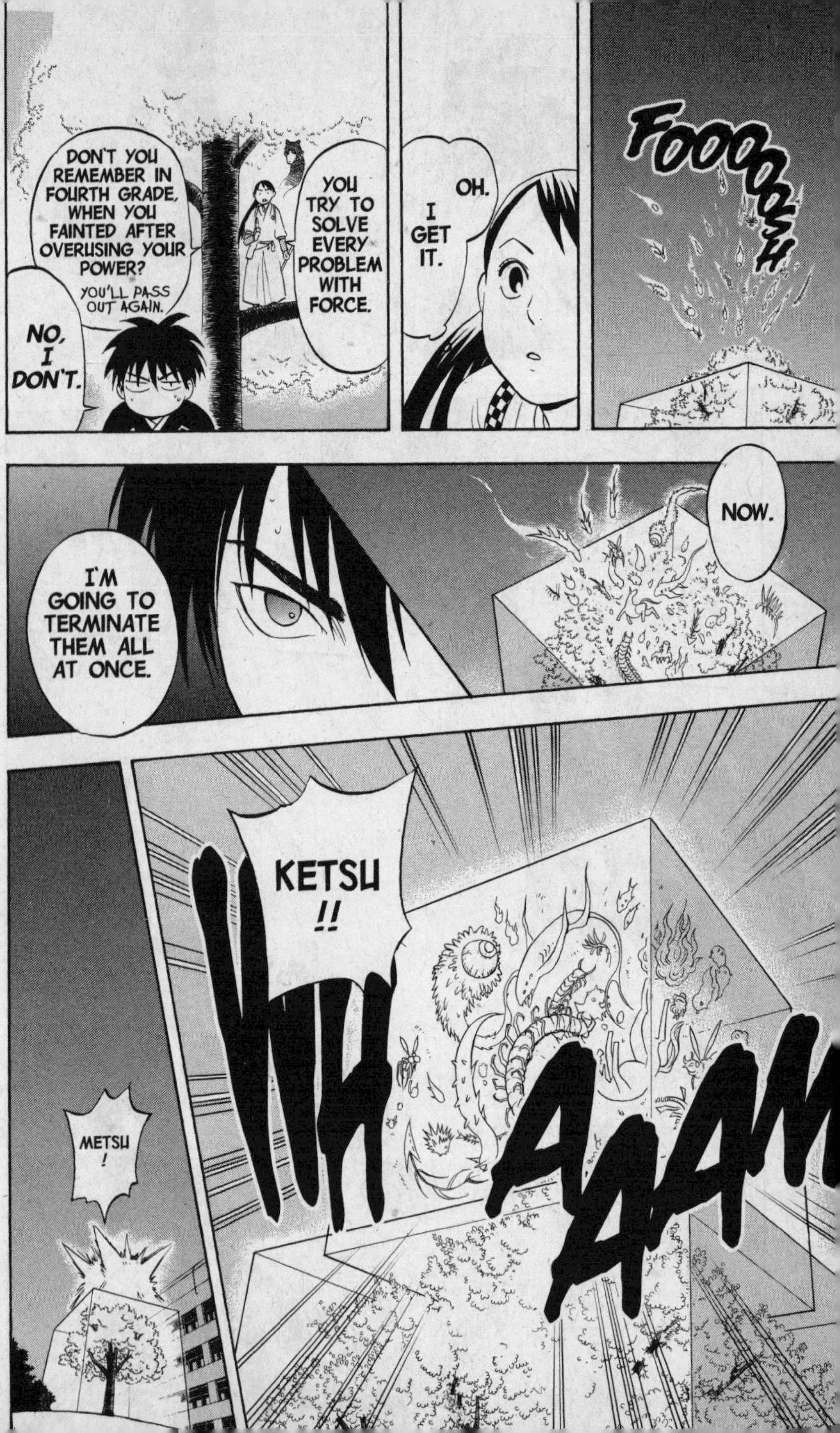
FOOOOOSH
OH.
I GET IT.
YOU TRY TO SOLVE EVERY PROBLEM WITH FORCE.
DON'T YOU REMEMBER IN FOURTH GRADE, WHEN YOU FAINTED AFTER OVERUSING YOUR POWER?
YOU'LL PASS OUT AGAIN.
NO, I DON'T.
NOW.
I'M GOING TO TERMINATE THEM ALL AT ONCE.
KETSU !!
WHAAAM
METSU !

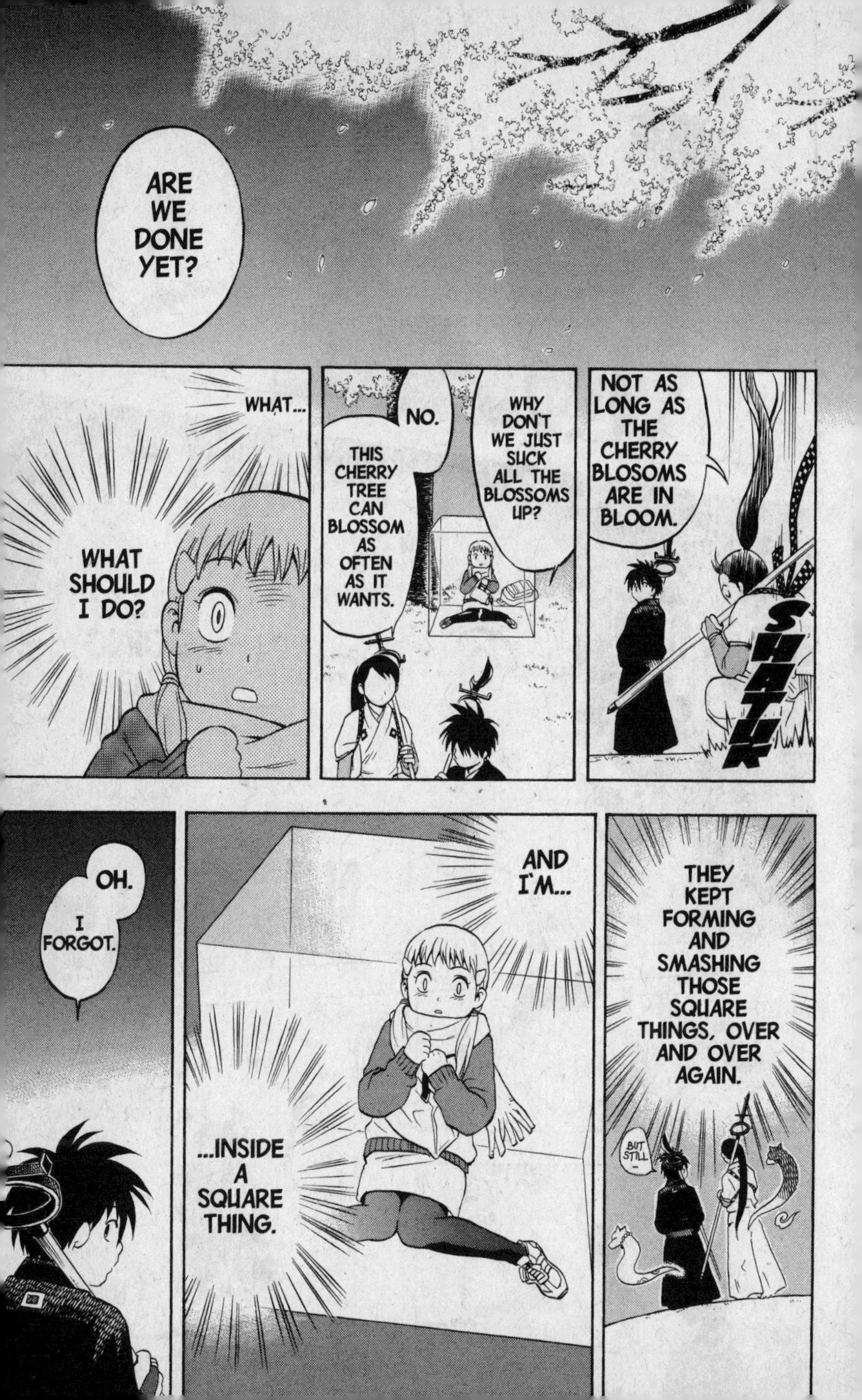
ARE WE DONE YET?
NOT AS LONG AS THE CHERRY BLOSOMS ARE IN BLOOM.
SHATUK
WHY DON'T WE JUST SUCK ALL THE BLOSSOMS UP?
NO.
THIS CHERRY TREE CAN BLOSSOM AS OFTEN AS IT WANTS.
WHAT...
WHAT SHOULD I DO?
THEY KEPT FORMING AND SMASHING THOSE SQUARE THINGS, OVER AND OVER AGAIN.
BUT STILL...
AND I'M...
...INSIDE A SQUARE THING.
OH.
I FORGOT.

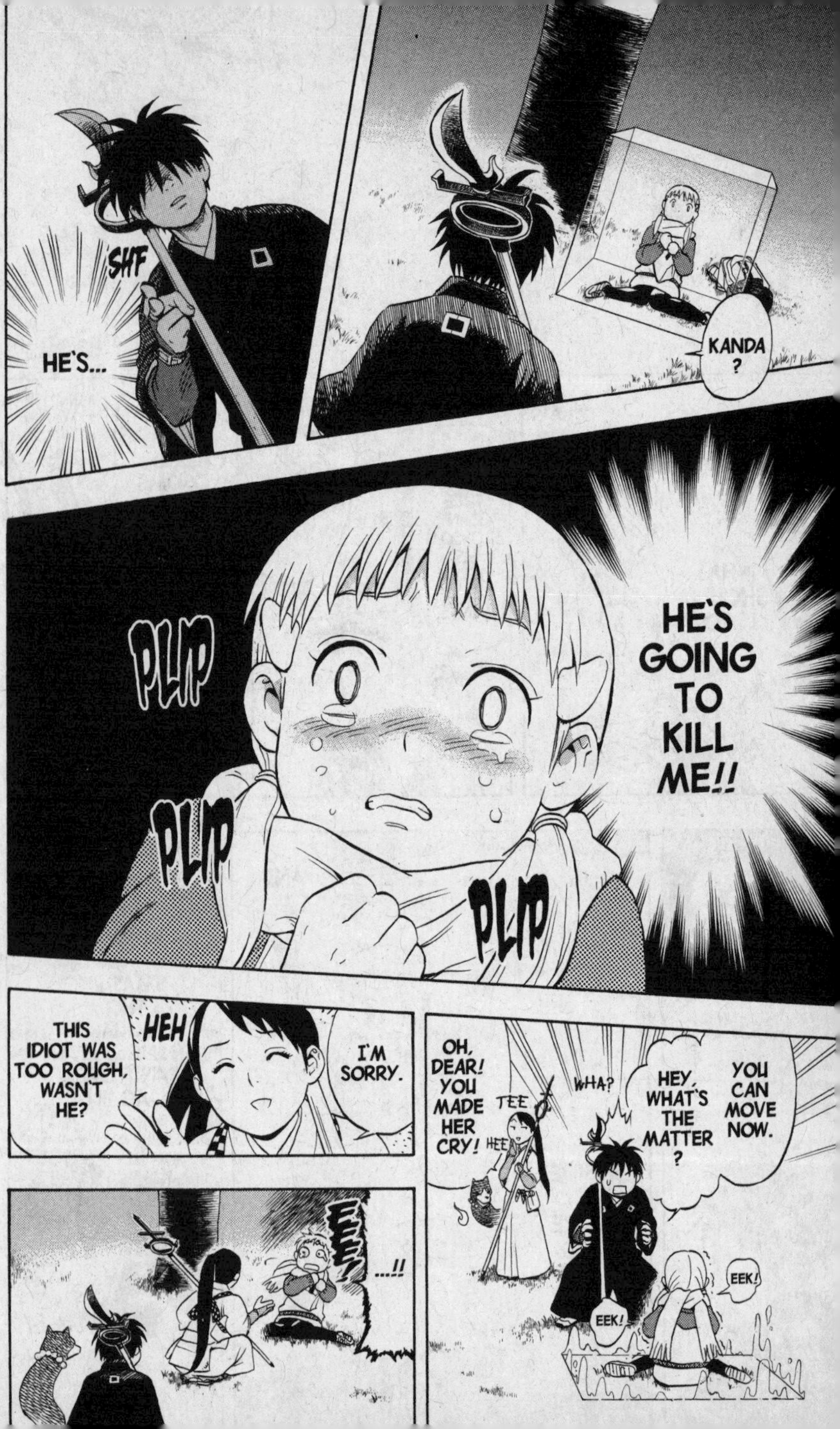
KANDA ?
SHF
HE'S...
PLIP
PLIP
PLIP
HE'S GOING TO KILL ME!!
YOU CAN MOVE NOW.
HEY, WHAT'S THE MATTER ?
WHA?
OH, DEAR! YOU MADE HER CRY!
TEE HEE
EEK!
EEK!
I'M SORRY.
HEH
THIS IDIOT WAS TOO ROUGH, WASN'T HE?
EEEE!
...!!

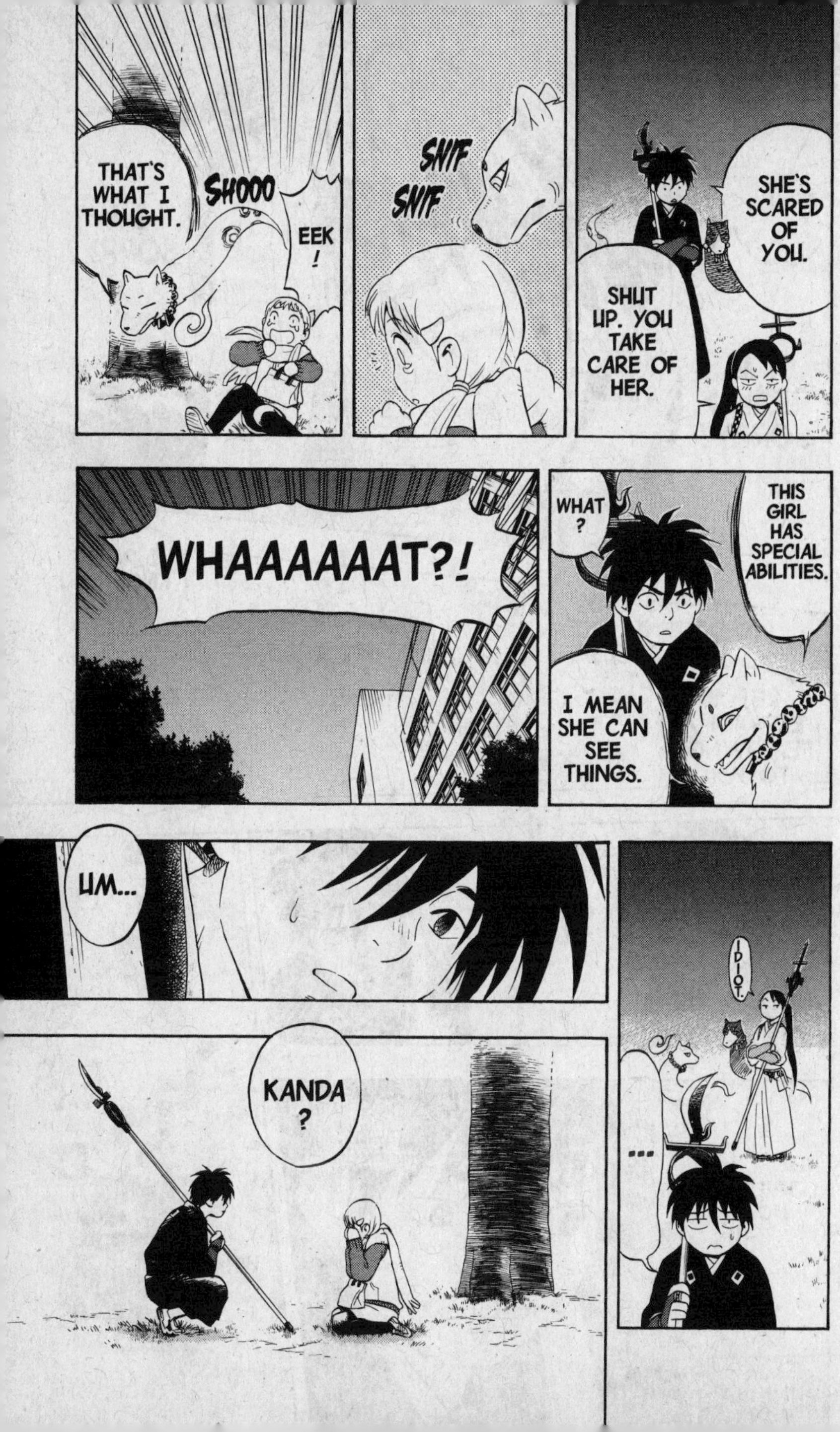
SHE'S SCARED OF YOU.
SHUT UP. YOU TAKE CARE OF HER.
SNIF
SNIF
THAT'S WHAT I THOUGHT.
SHOOO
EEK!
THIS GIRL HAS SPECIAL ABILITIES.
WHAT?
I MEAN SHE CAN SEE THINGS.
WHAAAAAAT?!
IDIOT.
...
UM...
KANDA?

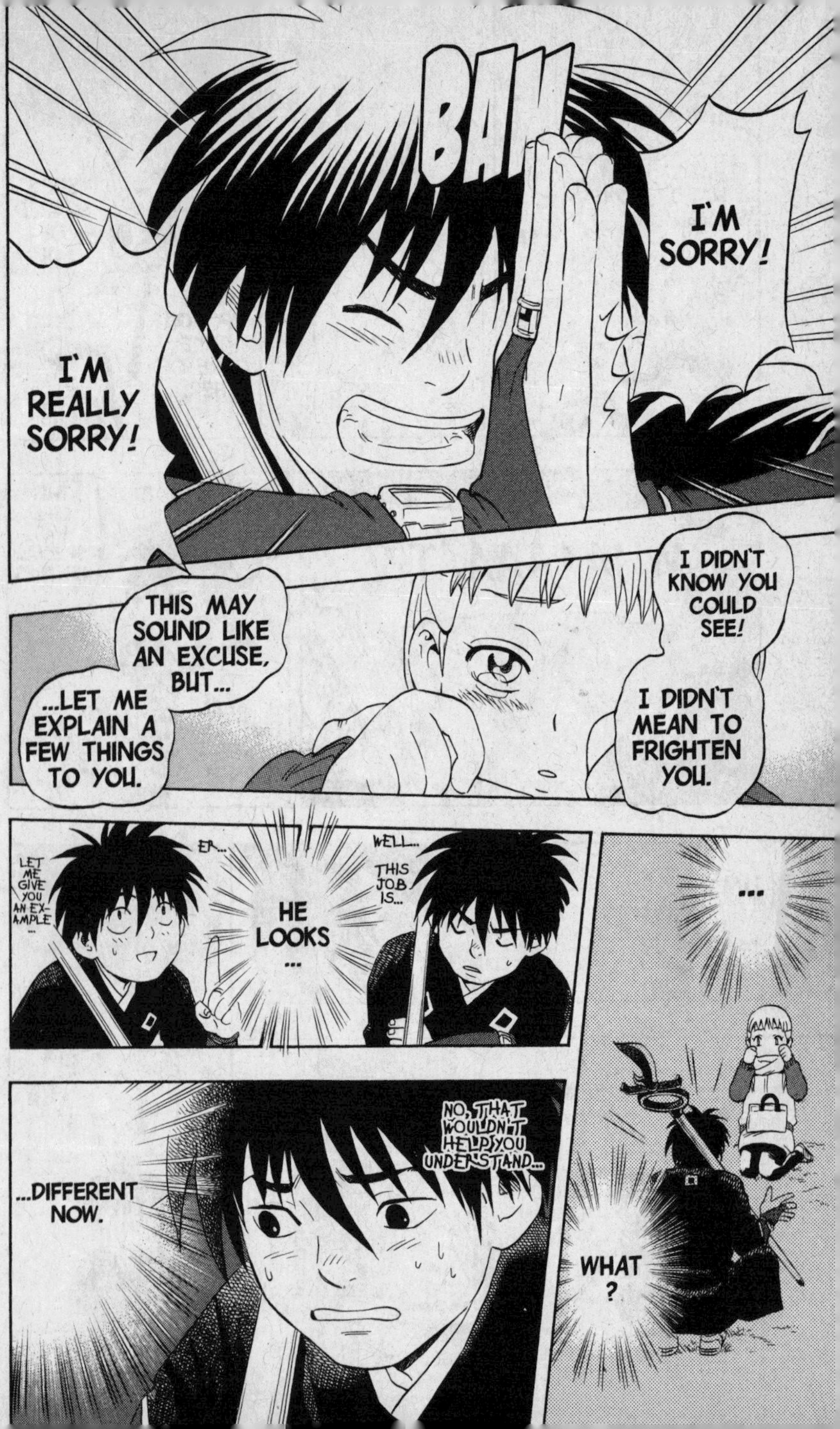
BAM
I'M SORRY!
I'M REALLY SORRY!
I DIDN'T KNOW YOU COULD SEE!
I DIDN'T MEAN TO FRIGHTEN YOU.
THIS MAY SOUND LIKE AN EXCUSE, BUT...
...LET ME EXPLAIN A FEW THINGS TO YOU.
...
WHAT ?
WELL... THIS JOB IS...
HE LOOKS ...
ER...
LET ME GIVE YOU AN EX-AMPLE ...
NO, THAT WOULDN'T HELP YOU UNDERSTAND...
...DIFFERENT NOW.

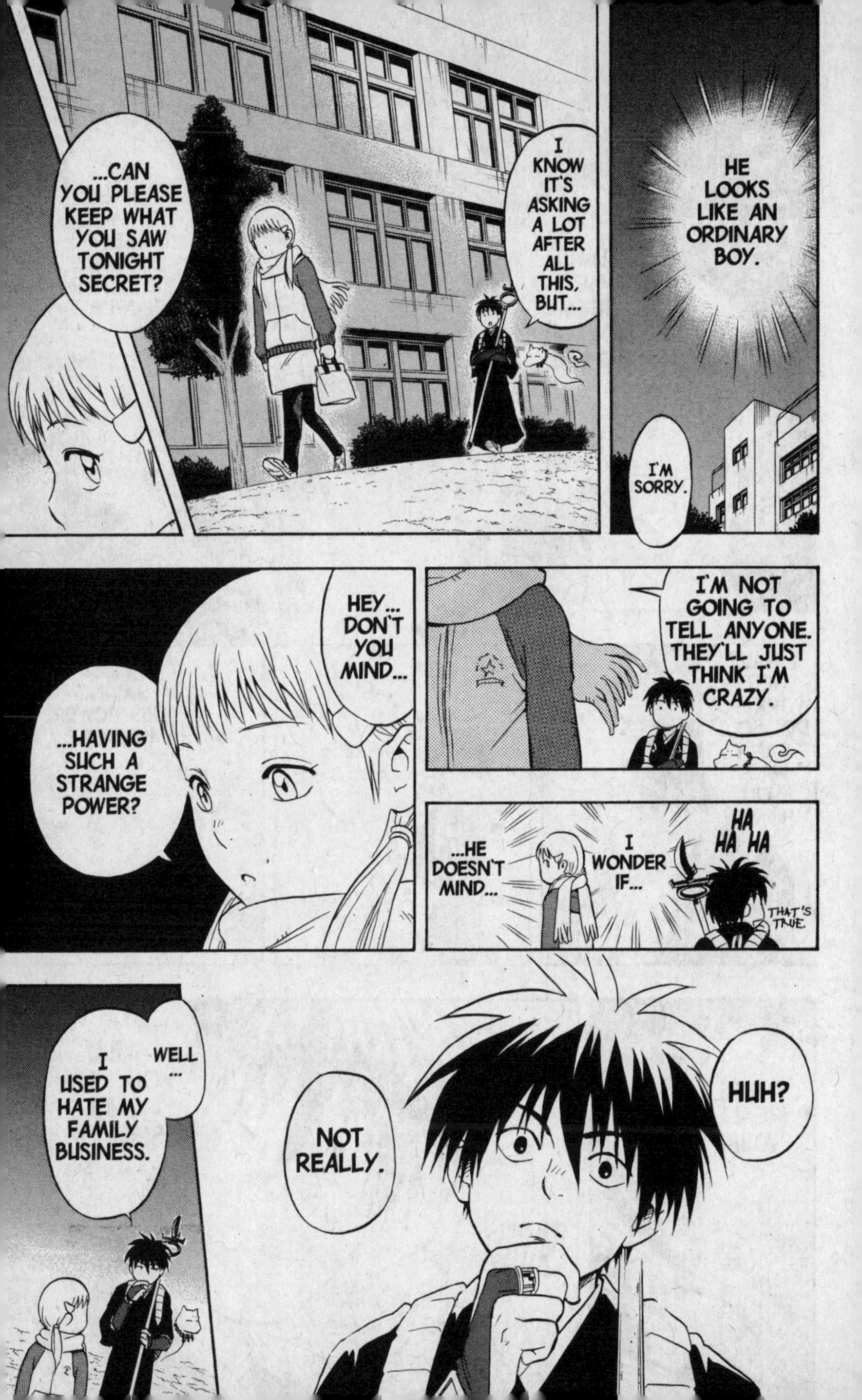
HE LOOKS LIKE AN ORDINARY BOY.
I'M SORRY.
I KNOW IT'S ASKING A LOT AFTER ALL THIS, BUT...
...CAN YOU PLEASE KEEP WHAT YOU SAW TONIGHT SECRET?
I'M NOT GOING TO TELL ANYONE. THEY'LL JUST THINK I'M CRAZY.
HA HA HA
THAT'S TRUE.
I WONDER IF...
...HE DOESN'T MIND...
HEY... DON'T YOU MIND...
...HAVING SUCH A STRANGE POWER?
HUH?
NOT REALLY.
WELL...
I USED TO HATE MY FAMILY BUSINESS.

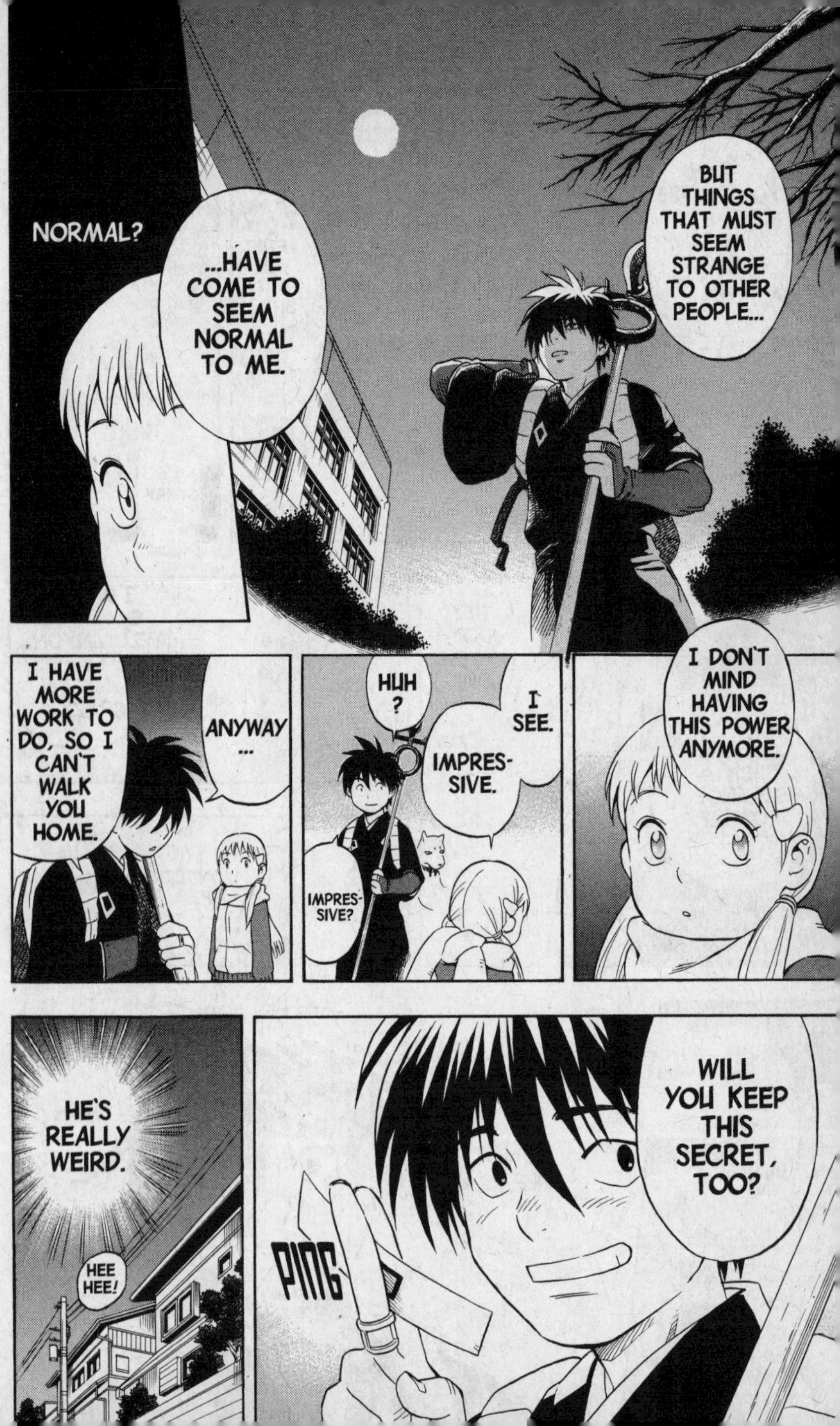
BUT THINGS THAT MUST SEEM STRANGE TO OTHER PEOPLE...
...HAVE COME TO SEEM NORMAL TO ME.
NORMAL?
I DON'T MIND HAVING THIS POWER ANYMORE.
I SEE.
IMPRES-SIVE.
HUH?
IMPRES-SIVE?
ANYWAY...
I HAVE MORE WORK TO DO, SO I CAN'T WALK YOU HOME.
WILL YOU KEEP THIS SECRET, TOO?
PING
HE'S REALLY WEIRD.
HEE HEE!

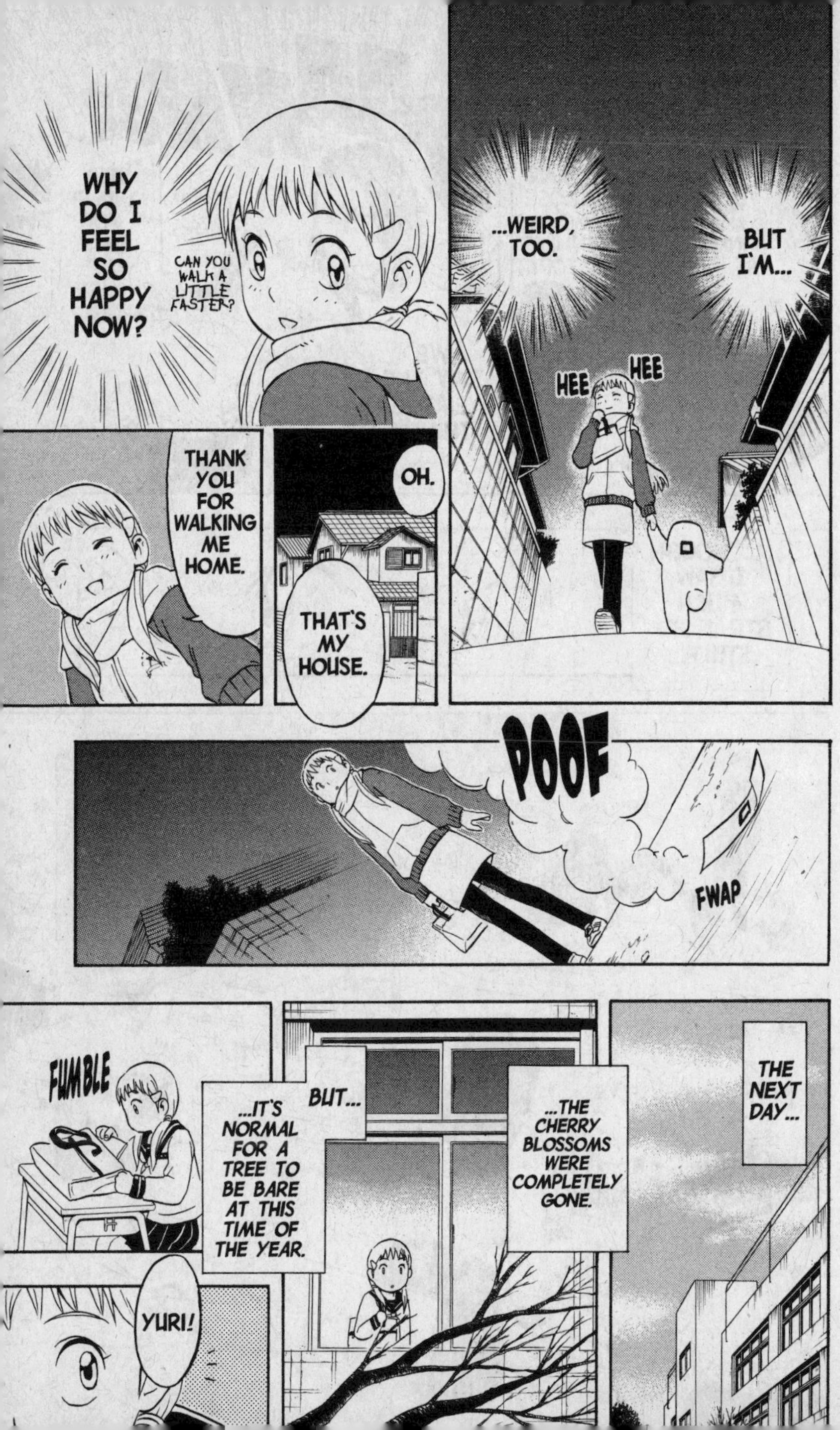
BUT I'M...
...WEIRD, TOO.
HEE HEE
WHY DO I FEEL SO HAPPY NOW?
CAN YOU WALK A LITTLE FASTER?
OH.
THAT'S MY HOUSE.
THANK YOU FOR WALKING ME HOME.
POOF
FWAP
THE NEXT DAY...
...THE CHERRY BLOSSOMS WERE COMPLETELY GONE.
BUT...
...IT'S NORMAL FOR A TREE TO BE BARE AT THIS TIME OF THE YEAR.
FUMBLE
YURI!

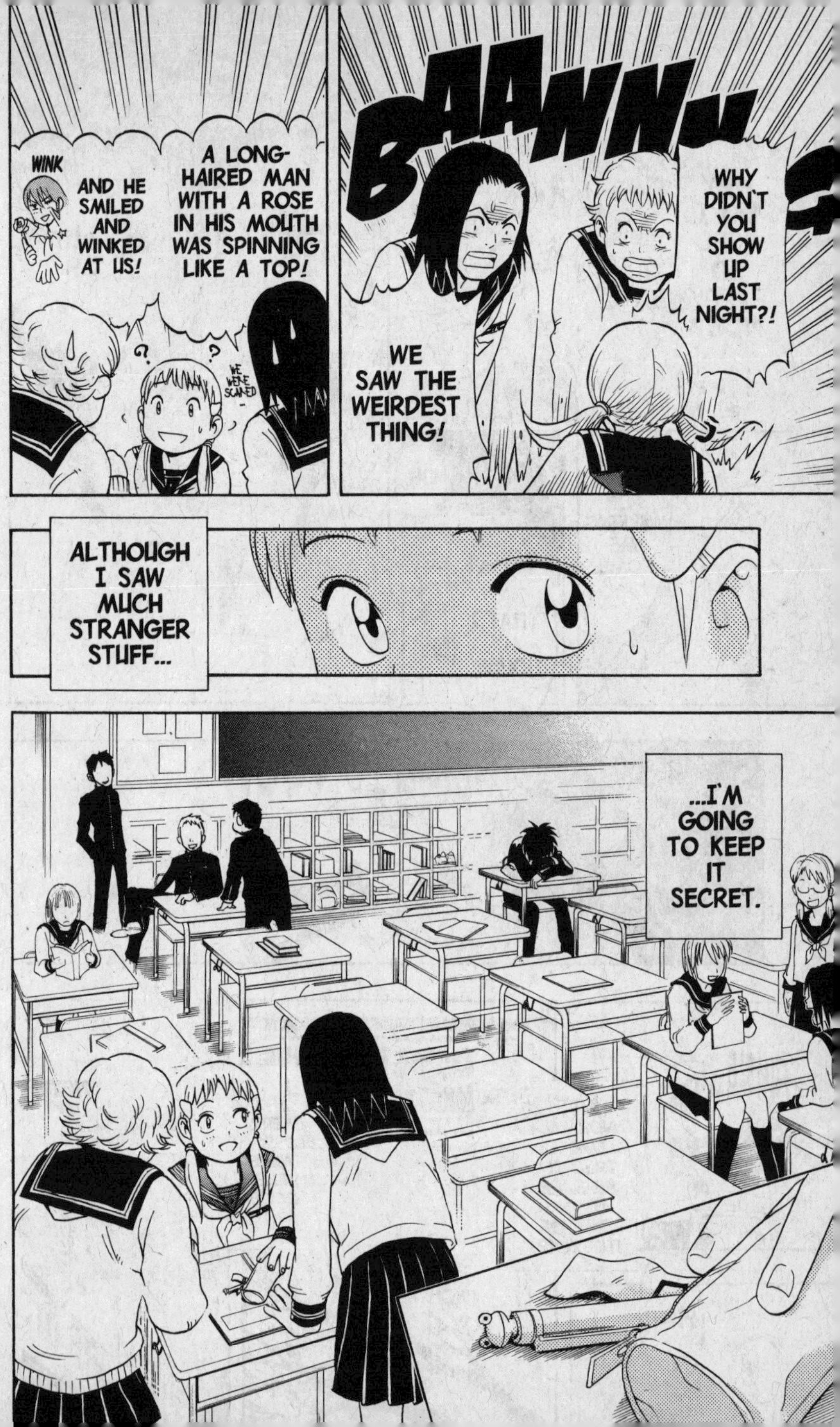

WHY DIDN'T YOU SHOW UP LAST NIGHT?!
WE SAW THE WEIRDEST THING!
A LONG-HAIRED MAN WITH A ROSE IN HIS MOUTH WAS SPINNING LIKE A TOP!
AND HE SMILED AND WINKED AT US!
WINK
WE WERE SCARED
ALTHOUGH I SAW MUCH STRANGER STUFF...
...I'M GOING TO KEEP IT SECRET.

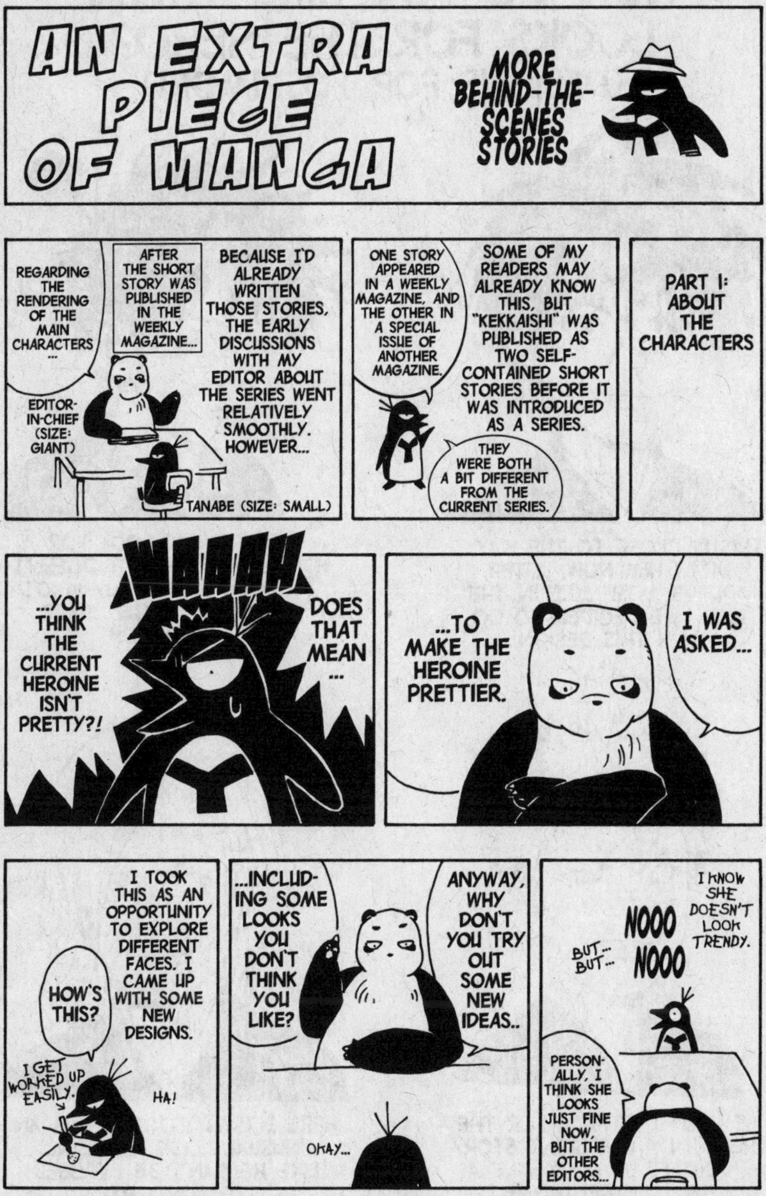
AN EXTRA PIECE OF MANGA
MORE BEHIND-THE-SCENES STORIES
PART 1: ABOUT THE CHARACTERS
SOME OF MY READERS MAY ALREADY KNOW THIS, BUT "KEKKAISHI" WAS PUBLISHED AS TWO SELF-CONTAINED SHORT STORIES BEFORE IT WAS INTRODUCED AS A SERIES.
ONE STORY APPEARED IN A WEEKLY MAGAZINE, AND THE OTHER IN A SPECIAL ISSUE OF ANOTHER MAGAZINE.
THEY WERE BOTH A BIT DIFFERENT FROM THE CURRENT SERIES.
BECAUSE I'D ALREADY WRITTEN THOSE STORIES, THE EARLY DISCUSSIONS WITH MY EDITOR ABOUT THE SERIES WENT RELATIVELY SMOOTHLY. HOWEVER...
AFTER THE SHORT STORY WAS PUBLISHED IN THE WEEKLY MAGAZINE...
REGARDING THE RENDERING OF THE MAIN CHARACTERS...
EDITOR-IN-CHIEF (SIZE: GIANT)
TANABE (SIZE: SMALL)
I WAS ASKED...
...TO MAKE THE HEROINE PRETTIER.
WAAAH
DOES THAT MEAN...
...YOU THINK THE CURRENT HEROINE ISN'T PRETTY?!
I KNOW SHE DOESN'T LOOK TRENDY.
NOOO NOOO
BUT... BUT...
PERSONALLY, I THINK SHE LOOKS JUST FINE NOW, BUT THE OTHER EDITORS...
ANYWAY, WHY DON'T YOU TRY OUT SOME NEW IDEAS..
...INCLUDING SOME LOOKS YOU DON'T THINK YOU LIKE?
OKAY...
I TOOK THIS AS AN OPPORTUNITY TO EXPLORE DIFFERENT FACES. I CAME UP WITH SOME NEW DESIGNS.
HOW'S THIS?
HA!
I GET WORKED UP EASILY.

HOW DO YOU LIKE THESE LOOKS FOR THE HERO?
(DESIGNS FOR YOSHIMORI)

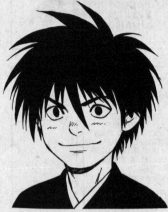

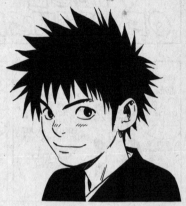

A TYPICAL LOOK FOR A MANGA HERO. IT DOESN'T LOOK LIKE A GUY WHO'D MAKE CASTLE CAKES, THOUGH.

THIS IS CLOSE TO THE WAY I DRAW HIM NOW. AFTER ADDING A TWINKLE IN THE EYES, WE DECIDED TO GO WITH THIS DESIGN.

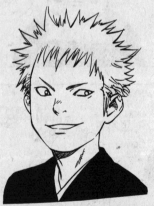

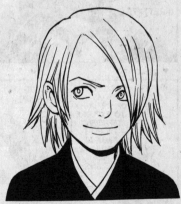

HERE I TRIED TO GIVE HIM AN UNUSUAL LOOK. HE LOOKS LIKE HE CAN'T BE EXPOSED TO SUNLIGHT.

I USED THIS FACE FOR THE HERO IN A DIFFERENT STORY. DOESN'T HE LOOK LIKE A JUVENILE DELINQUENT, THOUGH?

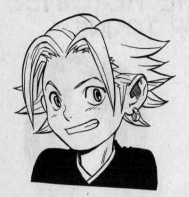

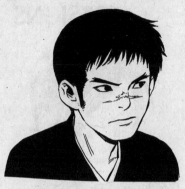

I DON'T LIKE AN EIGHTH-GRADER TO LOOK AS SAVAGE AS THIS.

THIS IS A CUTESY LITTLE TYPE. TOO MUCH LIKE AN ANIME CHARACTER, HUH?

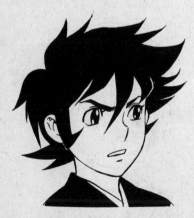

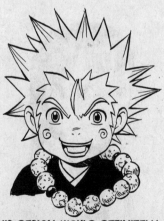

THIS DESIGN WOULD DEFINITELY BE FOR YOUNGER READERS THAN OUR TARGET AUDIENCE. HE LOOKS LIKE THE SORT OF ANIME CHARACTER WHO TRAVELS TO OTHER WORLDS.

DOESN'T THIS LOOK LIKE A CHARACTER IN AN OLD-TIMEY ANIME? IT HAS KIND OF A RETRO APPEAL. THE SIDEBURNS WOULD BE REVIVED LATER IN THE SERIES.

HOW DO YOU LIKE THESE LOOKS FOR THE HEROINE?
(DESIGNS FOR TOKINE)

THIS IS THE CLOSEST DESIGN TO THE ONE I CURRENTLY USE. I ENDED UP MAKING TOKINE LOOK A LITTLE OLDER THAN THIS.

THIS HAS THE LOOK OF AN OLD CHILDHOOD FRIEND, DOESN'T IT? THIS WAS A STRONG POSSIBILITY FOR TOKINE.

THIS HAS THE LOOK OF A GOOD GIRL FROM A TRADITIONAL FAMILY. SHE RADIATES TRADITION AND FORMALITY.

I PERSONALLY THINK THIS ONE LOOKS TOO YOUNG, BUT IT COULD BE A POSSIBLE CHOICE. SHE DOESN'T LOOK OLDER THAN YOSHIMORI AT ALL, THOUGH.

THIS IS A "RETRO GIRLY" STYLE (WHATEVER THAT MEANS). YOU DON'T USUALLY FIND THIS TYPE IN BOYS' MANGA, THOUGH.

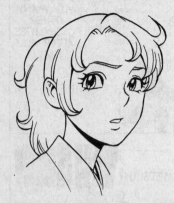

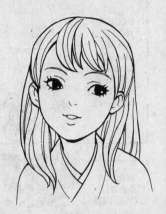

THIS IS A DESIGN YOU'D OFTEN FIND IN OLD ANIME. MY EDITOR TOLD ME THAT SHE LOOKS LIKE A WOMAN IN AN OLD-FASHIONED EROTIC MANGA. DO YOU THINK SO?

THIS ONE IS ABSOLUTELY NOT FOR BOYS' MANGA. SHE'D BE TOO MUCH FOR YOSHIMORI TO HANDLE. DOESN'T THIS GIRL LOOK VERY JAPANESE, THOUGH?

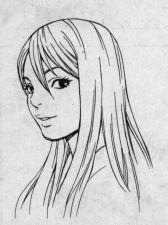

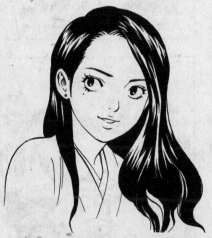

IN AMERICAN COMIC BOOKS, YOU SEE THIS TYPE VERY OFTEN. HOWEVER, SHE MIGHT LOOK TOO GROWN-UP FOR TOKINE'S CHARACTER.

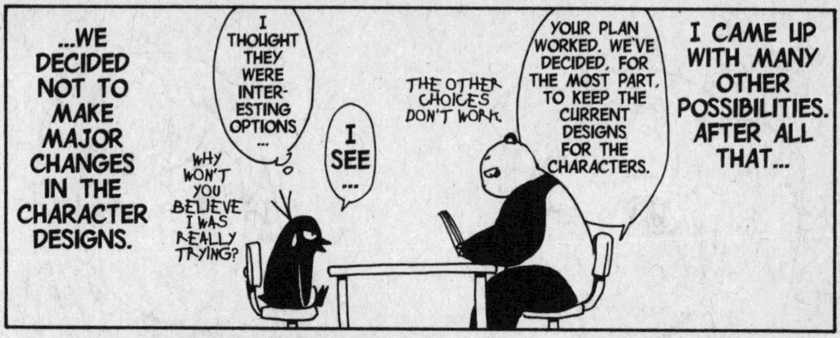
I CAME UP WITH MANY OTHER POSSIBILITIES. AFTER ALL THAT...
YOUR PLAN WORKED. WE'VE DECIDED, FOR THE MOST PART, TO KEEP THE CURRENT DESIGNS FOR THE CHARACTERS.
THE OTHER CHOICES DON'T WORK.
I SEE...
I THOUGHT THEY WERE INTERESTING OPTIONS...
WHY WON'T YOU BELIEVE I WAS REALLY TRYING?
...WE DECIDED NOT TO MAKE MAJOR CHANGES IN THE CHARACTER DESIGNS.

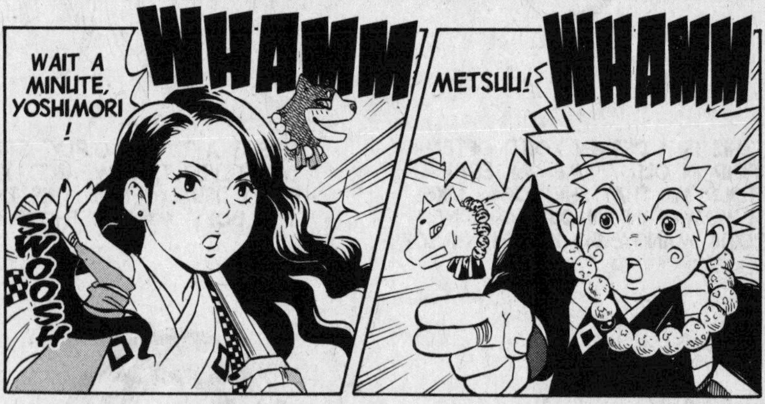
WHAMM
METSUU!
WHAMM
WAIT A MINUTE, YOSHIMORI!
SWOOSH

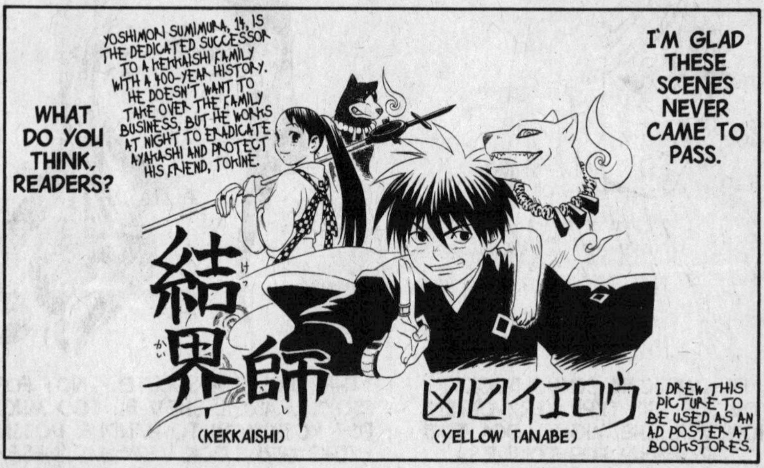
I'M GLAD THESE SCENES NEVER CAME TO PASS.
YOSHIMORI SUMIMURA, 14, IS THE DEDICATED SUCCESSOR TO A KEKKAISHI FAMILY WITH A 400-YEAR HISTORY. HE DOESN'T WANT TO TAKE OVER THE FAMILY BUSINESS, BUT HE WORKS AT NIGHT TO ERADICATE AYAKASHI AND PROTECT HIS FRIEND, TOKINE.
WHAT DO YOU THINK, READERS?
結界師
(KEKKAISHI)
田辺イエロウ
(YELLOW TANABE)
I DREW THIS PICTURE TO BE USED AS AN AD POSTER AT BOOKSTORES.

PART 2: ABOUT THE KEKKAISHI MAGIC
THE CONCEPT OF THE "KEKKAI" (PROTECTIVE WARD) HAS EXISTED IN JAPAN SINCE ANCIENT TIMES. KEKKAI JUTSU IS MY IDEA.
I CREATED THE TERM.
NORMALLY, A KEKKAI IS CONSIDERED SOMETHING LIKE A BARRIER OR SHIELD...
...THAT PROTECTS A PERSON OR ENCLOSES UNWANTED OBJECTS.
COO COO
HE'S DEFENDING HIMSELF.
HOW-EVER...
CAN'T WE FIGHT A BATTLE USING KEKKAI?
...AFTER HAVING THIS THOUGHT, I CAME UP WITH THE IDEA OF USING KEKKAI OFFENSIVELY AS WELL AS DEFENSIVELY.
THERE I CHOSE MY FAVORITE CUBIC AND RECTANGULAR PARALLELE-PIPED SHAPES FOR MY KEKKAI.
SHING
THE SHAPE IS SIMPLE AND PRACTICAL.
ALTHOUGH NOT TOO EXOTIC.
AFTER DETERMINING THE SHAPE OF THE KEKKAI, I INVENTED THE FOLLOWING KEKKAI MECHANISM.
"HOI" DESIGNATES THE TARGET.
VMM
"JOSO" DETERMINES THE LOCATION.
ZK
ZK
"KETSU" FORMS AND ACTIVATES A KEKKAI SHIELD.
I NAMED EACH STEP ACCORDINGLY.
WHAM
THE PROCEDURE RESEMBLES THE METHOD OF DRAWING A THREE-DIMENSIONAL SHAPE: LENGTH, WIDTH, AND HEIGHT.

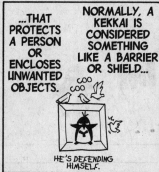

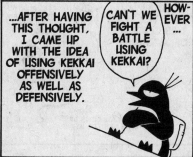

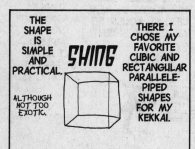

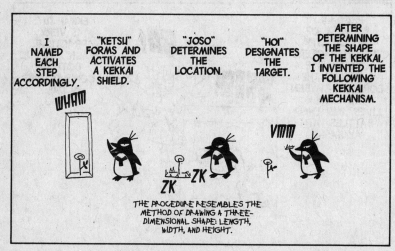

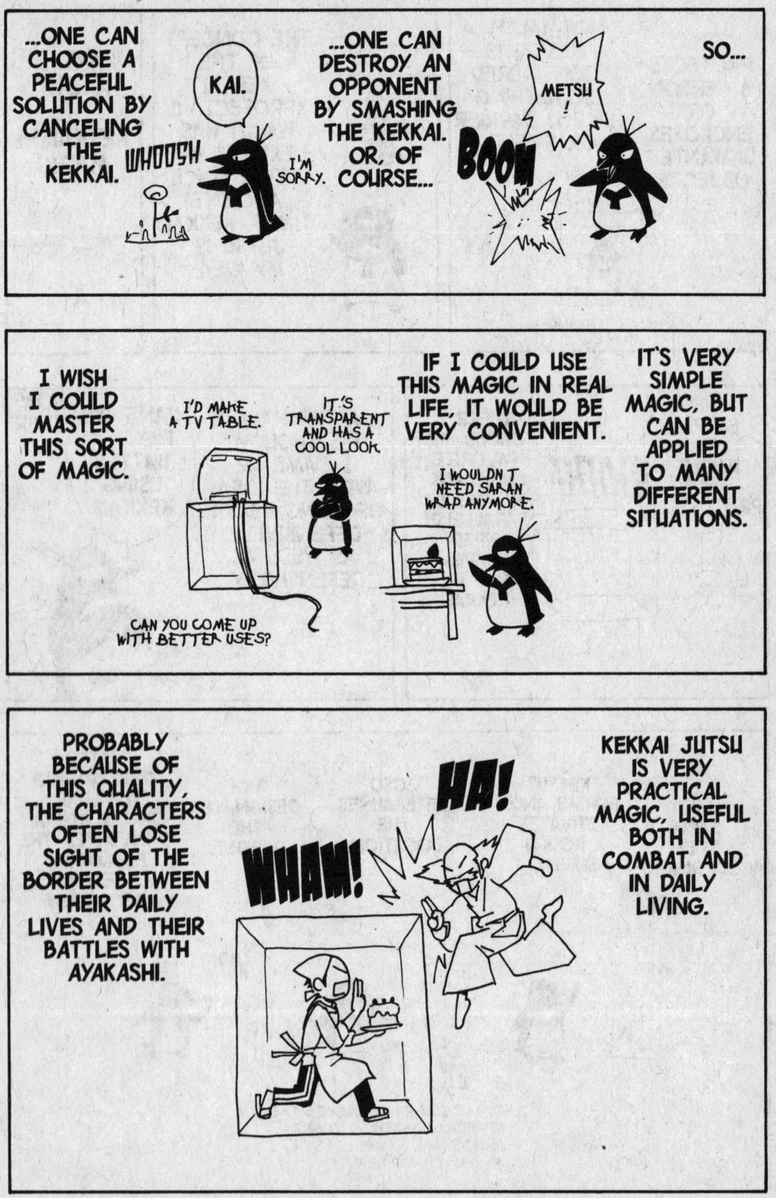
SO...
METSU!
BOOM
...ONE CAN DESTROY AN OPPONENT BY SMASHING THE KEKKAI. OR, OF COURSE...
I'M SORRY.
KAI.
...ONE CAN CHOOSE A PEACEFUL SOLUTION BY CANCELING THE KEKKAI.
WHOOSH
IT'S VERY SIMPLE MAGIC, BUT CAN BE APPLIED TO MANY DIFFERENT SITUATIONS.
IF I COULD USE THIS MAGIC IN REAL LIFE, IT WOULD BE VERY CONVENIENT.
I WOULDN'T NEED SARAN WRAP ANYMORE.
IT'S TRANSPARENT AND HAS A COOL LOOK.
I'D MAKE A TV TABLE.
I WISH I COULD MASTER THIS SORT OF MAGIC.
CAN YOU COME UP WITH BETTER USES?
KEKKAI JUTSU IS VERY PRACTICAL MAGIC, USEFUL BOTH IN COMBAT AND IN DAILY LIVING.
HA!
WHAM!
PROBABLY BECAUSE OF THIS QUALITY, THE CHARACTERS OFTEN LOSE SIGHT OF THE BORDER BETWEEN THEIR DAILY LIVES AND THEIR BATTLES WITH AYAKASHI.

WATERING THE PLANTS WITH A WATER BOTTLE
THAT SHOULD BE USED FOR MY PAINTS.

MESSAGE FROM YELLOW TANABE

On the morning *Kekkaishi* volume 1 went on sale, a pot of orchids was delivered to my house. It was a gift from a relative of mine, celebrating the title's release.

I was caught unprepared for such a thing and screamed, "It's...it's orchids!!"

Later, another flower shop phoned to tell me that they were delivering flowers to my house. The sender's name was unfamiliar to me. As I waited nervously, the flowers arrived. I screamed, "Orchids again!" It turned out to be another relative of mine (whom I don't know) sending more orchids.

Thank you, everyone.

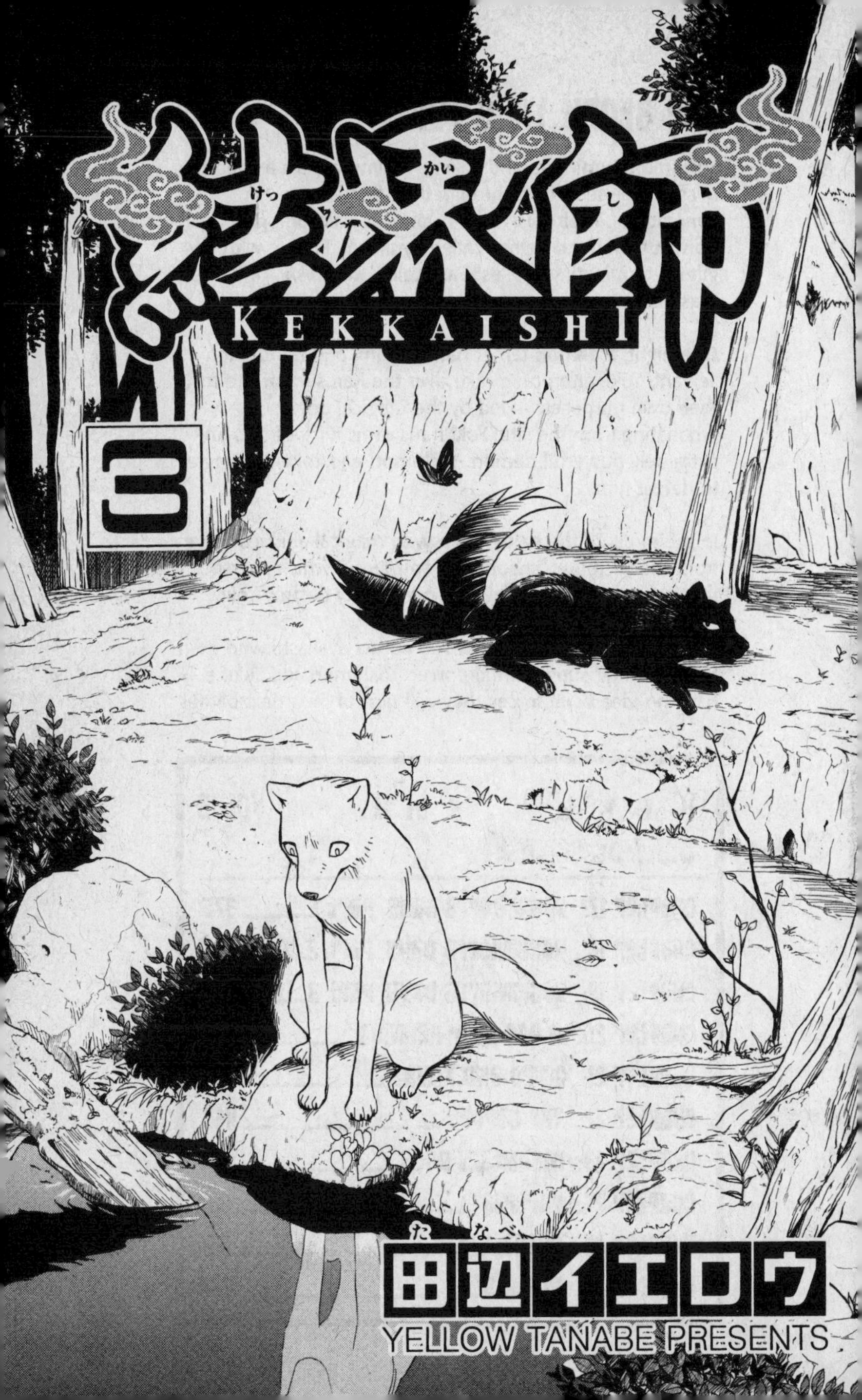
結界師
KEKKAISHI
3
田辺イエロウ
YELLOW TANABE PRESENTS

The Story Thus Far

Yoshimori Sumimura and Tokine Yukimura have a special mission, passed down through their families for generations. Their mission is to protect Karasumori forest from supernatural beings called *ayakashi*. People with this gift for terminating ayakashi are called *kekkaishi*, or barrier masters.

One night, a demon tamer named Yomi and her demon servant, Yoki, attempt to take over the Karasumori site for their own purposes. Aided by the magical power emanating from the site, Yoki transforms himself into an extremely powerful demon. Yoshimori and Tokine struggle to defeat him.

In the midst of the battle, men with magical abilities arrive from the secretive "shadow organization," which oversees the work of the kekkaishi, and mercilessly destroy Yoki.

The Karasumori site continues to attract ayakashi who wish to boost their supernatural power. Yoshimori and Tokine have no idea what forces they will face in their next battle!

KEKKAISHI VOL. 3

TABLE OF CONTENTS

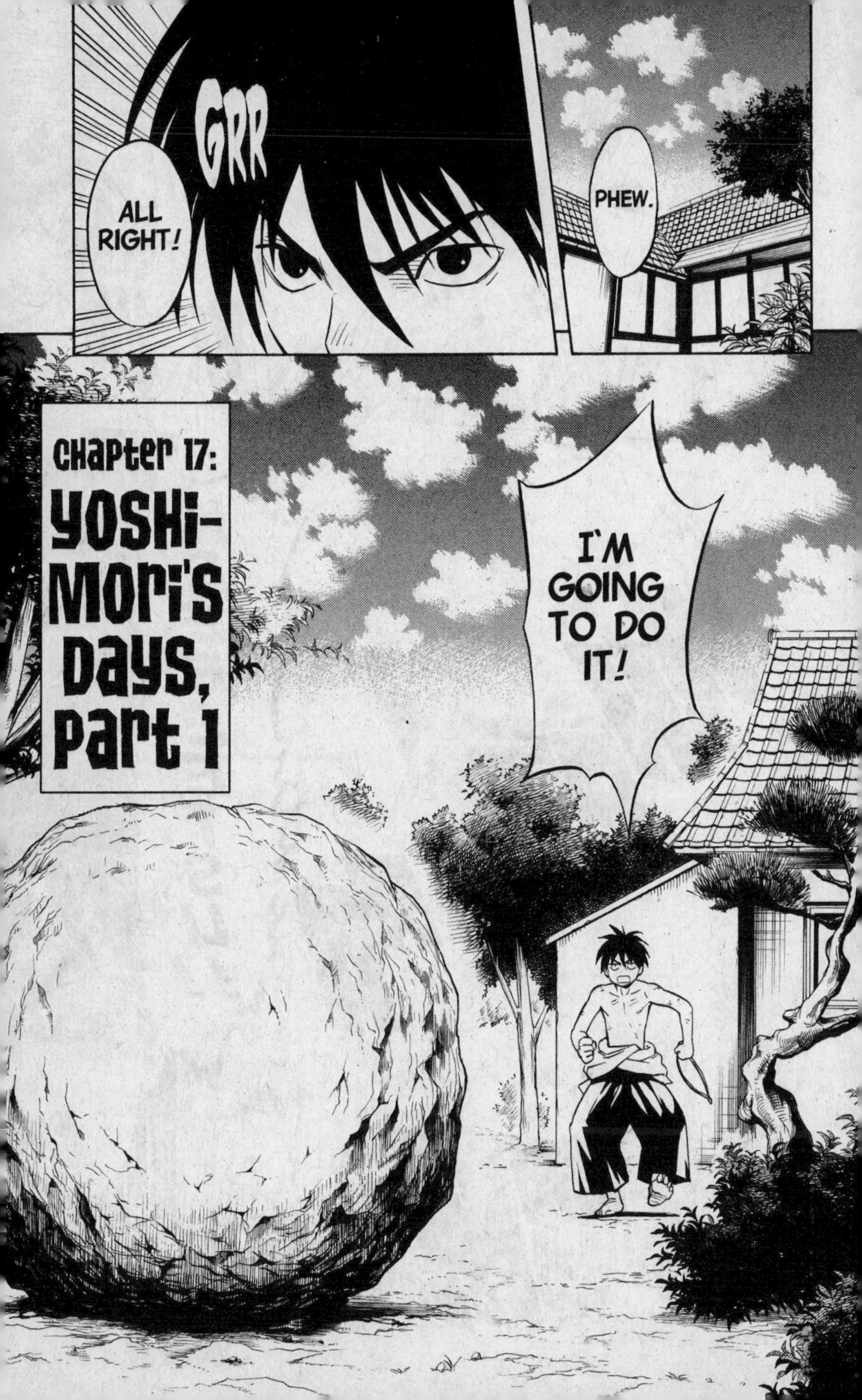
PHEW.
GRR
ALL RIGHT!
I'M GOING TO DO IT!
Chapter 17: Yoshimori's Days, Part 1

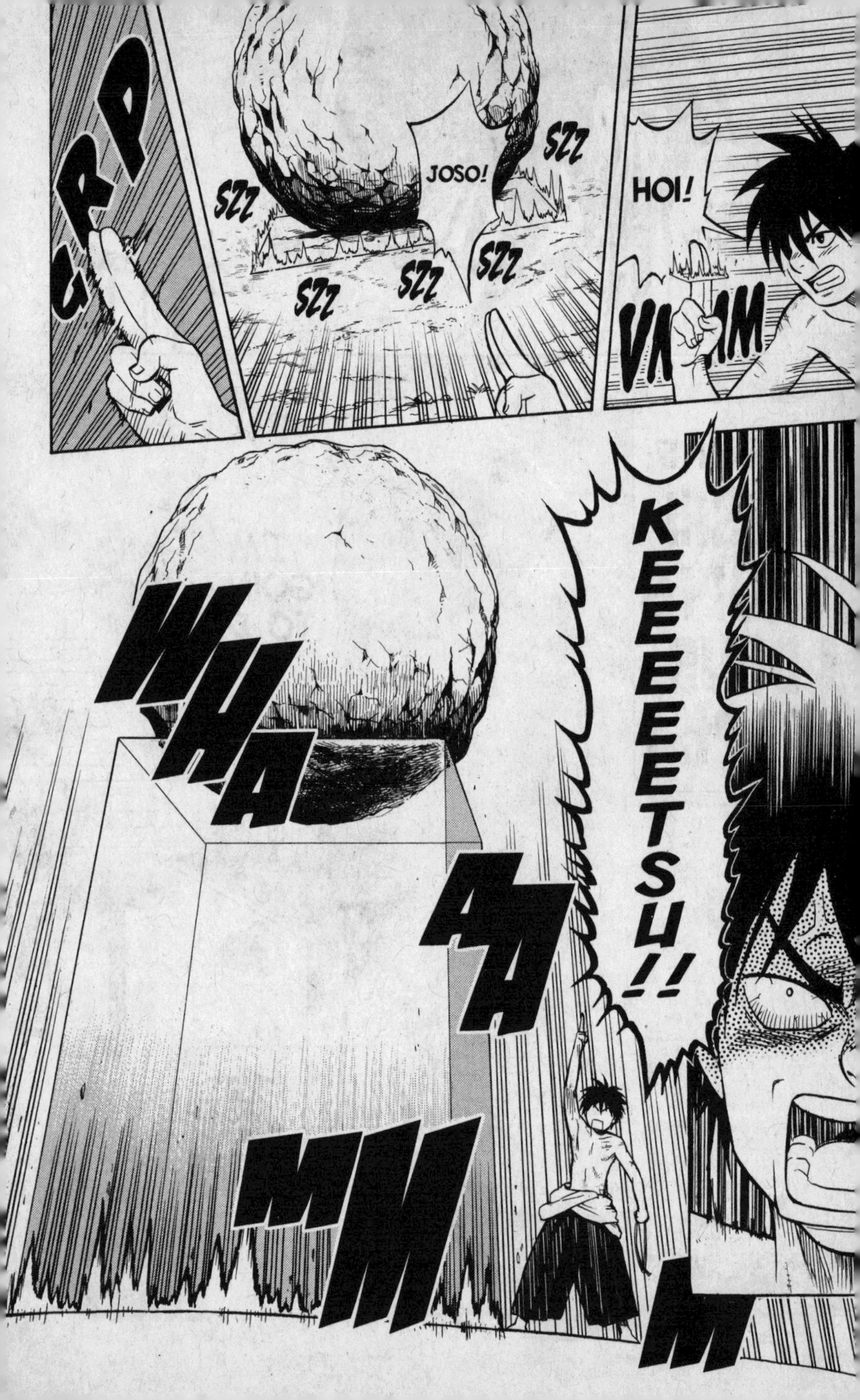
HOI!
VA AM
JOSO!
SZZ
SZZ
SZZ
SZZ
SZZ
GRP
KEEEEETSU!!
WHAAAMMMM

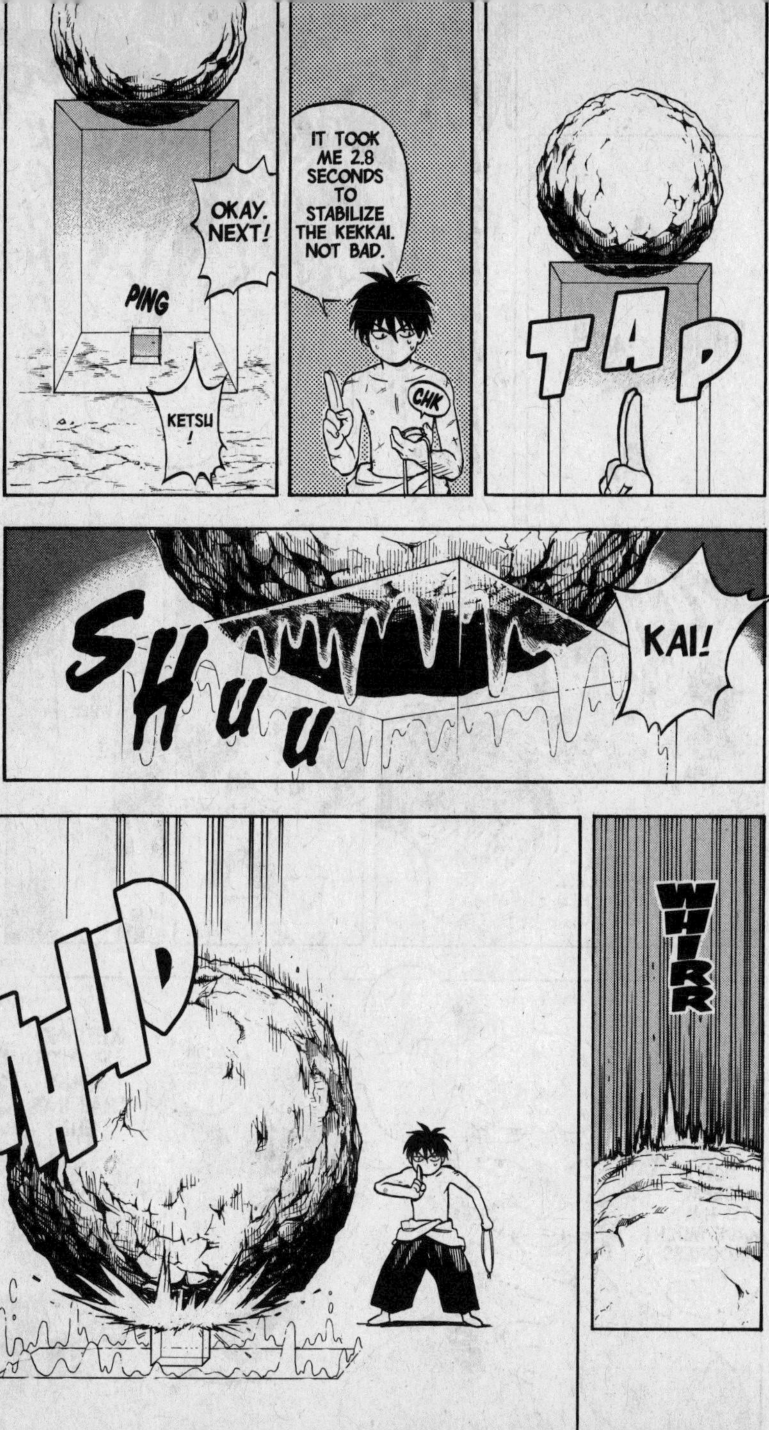
TAP
IT TOOK ME 2.8 SECONDS TO STABILIZE THE KEKKAI. NOT BAD.
CHK
OKAY. NEXT!
PING
KETSU!
KAI!
SHUUU
WHIRR
THUD

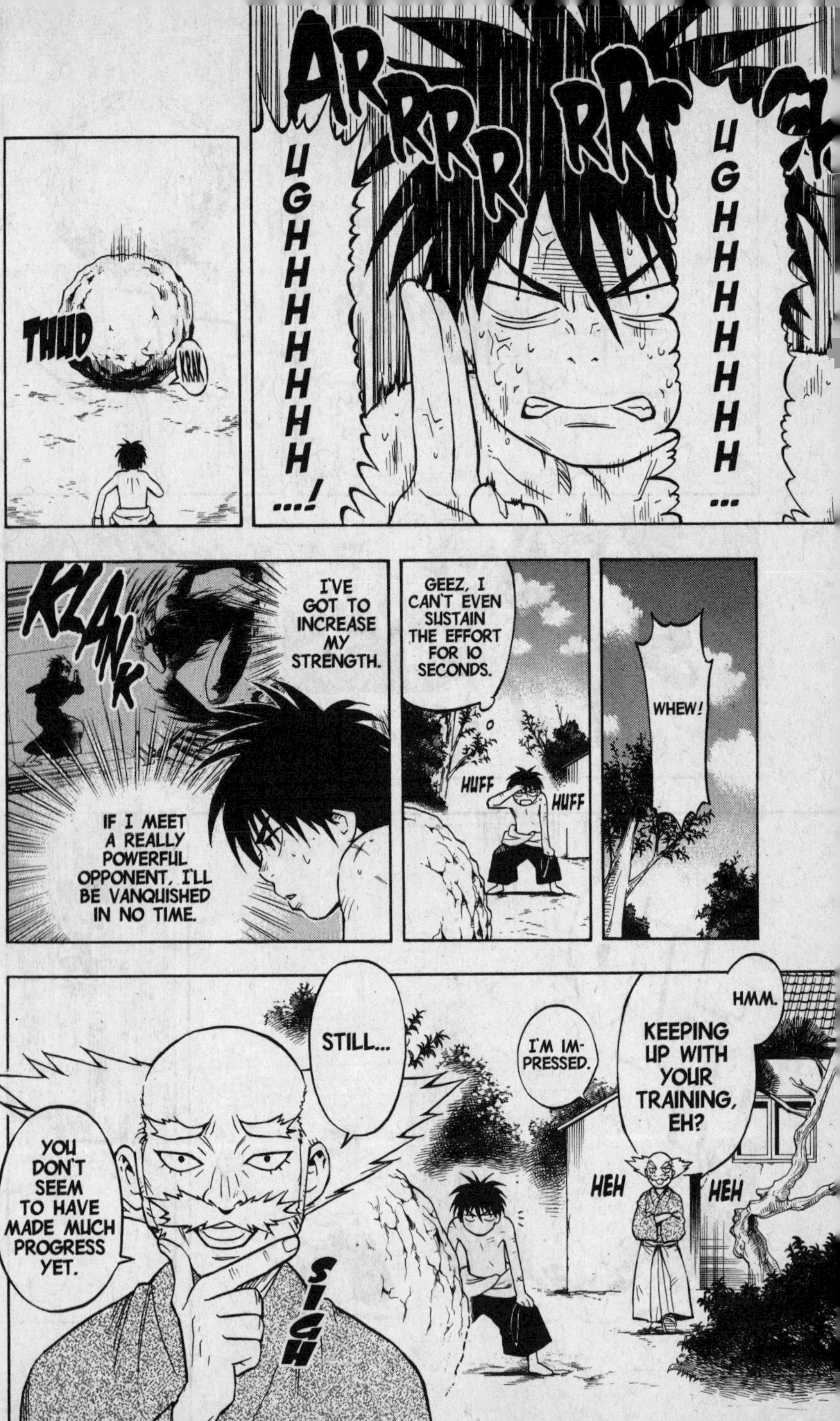

UGHHHHHHH...
UGHHHHHHH...!
THUD
KRAK
WHEW!
GEEZ, I CAN'T EVEN SUSTAIN THE EFFORT FOR 10 SECONDS.
HUFF
HUFF
I'VE GOT TO INCREASE MY STRENGTH.
IF I MEET A REALLY POWERFUL OPPONENT, I'LL BE VANQUISHED IN NO TIME.
KLANK
HMM.
KEEPING UP WITH YOUR TRAINING, EH?
HEH
HEH
I'M IMPRESSED.
STILL...
YOU DON'T SEEM TO HAVE MADE MUCH PROGRESS YET.
SIGH

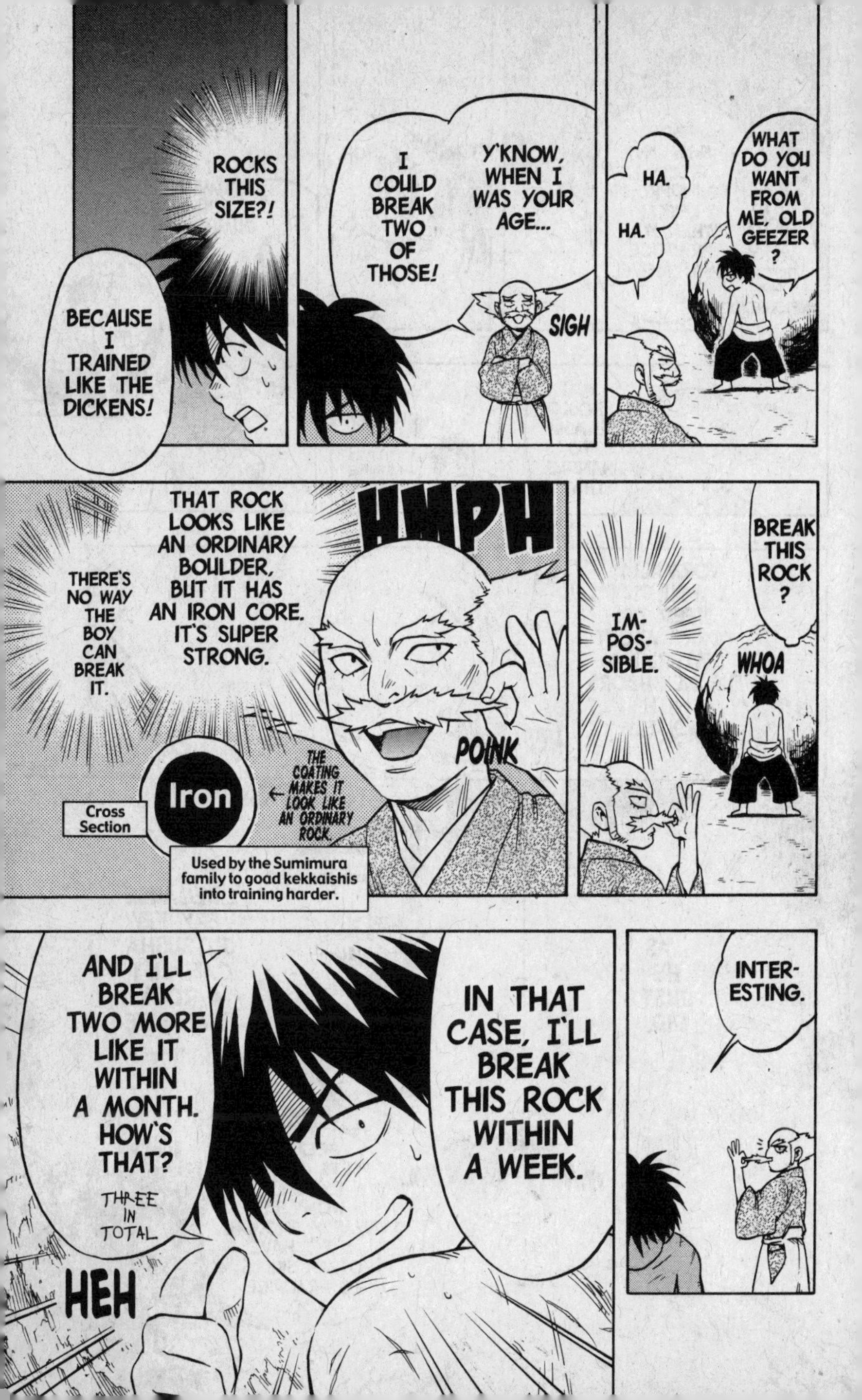
WHAT DO YOU WANT FROM ME, OLD GEEZER?
HA.
HA.
Y'KNOW, WHEN I WAS YOUR AGE...
I COULD BREAK TWO OF THOSE!
SIGH
ROCKS THIS SIZE?!
BECAUSE I TRAINED LIKE THE DICKENS!
BREAK THIS ROCK?
WHOA
IM-POS-SIBLE.
HMPH
THAT ROCK LOOKS LIKE AN ORDINARY BOULDER, BUT IT HAS AN IRON CORE. IT'S SUPER STRONG.
THERE'S NO WAY THE BOY CAN BREAK IT.
POINK
Iron
← THE COATING MAKES IT LOOK LIKE AN ORDINARY ROCK.
Cross Section
Used by the Sumimura family to goad kekkaishis into training harder.
INTER-ESTING.
IN THAT CASE, I'LL BREAK THIS ROCK WITHIN A WEEK.
AND I'LL BREAK TWO MORE LIKE IT WITHIN A MONTH. HOW'S THAT?
THREE IN TOTAL
HEH

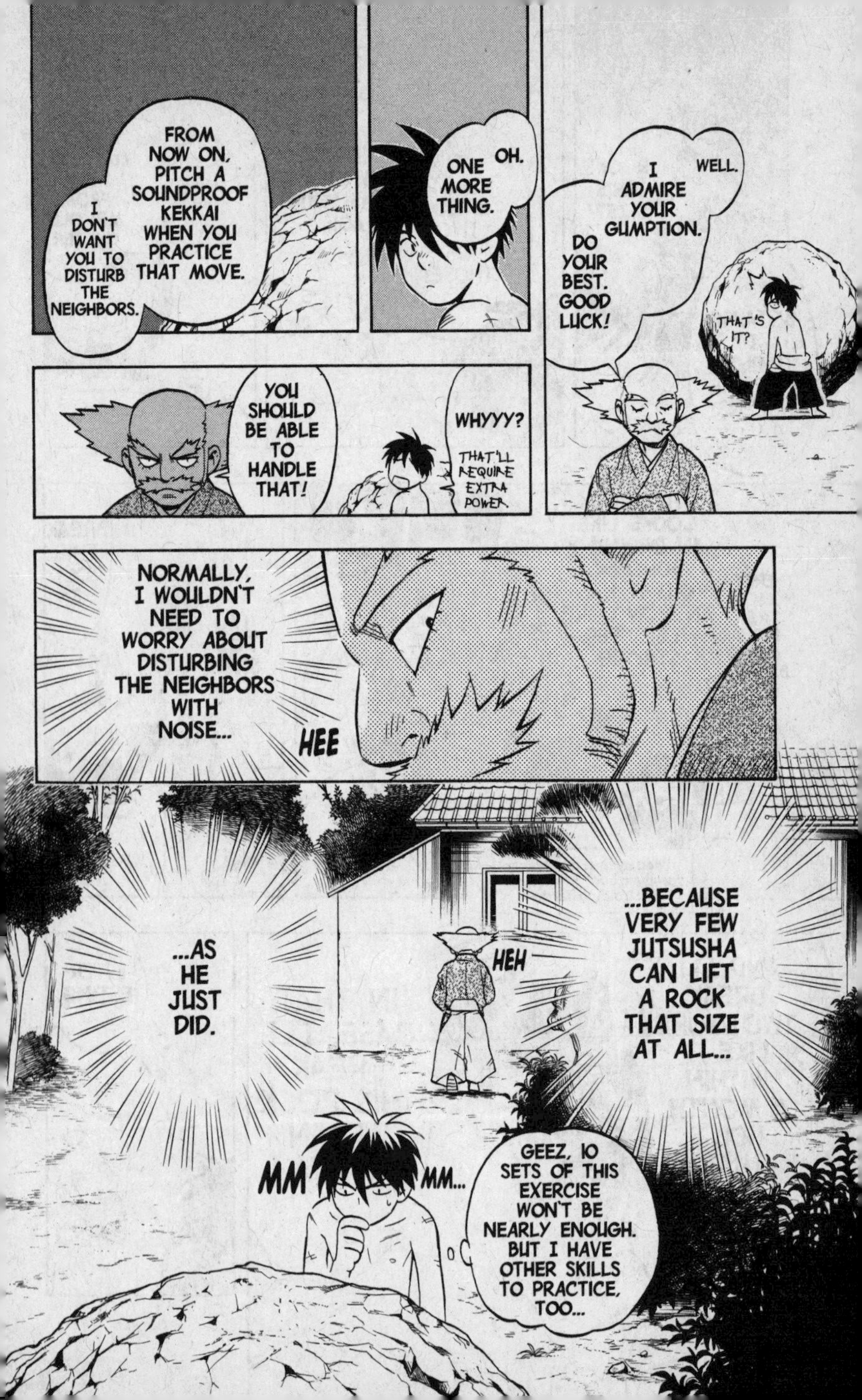
WELL. I ADMIRE YOUR GUMPTION.
DO YOUR BEST. GOOD LUCK!
THAT'S IT?
OH. ONE MORE THING.
FROM NOW ON, PITCH A SOUNDPROOF KEKKAI WHEN YOU PRACTICE THAT MOVE.
I DON'T WANT YOU TO DISTURB THE NEIGHBORS.
WHYYY?
THAT'LL REQUIRE EXTRA POWER
YOU SHOULD BE ABLE TO HANDLE THAT!
NORMALLY, I WOULDN'T NEED TO WORRY ABOUT DISTURBING THE NEIGHBORS WITH NOISE...
HEE
...BECAUSE VERY FEW JUTSUSHA CAN LIFT A ROCK THAT SIZE AT ALL...
HEH
...AS HE JUST DID.
MM
MM...
GEEZ, 10 SETS OF THIS EXERCISE WON'T BE NEARLY ENOUGH. BUT I HAVE OTHER SKILLS TO PRACTICE, TOO...

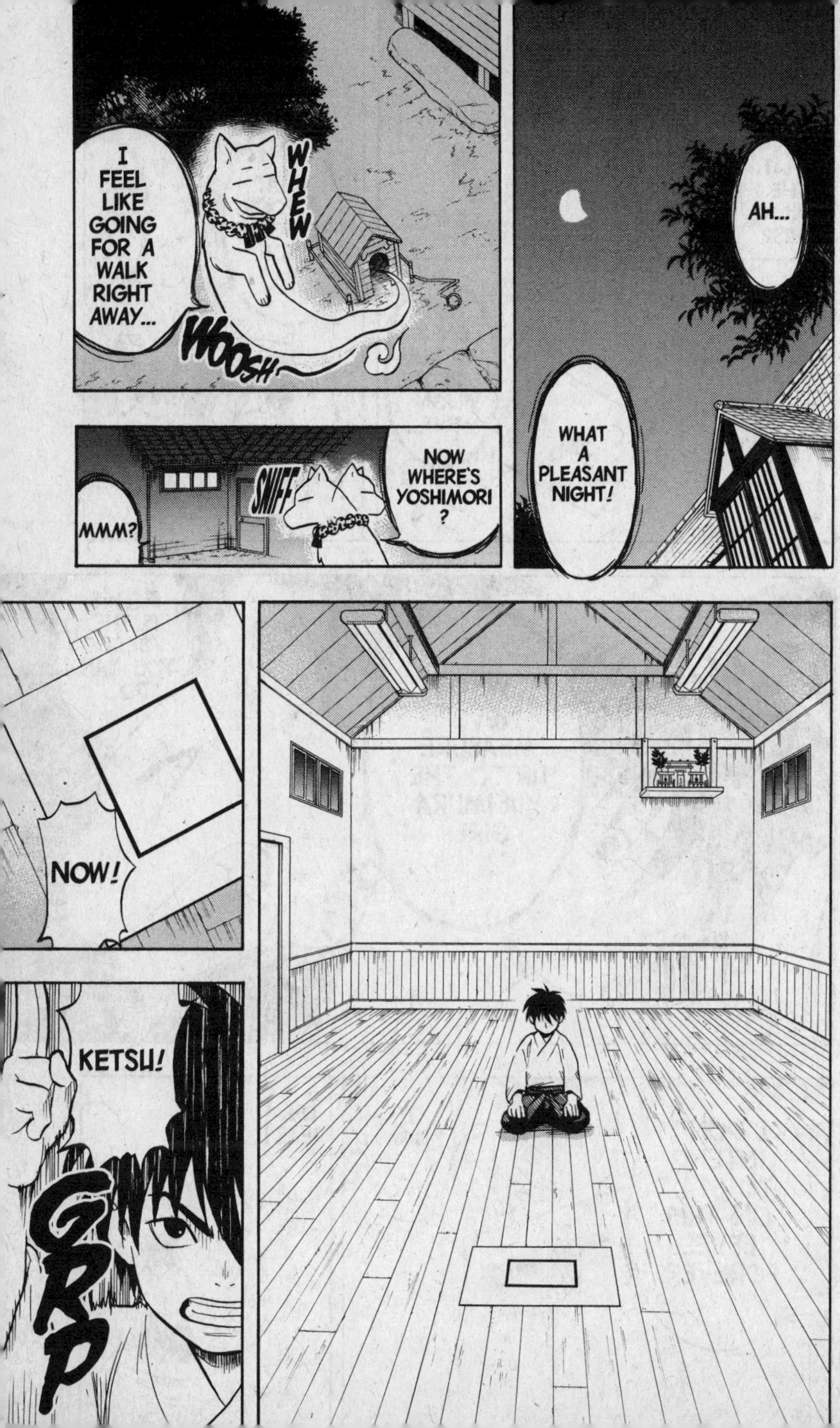
AH...
WHAT A PLEASANT NIGHT!
I FEEL LIKE GOING FOR A WALK RIGHT AWAY...
WHEW
WOOSH
NOW WHERE'S YOSHIMORI?
SNIFF
MMM?
NOW!
KETSU!
GRIP

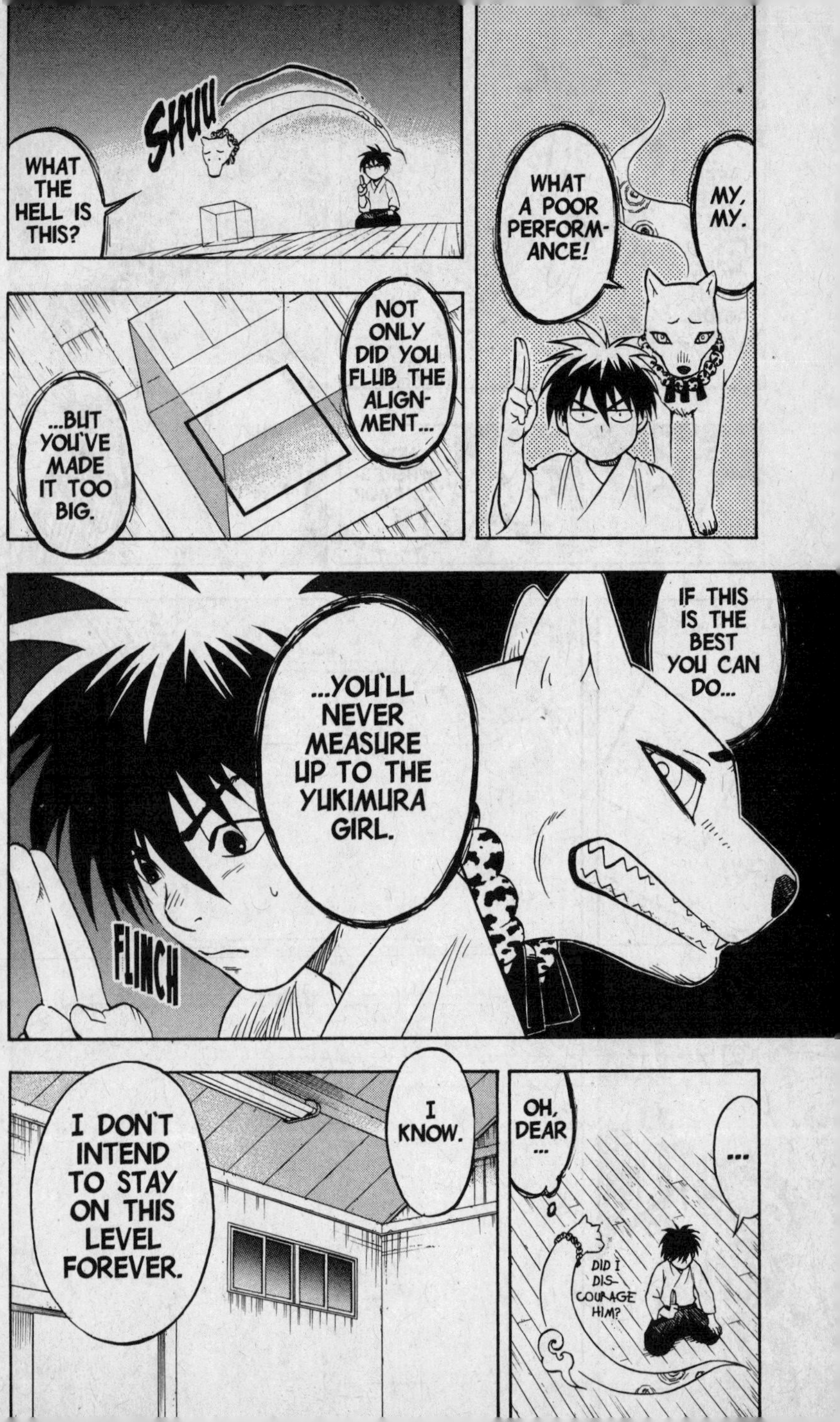
MY, MY.
WHAT A POOR PERFORMANCE!
SHUU
WHAT THE HELL IS THIS?
NOT ONLY DID YOU FLUB THE ALIGNMENT...
...BUT YOU'VE MADE IT TOO BIG.
IF THIS IS THE BEST YOU CAN DO...
...YOU'LL NEVER MEASURE UP TO THE YUKIMURA GIRL.
FLINCH
...
OH, DEAR...
DID I DISCOURAGE HIM?
I KNOW.
I DON'T INTEND TO STAY ON THIS LEVEL FOREVER.

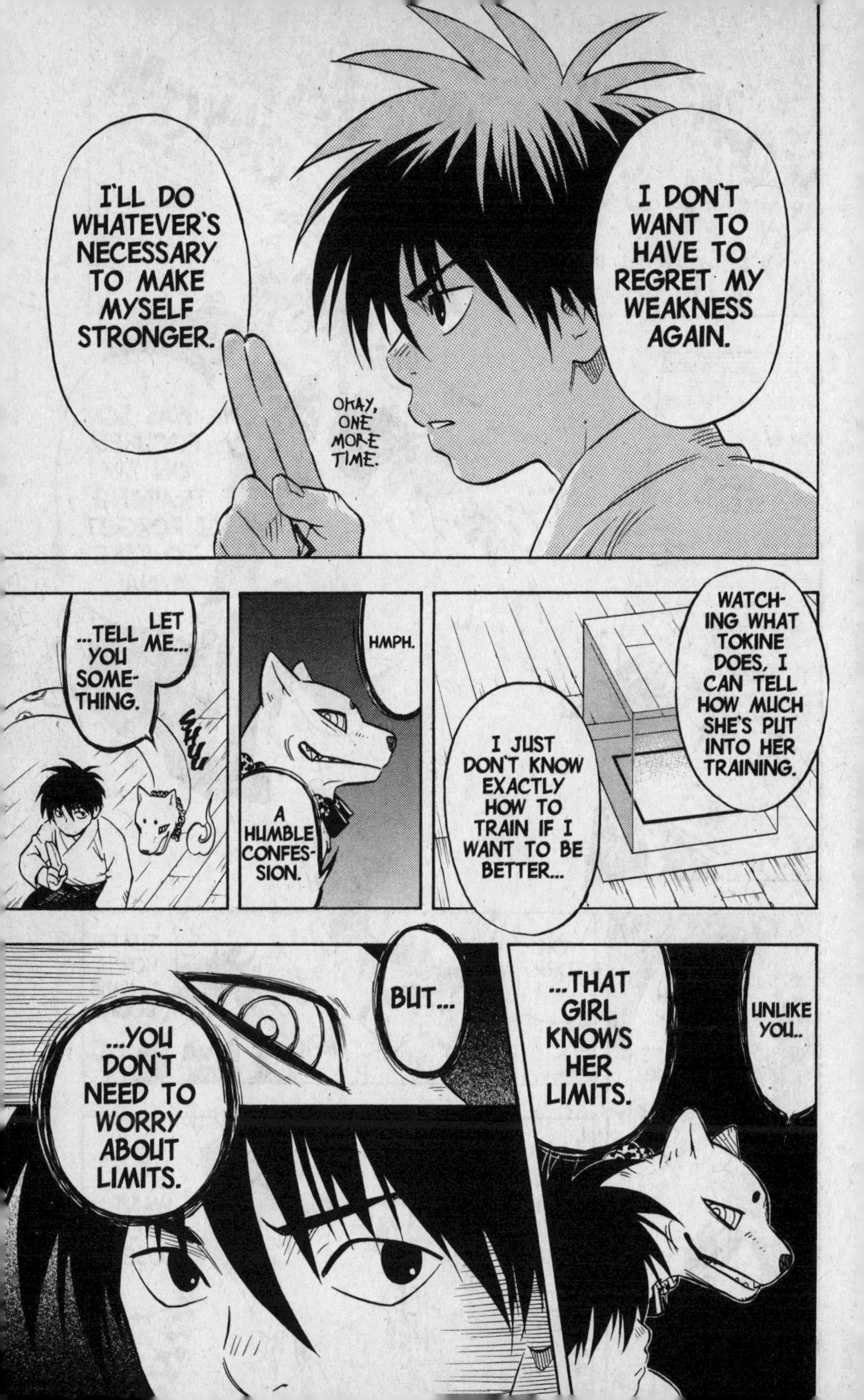
I DON'T WANT TO HAVE TO REGRET MY WEAKNESS AGAIN.
I'LL DO WHATEVER'S NECESSARY TO MAKE MYSELF STRONGER.
OKAY, ONE MORE TIME.
WATCHING WHAT TOKINE DOES, I CAN TELL HOW MUCH SHE'S PUT INTO HER TRAINING.
I JUST DON'T KNOW EXACTLY HOW TO TRAIN IF I WANT TO BE BETTER...
HMPH.
A HUMBLE CONFESSION.
LET ME...
...TELL YOU SOMETHING.
UNLIKE YOU..
...THAT GIRL KNOWS HER LIMITS.
BUT...
...YOU DON'T NEED TO WORRY ABOUT LIMITS.

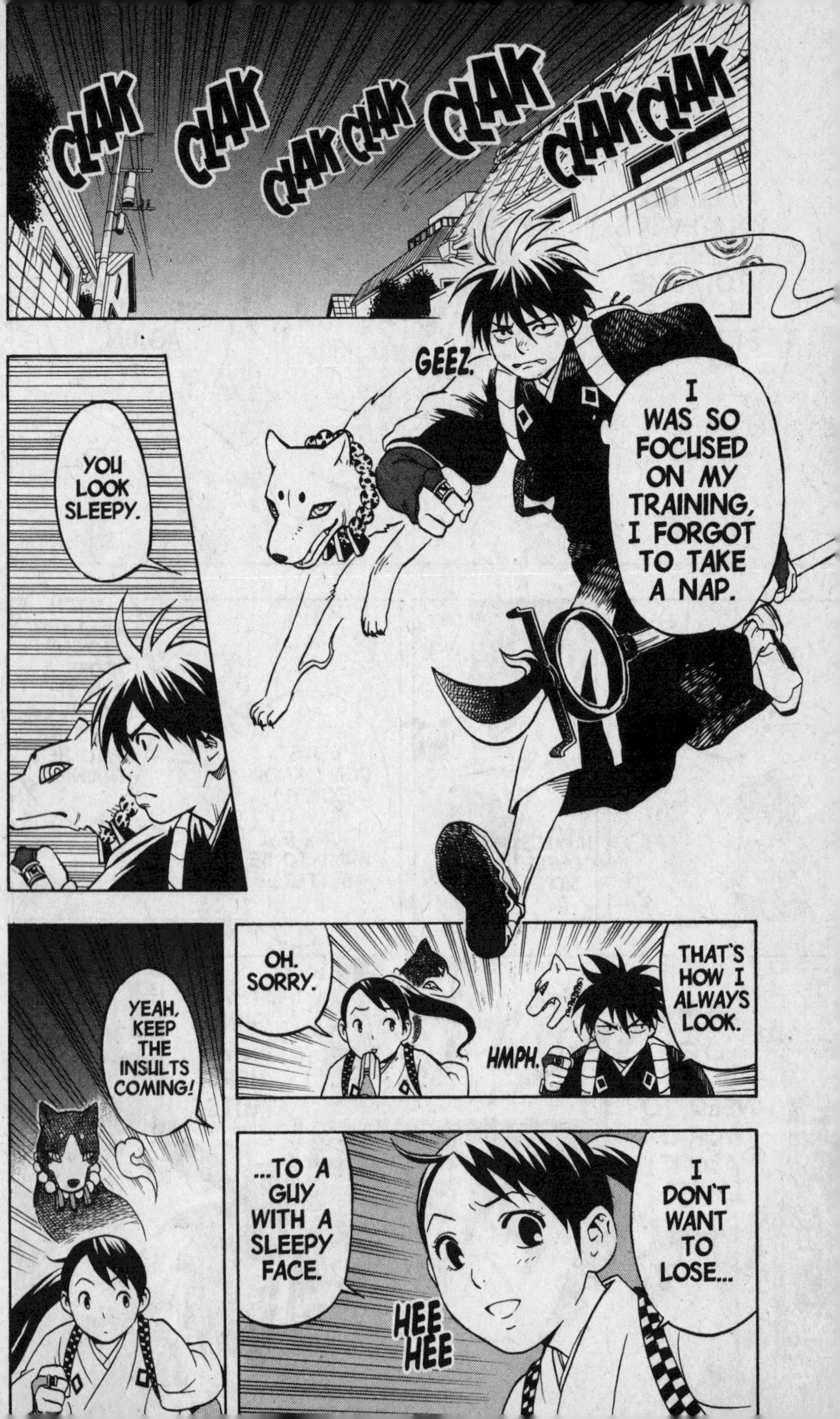
CLAK CLAK
CLAK
CLAK CLAK
CLAK
CLAK
I WAS SO FOCUSED ON MY TRAINING, I FORGOT TO TAKE A NAP.
GEEZ.
YOU LOOK SLEEPY.
THAT'S HOW I ALWAYS LOOK.
HMPH.
OH. SORRY.
YEAH, KEEP THE INSULTS COMING!
I DON'T WANT TO LOSE...
...TO A GUY WITH A SLEEPY FACE.
HEE HEE

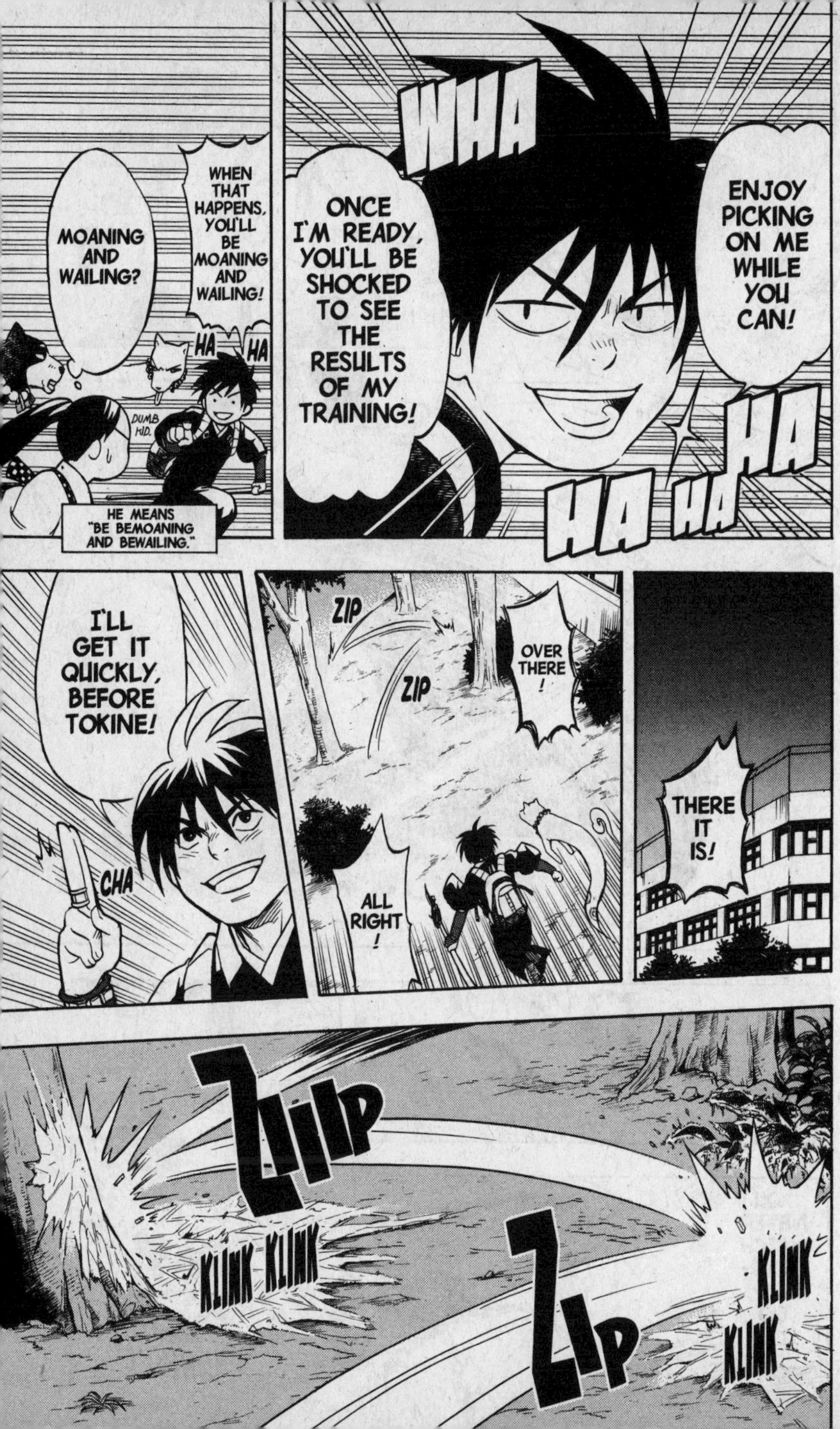
WHA
ONCE I'M READY, YOU'LL BE SHOCKED TO SEE THE RESULTS OF MY TRAINING!
ENJOY PICKING ON ME WHILE YOU CAN!
HA HA HA
WHEN THAT HAPPENS, YOU'LL BE MOANING AND WAILING!
HA HA
MOANING AND WAILING?
DUMB KID.
HE MEANS "BE BEMOANING AND BEWAILING."
THERE IT IS!
OVER THERE!
ZIP
ZIP
ALL RIGHT!
I'LL GET IT QUICKLY, BEFORE TOKINE!
CHA
KLINK KLINK
ZIP
ZIIIP
KLINK KLINK

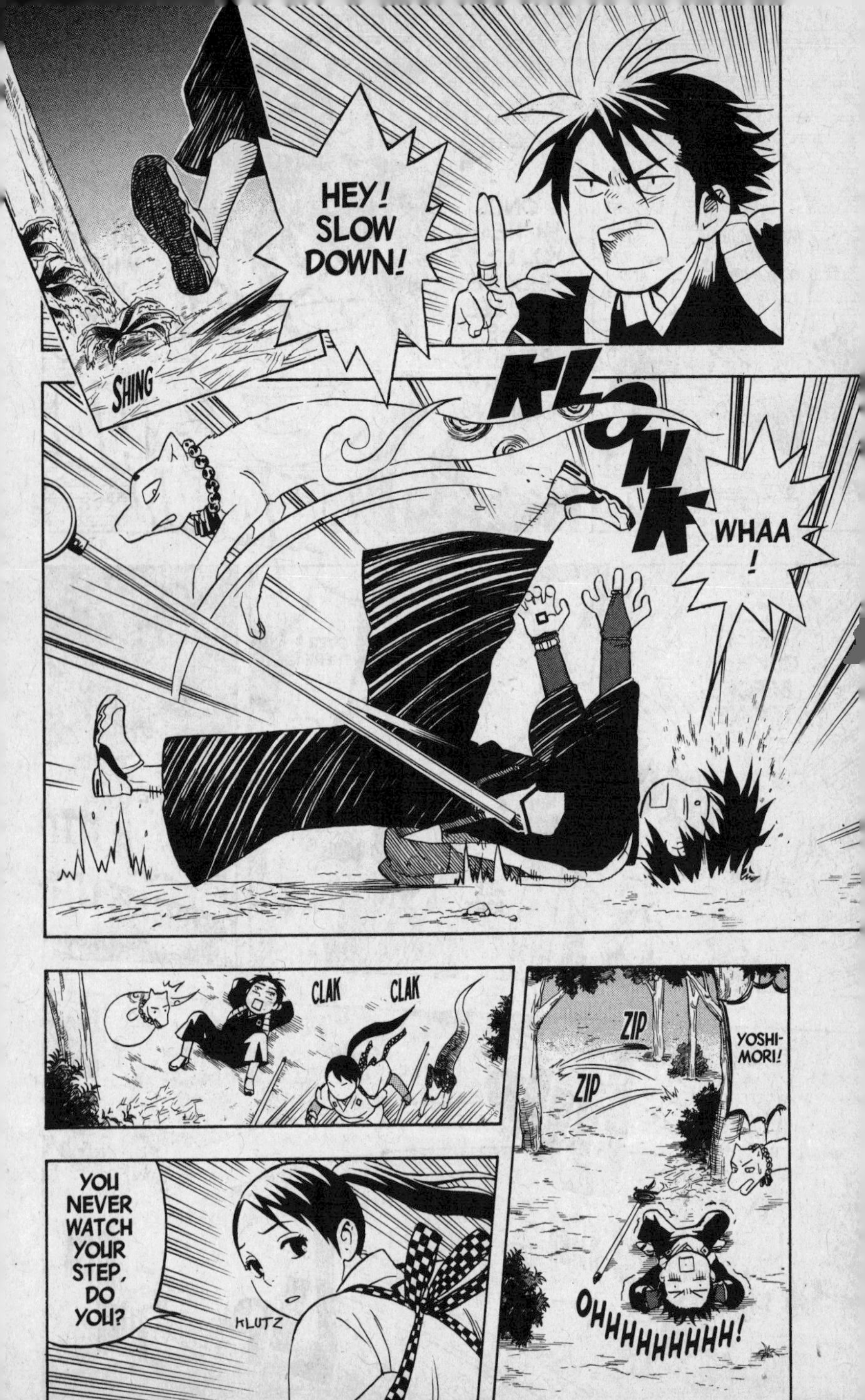
HEY! SLOW DOWN!
SHING
KLONK
WHAA!
ZIP
ZIP
YOSHIMORI!
OHHHHHHHHH!
CLAK
CLAK
YOU NEVER WATCH YOUR STEP, DO YOU?
KLUTZ

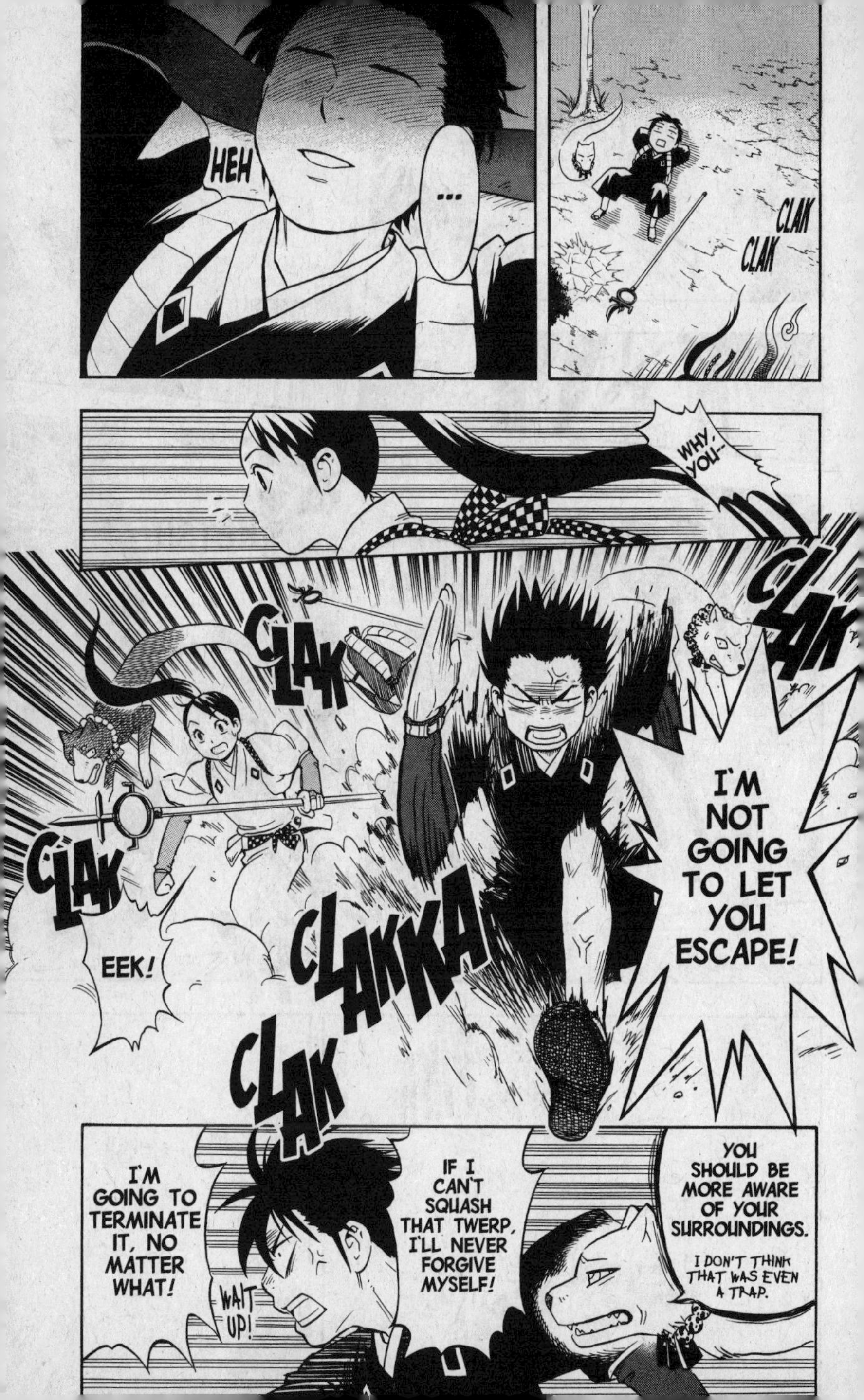
CLAK
CLAK
HEH
...
WHY, YOU--
CLAK
I'M NOT GOING TO LET YOU ESCAPE!
CLAK
CLAKKA
CLAK
EEK!
CLAK
YOU SHOULD BE MORE AWARE OF YOUR SURROUNDINGS.
I DON'T THINK THAT WAS EVEN A TRAP.
IF I CAN'T SQUASH THAT TWERP, I'LL NEVER FORGIVE MYSELF!
WAIT UP!
I'M GOING TO TERMINATE IT, NO MATTER WHAT!

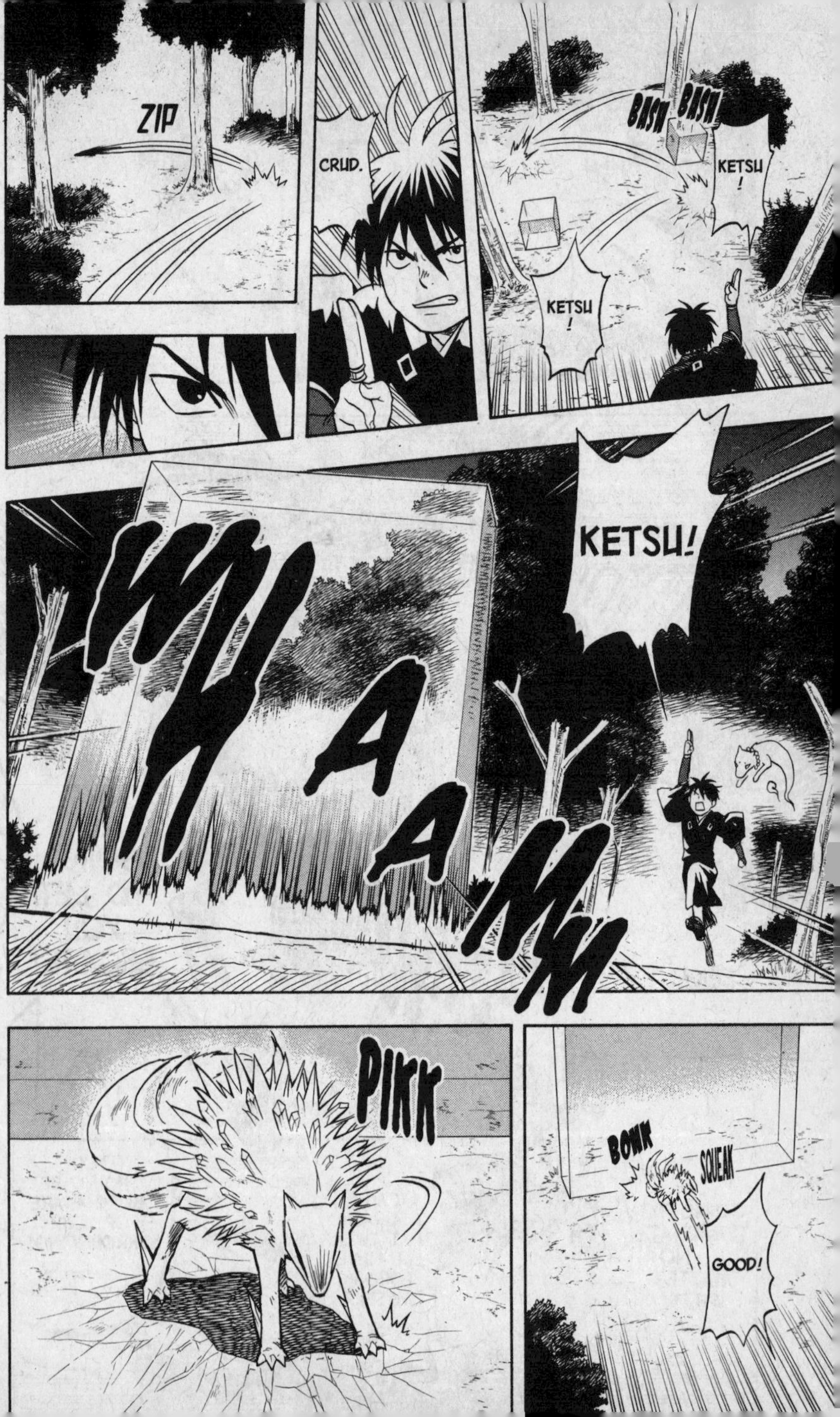
BASH
BASH
KETSU!
KETSU!
CRUD.
ZIP
KETSU!
WHAAAM
BONK
SQUEAK
GOOD!
PIKK

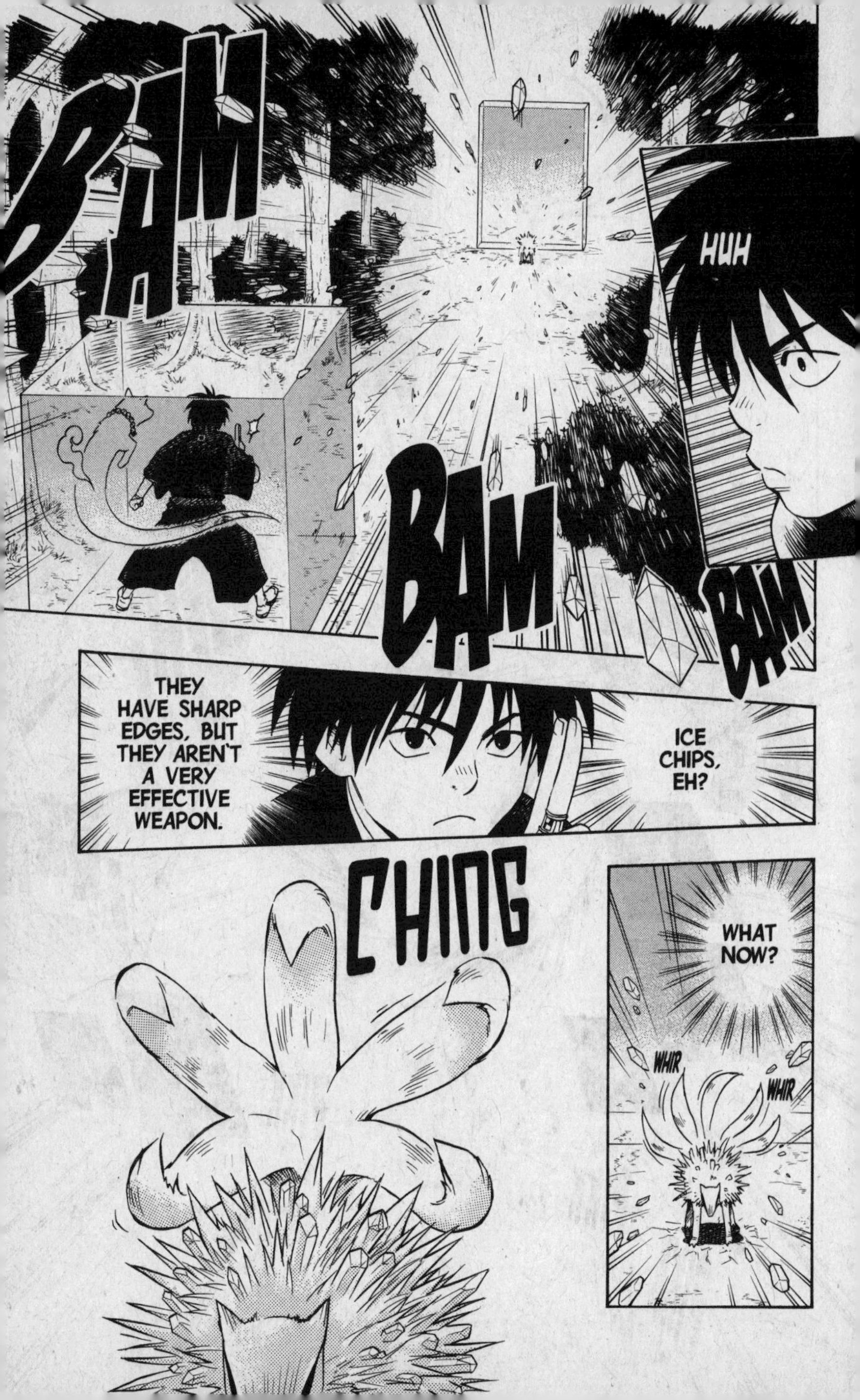
HUH
BAM
BAM
BAM
ICE CHIPS, EH?
THEY HAVE SHARP EDGES, BUT THEY AREN'T A VERY EFFECTIVE WEAPON.
WHAT NOW?
WHIR
WHIR
CHING

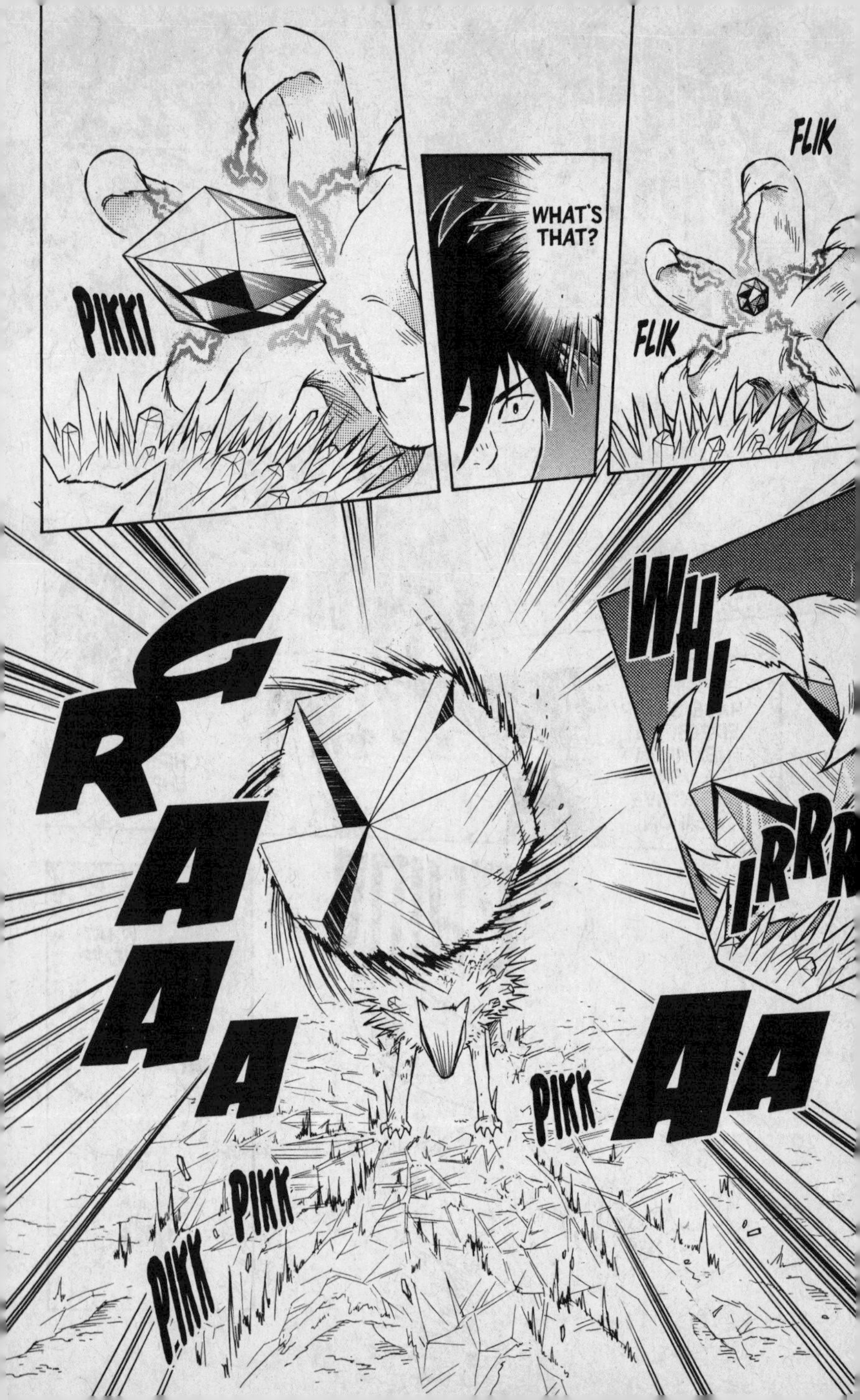
FLIK
FLIK
WHAT'S THAT?
PIKKI
WHIRRR
AA
PIKK
GRAAAA
PIKK
PIKK

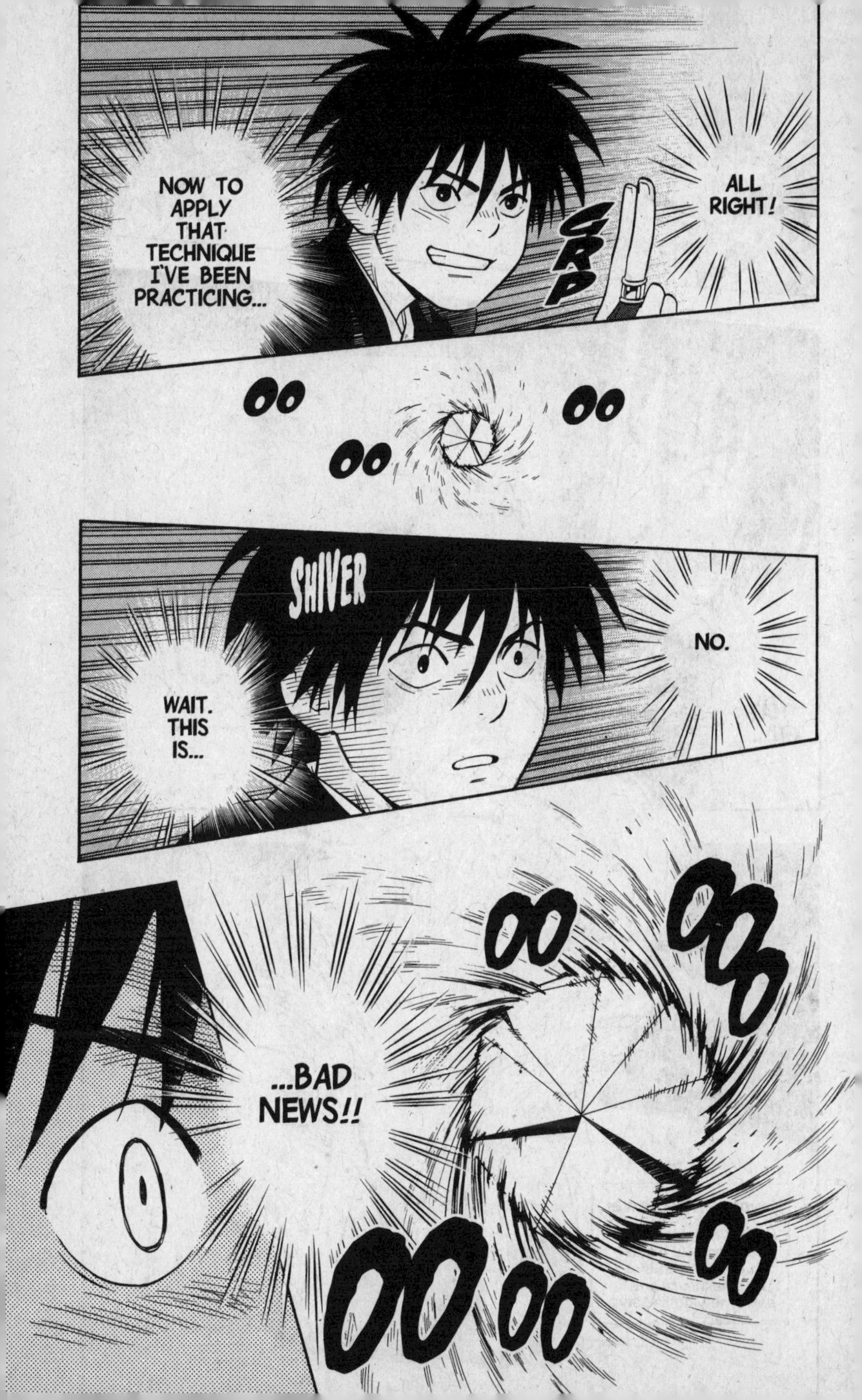
ALL RIGHT!
GRP
NOW TO APPLY THAT TECHNIQUE I'VE BEEN PRACTICING...
OO
OO
OO
NO.
SHIVER
WAIT. THIS IS...
OOO
OO
...BAD NEWS!!
OO
OOOOO

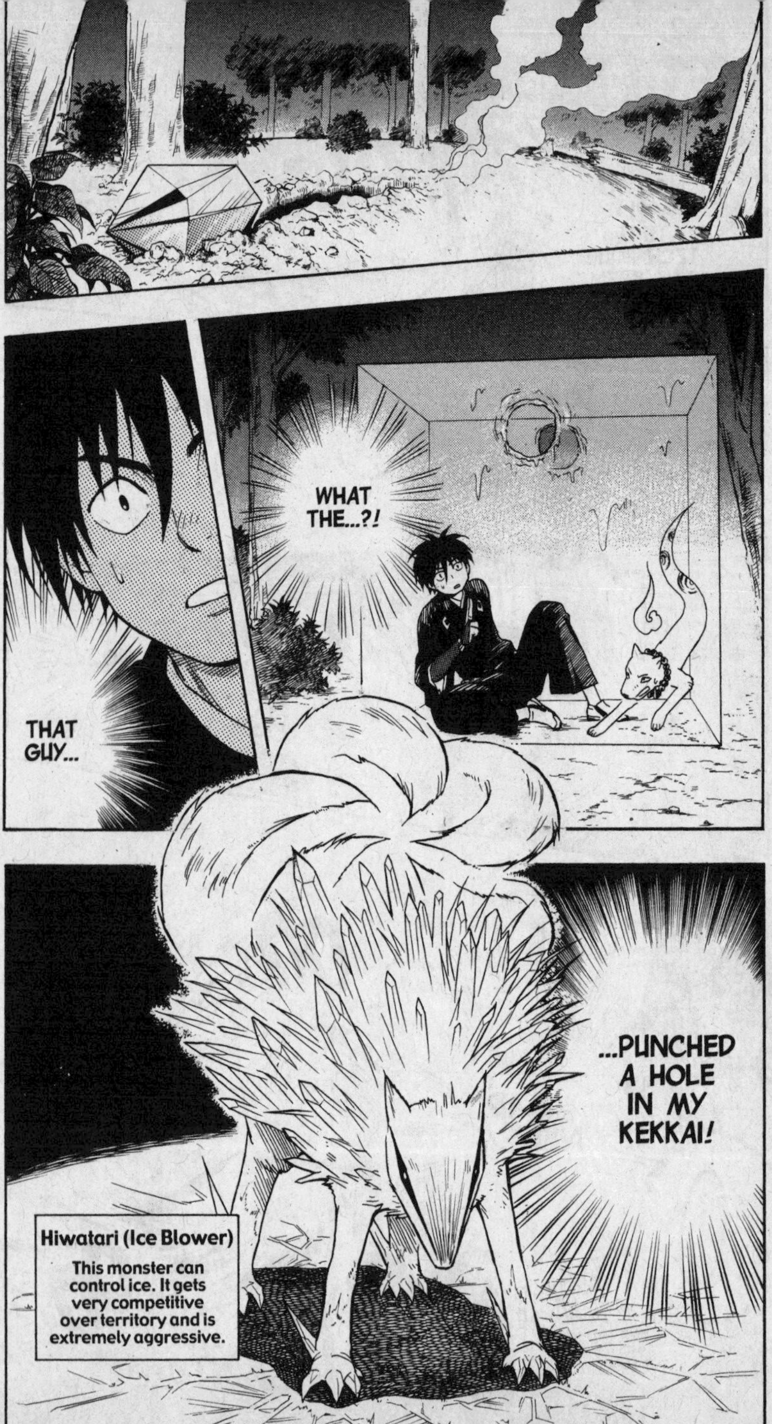
WHAT THE...?!
THAT GUY...
...PUNCHED A HOLE IN MY KEKKAI!
Hiwatari (Ice Blower)
This monster can control ice. It gets very competitive over territory and is extremely aggressive.

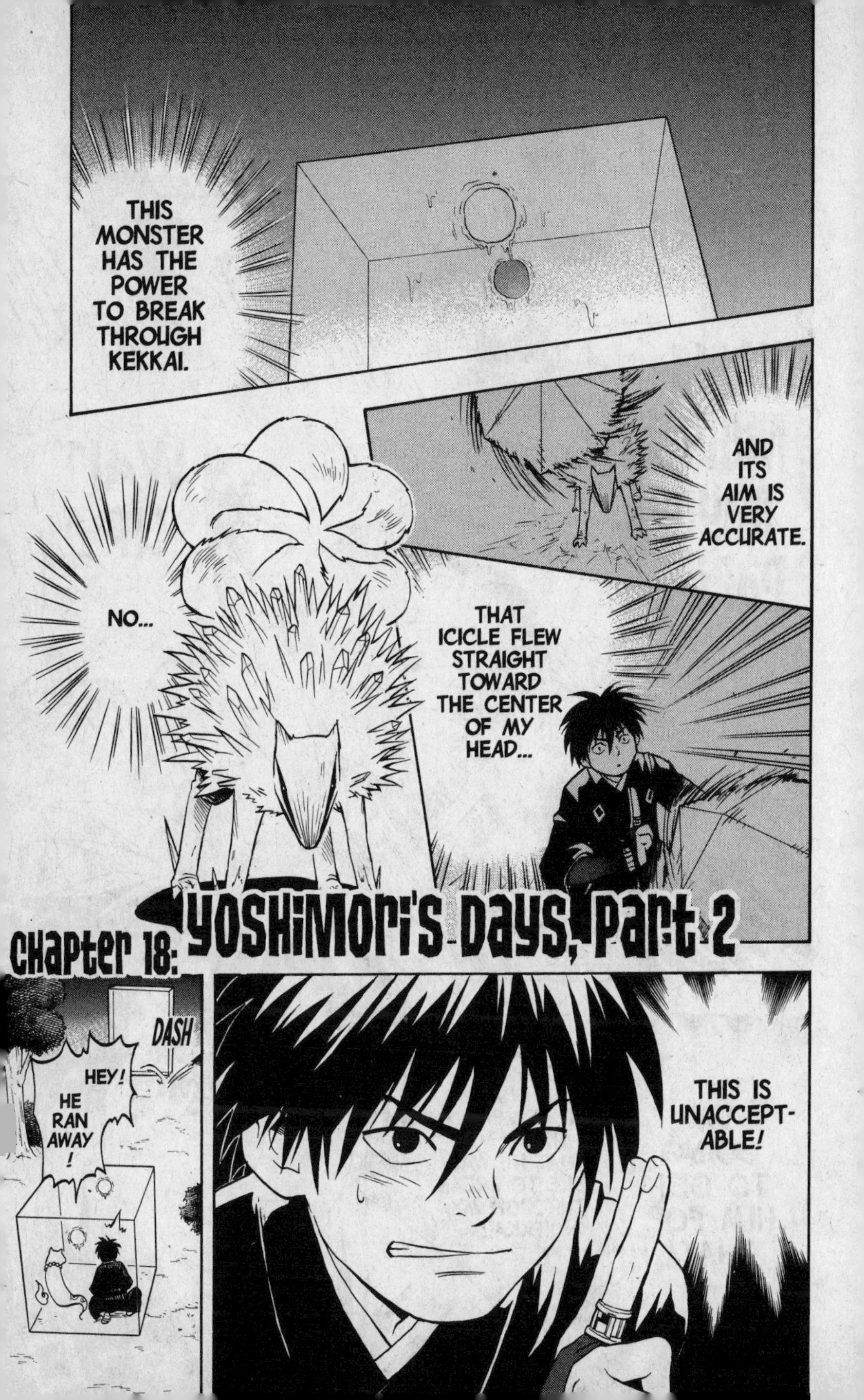
THIS MONSTER HAS THE POWER TO BREAK THROUGH KEKKAI.
AND ITS AIM IS VERY ACCURATE.
THAT ICICLE FLEW STRAIGHT TOWARD THE CENTER OF MY HEAD...
NO...
Chapter 18: Yoshimori's Days, Part 2
THIS IS UNACCEPTABLE!
DASH
HEY! HE RAN AWAY!

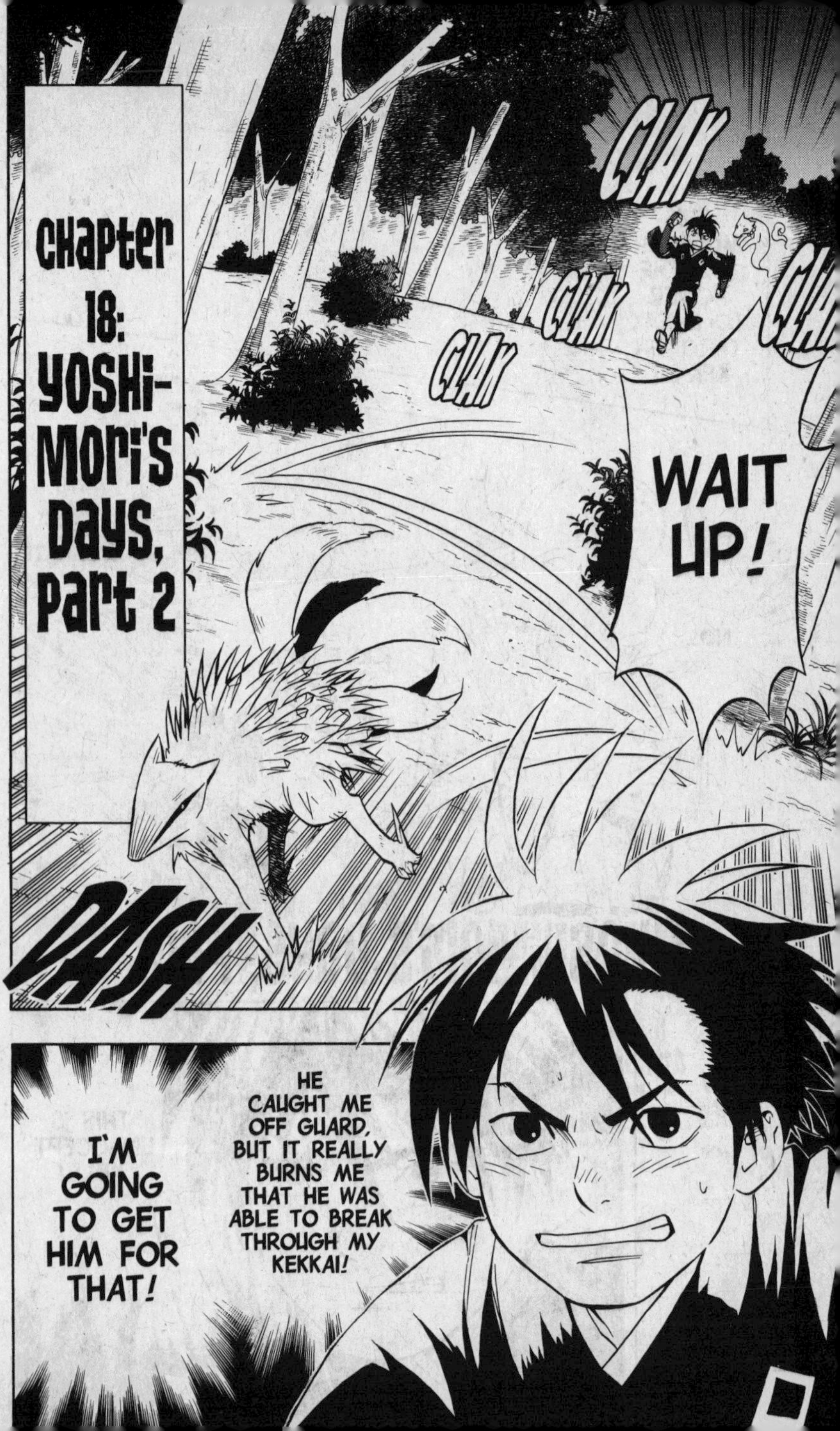
CLAK
CLAK
CLAK
CLAK
WAIT UP!
Chapter 18: Yoshimori's Days, Part 2
DASH
HE CAUGHT ME OFF GUARD, BUT IT REALLY BURNS ME THAT HE WAS ABLE TO BREAK THROUGH MY KEKKAI!
I'M GOING TO GET HIM FOR THAT!

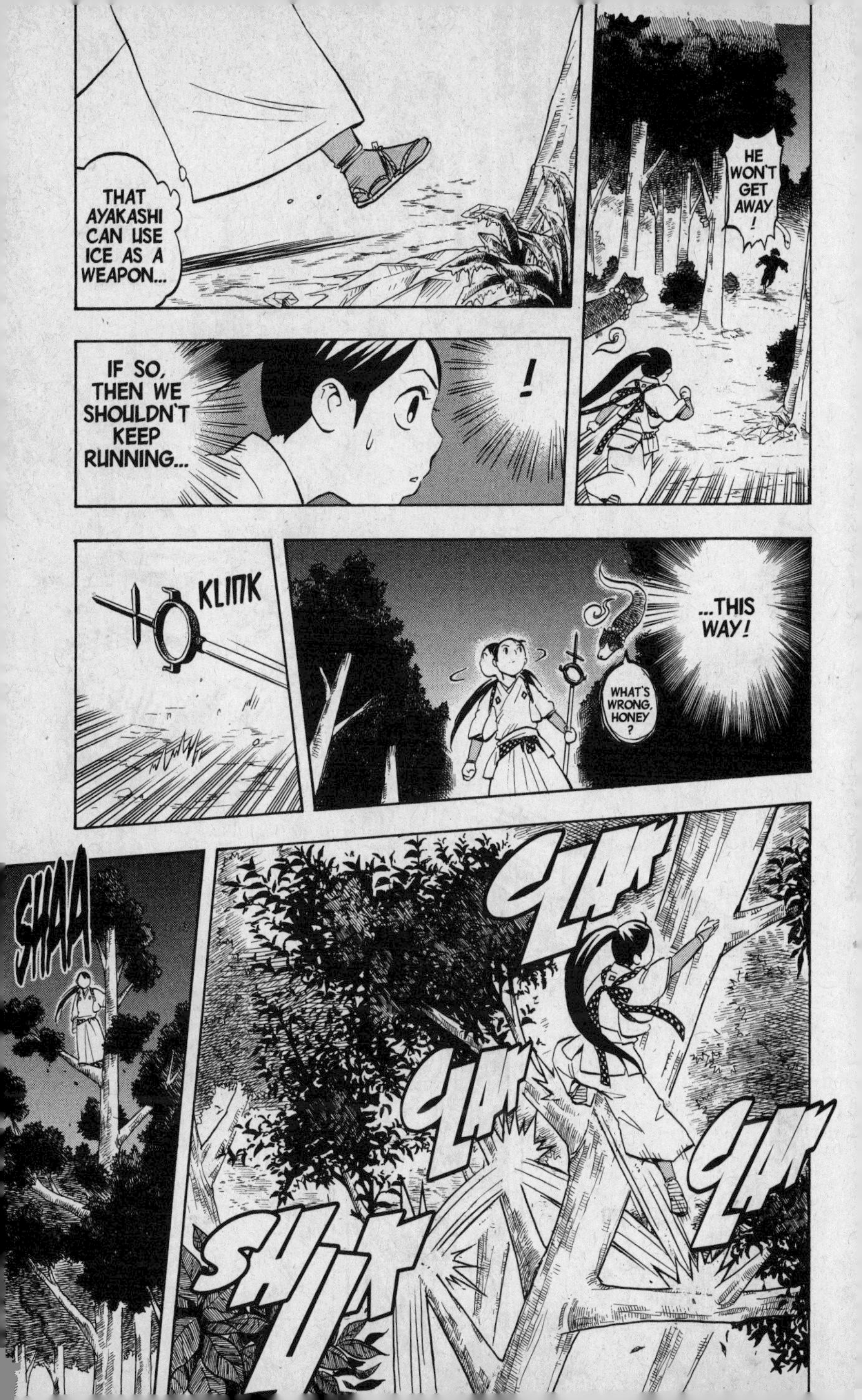
HE WON'T GET AWAY!
THAT AYAKASHI CAN USE ICE AS A WEAPON...
!
IF SO, THEN WE SHOULDN'T KEEP RUNNING...
...THIS WAY!
WHAT'S WRONG, HONEY?
KLINK
CLAK
CLAK
CLAK
SHIK
SHAA

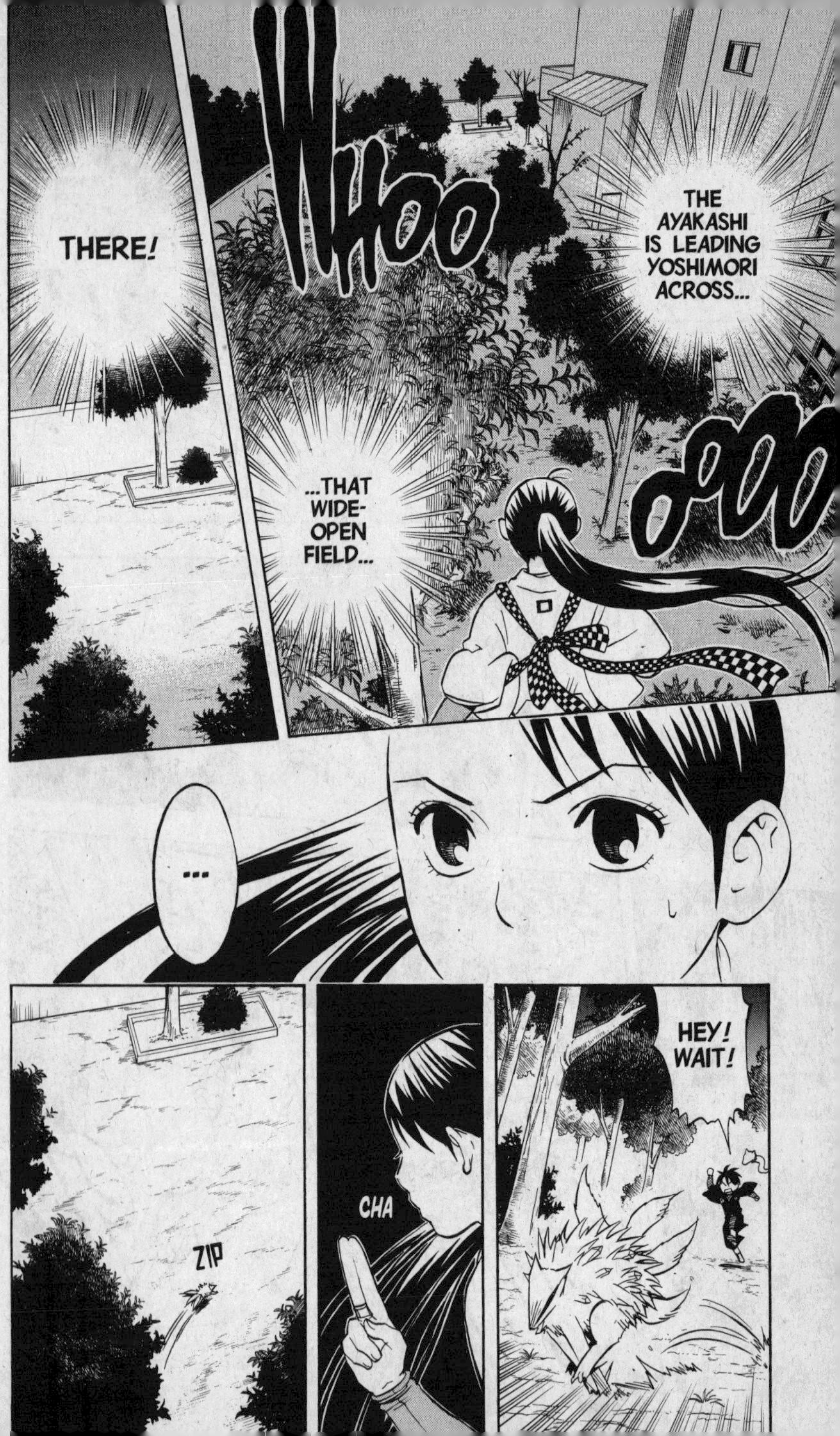

WHOO
OOOO
THE AYAKASHI IS LEADING YOSHIMORI ACROSS...
...THAT WIDE-OPEN FIELD...
THERE!
...
HEY! WAIT!
CHA
ZIP

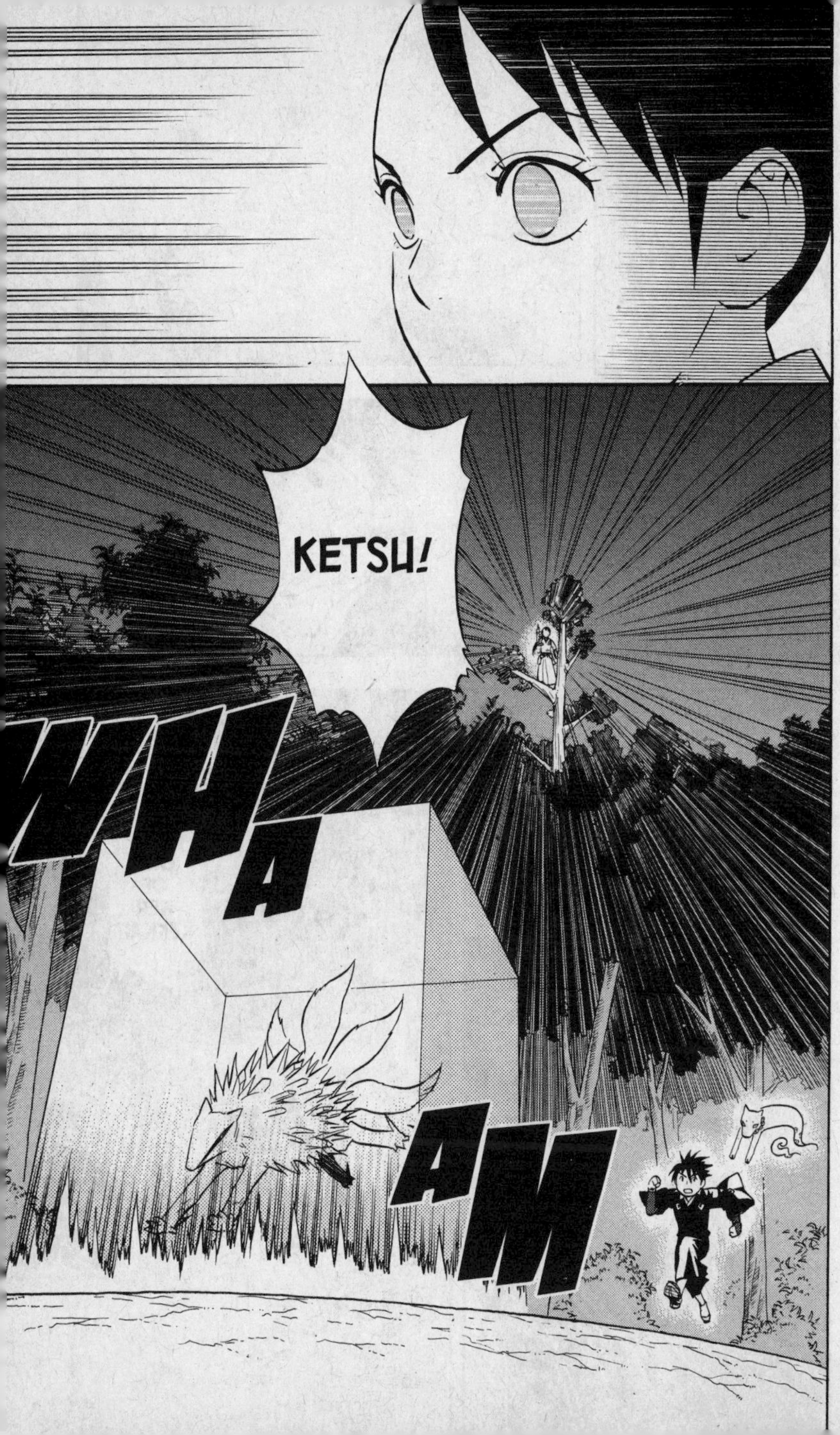
KETSU!
WHAAM

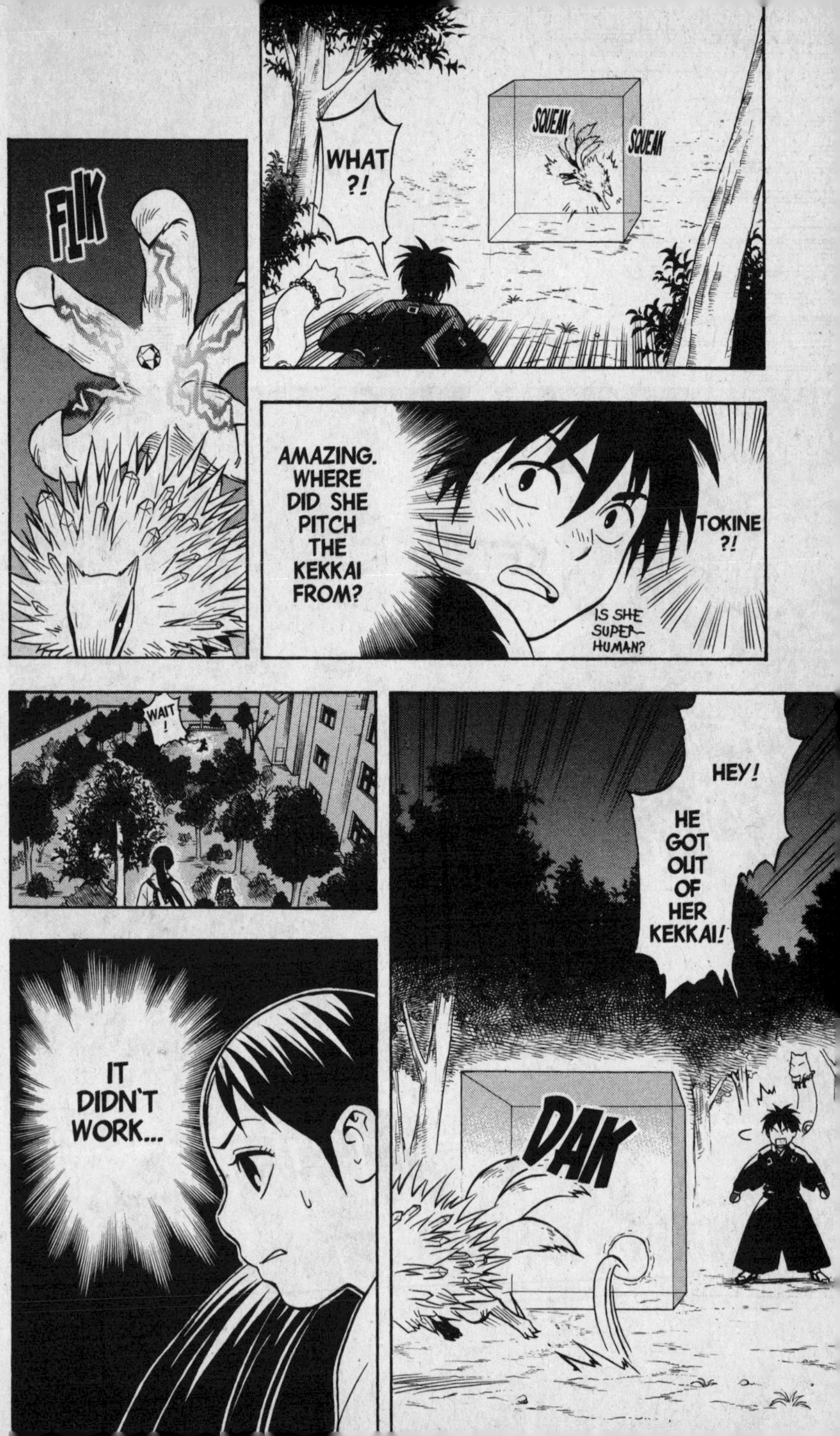
SQUEAK
SQUEAK
WHAT?!
TOKINE?!
IS SHE SUPER-HUMAN?
AMAZING. WHERE DID SHE PITCH THE KEKKAI FROM?
FLIK
HEY!
HE GOT OUT OF HER KEKKAI!
DAK
WAIT!
IT DIDN'T WORK...

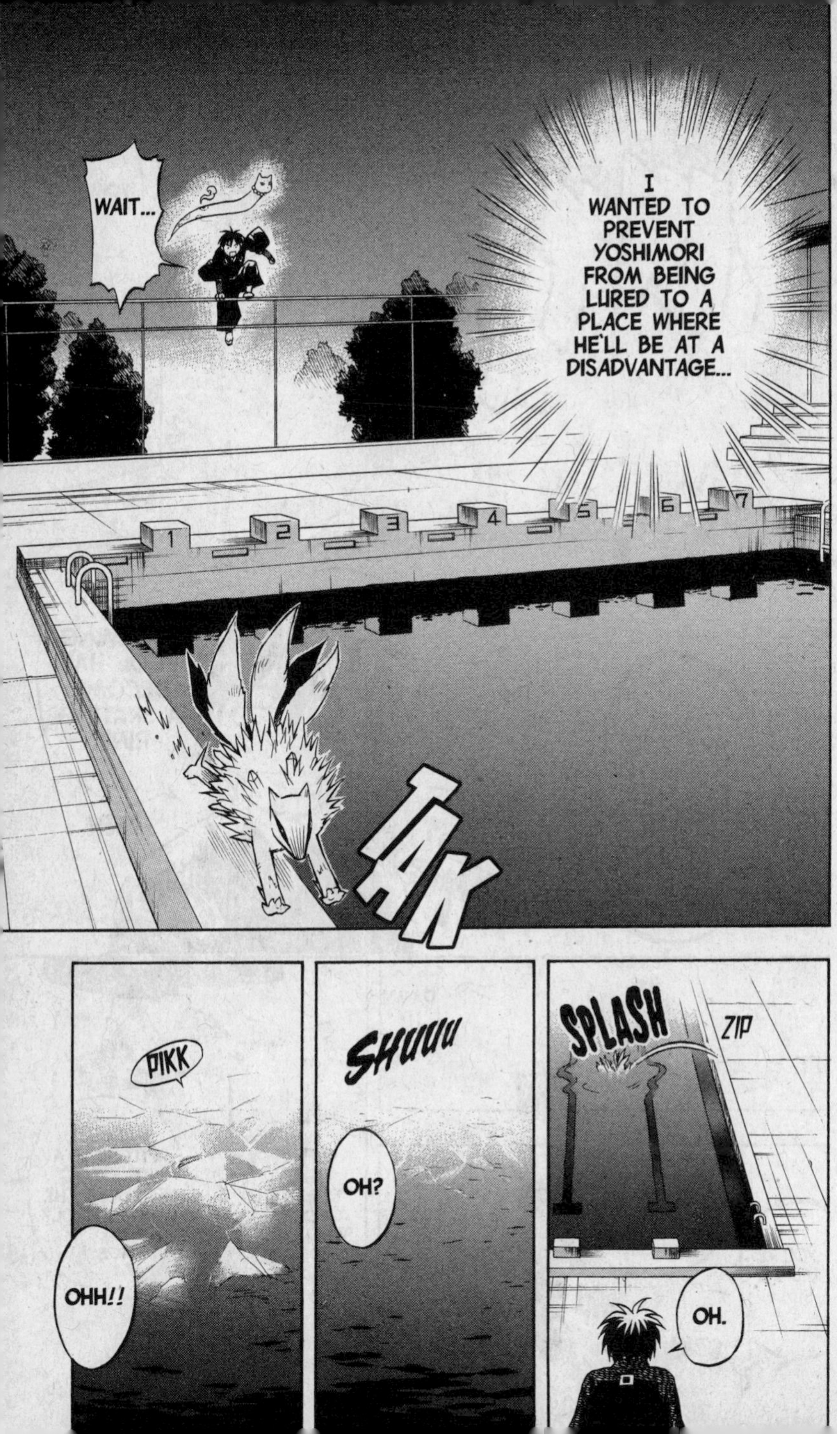
I WANTED TO PREVENT YOSHIMORI FROM BEING LURED TO A PLACE WHERE HE'LL BE AT A DISADVANTAGE...
WAIT...
1
2
3
4
5
6
7
TAK
SPLASH
ZIP
OH.
SHUUU
OH?
PIKK
OHH!!

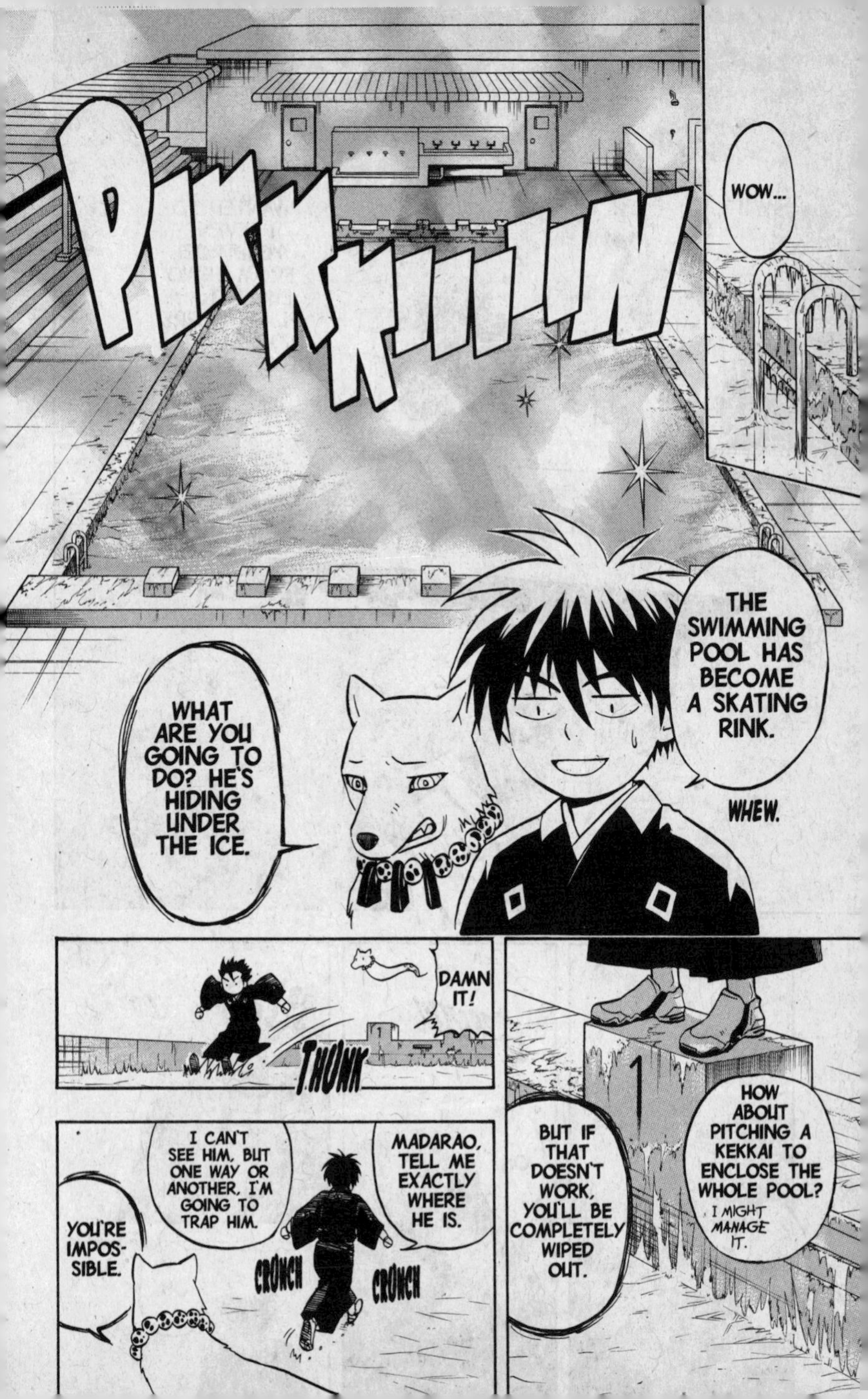
WOW...
PIKKIIIIIN
THE SWIMMING POOL HAS BECOME A SKATING RINK.
WHEW.
WHAT ARE YOU GOING TO DO? HE'S HIDING UNDER THE ICE.
HOW ABOUT PITCHING A KEKKAI TO ENCLOSE THE WHOLE POOL?
I MIGHT MANAGE IT.
BUT IF THAT DOESN'T WORK, YOU'LL BE COMPLETELY WIPED OUT.
DAMN IT!
THUNK
MADARAO, TELL ME EXACTLY WHERE HE IS.
I CAN'T SEE HIM, BUT ONE WAY OR ANOTHER, I'M GOING TO TRAP HIM.
CRUNCH
CRUNCH
YOU'RE IMPOSSIBLE.

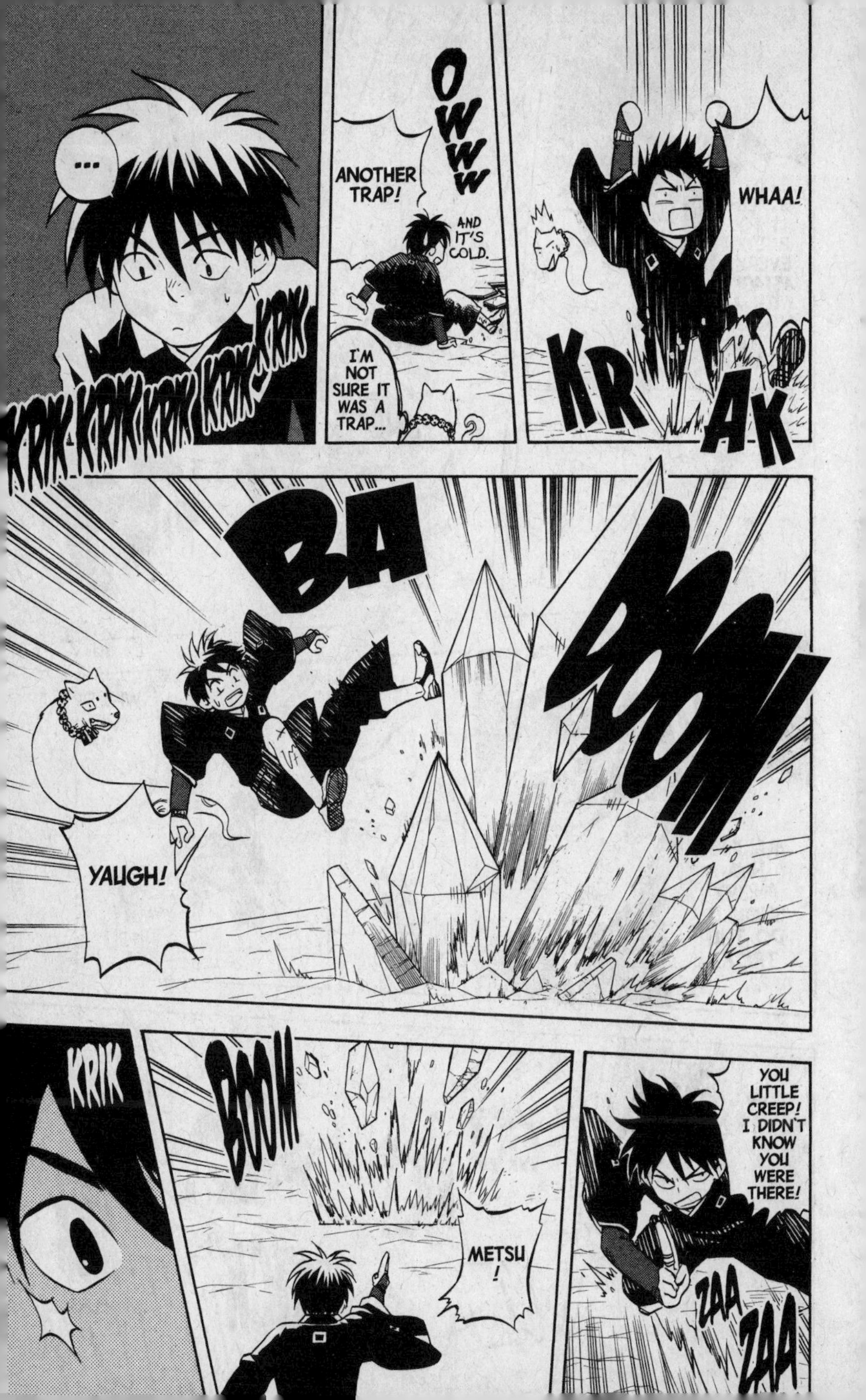
WHAA!
KRAK
OWWW
ANOTHER TRAP!
AND IT'S COLD.
I'M NOT SURE IT WAS A TRAP...
...
KRIK KRIK KRIK KRIK KRIK
BA BOOM
YAUGH!
YOU LITTLE CREEP! I DIDN'T KNOW YOU WERE THERE!
ZAA ZAA
BOOM
METSU!
KRIK

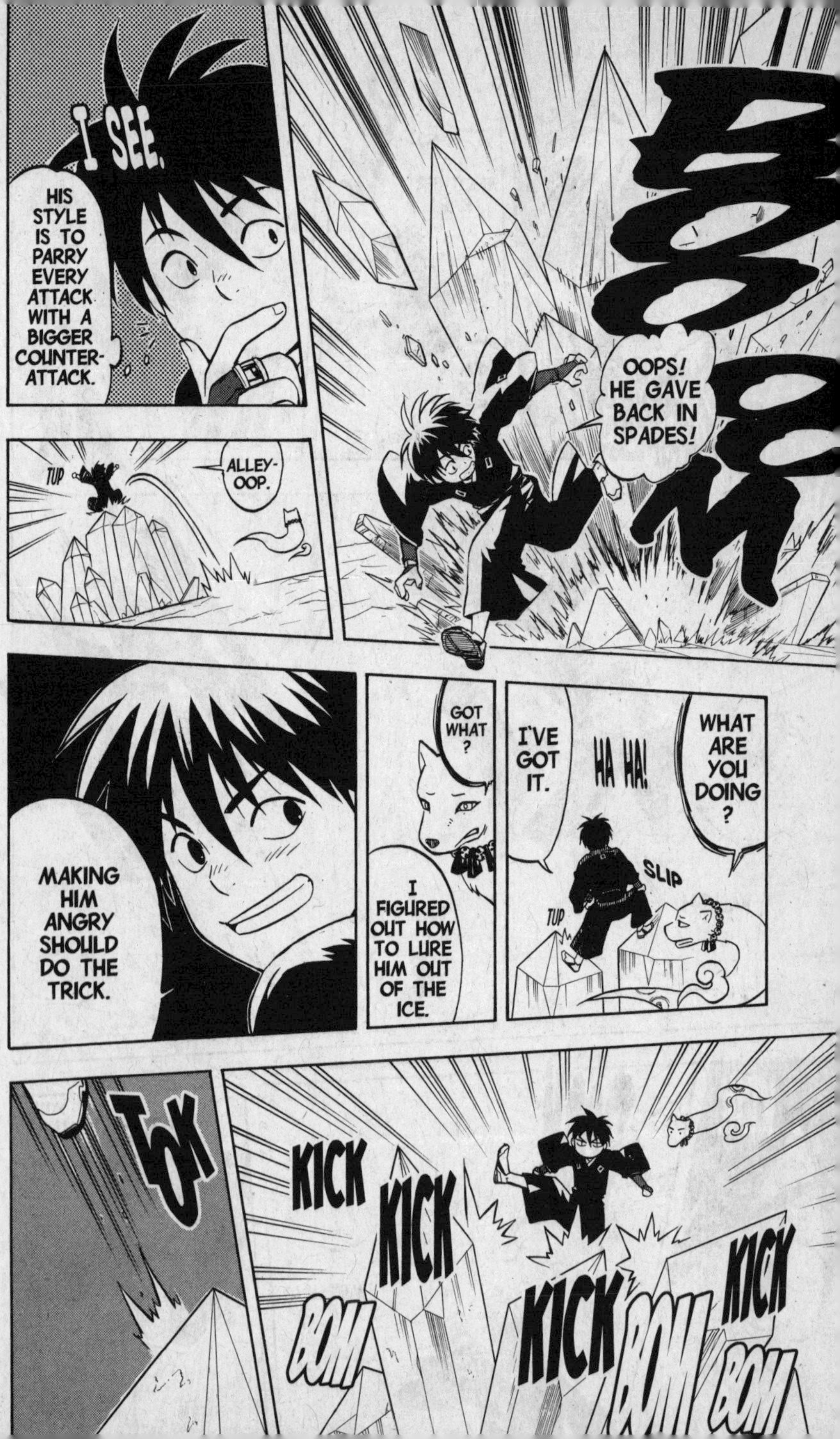
BOOM
OOPS! HE GAVE BACK IN SPADES!
I SEE.
HIS STYLE IS TO PARRY EVERY ATTACK WITH A BIGGER COUNTER-ATTACK.
TUP
ALLEY-OOP.
WHAT ARE YOU DOING?
HA HA!
I'VE GOT IT.
SLIP
TUP
GOT WHAT?
I FIGURED OUT HOW TO LURE HIM OUT OF THE ICE.
MAKING HIM ANGRY SHOULD DO THE TRICK.
KICK
KICK
KICK
KICK
BOM
BOM
BOM
BOM
TOK

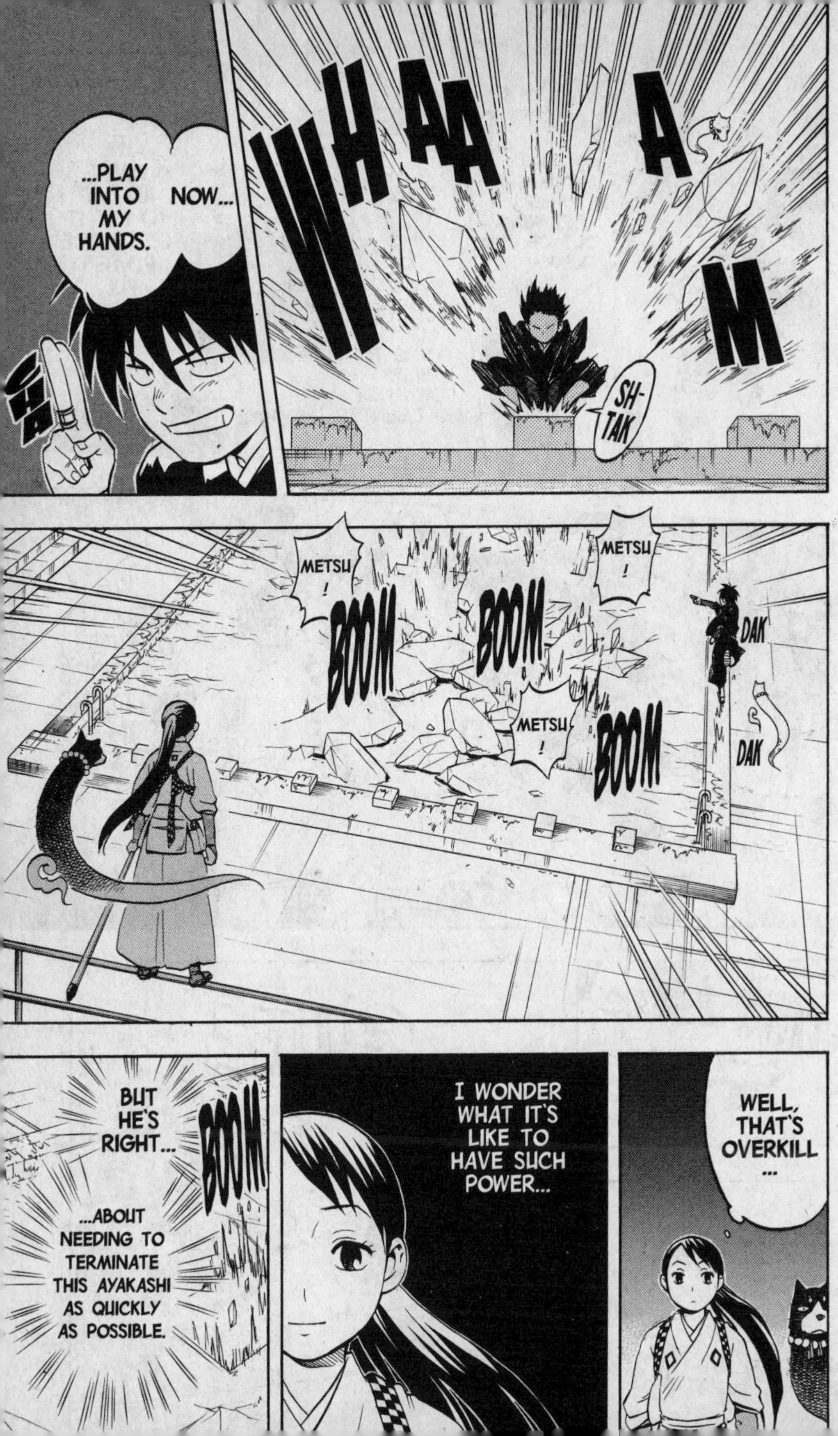
WHAAAAM
SH-TAK
NOW...
...PLAY INTO MY HANDS.
CHA
METSU!
DAK
DAK
BOOM
BOOM
METSU!
BOOM
METSU!
WELL, THAT'S OVERKILL...
I WONDER WHAT IT'S LIKE TO HAVE SUCH POWER...
BUT HE'S RIGHT...
BOOM
...ABOUT NEEDING TO TERMINATE THIS AYAKASHI AS QUICKLY AS POSSIBLE.

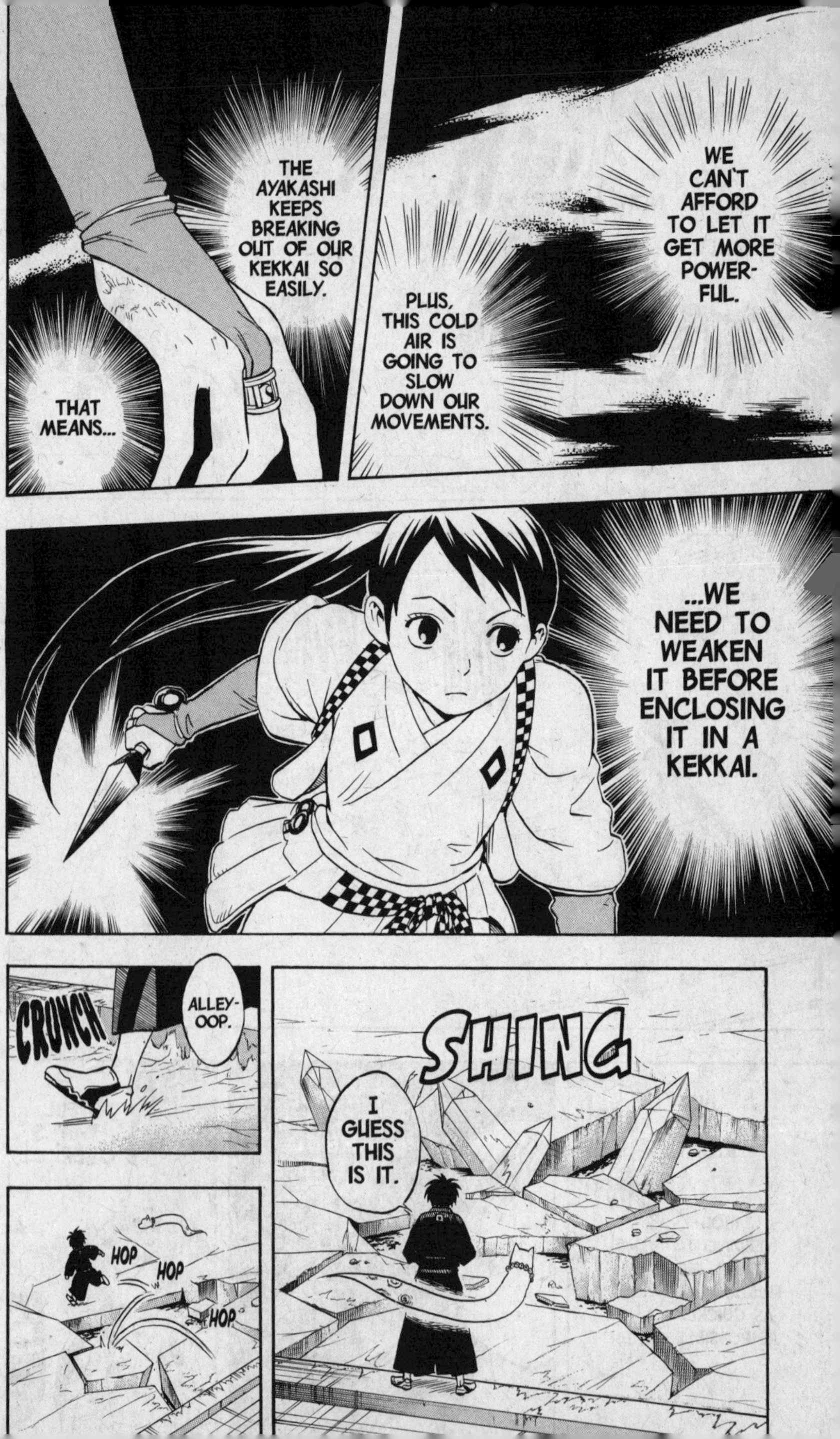
WE CAN'T AFFORD TO LET IT GET MORE POWER-FUL.
PLUS, THIS COLD AIR IS GOING TO SLOW DOWN OUR MOVEMENTS.
THE AYAKASHI KEEPS BREAKING OUT OF OUR KEKKAI SO EASILY.
THAT MEANS...
...WE NEED TO WEAKEN IT BEFORE ENCLOSING IT IN A KEKKAI.
SHING
I GUESS THIS IS IT.
ALLEY-OOP.
CRUNCH
HOP
HOP
HOP

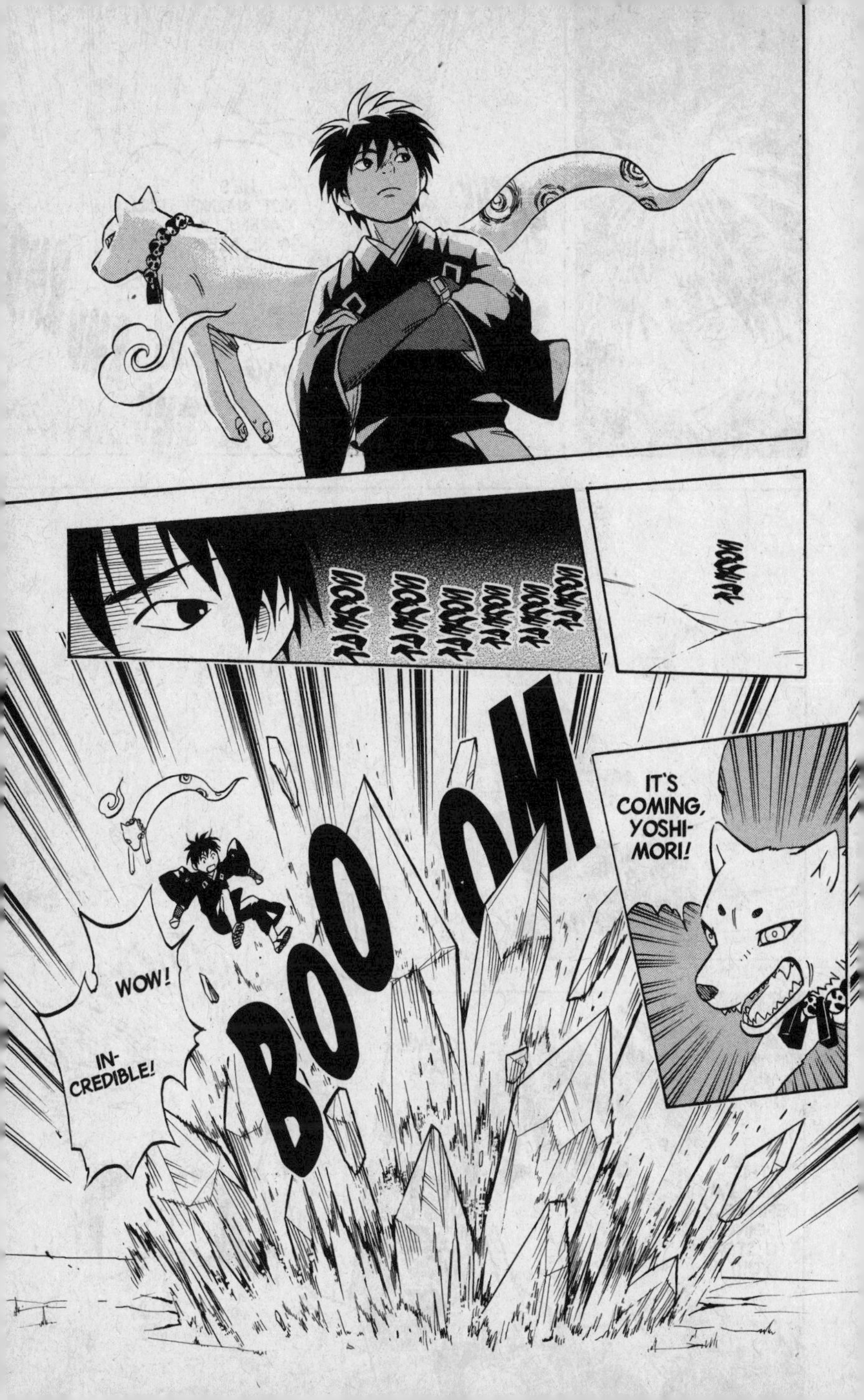
IT'S COMING, YOSHI-MORI!
BOOOM
WOW!
IN-CREDIBLE!

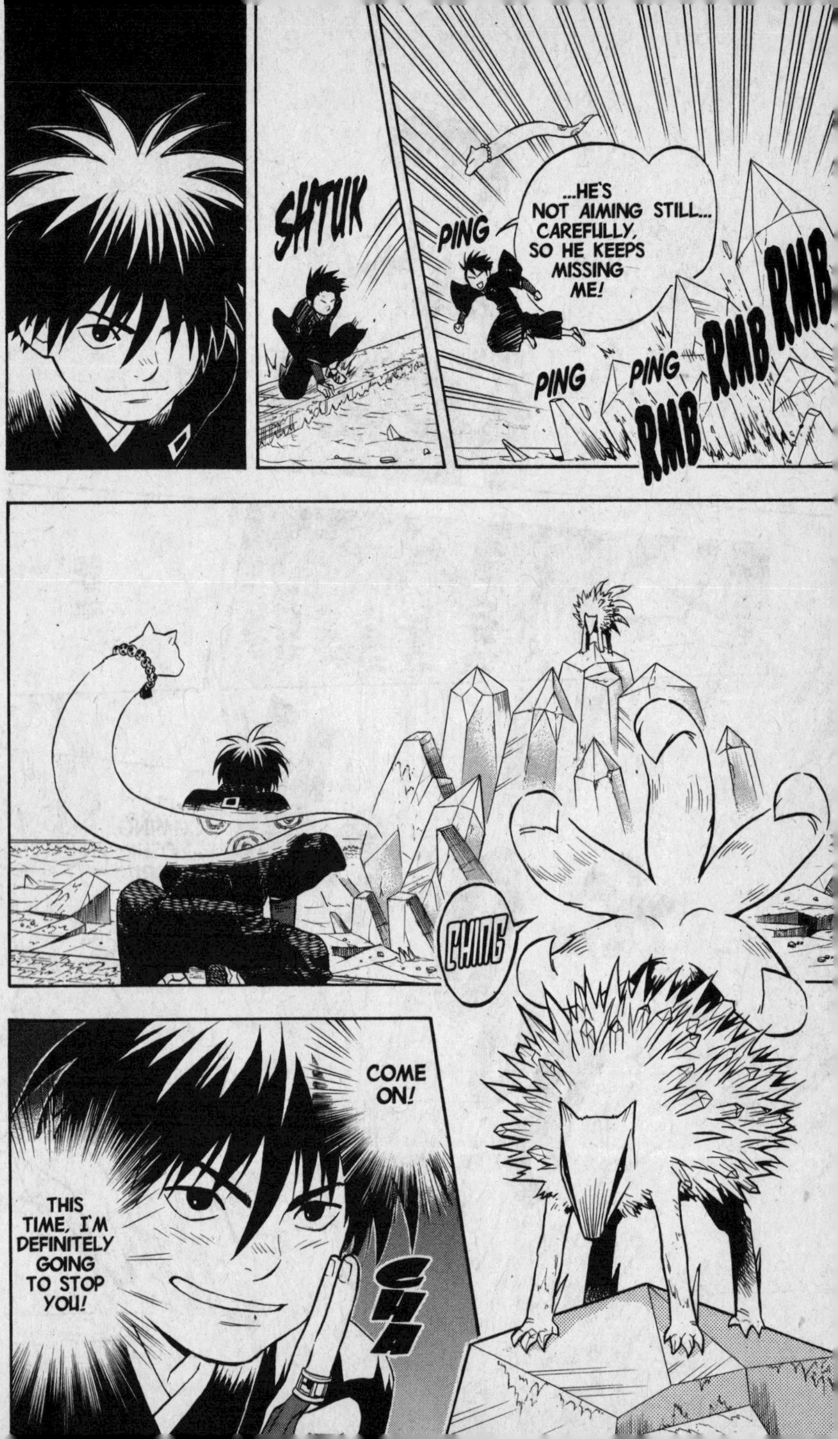
...HE'S NOT AIMING STILL... CAREFULLY, SO HE KEEPS MISSING ME!
PING
RMB RMB
RMB
PING
PING
RMB
SHTUK
CHING
COME ON!
THIS TIME, I'M DEFINITELY GOING TO STOP YOU!
CHA

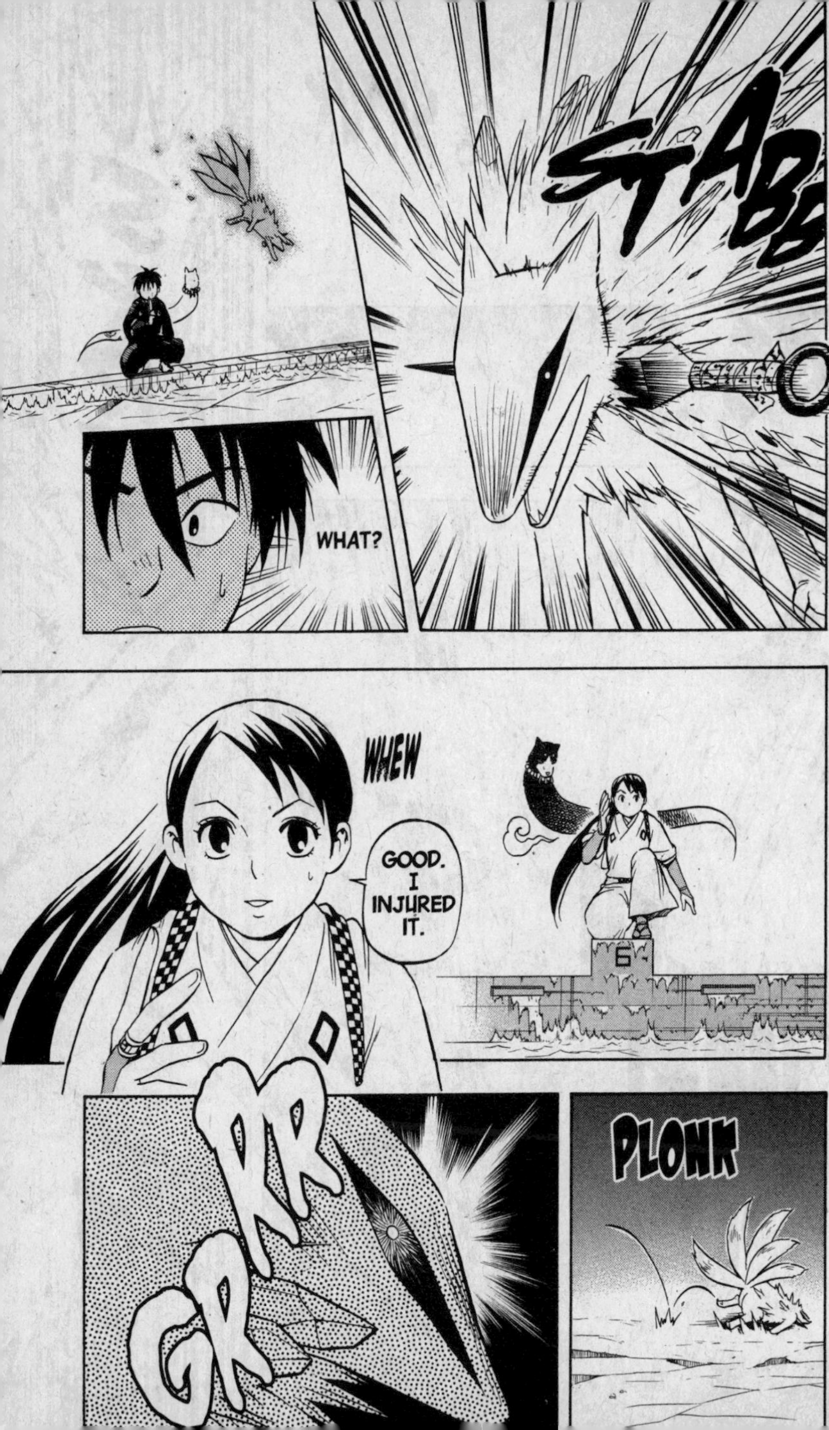
STABB
WHAT?
WHEW
GOOD. I INJURED IT.
PLONK
GRRR

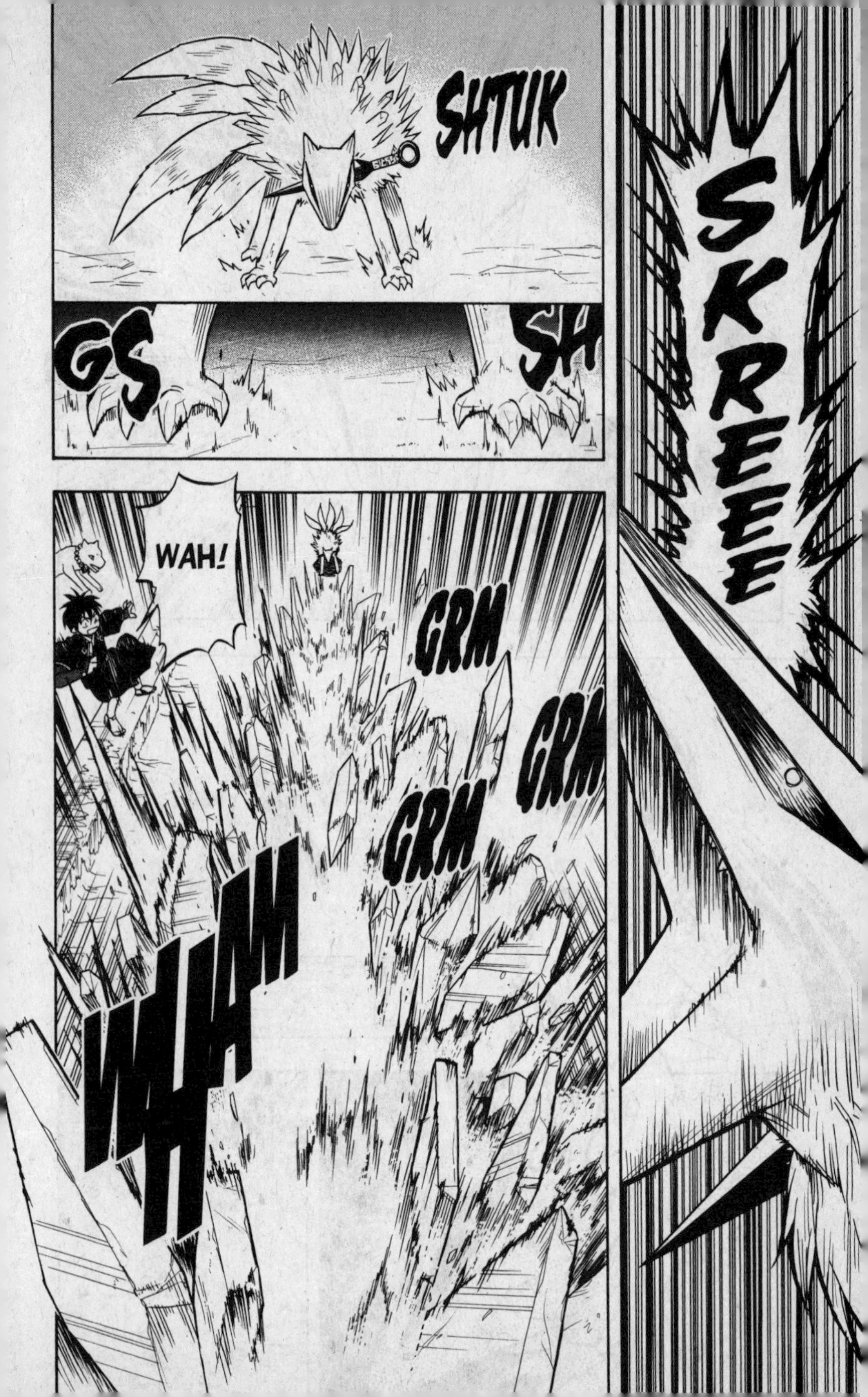
SKREEE
SHTUK
SH
GS
WAH!
GRM
GRM
GRM
WHAM

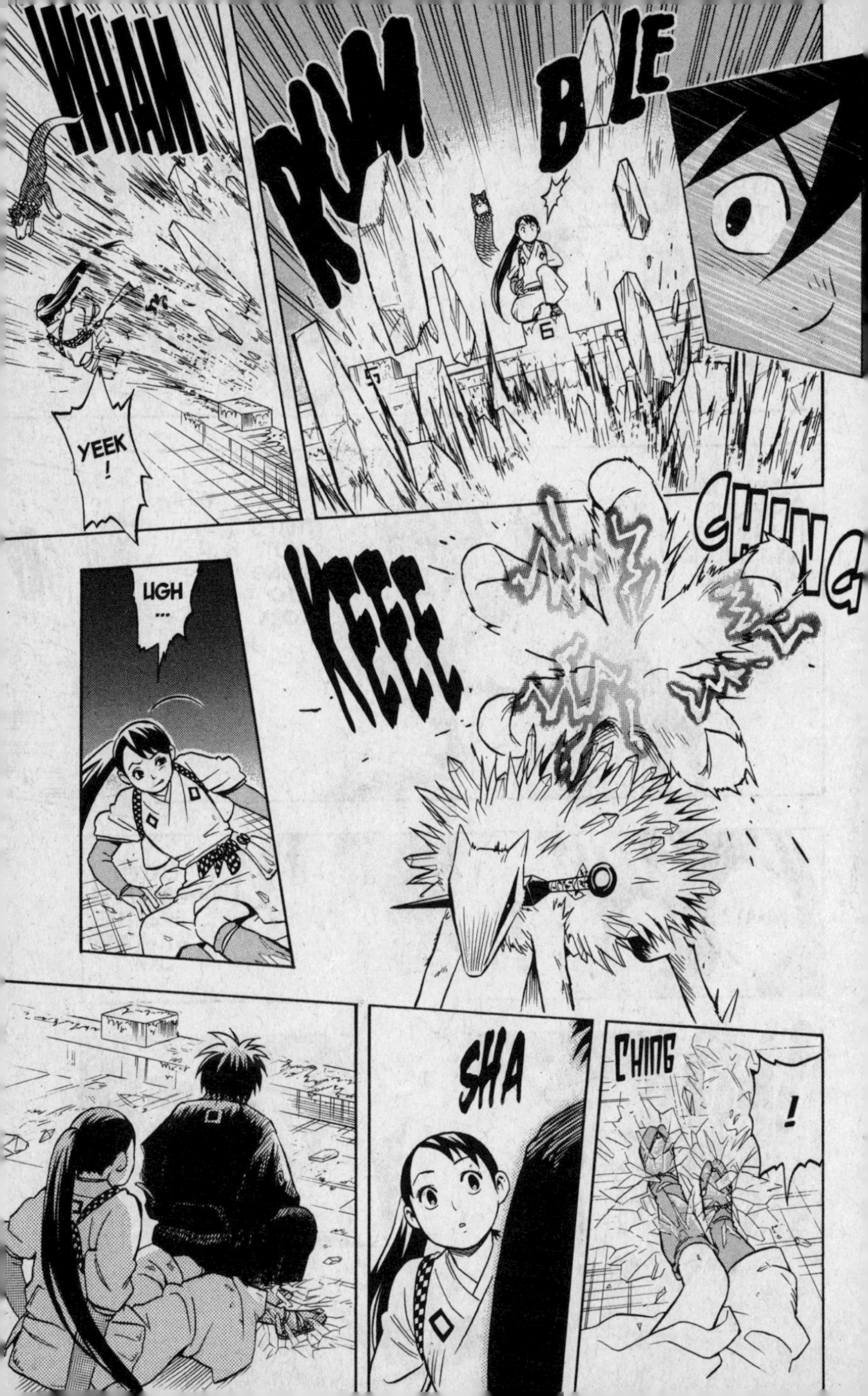
RUMBLE
WHAM
YEEK!
CHING
KEEE
UGH...
CHING
!
SHA

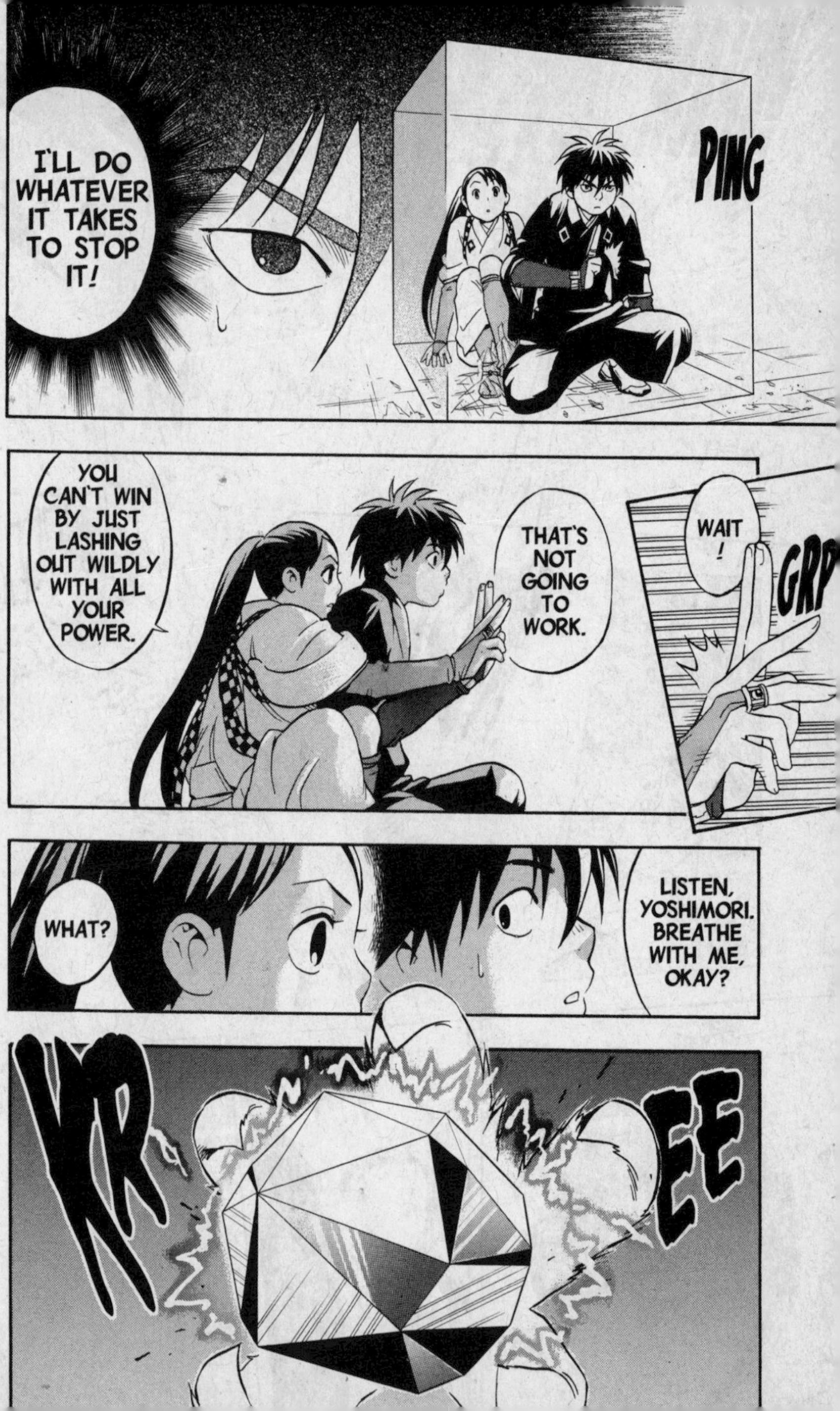
PING
I'LL DO WHATEVER IT TAKES TO STOP IT!
GRP
WAIT!
THAT'S NOT GOING TO WORK.
YOU CAN'T WIN BY JUST LASHING OUT WILDLY WITH ALL YOUR POWER.
LISTEN, YOSHIMORI. BREATHE WITH ME, OKAY?
WHAT?
EE
KR

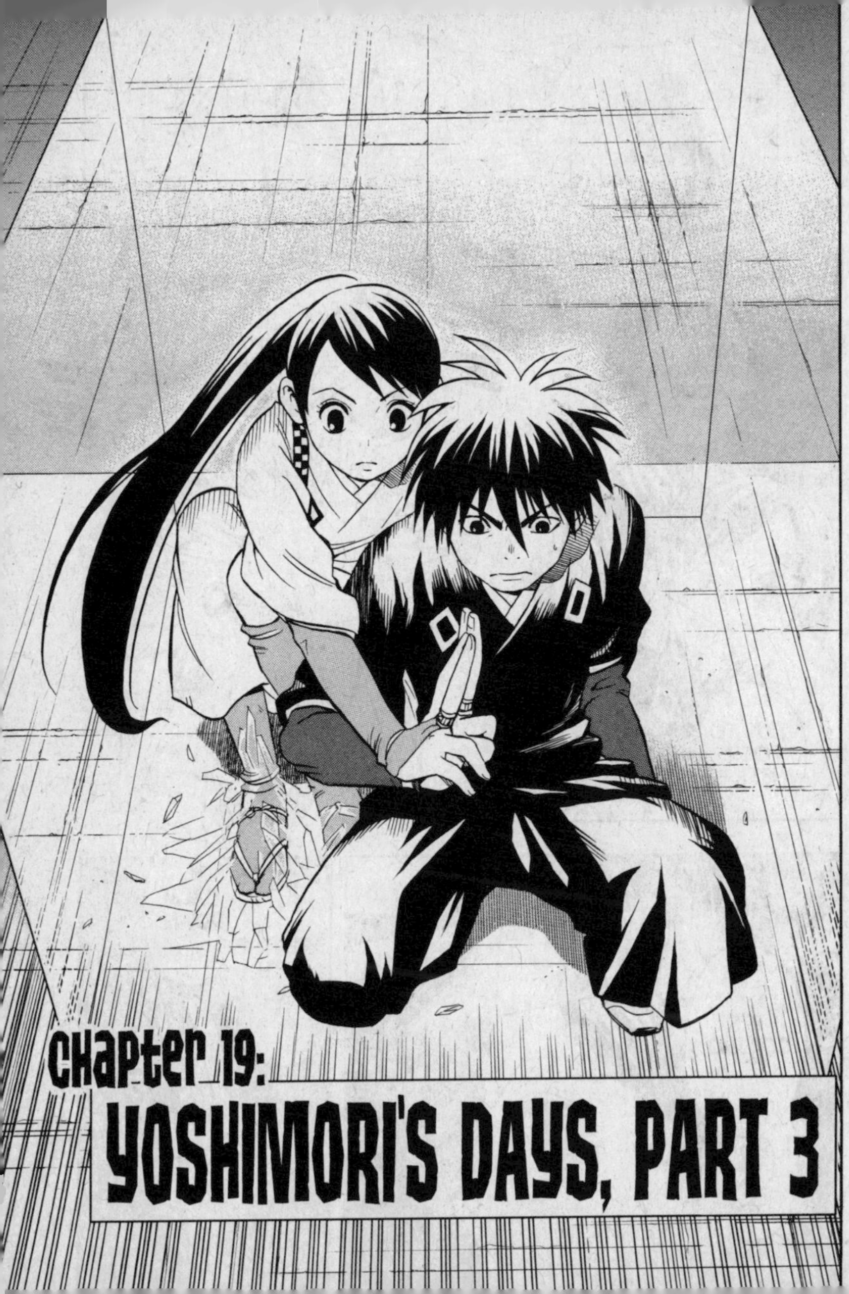
CHAPTER 19:
YOSHIMORI'S DAYS, PART 3

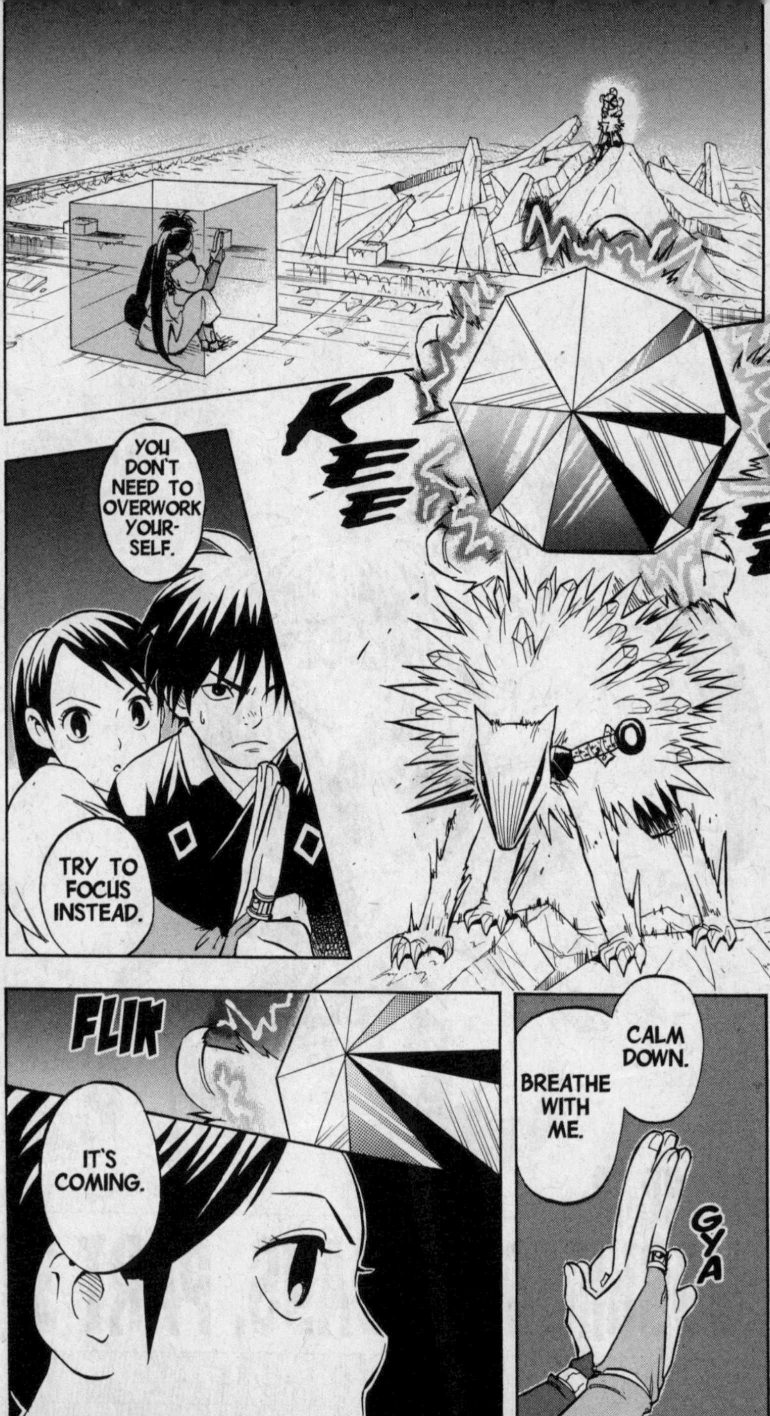
KEE
EE
YOU DON'T NEED TO OVERWORK YOUR-SELF.
TRY TO FOCUS INSTEAD.
CALM DOWN.
BREATHE WITH ME.
GYA
FLIR
IT'S COMING.

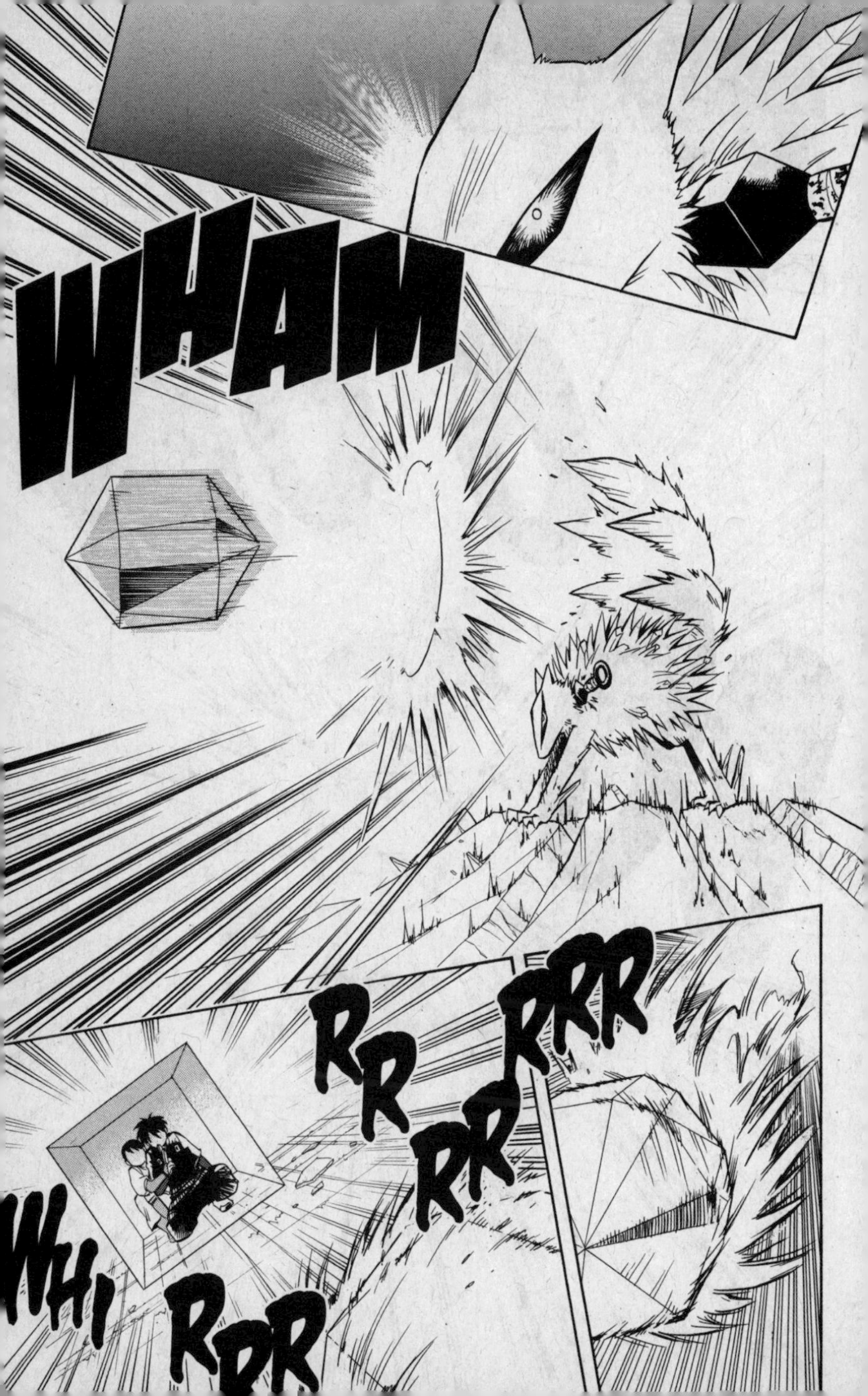
WHAM
RRRRRRRRR
WHIRRR

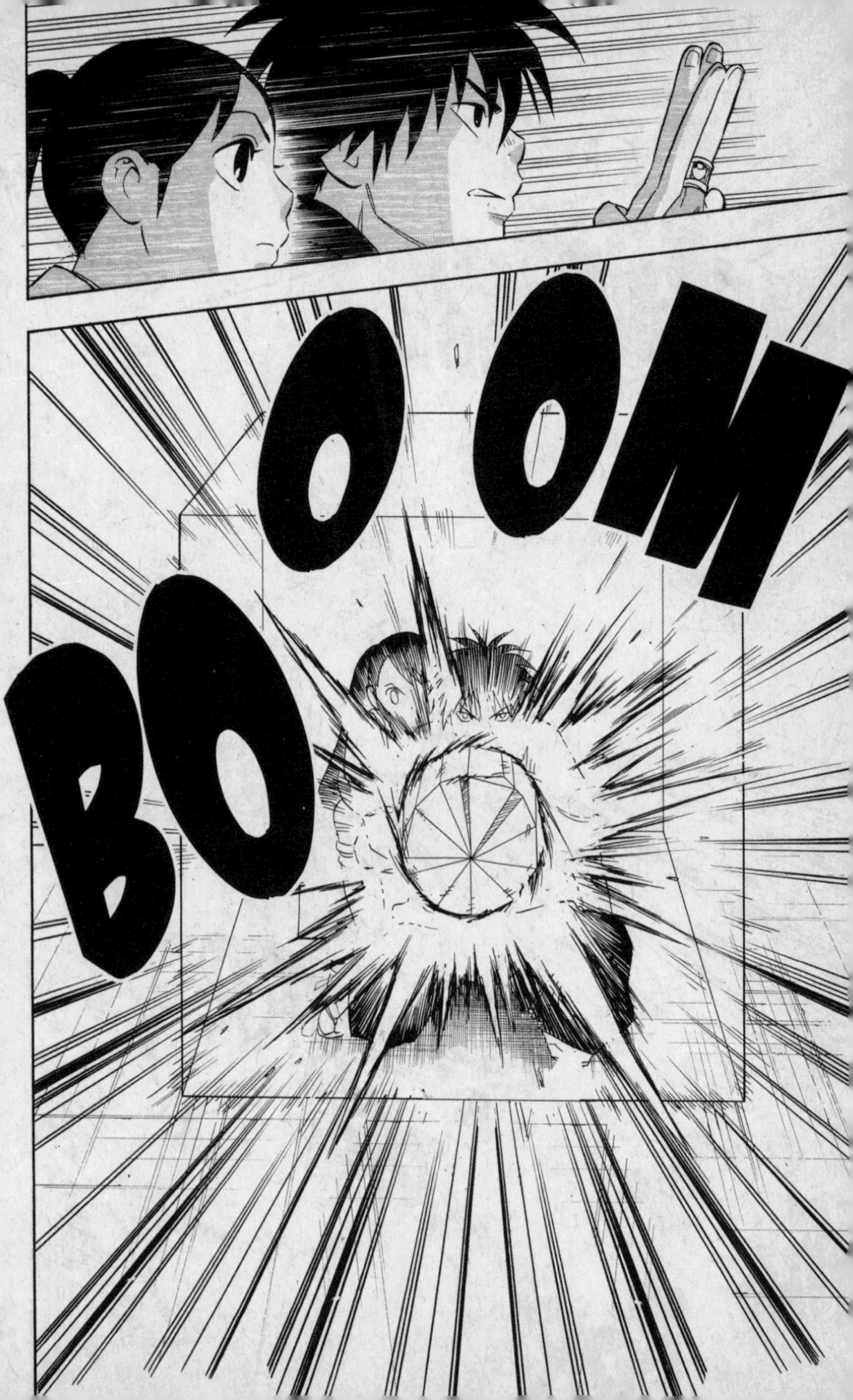
BOOOOM

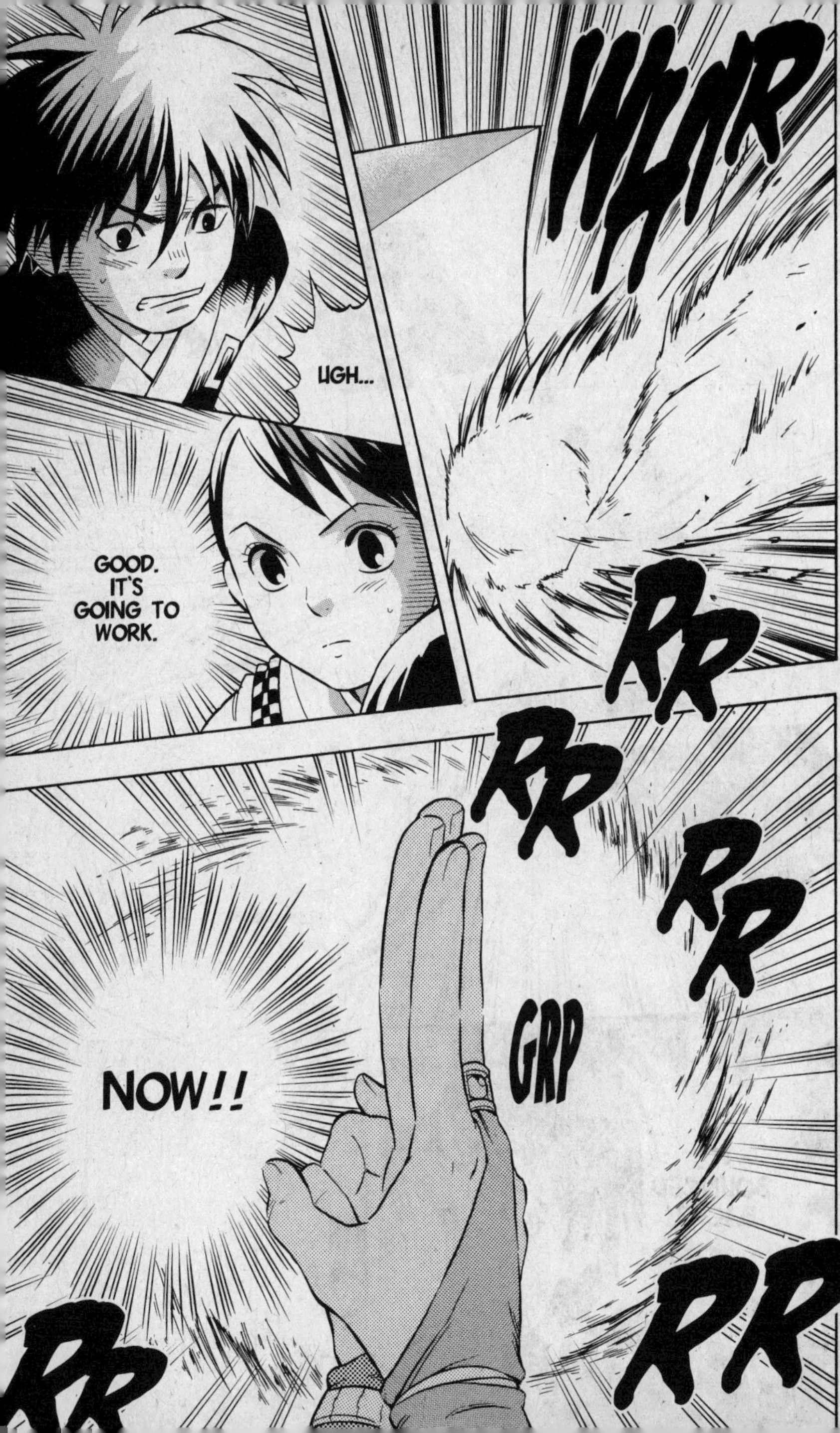
WHIR
RR
UGH...
GOOD. IT'S GOING TO WORK.
RR
RR
GRP
NOW!!
RRR
RR

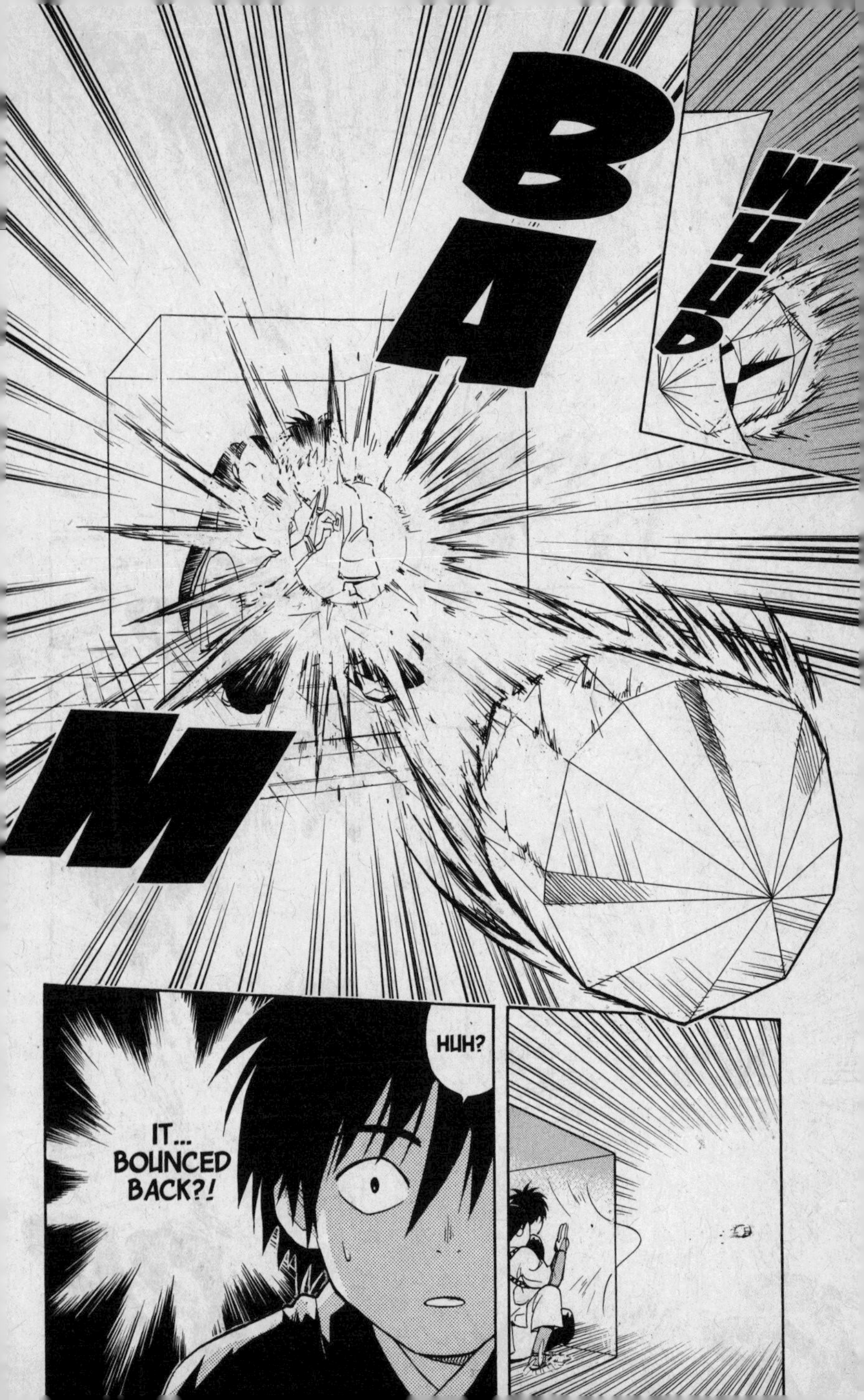
BAM
WHUD
HUH?
IT... BOUNCED BACK?!

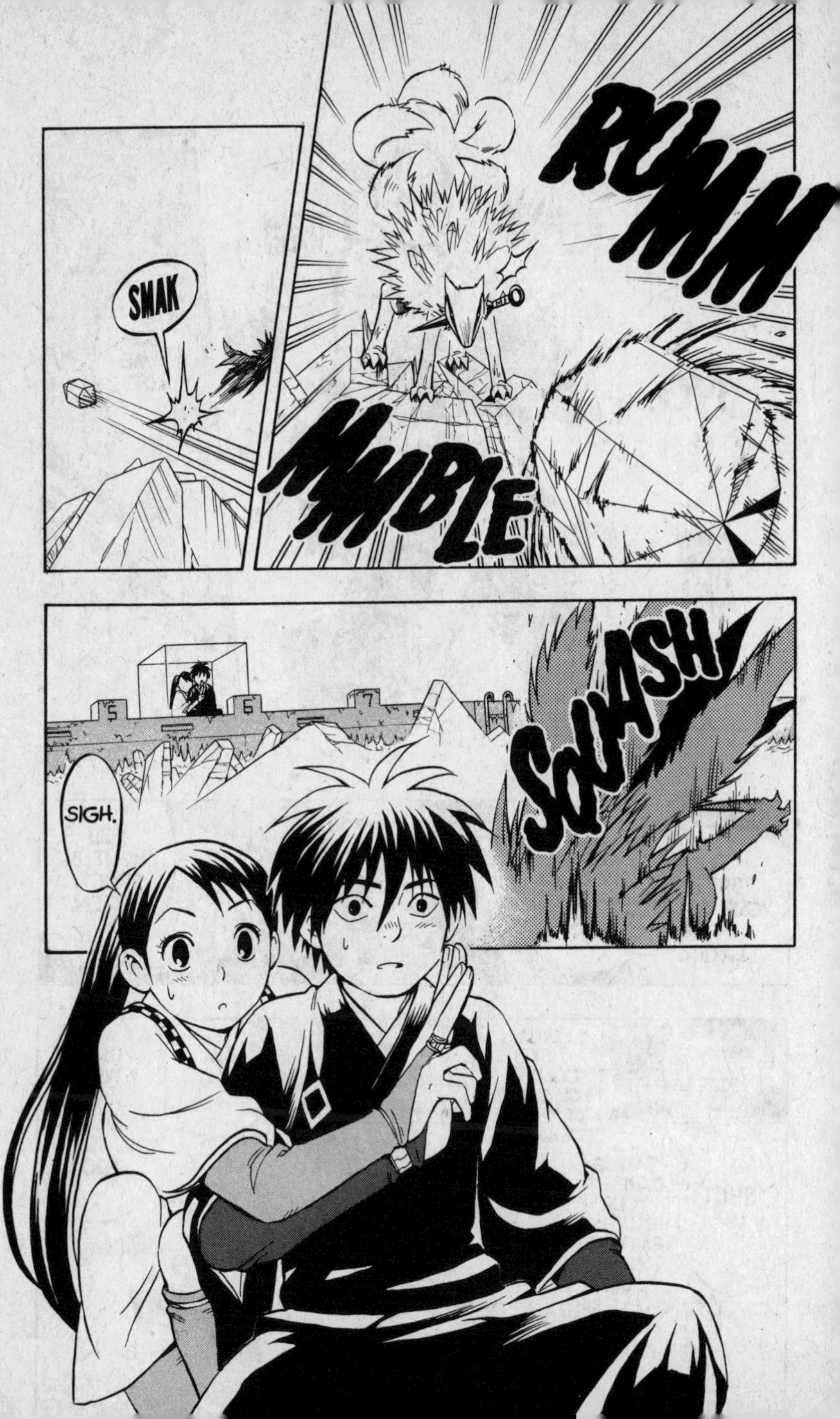
RUMMM
MMBLE
SMAK
SQUASH
SIGH.

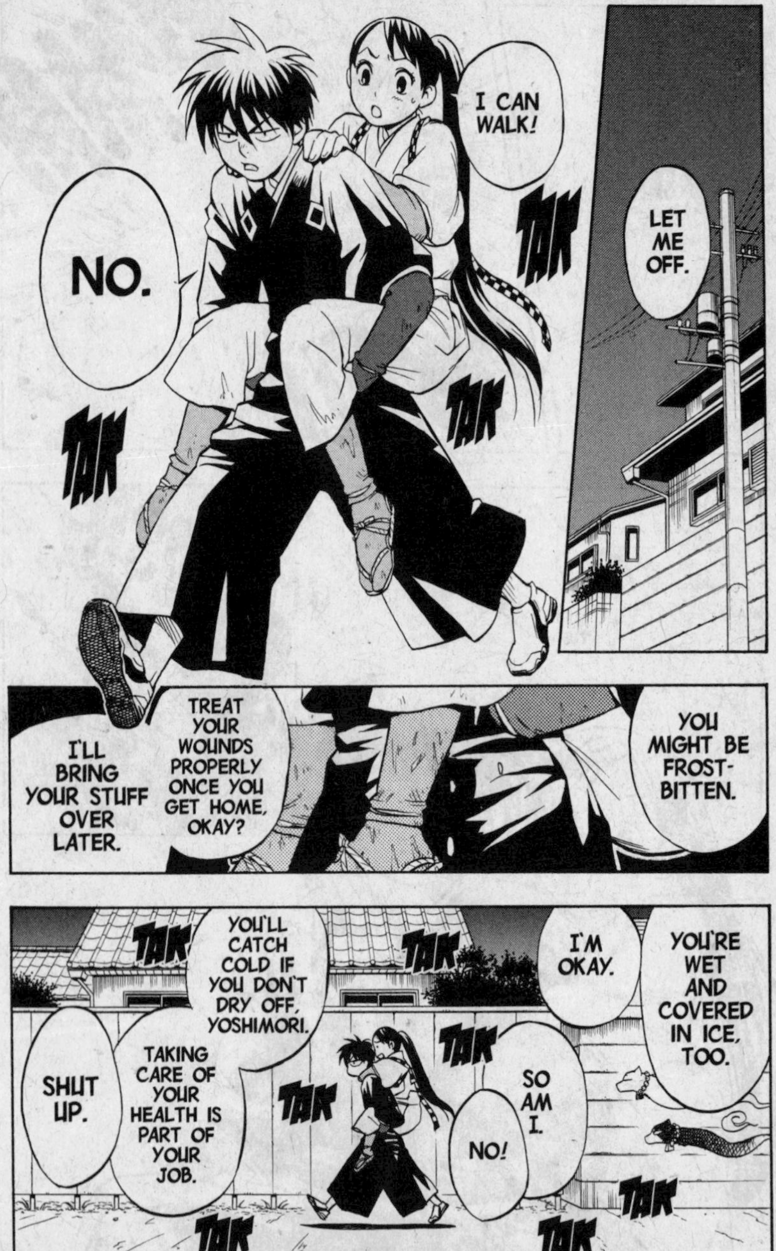
LET ME OFF.
I CAN WALK!
TAK
NO.
TAK
TAK
YOU MIGHT BE FROST-BITTEN.
TREAT YOUR WOUNDS PROPERLY ONCE YOU GET HOME, OKAY?
I'LL BRING YOUR STUFF OVER LATER.
YOU'RE WET AND COVERED IN ICE, TOO.
I'M OKAY.
SO AM I.
NO!
TAK
TAK
TAK
YOU'LL CATCH COLD IF YOU DON'T DRY OFF, YOSHIMORI.
TAK
TAKING CARE OF YOUR HEALTH IS PART OF YOUR JOB.
TAK
SHUT UP.
TAK
TAK

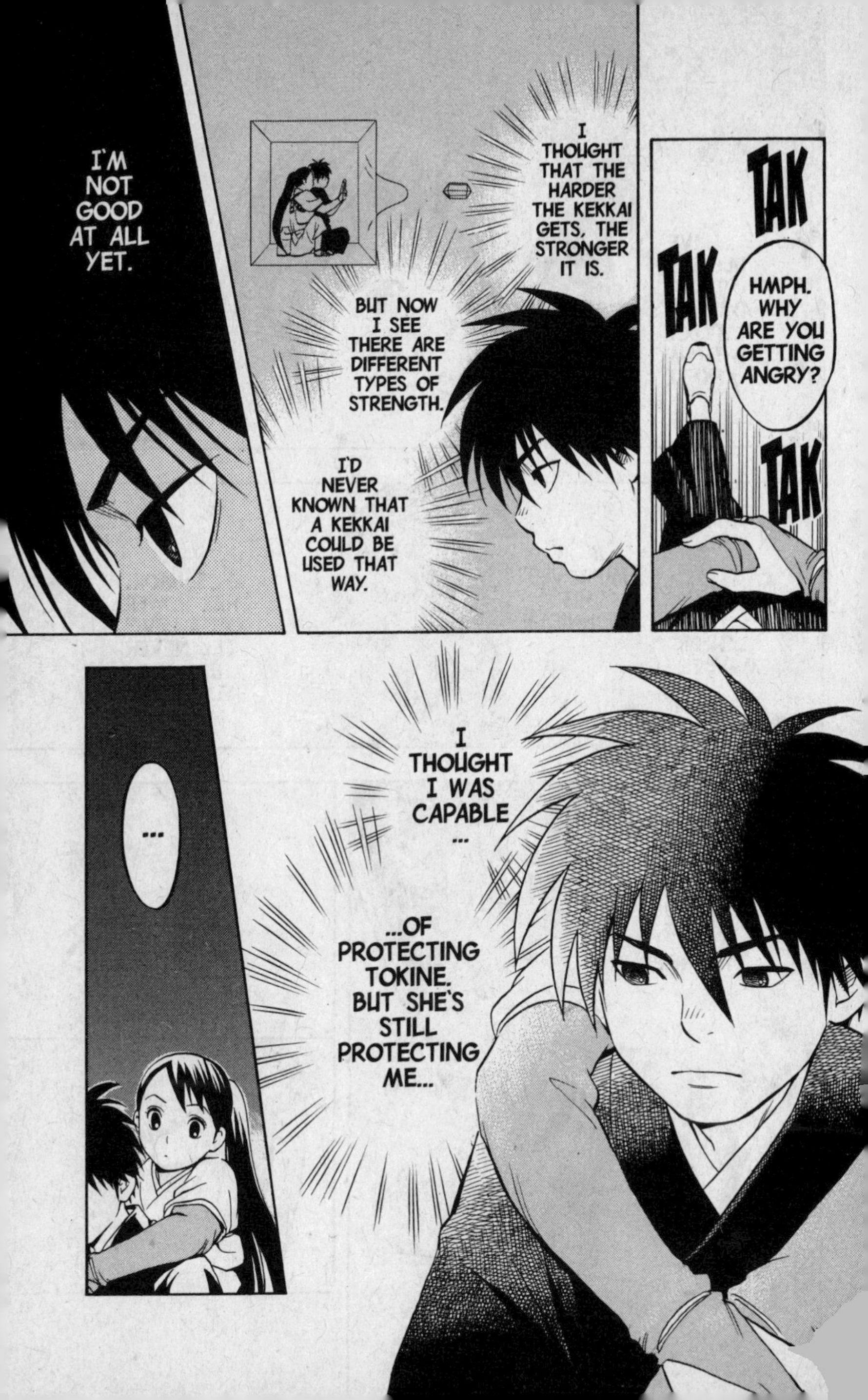
TAK
TAK
HMPH. WHY ARE YOU GETTING ANGRY?
TAK
I THOUGHT THAT THE HARDER THE KEKKAI GETS, THE STRONGER IT IS.
BUT NOW I SEE THERE ARE DIFFERENT TYPES OF STRENGTH.
I'D NEVER KNOWN THAT A KEKKAI COULD BE USED THAT WAY.
I'M NOT GOOD AT ALL YET.
I THOUGHT I WAS CAPABLE ...
...OF PROTECTING TOKINE. BUT SHE'S STILL PROTECTING ME...
...

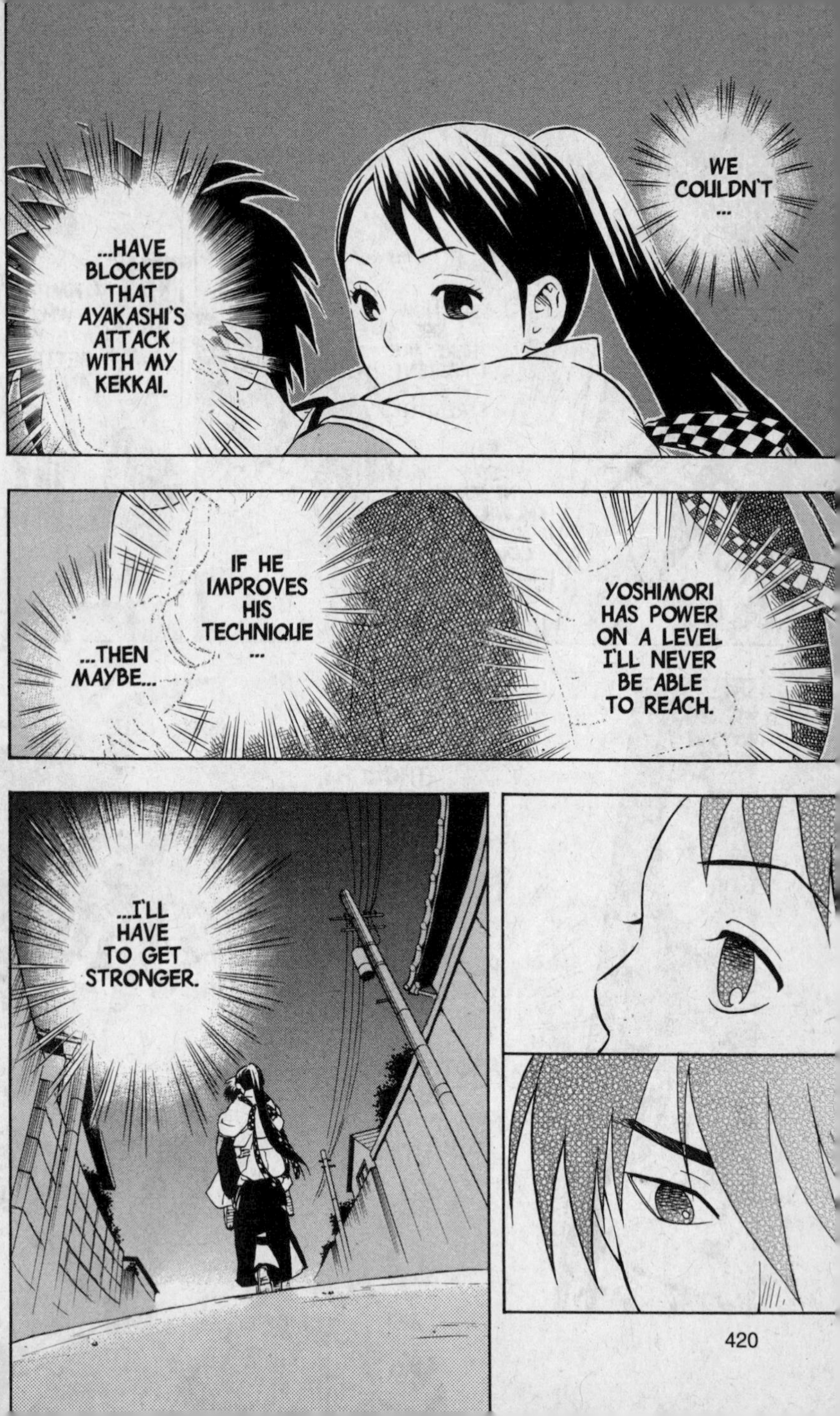
WE COULDN'T ...
...HAVE BLOCKED THAT AYAKASHI'S ATTACK WITH MY KEKKAI.
YOSHIMORI HAS POWER ON A LEVEL I'LL NEVER BE ABLE TO REACH.
IF HE IMPROVES HIS TECHNIQUE ...
...THEN MAYBE...
...I'LL HAVE TO GET STRONGER.

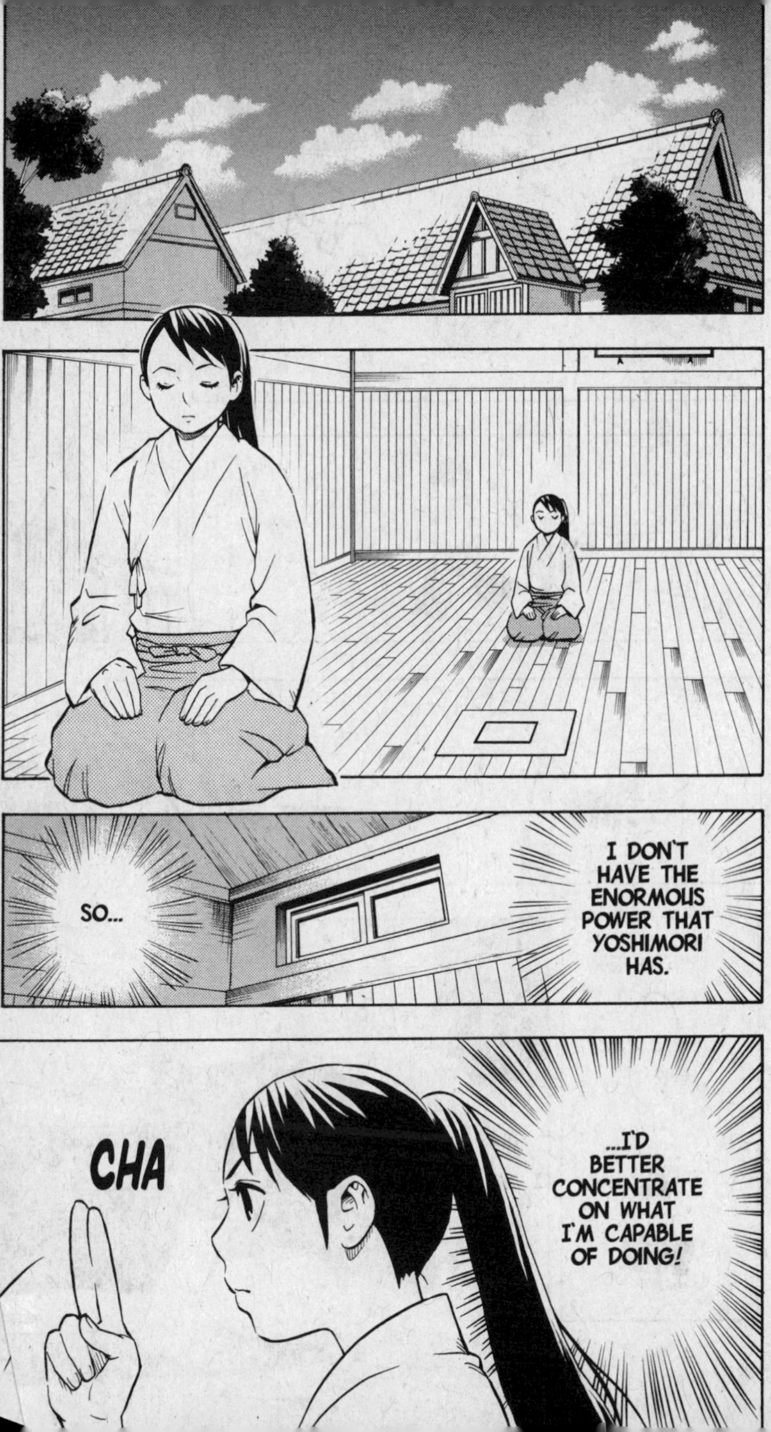
I DON'T HAVE THE ENORMOUS POWER THAT YOSHIMORI HAS.
SO...
...I'D BETTER CONCENTRATE ON WHAT I'M CAPABLE OF DOING!
CHA

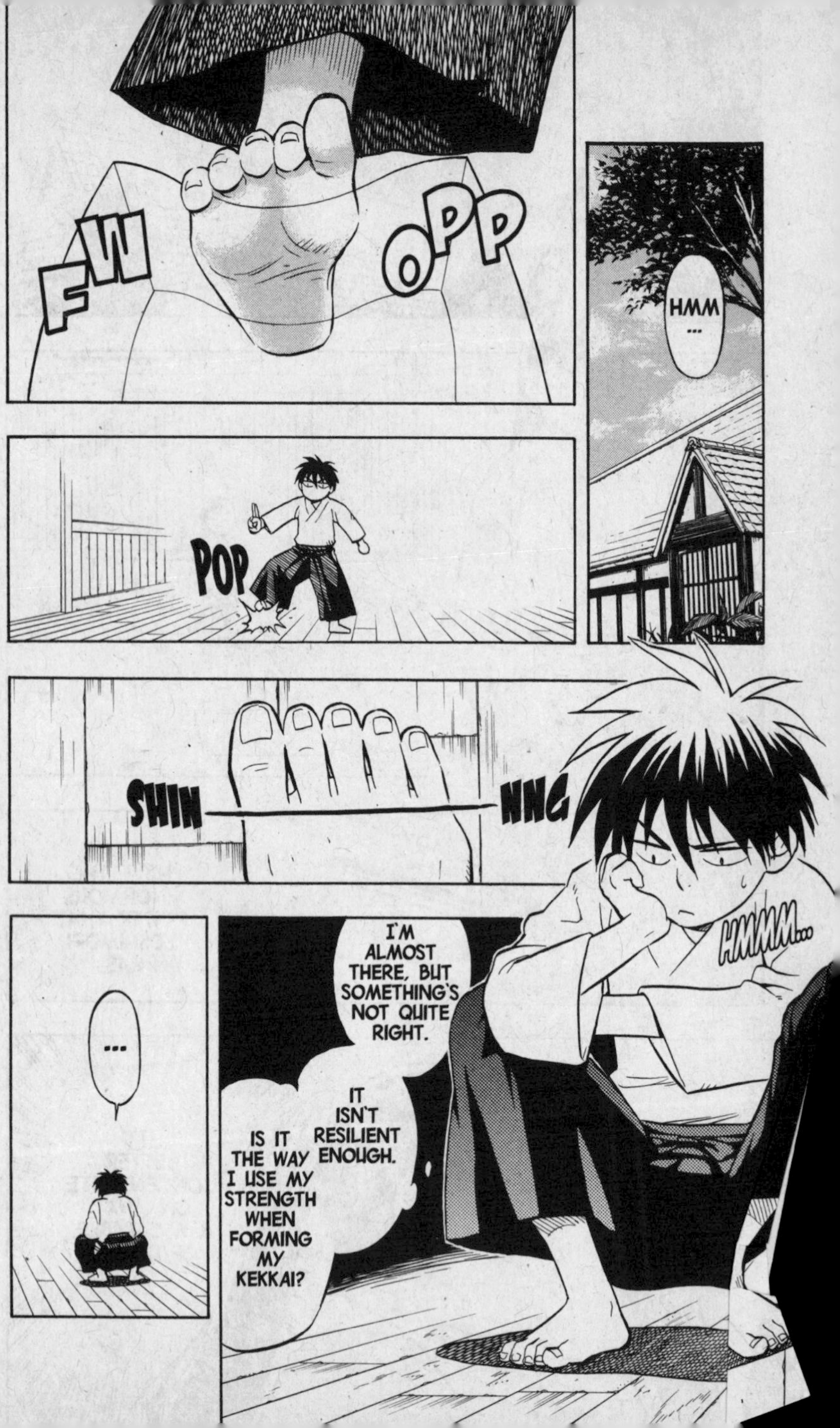
HMM...
FWOPP
POP
SHINNNG
HMMM...
I'M ALMOST THERE, BUT SOMETHING'S NOT QUITE RIGHT.
IT ISN'T RESILIENT ENOUGH.
IS IT THE WAY I USE MY STRENGTH WHEN FORMING MY KEKKAI?
...

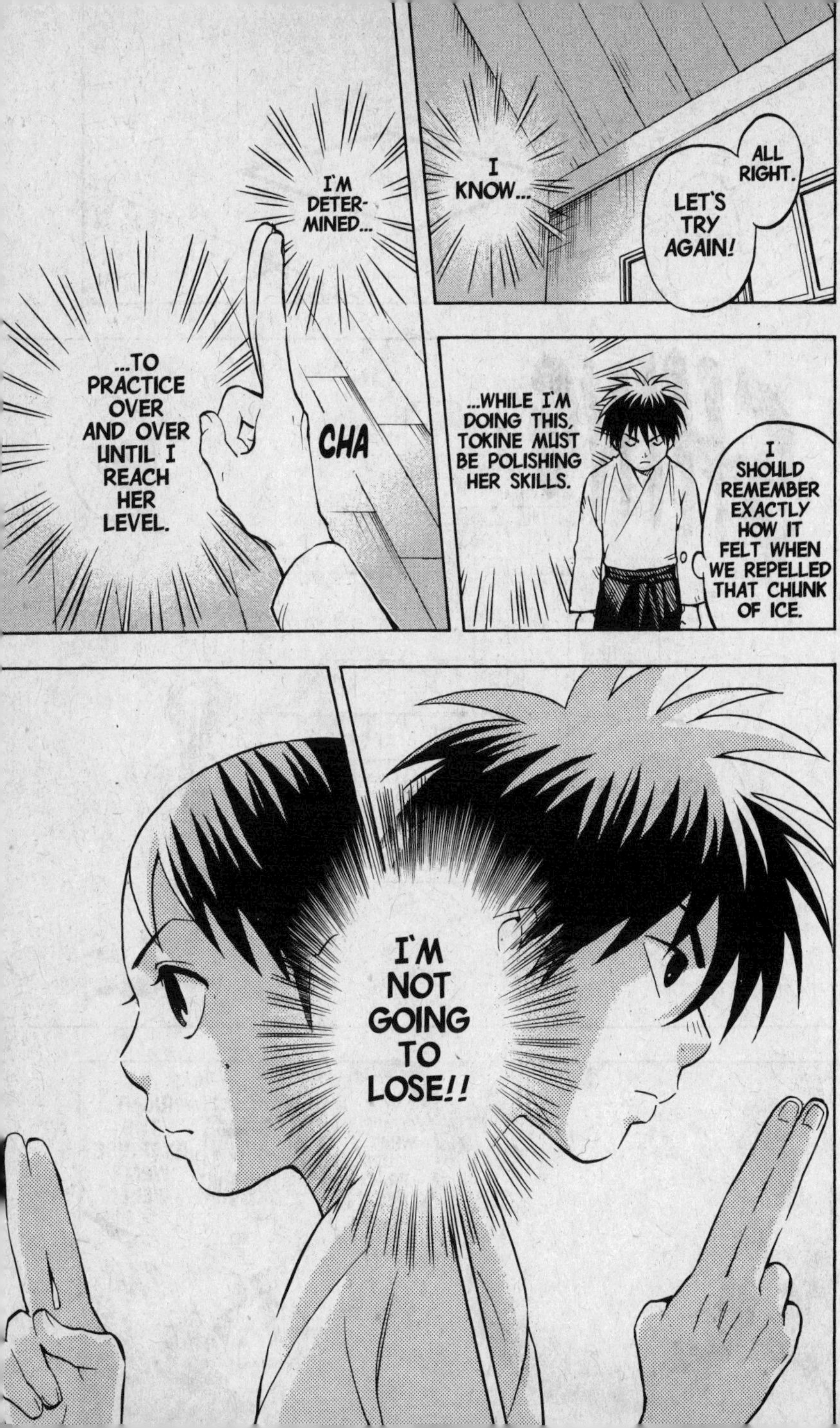
ALL RIGHT. LET'S TRY AGAIN!
I KNOW...
I SHOULD REMEMBER EXACTLY HOW IT FELT WHEN WE REPELLED THAT CHUNK OF ICE.
...WHILE I'M DOING THIS, TOKINE MUST BE POLISHING HER SKILLS.
I'M DETERMINED...
CHA
...TO PRACTICE OVER AND OVER UNTIL I REACH HER LEVEL.
I'M NOT GOING TO LOSE!!

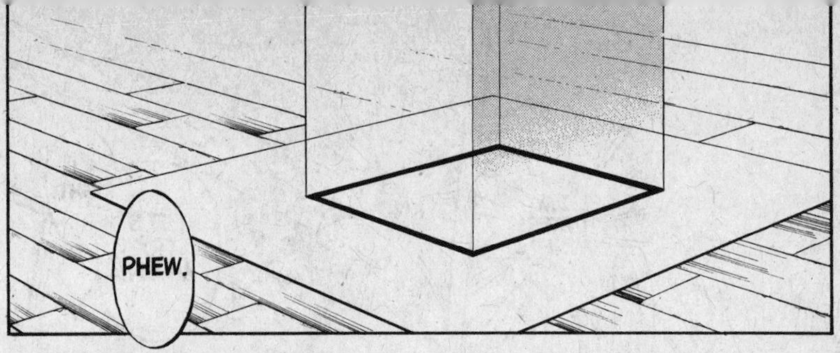
PHEW.

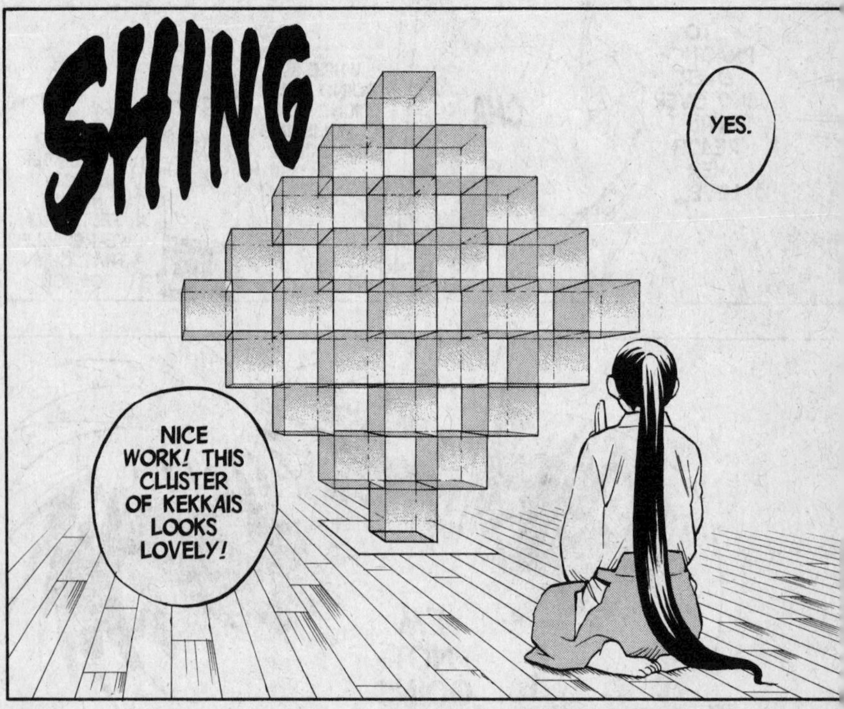
SHING
NICE WORK! THIS CLUSTER OF KEKKAIS LOOKS LOVELY!
YES.

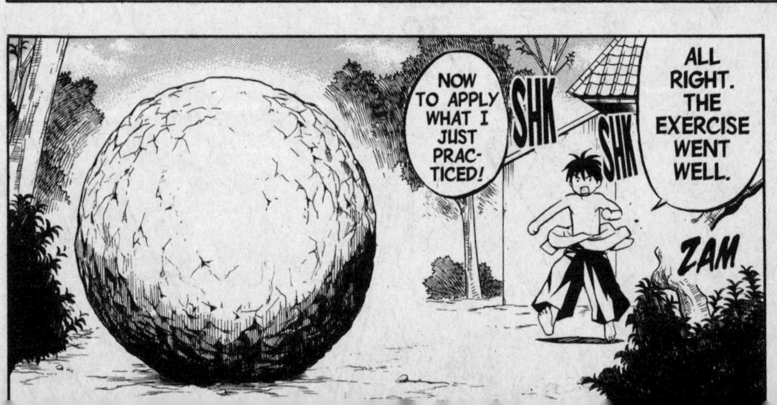
ALL RIGHT. THE EXERCISE WENT WELL.
SHK
SHK
NOW TO APPLY WHAT I JUST PRAC-TICED!
ZAM

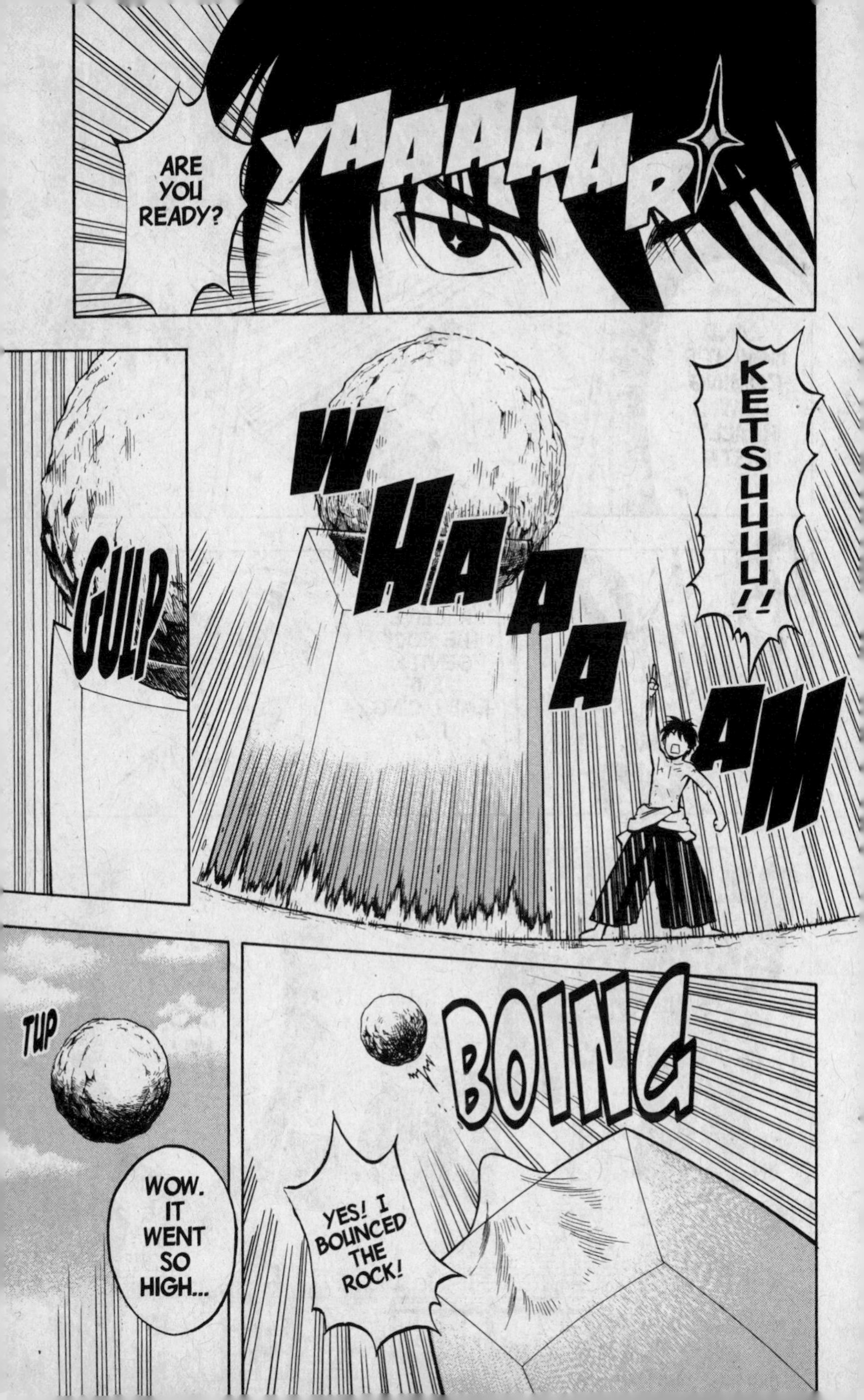
YAAAAAR
ARE YOU READY?
KETSUUUU!!
WHAAAAM
GULP
BOING
YES! I BOUNCED THE ROCK!
TUP
WOW. IT WENT SO HIGH...

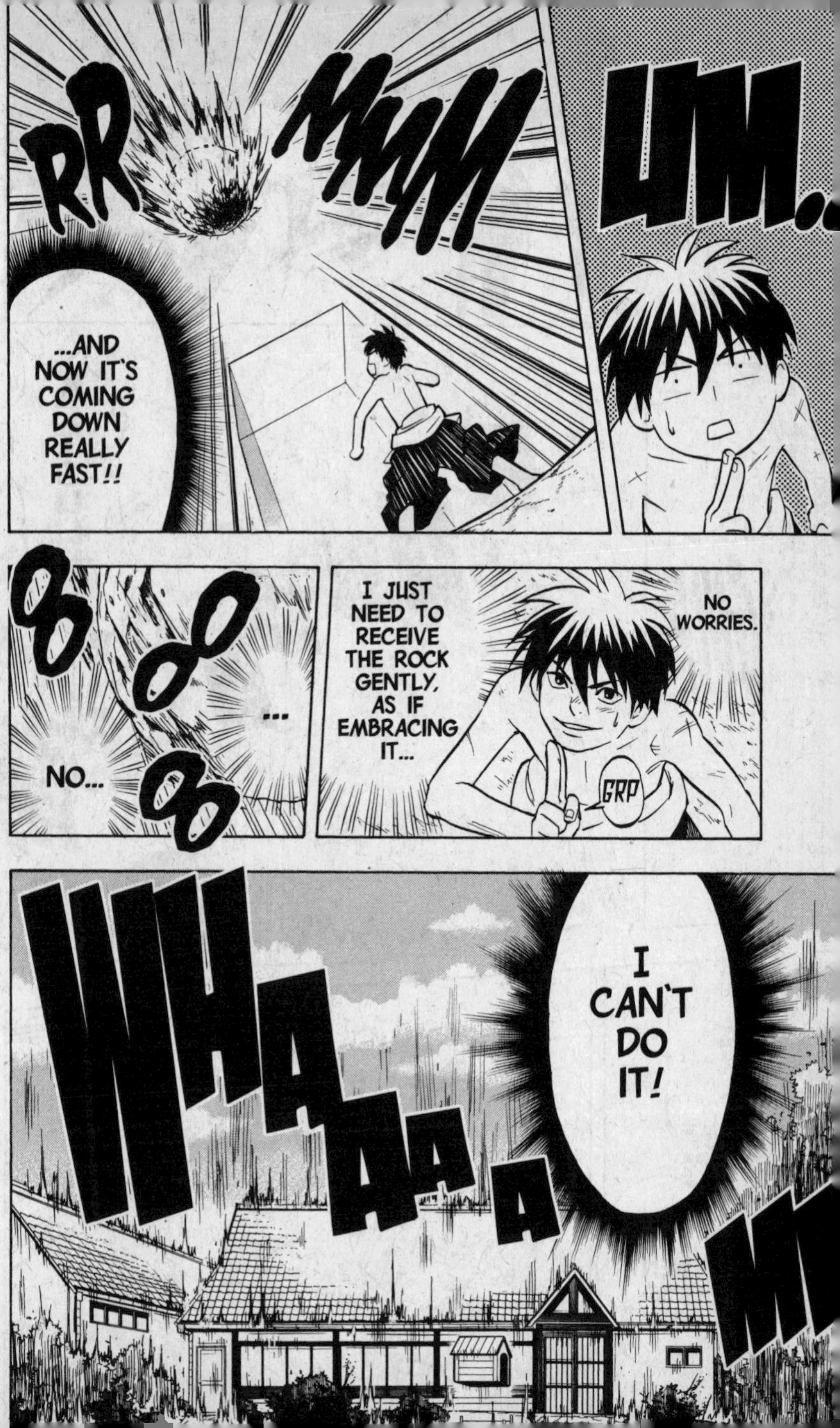
UM...
RRMMMM
...AND NOW IT'S COMING DOWN REALLY FAST!!
NO WORRIES.
I JUST NEED TO RECEIVE THE ROCK GENTLY, AS IF EMBRACING IT...
GRP
...
NO...
I CAN'T DO IT!
WHAAAAM

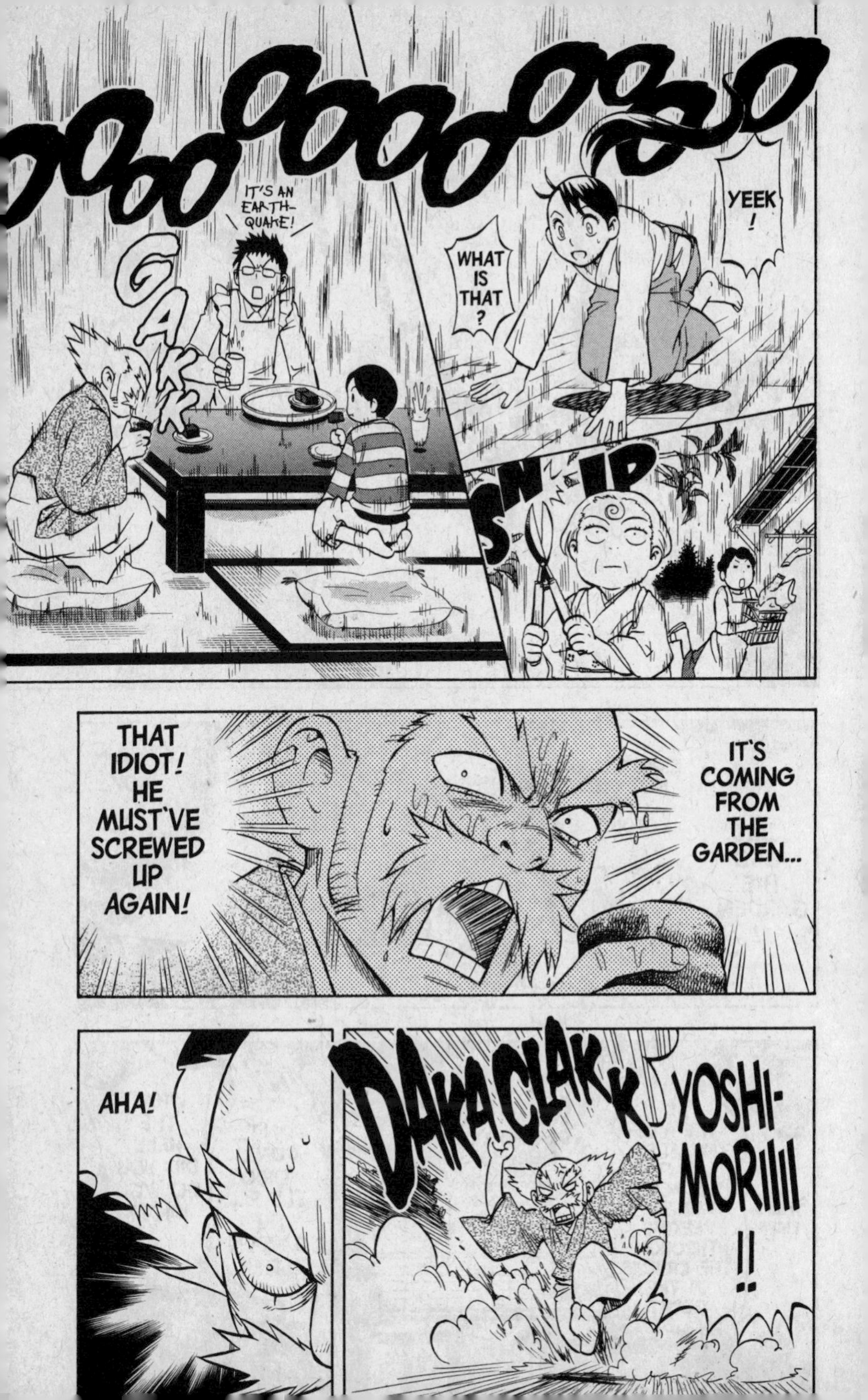
YEEK!
WHAT IS THAT?
IT'S AN EARTH-QUAKE!
GAK
SNIP
IT'S COMING FROM THE GARDEN...
THAT IDIOT! HE MUST'VE SCREWED UP AGAIN!
DAKACLAKK
YOSHI-MORIIII!!
AHA!

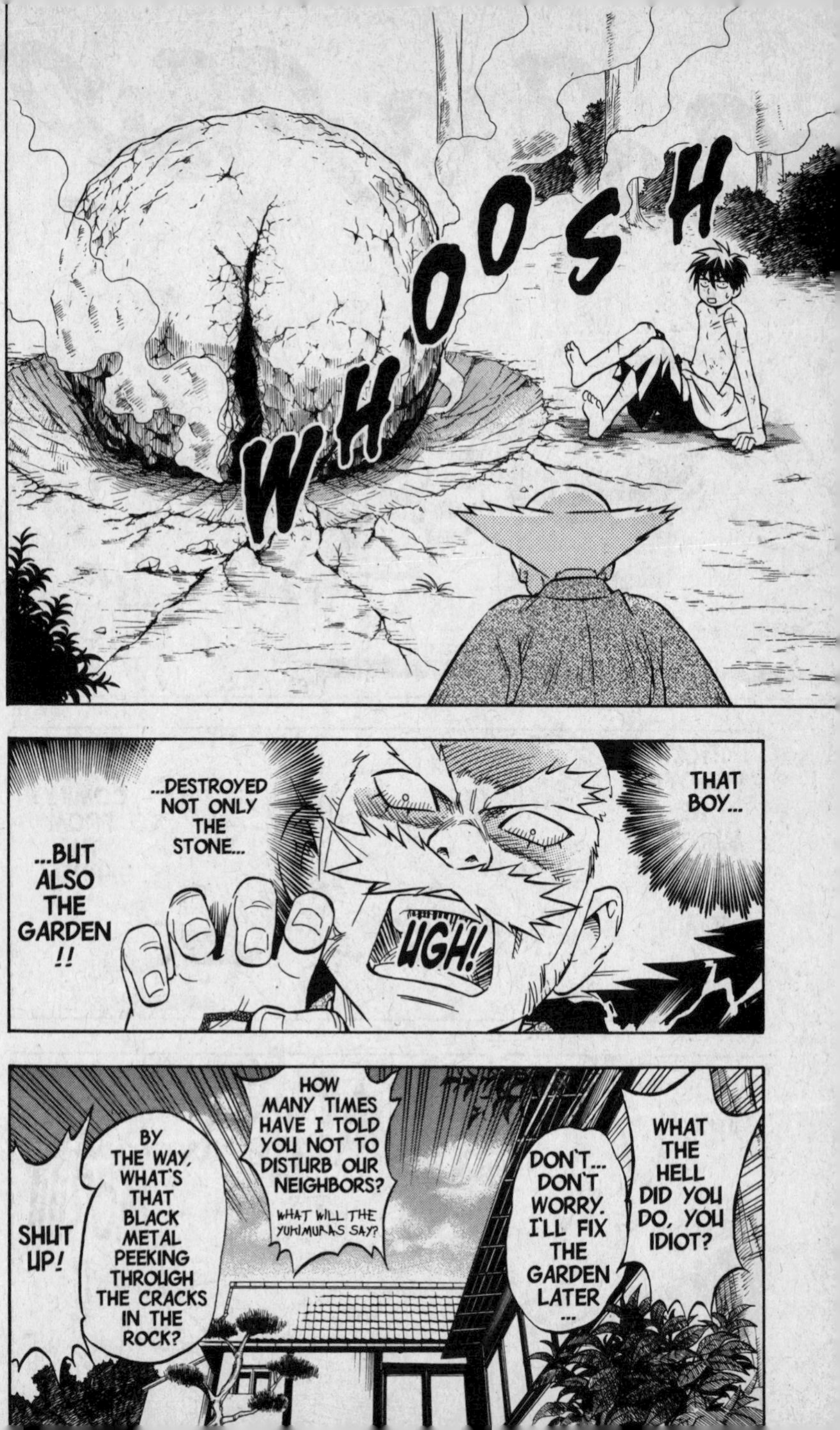
WHOOSH
THAT BOY...
...DESTROYED NOT ONLY THE STONE...
...BUT ALSO THE GARDEN!!
UGH!
WHAT THE HELL DID YOU DO, YOU IDIOT?
DON'T... DON'T WORRY. I'LL FIX THE GARDEN LATER...
HOW MANY TIMES HAVE I TOLD YOU NOT TO DISTURB OUR NEIGHBORS?
WHAT WILL THE YUKIMURAS SAY?
BY THE WAY, WHAT'S THAT BLACK METAL PEEKING THROUGH THE CRACKS IN THE ROCK?
SHUT UP!

Chapter 20: A 400-Year Reunion

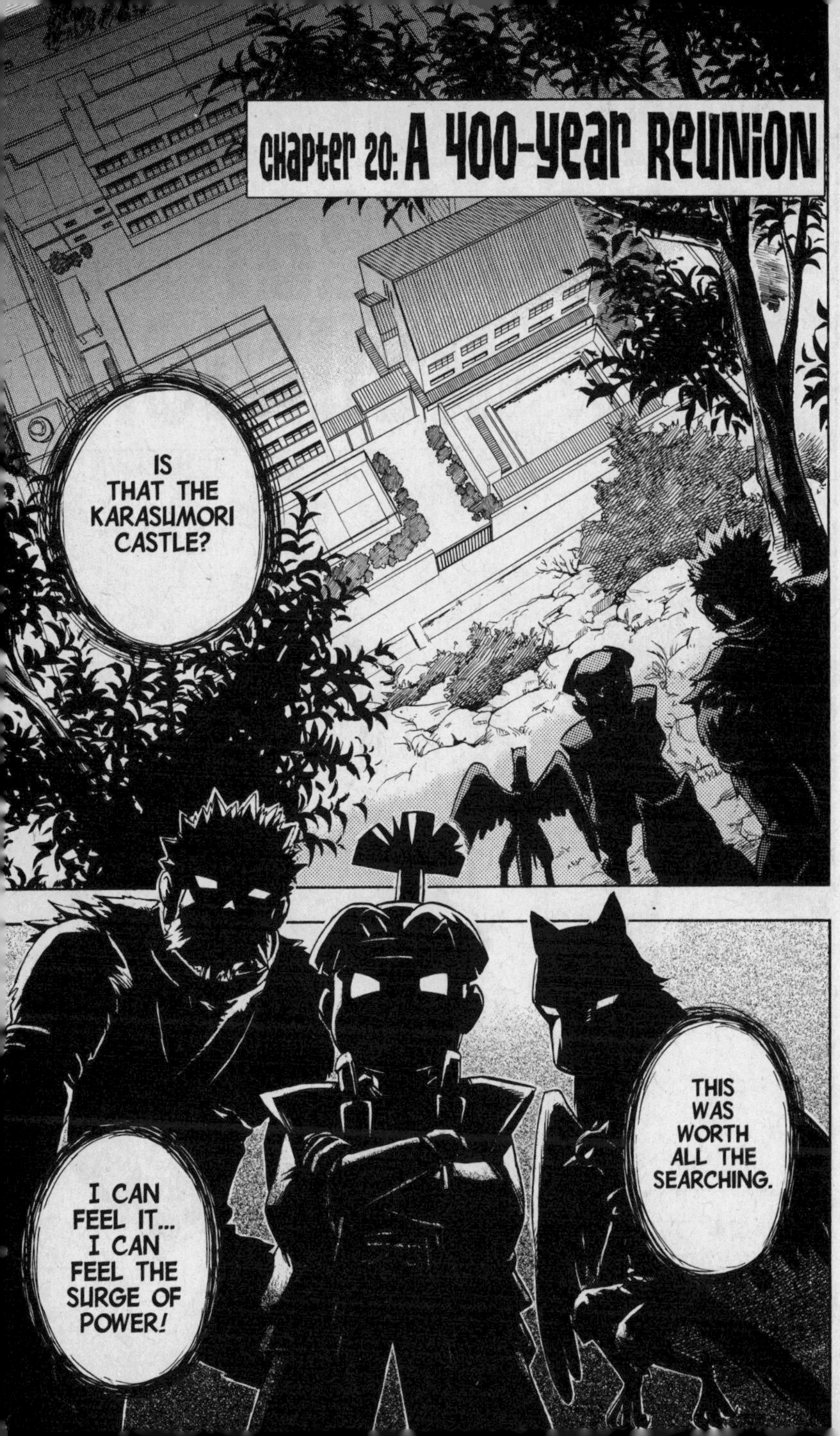

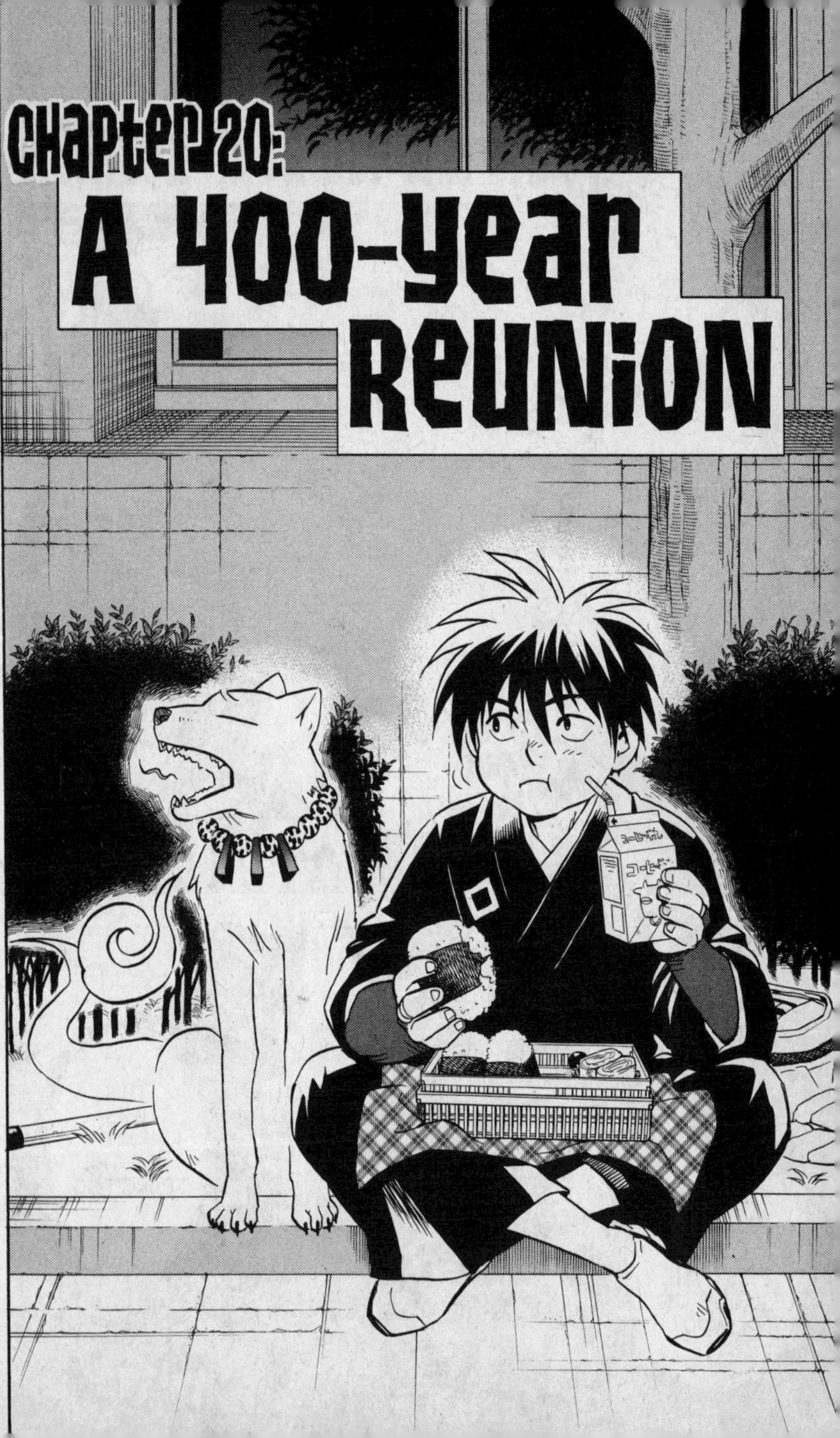
Chapter 20:
A 400-year Reunion

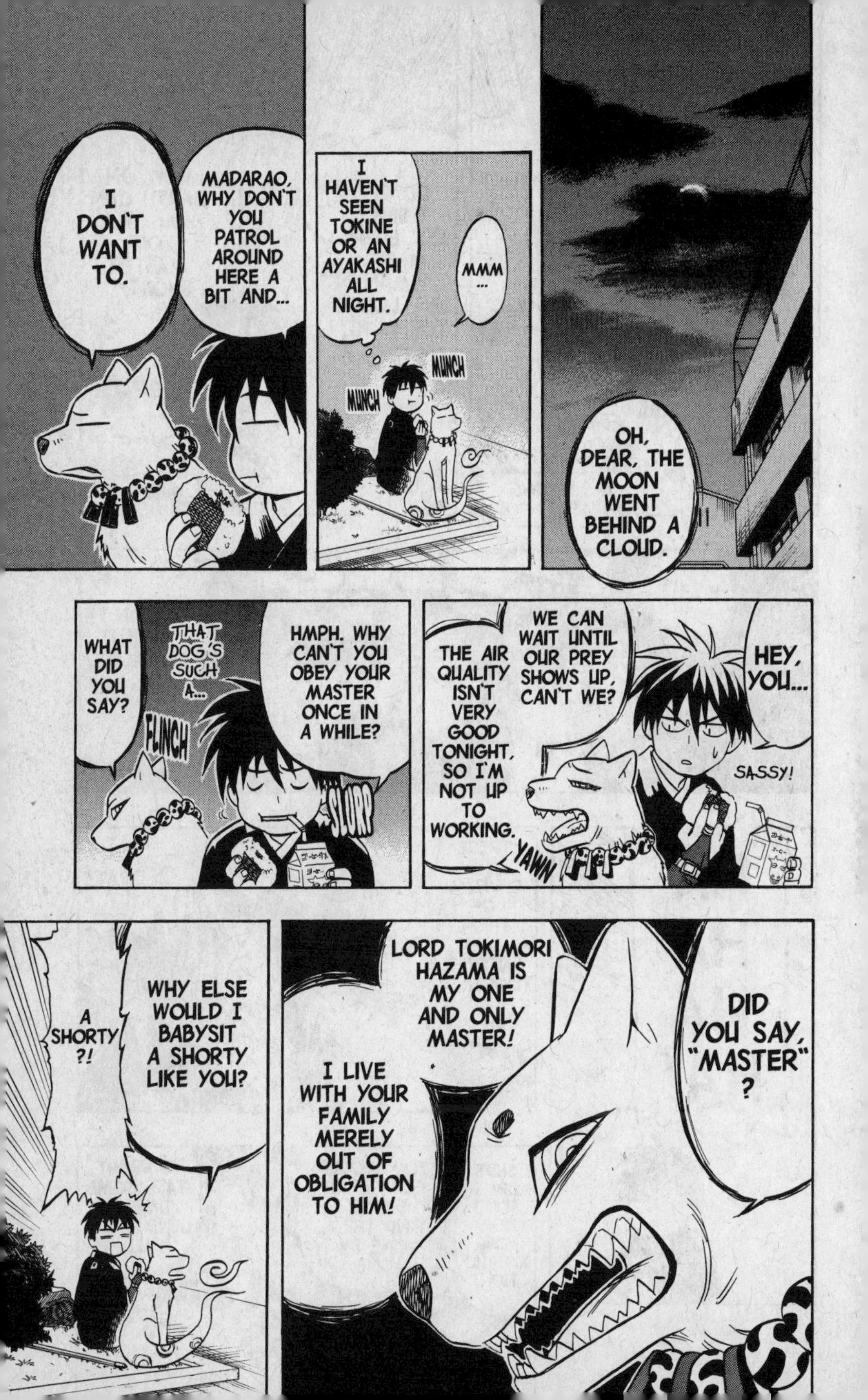
OH, DEAR, THE MOON WENT BEHIND A CLOUD.
I HAVEN'T SEEN TOKINE OR AN AYAKASHI ALL NIGHT.
MMM...
MUNCH
MUNCH
MADARAO, WHY DON'T YOU PATROL AROUND HERE A BIT AND...
I DON'T WANT TO.
HEY, YOU...
WE CAN WAIT UNTIL OUR PREY SHOWS UP, CAN'T WE?
THE AIR QUALITY ISN'T VERY GOOD TONIGHT, SO I'M NOT UP TO WORKING.
SASSY!
YAWN
HMPH. WHY CAN'T YOU OBEY YOUR MASTER ONCE IN A WHILE?
SLURP
THAT DOG'S SUCH A...
FLINCH
WHAT DID YOU SAY?
DID YOU SAY, "MASTER"?
LORD TOKIMORI HAZAMA IS MY ONE AND ONLY MASTER!
I LIVE WITH YOUR FAMILY MERELY OUT OF OBLIGATION TO HIM!
WHY ELSE WOULD I BABYSIT A SHORTY LIKE YOU?
A SHORTY?!

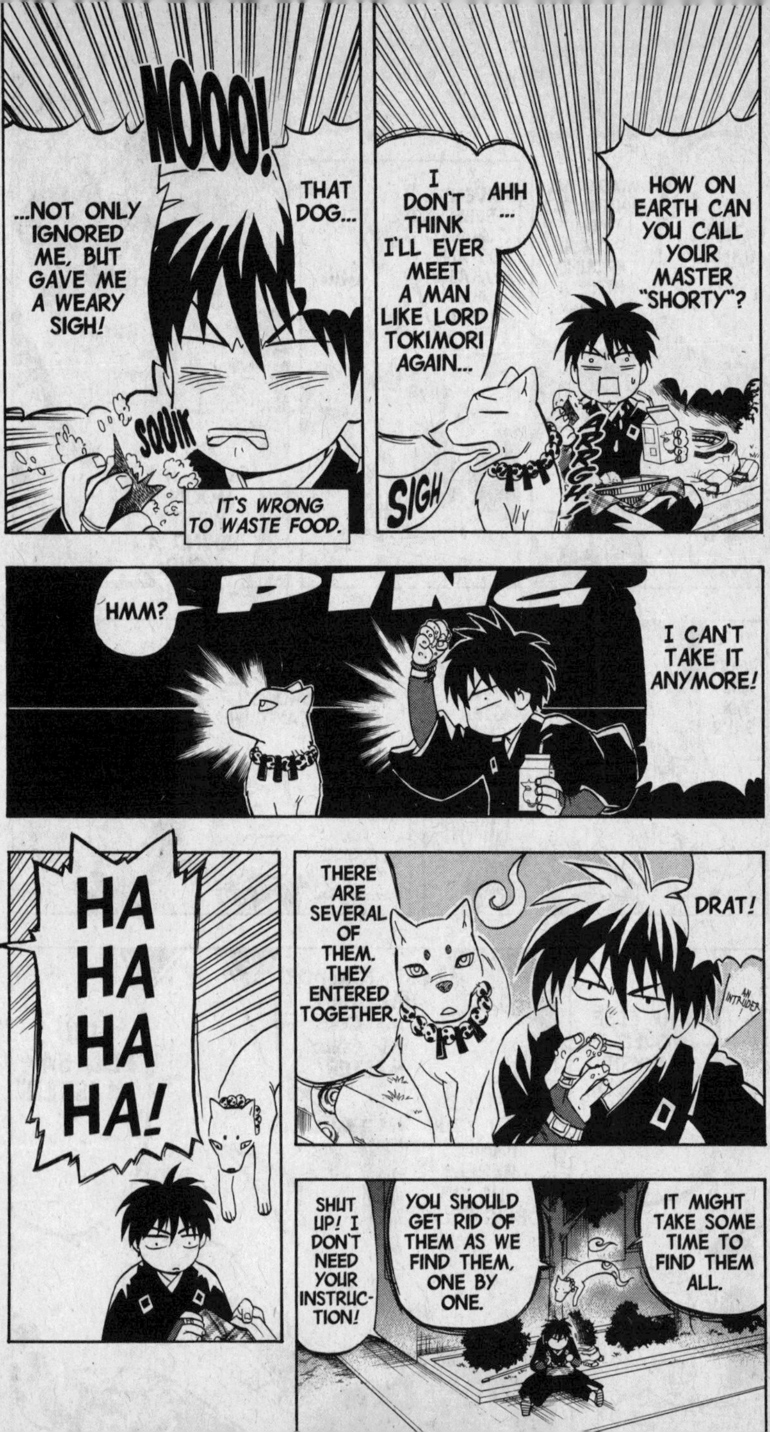
HOW ON EARTH CAN YOU CALL YOUR MASTER "SHORTY"?
AHH ...
I DON'T THINK I'LL EVER MEET A MAN LIKE LORD TOKIMORI AGAIN...
ARRGH
SIGH
NOOO!
THAT DOG...
...NOT ONLY IGNORED ME, BUT GAVE ME A WEARY SIGH!
SQUIK
IT'S WRONG TO WASTE FOOD.
I CAN'T TAKE IT ANYMORE!
PING
HMM?
DRAT!
AN INTRUDER!
THERE ARE SEVERAL OF THEM. THEY ENTERED TOGETHER.
IT MIGHT TAKE SOME TIME TO FIND THEM ALL.
YOU SHOULD GET RID OF THEM AS WE FIND THEM, ONE BY ONE.
SHUT UP! I DON'T NEED YOUR INSTRUCTION!
HA HA HA HA HA!

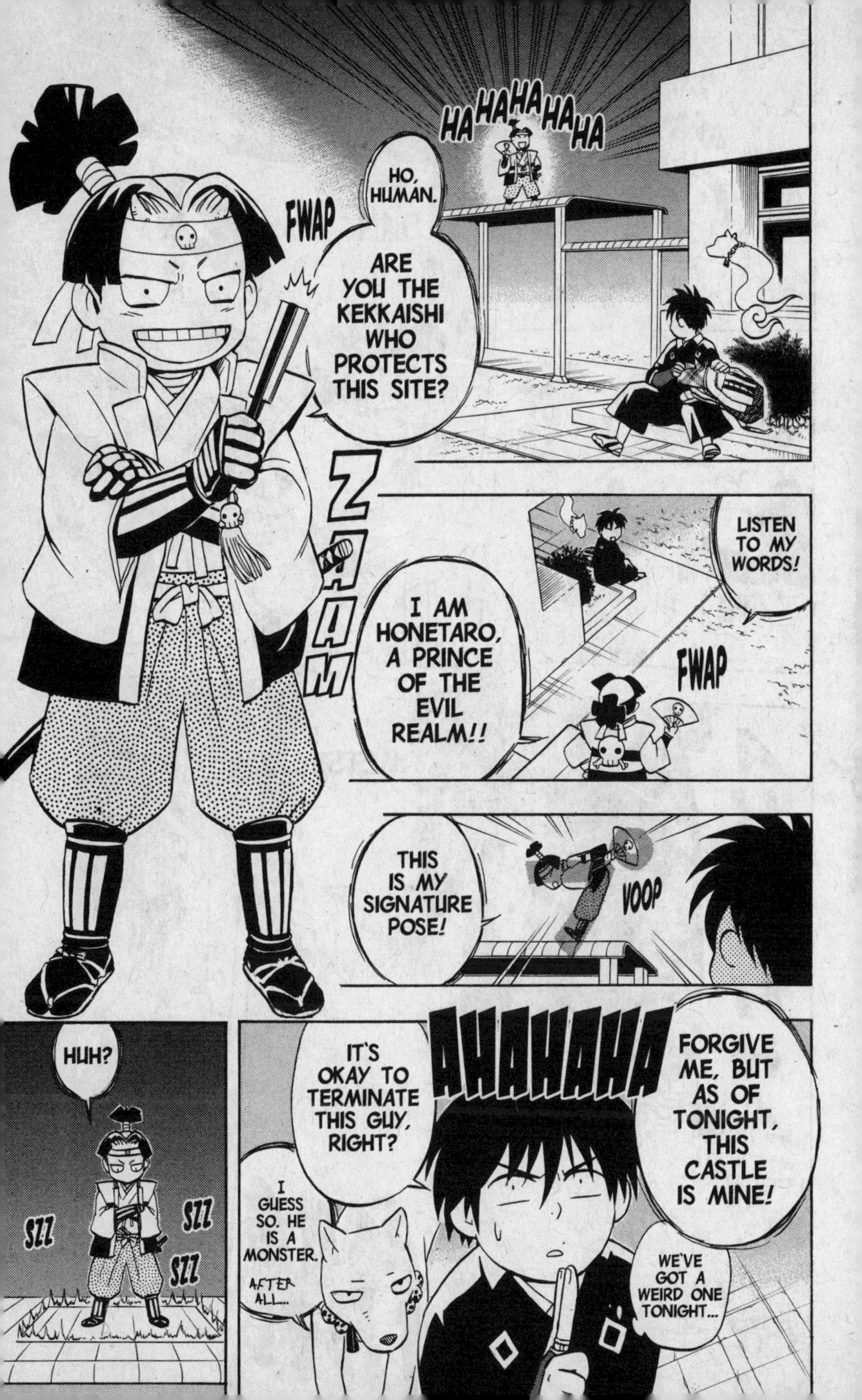
HAHAHAHAHAHA
HO, HUMAN. ARE YOU THE KEKKAISHI WHO PROTECTS THIS SITE?
FWAP
LISTEN TO MY WORDS!
I AM HONETARO, A PRINCE OF THE EVIL REALM!!
FWAP
THIS IS MY SIGNATURE POSE!
VOOP
ZAAAM
AHAHAHA
FORGIVE ME, BUT AS OF TONIGHT, THIS CASTLE IS MINE!
IT'S OKAY TO TERMINATE THIS GUY, RIGHT?
WE'VE GOT A WEIRD ONE TONIGHT...
I GUESS SO. HE IS A MONSTER.
AFTER ALL...
HUH?
SZZ
SZZ
SZZ

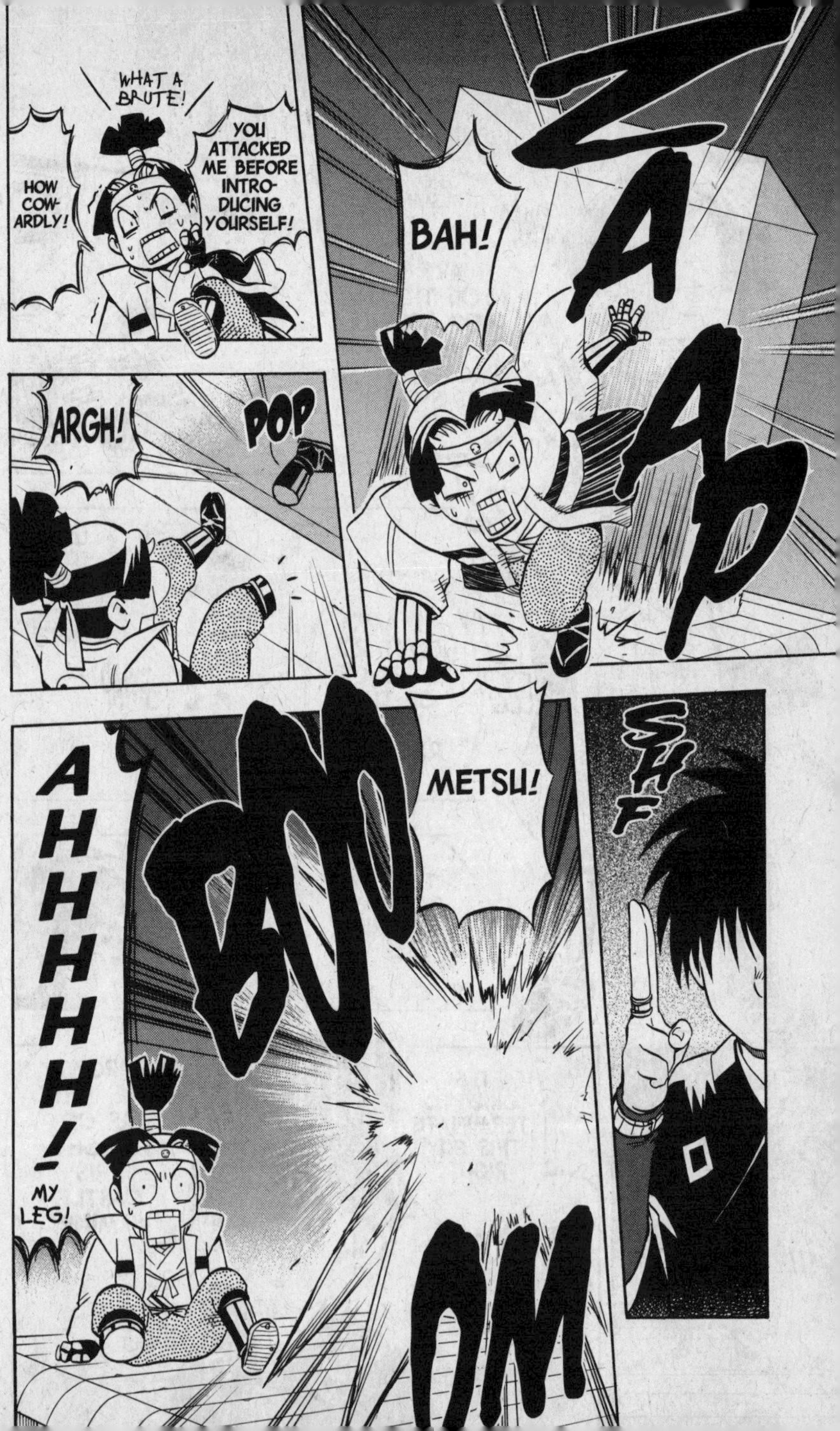
ZAAP
BAH!
WHAT A BRUTE!
YOU ATTACKED ME BEFORE INTRODUCING YOURSELF!
HOW COWARDLY!
POP
ARGH!
SHF
METSU!
BOOM
AHHHHH!
MY LEG!

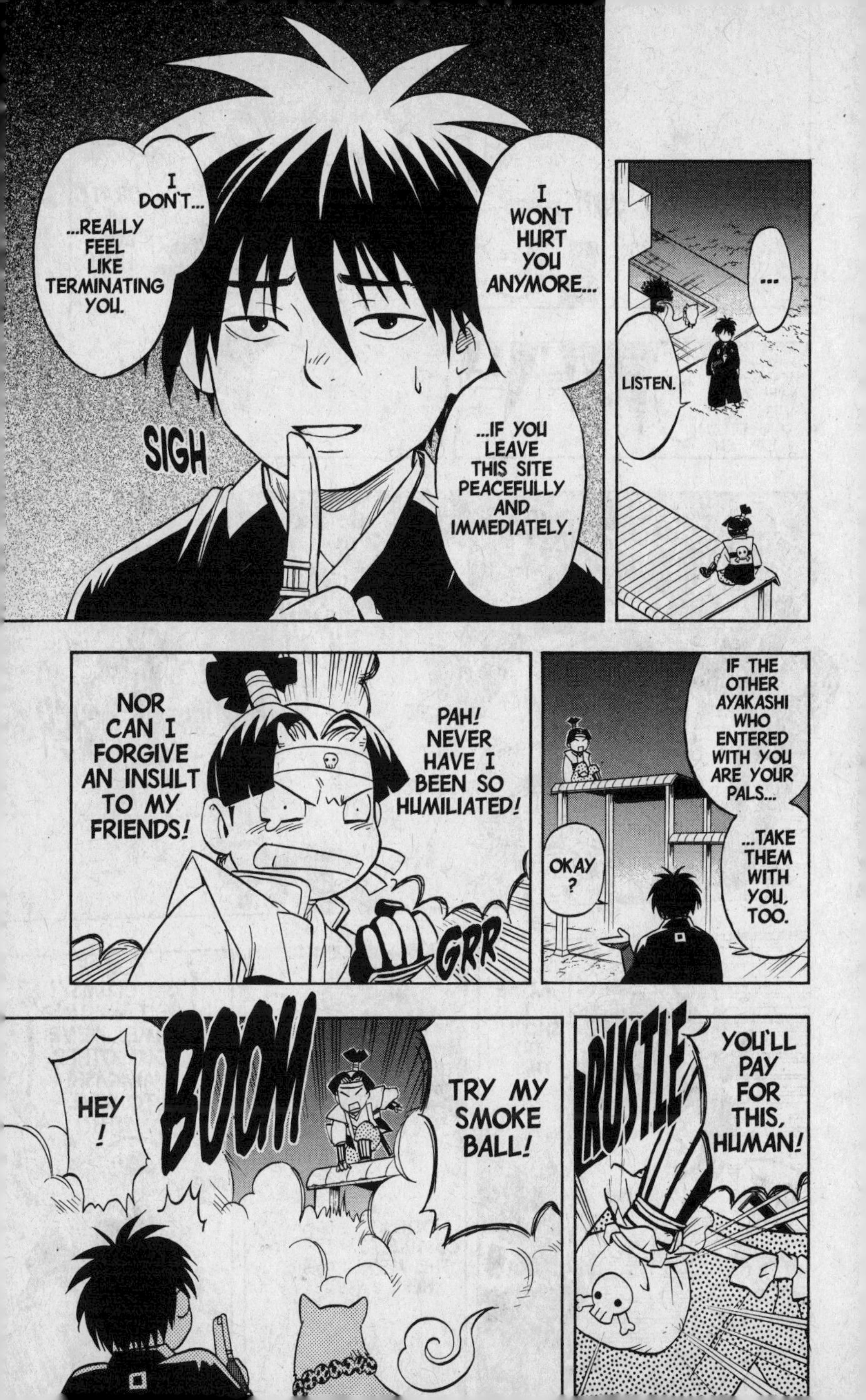
...
LISTEN.
I WON'T HURT YOU ANYMORE...
...IF YOU LEAVE THIS SITE PEACEFULLY AND IMMEDIATELY.
I DON'T...
...REALLY FEEL LIKE TERMINATING YOU.
SIGH
IF THE OTHER AYAKASHI WHO ENTERED WITH YOU ARE YOUR PALS...
...TAKE THEM WITH YOU, TOO.
OKAY?
PAH! NEVER HAVE I BEEN SO HUMILIATED!
NOR CAN I FORGIVE AN INSULT TO MY FRIENDS!
GRR
RUSTLE
YOU'LL PAY FOR THIS, HUMAN!
TRY MY SMOKE BALL!
BOOM
HEY!

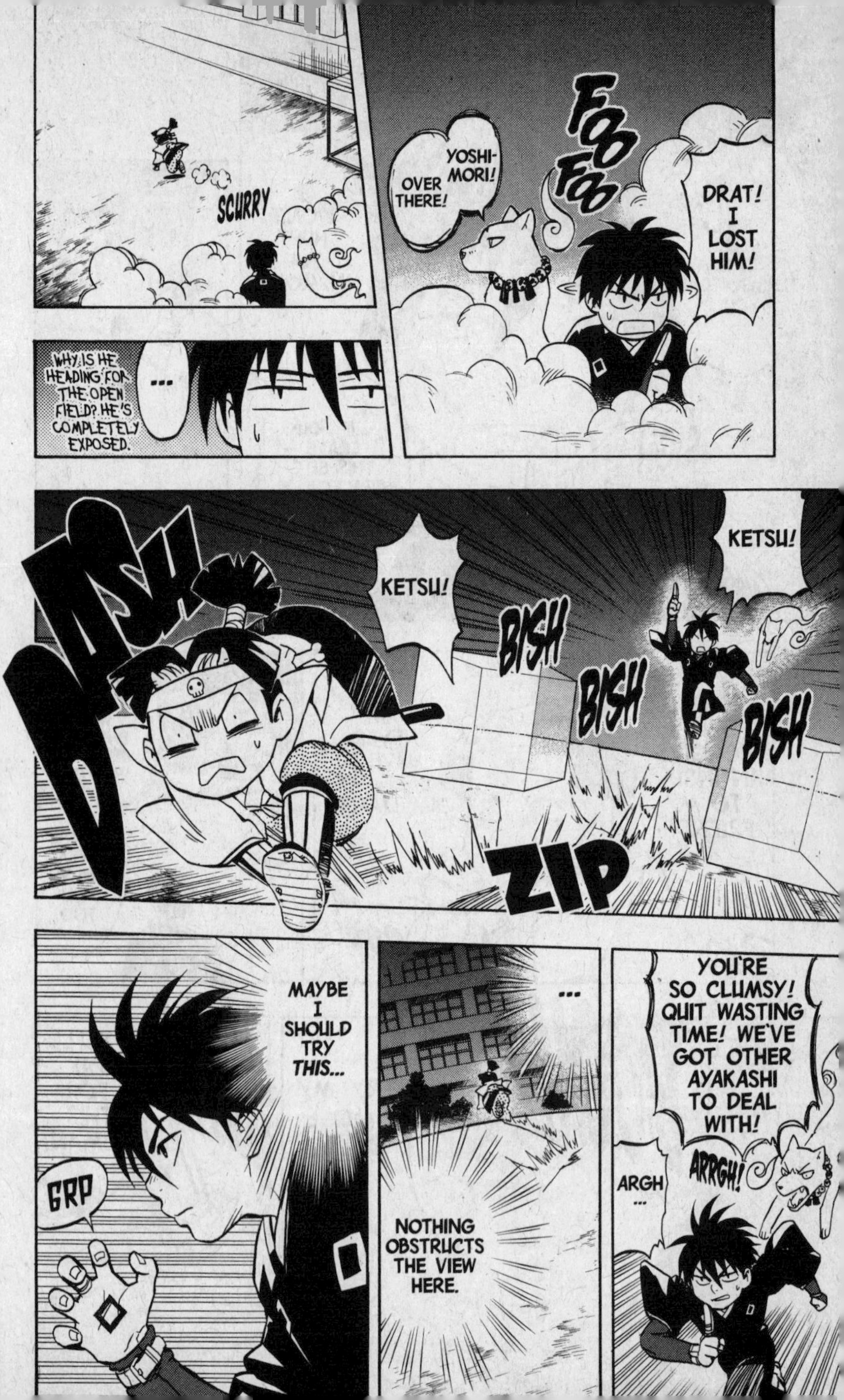
DRAT! I LOST HIM!
FOO FOO
YOSHI-MORI! OVER THERE!
SCURRY
...
WHY IS HE HEADING FOR THE OPEN FIELD? HE'S COMPLETELY EXPOSED.
KETSU!
BISH
BISH
BISH
KETSU!
DASH
ZIP
YOU'RE SO CLUMSY! QUIT WASTING TIME! WE'VE GOT OTHER AYAKASHI TO DEAL WITH!
ARRGH!
ARGH ...
...
NOTHING OBSTRUCTS THE VIEW HERE.
MAYBE I SHOULD TRY THIS...
GRP

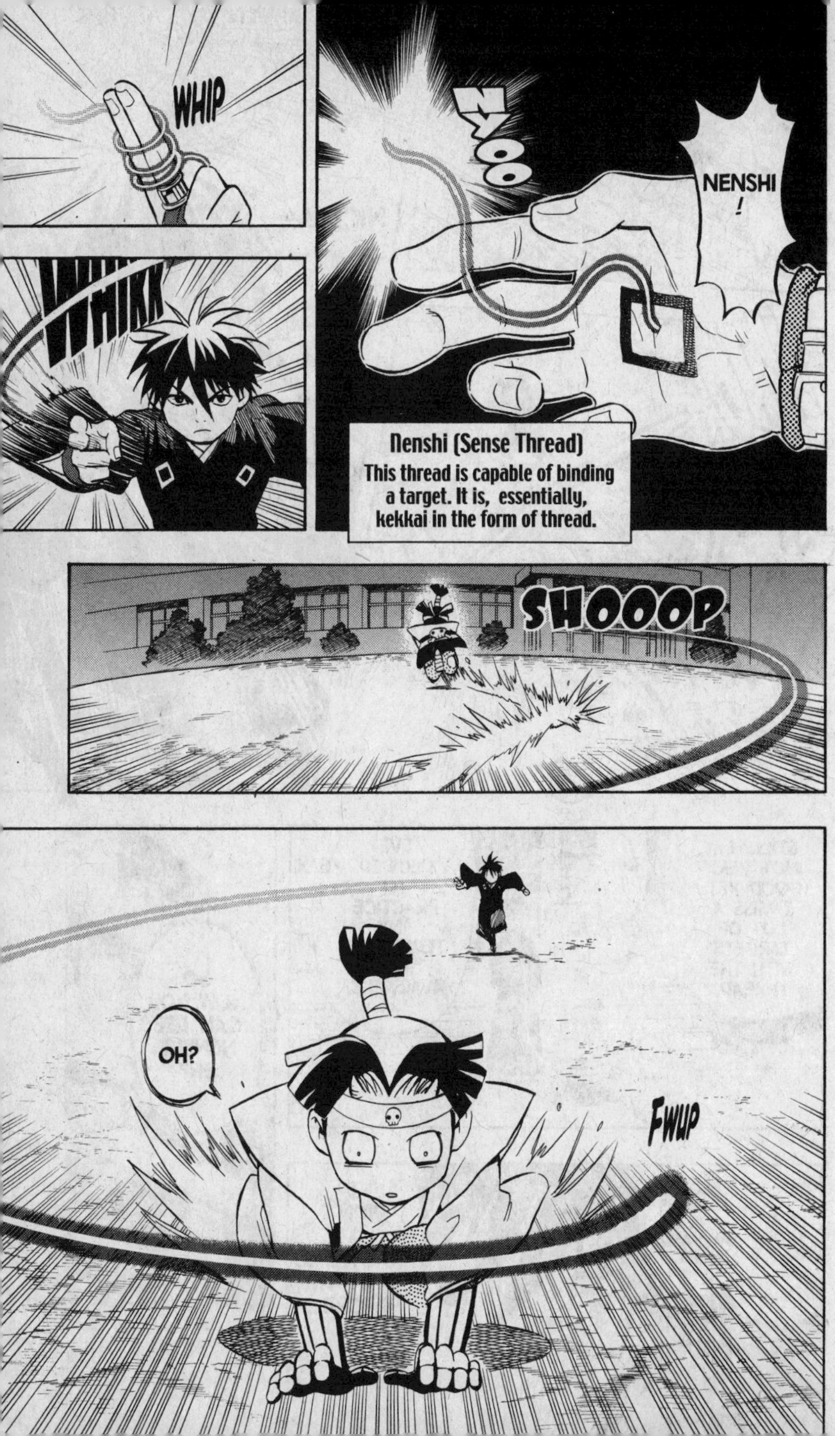

NYOO
NENSHI!
Nenshi (Sense Thread)
This thread is capable of binding a target. It is, essentially, kekkai in the form of thread.
WHIP
WHIRR
SHOOOP
OH?
FWUP

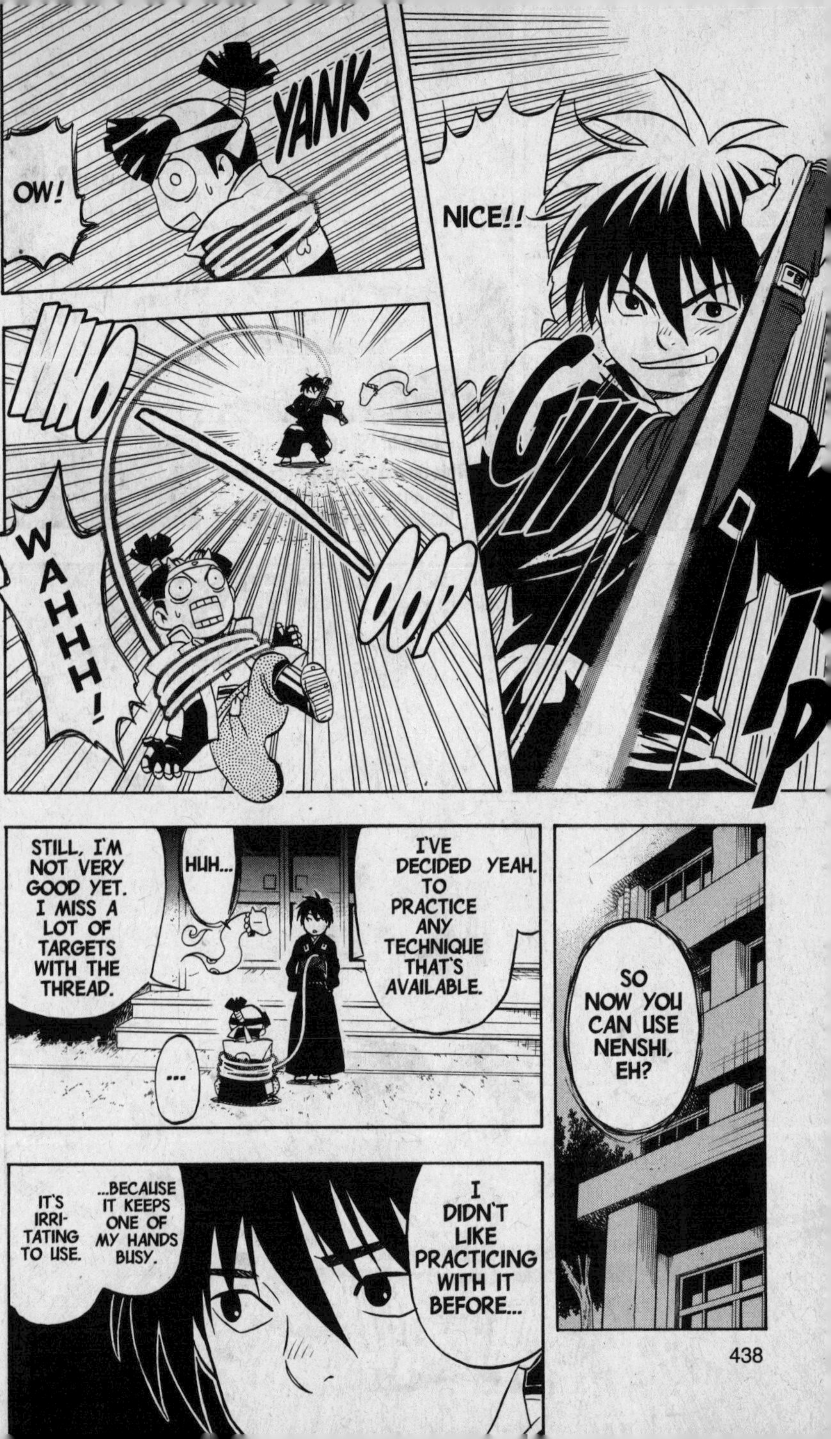
NICE!!
YANK
OW!
WAHHH!
SO NOW YOU CAN USE NENSHI, EH?
YEAH.
I'VE DECIDED TO PRACTICE ANY TECHNIQUE THAT'S AVAILABLE.
HUH...
STILL, I'M NOT VERY GOOD YET. I MISS A LOT OF TARGETS WITH THE THREAD.
...
I DIDN'T LIKE PRACTICING WITH IT BEFORE...
...BECAUSE IT KEEPS ONE OF MY HANDS BUSY.
IT'S IRRITATING TO USE.

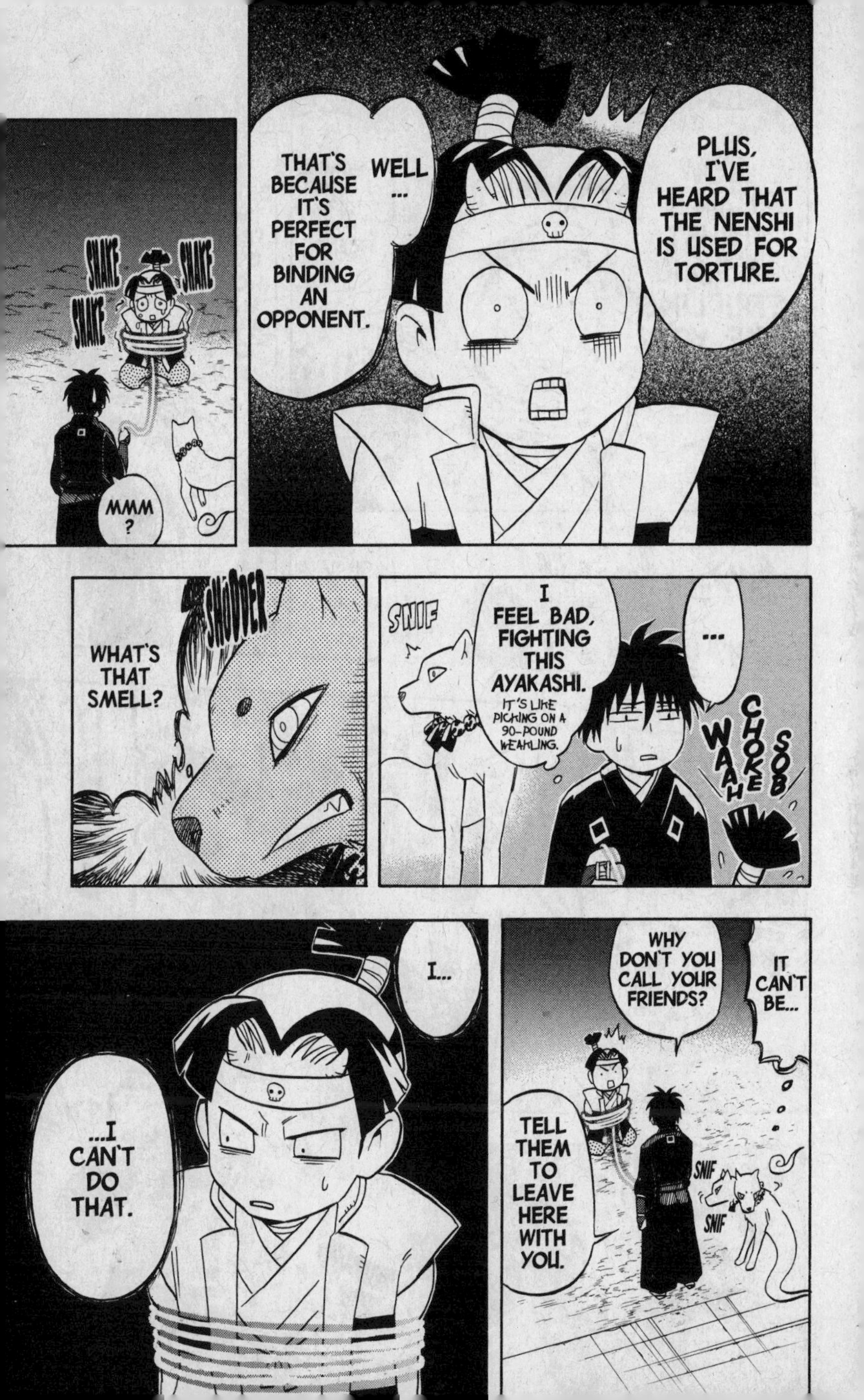
WELL ...
THAT'S BECAUSE IT'S PERFECT FOR BINDING AN OPPONENT.
PLUS, I'VE HEARD THAT THE NENSHI IS USED FOR TORTURE.
SHAKE
SHAKE
SHAKE
MMM ?
...
SNIF
I FEEL BAD, FIGHTING THIS AYAKASHI.
IT'S LIKE PICKING ON A 90-POUND WEAKLING.
WAAH
CHOKE
SOB
SHUDDER
WHAT'S THAT SMELL?
IT CAN'T BE...
WHY DON'T YOU CALL YOUR FRIENDS?
TELL THEM TO LEAVE HERE WITH YOU.
SNIF
SNIF
I...
...I CAN'T DO THAT.

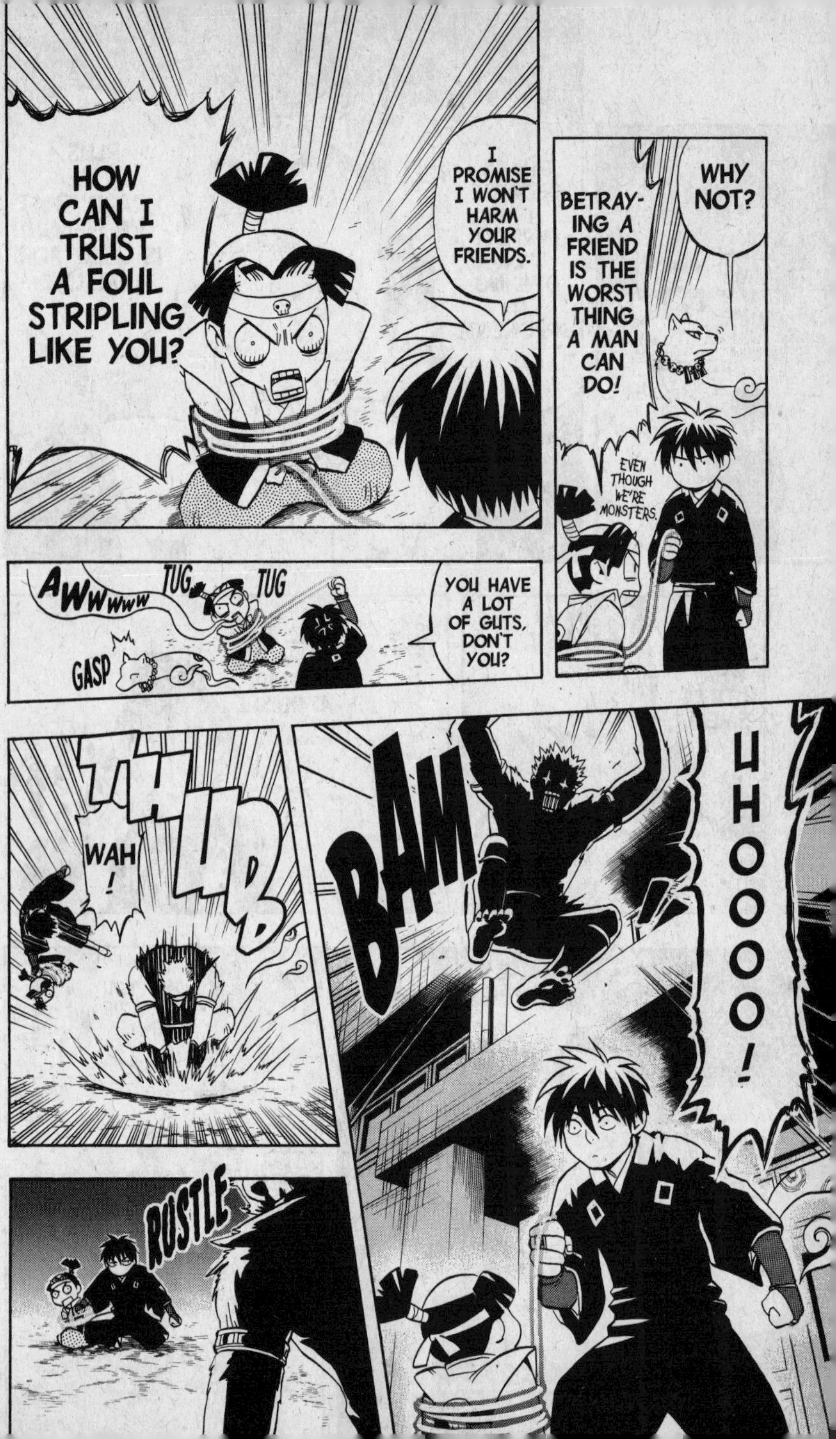
WHY NOT?
BETRAY-ING A FRIEND IS THE WORST THING A MAN CAN DO!
EVEN THOUGH WE'RE MONSTERS.
I PROMISE I WON'T HARM YOUR FRIENDS.
HOW CAN I TRUST A FOUL STRIPLING LIKE YOU?
YOU HAVE A LOT OF GUTS, DON'T YOU?
TUG TUG
AWWWWWW
GASP
UHOOOOO!
BAM
THUD
WAH!
RUSTLE

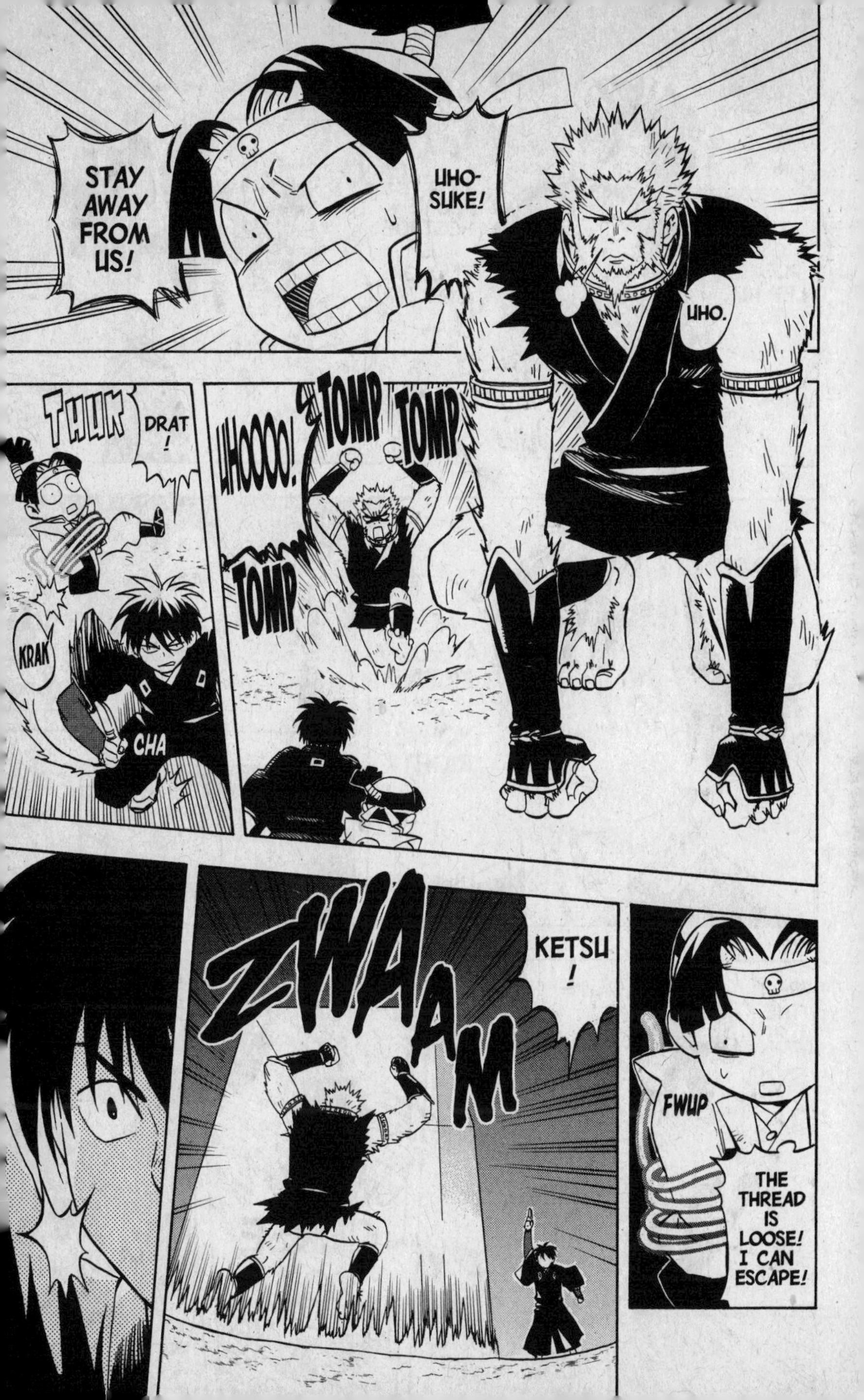
UHO-SUKE!
STAY AWAY FROM US!
UHO.
TOMP
TOMP
UHOOOO!
TOMP
DRAT!
THUK
KRAK
CHA
FWUP
THE THREAD IS LOOSE! I CAN ESCAPE!
KETSU!
ZWAAAM

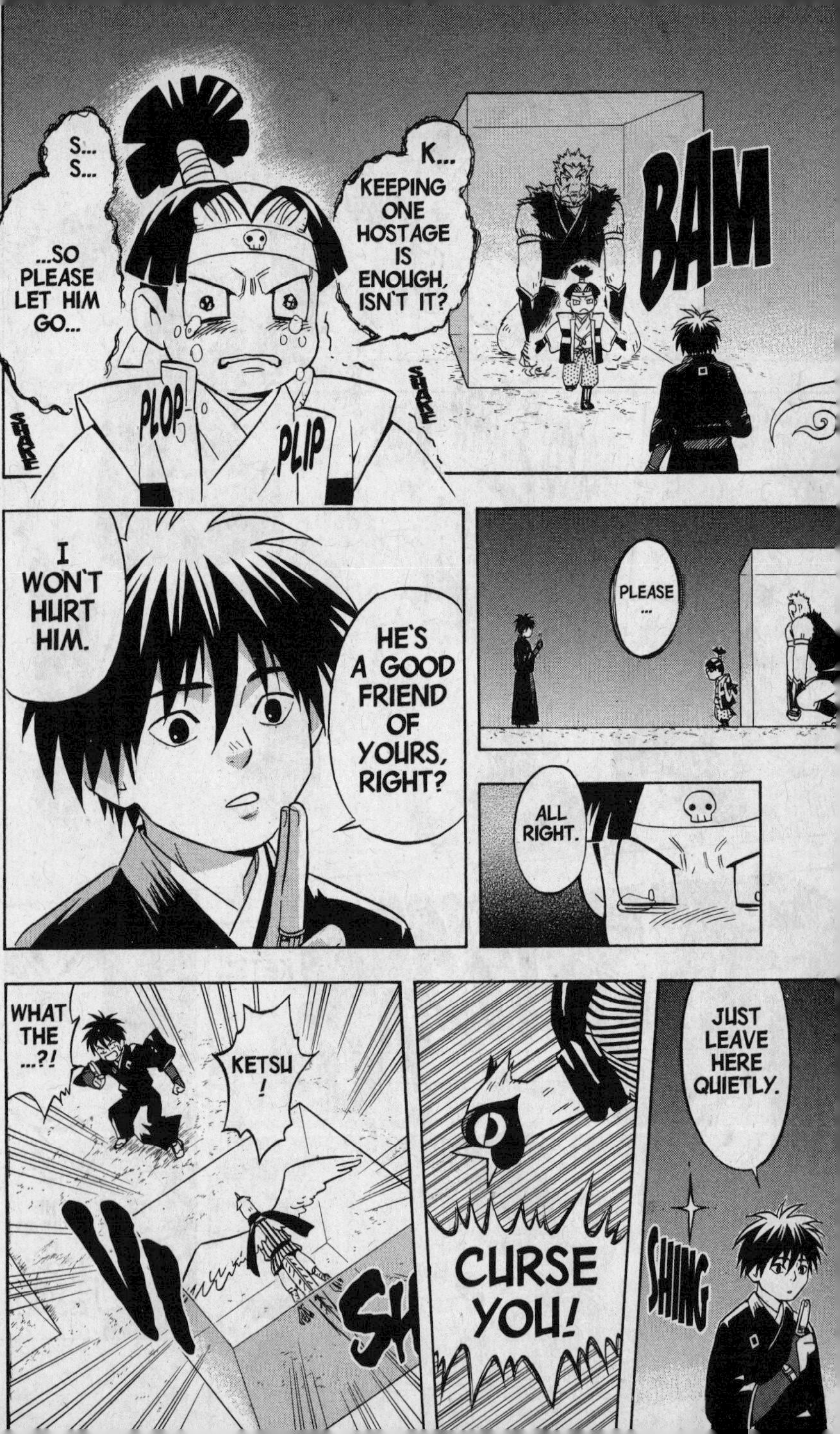
BAM
K... KEEPING ONE HOSTAGE IS ENOUGH, ISN'T IT?
S... S...
...SO PLEASE LET HIM GO...
SHAKE
PLOP
PLIP
SHAKE
PLEASE ...
ALL RIGHT.
HE'S A GOOD FRIEND OF YOURS, RIGHT?
I WON'T HURT HIM.
JUST LEAVE HERE QUIETLY.
SHING
CURSE YOU!
KETSU !
WHAT THE ...?!
SH

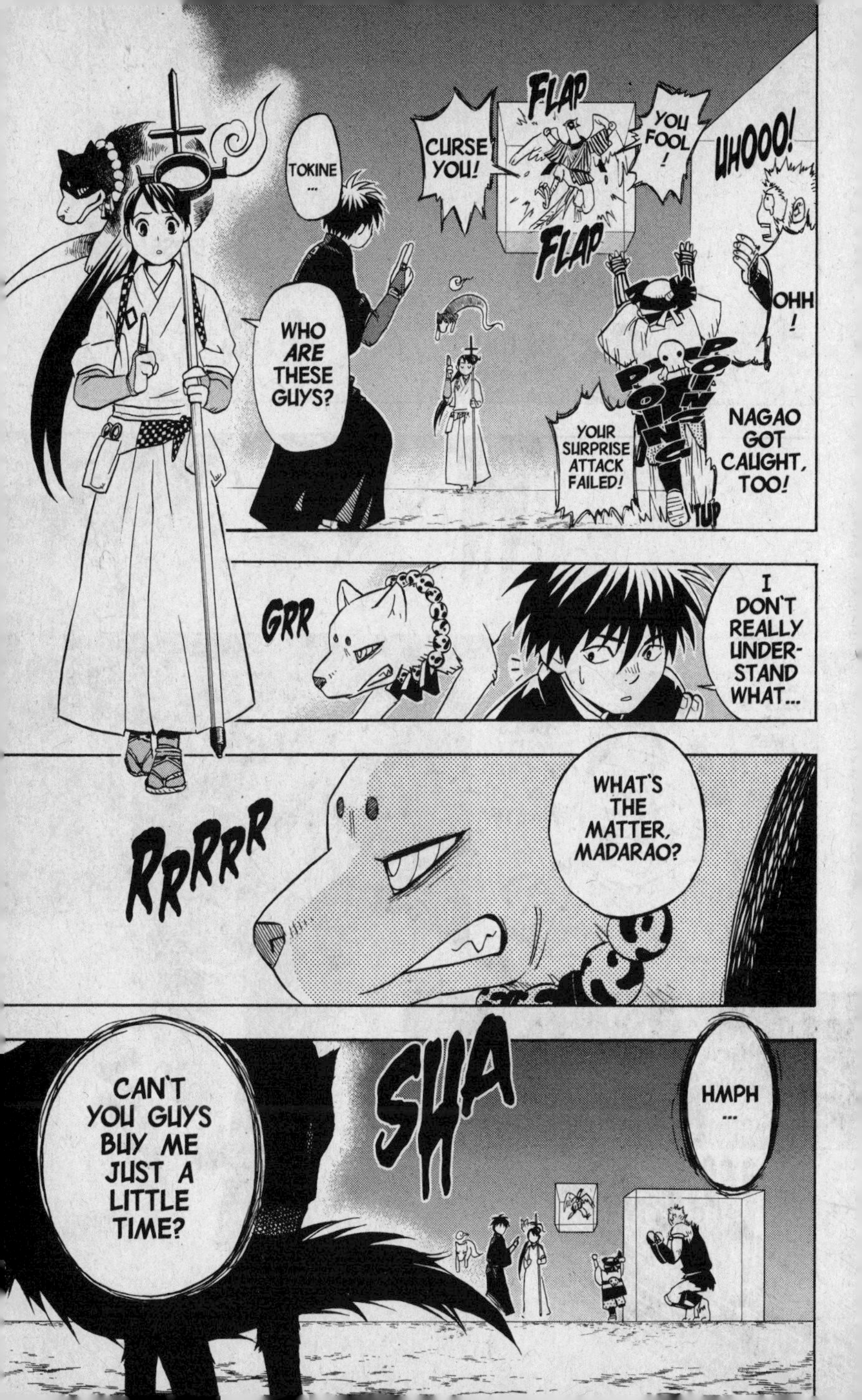
UHOOO!
YOU FOOL!
FLAP
CURSE YOU!
FLAP
OHH!
NAGAO GOT CAUGHT, TOO!
POING POING
YOUR SURPRISE ATTACK FAILED!
TUP
TOKINE...
WHO ARE THESE GUYS?
I DON'T REALLY UNDER-STAND WHAT...
GRR
WHAT'S THE MATTER, MADARAO?
RRRRR
HMPH...
SHA
CAN'T YOU GUYS BUY ME JUST A LITTLE TIME?

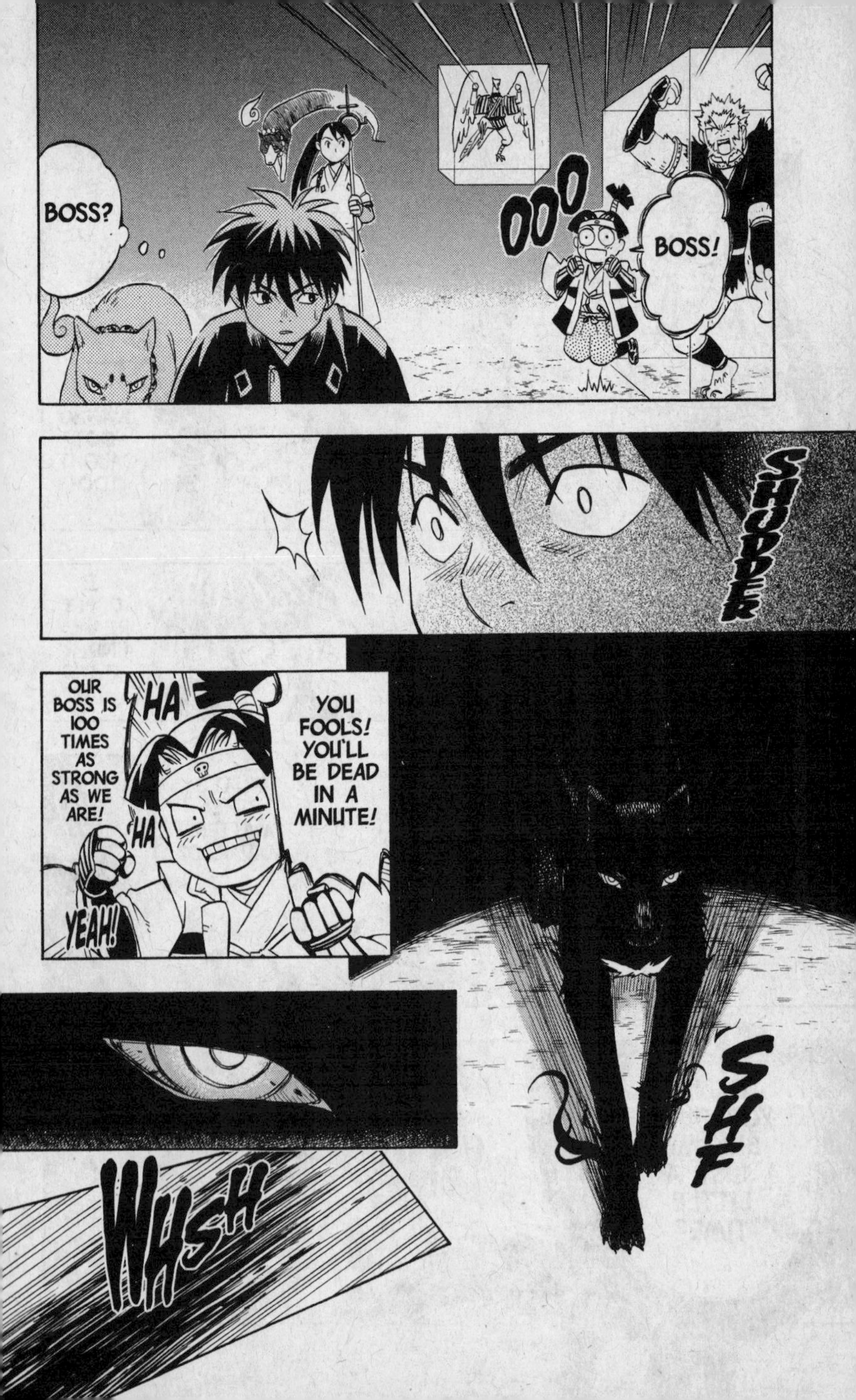
OOO
BOSS!
BOSS?
SHUDDER
SHF
YOU FOOLS! YOU'LL BE DEAD IN A MINUTE!
HA
OUR BOSS IS 100 TIMES AS STRONG AS WE ARE!
HA
YEAH!
WHSH

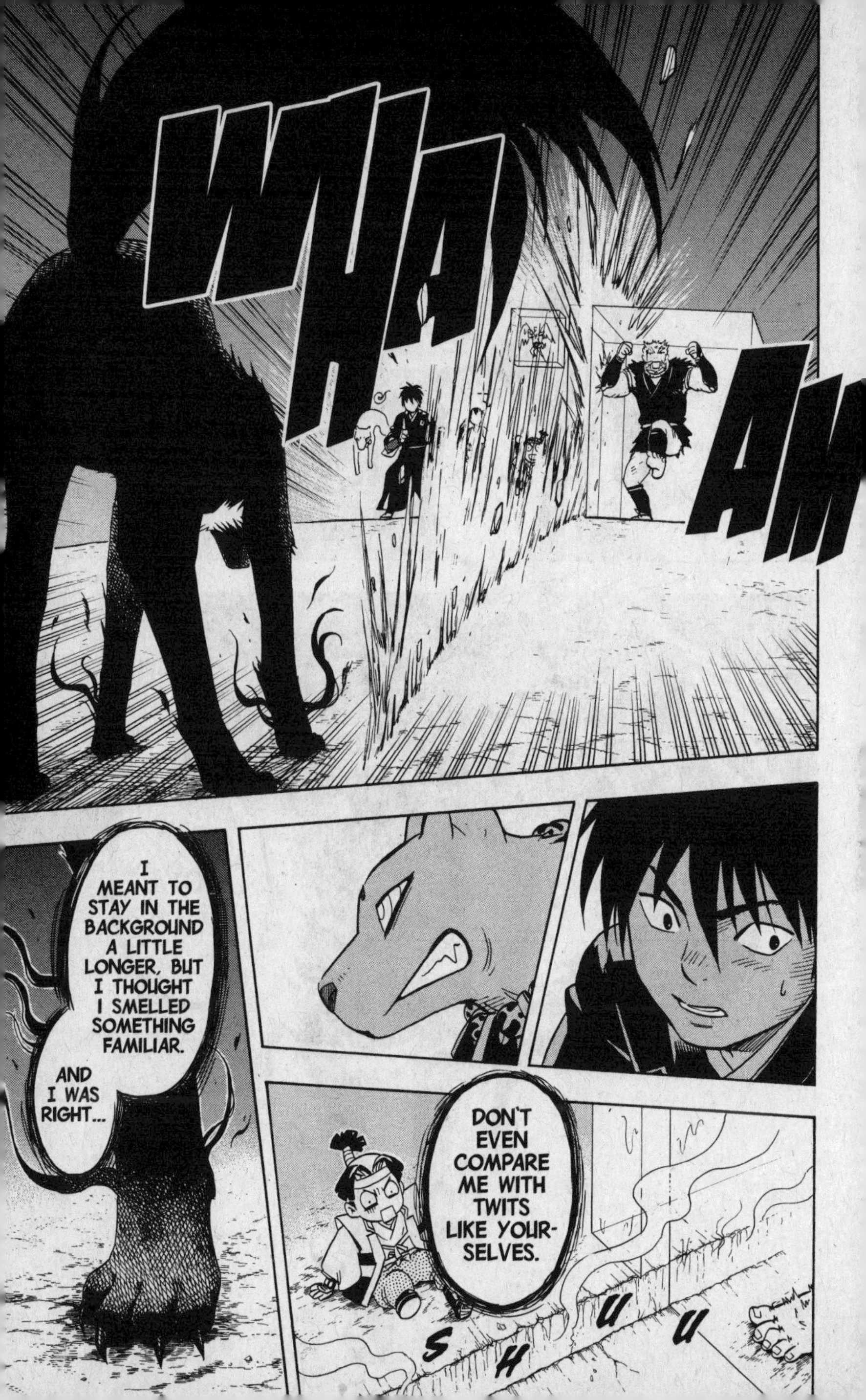
WHAAAH
I MEANT TO STAY IN THE BACKGROUND A LITTLE LONGER, BUT I THOUGHT I SMELLED SOMETHING FAMILIAR.
AND I WAS RIGHT...
DON'T EVEN COMPARE ME WITH TWITS LIKE YOUR-SELVES.
SHUUU

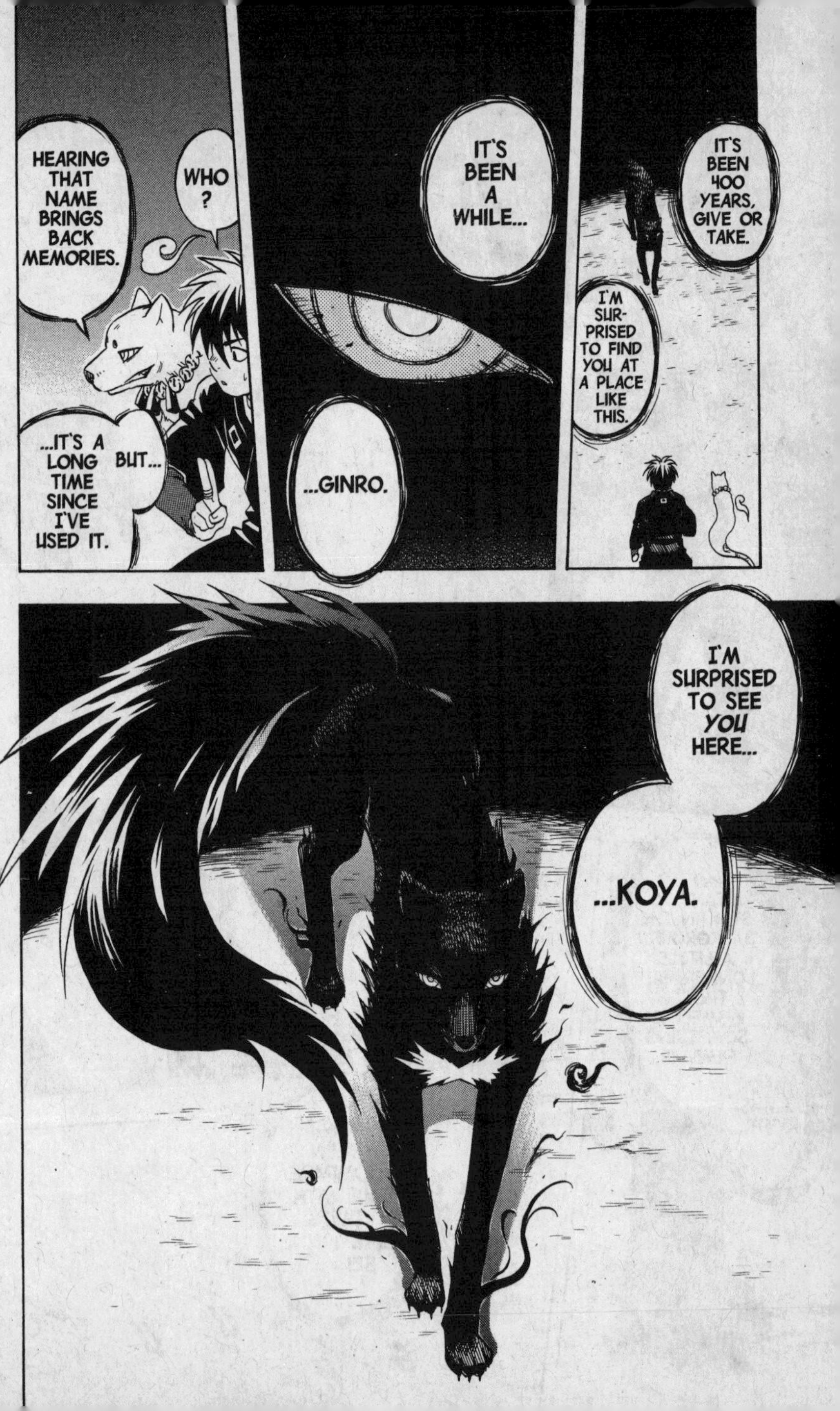
IT'S BEEN 400 YEARS, GIVE OR TAKE.
I'M SURPRISED TO FIND YOU AT A PLACE LIKE THIS.
IT'S BEEN A WHILE...
...GINRO.
WHO?
HEARING THAT NAME BRINGS BACK MEMORIES.
BUT...
...IT'S A LONG TIME SINCE I'VE USED IT.
I'M SURPRISED TO SEE YOU HERE...
...KOYA.

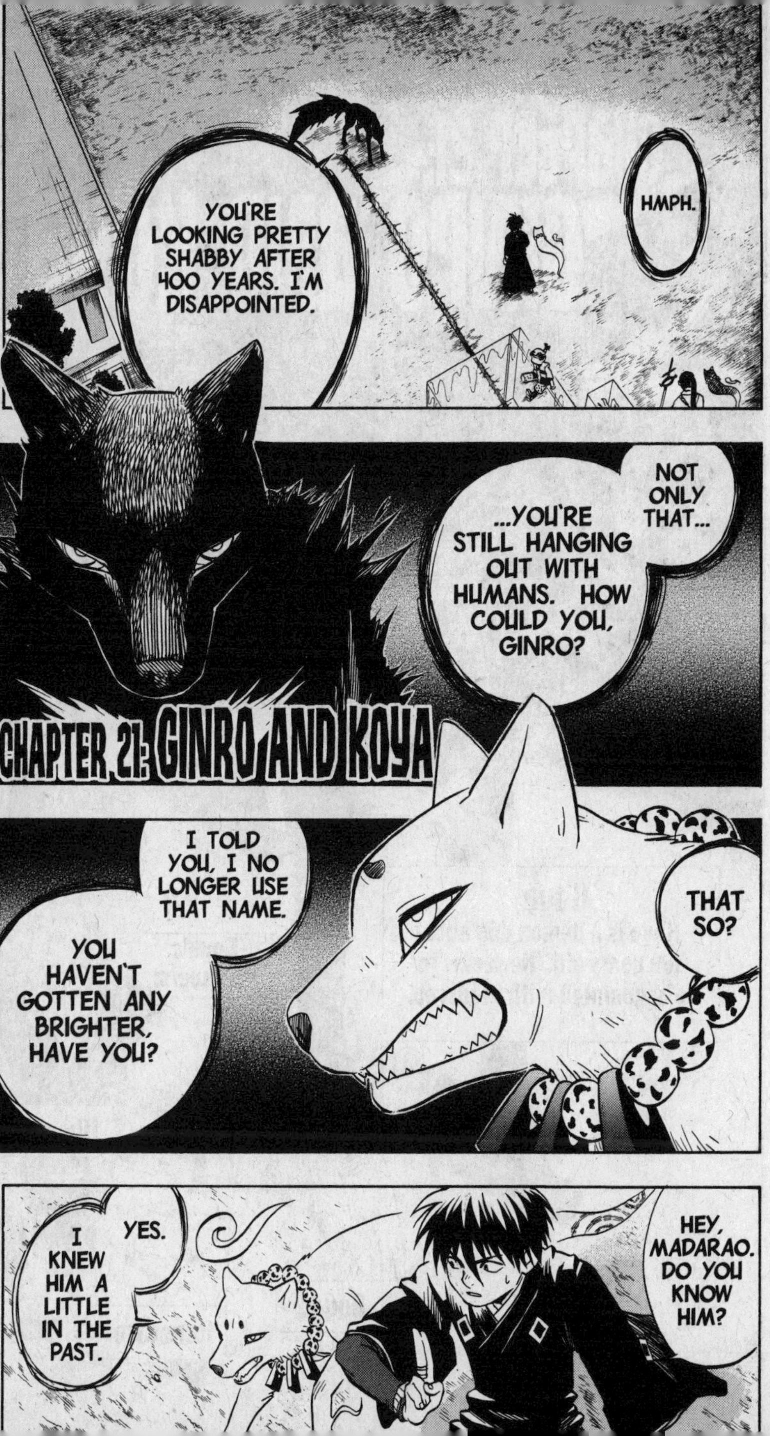
YOU'RE LOOKING PRETTY SHABBY AFTER 400 YEARS. I'M DISAPPOINTED.
HMPH.
NOT ONLY THAT...
...YOU'RE STILL HANGING OUT WITH HUMANS. HOW COULD YOU, GINRO?
CHAPTER 21: GINRO AND KOYA
THAT SO?
I TOLD YOU, I NO LONGER USE THAT NAME.
YOU HAVEN'T GOTTEN ANY BRIGHTER, HAVE YOU?
HEY, MADARAO. DO YOU KNOW HIM?
YES.
I KNEW HIM A LITTLE IN THE PAST.

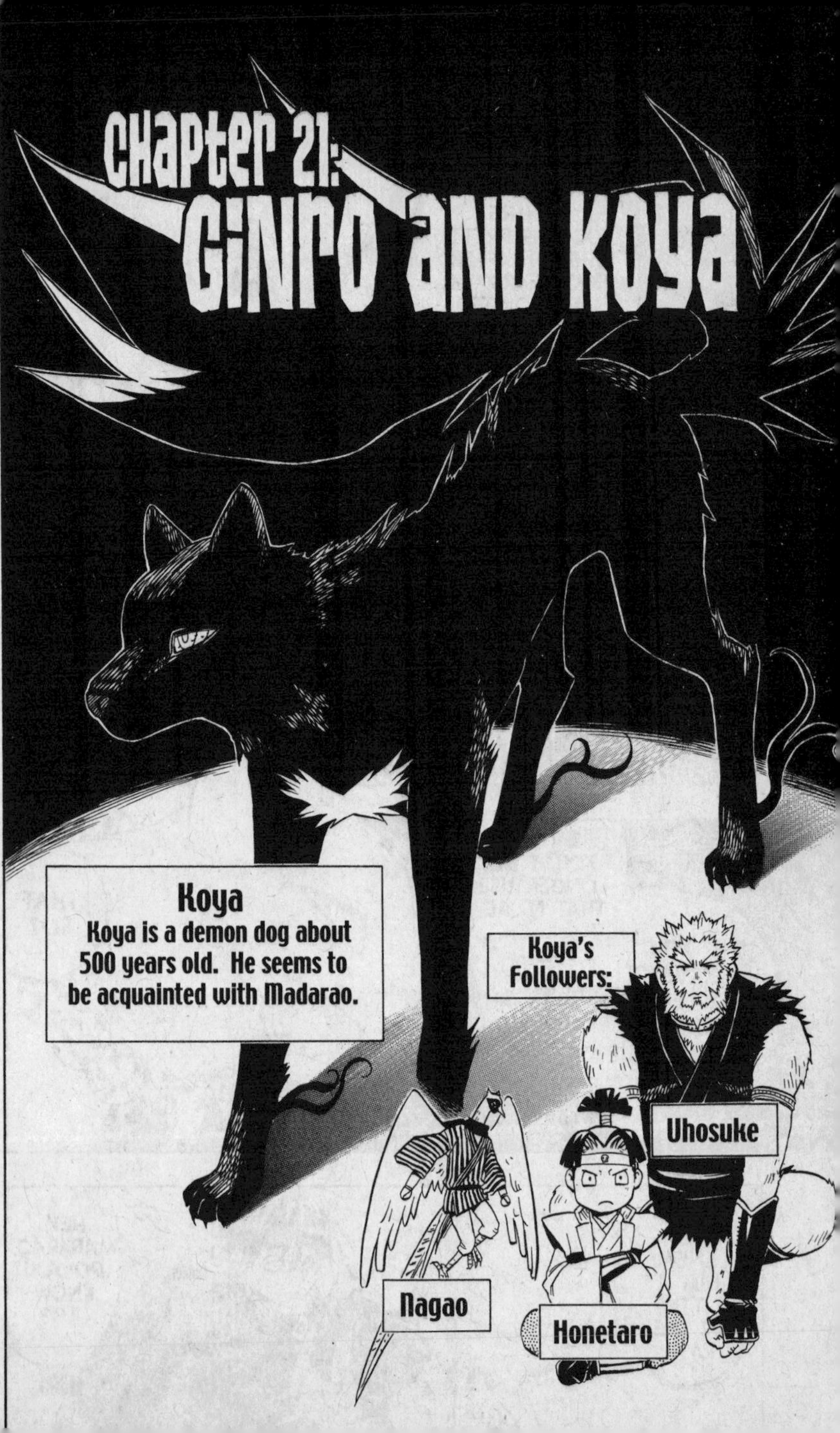
Chapter 21:
Ginro and Koya
Koya
Koya is a demon dog about 500 years old. He seems to be acquainted with Madarao.
Koya's Followers:
Uhosuke
Nagao
Honetaro

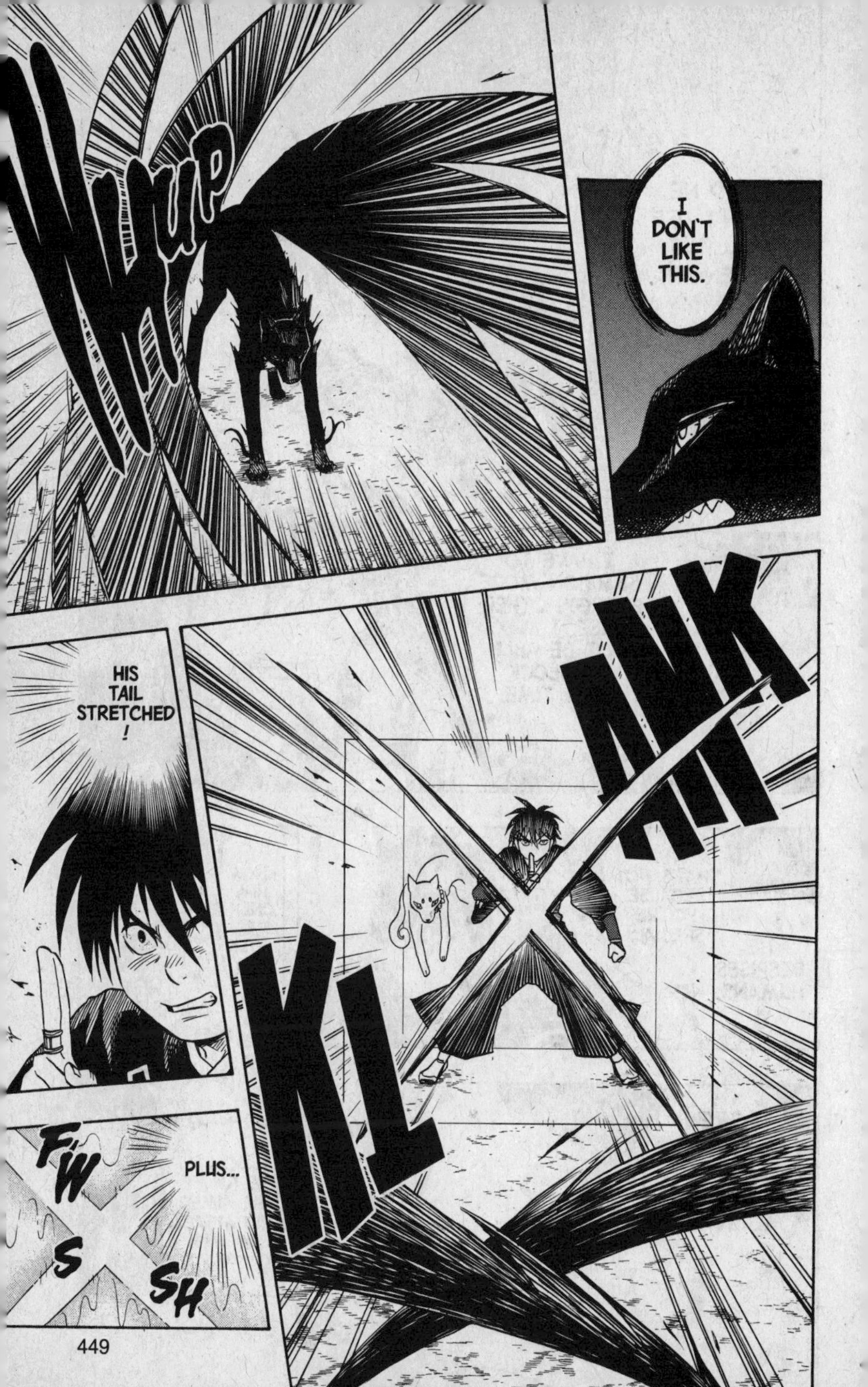
I DON'T LIKE THIS.
WHUP
KLANK
HIS TAIL STRETCHED!
FWSSH
PLUS...

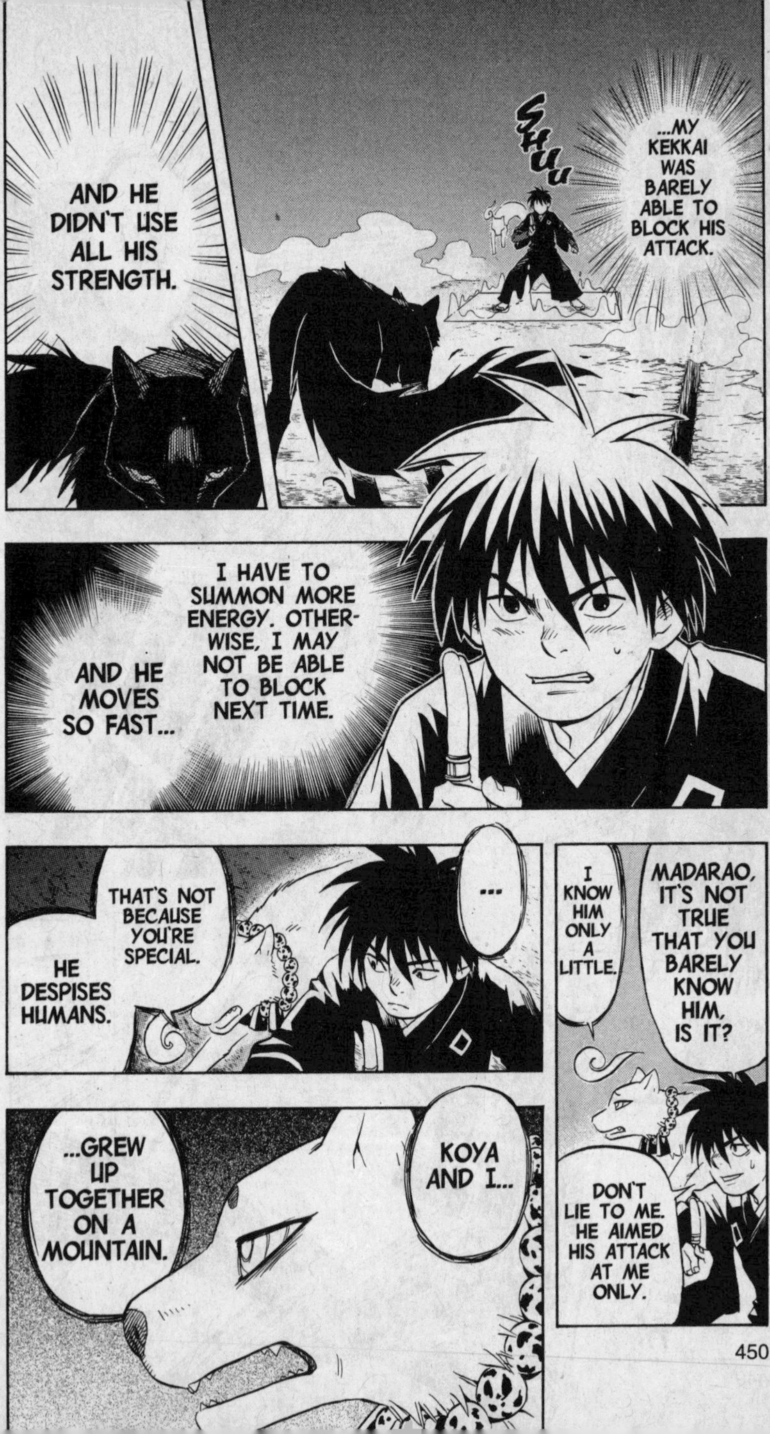
SHUUU
...MY KEKKAI WAS BARELY ABLE TO BLOCK HIS ATTACK.
AND HE DIDN'T USE ALL HIS STRENGTH.
I HAVE TO SUMMON MORE ENERGY. OTHER-WISE, I MAY NOT BE ABLE TO BLOCK NEXT TIME.
AND HE MOVES SO FAST...
MADARAO, IT'S NOT TRUE THAT YOU BARELY KNOW HIM, IS IT?
I KNOW HIM ONLY A LITTLE.
DON'T LIE TO ME. HE AIMED HIS ATTACK AT ME ONLY.
...
THAT'S NOT BECAUSE YOU'RE SPECIAL.
HE DESPISES HUMANS.
KOYA AND I...
...GREW UP TOGETHER ON A MOUNTAIN.

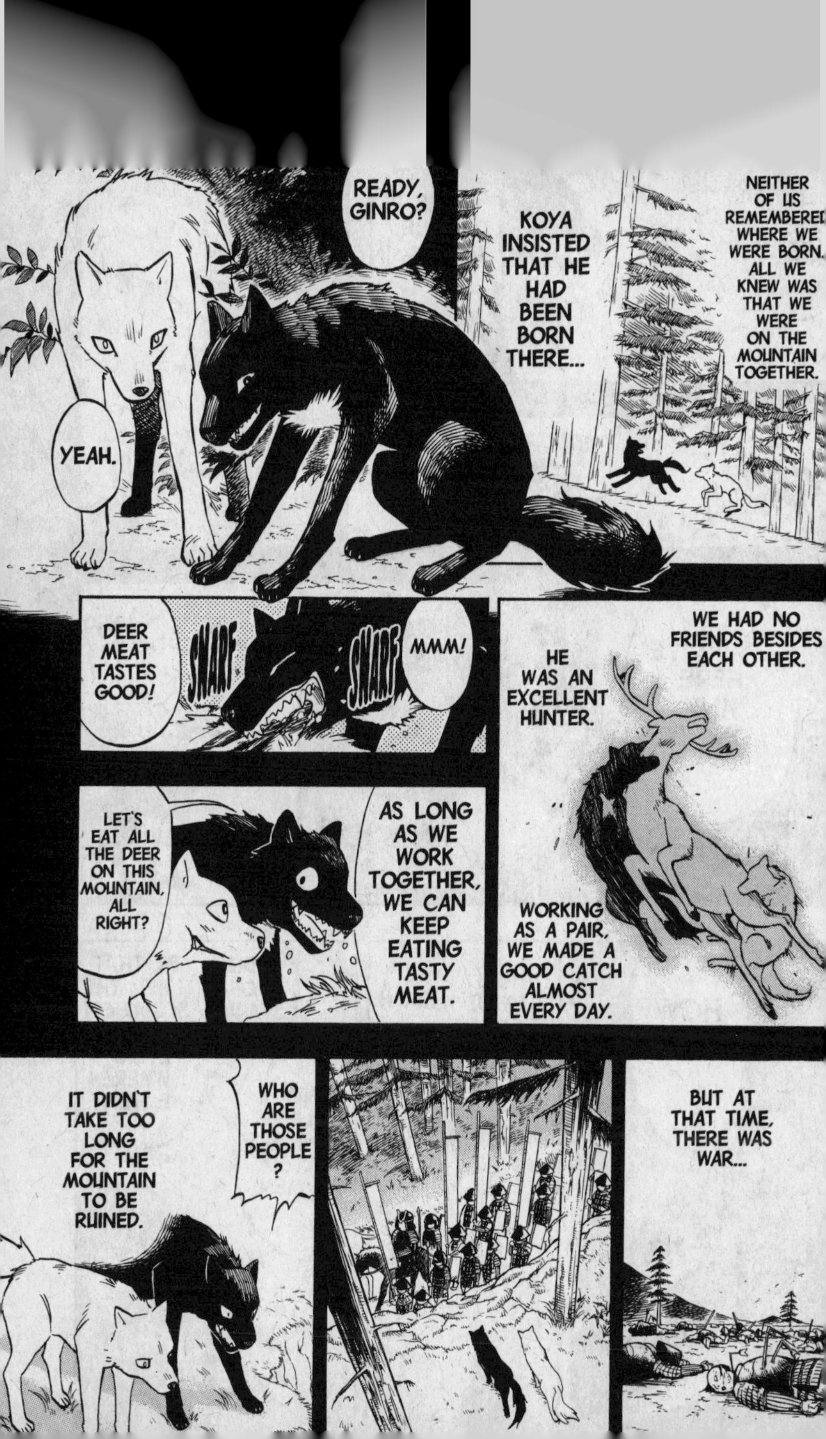
NEITHER OF US REMEMBERED WHERE WE WERE BORN. ALL WE KNEW WAS THAT WE WERE ON THE MOUNTAIN TOGETHER.
KOYA INSISTED THAT HE HAD BEEN BORN THERE...
READY, GINRO?
YEAH.
WE HAD NO FRIENDS BESIDES EACH OTHER.
HE WAS AN EXCELLENT HUNTER.
WORKING AS A PAIR, WE MADE A GOOD CATCH ALMOST EVERY DAY.
MMM!
SNARF
SNARF
DEER MEAT TASTES GOOD!
AS LONG AS WE WORK TOGETHER, WE CAN KEEP EATING TASTY MEAT.
LET'S EAT ALL THE DEER ON THIS MOUNTAIN, ALL RIGHT?
BUT AT THAT TIME, THERE WAS WAR...
WHO ARE THOSE PEOPLE?
IT DIDN'T TAKE TOO LONG FOR THE MOUNTAIN TO BE RUINED.

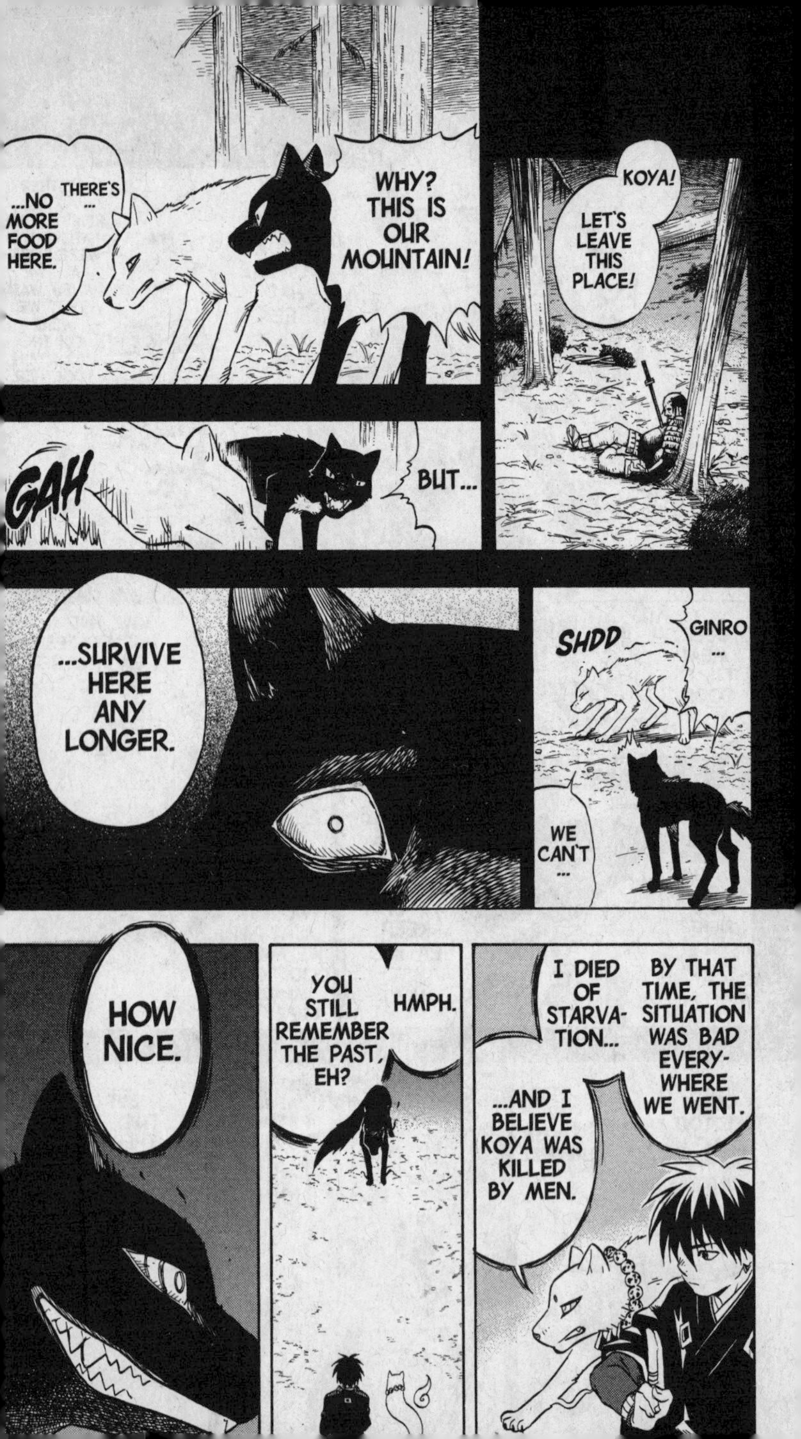
KOYA!
LET'S LEAVE THIS PLACE!
WHY? THIS IS OUR MOUNTAIN!
THERE'S ...
...NO MORE FOOD HERE.
BUT...
GAH
GINRO ...
SHDD
WE CAN'T ...
...SURVIVE HERE ANY LONGER.
BY THAT TIME, THE SITUATION WAS BAD EVERYWHERE WE WENT.
I DIED OF STARVATION...
...AND I BELIEVE KOYA WAS KILLED BY MEN.
HMPH.
YOU STILL REMEMBER THE PAST, EH?
HOW NICE.

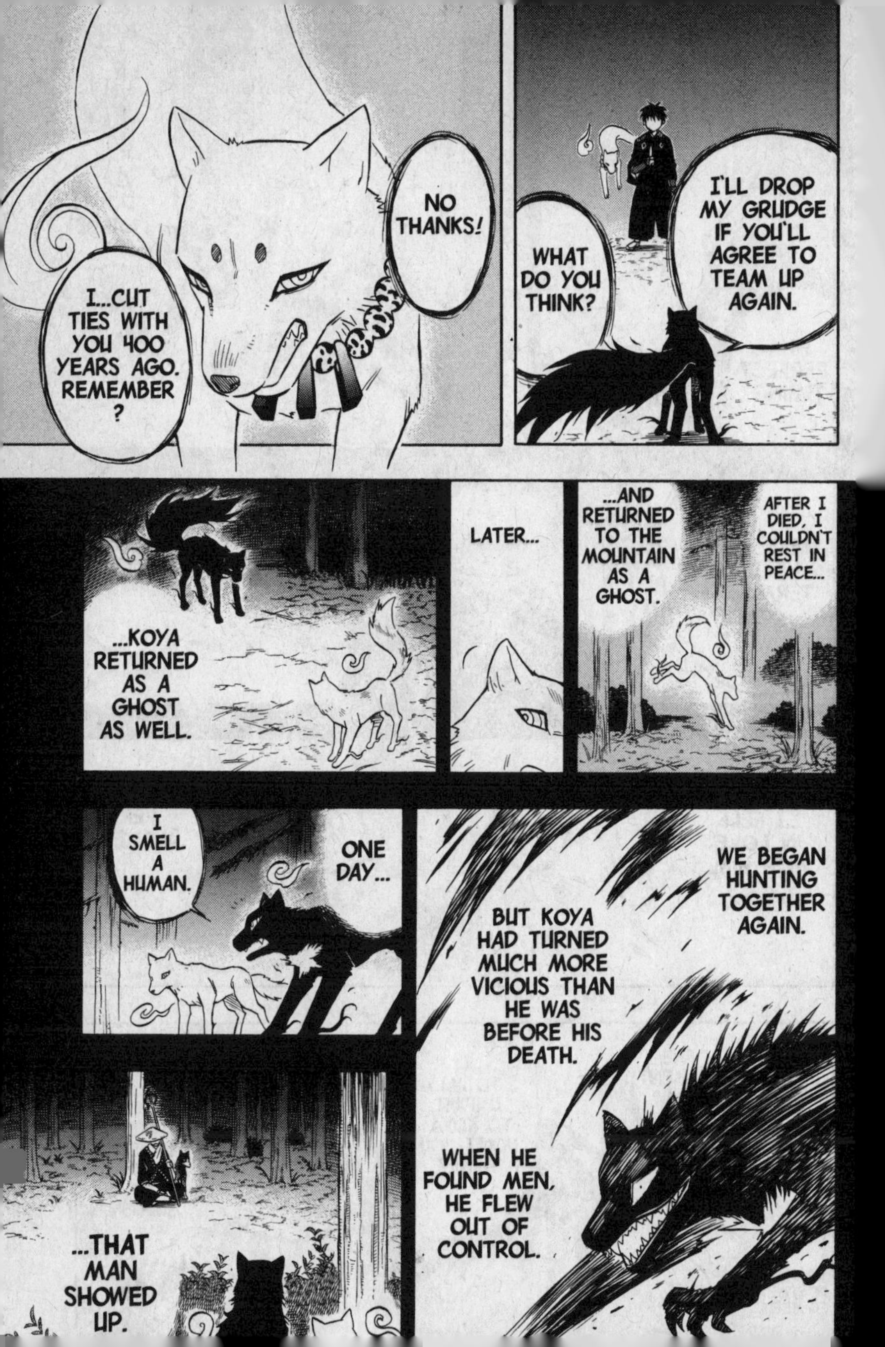
I'LL DROP MY GRUDGE IF YOU'LL AGREE TO TEAM UP AGAIN.
WHAT DO YOU THINK?
NO THANKS!
I...CUT TIES WITH YOU 400 YEARS AGO. REMEMBER?
AFTER I DIED, I COULDN'T REST IN PEACE...
...AND RETURNED TO THE MOUNTAIN AS A GHOST.
LATER...
...KOYA RETURNED AS A GHOST AS WELL.
WE BEGAN HUNTING TOGETHER AGAIN.
BUT KOYA HAD TURNED MUCH MORE VICIOUS THAN HE WAS BEFORE HIS DEATH.
WHEN HE FOUND MEN, HE FLEW OUT OF CONTROL.
ONE DAY...
I SMELL A HUMAN.
...THAT MAN SHOWED UP.

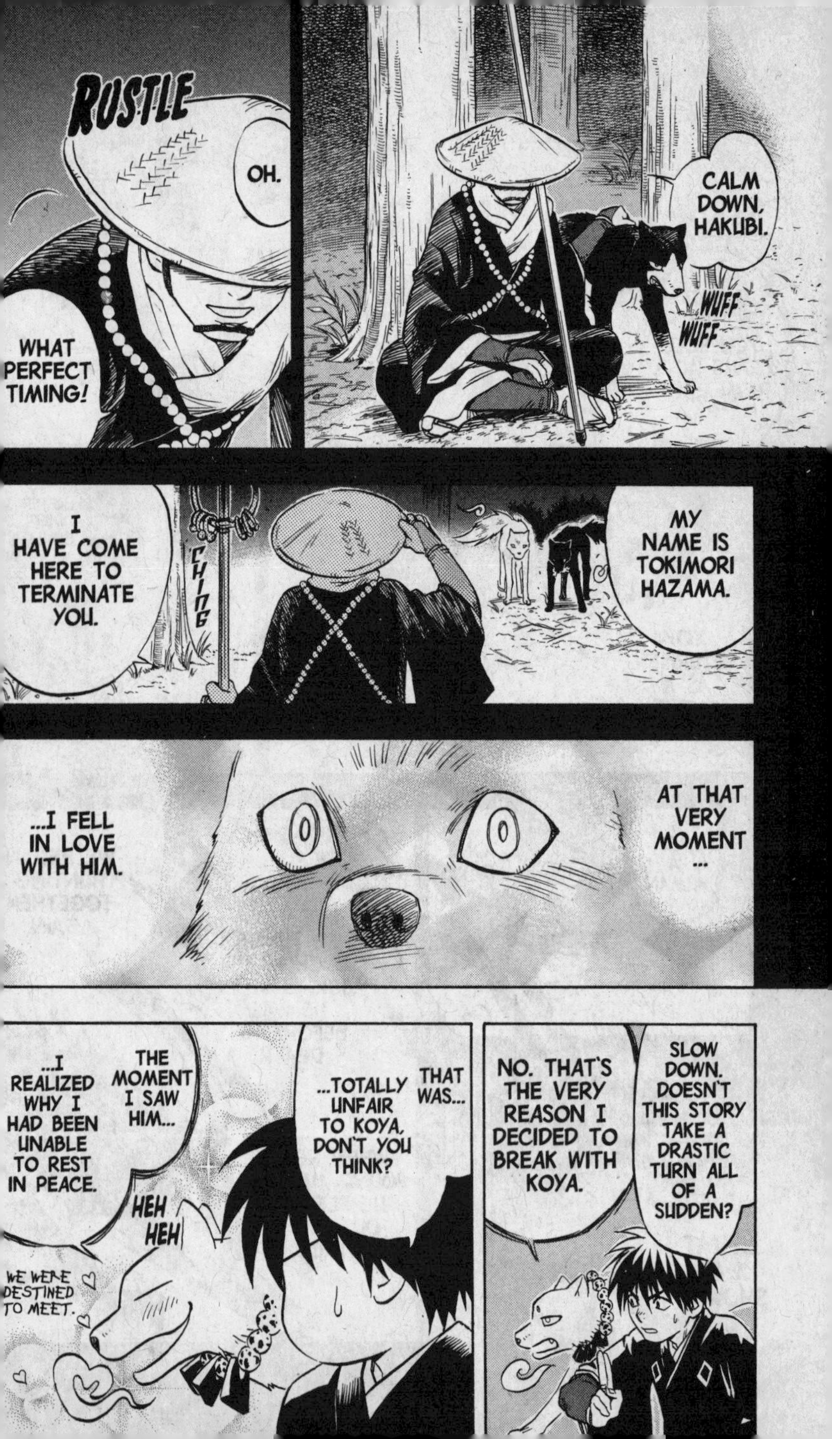
CALM DOWN, HAKUBI.
WUFF
WUFF
RUSTLE
OH.
WHAT PERFECT TIMING!
MY NAME IS TOKIMORI HAZAMA.
CHING
I HAVE COME HERE TO TERMINATE YOU.
AT THAT VERY MOMENT ...
...I FELL IN LOVE WITH HIM.
SLOW DOWN. DOESN'T THIS STORY TAKE A DRASTIC TURN ALL OF A SUDDEN?
NO. THAT'S THE VERY REASON I DECIDED TO BREAK WITH KOYA.
THAT WAS...
...TOTALLY UNFAIR TO KOYA, DON'T YOU THINK?
THE MOMENT I SAW HIM...
...I REALIZED WHY I HAD BEEN UNABLE TO REST IN PEACE.
HEH HEH
WE WERE DESTINED TO MEET.

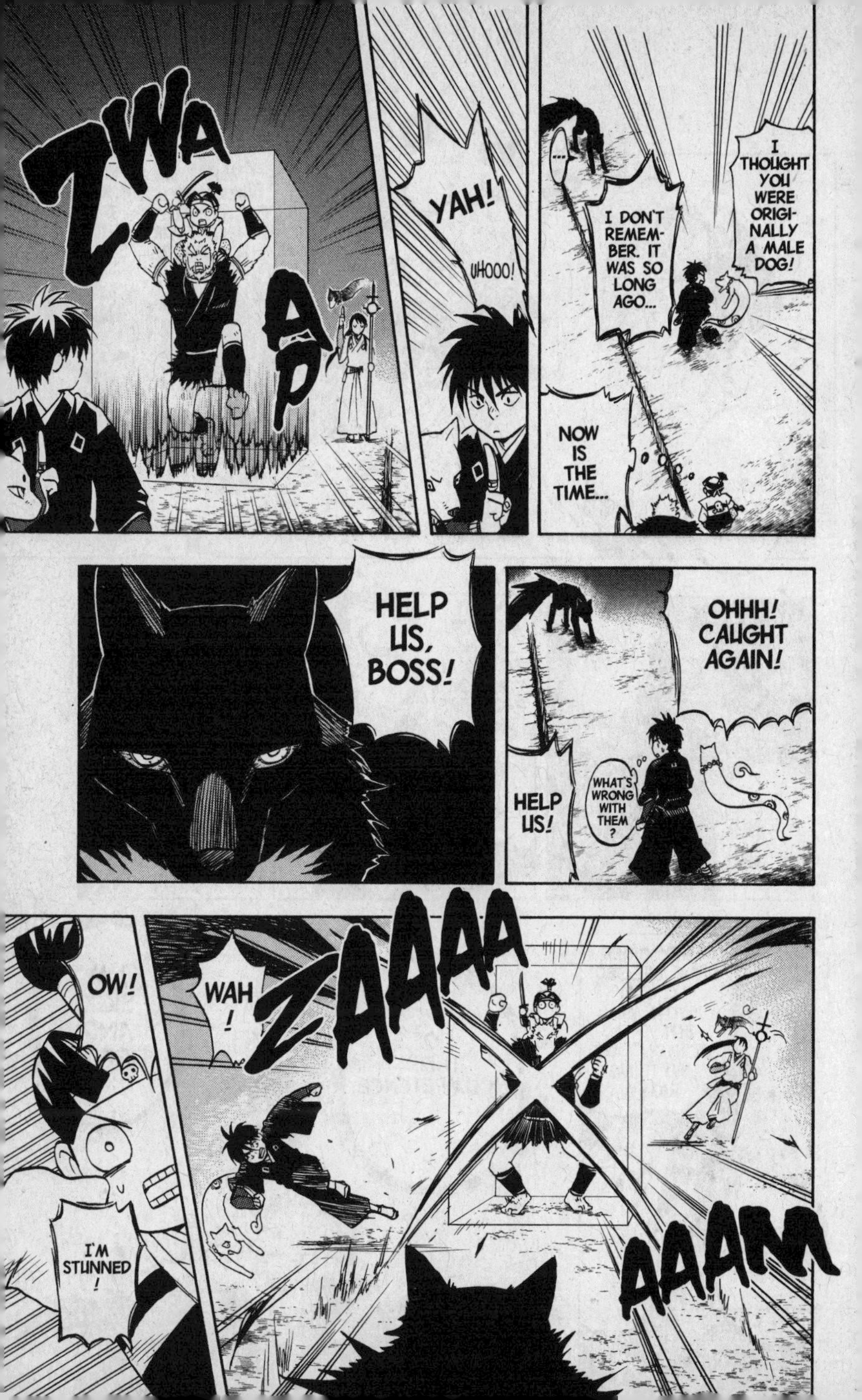
I THOUGHT YOU WERE ORIGINALLY A MALE DOG!
...
I DON'T REMEMBER. IT WAS SO LONG AGO...
NOW IS THE TIME...
YAH!
UHOOO!
ZWAAP
OHHH! CAUGHT AGAIN!
WHAT'S WRONG WITH THEM?
HELP US!
HELP US, BOSS!
WAH!
ZAAAA
AAAM
OW!
I'M STUNNED!

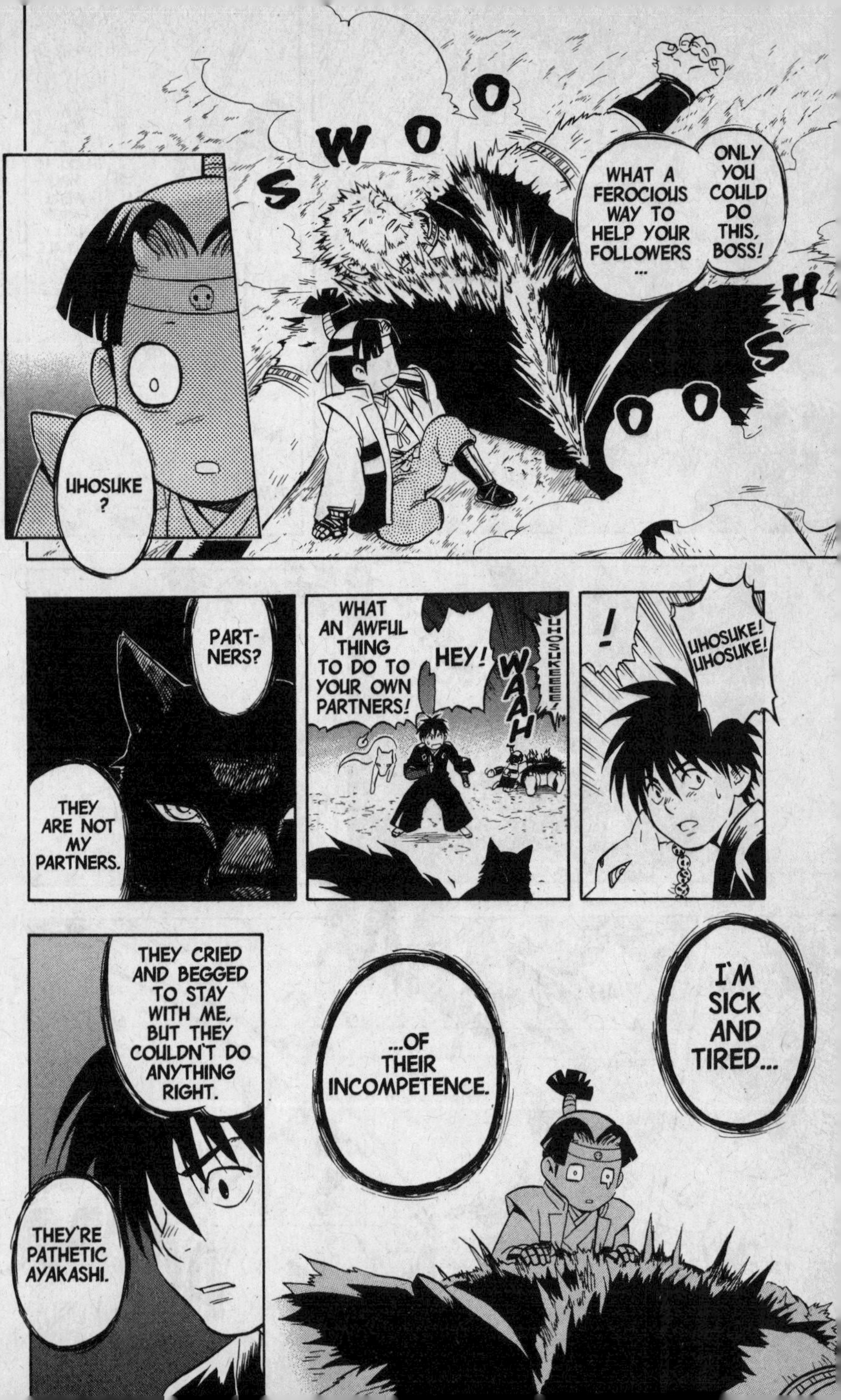
SWOOOOSH
ONLY YOU COULD DO THIS, BOSS!
WHAT A FEROCIOUS WAY TO HELP YOUR FOLLOWERS ...
UHOSUKE ?
!
UHOSUKE! UHOSUKE!
HEY!
WHAT AN AWFUL THING TO DO TO YOUR OWN PARTNERS!
UHOSUKEEEE!
WAAH
PARTNERS?
THEY ARE NOT MY PARTNERS.
I'M SICK AND TIRED...
...OF THEIR INCOMPETENCE.
THEY CRIED AND BEGGED TO STAY WITH ME, BUT THEY COULDN'T DO ANYTHING RIGHT.
THEY'RE PATHETIC AYAKASHI.

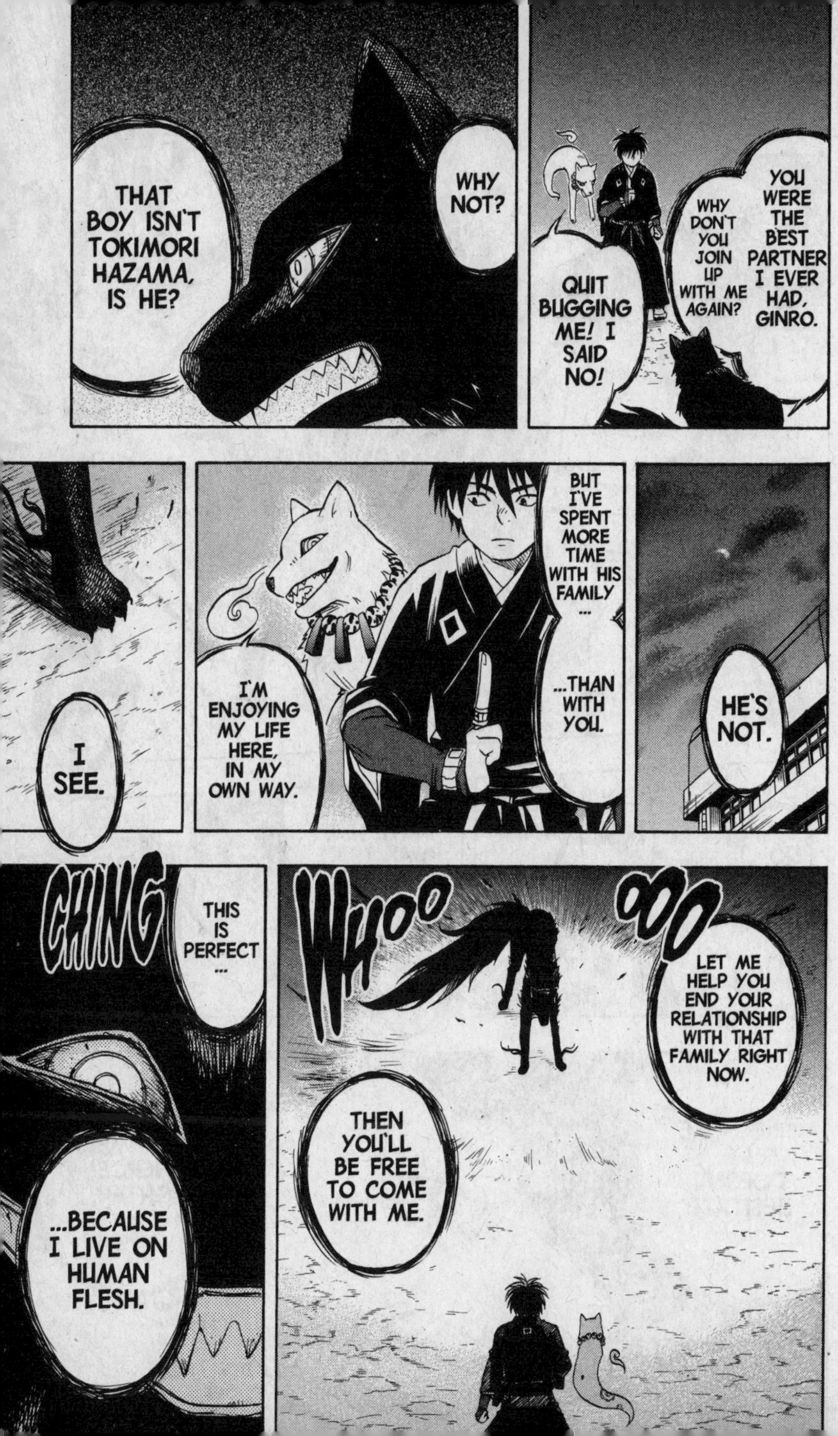
YOU WERE THE BEST PARTNER I EVER HAD, GINRO.
WHY DON'T YOU JOIN UP WITH ME AGAIN?
QUIT BUGGING ME! I SAID NO!
WHY NOT?
THAT BOY ISN'T TOKIMORI HAZAMA, IS HE?
HE'S NOT.
BUT I'VE SPENT MORE TIME WITH HIS FAMILY ...
...THAN WITH YOU.
I'M ENJOYING MY LIFE HERE, IN MY OWN WAY.
I SEE.
WHOO OOO
LET ME HELP YOU END YOUR RELATIONSHIP WITH THAT FAMILY RIGHT NOW.
THEN YOU'LL BE FREE TO COME WITH ME.
CHING
THIS IS PERFECT ...
...BECAUSE I LIVE ON HUMAN FLESH.

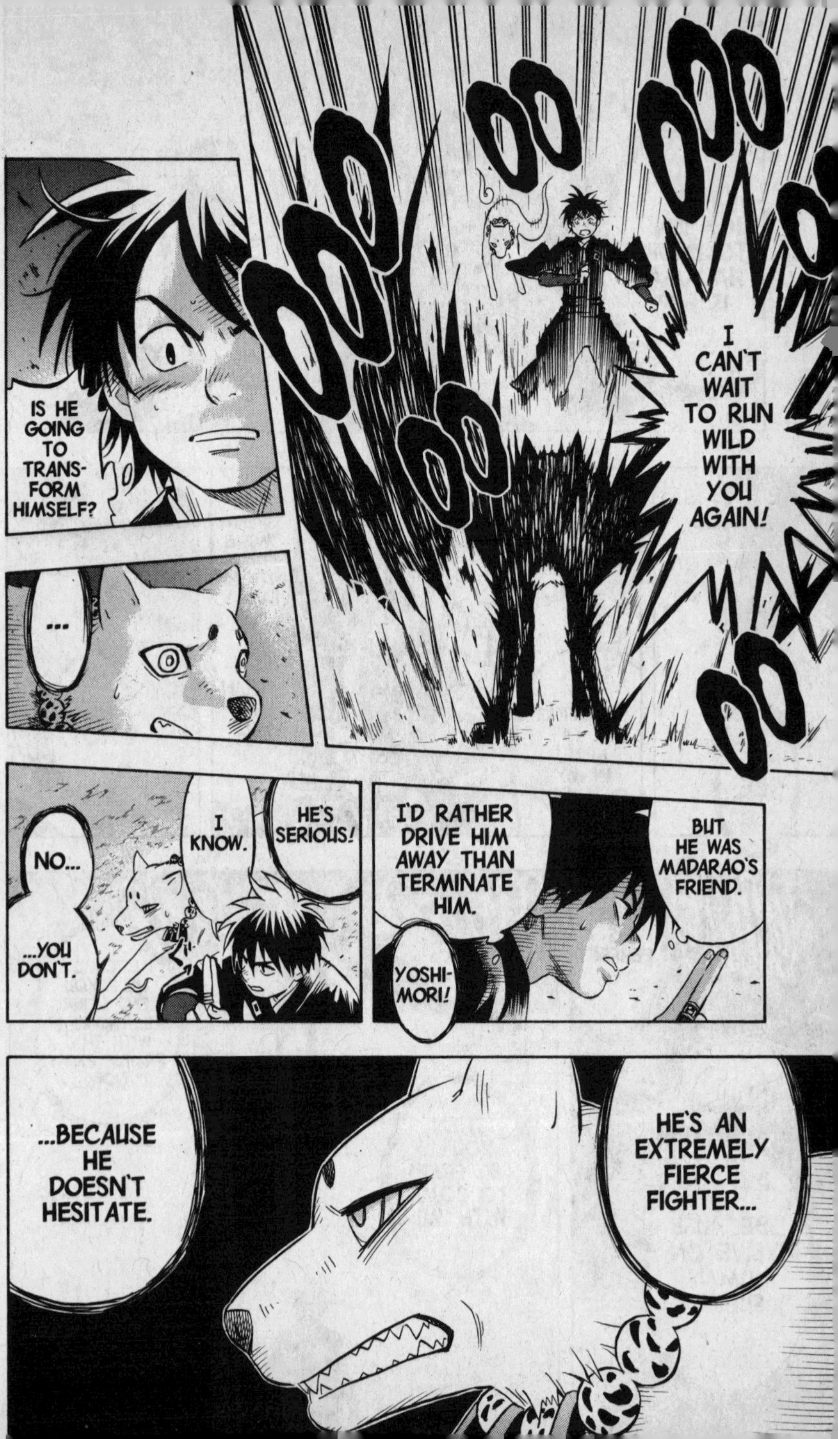
OOOOOOOOOOOOOO
I CAN'T WAIT TO RUN WILD WITH YOU AGAIN!
IS HE GOING TO TRANSFORM HIMSELF?
...
BUT HE WAS MADARAO'S FRIEND.
I'D RATHER DRIVE HIM AWAY THAN TERMINATE HIM.
YOSHIMORI!
HE'S SERIOUS!
I KNOW.
NO...
...YOU DON'T.
HE'S AN EXTREMELY FIERCE FIGHTER...
...BECAUSE HE DOESN'T HESITATE.

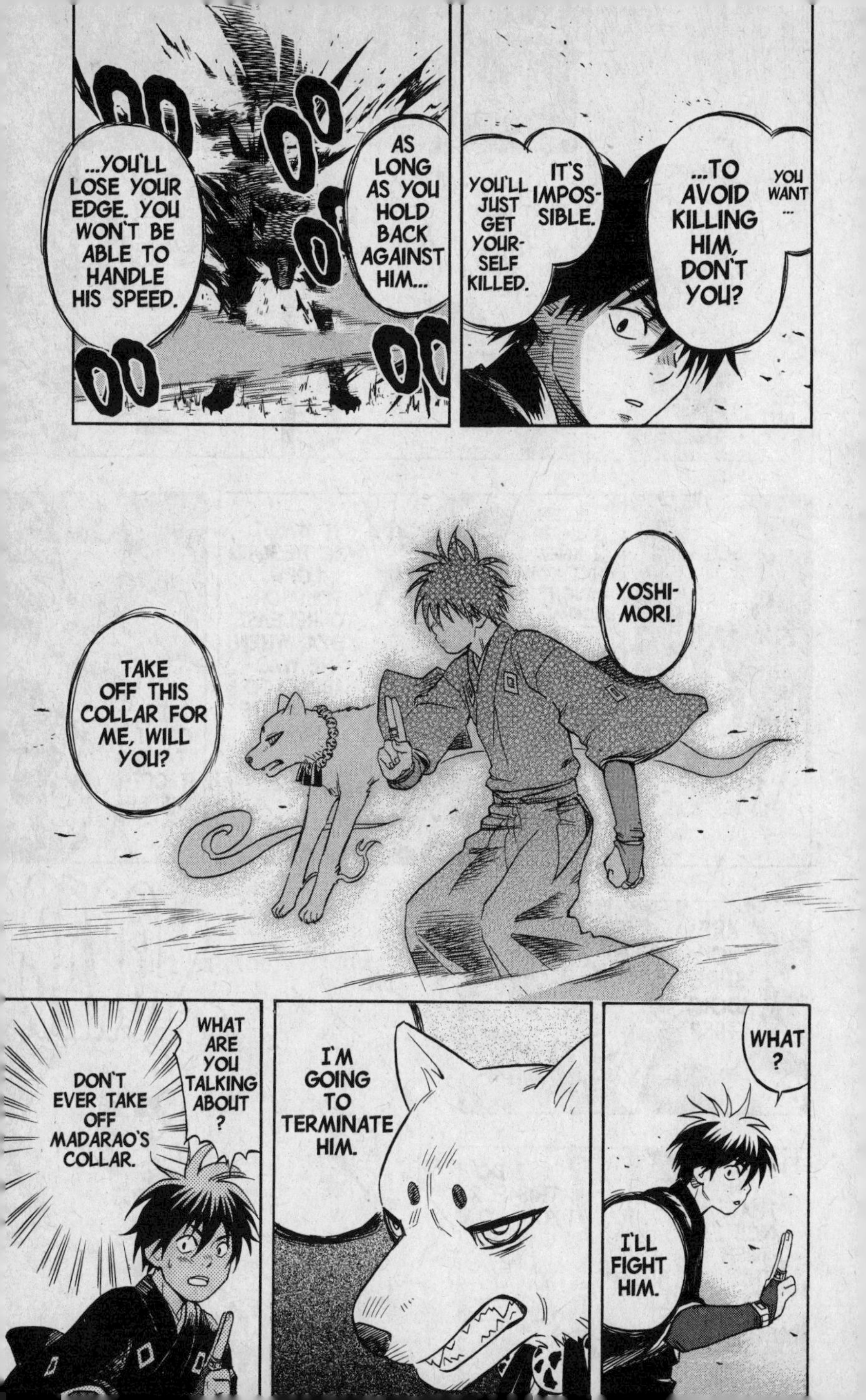
YOU WANT...
...TO AVOID KILLING HIM, DON'T YOU?
IT'S IMPOSSIBLE.
YOU'LL JUST GET YOURSELF KILLED.
AS LONG AS YOU HOLD BACK AGAINST HIM...
...YOU'LL LOSE YOUR EDGE. YOU WON'T BE ABLE TO HANDLE HIS SPEED.
YOSHIMORI.
TAKE OFF THIS COLLAR FOR ME, WILL YOU?
WHAT?
I'LL FIGHT HIM.
I'M GOING TO TERMINATE HIM.
WHAT ARE YOU TALKING ABOUT?
DON'T EVER TAKE OFF MADARAO'S COLLAR.

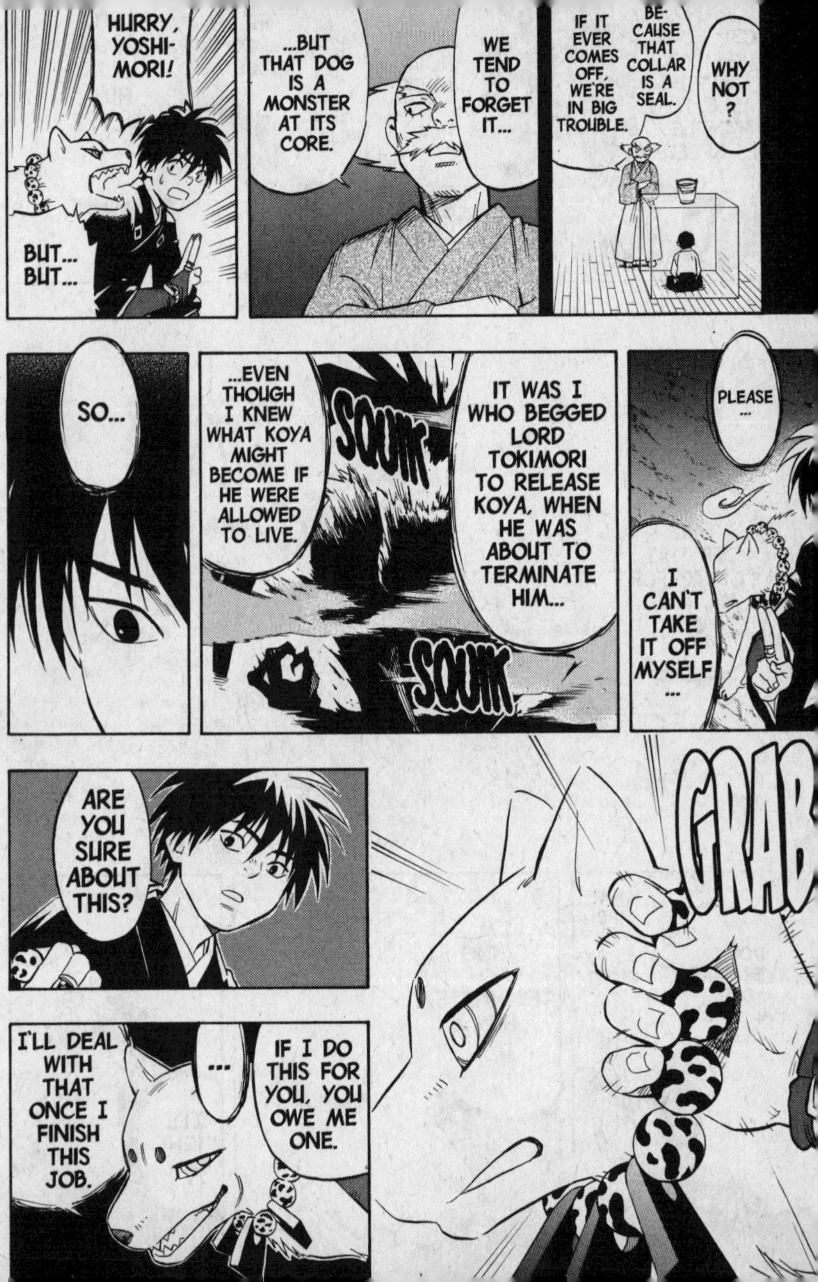
WHY NOT?
BECAUSE THAT COLLAR IS A SEAL.
IF IT EVER COMES OFF, WE'RE IN BIG TROUBLE.
WE TEND TO FORGET IT...
...BUT THAT DOG IS A MONSTER AT ITS CORE.
HURRY, YOSHIMORI!
BUT... BUT...
PLEASE...
I CAN'T TAKE IT OFF MYSELF...
IT WAS I WHO BEGGED LORD TOKIMORI TO RELEASE KOYA, WHEN HE WAS ABOUT TO TERMINATE HIM...
...EVEN THOUGH I KNEW WHAT KOYA MIGHT BECOME IF HE WERE ALLOWED TO LIVE.
SQUIK
SQUIK
SO...
GRAB
ARE YOU SURE ABOUT THIS?
IF I DO THIS FOR YOU, YOU OWE ME ONE.
...
I'LL DEAL WITH THAT ONCE I FINISH THIS JOB.

IT'S
A
NENSHI
...

WHOOO

MADARAO

KY
A

AAA

AA

AAA

SH

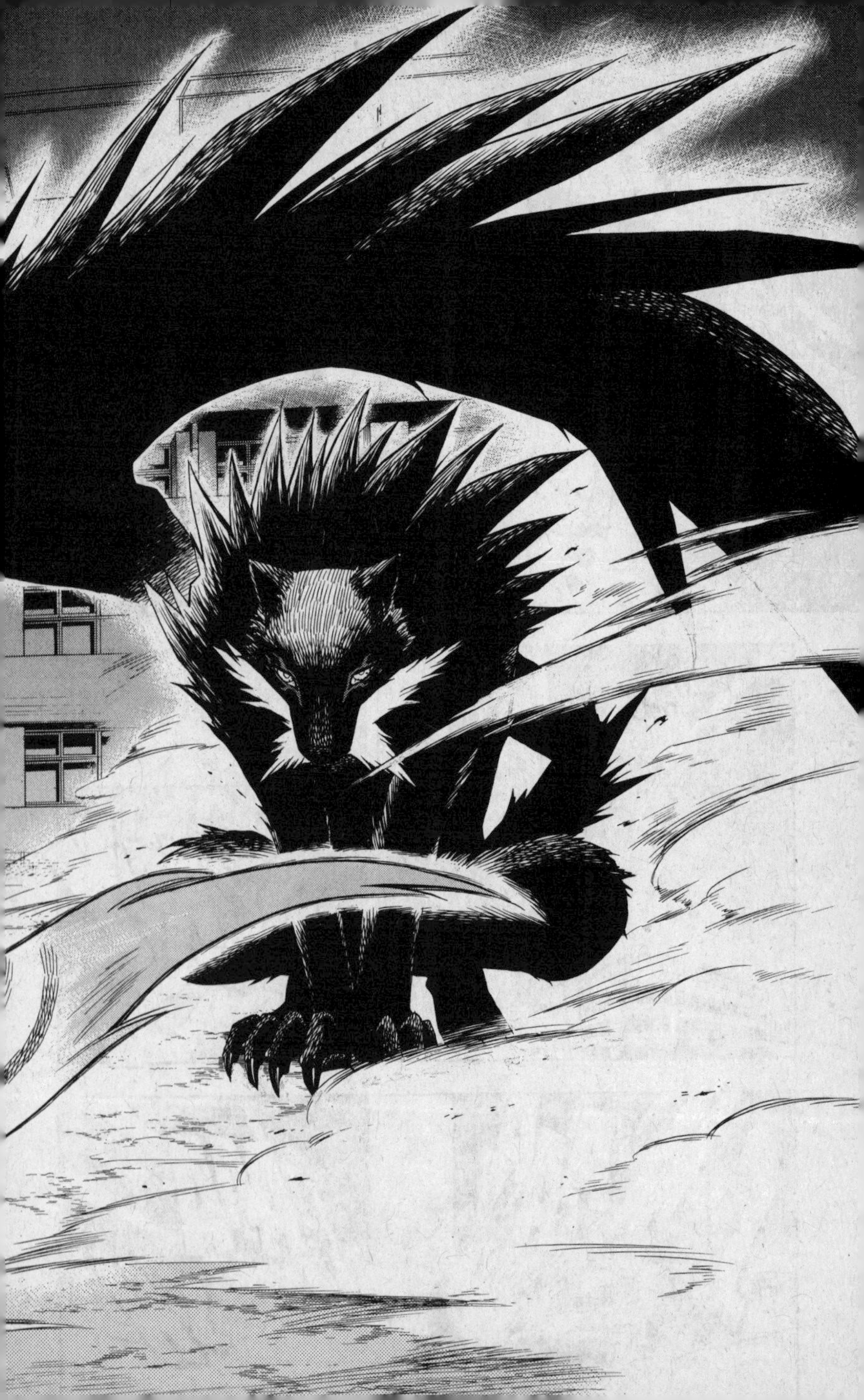

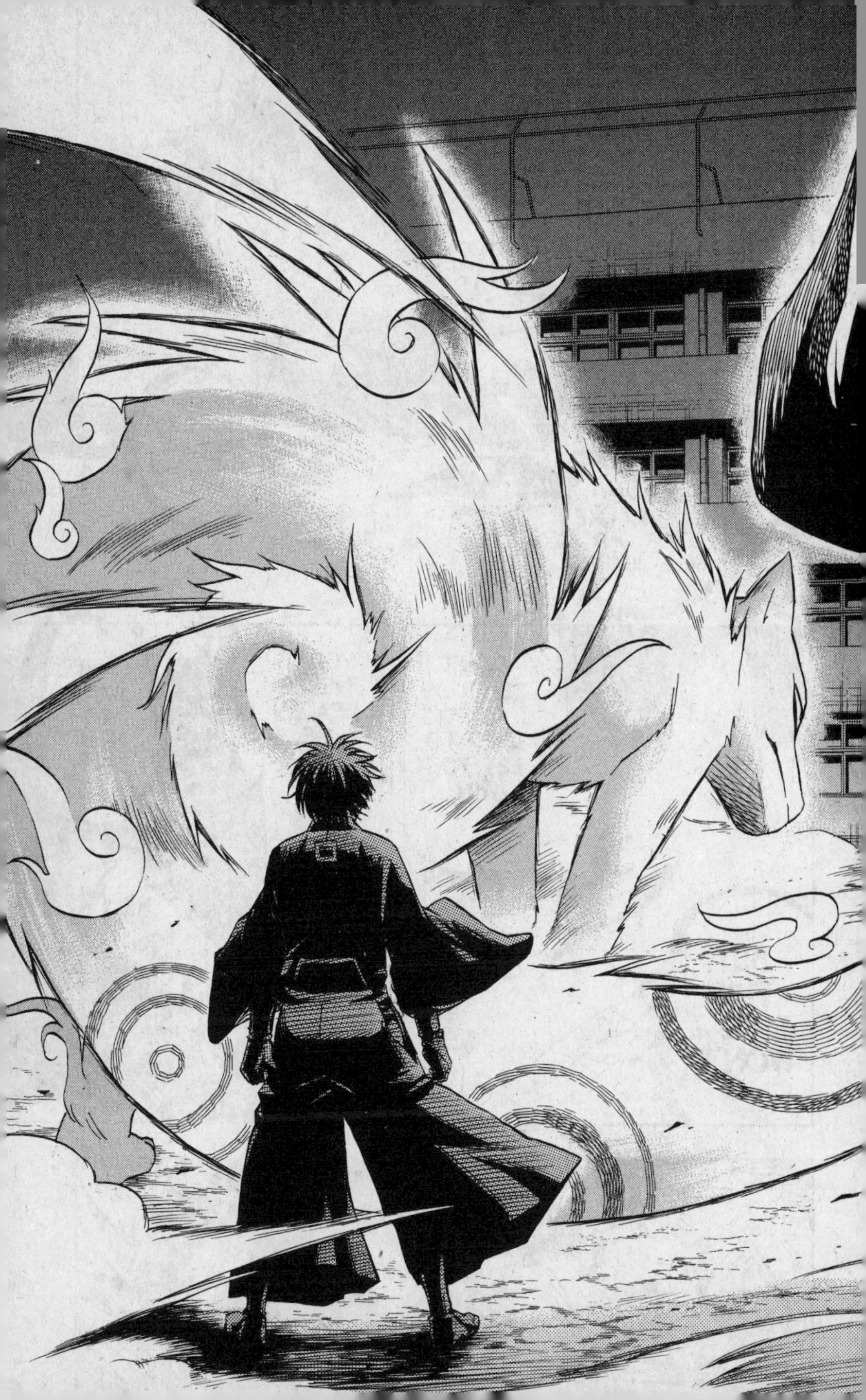

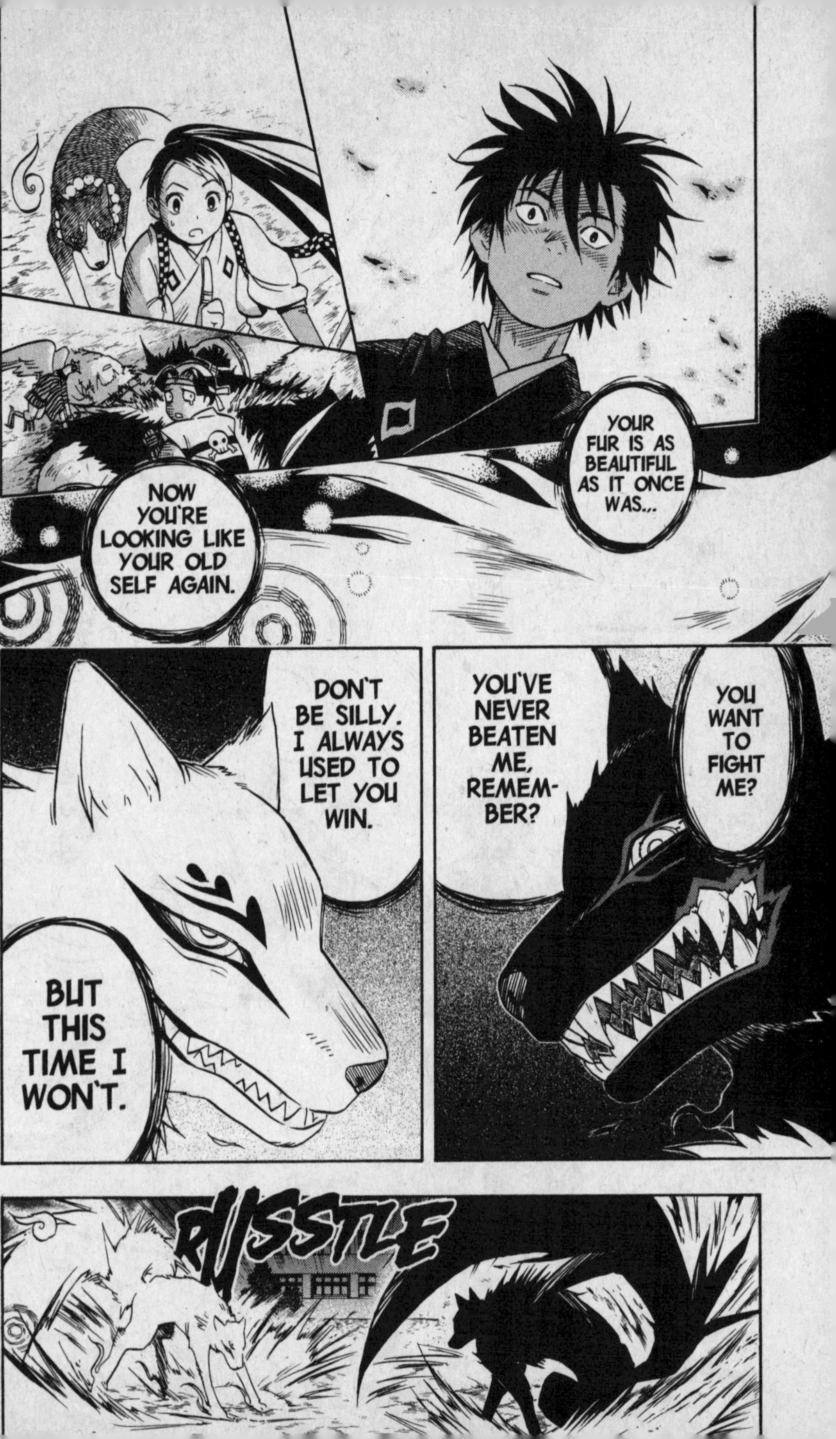
YOUR FUR IS AS BEAUTIFUL AS IT ONCE WAS...
NOW YOU'RE LOOKING LIKE YOUR OLD SELF AGAIN.
YOU WANT TO FIGHT ME?
YOU'VE NEVER BEATEN ME, REMEMBER?
DON'T BE SILLY. I ALWAYS USED TO LET YOU WIN.
BUT THIS TIME I WON'T.
RUSSTLE

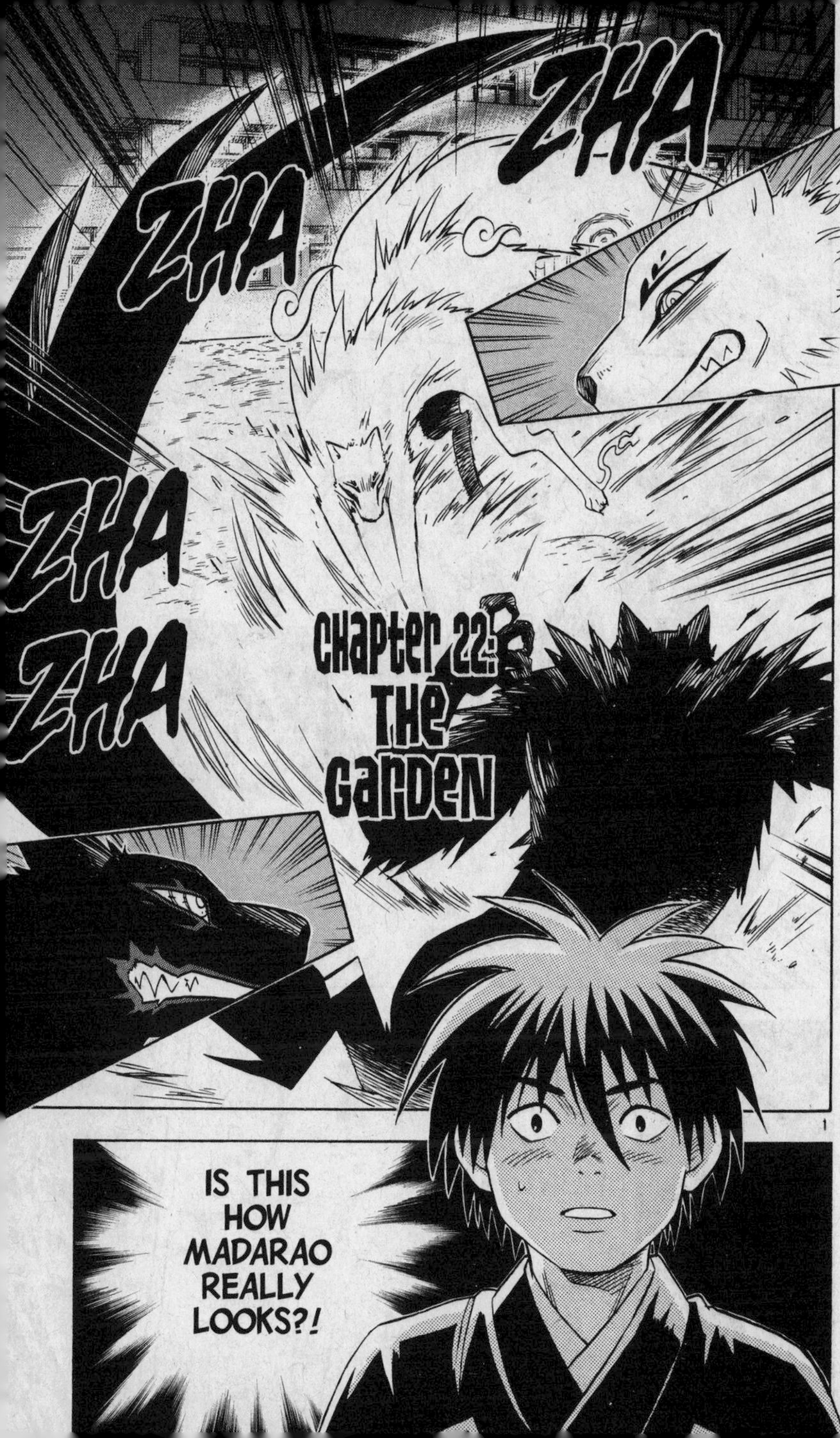
ZHA
ZHA
ZHA
ZHA
CHAPTER 22: THE GARDEN
IS THIS HOW MADARAO REALLY LOOKS?!

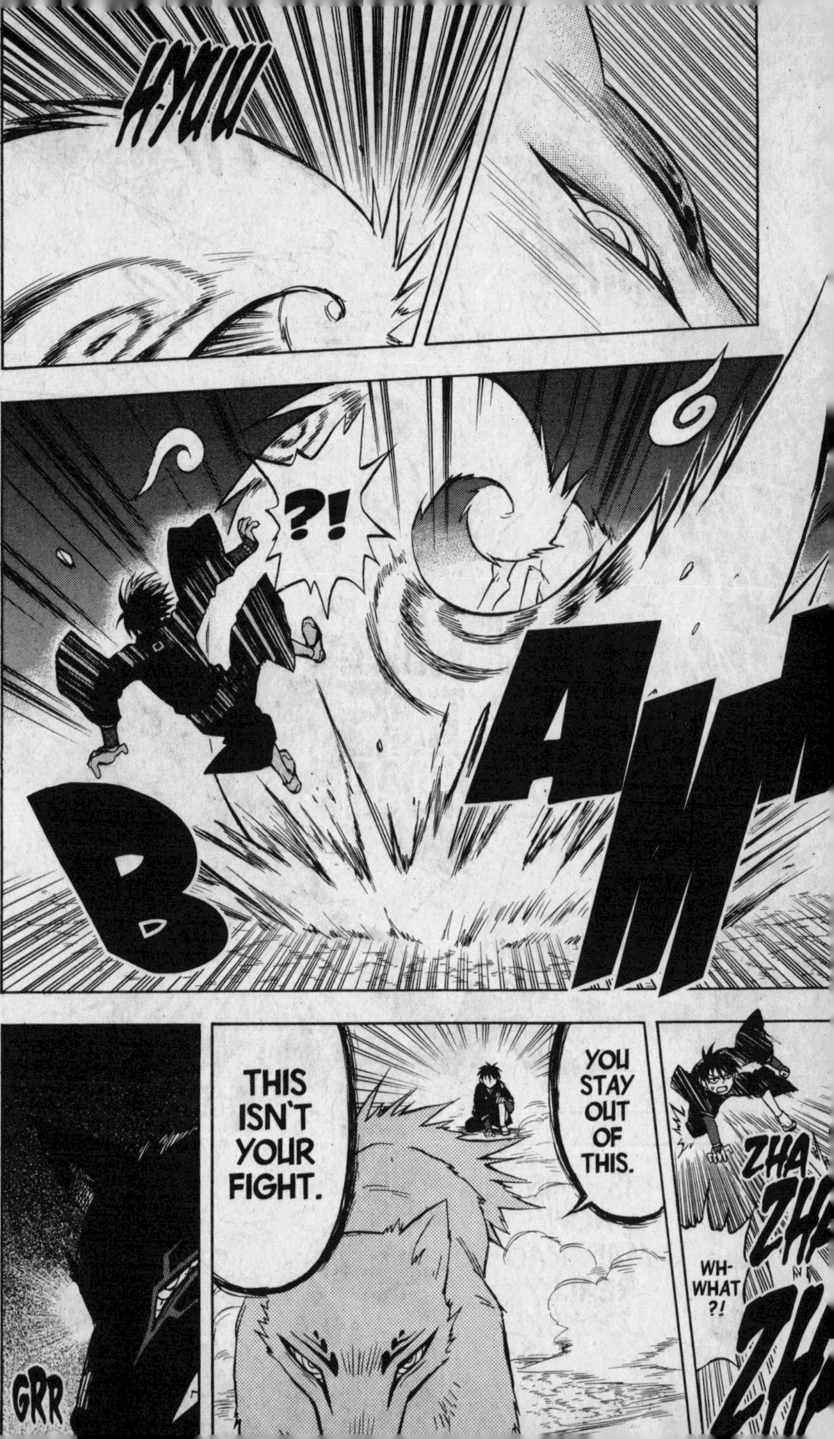
HYUU
?!
BAM
ZHA
WH-WHAT?!
YOU STAY OUT OF THIS.
THIS ISN'T YOUR FIGHT.
GRR

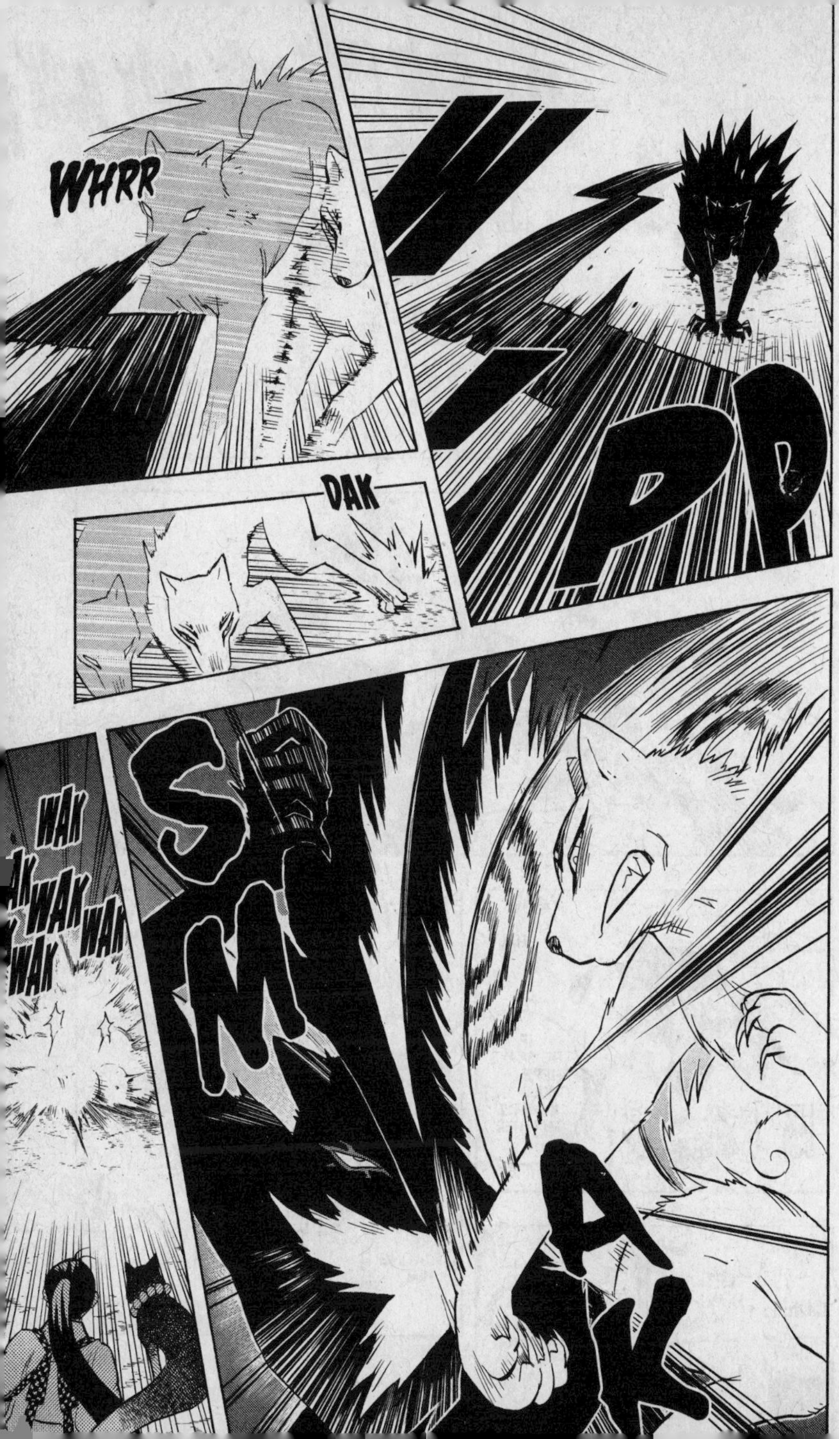
WHRR
DAK
SMACK
WAK WAK WAK WAK WAK

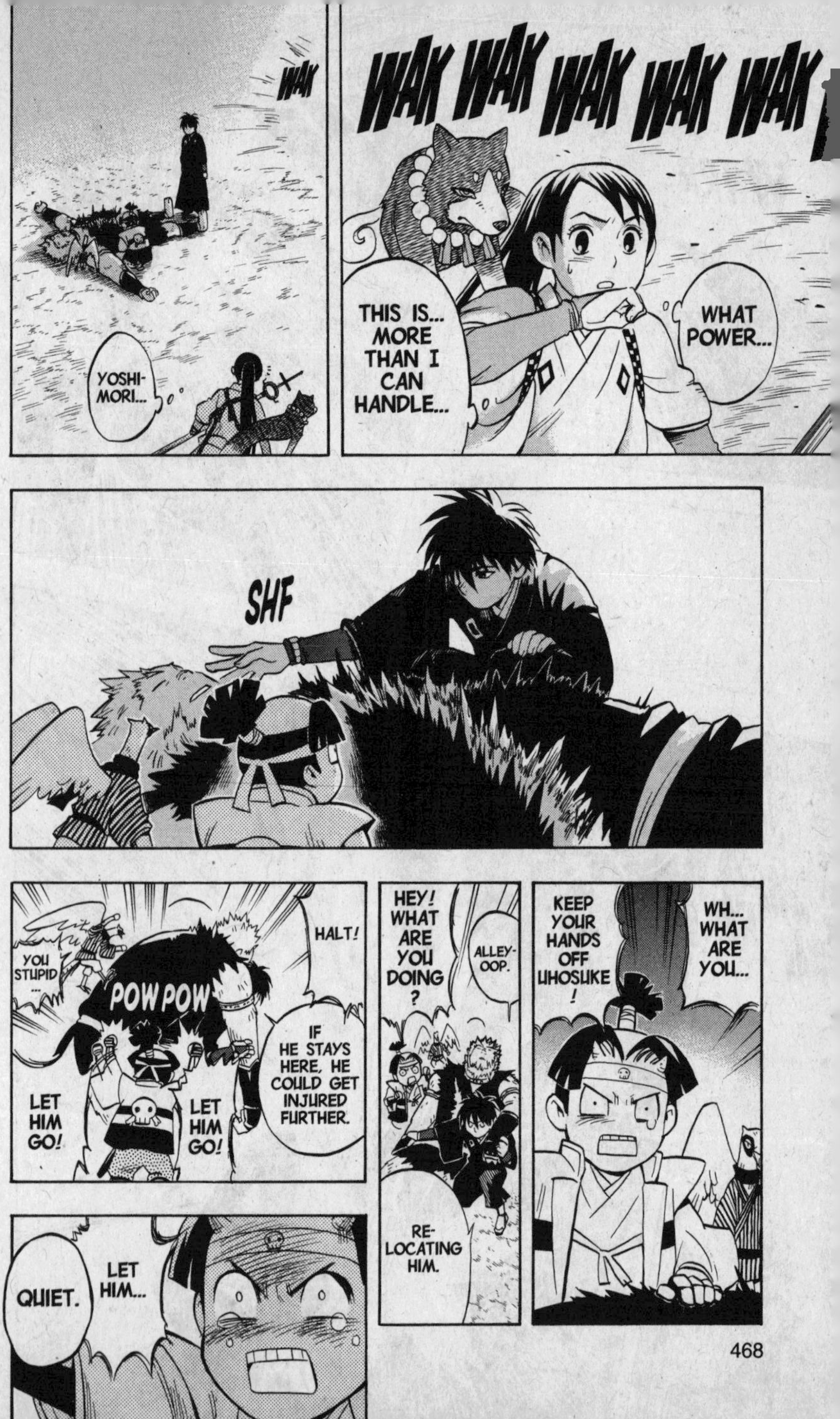
WAK WAK WAK WAK WAK
WHAT POWER...
THIS IS... MORE THAN I CAN HANDLE...
WAK
YOSHIMORI...
SHF
WH... WHAT ARE YOU...
KEEP YOUR HANDS OFF UHOSUKE!
HEY! WHAT ARE YOU DOING?
ALLEY-OOP.
RE-LOCATING HIM.
HALT!
IF HE STAYS HERE, HE COULD GET INJURED FURTHER.
POW POW
YOU STUPID...
LET HIM GO!
LET HIM GO!
LET HIM...
QUIET.

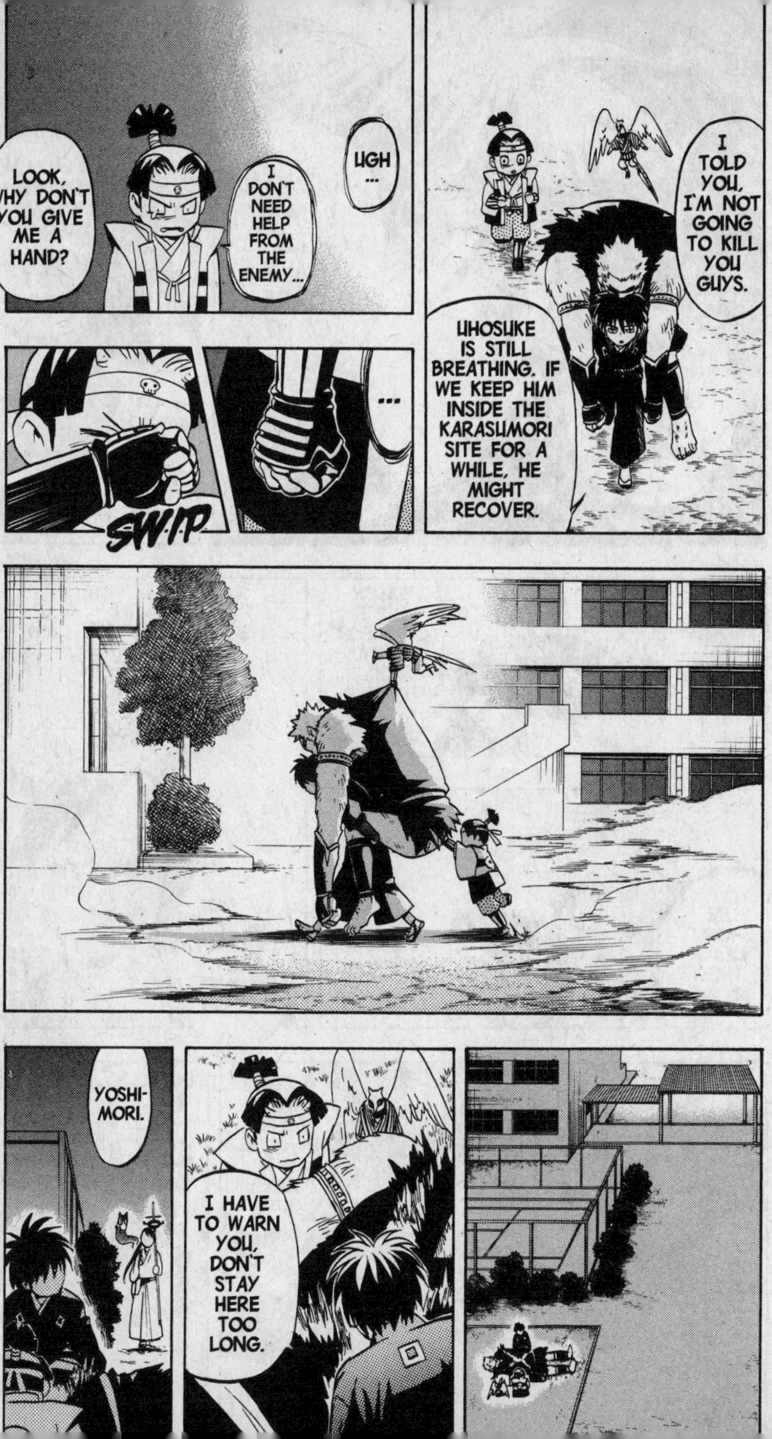
UGH...
I DON'T NEED HELP FROM THE ENEMY...
LOOK, WHY DON'T YOU GIVE ME A HAND?
...
SWIP
I TOLD YOU, I'M NOT GOING TO KILL YOU GUYS.
UHOSUKE IS STILL BREATHING. IF WE KEEP HIM INSIDE THE KARASUMORI SITE FOR A WHILE, HE MIGHT RECOVER.
I HAVE TO WARN YOU, DON'T STAY HERE TOO LONG.
YOSHI-MORI.

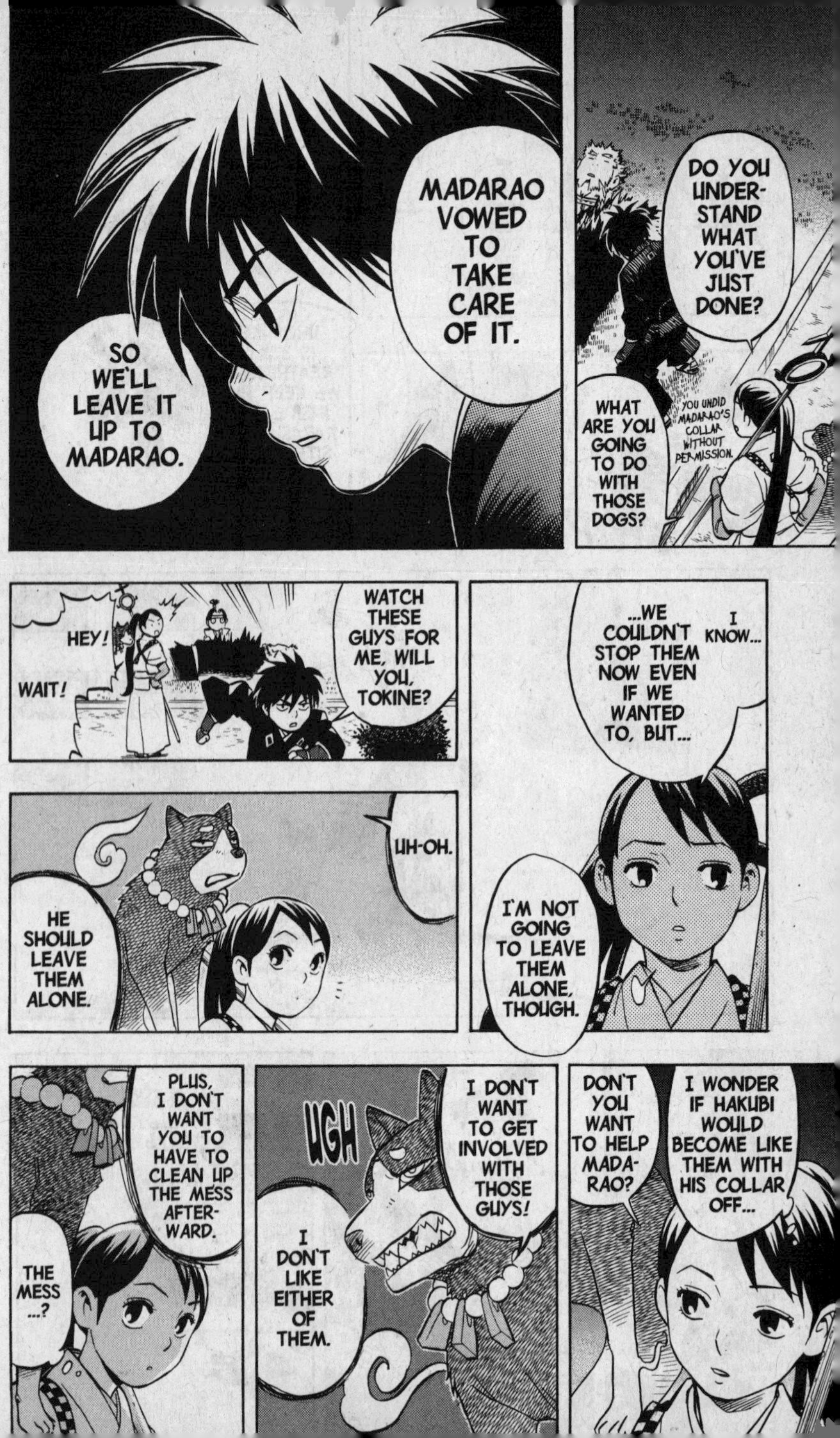
DO YOU UNDERSTAND WHAT YOU'VE JUST DONE?
YOU UNDID MADARAO'S COLLAR WITHOUT PERMISSION.
WHAT ARE YOU GOING TO DO WITH THOSE DOGS?
MADARAO VOWED TO TAKE CARE OF IT.
SO WE'LL LEAVE IT UP TO MADARAO.
WATCH THESE GUYS FOR ME, WILL YOU, TOKINE?
HEY!
WAIT!
UH-OH.
HE SHOULD LEAVE THEM ALONE.
I KNOW...
...WE COULDN'T STOP THEM NOW EVEN IF WE WANTED TO, BUT...
I'M NOT GOING TO LEAVE THEM ALONE, THOUGH.
I WONDER IF HAKUBI WOULD BECOME LIKE THEM WITH HIS COLLAR OFF...
DON'T YOU WANT TO HELP MADARAO?
I DON'T WANT TO GET INVOLVED WITH THOSE GUYS!
UGH
I DON'T LIKE EITHER OF THEM.
PLUS, I DON'T WANT YOU TO HAVE TO CLEAN UP THE MESS AFTERWARD.
THE MESS...?

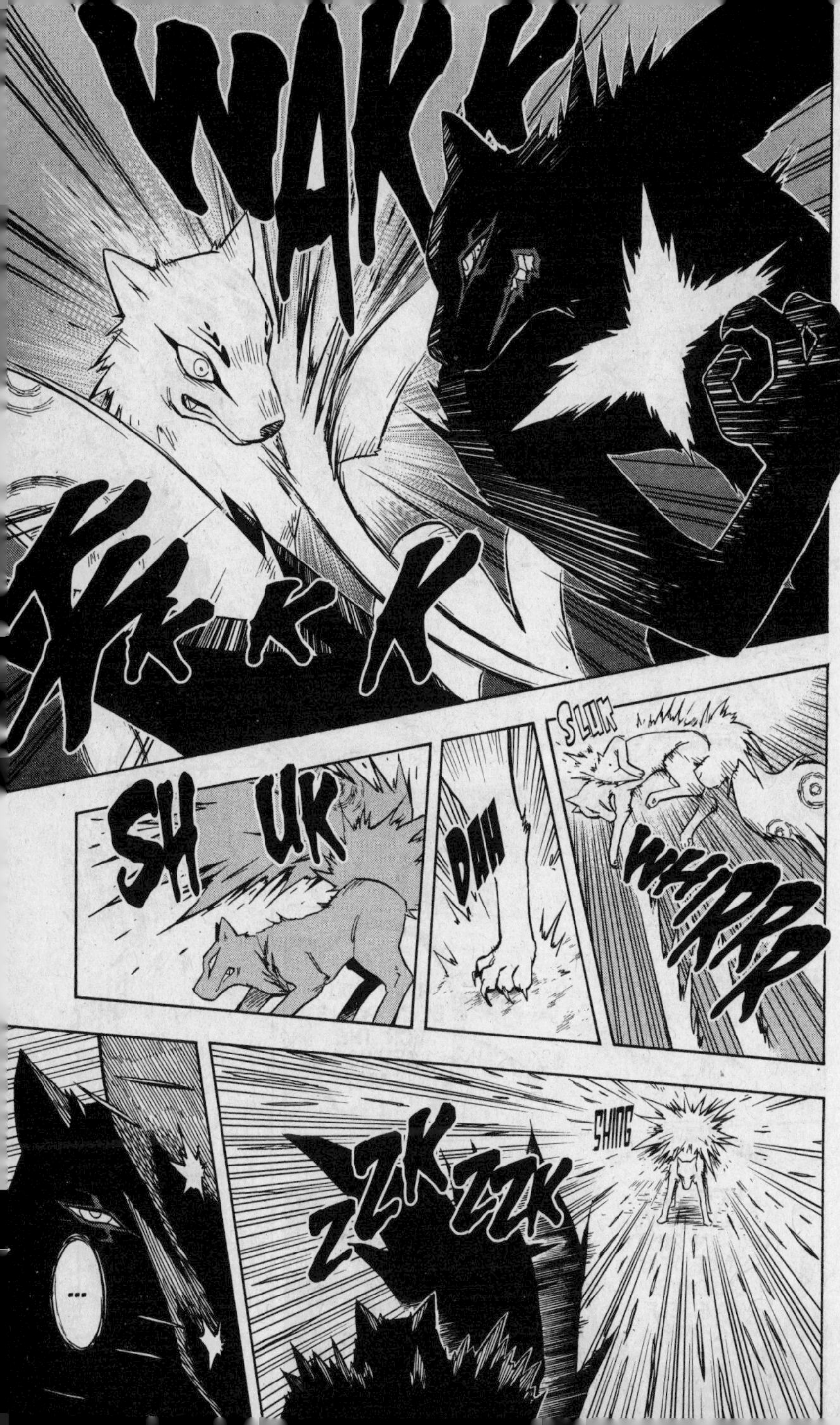
WAK
KKKKX
SLUR
WHIRRR
DAH
SH
UK
SHING
ZZK ZZK
...

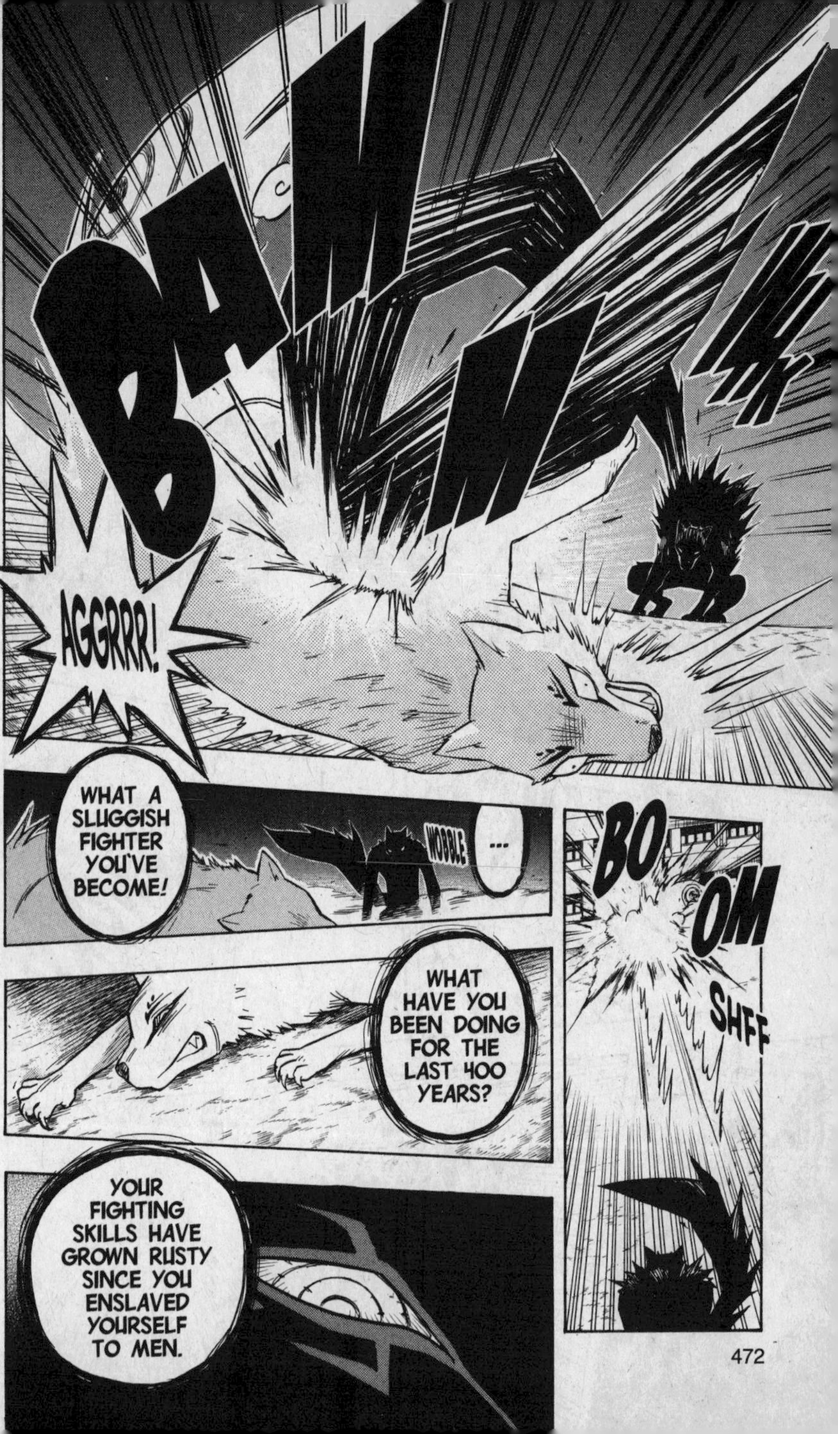
BAM
AGGRRR!
BOOM
SHFF
...
WOBBLE
WHAT A SLUGGISH FIGHTER YOU'VE BECOME!
WHAT HAVE YOU BEEN DOING FOR THE LAST 400 YEARS?
YOUR FIGHTING SKILLS HAVE GROWN RUSTY SINCE YOU ENSLAVED YOURSELF TO MEN.

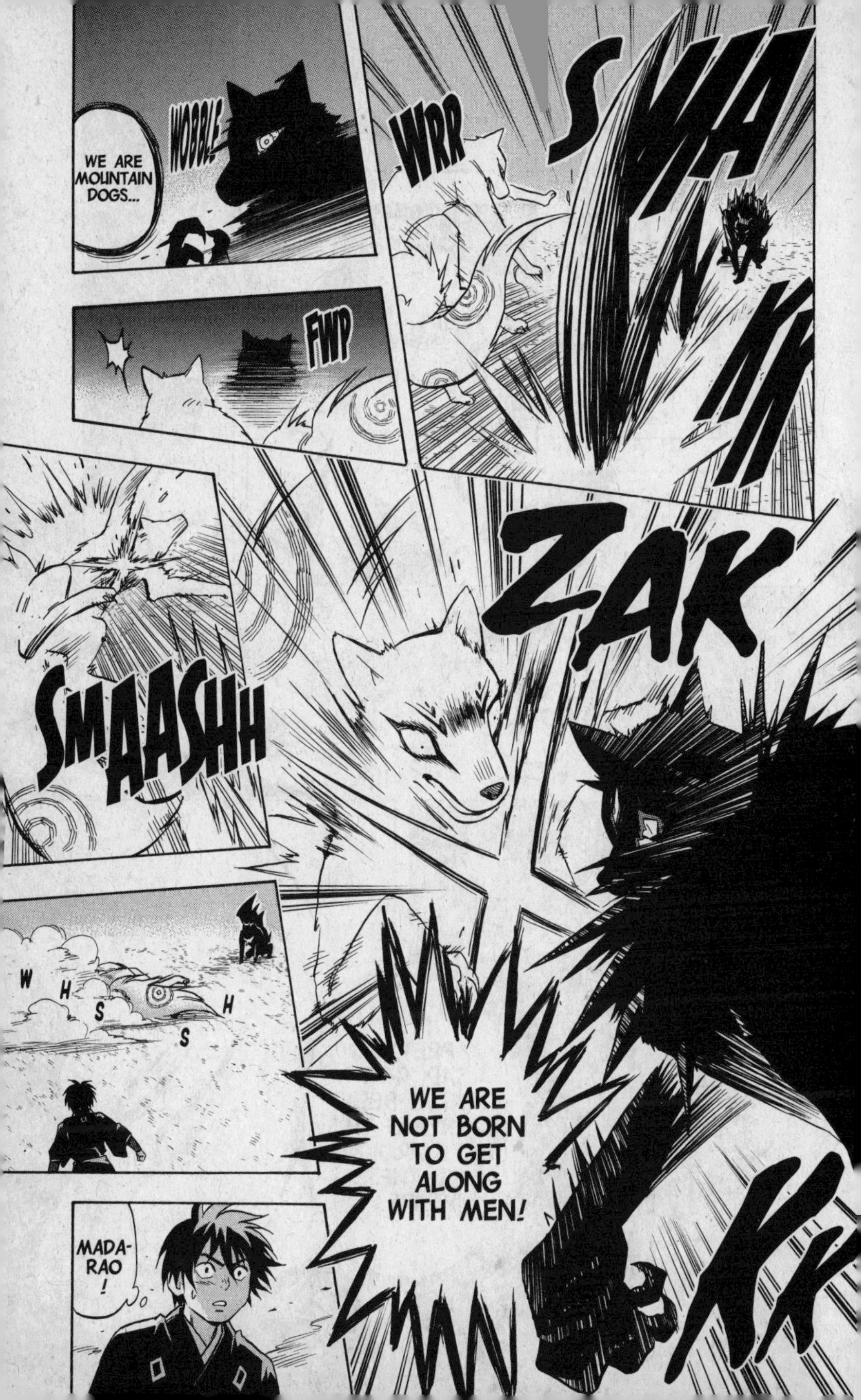
WRR
SWAAKK
WE ARE MOUNTAIN DOGS...
WOBBLE
FWP
ZAK
SMAASHH
WE ARE NOT BORN TO GET ALONG WITH MEN!
WHSSH
MADARAO!

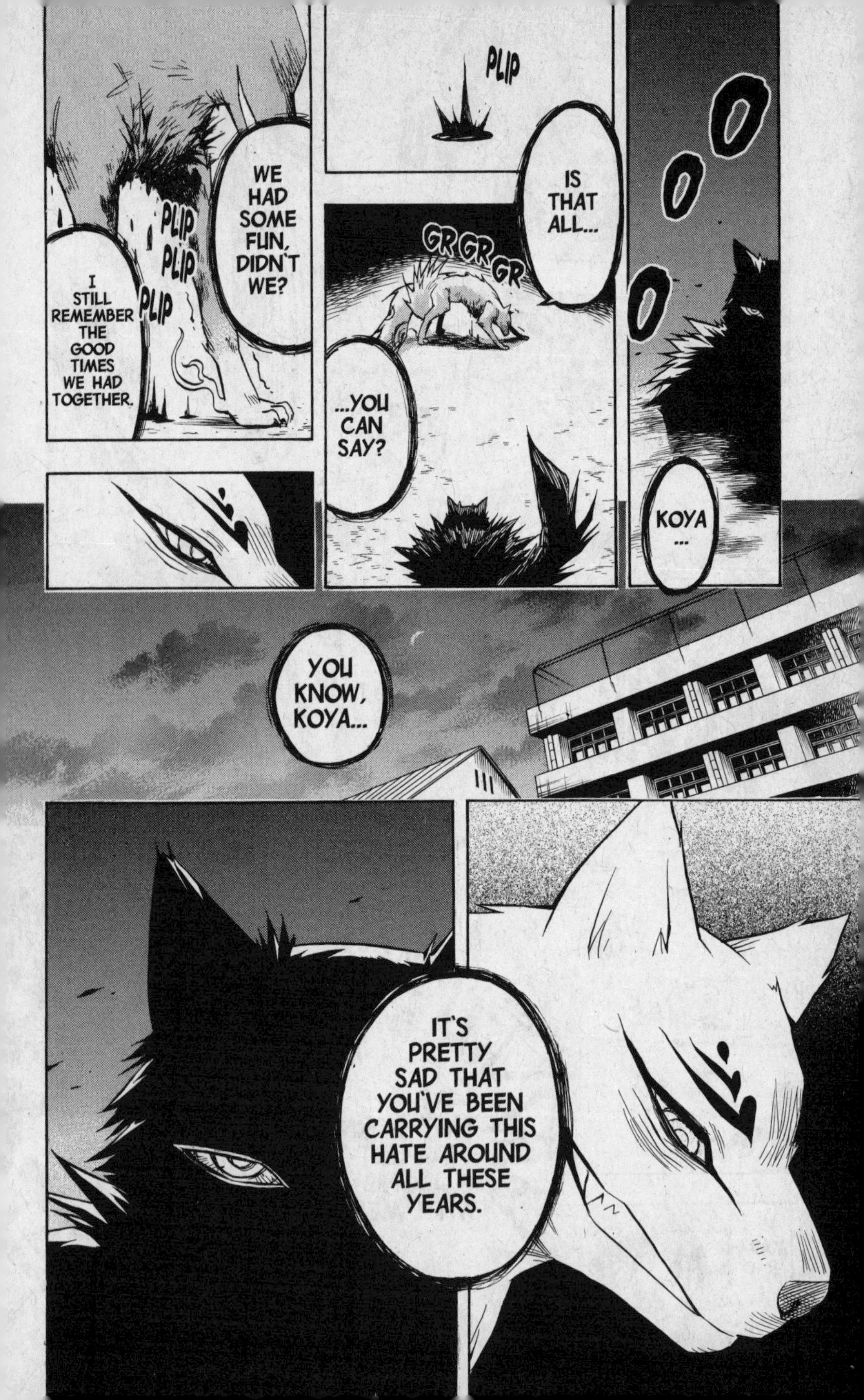
KOYA...
PLIP
IS THAT ALL...
GR GR GR
...YOU CAN SAY?
WE HAD SOME FUN, DIDN'T WE?
PLIP PLIP
PLIP
I STILL REMEMBER THE GOOD TIMES WE HAD TOGETHER.
YOU KNOW, KOYA...
IT'S PRETTY SAD THAT YOU'VE BEEN CARRYING THIS HATE AROUND ALL THESE YEARS.

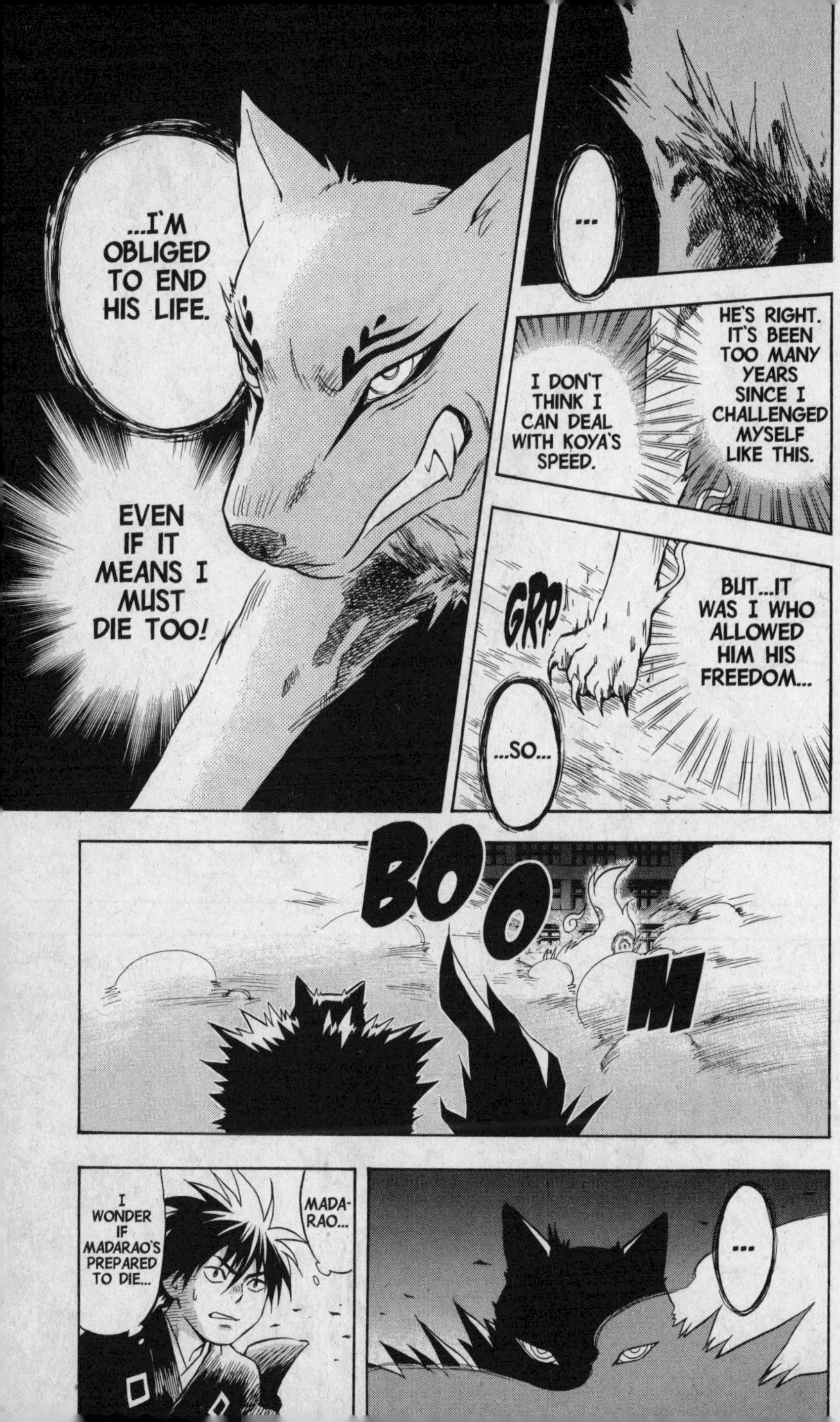
...
HE'S RIGHT. IT'S BEEN TOO MANY YEARS SINCE I CHALLENGED MYSELF LIKE THIS.
I DON'T THINK I CAN DEAL WITH KOYA'S SPEED.
BUT...IT WAS I WHO ALLOWED HIM HIS FREEDOM...
GRP
...SO...
...I'M OBLIGED TO END HIS LIFE.
EVEN IF IT MEANS I MUST DIE TOO!
BOOOM
...
MADARAO...
I WONDER IF MADARAO'S PREPARED TO DIE...

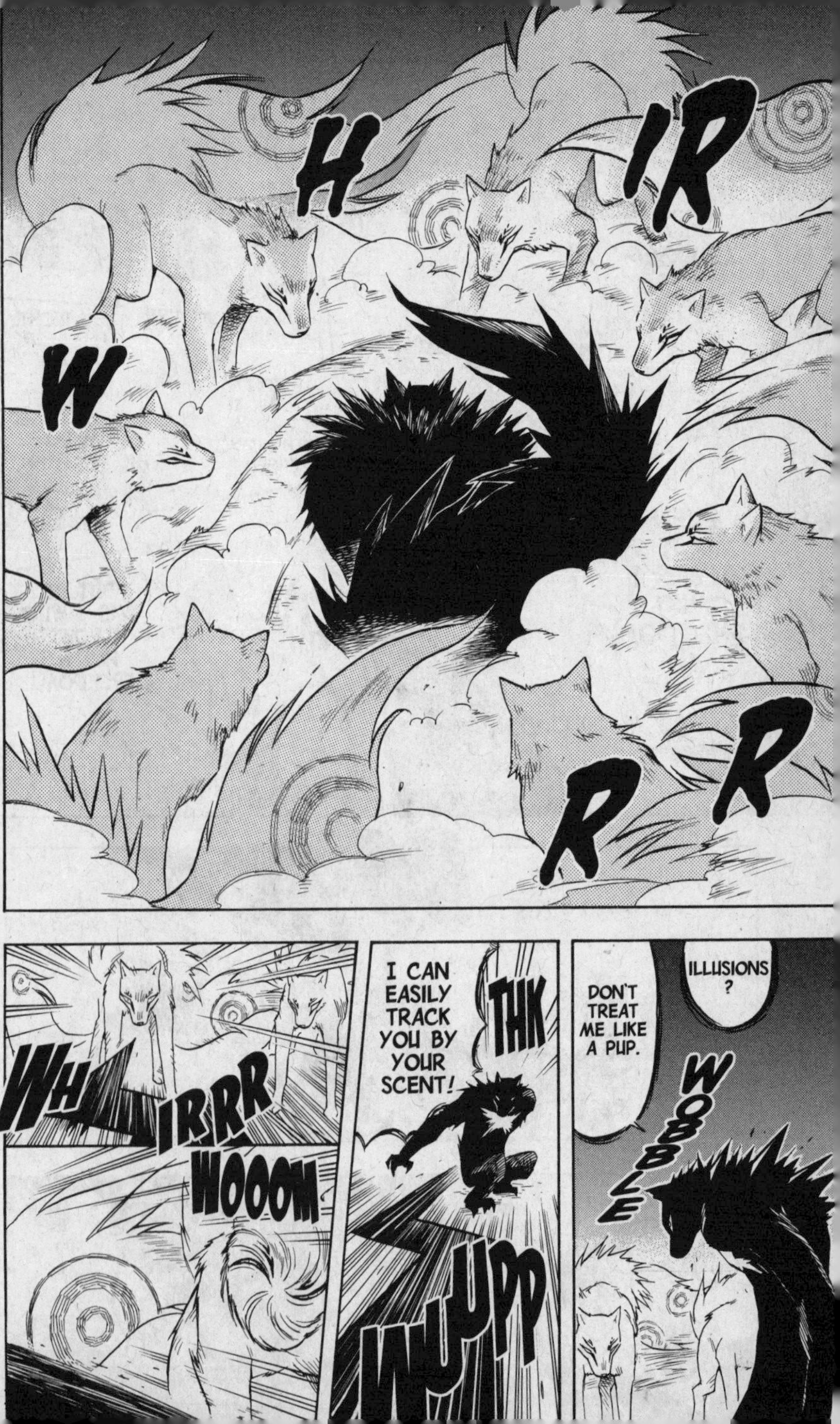
WHIRRR
ILLUSIONS?
DON'T TREAT ME LIKE A PUP.
WOBBLE
I CAN EASILY TRACK YOU BY YOUR SCENT!
THK
WHUPP
WHIRRR
WHOOOM

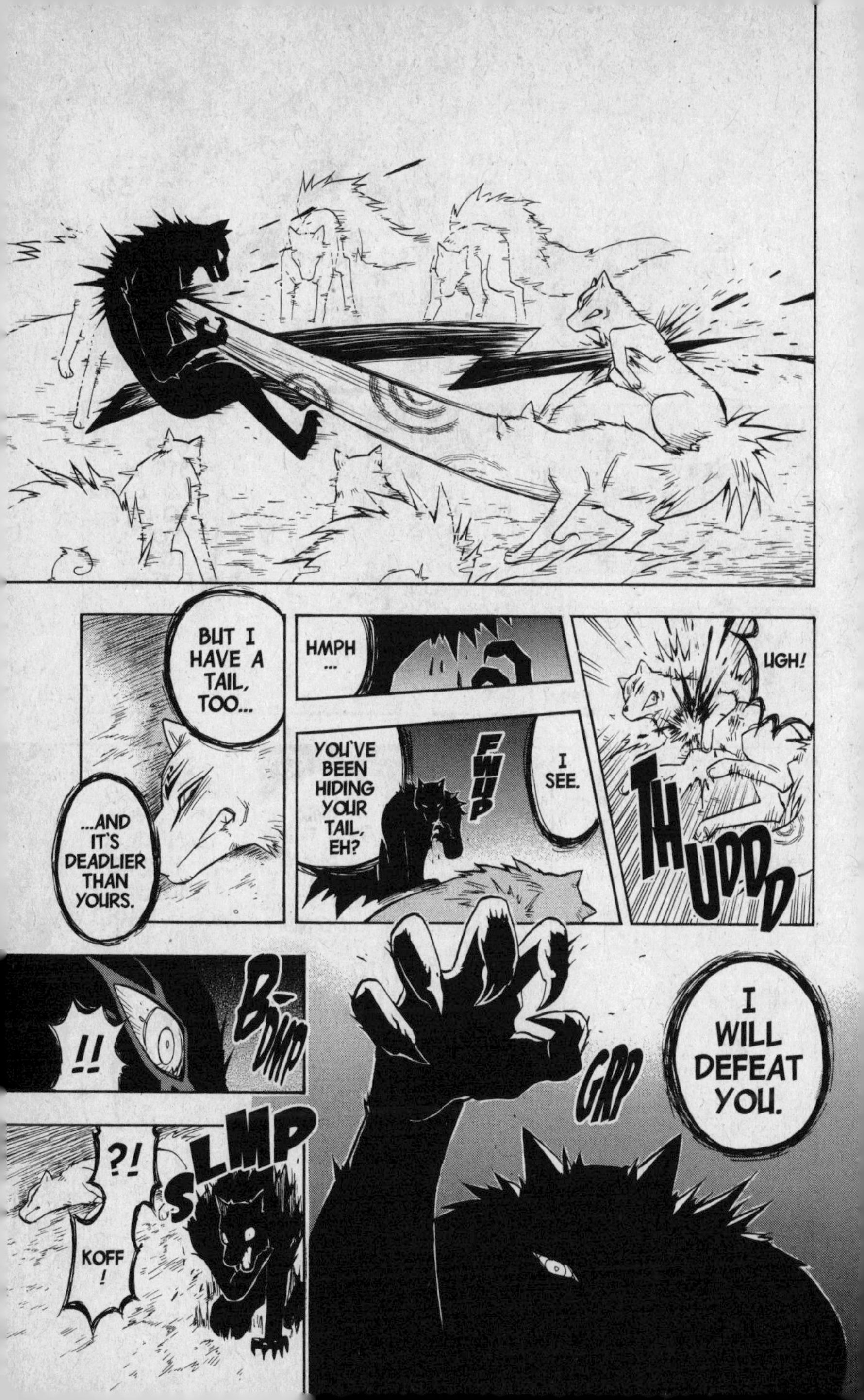
UGH!
THUDDD
HMPH ...
I SEE.
FWUP
YOU'VE BEEN HIDING YOUR TAIL, EH?
BUT I HAVE A TAIL, TOO...
...AND IT'S DEADLIER THAN YOURS.
I WILL DEFEAT YOU.
GRP
B-DMP
!!
SLMP
?!
KOFF!

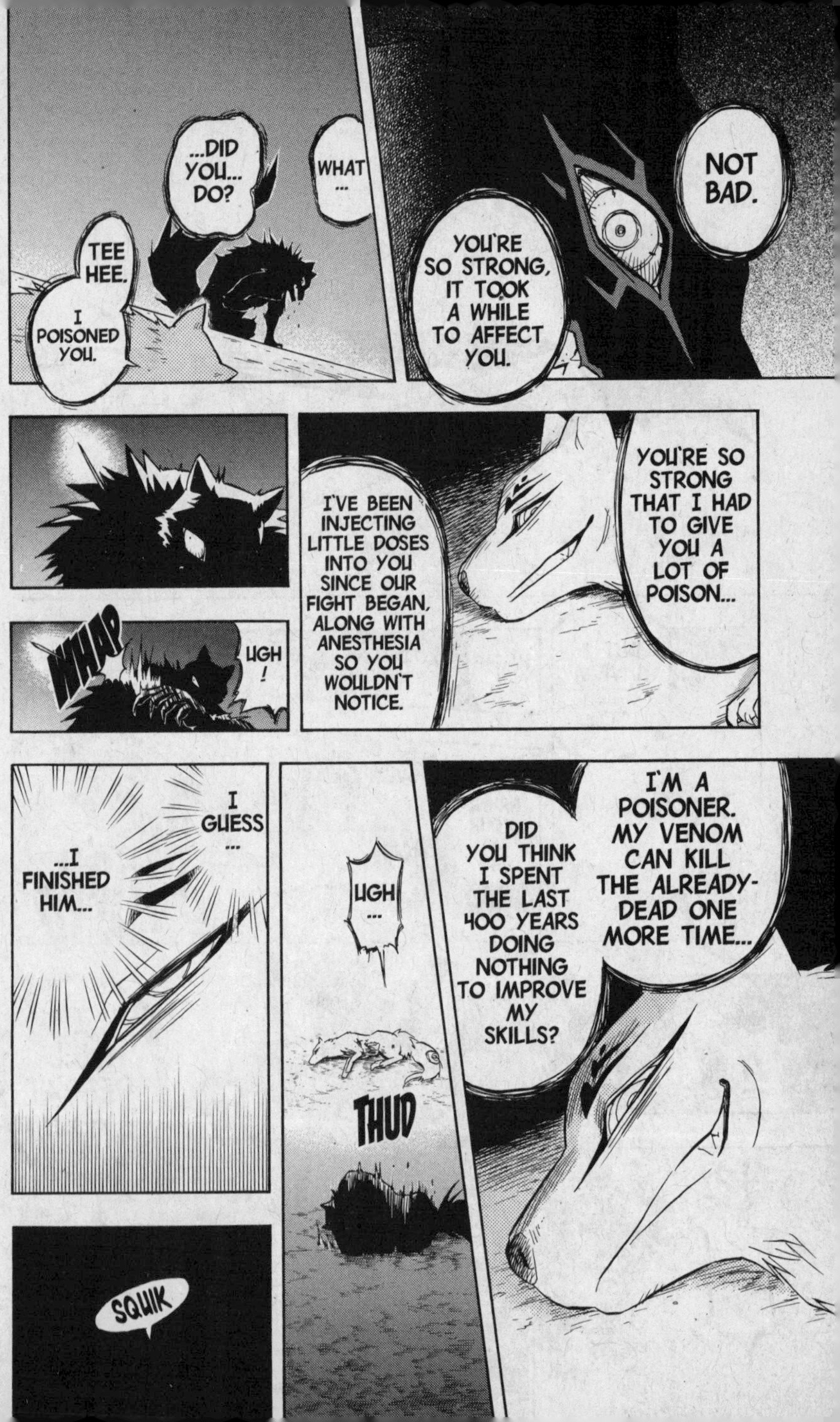
NOT BAD.
YOU'RE SO STRONG, IT TOOK A WHILE TO AFFECT YOU.
WHAT ...
...DID YOU... DO?
TEE HEE.
I POISONED YOU.
YOU'RE SO STRONG THAT I HAD TO GIVE YOU A LOT OF POISON...
I'VE BEEN INJECTING LITTLE DOSES INTO YOU SINCE OUR FIGHT BEGAN, ALONG WITH ANESTHESIA SO YOU WOULDN'T NOTICE.
WHAP
UGH !
I'M A POISONER. MY VENOM CAN KILL THE ALREADY-DEAD ONE MORE TIME...
DID YOU THINK I SPENT THE LAST 400 YEARS DOING NOTHING TO IMPROVE MY SKILLS?
UGH ...
THUD
I GUESS ...
...I FINISHED HIM...
SQUIK

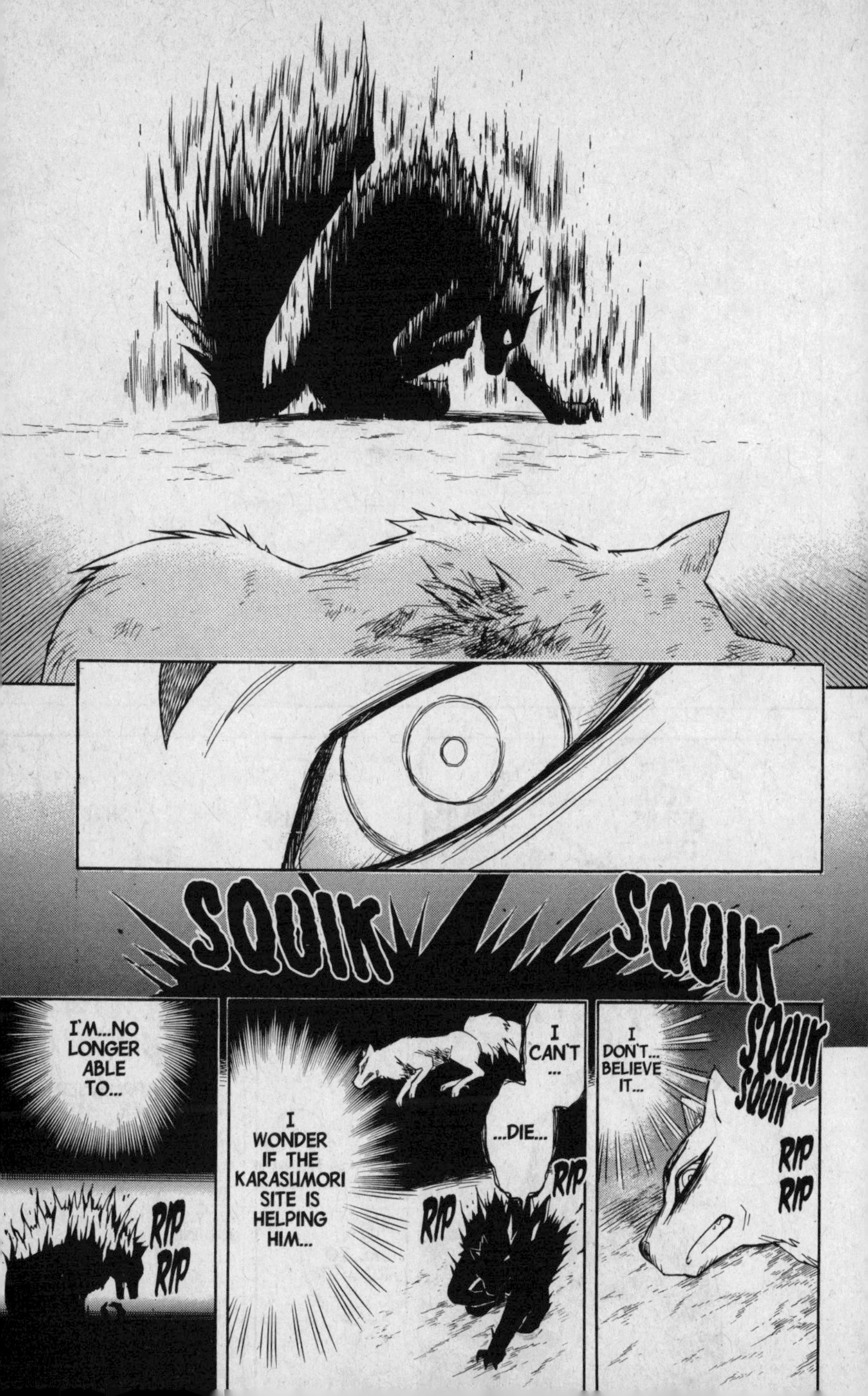
SQUIK
SQUIK
I DON'T... BELIEVE IT...
SQUIK
SQUIK
RIP
RIP
I CAN'T...
...DIE...
I WONDER IF THE KARASUMORI SITE IS HELPING HIM...
RIP
RIP
I'M...NO LONGER ABLE TO...
RIP
RIP

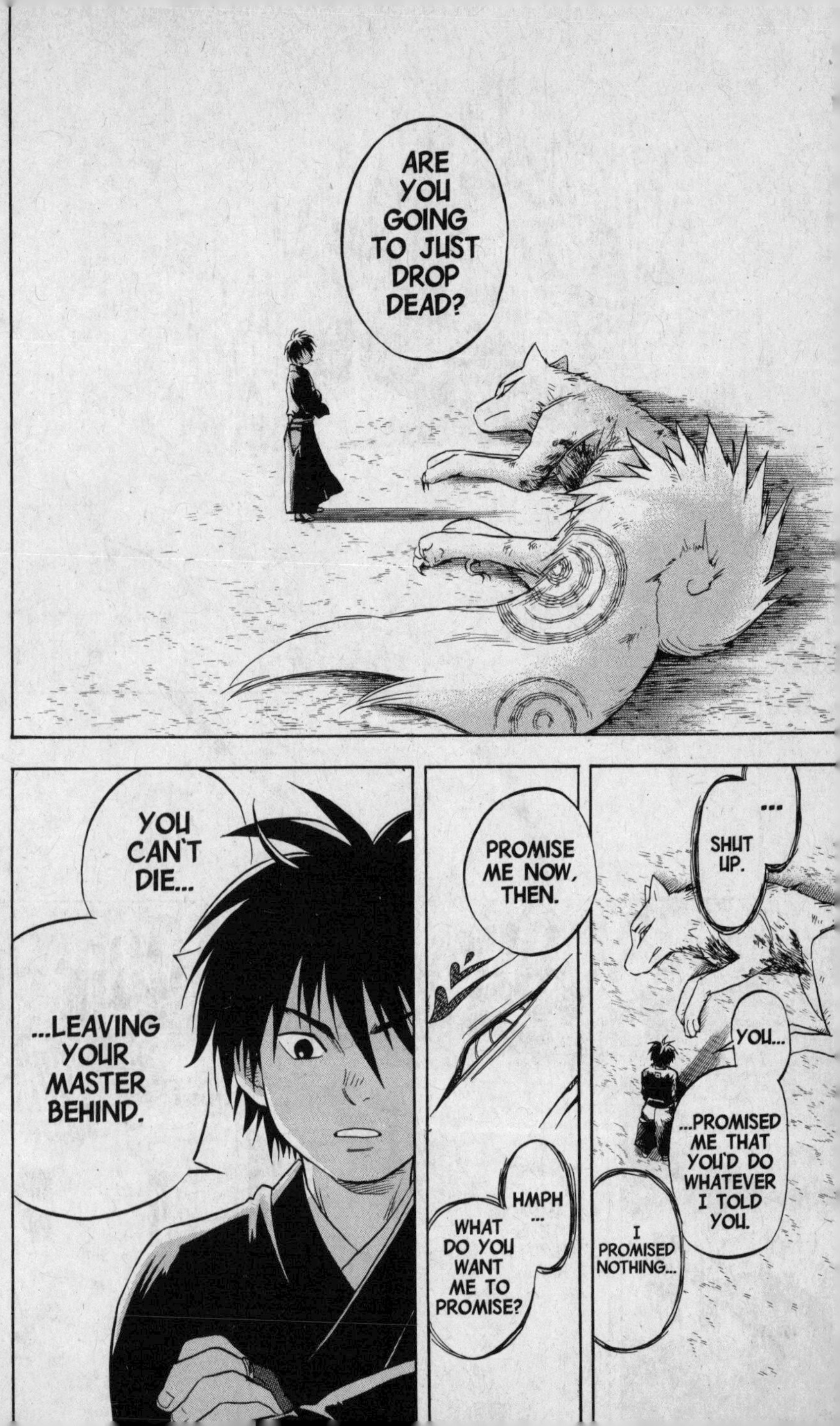
ARE YOU GOING TO JUST DROP DEAD?
...
SHUT UP.
YOU...
...PROMISED ME THAT YOU'D DO WHATEVER I TOLD YOU.
I PROMISED NOTHING...
PROMISE ME NOW, THEN.
HMPH...
WHAT DO YOU WANT ME TO PROMISE?
YOU CAN'T DIE...
...LEAVING YOUR MASTER BEHIND.

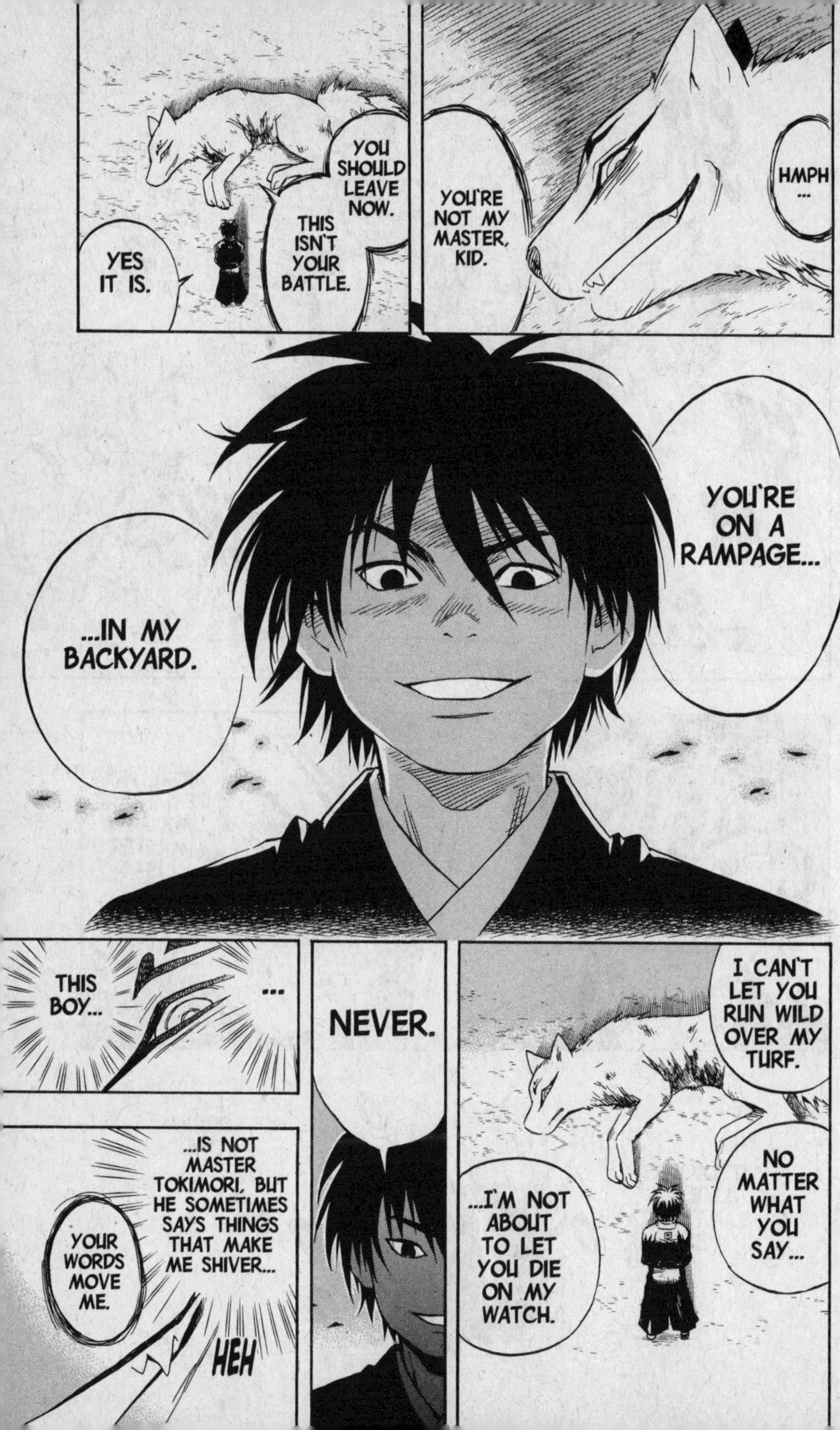
HMPH ...
YOU'RE NOT MY MASTER, KID.
YOU SHOULD LEAVE NOW.
THIS ISN'T YOUR BATTLE.
YES IT IS.
YOU'RE ON A RAMPAGE...
...IN MY BACKYARD.
I CAN'T LET YOU RUN WILD OVER MY TURF.
NO MATTER WHAT YOU SAY...
...I'M NOT ABOUT TO LET YOU DIE ON MY WATCH.
NEVER.
THIS BOY...
...
...IS NOT MASTER TOKIMORI, BUT HE SOMETIMES SAYS THINGS THAT MAKE ME SHIVER...
YOUR WORDS MOVE ME.
HEH

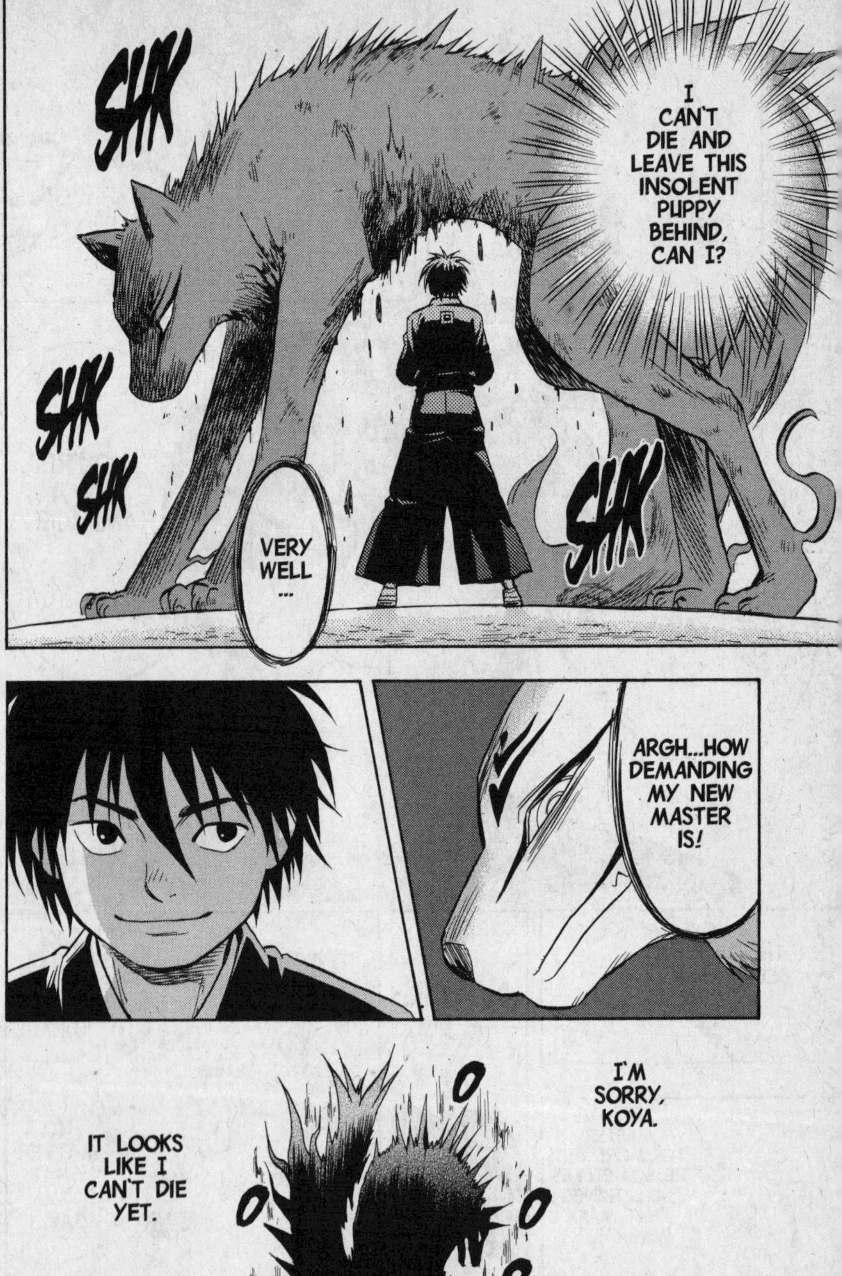
I CAN'T DIE AND LEAVE THIS INSOLENT PUPPY BEHIND, CAN I?
SHK
SHK
SHK
SHK
VERY WELL...
ARGH...HOW DEMANDING MY NEW MASTER IS!
I'M SORRY, KOYA.
IT LOOKS LIKE I CAN'T DIE YET.

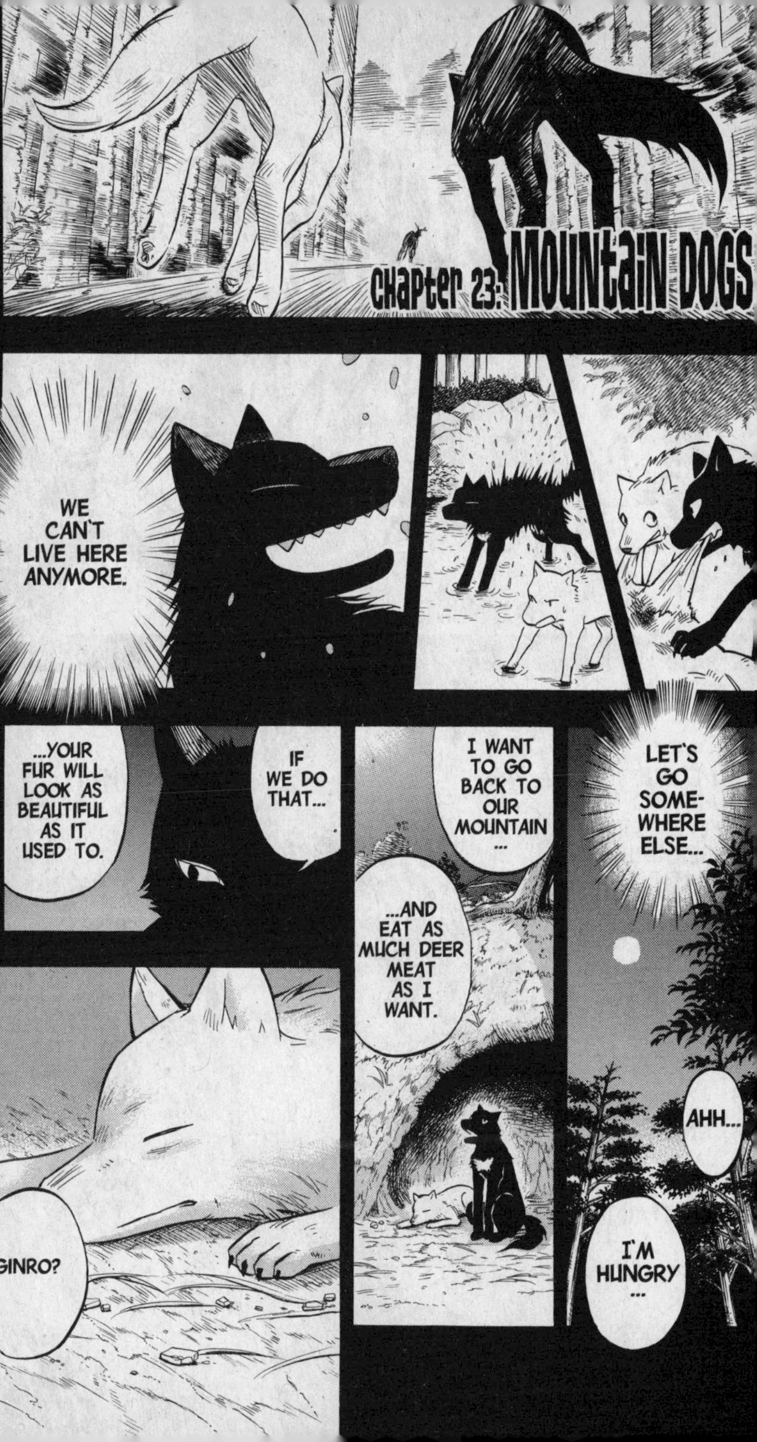
Chapter 23: Mountain Dogs
WE CAN'T LIVE HERE ANYMORE.
LET'S GO SOMEWHERE ELSE...
AHH...
I'M HUNGRY...
I WANT TO GO BACK TO OUR MOUNTAIN...
...AND EAT AS MUCH DEER MEAT AS I WANT.
IF WE DO THAT...
...YOUR FUR WILL LOOK AS BEAUTIFUL AS IT USED TO.
GINRO?

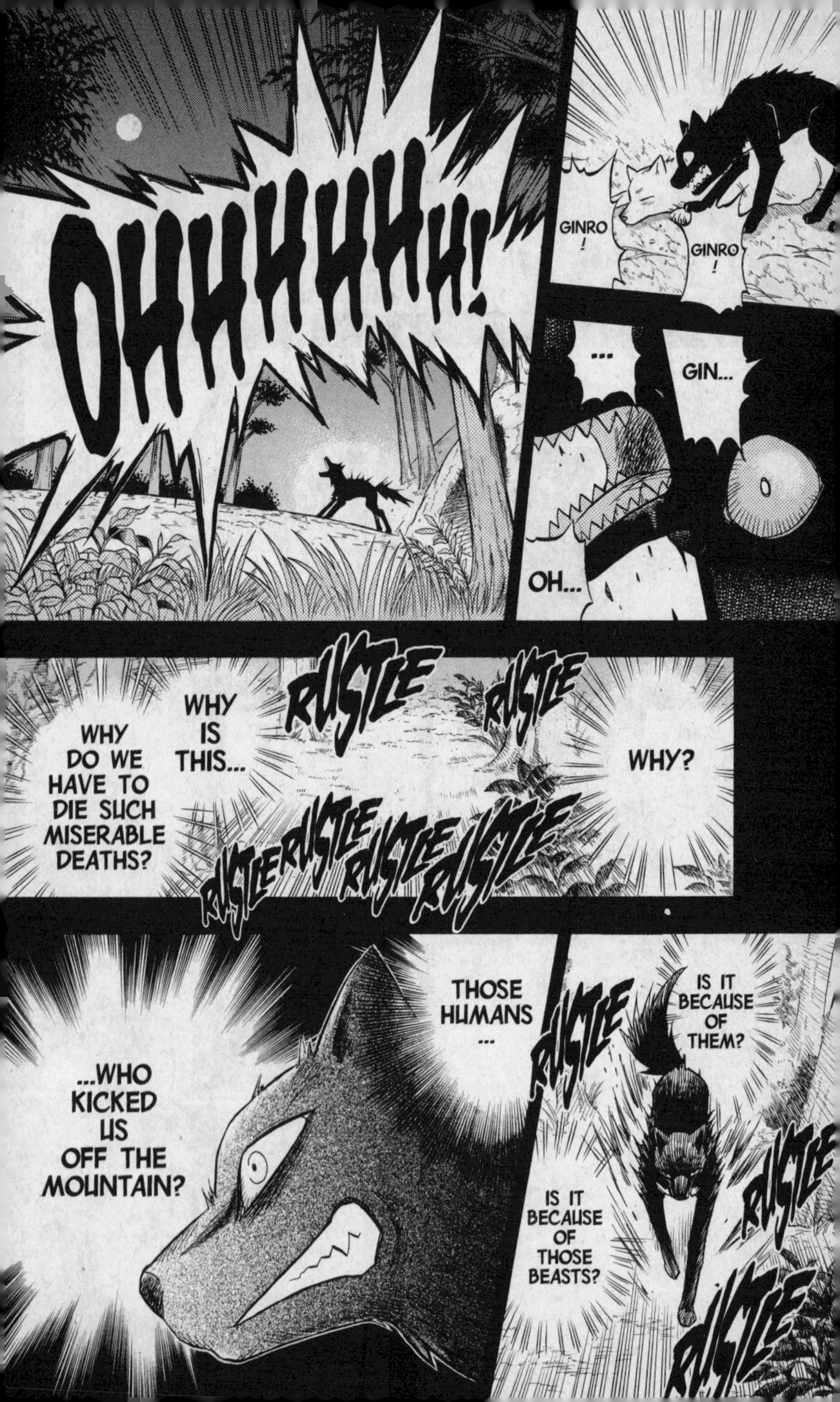
GINRO!
GINRO!
GIN...
...
OH...
OHHHHHHH!
WHY?
RUSTLE
RUSTLE
WHY IS THIS...
WHY DO WE HAVE TO DIE SUCH MISERABLE DEATHS?
RUSTLE RUSTLE RUSTLE RUSTLE
IS IT BECAUSE OF THEM?
RUSTLE
IS IT BECAUSE OF THOSE BEASTS?
RUSTLE
RUSTLE
THOSE HUMANS...
...WHO KICKED US OFF THE MOUNTAIN?

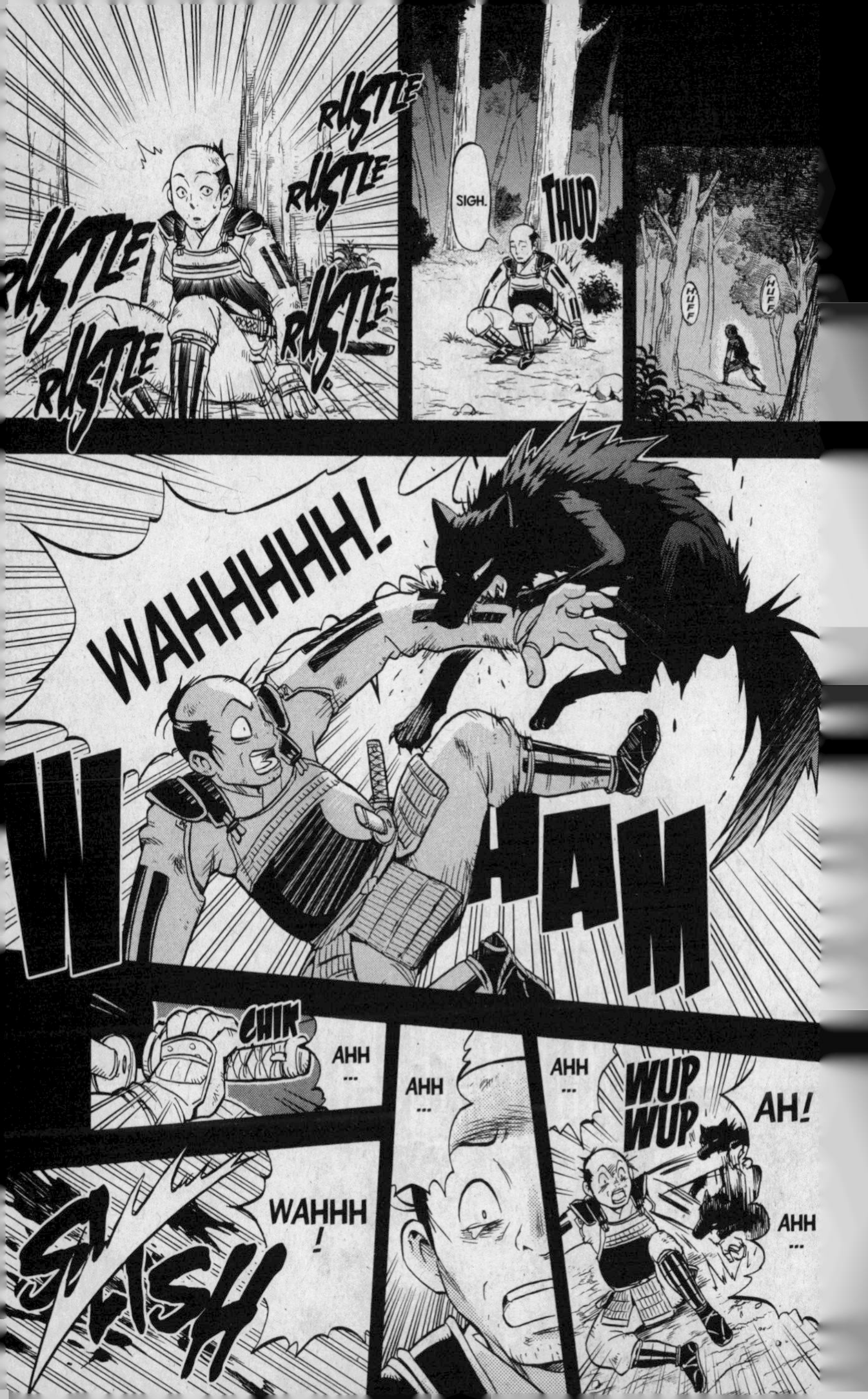
HUFF
HUFF
SIGH.
THUD
RUSTLE
RUSTLE
RUSTLE
RUSTLE
RUSTLE
RUSTLE
WAHHHHH!
WHAM
CHIK
AHH ...
AHH ...
AHH ...
WUP WUP
AH!
AHH ...
WAHHH!
SWISH

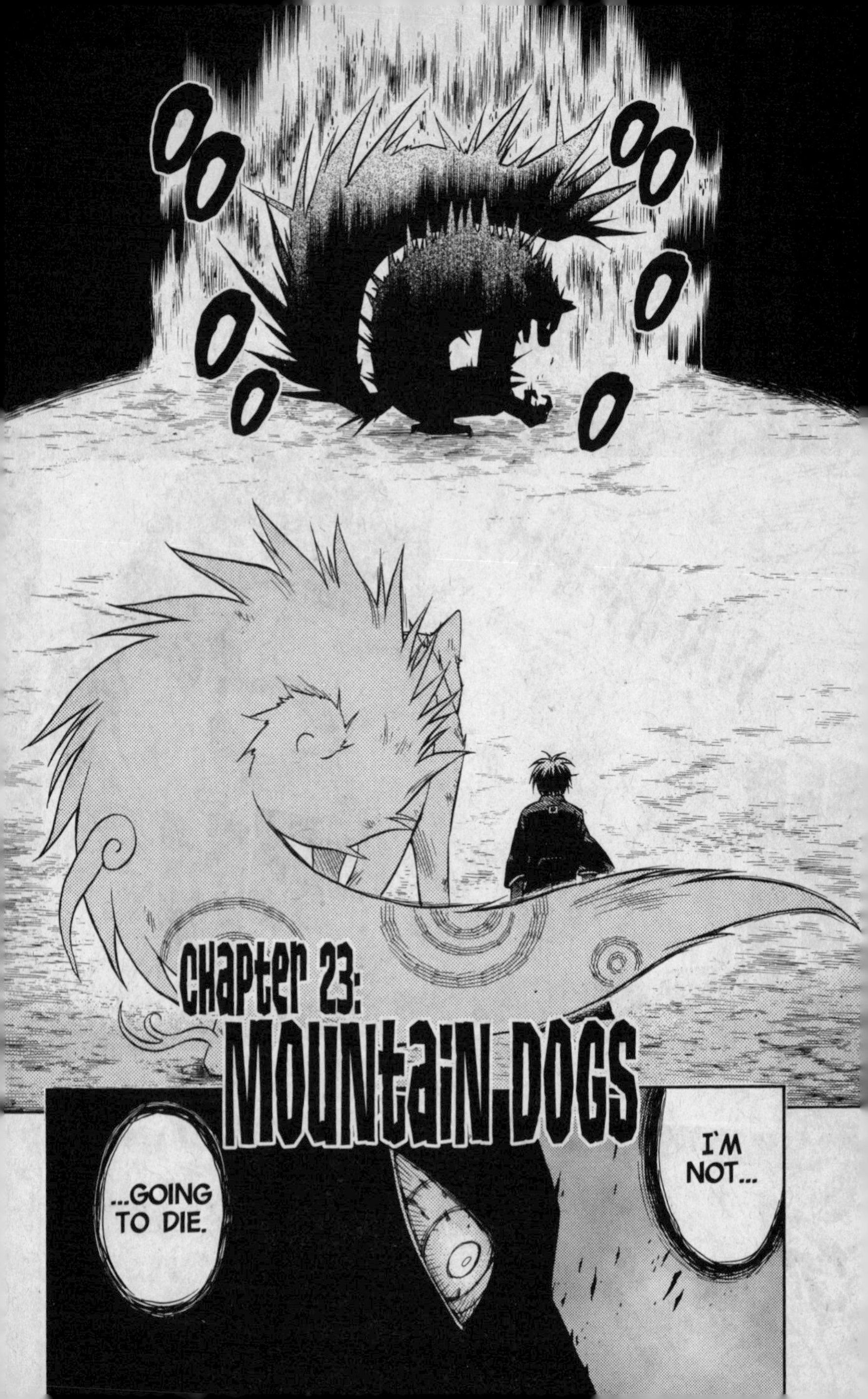
OOOOOO
OOOOO
CHAPTER 23:
MOUNTAIN DOGS
I'M NOT...
...GOING TO DIE.

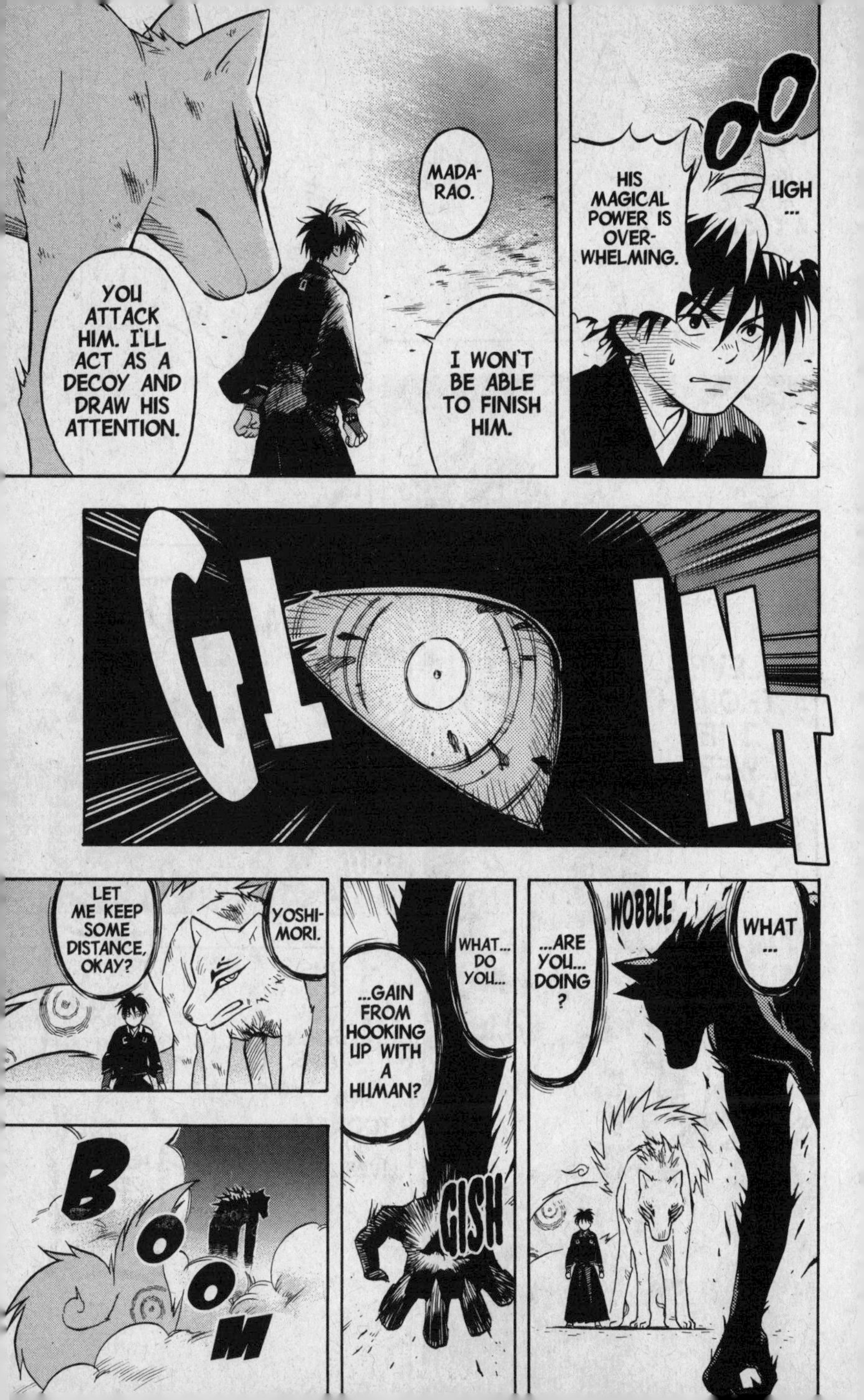
OO
UGH ...
HIS MAGICAL POWER IS OVER-WHELMING.
MADA-RAO.
I WON'T BE ABLE TO FINISH HIM.
YOU ATTACK HIM. I'LL ACT AS A DECOY AND DRAW HIS ATTENTION.
GLINT
WHAT ...
WOBBLE
...ARE YOU... DOING ?
WHAT... DO YOU...
...GAIN FROM HOOKING UP WITH A HUMAN?
GISH
YOSHI-MORI.
LET ME KEEP SOME DISTANCE, OKAY?
BOOM

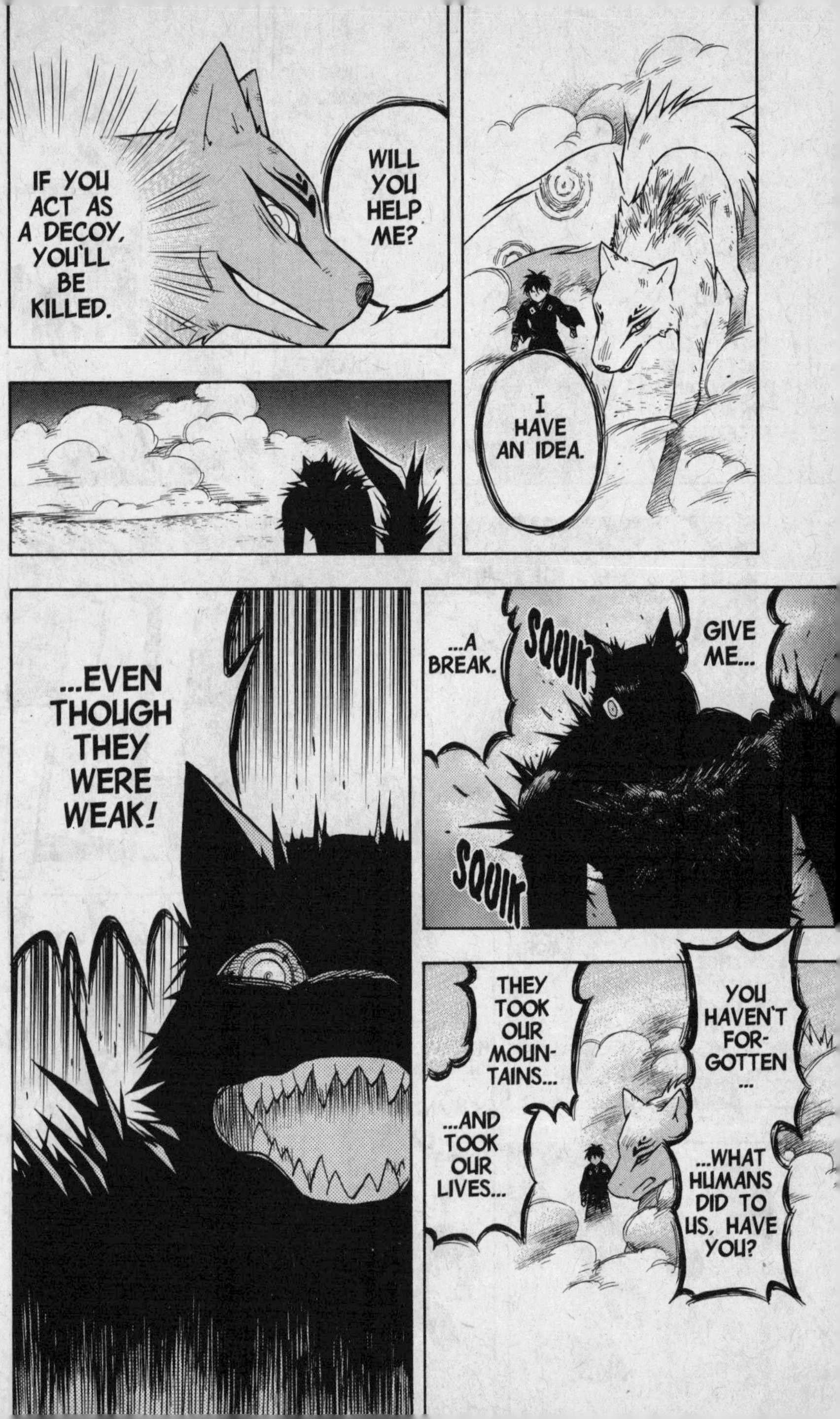
I HAVE AN IDEA.
WILL YOU HELP ME?
IF YOU ACT AS A DECOY, YOU'LL BE KILLED.
GIVE ME...
SQUIK
...A BREAK.
SQUIK
YOU HAVEN'T FOR-GOTTEN...
...WHAT HUMANS DID TO US, HAVE YOU?
THEY TOOK OUR MOUN-TAINS...
...AND TOOK OUR LIVES...
...EVEN THOUGH THEY WERE WEAK!

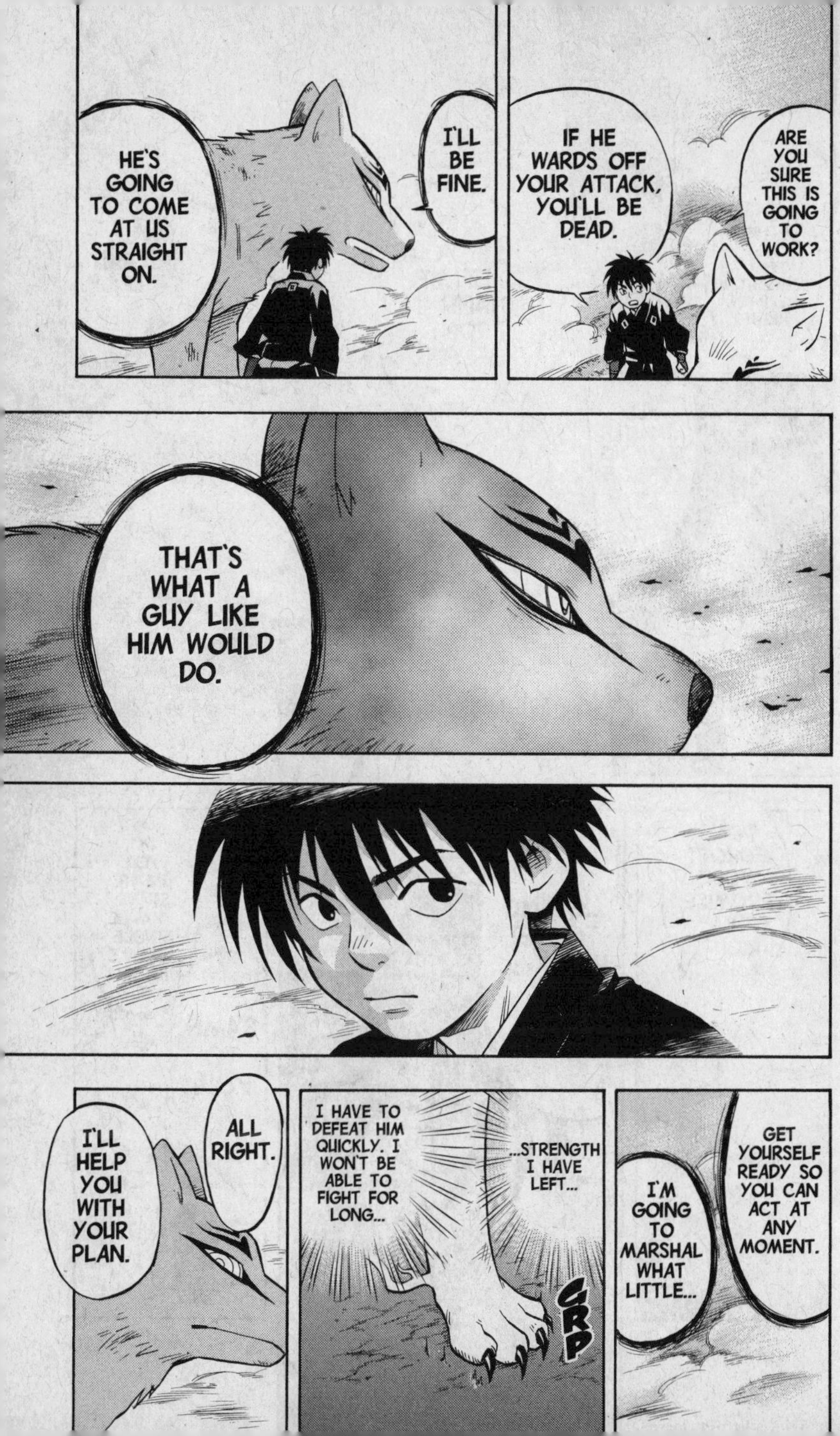
ARE YOU SURE THIS IS GOING TO WORK?
IF HE WARDS OFF YOUR ATTACK, YOU'LL BE DEAD.
I'LL BE FINE.
HE'S GOING TO COME AT US STRAIGHT ON.
THAT'S WHAT A GUY LIKE HIM WOULD DO.
GET YOURSELF READY SO YOU CAN ACT AT ANY MOMENT.
I'M GOING TO MARSHAL WHAT LITTLE...
...STRENGTH I HAVE LEFT...
GRP
I HAVE TO DEFEAT HIM QUICKLY. I WON'T BE ABLE TO FIGHT FOR LONG...
ALL RIGHT.
I'LL HELP YOU WITH YOUR PLAN.

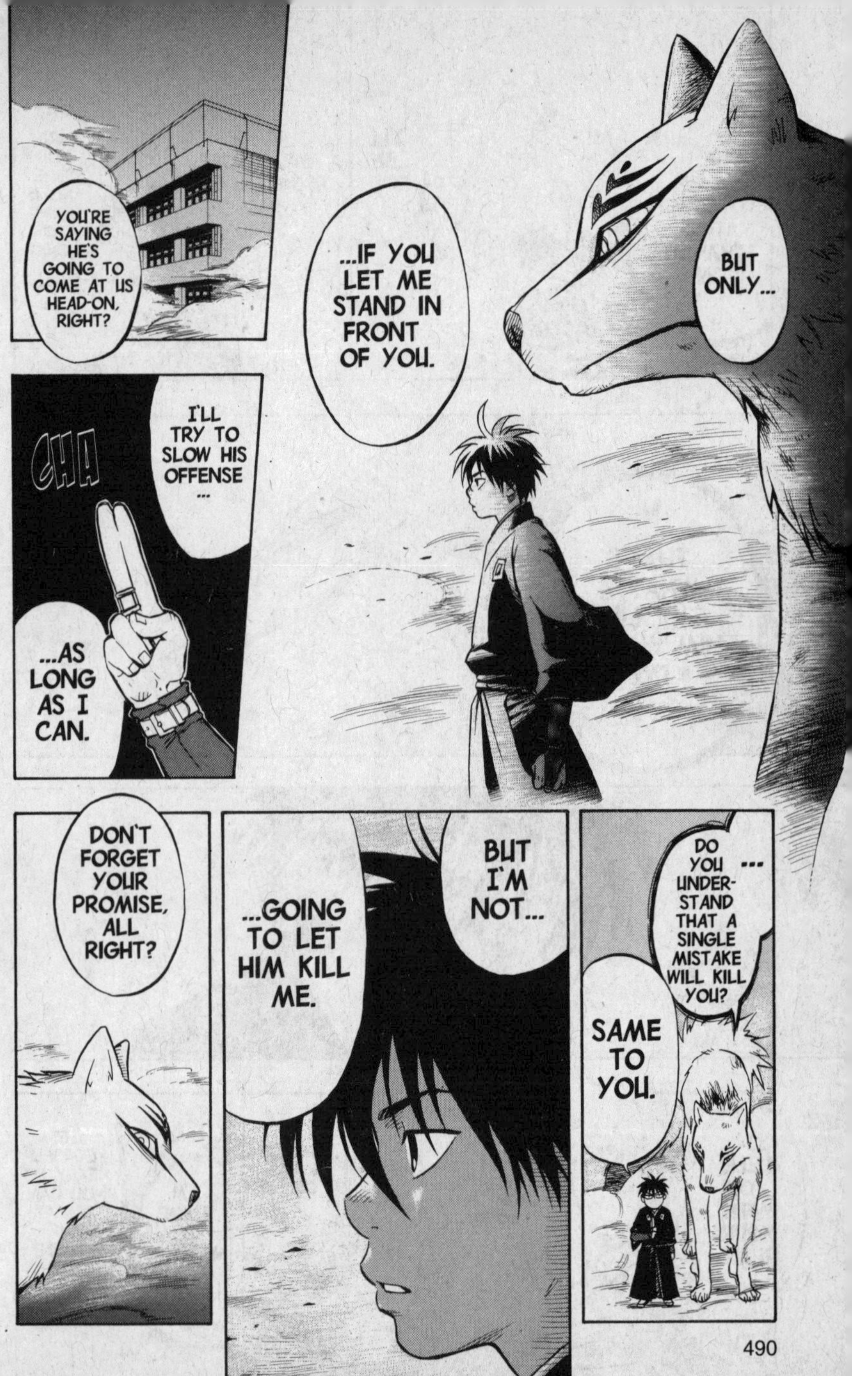
BUT ONLY...
...IF YOU LET ME STAND IN FRONT OF YOU.
YOU'RE SAYING HE'S GOING TO COME AT US HEAD-ON, RIGHT?
I'LL TRY TO SLOW HIS OFFENSE ...
CHA
...AS LONG AS I CAN.
DO YOU UNDER-STAND THAT A SINGLE MISTAKE WILL KILL YOU? ...
SAME TO YOU.
BUT I'M NOT...
...GOING TO LET HIM KILL ME.
DON'T FORGET YOUR PROMISE, ALL RIGHT?

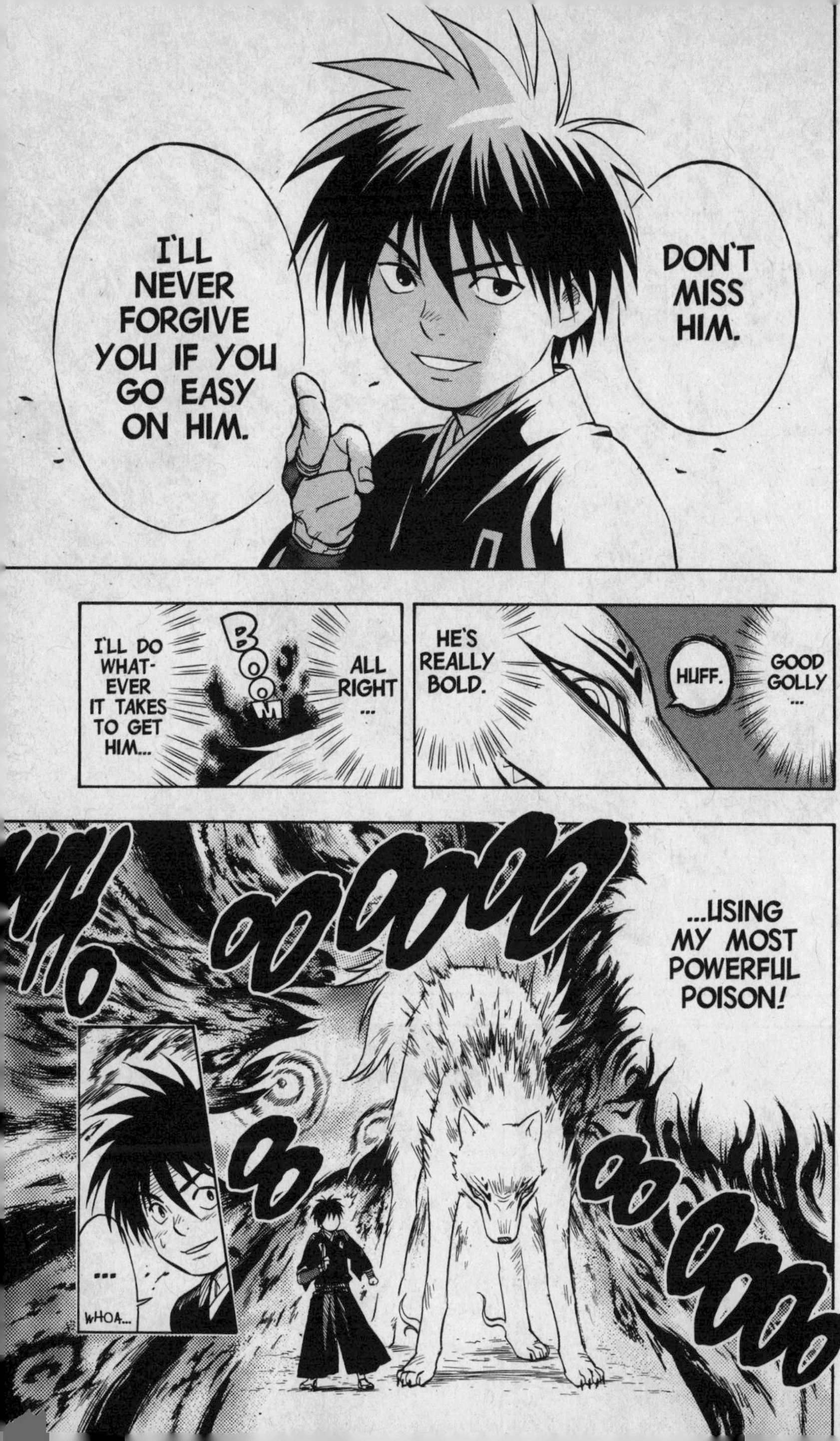
DON'T MISS HIM.
I'LL NEVER FORGIVE YOU IF YOU GO EASY ON HIM.
GOOD GOLLY ...
HUFF.
HE'S REALLY BOLD.
ALL RIGHT ...
BOOM
I'LL DO WHAT-EVER IT TAKES TO GET HIM...
...USING MY MOST POWERFUL POISON!
...
WHOA...

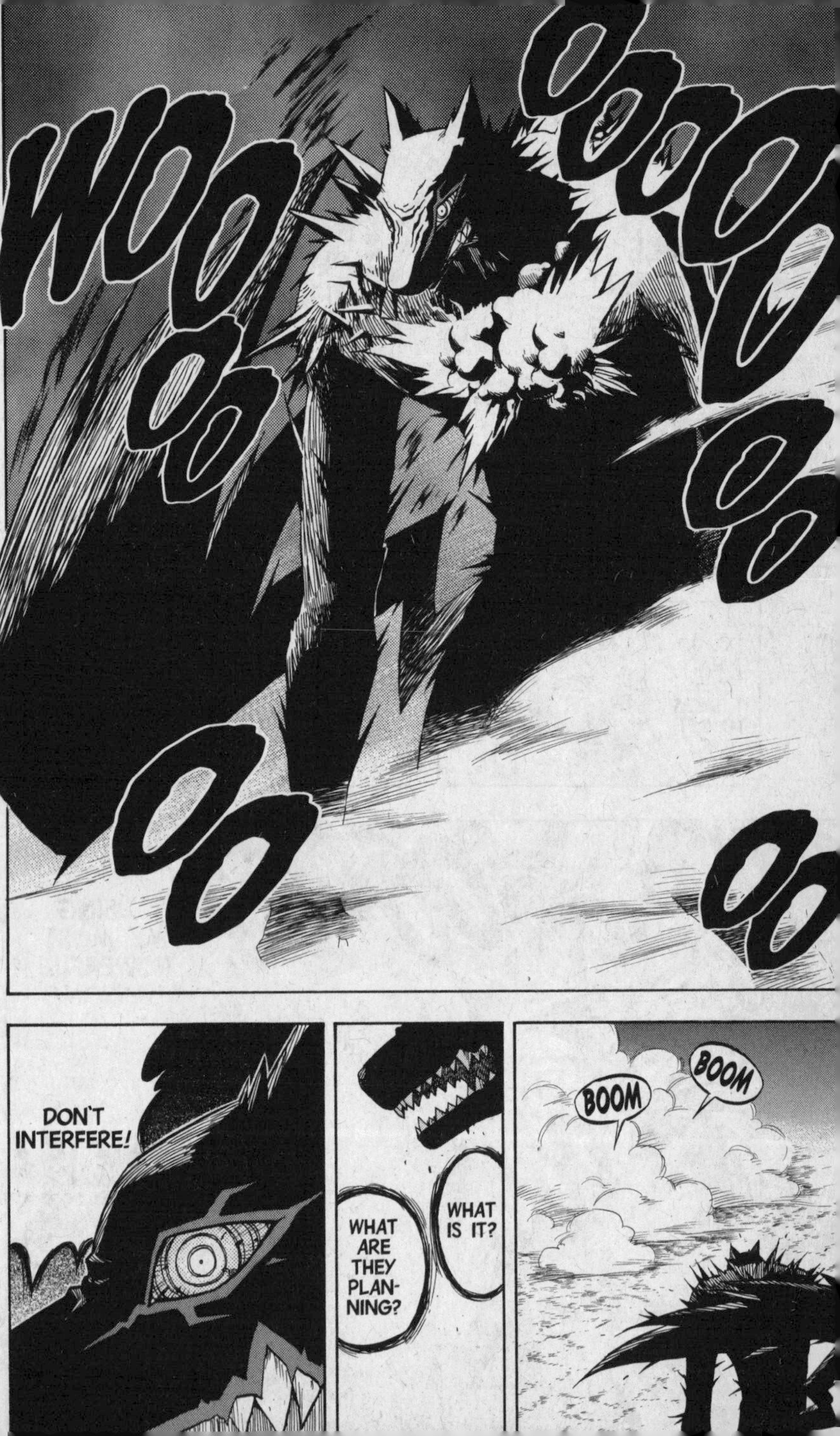
WOOOOOOOOOOOOOOOO
BOOM
BOOM
WHAT IS IT?
WHAT ARE THEY PLAN-NING?
DON'T INTERFERE!

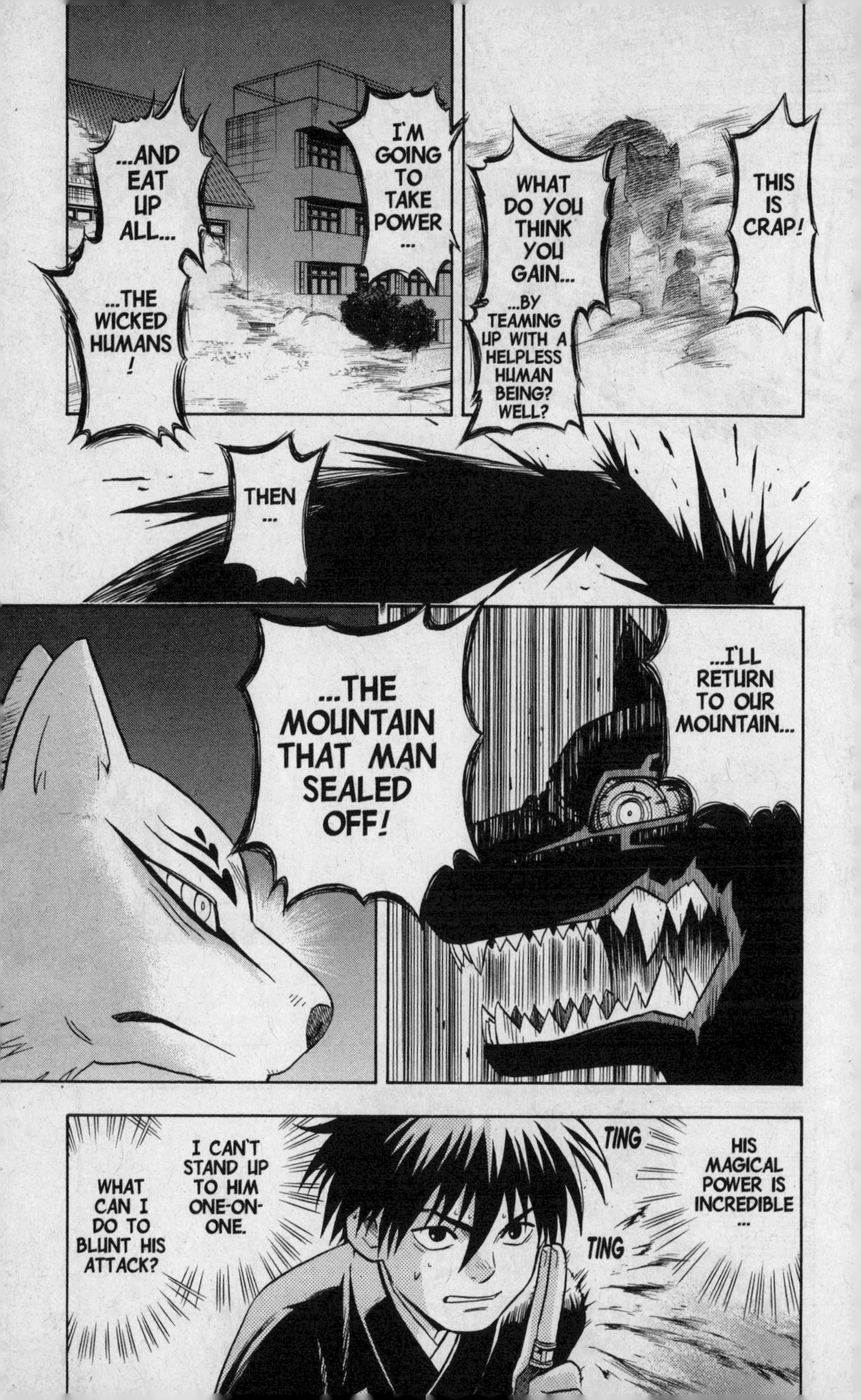
THIS IS CRAP!
WHAT DO YOU THINK YOU GAIN...
...BY TEAMING UP WITH A HELPLESS HUMAN BEING? WELL?
I'M GOING TO TAKE POWER...
...AND EAT UP ALL...
...THE WICKED HUMANS!
THEN...
...I'LL RETURN TO OUR MOUNTAIN...
...THE MOUNTAIN THAT MAN SEALED OFF!
HIS MAGICAL POWER IS INCREDIBLE...
TING
TING
I CAN'T STAND UP TO HIM ONE-ON-ONE.
WHAT CAN I DO TO BLUNT HIS ATTACK?

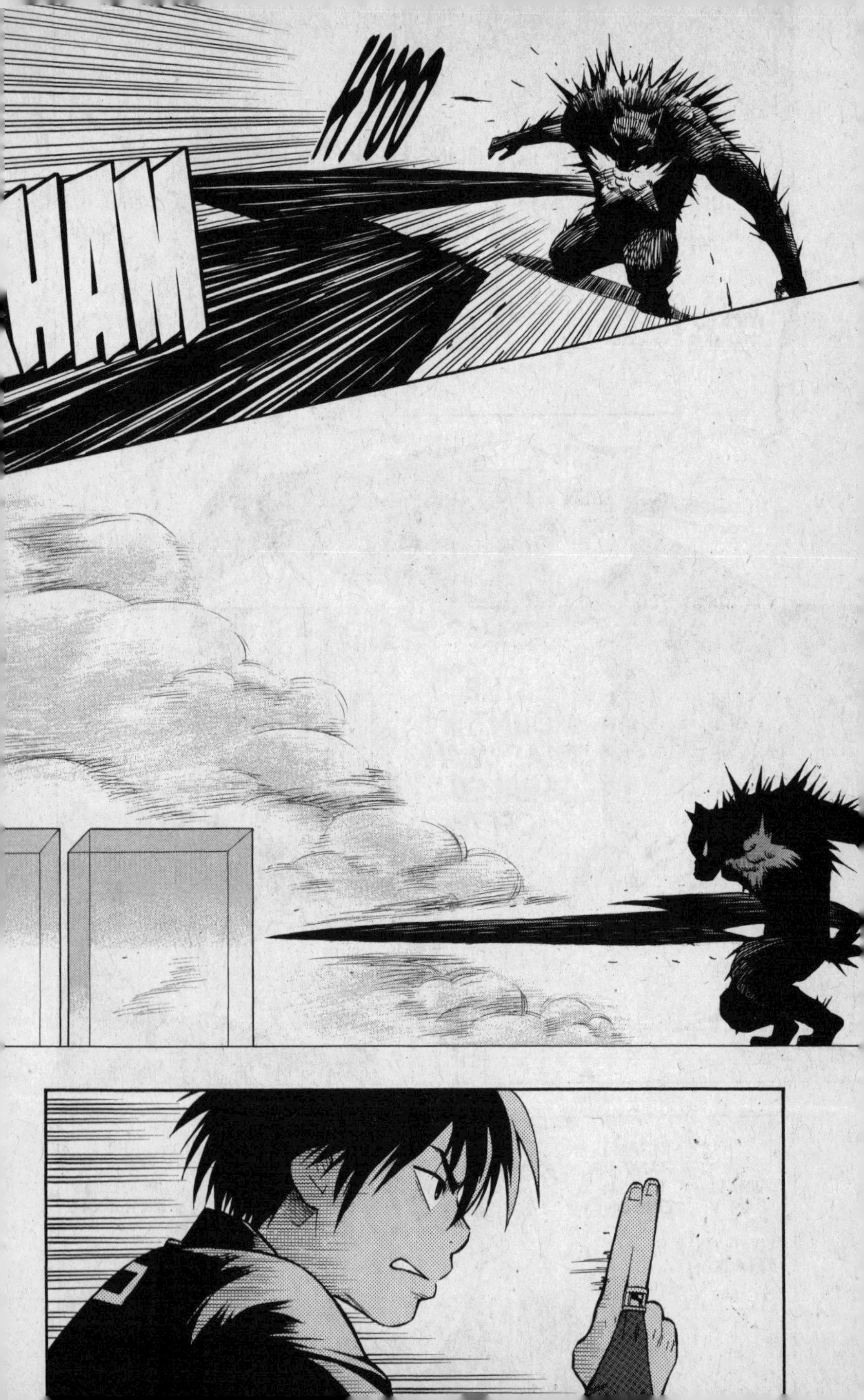
HYOO
HAM

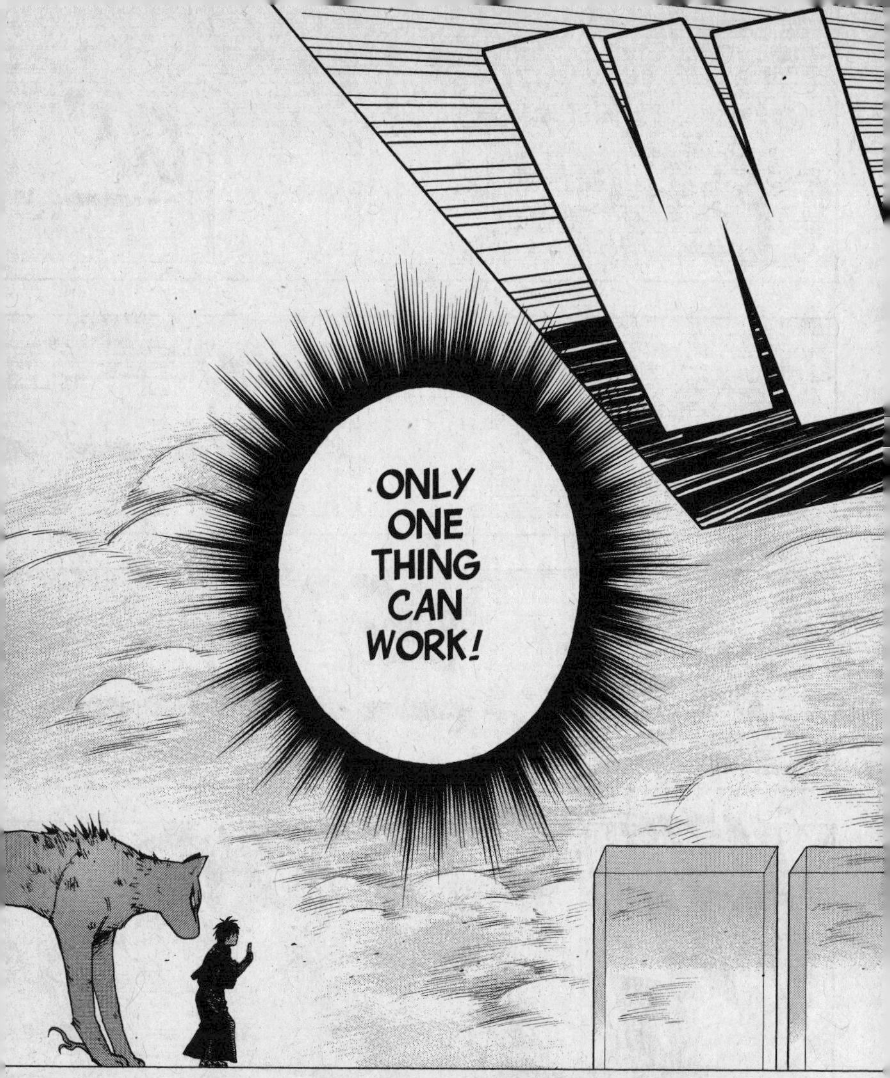
ONLY ONE THING CAN WORK!

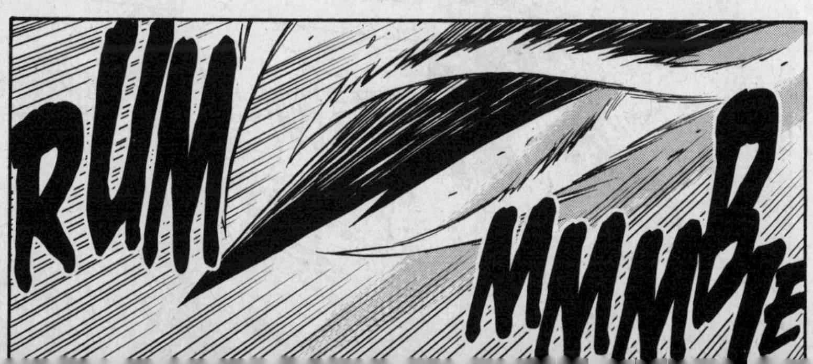
RUM
MMMBLE

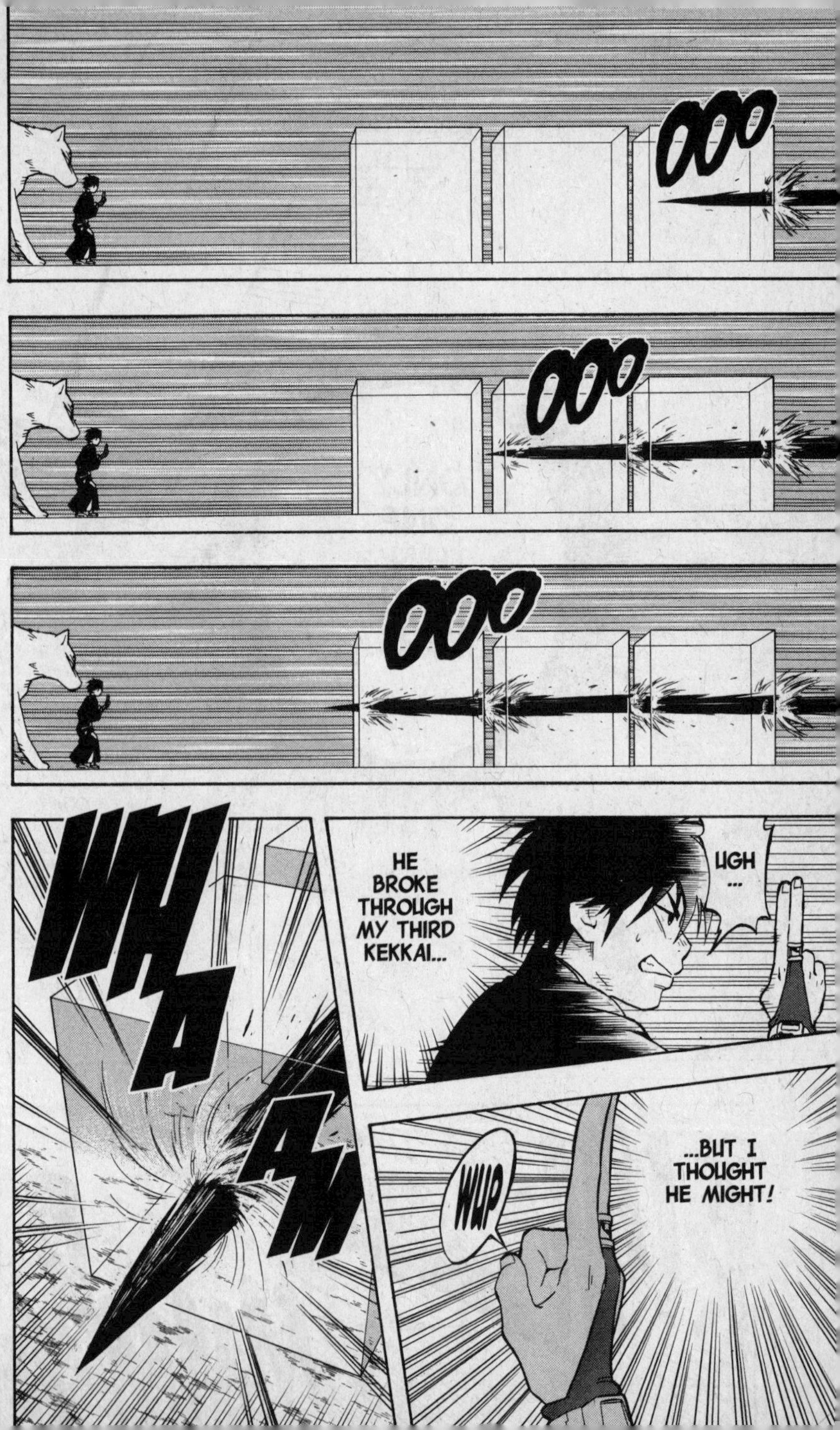
OOO
OOO
OOO
UGH ...
HE BROKE THROUGH MY THIRD KEKKAI...
...BUT I THOUGHT HE MIGHT!
WUP
WHAAM

I'M NOT GOING TO LET YOU GO.

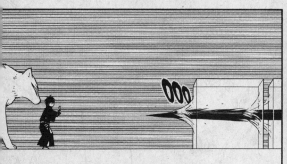

OOO

GIK GIK

WHAM

GOOD! HIS TAIL'S SLOWED DOWN!

MADA-RAO!

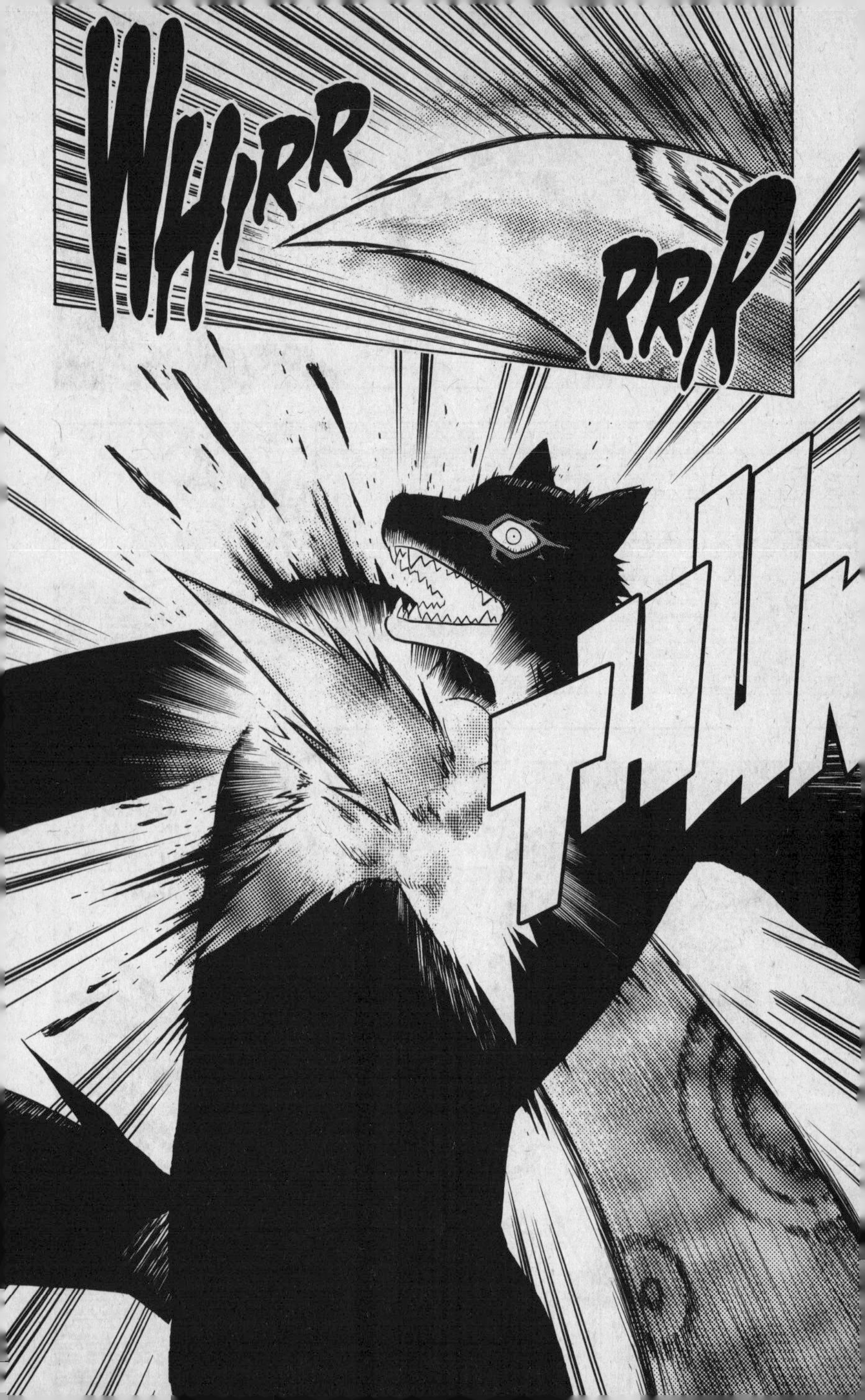
WHIRRRRR
THU

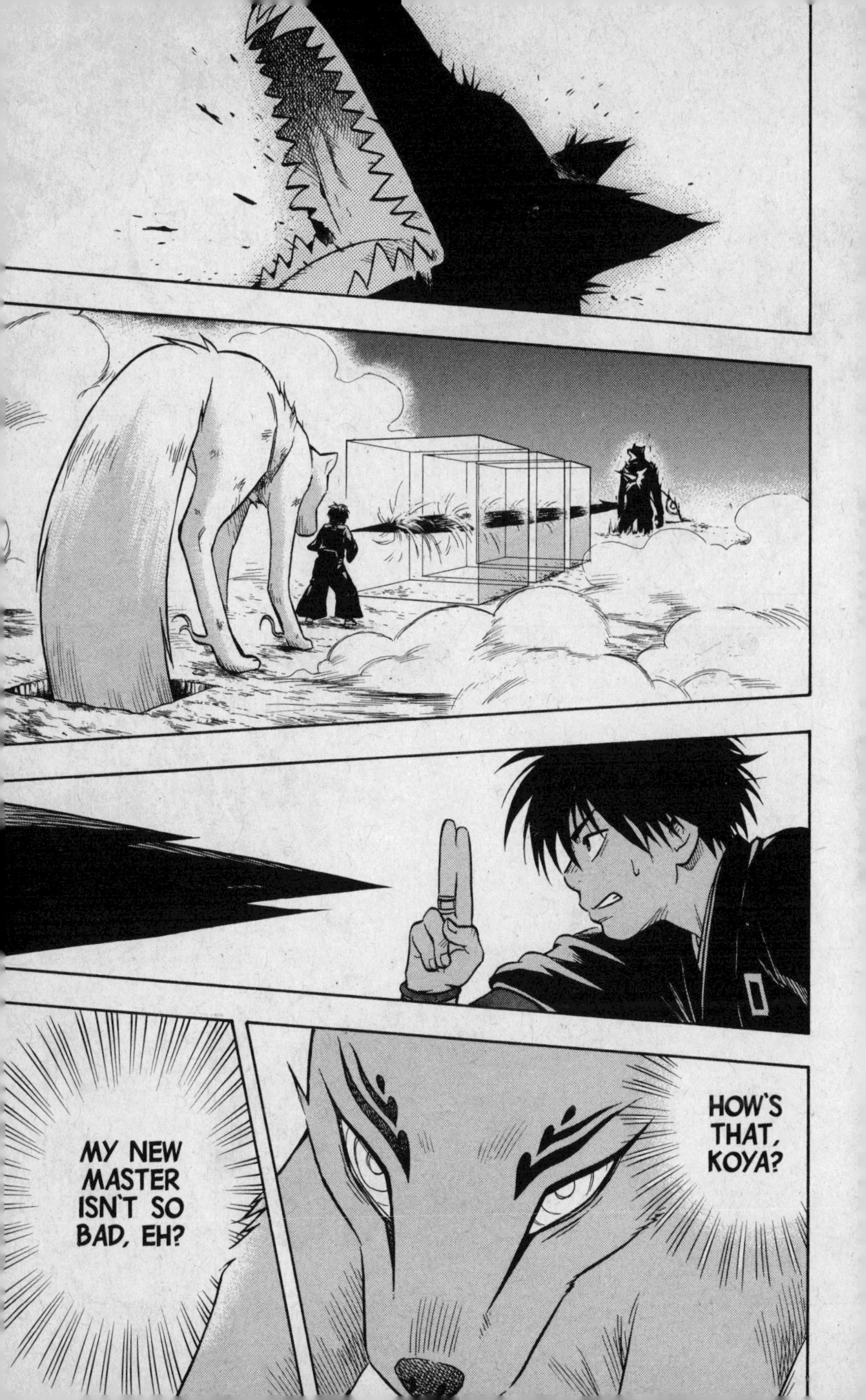
HOW'S THAT, KOYA?
MY NEW MASTER ISN'T SO BAD, EH?

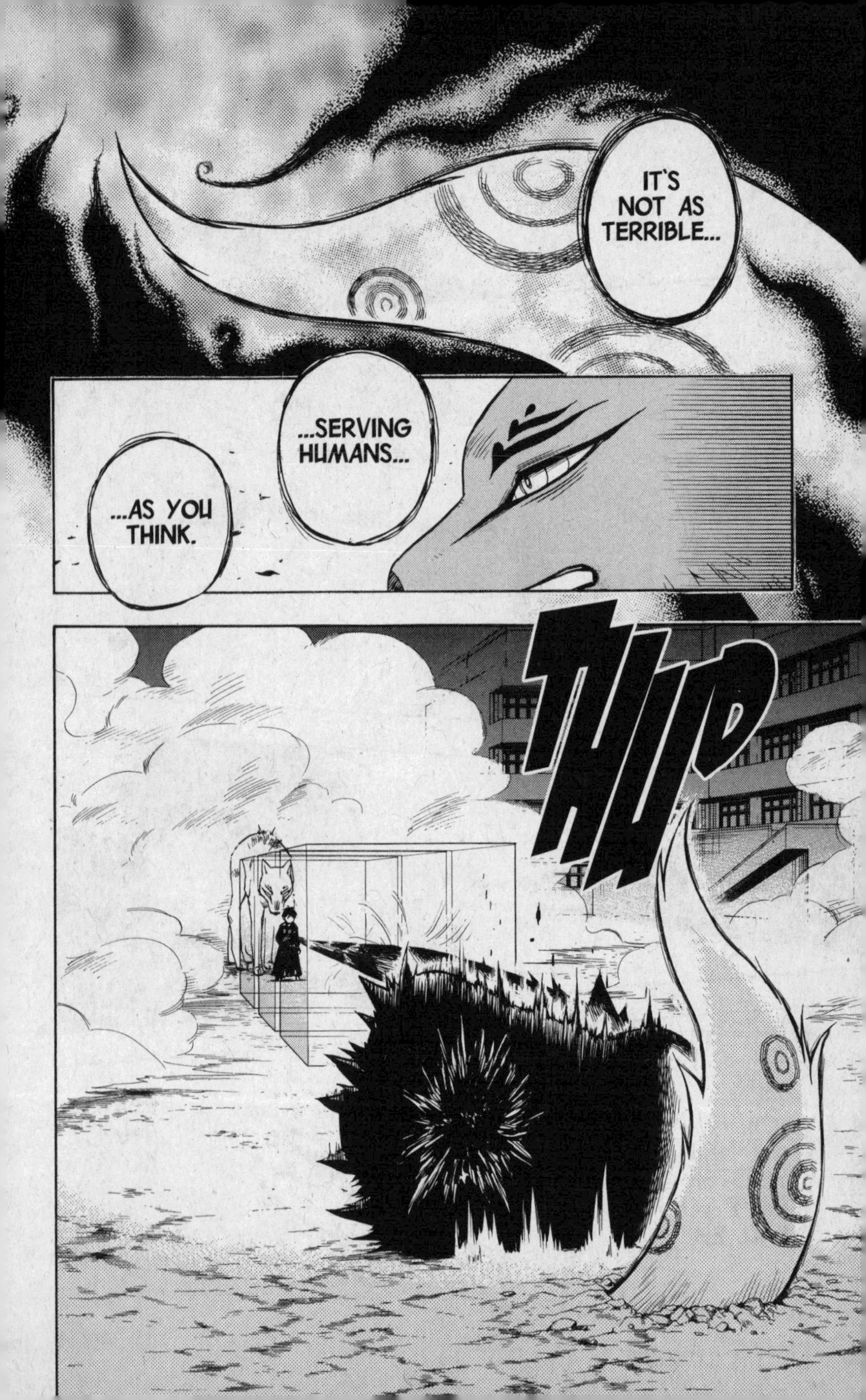
IT'S NOT AS TERRIBLE...
...SERVING HUMANS...
...AS YOU THINK.
THUD

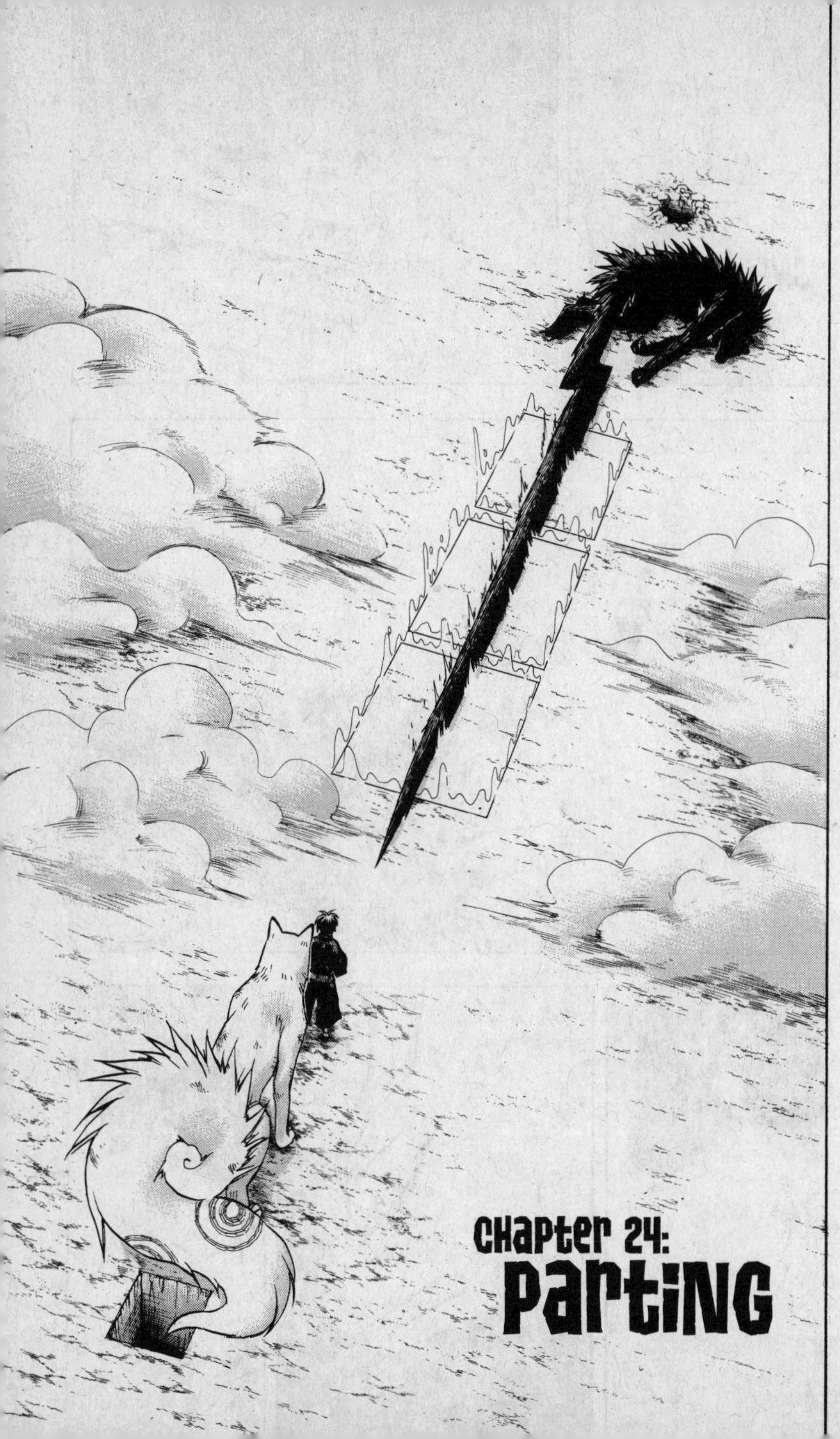
Chapter 24:
Parting

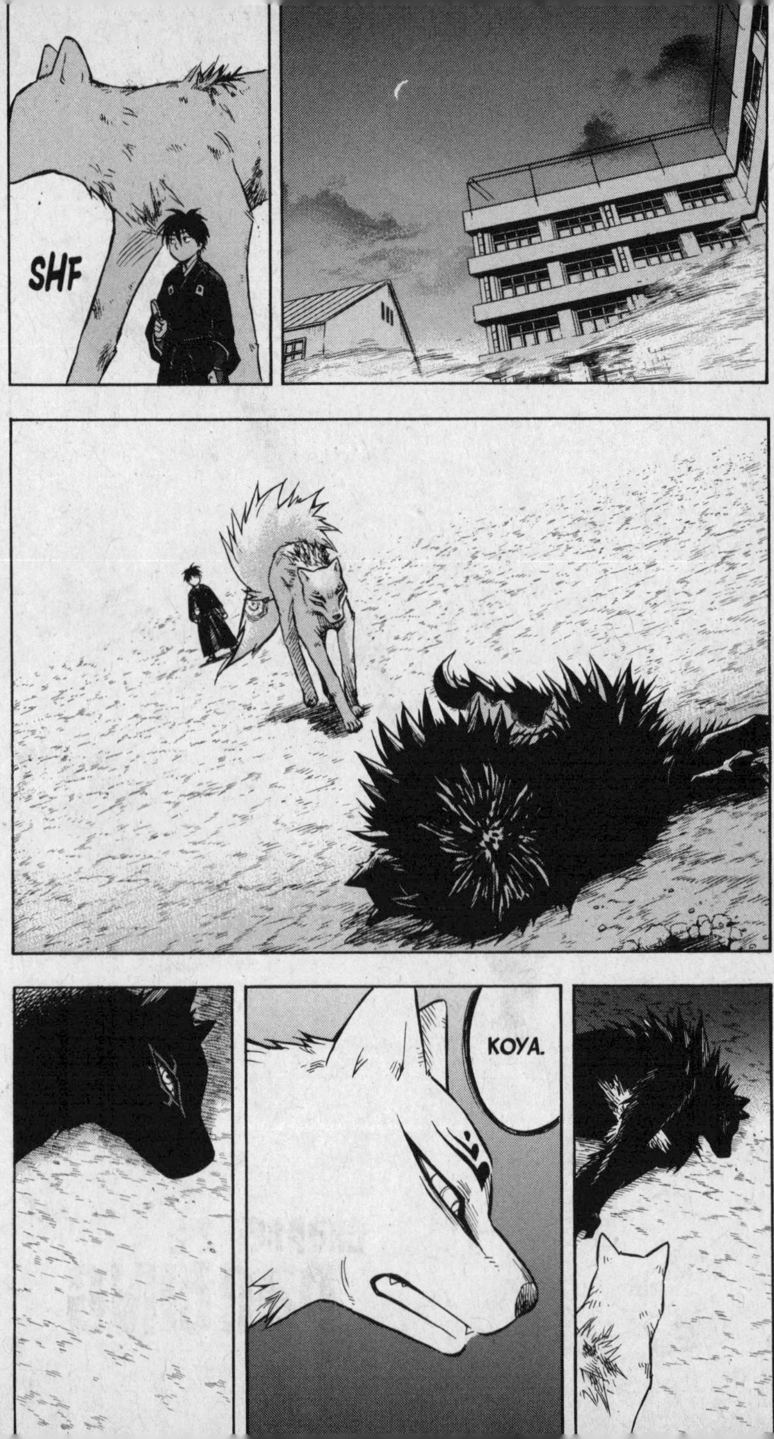
SHF
KOYA.

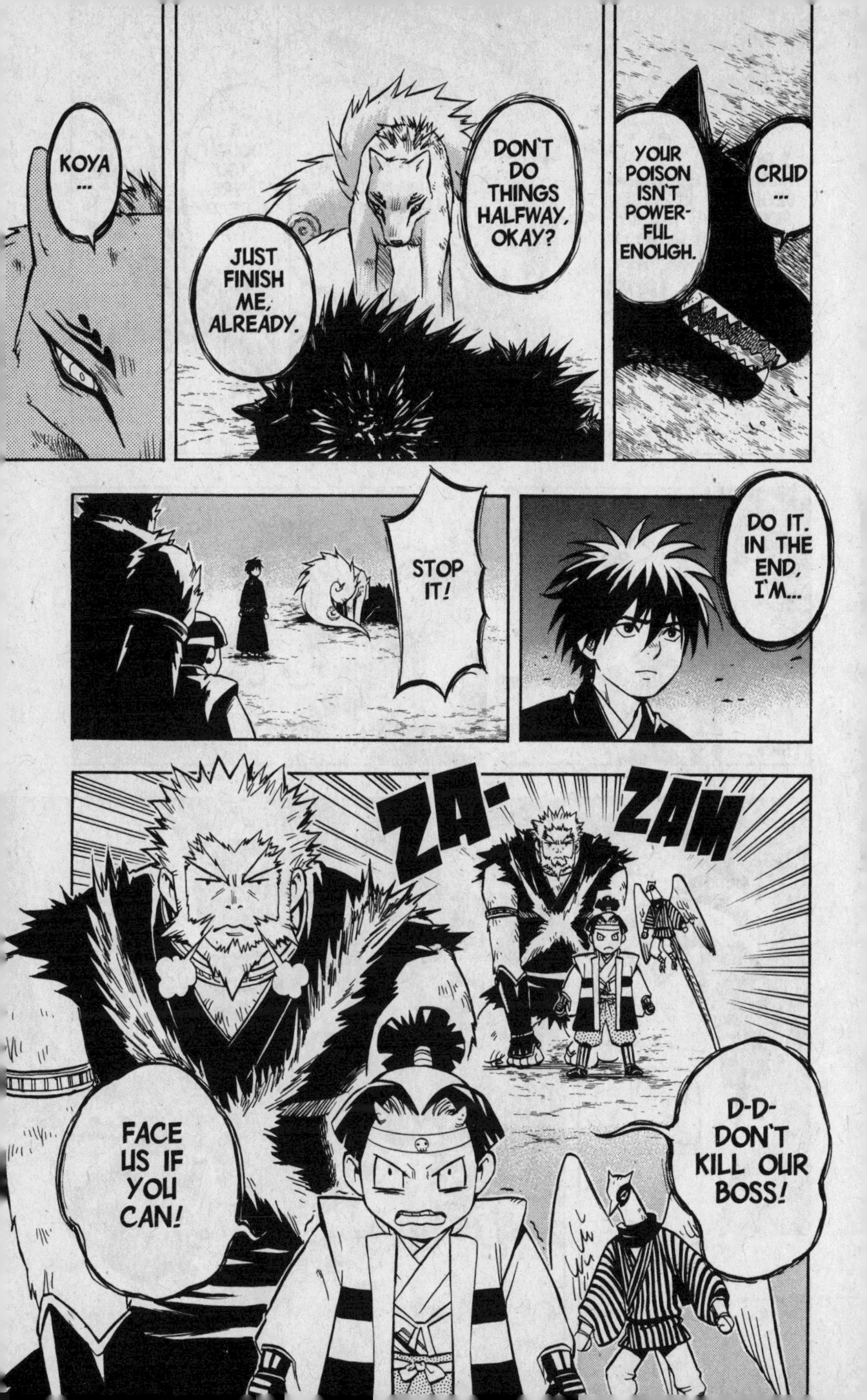
CRUD ...
YOUR POISON ISN'T POWER-FUL ENOUGH.
DON'T DO THINGS HALFWAY, OKAY?
JUST FINISH ME, ALREADY.
KOYA ...
DO IT. IN THE END, I'M...
STOP IT!
ZA-ZAM
D-D-DON'T KILL OUR BOSS!
FACE US IF YOU CAN!

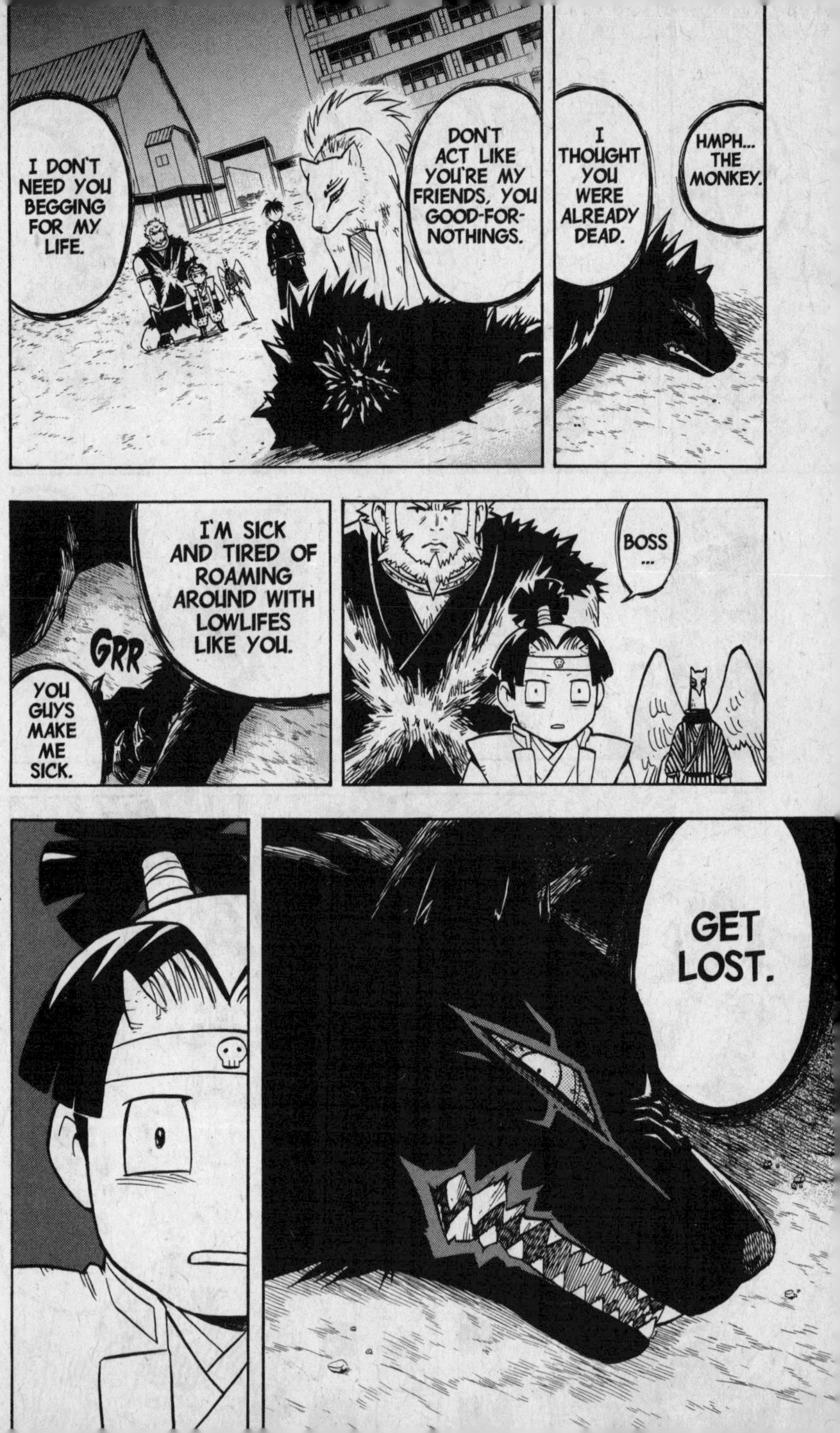
HMPH... THE MONKEY.
I THOUGHT YOU WERE ALREADY DEAD.
DON'T ACT LIKE YOU'RE MY FRIENDS, YOU GOOD-FOR-NOTHINGS.
I DON'T NEED YOU BEGGING FOR MY LIFE.
BOSS ...
I'M SICK AND TIRED OF ROAMING AROUND WITH LOWLIFES LIKE YOU.
GRR
YOU GUYS MAKE ME SICK.
GET LOST.

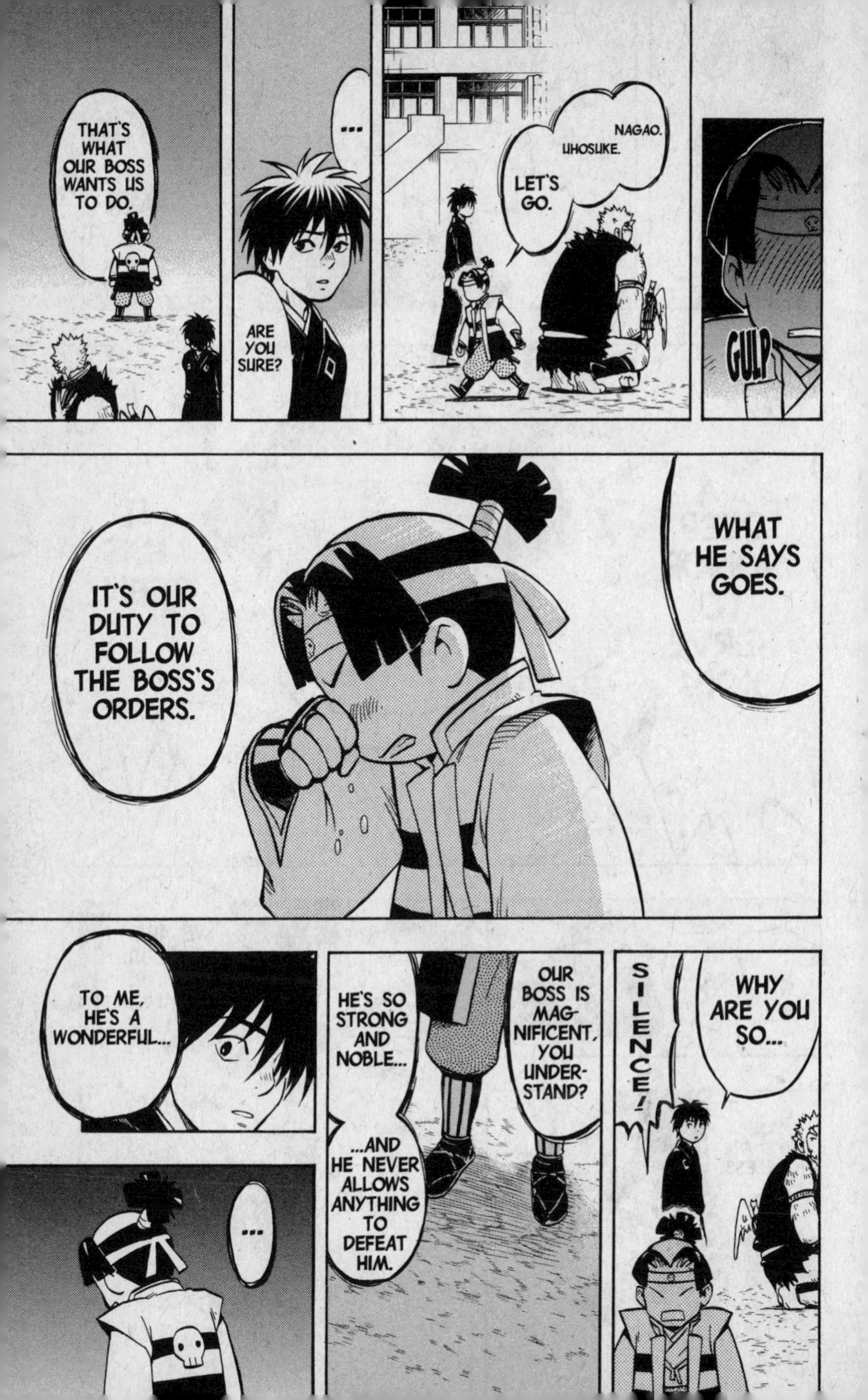
GULP
NAGAO.
UHOSUKE.
LET'S GO.
...
ARE YOU SURE?
THAT'S WHAT OUR BOSS WANTS US TO DO.
WHAT HE SAYS GOES.
IT'S OUR DUTY TO FOLLOW THE BOSS'S ORDERS.
WHY ARE YOU SO...
SILENCE!
OUR BOSS IS MAG-NIFICENT, YOU UNDER-STAND?
HE'S SO STRONG AND NOBLE...
...AND HE NEVER ALLOWS ANYTHING TO DEFEAT HIM.
TO ME, HE'S A WONDERFUL...
...

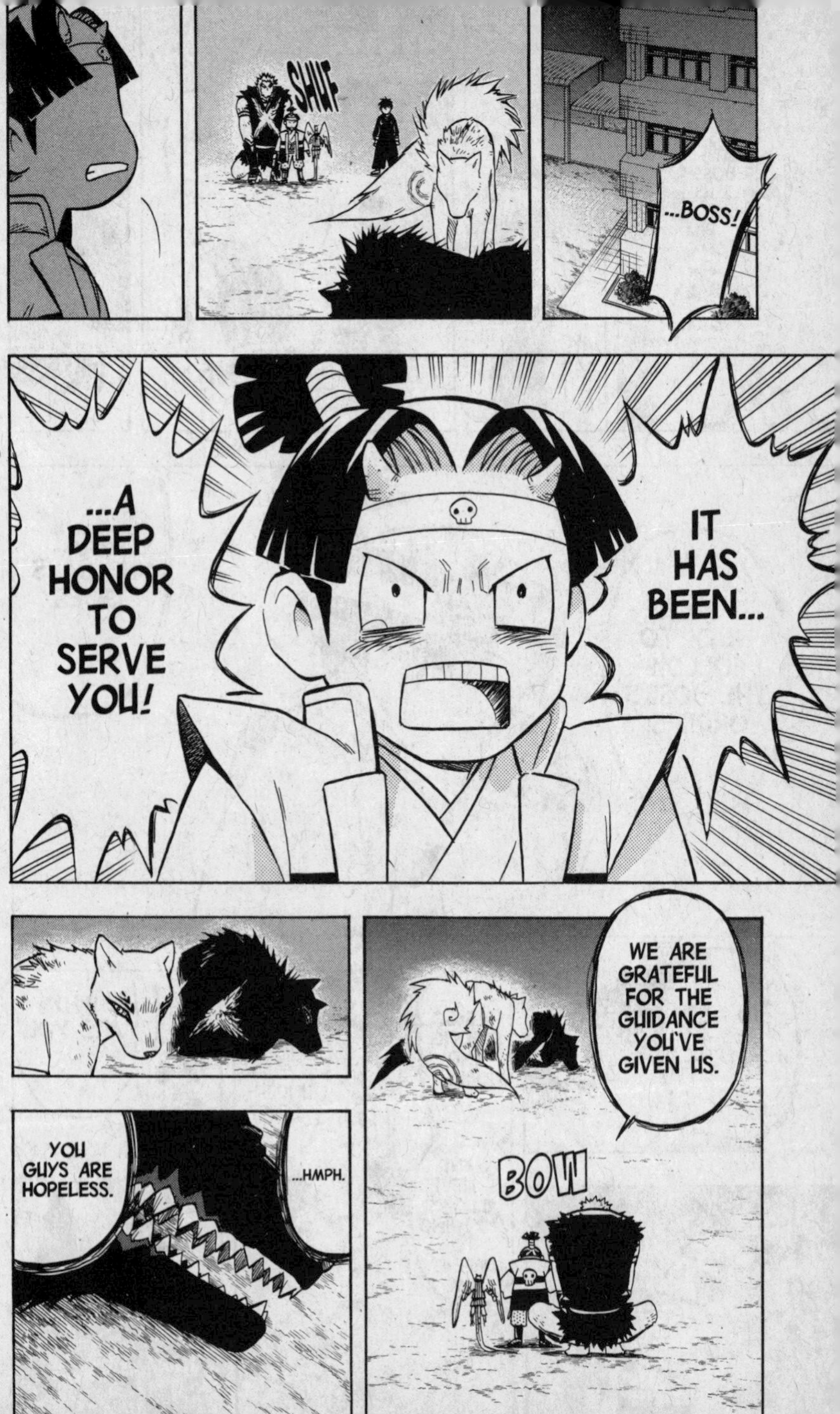
...BOSS!
SHUF
IT HAS BEEN...
...A DEEP HONOR TO SERVE YOU!
WE ARE GRATEFUL FOR THE GUIDANCE YOU'VE GIVEN US.
BOW
...HMPH.
YOU GUYS ARE HOPELESS.

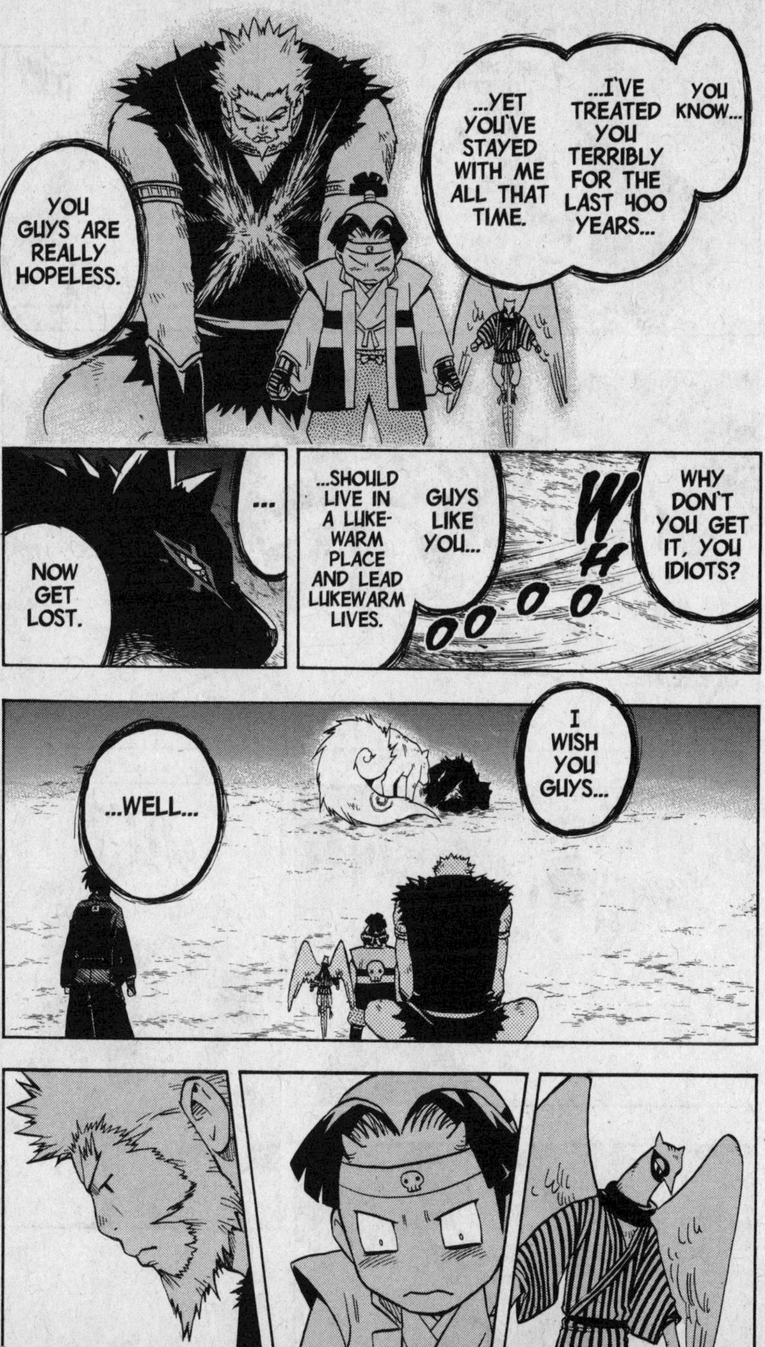
YOU KNOW...
...I'VE TREATED YOU TERRIBLY FOR THE LAST 400 YEARS...
...YET YOU'VE STAYED WITH ME ALL THAT TIME.
YOU GUYS ARE REALLY HOPELESS.
WHY DON'T YOU GET IT, YOU IDIOTS?
WHOOOOO
GUYS LIKE YOU...
...SHOULD LIVE IN A LUKE-WARM PLACE AND LEAD LUKEWARM LIVES.
...
NOW GET LOST.
I WISH YOU GUYS...
...WELL...

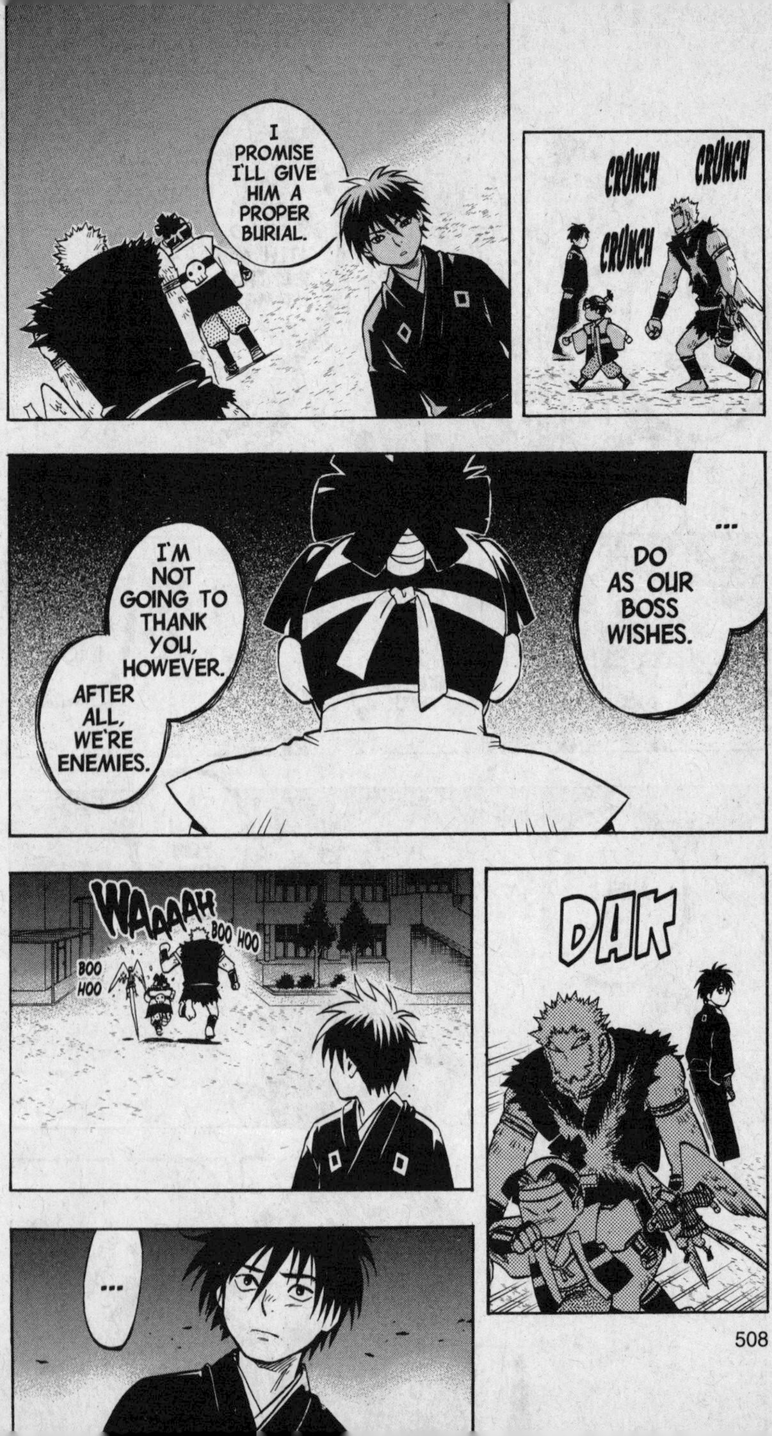
CRUNCH CRUNCH
CRUNCH
I PROMISE I'LL GIVE HIM A PROPER BURIAL.
... DO AS OUR BOSS WISHES.
I'M NOT GOING TO THANK YOU, HOWEVER. AFTER ALL, WE'RE ENEMIES.
DAK
WAAAAH
BOO HOO
BOO HOO
...

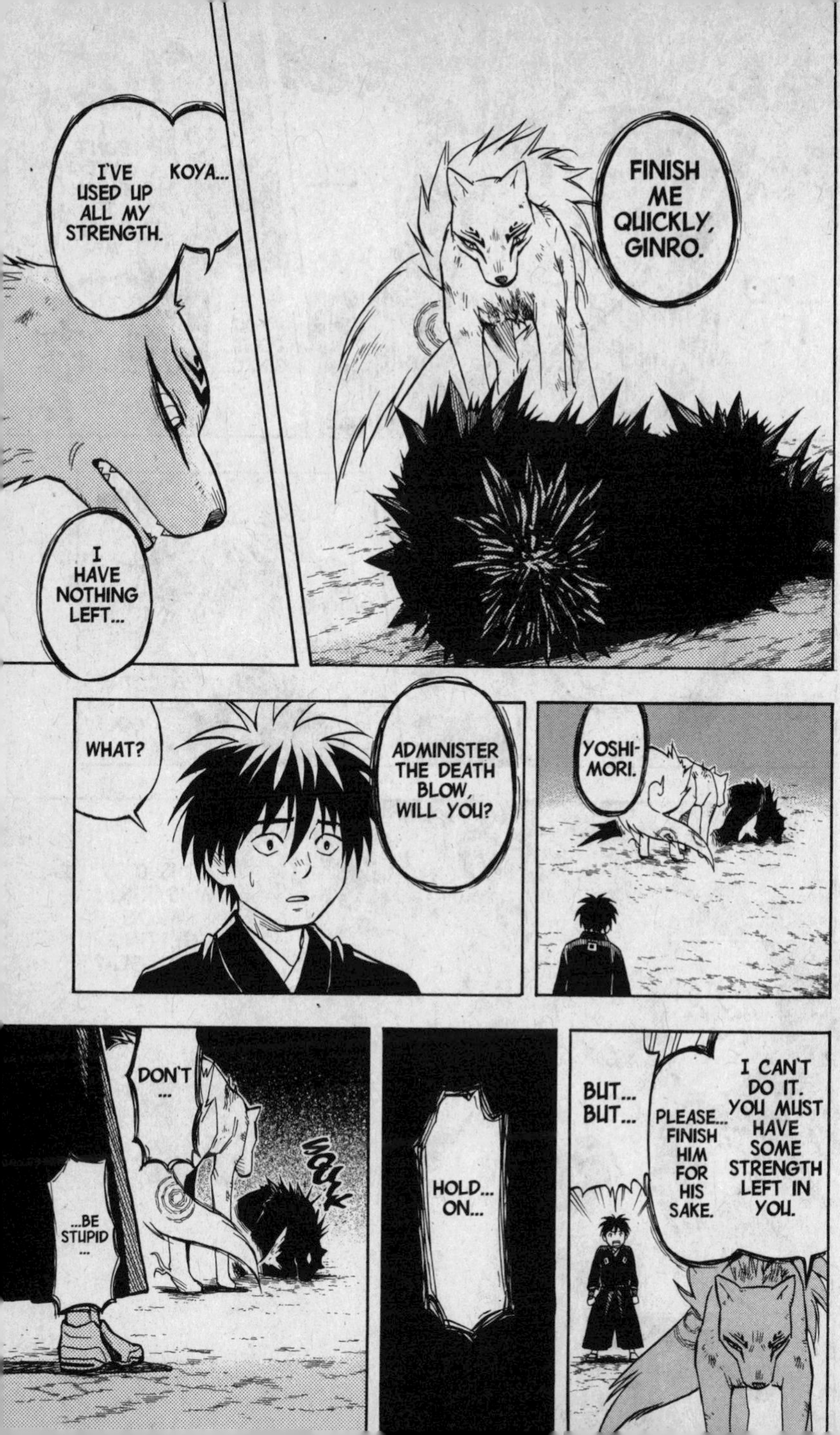
FINISH ME QUICKLY, GINRO.
KOYA...
I'VE USED UP ALL MY STRENGTH.
I HAVE NOTHING LEFT...
YOSHI-MORI.
ADMINISTER THE DEATH BLOW, WILL YOU?
WHAT?
I CAN'T DO IT. YOU MUST HAVE SOME STRENGTH LEFT IN YOU.
PLEASE... FINISH HIM FOR HIS SAKE.
BUT... BUT...
HOLD... ON...
DON'T ...
...BE STUPID ...

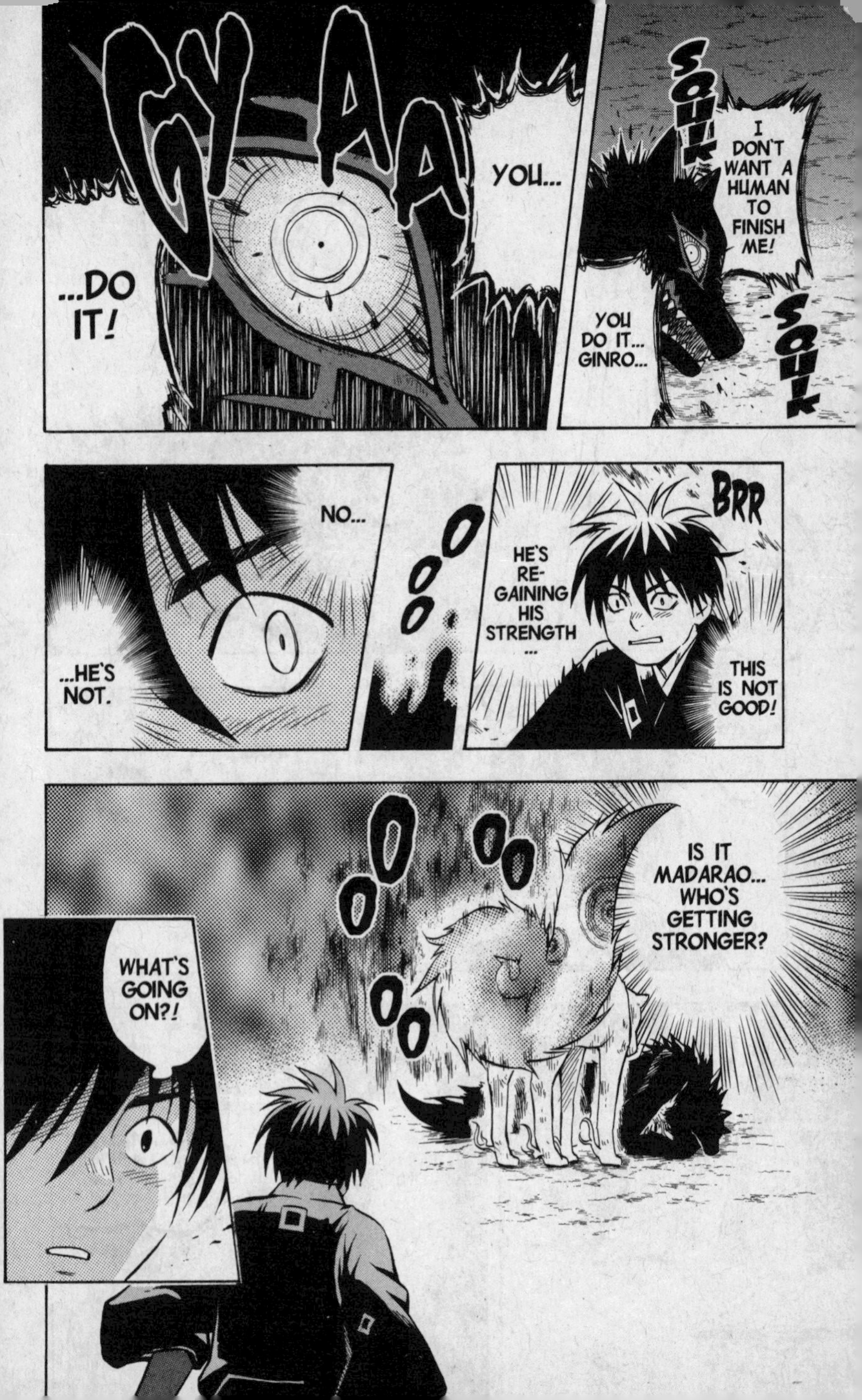
SOUIK
I DON'T WANT A HUMAN TO FINISH ME!
YOU DO IT... GINRO...
SOUIK
GYAA
YOU...
...DO IT!
BRR
HE'S RE-GAINING HIS STRENGTH ...
THIS IS NOT GOOD!
OOOO
NO...
...HE'S NOT.
IS IT MADARAO... WHO'S GETTING STRONGER?
OOOOOOO
WHAT'S GOING ON?!

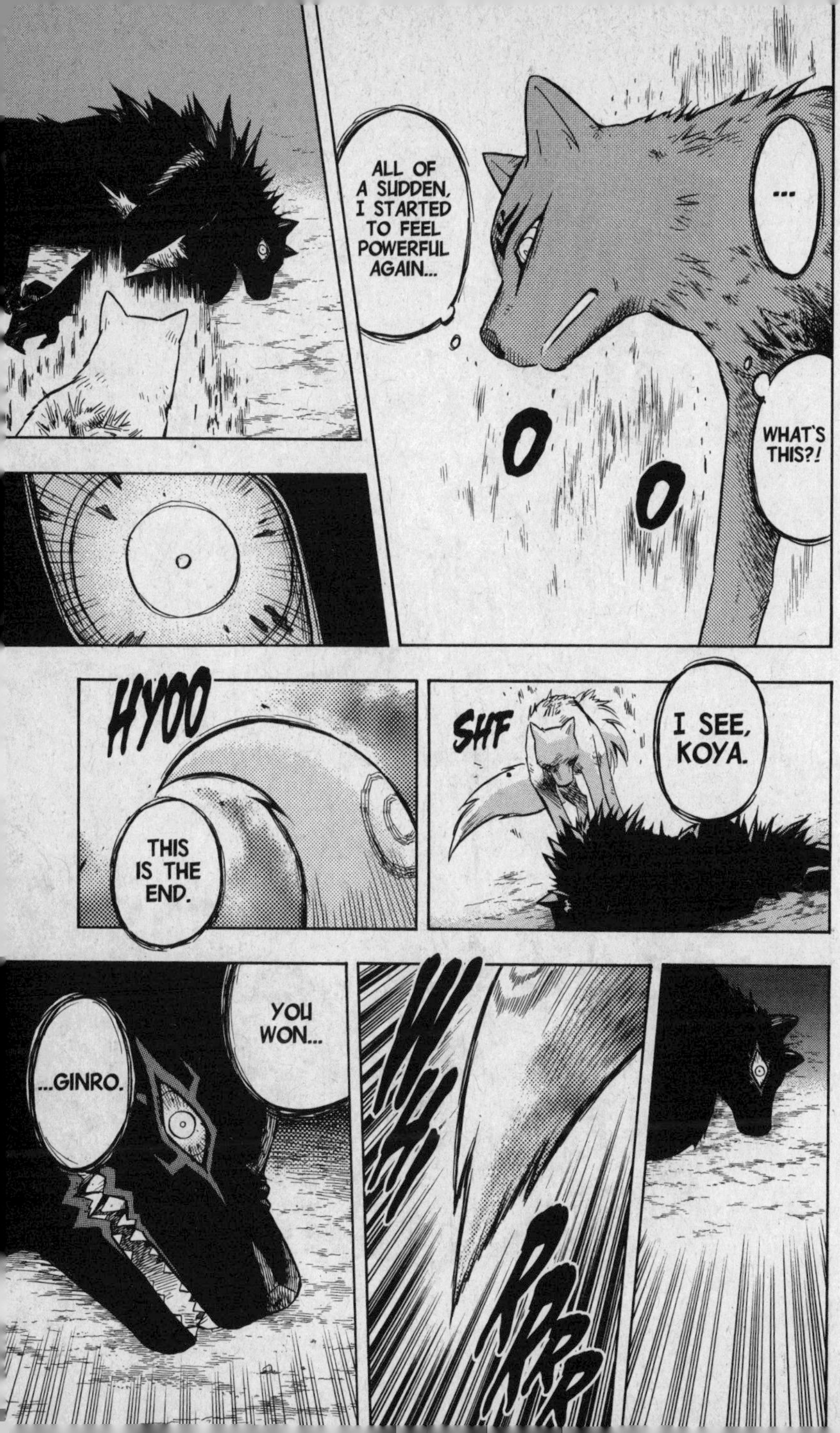
...
WHAT'S THIS?!
ALL OF A SUDDEN, I STARTED TO FEEL POWERFUL AGAIN...
I SEE, KOYA.
SHF
HYOO
THIS IS THE END.
YOU WON...
...GINRO.

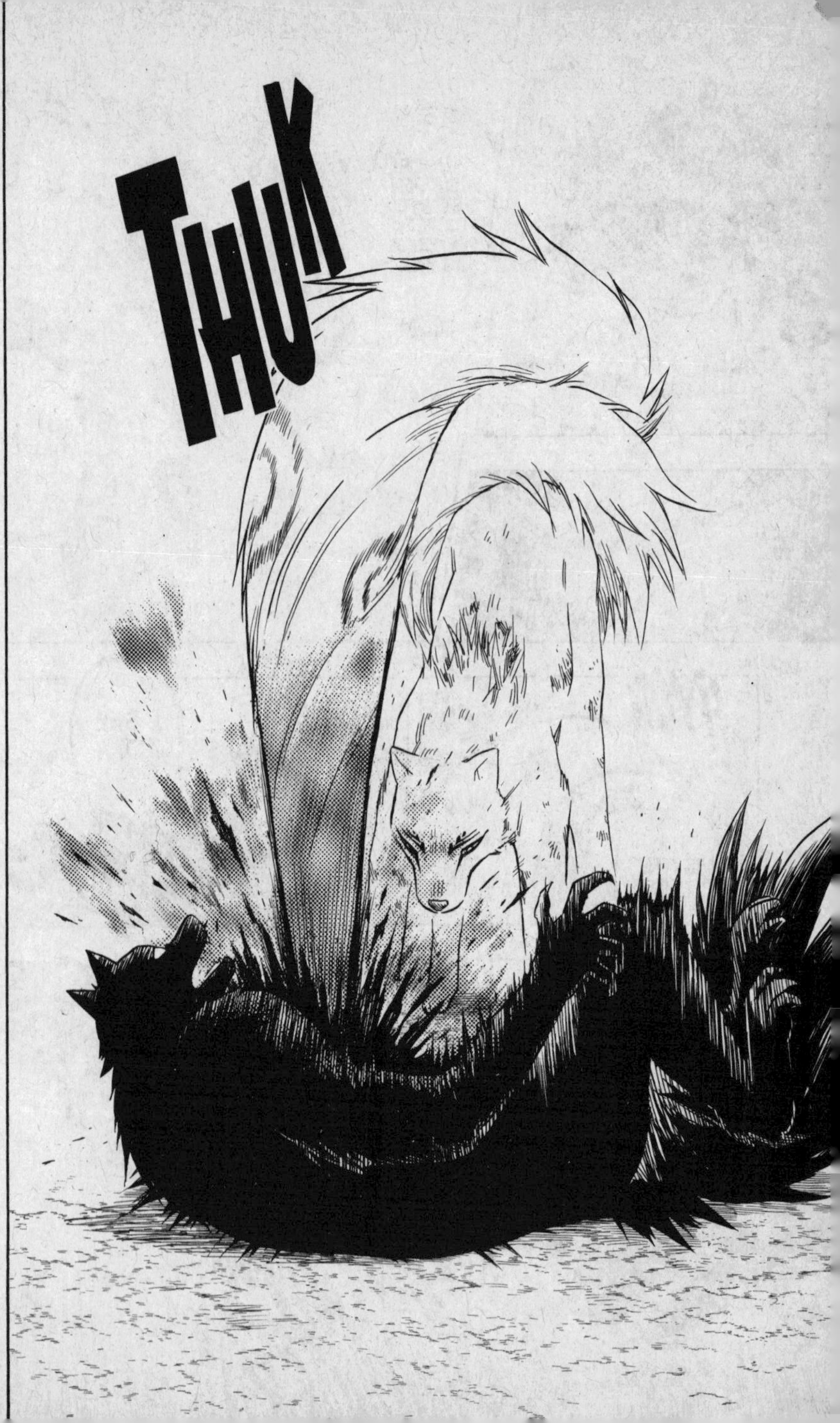
THUK

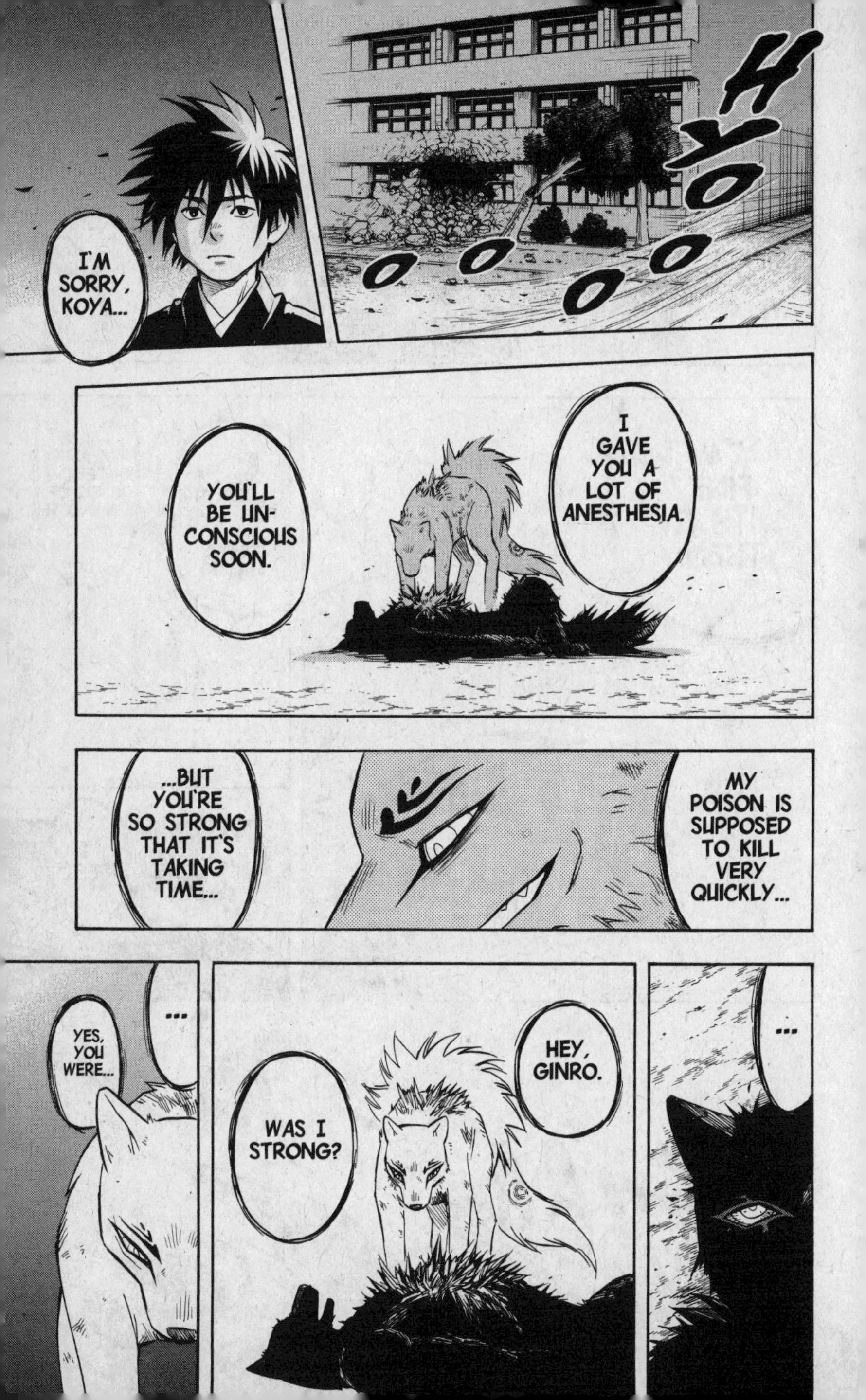
I'M SORRY, KOYA...
I GAVE YOU A LOT OF ANESTHESIA.
YOU'LL BE UN-CONSCIOUS SOON.
MY POISON IS SUPPOSED TO KILL VERY QUICKLY...
...BUT YOU'RE SO STRONG THAT IT'S TAKING TIME...
...
HEY, GINRO.
WAS I STRONG?
...
YES, YOU WERE...

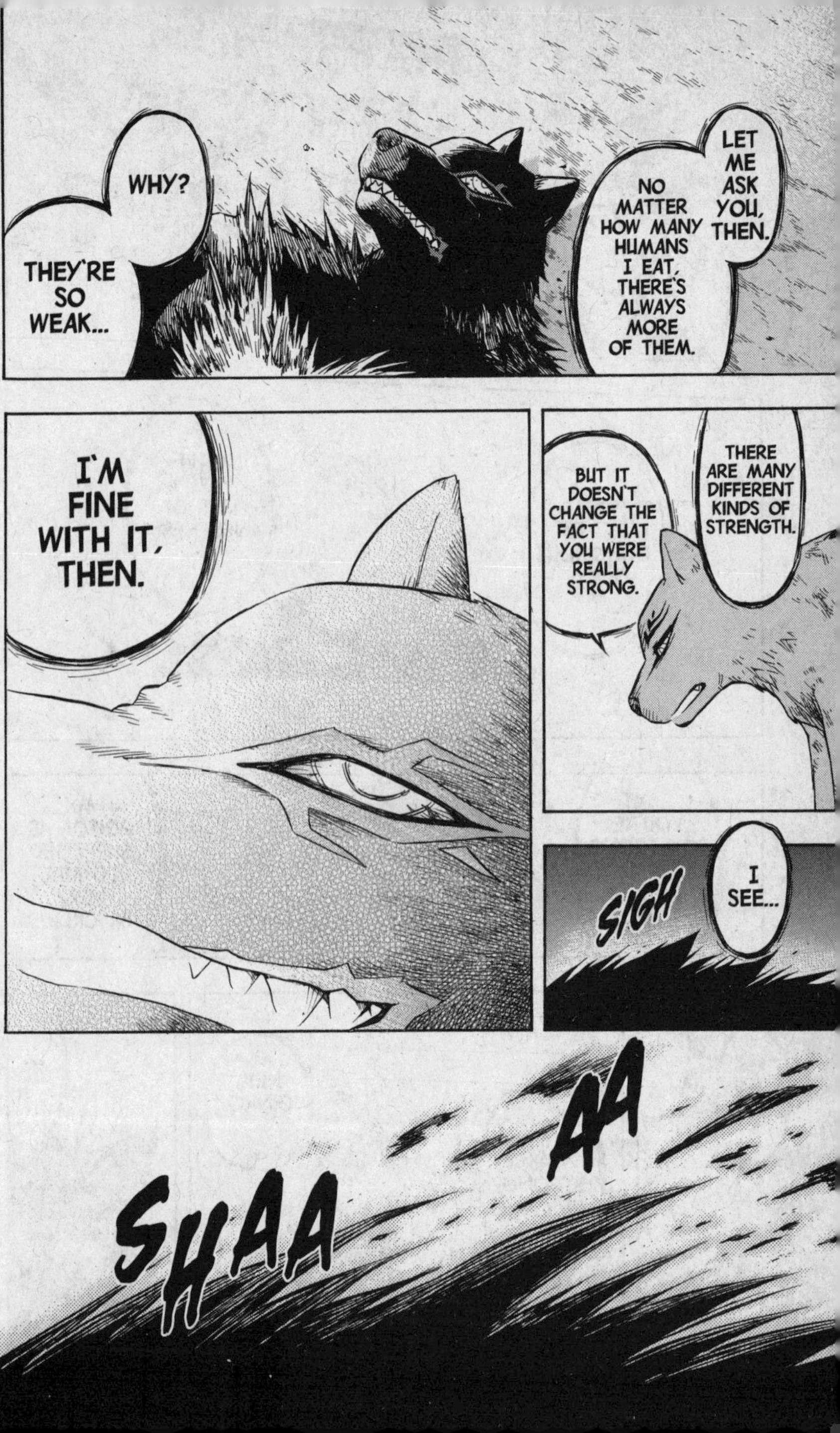
LET ME ASK YOU, THEN.
NO MATTER HOW MANY HUMANS I EAT, THERE'S ALWAYS MORE OF THEM.
WHY?
THEY'RE SO WEAK...
THERE ARE MANY DIFFERENT KINDS OF STRENGTH.
BUT IT DOESN'T CHANGE THE FACT THAT YOU WERE REALLY STRONG.
I SEE...
SIGH
I'M FINE WITH IT, THEN.
SHAA
AA

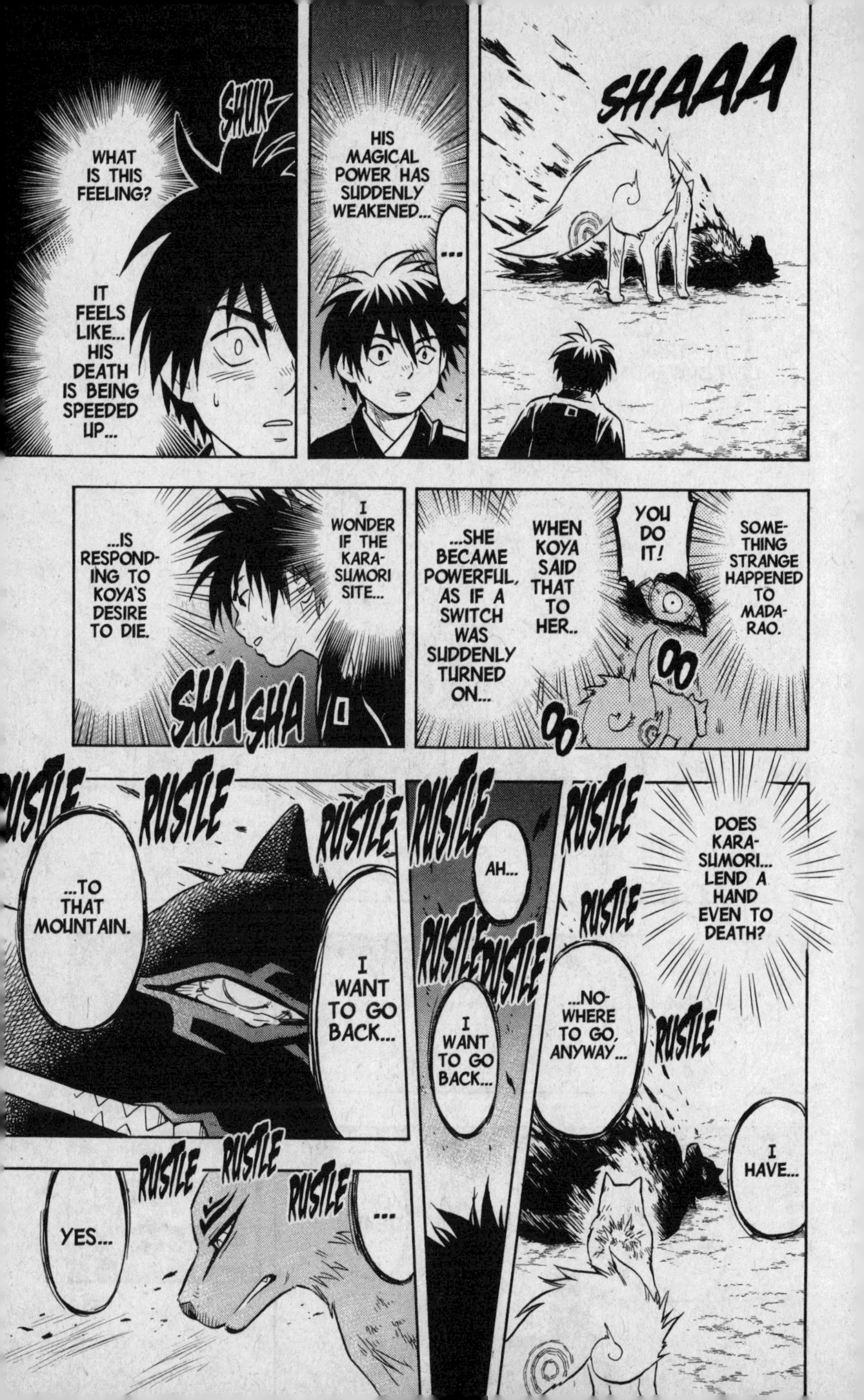
SHAAAA
HIS MAGICAL POWER HAS SUDDENLY WEAKENED...
...
SHUK
WHAT IS THIS FEELING?
IT FEELS LIKE... HIS DEATH IS BEING SPEEDED UP...
SOME-THING STRANGE HAPPENED TO MADA-RAO.
YOU DO IT!
WHEN KOYA SAID THAT TO HER..
...SHE BECAME POWERFUL, AS IF A SWITCH WAS SUDDENLY TURNED ON...
OO
OO
I WONDER IF THE KARA-SUMORI SITE...
...IS RESPOND-ING TO KOYA'S DESIRE TO DIE.
SHASHA
DOES KARA-SUMORI... LEND A HAND EVEN TO DEATH?
RUSTLE
RUSTLE
RUSTLE
I HAVE...
...NO-WHERE TO GO, ANYWAY...
RUSTLE
AH...
RUSTLE RUSTLE
I WANT TO GO BACK...
RUSTLE
RUSTLE
RUSTLE
I WANT TO GO BACK...
...TO THAT MOUNTAIN.
RUSTLE RUSTLE RUSTLE
...
YES...

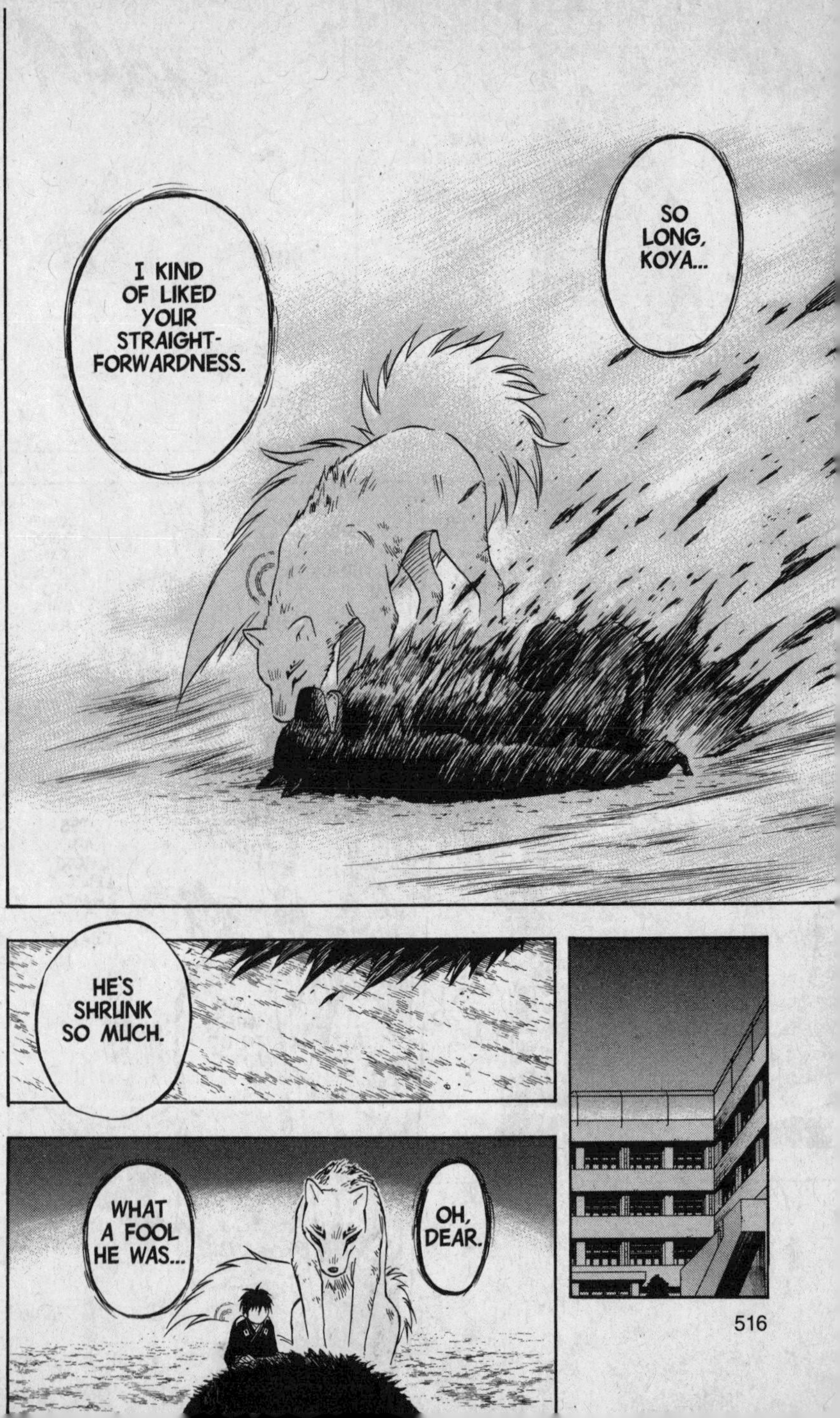
SO LONG, KOYA...
I KIND OF LIKED YOUR STRAIGHT-FORWARDNESS.
HE'S SHRUNK SO MUCH.
OH, DEAR.
WHAT A FOOL HE WAS...

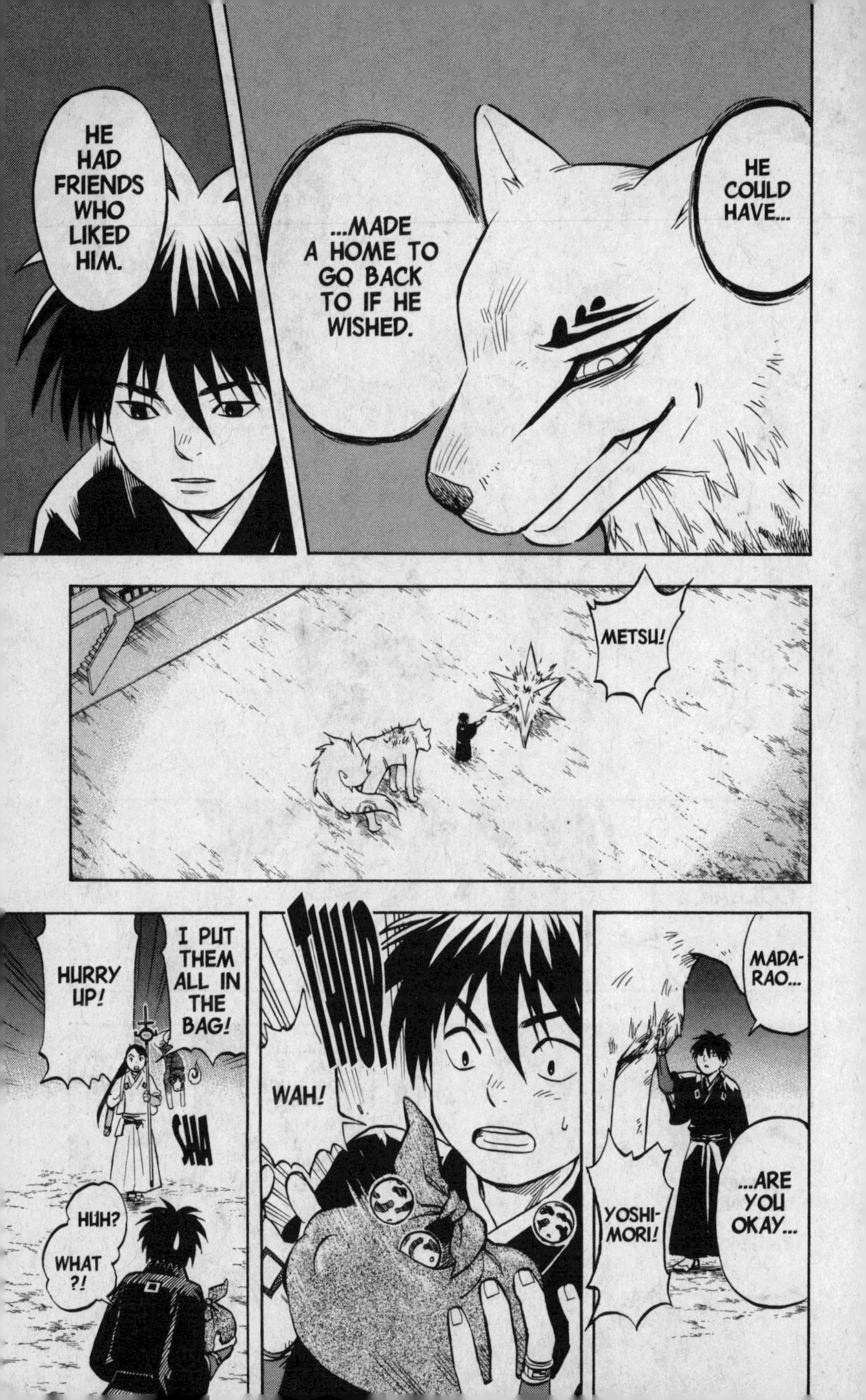
HE COULD HAVE...
...MADE A HOME TO GO BACK TO IF HE WISHED.
HE HAD FRIENDS WHO LIKED HIM.
METSU!
MADA-RAO...
...ARE YOU OKAY...
YOSHI-MORI!
THUD
WAH!
I PUT THEM ALL IN THE BAG!
HURRY UP!
SHA
HUH?
WHAT?!

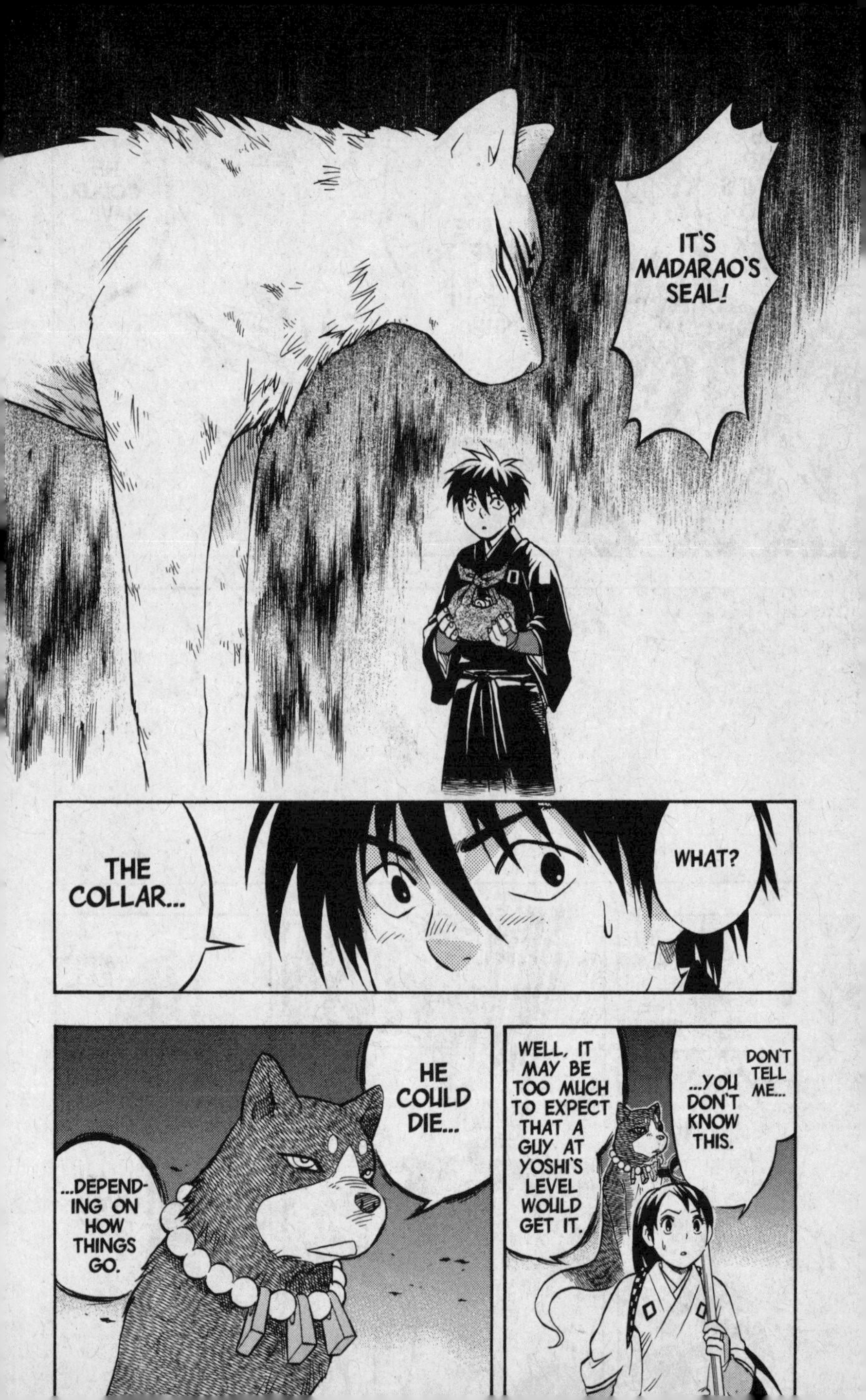
IT'S MADARAO'S SEAL!
WHAT?
THE COLLAR...
DON'T TELL ME...
...YOU DON'T KNOW THIS.
WELL, IT MAY BE TOO MUCH TO EXPECT THAT A GUY AT YOSHI'S LEVEL WOULD GET IT.
HE COULD DIE...
...DEPENDING ON HOW THINGS GO.

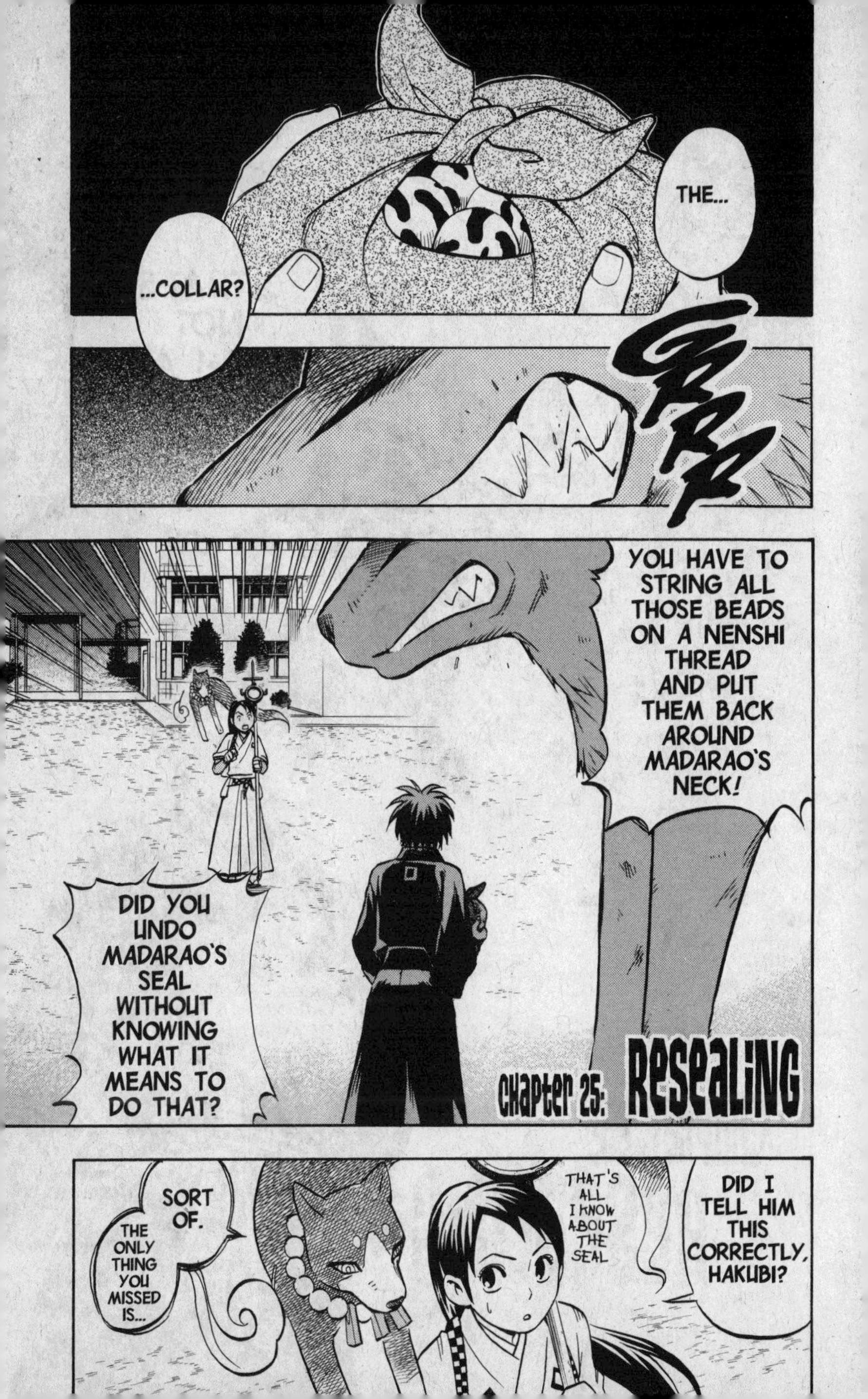
THE...
...COLLAR?
GRRR
YOU HAVE TO STRING ALL THOSE BEADS ON A NENSHI THREAD AND PUT THEM BACK AROUND MADARAO'S NECK!
DID YOU UNDO MADARAO'S SEAL WITHOUT KNOWING WHAT IT MEANS TO DO THAT?
Chapter 25: Resealing
DID I TELL HIM THIS CORRECTLY, HAKUBI?
THAT'S ALL I KNOW ABOUT THE SEAL
SORT OF.
THE ONLY THING YOU MISSED IS...

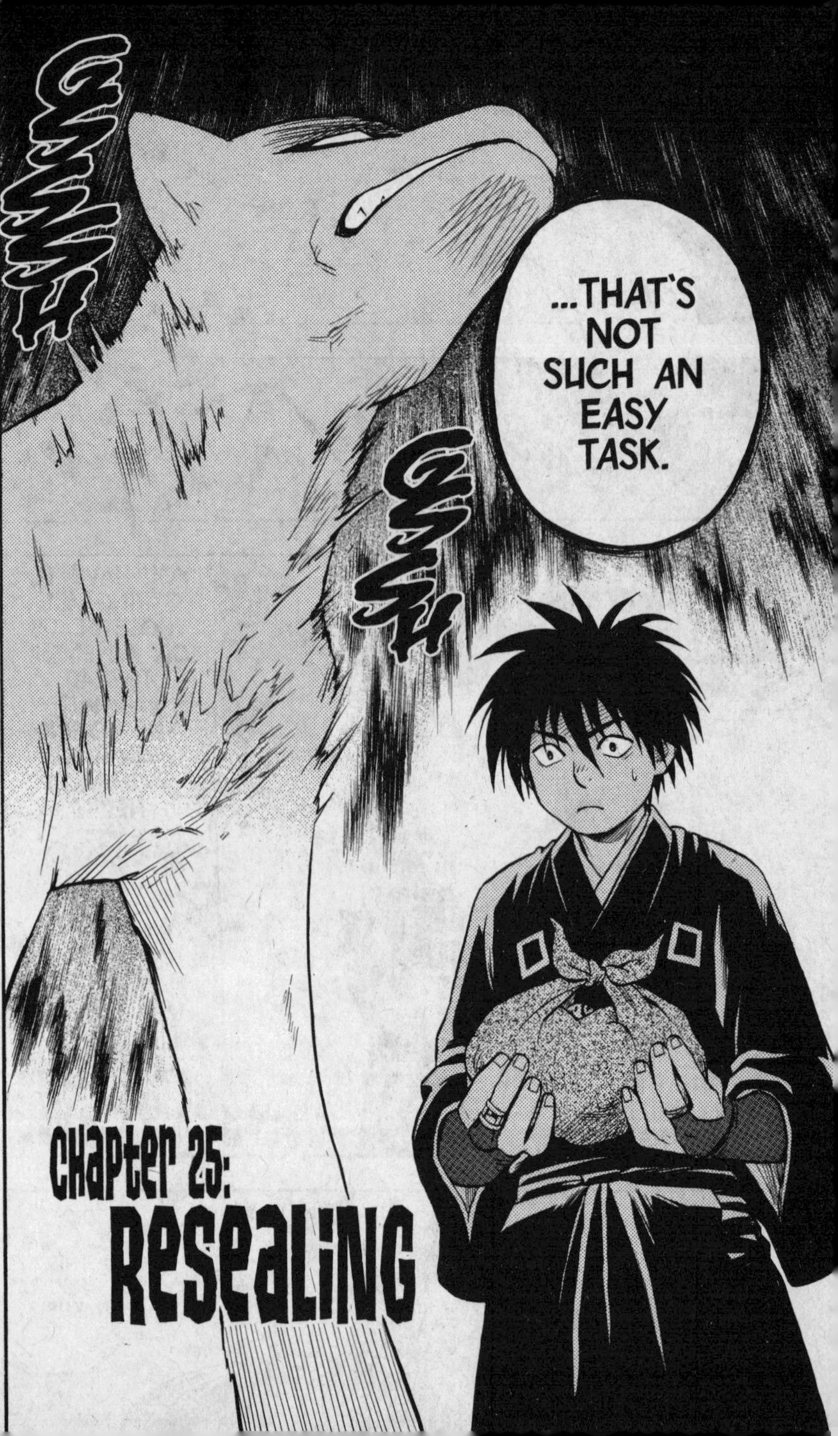
...THAT'S NOT SUCH AN EASY TASK.
Chapter 25:
Resealing

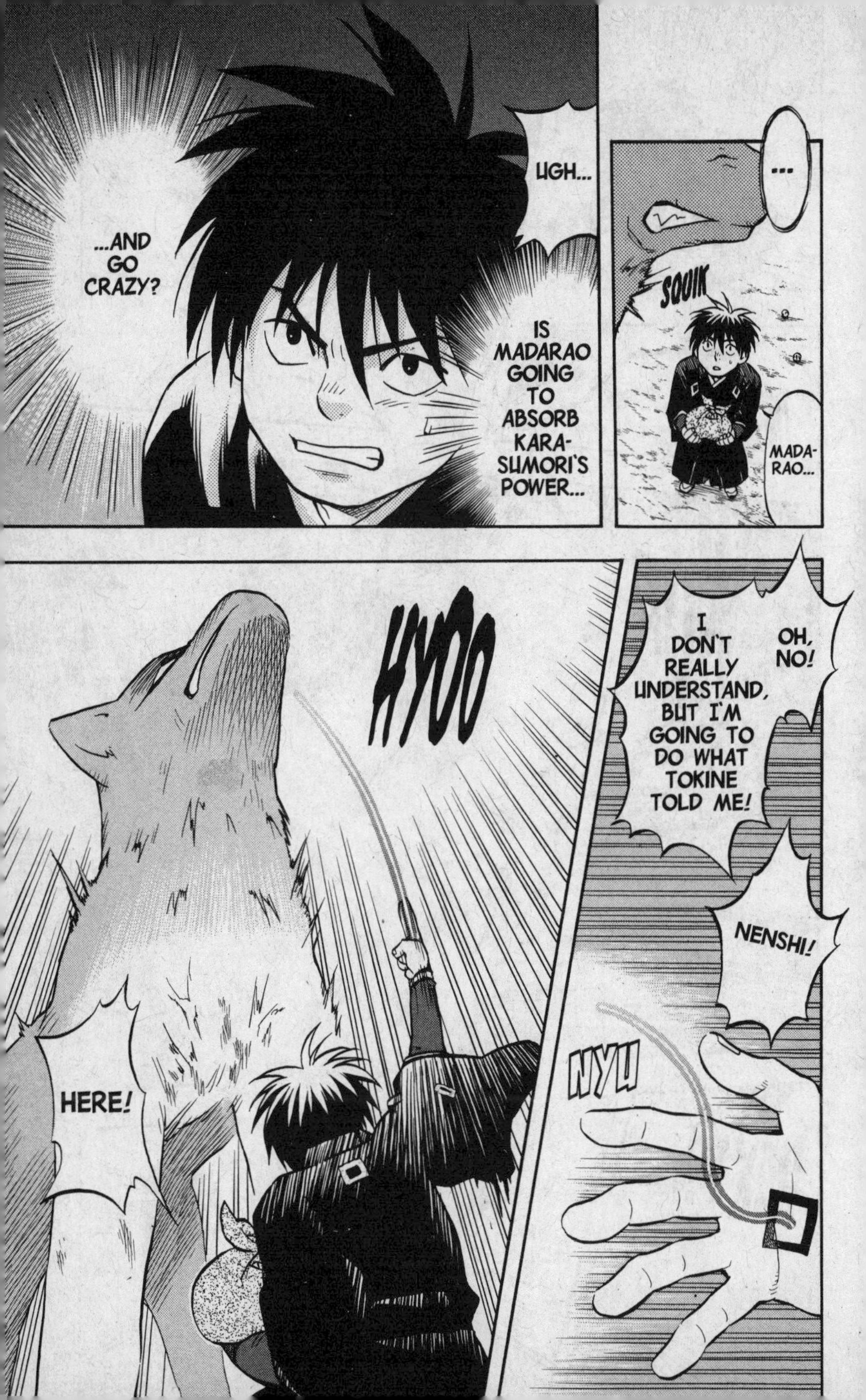
...
SQUIK
MADARAO...
UGH...
IS MADARAO GOING TO ABSORB KARASUMORI'S POWER...
...AND GO CRAZY?
OH, NO!
I DON'T REALLY UNDERSTAND, BUT I'M GOING TO DO WHAT TOKINE TOLD ME!
NENSHI!
NYU
HYOO
HERE!

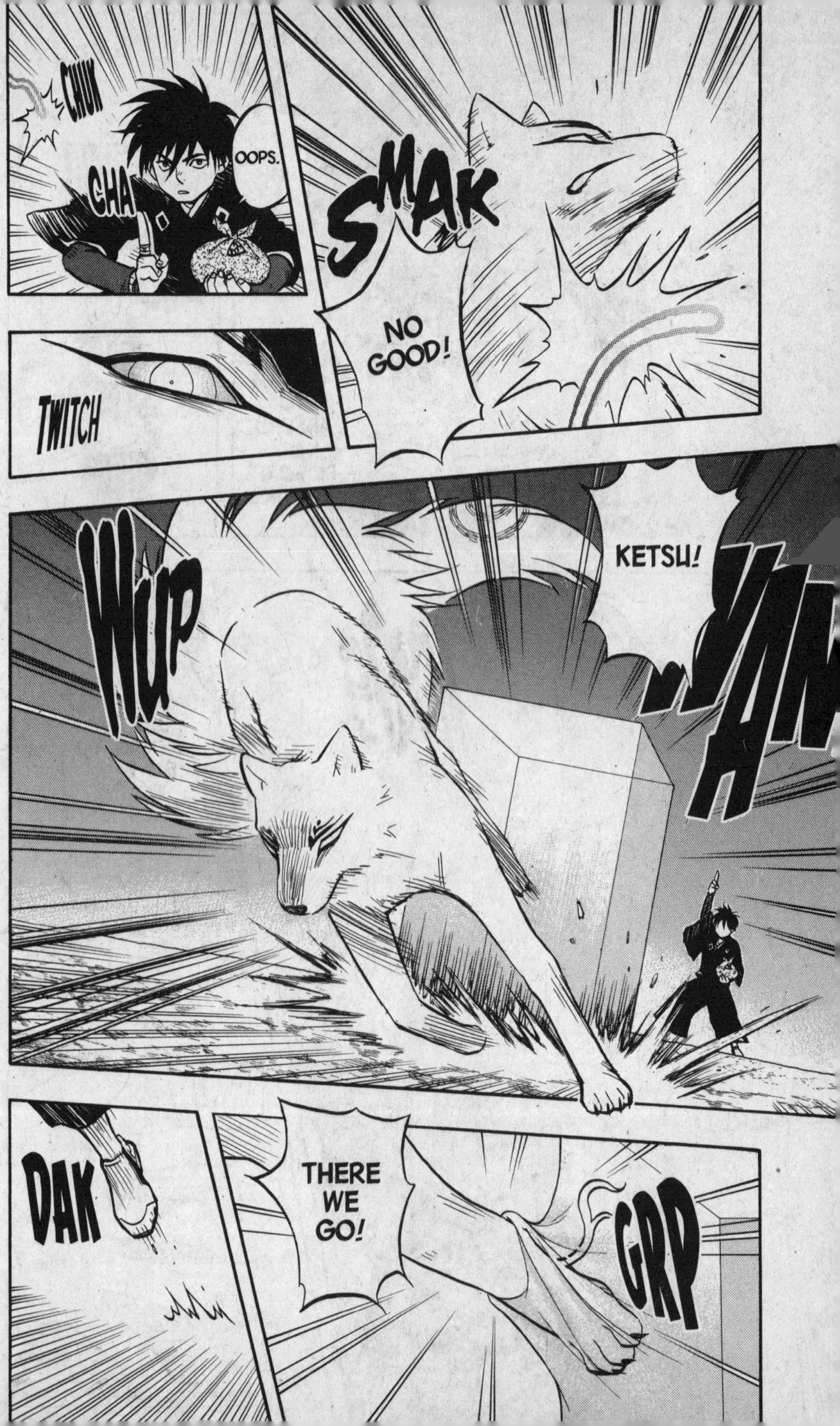
SMAK
NO GOOD!
CHUK
CHA
OOPS.
TWITCH
KETSU!
WUP
THERE WE GO!
GRP
DAK

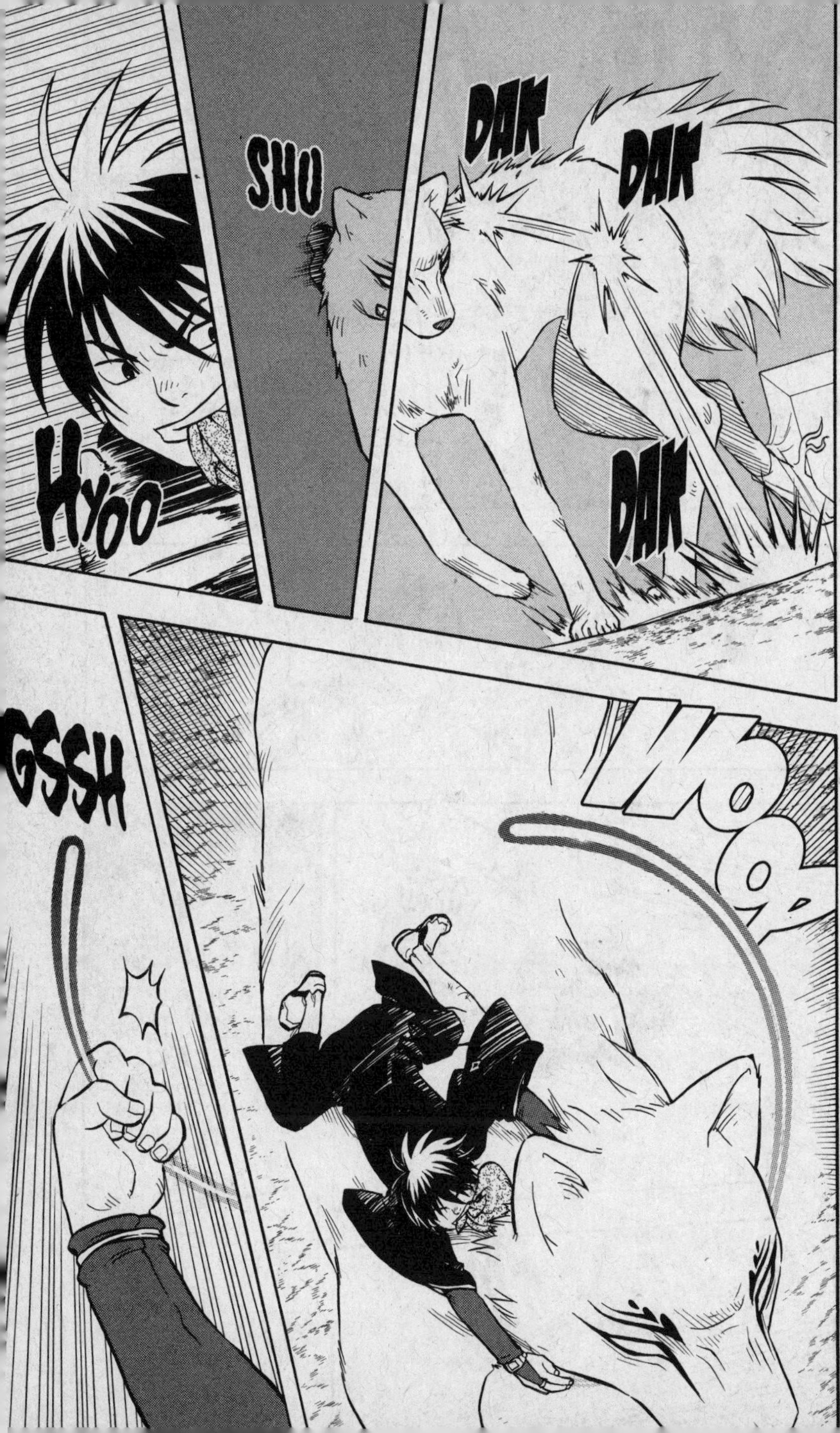
DAK
DAK
DAK
SHU
HYOO
WOO
GSSH

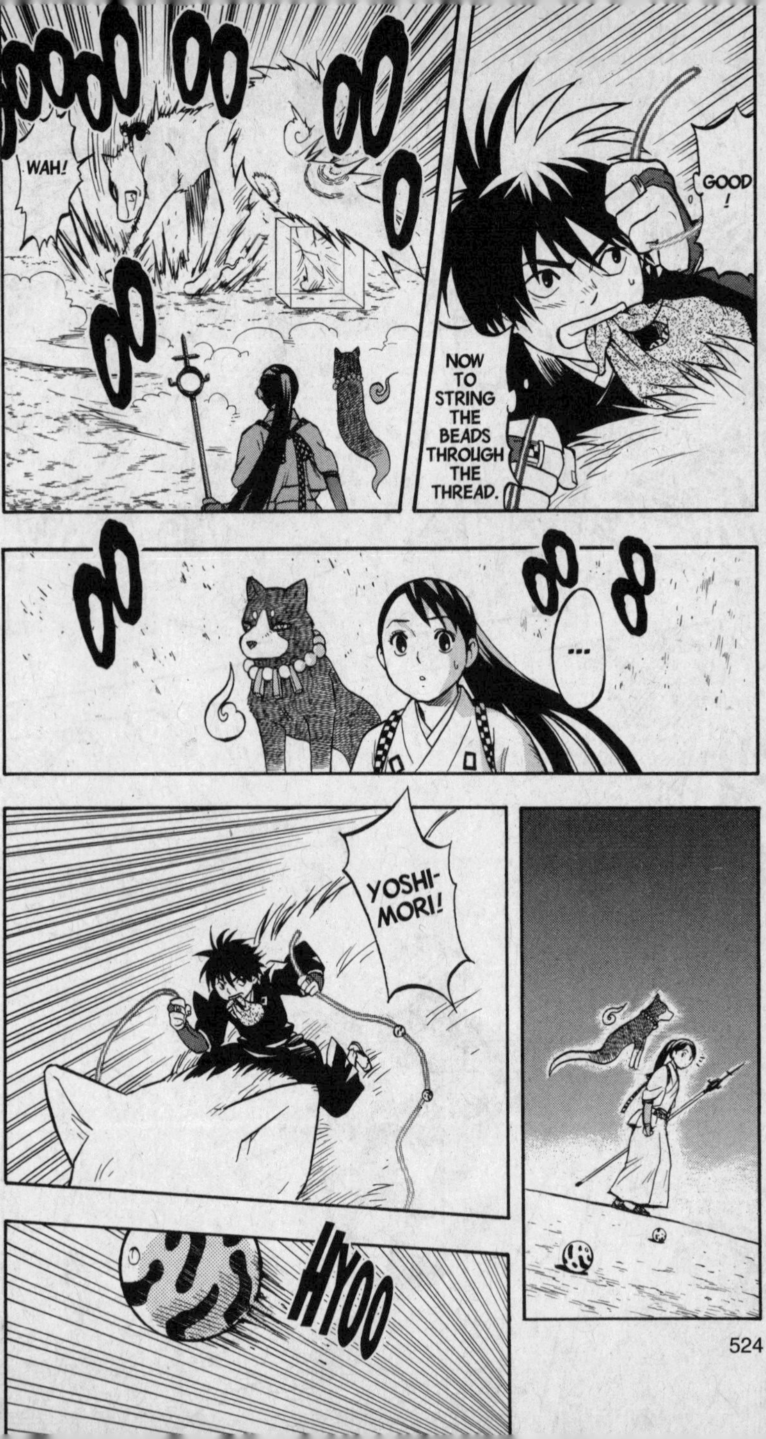
GOOD!
NOW TO STRING THE BEADS THROUGH THE THREAD.
OOOOO OO
OO
OO
WAH!
OO
OO
...
YOSHI-MORI!
HYOO

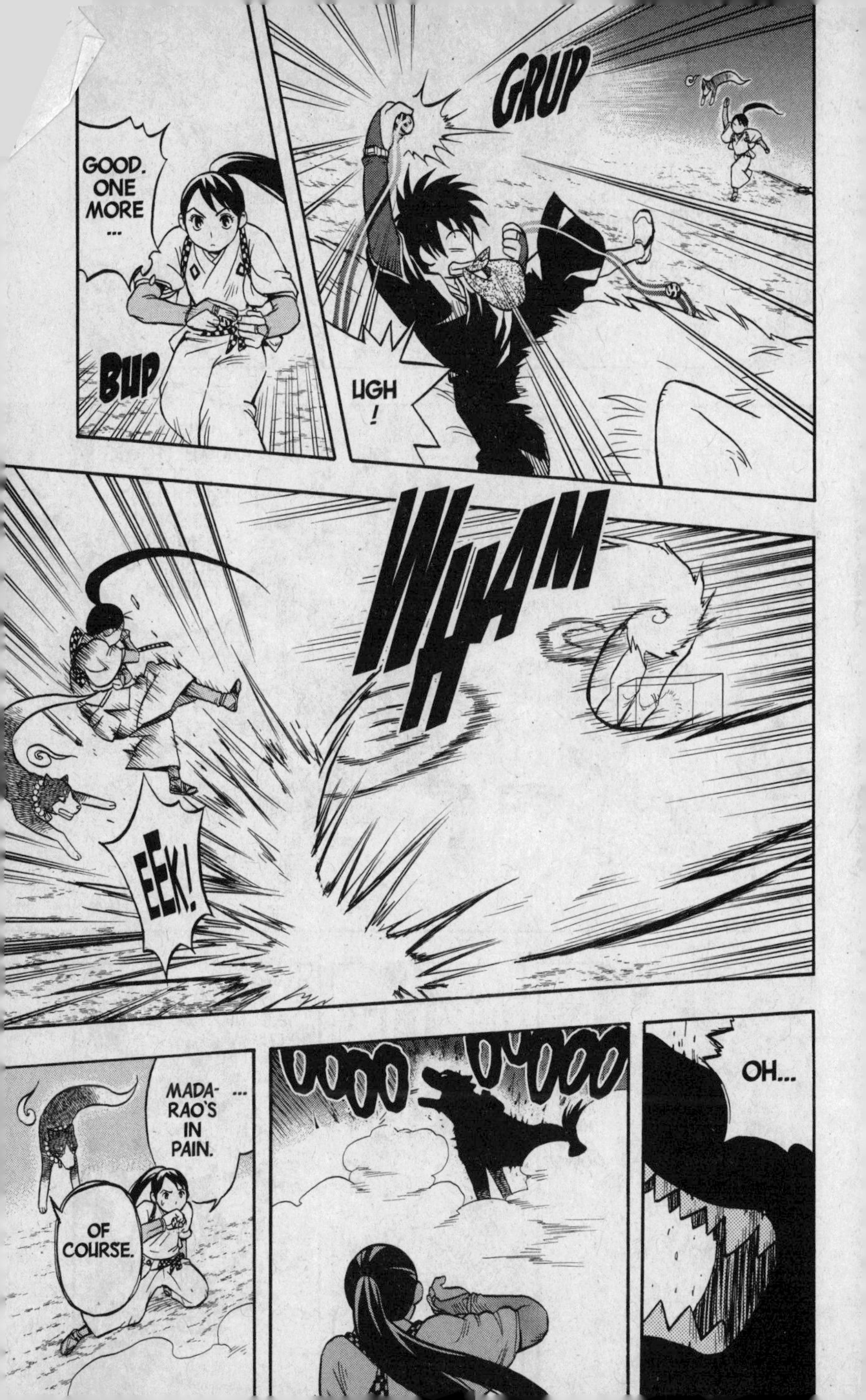
GRUP
UGH!
GOOD. ONE MORE ...
BUP
WHAM
EEK!
OH...
MADARAO'S IN PAIN. ...
OF COURSE.

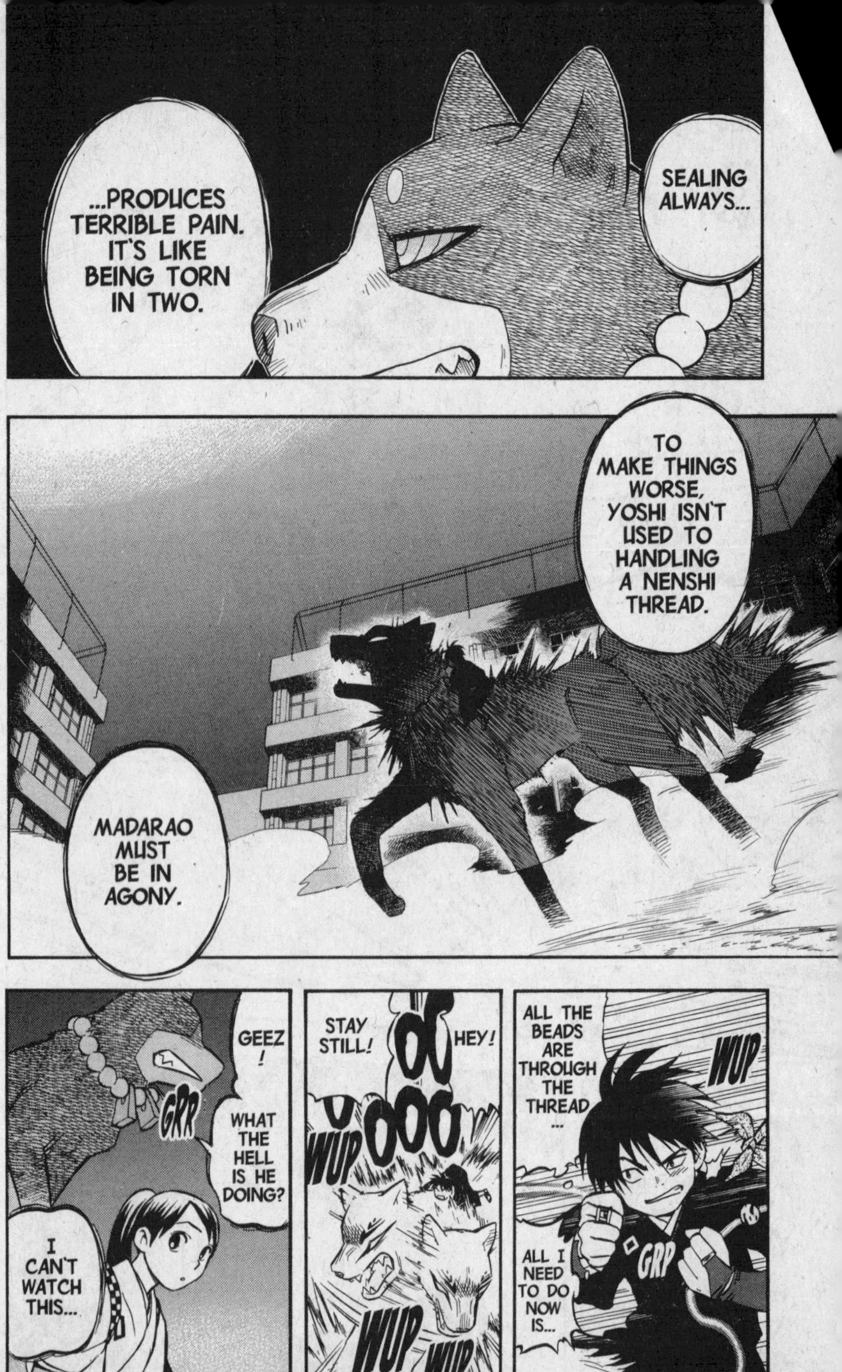
SEALING ALWAYS...
...PRODUCES TERRIBLE PAIN. IT'S LIKE BEING TORN IN TWO.
TO MAKE THINGS WORSE, YOSHI ISN'T USED TO HANDLING A NENSHI THREAD.
MADARAO MUST BE IN AGONY.
ALL THE BEADS ARE THROUGH THE THREAD...
WUP
GRP
ALL I NEED TO DO NOW IS...
HEY!
OOOOOO
STAY STILL!
WUP
WUP
WUP
GEEZ!
WHAT THE HELL IS HE DOING?
GRR
I CAN'T WATCH THIS...

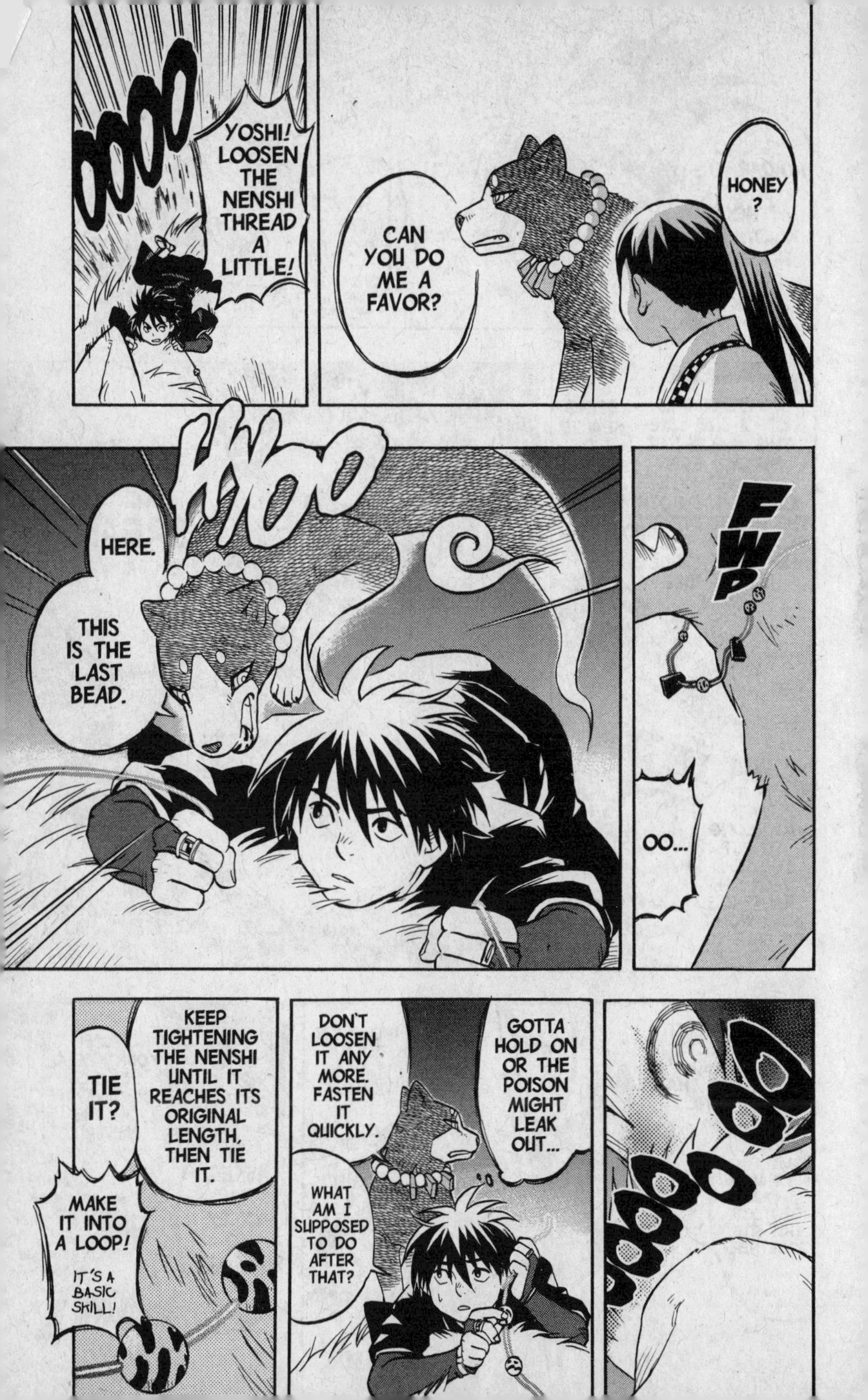
HONEY ?
CAN YOU DO ME A FAVOR?
YOSHI! LOOSEN THE NENSHI THREAD A LITTLE!
FWP
OO...
HYOO
HERE.
THIS IS THE LAST BEAD.
GOTTA HOLD ON OR THE POISON MIGHT LEAK OUT...
DON'T LOOSEN IT ANY MORE. FASTEN IT QUICKLY.
WHAT AM I SUPPOSED TO DO AFTER THAT?
KEEP TIGHTENING THE NENSHI UNTIL IT REACHES ITS ORIGINAL LENGTH, THEN TIE IT.
TIE IT?
MAKE IT INTO A LOOP!
IT'S A BASIC SKILL!

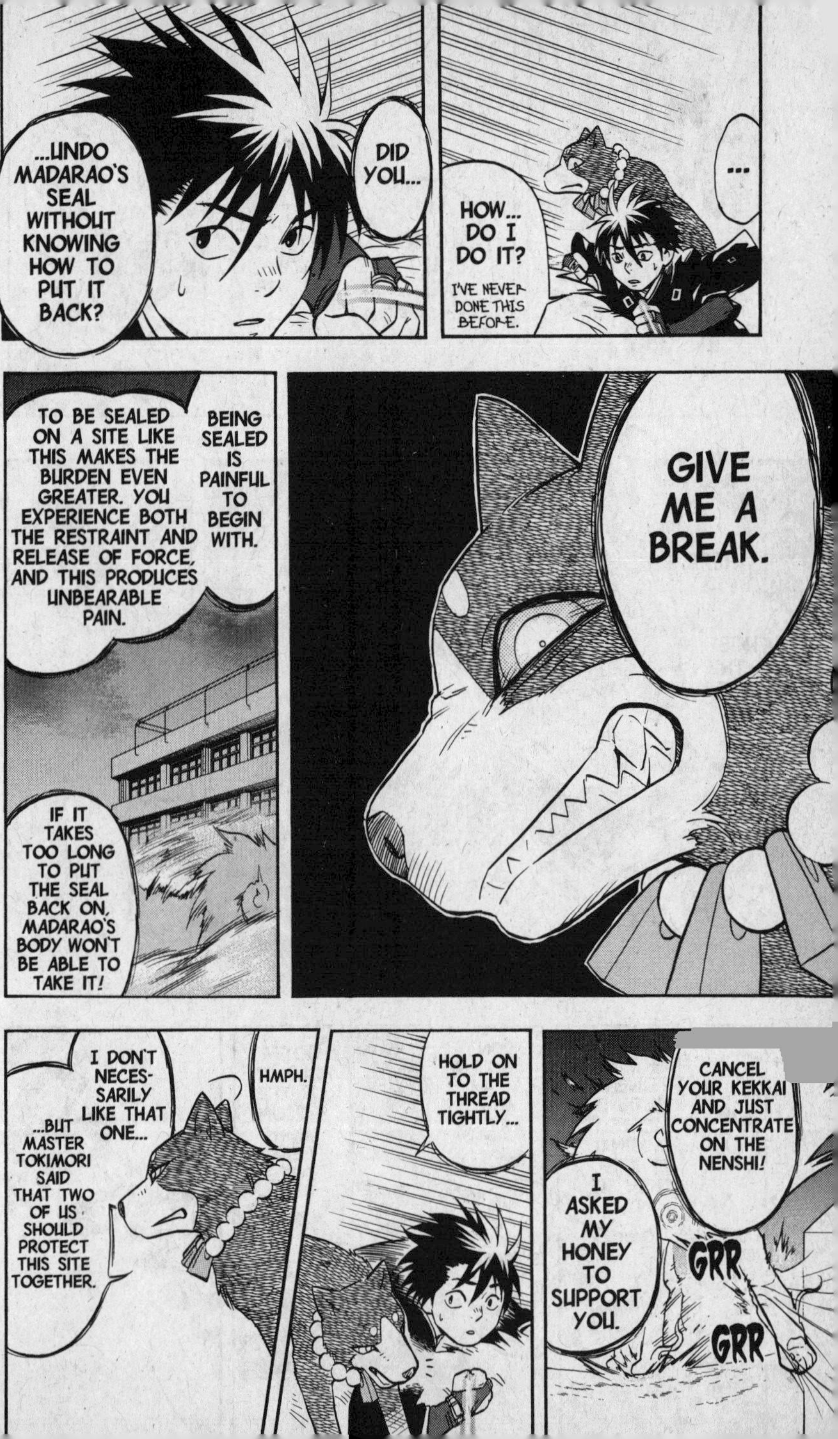
...
HOW... DO I DO IT?
I'VE NEVER DONE THIS BEFORE.
DID YOU...
...UNDO MADARAO'S SEAL WITHOUT KNOWING HOW TO PUT IT BACK?
GIVE ME A BREAK.
BEING SEALED IS PAINFUL TO BEGIN WITH.
TO BE SEALED ON A SITE LIKE THIS MAKES THE BURDEN EVEN GREATER. YOU EXPERIENCE BOTH THE RESTRAINT AND RELEASE OF FORCE, AND THIS PRODUCES UNBEARABLE PAIN.
IF IT TAKES TOO LONG TO PUT THE SEAL BACK ON, MADARAO'S BODY WON'T BE ABLE TO TAKE IT!
CANCEL YOUR KEKKAI AND JUST CONCENTRATE ON THE NENSHI!
I ASKED MY HONEY TO SUPPORT YOU.
GRR
GRR
HOLD ON TO THE THREAD TIGHTLY...
HMPH.
I DON'T NECES-SARILY LIKE THAT ONE...
...BUT MASTER TOKIMORI SAID THAT TWO OF US SHOULD PROTECT THIS SITE TOGETHER.

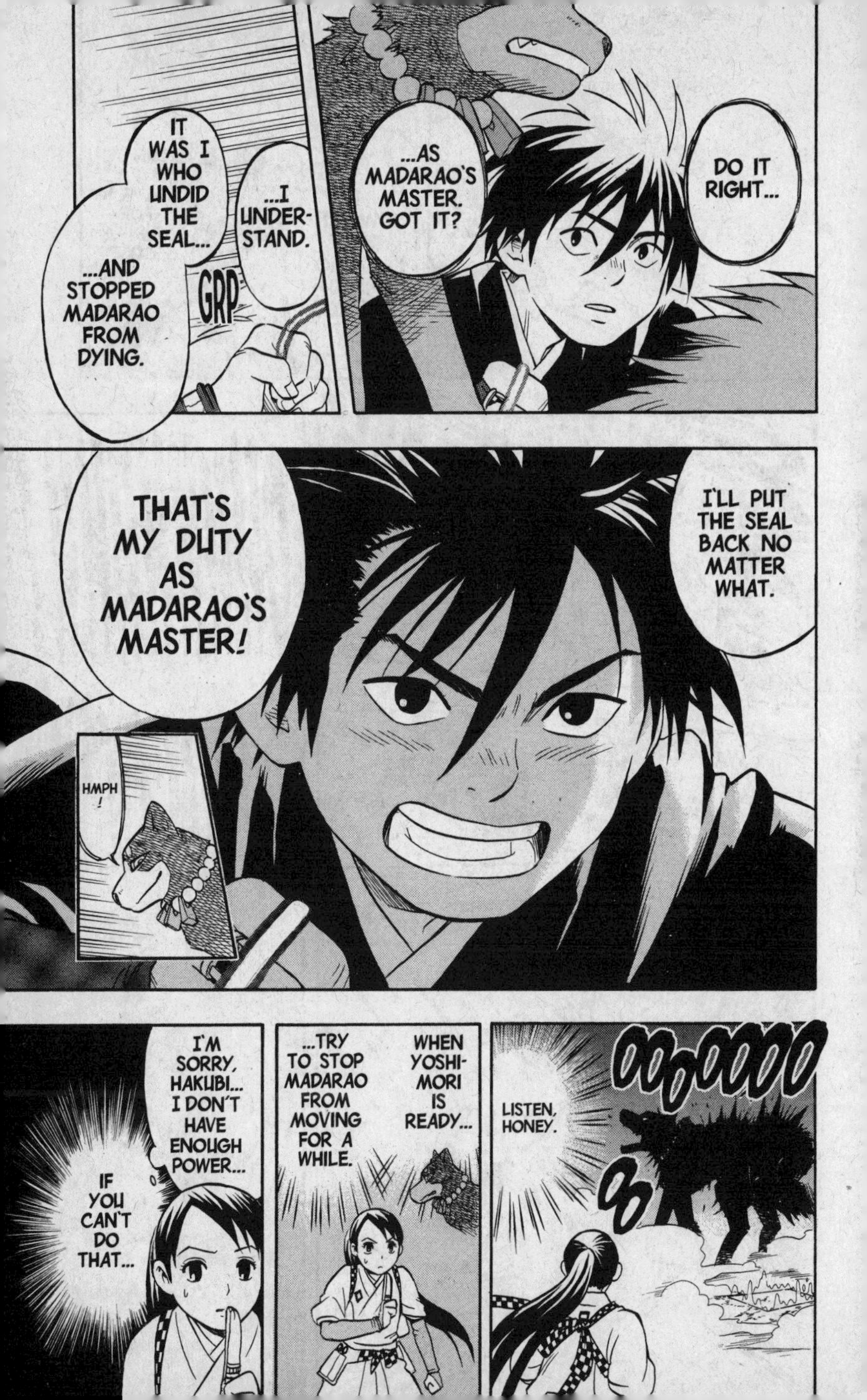
DO IT RIGHT...
...AS MADARAO'S MASTER. GOT IT?
...I UNDERSTAND.
GRP
IT WAS I WHO UNDID THE SEAL...
...AND STOPPED MADARAO FROM DYING.
I'LL PUT THE SEAL BACK NO MATTER WHAT.
THAT'S MY DUTY AS MADARAO'S MASTER!
HMPH!
OOOOOOO
LISTEN, HONEY.
WHEN YOSHIMORI IS READY...
...TRY TO STOP MADARAO FROM MOVING FOR A WHILE.
I'M SORRY, HAKUBI... I DON'T HAVE ENOUGH POWER...
IF YOU CAN'T DO THAT...

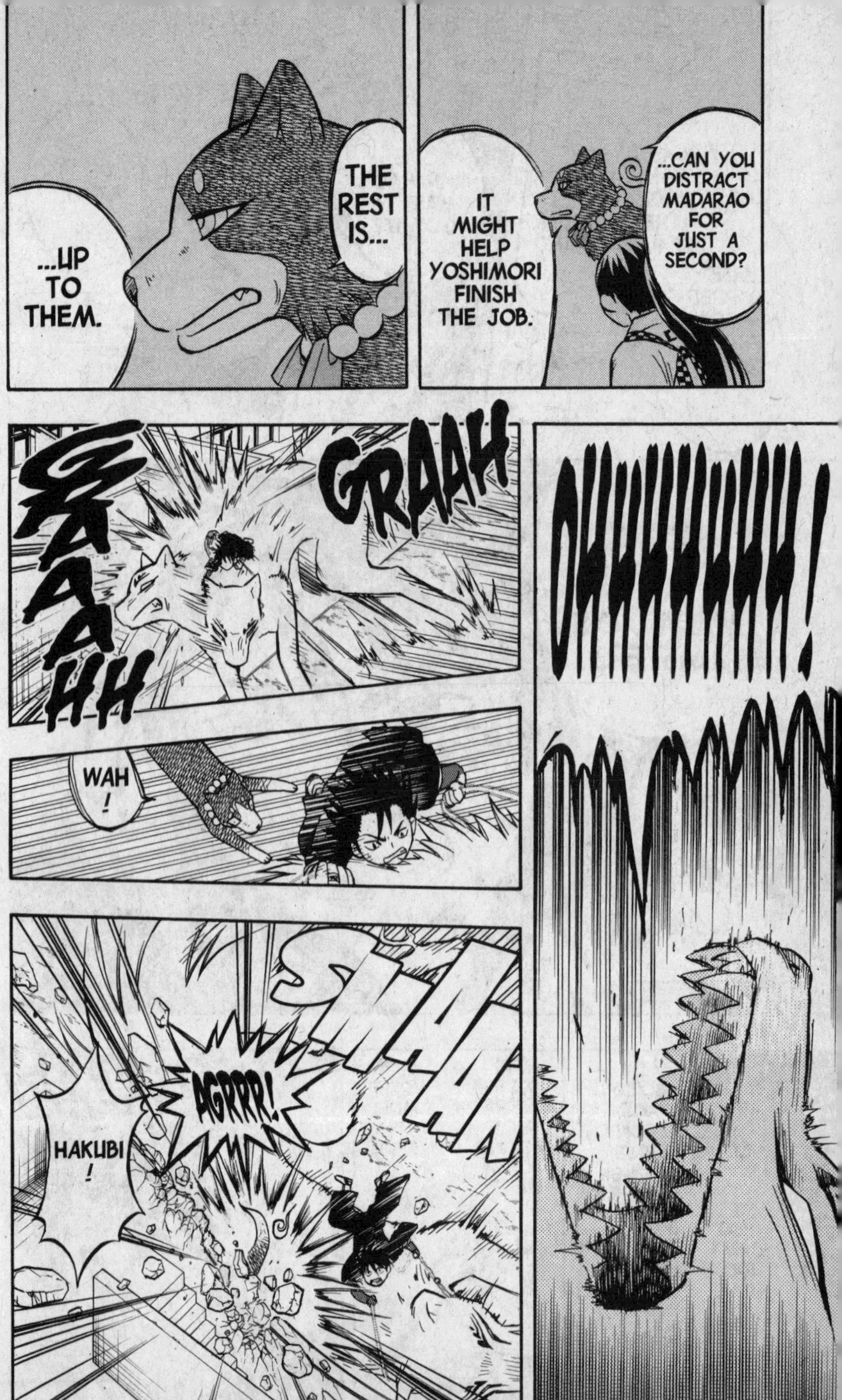
...CAN YOU DISTRACT MADARAO FOR JUST A SECOND?
IT MIGHT HELP YOSHIMORI FINISH THE JOB.
THE REST IS...
...UP TO THEM.
OHHHHHHHH!
GRAAH
GRAAAHH
WAH!
SHAA
AGRRR!
HAKUBI!

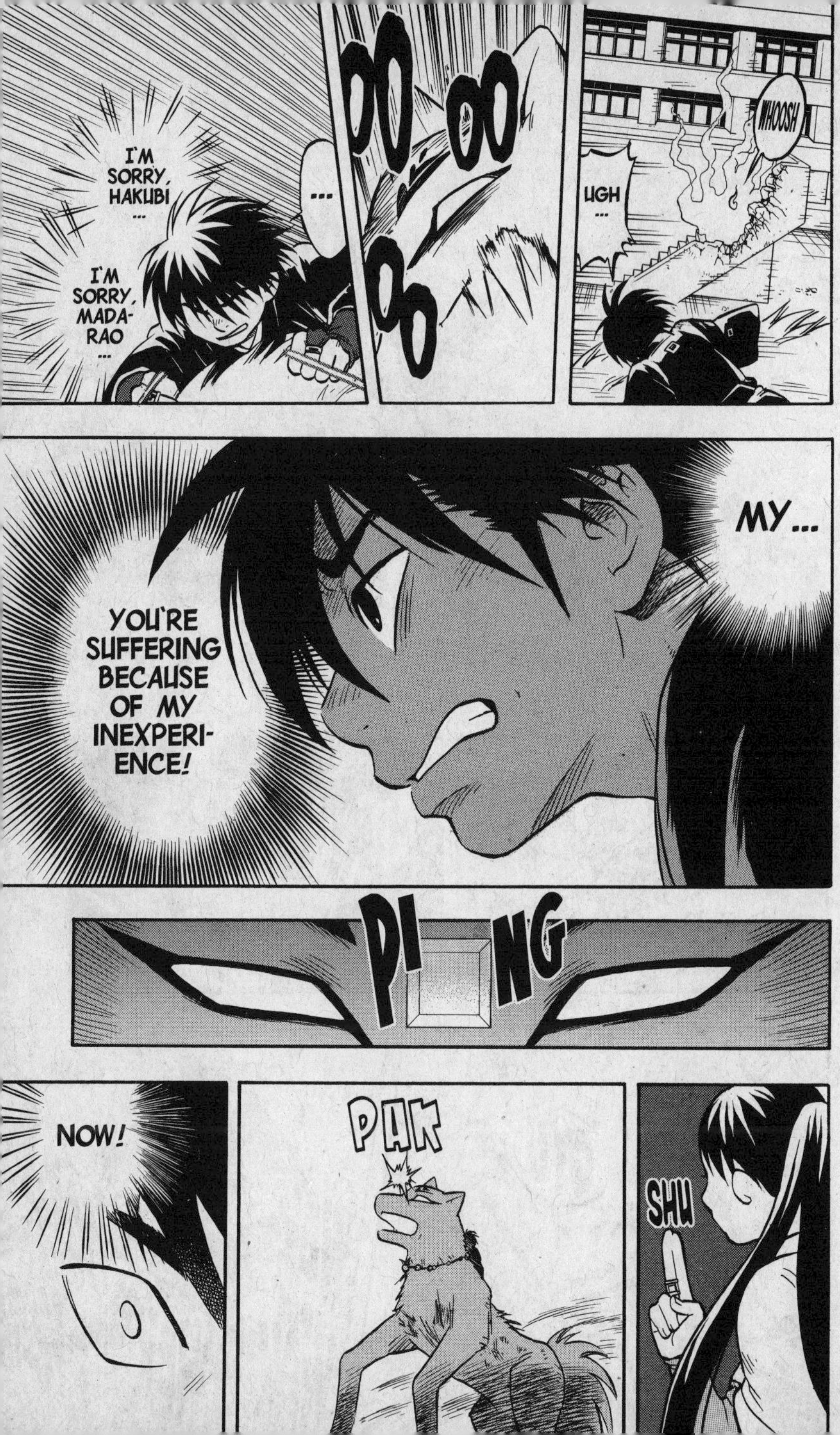
WHOOSH
UGH ...
...
I'M SORRY, HAKUBI ...
I'M SORRY, MADARAO ...
MY...
YOU'RE SUFFERING BECAUSE OF MY INEXPERIENCE!
PING
SHU
PAK
NOW!

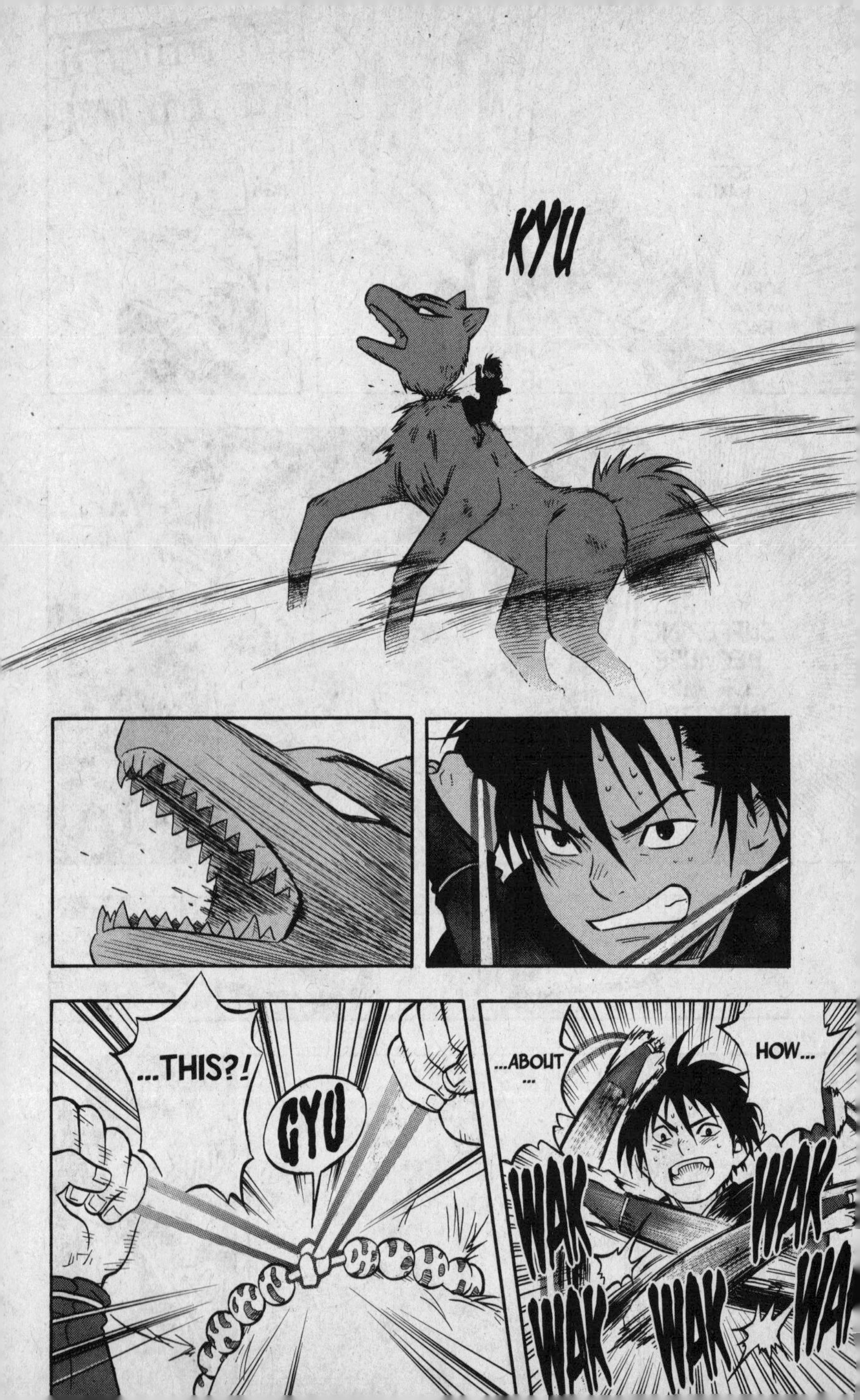
KYU
HOW...
...ABOUT
...
WAK
WAK
WAK
WAK
...THIS?!
GYU

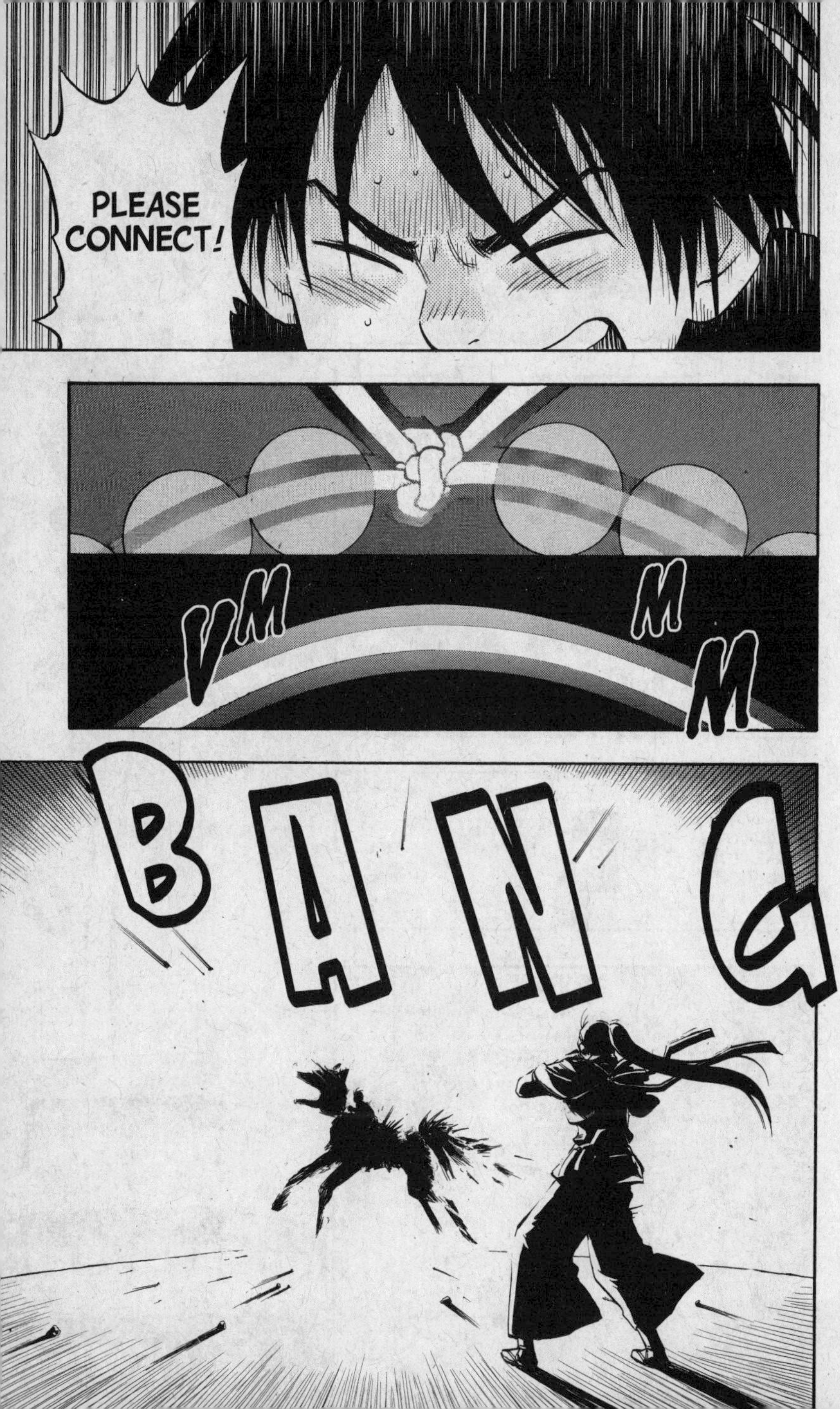
PLEASE CONNECT!
VM
M
M
BANG

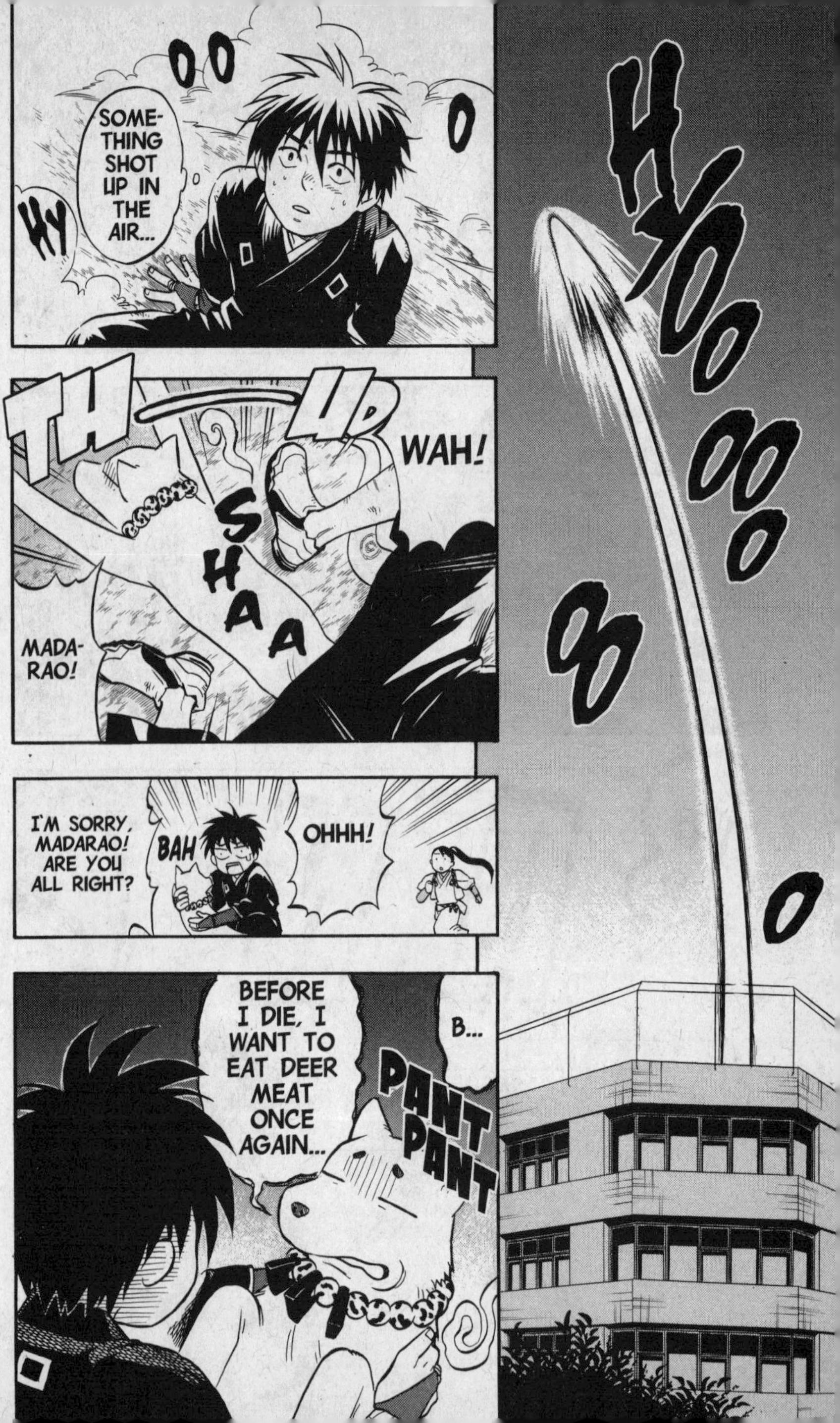
HYOOOOOOOOO
HY
OOO
SOME-THING SHOT UP IN THE AIR...
THUD
WAH!
SHAAA
MADARAO!
OHHH!
I'M SORRY, MADARAO! ARE YOU ALL RIGHT?
BAH
B...
BEFORE I DIE, I WANT TO EAT DEER MEAT ONCE AGAIN...
PANT PANT

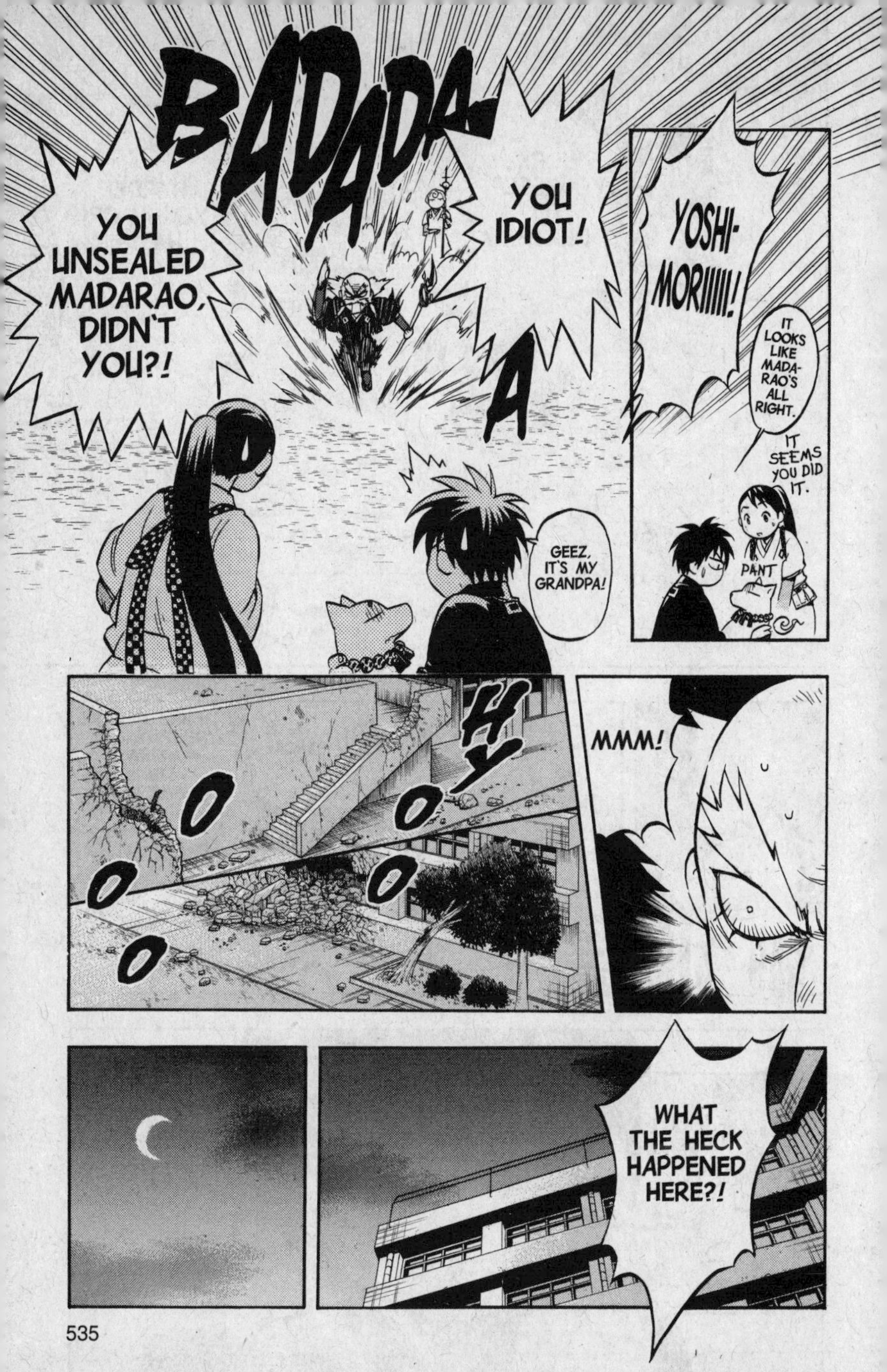
YOSHI-MORIIIIII!
IT LOOKS LIKE MADARAO'S ALL RIGHT.
IT SEEMS YOU DID IT.
PANT
BADADA
YOU IDIOT!
A
YOU UNSEALED MADARAO, DIDN'T YOU?!
GEEZ, IT'S MY GRANDPA!
MMM!
HYOOOOO
WHAT THE HECK HAPPENED HERE?!

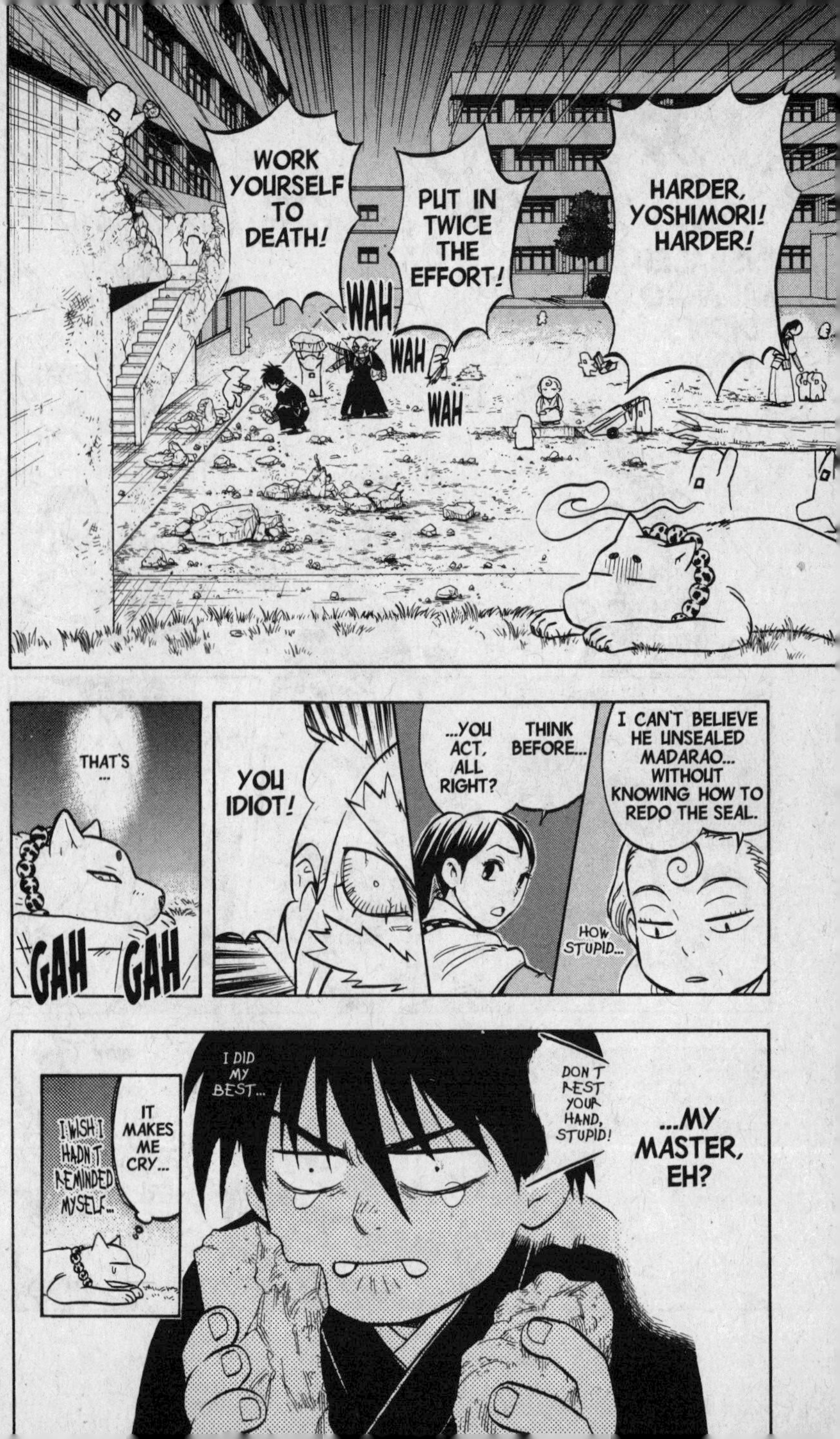
HARDER, YOSHIMORI! HARDER!
PUT IN TWICE THE EFFORT!
WORK YOURSELF TO DEATH!
WAH
WAH
WAH
I CAN'T BELIEVE HE UNSEALED MADARAO... WITHOUT KNOWING HOW TO REDO THE SEAL.
THINK BEFORE...
...YOU ACT, ALL RIGHT?
YOU IDIOT!
HOW STUPID...
THAT'S ...
GAH GAH
...MY MASTER, EH?
DON'T REST YOUR HAND, STUPID!
I DID MY BEST...
IT MAKES ME CRY...
I WISH I HADN'T REMINDED MYSELF...

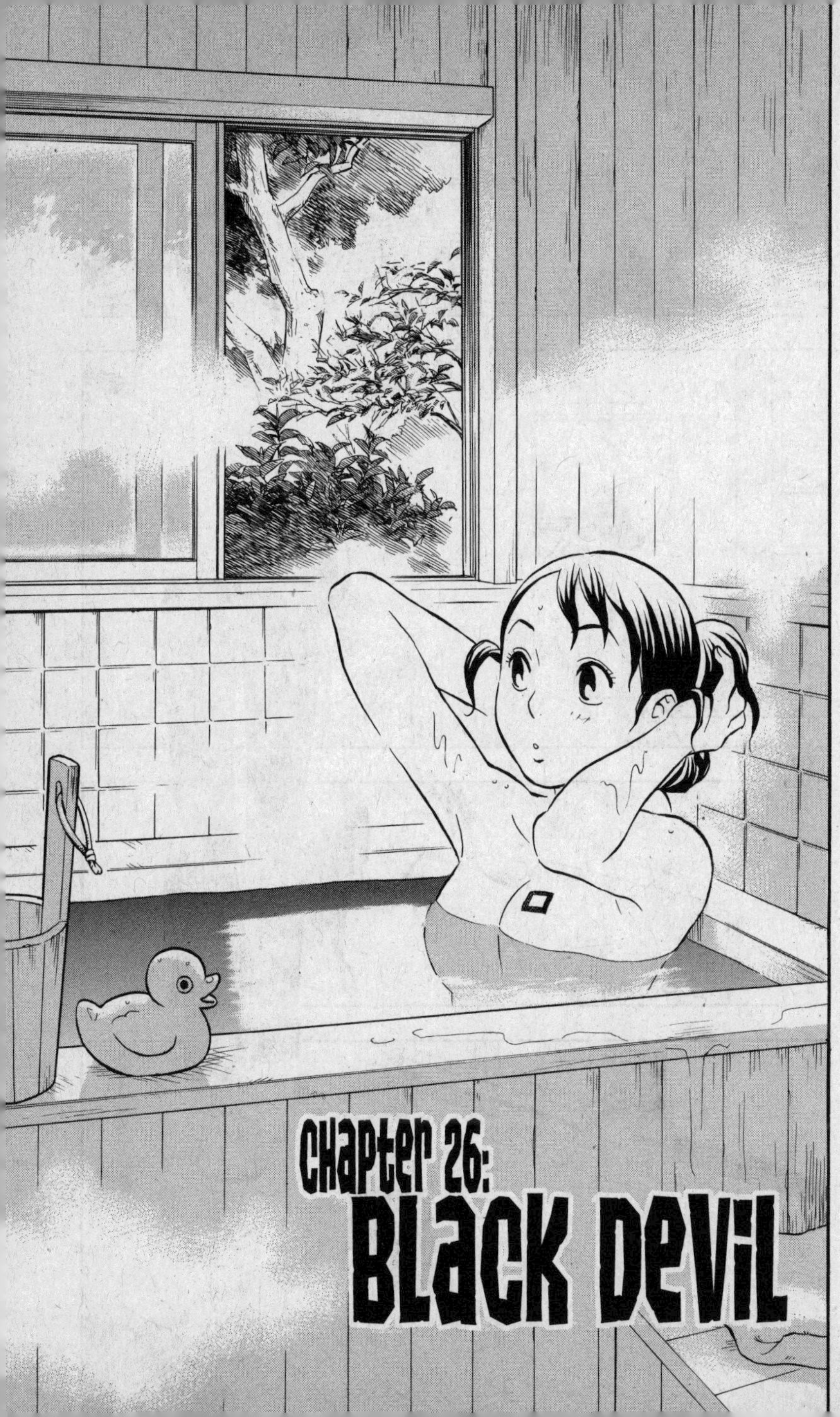
CHAPTER 26:
BLACK DEVIL

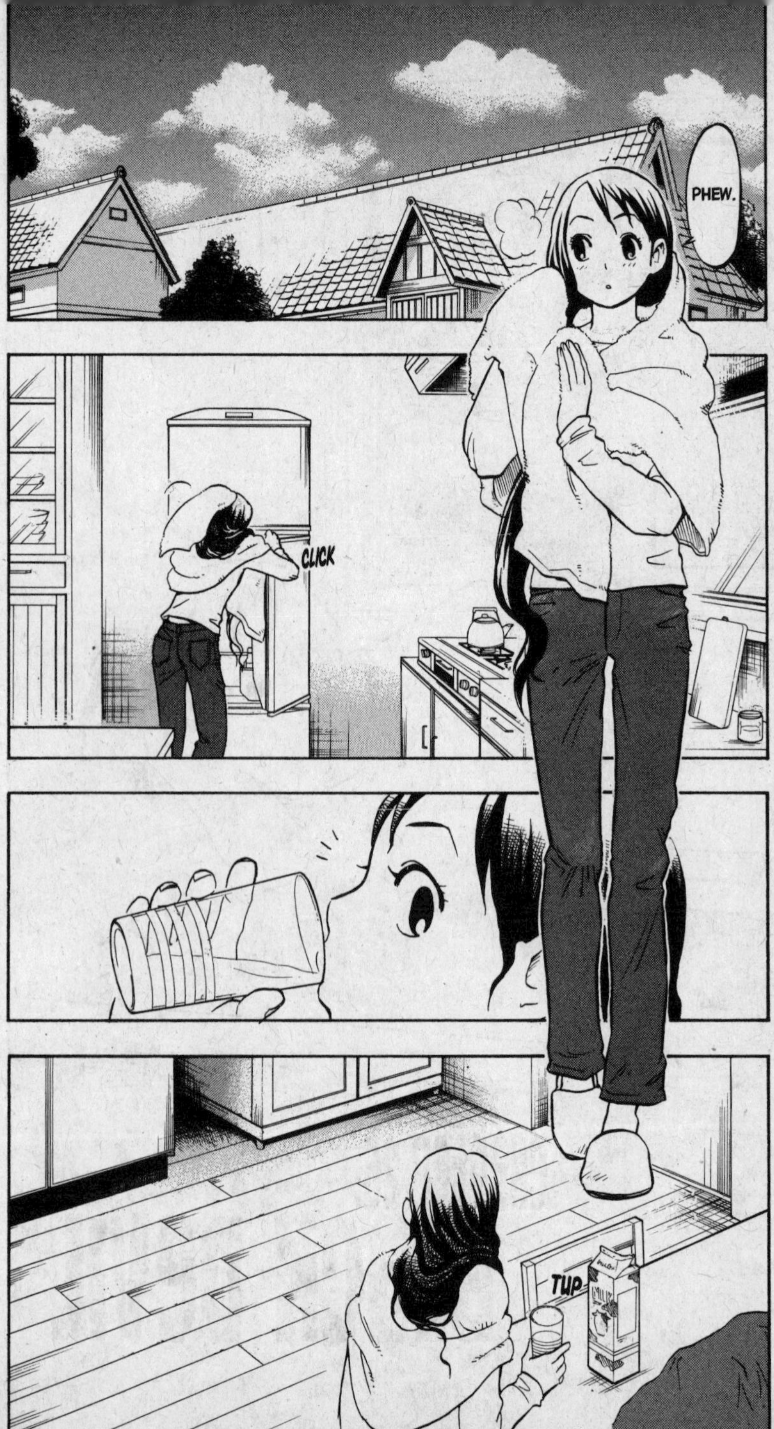
PHEW.
CLICK
TUP

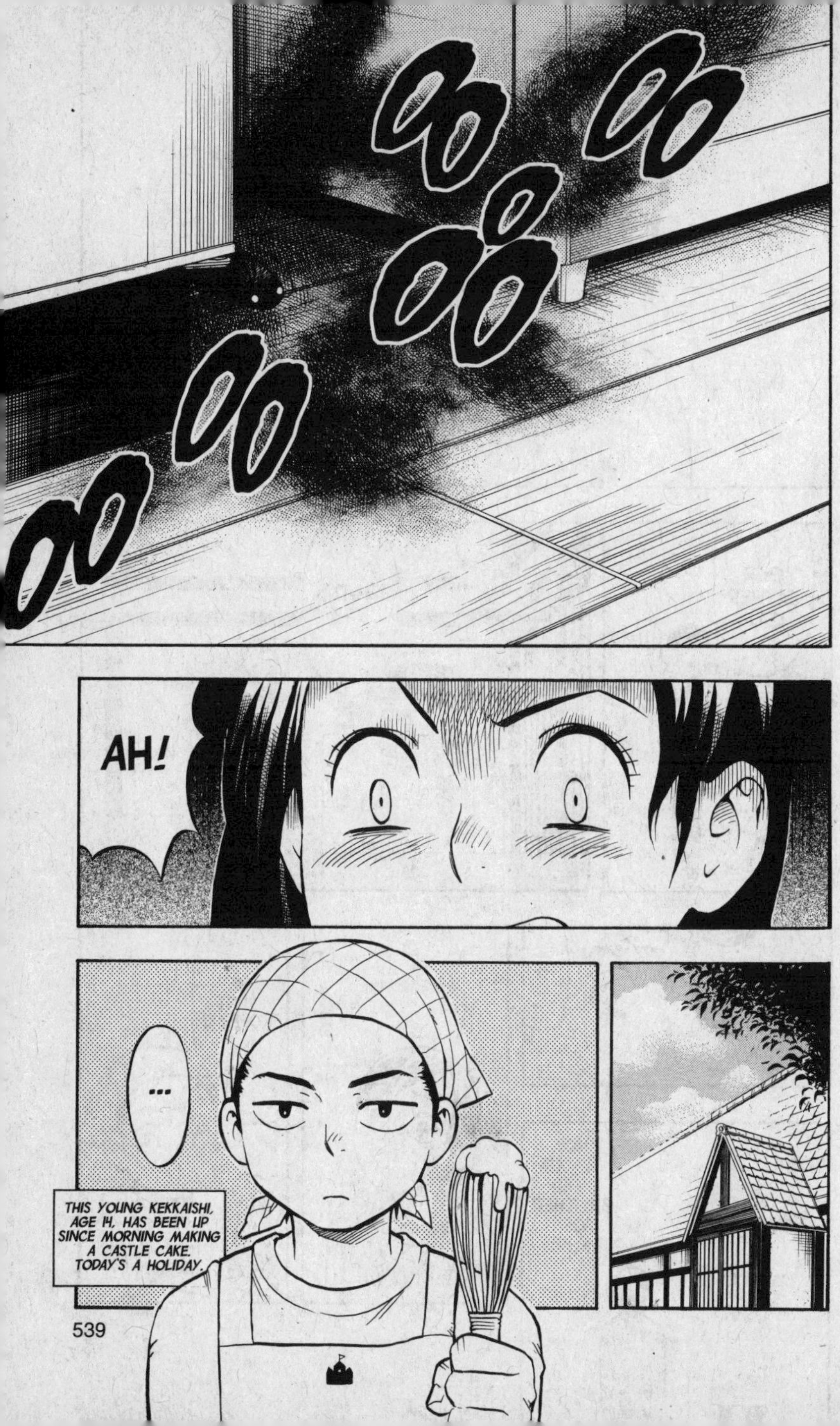
AH!
...
THIS YOUNG KEKKAISHI, AGE 14, HAS BEEN UP SINCE MORNING MAKING A CASTLE CAKE. TODAY'S A HOLIDAY.

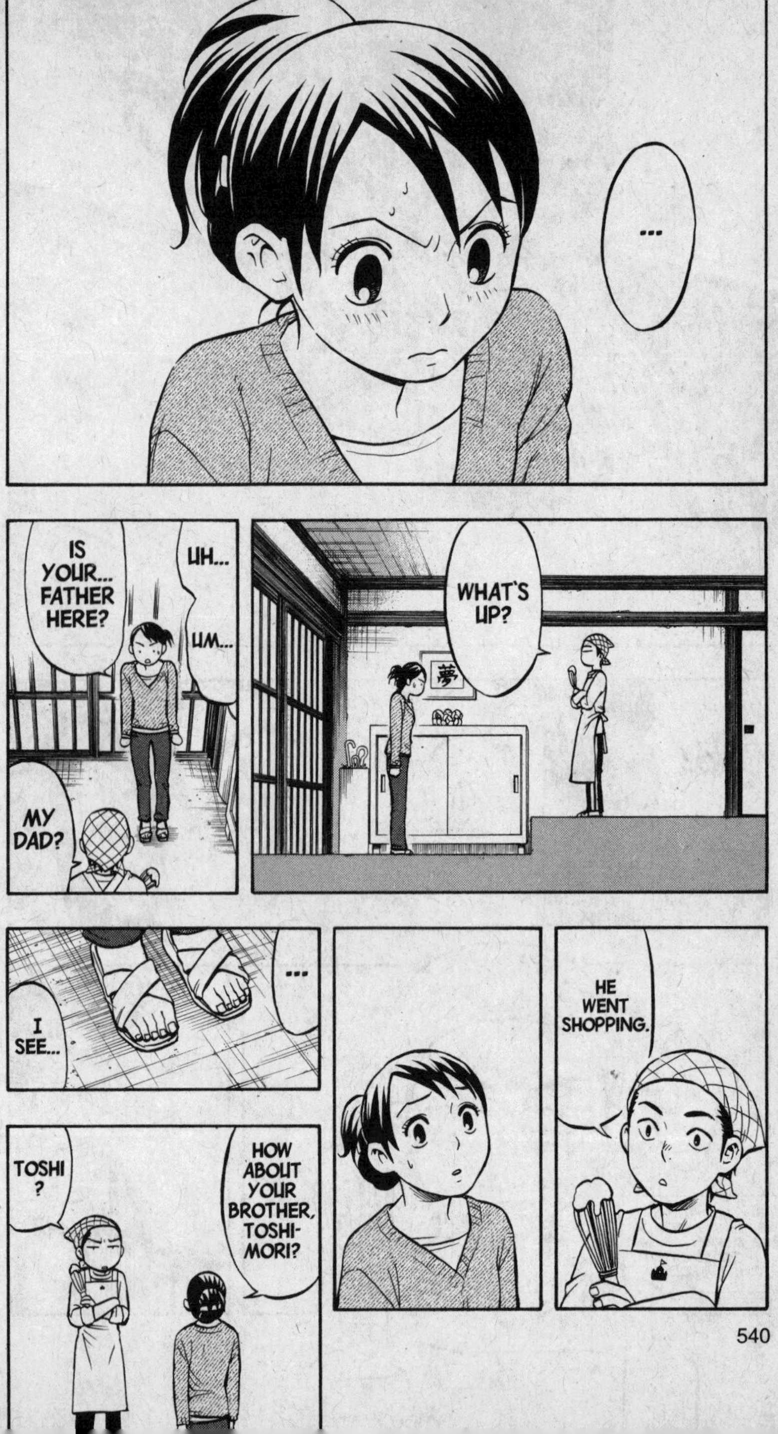
...
WHAT'S UP?
UH...
UM...
IS YOUR... FATHER HERE?
MY DAD?
HE WENT SHOPPING.
...
I SEE...
HOW ABOUT YOUR BROTHER, TOSHI-MORI?
TOSHI?

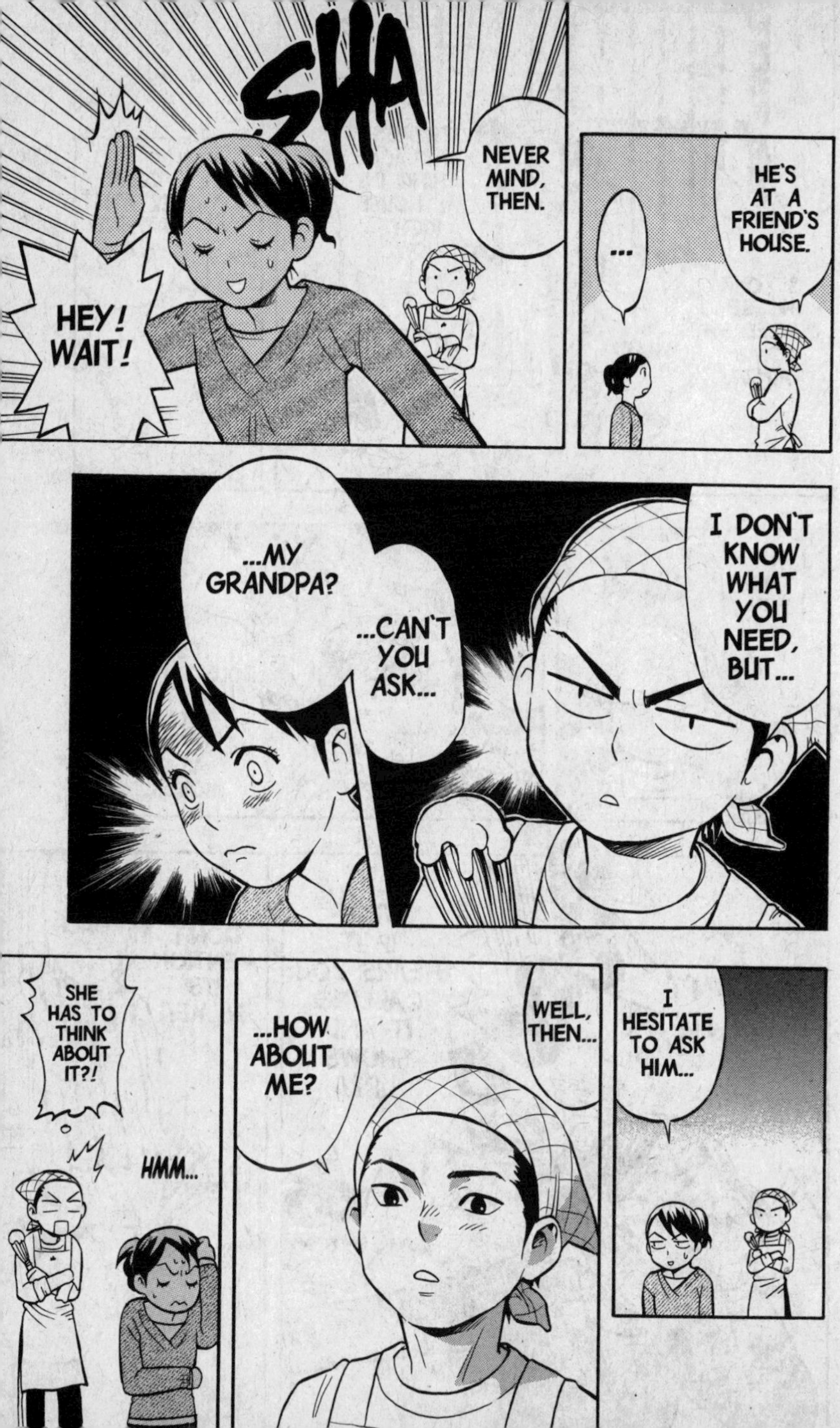
HE'S AT A FRIEND'S HOUSE.
...
NEVER MIND, THEN.
SHA
HEY! WAIT!
I DON'T KNOW WHAT YOU NEED, BUT...
...CAN'T YOU ASK...
...MY GRANDPA?
I HESITATE TO ASK HIM...
WELL, THEN...
...HOW ABOUT ME?
SHE HAS TO THINK ABOUT IT?!
HMM...

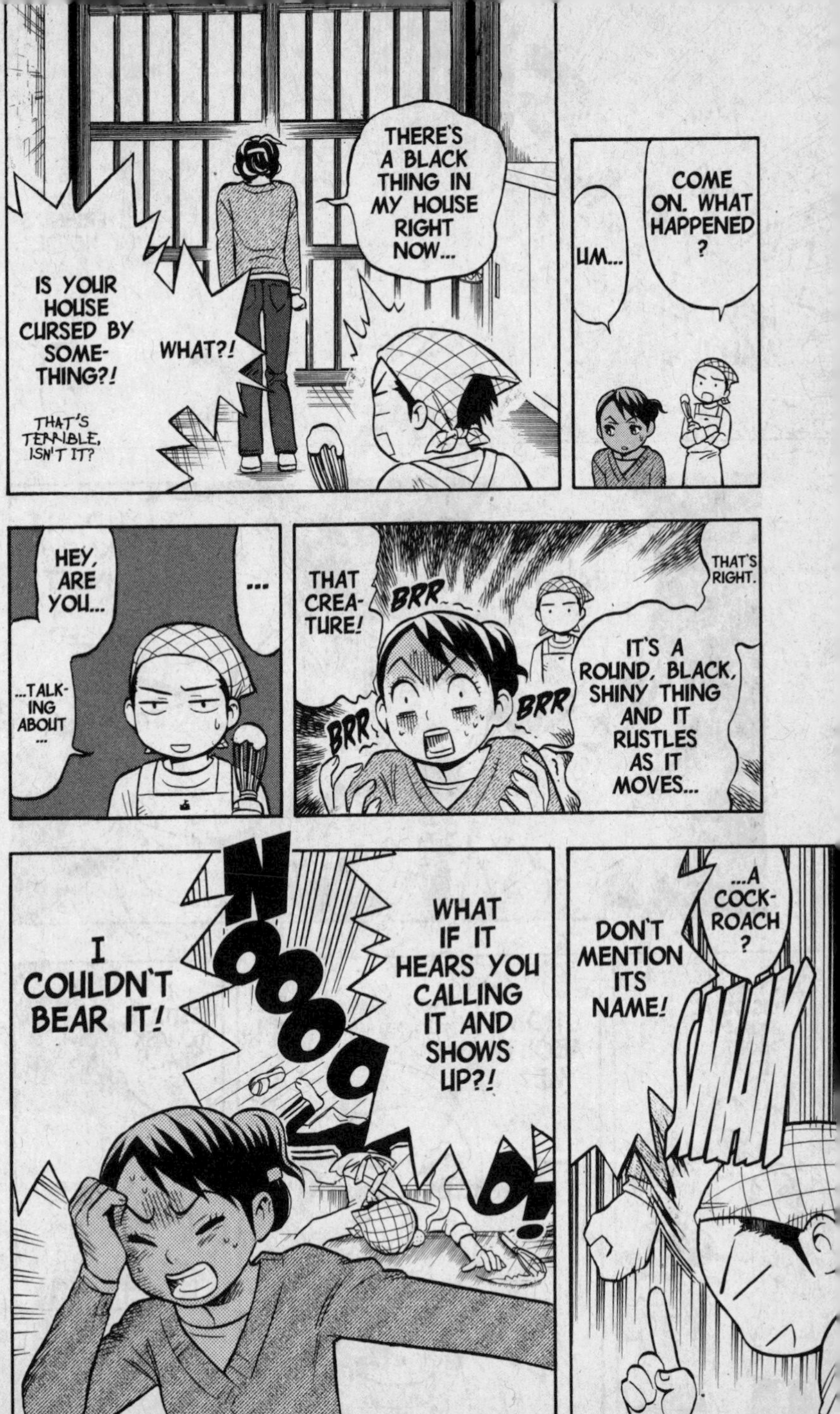
COME ON. WHAT HAPPENED?
UM...
THERE'S A BLACK THING IN MY HOUSE RIGHT NOW...
WHAT?!
IS YOUR HOUSE CURSED BY SOME-THING?!
THAT'S TERRIBLE, ISN'T IT?
THAT'S RIGHT.
IT'S A ROUND, BLACK, SHINY THING AND IT RUSTLES AS IT MOVES...
THAT CREA-TURE!
BRR
BRR
BRR
...
HEY, ARE YOU...
...TALK-ING ABOUT ...
...A COCK-ROACH?
DON'T MENTION ITS NAME!
WHAM
WHAT IF IT HEARS YOU CALLING IT AND SHOWS UP?!
NOOOO!
I COULDN'T BEAR IT!

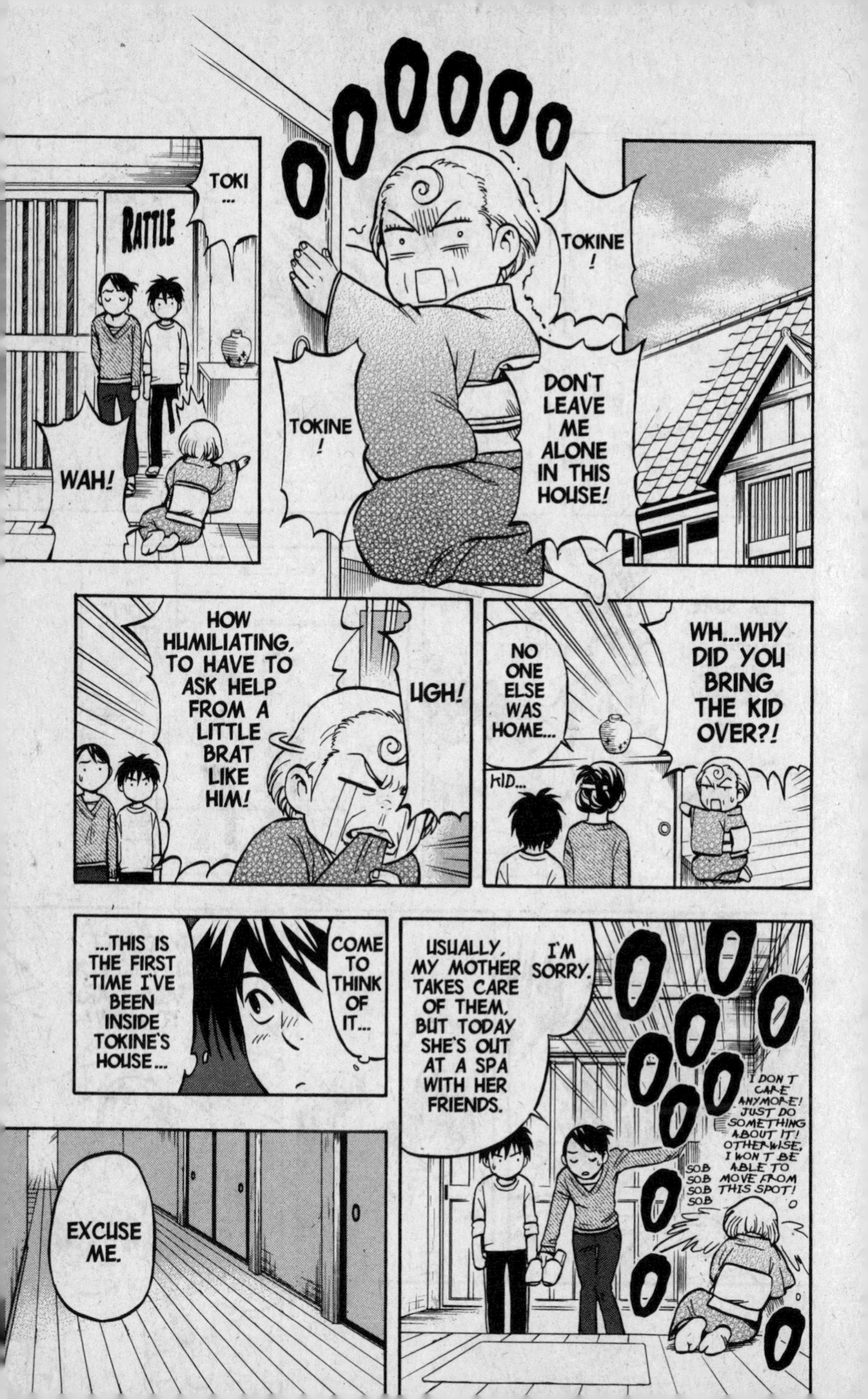
TOKINE!
DON'T LEAVE ME ALONE IN THIS HOUSE!
OOOOOOO
TOKINE!
TOKI...
RATTLE
WAH!
WH...WHY DID YOU BRING THE KID OVER?!
NO ONE ELSE WAS HOME...
KID...
UGH!
HOW HUMILIATING, TO HAVE TO ASK HELP FROM A LITTLE BRAT LIKE HIM!
I'M SORRY.
USUALLY, MY MOTHER TAKES CARE OF THEM, BUT TODAY SHE'S OUT AT A SPA WITH HER FRIENDS.
I DON'T CARE ANYMORE! JUST DO SOMETHING ABOUT IT! OTHERWISE, I WON'T BE ABLE TO MOVE FROM THIS SPOT!
SOB SOB SOB SOB
COME TO THINK OF IT...
...THIS IS THE FIRST TIME I'VE BEEN INSIDE TOKINE'S HOUSE...
EXCUSE ME.

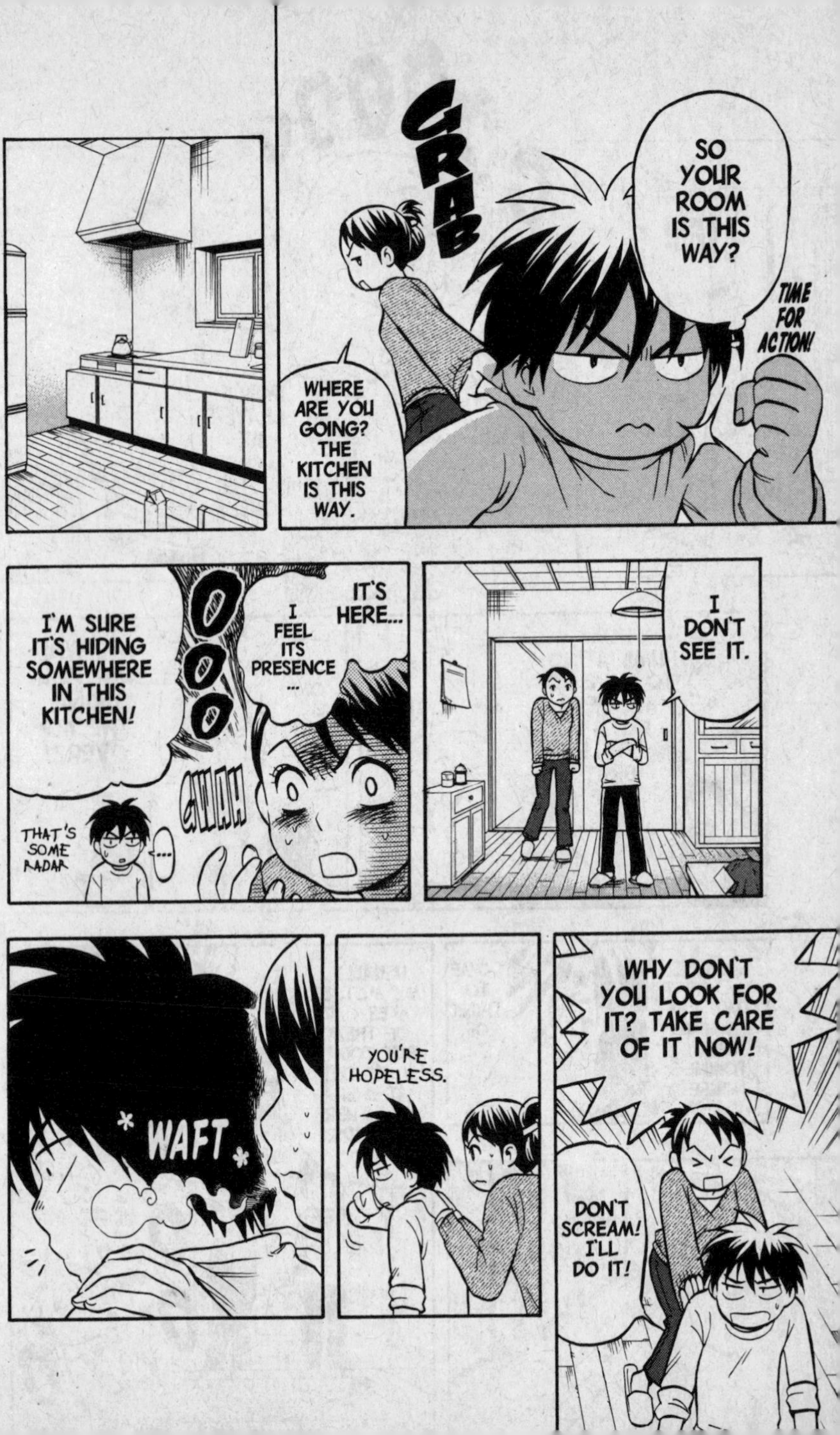
GRAB
SO YOUR ROOM IS THIS WAY?
TIME FOR ACTION!
WHERE ARE YOU GOING? THE KITCHEN IS THIS WAY.
I DON'T SEE IT.
IT'S HERE...
I FEEL ITS PRESENCE...
I'M SURE IT'S HIDING SOMEWHERE IN THIS KITCHEN!
GWAH
...
THAT'S SOME RADAR
WHY DON'T YOU LOOK FOR IT? TAKE CARE OF IT NOW!
DON'T SCREAM! I'LL DO IT!
YOU'RE HOPELESS.
WAFT

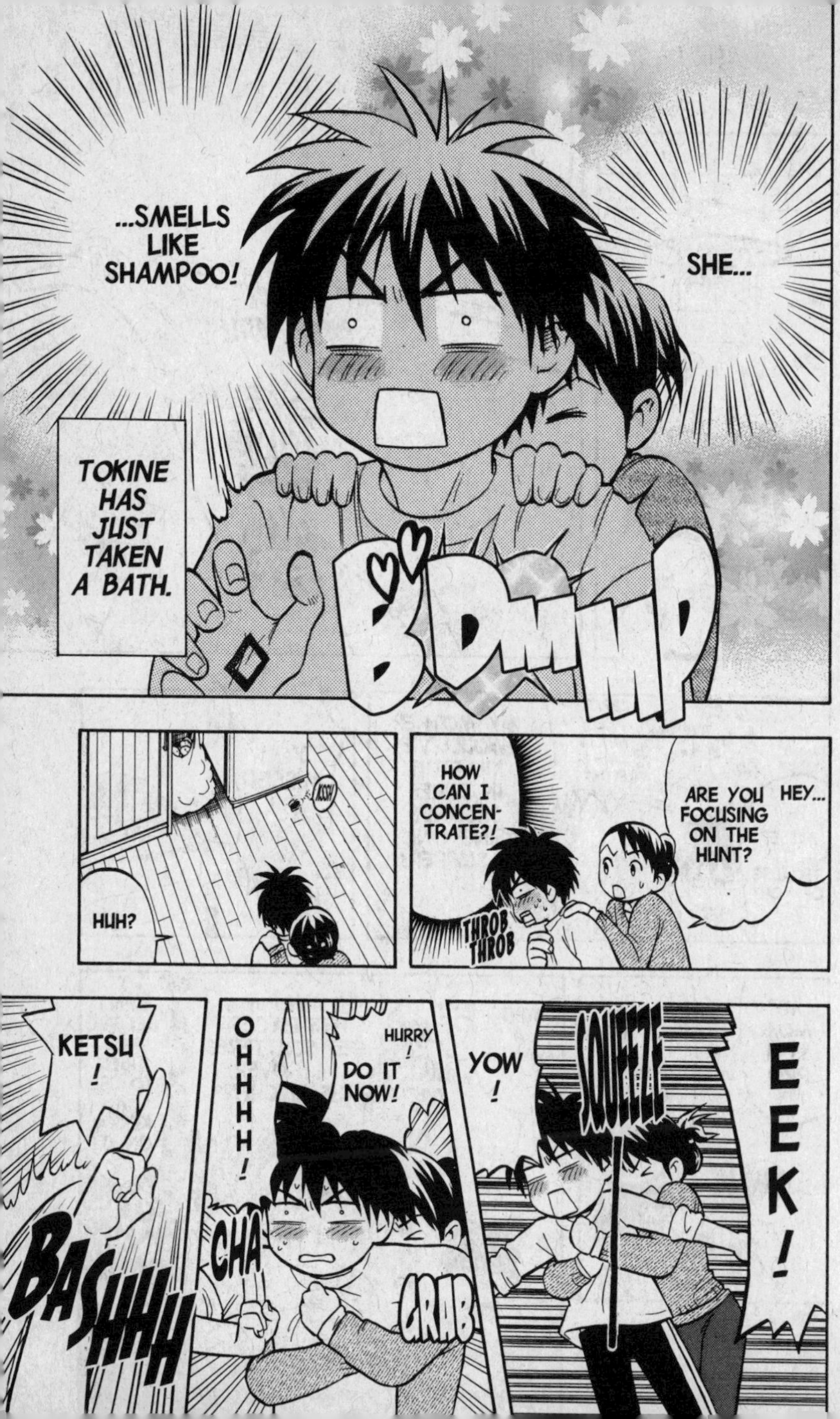
SHE...
...SMELLS LIKE SHAMPOO!
TOKINE HAS JUST TAKEN A BATH.
HEY...
ARE YOU FOCUSING ON THE HUNT?
HOW CAN I CONCEN-TRATE?!
THROB THROB
KSSH
HUH?
EEK!
SQUEEZE
YOW!
HURRY! DO IT NOW!
OHHHHH!
GRAB
CHA
KETSU!
BASHHH

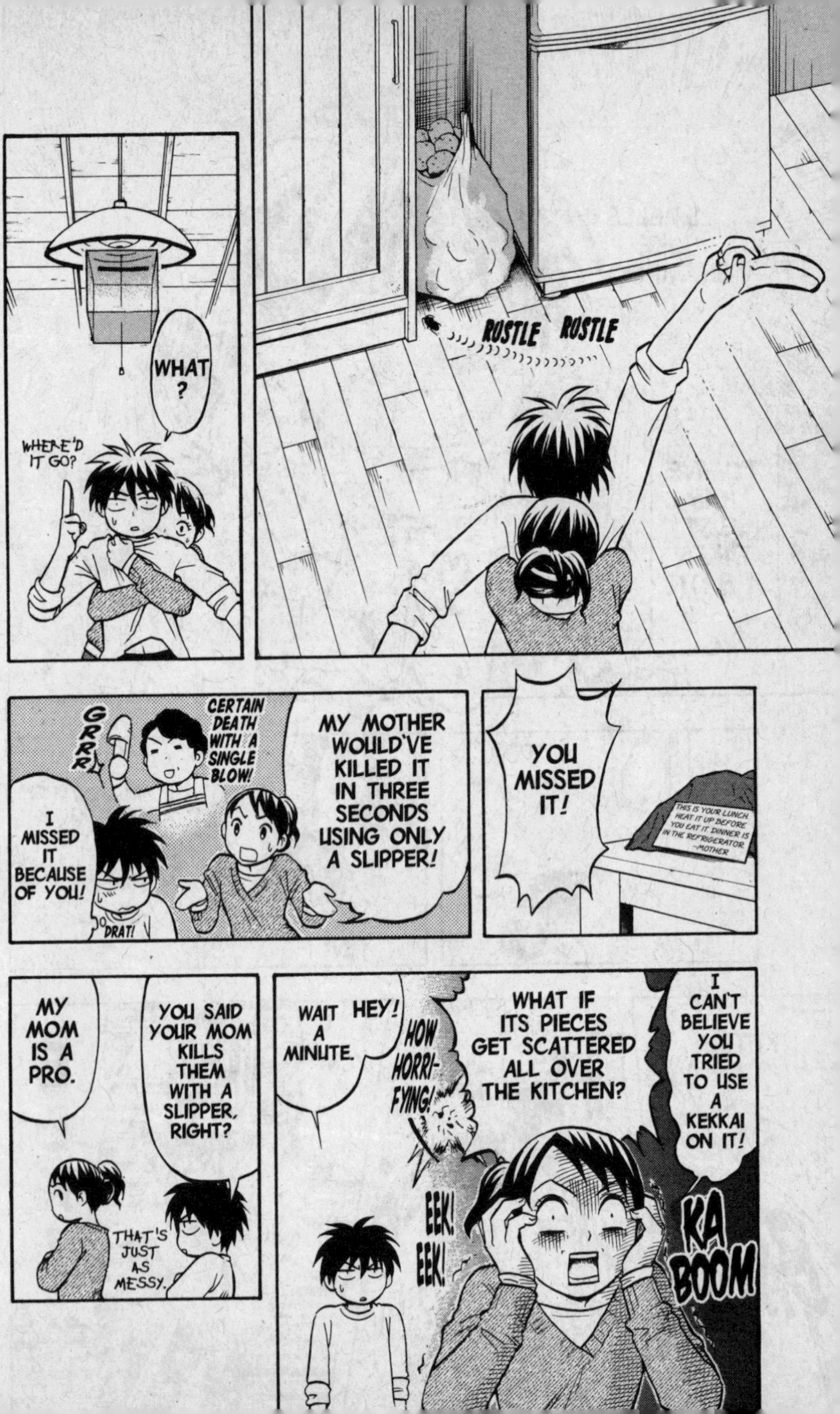
RUSTLE RUSTLE
WHAT ?
WHERE'D IT GO?
YOU MISSED IT!
THIS IS YOUR LUNCH. HEAT IT UP BEFORE YOU EAT IT. DINNER IS IN THE REFRIGERATOR. ~MOTHER
MY MOTHER WOULD'VE KILLED IT IN THREE SECONDS USING ONLY A SLIPPER!
CERTAIN DEATH WITH A SINGLE BLOW!
GRRR
I MISSED IT BECAUSE OF YOU!
DRAT!
I CAN'T BELIEVE YOU TRIED TO USE A KEKKAI ON IT!
KA BOOM
WHAT IF ITS PIECES GET SCATTERED ALL OVER THE KITCHEN?
HOW HORRI-FYING!
EEK! EEK!
HEY!
WAIT A MINUTE.
YOU SAID YOUR MOM KILLS THEM WITH A SLIPPER, RIGHT?
MY MOM IS A PRO.
THAT'S JUST AS MESSY.

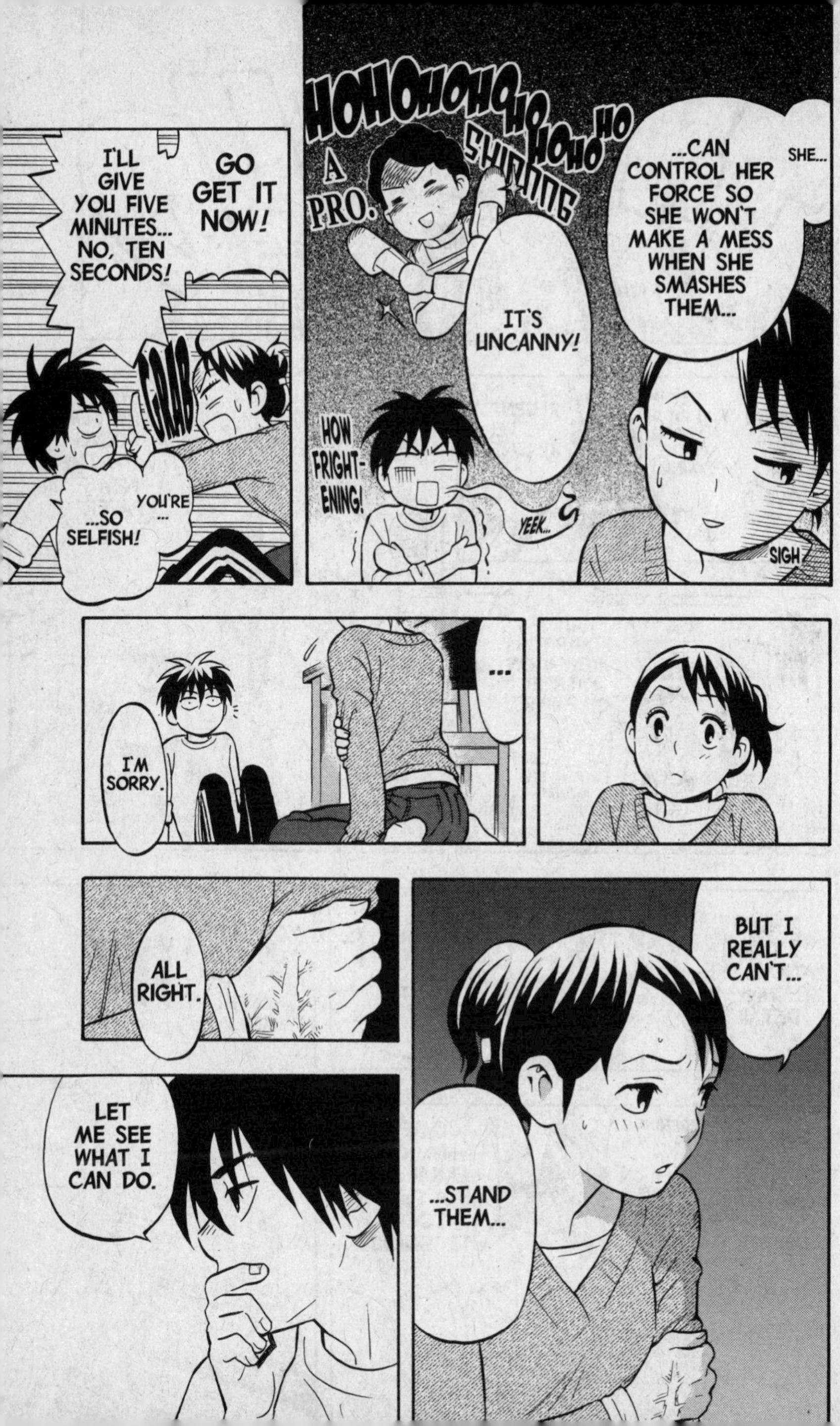
SHE...
...CAN CONTROL HER FORCE SO SHE WON'T MAKE A MESS WHEN SHE SMASHES THEM...
HOHOHOHOHOHOHOHO
A PRO.
SHINING
IT'S UNCANNY!
HOW FRIGHT-ENING!
YEEK...
SIGH
GO GET IT NOW!
I'LL GIVE YOU FIVE MINUTES... NO, TEN SECONDS!
GRAB
YOU'RE ...
...SO SELFISH!
...
I'M SORRY.
BUT I REALLY CAN'T...
...STAND THEM...
ALL RIGHT.
LET ME SEE WHAT I CAN DO.

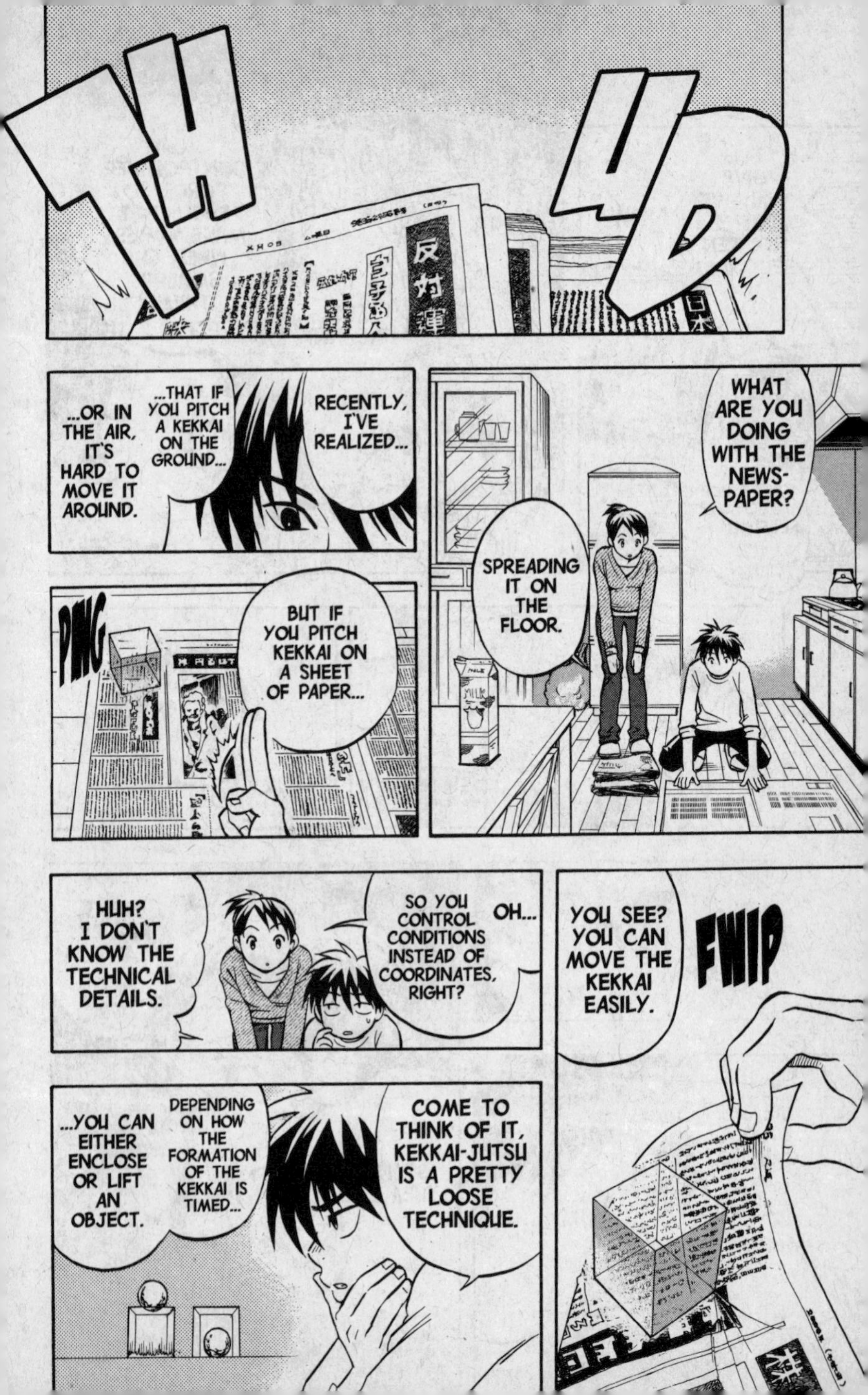
THUD
WHAT ARE YOU DOING WITH THE NEWS-PAPER?
SPREADING IT ON THE FLOOR.
RECENTLY, I'VE REALIZED...
...THAT IF YOU PITCH A KEKKAI ON THE GROUND...
...OR IN THE AIR, IT'S HARD TO MOVE IT AROUND.
BUT IF YOU PITCH KEKKAI ON A SHEET OF PAPER...
PING
YOU SEE? YOU CAN MOVE THE KEKKAI EASILY.
FWIP
OH...
SO YOU CONTROL CONDITIONS INSTEAD OF COORDINATES, RIGHT?
HUH? I DON'T KNOW THE TECHNICAL DETAILS.
COME TO THINK OF IT, KEKKAI-JUTSU IS A PRETTY LOOSE TECHNIQUE.
DEPENDING ON HOW THE FORMATION OF THE KEKKAI IS TIMED...
...YOU CAN EITHER ENCLOSE OR LIFT AN OBJECT.

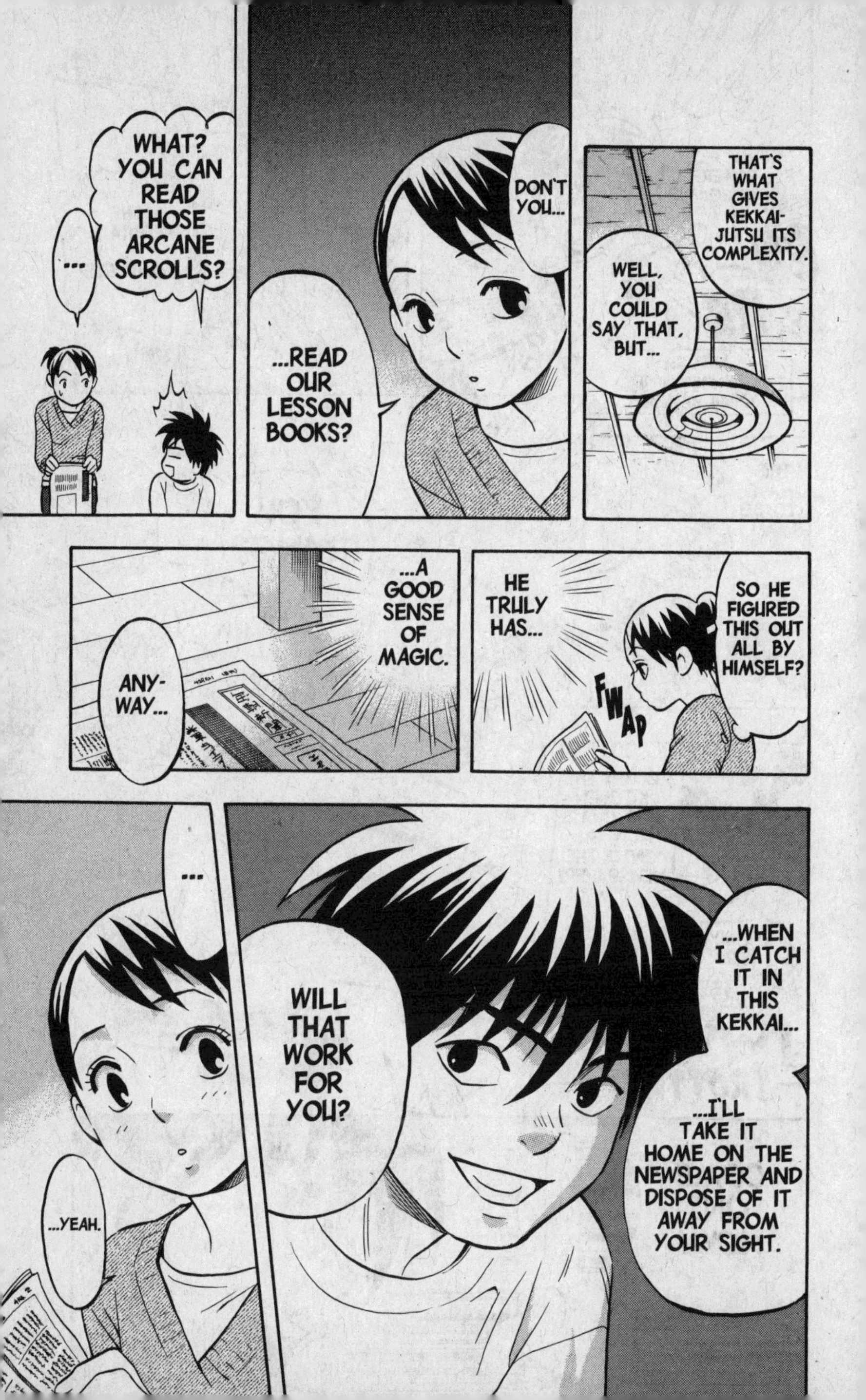
THAT'S WHAT GIVES KEKKAI-JUTSU ITS COMPLEXITY.
WELL, YOU COULD SAY THAT, BUT...
DON'T YOU...
...READ OUR LESSON BOOKS?
WHAT? YOU CAN READ THOSE ARCANE SCROLLS?
...
SO HE FIGURED THIS OUT ALL BY HIMSELF?
FWAP
HE TRULY HAS...
...A GOOD SENSE OF MAGIC.
ANY-WAY...
...WHEN I CATCH IT IN THIS KEKKAI...
...I'LL TAKE IT HOME ON THE NEWSPAPER AND DISPOSE OF IT AWAY FROM YOUR SIGHT.
WILL THAT WORK FOR YOU?
...
...YEAH.

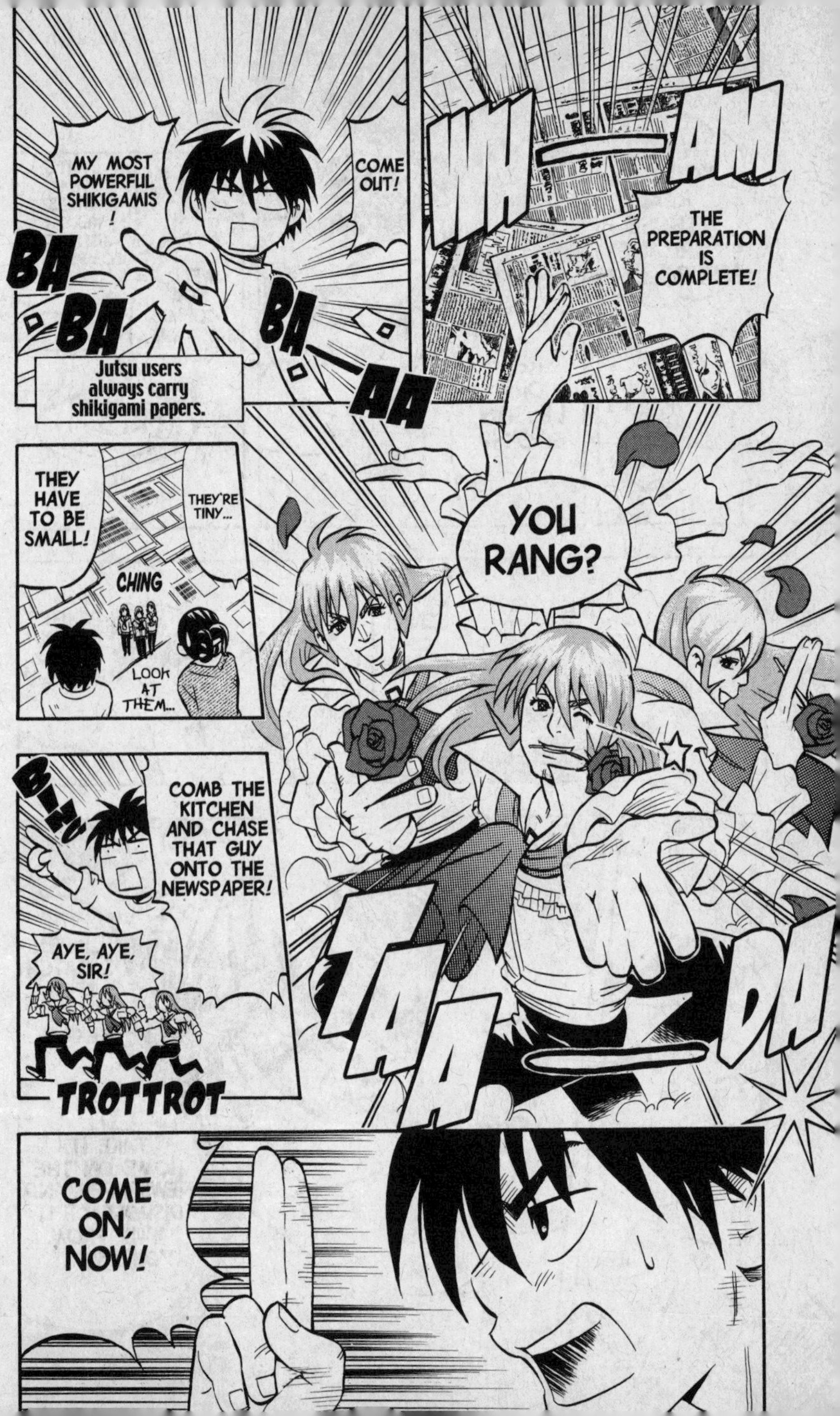
WHH—AM
THE PREPARATION IS COMPLETE!
COME OUT!
MY MOST POWERFUL SHIKIGAMIS!
BA BA BA—AA
Jutsu users always carry shikigami papers.
YOU RANG?
TA A—DA
THEY'RE TINY...
THEY HAVE TO BE SMALL!
CHING
LOOK AT THEM...
COMB THE KITCHEN AND CHASE THAT GUY ONTO THE NEWSPAPER!
BIZU
AYE, AYE, SIR!
TROTTROT
COME ON, NOW!

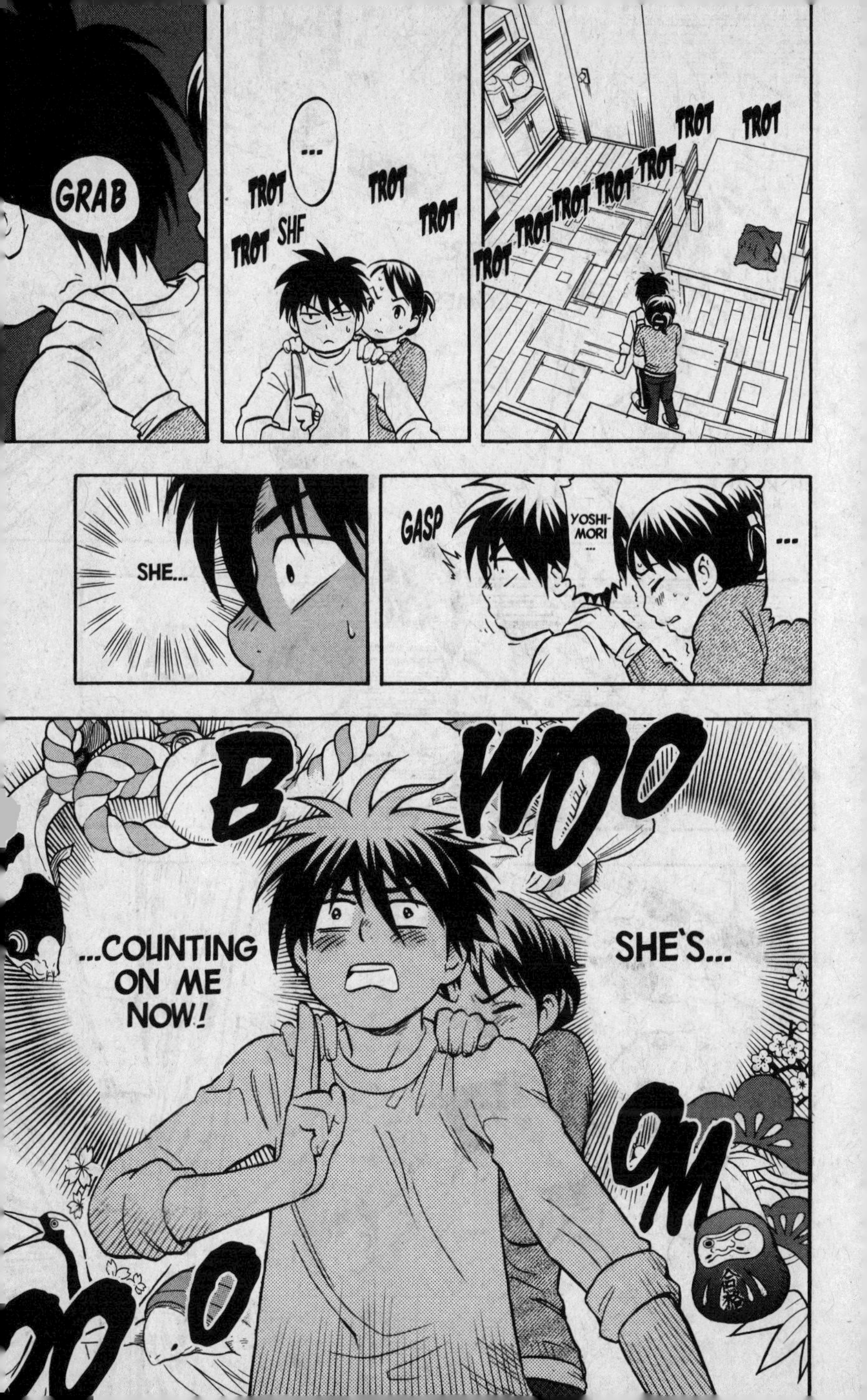
TROT TROT TROT TROT TROT TROT TROT TROT
...
TROT
TROT
SHF
TROT
TROT
GRAB
GASP
YOSHI-MORI...
...
SHE...
BWOOOM
SHE'S...
...COUNTING ON ME NOW!

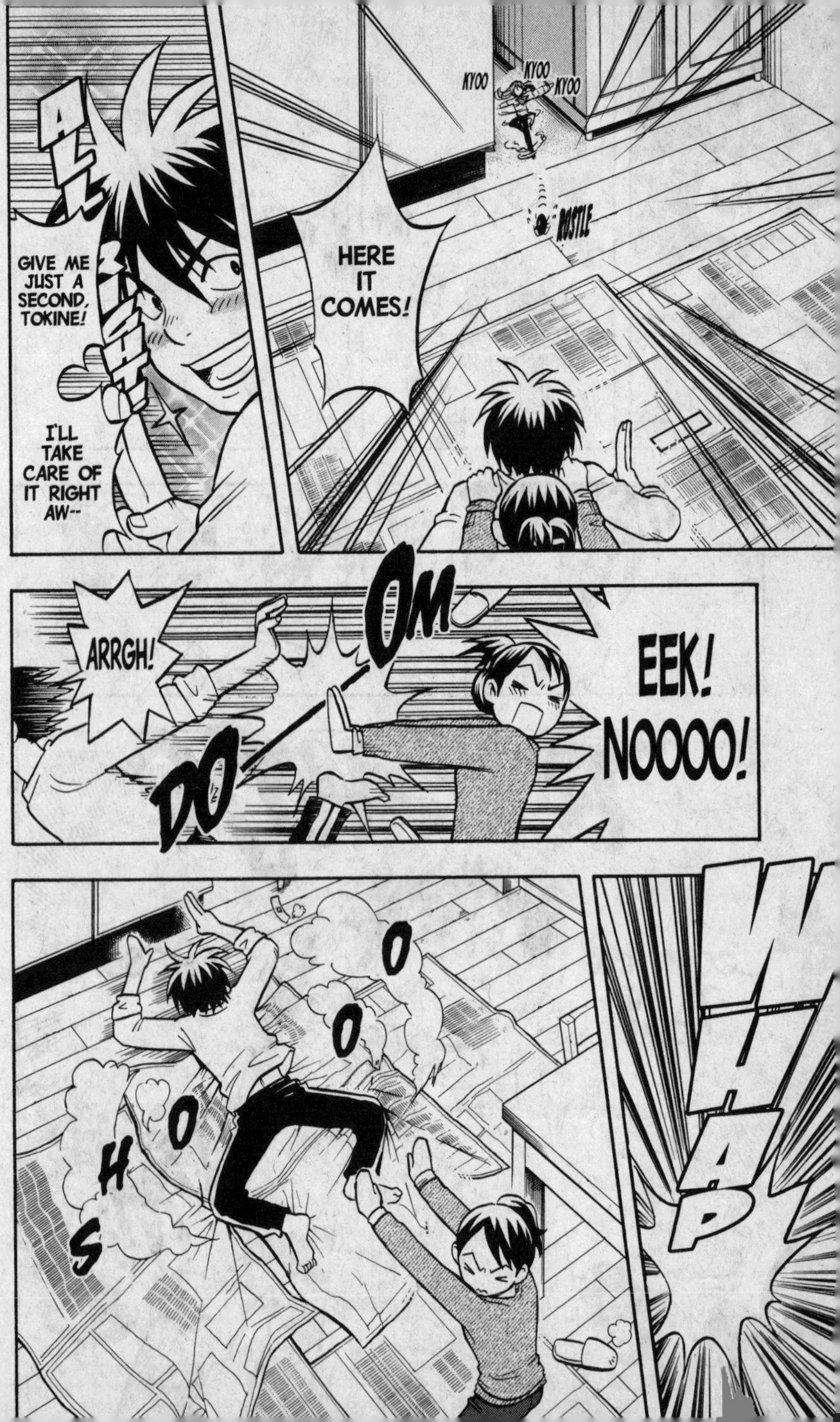
KYOO
KYOO
KYOO
RUSTLE
HERE IT COMES!
ALL RIGHT!
GIVE ME JUST A SECOND, TOKINE!
I'LL TAKE CARE OF IT RIGHT AW--
EEK! NOOOO!
DOOM
ARRGH!
WHAP
SHOOOO

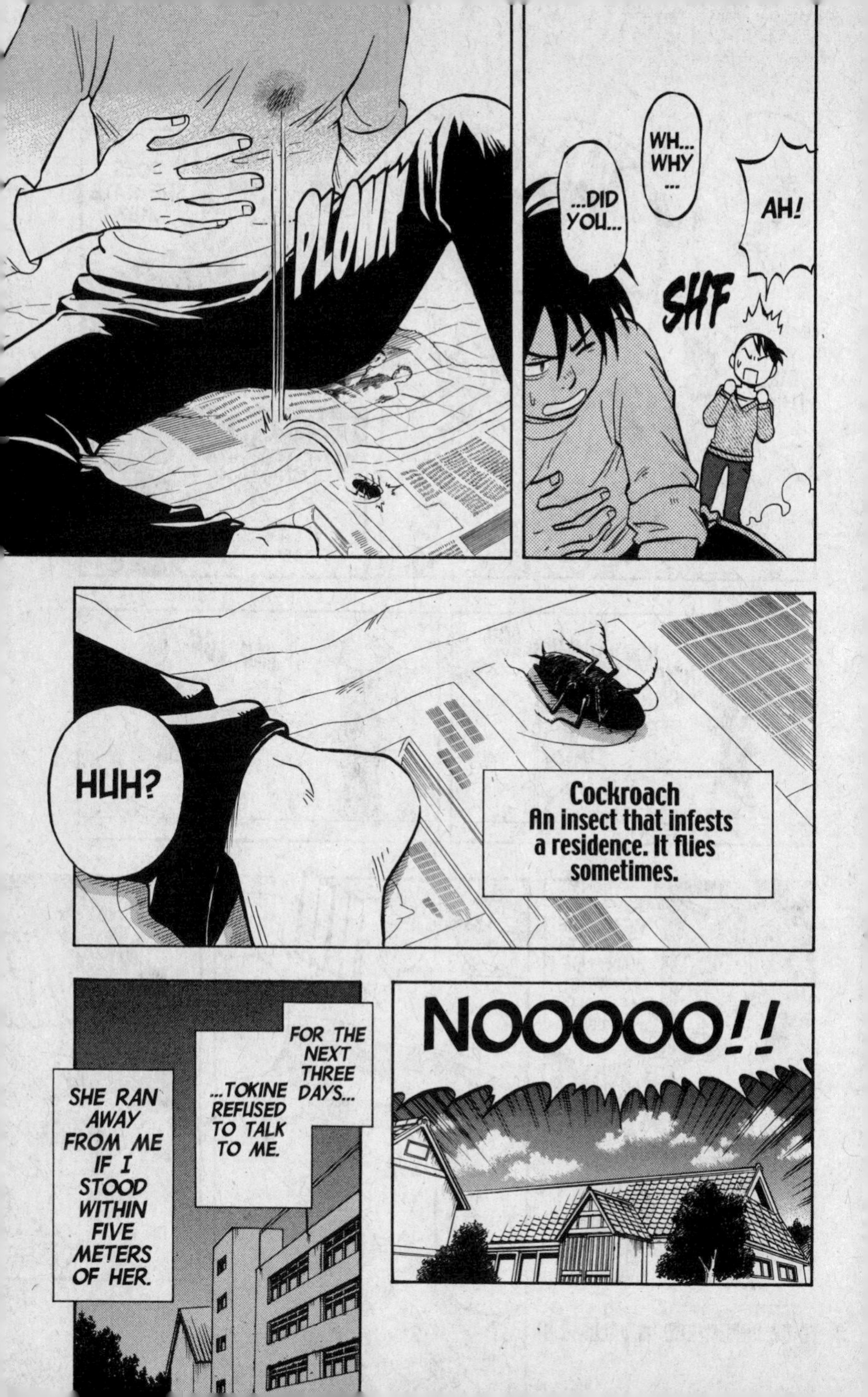
AH!
SHF
WH... WHY ...
...DID YOU...
PLONK
HUH?
Cockroach
An insect that infests a residence. It flies sometimes.
NOOOOO!!
FOR THE NEXT THREE DAYS...
...TOKINE REFUSED TO TALK TO ME.
SHE RAN AWAY FROM ME IF I STOOD WITHIN FIVE METERS OF HER.

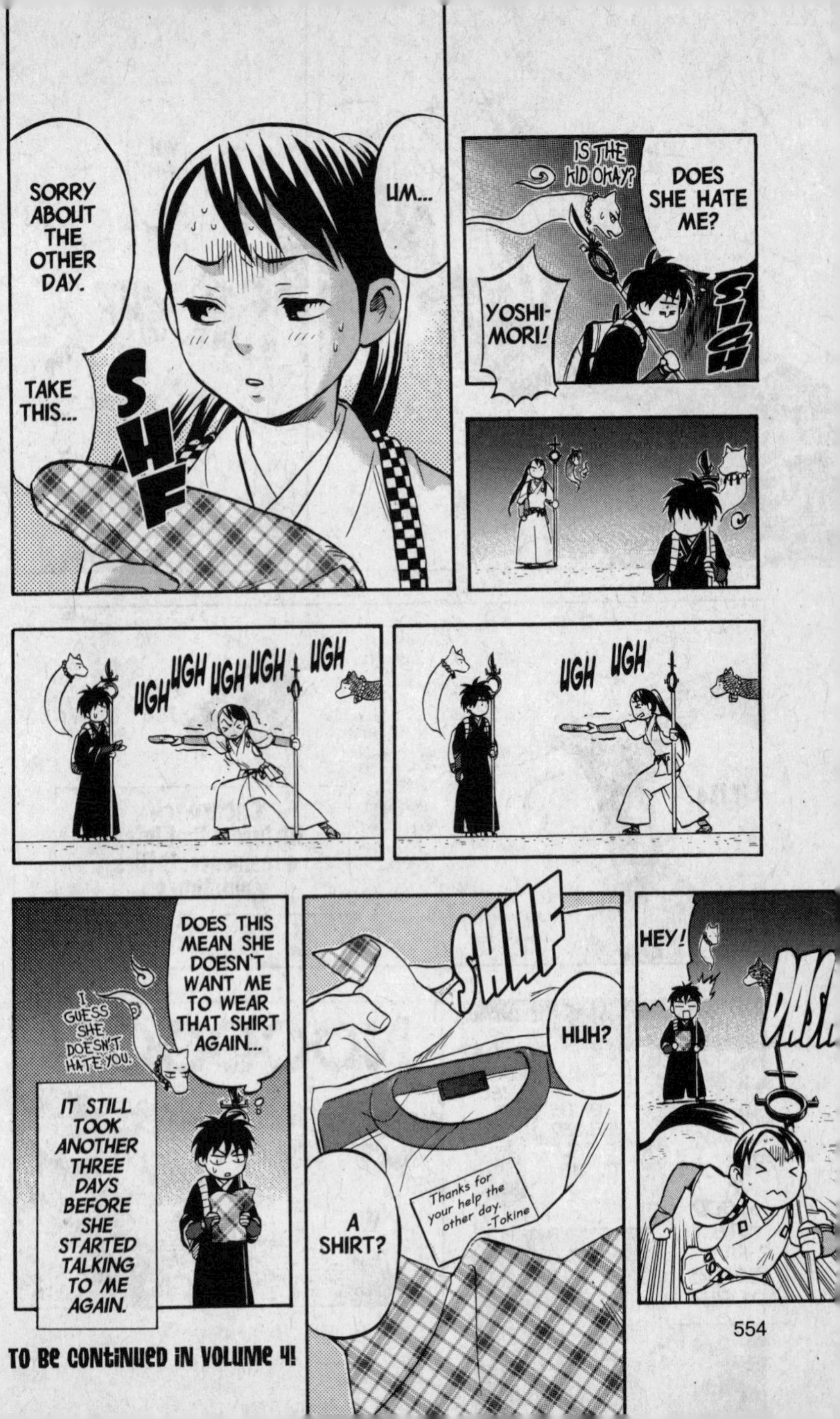
IS THE KID OKAY?
DOES SHE HATE ME?
SIGH
YOSHI-MORI!
UM...
SORRY ABOUT THE OTHER DAY.
TAKE THIS...
SHF
UGH UGH
UGH UGH UGH UGH UGH
HEY!
DASH
SHUF
HUH?
Thanks for your help the other day. -Tokine
A SHIRT?
DOES THIS MEAN SHE DOESN'T WANT ME TO WEAR THAT SHIRT AGAIN...
I GUESS SHE DOESN'T HATE YOU.
IT STILL TOOK ANOTHER THREE DAYS BEFORE SHE STARTED TALKING TO ME AGAIN.

TO BE CONTINUED IN VOLUME 4!

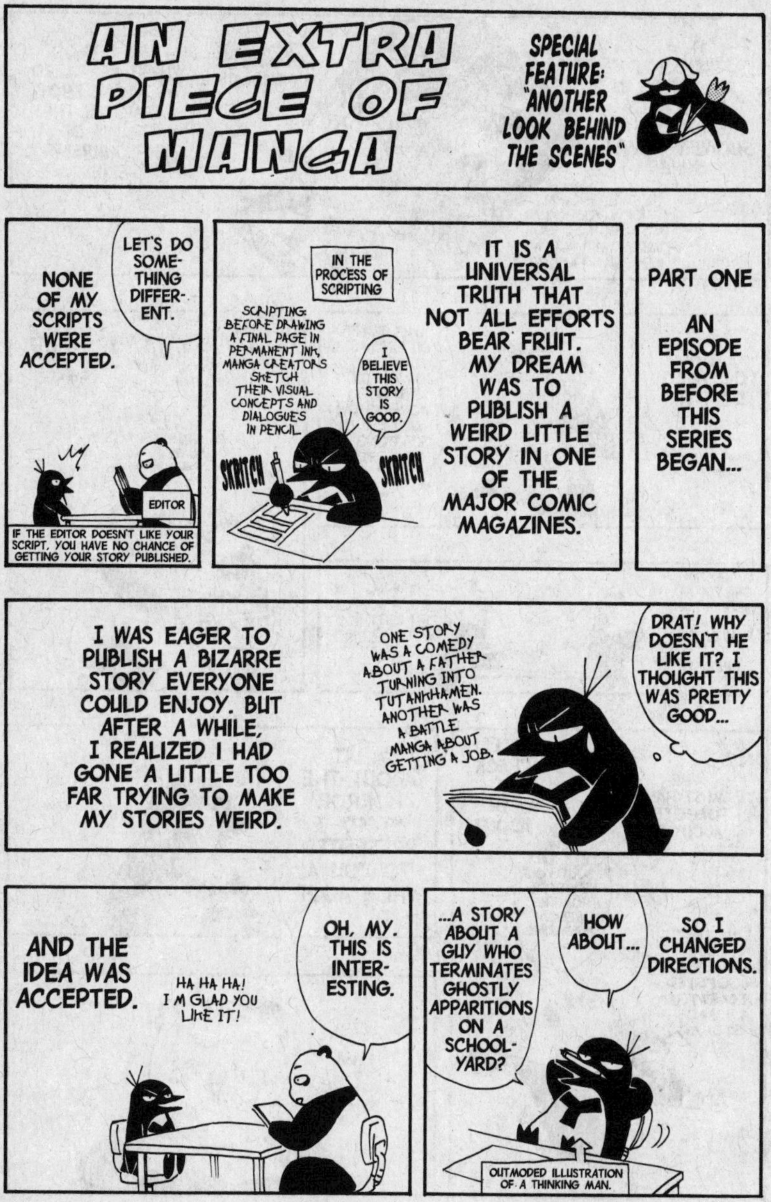
AN EXTRA PIECE OF MANGA
SPECIAL FEATURE: "ANOTHER LOOK BEHIND THE SCENES"
PART ONE
AN EPISODE FROM BEFORE THIS SERIES BEGAN...
IT IS A UNIVERSAL TRUTH THAT NOT ALL EFFORTS BEAR FRUIT. MY DREAM WAS TO PUBLISH A WEIRD LITTLE STORY IN ONE OF THE MAJOR COMIC MAGAZINES.
IN THE PROCESS OF SCRIPTING
SCRIPTING: BEFORE DRAWING A FINAL PAGE IN PERMANENT INK, MANGA CREATORS SKETCH THEIR VISUAL CONCEPTS AND DIALOGUES IN PENCIL.
I BELIEVE THIS STORY IS GOOD.
SKRITCH
SKRITCH
LET'S DO SOMETHING DIFFERENT.
NONE OF MY SCRIPTS WERE ACCEPTED.
EDITOR
IF THE EDITOR DOESN'T LIKE YOUR SCRIPT, YOU HAVE NO CHANCE OF GETTING YOUR STORY PUBLISHED.
DRAT! WHY DOESN'T HE LIKE IT? I THOUGHT THIS WAS PRETTY GOOD...
ONE STORY WAS A COMEDY ABOUT A FATHER TURNING INTO TUTANKHAMEN. ANOTHER WAS A BATTLE MANGA ABOUT GETTING A JOB.
I WAS EAGER TO PUBLISH A BIZARRE STORY EVERYONE COULD ENJOY. BUT AFTER A WHILE, I REALIZED I HAD GONE A LITTLE TOO FAR TRYING TO MAKE MY STORIES WEIRD.
SO I CHANGED DIRECTIONS.
HOW ABOUT...
...A STORY ABOUT A GUY WHO TERMINATES GHOSTLY APPARITIONS ON A SCHOOLYARD?
OUTMODED ILLUSTRATION OF A THINKING MAN.
OH, MY. THIS IS INTERESTING.
HA HA HA! I'M GLAD YOU LIKE IT!
AND THE IDEA WAS ACCEPTED.

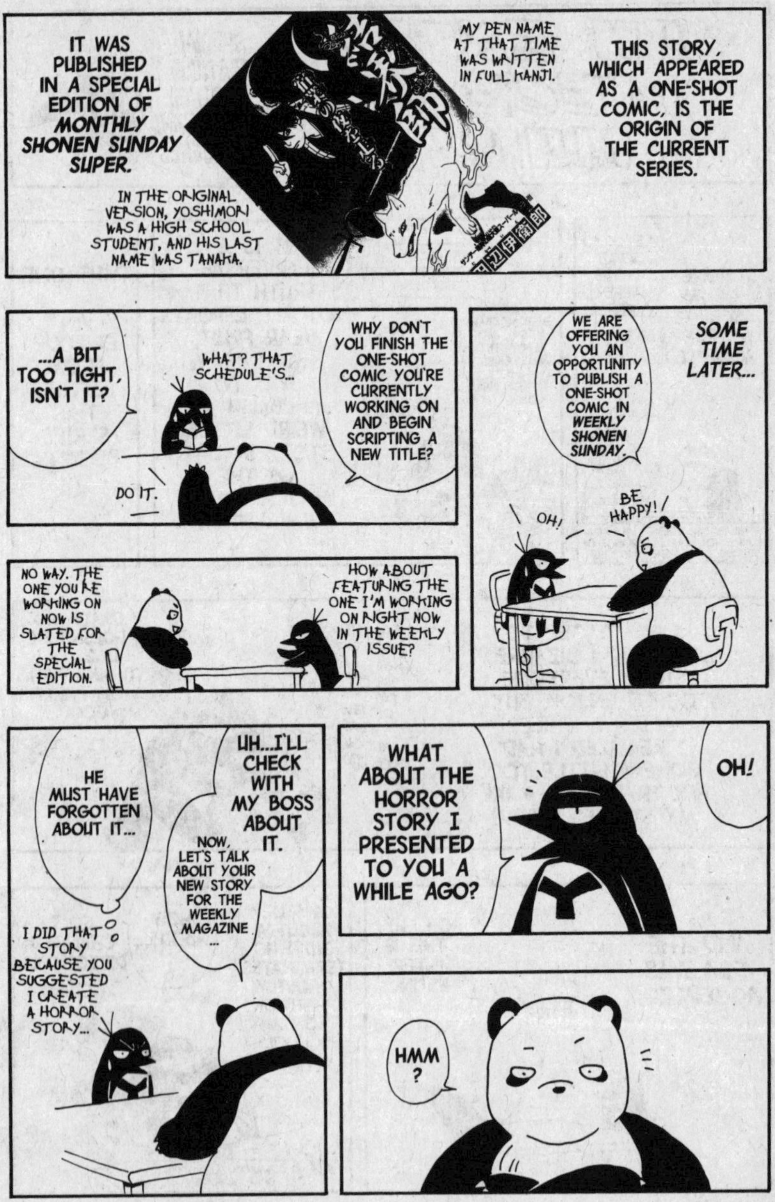
THIS STORY, WHICH APPEARED AS A ONE-SHOT COMIC, IS THE ORIGIN OF THE CURRENT SERIES.
MY PEN NAME AT THAT TIME WAS WRITTEN IN FULL KANJI.
IT WAS PUBLISHED IN A SPECIAL EDITION OF MONTHLY SHONEN SUNDAY SUPER.
IN THE ORIGINAL VERSION, YOSHIMORI WAS A HIGH SCHOOL STUDENT, AND HIS LAST NAME WAS TANAKA.
SOME TIME LATER...
WE ARE OFFERING YOU AN OPPORTUNITY TO PUBLISH A ONE-SHOT COMIC IN WEEKLY SHONEN SUNDAY.
BE HAPPY!!
OH!
WHY DON'T YOU FINISH THE ONE-SHOT COMIC YOU'RE CURRENTLY WORKING ON AND BEGIN SCRIPTING A NEW TITLE?
WHAT? THAT SCHEDULE'S...
...A BIT TOO TIGHT, ISN'T IT?
DO IT.
HOW ABOUT FEATURING THE ONE I'M WORKING ON RIGHT NOW IN THE WEEKLY ISSUE?
NO WAY. THE ONE YOU'RE WORKING ON NOW IS SLATED FOR THE SPECIAL EDITION.
OH!
WHAT ABOUT THE HORROR STORY I PRESENTED TO YOU A WHILE AGO?
HMM?
UH...I'LL CHECK WITH MY BOSS ABOUT IT.
NOW, LET'S TALK ABOUT YOUR NEW STORY FOR THE WEEKLY MAGAZINE...
HE MUST HAVE FORGOTTEN ABOUT IT...
I DID THAT STORY BECAUSE YOU SUGGESTED I CREATE A HORROR STORY...

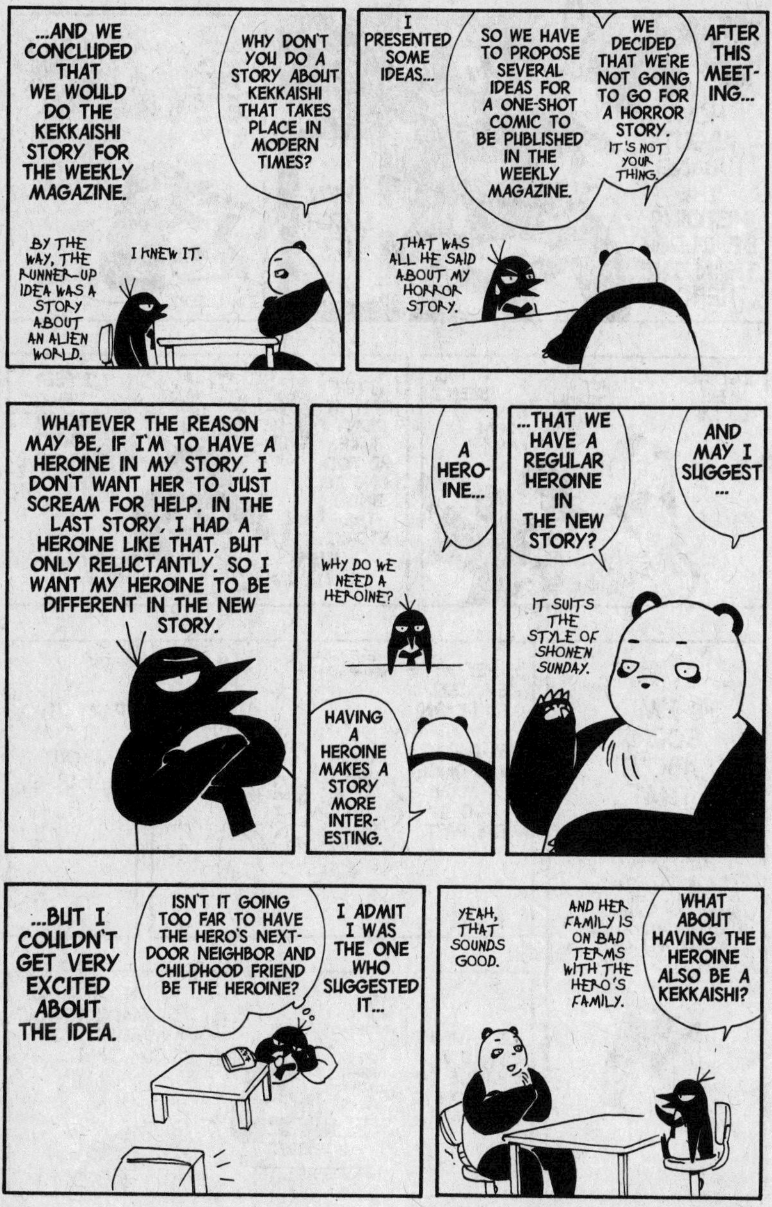
AFTER THIS MEETING...
WE DECIDED THAT WE'RE NOT GOING TO GO FOR A HORROR STORY.
IT'S NOT YOUR THING.
SO WE HAVE TO PROPOSE SEVERAL IDEAS FOR A ONE-SHOT COMIC TO BE PUBLISHED IN THE WEEKLY MAGAZINE.
I PRESENTED SOME IDEAS...
THAT WAS ALL HE SAID ABOUT MY HORROR STORY.
WHY DON'T YOU DO A STORY ABOUT KEKKAISHI THAT TAKES PLACE IN MODERN TIMES?
...AND WE CONCLUDED THAT WE WOULD DO THE KEKKAISHI STORY FOR THE WEEKLY MAGAZINE.
I KNEW IT.
BY THE WAY, THE RUNNER-UP IDEA WAS A STORY ABOUT AN ALIEN WORLD.
AND MAY I SUGGEST...
...THAT WE HAVE A REGULAR HEROINE IN THE NEW STORY?
IT SUITS THE STYLE OF SHONEN SUNDAY.
A HEROINE...
WHY DO WE NEED A HEROINE?
HAVING A HEROINE MAKES A STORY MORE INTERESTING.
WHATEVER THE REASON MAY BE, IF I'M TO HAVE A HEROINE IN MY STORY, I DON'T WANT HER TO JUST SCREAM FOR HELP. IN THE LAST STORY, I HAD A HEROINE LIKE THAT, BUT ONLY RELUCTANTLY. SO I WANT MY HEROINE TO BE DIFFERENT IN THE NEW STORY.
WHAT ABOUT HAVING THE HEROINE ALSO BE A KEKKAISHI?
AND HER FAMILY IS ON BAD TERMS WITH THE HERO'S FAMILY.
YEAH, THAT SOUNDS GOOD.
I ADMIT I WAS THE ONE WHO SUGGESTED IT...
ISN'T IT GOING TOO FAR TO HAVE THE HERO'S NEXT-DOOR NEIGHBOR AND CHILDHOOD FRIEND BE THE HEROINE?
...BUT I COULDN'T GET VERY EXCITED ABOUT THE IDEA.

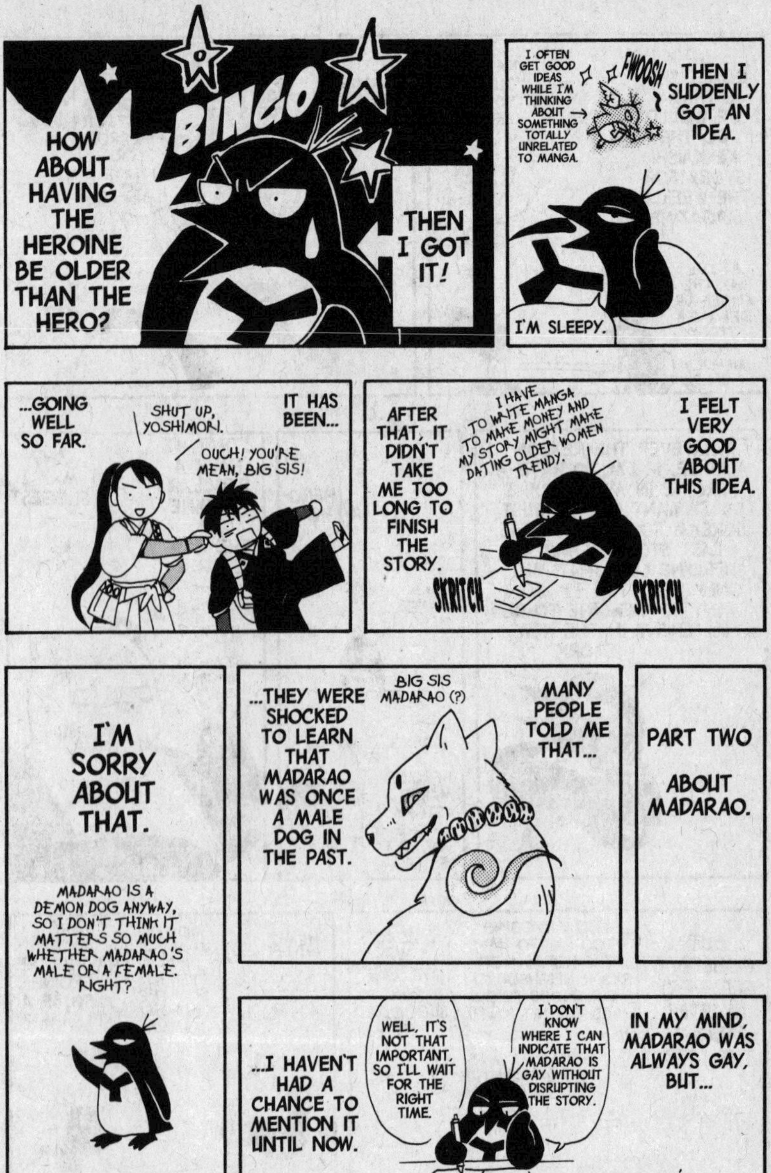
THEN I SUDDENLY GOT AN IDEA.
FWOOSH
I OFTEN GET GOOD IDEAS WHILE I'M THINKING ABOUT SOMETHING TOTALLY UNRELATED TO MANGA.
I'M SLEEPY.
THEN I GOT IT!
BINGO
HOW ABOUT HAVING THE HEROINE BE OLDER THAN THE HERO?
I FELT VERY GOOD ABOUT THIS IDEA.
I HAVE TO WRITE MANGA TO MAKE MONEY AND MY STORY MIGHT MAKE DATING OLDER WOMEN TRENDY.
AFTER THAT, IT DIDN'T TAKE ME TOO LONG TO FINISH THE STORY.
SKRITCH
SKRITCH
IT HAS BEEN...
...GOING WELL SO FAR.
SHUT UP, YOSHIMORI.
OUCH! YOU'RE MEAN, BIG SIS!
PART TWO
ABOUT MADARAO.
MANY PEOPLE TOLD ME THAT...
BIG SIS MADARAO (?)
...THEY WERE SHOCKED TO LEARN THAT MADARAO WAS ONCE A MALE DOG IN THE PAST.
IN MY MIND, MADARAO WAS ALWAYS GAY, BUT...
I DON'T KNOW WHERE I CAN INDICATE THAT MADARAO IS GAY WITHOUT DISRUPTING THE STORY.
WELL, IT'S NOT THAT IMPORTANT, SO I'LL WAIT FOR THE RIGHT TIME.
...I HAVEN'T HAD A CHANCE TO MENTION IT UNTIL NOW.
I'M SORRY ABOUT THAT.
MADARAO IS A DEMON DOG ANYWAY, SO I DON'T THINK IT MATTERS SO MUCH WHETHER MADARAO'S MALE OR A FEMALE. RIGHT?

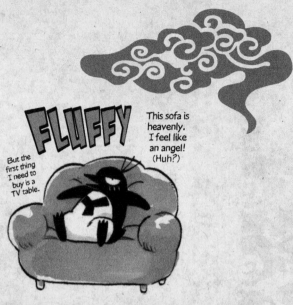

This sofa is heavenly. I feel like an angel! (Huh?)
FLUFFY
But the first thing I need to buy is a TV table.

MESSAGE FROM YELLOW TANABE

There are always things that we don't immediately need, but we think it would be nice to have. There are also those things that we don't necessarily need but we want to have anyway.

Right now for me, a sofa is one of those types of things. I think it would help me to relax. Actually, what I really want is spare time to sleep. I would sleep three days a week if I could.

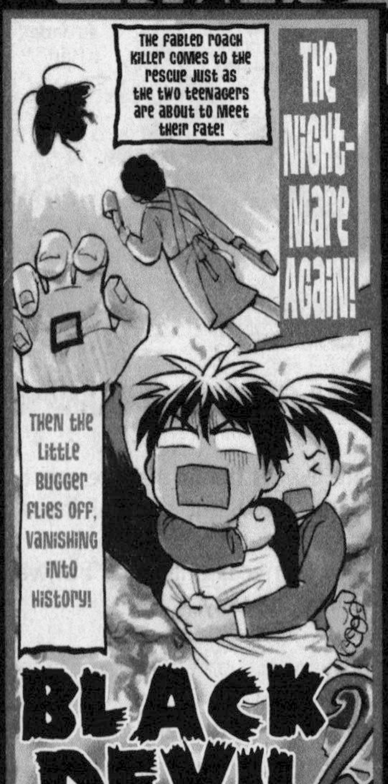
THE NIGHTMARE AGAIN!
The fabled roach killer comes to the rescue just as the two teenagers are about to meet their fate!
Then the little bugger flies off, vanishing into history!
BLACK DEVIL 2

Don't miss the next Kekkaishi 3-in-1, containing vols. 4, 5, and 6!

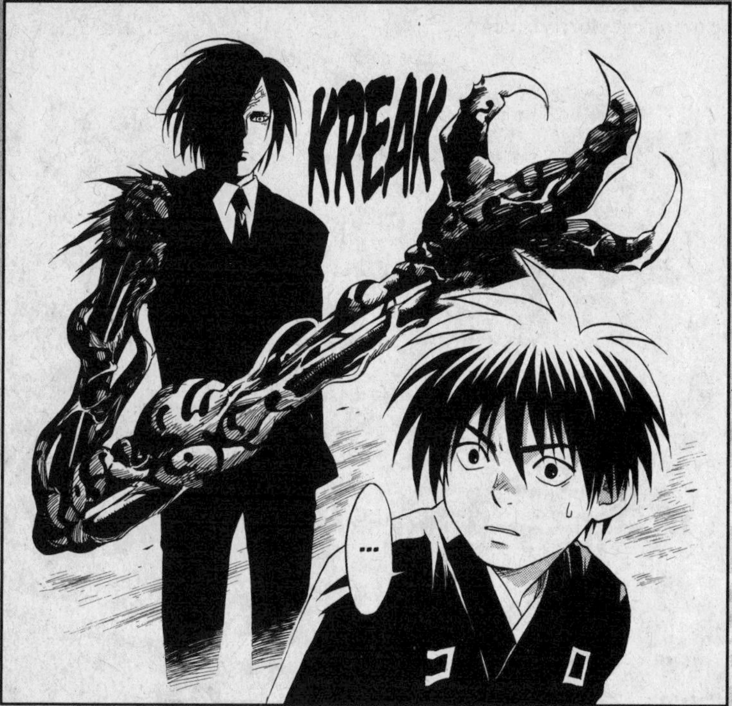
KREAK
...

Sibling feuds and rivalry abound at Karasumori! First, a ghost pastry chef must resolve unresolved issues with his flesh-and-blood brother. Next Yoshimori's big brother, Masamori, makes him feel small. And then the Shadow Organization, a secret cabal charged with protecting mortals from magic, sends an aloof operative named Gen to "help out" at the mystical site. Why is everyone picking on Yoshimori...?!

Available NOW!

At Your Indentured Service

Hayate's parents are bad with money, so they sell his organs to pay their debts. Hayate doesn't like this plan, so he comes up with a new one—kidnap and ransom a girl from a wealthy family. Solid plan… so how did he end up as her butler?

Find out in *Hayate the Combat Butler*— buy the manga at store.viz.com!

InuYasha

Read the action from the start with the original manga series

Full color adaptation of the popular TV series

The Art of
InuYasha

Original Illustrations by
Rumiko Takahashi

Art book with cel art, paintings, character profiles and more

TV SERIES & MOVIES ON DVD!

See more of the action in *Inuyasha* full-length movies

www.viz.com
inuyasha.viz.com

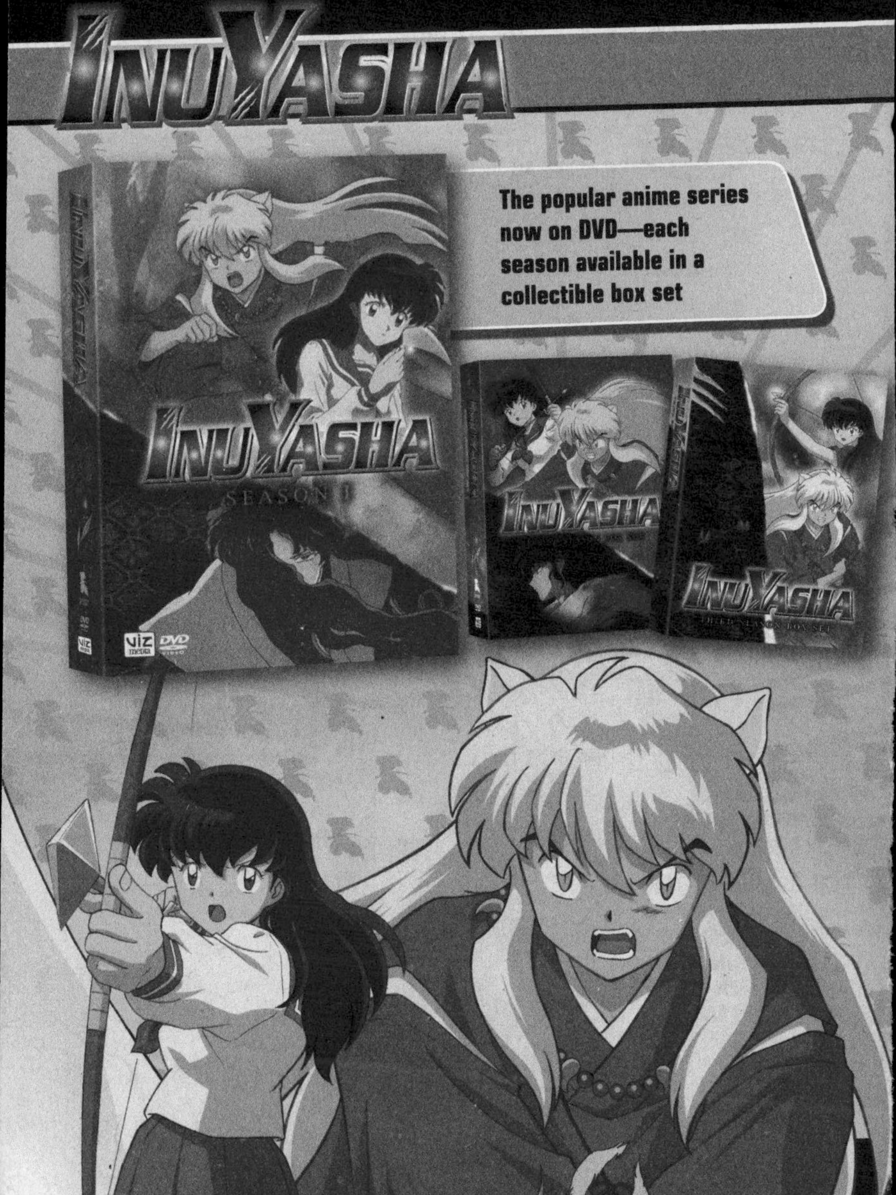

InuYasha
The popular anime series now on DVD—each season available in a collectible box set
InuYasha
Season 1
InuYasha
InuYasha
viz media
DVD

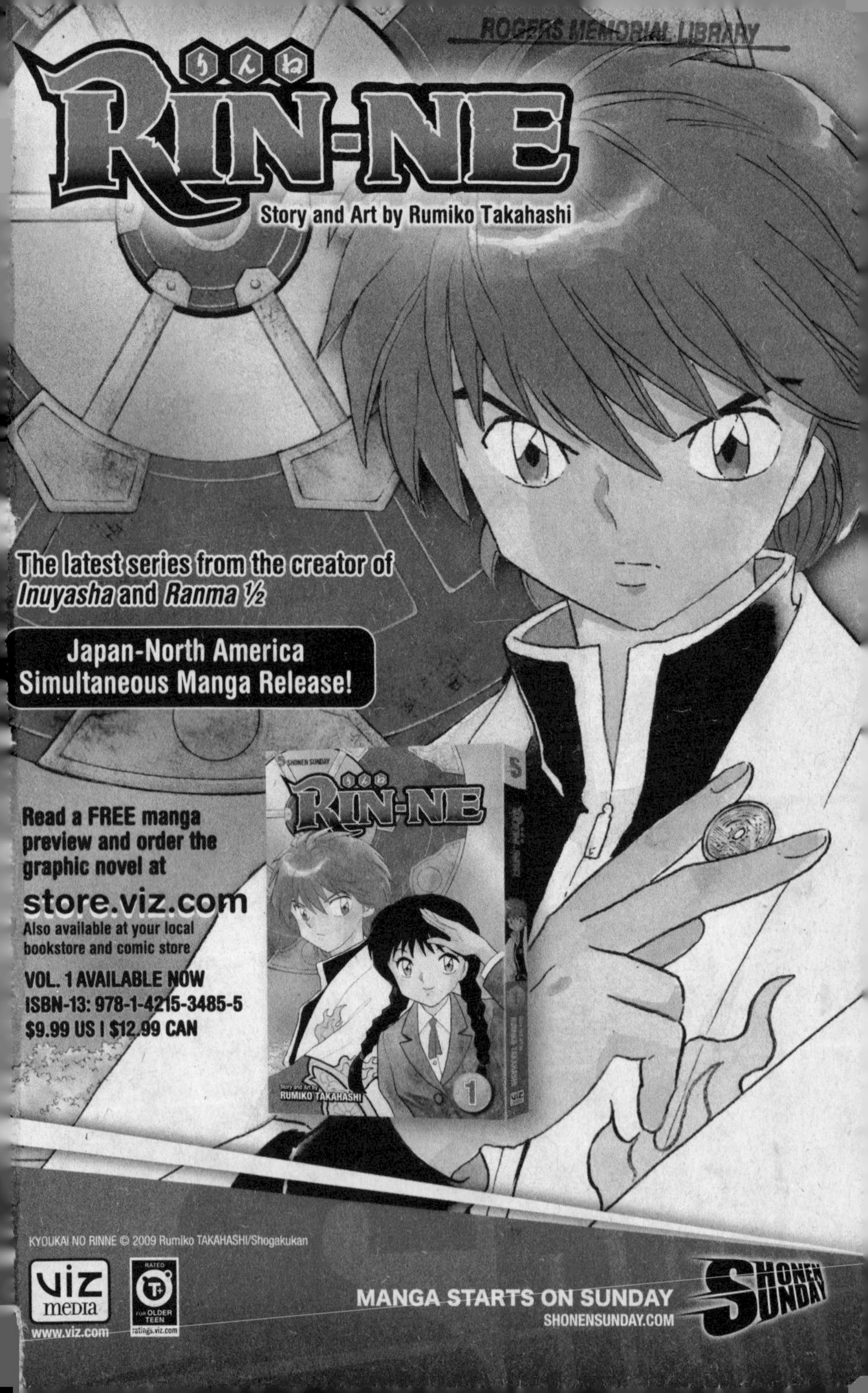
ROGERS MEMORIAL LIBRARY
りんね
RIN-NE
Story and Art by Rumiko Takahashi
The latest series from the creator of *Inuyasha* and *Ranma ½*
Japan-North America Simultaneous Manga Release!
SHONEN SUNDAY
RIN-NE
Story and Art by RUMIKO TAKAHASHI
1
Read a FREE manga preview and order the graphic novel at
store.viz.com
Also available at your local bookstore and comic store
VOL. 1 AVAILABLE NOW
ISBN-13: 978-1-4215-3485-5
$9.99 US | $12.99 CAN
KYOUKAI NO RINNE © 2009 Rumiko TAKAHASHI/Shogakukan
viz media
www.viz.com
RATED T+ FOR OLDER TEEN
ratings.viz.com
MANGA STARTS ON SUNDAY
SHONENSUNDAY.COM
SHONEN SUNDAY